MARKETING

McGraw-Hill Series in Marketing

MARKETING

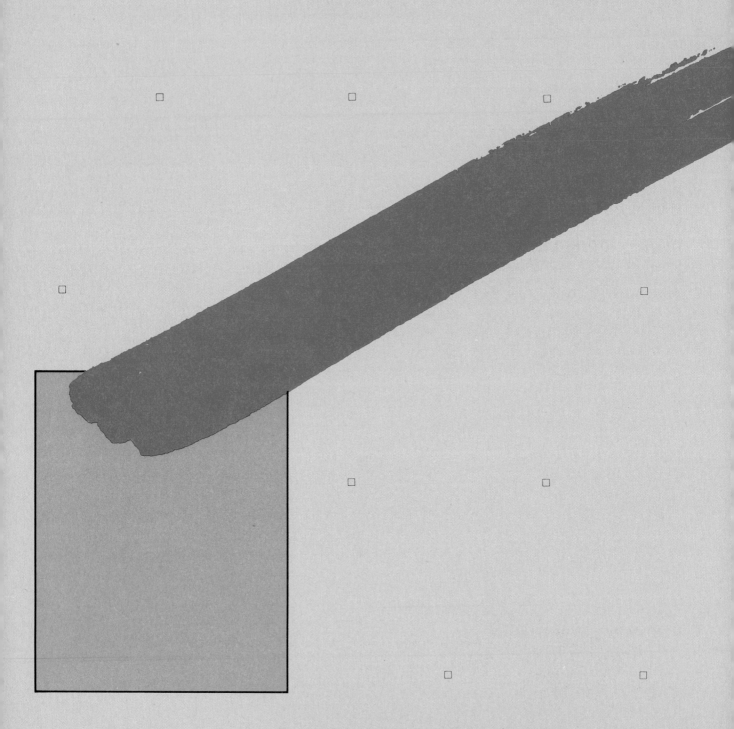

PETER D. BENNETT

**In collaboration with Robert P. Lamm
and Robert A. Fry**

McGRAW-HILL BOOK COMPANY
New York   St. Louis   San Francisco   Auckland   Bogotá   Caracas
Colorado Springs   Hamburg   Lisbon   London   Madrid   Mexico
Milan   Montreal   New Delhi   Oklahoma City   Panama   Paris
San Juan   São Paulo   Singapore   Sydney   Tokyo   Toronto

To Mary Lou, Bonnie Kathleen, and Blythe

1 2 3 4 5 6 7 8 9 0 K G P K G P 8 9 3 2 1 0 9 8

ISBN 0-07-004721-9

This book was set in Garamond Book by Waldman Graphics, Inc.
The editors were Daniel Kaizer, Sam Costanzo,
Sheila Gillams, and Michael Asher;
the production supervisor was Diane Renda.
Drawings were done by Caliber Design Planning, Inc.
Arcata Graphics/Kingsport was printer and binder.

Library of Congress Cataloging-in-Publication Data

Bennett, Peter D.
  Marketing / Peter D. Bennett in collaboration with Robert P. Lamm
and Robert A. Fry.
     p.   cm.—(McGraw-Hill series in marketing)
  Bibliography: p.
  Includes index.
  ISBN 0-07-004721-9
  1. Marketing. I. Lamm, Robert P. II. Fry, Robert A.
III. Title. IV. Series.
HF5415.B4293 1988   87-17335
658.8—dc19   CIP

Acknowledgments for part-opening photos:

Part One: Copyright © Jeff Smith.

Part Two: Copyright © Gabe Palmer/The Stock Market.

Part Three: Copyright © Karen Leeds/The Stock Market.

Part Four: Photo by Gerard Amsellum. Choreography by Maguy Marin as danced by The Lyon Opera
               Ballet. Graphic design by Perez/Griffin Graphics.

To the memory of my friend

and colleague

Rob Fry

ABOUT THE AUTHOR

PETER D. BENNETT (Ph.D., University of Texas at Austin) is Professor of Marketing at the Pennsylvania State University, where he has done research on consumer behavior and taught marketing for over twenty years. Professor Bennett has been widely published in professional books, magazines, and journals (including *Journal of Marketing, Journal of Consumer Research,* and *Journal of Marketing Research*), and has coauthored a consumer behavior textbook. He has been vice president of both the Marketing Education and Marketing Management Divisions of the American Marketing Association, and has recently edited the AMA's official dictionary of marketing terms. He was an IBM marketing representative before entering an academic career, and has since served as a consultant to a number of businesses, among them Kodak, Westinghouse, and Herman Miller. Dr. Bennett has taken a special interest in teaching introductory marketing throughout his career—he still teaches hundreds of students each semester at Penn State.

ROBERT A. FRY and ROBERT P. LAMM, New York–based professional writers with extensive textbook writing experience, collaborated with Dr. Bennett on this book. Rob Fry worked in college publishing for 30 years, as editor, marketing manager, sales representative, and writer. Until his death in 1986, he worked on this book with Pete Bennett. Bob Lamm's work has appeared in more than 30 periodicals in the United States, Canada, and Great Britain. He collaborated with Richard T. Schaefer on the successful textbook *Sociology.*

CONTENTS
IN BRIEF

CONTENTS

xiii

PREFACE

Economics is about exchange—people, businesses, and other organizations exchanging one thing for another. Production is about making that something of value which is exchanged. Accounting is about recording and reporting exchanges. *Marketing* is about making those exchanges happen, and about establishing the environment in which they can happen. In the very crude economies that characterized human existence before the twentieth century, and that still do exist in many parts of the world, marketing is not central to exchange. But in our current economic order, which happily involves making many economic choices, the role of marketing is central.

This book is designed to help the student learn about marketing in this fundamental way, leading toward an understanding of the full scope of marketing principles and practices in the modern world. The text is thorough, at a level of rigor appropriate to the student being formally introduced to the subject for the first time, and it is written specifically to make the subject both lively and interesting.

Approach

Any book must bear the stamp of its author's particular approach to the subject. After over a quarter of a century of teaching marketing, I am fully persuaded that students learn marketing best by seeing how it is done by the most sophisticated and effective marketing organizations. After an equal number of years working in and with marketing organizations—both effective and ineffective—I have developed solid views about what makes for sophisticated marketing.

The approach of the best marketers can be described in two ways. It includes a disciplined process, and it involves a particular content. The **process** must begin with **analysis** of markets and the environments in which marketing operates. It proceeds to planning marketing efforts to reach organizational goals, and on to the implementation of those plans. The process ends with a mechanism for **control,** or an evaluation of how well plans have been implemented. The **content** is that which is planned and implemented—the key decisions and actions of the marketing organization. This encompasses the products to be marketed, the prices charged for those products, how those products are distributed, and how they are promoted. These subplans, the so-called "4-Ps" (product, place, price, promotion), comprise the detail of marketing.

In addition to this view of the process and content of marketing, a strong aspect of this book's approach to marketing is its focus on competition. The essence of marketing is choices and about how organizations attempt to influence those choices. When competitors also attempt to influence those choices, marketing is more likely to take a leading role. There is much being said these days about marketing warfare. While "warfare" is often an exaggeration, there are competitive battles going on between the colas, the personal computers, and a host of other products. Marketing strategy is often at the heart of competitive strategy, and so those competitive battles are a major part of marketing.

This fundamental orientation to the world of marketing has guided the development of the book and has led to a number of its key features:

Action-oriented: Serious scholarship in the discipline of marketing constantly pushes back the frontiers of our understanding of the subject. However, scholarly treatise is not the focus of this principles book. Beginning students learn the fundamentals by seeing how successful organizations *do* marketing. The book is therefore liberally sprinkled with real marketing examples. All the concepts in the book are illustrated with examples of marketing decisions by *real* companies or other organizations.

Environmental: Of all of the various functions of an organization, from production to accounting, marketing is the one in most contact with the external environment. The influences of consumers and customers; of governments; of competitors; and of changes in technology, the economy, and the larger society are felt first and most directly in an organization's marketing efforts. The effects of these environmental forces permeate the entire book; and there is a chapter devoted directly to what managers can do to anticipate, plan for, and *manage* change in these environments.

Strategic: This book is not just about the day-to-day things marketing organizations do—rather, it views those practices in the light of the marketer's larger goals. The strategic orientation of the book places a strong emphasis on the role of marketing in the overall strategy of the corporation or other organization. As more and more organizations become market-focused, that role is central.

Complete: Modern, sophisticated marketing, as practiced by private firms that manufacture physical consumer products, has become a model for how marketing is done in other organizations. This book treats the marketing of services together with that of physical products, and also discusses industrial and business marketing throughout. It includes the marketing carried out by nonprofit organizations as well as business firms. And, it describes not just the domestic marketing of U.S. firms—it is global in its coverage.

Engaging: Marketing can be, and should be, an interesting subject to study. This book is unique among "principles of marketing" texts in the way it was written. As the author, the marketing expert, I wrote it all first. After that, it was completely rewritten by Rob Fry and Bob Lamm, who both worked very closely with me. These men brought to the book their special expertise as professional writers. The result is a crisp, lucid style that is easy to read, but that doesn't detract one bit from the rigor of the treatment.

Aids to Learning

In developing the text, we have paid constant attention to ways to help students learn marketing. These include:

Vignettes: Each chapter opens with a description of an organization and its marketing problem. Each is a lively story that raises the issues dealt with in the chapter. It *invites* the student into the chapter material.

Boxes: Throughout the text are a number of brief lively discussions about specific organizations or issues. Some carry the heading Competition in Marketing to highlight one theme of the book. Others are labeled Marketing Issues. These reflect the dynamic and changing nature of marketing. They focus on issues that are still being debated—issues which the students can decide about for themselves. Other boxes are of a more general nature. All are there to both engage and add perspective without detracting from the solid treatment in the text proper.

Figures and Exhibits: Whenever it is appropriate, we present material in diagramatic or tabular form. These brief figures or exhibits are designed to help the student grasp the material more easily and more thoroughly.

Photographs: There are over 250 color photographs in the text, each chosen because of its vivid visualization of the text. Each of these photographs is presented with a meaty caption that drives home its teaching and learning purpose.

End-of-Chapter Material: Each chapter ends with a numbered set of summary statements that captures "in a nutshell" a whole section of the chapter. These are followed by a set of review questions that challenge the student to go beyond the examples in the chapter. They ask the student to think about the material in the chapter and to apply the concepts. Also included at the end of chapters is a set of key terms, each of which appears in the text in **boldface** type. At the end of the book is a Dictionary of Marketing Terms, with definitions of each of these key terms.

Cases: At the end of each major part or subpart of the book are case studies of real companies or other organizations. These are designed to provide a well developed situation which requires the application of marketing concepts in the text. They can be a valuable source of class discussion or form the basis of the instructor's lecture. However used, the cases will help make the concepts meaningful by showing how they apply in a real situation.

An important aid to learning available to students is the *Student Study Guide,* prepared by this author and Dr. A. Jackson McCormack. This guide is designed with one purpose in mind—to help the student learn the material and make the best possible grade in the course. Each chapter contains an *overview* that vividly describes the central purpose of the chapter in the text, an extended *summary* of the text chapter's contents that pays particular attention to the text's key terms, a wide variety of test *exercises,* a *checklist* of main chapter concepts, and some case *applications.* The test exercises include thought completion (fill-in), matching, multiple choice, and true-false.

Aids to Teaching

Test Bank: The test bank features over 2500 multiple choice, true-false, and fill-in questions. The multiple choice questions require factual recall, as well as conceptual application. Each chapter has 2 or 3 sets of application questions in which some brief data are given (a sort of mini-case); questions follow requiring students to apply specific marketing concepts to the information given. The entire test bank has been edited by Dr. William Kline, the former Director of Test Development of the California Testing Bureau, and a leading expert in objective testing. Dr. Kline, who has a Ph.D. in Psychometrics from Princeton, has been a professional writer and editor of objective tests for over 30 years. He has personally assured the quality of every test question.

Instructor's Manual: Prepared by Daryl McKee (Louisiana State University), the Instructor's Manual features a brief outline of each chapter, an extended lecture outline for each chapter's topic, and many "instructor's notes." These notes provide a wealth of stories, examples, and exercises for the instructor to enhance classroom instruction. The Instructor's Manual also features in-depth answers to the review questions at the end of each text chapter and analysis of each of the book's cases.

Overhead Transparencies: Prepared by Les Dlabay (Lake Forest University), these four-color transparencies consist of advertisements and original line art. Each of the 150 OHTs (100 of which are not in the text) is accompanied by a set of teaching notes, with background of the transparency and suggestions for classroom use.

Video Tapes: Adopters of the book have available video tapes that consist of clusters of commercial advertisements that exemplify essential marketing concepts. These up-to-date commercials have been specifically selected for use in Principles of Marketing classes by Ron Herr of Southeast Missouri State University, who has utilized video tapes in his classroom instruction for the last 10 years. Professor Herr has also written a manual for these tapes, which gives background for each commercial and specific suggestions for their classroom use.

Larréché MARKOPS—A Marketing Operations and Strategy Simulation: This simulation, developed by Jean-Claude Larréché, allows students to make marketing mix, portfolio, segmentation, and positioning decisions under competitive situations.

Business Week Reader: A collection of recent articles from *Business Week* that covers important marketing concepts. The articles were selected by Charles Futrell of Texas A&M University.

Acknowledgments

A book such as this one owes a debt of gratitude to a host of people. A deep debt is owed to the past, to all those scholars and practitioners who have developed and written about modern marketing practices. If we stand tall at the end of the twentieth century, it is because we are standing on the shoulders of giants. In my own case, those giants include professors I have studied with, and the authors whose writings I have read.

The most diverse, but perhaps the deepest, gratitude I owe is to my students of almost three decades of teaching. As I have sought to help them learn about marketing, they have taught me about how to teach and about what really matters to students. All of that has gone into the preparation of this book.

I wish to thank my colleagues in the two universities at which I have taught, Penn State University and The University of Texas at Austin. In reality, there is a whole nation of colleagues who have influenced my understanding of marketing who cannot be thanked individually. They know who they are. I do wish to thank those colleagues in the marketing profession who have taken the time and effort to read and critique drafts of this book. I would not put on them any of the responsibility for any errors that may persist, but their guidance at various stages has made the book better than it would otherwise have been. They include:

Rolph Anderson
Drexel University

David Andrus
Kansas State University

Peter Bloch
Louisiana State University

Paul Dion
University of Minnesota at Duluth

Ronald Dornoff
University of Cincinnati

Michael Fowler
Brookdale Community College

Cathy Goodwin
California State University at Chico

Richard Goodwin
Broward Community College

Greg Gundlach
University of Tennessee

Jon Hawes
University of Akron

Don English
Winona State University

Marye Hilger
University of Texas

Carol Kaufman
Rutgers University

Priscilla LaBarbera
New York University

James Maskulka
Lehigh University

Wayne Norvell
Kansas State University

Thomas O'Connor
University of New Orleans

Allen Smith
Florida Atlantic University

Ronald H. Herr
Southeast Missouri State University

Vernon Stauble
California State Polytechnic University

Gerald Stiles
Mankato State University

Gerald Tellis
University of Iowa

Paul Thistlethwaite
Western Illinois University

Robert Thompson
Indiana State University

Erhard Valentin
Weber State College

I would also like to thank my dean and good friend, Eugene J. Kelley. In his support for my research and writing over the years, he has acted as mentor and cheer leader and proved an understanding administrator when those efforts took so much of my time. He is a respected marketing scholar himself, and has influenced my views of the discipline.

No book is complete without the people at the publishing company who make so many things happen. My editor, Daniel Kaizer, shoved, prodded, pleaded, questioned, and supported me throughout the last two years. His talent, as well as his good humor, made the process bearable. Sam Costanzo played a key role in guiding the overall development of the total package of text and supplements. The production process was ably guided by Sheila Gillams. The total photography program is the result of the creative Inge King.

A special thank you is due to Roger Emblen, now a Denver stock broker. Roger is the person, more than any other, who convinced me that I should write this book, and I have learned to agree with him.

There are a number of people who gave of their time and talent in getting the details of the project done. Joan Kerstetter, Sue Rinehart, and Tina Jones typed and retyped manuscript. Graduate students who provided assistance with a number of sections of the book included Xiao-hong Sun and Christine Perintino. I also appreciate the help and support of the Browns, and others around Chaffey's Lock.

It would not do to fail to point out my deep debt of gratitude to the late Rob Fry, and to Bob Lamm, for the use of their writing talent to make the book not only clear, but lively and interesting to read. Their hands can be seen throughout the book.

Finally, I thank my family for the love and support they showed to me during the writing of the book. My wife of 35 years, Mary Lou Bennett, has been a constant support, as have my two daughters, Kathy and Blythe.

Peter D. Bennett

MARKETING

1

Jerry W. Meyers/Stock, Boston

MARKETING: A PHILOSOPHY OF BUSINESS

SPOTLIGHT ON

☐ Why marketing is viewed as a philosophy of business

☐ Different definitions of marketing proposed by economists, marketing scholars, and marketing practitioners

☐ The basic principles of the modern marketing concept

☐ How marketing philosophy evolved from a product orientation to a societal marketing orientation

☐ How the managerial framework of analyzing, planning, implementing, and controlling provides a basis for marketing action

☐ Key marketing concepts which are often misunderstood or confused

The PC, International Business Machine's (IBM's) personal computer, has certainly been the marketing success story of the 1980s. When IBM introduced the PC in mid-1981, over 150 companies had already jumped into the lucrative personal microcomputer market. Nevertheless, within 2 years IBM had seized more than 26 percent of the annual market. By the beginning of 1984, about 750,000 PCs were in use worldwide. By 1985, IBM had captured approximately half the world market, far surpassing such strong competitors as Apple and Tandy Corporation (Radio Shack). The triumph of the PC offers important lessons for contemporary marketers.

Before any product was designed, IBM's market researchers carefully and accurately pinpointed what potential buyers wanted: a machine that (1) was "user friendly" and would not frighten those who lacked computer experience and technical training; (2) was priced within reach of individual buyers and small businesses; (3) was backed by an established company with a reputation built on service; (4) could communicate with other, larger computers—mainly IBM mainframes; and (5) could run a full range of software programs. IBM's special-projects team, based in Boca Raton, Florida, devised just the product to meet those needs. The original PC was a useful (even admirable) product, but it offered no stunning technological advances over competitive machines like the Apple II. It did, however, provide PC buyers with both a sense of security about their purchase and an unmatched selection of programs to run.

To sell the PC, IBM made major changes in its distribution philosophy. In the past, the company had relied exclusively on its own sales force to sell to businesses, but the PC was aimed at individuals as well as businesses. As a result, IBM not only arranged to place the machines with Sears Business Centers and several retail computer chains, it also opened a number of its own retail outlets.

The use of the "little tramp" character in IBM advertising has been an effective way to appeal to people who might find computers hard to understand, or even frightening. (Courtesy of IBM.)

The PC's original price—in the $3000 to $5000 range—was apparently neither too high nor too low. Apple chose to price its answer to the IBM challenge, its Lisa model, at around $10,000, obviously far above the cost of the PC. As more sophisticated models (the AT and the XT) were developed, IBM began to cut its price on the original PC, thereby forcing Apple and a host of competitors to cut their prices and profit margins.

Finally, IBM's well-executed promotional campaign, estimated to cost $36 million, made a favorable and lasting impression on buyers. The advertising agency of Lord, Geller, Federico, Einstein came up with a surprising choice as "spokesperson" for the campaign: the clumsy but lovable "little tramp" first created by silent film legend Charlie Chaplin. According to Charles Pankenier, IBM's director of communications for the PC, this friendly image "stands fear of technology on its head and helps the PC open up a new technological world for the nontechnician." The advertising campaign also softens people's perceptions of IBM as an efficient but detached giant. The fallible little tramp with his cherished red rose brings a hint of a smile to IBM's stern corporate face.

By 1986, a number of competitors, mostly from the Far East, made copies, or clones, of the IBM PC and priced them well below the PC. In the spring of 1987, IBM introduced a whole new line, the PS/2, which contained many hard-to-copy features. Once again, competitors have found IBM a formidable opponent.

Sources: Myron Magnet, "How to Compete with IBM," *Fortune,* Feb. 6, 1984, pp. 58–71; "Personal Computers: And the Winner Is IBM," *Business Week,* Oct. 3, 1983, pp. 75–95; "The Colossus That Works: Big Is Bountiful at IBM," *Time,* July 1983, pp. 44–54; "IBM: More Worlds to Conquer," *Business Week,* Feb. 18, 1985, pp. 84–98; Geoff Lewis, "IBM's New PCs: Homegrown and Harder to Clone," *Business Week*, April 13, 1987, p. 71.

From the moment you reach for your alarm clock in the morning until you turn off your bedroom light at night, you are in continuous and unavoidable contact with products—goods, services, and ideas—that have been created or enhanced by marketers all over the world. The products of **marketing** add variety to life by presenting us with options from cradle to grave. However, many people misunderstand the goals and methods of marketing, perhaps because marketing encompasses so much that is seemingly familiar.

The introduction of the IBM PC was a phenomenal success largely because IBM managers—led by Don Estridge, president of the Entry Systems Division—effectively accomplished the fundamental process of marketing. The team charged with the development of the PC carefully analyzed the needs of chosen markets—both individuals and organizations—and came up with the concept for the PC. Plans for pricing, distributing, and promoting the PC were smartly executed, and impressive sales figures were the result.

Actually, the PC was only one addition to a long string of marketing successes for IBM, a company well-known for its commitment to marketing. As Peter Drucker observed many years before the introduction of the PC:

> Among American manufacturing companies the outstanding practitioner of the marketing approach may well be IBM; and IBM is also the best example of the power of marketing. IBM does not owe its meteoric rise to technological innovation or product leadership. It was a Johnny-come-lately when it entered the computer field, without technical expertise or scientific knowledge. But while the technological

leaders in the early computer days, Univac, GE, and RCA, were product-focused and technology-focused, the punch-card sales people who ran IBM asked: "Who are the customers? What is value for them? How do they buy? And what do they need?" As a result, IBM took over the market.[1]

IBM's leadership in its industry—like the leadership of many successful firms in other industries—can be attributed directly to the priority IBM gives to marketing in its corporate philosophy. The most successful modern organizations view marketing not only as a process but also as a philosophy of business.

We begin Chapter 1 by examining marketing as a way of thinking about business. We then study definitions of marketing offered by economists, marketing scholars, and marketing practitioners, although we use the latter's perspective throughout this book. An overview of marketing provides a "road map" of the book. Finally, we discuss a few important and often misunderstood concepts that are used throughout this book.

THE MARKETING PHILOSOPHY

Thomas J. Watson, Sr., founded IBM and served as its first president during the early decades of this century. Before founding IBM, Watson was the national sales manager of NCR Corporation. The following story illustrates his firm belief in the marketing philosophy:

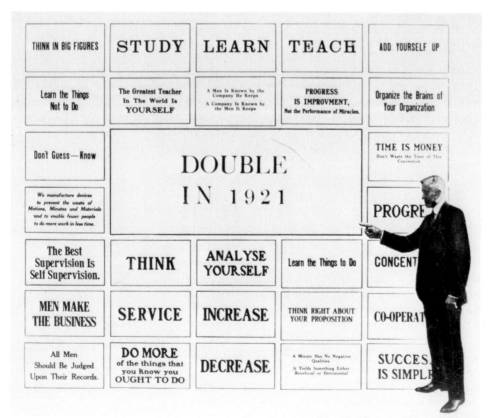

Thomas J. Watson, Sr., founded one of the most successful companies in the world. He built IBM's success on the principle of customer satisfaction. He insisted that everyone in the company pay attention to customers' needs. (Courtesy of IBM.)

On the front table there were eight or ten piles of papers, identifying the source of problems: "manufacturing problems," "engineering problems," and the like. After much discussion, Mr. Watson, a big man, walked slowly to the front of the room and, with a flash of his hand, swept the table clean and sent papers flying all over the room. He said, "There aren't any categories of problems here. There's just one problem. Some of us aren't paying enough attention to our customers." He turned crisply on his heel and walked out, leaving 20 fellows wondering whether or not they still had jobs.[2]

The marketing philosophy of business assumes that an organization can best survive, prosper, and profit by identifying and satisfying the needs of its customers. Since marketing is that function which is in most direct contact with the customer, its role in satisfying the customer is central. But the customer—not marketing—is the organization's ultimate dictator. As Thomas Watson suggested, paying attention to the customer is at the heart of the marketing philosophy.

Sears is one well-known company which has dramatized its commitment to the marketing philosophy of business in an unusual way. During staff meetings at Sears headquarters in Chicago, an empty chair sits conspicuously in the conference room. Painted on the chair are the words, "The Customer." This symbolic presence reminds Sears managers who their ultimate boss is.[3]

As we will see throughout this book, it is not only profit-seeking companies who practice the marketing philosophy. Many not-for-profit organizations—among them the Cleveland Orchestra, the U.S. Navy, the Democratic party, and San Antonio's Trinity University—may be said to practice marketing as a philosophy of business. When New York City's Metropolitan Opera needed a general manager to lead the company through the last half of the 1980s, it chose an experienced marketing executive: Bruce Crawford, president of the large international advertising agency of Batten, Barton, Durstine, and Osborne. Like others in charge of not-for-profit organizations, the trustees of the Metropolitan Opera recognized that in today's competitive world, skillful marketing is essential for the survival of *any* large organization (and many smaller ones as well).

This chair sits in the boardroom of Sears, Roebuck & Company. It is there to remind all Sears managers that their real boss—the one who has the final say about their success—is the customer. (Photo courtesy of Sears, Roebuck & Co.)

■ DEFINING MARKETING ■

It is customary to define the subject matter of a textbook early in the first chapter. However, defining marketing presents a problem: Which definition you get depends on who you ask. This book looks at marketing from the action perspective of the marketing manager, or the practitioner of marketing. Before proceeding to the definition from that perspective, however, let us discuss the definitions of marketing offered by economists and by marketing scholars.

□ *The Perspective of Economists*

If you ask an economist to define marketing, he or she will undoubtedly give you an answer that speaks of the process of exchange and of the utilities that buyers receive from sellers in this exchange process.

EXCHANGE   Marketing deals with the motivations and actions of people who make exchanges, that is, buyers and sellers. An **exchange** is a transaction between two or more people, groups, or organizations in which each party gives up something of value and receives something of value. At the highest level, exchange may involve the sale of U.S. grain to the Soviet Union, the negotiation of a new contract

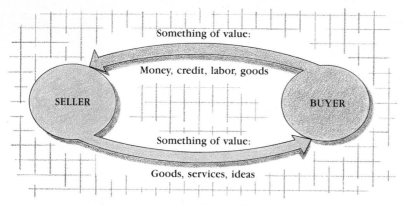

Figure 1-1 *The exchange process.* Exchange involves at least two parties, most commonly a buyer and a seller. The buyer usually gives up money or promises to pay money in the future (credit). In bartering, buyers may give up their labor or goods to be traded. The seller usually gives up goods, services, or ideas (what we define as products). In modern economies, both buyer and seller are presumed to consider what they receive in the exchange to be of equal or greater value than what they give up.

between the United Auto Workers and the major car manufacturers, or a loan to Nigeria from the International Monetary Fund. But an exchange may also be quite simple and ordinary, as when you purchase a new shirt or trade record albums with a friend. The presumption in any exchange is that all parties receive something whose value equals or is greater than the value of what they give up. The buyer usually receives a product or service; the seller usually receives money. Figure 1-1 offers a simplified view of the exchanges that occur between buyer and seller.

A **product** is anything an organization offers for exchange that satisfies a consumer need. In marketing terms, a product may be a tangible good (a car or a coat), an intangible benefit in the form of a service (dry cleaning or fire insurance), or even an idea that offers some benefit (to stop smoking). In many cases, the product may be perceived by both parties in the exchange as a combination of a good, a service, and an idea. For example, if you have the money to exchange for a Mercedes-Benz, the product you buy is a physical good (a car), a service (the warranty), and an idea (an image of luxury and success). For an exchange to succeed, it must lead to utility for the consumer.

UTILITY **Utility** is a measure of the satisfaction obtained through the receipt of something of value in an exchange. It is, in fact, the goal—if not always the result—of the exchanges that we make every day. As consumers, we gain satisfaction when we see a movie, drive a smoothly running car out of the repair shop, or bite into a Big Mac. Utility is whatever makes such things valuable to us—presumably more valuable than the money we exchange for them. But what makes a product useful? Marketing scholars have identified four types of utility associated with a product's form, place, time, and possession.

Form Utility A product first provides **form utility,** which is the usefulness attributable to the form or design of something received. Iron ore is processed and made into steel axles, steam irons, cookware, and building beams; silicon is worked into semiconductor chips, which are assembled into microcomputers; lambs' wool and polyester are fabricated into cloth. Lawyers draft wills, plastic surgeons perform face-lifts, and college professors deliver lectures. In all these cases, raw materials or skills which have no value to us as they exist—what would you do with a ton of iron ore?—are transformed into products (goods, services, and ideas) that have use and are therefore valuable.

Providing form utility is shared among a firm's marketing, research and development, and manufacturing arms. Marketing's essential role in this process is to provide critical information about what people want, so that research and development and manufacturing can create the form that is wanted.

Place Utility   If the product is not where the consumer wants or needs it, it has no **place utility**, the usefulness gained when something of value is received where it is wanted. A car built in Japan, Sweden, or even Detroit has no value for a person who lives in Colorado until that car is transported there. To gain expanded place utility, Texas grapefruit and Alaskan crabmeat are shipped around the world.

Place utility is important both for products and for services. When someone hits your car or robs you, you need an insurance adjuster (and possibly a doctor) who is nearby, not in a distant office in another state. Pace University in New York City advertises its place utility through posters in the subway system: "We have five locations so you can put your energy into getting ahead. Not getting to class."

Time Utility   Products must be available not only where the consumer wants them but also when they are wanted. In other words, products must have **time utility**, the usefulness gained when something of value is received when it is wanted. Successful marketers plan carefully to ensure the availability of their products at the proper time. Swimsuits are typically manufactured in the winter and later stored in retail outlets in time for display in June. Textbooks must be in college bookstores by the day that school opens. Gefilte fish and matzos must be on supermarket shelves before Passover; freshly cut trees must be ready for sale shortly before Christmas. In all these examples, time is everything. A product without time utility cannot be used; if the product is perishable, it may become useless.

Possession Utility   Armour hams in a supermarket meat case, a Toyota Supra in a dealer's showroom, a dentist replacing fillings at a clinic—none of these products or services has value unless it can be bought and owned, consumed, or used

Cranapple juice is produced in the state of Washington, but people all over the country want to buy it. The marketing system, involving the physical movement of the product, as well as the retail system where consumers can buy it, adds the place, time, and possession utility to the basic product. (Left: Copyright © 1985 José Fernandez/Woodfin Camp & Assoc. Right: By Ken Karp.)

at the owner's discretion. Consumers must be able to own or use the products that they need. Consequently, a marketing exchange must give a product **possession utility,** the usefulness gained with the transfer of ownership of a good, or the actual provision of a service. Although you may squeeze a melon in the grocery store, you may not eat it unless you buy it first!

Marketing provides possession utility by providing the system through which the title to products and services is transferred—primarily the retailing system for consumer products. The satisfaction that a consumer receives from an exchange is the sum of the four utilities of form, time, place, and possession.

☐ *The Perspective of Marketing Scholars*

Instead of asking economists to define marketing, you might decide to ask serious students of marketing who have made important scholarly contributions to the field to define the term. These scholars are often professors of marketing, like the instructor in your course. Some are consultants who advise business firms and not-for-profit organizations about how to market. Three scholars have had a particularly strong influence on contemporary marketing: Peter Drucker, Theodore Levitt, and Thomas Peters.

PETER DRUCKER ON MARKETING   In his writings over several decades, Peter Drucker has emphasized the importance of keeping the customer at the center of management's attention. At one point, he observed: "There is only one valid definition of business purpose: *to create a customer.*"[4] The customer determines whether a business will survive and prosper.

Drucker believes that successful organizations devote themselves to identifying and offering products that satisfy the wants and needs of consumers. He concludes that a business has only two fundamental activities: innovation and marketing. Through innovation, companies continuously replace products with new products that better satisfy customers' needs. The function of marketing is to *identify* these changing needs so that innovative products can be developed to meet them. Drucker views marketing as the "central dimension" of the entire business: "It is the whole business seen from the point of view of its final result, that is from the customer's point of view."[5]

Two central lessons stressed by Drucker have shaped the thinking of today's marketing scholars:

1. The primary responsibility of any business is to identify and meet customers' needs. The best technology is simply the technology which best satisfies those needs.
2. Marketing is special work with its own particular set of activities; consequently, marketing specialists are needed to handle that work. At the same time, marketing must be the concern of *everyone* in an organization and must permeate the thinking of all managers.

THEODORE LEVITT ON MARKETING   Almost 30 years ago, Theodore Levitt of Harvard University wrote an article, "Marketing Myopia," that became a classic statement of modern marketing philosophy.[6] Using the image of nearsightedness to comic effect, Levitt set out to dramatize the positive value of a more farsighted marketing orientation. Businesses, Levitt said, suffer from myopia when they fail to ask themselves the question, "What business are we in?"

Defining a business in terms of the product made and sold is an easy answer.

Peter Drucker has long been one of the most respected commentators on business management. Central to much of his teachings and writings is the message that the only ultimate purpose of a business is to satisfy customers. (The Claremont Graduate School, Claremont, Ca.)

Since 1960, the most influential single article about marketing has been "Marketing Myopia" by Theodore Levitt, of Harvard Business School. Levitt sounded a warning of the dangers of managers keeping their attention on the products they make rather than on the needs of the customers who are satisfied by those products. (News Bureau, Harvard Business School.)

But, as Levitt wrote elsewhere, customers buy "quarter-inch holes, not quarter-inch drills."[7] Therefore, in his view, the more appropriate answer to the question lies in whatever needs of the customer are satisfied—or, put a little differently, in the service provided to the customer. As Levitt points out:

> The railroads did not stop growing because the need for passenger and freight transportation declined. That grew. The railroads are in trouble today not because the need was filled by others (cars, trucks, airplanes, even telephones), but because it was not filled by the railroads themselves. They let others take customers away from them because they assumed themselves to be in the railroad business rather than in the transportation business. The reason they defined their industry wrong was because they were railroad-oriented instead of transportation-oriented; they were product-oriented instead of customer-oriented.[8]

Had the railroads answered the question of "What business are we in?" from the *customer's* point of view, today's airlines might be named Penn Central or Baltimore and Ohio instead of TWA and United. Levitt has also used the example of the motion picture industry to illustrate his point. Had film executives of the 1940s and 1950s identified their business as entertainment rather than movies, today's television networks might be MGM, Disney, and Paramount instead of NBC, ABC, and CBS. At one time, the three television networks were simply radio networks, but they were wise enough to see that television represented an opportunity rather than a threat. In Levitt's terms, the networks were not suffering from myopia.

Levitt's message to students of marketing is clear: Organizations that define themselves in terms of their products—rather than their markets or consumers' needs—do so nearsightedly and at their own peril.

THOMAS PETERS ON MARKETING   One of the most important business books published in the 1980s was *In Search of Excellence* by Thomas J. Peters and Robert H. Waterman, Jr.[9] It was followed a few years later by *A Passion for Excellence* by Thomas J. Peters and Nancy Austin.[10] Both books report on extensive research into what distinguishes excellent companies from ordinary ones; a key factor identified in the research is how different companies treat their customers. Apparently, Peter Drucker's lessons have had their impact over the years, at least to the point that nearly everyone gives lip service to keeping the customer's needs foremost. However, Peters and Waterman did conclude that "the excellent companies *really are* close to their customers.... Other companies talk about it; the excellent companies do it."[11]

Some experts have criticized *In Search of Excellence* for oversimplifying its analysis, but Peters and Austin conclude that the earlier work did not simplify matters enough:

> In the private or public sector, in big business or small, we observe that there are only two ways to create and sustain superior performance over the long haul. First, take exceptional care of your customers (for chicken, jet engines, education, health care, or baseball) via superior service and superior quality. Secondly, constantly innovate. That's it. There are no alternatives in achieving long-term superior performance, or sustaining strategic competitive advantage, as the business strategists call it.[12]

Peters insists that firms that take care of customers and innovate constantly consistently win competitive battles, hold leading shares of the markets in which they compete, and produce top financial returns for their stockholders.

Thomas J. Peters was the co-author of what many think are the two most important management books of the 1980s, *In Search of Excellence* and *A Passion for Excellence*. These books show that close attention to the needs of customers makes excellent organizations excellent. (Chris Petersen Photography, courtesy of Harper & Row.)

In the early twentieth century, Peter Drucker gave us the concept of focusing on satisfying the customer. In the middle of the century, Theodore Levitt provided stark examples of what could happen to firms that failed to maintain this focus. In the latter part of the century, Thomas Peters has underscored the benefits realized by excellent companies which follow the modern marketing philosophy.

☐ *The Perspective of Marketing Practitioners*

After asking economists and marketing scholars how marketing should be defined, you might decide to ask people who are *doing* marketing to define it. Not surprisingly, most would offer a definition based on their own day-to-day activities. Certainly, much is to be learned from the views of economists and marketing scholars, but this book deals with marketing as it is actually conducted in the real world.

The definition that comes closest to marketing action is the official definition offered by the American Marketing Association (AMA), the nation's largest and most prestigious association of marketing practitioners and professors:

> Marketing is the process of planning and executing the conception, pricing, promotion, and distribution of ideas, goods, and services to create exchanges that satisfy individual and organizational goals.[13]

This definition is particularly useful because it deals directly with (1) marketing as a managerial process, (2) the purpose of marketing—goal satisfaction, and (3) how the marketing process works—marketing actions. Moreover, while attempting to clarify the definition of marketing, the AMA is at the forefront of efforts to develop professional and ethical standards for marketers (see Box 1-1).

The AMA's definition of marketing includes two of the four major steps in the marketing management process: planning and implementation. However, two steps are missing: analysis (which comes before plans can be drawn) and control (which comes after implementation, when marketers examine whether they have met their goals). Since this very marketing management process is the organizing principle of this book, we will elaborate on it more fully when we provide an overview of the book at the end of this chapter.

☐ *The Marketing Concept*

The most important idea in contemporary marketing thought and practice is the **marketing concept:** Business organizations achieve their profit and other goals by satisfying consumers.[14] To apply this concept, an organization must meet three basic conditions. First, it must truly believe in the customer's importance. As noted earlier, many companies give lip service to this idea; no manager wants to be caught saying that customers are not important. By contrast, a genuine customer orientation demands a fervent commitment of people, time, and monetary resources to implement this orientation.

Second, marketing efforts must be integrated. Specific and measurable goals should be set; all marketing activities should be coordinated. If various departments follow their own private agendas in conducting marketing activities, the organization may lose sight of customers' needs.

Finally, management must accept the assumption that profit goals will be reached through satisfied customers. Clearly, the path to profit is not a simple one; all business firms compete within a complex environment that demands astute management of organizational resources and efforts. Nevertheless, managers must have confidence that if they meet real needs by offering quality products at fair

Is marketing a profession? Should it attempt to emulate established professions such as medicine, law, and accounting? Should standards of education and experience be established for the licensing of individuals as certified public marketers (CPMs) just as they are for certified public accountants (CPAs)? These questions have been debated within the American Marketing Association over the last 25 years.

Currently, there is little agreement within the AMA as to what standards would be appropriate in licensing a CPM. Some AMA members contend that it is difficult or even impossible to devise licensing standards because of the breadth and complexity of marketing. After all, they suggest, both the research analyst dealing with models of consumer behavior and the salesperson in a shoe store are involved in marketing. For other AMA members, however, this argument seems little more than an excuse—a convenient way to avoid the challenging task of discussing and drafting professional standards.

Clearly, when compared to older and better recognized professions, marketing has a long way to go. But marketers continue working toward the goal of becoming a respected profession. As one critical element in this process, the AMA adopted the following code of ethics:

> As a member of the American Marketing Association, I recognize the significance of my professional conduct and my responsibilities to society and to the other members of my profession.

1. By acknowledging my accountability to society as a whole as well as to the organization for which I work.
2. By pledging my efforts to assure that all presentations of goods, services, and concepts be made honestly and clearly.
3. By striving to improve marketing knowledge and practice in order to better serve society.
4. By supporting free consumer choice in circumstances that are legal and are consistent with generally accepted community standards.
5. By pledging to use the highest professional standards in my work and in competitive activity.
6. By acknowledging the right of the American Marketing Association, through established procedure, to withdraw my membership if I am found to be in violation of ethical standards of professional conduct.

This code of ethics, while certainly admirable, has been criticized as being too general. An AMA task force, well aware that professionalism requires more precise ethical standards, has drafted a more detailed code with 22 specific points covering general issues of competence, professional conduct, responsibilities of the marketer, honesty and fairness, rights of the consumer, and organizational relationships. As of 1987, this revised code of ethics was under consideration by AMA members. ■

Source: Marketing News, May 9, 1986, p. 1. Code of ethics reprinted by permission of the American Marketing Association.

prices, their companies will make money. Similarly, not-for-profit organizations will achieve their financial and other goals if they satisfy their customers and members. Figure 1-2 illustrates these three pillars of the marketing concept, which are necessary conditions in creating satisfactory exchanges and in making marketing a true philosophy of business.

Although the marketing concept is a necessary reminder of the important messages of Drucker, Levitt, and Peters—keep customers' needs first—it must be applied carefully. Some firms have gone too far by failing to bring out innovative products because customers don't already know that they need them.[15] Indeed, it can be quite difficult for marketers to determine what consumers' needs are; consumers themselves may not be certain. Consequently, following the marketing concept is more easily said than done.

☐ *The Marketing Mix*

Through application of the marketing concept, a company develops its **marketing mix** (see Figure 1-3). The marketing mix includes the four major elements of

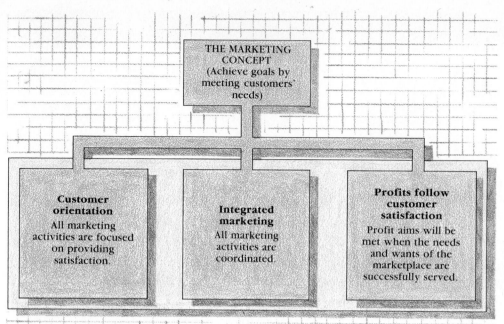

Figure 1-2 *Key assumptions of the marketing concept.*

THE MARKETING CONCEPT
(Achieve goals by meeting customers' needs)

Customer orientation
All marketing activities are focused on providing satisfaction.

Integrated marketing
All marketing activities are coordinated.

Profits follow customer satisfaction
Profit aims will be met when the needs and wants of the marketplace are successfully served.

marketing programs: product conception (and development), pricing decisions, promotion of the product, and distribution to consumers. These four elements comprise the content of marketing plans and a major portion of this book.[16]

For marketing planning to succeed, each component of the marketing mix must be on target. The desired level of exchange will not be reached if the product

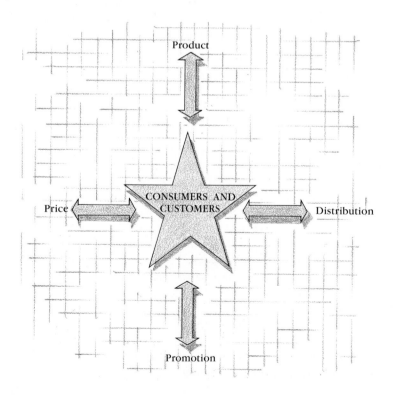

Product

Price

CONSUMERS AND CUSTOMERS

Distribution

Promotion

Figure 1-3 *Components of the marketing mix.* Plans for the marketing mix integrate marketers' efforts to provide a wanted product at an appropriate price, to promote the product creatively and effectively, and to distribute the product through an efficient system. Consumers and organizational customers remain at the heart of all such plans.

BOX 1-2 Marketing Mousetraps and Light Bulbs

For as long as students have enrolled in marketing classes, teachers have been telling the old story which concludes "if you make a better mousetrap, the world will beat a path to your door." According to this view, offering the right product is a guarantee of success. Kevin Keating, founder of Diolight Technology Incorporated, thought this way when he helped to invent a light bulb that lasts, on average, 6 years and 10 months if used continuously and 50 years if burned only 2 or 3 hours per day. "Once we started making them," Keating admits, "I thought all the work was done." But the difficulties faced by Diolight in selling its long-lasting bulbs demonstrate that having "a better mousetrap" is not necessarily enough. In today's competitive business world, a fully effective marketing mix is essential.

When Diolight began its sales efforts in mid-1983, it assumed that customers would rush to buy the new bulbs—even at a cost of $4.99 or $5.99. But resistance was immediately apparent from bartenders, who typically commented: "OK buddy, if this is such a great light bulb, how come GE doesn't make it?" Diolight soon came to realize that it had three problems: price, credibility, and lack of interest. Few owners of small businesses thought much about light bulbs; when they did, they were in no rush to spend $5.99 for a light bulb from a company that they had never heard of. Diolight next targeted corporate purchasing agents and began canvassing them by telephone—again with little success. Eventually, after a disappointing sales performance in its first year, Diolight finally realized that its new light bulbs were too expensive for general use. Yet these bulbs were a desirable specialty product for hard-to-reach places where it is difficult to change a bulb and for certain situations where aesthetics is especially important (as on a sign or a chandelier, where one burned-out bulb can ruin the entire effect).

Through a clever marketing campaign—with press releases promoting the "household light bulb that is guaranteed to last forever"—Diolight launched a media boom. It began with a video feature on the Cable News Network in mid-1984 and a subsequent article in *USA Today*. In 1985, Diolight's press releases led to 50 newspaper articles, 50 pieces in trade and consumer magazines, 7 television features, and 300 radio interviews with Keating. According to one Diolight executive, the chief benefit of this promotional blitz was the kind of credibility that advertising cannot buy.

By early 1986, Diolight's sales network had expanded to 125 distributors in all 50 states. In the fiscal year ending October 1, 1985, the company sold more than half a million light bulbs and generated revenues of more than $800,000. For fiscal 1986, Diolight projects unit and dollar sales twice as high. Yet, even if things continue to go well for Diolight, founder Kevin Keating will undoubtedly remember the difficult years of the mid-1980s. If pressed, he may even admit that "if you make a better light bulb, the world *will not* beat a path to your door."

Source: Tom Richman, "How Do You Sell a Light Bulb That Never Burns Out?" *Inc.,* March 1986, pp. 90–94.

does not match consumers' needs, if it is priced too high or low, if it is promoted poorly, or if it is distributed improperly. As Box 1-2 illustrates, having a good product—even an exceptional product—is no guarantee of success. To compete effectively in today's business world, marketers require a carefully planned and fully satisfactory marketing mix.

THE DEVELOPMENT OF MODERN MARKETING PHILOSOPHY

Marketing scholars have identified four main approaches to business: product orientation, sales orientation, marketing orientation, and societal marketing orientation (see Exhibit 1-1). As we will see, product and sales orientations do not place the customer at the center of an organization's strategy. Although certain firms still use these two approaches, we will view them primarily as historical phenomena.

EXHIBIT 1-1	Four Business Orientations		
Orientation	Focus	Methods	Goals
Production	Goods	Lower prices, production efficiency	Profit through high sales volume
Sales	Seller needs	Selling and promoting	Profit through high sales volume
Marketing	Customer needs	Integrated marketing	Profit through customer satisfaction
Societal marketing	Social needs	Integrated and socially responsible marketing	Profit through customer satisfaction within socially responsible constraints

☐ *Product Orientation: Make What You Know How To Make*

Exchange has taken place ever since humans agreed to satisfy their needs by means other than brute force, but it was not until the mid-eighteenth century that labor specialization and mass-production techniques brought about massive increases in productivity and lower prices for goods. From the industrial revolution until the 1920s and 1930s—often called the "production era"—the product orientation came into full flower. In this period, demand generally exceeded supply; producers could expect to sell whatever they could make.

According to the **product orientation,** consumers have little product choice. If a product is available and if consumers can afford it, they will purchase it. As a

In the early decades of the twentieth century, the key to business success was efficient production. There was so much un-satisfied demand that this kind of production orienta-tion led to success, as in this factory where Henry Ford made his famous "Model T." In today's economy, consumers are more demanding—wanting more models, body styles, and colors than the Model T offered. (Courtesy of the Ford Motor Company.)

philosophy of business, product orientation focuses primarily on a firm's own resources and products. Management strives to improve production efficiency and to lower prices in the belief that profits result from lowered manufacturing costs. One of the most famous disciples of product orientation was carmaker Henry Ford. Ford initially produced only one model in one color—the black Model T—thereby reducing his unit price and putting the customer's price within reach of many U.S. families.

More recently, makers of television sets, air conditioners, food processors, and digital watches have adopted a product orientation. These manufacturers lowered production costs—and, in turn, prices—to appeal to a wide range of consumers. Texas Instruments, for example, succeeded for a time in garnering a large share of the market for small electronic calculators by using rapidly advancing technology to lower costs and prices. However, few firms follow a pure product orientation in the 1980s. Initially, demand exceeded supply for the products mentioned above, but clever later entries in these markets quickly expanded consumers' choices and forced the original producers to shift to a sales orientation.

☐ Sales Orientation: Get Rid Of What You Have

A **sales orientation** focuses primarily on how a firm promotes and sells its products. If management is sales-oriented, it assumes that customers will not buy a product (or will not buy enough of it) unless intensive persuasive promotional efforts induce them to buy. The sales orientation had its heyday between the 1930s and 1950s, a period known as the "sales era." Except for the years during and immediately after World War II, supply generally exceeded demand during this period. Many firms developed large sales staffs and concentrated their efforts on advertising and promotion, although management continued to focus on the product rather than on consumers.

Certain industries still favor the sales approach, among them encyclopedia publishing, life insurance, and magazine subscriptions. Companies using hard-sell techniques argue that their methods "help" consumers to discover unrealized wants and needs. These firms insist that their central concern is the consumer's welfare, but the truth of this claim varies widely.

☐ Marketing Orientation: Have What You Can Get Rid Of

As an important step forward from the sales orientation, a **marketing orientation** focuses primarily on satisfying consumers' needs. This is the heart of the marketing concept: identifying and offering products that will satisfy customers. Indeed, as Peter Drucker has stated, the purpose of marketing is to make selling superfluous. According to this ideal, you should not need to persuade consumers that they want and need your product. If your marketing efforts have been on target, you will have exactly what the consumers want, and they will take the goods away from you.

Of course, this ideal is easier to write in a textbook than to put into practice in the competitive world of business. Marketers must correctly identify their **target markets** (the specific groups of consumers that they propose to serve). Then they must correctly identify what these markets want, correctly describe what is wanted to the design and production departments, and see to it that what is produced is actually what is wanted. All these steps are essential in applying a marketing orientation and satisfying the needs of consumers.

There is no doubt that as consumers people enjoy the benefits of disposable bottles and cans, and other such conveniences. But, as citizens, they do not like littered highways. The societal marketing orientation calls for managers to consider both of these issues. (Copyright © Luis Villota/The Stock Market.)

☐ *Societal Marketing Orientation: Have What You Can Get Rid Of—Responsibly*

A **societal marketing orientation** adds an additional consideration to the marketing concept: the impact of a firm's activities on society's well-being. Products (and especially the by-products of manufacturing or processing) may not always further the long-term interests of consumers even though they satisfy immediate wants. No-return bottles consume resources and intensify litter problems; refinery by-products may pollute the atmosphere; certain processed foods have little nutritional value.

The last two decades have seen wide and sometimes intense debate regarding the possible negative effects of marketing on society as a whole and on individuals. It is unfortunate but true that socially responsible marketing can be costly. Automobile pollution controls, for example, are expensive to manufacture and install. Additional production costs lead to higher prices for consumers and lower profits for manufacturers. Moreover, companies may find it difficult to compete in the marketplace if they fail to produce popular (but possibly harmful) goods. Many consumers *want* no-return bottles and processed foods with little nutrition. If firms reduce their profit goals, they may endanger their survival and thus cause harm to their stockholders (who are also consumers).[17]

Some firms have attempted to implement the societal marketing concept by considering the needs of all their "stakeholders"—that is, all persons who have a stake in the business. Among these stakeholders are *c*onsumers, *o*wners, the *p*ublic, and the firm's *e*mployees: These companies recognize the need to *cope* with all four groups.

Perhaps the best hope for an acceptable compromise between the goal of social responsibility and the need for profits lies in the combined efforts of businesses and consumers. For their part, consumers must learn to think realistically about the difficulties of making and selling products that have no negative side effects. When the public wants and is ready to pay for air bags to protect automobile passengers during accidents, automakers will undoubtedly produce cars with air bags. However, marketers must learn to regard societal concerns as opportunities rather than problems. In the future, some innovative marketers may reap handsome profits by offering new and improved products that enhance societal well-being while satisfying the immediate needs of consumers.

■ *CLARIFYING SOME KEY CONCEPTS* ■

Even if the formal study of marketing is new to you, your everyday experiences as a consumer have undoubtedly given you certain knowledge and opinions about products, salespeople, advertising, brand names, and other aspects of marketing. Many of these facts and opinions may be accurate, but others may need clarification. Be wary as you study marketing, because many conclusions that seem common sense reflect much research, thought, and hard work.

☐ *Customers and Consumers*

Consider a manufacturer of candy bars, say, Hershey. This marketer competes with Mars and other producers of sweets. Who are Hershey's customers and consumers? Discussion of the marketing of consumer products traditionally identifies the consumers as the end users of the product purchased (those persons who buy and eat Hershey bars). By contrast, the customers are the wholesalers, retail stores, and chains in which consumer products such as Hershey bars are displayed. Marketers view these intermediaries as "customers" because their sales staffs can call on customers directly.

If you asked consumers of Hershey bars what their real needs are, you might get answers relating to sweetness, chocolate, or just "yummy." However, if you asked Hershey's customers what their real needs are, many might tell you about profit per square foot of display space. Marketers of consumer products must satisfy both consumers and customers if the overall marketing mix is to be successful.

The need to understand the differences between consumers and customers is no less important in the marketing of industrial products. Consider a marketer of audio-visual equipment to a college or university. The consumer/end user in this case is the faculty member who uses the equipment in teaching. The customer is the college's purchasing department. They have different needs, and marketers must pay attention to both.

☐ Marketing and Selling

Isn't "marketing" just a fancy word for selling? Actually, this is a common misconception. Selling is the process of persuading someone to do something—buy whatever you wish to sell. Marketing, however, requires figuring out what people want and then having it available when and where they need it.

Selling relies on a short-range philosophy: How do you get the consumer to buy what is currently available? Marketing takes a long-range view: How can you change the product or service to more effectively meet the needs of consumers? Similarly, selling tends to be rather narrowly focused on what can be done to promote the product. Marketing involves research structured to find out what consumers want, what segments of the market exist, and how the product should be distributed, priced, and promoted. These fundamental differences illustrate that marketing is *not* a fancy word for selling; it is a dramatically different, much more complex, long-range philosophy of business.

☐ Macromarketing and Micromarketing

Theoreticians who measure, explain, and predict the performance of national and international economies—focusing on the relationships among large units within these systems—are known as **macroeconomists.** They study such factors as the total income of all laborers or the total number of persons employed throughout the U.S. economy. Macroeconomists at the Federal Reserve Board attempt to predict how increasing the nation's money supply will affect inflation, or how government borrowing will affect borrowing by private business.

Certain marketing scholars also analyze phenomena on a grand scale—looking, for example, at the buying behavior of homeowners or the effects of internal population shifts on the supermarket industry. **Macromarketers** examine processes whereby exchanges are created to satisfy the needs and wants of individuals and organizations within a national marketing system. Figure 1-4 shows such a system of individuals and groups (such as consumers, investors, workers, business firms, and government); of markets (product and resource markets); and of flows (resources, goods and services, money, and information).

In the national marketing system of the United States, consumers who want goods and services go to product markets to purchase them (in exchange for money). Consumers get their money by going to resource markets, where they exchange their resources (labor, land, capital) for income (wages, rent, interest, and dividends). The U.S. business firms produce what consumers want in much the same way. They go to resource markets for capital, labor, and raw materials; then they sell their products to consumers in exchange for money (which the sellers also need).

All the exchanges within a national marketing system depend on communication. Sellers need to know what consumers want; consumers need to know what products are available, where they can be purchased, and at what price. Sellers and consumers also need information to make exchanges in resource markets. Moreover, this flow among individuals and groups must include the government. To varying degrees, government regulates the numerous exchange processes, provides a number of services (such as law enforcement and Social Security), and collects taxes to pay for its services. Exchange, therefore, is at the heart of a national marketing system. All the individuals and groups who enter resource and product markets are seeking to exchange what they have in return for utility and satisfaction.

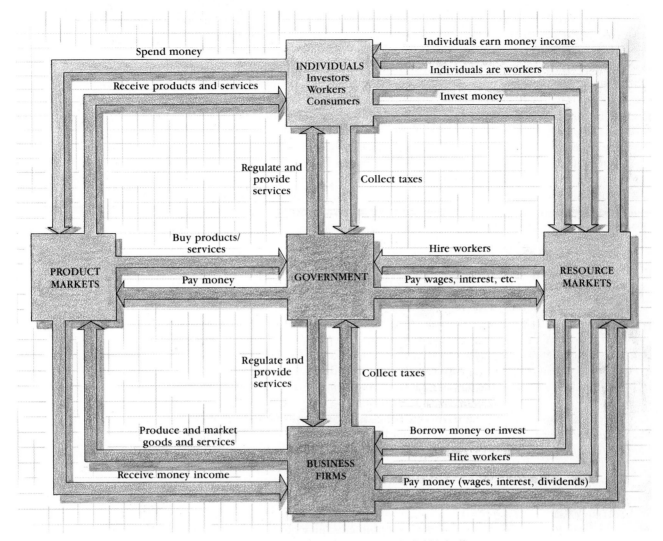

Figure 1-4 *National marketing system.* In the U.S. marketing system, individuals (functioning as investors, workers, and consumers), business firms, and governments interact not only with each other but also with product markets and resource markets.

In contrast to macromarketing, **micromarketing** deals with how individual organizations solve their particular marketing problems. Examples of micromarketing include Procter & Gamble's introduction of a new brand of soap, and K mart's decision to reduce its prices on more expensive items. This book focuses on the micromarketing decisions of individual companies and organizations.

☐ *Competition*

A special note concerning competition will help you to better understand marketing. As noted throughout this chapter, the marketing process can be followed by any organization, including not-for-profit groups. However, marketing has had and continues to have its major expression within the private sector.

The extent to which marketing has been accepted as the driving force in the business world is directly related to the extent to which competitive forces are operating. In an industry where government regulation limits competition—as when airline fares and routes were dictated by the government—you find an industry with little need for marketing. Where you find an organization whose customers are "captive"—as residents are in an area with only one hospital—you will not find marketing thinking. However, where you find any industry (or not-for-profit organization) whose consumers and clients are free to choose among competing groups for their time, money, or attention, there will certainly be marketing.

Deregulation of such industries as banking and airlines has brought a noticeable increase in use of the marketing concept. More than ever, marketing stands as the dominant philosophy of business in the United States and is becoming more influential across the world. With this in mind, the importance of studying marketing should be quite apparent.

■ OVERVIEW OF THE BOOK ■

Contemporary marketing involves a dynamic set of actions by a large number of participants: buyers and sellers, advertisers and readers, merchants and wholesalers, and many more persons. Because the marketplace is constantly changing, any attempt to pick it apart and closely examine one element must be somewhat artificial even if necessary in writing a textbook. As you study individual chapters and topics in this book, keep in mind the larger picture of the complex, competitive business world.

The logic and organization of this book is based on the managerial marketing process. As noted earlier, this process has four basic steps: (1) analysis of the market and the environment; (2) planning for the marketing actions of the organization, (3) implementing marketing plans, and (4) controlling steps to determine if marketing goals have been met.

☐ Analysis

The major subjects of *analysis* are the environments in which an organization operates, the needs and wants of consumers and organizational buyers, and their buying behavior. Chapter 2 explores the changing environments of marketing—populations, the economy, culture, political and legal issues, and others. It focuses on the firm's need to monitor those environments.

The next three chapters discuss the analysis of markets. Chapters 3 and 4 deal with consumer behavior, including the social and cultural forces which help explain such behavior, and the ways in which ultimate consumers—individuals and households—go about making consumption decisions. Chapter 5 is devoted to the buying behavior of organizational buyers—in business, industry, and government, where buying is not for personal reasons, but for carrying out organizational objectives.

The final chapter in the analysis part of the book focuses on the process of gathering information which is the subject of analysis. Marketing research and information system design is critical to effective customer-oriented marketing.

☐ Planning

The second part of the book deals with the use of the analyses carried out in the process of *planning* marketing mix programs. Planning begins with the process of segmenting large, dissimilar markets into smaller, more similar groups—the topic of Chapter 7. Also included in that chapter is a discussion of positioning products—primarily concerned with how competitive products or brands are perceived by consumers.

Following that are two chapters on the planning process itself. Chapter 8 treats the high-level strategic planning process of the total organization, but concentrates primarily on the role of marketing in that total-company process of setting organizational-level strategies and goals. This is followed by Chapter 9, which deals with the more tactical-level planning of the elements of the marketing mix programs themselves.

☐ *Implementation*

The bulk of this book—Chapters 10 through 21—focuses on *implementation*, or what people *do* to make marketing work. Implementation is explained in terms of the four elements of the marketing mix: product, distribution, pricing, and promotion. The first two chapters are devoted to the management and development of products—they emphasize that products include not just physical goods, but also services and ideas.

Chapters 12, 13, and 14 discuss the second marketing mix element, distribution. The building blocks of marketing channels of distribution are the many institutions, predominantly wholesalers and retailers, that are available to play their role in the marketing process. Chapter 12 sets out the structure of institutions, and the process of welding those institutions into effective channels is the topic of Chapter 13. Chapter 14 is devoted to the physical distribution of products, such as transporting and storage of inventories.

The third element of marketing mix programs is that of pricing. Chapter 15 reviews an economic theory of pricing that is particularly useful for the actual price determination process, which is the topic of Chapter 16.

The final aspect of implementation is that of promotion—the efforts marketers make to communicate with the market. The overall promotion process, as well as some specialized promotional methods, make up Chapter 17. Chapter 18 focuses specifically on advertising, the major method of mass communication used by marketers. The personal selling process is the topic of the next two chapters. Chapter 19 considers the process from the point of view of the sales manager, and Chapter 20 deals with the role of the individual who is the closest to the customer, the sales representative, or as we will refer to the role, the manager of a sales territory.

☐ *Control*

Chapter 21 is devoted to the means by which organizations *control* the marketing process. It discusses the need to see how well the organization is able to achieve its goals and objectives. This chapter, then, completes the cycle that underlies the structure of the book—analysis, planning, implementation, and control.

The final part of the book is devoted to discussion of how marketing is, or should be, practiced in some special settings. Chapter 22 discusses some of the major problems and opportunities of marketing on a global basis. Finally, Chapter 23 presents a discussion of how marketing is beginning to make headway in some newer settings. Many organizations, mostly in the not-for-profit sector of the economy, have just begun to realize the power of the marketing concept. They are the focus of the last chapter.

SUMMARY

1. The marketing philosophy of business assumes that an organization can best survive and prosper by identifying and satisfying the needs of its customers.
2. In marketing terms, a product may be a tangible good, an intangible benefit in the form of a service, or even an idea that offers some benefit.
3. Marketing scholars have identified four types of utility associated with a product's form, place, time, and possession.
4. According to Peter Drucker, the only valid definition of business purpose is to create a customer.
5. Theodore Levitt called on organizations to clearly define their businesses and to focus on markets (consumers) rather than products.
6. Thomas Peters insists that care of customers and constant innovation characterize truly excellent companies.
7. The marketing concept has three basic conditions: (1) the organization must truly believe in the customer's importance; (2) the organization must integrate its marketing efforts; and (3) management must accept the assumption that profits will follow consumer satisfaction.
8. The marketing mix includes the four major elements of marketing programs: product conception (and development), pricing decisions, promotion of the product, and distribution to consumers.
9. A societal marketing orientation adds an additional consideration to the marketing concept: the impact of a firm's activities on society's well-being.
10. The marketing managerial process has four basic steps: (1) analysis of the market and the environment; (2) planning for the marketing actions of the organization; (3) implementing marketing plans; and (4) controlling steps to determine if marketing goals have been met.
11. The extent to which marketing has been accepted as the driving force in the business world is directly related to the extent to which competitive forces are operating.

☐ Key Terms

exchange	marketing mix	product orientation
form utility	marketing orientation	sales orientation
macroeconomists	micromarketing	societal marketing orientation
macromarketers	place utility	time utility
marketing	possession utility	utility
marketing concept	product	

☐ Chapter Review

1. Why would many agree with Peter Drucker's statement that IBM is an example of the power of marketing?
2. Explain why not-for-profit organizations should be concerned about effective marketing.
3. Why do we use the term "product" to apply to more than physical goods?
4. What is the marketing responsibility for providing form, time, place, and possession utilities?
5. What does the phrase "marketing myopia" mean?
6. How does a marketing orientation differ from production, sales, and societal marketing orientations?
7. Describe the four elements of the marketing mix.
8. Distinguish between consumers and customers.
9. What are the major differences between selling and marketing?
10. How does macromarketing differ from micromarketing?

☐ *References*

1. Peter F. Drucker, *People and Performance* (New York: Harper's College, 1977), p. 91.
2. Thomas J. Peters and Robert H. Waterman, Jr., *In Search of Excellence* (New York: Harper & Row, 1982), p. 159.
3. "Sears' Sizzling New Vitality," *Time,* Aug. 20, 1984, pp. 82–90.
4. Peter F. Drucker, *Management: Tasks, Responsibilities, Practices* (New York: Harper & Row, 1974), p. 61.
5. Drucker, op. cit., p. 91.
6. Theodore Levitt, "Marketing Myopia," *Harvard Business Review,* July–Aug. 1960.
7. Theodore Levitt, *The Marketing Mode* (New York: McGraw-Hill, 1969), p. 1.
8. Levitt, op. cit., p. 45.
9. Peters and Waterman, op. cit.
10. Thomas J. Peters and Nancy Austin, *A Passion for Excellence* (New York: Random House, 1985).
11. Peters and Waterman, op. cit., p. 156.
12. Peters and Austin, op. cit., p. 4.
13. Ernest F. Cooke, C. L. Abercrombie, and J. Michael Rayburn, "Problems with the AMA's new definition of marketing offer opportunity to develop an even better definition," *Marketing Educator*, vol. 5, no. 2, Spring 1986, p. 1.
14. Franklin S. Houston, "The Marketing Concept: What It Is and What It Is Not," *Journal of Marketing*, vol. 50, Apr. 1986, pp. 81–87.
15. Peter C. Riesz, "Revenge of the Marketing Concept," *Business Horizons*, June 1980, pp. 49–53; Roger C. Bennett and Robert G. Cooper, "The Misuses of Marketing: An American Tragedy," *Business Horizons*, Nov.–Dec. 1981, pp. 51–61.
16. Benson P. Shapiro, "Rejuvenating the Marketing Mix," *Harvard Business Review*, Sept.–Oct. 1985, pp. 28 ff.
17. John F. Gaski, "Dangerous Territory: The Societal Marketing Concept Revisited," *Business Horizons*, July–Aug. 1985, pp. 42–47.

PART

ONE

ANALYSIS FOR MARKETING PLANNING

Analysis separates a whole into its distinctive parts for individual study; it is necessarily the first step in applying the marketing concept. Before marketers can devise their plans and act on them, they must focus on markets and gather information to analyze what buyers need and want.

Chapter 2 looks outside the marketing organization to examine the marketing environments that most marketers face but do not directly control. The chapter emphasizes the need to manage change and to monitor trends in these external environments. Six marketing environments are explored in detail: demographics, the economy, technology, politics and the law, culture, and competition.

Chapters 3 through 5 describe market analysis. In particular, Chapters 3 and 4 examine social and psychological influences on consumers' buying decisions through an interdisciplinary approach; these chapters survey contemporary theory and research from the disciplines of cultural anthropology, sociology, and psychology. Chapter 5 goes beyond analysis of consumer markets to characterize the buying decisions of organizations.

Finally, Chapter 6 shows how marketers collect and use information; it explores the techniques, procedures, and findings of marketing analysis. Although properly devised research is the foundation of analysis, the results of any research must be integrated into the organization's entire marketing information system, thereby linking the analysis phase to planning.

2

MONITORING THE ENVIRONMENT

Copyright © Jon Feingersh 1986/The Stock Market.

SPOTLIGHT ON

☐ How controllable and uncontrollable variables affect marketing

☐ The importance of managing change

☐ The difficulties of monitoring the marketing environment

☐ Analyzing the projected effects of demographic shifts, economic trends, technological advances, government legislation, cultural changes, and competitive plans and actions

The future of the U.S. tobacco industry is quite uncertain: The surgeon general and other health officials have issued increasingly serious warnings about the perils of cigarette smoking, and smoking is being banned in a growing number of workplaces, restaurants, and retail stores. Although cigarette smoking and tobacco production will not be outlawed in the immediate future, a long-range reduction in cigarette sales is likely.

These developments have been followed carefully by managers of the two giants of the tobacco industry: Philip Morris (which offers Marlboro, Benson & Hedges, Merit, and Virginia Slims cigarettes) and R. J. Reynolds (best-known for Winston, Salem, and Camel cigarettes). Both tobacco producers have been working for some years to reduce their dependence on cigarette sales. Philip Morris owns the Miller Brewing Company, and R. J. Reynolds is the parent company of Del Monte Foods, Heublein (liquors), and Kentucky Fried Chicken. In 1985, the North Carolina–based firm paid almost $5 billion to acquire the food giant Nabisco Brands. Not to be outdone, Philip Morris spent over $5 billion to acquire Nabisco's competitor, General Foods.

By looking ahead, anticipating changes, and taking early and decisive actions, managers at R. J. Reynolds and Philip Morris are attempting to ensure healthy futures for their companies. They are well aware that consumers may stop smoking but are unlikely to stop eating.

Source: Christy Marshall and Mitchell J. Shields, "PM Challenges RJR to a Retail Food Fight," *Adweek,* Oct. 7, 1985, pp. 1, 4.

Humans are unique in that they wonder about, anticipate, and plan for the future. They even study the strange world of history to learn from the past. Humans try to shape their own destinies; sometimes they succeed, and sometimes they do not.

Like the managers and planners at Philip Morris and R. J. Reynolds, college students must constantly adjust to changes, look ahead, and make choices. A student's faculty adviser may suddenly accept a position at another school; a nearby university may begin a new and attractive program for transfer students; the nation's business schools may decide that all applicants should meet stiffer requirements for admission. As they plan for their careers and later lives, college students can control *some* of the changing forces and circumstances around them, and in some cases they can find ways to adapt to those factors which are beyond their immediate control.

We begin Chapter 2 by explaining why marketing organizations must distinguish between controllable and uncontrollable variables. We then summarize the importance of management of change, which is based on monitoring the "environments—or marketing arenas—in which uncontrollable forces operate. The remainder of the chapter describes marketing's major external environments: demographics, the economy, technology, politics and legal considerations, culture, and competition. Throughout Chapter 2, we focus on how managers study these environmental forces and incorporate their resulting knowledge into their planning efforts.

CONTROLLABLE AND UNCONTROLLABLE VARIABLES

Those in charge of marketing Jell-O desserts at Philip Morris's General Foods unit have a great deal of control over their product, their distribution, their pricing, and their promotion—the elements that make up Jell-O's marketing mix. They also control their choice of target markets (consumers), suppliers, and their own objectives and organization. **Controllable variables** are directly or primarily under the control of the marketing organization. General Foods can add a new flavor to the Jell-O line, raise or lower the product's price, add or drop distributors, and hire and fire advertising agencies. They can even choose to stop making and selling Jell-O (highly unlikely) and devote their resources to other products.

Marketing mix factors are considered variable because they can be changed in response to changes in the firm's external environment. **Uncontrollable variables** are forces outside the organization over which managers have little or no control over the short term. We group uncontrollable variables into several environments—marketing arenas with some common characteristics. Economic recessions, changes in consumer tastes, and new competitive products are examples of uncontrollable variables.

Marketers do not simply throw up their hands in despair when faced with uncontrollable variables. They keep careful tabs on trends in external environments and lay out plans to deal with various possibilities. In an economic recession, Jell-O's marketing managers know they will face consumer price resistance and the need for stringent cost controls on their entire marketing mix. By contrast, prosperity may present opportunities for introduction of new products and expansion into new international markets. External variables may not be controllable, but they can be "managed" by anticipating and planning for change. As Zeithaml and Zeithaml suggest, managers should not view their environments as uncontrollable; rather, managers should be proactive (that is, entrepreneurial) in their management of change.[1]

THE MANAGEMENT OF CHANGE

One foundation of good marketing is the effective management of change. In spite of the serious warnings that the rapid rate of change in the modern world threatens us all with "future shock," the better managed companies *manage* change instead of being *shocked* by it.[2]

Change occurs more rapidly than it used to. Only 50 years ago (a short time in the history of humanity), there were no jet airplanes, television sets, communications satellites, laser beams, or computers. The two-parent family was the norm; the U.S. dollar was the world's monetary standard; the policies of world governments, although changeable, evolved more slowly. Social and cultural institutions seemed stable, and fewer competitors sought the consumer's dollar.

Writers Peter Drucker and Alvin Toffler foresaw this ever-increasing rate of change. For the most part, they predicted correctly that organizations would have to respond quickly to change. In periods of great change, organizations must be responsive, or they will miss opportunities and face threats to their existence.

Marketing managers, like most people, are too apt to view a change in their environments as a crisis, portending threat or danger, but managers would do well to recall that the Chinese language represents the concept of crisis through a combination of two characters—one signifies danger, and the other signifies opportunity. Managers should anticipate not only the threats inherent in change but also the new opportunities.

Change can be predicted only through active monitoring of external environments and identifying of the forces most likely to bring about environmental change. With this in mind, high-level executives attempt to anticipate and manage change in line with the marketing concept of keeping products attuned to the needs and desires of customers.[3]

■ THE NEED TO MONITOR ENVIRONMENTS ■

At its best, **environmental monitoring** consists of a systematic group of activities designed to anticipate changes in external variables that will affect the organization's ability to meet its goals. Of a firm's many functions, marketing is most directly

Change is the only constant. The technological change that brought the first crude sound into isolated farms early in the century continues to progress. The early TV sets of the 1940s, with their small-sized black and white pictures, had become full-screen color sets by the mid-sixties, but were still expensive. The cost of electronic equipment has now dropped so that many college students have not only their own TVs, but compact disk stereos, tape decks, and other electronics. (Clockwise from top, left: National Archives; Culver Pictures; Jonathan Lipkin; The Bettmann Archive.)

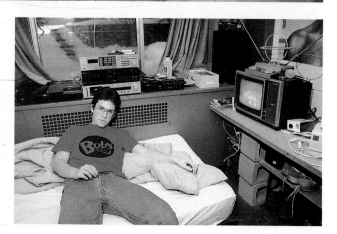

affected by environmental factors. Marketing is specifically charged with the responsibility of dealing with the world outside the organization, and most important are the consumers or organizational buyers. In general, the competitive pressures of the external environment are first experienced in marketing and then reverberate into other departments such as production or finance. Consequently, marketing assumes responsibility for external monitoring in most organizations.

External variables affect an organization both directly and through its customers. In fact, an underlying aim of environmental scanning is to forecast just how change will influence buyers' perceptions and behaviors. To practice the marketing concept, organizations increasingly must provide for formal environmental monitoring. As an example, economic conditions, government regulations, and competition have combined to produce wide-ranging changes in how U.S. consumers seek health care. Those hospitals that foresaw the rise of health maintenance organizations (HMOs), neighborhood clinics, and excess bed capacity are far ahead of their competitors in attracting patients and adjusting the services they offer to changing consumer needs.

■ THE MONITORING PROCESS ■

In Figure 2-1, we use the example of a cola marketer to illustrate the steps through which a firm proceeds in determining which environmental variables it should monitor. Each variable will be more or less important to different firms. Once a firm has decided which variables it will monitor, the company then must assess important trends. In the example presented, the cola marketer has identified growing concern about body weight as a major social trend that could impact on target markets. This trend is projected (the number of weight-conscious consumers will reach z millions by 1994), and its impact is assessed in terms of both problems (sales of regular cola will drop) and opportunities (sales of low-calorie cola may increase). Ideally, the environmental monitoring process guides the marketer into specific decisions that avoid problems and exploit opportunities (in this case, by introducing a new diet cola).

Environmental monitoring can become extremely complex. Marketers may wish to study literally hundreds of economic variables (interest rates, unemployment data, and so forth) and dozens of technological or cultural variables. Consequently, many firms employ special experts—for example, John Naisbitt, author of the popular book *Megatrends*—to assist them in this monitoring process. (Note, however, that many businesspeople question the need for such "expert advice.")[4]

Clearly, it is impossible to carefully monitor hundreds of potential variables. Marketers must determine which variables are most important for their particular industries and firms to monitor.[5] For example, two of the leading firms marketing office furniture are Herman Miller and Steelcase. Both companies are especially interested in general trends affecting the industry, studying measures of such variables as white-collar employment and new building permits. Both firms also monitor the competitive environment by studying each other.

In the following sections, we will discuss six external environments separately, although their effects on marketing organizations and consumers are most often combined (see Figure 2-2). Certain forces are more relevant to a particular organization than others, but few marketers can ignore the continuing changes presented by these external variables.

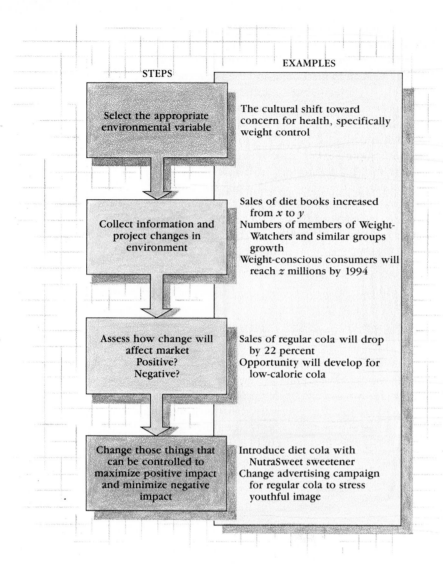

STEPS	EXAMPLES
Select the appropriate environmental variable	The cultural shift toward concern for health, specifically weight control
Collect information and project changes in environment	Sales of diet books increased from x to y Numbers of members of Weight-Watchers and similar groups growth Weight-conscious consumers will reach z millions by 1994
Assess how change will affect market Positive? Negative?	Sales of regular cola will drop by 22 percent Opportunity will develop for low-calorie cola
Change those things that can be controlled to maximize positive impact and minimize negative impact	Introduce diet cola with NutraSweet sweetener Change advertising campaign for regular cola to stress youthful image

Figure 2-1 *The process of environmental monitoring.* In beginning environmental monitoring, a marketer must examine the hundreds of forces outside the control of the firm and must carefully select those which will impact the firm's business. Data must then be collected and built into a forecast of the chosen trend, suggesting where that environment is heading. Next the marketer will try to assess what impacts—both positive and negative—that change will have on the market under study. Finally, the firm will consider what actions it can take to alter the controllable factors—product, price, distribution, and promotion—to maximize the positive impact of the change and minimize the negative impact. Through such activities, a marketer engages in management of change.

THE DEMOGRAPHIC ENVIRONMENT

We begin with a look at the external variable most directly reflective of consumers: **Demography** is the study of the changing characteristics of human populations—factors such as vital statistics, growth, size, density, and distribution. **Demographics** is a catchall term referring to population studies and their statistical results. Marketers are vitally concerned with analysis of demographic trends, since people are the most important component of every market. These demographic trends are used to forecast changes in consumer behavior.[6]

Of the various environments that we will discuss, the demographic environment is the easiest to monitor with some accuracy. Believable data are readily available, and most demographic changes are predictable over a relatively long time. For example, using data from the U.S. Bureau of the Census, university and college administrators can predict certain characteristics of their target market approximately 18 years in advance. Marketers of almost all products have time to respond

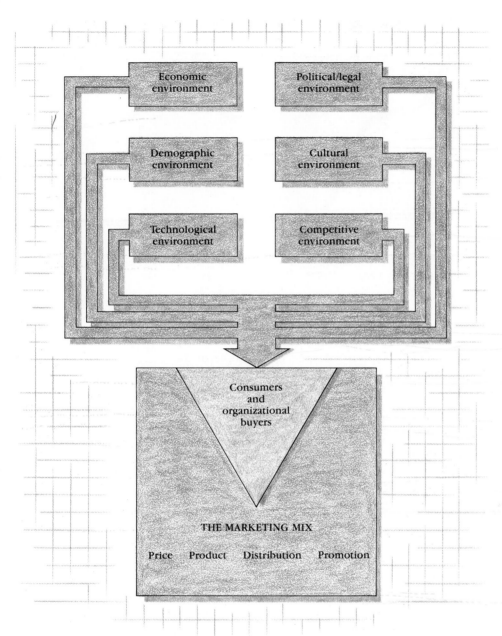

Economic environment

Political/legal environment

Demographic environment

Cultural environment

Technological environment

Competitive environment

Consumers
and
organizational
buyers

THE MARKETING MIX

Price   Product   Distribution   Promotion

Figure 2-2 *The external environments of marketing.* The external environments (uncontrollable variables) affect both potential buyers and the marketing organization itself. Modern marketers monitor and analyze trends in these environments to manage change.

to demographic changes because they evolve more slowly than do changes in other environments.

Hundreds of demographic characteristics can be and are measured and studied. Demographic data can be obtained for such wide-ranging issues as the number of babies born to currently incarcerated females, the county location of U.S. households in which the first language is Chinese, or the number of deaths by drowning in the home. For purposes of this discussion, we have chosen to analyze three variables that are central to marketing planning: births and population growth, shifting age structure, and where people choose to live. In Chapter 3, we will look at another demographic variable, changing household composition.

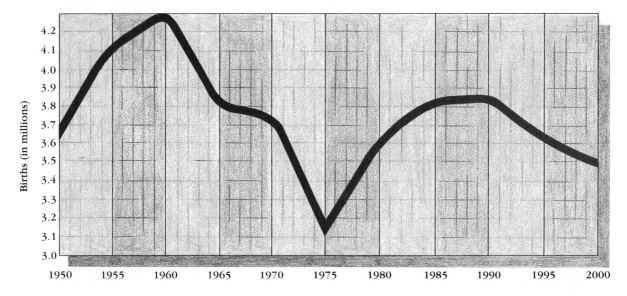

Population Size

The most fundamental demographic statistic is the size of the overall population—which directly reflects the birthrate and death rate. The **birthrate** of the United States—the number of births that occur in a given year per 1000 people in the population—has fluctuated dramatically in the last 40 years. As Figure 2-3 indicates, the number of births reached a high point in 1960, producing what is known as the "baby-boom" generation (those people now in their late twenties to mid-forties). As a result of changing attitudes toward family size, the introduction of reliable contraceptives, and the legalization of abortion, the number of births dropped to a low of a little over 3 million per year in 1975. Since that time, the large baby-boom generation has reached child-bearing age, and the number of births per year has gradually increased. Beginning around 1990, the Census Bureau projects another decline in the birthrate of the United States.

According to current forecasts, the population of the United States will continue to rise, reaching the 300 million figure around the year 2030 (see Figure 2-4). This forecast is based on three assumptions:

- The **fertility rate** of the United States—the average number of births per woman—will stabilize at 2.1 births, approximately the replacement level.
- The **death rate**—the number of deaths that occur in a given year per 1000 people in the population—will decline. Effective medical care and improved health practices will allow more Americans to live longer lives.
- Immigration into the United States will remain stable at slightly fewer than 500,000 persons per year. Most immigrants will come from Latin America and Asia.

Although population growth has slowed in the world's technologically advanced nations, the growth rate in the world's developing nations is projected at more than 2 percent per year. If such growth continues, the world population is expected to double from the 1977 figure of 4.1 billion to over 8 billion by about 2010.

Few marketers can consider the entire population of the world—or of a single nation—as a target market. Infants cannot buy stocks and bonds or exercise equip-

Figure 2-3 *U.S. births: 1950 to 2000 (projected).* The number of births in any year forecasts the consumption of diapers for the immediate future, university enrollments for about 18 years later, and, as the figure shows, the number of births (occurring in the late 1970s and 1980s) to women who were part of the U.S. baby boom in the late 1940s and early 1950s. (From U.S. Bureau of the Census.)

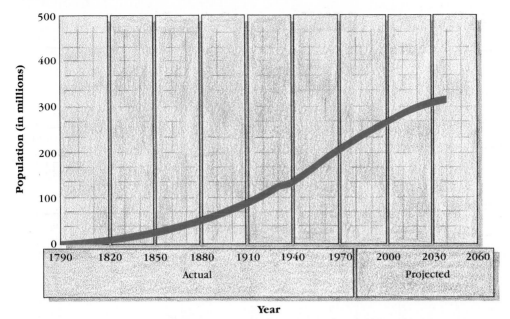

Figure 2-4 *U.S. population growth for selected years: 1790–2040 (projected).* The U.S. Bureau of the Census bases population projections on three different estimated fertility rates (noted on the figure as Series 1, Series 2, and Series 3). Depending on which proves to be most accurate, the nation's population could reach 400 million persons by the year 2030 or could hold at a much lower figure of about 250 million persons. The middle line on the chart, assuming 2.1 births per woman, seems to represent the most realistic projection: a population of 300 million Americans in the year 2030. (From U.S. Bureau of the Census.)

ment; the elderly purchase few rock music videos. Consequently, marketers focus on the numbers of people in age groups who are the predominant buyers of their products. Burger King and Wendy's do not add food outlets because the overall U.S. population is growing; rather, they add outlets where the number of families with young children and teenagers is growing.

☐ *Age Structure*

Articles in the mass media frequently refer to the "graying of America" to point out that the United States is growing older, that is, the proportion of older people in the U.S. population is increasing while the proportion of young people is declining. Figure 2-5 projects the changing age composition of the nation through the year 2000.

The population is also graying in other advanced nations of the world such as Great Britain, Japan, and most of the northern European and Scandinavian countries. In West Germany, for example, the median age of the population is already 37. As medical technology spreads, health care improves, and the use of contraceptives is more widely accepted, birthrates of developing nations will decrease, and the average age of their populations will rise.

Marketers face difficulties in developing products geared to older persons. In general, retirement incomes are lower than those earned in earlier years, leaving many elderly Americans with few discretionary funds. In addition, many older men and women are in better health than elders of previous generations; as a result,

Improvements in health care have led to longer lives, and thus more elderly people in our society. These same changes in health care, as well as changes in attitudes, have led many grandparents out of the rocking chair and into the street. The *quality* of these longer lives is changing. (Copyright 1984 Sylvia Johnson/ Woodfin Camp & Assoc.)

they are likely to prolong "youthful" lifestyles and buying behaviors. Finally, products specifically viewed (or labeled) as "for the elderly" may carry the burden of **ageism** (prejudice and discrimination against the elderly) in a society which reveres youth and sees aging as a negative and frightening experience.

☐ *Geographic Centers of Population*

In recent years, three important trends in population movement have become apparent in the United States. First, the southern and western states are experiencing more population growth than is the rest of the nation (see Figure 2-6). This trend is expected to continue, though the rate of growth in the South and the West may slow somewhat. Through the year 2000, the states of Wyoming, Nevada, Arizona, Utah, Florida, and Texas will experience the largest gains in population. Significant population losses will be evident in Washington, D.C., New York, Pennsylvania, and Massachusetts.

Second, we are an increasingly mobile people. It is estimated that, in any year, one out of five Americans changes residences. Between 1975 and 1980, 46.4 percent of people over 5 years old moved. People between the ages of 20 and 29 were most likely to move.

Third, much internal migration takes place between metropolitan areas, suburbs, and nonmetropolitan areas. Americans are still moving into central cities, but about twice as many people leave central cities as enter them. In general, the pattern of migration is away from central cities to the suburbs and then on to the "exurbs" even farther away.

Although demographic changes are significant mostly for the long term, they must be carefully monitored by marketers. If a change in demographic patterns is identified early, an organization can adjust its marketing strategy and plans. Population shifts are important to industrial product marketers and even more important to marketers of consumer products. After all, marketers have to go where their customers are.

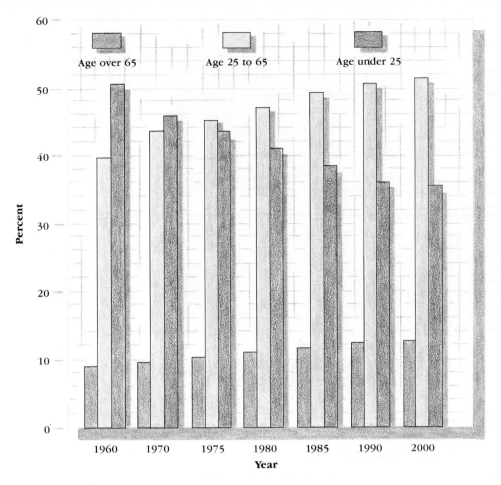

Figure 2-5 *Age distribution of U.S. population from 1960 to 1984 and projections to 2000.* According to projections, the proportion of Americans aged 65 years and over will continue to rise in the period 1985 to 2000; the proportion of Americans under 25 years of age will continue to decline. (Data from U.S. Bureau of the Census, *Statistical Abstract of the United States, 1986,* 106th ed., 1985, pp. 24–25.)

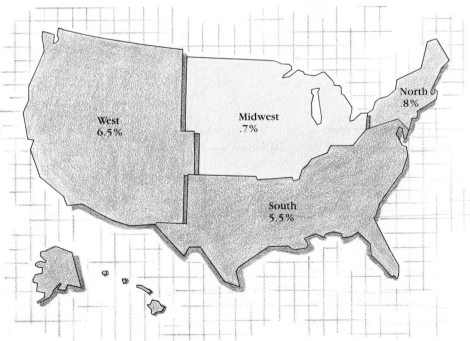

Figure 2-6 *Regional change in population.* Marketers need to know where their customers are and how to get products to them, and therefore they study carefully data on regional population changes. The illustration shows the percent change of the U.S. resident population from 1980 to 1983. (U.S. Bureau of the Census, *Statistical Abstract of the United States, 1986, 106th ed., 1985,* p. xvii.)

One major demographic change has made scenes like this one very common. Moving from one city to another is common; but moving from one house to another has increased even more. (Copyright © George Ancona/International Stock Photo.)

Note that a major population shift, such as the migration to the Sunbelt, has enormous impact on the types of products that consumers need. People moving from Minnesota or Maine to Arizona will not need heavy coats or heating systems; they will need air conditioners and suntan oil. Moreover, people tend to adopt the prevailing tastes of their new communities. In California, slightly half of all automobiles sold are imports, although the national figure is only 27 percent. Thus, when transplanted easterners and southerners living in California find that they need new cars, they may decide that an import is preferable.

ECONOMIC ENVIRONMENT

In Chapter 15, we will examine the impact of economic laws and theories on price setting within the individual organization. Here, we take a broader, but simple and selective, look at the larger effects of the economy—the macroeconomic environment—on marketing organizations.

From industry to industry and from firm to firm, the meaning and actual effect of different factors and indicators in the economic environment will vary. To complicate matters, economists and statisticians follow hundreds of variables in the macroenvironment and often project trends with sophisticated mathematical models. We have chosen three of the most fundamental economic variables to investigate, variables that affect the ability of almost all firms to market their products: the gross national product, consumers' disposable and discretionary incomes, and interest and inflation rates. Although we look at these economic indicators primarily as they affect the macroeconomic environment of the United States, these indicators are used as signposts by economists in all countries.

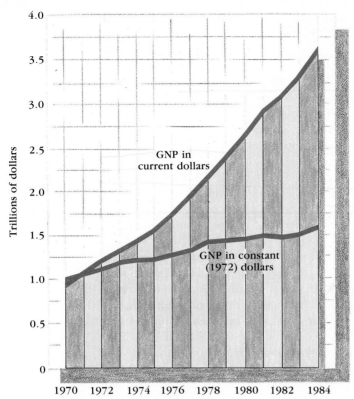

Figure 2-7 *Gross national product in current and constant dollars.* Gross national product (GNP) is a very broad and general indicator of the health of the nation's economy. When measured in current dollars, the GNP reflects actual prices as they exist in each year. Measurement in constant dollars reflects the actual data adjusted to the prices of an arbitrarily chosen previous year. The GNP does not measure a number of factors important to marketers, such as income or ability to buy. It is the figure most frequently cited to express the total activity of an economy. (From U.S. Bureau of the Census, *Statistical Abstract of the United States, 1986,* 106th ed., 1985, p. 392.)

☐ *Gross National Product*

Since the 1930s, the U.S. Department of Commerce has been charged with charting the nation's financial health. The most fundamental measure of the economy's over-all performance is the **gross national product (GNP)**—the total market value of all goods and services produced in an economy in a given year.

The GNP is typically expressed in two ways. Measured in **current dollars,** the GNP reflects actual prices as they exist each year; measured in **constant dollars,** GNP reflects the actual data adjusted to the prices of an arbitrarily chosen previous year. Figure 2-7 charts the movement of the GNP of the United States in both current and constant dollars. The use of constant dollars compensates for the effects of inflation (the long-run, upward trend of prices above the real value of output) and thus allows a more direct view of economic growth.

Although GNP is a very broad indicator of the state of the nation's economy, it has significant drawbacks. It does not take into account the growth of leisure time, the quality and variety of goods and services, or the distribution of total output among society's members—all factors of concern to marketing planners. Individual and household income serve as more useful barometers to monitor.

☐ *Personal Income*

Personal income is total income received by people from all sources. It is usually reported either per capita or per household and is important to marketers because it is a crucial measure of consumers' buying power.

Personal income is also described in more specific ways. Since people must pay taxes out of their incomes, income is also reported as **disposable income,** the amount left after taxes. In addition, government statisticians report on **discretionary income,** money left after people pay not only for taxes but also for such necessities as food, shelter, and clothing. To marketers of bread and milk, the amount of disposable income remaining to an individual or household is an important economic indicator; producers of stereos and microwave ovens find data on discretionary income more useful.

Americans spend about 95 percent of their disposable income for personal consumption and save the rest. Of the money spent for personal consumption during the last several decades, an increasing amount has been devoted to services rather than goods. Although every household has slightly different spending priorities, on average about $70 out of every $100 goes for necessities—food, housing, transportation, household operations, and medical care. Figure 2-8 breaks down the amount consumers spend on personal consumption for various goods and services.

Marketers find it valuable to monitor the per capita personal income of the United States; it rose from $7584 in 1979 to $13,876 in 1985. For most purposes, however, the household is the more common spending unit. Unfortunately, using a single figure such as per capita income or even data on family or household incomes reveals an inherent problem for marketing analysts: All groups are included; overall figures do not illuminate meaningful differences between different individuals, households, or families.

As a result, marketers find it useful to combine economic and demographic data. For example, the average family income in the United States in 1984 was $24,433. Looking specifically at the variable of educational background, however, the average family income ranged from $13,319 for families whose head had less than an eighth-grade education to $46,656 for families whose head had 5 or more years of college. In terms of race, average family income was $27,700 for whites but only $15,400 for blacks. In terms of occupation, workers in private households (mostly maids) earned less than $8000 on average, whereas managers earned about $43,000.[7]

Organizational marketers monitor that portion of the GNP not captured by personal income and expenditures. Business investments account for around 16 percent of the nation's output and government purchases for 20 percent; the remaining two-thirds go to consumer purchases. Of course, industrial marketers must also follow trends in consumer spending, since so much of their business rests on demand by final consumers.

☐ *Inflation and Interest Rates*

The general health of the economy can also be gauged by the rate of inflation and the rates of interest consumers and businesses are charged by lenders. **Inflation** is the rise in the general price level of all goods and services. Looked at another way, it is a decline in the purchasing power of a unit of money. Consequently, when the inflation rate is high, consumers and businesses cannot purchase as much as when

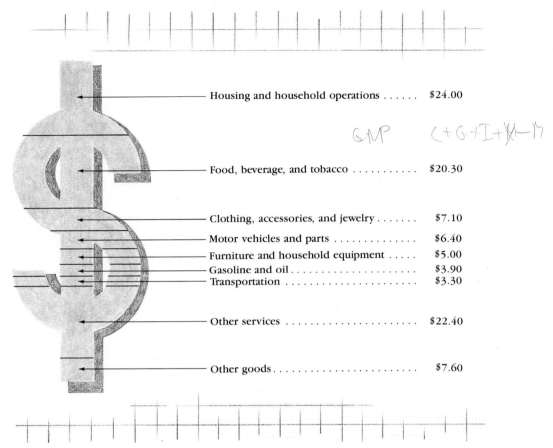

Housing and household operations	$24.00
Food, beverage, and tobacco	$20.30
Clothing, accessories, and jewelry	$7.10
Motor vehicles and parts	$6.40
Furniture and household equipment	$5.00
Gasoline and oil	$3.90
Transportation	$3.30
Other services	$22.40
Other goods	$7.60

GNP   C + G + I + X − M

Figure 2-8 *What Americans spend for personal consumption.* In spending on goods and services, Americans spend the highest proportion of their consumer dollars on food and beverages, housing, household operations, and other services. (Data from U.S. Bureau of the Census, *Statistical Abstract of the United States, 1986,* Washington, D.C., 1985, p. 435.)

inflation is low. Marketers are thus strongly affected by the ups and downs of inflation. Figure 2-9 illustrates the rate of inflation in the United States since 1960. In times of high inflation, consumers are likely to postpone the purchase of durable goods such as major appliances, cars, and homes.

Interest is the price paid for loaned funds over a period of time, usually expressed as a percentage per year. Rising interest rates reduce the willingness and ability of consumers to make purchases and businesses to make investments. From 1979 to 1982, high rates of inflation and interest contributed to a **recession**—a downward phase of a business cycle resulting in a falling off of business and consumer optimism. In the mid-1980s, inflation declined from over 10 percent per year to under 5 percent while interest rates fell from well over 10 percent to roughly 6 or 7 percent. These changes gave the U.S. economy a major lift.[8]

Anticipating changes in inflation and interest rates is quite difficult because such changes are produced by a complex set of causes. Nevertheless, economists continually attempt to project the courses of inflation and interest rates; marketers must heed such predictions, since consumer demand is so directly affected by the overall health of the economy.

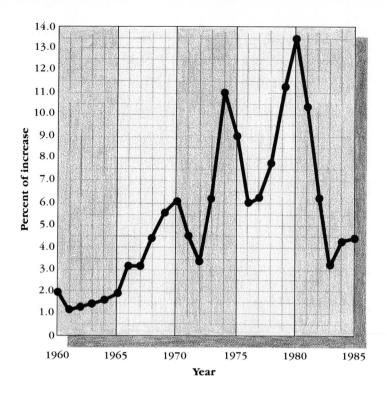

Figure 2-9 *Changes in consumer price index: 1960 to 1988 (projected).* Consumer price index reflects the change in the price of a basket of goods over time and is the most common measure of inflation in the United States. According to these projections, the consumer price index will rise by more than 5 percent per year from 1985 to 1988. (From The White House, *The Economic Report of the President*, Feb. 1985.)

■ TECHNOLOGICAL ENVIRONMENT ■

In the 1930s, Chester Carlson, a patent attorney and amateur physicist, spent several years dabbling in his New York City kitchen, developing a process he called "electrophotography." Today we know that process (basically the use of static electricity to make instant copies of documents on plain paper) as Xerography. Carlson made his first successful copy in 1938, but selling his process was much more difficult than inventing it. Carlson approached more than 20 companies—including RCA, IBM, Remington Rand, and General Electric—and was turned down by all of them. Finally, in 1947, a small company from Rochester, New York, named Haloid agreed to develop this process commercially; Carlson joined Haloid as a consultant. It took until 1959 before the firm's scientists produced a dramatic breakthrough: a dependable, easy-to-use document copier. In 1961, Haloid changed its name to Xerox, and today it is one of the largest corporations in the United States.[9]

Although a commercially viable copying machine took many years to develop, Haloid's striking success clearly justified its early interest in Chester Carlson's invention. By contrast, more than twenty other firms—some much more powerful than Haloid—failed to see the dynamic marketing potential of photocopying. The success of Haloid (and its emergence as Xerox) underscores the need for contemporary business firms to recognize the threat and opportunity of technological change. To do so, they must carefully monitor the technological environment.

The seventies and eighties produced astonishing leaps in technological growth. We sent a man to the moon (and dumped some of our garbage there). Engineers at Intel built the first microprocessor chip in 1970. The first personal computer—the ALTAIR 8800—was put on the market for hobbyists in 1974; by 1989, manufacturers are expected to sell around $25 billion worth of personal computers.[10]

Technological advances have had substantial effect on the variety of goods and services available to consumers. For example, digital watches now account for a substantial share of all timepieces sold. Digital recordings offer a new level of fidelity and clarity. Digital television is on the horizon.

Technology often produces new products and markets, but it can also promote their demise: Xerography was a hard blow to manufacturers of carbon paper and mimeograph machines. Technology often affects the production of traditional products. Armstrong Nurseries, which sells one rose bush in five on the U.S. market, is now producing plants by a startlingly new technique: Instead of painstakingly breeding hybird roses in soil, Armstrong is using laboratory techniques to produce roses in test tubes. Grown from a small number of cells from the specimen "mother" rose, those plants, unlike those bred by conventional means, are perfect copies of their parent.

Organizations must monitor those technologies most likely to affect their goals and efforts. Here we will briefly examine three wide-ranging technologies that are having and will have dramatic impact on most of our lives. These technologies—microelectronics, robotics, telecommunications—seem destined to affect the futures of many marketing organizations.

☐ *Microelectronics*

The microelectronics revolution is characterized by ever-increasing miniaturization, speed, and power of electronic devices and by decreasing product costs. Symbolized by the microprocessor—the computer on a chip—microelectronic components are getting smaller, faster, and cheaper at an astonishing rate. The use of digital, solid-state products in toys, watches, and automotive controls seems to be only the beginning of the spread of microprocessors into fields as diverse as home energy management, medical diagnostics, and computer-assisted instruction. The implications of new microelectronic technology for marketers seem to be most far-reaching in the areas of new product development, modification of existing products and techniques for making them, and product pricing. As Peter Schwartz, director of the strategic environment center at SRI International, a California research organization, noted at the beginning of the 1980s, "we're about where oil was in 1870—trying to use petroleum as a substitute for whale oil. It's the fuel for a new, information economy."[11]

☐ *Robotics*

In the late 1980s and early 1990s, few Americans can expect to have R2D2-like servants in their homes. Yet, on automotive assembly lines in the United States, Western Europe, and Japan, robots are currently spot welding and performing inspection functions. A *robot* is any machine that performs jobs previously assigned to human beings, is self-operating, and is "intelligent" (that is, contains electronic logic in the form of a microcomputer). For obvious reasons, robot development is closely tied to advances in microelectronics.

Depending on the needs of the manufacturer, robots can be programmed to handle different functions. Thus far, they have been used primarily for repetitive, dangerous, or unpleasant jobs. However, in the future, robots will take away jobs that human workers want and need.[12] Optimistic forecasters suggest that the total number of jobs available for U.S. workers will not decline. Rather, they argue (or at least hope) that the use of robots will increase productivity, which will in turn lead to economic growth and new jobs. Even if this proves to be true, massive

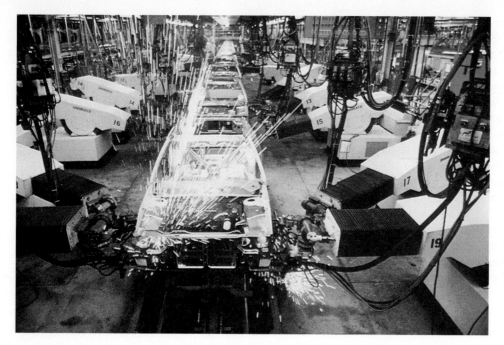

Computer-programmed robots are responsible for doing most of the welding of automobiles that had been done by human beings just a few years ago. The impact of this kind of technological change on consumers and on markets must be considered in analyzing marketing environments. (Copyright © Tom Mc-Hugh/Photo Researchers, Inc.)

retraining programs for factory and office workers will be needed as automation and robot technology spread.

Increasing use of robots within the U.S. economy will have profound marketing implications. Product quality of manufactured goods should improve; after all, robots do not make mistakes or allow shoddy goods to leave the assembly line! Distribution and warehousing of products will become highly automated, allowing marketers to move products to buyers with greater efficiency. In the field of financial services, the use of automated teller machines will continue to increase.

☐ *Telecommunications*

Sweeping changes in how we talk to each other are also tied to advances in microelectronics. Telecommunications is a blanket term for the electronic transmission of data through wires, cables, fiber optics, or broadcast. From telephone service and equipment to satellite broadcast of television shows, many of the world's largest corporations are involved in the development of new kinds of telecommunications services. Those not directly involved in selling telecommunications will be major users of the new services.

Futurists see a time, not too many years hence, when every home and business will be linked in a worldwide communications grid. This "electronic cottage" technology, predicted by Alvin Toffler, will fundamentally change the way people shop, bank, work, and communicate, since it will permit them to do all these things from the comfort of their homes.[13] "Videotex," a generic label applied to home information retrieval and communications systems, is a new industry in the making. By the mid-1990s several million homes in the United States will be linked to computer data banks through personal computers, telephones, and cable television networks.

Marketers will be deeply involved in this telecommunications revolution. If consumers wish to shop at home, perhaps for a refrigerator, they will be able to view various models on their television screens and will receive promotional and information messages about different brands. Consumers will then be able to order an appliance by punching certain buttons on their telephones or computer terminals. Payment may even be made through a checkless electronic transaction.

Currently, many marketers are attempting to determine whether Americans will want to use this new technology to make consumer purchases.[14] If the so-called telecommunications revolution is accepted by consumers, marketers will have to adjust their marketing mixes for new methods of promoting, selling, delivering, and pricing their products. Moreover, telecommunications equipment and services will become desirable new products that must themselves be marketed.

In response to changes in microelectronics, robotics, telecommunications, and other areas, many large corporations have created technology assessment and forecasting groups. These groups may be staffed by senior managers who monitor specific aspects of technology through scientific papers, contacts with customers and distributors, and the mass media. Typically, combined reports on technological advances are made to top-level management on both a regular and an as-needed basis.[15] Some companies may establish monitoring groups for areas in need of special attention. Thus, in addition to their overall technology forecasting efforts, RCA, 3M, Corning Glass, and IBM have set up systems to monitor advances in Japanese technology.[16]

■ POLITICAL/LEGAL ENVIRONMENT ■

On the national level, four important forces are at work in the political/legal environment: (1) Congress enacts laws; (2) federal agencies regulate business; (3) federal courts interpret the Constitution and set precedents; and (4) interest groups representing business and citizens' organizations attempt to influence public policy by lobbying officials and filing lawsuits. Marketers must monitor all these forces and try to anticipate changes in the political/legal environment. The most essential questions in this monitoring process are: Will a certain law be enacted? Will a certain law be repealed? How will a law be enforced?

Historically, the first groups of laws affecting businesses and marketing organizations were aimed at defending free enterprise—that is, at preserving competition. Beginning with the Sherman Act of 1890, several laws have been enacted to ensure that no firm is able to dominate a market so powerfully that it eliminates opportunities for other companies to operate. The antitrust division of the U.S. Department of Justice is charged with instituting legal action to prevent the growth of monopolies. As part of the administrative branch of the federal government, this division tends to reflect the politics of the President. Consequently, it is much less active under a conservative Republican (such as Ronald Reagan) than under a more liberal Democrat (such as Jimmy Carter).[17] Federal courts can also act to preserve competition; by ruling on the application of antitrust laws, the courts interpret such laws and set precedents which can be as important as the laws themselves.

Another set of laws is designed to protect business competitors from one another. The Robinson-Patman Act of 1936 sought to prohibit price discrimination against wholesalers and retailers who buy the same merchandise. This law has been called the "anti-A&P law," since it was intended to help small stores to remain competitive with large chains. Such regulatory legislation does not always benefit consumers; prices may remain higher than they would have been under unregulated competition. Exhibit 2-1 summarizes the key legislative acts intended to preserve competition and protect competitors.

Exhibit 2-1 **Key Legislation Aimed at Preserving Competition and Protecting Competitors**

Law (Year)	Purpose
Sherman Antitrust Act (1890)	Prohibits monopolies and restrains trade in foreign and interstate commerce
Clayton Act (1914)	Prohibits specific anticompetitive practices
Federal Trade Commission Act (1914)	Establishes regulatory commission with cease and desist powers against unfair competitive practices
Robinson-Patman Act (1936)	Prohibits price discrimination (with certain defenses allowed) against channel members purchasing the same merchandise
Wheeler-Lea Act (1938)	Prohibits unfair and deceptive acts and practices regardless of whether competition is injured; gives Federal Trade Commission (FTC) jurisdiction over food and drug advertising
Celler-Kefauver Act (1950)	Prohibits mergers with or acquisition of other firms if such acts will substantially lessen competition
Consumer Foods Pricing Act (1975)	Prohibits the use of price maintenance agreements among manufacturers and resellers in interstate commerce

Exhibit 2-2 **The Move toward Deregulation**

Year	Steps Taken
1968	The Supreme Court's *Carterfone* decision permits non-AT&T equipment to be connected to the AT&T system.
1969	The Federal Communications Commission (FCC) gives MCI the right to hook its long-distance network into local phone systems.
1970	The Federal Reserve Board (Fed) frees interest rates on bank deposits over $100,000 with maturities of less than 6 months.
1974	The Justice Department files an antitrust suit against AT&T.
1975	The Securities and Exchange Commission (SEC) orders brokers to cease fixing commissions on stock sales.
1977	Merrill Lynch offers the cash management account, thereby competing more closely with commercial banks.
1978	Congress deregulates the airlines.
1979	The FCC allows AT&T to sell nonregulated services, such as data processing.
1980	The Fed allows banks to pay interest on checking accounts.
1980	Congress deregulates trucking and railroads.
1981	Sears Roebuck becomes the first one-stop financial supermarket, offering insurance, banking, and brokerage services.
1982	Congress deregulates intercity bus services.
1984	AT&T divests itself of its local phone companies.

Source: "Deregulating America: The Benefits Begin to Show—in Productivity, Innovation, and Prices," *Business Week*, Nov. 28, 1983, pp. 80–81.

In the last 20 years, still another group of laws has been passed to encourage renewed competition in a number of major industries. Through such legislation, actions of regulatory agencies, and judicial decisions, policymakers have opened the way for new competitors to emerge in the fields of transportation, financial services, and telecommunications. Exhibit 2-2 summarizes these regulatory actions.

As an outgrowth of the consumerism movement of the 1960s and 1970s, a final group of statutes has been enacted to set higher standards for manufacturers and lenders. These laws establish safety standards for products; protect the natural environment; prohibit deceptive marketing practices; and require fairness, privacy, and nondiscrimination in credit reporting and investigations (see Exhibit 2-3).

Marketers must carefully monitor the enactment, repeal, and enforcement of federal, state, and local laws. They must anticipate and closely scrutinize regulations issued by federal regulatory agencies. Marketers must also follow the course of court cases relevant to the laws and regulations affecting their business operations.

At a far-reaching level, marketing planners must be students of the nation's political climate. Beginning with the election of Ronald Reagan and the Republican takeover of the U.S. Senate in 1980, the eighties saw a pronounced trend toward the election of "conservative" public officials. In general, conservatives are expected to be sympathetic to business interests; they often press for restricted (rather than expanded) governmental regulation of business practices. Of course, political trends tend to come in cycles, and U.S. voters may swing back to a stance favoring more "liberal" officials. If marketing planners correctly anticipate political changes, they can project the likely actions of legislators and other policymakers.

A very small child could choke on this toy. In order to foster protection of consumers, the government passes laws that require marketers to warn them of these dangers; just how these laws apply to their organizations is part of the manager's environmental monitoring task. (Ken Karp.)

■ CULTURAL ENVIRONMENT ■

The cultural environment is one of the most difficult to monitor, because changes in values and attitudes and lifestyles are not easily measured in reassuringly quantifiable ways. Cultural values—and the behaviors that reflect those values—are perhaps most clearly seen in the changes in various relationships. A list of such relationships that are relevant to marketing plans could be almost limitless but would almost certainly include interactions between the following:

Women and men
Majority and minority
Individuals and institutions
Parents and children
Economics and ecology
Work and leisure
Consumers and producers
Business and society

The objectives of cultural monitoring, then, are to identify trends that are developing in such relationships and to analyze the significance of these changes for the marketing organization. Obviously, different cultural trends, such as the growing popularity of "lite" food and beverage products (see Box 2-1), will affect different marketing organizations.

Broad-based cultural changes evolve slowly; thus, planners have some lead time to consider future actions. But cultural trends must be closely watched for two primary reasons. First, cultural changes directly influence the desires of con-

Exhibit 2-3 — Key Legislation Protecting Consumers

Law (Year)	Purpose
Meat Inspection Act (1906)	Demands sanitary practices in meat packing and shipping in interstate commerce
Pure Food and Drug Act (1906)	Prohibits adulteration and mislabeling of foods, drugs, cosmetics, or therapeutic devices; establishes the Food and Drug Administration (FDA)
Wool Products Labeling Act (1939), Fur Products Labeling Act (1951), Flammmable Fabrics Act (1953), Textile Fiber Identification Act (1958)	Require correct labeling of wool, fur, and textile products and prohibit sale of dangerously flammable products
Automobile Information Disclosure Act (1958)	Requires automobile manufacturers to post suggested retail prices ("sticker" prices) on new passenger cars
Kefauver-Harris Drug Amendments (1962)	Requires that (1) drugs be labeled with their generic names, (2) new drugs be pretested, and (3) new drugs be approved for marketing by FDA
National Traffic and Safety Act (1966)	Provides for establishment of safety standards for automobiles and tires
Fair Packaging and Labeling Act (1966)	Requires accurate labeling of certain consumer products
Child Protection Act (1966)	Bans the sale of potentially hazardous toys
Cigarette Labeling and Advertising Acts (1966, 1969)	Requires cigarette manufacturers to label cigarettes as harmful to health and bans radio and television advertising
Truth-in-Lending Act (1968)	Requires full disclosure of credit and loan terms and rates
National Environmental Policy Act (1969)	Establishes a national policy on the environment; Environmental Protection Agency (EPA) established in 1970
Fair Credit Reporting Act (1970)	Regulates the reporting and use of credit information
Consumer Product Safety Act (1972)	Establishes the Consumer Product Safety Commission with power to regulate the marketing of products ruled unsafe by the commission
Magnuson-Moss Consumer Product Warranty Act (1975)	Regulates warranties and sets disclosure requirements
Consumer Education Act (1978)	Establishes the Office of Consumer Education; supports research projects designed to provide consumer education to the public

sumers. For example, in recent decades the dominance of the U.S. nuclear-family model (two parents living together with their children) has been eroded. There are more single-person households, childless parents, and single-parent families, and they often require and demand new types of goods and services. For example, single men and women may live alone in highly cramped apartments and therefore will

Box 2-1 The "Lite" Decade of the 1980s

Since 1982, more than 350 "lite" or "light" products have been added to the shelves of U.S. supermarkets and liquor stores. Consumers can now purchase lite beer, lite salad dressing, light natural cheeses, light sour cream, light wheat and white breads, lite catsup, lite pancakes, lite cola, and even lite ice cream (only 100 calories per scoop). According to a 1986 report by the Food and Drug Administration, lite foods have become "one of the fastest growing segments of the American food industry."

Yet the cultural trend toward lite products goes far beyond food and beverages. Americans can wash their hair with lite shampoo and can spray their apartments with light aerosol air freshener (less than half the perfume of most sprays). They can listen to light music (where the heavy bass line has been removed) and can quickly master novels such as *Moby Dick* through highly abridged "light literature" (audiocassette tapes offer "Ten Classics in Ten Minutes").

According to sociologists, "lite" began as a marketing term used to denote dietetic food products. In terms of food and beverages, "lite" (or "light") currently refers to some degree of reduction in calories, fat, salt, sugar, or alcohol. Taking a broader perspective, however, the "lite" revolution appears to reflect a cultural trend of the 1980s whereby Americans are seeking easy and instant answers to their needs and problems. For example, instead of committing oneself to the stresses of a long-term weight-reduction program involving exercise and careful dieting, a person can switch from regular beer to lite beer and hope that this change will be sufficient.

Certainly for marketers, the growing public demand for lite products represents an important cultural trend. Lite offerings have flooded the marketplace because business firms have seen an opportunity to launch new products and to challenge traditionally dominant products. Interestingly, however, the cultural change leading to more and more lite products has led to changes in the political/legal environment confronting marketers. In 1986, Congress began consideration of legis-

Whether it is spelled "Light" or "Lite," the extent of the movement toward this kind of product is still not known. This trend is directly responsive to the social change that makes many people in this country concerned with health and a slender body. (Ken Karp.)

lation setting specific standards for a food product to be labeled "lite," "light," "lean," or "low-fat." At the same time, the federal Bureau of Alcohol, Tobacco, and Firearms announced that it would attempt to determine what constitutes "light" or "lite" in alcoholic beverages. Whereas marketers have thus far been free to label products "lite" whenever they please—and some have conveyed the *misleading* impression that their products are light in calories—greater consumer awareness and closer scrutiny by policymakers may lead to new and tougher restrictions on the marketing of so-called lite products.

Sources: William R. Greer, "In the 'Lite' Decade, Less Has Become More," *New York Times*, Aug. 13, 1986, pp. A1, C10; Irvin Molotsky, "U.S. to Define 'Light' Alcohol Beverages," *New York Times*, Aug. 13, 1986, p. C10; Martin Friedman, "Nobody's Taking 'Lite' Lightly," *Adweek*, Aug. 18, 1986, p. 28.

need smaller appliances (such as combination washer/dryers). Such individuals will also prefer that certain food items be marketed in smaller package sizes to reduce spoilage.

Second, cultural trends may significantly influence the external pressures with which marketers must contend. In the 1960s, spurred by the work of Ralph Nader and his associates, a consumer movement for safer products and tougher liability standards arose across the United States. At the same time, citizens' groups became increasingly active in efforts to protect the natural environment from pollution and from unfettered exploitation. Companies that did not anticipate these changes in cultural values paid dearly for their lack of foresight. When environmentalists initially proposed greater pollution controls of U.S. cars, no one listened. Eventually, however, legislation was passed—often to the dismay of both manufacturers and consumers—which mandated the installation of catalytic converters in new cars, a major switchover to unleaded gas, and federal guidelines concerning the average miles per gallon for entire fleets of new cars.

Here we look at three continuing cultural shifts that affect many marketing organizations, or at least those heavily involved in marketing products to industrialized nations: (1) the changing roles of women and men, (2) the emergence of variations in family structure, and (3) the increase of leisure time.

Figure 2-10 *Women continue to enter the work force.* According to projections, the proportion of women in the paid labor force of the United States will continue to rise. (From *Sales and Marketing Management,* Oct. 26, 1981, p. 9; current data from U.S. Bureau of the Census, *Statistical Abstract of the United States: 1986,* 1985, p. 392.)

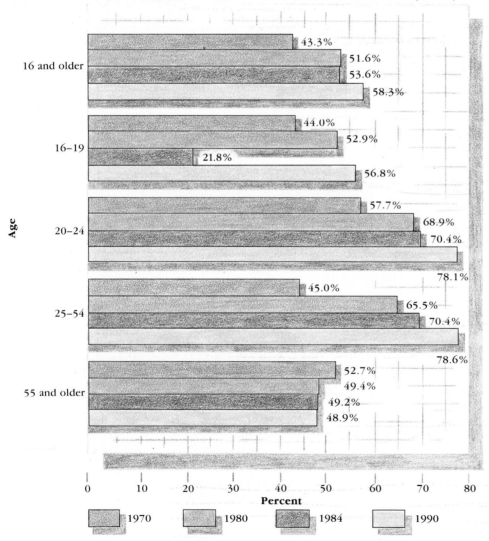

☐ *Changing Sex Roles*

A key cultural trend is the dramatic increase of women in the work force. Over the last three decades, the percentage of women over age 16 in the work force has risen dramatically. As projected in Figure 2-10, by 1990 more than 78 percent of women ages 20 through 54 will be found in the U.S. labor force.

The increase in working women has far-reaching social implications. First, the number of two-earner households has increased steadily—from about 21 million in 1977 to 27 million in 1985—and is projected to reach 29 million in 1990. Two wages can usually be translated into more disposable and discretionary income. And working mothers have created a demand for new products; most obvious are child-care services and time-saving appliances.[18]

Second, shifts have occurred in the patterns of how buying decisions are made and who actually makes purchases. Increasing numbers of men are doing their families' food shopping; so, too, are teenage daughters and sons.[19] Given the time pressures that they face, working women become less involved in food shopping and cooking and tend to spend money on services that save them time.[20] Insurance brokers and automobile dealers now find that a rising proportion of their customers are female. The steady increase in women workers has forced marketers to adjust their marketing research and product design. For example, Detroit's automakers are offering vans and minivans with lower, easier access. Promotional messages for new cars are being designed to appeal to both sexes.

☐ *Variations on the Traditional Household*

Divorced people with children and married couples without children represent an increasing percentage of family households. In addition, the number of unmarried couples living together and of one-person households has risen drastically in the last 15 years or so. These variations from the traditional family composition are forcing marketers of family-oriented products to fashion new products and to develop new selling appeals for existing products.

These trends are demographic, but their implications are more than demographic. They represent changes in values, attitudes, and lifestyles that should be monitored. For example, not only do singles want smaller living quarters and food portions, they also are likely to have different attitudes about spending their discretionary income—for gourmet foods, sports cars, home entertainment, investment, and travel.[21] And all households, traditional or not, are affected by another important social trend: increased leisure time.

☐ *Leisure Time and Our Use of It*

In 1947, the average worker spent a little over 40 hours a week on the job; today the average worker puts in about 36 hours a week. That 4-hour-per-week drop multiplied by well over a 100 million of us adds up to almost 500 million hours a week to be disposed of in some way—bowling, mowing the grass, playing cards or the stock market. We have a lot more time to spend, and we spend more and more money on that time. In 1960, Americans spent just under $40 billion for leisure and cultural activities. By 1983, that figure had reached $141 billion, or 6.6 percent of personal consumption expenditures. Figure 2-11 gives a broad breakdown of where leisure dollars go.

Marketers of leisure-time goods and services are concerned with monitoring changes in the way consumers spend their money. An upsurge in the popularity of bowling would represent an opportunity for manufacturers of bowling balls, pins, and other equipment as well as for bowling alley operators. Such an increase, how-

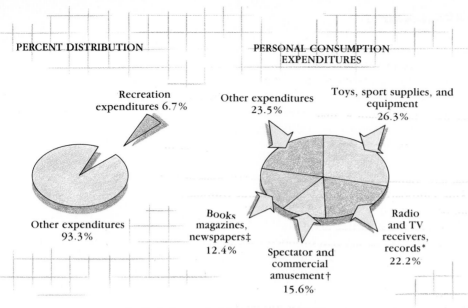

Recreation expenditures 6.7%

Other expenditures 23.5%

Toys, sport supplies, and equipment 26.3%

Other expenditures 93.3%

Books magazines, newspapers‡ 12.4%

Spectator and commercial amusement† 15.6%

Radio and TV receivers, records* 22.2%

Figure 2-11 *Personal consumption expenditures for recreation: 1983.* Americans spend a healthy amount on recreation, and marketers of sporting goods, toys, books, and entertainment equipment follow recreational spending closely. (From U.S. Bureau of the Census, *Statistical Abstract of the United States: 1986,* Washington, D.C., 1985, p. 226.)

* Includes musical instruments and radio and TV repair.

† Includes admissions to spectator amusements, commercial participant amusement, and panmutual net receipts.

‡ Includes maps and sheet music.

ever, would probably represent a threat to producers of products for alternative sports. The leisure time available to citizens of industrialized nations should continue to rise, providing great possibilities for marketers who can forecast how people will spend that leisure time.

Leisure time grows as the time we spend working declines. Since much of our work is more sedentary in nature, we are finding ways to spend our leisure time and our money now. Home gym equipment like that used by these exercisers is one of the fastest growing product classes in the economy. (Karl Schumacher/Time Magazine.)

COMPETITIVE ENVIRONMENT

Charles Strang, chair of Outboard Marine Corporation, believes in watching his competitors closely. Outboard, the world's largest producer of motors for small boats, markets the two strongest brand names in the business: Johnson and Evinrude. In the early 1970s, Outboard had some 40 percent of the worldwide market. But in March of 1972, Strang got wind that Japanese manufacturers were planning to compete in the outboard motor market in a big way. He dashed off to the Tokyo boat show. "I was startled to see one Yamaha motor that was a dead copy of one of ours," he recalls.

By 1978, Suzuki, Honda, and Yamaha had 15 percent of the U.S. market and 40 percent in Europe, knocking Outboard down to 28 percent. But Outboard had time to plan and take action. Strang cut prices, reorganized distributorships, and ended a long internal rivalry between the Evinrude and Johnson divisions. By 1982, the Japanese companies' share in the U.S. market had dropped back to 10 percent. In Europe, Outboard had gone back up to a 35 percent market share, and the Japanese manufacturers had fallen to 25 percent. Outboard apparently had emerged from the battle with clear sailing ahead.[22]

This same theme—whether pitting U.S. firms against foreign competitors or simply against other domestic rivals—has led some to suggest that marketing is similar to war. According to this argument, the secret to competition is to think like the military.[23] Many others see this as an extreme view but accept that competition is central to what marketing is all about.[24] Such debate has sparked interest in how marketers conduct competitive analyses.[25]

Identifying Competitors

Identifying competitors isn't as simple as it may seem. For example, Owens-Corning manufactures fiberglass-based shingles for roofing. Just who are the company's competitors? Other companies which also manufacture fiberglass shingles—Manville, Georgia-Pacific, Jim Walter, Certain-Teed, and Bird—are **brand competitors,** filling the same need as Owens-Corning. These are the competitors that Owens-Corning will want to monitor most closely, but there are other, less obvious, competitors for the shingles buyer's dollar. Organizational buyers and homeowners may prefer more traditional asphalt and felt-paper shingles. These are **product competitors,** filling a need with a slightly different offering. A firm's brand competitors may also be its product competitors, but this is not always the case.

Generic competitors do not offer customers either direct brand or even product form alternatives but do compete for customers' available funds by providing different solutions for a particular need. For example, window manufacturers, driveway repair services, and plumbers are generic competitors in that they compete for households' home repair budgets. A family may be able to afford installation of an entirely new set of windows only if it delays needed kitchen plumbing work for another year or two. In comparison with brand and product competitors, generic competitors are the most difficult to identify and monitor.

Whatever a firm's business, it faces the demanding work involved in monitoring diverse categories of competitors. Nevertheless, marketers must remain aware of all possible rivals for a consumer's dollars. As part of this effort, they must be wary of potential entrants into a market and possible new technologies to replace a market.[26] Although such wide-ranging monitoring is a priority, any firm's competitive monitoring will focus most sharply on its closest rivals—brand competitors.

☐ *Key Competitive Factors*

Most marketing organizations will hone in on several key brand competitors. A simple analysis of a competitor's characteristics can provide a useful basis for monitoring. A competitive analysis should include a careful look at a competitor's past strategy, marketing mix, resources, and future strategy.[27]

PAST STRATEGY The first step in a competitive analysis is to reconstruct a competitor's past strategy—its overall plan for meeting marketing goals and objectives. A firm's strategy can be learned from annual reports, management's public speeches and interviews, and media coverage. The key question is: "Has the competitor implemented publicized plans?" Any deviation between strategy and implementation may point to weaknesses that can be exploited.

Many firms have, in fact, followed stated strategies—such as "technological leadership"—while neglecting aggressive action in other important areas such as manufacturing and marketing. Such firms become vulnerable to competitors with more balanced plans. For example, by relying for many years on a strategy based on technological leadership, Polaroid gained a commanding lead in the development of instant photography. However, Polaroid's managers neglected the equally critical area of maintaining good dealer relations. Kodak took advantage of this competitive weakness in distribution by waging aggressive campaigns to assist dealers in promoting Kodak products.

MARKETING MIX How does a competitor conceive and design its products? How does it produce them? Distribute them? Promote them? Is its marketing mix strong in certain areas and weak in others? These questions are extremely important in assessing a firm's competitive environment. If Owens-Corning's competitors spend lavishly on advertising and sales force promotion but do not attend to product quality, these factors will substantially influence Owens-Corning's own marketing mix strategy.

Keeping tabs on a competitor's marketing mix will depend heavily on accurate and timely feedback from a firm's sales force. Ongoing reports on a competitor's marketing mix should be an integral part of the marketing feedback system. Sales representatives will learn of new products, discounts, and distribution arrangements during their regular sales calls. Moreover, talks with wholesalers and retailers in a firm's distribution system can provide up-to-date information about a competitor's pricing policies and structure. Finally, any competitor's advertising is public and out there for the world (and its competitors) to see. By monitoring how a competitor orchestrates its marketing mix, a firm can predict with some accuracy how its competitor will handle even a closely guarded, breakthrough product.

RESOURCES If our competitor is a publicly held corporation, by buying one share of stock, we can receive its annual report and have a fair idea of where it stands financially. Is it cash-rich and able to move quickly to take advantage of opportunities, or is it deeply in debt and vulnerable to threats? One of Owens-Corning's competitors, Manville, has spent some years under protection from its creditors through Chapter 11 of the federal bankruptcy laws (because of thousands of lawsuits stemming from health injuries to its workers in the asbestos business). It is safe to assume that these lawsuits will tie up some of Manville's financial resources as well as the attention of the firm's management.

9. Cultural trends directly influence the desires of consumers and may shape the external pressures confronting marketers.
10. Typically, competitive monitoring will include analysis of past strategy, marketing mix, resources, and future strategy.
11. In the future, marketers may develop more sophisticated and accurate tools to assist their environmental monitoring.

☐ Key Terms

ageism	demography	gross national product
birthrate	death rate	inflation
brand competitors	discretionary income	interest
constant dollars	disposable income	personal income
controllable variables	environmental monitoring	product competitors
current dollars	fertility rate	recession
demographics	generic competitors	uncontrollable variables

☐ Chapter Review

1. Explain how marketing variables that are controllable differ from those that are not. Would a shift in consumer preferences to decaffeinated coffees from regular coffees be controllable?

2. In what ways can IBM's introduction of its personal computer be seen as effective management of change?

3. Why do marketing organizations need to monitor external environments? By monitoring those environments, can marketers control them?

4. What is the prime source of demographic information that is useful to marketing analysis? Cite some opportunities and threats to marketers resulting from the aging of the U.S. population.

5. Speculate on some possible technological advances that would affect marketers of color television sets. If you predict a certain technical improvement to be commercially viable in the year 1995, what steps might the television marketers take now?

6. Why are cultural trends so difficult to predict? Identify some cultural and demographic trends that may affect marketers of children's toys.

7. What types of competitors might someone opening a new pizza parlor have to contend with? In what ways does a pizza parlor compete with an oriental take-out restaurant?

☐ References

1. Carl P. Zeithaml and Valerie A. Zeithaml, "Environmental Management: Revising the Marketing Perspective," *Journal of Marketing*, vol. 48, Spring 1984, pp. 46–53.
2. Alvin Toffler, *Future Shock* (New York: Bantam Books, 1970).
3. Gene R. Laczniak and Robert F. Lusch, "Environment and Strategy in 1995: A Survey of High-Level Executives," *Journal of Consumer Marketing*, vol. 3, Spring 1986, pp. 27–45.
4. Myron Magnet, "Who Needs a Trend-Spotter?" *Fortune*, Dec. 9, 1985, pp. 51–56.
5. Roberto Friedmann and Warren French, "Beyond Social Trend Data," *Journal of Consumer Marketing*, Fall 1985, pp. 17–21.
6. John M. McCann and David J. Reibstein, "Forecasting the Impact of Socioeconomic and Demographic Change on Product Demand," *Journal of Marketing Research*, vol. XXII, Nov. 1985, pp. 415–423.
7. Bryant Robey, "Earning Power Pays—for Some," *Adweek*, Oct. 28, 1985.
8. Arthur M. Louis, "America's New Economy," *Fortune*, June 23, 1986, pp. 18–28.
9. Milton Moskowitz, Michael Katz, and Robert Levering (eds.), *Everybody's Business: An Almanac* (New York: Harper & Row, 1980), pp. 416–417.
10. "Software: The New Driving Force," *Business Week*, Feb. 27, 1984, p. 75.
11. "The Microchip Revolution: Piecing Together a New Society," *Business Week*, Nov. 10, 1980, p. 97.

12. Donald H. Sanders, *Computers Today*, 2d ed. (New York: McGraw-Hill, 1985), p. 406.

13. Alvin Toffler, *The Third Wave* (New York: Bantam Books, 1980).

14. George P. Moschis, Jac L. Goldstucker, and Thomas J. Stanley, "At-Home Shopping: Will Consumers Let Their Computers Do the Walking?" *Business Horizons*, Mar.–Apr. 1985, pp. 22–29.

15. David A. Aaker, "Organizing a Strategic Information Scanning System," *California Management Review*, vol. XXV, no. 2, Jan. 1983, pp. 76–83.

16. "America Starts Looking Over Japan's Shoulder," *Business Week*, Feb. 13, 1984, pp. 136–140.

17. Ben M. Enis and E. Thomas Sullivan, "The A.T.&T. Settlement: Legal Summary, Economic Analysis, and Marketing Implications," *Journal of Marketing*, vol. 49, Winter 1985, pp. 127–136.

18. Peter Francese, "Daycare's Importance Grows," *Advertising Age*, Mar. 6, 1986, p. 50.

19. Ronald D. Michman, "The Male Queue at the Checkout Counter," *Business Horizons*, May–June 1986, pp. 51–55.

20. Ralph W. Jackson, Stephen W. McDaniel, and C. P. Rao, "Food Shopping and Preparation: Psychographic Differences of Working Wives and Housewives," *Journal of Consumer Research*, vol. 12, June 1985, pp. 110–113; Don Bellante and Ann C. Foster, "Working Wives and Expenditure on Services," *Journal of Consumer Research*, vol. 11, Sept. 1984, pp. 200–207.

21. Joann S. Lublin, "Staying Single: Rise in Never-Marrieds Affects Social Customs and Buying Patterns," *Wall Street Journal*, May 28, 1986, pp. 1, 18.

22. Barbara Rudolph, "Why Putt-Putt Isn't Sputter-Sputter," *Forbes*, June 7, 1982, pp. 51–52.

23. Al Reis and Jack Trout, *Marketing Warfare* (New York: McGraw-Hill, 1986).

24. Larry J. Rosenberg and James H. Van West, "The Collaborative Approach to Marketing," *Business Horizons*, Nov.–Dec. 1984, pp. 29–35; Barton A. Weitz, "Introduction to Special Issue on Competition in Marketing," *Journal of Marketing Research*, vol. XXII, Aug. 1985, p. 229–236.

25. George M. Zinkham and Betsy D. Gelb, "Competitive Intelligence Practices of Industrial Marketers," *Industrial Marketing Management*, vol. 14, Nov. 1985, pp. 269–275.

26. Michael E. Porter, *Competitive Strategy: Techniques for Analyzing Industries and Competitors* (New York: Free Press, 1980).

27. The following four sections are based in large part on William E. Rothschild. *Putting It All Together* (New York: AMACOM, 1976), chap. 5.

28. John J. Brock, "Competitor Analysis: Some Practical Approaches," *Industrial Marketing Management*, vol. 13, Oct. 1984, pp. 225–231.

29. Florence R. Skelly, "Using Social Trend Data to Shape Marketing Policy: Some Do's and a Don't," *Journal of Consumer Marketing*, Summer 1983, pp. 14–17.

30. Steven E. Prokesch, "Keeping Tabs on Competitors," *New York Times*, Oct. 28, 1985, pp. D1, D4.

3

ANALYZING INFLUENCES ON CONSUMER BEHAVIOR

Copyright © 1984 Jeff Smith.

SPOTLIGHT ON

☐ Understanding consumer behavior as a buying process

☐ How the values of a culture or its subcultures affect consumer behavior

☐ Identifying aspects of social-class membership that are useful in predicting consumer behavior

☐ How reference groups influence people's buying decisions

☐ Why marketers pay special attention to the family as a reference group

☐ Analyzing self-concept as an external influence on buying behavior

Each year, Americans exchange over 7 billion greeting cards, including 2.7 billion Christmas cards, 1.5 billion birthday cards, and 900 million valentines. The other 1.9 billion cards commemorate weddings, anniversaries, new births, and vacations; express sympathy concerning illnesses or deaths; or simply convey the message that we are thinking of someone. Americans spend about $2.5 billion per year on greeting cards; such cards constitute 40 percent of all mail flowing between households.

Marketers recognize that Americans are fond of using greeting cards to express love, happiness, and sorrow. Indeed, the greeting-card industry calls itself the "social expression" business. Frank Braconi, director of research at Business Trends Analysts, notes: "No question, Americans are the biggest social expressers in the world. People in the habit of social expression can zip hundreds of cards a year." On the average, each American purchases about 25 cards per year.

Who are the heaviest social expressers? Women buy at least 80 percent of all greeting cards; consequently, most cards are designed to appeal to women. People in the northeastern and northcentral regions of the nation buy more cards than the average American; southerners purchase 30 percent fewer. Committed card users tend to live in their own homes, to live in the suburbs, and to come from large families. They are between 35 and 54 years old and have an average household income of $30,000. The national fascination with greeting cards is not as strong among persons with higher and lower incomes.

After a decline in the 1970s, greeting-card sales have rebounded in the 1980s, perhaps indicating a renewed interest in "tradition." Hallmark is currently the leading marketer of greeting cards with a 40 percent market share. American Greetings holds a 26 percent share, and 10 percent of sales go to Gibson Greeting Cards. Some 150 small companies—many of which feature "alternative" cards with offbeat or risqué humor—account for remaining purchases.

To take advantage of a growing market as the baby-boom generation reaches middle age and develops a card-sending habit, card makers are diversifying their offerings. New cards include holograms on die-cut specialty cards; "activity" cards with games and puzzles; cards that deliver electronic musical messages; and (for $10) a perfumed card with a small vial of Revlon's Jontue perfume tucked inside.

Contemporary cards reflect the changing values and lifestyles evident in the United States. For example, wedding anniversary cards are available for parents and stepparents, and some Mother's Day cards are addressed to "my other mother" or to "someone who's been like a mother to me." Whereas greeting cards were traditionally quite sentimental, demand for humorous and even insulting cards has shown a marked increase. Bittersweet cards convey such sentiments as "Do you remember that wonderful time when . . . Oh, never mind. That wasn't you." Curiously, greeting cards do not reflect the racial and ethnic diversity of the nation. Whereas blacks comprise about 13 percent of the U.S. population and Hispanics about 7 percent, only 3 percent of greeting cards feature black or Hispanic characters.

Sources: "The New Greeting Cards: Slick, Sassy—and Strange," *Business Week*, Dec. 16, 1985, pp. 49, 52; Teresa H. Barker, "Hallmark Responds to Life Style," *Advertising Age*, April 9, 1984, pp. 10, 59; Bernice Kanner, "Love for Sale," *New York*, Feb. 20, 1984, pp. 24–28.

Should you buy Head skis? A hamburger at Burger King? Kellogg's All-Bran cereal? A Toyota Corolla car? A humorous or sentimental card for your mother's birthday? You don't make buying decisions in a vacuum. A number of forces—the opinions of others, your own self-image, and events at the time and place of purchase—influence how you perceive a particular product. Your family may have a tradition of sending humorous cards; if so, you probably won't even consider purchasing a card with a serious message.

In Chapter 3, we focus our attention on the social factors that influence buying decisions: cultures and subcultures, social-class standing, and reference-group membership (especially family membership). In addition, we explore how consumer behavior is affected by one's self-concept and such factors as personality and lifestyle. Finally, we examine aspects of the buying situation itself that may influence your perceptions and decisions.

The people at Hallmark understand the influences on card buyers; the success of their products attests to that knowledge. All marketers need a basic knowledge of the sociological and psychological factors that influence consumer behavior. Chapter 4 explores the psychological (or personal) factors that determine consumer behavior.

■ INFLUENCES ON CONSUMER BEHAVIOR ■

To apply the marketing concept, firms in the greeting-card industry must base their efforts on the needs and desires of customers. Marketers must learn what types of products people want; marketers also need to understand how, when, where, and why consumers buy. Only by analyzing both social and psychological influences on consumer behavior can marketers understand people's buying decisions and reliably provide the utilities of form, time, place, and possession.

☐ The Marketing Concept and Consumer Behavior

The formal study of consumer behavior as a separate marketing discipline really began in the early 1960s. The work of John B. McKitterick, Fred J. Borsch, and Robert J. Keith, then president of Pillsbury, did much to spread the marketing concept in the late 1950s.[1] In 1960, Theodore Levitt's ground-breaking article "Marketing Myopia" (see Chapter 1) directed marketing scholars and practitioners to the idea that an understanding of consumer behavior is essential to the satisfaction of consumers' needs. Adapting concepts from sociology, social psychology, and cultural anthropology, marketing scholars began extensive research into factors that affect buying decisions. Today, the undergraduate marketing curriculum often includes a separate course in consumer behavior, and the topic is an important postgraduate specialty as well. This situation reflects the rise of the marketing concept, which dictates that consumers be the focus of all marketing efforts.

Consumer behavior, then, encompasses all the "acts of individuals that involve buying and using products, including the decision processes that precede and determine these acts."[2] Although the factors that precede and determine consumer behavior are a combination of external and internal influences which interact constantly, it is helpful to analyze them as separate elements.

☐ Consumer Behavior as Problem Solving

We all buy consumer products almost every day. The process of buying involves making many decisions; from the standpoint of marketing, it can be viewed as a

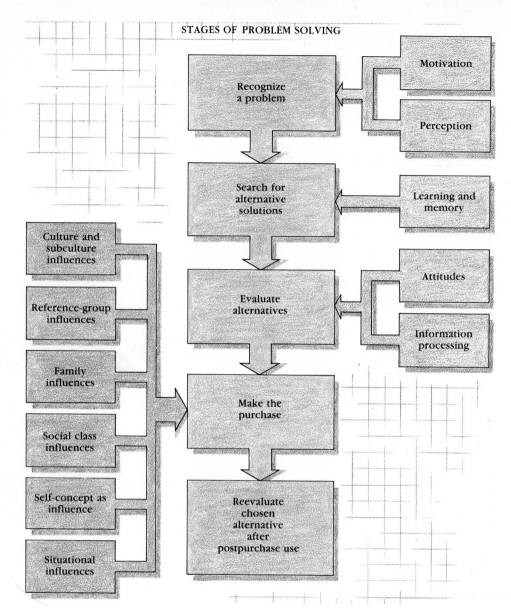

Figure 3-1 *Consumer problem-solving model.* The center of the figure shows the steps in the consumer problem-solving or decision-making process. The boxes on the left illustrate those influences on the process that are external to the individual. The influences on the right are internal, or psychological, and tend to influence the process at very specific stages, as the arrows indicate.

problem-solving process. The central column of Figure 3-1 illustrates a generic process of five stages through which we pass to solve problems and buy consumer goods.

The first stage occurs when you become aware that you have a problem that a purchase might solve. This may be as simple as noticing that you have run out of breakfast cereal, tissues, or blank tapes for your videocassette recorder. However, this realization may be much more complex, as when you decide that you are unhappy with your living room furniture and need to redecorate.

In the second stage, you begin your search for alternative solutions, such as various brands of breakfast cereal. You may conduct this search internally in your own memory ("Which brand was it that I ate last week and enjoyed so much?"), or you may engage in an external search by visiting one or more stores to examine the brands they offer. Then, in the third stage of this buying process, you evaluate the alternatives. You weigh one against the other, compare them on various features, and try to decide which alternative will best solve the problem you have recognized.

The fourth stage is the actual purchase of the product—the result of your evaluation. After purchase, you use the product and then generally go through a final postpurchase stage of reevaluating the alternative you have chosen. Was the cereal as good as you remembered? Are you satisfied with your new living room furniture? After spending money on a purchase, it is natural to think about whether you made the right choice.

In reality, the consumer problem-solving process can be extremely complex. Marketers know that understanding how consumers make such decisions is very important in designing products and developing marketing mixes that best satisfy customers. Researchers have found that many important psychological and social factors influence this process. The boxes shown on the left of Figure 3-1—culture and subculture influences, reference-group influences, family influences, social-class influences, self-concept as influence, and situational influences—represent the *external* forces which shape consumers' problem solving. The boxes on the right of the figure represent *internal* processes that are going on as you make your decision.

In this generalized model, four of the factors on the left—culture, class, reference groups, and family—are considered social influences. Self-concept is a psychological influence, and the sixth factor affecting the buying process is **situational influences**. This broad term refers to any factor surrounding a purchase that may shape the outcome. Use of such a broad term underscores the imprecise nature of our model of buying behavior. We offer generalizations about the other factors identified above, but we recognize that any such influences may be rendered invalid by unexpected circumstances (situational influences) which arise at the time of purchase.

Marketing researchers examine all these factors, which often overlap, to learn how and why consumers respond to an organization's products. As we look more closely at the external factors shown in Figure 3-1, consider how they influence your own buying behavior.

◼ ANALYZING CULTURES AND SUBCULTURES ◼

We are all creatures of the particular culture into which we were born and in which we live. **Culture** encompasses all the things, abilities, and ideas that human beings use, do, know, and believe—everything that one generation of a society transmits to the next. **Material culture** consists of all the tangible things that human beings make, use, and give value to—dugouts and dirigibles, totem poles and temples, rockets and rosary beads. **Nonmaterial culture** is abstract but equally important; it comprises the values, beliefs, and rules by which a society directs people's interactions. Protestantism, communism, and nonverbal communication are examples of nonmaterial culture.

There can be broad differences between the cultures of various societies, but there are also differences within any culture. Each culture harbors **subcultures**—groups that share the values and artifacts of the larger society but also have distinctive practices, preferences, and beliefs. Senior citizens living in housing for the elderly, test pilots working for the military, members of rural communes, and circus performers are all examples of what sociologists refer to as subcultures. Christianity is the dominant religion in the culture of the United States; Mormons and Jehovah's Witnesses may be viewed as subcultures within the larger Christian culture. Because of the important differences within any culture, marketers must be aware of diverse subcultures—examining them individually and on their own terms.

In general, marketers wish to avoid conflict with broadly accepted cultural standards. Thus, certain services (such as hired killings) are not marketed at all. Other services opposed by a substantial number of people, such as abortions, need to be marketed with great care.[3] If advertising is to be used—for example, a public service message for a health clinic that performs abortions—it must be done tastefully. The clinic will not want to advertise its services with a message that incites opposition.

In most instances, of course, awareness of cultural values and sensitivity to those values will allow marketers to avoid damaging conflicts. Simply by studying the fashions people wear and the advertising used on television, marketers can develop a good picture of a culture's most cherished norms and values.[4]

Values: The Keys to Culture

Understanding a culture means understanding its **values**—shared standards of what is acceptable and unacceptable, good and bad, desirable and undesirable. Values are abstract, very general concepts that are expressed by **norms**—rules and guidelines setting forth proper attitudes and behaviors for specific situations. In the United States and Canada, for example, the culture places a high value on literacy; therefore, our norms specify compulsory formal education for every child up to a certain age. This, in turn, creates a great need for teachers, educational materials, and supplementary services. The norms of mass education directly affect marketers of textbooks, desks, athletic equipment, and band instruments; marketers of hand-held calculators, pencils, typewriters, and personal computers and software are affected indirectly.

CENTRAL AND PERIPHERAL VALUES   What do you want to be in 10 or 20 years? Successful in your career? Happily married? A proud parent? What do you want out of life? What will give your life meaning? Your answers to these questions are influenced strongly by your central, or core, values. **Central values** are the deeply held enduring beliefs that guide our actions, judgments, and specific behaviors and that support our efforts to realize important aims.[5] One central value held by many Americans is good health. The current emphasis on health and physical fitness underlies decisions about behavior in general and about buying and consumer behavior in particular.

Although not as deeply embedded or as fundamental as central values, our **peripheral values** reflect our central values. If you value your health, you may value regular exercise and a low-salt, low-cholesterol diet. You may also abstain from smoking cigarettes and drinking alcoholic beverages. These peripheral values will support the central value of maintaining good health.

As Figure 3-2 illustrates, our peripheral values become evident in the kinds of goods and services that we buy. Use of diet supplements and vitamins, purchase of running shoes, and membership in a health club all express peripheral values. Interestingly, information concerning products *not* purchased also reveals peripheral values. Health-conscious Americans express peripheral values by avoiding consumption of cigarettes, liquor, coffee, and candy.

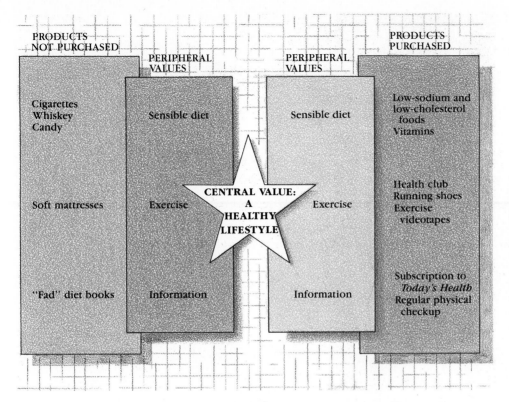

Figure 3-2 *Central and peripheral values.* Deeply held "central" values have an important impact on consumer purchases and lead to other less fundamental values (peripheral values) which shape our buying decisions. We may prefer certain products because they help us express our values; we may avoid others because they conflict with our values.

Although consumers' central values cannot be observed directly, they are fundamental to peripheral values (which are reflected in purchased products). Marketing analysts seek to understand both central and peripheral values. Thus, Adidas, as a marketer of running shoes, will appeal directly to the central value of "good health." By contrast, marketers of Marlboro cigarettes will avoid raising issues of health; they are well aware that certain segments of the market (the health conscious) have little interest in tobacco products.

SOCIALIZATION AND ACCULTURATION   The analysis of consumer behavior also requires an understanding of socialization and acculturation. **Socialization** is the process through which we learn the entire range of physical, intellectual, and social skills needed to function as members of our society. The most important agents of socialization in Western culture are the family, the schools, peer groups, and the mass media.

How and where do potential customers in a large market learn their culture? Are they socialized in large or small households? In religious or nonreligious families? At public or private schools? In what types of peer groups? What exposure to products do they receive through the mass media? Such questions are critically important to marketers, since socialization of any sort influences a person's perception of a product.

For example, clothing manufacturers are now designing tailored suits for female executives, because they realize that working women are under peer pressure to project an image of efficiency. Advertising for such apparel typically presents the model in a position of responsibility and taking action. Appeals to successful working

As more women join the management ranks, ads such as this one attempt to let them know how they should dress, as well as where they can buy. It is part of learning the values of the culture of which they are becoming a part. (Courtesy of Ephron, Raboy, Tsao & Kurnit Advertising, Inc.)

women must be rooted in an awareness of how these women are socialized within today's business world.

The process of learning the values and norms of a culture other than the culture in which one was first socialized is called **acculturation**. Recent immigrants from Mexico, the Philippines, and Korea undergo acculturation—including the most difficult process of learning a new language—when they come to the United States. Marketers seeking to reach consumers who are going through acculturation need to understand the difficulties and insecurities that arise in that process. For example, New York's Con Edison power company employs Chinese- and Korean-speaking customer-service clerks to help recent immigrants with their accounts. The clerks use both English and the customer's native language in solving problems.

☐ *Influences of Subcultures*

The United States has often been called a melting pot, but a better analogy might be to a checkerboard or a salad bowl. Although immigrants do become acculturated within U.S. society, they not only retain various norms of their native cultures but also contribute some of their customs to the evolving culture of the United States. Pizzas, tacos, and blintzes—each indigenous to a native culture—are now marketed nationwide.

Although certain subcultural traits can persevere and coexist happily within a dominant culture, those which differ radically from the dominant culture cannot be tolerated. Subcultures whose values are in conflict with those of the wider society are called **countercultures**. For example, the subcultural world of drug dealers and drug addicts is a counterculture whose norms are widely condemned by the larger U.S. culture.

MAJOR TYPES OF SUBCULTURES Sociologists and anthropologists typically divide subcultures into three types: racial groups, ethnic groups, and regional groups. Membership in a **racial group** is determined by genetically transmitted, physically observable traits to which people attach social meaning, both within the group and outside it. Membership in an **ethnic group**, however, is determined by culturally transmitted, learned traits. Thus, racial groups are not considered ethnic groups. For one thing, they are too large and too widespread to have recognizable, homogeneous cultures that can be transmitted. Some racial subgroups do share certain cultural characteristics, such as language patterns; to the extent that their members share culturally transmitted traits, racial subgroups may be viewed as ethnic groups. Ethnic groups are also determined by common religion or national origin. Finally, a **regional group** is so classified because its members exhibit certain values and tastes that are prevalent within their geographic area.

Racial Groups Blacks constitute the largest racial minority group in the United States, numbering roughly 28.5 million persons and representing about 13 percent of the population.[6] Most black Americans have been socialized within the majority culture; their tastes and behaviors therefore reflect those of the larger society. Marketers are interested in any distinctive behaviors exhibited by members of a racial group. Importantly, these behaviors are transmitted by culture, not by genes; they are learned, not inherited. The issue of marketing to blacks is discussed further in Box 3-1.

Even though they may be well integrated into the dominant culture, members of subcultures often retain many of their own ways of living. The chances are very slight that the foods being eaten by this group of Hispanic-Americans would be the same as those eaten by a Polish-American group. (Copyright © by Stephanie Maze 1985/Woodfin Camp & Assoc.)

BOX 3-1 MARKETING ISSUES: Should Marketers Target Blacks?

There is little doubt that black Americans represent a desirable target market for business firms. According to Bryon Lewis, chair of the board of New York's Uniworld Group, blacks have a gross national product of $205 billion per annum and represent "one of the fastest growing consumer segments in the country, both in terms of population . . . and income." Yet the marketing community remains divided over a fundamental issue: Should marketers concentrate on segmented appeals to blacks? Or should they instead reach black consumers simply through general marketing campaigns aimed at *all* Americans?

McDonald's has made special appeals to black customers, particularly through national advertising campaigns devised by Burrell Advertising, a black-owned agency in Chicago. Among the award-winning Burrell spot commercials are one in which black children jump rope "double-dutch" style and another in which a young black man escorts his grandmother to McDonald's. Noting its competitor's success in such advertising efforts, Wendy's followed suit and hired an agency specializing in marketing to blacks. "We want the black community to know they're important to us," stated an executive for Wendy's. By contrast, Xerox does not have a separate campaign for the black market. Company spokesperson Peter Hawes suggests that "the people we are trying to reach are businesspeople. We don't sell to them as whites, blacks or any other racial or ethnic group. We sell to them as businesspeople."

These contrasting approaches symbolize the continued debate over whether to appeal to blacks *as blacks*. Some blacks within the marketing industry—particularly those involved in advertising agencies specializing in the Afro-American market—argue that the prejudices and ignorance of (overwhelmingly white) corporate marketing and advertising executives lead to misleading assumptions about black consumer behavior. Lafayette Jones, president of a market consultancy firm in Los Angeles, notes that certain brands attract large percentages of black consumers, yet marketing managers often fail to exploit this competitive advantage. Jones believes that "tomorrow's products will most likely be targeted to highly defined segments." Consequently, in his view, marketers should make specific and thoughtful appeals to the black consumer.

Thus far, however, most marketing experts remain skeptical that race is, in fact, an important marketing variable. James Spanier, senior vice president with a New York ad agency, points out: "Our research has found that the difference among black consumers between the better educated, more affluent and the poorer, less educated was greater than the differences between middle class whites and middle class blacks." If this widely accepted view is correct—if class is a far more important variable than race in influencing buying behavior—then the argument for marketing appeals to blacks *as blacks* is significantly undercut.

Obviously, there is no simple answer to the question about how best to target blacks. Much more research is needed to clarify the influences on the consumer behavior of black Americans.

Sources: W. Franklin Joseph, "Despite Growth in Market, Strong Resistance Continues," *Advertising Age*, Aug. 25, 1986, pp. S1, S2; Ronald Alsop, "Firms Still Struggle to Devise Best Approach to Black Buyers," *Wall Street Journal*, Oct. 25, 1984, p. 35; Lafayette Jones, "An Uncompromising Challenge," *Advertising Age*, Nov. 29, 1982, pp. M-12, M-14; B. G. Yovovich, "Marketing to Blacks: The Debate Rages On," *Advertising Age*, Nov. 29, 1982, pp. M-9, M-10.

Ethnic Groups The largest ethnic groups in the United States are made up of people who have been socialized to identify with a particular national origin or to practice a particular religion. Millions of Americans describe themselves as having a foreign ancestry or a combination of ancestries—German, English, Irish, Italian, and Polish were mentioned most often in the 1980 census.[7] Like race, however, ethnicity is significant for marketers only to the degree that it explains an individual's behavior as a consumer. Many Americans of foreign ancestries do not identify with their ethnic backgrounds; as a result, a person's degree of acculturation becomes quite important. Some recent immigrants may quickly adopt U.S. customs and values, whereas a fourth-generation citizen may steadfastly honor the heritage and traditions of long-deceased ancestors.

Regional Groups   There is less controversy in categorizing consumers by region than by race or ethnicity, but the same dangers arise: Generalizations are suspect because they overlook the exceptions and individual differences that exist. Even so, marketers have solid evidence that people in different geographic areas exhibit identifiable tastes and preferences that may be important in analyzing markets. For example, most Texans like their beer served icy cold (32° Fahrenheit); most New Yorkers prefer bitter-tasting brews. In the Southwest, Mexican and "Tex-Mex" food has long been popular; elsewhere it is an occasional treat. Iced tea is a daily beverage in warm southern states, but is consumed much less often in the North.

■ ANALYZING SOCIAL CLASSES ■

Every human society maintains a system of **social stratification**, or layering, through which members are assigned ranks, grades, or positions. This system is transmitted from one generation to the next by agents of socialization such as the family, the schools, and religion. Social stratification inevitably brings with it social inequality—that is, persons in the lower strata have limited access to money, power, and prestige. Thus, physicians are highly regarded and rewarded in our society, but hospital janitors are not, even though both groups contribute to the well-being of patients.

Social stratification has both economic and noneconomic dimensions. It is quite clear, for example, that income is not the only difference in the position of physicians and janitors. The insights of economics can assist us in understanding how differing levels of income influence consumer behavior, but we must turn to sociology to better understand the impact of noneconomic dimensions such as status. By analyzing the bases of social stratification and the resulting social groups within a culture (or subculture), marketers can improve their ability to define and analyze target markets.

☐ Bases of Stratification

Every member of society holds one or more socially defined positions known as **statuses**. Most of us occupy more than one status at the same time; thus, a woman may simultaneously be a daughter, a lawyer, and a mother. But one status is likely to dominate the others at any particular time; this is called a *master status*. One's master status can change several times over the course of a life.

Every status has its **roles**—a set of proper behaviors specified by culturally defined rules. The office of U.S. Senator is a status; once a person becomes a senator, he or she is expected to fulfill certain roles associated with that status. A senator may have legislative roles (as a member of certain committees and when the Senate convenes to consider legislation), political roles (as a leading figure in the Democratic or Republican party within the senator's home state), and ceremonial roles (appearing at parades and dedications). Of course, certain behaviors are considered improper for a U.S. Senator, among them frolicking in the Tidal Basin by moonlight and accepting bribes from foreign agents.

Systems of social stratification, which are enforced through the assignment of statuses and roles, can be classified as either open or closed to **social mobility** (the ability of a person or a category of people to move from one level to another within the system). Hindu society in India traditionally maintained a closed system of castes: Those born into a caste were expected to stay in it all their lives. By contrast, the United States is a more open society. People are born into the strata that their parents occupy; however, either through their own efforts or chance circumstances, they can move from one social class to another.

A **social class** is made up of people who share similar opportunities, economic positions, lifestyles, attitudes, and behaviors. Stratification by class occurs in all industrial societies. Even Marxist societies like the Soviet Union, which theoretically are committed to the abolition of class inequalities, have definable social classes based on the values assigned to statuses and roles.

Social Classes in the United States

In the 1940s, F. Lloyd Warner of the University of Chicago devised a six-class description of U.S. society that has been widely used by sociologists and students of consumer behavior alike.[8] In recent years, that system has been refined and revised as shown in Exhibit 3-1.[9] Although the figures are neither exact nor static, the percentage in each of the six classes and the descriptions of class characteristics are useful in analyzing target markets. The buying power and buying behavior of people in each class can be characterized broadly, although overlap exists between certain classes. There can also be a wide range of incomes, taste, and behavior within any particular class. Consequently, this six-class model must be used with great care in making marketing decisions.

THE MIDDLE AMERICANS   The middle class and the working class, considered together, make up approximately two-thirds of U.S. consumers—the mass market

EXHIBIT 3-1	Class Structure in the United States: A Six-Class Model

Upper Class

Capitalist class (1%): Their investment decisions shape the national economy; income mostly from assets, earned and/or inherited; prestigious university connections.
Upper-middle class (14%): Upper managers, professionals, owners of medium-size businesses; college-educated; family income ideally runs nearly twice national average.

Middle Class

Middle class (33%): Middle-level white-collar, top-level blue-collar; education past high school typical; income somewhat above national average.
Working class (32%): Middle-level blue-collar, lower-level white-collar; income runs slightly below national average; education is also slightly below.

Marginal and Lower Class

Working poor (11–12%): Below mainstream U.S. living standard, but above the poverty line; low-paid service workers, operatives; some high school.
Underclass (8–9%): Depend primarily on welfare system for sustenance; living standard below poverty line; not regularly employed; lack schooling.

Note: Percentage figures for each social class are not absolute and may vary slightly from one study to another. However, these percentages are within an acceptable range and are useful for purposes of marketing analysis.

Source: Richard P. Coleman, "The Continuing Significance of Social Class to Marketing," *Journal of Consumer Research*, vol. 10, Dec. 1983, p. 267. This class structure was abstracted by Coleman from chap. 11, "The American Class Structure: A Synthesis," in Dennis Gilbert and Joseph A. Kahl, *The American Class Structure: A New Synthesis* (Homewood, Ill.: Dorsey, 1982).

so ardently pursued by marketers of most consumer products. In targeting groups within these classes, marketers should remember that income alone is almost useless as a determinant of social class. Labor unions, among other factors, have raised the income of workers to a level comparable to that of the traditional middle class. Although many middle-class people have higher incomes than many in the working class, the reverse is also true. Marketing analysts differentiate the two groups in terms of lifestyles, aspirations, tastes, and family values. Rather than income, they examine differences in general world views, in family relationships, and especially in the lifestyles of women, who are the principal makers of buying decisions.[10]

VARIATIONS IN CLASS BEHAVIOR   A study of car ownership by social class revealed that 40 percent of families in upper-status groups and 25 percent in the middle classes owned imported cars, either economy or luxury models, whereas less than 10 percent of the working class had purchased these generally smaller, less expensive, and more fuel-efficient vehicles. Apparently working-class men were not ready to give up large, heavy, ornate cars. Working-class pride in U.S. industrial accomplishment was also a factor in car-buying decisions. The better-educated upper classes were less influenced by such attitudes and more influenced by the lower cost of the imported cars, a phenomenon that had not been predicted.[11]

Another surprising example of variable class behavior is found in the use of money-saving coupons to purchase food and household goods. Although the working poor and the underclass need the savings that coupons would bring, they use them less frequently than do the middle and upper-middle classes. Many members of the urban lower class must shop in local stores that do not accept the coupons. In addition, members of the working poor and underclass do not regularly read the newspapers in which these coupons appear.

☐ Determinants of Social Class

Various and often interrelated factors affect class membership. Race, religion, kinship connections, ethnic origin, and lifestyle affect how people judge their own class placement as well as how social scientists rank them. The most influential determinants of social-class membership are occupation, education, and income.

OCCUPATION   When you meet someone for the first time, you probably first ask the person's name and then ask "What kind of work do you do?" The answer to the second question tells you a great deal about that person. Analysts of consumer behavior consider occupation the best single indicator of social class.[12] In general, prestige ratings of occupations coincide with assumptions about salary or other monetary rewards, level of education, and political or social power.

Exhibit 3-2 shows the prestige rankings assigned by Americans to some 38 occupations. As you can see, prestige ranking often, but not always, coincides with a high income. Physicians and lawyers enjoy both prestige and high salaries, but a funeral director (moderate prestige score of 52) may make more money than a college teacher (second-highest prestige score of 78).

EDUCATION   More education generally means higher social standing. People holding doctorates do not abound in the lower classes; a baccalaureate degree is almost a prerequisite for placement in the contemporary middle class. Those Americans graduating from a prestigious university are likely to belong to—or be able to enter—the two highest social classes.

Education is the most common avenue for social mobility in almost all nations.

EXHIBIT 3-2　Prestige Ranking of Occupations

In a series of national surveys conducted between 1972 and 1984 by the National Opinion Research Center, occupations were ranked in terms of prestige. The highest possible score was 90, the lowest 10.

Occupation	Score	Occupation	Score
Physician	82	Bank teller	50
College teacher	78	Electrician	49
Lawyer	76	Police officer	48
Dentist	74	Insurance agent	47
Bank officer	72	Secretary	46
Airline pilot	70	Air traffic controller	43
Clergy	69	Mail carrier	42
Sociologist	66	Owner of a farm	41
Secondary-school teacher	63	Restaurant manager	39
Registered nurse	62	Automobile mechanic	37
Pharmacist	61	Baker	34
Elementary-school teacher	60	Sales clerk	29
Accountant	56	Gas-station attendant	22
Painter	56	Waiter and waitress	20
Librarian	55	Laundry operator	18
Actor	55	Garbage collector	17
Funeral director	52	Janitor	16
Athlete	51	Usher	15
Reporter	51	Shoeshiner	12

Source: National Opinion Research Center, 1984.

In Japan and Sweden, as well as in Canada and the United States, attending college is the most frequently employed means of moving from the blue-collar working class to the white-collar middle class. In general, those who pursue graduate education aspire to enter the professional upper-middle class.

INCOME　Most Americans equate income and social class; indeed, a general overall correlation between the two does exist. However, that correlation is not as high as most people believe. We have already seen that some working-class people earn more money than many white-collar workers of the middle class. In fact, a truck driver who belongs to the Teamsters Union may earn more than most editors at publishing houses, who are generally considered to be in the middle class. Some participants in the "underground economy"—drug dealers and prostitutes, for example—have large incomes but low social status.

How a person is paid is an auxiliary determinant of social class. Those in the working class typically receive hourly wages; middle-class workers commonly get weekly or biweekly salaries; members of the upper-middle class usually earn monthly salaries or fees; many in the highest social class derive their incomes from inherited or earned assets. In the underclass, the most frequent source of income may be a welfare check.

In some circumstances, however, income does not indicate social class. Some households earn far more than the average income for the class in which they belong. This is happening increasingly because of second and third jobs within a single household; when additional family members join the work force, their occupations are usually not of a higher status than that of the primary income earner. If fact, second and third jobs within a household are more common in families of a lower status. Families with multiple incomes may move to the highest income

The most important cue to social status is the occupation one holds. In the United States, a judge, for instance, is nearly always ascribed a higher social ranking than a waiter or waitress. (Left: Copyright © by John Maher/The Stock Market. Right: Copyright © by Jim Wilson 1986/Woodfin Camp & Assoc.)

levels within their class, but their social class standing almost always remains the same.[13]

Within each social class, families are said to be overprivileged, average, or underprivileged, according to their income. As Richard Coleman has pointed out, a working-class family with a greater-than-average income is more accurately classified as "overprivileged working class" than as "average middle class."[14] But whether a family's income goes up or down, other factors, such as education and occupation, tend to hold its behaviors to the norms of its class. People continue to live in the same kind of neighborhood, to buy the same kind of car, and to enjoy the same recreation as other members of their class, no matter what their income.

☐ *Class, Income, and Buying Behavior*

Which is the better predictor of buying behavior: social class or income? Some research studies from the past two decades indicate that income is the more accurate predictor; others find for social class.[15] Most researchers today argue that marketing analysis should investigate the combined effects of class and income on buying behavior. In many cases, analysts must determine which factor is more predictive for a particular product. For example, differences in purchases of clothing and home furnishings have been found to be strongly related to differences in social class, whereas income is a better predictor of purchases of black-and-white television sets as well as air travel.[16]

This question—whether social class or income is a more useful predictor of buying behavior—is important to marketers partly because specific appeals are made to consumers based on their incomes and class backgrounds. Box 3-2 shows how a major stock brokerage firm, Dean Witter Reynolds, attempted to target potential blue-collar clients.

Only 20 percent of Americans currently employ a stock broker. With this in mind, Dean Witter Reynolds, the brokerage arm of Sears, Roebuck & Company, has gone after the other 80 percent. The firm's ad agency—Lord, Geller, Frederico, Einstein—developed a special marketing campaign with the theme, "Everybody's Somebody at Dean Witter."

Most Wall Street advertising aims directly at the nation's financial and social elite. Not surprisingly, most blue-collar Americans (and some members of the middle class) do not identify well with the mansions, tuxedos, and cocktail parties that form the background for typical financial ads. Consequently, Dean Witter's print ads in major newspapers and magazines read, in part: "You don't have to be somebody special to be somebody special. Whether you sit at the head of a corporation or just at the head of your own dinner table, we believe you're entitled to the same things." This campaign was designed to convince middle- and working-class Americans that people of *their* class could save and invest wisely in the stock market—with the assistance, of course, of a Dean Witter broker.

By tapping a market segment virtually ignored by other brokers, Dean Witter avoided the heavyweight competition for wealthy investors involving Shearson Lehman, Merrill Lynch, Smith Barney, E. F. Hutton, and Prudential Bache. Dean Witter holds an important competitive advantage in attracting middle- and working-class customers because of its Sears tie-in, its access to Sears's mailing lists and card holders, and its in-store locations.

Thus far, however, Dean Witter's ambitious campaign has yet to demonstrate its success. Although the company has registered steady increases in the number of branch offices and account executives, it lost $32.7 million in 1984. While 1985 was an extremely profitable year for most Wall Street firms, Dean Witter's profits were a modest $13.1 million. According to projections, the firm was expected to show substantial losses for 1986.

Analysts remain divided on the wisdom of Dean Witter's move into consumer financing. John Landschulz, an analyst with a Chicago firm, states: "We're not going to really know for a few years how well it will work out, but it looks good to me." By contrast, Spencer Nilson, publisher of a newsletter about the credit-card industry, suggests that Sears and Dean Witter will have to pull back from the consumer financial business: "In 18 months they'll have to fold it."

Sources: Philip H. Doughterty, "Witter's Campaign for Savers," *New York Times,* Dec. 19, 1985, p. 30; Robert A. Bennett, "Toughing It Out at Dean Witter," *New York Times,* Oct. 5, 1986, sec. 3, pp. 1, 30.

ANALYZING REFERENCE GROUPS

We look to others for guidance in how to dress, speak, work, and spend our leisure time. We look to others to guide or reinforce our basic beliefs and attitudes about ethics, morality, politics, and general behavior. Those others, the groups we use to measure the acceptability of what we do, are termed "reference groups."

Characteristics of Reference Groups

Reference groups give us standards of comparison against which to measure our own values, attitudes, and actions. All of us are influenced by a number of reference groups; these groups vary in size, formality, and impact on members. Reference groups that are small and informal have the greatest influence on people's behavior and on our buying decisions. One such group is our family; another is the group of friends with whom we spend our leisure time. These groups tend to have more influence on us than do larger organizations to which we belong, such as professional and business associations.

Some reference groups have formal membership requirements; members may be expected to pay dues or even to wear specific uniforms to meetings. Less formal groups are held together not by formal rules but instead by the informal under-

standings shared by friends with similar interests. For example, a group of actors who enjoy a regular bowling night may all be aware of an informal group norm: Everyone should be supportive of less experienced bowlers and avoid becoming too competitive. The degree of structure or formality often overlaps with the size of a reference group. One's family is both small and informal, whereas a student government or a trade union is both large and formal.

Reference-Group Influences

Reference groups have been found to wield enormous influence on buying behavior. How does a group influence behavior? To sociologists, a **group** is defined as two or more people, with related statuses and roles, who interact on the basis of shared expectations about each other's behavior. In other words, groups are not simply aggregates of people who happen to be at the same place at the same time, such as riders on a city bus.[17] A group influences its members primarily through the roles and the behavioral norms expected of them.

ROLES AND ROLE EXPECTATIONS   One large group to which you now belong is the student body of your college or university. Your status as a student casts you in several different roles. To your professors, you play the role of learner; to most of your fellow students, your role is that of a peer; to the person you live with, you play the part of a roommate. People in all the groups to which you belong expect certain things in terms of your role performance. Insofar as you mold your behavior in terms of these **role expectations**, groups influence your thoughts and actions as you play your various roles.

NORMS AND CONFORMITY   Just as the larger society establishes norms—the rules that establish proper behavior in particular situations—groups within society establish their own rules of behavior. Norms are an important mechanism through which groups influence the behavior of their members. If you went to church in dirty jeans and a torn T-shirt, the other people there would be understandably shocked and angry at you. In fact, one of the major functions of any group is to exert pressure on its members to conform to norms. When a group member breaks a written or an unwritten rule (dressing inappropriately, smoking in the locker room, or hogging the professor's attention), the group punishes that behavior by various means, both subtle and obvious. A formal, obvious means of punishment is banishment from the group.

Reference groups may be either formal or informal. The group of two on the left is a purely informal friendship group—usually the one with the greatest influence on our behavior. The group on the right is a formal one in that membership is open only to those who made the University of Texas basketball team in that year. Both are primary groups because they bring their members into face-to-face contact. (Left: Copyright © by Nancy Dudley 1982/ Stock, Boston. Right: Copyright © by Bob Daemmrich.)

Just as deviant behavior is punished by a group, normative behavior, or conformity, is rewarded. The more normative one's behavior, the higher one's status in the group is likely to be. The man or woman elected president of the local Chamber of Commerce is likely to be a person who believes in the norms of the organization and plays leadership roles according to the group's expectations.

Group influences become quite complicated. Each of us occupies many statuses—student, daughter, employee, team captain, sweetheart, and Baptist, for example—and we play multiple roles within each of those statuses. Because we belong to so many groups, we are also subject to many sets of norms, and those norms are apt to conflict with each other. Playing all our roles and conforming to all relevant norms is extremely difficult; the fact that most of us do so with relative success is a tribute to human adaptation.

☐ *Group Influences on Consumer Behavior*

A group can have great impact on the products its members buy, although this varies from group to group and from product to product.[18] If you belong to a ski club, for example, the brand of skiis you have is likely to be determined by the opinions frequently voiced by the group. Most group influences are subtle. If a young man's friends favor a "preppie" look, the chances are that he owns at least one Izod shirt along with a pair of Bass Weejun loafers—even though no one told him to buy them.

The characteristics of a product influence the extent to which individuals will consider the norms and opinions of reference groups in making purchase decisions. The first question is whether to buy a product. For products which are essentially necessities, group influence is quite weak or nonexistent. For example, we do not need group influence to tell us whether to buy a wristwatch or a refrigerator. (Note that what we casually call a "necessity" today was considered a luxury by earlier generations of Americans and still is in many contemporary societies.) When considering the purchase of luxuries, by contrast, we find more group influence. Our

Check the dress of this group of college-age people. It is not surprising to find the similarity in shoes, jeans, and even rugby-type shirts, given the year this picture was taken. People tend to conform to the norms of their important reference groups in dress as well as other matters. (Mimi Forsyth/Monkmeyer.)

Analysis for Marketing Planning

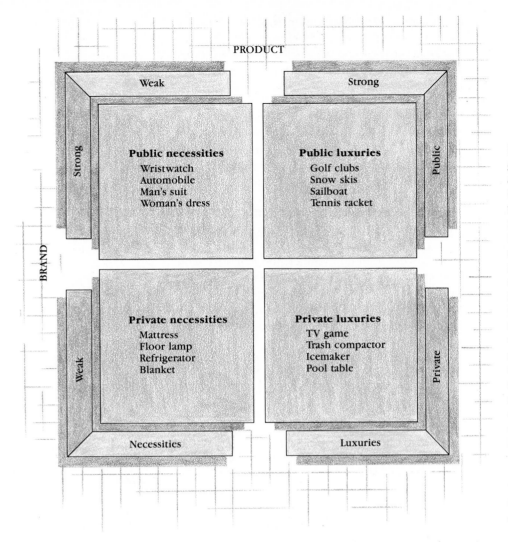

Figure 3-3 *Reference-group influences on product and brand choices.* Group influences on whether people buy or do not buy a product (regardless of the brand) typically are weak for necessities (the two left boxes) and are relatively strong for luxuries (the two right boxes). Those influences on what *brand* to buy are weak for products which are consumed privately (the bottom two boxes) and are strong for products consumed in public (the top two boxes). (Adapted from William D. Bearden and Michael J. Etzel, "Reference Group Influence on Product and Brand Purchase Decisions," *Journal of Consumer Research,* vol. 9, Sept. 1982, pp. 183–194.)

friends may shape our decision to buy a sailboat as opposed to a canoe and camping equipment.

If we decide to buy a product, the groups' influence on what brand we buy differs according to how conspicuous is the product's use. For products which we consume *publicly*—where the product and even the brand may be evident to those we care about—reference group influence is sometimes strong. Some examples might include our clothing, our jewelry, and our living room furniture. By contrast, the brands of some products (such as an ice maker) are rarely seen by our friends. In many cases, even the product may not be seen by others. For these privately consumed products, group influence is fairly weak.

Figure 3-3 depicts products which fall into one or another of four categories: public necessities, public luxuries, private necessities, and private luxuries. Of course, group influence is weakest for private necessities (the lower left box in the figure) and strongest for public luxuries (the upper right box).

☐ *Opinion Leadership*

An **opinion leader** is someone in a group to whom other members look for expert advice, usually on particular subjects. Within a friendship group consisting of ten women, everyone may look to one woman for information about fashion. She reads *Women's Wear Daily* every day and often reads *Vogue* and *Harper's Bazaar*. Another woman in the group owns her own software company; everyone looks to her for advice about what computers and software to buy. Leaders can also influence members *not* to buy products in their domain of leadership.[19]

The rather obvious notion that opinion leaders exert a great influence on the buying behavior of other group members is buttressed by the **two-step flow of mass communications**.[20] Information flows down from the mass media to opinion leaders (step 1), who pass it horizontally to other members of their groups (step 2). An older view held that mass communication was a "trickle-down" process—that information about trends trickled down from the higher classes to the lower classes. Subscribers to this theory believed they could predict the buying patterns of the masses by watching the adoption of new products among the elite. Most communications theorists now agree, however, that the two-step flow thesis best describes how mass communication actually occurs.

One other type of opinion leader is *not* a group member: the celebrity who endorses products. Celebrities serve as a kind of aspirational group. Consumers believe that model Cheryl Tiegs must know something about style; perhaps if they follow her advice, they may also share her good looks. By the same token, Lee Iacocca, the man who turned Chrysler around, must know *something* about building a good car.

Figure 3-4 *Interrelatedness of nuclear and extended family structures.* John begins life within his nuclear family of orientation, which is embedded in his extended family. When older, John leaves this first nuclear family and—through his marriage to Mary—creates a new nuclear family, the family of procreation. The first family is John's father's and mother's family of procreation; the second is John's and Mary's family of procreation. Members of these families—along with various grandparents, uncles, aunts, and cousins—constitute John's extended family.

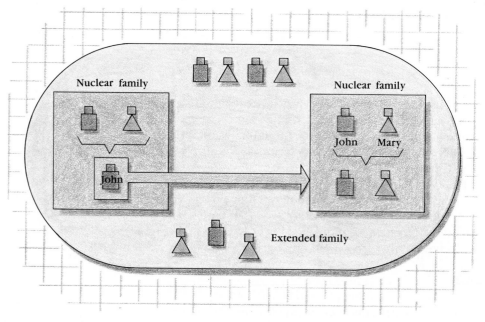

□ *The Family as Reference Group*

Marketers pay special attention to the family as a reference group because it is there that the young are socialized and endowed with their initial social status. Analysts of consumer behavior often address the family as a consumption unit as well, because families make group purchasing decisions and shape the consuming behavior of their members—often for life.

FAMILY STRUCTURES   In most societies, individuals are members of a number of kinds of families. They are members simultaneously of an extended family and a nuclear family. They are members at different times of two kinds of nuclear families—the family of orientation and the family of procreation. Figure 3-4 illustrates these family structures and how they relate to each other.

The basic family form is the **nuclear family**—two parents and their children. The nuclear family is found in all societies, and forms the basis for all other family structures. The **extended family** includes relatives other than parents and their children, spans all generations of living members, and derives from the nuclear family. Extended families may include grandparents and great-grandparents, aunts and uncles, cousins, step-relatives, and in-laws. In the United States, members of extended families once lived together or near each other and formed cooperative units. Today, however, ease of mobility has diminished the cohesiveness of the extended family. Yet it remains important in the socialization process and in its influence as a reference group, particularly among certain ethnic groups.

The **family of orientation** is the one into which an individual is born, the family that cares for and socializes us as children and gives us our initial class status. Later, we ourselves may establish a **family of procreation** by choosing a mate and rearing children (and thereby also providing a family of orientation and a nuclear family for the next generation).

This picture shows an extended family. It includes the grandparents, with their two grown children and their spouses, and the children of those two couples. Although it is no longer common to find extended families such as this living together in the United States, they are important groups that shape consumer behavior. (Copyright © by Michal Heron 1982/Woodfin Camp & Assoc.)

HOUSEHOLDS AND FAMILIES   The Census Bureau classifies the nation's more than 80 million households into one of three general forms. **Family households** consist of two or more persons living together who are related by marriage or birth. A married couple, with or without children in the home, is still the most common kind of family household. Other family households include a single parent with one or more children, or a variation of family members living together (such as two sisters who share a residence).

Two or more unrelated persons sharing living quarters constitute a **nonfamily household.** Members may be roommates or may be nonmarried couples of the opposite or the same sex. An individual who lives alone in a separate residence is classified as a **single-person household.**

Exhibit 3-3 summarizes certain changes in U.S. households from 1970 to 1985. Most notable are the increases in single-parent families and nonfamily households—generally at the expense of married couple families. These shifts result from increases in the number of marriages that end in divorce, in the number of couples who choose not to have children, in the number of same-sex couples, and in the number of people who live alone.

Nontraditional households function as reference groups in many of the same ways that traditional families do—as consumption units and as influences on the buying behavior of individual members. Viewed from a marketing perspective, however, nonfamily households and single-parent families have certain distinctive needs. For example, they may prefer food packaged in smaller quantities and smaller living accommodations.

SPOUSE INFLUENCES ON CONSUMER BEHAVIOR   Even today, many television commercials still feature women comparing their wash and men sniffing engine oil. Reflecting traditional sex roles, research suggests that wives make buying decisions concerning household products and husbands decide when to trade in the car and which power tools to buy. Both partners confer on buying decisions about furniture, vacations, and toys for the children. Figure 3-5 presents breakdowns on spouse involvement in various decisions.

EXHIBIT 3-3	The Changing Character of U.S. Households, 1970–1985

Data show the dramatic increase in nonfamily and single-person households in the United States from 1970 to 1985 and the decrease in average household size during the same period.

| Type of Unit | Numbers (in thousands) | | | Percent Change | |
	1970	1980	1985	1970–1980	1980–1985
Total households	63,401	80,776	86,789	27.4	7.4
Average size	3.14	2.76	2.71	—	—
Family households	51,456	59,550	62,706	15.7	5.3
Married couple	44,728	49,112	50,350	9.8	2.5
Male householder	1,228	1,733	2,228	41.1	28.6
Female householder	5,500	8,705	10,129	58.3	16.4
Nonfamily households	11,945	21,226	24,082	77.7	13.5
Male householder	4,063	8,807	10,114	116.8	14.8
Female householder	7,882	12,419	13,968	57.6	12.5
One person	10,851	18,296	20,602	68.6	12.6

Source: U.S. Department of Commerce, *Statistical Abstract of the United States: 1986* (Washington, D.C., 1986), p. 39.

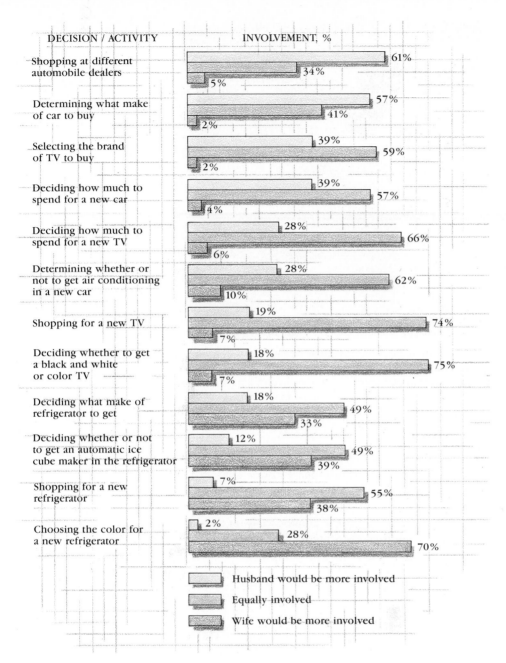

DECISION / ACTIVITY   INVOLVEMENT, %

Shopping at different automobile dealers
- 61%
- 34%
- 5%

Determining what make of car to buy
- 57%
- 41%
- 2%

Selecting the brand of TV to buy
- 39%
- 59%
- 2%

Deciding how much to spend for a new car
- 39%
- 57%
- 4%

Deciding how much to spend for a new TV
- 28%
- 66%
- 6%

Determining whether or not to get air conditioning in a new car
- 28%
- 62%
- 10%

Shopping for a new TV
- 19%
- 74%
- 7%

Deciding whether to get a black and white or color TV
- 18%
- 75%
- 7%

Deciding what make of refrigerator to get
- 18%
- 49%
- 33%

Deciding whether or not to get an automatic ice cube maker in the refrigerator
- 12%
- 49%
- 39%

Shopping for a new refrigerator
- 7%
- 55%
- 38%

Choosing the color for a new refrigerator
- 2%
- 28%
- 70%

☐ Husband would be more involved
☐ Equally involved
☐ Wife would be more involved

Figure 3-5 *Spousal involvement in selected household decisions.* Husbands and wives are equally involved in most decisions concerning cars and household appliances. Husbands are typically more involved in brand choice of cars, whereas wives take the more active role in shopping for a new television set. (Adapted from Harry Davis, "Research Explores Further Aspects of Family Purchasing Power," *Marketing Today,* vol. 16, no. 1, 1978, p. 2.)

As conventional sex roles continue to weaken—and more and more women enter the U.S. work force—buying-decision patterns in the nation are also changing. For example, some 40 percent of car-purchase decisions are now being made by women. Automakers are therefore scrambling to appeal to women, both in product design and advertising. One result of such shifting patterns is that neither husbands nor wives are very skillful at predicting what their spouse prefers to buy.[21] Marketing researchers will have to anticipate future decision-making patterns if they are to effectively design and promote products for households of the future. Perhaps the only sure bet is that income-earning women will insist on more involvement in buying decisions than did the full-time homemakers of past decades.

Traditional sex roles have had an important impact on consumer behavior. As they change, however, marketers must be aware of that change. For instance, it was once considered appropriate to consistently show males explaining complicated things such as cars to females. The new woman is just as likely to be offended by this portrayal of traditional sex roles. (Copyright © by Richard Hackett/International Stock Photo.)

INFLUENCE OF CHILDREN ON CONSUMER BEHAVIOR   Married Americans are choosing to bear fewer children. The birthrate per 1000 persons in the population was 15.7 in 1984, compared with 18.4 in 1970 and 23.7 in 1960.[22] Although U.S. families are becoming smaller, children continue to play an important role in certain family buying decisions. As a glance at the commercials on Saturday morning television programs quickly reveals, marketers are well aware of the value of appealing to children.[23]

Teenagers are likely to become involved in decisions to purchase home computers, stereo systems, and even automobiles. In such instances, marketers realize that although parents eventually make actual buying decisions, their children can exert an important influence. Of course, the extent of children's decision-making influence varies from product to product (and from family to family); it will depend not only on the age of the children but also on the values of their parents.

THE FAMILY LIFE CYCLE: A CHANGING CONCEPT   For at least 50 years, marketers have used the concept of the **family life cycle**—the recognition of various stages in family life, each with its own characteristics—in analyzing and predicting the consumer behavior of families. Figure 3-6 details the stages in the life cycles of various kinds of families. Moving horizontally through the boxes in the center of the figure are the stages of the traditional family life cycle. Other paths through the figure indicate the stages for divorced people (with or without children) and for married people without children.

Buying behavior and consumption vary according to the stage in the family life cycle. Young married couples without children frequently buy to set up their

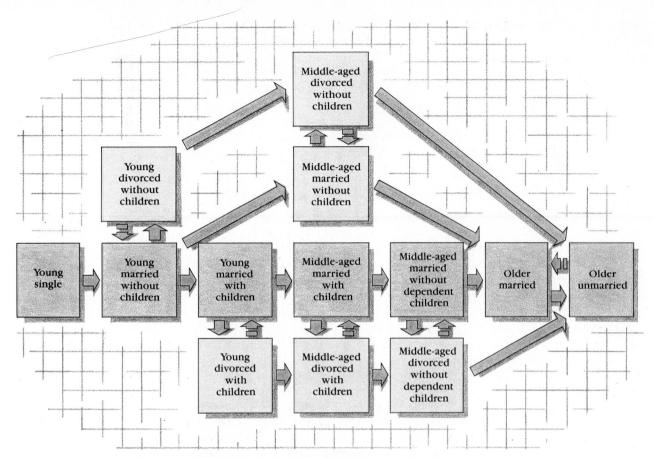

Figure 3-6 *Modern family life cycle.* The middle (green) path going straight across shows the traditional (and still dominant) pattern of U.S. family life; the upper paths lay out the childless life cycle; the lower path traces the progression of divorced families with children. (From Patrick E. Murphy and William A. Staples, "A Modernized Family Life Cycle," *Journal of Consumer Research,* vol. 6, June 1979, p. 17.)

home, shopping for furniture, refrigerators, and recreational equipment. Once children arrive, the couple's purchases change. Not only do they begin to buy baby food, disposable diapers, and toys, but they become more attracted to station wagons and vans than to compact cars. Many new parents also begin to put aside money for their children's education.

Marketers find that the stage in the family life cycle often predicts consumer behavior better than age does. One couple may postpone having children until their middle thirties; another may begin their family in their middle twenties. Thus, even though the couples are 10 years apart in age, they are at the same stage of the family life cycle and exhibit similar buying behavior. Marketers should be aware of important nuances, however. Even though the two couples purchase the same kinds of items, the older couple (having worked 10 years longer) may be better able to afford more expensive products.

Two groups that do not participate in the family life cycle are growing fast enough to demand the attention of marketers: nonfamily households made up of unmarried couples and one-person households. Although some of these people are divorced and will remarry, others will remain single. As shown in Exhibit 3-3, the number of such households has grown at an enormous rate. Among the important considerations this increase raises for marketers are that unmarried couples are far less likely than their married counterparts to have children and that single people look to reference groups other than their families for guidance in buying decisions.

A concept closely related to the family life cycle is that of change in *life status.* This concept extends life changes beyond those that mark stages in the life cycle (marriage, birth of children, divorce, death of spouse) to other major status changes (taking a new job, loss of a job, broken engagement, and so forth). These stress-producing life changes trigger shifts in buying behavior, including brand choices.[24]

■ *ANALYZING SELF-CONCEPT* ■

We have seen that external factors—culture, social class, and reference groups—influence buying behavior. However, a person's own characteristics play a role in shaping that behavior. Although a person's self-concept exists inside his or her mind, marketers analyze it as an external influence on buying behavior because it is formed in relation to the outside factors considered in this chapter. In other words, our self-concepts reflect the influences of culture, social class, and reference groups. In addition, certain personality traits and lifestyles shape or reflect our self-concept and thus influence buying behavior.

□ *Self-Concept*

Most of us are a bit like Walter Mitty, the James Thurber character who fantasizes a secret life full of adventure and beautiful women but who is, in fact, a casualty of daily routine, a likeable nobody. Like Mitty, we all have an **ideal self-concept**—a view of ourselves as we would like to be. Fortunately, though, most of us temper that fantasy with a **real self-concept**—a more realistic appraisal of who we are and what we can accomplish.[25] Many people have a third self-image: an **others self-concept** or looking-glass self. That is, they see themselves as they believe others see them. It is probably safe to say that the more aligned these three self-concepts are, the more integrated our personalities are and the happier we are.

Mental health considerations aside, the self-concept is important to marketers because consumers tend to buy goods and services that express or enhance the self in any of its guises. Conflict among people's ideas of self will place opposing pressures on their buying decisions. For example, a Dodge minivan might be most consistent with your real self-concept; a red Ferrari sports car might best express your ideal self-concept; and a black four-door Saab Turbo car might live up to the image of understated success that you think others have of you. A crucial challenge in designing marketing messages—whether commercial advertising, informative press releases, or labels on packaging—is to appeal to the self-concepts of members of target market groups in a way that reconciles an individual's three self-images (or, at a minimum, does not put these self-images at odds).

Both marketers and psychologists have had mixed results in conducting and applying self-concept research.[26] In addition to the obvious difficulty in determining which self-image might be ascendant in a particular buying situation, no one can suggest whether that pattern would be true of all persons in the same situation and whether it would apply to other situations as well. Nevertheless, a specific marketer of a particular product may—through intuition, research, or imagination—discover which message most effectively matches or disrupts people's self-concepts. Any

organization that can find ways to understand and enhance consumers' self-images will hold a distinct competitive advantage. For example, Sylvester Stallone's *Rambo* films certainly appeal to the fantasy images of U.S. and foreign audiences. They may also attract ticket buyers who enjoy an others self-concept of action and power. People's real self-concepts may be swept away by the dynamic nature of this entertainment product.

Personality Traits

Personality is the composite of a person's patterned, enduring, and interacting characteristics. In general, how these traits are organized determines how a person responds to stimuli. Certain traits dominate others, and therefore we commonly label people as aggressive or compliant, obnoxious or charismatic, friendly or aloof.

A great deal of research into the effects of dominant personality traits on consumer behavior was carried out in the 1950s. Marketers hoped to achieve substantial insights into why people bought certain products and not others, but studies to determine the personalities of owners of Ford and Chevrolet cars, for example, produced conflicting results.[27] Research of this kind continues, but personality test results have not been reliable predictors of buying behavior.[28] Nor have marketers been able to isolate large enough groups of people with similar personalities to constitute identifiable market segments. When researchers have focused on more specific (and less abstract) traits, the results have been somewhat better.[29]

EXHIBIT 3-4	Common Measures of Lifestyle Analysis		
Activities	**Interests**	**Opinions**	**Demographics**
Work	Family	Themselves	Age
Hobbies	Home	Social issues	Education
Social events	Job	Politics	Income
Vacation	Community	Business	Occupation
Entertainment	Recreation	Economics	Family size
Club membership	Fashion	Education	Dwelling
Community	Food	Products	Geography
Shopping	Media	Future	City size
Sports	Achievements	Culture	Stage in life cycle

Source: Joseph T. Plummer, "The Concept and Application of Life-Style Segmentation," *Journal of Marketing,* Jan. 1974, p. 34.

☐ *Lifestyle Analysis*

Although personality research has not provided a basis for market segmentation, it has been helpful in studying and understanding people's preferences. **Lifestyles** are preferred patterns of living as expressed in a person's activities, interests, and opinions, taken as a whole. Lifestyle analysis and measurement, or **psychographics,** groups consumers according to their general beliefs, how they spend their time, the importance of material things in their lives, and such demographic characteristics as income and education.[30] Exhibit 3-4 lists some of the dimensions measured in psychographics.

EXHIBIT 3-5	Groups Defined in the Values and Lifestyles System	
Population Segment	**Description**	**Percentage of the Population**
Belongers	Patriotic, stable, and sentimental traditionalists of any age, who are content with their lives	33
Achievers	Prosperous and self-assured middle-aged materialists	25
Emulators	Ambitious young adults trying to break into the system	10
"I-am-me" group	Impulsive and experimental young adults who are a bit narcissistic and unconventional	5
Experiential group	Adults, generally young, who are slightly more people-oriented and more directed toward inner growth	7
Societally conscious	Mature, successful, mission-oriented people who like causes and have chosen to live simply	9
Survivors	Old people who are poor, with little optimism about the future	4
Sustainers	Those who are having a hard time making ends meet and who are resentful about their condition	7

Source: William Meyers, "Of Belongers, Achievers, Survivors, et al.," *The New York Times,* Dec. 5, 1982, p. F29.

All of us attach psychographic labels to people: We say that someone is an "artistic" type, or an "athletic" type, or an "outdoors" type, or an "intellectual." Market researchers construct psychographic profiles with more care than we do, giving lengthy, carefully developed questionnaires to many respondents before arriving at any conclusions.[31] The use of lifestyle profiling owes much to the pioneering work of William Wells and Joseph Plummer at the advertising agency of Needham, Harper and Steers in Chicago.[32] They identified five distinctive lifestyle groups for both men and women. The more recent Values and Lifestyles System (VALS), developed at the Stanford Research Institute, isolates the eight lifestyle groups shown in Exhibit 3-5. Plummer, now executive vice president for research at Young & Rubicam, believes that the new system gets marketers closer to the people they are trying to reach.

How do marketers use lifestyle profiles? When one VALS analysis indicated that the "belongers," traditionally the best customers of U.S. automakers, were losing faith in the quality of domestic cars, Young & Rubicam developed a series of high-visibility, "new wave" television commercials for Lincoln-Mercury to attract younger belongers.[33] Companies have also found it useful to study the lifestyles of people who buy their products regularly. For example, beer marketers often use such studies to select the images and messages for their advertising. Most marketing managers are now aware of the value of lifestyle research and use it along with demographic data on consumers.[34] In Chapter 7, we will show how psychographic studies are helpful in identifying and understanding target market segments.

■ SITUATIONAL INFLUENCES ■

Even when marketers can pin down the potential buying behaviors of a target market through careful analysis of culture, social class, reference groups, and self-concept, various kinds of **situational influences** (events beyond their control) can sway consumers' behavior from the expected path. If you decide, for instance, to buy a particular personal computer and then discover that it will take 3 months to get the software you want, you may turn to another brand whose programs are available now. And if, on the day you go to buy a new Mercury Lynx car, the Pontiac auto dealer across the street announces a $500 rebate on a similarly priced Firebird car, you may decide that the Pontiac is the car you want after all. Or if you are just in a particularly bad (or good) mood, your buying behavior may be affected.[35]

Marketers cannot control the buying situation—or competitors' actions—to ensure that consumers will behave as analysis indicates, but they can try to eliminate or weaken the impact of unpredictable events, and sometimes they can even take advantage of the unexpected. No amount of analysis guarantees success. But analysis does help marketers to identify who their most likely customers are and to present their products in the most persuasive way—barring unforeseen events. By designing a marketing mix that reinforces the various cultural and sociological influences on consumers, marketers hope to lessen the impact of situational factors.

■ SUMMARY ■

1. Marketing scholars and practitioners believe that an understanding of consumer behavior is essential to the satisfaction of consumers' needs.
2. The main sociological (or external) influences on consumer behavior are culture, social

class, reference groups (including the family), self-concept, certain lifestyle factors, and the buying situation itself.

3. Consumer behavior is shaped by the dominant culture of a society as well as by its subcultures.

4. A society's values are expressed through its norms and are transmitted through the processes of socialization and acculturation.

5. Sociologists and anthropologists typically divide subcultures into three types: racial groups, ethnic groups, and regional groups.

6. Differences among people lead to social stratification and, inevitably, to social inequality.

7. Systems of social stratification, which are enforced through the assignment of statuses and roles, can be classified as either open or closed to social mobility.

8. The middle class and the working class, considered together, make up approximately two-thirds of U.S. consumers—the mass market so avidly pursued by marketers of most consumer products.

9. The most influential determinants of social-class membership are occupation, education, and income.

10. Reference groups give us standards of comparison against which to measure our own values, attitudes, and actions.

11. Marketers pay special attention to the family as a reference group because it is there that the young are socialized and endowed with their initial social status.

12. The last 15 years have seen a dramatic increase in the number of single-parent families and nonfamily households in the United States.

13. For at least 50 years, marketers have used the concept of the family life cycle in analyzing and predicting the consumer behavior of families.

14. The self-concept is important to marketers because consumers tend to buy goods and services that express or enhance the self in any of its guises.

15. Even when marketers are able to pin down the potential buying behaviors of a target market through careful analysis of culture, social class, reference groups, and self-concept, various situational influences beyond marketers' control can sway consumers' behavior from the expected path.

☐ *Key Terms*

acculturation
central values
consumer behavior
counterculture
culture
ethnic group
extended family
family household
family life cycle
family of orientation
family of procreation
group
ideal self-concept
lifestyle

material culture
nonfamily household
nonmaterial culture
norms
nuclear family
opinion leader
others self-concept
peripheral values
personality
psychographics
racial group
real self-concept
reference group
regional group

role expectations
roles
single-person household
situational influences
social class
socialization
social mobility
social stratification
status
subcultures
two-step flow of mass
    communications
values

☐ *Chapter Review*

1. Why is the study of consumer behavior the foundation of the marketing concept? Which external factors are important in analyzing consumer behavior?

2. How might a central value such as the importance of education be expressed in buying behavior? Which products might be sought by a person who values education highly? Which products might be rejected?

3. Why are genetically transmitted social characteristics generally not suitable bases for

identifying target markets? To what extent is ethnicity important as a subcultural influence on buying behavior?

4. Why is occupation considered a more significant determinant of social-class membership than income?

5. Give examples of how reference groups influence your behavior as a consumer.

6. Why is the family such an important reference group? How does the presence or absence of children influence a family's buying behavior?

7. Is buying behavior influenced more by one's real self-concept or by one's ideal self-concept? Give examples to support your view.

8. Name a product that could be used by both sexes but that is aimed at either males or females. Does gender identification influence your use or rejection of this product?

9. List the external factors that most strongly influence your behavior as a consumer. Which subcultural groups and reference groups do you identify with? Which social class? To what extent does family life influence you?

References

1. John B. McKitterick, "What Is the Marketing Management Concept?" *The Frontiers of Marketing Thought and Action* (Chicago: American Marketing Association, 1957), pp. 71–82; Fred J. Borch, "The Marketing Philosophy as a Way of Business Life," *The Marketing Concept: Its Meaning to Management,* Marketing Series no. 99 (New York: American Management Association, 1957), pp. 3–5; Robert J. Keith, "The Marketing Revolution," *Journal of Marketing,* Jan. 1960, pp. 35–38.

2. James F. Engel and Roger D. Blackwell, *Consumer Behavior,* 4th ed. (Hinsdale, Ill.: Dryden, 1982), p. 9.

3. Aubrey Wilson and Christopher West, "The Marketing of 'Unmentionables,'" *Harvard Business Review,* Jan.–Feb. 1981, pp. 91–102.

4. Grant McCracken, "Culture and Consumption: A Theoretical Account of the Structure and Movement of the Cultural Meaning of Consumer Goods," *Journal of Consumer Research,* vol. 13, June 1986, pp. 71–84.

5. Milton Rokeach, *The Nature of Human Values* (New York: Free Press, 1973).

6. U.S. Department of Commerce, *Statistical Abstract of the United States: 1986* (Washington, D.C., 1986).

7. Andrew Hacker, *U/S: A Statistical Portrait of the American People* (New York: Viking, 1983), p. 46. Hacker's data are drawn from the 1980 census.

8. Lloyd Warner and Paul S. Lunt, *The Social Life of a Modern Community* (New Haven, Conn.: Yale University, 1941).

9. Richard P. Coleman, "The Continuing Significance of Social Class to Marketing," *Journal of Consumer Research,* vol. 10, Dec. 1983, pp. 265–280; Dennis Gilbert and Joseph A. Kahl, *The American Class Structure: A New Synthesis* (Homewood, Ill.: Dorsey, 1982), chap. 11; Richard P. Coleman and Lee P. Rainwater with Kent McClelland, *Social Standing in America: New Dimensions of Class* (New York: Basic Books, 1978), chaps. 8, 9, 10.

10. Coleman, ibid., p. 270.

11. Peter D. Bennett and Harold H. Kassarjian, *Consumer Behavior* (Englewood Cliffs, N.J.: Prentice-Hall, 1972), pp. 115–118.

12. Engel and Blackwell, op. cit., pp. 113–114.

13. Coleman, op. cit., p. 274.

14. Coleman, ibid.

15. Louis V. Dominguez and Albert L. Page, "Stratification in Consumer Behavior Research: A Re-examination," *Journal of the Academy of Marketing Science,* vol. 9, Summer 1981, pp. 250–271; Charles M. Schaninger, "Social Class versus Income Revisited: An Empirical Investigation," *Journal of Marketing Research,* vol. 18, May 1981, pp. 192–208.

16. Engel and Blackwell, op. cit., pp. 133–134.

17. Ian Robertson, *Sociology,* 2d ed. (New York: Worth, 1981), pp. 82–83.

18. Peter H. Reingen, Brian L. Foster, Jacqueline Johnson Brown, and Stephen B. Seidman, "Brand Congruence in Interpersonal Relations: A Social Network Analysis," *Journal of Consumer Research,* vol. 11, Dec. 1984, pp. 771–783.

19. Dorothy Leonard-Barton, "Experts as Negative Opinion Leaders in the Diffusion of a Technological Innovation," *Journal of Consumer Research,* vol. 11, Mar. 1985, pp. 914–926.

20. Elihu Katz, "The Two-Step Flow of Communications: An Up-to-Date Report on a Hypothesis," *Public Opinion Quarterly,* Spring 1957, pp. 61–78; Elihu Katz and Paul F. Lazarsfeld, *Personal Influence: The Part Played by People in the Flow of Mass Communications* (New York: Free Press, 1955).

21. Harry L. Davis, Stephen J. Hoch, and E. K. Easton Raysdale, "An Anchoring and Adjustment Model of Spousal Predictions," *Journal of Consumer Research,* vol. 13, June 1986, pp. 25–37.

22. U.S. Bureau of the Census, *Statistical Abstract of the United States, 1986,* 106th ed. (Washington, D.C., 1986), p. 56.

23. Russell Belk, Robert Mayer, and Amy Driscoll, "Children's Recognition of Consumption Symbolism in Children's Products," *Journal of Consumer Research,* vol. 10, Mar. 1984, pp. 386–397.

24. Alan R. Andreasen, "Life Status Changes and Changes in Consumer Preferences and Satisfaction," *Journal of Consumer Research,* vol. 11, Dec. 1984, pp. 784–794.

25. M. Joseph Scigy, "Self-Concept in Consumer Behavior: A Critical Review," *Journal of Consumer Research,* vol. 9, Dec. 1982, pp. 287–300.

26. J. Paul Peter, "Some Observations on Self-Concept in Consumer Behavior Research," in Jerry C. Olson (ed.), *Advances in Consumer Research,* vol. 7 (Ann Arbor, Mich.: Association for Consumer Research, 1980), pp. 625–626.

27. Bennett and Kassarjian, op. cit., pp. 69–71.

28. Harold H. Kassarjian, "Personality and Consumer Behavior: A Review," *Journal of Marketing Research,* Nov. 1971, pp. 409–418; and Harold H. Kassarjian and Mary Jane Sheffet, "Personality and Consumer Behavior: An Update," in Harold H. Kassarjian and Thomas S. Robertson (eds.), *Perspectives in Consumer Behavior,* 3d ed. (Glenview, Ill.: Scott, Foresman, 1981), p. 180.

29. Russell W. Belk, "Materialism: Trait Aspects of Living in the Material World," *Journal of Consumer Research,* vol. 12, Dec. 1985, pp. 265–280.

30. Joseph T. Plummer, "The Concept and Application of Life Style Segmentation," *Journal of Marketing Research,* Jan. 1974, p. 33.

31. Avraham Shama, "The Voluntary Simplicity Consumer," *Journal of Consumer Marketing,* Fall 1985, pp. 57–63.

32. William D. Wells (ed.), *Life Style and Psychographics* (Chicago: American Marketing Association, 1974).

33. William Meyers, "Of Belongers, Achievers, Survivors, et al.," *The New York Times,* Dec. 5, 1982, p. F29.

34. "Lifestyles: Survey Finds Advertisers Confused," *Adweek,* Sept. 30, 1985, p. 84.

35. Meryl Paula Gardner, "Mood States and Consumer Behavior: A Critical Review," *Journal of Consumer Research,* vol. 12, Dec. 1985, pp. 281–300; and Joseph A. Cote, "The Person by Situation Interaction Myth: Implications for the Definition of Situations," in Richard J. Lutz (ed.), *Advances in Consumer Research* (Provo, Utah: Association for Consumer Research, 1986), pp. 37–41.

4

UNDERSTANDING CONSUMERS' DECISION PROCESSES

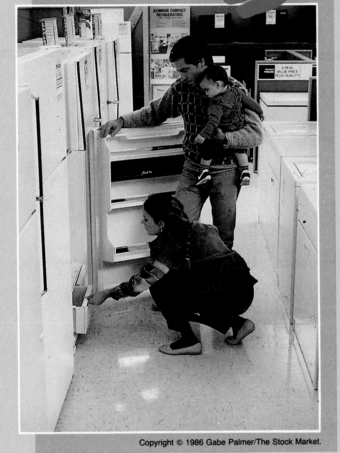

Copyright © 1986 Gabe Palmer/The Stock Market.

SPOTLIGHT ON

☐ Steps in the consumer problem-solving process

☐ Assessment of the needs and benefits that motivate consumers

☐ Selectivity of perception

☐ Role of learning in a consumer's search for information

☐ Development of brand loyalty

☐ Impact of attitudes on buying behavior

☐ Models of information processing

☐ Consumers' postpurchase perceptions and actions

Like an increasing number of U.S. women, Ruth Grossman returned to the paid labor force in her forties after her children left home for college. Ruth eventually took classes and passed her state real estate exam, joined Associated Realty, and had impressive success selling houses in her first year on the job. During this year, Ruth's 1979 Buick car was beginning to show its age and required extensive and expensive repairs. It was time for a new car.

Ben Grossman, Ruth's husband, encouraged her to tackle the purchase on her own. After overcoming initial nervousness, Ruth sat down with a yellow legal pad and drafted a set of criteria for her new car. Practicality for work was Ruth's first criterion. To ferry prospective clients around to look at homes, the car had to be comfortable and roomy. A four-door sedan or a station wagon seemed the logical choices.

Consumers' perceptions of the car were next on Ruth's list. The car should convey an image of moderate affluence—impressive enough to make customers feel that they were dealing with a competent and established agent, but not ostentatious or grand enough to intimidate middle-class clients. Only in Beverly Hills do real estate agents drive Rolls-Royces.

Ruth wanted her new car to fit in with her own self-concept. It would be unpleasant to deal with teasing from neighbors, members of her synagogue, or her daughters. Ideally, the car should reflect who she is. In addition, Ruth wanted a domestic car. Even though Japanese and European cars were increasingly popular in her community, Ruth felt safer buying a car from one of the "big three" automakers: General Motors, Ford, and Chrysler.

Her list complete, Ruth began to check the prices of cars advertised in local newspapers and on television. Ben gently reminded her that—owing to her success at Associated Realty—Ruth could afford virtually any car being advertised. However, Ruth settled on a top price of $15,000. A number of models fit her criteria, but only three "felt right" to her: a Mercury Sable, an Oldsmobile Ninety-Eight, and a Chrysler Newport.

Ruth then visited the three dealerships, gathering promotional literature to read. She was treated courteously by two of the dealers; at the third, she left with the distinct impression that the salesman could not believe that a "nice middle-aged lady" would actually buy a car on her own. His attitude was especially unfortunate, because his agency was offering a 1-month special interest rate on financing.

After an evening of discussion with Ben and careful reading of the three brochures, Ruth went to bed undecided. When she awoke the next morning, a picture of the maroon, four-door sedan in the Oldsmobile dealer's showroom popped into her mind. That afternoon, she signed the necessary papers, and was soon the owner of a sparkling new Oldsmobile Ninety-Eight, complete with air conditioning and a stereo cassette deck.

When Ruth Grossman buys a jar of peanut butter or a nighttime cold remedy, she gives little conscious thought to her choice. Such decisions—generally made in an instant with little or no influence from social or cultural forces—are classified

Consumers show different degrees of involvement in the purchases they make. For most of us, the decision process used in buying low-involvement products such as milk is much simpler than that used in buying a product such as a yacht, a high-involvement purchase. For marketers studying consumer behavior, the challenge is to discover the degree of involvement the target market has in their company's product. (Left: Copyright © by Patrick L. Pfister/Stock, Boston. Right: Copyright © by Dean Abramson/Stock, Boston.)

as **low-involvement decisions** by those who study consumer behavior. In such low-involvement purchases, consumers follow rather simple rules of decision making that produce a satisfactory result with a minimum of effort.[1] For example, when Ruth buys peanut butter, she always buys "chunky," which Ben loves. When she buys a cold remedy, she buys whichever is on sale, since she finds them all equally effective.

By contrast, Ruth's purchase of a new Oldsmobile is classified as a **high-involvement decision**—one that generally involves a large sum of money, has personal relevance, demands a search for information, and produces some degree of anxiety about the correctness of the product chosen. In high-involvement purchases, consumers follow more complex rules of decision making than those they use in low-involvement decisions. Thus, Ruth Grossman was interested in the most practical car available—if it also conveyed an image of moderate affluence, fit in with her self-concept, was made by a U.S. manufacturer, and cost no more than $15,000. No simple rule could express these varied criteria.

Most research on consumer behavior has focused on how important, high-involvement purchases are made. Such decisions involve a series of observable and definable steps. As a result, the process of decision making can be traced by marketing researchers. In this chapter, we will primarily study high-involvement decisions. However, remember that even when consumers do not pass formally through definable steps of decision making—as in simple, low-involvement decisions—they may nevertheless go through an unconscious process as they decide which goods and services to buy.

Chapter 4 begins by examining the internal processes that influence buying decisions. We show how these processes come into play as consumers recognize a problem, search for alternative solutions, and evaluate alternatives. Particular attention is devoted to how consumers learn about products and evaluate information. Finally, we examine influences on the purchase decision and on consumers' post-purchase behavior.

UNDERSTANDING THE CONSUMER BUYING PROCESS

A **stimulus** is anything that elicits or accelerates a physiological or psychological activity. When you decide, for example, to buy a Snickers candy bar (a low-involvement purchase), your decision is actually a response to various stimuli: hunger, the need for increased blood sugar, your personal taste in candy bars, a special display near a cash register. But when you shop for a video system, a college to attend, or a new home in the suburbs, your high-involvement decision is influenced by a large number of complex stimuli. Not only do major purchases involve more money than do simple ones, they also usually have profound effects on your life. Consequently,

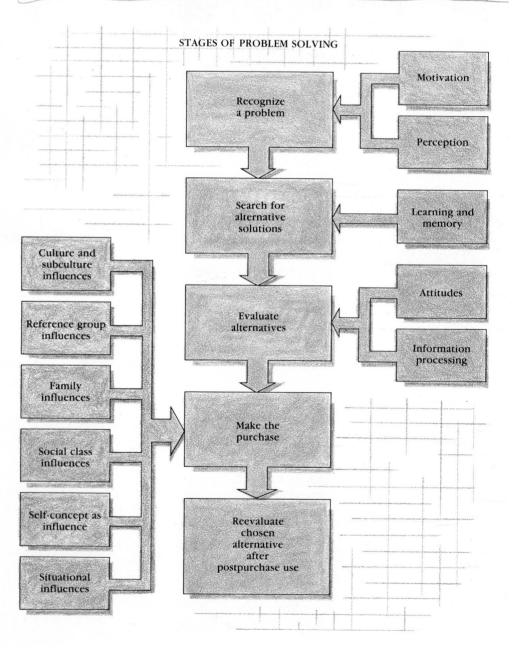

Figure 4-1 *Consumer decision process.* The process by which consumers reach decisions is illustrated in the central portion of the figure. We repeat here the external (social) influences on that process, as discussed in Chapter 3. However, in this chapter, we will concentrate on the internal (psychological) influences highlighted in the right-hand portion of the figure.

you must absorb and process a barrage of stimuli, and your buying decision (unlike a snap judgment about a candy bar) is likely to take time.

In Chapter 3, we examined the external (or social) stimuli that influence buying behavior: culture and subcultures, social class, the family and other reference groups, self-concept, and lifestyle. In this chapter, we investigate the internal processes that affect buying decisions: motivation, perception, learning and memory, attitude formation and change, and information processing. Figure 4-1 illustrates how these influences act on the consumer problem-solving process.

Since internal influences tend to affect the buying process at particular stages, we will structure our discussion around the five stages themselves: (1) recognition of problem, (2) search for alternative solutions, (3) evaluation of alternatives, (4) actual purchase, and (5) postpurchase behavior. The internal stimuli that trigger your decision to buy or reject a product take place within your mind. Whether you choose a movie or a motorcycle, you will move from recognition of a problem (or realization of a need) to a purchase and then to some satisfaction (or lack of satisfaction).

■ RECOGNITION OF A PROBLEM ■

In many low-involvement purchases—buying breakfast cereal, tissues, or the morning newspaper—you move through the stages of the consumer decision-making process so quickly that your behavior cannot be analyzed in depth. Consequently, for purposes of analysis, let us use an example involving a more complex purchase: your trip to a faraway city for the New Year's Day bowl game in which your school's football team is playing. This purchase decision involves a travel mode, a hotel stay, and other substantial expenditures. Since it will take you to an unfamiliar location, you will have to search for helpful information.

As soon as word gets out that your school has accepted the invitation to play in the bowl game, marketers from the travel agencies near you (and hotels and other businesses in the bowl city) will begin attempts to influence your behavior. They know that you have a basic problem: You want to see the game but are not living where it will be played. In their attempts to influence how you view your problem—and how you view the solutions that they are offering—these marketers will draw on their understanding of your motivation and your perception.

□ Motivation

To understand why and how consumers buy, we first must grasp **motivation**, our impulses to take action and the internal and external forces that energize, mobilize, and direct our behavior toward goals. Three theoretical assumptions about human motivation are particularly significant to marketers:

■ We seek pleasure and avoid pain.
■ We are born with certain fundamental needs and with drives to fulfill higher needs.
■ We naturally want to reduce—or, sometimes, enhance—the tension caused when needs and drives are frustrated.

Whatever the origins of the forces that urge us to action, motivating factors probably work together. The important point is that our motivations direct our behavior toward fulfilling our various needs and drives or toward reducing tension

In an affluent society, most people's interest moves beyond their basic biogenic needs, such as hunger and thirst. It is still sometimes useful, however, for marketers to appeal to a basic need like hunger. Burger King did this with its successful advertising campaign theme, "Aren't you hungry for Burger King now?" (Courtesy of Burger King.)

when the environment prevents satisfaction. In seeking to satisfy consumers' needs, marketers must consider whether those needs are biogenic or psychogenic in nature.

BIOGENIC NEEDS   Humans share some needs with lower organisms. Practically all living creatures need food, water, and protection from extreme temperature. Such **biogenic needs** are inborn; they have their genesis in the physiology of the organism. Ducks and donkeys also have these needs, just as they have a need for sex. But in human beings the need for sex, although rooted in biology, is conditioned by culture and learning. Unlike animals in nature, human beings can choose not to have sexual relations. Sex, therefore, is not vital to a person's survival—even though it *is* essential to the survival of the species. The human need for sex, although biological in nature, is just as much a social and psychological need.

Marketers seek to appeal, subtly or directly, to consumers' biogenic needs, those rooted in physiology. Although we could live on a diet of soybean by-products, most people prefer hamburgers and fried chicken, as the marketers at Burger King and Kentucky Fried Chicken well know. (Burger King appealed to the simplest of needs with the question, "Aren't you hungry—for Burger King now?") And although we could stay alive by drinking water from any puddle that was not polluted, Perrier, Evian, and a host of competing bottled waters offer to fulfill needs that go beyond simple thirst—promising purity, sparkle, taste, and especially status. Actually, no needs are purely physiological needs—food and even water (thirst) have social overtones. Thus, marketers satisfy needs that spring not only from our biology but also from our psychology.

PSYCHOGENIC NEEDS   Needs which arise from learning and socialization are considered **psychogenic needs**. Infants are not born needing power, approval, prestige, and the like. Such needs begin to form as cognition (the ability to recognize, remember, and learn) develops and the child becomes aware of people and events outside the crib. Individual and social experience—and what we make of it—moves us beyond biological needs to psychological ones. The need for various types of status, for example, is learned through interactions with members of one's culture, social class, and reference groups.

Marketers of products that lend status to their owners—Mercedes-Benz automobiles, Chivas Regal scotch whiskey, Tiffany silver, and membership in exclusive clubs—may capitalize on psychogenic needs, but they cannot create them. Such needs are already formed. An advertisement for a luxury product may appeal to those who seek status—for example, by picturing elegant people on a lush lawn in front of a mansion—but such ads do not inspire a need for status. Rather, they suggest that the product will satisfy a need that already exists.

Needs may be very complex. For example, we have a biogenic need to maintain body temperature within a tolerable range. Clothing is therefore essential in cold climates but not when the temperature approaches 98° Fahrenheit. We wear clothes because our culture decrees that civilized adults cover their bodies. Further than that, our folkways press all manner of dress requirements on us. Why, for example, must men wear neckties to the office? In the eighteenth century, men wrapped cloths around their necks not only for warmth but also to keep food off their coats—it was easier to launder the cloth than to clean the coat. Dry cleaning has changed that, and the necktie is now purely decorative. Nonetheless, the need to conform motivates millions of men to buy even more millions of neckties every year. Status tie makers like Christian Dior, John Weitz, and Countess Mara did not originate the need to wear ties; they merely satisfy a psychogenic need to conform to society's customs with style.

Whether a need is biogenic, psychogenic, or both, it is not always activated. Needs exist within us, and we act on them when a stimulus motivates us to do so. The challenge for marketers is to identify a target market's needs and then to create a stimulus that motivates consumers in that market to act and satisfy their needs.

We can get from one place to another on buses or subways, or with a 10-year-old used car. But when we buy a car like a Rolls-Royce, we are meeting more than our transportation needs. The purchase is based in such psychogenic needs as the need for status. These needs are learned. (Copyright © Burt Glinn/Magnum.)

NEEDS AND BENEFITS   The **benefits** of a product or marketing mix are those attributes which satisfy the perceived needs of a target market and stimulate those consumers to act. In short, benefits *motivate* consumers, making them aware of the marketer's offering, attracting them to it, and encouraging exchange.

Consider the benefits of humble toothpaste, for instance. Clean, healthy teeth and gums are considered a biogenic necessity in Western culture, a need that can be satisfied with simple baking soda and a relatively new toothbrush. But most consumers seek more than dental hygiene in selecting a toothpaste. Crest, for example, was the first toothpaste to contain stannous fluoride, a decay preventer. This appealed to consumers who understood that tooth decay undermines oral health; today many brands of toothpaste offer the benefits of stannous fluoride. A newly formulated Crest now provides the benefits of pyrophosphate, which combats the buildup of tartar, and Dentagard includes an abrasive agent that removes plaque.

Some consumers, however, seek still other benefits from their toothpaste. Those who want whiter teeth may turn to Ultra-Brite, which claims to keep teeth whiter, or to Topol, which claims to remove tobacco stains. Both make a person more attractive, a social, learned need. Close-up offers a fresh, kissable mouth, that is, sex appeal, a complex psychogenic need demanding no decay, no stains, *and* fresh breath. The marketers of Crest (Procter & Gamble), Ultra-Brite (Unilever), Topol (Jeffrey Martin, Inc.), and Close-Up (Colgate-Palmolive) have identified different psychogenic needs and therefore offer differing benefits.

Biogenic needs, psychogenic needs, or both in combination motivate consumers toward obtaining the benefits that fill their needs—a fundamental premise of consumer behavior. But marketers must go beyond simple identification of needs, because needs change, both in their nature and in their priorities.

THE HIERARCHY OF NEEDS   The most widely used theory of needs is probably that of psychologist Abraham Maslow.[2] Maslow's **hierarchy of needs** estab-

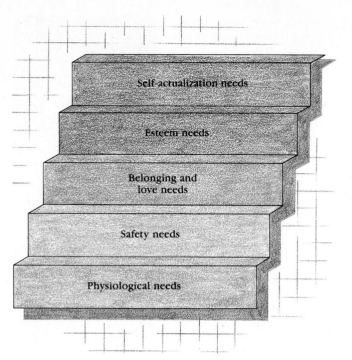

Figure 4-2 *Maslow's hierarchy of needs.* According to Abraham Maslow's hierarchy of needs, lower-level needs (such as physiological and safety needs) become less important as higher-level needs enter phases of dominance, although various needs will overlap. (From Abraham H. Maslow, *Motivation and Personality,* New York: Harper & Row, 1954.

lishes five basic classes: physiological needs, the need for safety, the need for belonging and love, the need for esteem, and the need for self-actualization. These needs are ranked according to priority; Figure 4-2 presents this structure of needs. According to this model, a starving person will be primarily concerned with obtaining food, rather than with the need for safety, love, or esteem. However, as each lower need is at least partly satisfied, the next need in the hierarchy will become dominant. When biological needs are fulfilled, for example, the need for safety becomes the overriding human goal. Various needs will overlap, and lower needs will never completely disappear. However, when the need for self-actualization (realizing one's full potential as a human being) finally becomes most powerful, physiological needs will assume a lower priority, since they can usually be satisfied.

Marketing analysis often takes account of the ascendancy of some needs over others. Ultra-Brite and Close-Up toothpastes are aimed at teenagers and young adults, a market segment with strong needs for belonging and love. Crest targets families with children as its primary market segment, capitalizing on physiological and safety needs ("Aren't your kids worth Crest?"). And although food satisfies a lower-level physiological need, marketers of food products generally do not aim their offerings at those who are starving; rather, they address higher psychogenic needs. Premium-priced items containing all-natural ingredients appeal to needs for safety and belonging (caring for one's family), and prime meats and costly herbs satisfy the need for self-esteem (having the best that money can buy). When McDonald's tells consumers, "You deserve a break today," it is certainly not aiming at our lowest need to satisfy hunger. Marketers have learned to look more deeply at people's needs and the kinds of benefits that will satisfy them.

Individuals' need structures are often reflected in the lifestyle they choose. In Chapter 7, we will see how these choices result in identifiable market segments to which marketers address their efforts and appeals.

Consumers tend to relate the benefits of products to their own needs. Heavy smokers see the benefit of Topol as a tobacco-stain remover. Crest users seek the benefit of decay prevention, and Close-Up and Ultra-Brite users seek the benefits of fresher, more kissable breath. (Ken Karp.)

Perception

To want a product enough to seek it out in the marketplace, we must become aware both of its existence and of our desire or potential use for it. The process of becoming aware of phenomena—whether internal or external, tangible or intangible—is called **perception**. It begins when any of the hundreds of millions of cells in our six sensory systems respond to stimulus, but these responses cannot be called "perception" until the 50 billion or so neurons in the brain somehow process sensory input so that we become aware of it and assign it meaning.[3]

What is meaningful to one person, of course, may escape the notice of another. Although it cannot be proved, it seems safe to say that our perceptions are unique. One shopper studying a display of frozen dinners may perceive Lean Cuisine entrees as a diet aid; another, attracted by the colorful photograph of Sole Florentine, may see a tempting treat; a third shopper may notice the price and then move quickly along to find Swanson's less expensive frozen foods. Why should the same phenomenon—a package of frozen food—be perceived differently by three different people?

THE SELECTIVITY OF PERCEPTION   Because we can detect only so much sensory information and can attend to even less, our perceptual processes are by necessity selective. Suppose you are standing on a street corner waiting for the light to change; all the traffic looks pretty much alike—dirty gray, green, blue, and brown cars, maybe a red truck. Your perceived responses to this scene may be "cars," "going someplace," "I wish they'd stop." Then your gaze fixes on a mint-condition 1932 Rolls-Royce Silver Phaeton, and your perceptions change.

Perception has to do with how we deal with incoming stimuli. The black box of the mind uses the processes of **selective attention, selective distortion**, and **selective retention** to sort out and deal with a manageable amount of stimuli.

SELECTIVE ATTENTION   Your eyes quickly pick out a grand old car, and for a moment you see nothing else. More than just a car, you perceive timeless elegance, superior engineering, beauty, great cost, and painstaking maintenance—along with wealth, power, and sophistication. After a good look at the antique Rolls, however, a new brown Volkswagen Jetta may catch your eye. It is, after all, more in line with your experience and your pocketbook.

We tend to perceive those things that are both meaningful to us and consistent with our experiences and beliefs. You attend to the Rolls-Royce first because it represents a familiar ideal; you select the Jetta next because it is consistent with your lifestyle. If the mind did not filter the billions of stimuli in our environment, allowing only selected details into consciousness, our black box circuits would overload. Consequently, marketers do not expect, for example, that consumers will attend to all the products on the shelves of a supermarket as they walk down the aisles. Marketers design special packaging and even display cases so that their products will stand out amidst hundreds of supermarket items.

The ability to perceive selectively and to screen out most irrelevant stimuli keeps human beings sane and functional. Selectivity is a basic principle of human behavior. It is of constant interest to students of consumer behavior and, indeed, to all marketers.

SELECTIVE DISTORTION   Not only do consumers attend selectively, they tend to distort the information that they perceive to conform to their existing beliefs and attitudes. To test your own perception, follow the instructions in Figure 4-3. If your family likes its Zenith televison set and a friend tells you not to buy Zenith products, you may think that you heard the remark wrong. Or you may decide that your friend doesn't know anything about Zenith products and probably knows very little about television sets in general. A fast-food chain's commercial may claim that its flame-broiled hamburgers are tastier and better for you than fried hamburgers, but if you prefer a competitor's hamburgers, you may distort this news and believe that the hamburgers *you* buy are broiled. We frequently alter information to fit

Figure 4-3   *Perception.* The figure in (c) is ambiguous. If you cover up (b), both (a) and (c) will look like an old woman in profile; but if you cover up (a), then (b) and (c) will both look like a young woman whose face is turned away. Try showing (c) to a friend while covering up both other drawings. Ask, "What do you see?" And then: "Do you see anything else?" Then show each of the other drawings.

(a)   (b)   (c)

with our existing views. Jarring information is psychologically uncomfortable, and so we unconsciously process it into a perception that we can accept.

The process of selective distortion is evident not only in marketing of consumer goods but also in industrial marketing. When calling on customers who are previous buyers of a firm's industrial product, a salesperson will tend to selectively distort information to make it consistent with the clients' previous buying decisions. Ideally, the information provided will allow the clients to confirm the wisdom of their previous choices. By contrast, when attempting to make a sale to a client who has traditionally chosen a competitive brand, a salesperson faces an uphill battle—partly because the client may selectively distort information to maintain the status quo.

SELECTIVE RETENTION   Just as the mind selects and shapes the incoming information that it attends to, it also retains only those perceptions that are consistent with existing psychological patterns. Consumers who want a new lawn mower, a 35mm camera, or a tax-free investment fund seek out information about those products and retain the knowledge that they believe is important. Consumers with no need for these items are unlikely to remember details about them even if they initially paid attention to the product.

The selectivity of attention, distortion, and retention challenges the abilities of marketers to communicate effectively. These factors account for the repetition and other attention-getting devices built into promotional messages. Advertising agencies invest a great deal of effort and money to catch consumers' attention with messages that overcome negative distortions and stick in the mind. The combined words, music, and visual effects of the best television commercials achieve these ends.

We pay attention to advertisements when we are already interested in a product. People considering the purchase of a new car are more likely to pay attention to auto advertising than are those who have no interest in such a purchase. We are also more likely to retain messages that reinforce existing beliefs. If we believe that Volkswagen is a solid, dependable, economical car, promotions featuring the gas-saving features of a Hyundai from Korea or a Yugo from Yugoslavia may pass us by without being "filed away" in our black boxes. Interestingly, we tend to distort incoming messages when they do not support existing beliefs. If we already believe that a Volkswagen is a cheap car that is not likely to hold up over time, we may place a negative interpretation on Volkswagen price appeals ("Of course it's less expensive than my car; it falls apart in two years!").

Clearly, perception is a process of placing information in a framework consistent with our backgrounds, personalities, knowledge, and prejudices. The more marketers learn about perception—and a great deal remains unclear or in dispute (see Box 4-1)—the better they can tailor messages that will have the desired perceptual penetration and impact.

■ SEARCH FOR ALTERNATIVE SOLUTIONS ■

After you realize that you have a problem that purchase behavior can possibly solve, you will normally go to the next stage of the consumer buying process and search for alternative solutions. To get to the bowl game, you can drive, take a train or bus, or fly. Each alternative involves further choices; for example, you can fly by buying your own ticket or by joining a tour group being formed by a local travel

BOX 4-1   MARKETING ISSUES: Subliminal Perception

Can advertisers gain power over a consumer's thoughts and actions by assaulting the consumer with sexual images that the conscious mind cannot detect? Can such "subliminal" messages exert a sinister influence over unsuspecting Americans? Marketing scholars and advertising experts scoff at such suggestions, yet one of the prime defenses of this view—Wilson Bryan Key's book *Subliminal Seduction*—has sold nearly 1 million copies.

According to Walter Weir, an associate professor of journalism at Temple University, the term "subliminal advertising" was invented by Jim Vicary in 1957. Vicary, the owner of a struggling research business, claimed that he had discovered a means of advertising subliminally with powerful effect by flashing messages on a screen so rapidly that they could not be seen consciously but could be absorbed by the unconscious mind. Vicary insisted that he had substantiated this new and effective advertising technique through a test at a New Jersey movie theater in which messages were flashed instantaneously on the screen to induce viewers to buy Coca-Cola and popcorn. However, Henry Link, president of Psychological Corporation, challenged Vicary to repeat the test under agreed-upon controls and supervision by an independent research firm. Vicary accepted the challenge, the testing revealed no increase in sales of either Coke or popcorn, and Vicary was forced to admit that he had fabricated the results of his original "test" in the hopes of assisting his failing research business.

Allegations concerning subliminal advertising surfaced again in the early 1970s, with the publication of *Subliminal Seduction* and other works by Wilson Bryan Key. Key argues that a wide assortment of television commercials and print advertisements contain hidden sexual messages. For example, Key claims that Ritz crackers have a mosaic of the letters *S E X* embedded on both sides of each cracker, and that the same letters are frequently embedded on ice cubes appearing in photographs used for liquor advertising. Key insists that each of his readers "has been victimized and manipulated by the use of subliminal stimuli directed into his unconscious mind by the mass merchandisers of media."

Marketing experts have widely attacked Key's sweeping and sensationalistic assertions about the prevalence and power of subliminal advertising messages. Many have charged that Key has offered doctored photographs with added subliminal messages never used in actual advertisements. Their criticisms have been fueled by a study conducted by Professor Jack Haberstroh of Virginia Commonwealth University. Haberstroh and two of his students interviewed art directors of ad agencies which created the advertisements identified by Key as containing subliminal messages. The interviews revealed no evidence that there had been implanting of specific and hidden sexual messages in advertising. Moreover, Haberstroh analyzed the baking process used to prepare Ritz crackers and found that the embedding of cracker bottoms with *any* type of message is virtually impossible.

Haberstroh concludes that advertising professionals have too often ignored Key's charges, thereby allowing gullible Americans to be persuaded by these conspiratorial allegations. "It is," suggests Haberstroh, "an issue about which we must no longer remain mute." Replying in a 1984 editorial, the editors of *Advertising Age* argued that "remaining mute, in this instance, only means that advertising professionals have better things to do with their time." Thus, although some Americans continue to be alarmed by the dangers of subliminal advertising, most advertising experts feel that the entire issue is ludicrous and hardly deserves a serious response.   ▪

Sources: Wilson Bryan Key, *Subliminal Seduction* (New York: Signet, 1973), p. 1; "Scrutinizing 'Subliminal' Ads," *Advertising Age*, Sept. 24, 1984, p. 18; Walter Weir, "Another Look at Subliminal 'Facts,'" *Advertising Age*, Oct. 15, 1984, p. 46.

---

agency. There are also many alternatives as to where to stay in the bowl city—ranging from an expensive hotel where the football team is staying to the local YMCA.

In the process of searching for solutions, you will generally engage in both an internal search of your own memory and an external search for information from both commercial and independent sources. We can best understand the internal search by referring to psychological theories of learning and memory.

☐ *Internal Search for Information*

From the day we are born, we sense our environment. As our nervous systems begin to process sensations, experiences penetrate our awareness and become perceptions. As our nervous systems develop and we are able to have expanded new perceptions, we begin to find increasing meaning in our experiences. In short, we learn.

Psychologists broadly describe **learning** as relatively permanent changes in thought and behavior that result from experience. Learning requires **memory,** the ability to summon past thoughts and events to mind. The two processes are intertwined: We must remember to learn, and we must have learned to remember. Marketers need to know as much as possible about how consumers perceive products, how they learn about them, how they learn to avoid or seek them, and how they remember them.

HOW WE LEARN   Most of us are familiar with the kind of learning that has been termed **classic (respondent) conditioning.** This is a **stimulus-response (SR) theory** which holds that organisms learn first to associate an original stimulus with another, adjacent stimulus and then to respond to that second "conditioned" stimulus with the behavior formerly induced by the original stimulus.

Ivan Pavlov established the existence of this kind of learning (and thereby won the Nobel Prize in 1904) by conditioning dogs to salivate upon hearing a bell, the sound of which had previously been associated with the presentation of food. Through conditioning, the dogs came to salivate when they heard only the bell—even without food (the original stimulus). Similarly, some of us demonstrate a conditioned response if we cannot go to sleep without the sound of a radio or television. Such learning usually involves the association of some reflex behavior (sleep) with a neutral stimulus (the sound). Researchers continue to study classical conditioning.[4]

Of more relevance to students of consumer behavior is **operant conditioning,** in which we learn not simply to respond to stimuli but also to perform operations on our environment; that is, we actively manipulate things to produce desired consequences or to avoid undesired ones. This concept holds that learning results not in habitual responses but in mental structures—systems of thinking about our experiences. If you are hungry in the morning, your thinking might go like this: "I'm hungry for breakfast. My parents used to give me Raisin Bran in the morning. I remember that I liked it and I felt good after eating it. I think I'll buy some." This entire sequence occurs almost instantaneously as a single thought, of course, composing a mental structure that you use for thinking about breakfast cereal. Consumer behavior leans heavily on the learning brought about through operant conditioning, which involves voluntary responses and expresses both biogenic and psychogenic needs.

SIMPLIFIED BEHAVIORAL MODEL OF THE LEARNING PROCESS   The steps detailed in Figure 4-4 provide an oversimplified but workable picture of the learning process. It begins with a need or drive and stimulus and cues, followed by response, reinforcement, and (further) learning.

As we become aware of needs, stimuli may emerge that suggest a way to reduce or eliminate those needs. If you notice that the lining is falling out of your winter jacket, a window display of down-filled coats on preseason sale will remind you that it is time to get a new one. Or a stimulus may trigger the recognition of a need. A sharp temperature drop suddenly makes you aware that your coat has

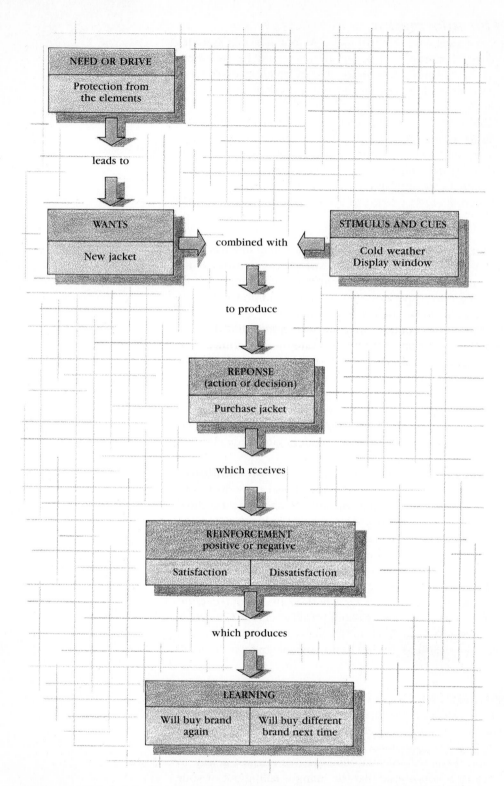

Figure 4-4 *Consumer learning process.* Stimuli combine with needs to produce action (a purchase). Satisfaction or dissatisfaction with the purchase produces learning which influences future purchases.

seen better days. Whatever the original stimulus and its supporting **cues**—the minor stimuli that shape your response, you will respond, either by buying a new coat or by deciding to get through one more winter with the old one.

If you buy the coat and are happy with it, your behavior is reinforced positively; you are likely to buy the same brand and/or shop in the same store again. If you are not satisfied with the purchase, however, negative reinforcement may steer you from that brand or store in the future. Marketers try to increase the likelihood of positive reinforcement and to reduce the chance of negative reinforcement.[5]

DEVELOPMENT OF BRAND LOYALTY   **Brand loyalty,** the habit of repeatedly purchasing the same brand of a product, develops through learning. Because marketers obviously hope to establish brand loyalty, they bend every effort toward associating their products with powerful consumer needs by developing motivating cues and attempting to ensure positive reinforcement. Of course, products of superior quality tend to generate consumer satisfaction; such positive reinforcement encourages brand loyalty. Whatever the source of their rewards, however, satisfied consumers do translate their satisfaction into repeat purchases, just as the negative reinforcement resulting from dissatisfaction pushes consumers toward other brands.

Advertisers speak of a brand's "franchise," referring to a core of brand-loyal customers. In general, the promotional money spent on media advertising is designed to expand and solidify that loyal core. Promotional efforts are also intended to break down a competitor's core of loyal customers.[6] The issue of brand loyalty is examined further in Box 4-2.

LEARNING AND THE SEARCH FOR INFORMATION   How far will people go in their search for information about a product? In part, the answer depends on how much they have already learned about it. As consumers gain knowledge about a product class—paper towels, for example—they begin to narrow down the range

Among those sources of information that have a strong impact on consumers' decisions are the informal sources over which the marketer has no control. Perhaps the most powerful of these is the "word-of-mouth" communication that takes place between neighbors, or friends, where the assumption is that neither friend has anything to gain by not being honest with the other. (Copyright © by Junebug Clark 1982/Photo Researchers, Inc.)

of acceptable alternatives. After testing several towel brands, they learn that unbranded, generic products are cheaper than national brands such as Bounty or Viva. However, they also learn that the more expensive brands are stronger, are more absorbent, and come in a range of colors and patterns. Ultimately, most buyers reject certain brands, accept two or three, and prefer a particular brand.

The search for information about a product class typically has three stages: extensive problem solving, limited problem solving, and routinized response.[7] Young people buying their first car usually undertake a fairly extensive search for information, comparing makes and models and matching this information with peer-group opinions and their own self-images. With no narrowly defined set of alternatives at this stage, buyers are more likely to generalize—considering all Chrysler products equally acceptable, for example—than to discriminate by perceiving certain qualities in Dodges that Plymouths do not have.

A stage of limited problem solving follows extensive problem solving. With more experience, buyers learn to discriminate among products and develop certain brand loyalties. They seek less information because they are now more likely to choose among a narrowed range of alternatives.[8] Buyers of new cars reduce their search for information with each succeeding purchase, since their experience with each previous car reinforces them positively or negatively.[9] For some products, consumers ultimately reach a stage of routinized response, habitually choosing their preferred brand without searching for new information. If a car buyer has been

tional tie to the long-accepted Coke taste, which seemed to summon fond memories of childhood days. Clearly, Coca-Cola could not count on behavioral loyalty to the Coke name if it changed the taste of the product and thereby disrupted consumers' emotional attachments to the past.

Despite the compelling efforts of Coca-Cola loyalists, some marketing experts view brand loyalty as a dying phenomenon—especially as competition becomes more intense through introduction of new products and an increase in aggressive price promotions.

Degrees of Brand Loyalty
According to a study conducted by the J. Walter Thompson advertising agency, brand loyalty varies depending on the product.

High-Loyalty Products	Medium-Loyalty Products	Low-Loyalty Products
Cigarettes	Cola drinks	Paper towels
Laxatives	Margarine	Crackers
Cold remedies	Shampoo	Scouring powder
35mm film	Hand lotion	Plastic trash bags
Toothpaste	Furniture polish	Facial tissues

Source: Anne B. Fisher, "Coke's Brand-Loyalty Lesson," *Fortune,* Aug. 5, 1985, p. 46.

When People's Express fell into financial crisis in mid-1986, few passengers seemed to care whether the discount airline survived. Although People's Express had saved travelers billions of dollars in lower air fares, most customers felt no special obligation to the airline. "Who cares about an airline? They are all miserable to fly on," stated one People's Express passenger.

Still other marketing experts challenge the view that brand loyalty is dying. Instead, they suggest, brand loyalty can vary dramatically depending on the product. Current marketing research indicates that the higher the level of consumer involvement in purchase decisions, the stronger the resulting brand loyalty. One of the leading ad agencies in New York, J. Walter Thompson, studied consumer loyalty to brands in 80 product categories. Researchers measured the degree of brand loyalty by asking consumers if they would switch brands for a 50 percent discount. Cigarette smokers were among the *least* likely to switch, making them the most brand-loyal group in the survey (see accompanying table). Users of paper towels, plastic trash bags, and facial tissues were among the most likely to switch brands. ■

Sources: Mark N. Vamos, "Harley-Davidson Rides a Marketing Tightrope," *Ad Forum,* Jan. 1984, pp. 27–28; Anne B. Fisher, "Coke's Brand-Loyalty Lesson," *Fortune,* Aug. 5, 1985, pp. 44–46; John Koten, "Product Loyalty Lasts as Long as the Best Price," *Wall Street Journal,* Aug. 7, 1986, p. 21.

satisfied with the four different Pontiacs she owned during the past 15 years, her next car is likely to be a Pontiac.

The time required for these stages of learning and information search varies with the product class. You can quickly find out all you need to know about paper towels or peanut butter, but learning about automobiles or personal computers can take years. Importantly, such learning about products can begin at a very young age. Even girls 9 to 10 years old are affected by advertisements for brands of lipstick.[10]

MEMORY AND INFORMATION SEARCH   Consumers who set out to satisfy a need or want by buying a product usually tap their own memories first. They search internally to retrieve all relevant information. The efficiency with which we make daily buying decisions indicates that the process is all but instantaneous when considering relatively inexpensive, low-risk items. We seldom need to conduct research about which toothpaste to buy, which notebook, or which gasoline. Our stored experiences with such items allow us to make choices quickly and with little mental effort. Often we store this information in memory along with a brand name—a most useful buying tool. (And even though you may not know the brand name of the notebooks you buy, you probably recognize their covers and know where to find them in the campus bookstore.)

Even for costlier purchases with a higher perceived risk, consumers usually conduct an internal search before an external one. Before shopping for a new television set, you comb your memory for impressions of the sets owned by your family and friends. You think about picture quality, the looks of various models, repair or service problems that you have heard about, and comments that peers have made about different brands. This internal search lays the foundation for your external search, during which you check advertisements for features and prices, hunt for sales, and narrow your list of possibilities.

☐ External Search for Information

After you have searched your own memory for solutions to your problem, you often feel a need for further information. At this point, you will probably begin an external search for information. Returning to the example involving the bowl game, you may call or visit the travel agency offering the package tour to the bowl city. Or you may seek out a friend who lives near that city and ask about restaurants, bars, and hotels. Consumers seek external information both from marketers and from independent sources.

MARKETER-DOMINATED SOURCES   Marketers design and control descriptive information about their products through such means as labels, advertising, publicity, and salespeople. In fact, the entire promotion component of the marketing mix is aimed at communicating effectively with the target markets. In general, marketer-dominated information sources are grouped into personal, face-to-face communication and impersonal, mass-media approaches.

The salespeople in retail stores and service agencies are the chief personal sources of product information. Consumers deciding on a new dishwasher can ask sales personnel about load capacity, voltage requirements, servicing provisions, and special features. Salespeople, in turn, point out salient features in various models and provide pricing and rebate information. Almost 3 million consumers call General Electric's Louisville-based tollfree telephone number every year. According to N. Powell Taylor, manager of the General Electric Answer Center: "Many of the calls we receive are from consumers looking for information before they purchase a home appliance. We don't try to sell them GE's products in particular, but give them comparison information so they can make their buying decisions."[11]

Impersonal sources of information controlled by the marketer include print advertising, television and radio commercials, promotional booklets, posters detailing special offers and rebates, and operating instructions. Consumers undoubtedly perceive that marketer-dominated information is intended to create favorable impressions for the product in question. As such, advertising messages are assigned less legitimacy and believability than is information coming from independent sources.

INDEPENDENT SOURCES   The most influential sources of information independent of the marketer are the opinions of reference-group members. People commonly seek product advice from their friends, their families, and especially the opinion leaders in their reference groups. Such word-of-mouth judgments exert a powerful influence on many consumer decisions. For example, regardless of all promotional efforts, bad "word of mouth" can quickly kill a new motion picture. Independent sources of information are particularly important for innovations, which are discussed in detail in Chapter 11.

Media news sources are another important supplier of consumer information. Certain newspapers—the *Washington Post, The New York Times,* the *Los Angeles*

Times, the *Louisville Courier Journal*—add their own authority to the subjects they cover. (This is true to a lesser extent of all newspapers.) Consumers tend to believe what they read about a product, whether it is positive or negative. Magazines aimed at particular market segments also lend expert approval to the products they feature. For example, shelter magazines, such as *Architectural Digest, Better Homes and Gardens,* and *Southern Living,* tacitly endorse home furnishings. Finally, among a host of consumer affairs publications, *Consumer Reports* magazine, which rates various products in unbiased tests, stands out as a potent source of product information.

EXTENT OF OUTSIDE SEARCH   Marketers seek to understand how far consumers will go in their search for outside information. The amount of effort expended usually corresponds to the dollar amount of the purchase or to its personal or financial importance to the buyer. Automobiles, clothing, major appliances, homes, and investment services (high-involvement items) are products that consumers investigate at great length, carefully comparing prices and other features of alternatives. Because customers do make comparisons, marketers often provide careful and specific product information.

On occasion, consumers undertake relatively extensive research on less costly, less important items. People who are already familiar with a product will search more (and more efficiently) for information before making a new purchase.[12] The amount of time we spend in the supermarket reading label information about how many ounces we are getting per dollar and about nutritional benefits of a food product represent an effort not typically required in the purchase of a pack of gum or a felt-tipped pen.

■ PERCEIVED RISK AND BUYING BEHAVIOR ■

In addition to providing information about products for consumers, marketers assess the amount of risk consumers attach to the purchase of an item. Perceived risk enters the buying process when consumers are uncertain about their buying goals. One might evaluate an upcoming vacation and ask: "Do I want to just relax or to run around sight-seeing?" If the decision is to sightsee, the next question might be: "Will I be more satisfied with a trip to Paris or to the Canadian Rockies?" Even when that decision is made, there may be doubts concerning adverse consequences ("Will the weather in Paris be cold and rainy?"). If one or more of these conditions exist, the consumer must deal with the **perceived risk** that an incorrect buying decision may result in undesired consequences.

The amount of risk perceived is greater, in general, when contemplating an expensive purchase. For example, buying a new home while interest rates are especially high and real estate taxes are rising is likely to increase your perception of risk. Whether real or imaginary, however, a perceived risk is often a major influence on buying decisions. Usually, the perception of risk arises either from uncertainty that the product will match the buying goals ("If I buy a motorcycle to replace my car, will I still be able to get to work on time?") or from fear of consequences relating to the product's performance and quality and its ability to fulfill social and psychological needs ("Will it be dangerous to ride my motorcycle to work in the midst of rush-hour traffic?").[13]

Perceived risk may be physical, financial, or social. A perception of physical risk may intrude on the decision to buy a motorcycle rather than a new car. Questions of physical risk also arise in the purchase of over-the-counter or prescription drugs. Is the seal on the aspirin bottle broken? Will the antibiotic produce uncomfortable or dangerous side effects?

Perceived financial risks accompany almost any large purchase. Are tax-free municipal bonds a sound investment? Would a money market fund be more lucrative? Will future environmental regulations forbid building on a piece of waterfront land? Will the higher price of a Maytag washer be "money well spent"?

A purchase may also entail social risks. If you select the wrong bottle of wine in an expensive restaurant, your selection may elicit a condescending glare from the wine steward. If you install a swimming pool in your backyard, your middle-class neighbors may be jealous and insist that you are simply "showing off."

Marketers are aware of the many uncertainties and possible negative consequences that consumers weigh when making purchase decisions. Whenever possible, marketers attempt to reduce or eliminate troublesome perceptions of risk. Money-back guarantees, offers to exchange unsatisfactory merchandise, marketing communications that emphasize product quality and desirability—all are attempts by marketers to decrease levels of perceived risk. After all, the less risk involved in the purchase, the more likely that the consumer will make the purchase and be satisfied afterward.

■ *EVALUATION OF ALTERNATIVES* ■

Your work isn't over once you have identified various ways to travel to the bowl game, along with various places to stay and to eat while there. Now you must weigh the alternatives and decide which is the best: Which one should you choose to purchase? Is the package deal offered by the travel agency really worth the money? Or would you be better off driving with a few friends (thereby sharing travel expenses), staying in a less-than-elite hotel, and spending some of the money you save on some wonderful meals and entertainment?

In making purchase decisions, you will almost always base your choices partly on the attitudes you have developed—including your attitudes toward the set of available brands. For example, if you have a general attitude that budget hotels are good (or bad) places to stay, it will shape your plans for attending the bowl game. At this stage of the consumer problem-solving process, consumers bring together many external and internal influences to arrive at the most desirable choice. They accomplish this through what is called "information processing."

☐ *Attitudes*

"I hate turnips. I love icy cold beer. Toyotas are the greatest. Madonna is a great entertainer, but a second-rate singer." Statements like these express attitudes. An **attitude** is a predisposition toward some aspect of the world that is positive or negative but never neutral (a neutral attitude is no attitude). Psychologists and marketers know that consumers' attitudes are mixtures of beliefs, feelings, and tendencies toward behavior. Marketers seek first to establish favorable beliefs about their products in the minds of consumers. These lead to positive emotional responses which, in turn, should result in an inclination to purchase.

Attitudes are learned, and they can be changed—but rarely easily. Changing consumers' attitudes about a product is usually a time-consuming and costly proposition. First impressions in product promotion are very important, since they quickly solidify into attitudes. A newspaper advertisement for a movie may create

At the time United Airlines took over the routes in the Far East from Pan Am, they used creative ads such as this one to appeal to consumers. They were trying to turn consumers' negative attitudes toward Pan Am, from whom they had purchased the routes, into the positive attitudes they had from dealing with United—the "friendly skies" airline. (Courtesy of Leo Burnett USA.)

an attitude ("that has to be another creepy horror film") that may not be changed despite favorable comments from peers.

Even though marketers spend great effort on researching attitudes and trying to influence them, attitudes are not always predictive of buying behaviors. You may have a favorable attitude toward both Jaguar and Chevrolet Sprint automobiles, yet you may have no intention of buying either one.

Many advertising and promotion activities are aimed at creating favorable attitudes toward a new product or changing negative attitudes toward an existing product. When United Airlines took over Pan Am's routes from the United States to the Pacific, magazine advertising headlines proclaimed "A Fresh Breeze across the Pacific." Customers had to know (believe) that they could now choose United. The ads offered a number of positive reasons for having a favorable attitude toward United—"You'll enjoy United's Royal Pacific Service," and "Best of all, you'll be flying with a friend. United Airlines." Copy ended with the traditional urge to action: "Call United or your travel agent." Such advertising may not immediately change a business flier's negative attitude toward United, but it may trigger a change that will come to fruition later.

Attitudes and Choice Limitation—The Evoked Set

Besides hoping to foster positive attitudes or to neutralize negative ones toward a particular product, marketers recognize that attitudes lead consumers to limit their acceptable choices within an entire product class. Rather than considering *all* available laundry detergents, television sets, or optometrists, consumers narrow their buying decision to an **evoked set** of choices.[14] Some circumstances limit the evoked set. For example, consumers may be unaware of some brands; they may eliminate brands at the high and low ends of the price range; they may require certain specific product features; and they may be persuaded by marketers' efforts to consider some previously unknown or less favored brand.

Suppose you set out to buy a new typewriter with $500 that you saved from your summer job. Two brands are already outside your price range—the IBM Selectric II and the Xerox Memorywriter—and they will not be included in your evoked set of choices. Nor will you consider any typewriter that is not self-correcting or not portable, two features you require.

Because your experience with typewriters is limited, an internal search through your memory yields little information. But your external search at a local office-machine store and your talks with friends reveal that three brands make up your evoked set: the Smith-Corona 450 Messenger, the Olivetti-Praxis 35, and the Brother CE-70. When you check the Consumers Union *Buying Guide,* you discover one more previously unfamiliar brand: the Canon Typestar 5. Your evoked set of choices now includes four brands that are self-correcting, portable, and within your price range. You have moved from little or no awareness of these brands to a point where they seem equally satisfactory. If your attitudes toward each brand are similar, you will have to evaluate additional information (price, warranty, other features) to reach a buying decision.

Information Processing and Evaluation

Perceptions, learning, and attitudes do come together, finally, to motivate and inform people's buying decision. Consumers use fairly predictable patterns to apply the information they have acquired and to evaluate the alternative products that fit within their evoked set of choices.

Several models, or decision rules, have been proposed to describe how consumers evaluate information.[15] Each model assumes (1) that the products which fit into an evoked set have attributes that are important to the prospective buyer and (2) that the buyer can evaluate those attributes. Besides these assumptions, remember that the models outline formal, logical, conscious processes. In real life—inside the black box—the evaluation of information is not so neat or orderly. Evaluation is a cognitive process and, as such, is often vague and contradictory.

A Case Study of Information Processing

Spencer Lofton, a young man of high musical standards but more modest means, has decided to buy an audiocassette deck. Four attributes are essential to Spencer: a fair price, an automatic tape-reverse feature, off-the-air recording capability, and compactness and light weight. He has measured numerous cassette decks by these standards and, after extensive internal and external information searches, has narrowed the evoked set to four brands: Sony, Pioneer, Technics, and Toshiba. On what basis will he make a decision? If he is like most consumers, Spencer will process and evaluate information by using a compensatory or noncompensatory model.

EXHIBIT 4-1

EXHIBIT 4-1 **Example of the Compensatory Model
of Information Processing**

In the compensatory model of information processing, the consumer considers each attribute
(such as fair price) for each brand. A brand is given a total score based on the total of its rating
times weight on each attribute.

Attributes	Attribute Weight	Sony	Pioneer	Technics	Toshiba
Fair price	4	6	4	6	6
Compactness and light weight	2	5	5	2	1
Automatic tape reverse	1	3	5	7	1
Off-the-air recording capability	3	4	4	2	5

Product	Calculations	Total
Sony	(4) (6) + (2) (5) + (1) (3) + (3) (4) =	49
Pioneer	(4) (4) + (2) (5) + (1) (5) + (3) (4) =	43
Technics	(4) (6) + (2) (2) + (1) (7) + (3) (2) =	41
Toshiba	(4) (6) + (2) (1) + (1) (1) + (3) (5) =	42

Source: Adapted from Brian Sternthal and Samuel Craig, *Consumer Behavior: An Information Processing Perspective* (Englewood Cliffs, N.J.: Prentice-Hall, 1982), pp. 142–143.

THE COMPENSATORY MODEL   The **compensatory model** of information processing assumes that consumers judge a limited number of product attributes, that the attributes vary in importance to the consumer, and that strength in one area compensates for weakness in another. To apply this decision rule, Spencer first weighs the relative importance of each attribute. For him, a fair price is most important, and so he assigns it a weight of 4. Off-the-air recording capability is almost as important as the price; Spencer gives that attribute a 3. He rates compactness/light weight as a 2; the least important required attribute—the automatic tape reverse—gets a 1.

Next, Spencer has to rank each of the brands in his evoked set according to how well it satisfies his four requirements. He decides to use a 7-point scale for this (7 = best; 1 = worst), as shown in Exhibit 4-1. The total scores for each brand are derived by multiplying its rating times the weight of the attribute. Given these totals, Spencer should buy the Sony tape deck (49 points); all other brands come in at least 6 points lower.

The compensatory model is sometimes called the *value-expectancy model;* "value" refers to the relative (weighted) importance of each attribute, and "expectancy" refers to the rating each brand receives on each attribute. Whatever name is used, however, the model is compensatory because a high score for one attribute may offset (or compensate for) a low score for another, depending on the weight of each attribute. In Spencer's case, the fair price of the Sony machine compensated for its low rating on tape reverse; he valued a fair price more than the reversing feature.

As this example shows, the compensatory model can be difficult to apply—especially if the evoked set and important attributes are not strictly limited. This model would be useless, for example, in evaluating all possible attributes of all possible cars. The consumer might suffer from information overload if such a complex model were used for a buying evaluation.[16]

THE NONCOMPENSATORY MODEL   With a **noncompensatory model** of information processing, a high rating for one attribute does not offset a low rating for another. If several products score equally on the most important criterion, the decision must be made by assessing the other criteria in terms of their importance. Consequently, the basic decision rule is to choose whichever brand exceeds the others by the greatest amount for a selected attribute.[17] Returning to the example above, Spencer rated fair price as his most important attribute; Sony, Technics, and Toshiba are tied on this standard. He would then move to his second-ranked attribute: off-the-air recording capacity. With a score of 5 for this feature, the Toshiba cassette deck would be selected.

Of these two models, the compensatory model is more difficult in a cognitive sense. As a result, consumers are likely to use the compensatory model only when making high-involvement purchases (such as a new car). By contrast, consumers will often switch to the noncompensatory model when making decisions which carry little perceived risk.[18]

Whichever information-processing model is used, the number of choices in the evoked set must be small enough to manage. The number of attributes must also be restricted, and each must be important to the buyer. Although most consumers actually process information in a less formal and more personal manner than these models propose, marketers nevertheless find the models to be useful in testing and fine-tuning their offerings.

☐ *Influencing Consumers' Decisions*

A marketer who understands how consumers gather, process, and evaluate information in moving toward a purchase may be able to influence events inside the black box. If nothing else, an understanding of how consumers process information may make it possible to heighten awareness of the product so that it may be included in the target market's evoked set. Following are some illustrations of how a focus on consumers' information processing might be put to use in designing and promoting products:[19]

- Market research can identify which needs and benefits are truly important to most consumers in the target market, guiding not only the design of the product but also its distribution, pricing, and promotion. The entire marketing mix should match consumers' primary needs; the product's benefits should be promoted to make consumers aware of the satisfaction that a purchase will bring.
- If a product is good enough and consumers are aware that it exists, promotion may simply remind customers to keep the product within their evoked set. A magazine advertisement for Kellogg's Corn Flakes is designed primarily not to increase the market share of this well-known product but rather to remind consumers that Corn Flakes should be included in their set of choices.
- If analysis and research indicate that target markets want a particuar benefit—such as stereophonic sound on television sets—the high cost of redesigning a product may be warranted. The product may be excluded from consideration if a newly desired benefit is not offered.
- The compensatory model of information processing makes it worthwhile to attempt to influence consumers' ideas about the relative importance of product attributes. For example, if competing videocassette recorders are generally smaller and lighter than those offered by a firm, the firm may use promotion to emphasize that its machine is the easiest to operate of all recorders on the market and that this benefit is far more important than the size or weight of the machine.

(Think of how distressing it will be to discover that you have accidentally erased the ending of your favorite movie because your recorder is so complicated to operate!)

■ Research may show that consumers' beliefs are inaccurate. If people wrongly believe that the product is more expensive than competing brands, promotion should emphasize price in an effort to alter mistaken perceptions.

■ Consumers may overlook an important benefit or may underestimate its importance. Calling attention to the neglected attribute may allow reinstatement of the product in the target market's evoked set.

■ PURCHASE ■

Information processing leads to purchase *intentions,* not necessarily to an actual exchange. Much can happen to change the minds of even the most well-informed consumers as they move from awareness of the product to deciding to buy it. Their information processing itself may be erroneous. Everyone makes mistakes, and it is easy to proceed on the basis of false or mistaken information. We may misunderstand promotion or other information sources, causing us wrongly to include or exclude products from our evoked set. And even if we conduct careful, accurate searches for information, we may misuse it in applying whatever decision rule we enforce. In addition to these possibilities, the external influences described in Chapter 3 and the situational factors at the point of purchase may alter our buying intentions.

Let's say that you are ready to make your final purchase decisions about how to get to the New Year's Day bowl game, where to stay, and so forth. At this point, the external influences discussed in Chapter 3 will affect your choices. Reference groups and opinion leaders may shape the final outcome of your decisions. For example, just as you have neared a decision to book the package deal with the local travel agency, your roommates tell you that it would be a big mistake, that you'll be stuck with a whole bunch of strangers that you probably won't like. Such feedback can quickly alter our purchase intentions.

However, you decide to ignore your roommates' advice, and you book the package tour anyway. Then, just before you head downtown to visit the travel agency, a friend calls to say that she and her roommates have decided to rent a car, drive to the bowl city, and share the cost of a hotel suite near the beach. But they need one more person to share the expenses: are you interested? This is one example of a situational factor that can come between the consumer's intent and the final purchase outcome.

Marketers try to minimize situational factors by so effectively preselling their products that later events have little impact on purchase decisions. Or they may create or capitalize on situational events through promotion and pricing strategies that encourage people to switch to their product.[20]

■ POSTPURCHASE BEHAVIOR ■

After all relevant information is processed, the consumer exchanges money for a product. But the marketer's concern does not end when the consumer walks out of the store with a package. Consumer behavior continues, in the form of postpurchase behavior. Once consumers have used their new purchase a few times, they will feel some degree of satisfaction or dissatisfaction. A purchase that lives up to expectations is largely satisfactory. One that does not meet expectations may simply lead to disappointment, but it may also lead to some public or private action by the buyer.

A satisfied customer is a marketer's best friend. If you feel that a new purchase has all the attributes you were seeking when you made your decision, you are likely to extend these positive feelings toward other products sold by the manufacturer. And because you have searched out so much information and weighed your alternatives carefully, you have probably become an expert in the eyes of your friends. You are now an opinion leader who can influence the purchase decisions of your peers.

However, if your level of dissatisfaction is strong, you will take one of the courses illustrated in Figure 4-5: You may keep the product, remain unhappy, but take no action; you may try to return the purchase and get a replacement or your money back. You will certainly warn your friends about the product and be wary of purchasing the company's wares again. Indeed, you may generalize your dissatisfaction to all other products sold by that marketer.

Any important purchase will almost invariably produce what the noted U.S. psychologist Leon Festinger has termed **cognitive dissonance**—the psychological discomfort produced by doubts abut the wisdom of something we have done (in this case, our purchase decision).[21] In the marketing context, cognitive dissonance produces questions like "Was this the best product for the price?" "Would I have been more satisfied with other choices?" "Was my evaluation process correct?" "Where did I go wrong? Is it the product, or is it me?"

Because cognitive dissonance is uncomfortable, consumers try to reduce their doubts by justifying their purchase in some way. They may look for more external information that confirms their choice: New car owners pay closer attention to advertising for the brand they have purchased than they do to that for competing makes.[22] They may change the order of importance they give to the product's attributes. They may seek confirmation that the alternatives they did not choose are even worse than they originally thought. Or they may reinterpret their own reactions and even their images of themselves to relieve their anxiety.

To conclude our use of the bowl-game example, you have finally decided to accept your friend's offer. You will drive to the bowl city with her and her roommates and will share the costs of a hotel suite with them. You go to their apartment and give them $50 for your share of the deposit on the hotel suite. But, after leaving, you begin to have second thoughts: Is this really the best choice? Will I enjoy spending 3 days with these people? Will driving with them be safe? Are any of them likely to drink while driving? Your natural tendency will be to try to convince yourself that the decision you made was the right one.

Astute marketers are increasing their efforts to help consumers reduce cognitive dissonance and to reinforce buyers' satisfaction with their purchases. Whirlpool Corporation maintains a toll-free number—the "Cool-Line"—that consumers can call with complaints and questions for Whirlpool staffers. Such an arrangement allows consumers to engage in what Ralph Day has called "complaining behavior."[23] Consumers who are dissatisfied with a Whirlpool appliance have the opportunity to ventilate their complaints; in some instances, conversation with a knowledgeable and pleasant employee may defuse a consumer's grievances. More companies are beginning to see the strategic importance of consumer-complaint handling.[24]

Much automobile advertising aims at reinforcing car buyers' satisfaction with their purchases. Nissan describes its 300ZX as "awesome"; Oldsmobile touts its

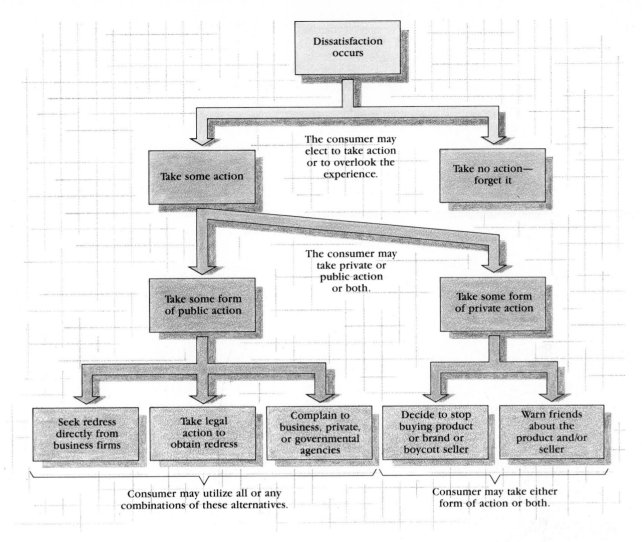

The consumer may elect to take action or to overlook the experience.

The consumer may take private or public action or both.

Consumer may utilize all or any combinations of these alternatives.

Consumer may take either form of action or both.

Calais 500 as a "winner"; BMW wants its customers to be convinced that they have bought "the ultimate driving machine." If the buyers of these cars feel certain that they made the right decisions, they will "spread the word" and assist the overall marketing effort for these products.

■ *SUMMARY* ■

1. Most research on consumer behavior has focused on the way in which important, high-involvement purchases are made.
2. Motivation consists of internal and external factors that direct our behavior toward goals and toward fulfilling needs.
3. Benefits *motivate* consumers, making them aware of the marketer's offering, attracting them to it, and encouraging exchange.
4. Perceptual processes are selective; we attend to only a small percentage of the stimuli to which we are exposed.
5. Marketers need to know as much as possible about how consumers perceive products, how they learn about them, how they learn to avoid or seek them, and how they remember them.

Figure 4-5 *Alternatives available to consumers when dissatisfied with a purchase.* Dissatisfied consumers have many alternatives, including taking public action, taking private action, taking both public and private action, and taking no action whatsoever. (From Ralph L. Day and E. Laird Landon, Jr., "Toward a Theory of Consumer Complaining Behavior," in A. G. Woodside et al., *Consumer and Industrial Buying Behavior,* 1977.)

6. The search for information about a product class typically has three stages: extensive problem solving, limited problem solving, and routinized response.

7. Perceived risk is present in almost all important purchases and has two elements: uncertainty and consequences. Perceived risk may be physical, financial, or social.

8. Consumers' attitudes toward a product class produce an acceptable group that makes up a consumer's evoked set.

9. Consumers are likely to use the compensatory model of information processing only when making high-involvement decisions. By contrast, consumers will often switch to the noncompensatory model when making decisions which carry little perceived risk.

10. Product evaluations lead consumers to purchase intentions, but new factors can still enter the picture, changing the decision.

11. Important purchases almost always produce cognitive dissonance—a psychological discomfort produced by doubts as to the wisdom of the purchase decision. Consumers will try to reduce this discomfort by seeking reinforcement as to the aptness of their choice.

☐ Key Terms

attitudes
benefits
biogenic needs
brand loyalty
classic (respondent) conditioning
cognitive dissonance
compensatory model
cues
evoked set

hierarchy of needs
high-involvement decisions
learning
low-involvement decisions
memory
motivation
noncompensatory model
operant conditioning

perceived risk
perception
psychogenic needs
selective attention
selective distortion
selective retention
stimulus
stimulus-response theory

☐ Chapter Review

1. What are the steps in an analytical approach to consumer behavior?

2. In what ways do biogenic and psychogenic needs differ?

3. What is meant by a "hierarchy of needs"?

4. Can you explain why perception is a selective process by analyzing your own reaction to television commercials?

5. Why do consumers perceive risk in their important buying decisions? What risks are encountered in buying a new automobile?

6. What do internal and external searches for information involve?

7. What components make up your attitudes toward a product you are considering for purchase? Why is the topic of attitude change so important to marketers?

8. Why is actual information processing less formal than the models used to describe it?

9. If you should be dissatisfied with a newly purchased television set, what steps might you take?

☐ References

1. Wayne D. Hoyer, "An Examination of Consumer Decision Making for a Common Repeat Purchase Product," *Journal of Consumer Research*, vol. 11, Dec. 1984, pp. 822–829. See also Gilles Laurent and Jean-Noel Kapferer, "Measuring Consumer Involvement Profiles," *Journal of Marketing Research*, vol. XXII, Feb. 1985, pp. 41–53; Judith Lynne Zaichowsky, "Measuring the Involvement Construct," *Journal of Consumer Research*, vol. 12, Dec. 1985, pp. 341–352.

2. Abraham Maslow, *Motivation and Personality* (New York: Harper & Row, 1954), p. 92.

3. Wilbert J. McKeachie and Charlotte L. Doyle, *Psychology* (Reading, Mass.: Addison-Wesley, 1966), p. 171.

4. Frances K. McSweeney and Calvin Bierley, "Recent Developments in Classical Conditioning," *Journal of Consumer Research*, vol. 11, Sept. 1984, pp. 619–631; Calvin Bierley,

Frances K. McSweeney, and Renee Vannieuwkerk, "Classical Conditioning of Preferences for Stimuli," *Journal of Consumer Research,* vol. 12, Dec. 1985, pp. 316–323.

5. Blaise J. Bergiel and Christine Trosclair, "Instrumental Learning: Its Application to Consumer Satisfaction," *Journal of Consumer Marketing,* Fall 1985, pp. 23–28.

6. Tod Johnson, "The Myth of Declining Brand Loyalty," *Journal of Advertising Research,* vol. 24, Feb.–Mar. 1984, pp. 9–17.

7. John A. Howard and Jagdish N. Sheth, *The Theory of Buyer Behavior* (New York: Wiley, 1969), pp. 145–150.

8. Peter D. Bennett and Harold H. Kassarjian, *Consumer Behavior* (Englewood Cliffs, N.J.: Prentice-Hall, 1972), p. 36.

9. Peter D. Bennett and Robert M. Mandell, "Prepurchase Information Seek Behavior of New Car Purchasers—The Learning Hypothesis," *Journal of Marketing Research,* vol. V, Aug. 1968, pp. 430–433.

10. Gerald J. Gorn and Renée Florsheim, "The Effects of Commercials for Adult Products on Children," *Journal of Consumer Research,* vol. 11, Mar. 1985, pp. 962–967.

11. Laurie Freeman, "Marketers Keep in Touch with Toll-free Phoning," *Advertising Age,* Oct. 29, 1984, p. 71.

12. Merrie Brucks, "The Effects of Product Class Knowledge on Information Search Behavior," *Journal of Consumer Research,* vol. 12, June 1985, pp. 1–16.

13. Donald F. Cox (ed.), *Risk Taking and Information Handling in Consumer Behavior* (Boston: Division of Research, Graduate School of Business Administration, Harvard University, 1967), pp. 5–6.

14. John A. Howard, *Marketing Management: Operating, Strategic, and Administrative,* 3d ed. (Homewood, Ill.: Irwin, 1973), pp. 62–71.

15. David L. Loudon and Albert J. Della Bitta, *Consumer Behavior: Concepts and Applications,* 2d ed. (New York: McGraw-Hill, 1984), pp. 628–633; Brian Sternthal and C. Samuel Craig, *Consumer Behavior: An Information-Processing Perspective* (Englewood Cliffs, N.J.: Prentice-Hall, 1983), pp. 142–149; James F. Engel and Roger D. Blackwell, *Consumer Behavior,* 4th ed. (Hinsdale, Ill.: Dryden, 1982), pp. 421–422; J. Paul Peter and Jerry C. Olson, *Consumer Behavior: Marketing Strategy Perspectives* (Homewood, Ill.: Irwin, 1987), pp. 247–250.

16. For a discussion of whether information overload can (and does) take place, see Jacob Jacoby, "Perspectives on Information Overload," *Journal of Consumer Research,* vol. 10, March 1984, pp. 432–435; and Naresh K. Malhotra, "Reflections on the Information Overload Paradigm in Consumer Decision Making," *Journal of Consumer Research,* vol. 10, Mar. 1984, pp. 436–440.

17. Loudon and Della Bitta, op. cit., p. 630.

18. David Grether and Louis Wilde, "An Analysis of Conjunctive Choice: Theory and Experiments," *Journal of Consumer Research,* vol. 10, Mar. 1984, pp. 373–385.

19. Based in part on Harper W. Boyd, Jr., Michael L. Ray, and Edward C. Strong, "An Attitudinal Framework for Advertising Strategy," *Journal of Marketing,* Apr. 1972, pp. 27–33.

20. Joseph A. Cote, James McCullough, and Michael Reilly, "Effects of Unexpected Situations on Behavior-Intention Differences: A Garbology Analysis," *Journal of Consumer Research,* vol. 12, Sept. 1985, pp. 188–194.

21. Leon Festinger, *A Theory of Cognitive Dissonance* (Stanford, Calif.: Stanford University, 1957).

22. D. Erlich, I. Guttman, P. Schonbak, and J. Mills, "Post-Decision Exposures to Relevant Information," *Journal of Abnormal and Social Psychology,* Jan. 1957, pp. 98–102.

23. Ralph L. Day and E. Laird Landon, Jr., "Toward a Theory of Consumer Complaining Behavior," in Arch G. Woodside, Jagdish N. Sheth, and Peter D. Bennett (eds.), *Consumer and Industrial Buying Behavior* (New York: Elsevier North-Holland, 1977), pp. 425–437.

24. Mary C. Gilly and Richard W. Hansen, "Consumer Complaint Handling as a Strategic Marketing Tool," *Journal of Consumer Marketing,* Fall 1985, pp. 5–16.

5

ANALYZING ORGANIZATIONAL MARKETS

Copyright © 1984 Jeff Smith.

SPOTLIGHT ON

☐ Classification of organizational markets

☐ Difficulties in pinpointing the size and scope of organizational markets

☐ Standard Industrial Classification (SIC) system

☐ Marketing to organizations contrasted with marketing to consumers

☐ Personal selling and professional buying in organizational marketing

☐ Steps in the buy-phase concept

☐ Classification of organizational buying tasks

☐ People's roles within the buying center

Can the Goliath of the telephone industry be defeated by its competitors? Despite losing its monopoly over long-distance services, American Telephone and Telegraph (AT&T) remains the dominant force in the industry. But MCI Communications Corporation has become the feisty number-two vendor and is making inroads into AT&T's domain.

Initially, MCI concentrated on consumer markets and signed up almost 3 million customers. However, MCI finally could not ignore a crucial fact: Organizations account for close to 40 percent of all long-distance revenues. In an effort to change its strategic thrust to organizational marketing (commonly called "industrial" or "business-to-business" marketing), MCI dropped its series of irreverent television commercials featuring comic Joan Rivers. A new advertising campaign emphasizing MCI's reliability was developed to appeal to buyers for organizational accounts.

Although it remains only a fraction of AT&T's size, MCI has grown rapidly in the 1980s by astutely exploiting its distinctive advantages:

- MCI and other smaller carriers have enjoyed a several-year price advantage over AT&T. The Federal Communications Commission nurtured these carriers by granting large discounts on connection fees to local telephone networks. However, these discounts are being phased out, and MCI will therefore lose much of its price advantage.
- In 1985, MCI bought Satellite Business Systems (SBS) from International Business Machines (IBM). IBM received 16 percent of MCI's stock in return, thus becoming MCI's largest stockholder. Certain joint marketing ventures to large accounts are planned; MCI certainly hopes that IBM's marketing clout and reputation for quality will help convince organizational buyers to switch from AT&T to MCI.
- MCI received more than $200 million—much less than they wanted—in an antitrust settlement with AT&T. In addition, MCI is receiving more than $100 million worth of advanced equipment. Since MCI is relatively debt-free, it will have a substantial hoard of cash to finance new marketing efforts against AT&T.

Despite MCI's advances and its competitive advantages, AT&T has held its position as the "king" of the long-distance industry. In fact, in early 1987, AT&T's market share stood at 86 percent, compared to less than 5 percent each for MCI and Sprint. AT&T has maintained its lead over its competitors because of its impressive resources for marketing long-distance services:

- AT&T has an easier marketing task: It needs merely to hold its customers rather than to woo them away from competitors. One accountant explained why it took him "about a minute" to decide how to vote in the phone election: "[With AT&T] I knew what I had. The other companies were question marks."
- AT&T's sales force is some 10,000 people strong. The company can assign a dozen consultants to a major organizational account. AT&T's sales representatives can therefore concentrate on decision makers at all levels in the buying organization—from top-level managers to equipment users.

AT&T
The right choice.

MCI
COMMUNICATIONS
FOR THE NEXT 100 YEARS.℠

■ AT&T is aggressively cutting prices, especially for its overseas services, thus largely negating MCI's price advantage.

The phone wars are expected to continue in the coming years. AT&T will probably remain far and away the industry leader in long-distance services. However, MCI hopes to gain its own healthy and profitable share of the long-distance business. Even if Goliath cannot be defeated, there is a chance that he will have to give a little ground.

Sources: "The Long-Distance Warrior," *Business Week,* Feb. 17, 1986, pp. 86–94; Stuart Gannes, "The Phone Fight's Frenzied Finale," *Fortune,* April 14, 1986, pp. 52–54, 58, 60; Francine Schwadel, "Calling Long Distance: User Vote Shows Strong Support for AT&T," *The Wall Street Journal,* Aug. 22, 1986, p. 17; "AT&T is Eating 'Em Alive," *Business Week,* Feb. 16, 1987, pp. 28–29.

We all have buying experiences as consumers, yet few of us have any reason to understand how organizations make buying decisions. Organizational purchasing differs from consumer purchasing in that it is planned and carried out by trained professional buyers. Each type of organization has distinctive buying needs and styles and uses its purchases differently. To serve the needs of an organizational customer, marketers must thoroughly understand the organization's structure and buying purpose, the pressures confronting organizational buyers, and the special characteristics of organizational buying behavior.

Thus, if attempting to sell long-distance services to Emerson Electric or Macy's department stores, both AT&T and MCI would lay out careful marketing plans. Those individuals involved in the buying decision would be identified, their particular needs would be addressed, and the likely steps in the organization's buying process would be charted. A major purchase decision (such as an organization's switch from AT&T to MCI or vice versa) could take months or even years.

Chapter 5 categorizes the different organizational markets and describes the federal government's Standard Industrial Classification (SIC) system. It then analyzes the special characteristics of organizational marketing. Finally, the buy-phase concepts (steps) of such purchasing are explored, along with the types of buying tasks and the role of the buying center.

TYPES OF ORGANIZATIONAL MARKETING

Marketing to organizations differs significantly from marketing to consumers. Organizational buyers have different motives, display different behaviors, and evaluate products more formally than do individual consumers. For example, in most consumer markets, the buying unit (normally an individual or household) plays a rather passive role in responding to the offerings of a marketing organization. By contrast, many buyers in organizational markets take a very active role, as when the Department of Defense specifies what it wants in a new fighter jet or when an automobile company buys robotic devices designed especially to weld auto bodies.[1] Despite such differences, *all* marketers (including those serving organizations) must ascertain what customers need and must promote and sell products in ways that satisfy their buyers. In other words, the marketing concept is the foundation of organizational marketing, just as it is central to consumer marketing.[2]

To understand what is different in marketing to organizations, we will examine the broad types of organizational sellers and buyers. Until recently, any form of nonconsumer marketing was called "industrial marketing," a phrase that suggests the buying and selling of heavy physical goods. To reflect the size and variety of nonconsumer marketing more accurately, however, marketing scholars in the 1980s have come to use the blanket term "organizational marketing."

Sometimes less precisely called "business-to-business marketing," **organizational marketing** includes all marketing efforts directed at buyers for formal institutions, including industrial, service, reseller, government, and not-for-profit groups. (Exhibit 5-1 lists representative buyers in each of these five classes.) Kodak, for example, sells laboratory and medical instruments to large corporations as well as to not-for-profit universities, and some universities sell on- or off-campus management-training seminars to a variety of businesses.

☐ *Buying Purposes of Organizational Markets*

Although organizational buyers make their decisions in varying ways, we will take a consistent approach to purchase steps. It is useful, however, to differentiate among these markets in terms of their *reasons* for buying, that is, the purpose to which they put their purchases.

INDUSTRIAL MARKETS   Inland Steel buys iron ore to make steel; J. P. Stevens buys cotton to weave fabrics for sheets and towels; Bechtel Corporation buys construction equipment and supplies to build dams, subway systems, and nuclear power plants. These companies and others like them are considered **industrial markets,** markets that buy goods to produce goods.

Industrial buyers for firms engaged in mining, agriculture, construction, and manufacturing—the producers of physical commodities, structures, or goods—purchase raw materials, heavy equipment, and components from other industrial firms to produce and sell products. These products may be for further fabrication or for industrial and consumer use. Of course, like companies of all types, these buyers also buy many types of products to maintain their own internal operations.

SERVICE MARKETS   The **service market** includes all organizations that buy to produce services. They purchase goods (computers, aircraft, buildings, com-

EXHIBIT 5-1	Representative Buyers in Organizational Markets

Organizational markets are categorized by the customer's type of business rather than by the product being marketed. Thus, as a manufacturer of tractors, Caterpillar is in the industrial market; as a retailer, Sears is in the reseller market.

Industrial Market	Service Market	Reseller Market	Government Market	Not-for-Profit Market
Caterpillar Tractor	Equitable Life Insurance	Federated Department Stores	Defense Personnel Support Center	Denver Symphony
Kellogg's	Club Med International	Sears	Bay Area Rapid Transit (BART), San Francisco	The Smithsonian Institution
Data General	Fotomat	Kroger's	U.S. Bureau of the Census	Political action committees (PACs)
E. J. Gallo	Northwest Orient Airlines	L. L. Bean	Texas Highway Department	Alley Theater (Houston)
Digital Equipment	Hyatt Hotels Corporation	McKesson	Los Angeles Board of Education	American Cancer Society

Many companies that market products directly to consumers also market them to organizational users who buy them for their own purposes. Vidal Sassoon, and others, market their products through motels such as Great Western, which buys to enhance their customers' satisfaction with the service they sell. (Courtesy of Guest Supply.)

munications systems) or other services (security, maintenance, data processing) to generate and maintain the services that they sell. Service organizations include banks, hotels, insurance companies, airlines, and entertainment firms. Delta Airlines buys or leases aircraft from Boeing; Hyatt Hotels buys small bars of soap from Colgate-Palmolive.

RESELLER MARKETS Wholesalers and retailers are examples of **reseller markets,** firms that acquire goods and services to sell them again. Insofar as they purchase products to maintain their own operations—cash registers, trucks, and warehouses, for example—resellers buy very much as industrial and service firms do. In fulfilling their roles as resellers, however, wholesalers and retailers have special concerns as buyers, such as markup percentages and inventory and selling costs. Department stores such as Macy's and Burdine's are major buyers of goods that will be resold to consumers. Many food stuffs pass first through wholesaler's hands on the way to retailers. Chapter 12 will examine reseller operations in detail.

GOVERNMENT MARKETS Each year, the federal government buys over $160 billion worth of goods and services, expenditures that exceed 5 percent of the nation's $3 trillion gross national product. "Too complex to deal with easily but too big to ignore entirely—that's the federal government as a buyer," noted one marketing expert.[3]

Federal government purchases range from aircraft carriers and their fighter complements to computer systems (see Box 5-1), food services, and paper clips. State and local governments collectively spend almost as much on goods and services as does the federal government; they spend most heavily for education in all its forms. These **government markets**—federal agencies, including the military;

state units; and local authorities, including school districts and law enforcement groups—purchase or lease goods and services to carry out their mandated functions and to further the public purpose.

Selling to the federal government, and to some degree to all government markets, differs from selling to business markets in subtle and not-so-subtle ways. Stringent packaging demands, voluminous paperwork, and quality-assurance requirements characterize government ordering. In addition, more than half of all federal contracts are negotiated on a noncompetitive basis; only 38 percent are awarded competitively to bidding vendors.[4] Finally, marketers who would sell to government must be sensitive to the opinion of the public; it is we the people who, through elected officials and their appointees, ultimately authorize government spending.

NOT-FOR-PROFIT MARKETS   Universities, public hospitals, museums, foundations, and charitable organizations buy and sell in ways similar to business organizations. These **not-for-profit markets,** or "institutional" markets, exist to serve society. They buy primarily to maintain and facilitate internal operations and to produce their services; they usually order through purchasing centers under stated purchasing policies.

Some institutions that are perceived as operating not-for-profit do, indeed, seek profits. For example, about 15 percent of all general hospitals in the United States are investor-owned, profit-seeking institutions.[5] Many trade and technical schools are also privately owned and seek to earn a profit. Marketing to institutions such as these, however, does not differ substantially from marketing to not-for-profit operations.

The Size and Scope of Organizational Markets

Organizational selling and buying involves dollar amounts in the millions, or even billions. Yet it is difficult to trace all these expenditures. Governments at federal, state, and local levels employ approximately 16 million people; over 15,000 motion-picture theaters cater to Americans; the annual value of agricultural products exceeds $100 billion; and the United States's 2 million retailers exceeded sales of $1.5 trillion in 1986.

Given the number and variety of all these exchanges, the total dollar amount involved in organizational marketing is impossible to pin down. Data on market sizes are not always dependable. When resellers are involved, the dollar value of a single purchase may be counted several times. Income and expenditures in the service and not-for-profit sectors are not always clear. In the face of these uncertainties, one estimate puts the dollar volume of all organizational purchases at about three times the amount of estimated retail sales.[6]

The Standard Industrial Classification System

Fortunately for marketing managers, accurate information is available for specific industries and geographic locations. For example, a manufacturer of fabricated structural metal for buildings can identify the number of firms that might be potential customers (and how much steel these firms use) in any county in the United States, mainly by referring to the Standard Industrial Classification (SIC) system. The Federal Office of Management and Budget's **Standard Industrial Classification Manual** classifies every kind of economic activity in the United States, using a four-digit system to assign increasingly explicit code numbers to each economic unit. First the *Manual* identifies 10 major categories by means of two-digit numbers:

01–09: Agriculture
10–14: Mining
15–19: Construction
20–39: Manufacturing
40–49: Transportation and public utilities
50–59: Wholesale and retail trade
60–69: Finance, insurance, and real estate
70–89: Services
90–98: Governments
99:     Other

After assignment to one of these broad groups, industries are classified more specifically into three- and four-digit categories. For example, a manufacturer of paper for books who wants information about potential marketers could proceed from major group 27—printing, publishing, and allied industries—to product code 2732, book printing. For more specific information, the paper manufacturer can then turn to the *Census of Manufacturers.* A fifth digit groups the textbook-printing industry. Sixth and seventh digits identify paper-buying markets even more specifically: Code 27323-14 identifies hardbound college-level textbooks (like the one you are reading).

And what can the paper marketer do with that classification? Using the *Census of Manufacturers* and other government publications such as the *Census of Business* and *County Business Patterns*—as well as nongovernmental sources such as *Sales & Marketing Management's Survey of Industrial Purchasing Power* or Dun and Bradstreet's *Market Identifiers*—one can obtain useful information about the

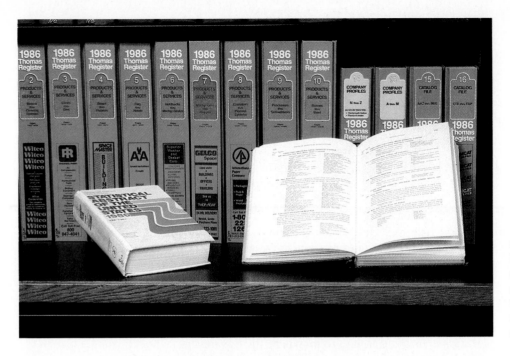

Organizational marketers have many sources of secondary information available to them to guide their efforts to target their marketing efforts. These are just a few. (Ken Karp.)

number and size of potential customers, their locations, and their potential purchases. These specific data enable marketers not only to pinpoint sales potential in their target markets but also to break those markets down even further into target market segments for which marketing mixes can be fine-tuned.

SPECIAL CHARACTERISTICS OF ORGANIZATIONAL MARKETING

After research and identification of target markets, organizational marketers need to consider a number of factors that distinguish organizational from consumer marketing.

Derived Demand

The demand for industrial goods and services derives from demand for other products. Markets for electric-power generators depend on consumer markets for electricity. A demand for automobiles creates a market for carburetor sales, which, in turn, rests on the availability of valves. Thus, **derived demand** is based on expectations of upcoming demand for other industrial or consumer products.

When manufacturers of household appliances foresee a rise in demand for microwave ovens, for example, they search out, buy, and install the necessary plant equipment in advance of projected consumer demand. Mills buy their silk yarn and retool their looms to weave black satin for shipment to cutting rooms and sewing factories a year or more before New York's Seventh Avenue designers have publicly endorsed black satin, and 2 years before any woman steps out in black satin.

Sometimes industrial manufacturers attempt to stimulate consumer demand for their customers' products to induce derived demand. For example, Monsanto, a company that extrudes acrylics, runs ongoing consumer advertising to persuade consumers to ask for children's clothing made of their materials.

☐ Geographical Concentration

Oil refineries are heavily concentrated in Texas, Oklahoma, and Louisiana; insurance companies abound in Connecticut; many federal purchasing agencies are situated in the District of Columbia and nearby Maryland and Virginia.

Industrial, business, and government markets tend to cluster geographically. Manufacturers of assembled products may locate near their sources of supply; thus, makers of computer components have proliferated in "Silicon Valley" in northern California. Bausch and Lomb, one of the prime manufacturers of fine-ground glass lenses used in cameras, is located in Monroe County, New York—as is a major customer, Eastman Kodak. Historically, industrial markets grew up near the sources of the raw materials that they use. The petroleum industry was built literally on top of underground oil.

Cost and ease of transportation can figure in the location and concentration of industrial markets. Manufacturing first appeared around seaports and in cities along inland waterways, then followed the path of railroads, and eventually followed the nation's highways. More recently, certain industries have established their offices close to major airports. Physical factors may also impel geographical concentration: The climate of northern California is ideally suited to growing grapes for wine, whereas grapefruit growers need the warm climates of southern Florida and Texas.

Consumer markets are widely dispersed; indeed, they are everywhere, but if marketers wish to sell to organizational markets, it pays to be where the business is.

☐ Vertical and Horizontal Markets

Markets for industrial products are organized either vertically or horizontally, according to the nature and use of a product. Products in **vertical markets** are tailored for specific industries; for example, industrial looms are sold only to textile mills, and oil rigs are sold only to drillers. By contrast, products in **horizontal markets** are sold to a wide range of industries. Among the products sold in horizontal markets are word processors, photocopying equipment, typewriters, telephones, and food services.

Marketers who serve vertical markets often focus on a few major accounts. Consequently, losing even one account can be a disaster. Manufacturers of auto carburetors have no markets other than automakers; a manufacturer that loses General Motors as a customer may be in serious trouble. Marketers who serve horizontal markets, however, design marketing mixes for each of their market segments. In a typical horizontal market, institutional food service marketers offer different products, prices, and distribution systems to various customers. They may develop different promotions for their buyers—schools, colleges, hospitals, and business firms—since each type of buyer has different needs.

☐ Large Sales

Consumer markets depend on pleasing millions of individual buyers, that is, they succeed through volume. However, although any one consuming household may devote 100 percent of its purchases to a single brand of a product like peanut butter, organizational buyers often wish to maintain more than one source of supply and therefore split their purchases.[7] Organizational marketers typically focus their efforts on a few major (often multimillion-dollar) buyers. Boeing, Lockheed, Rockwell International, and McDonnell-Douglas compete fiercely for military contracts because each fighter bomber means millions of dollars in profits and thousands of jobs. With such huge sales potentials, organizational marketers lobby for contracts at all levels of government and support sophisticated selling teams which pursue major accounts.

☐ *More Direct Channels of Distribution*

The largest proportion of consumer products are sold through a complex structure of wholesalers and retailers who separate the producer and the consumer. A candy bar, for example, will be sold to several kinds of wholesalers or food brokers. These wholesalers will sell some candy bars to retail grocers, some to drugstores, some to vending machine operators. These buyers, in turn, will sell the candy bars to their customers, who operate various types of retail establishments selling goods to consumers.

In the bulk of organizational marketing, however, sellers and buyers are more directly linked. When dealing with very large purchasers, marketers can make direct sales rather than go through industrial distributors or other intermediaries. Of course, certain products sold to organizational buyers are commonly sold through one or two tiers of wholesalers. We will discuss organizational channels of distribution in more detail in Chapter 13.

☐ *Emphasis on Personal Selling*

Because they have relatively few buyers who place large orders, organizational marketers have traditionally emphasized personal selling over advertising within the promotional element in the marketing mix. A good sales representative can tailor presentations and can call different product features to the attention of different persons involved in a purchase. With immediate customer feedback, the representative can adjust the promotional message on the spot. Of course, no such instant feedback is possible when using advertising.

In recent years, marketers have begun to employ more advertising to organizations. For example, "business-to-business" print advertising—placed largely in trade and business journals—aims to establish a company's reputation for stability, service, and quality (see Box 5-2). In some markets, sellers use the mass media to reach out both to organizational buyers and to the consumers who purchase their goods or services. Express mail services such as Federal Express, Emery Airfreight, and the U.S. Post Office square off regularly against each other in prime-time television commercials. And even though mailroom personnel may follow company policy with regard to overnight mail, employees at all levels of an organization may request and receive a specific service. Thus, organizational marketers often employ consumer-like campaigns, at least for their commercial services.

Organizational marketers may advertise quite differently when they aim a major selling campaign at key people within a buying organization. When 3M Company introduced its E.T. electronic typewriter, for example, its marketers directed different print campaigns to office managers, purchasing agents, and secretaries within the target company.[8] Again, however, although there has been an increase in such use of advertising, personal selling remains the fundamental promotional technique in marketing to organizations.

☐ *Professional Buying*

Organizations frequently carry out their purchasing more systematically than do most consumers. Purchasing agents are trained professionals who must continue their training in buying procedures, negotiation, materials management, and the legal aspects of buying. Some 70 percent of purchasing agents belong to one or

The Ethyl Chemicals Group developed an advertising campaign which uses toy fire engines, ships, and trucks to promote its chemical products. "The toys were basically a way of getting attention," notes a marketing executive for Ethyl. "Favorite pictures for chemical ads are valves, beakers, flasks, and so on. . . . You get so fed up seeing those things that you choke."

Peterbilt, a California truck manufacturer, used an unusual "floating trucks" ad campaign to help market its trucks to both large fleets and individual owners. A Peterbilt executive explains: "We want a visually strong and dramatic image because we are perceived as a premium product." The floating trucks campaign differs from conventional heavy-equipment ads, which generally rely on straightforward product shots.

Organizational marketers continue to emphasize personal selling within the overall marketing mix, but advertising has seen increasing use in recent years. The effectiveness of such business-to-business advertising rests on a number of factors:

1. Business-to-business ads must capture the attention of people involved in buying decisions. Ethyl's toys and Peterbilt's floating trucks are designed to stand out amid the often-predictable advertising used by other marketers of industrial goods.

(Continued on next page)

Buy bromine and bromine chemicals from Ethyl—we won't leave you high and dry.

One risk you don't have to run in your business is an interruption in your supply of bromine or bromine chemicals — when your supplier is Ethyl.

Ethyl has access to the largest known underground reserve of bromine in the world and we have the resources to get it above ground fast. To sell now as elemental bromine — or as brominated flame retardants, bromine chloride, hydrobromic acid, calcium bromide, zinc bromide, sodium bromide, methyl bromide or ethylene dibromide.

With over half a century of experience in bromine and its derivatives, we may have processes to make new products or answers to questions you haven't yet thought of. And we're taking the action needed to acquire more half centuries of experience.

In the past couple of years we have added to our product line bromine chloride, hydrobromic acid, sodium bromide, methyl bromide and seven flame retardants; expanded the alkali bromides plant; drilled many new bromine-rich brine wells. From bromine deposits to the production of over 30 bromine-based commercial chemicals, Ethyl is your complete and independent source.

If you're planning your business for the next decade and beyond, talk to the company whose actions and plans in bromine and bromine chemicals are already decades into the future: Ethyl.

For more information, write or call Ethyl Corporation, Chemicals Group, 451 Florida Blvd., Baton Rouge, LA 70801; (800) 535-3030. In Louisiana (504) 338-7556.

Ethyl Chemicals Group

We make it better for you.

Like nothing on earth

Peterbilt's new 4-point cab air suspension: remarkably smooth and stable.

That's because it's engineered like no other suspension system made. In fact, the only thing our Model 362 4-point cab air suspension has in common with competing designs, is its name.

Exclusive anti-roll bar cuts cab sway, even when cornering.

By combining a stout 1.25" anti-roll bar with our patented damper/snubber system, Peterbilt engineers have cut cab sway to virtually imperceptible levels. The result? No exaggerated side-to-side front-to-back cab motion so common to other 4-point suspensions. Cab stability and handling is excellent — even when cornering.

And since a suspended Model 362 cab sits only ⅜" higher than a standard 362 cab, we've also eliminated the need for special cab skirts, and expensive, unreliable modified linkages. In addition, the entire suspension weighs less than half of the nearest competing design.

500,000 mile cab warranty.

After putting a suspended Model 362 cab through 40 hours of brutal shake testing, not a single loose fastener was discovered. In fact, it does such a good job of protecting equipment against damage, we're able to offer a 500,000 mile cab warranty on all Model 362's with the 4-point suspension system.

Comfort, handling, reliability: it's all there. Call 800-447-4700.

Think of it. No unnerving cab sway. No expensive repairs on unfamiliar, modified linkages. An extended cab warranty. Increased resale value. And a ride that's remarkably smooth — but not at the expense of handling. Peterbilt's Model 362 4-point cab air suspension performance and value no other competing design can match. Just call 800-447-4700 for more information and the name of the Peterbilt dealer nearest you.

Peterbilt
A DIVISION OF PACCAR
Peterbilt Motors Company
38801 Cherry Street
Newark, CA 94560

Business-to-business advertising has traditionally been rather matter of fact—even boring. Recent ads, such as those by Ethyl Chemicals and Peterbilt trucks, use some of the same kinds of creative efforts found in consumer advertising to get audience attention. (Top: Ethyl Corporation. Bottom: Pinne', Garvin, Herbers & Hock, Inc.)

more professional associations; one such association awards the title of certified purchasing manager (CPM) to qualified agents who pass the prescribed course.[9]

Professional buyers have developed a number of formal methods of purchasing. For instance, almost two-thirds of buying organizations use a formal system of placing potential vendors on an approved vendor list.[10] Many firms develop systems for investigating multiple sources of information before they make major purchases.[11] Perhaps one of the clearest examples of the need for highly rational and professional decision making occurs when organizational buyers decide whether to purchase a product or to make it themselves.[12]

Organizational buying is most often based on logic and analysis—on comparisons between price on the one hand and product quality, service, and delivery schedules on the other. At times, however, purchasing agents will disregard their prescribed routines and will buy from companies with whom they have long-standing and positive relationships—even though other vendors offer somewhat lower prices. These and other less rational buying processes occur with some frequency.

Reciprocity

Another practice not encountered in consumer marketing but somewhat common in organizational marketing is **reciprocity** (or mutual give-and-take). In the world of organizational marketing, this principle translates into "You buy from me, and I'll buy from you," or, less specifically, "You do something for me, and I'll do something for you." This dynamic may occur when a trucking company buys its computers from a company which uses its trucking services.

Reciprocity is most commonly encountered when the products in question are commodities with little variance in price from one manufacturer to another—paper cartons are an example. Note that reciprocity is illegal when it can be shown to restrain trade. Although it remains fairly common, most executives and purchasing agents object to reciprocity, viewing it as a bad business practice.

Leasing

Some organizational buyers choose to lease equipment rather than purchase it outright. Leasing has several advantages for both the lessee and the lessor. Lessors end up with a product placement with a customer who could not afford the initial purchase; at the very least, they have found users of their products who can pay for the privilege. Lessees can keep their capital, receive the latest models, enjoy

This photograph shows a fairly typical sales situation—a Union Camp carton sales agent explaining the values of his product to a customer with a packaging problem. The packaging used in the production of millions of tubes of toothpaste, or millions of any other product, is a major cost. A fraction of a penny per package, or an agreement of delivery schedules, can be the subject of intense negotiation before the final sale is determined. (Copyright © by Craig Hammell/The Stock Market.)

beneficial service contracts, buy at reduced prices at the end of a lease, and gain certain tax advantages.

Leasing is most common when large capital goods are involved—in other words, when a substantial investment would be necessary for purchase. For example, it is quite common for customers to lease large mainframe computers rather than buy them outright. In fact, during the early days of computer use, IBM refused to sell its products and insisted on leasing arrangements.

☐ *Negotiation and Bidding*

Although consumers may negotiate the price of a used car, or even the cost of a zucchini, it is not common for U.S. consumers to negotiate the cost of goods and services. However, when organizations buy and sell, they frequently negotiate over both price and product specifications. If marketers can learn about a customer's new product while it is still under development, they can influence its specifications even before negotiations begin. They may negotiate a lower price, for example, if the buyer is willing to accept a less durable product or less service. In those situations where both the buyer and seller hold considerable bargaining power, and where the purchase is an important one, negotiation can be a major aspect of the interaction between the parties. The negotiating styles of the two sides can range from confrontational to collaborative; most buyers claim to favor the latter.[13]

Prospective buyers frequently solicit and compare bids from many vendors. The federal government conducts almost 40 percent of purchasing, for instance, on a bid basis. In **open bidding** situations, prospective suppliers are allowed to examine their competitor's proposals. In **closed bidding,** contract terms are kept secret, and suppliers are expected to make their best bids first. Bids for government business are usually closed; government buyers are often required to accept the lowest bid.[14]

ANALYZING ORGANIZATIONAL BUYING

Like individual consumers, organizational buyers go through a number of steps and are influenced by various psychological processes in reaching buying decisions. Organizations, however, are more formal, analytical, and systematic in reaching their decisions. This section differentiates the somewhat formal sequential behaviors of organizational buyers from the more informal internal processes that individual consumers go through.

Organizational buying behavior is the decision-making process by which a buying group establishes the need for goods and services and identifies, evaluates, and chooses among alternative brands and suppliers.[15] Of course, not all organizations and industries have the same buying practices and procedures, just as no two consumers are identical. But one useful descriptive model isolates seven phases, or steps, involved in organizational purchasing. Although some organizations establish more stages and others use a simpler process, marketers that serve an organization must understand not only its buying process but also how its customers make purchases.

The Buy-Phase Concept

The **buy-phase concept** views organizational purchasing as a series of sequential steps proceeding from recognition of a need through evaluation of the product's performance in satisfying that need (see Exhibit 5-2). This approach is particularly useful when the purchase involves products and suppliers that are new or unfamiliar to the customer.[16] The formality of procedures and the specific steps involved depend on the size and structure of the organization, the nature of the product needed, and the buying situation. In general, however, organizations move from

EXHIBIT 5-2	Major Stages of Organizational Buying Behavior (Buy Phases)

Just as consumers pass through stages in their purchase decision process, organizational buyers pass through a number of distinct phases. However, organizational buyers tend to be more formal in their buying process.

1. Recognition of problem or need

2. Identification and description of product's characteristics

3. Search for qualified suppliers

4. Acquisition and analysis of suppliers' proposals

5. Evaluation of proposals and selection of suppliers

6. Selection of an order routine

7. Evaluation of performance

Adapted from Patrick J. Robinson, Charles W. Faris, and Yoram Wind, *Industrial Buying and Creative Marketing* (Boston: Allyn & Bacon, 1967), p. 14.

The makers of a variety of consumer products buy ingredients to make those products. When Searle developed NutraSweet sweetener, one marketing task was to convince the users of sweeteners that this new development would improve their products. This included their efforts to help the organizational buyers recognize that need. (Ken Karp.)

recognizing a problem or need to searching for a product that solves or satisfies it, to selecting a supplier and an ordering procedure, to evaluating results. The sequence itself is not so different from consumers' buying behavior, but the formality and complexity of the various buy phases make organizational purchasing a professional endeavor.

PHASE 1: RECOGNITION OF PROBLEM OR NEED Sometimes events in the customer's organization—the discovery of worn or outdated equipment, an opportunity for cost savings, dissatisfaction with a previous purchase—may trigger the organization's recognition of a problem or need. But events outside the organization can also serve as triggers. The announcement of a new product, a conversation with a supplier's sales representative, a magazine ad, or a display at a trade show may spark the idea for a new purchase. Marketers try to understand their organizational customers' problems, and they use promotion programs to stimulate the recognition of needs.

In the early 1980s, for example, soft-drink marketers recognized that a health-conscious public would find their products more acceptable if they removed some ingredients recently found to be health-threatening. It was time to get rid of caffeine and to replace saccharin. Royal Crown introduced the first caffeine-free cola, and 7-Up capitalized on the fact that it never *had* contained caffeine ("never had it . . . never will"). Coca-Cola and Pepsi-Cola also moved to put caffeine-free products on the market as quickly as possible, but makers of diet soda were left staring at the link between low-calorie saccharin and cancer.

At just about this time, the Food and Drug Administration approved the use of aspartame as a low-calorie sweetener. Although more expensive than saccharin, aspartame has no aftertaste and—more important—no correlation with cancer. G. D. Searle Company, the manufacturer of aspartame, took action and prompted need recognition among soft-drink marketers by advertising heavily both to bottlers and to consumers. Searle recognized and seized an extremely profitable marketing opportunity, and its gain was the saccharin sellers' loss. Sales of aspartame reached a sweet $100 million in the first year of approved use.

**PHASE 2: IDENTIFICATION AND DESCRIPTION OF PRODUCT'S CHAR-
ACTERISTICS**   Once a problem or need is recognized, some notion of a product
to solve that problem or satisfy that need comes to mind. This image, in turn, should
suggest some of the characteristics of that product. For example, if the question is
"How do we join these two parts together?" various options arise—welding, riveting, bolting, or bonding—depending on the materials involved. If the problem is
identified as "How do we best rivet these two parts together?" the description of
characteristics will deal only with riveting technology.

Early in this buy phase, various specialists in the organization consider the
product's general characteristics. Designers for a manufacturer of personal computers might, at this stage, discuss required features and performance standards for
the microprocessors they will need to fabricate the new product. Once the general
characteristics of the product are described, more specific plans are made for the
components that will make these features possible. The manufacturer then translates
the desired features into detailed specifications, seeking advice from engineers,
designers, consultants, and other specialists in research, development, production,
and sales, depending on the nature of the product.

At this stage, organizational marketers who know a buying company's plans
may be able to influence its decisions about product specifications, perhaps in favor
of their own products. One of the most creative aspects of marketing to organizations lies in helping the buyer to design product specifications. Qualified
marketers may even be invited to participate in value analysis, a process described
in Exhibit 5-3.

Some organizational buying situations call for highly
complex statements of needs, which often require detailed engineering specifications for plant and equipment
designed especially for the customer. The marketer's involvement in writing these specifications introduces a
distinct competitive advantage. (Copyright © by John
Zoiner/International Stock Photo.)

| EXHIBIT 5-3 | Value Analysis |

As a company develops new-product specifications, it may assign a value-analysis engineering team to the project. **Value analysis** is a cost-reduction program in which customers study each component of a supplier's product to determine whether it can be redesigned, standardized, or produced more cheaply. The customer analyzes whether each component will deliver the desired performance at a reasonable cost. If the rotors in an electric motor outlast the other parts, then their performance exceeds requirements, and cheaper rotors may be used.

A value-analysis team at Ford Motor Company may be asked to "reengineer" a carburetor that Ford buys for its Econoline vans from an outside supplier. The team rethinks its design, its materials, and perhaps its manufacture in an effort to determine whether it can be made more efficiently at a lower cost while still meeting performance specifications.

Value analysis can mean real savings to organizational buyers. Sellers may also present their own value analyses of a product, establishing that their product is the superior item for the price. The increasing use of computer-assisted design and manufacturing will make value analysis more sophisticated and precise, giving organizational buyers the engineering expertise that may lead to changes in the seller's product.

Sources: Anthony R. Tocco, "Value Engineering (Value Analysis)," in Carl Hayel (ed.), *The Encyclopedia of Management,* 2d ed. (New York: Van Nostrand-Rheinhold, 1973), p. 1084; Vincent G. Reuter, "What Good Are Value Analysis Programs?" *Business Horizons,* March–April 1986, pp. 73–79.

PHASE 3: SEARCH FOR QUALIFIED SUPPLIERS   During this third buy phase, the organization's purchasing agent, in consultation with appropriate staff members, seeks qualified suppliers of the product described in phase 2. This search may be exhaustive or limited, depending on previous experience in the area, the complexity of the product, the importance and cost of the purchase, the financial stability of suppliers, and any risk perceived by the buying organization. As the search continues, the list of potential suppliers is narrowed until only acceptable choices remain. (This group of suppliers is like the evoked set of acceptable products which consumers evaluate in making a purchase.) The final number of contenders depends, among other things, on the total number of suppliers available, the company's policies, and the magnitude of the purchase.

PHASE 4: ACQUISITION AND ANALYSIS OF SUPPLIERS' PROPOSALS
The product specifications drafted in the second buy phase are formally articulated in this phase so that suppliers can make their bids. The buying organization often puts out a formal request for proposals; suppliers then submit detailed written plans and may also present them orally. The marketing organization uses this opportunity to promote its products in their best light, emphasizing price, service, durability, or any other benefits that establish the superiority of its offerings over those of competitors.

PHASE 5: EVALUATION OF PROPOSALS AND SELECTION OF SUPPLIERS   During this stage the marketer's promotional efforts either pay off or don't. The buying organization performs a **vendor analysis,** systematically evaluating and rating prospective suppliers. Suppliers whose proposals are generally comparable are rated in terms of price and quality, reputation, support services, promised delivery time, and personal relations with the buyer.

Before making a final decision, buyers may negotiate for even better terms and prices. A single supplier may emerge with the entire order, or the buyer may decide to use several suppliers. This avoids dependence on one supplier and allows the organization to compare different sellers' service, scheduling, and overall performance.

PHASE 6: SELECTION OF AN ORDER ROUTINE   The details of the transaction are completed during this phase. Packing and shipping methods, credit and payment terms, and service agreements are all settled as is the important question of who holds inventory. Under a "just-in-time inventory plan," or a "stockless purchase plan," the seller may agree to hold items until the buyer needs them, promising delivery on 2 days' notice. This reduces the buyer's inventory costs and keeps valuable warehouse space available for other needed products. When the sale involves items that are reordered frequently, the vendor may offer a "blanket contract," agreeing to supply the products as needed during the period covered. A supplier of maintenance tools for a large city government, for example, might be linked by computer with the city's warehouse. When stock of any given item falls below a certain point, the computer automatically prints an order to the vendor. Blanket contracts encourage use of a single supplier and make it more difficult for new marketers to compete for the sale.[17]

PHASE 7: EVALUATION OF PERFORMANCE   Like individual consumers, organizational buyers follow up on their purchases, but their postpurchase activities are more formal, specific, and visible.

During this final buy phase, the product's quality and performance are evaluated periodically. Suppliers of parts to General Motors, for example, are checked out continuously for the rate of on-time deliveries, the percentage of products that fail to meet quality standards, and the timely servicing of equipment, among other things. Any vendor whose products fall short may find its contracts up for review, and the entire buying process may be reopened.

Performance evaluation benefits suppliers as well as buyers, for it ensures that quality standards are maintained and thus enhances the buyer's satisfaction. Ongoing business is the likely result, so sellers should look positively on evaluation programs.[18] As buyers determine and report how satisfied they are, suppliers can learn more about the customers' needs and requirements, allowing them to compete even more effectively.

☐ The Categories of Buying (Buy Classes)

Marketers who understand their customers' buying situations find themselves able to assist the buyer while promoting their own products and cementing the cordial relationships that result in sales. Marketing scholars often use a "buy grid" to classify buying situations into three categories: the new task, the straight rebuy, and the modified rebuy.[19]

THE NEW TASK   The most difficult situation for the buyer arises when an unfamiliar problem with an old product or the need for a new product generates a situation of **new-task buying.** In this case the buyer must gather as much information as possible to define the need, describe the product that meets the need, and work up new-product specifications. In addition, the new task usually requires a time-consuming consideration of suppliers and detailed negotiations with the final candidates for the contract.

New-task buying typically involves each of the seven steps, or buy phases, that we examined. Depending on the cost of the product and the scope of the problems to be solved, new-task buying may require advice from technical, financial, legal, and sales specialists as well as from management—in addition to the recommendation of those directly involved with acquiring and using the product.

As an example of new-task buying, consider a hospital's purchase of a computer-aided tomography (CAT) scanner—a device that x-rays tiny slices of body structures and then combines the thousands of shots into a composite picture. The scanner can pinpoint stroke-induced brain damage and also provide valuable diagnostic information about vascular structures and other soft-tissue organs. Central General, the largest of three hospitals in a medium-sized midwestern city, plans to share the CAT scanner with other local institutions. The need has been recognized: The hospital can vastly improve its diagnostic work and make it available to the entire community. Moreover, the product that meets that need has been generally identified: a third- or fourth-generation scanner, with high resolution and thin-sectioning capabilities.

To characterize and write specifications for so important a purchase, the chief-of-staff and the hospital administrator appoint a committee under the direction of the senior radiologist. One of the members, Central General's purchasing agent, will record all the information that the group gathers and will summarize it prior to a final decision. Each member has assigned tasks. Some will canvass the hospital services other than radiology that will use the scanner or refer to its output: neurosurgery, cardiology, orthopedics, neurology, ophthalmology, oncology, and so on. Others will identify the CAT units available, set up interviews with potential vendors, and check out the reputation of each manufacturer with several hospitals in Chicago.

After 8 weeks and as many committee meetings, several units are rejected as too difficult to service and too crude in imaging capability. Positron tomography, a technologically different option, has also been ruled out. Three units remain in contention (the committee's evoked set). Marketing representatives and technical specialists are invited to make formal presentations to the committee. Marketers from General Electric will present the advantages of its model 8800; those from Varian will promote its model 360; the group from Siemens will push for its Somatom 2.

Owing to its wide range of functions and convenient service provisions (and because the model received high marks from current users), the committee votes, with only one dissent, for the GE CT/T 8800. The chief of staff and the head radiologist, who share the burden of the final choice, concur in this decision. At a subsequent lunch hosted by GE's regional sales manager, the purchasing agent talks through the details of shipping, billing, and servicing. That afternoon, the purchasing agent meets with the GE technical staff and the hospital's chief of building maintenance to plan the subcontracting needed to build a suitable room for the new equipment.

The cost of a CAT scanner is between $3 and $4 million; typically, such expensive purchases are made through the kind of deliberative and collective process described above. The better informed marketers are about the customer's buying procedures and decision makers, the better their chances for a successful sales effort.

THE STRAIGHT REBUY   At the opposite end of the scale of difficulty, a **straight rebuy** (sometimes called a "reorder") is a routine purchase with which a buyer has had substantial experience. The buyer's knowledge of the product means that there is little need to look for alternative vendors. Purchase criteria and terms are well established, and the buyer is likely to handle the purchase with only routine approvals through customary channels.

The purchasing agent at Central General, for example, buys hundreds, perhaps thousands, of items every month. Articles such as surgical gloves, rubber tubing, electronic thermometers, and paper cups are routinely reordered without approval from the hospital management.

THE MODIFIED REBUY   Time and events can alter the nature of a straight rebuy. Availability of new products, changes in purchasing criteria, and dissatisfaction with the existing product, among other factors, can give rise to a modified rebuy. In between the straight rebuy and a new purchase, a **modified rebuy** has certain qualities of each. The need for a new purchase is obvious, but some consultation and description of the new product are necessary. A limited search for new suppliers is often undertaken; negotiations with the present supplier and possible new suppliers are apt to be extensive.

Let us suppose that Central General is opening a new intensive-care ward in 3 months and will need additional help and rigorous cleaning procedures. Indeed, the chief of staff has already complained about poor hygiene in the maternity and postsurgical wards. At just this time, the hospital's contract for janitorial services comes up for renewal. This situation transforms what might have been a straight rebuy into a modified rebuy. Although the purchasing agent knows about janitorial services, the new requirements of the intensive-care unit and the complaints about the current vendor suggest that the contract should be reopened for bids. The chief of staff, the hospital administrator, and the head nurse in the new intensive-care unit must be consulted. The purchasing agent will investigate new suppliers while urging the present supplier to upgrade performance.

☐ Analyzing the Buying Center

In making decisions about the purchase of a new missile launcher, the U.S. Army command considers the recommendations of full-time groups of experts in weaponry, ballistics, military strategy, production, and cost control. Hilda and Hank Garber, who own Garber's Hardware in New York City, confer with their nephews Tom and George—and perhaps with one or two senior employees—about purchasing a photocopying machine, a new sign, or an ad in the local Greenwich Village newspaper. The people who participate in purchase decisions, whether the Army's hundreds or the Garbers and their relatives, are referred to collectively as a **buying center.**

When a buying center is established as a special committee, its members are easy to identify and sellers can assess each member's influence. However, in most cases buying centers are not formal committees; they are informal groups of different people called together at different times for different purposes. Consequently, they are rarely found in organization charts. The group is formed to reach a major decision in one area or another and is then disbanded. Members come and go as their roles vary with different buy phases; because of their various perspectives, their opinions may conflict. For this reason, compromise is a hallmark of group buying recommendations and decisions. In any buying center, individuals or groups of people normally assume one or more of five important roles. They may function as users, influencers, deciders, buyers, or gatekeepers.

USERS   Users are those people within an organization who actually put a purchased product to work. They may initially suggest a product or the need for one

Members of a buying center, often from different departments in the organization, hold meetings both before and after the salespeople make their presentations. They often must settle their disagreements about which supplier would be best to solve their problem. (Copyright © by Lawrence Migdale 1986.)

and may help draft specifications for the product. Someone who puts information into a computer terminal is the *user* of that terminal. But a user may also be someone who uses a product in the fabrication of the company's own product. The person who installs compressors purchased from an outside supplier for a refrigerator manufacturer is the user of that compressor in one organizational sense. The person who eats in a company cafeteria run by a contracted food service is an organizational user in another sense. A compressor installer or a regular patron of the lunchroom may assume the user role on an ad hoc committee looking into new purchases in one area or the other.

INFLUENCERS   Any number of people, directly or indirectly participating in the work of the buying center, may be decision **influencers**—people whose expertise or opinions have a direct bearing on the purchase decision. In a complex purchase—buying a group of robots for a truck assembly line, for example—influencers might include any combination of design engineers, safety engineers, assembly-line managers (also users), workers' groups, the building maintenance superintendent, the chief of materials management, a corporate financial officer, a representative of the organization's bank, and perhaps even an outside consulting firm.

Who the influencers are varies according to the cost and complexity of a purchase, but technical personnel who draft specifications and evaluate available products are particularly influential. Some influencers may be obvious, but others operate so informally that their involvement and degree of influence is hard to identify.[20]

DECIDERS   Those who have the power and the responsibility to approve a product and select final suppliers are **deciders.** For complex purchases, a committee may make the decision; for large investments, the chief executive may become involved; for the purchase of a word processor, the "using" secretary may make the choice. Whoever the deciders are, they will be the recipients of the sales representative's most persuasive attentions.

BUYERS   Those who carry out the formal arrangements for purchase, service, delivery, and financial terms are the **buyers.** Buyers are not always deciders. For significant purchases, the purchasing agent may simply handle the arrangements for the purchase—the postdecision buy phases. For routine purchases and rebuys, the purchasing agent is likely to act as both decider and buyer.

GATEKEEPERS   Gatekeepers are those who can control information flow to members of the buying center—and to prospective suppliers. Purchasing agents, who decide which sales representatives are allowed access to users, influencers, and deciders, often have such power. The secretaries of buying-center members may also act as gatekeepers, granting access selectively to people and to information. Although the power of gatekeepers often lies below the surface, it is extremely effective.

IMPLICATIONS FOR MARKETERS   The marketer's job is relatively simple when the buying center consists of just one person, as when a purchasing agent buys a commodity such as paper towels or light bulbs. It becomes increasingly difficult as the buying center consists of more and more people with varying degrees of influence who may or may not play multiple roles. In approaching a buying center, marketers must be able to answer four basic questions:

1. Who comprises the buying center?
2. What influence does each member exert over the decision?
3. What product evaluation criteria does each member use, and how are those criteria applied to prospective suppliers?
4. What is the best way to communicate persuasively with members of the buying center?[21]

Identifying the important influencers and the real decider is not always easy, but marketers who establish good relationships with gatekeepers and influencers have an advantage as they deal with the buying center. Many buying decisions are made by a single individual (such as the purchasing agent) and others by a group (the buying center).[22] Effective selling involves knowing when an individual is making such decisions and when a group is. As we will see in Chapter 20, a primary task of professional sales representatives is the planning and execution of sales campaigns directed to multimember buying centers.

Techniques for reaching consumer and organizational markets differ enough so that many experts question the validity of treating them both in a single textbook or course. Although we agree that some of these differences are quite important, we nevertheless must emphasize that marketing concepts and skills apply to both consumer and organizational markets. Consequently, many men and women are able to shift from consumer to organizational marketing and enjoy success in both areas. Throughout this book, we use both consumer and organizational examples to illustrate the application of marketing principles.

■ SUMMARY ■

1. Organizational purchasing differs from consumer purchasing in that it is planned and carried out by trained professional buyers.
2. The marketing concept is the foundation of organizational marketing, just as it is central to consumer marketing.

3. Organizational marketing includes all marketing efforts directed at buyers for formal institutions, including industrial, service, reseller, government, and not-for-profit groups.

4. One estimate puts the dollar volume of all organizational purchases at about three times the amount of estimated retail sales.

5. The government-sponsored *Standard Industrial Classification Manual* classifies every kind of economic activity in the United States through a four-digit system.

6. The demand for industrial goods and services derives from demand for other products.

7. Industrial, business, and government markets tend to cluster geographically.

8. Marketers who serve vertical markets often focus on a few major accounts. Losing even one account can be a disaster.

9. Because their relatively few buyers place large orders, organizational marketers have traditionally emphasized personal selling over advertising within the promotional mix.

10. Some organizational buyers choose to lease equipment rather than purchase it outright.

11. When organizations buy and sell, they frequently negotiate both price and product specifications.

12. Under the buy-phase concept, organizational purchasing is a series of sequential steps, particularly when the purchase involves a new and unfamiliar product.

13. In sequence, the buy phases are (1) recognition of a problem or need; (2) identification and description of a product's characteristics; (3) search for qualified suppliers; (4) acquisition and analysis of suppliers' proposals; (5) evaluation of proposals and selection of suppliers; (6) selection of an order routine; and (7) evaluation of performance.

14. A modified rebuy has certain qualities of both the straight rebuy and a new purchase.

15. In any buying center, individuals or groups of people may function as users, influencers, deciders, buyers, or gatekeepers.

☐ Key Terms

buyers
buying center
buy-phase concept
closed bidding
deciders
derived demand
gatekeepers
government markets
horizontal markets

industrial markets
influencers
modified rebuy
new-task buying
not-for-profit markets
open bidding
organizational buying behavior
organizational marketing
reciprocity

reseller markets
service market
Standard Industrial Classification Manual
straight rebuy
users
value analysis
vendor analysis
vertical markets

☐ Chapter Review

1. What basic purpose does each of the five kinds of organizational markets have in making purchases? Are government markets and not-for-profit markets less constrained than other organizational buyers in reaching purchase decisions?

2. Explain how the manufacturer of aluminum window frames might use the *SIC Manual* in estimating the size of potential industrial markets.

3. What are some of the characteristics that might differentiate the marketing of Kellogg's Raisin Bran to consumers from the marketing of cereal grains to Kellogg's?

4. Of the seven steps listed for the buy-phase concept, which might be eliminated in a straight or modified rebuy?

5. What kinds of employees and roles might be represented in the buying center of an insurance company that is interested in a new telephone-switching system? How might these employees and roles change if the purchase involved a new fleet of cars for the company's sales force?

6. Why are industrial markets characterized by derived demand?

7. Is reciprocity legal in organizational marketing? Why might it be practiced?

References

1. Personal correspondence with Dr. Irwin Gross, managing director of the Institute for the Study of Business Markets, Pennsylvania State University, 1986.
2. For another view, see Edward F. Fern and James R. Brown, "The Industrial/Consumer Marketing Dichotomy: A Case of Insufficient Justification," *Journal of Marketing,* vol. 48, Spring 1984, pp. 66–77.
3. Warren H. Suss, "How to Sell to Uncle Sam," *Harvard Business Review,* Nov.–Dec. 1984, p. 136.
4. Ibid., p. 137.
5. "Report Says Hospital Chains Rely on High Fees for Profit," *The New York Times,* Aug. 11, 1983, p. A14.
6. Frederick A. Russ and Charles A. Kirkpatrick, *Marketing* (Boston: Little, Brown, 1982), p. 176.
7. Barbara Bund Jackson, "Build Customer Relations That Last," *Harvard Business Review,* Nov.–Dec. 1985, pp. 120–128.
8. Joanne Cleaver, "There's a New Way to Do Business (to Business)," *Advertising Age,* June 20, 1983, pp. M-9, M-24.
9. Larry Guinipero and Gary Zenz, "Impact of Purchasing Trends on Industrial Marketers," *Industrial Marketing Management,* vol. 11, Feb. 1982, pp. 17–23.
10. Ralph W. Jackson and William M. Pride, "The Use of Approved Vendor Lists," *Industrial Marketing Management,* vol. 15, Aug. 1986, pp. 165–169.
11. Rowland T. Moriarty, Jr., and Robert E. Spekman, "An Empirical Investigation of the Information Sources Used during the Industrial Buying Process," *Journal of Marketing Research,* vol. XXI, May 1984, pp. 137–147.
12. Erin Anderson and Barton A. Weitz, "Make-or-Buy Decisions: Vertical Integration and Marketing Productivity," *Sloan Management Review,* Spring 1986, pp. 3–19.
13. See Stephen W. Clopton, "Seller and Buying Firm Factors Affecting Industrial Buyers' Negotiation Behavior and Outcomes," *Journal of Marketing Research,* vol. XXI, Feb. 1984, pp. 39–53.
14. David E. Gumpert and Jeffrey A. Timmons, "Penetrating the Government Procurement Maze," *Harvard Business Review,* vol. 60, no. 3 (Sept.–Oct. 1982), pp. 14–23.
15. Adapted from Frederick E. Webster, Jr., and Yoram Wind, *Organizational Buying Behavior* (Englewood Cliffs, N.J.: Prentice-Hall, 1972), p. 2.
16. Patrick J. Robinson, Charles W. Faris, and Yoram Wind, *Industrial Buying and Creative Marketing* (Boston: Allyn & Bacon, 1967), p. 14.
17. H. Lee Matthews, David T. Wilson, and Klaus Backhaus, "Selling to the Computer-Assisted Buyer," *Industrial Marketing Management,* vol. 6, Oct. 1977, pp. 307–315.
18. Christopher P. Puto, Wesley E. Patton, III, and Ronald H. King, "Risk Handling Strategies in Industrial Vendor Selection Decisions," *Journal of Marketing,* vol. 49, Winter 1985, pp. 89–98.
19. Joseph A. Bellizzi and Phillip McVey, "How Valid Is the Buy-Grid Model?" *Industrial Marketing Management,* vol. 12, Feb. 1983, pp. 57–62.
20. Webster and Wind, op. cit., p. 6.
21. Rowland T. Moriarty and Morton Galper, *Organizational Buying Behavior: A State-of-the-Art Review and Conceptualization* (Cambridge, Mass.: Marketing Science Institute, 1978), p. 25.
22. W. E. Patton, III, Christopher P. Puto, and Ronald H. King, "Which Buying Decisions Are Made by Individuals and Not by Groups?" *Industrial Marketing Management,* vol. 15, May 1986, pp. 129–138.

6

Ellis Herwig/The Picture Cube.

GATHERING MARKETING INFORMATION

SPOTLIGHT ON

☐ How marketing managers use informal and formal sources of information

☐ Components and workings of a marketing information system

☐ Why companies do or do not commit resources to a marketing research effort

☐ Steps in the marketing research process

☐ How marketers gather and use primary and secondary data

☐ Managing and budgeting for marketing research

"We surveyed women to find if they had the problem for which we had the solution." Scientists at Elizabeth Arden, a subsidiary of the pharmaceutical giant, Eli Lilly, developed a new chemical with some interesting properties. However, they wondered whether there was a market for the new substance, Primilin II. Primilin II can stop the oils in lipsticks from seeping into the rhytides (the vertical lines above, below, and around lips). Many cosmetics users were unaware that they had a problem with "bleeding" until they were probed in Arden-sponsored focus groups (small groups of consumers gathered to discuss a product or idea). Women indeed *did* have this problem: A survey of 1200 women pointed to unusually strong interest in a product to cure "lipstick bleeding."

Arden introduced Lip-Fix, a treatment cream, in 1983. It was the most successful new-product introduction in cosmetic history. Arden believed that Lip-Fix had not simply opened a new product category; it had expanded consumer receptivity to repair products. As a result, they developed Eye-Fix, a cream to prevent eye-shadow from drying, flaking, fading, and caking.

Once again, Arden used focus groups to fine-tune the product and to develop packaging and advertising ideas. Then Eye-Fix was subjected to the ultimate test: More than 350 people were asked to use the product for 3 to 4 weeks. "In the early focus groups, we made sure we were slaying the right dragon," noted John Cella, Arden's director of research. "Now we wanted to answer the ultimate make-or-break question. In marketing I think they call it 'Do the dogs like the dog food?'"

In this case, Arden had developed another winner. When asked to surrender Eye-Fix, 90 percent of those in Arden's test groups preferred to keep it. Research had helped Arden to find the market for Eye-Fix and had helped the market to discover this popular new product.

Source: Bernice Kanner, "Putting in the Fix," *New York,* Apr. 16, 1984, pp. 17–20.

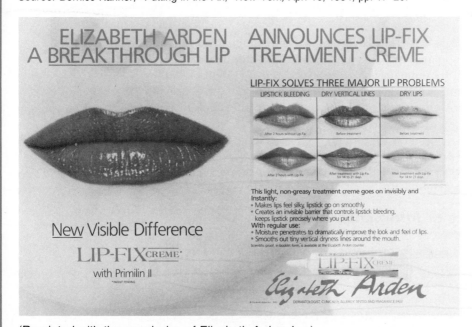

(Reprinted with the permission of Elizabeth Arden, Inc.)

The marketing concept is based on two fundamental assumptions: (1) that marketers know with assurance (or at least can find out) what buyers needs are and (2) that marketers know how, when, where, and why consumers and organizational buyers make their purchase decisions. Marketers at Elizabeth Arden were not certain that they had a market for the new substance that their research staff had developed; consequently, they gathered **information,** which suggested that consumers wanted products like Lip-Fix and Eye-Fix. Had this research shown otherwise, Arden would have had to continue searching for a use for Primilin II or consider dropping marketing plans for the chemical.

Of course, to what extent marketers know buyers needs "with assurance" is relative. No amount of information can guarantee a correct marketing decision. However, information about the marketplace and competitive offerings provides vital support for the decisions that marketers must make. Reliable information increases the probability that marketing decisions will be correct and ultimately beneficial for the company.

As we pointed out in Chapter 1, marketing management strikes a fine blend between art and science. Most marketing decisions are based on the manager's own experience and judgment without the benefit of research. Such decision making represents the art of marketing. By contrast, when faced with decisions of great importance, managers generally ask for more information. Gathering, interpreting, and reporting that information represents the most scientific aspect of marketing.

Chapter 6 begins by examining the importance of informal and formal sources of information as the basis of marketing decisions. We next describe the makeup and workings of a modern marketing information system, paying particular attention to the scope and methods of marketing research and to important considerations in managing marketing functions. Finally, we summarize the prospects for marketing research.

■ INFORMATION AND DECISION MAKING ■

Information does not make marketing decisions; rather, it helps managers make decisions. For example, Burger King officials compiled encouraging information concerning mustard burgers, a new product under development: Texans simply loved them! But there was discouraging information as well: Residents of other states had little interest in mustard burgers. Burger King wisely tested reactions to the new product across the United States and decided *not* to introduce mustard burgers, avoiding a potentially costly mistake. By contrast, marketing information supported Elizabeth Arden's decision to introduce Eye-Fix, resulting in millions of dollars in new revenues and profits. In making important marketing decisions, managers at Burger King, Elizabeth Arden, and other companies rely on both formal and informal sources of information.

☐ *Informal Sources of Information*

The bottom of Figure 6-1 depicts the many informal sources of information that affect a marketing manager's decisions. **Informal information** is that mixture of unorganized and irregular daily communications which flows to most of us in contemporary society. Friends, coworkers, and the media provide information that we process unconsciously but that nonetheless we assimilate into our personal "data banks." Typical informal information has certain characteristics:

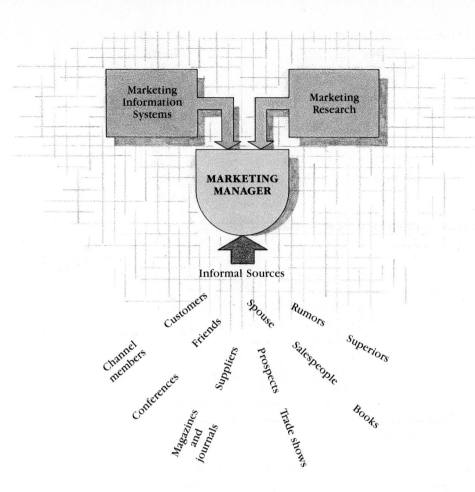

Figure 6-1 *Formal and informal information flows.* Marketing managers use formal and systematic flows of information obtained from well-designed information systems and from scientifically conducted marketing research. Marketing decisions are also influenced by informal flows of information that may be inaccurate, biased, incomplete, conflicting, or "fuzzy."

- It is not transmitted or received in any systematic way.
- Its quality and accuracy vary greatly.
- It is more often oral than written.
- In many cases, it is not consciously sought by the receiver.
- It is not under the control of the receiver.
- It is often biased.

In spite of these seemingly negative characteristics, informal information plays a major role in people's decisions. Decision makers cannot escape informal information, and it is likely to continue as part of input into decisions as long as human beings are making choices. Nothing is inherently correct about formal sources of information, the topic of the bulk of this chapter, and nothing is inherently wrong with informal sources. Formal sources support the scientific end of marketing decision making; informal sources support the art of marketing.

Formal Sources of Information

Most large business organizations maintain information systems designed to support the general information needs of managers in all areas—accounting, manufacturing, personnel, finance, general management, as well as marketing. **Formal information** is designed as such by the organization and is received in a planned and systematic

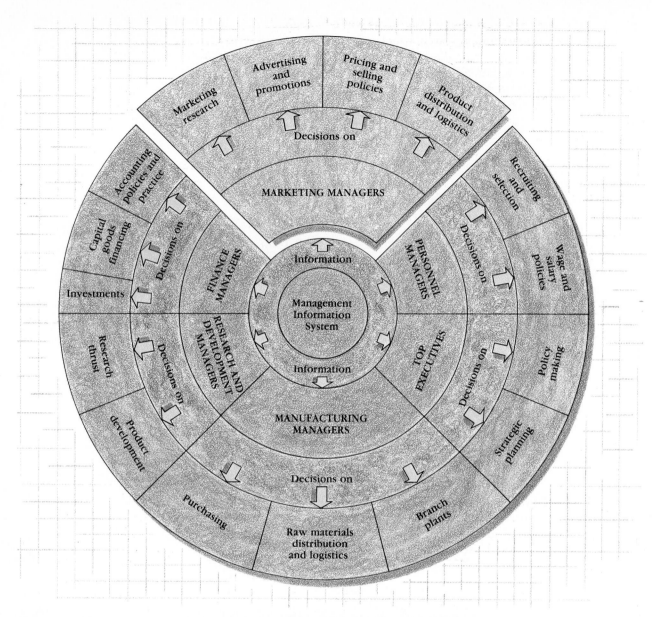

Figure 6-2 *The scope of a management information system.* The marketing information system (shown in blue) is only a component of the overall management information system. However, it is a vital component because it gives the entire organization a meaningful existence. (From Donald H. Sanders, *Computers Today*, 2d ed., New York: McGraw-Hill, 1985, p. 366.)

manner on a scheduled basis. Typically, formal procedures for generating and receiving marketing information are part of the organization's overall **management information system** (MIS). The scope of a typical system is shown in Figure 6-2. Marketing managers, along with their colleagues in production and finance, are major users of the MIS.[1]

Typical reports generated by a MIS include such items as sales and costs, environmental activities, and progress toward achieving goals. From time to time, results of marketing research into specific areas will be integrated into the overall information system. Marketing research, which applies in-depth analysis to a specific problem or opportunity, is properly viewed as a component of the total MIS.

Robert Williams, a pioneer in the establishment of information systems, likened the difference between marketing research and an information system to that between a flash bulb and a candle. Marketing research, like a flashbulb, illuminates an issue brightly but briefly. An MIS, however, offers less brilliant but continuous exposure, like a candle, allowing marketers to monitor the results of their actions over long periods.[2] Certain reports—sales, costs, deviations from plans—arrive on a regular basis. The results of actions based on these reports—for example, a price change or a sales forecast adjustment—are fed back into the data bank. The information found in subsequent reports is then adjusted. In other words, users of the information must provide input and interact with the system.

■ *MARKETING INFORMATION SYSTEMS (MKIS)* ■

The **marketing information system** (MKIS) is contained within the MIS; it uses the same computer hardware and a great deal of the same software. In fact, the MIS and the MKIS differ only in their applications. The MKIS is a continuously interacting structure of people, machines, and procedures that produces information pertinent to marketing decisions.[3]

□ *Components*

A typical MKIS, diagrammed in Figure 6-3, has at least four components. The basic **MKIS data bank** (probably handled by a mainframe computer or powerful mini-

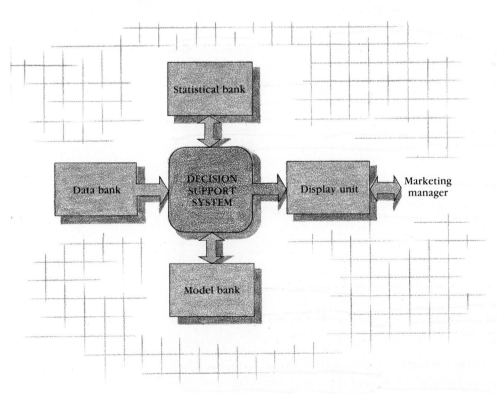

Figure 6-3 *Components of a marketing information system.* A marketing information system is essentially the same as a decision support system designed to support marketing decisions. Some mechanism—the display unit (recently often a computer terminal)—allows the manager to interact with the system's data, models, and statistical tools.

computer) receives and stores almost all data flowing into the system. The **MKIS statistical bank** contains programs for performing routine computations like advertising spending projections and sales tracking. Simple statistics may be performed through the statistical bank; more sophisticated analysis can be performed with the capabilities of the **MKIS model bank.** Operations research programs allow managers to ask "what if" questions from a model which simulates a market, for example. What will a price increase do to sales volume? Will a lower level of promotion expenditures seriously affect sales? The fourth component is a simple and familiar **display unit** or workstation, which provides the information to managers on a display screen or through use of a printer.

Some large organizations now have an additional component that greatly increases the usefulness of the MKIS. A **decision support system** (DSS) is software that enables managers with little computer training to use other banks from their own terminals. A DSS provides on-line access to data, statistical, and model banks for individual managers; nearly instantaneous results; and user-friendly software for easy manipulation of data.

Marketing managers for a large packaged-goods company used a DSS to quickly solve a major problem. One morning, the executive vice president of one of the nation's largest supermarket chains announced unexpectedly that he planned to drop 23 of the food packager's products because of poor sales. Marketers for the packager immediately retrieved information which showed that competing chains were doing quite well with the items in question. These retailers were taking lower markups on the products and were providing greater advertising support. Marketers then showed the retailer how many additional gross margin dollars might be realized if he raised sales volume to competitors' levels with a lower markup. The retailer accepted this suggestion and agreed to adjust the chain's pricing and promotion of the products. Saving the account became possible because a DSS was available—and the problem was solved before lunchtime.[4]

The development of DSSs has been aided by the appearance of "fourth-generation" computer languages. Although these languages are more complex than third-generation languages like COBOL and FORTRAN, a manager doesn't have to understand a fourth-generation language to use a DSS.[5] Further advances are being made in the "expert systems" branch of **artificial intelligence** (AI)—the science of getting computers to simulate human thought processes. An **expert system** is a software package that includes a stored base of knowledge in a specialized area and can probe this knowledge base and make decision recommendations. To develop an expert system, researchers pick the brains of specialists in an area to extract and structure the knowledge for programming. Doctors are using expert systems for diagnosis, and geologists use them for searching for mineral deposits. Expert systems are in their infancy, but future systems may provide great assistance in making marketing decisions.[6]

☐ *Sources*

The sources that feed a full-blown information system will vary, of course, from organization to organization. For the most part, **MKIS information flows** comprise scheduled information flows from internal and external sources, marketing intelligence networks, and marketing research findings. Figure 6-4 shows how information from these sources flows into the MKIS.

SCHEDULED INFORMATION FLOWS On a regular basis—daily, weekly, monthly, or quarterly—records of sales (units and revenues), operating and man-

INTERNAL SOURCES

Scheduled reports
Exception reports

EXTERNAL SOURCES

Syndicated services
Marketing
Intelligence
Networks
Marketing research

MKIS

Figure 6-4 *Information sources for the MKIS.* Examples of internal flows within the MKIS include monthly sales reports showing which customers are buying which products or inventory reports warning of a stockout of certain products. Two examples of external flows are weekly data received from SAMI (Selling-Areas Marketing Inc.) on warehouse withdrawals and the results of a specially commissioned study of consumer attitudes.

ufacturing costs, and inventory activity flow to managers at appropriate levels. Typically, these internal reports are produced under the direction of the corporate management information unit. For example, a San Diego–based regional manager for Pillsbury's grocery products division may receive a weekly sales printout for all "dry," shelf-stable products, showing revenues and unit sales for each product. That report may be broken down by sales territory and may include a comparison of sales for the same week a year ago. The report may also measure progress toward an established fiscal year sales goal by product, territory, and region. The sales vice president, based in Pillsbury's Minneapolis headquarters, will receive a weekly summary for each region.

Marketers may also purchase scheduled reports from private **syndicated research services.** Such reports spell out what consumers are buying and how a product (and competing brands) is faring in the marketplace. A. C. Nielsen Company (of television ratings fame) sells bimonthly reports on market shares, prices, stockouts, and the percentage of stores carrying each brand (based on a sample of over 1500 stores). The Nielsen surveys also measure how much retail shelf space is given over to individual products and brands. Competition sales are included in these reports. Selling-Areas Marketing Incorporated (SAMI) sells reports on withdrawals from supermarket warehouses for shipments to stores, including the movement of competitors' products.

Market data based on **purchase diaries** are also available. Shoppers in a sample of households keep detailed personal records of household purchases, noting brands, prices, product sizes, sales promotions, and so on. Nielsen, SAMI, and the Market Research Corporation of America (MRCA) are some of the largest firms compiling and selling marketing information. However, a number of other, smaller companies prepare and distribute various marketing performance reports, usually keyed to specific industries.

MARKETING INTELLIGENCE NETWORKS Most scheduled information flows tell managers what *has* happened, but managers also need to know what is happening and, more important, what is going to happen. A **marketing intelligence network** is a set of procedures and sources designed to monitor the organization's external environments—particularly the competitive environment.

[margin handwritten note: Competitive environment + environmental monitoring]

Some companies have established formal departments of marketing intelligence. These offices monitor a variety of publications and abstract relevant news and trends, and prepare regular reports on environmental trends for marketing managers. Intelligence reports emphasize competitors' actions and likely actions; they may summarize legislative and government agency activity and economic trends. Intelligence departments may also coordinate the efforts of internal committees of line managers who are assigned specific areas to monitor. These marketing intelligence units are an example of how the environmental monitoring discussed in Chapter 2 is carried out.

The Aluminum Company of America (ALCOA) maintains a Competitive Information Center, and IBM's Commercial Analysis Division has long been regarded as a model marketing intelligence operation. Holiday Inns, GTE's Sylvania Division, and Quaker Oats are other firms that maintain intelligence departments as key elements in an overall MKIS.

GATHERING SPECIAL INFORMATION: MARKETING RESEARCH In general, marketing research is performed on a one-time basis to address a specific problem or question, but such research is best treated as one more information source for the MKIS. Information gleaned in marketing research projects should be integrated into the databases of the MKIS. For example, if a marketing research study reveals that three new competitors are entering the market, that information should be quickly plugged into the MKIS databases and should be reflected in other reports.

◼ MARKETING RESEARCH ◼

The motivations, needs, attitudes, and buying decisions of consumers and organizational buyers are the focus of most marketing research efforts. Such research is labeled "market research" because it investigates and analyzes specific target markets—the growth or decline of the market for wet cat food, for example.

Market research is, however, only one area of the larger field of **marketing research**—"the systematic and objective research for and analysis of information relevant to the identification and solution of any problem in the field of marketing."[7] The first key word in this definition is "systematic"—ordered rules guide the conduct of marketing research, rules based on the scientific method that directs research in all areas. "Objective" is the second key word, indicating that the research should be bias-free and should not seek information supporting any particular position or decision alternative. The third key part of the definition is the phrase "any problem in the field of marketing." In addition to examining markets, marketing research encompasses a wide range of endeavors, including such projects as studies of alternative systems for transporting goods, the effects of various price levels on the demand for products, the effectiveness of sales representatives' persuasive techniques, and the best ways to organize a marketing operation.

☐ *Early Marketing Research*

In 1911, Curtis Publishing Company, publisher of the *Saturday Evening Post,* formed the first "commercial research" unit. Research department head Charles Coolidge Parlin made his mark by convincing Campbell Soup Company executives to advertise in his publication. Parlin collected garbage from Philadelphia's blue-collar neighborhoods and was able to prove that the *Post*'s working-class readers were heavy users of canned soup. Campbell's managers had believed that only the wealthy could afford to buy soup instead of making it from scratch. Parlin's research—unorthodox, but effective—convinced the soup company that the *Post* reached the right audience.[8]

The first books on marketing research were published in the 1920s, but growth of both independent and corporate research units was slow until after World War II. Beginning in the 1950s, however, the emergence of the marketing concept led to a rapid rise in the call for trained researchers and the spread of marketing research capabilities within organizations. Figure 6-5 illustrates the growth of new corporate marketing research organizations. Of the 426 companies reporting that they had marketing research departments, 39 percent were started in the 5 years from 1978 to 1983. A sizable majority were formed in the most recent 15-year period.

Outside the corporate setting, independent marketing research firms and marketing research departments of advertising agencies specialize in conducting research for corporate marketers and other clients. Both the number and variety of these organizations have grown very rapidly since the 1950s; their billings are

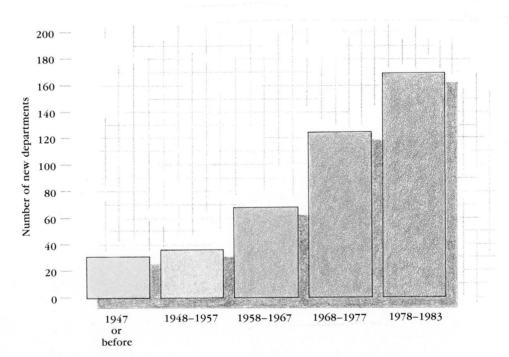

Figure 6-5 *New marketing research departments (to 1983).* Every 5 years the American Marketing Association reports on the formation of new marketing research departments. Recent 5-year periods have seen a dramatic increase in the number of departments, suggesting that research is still being established as a fixture of marketing efforts. (From Dik Warren Twedt, ed., *1983 Survey of Marketing Research,* Chicago: American Marketing Association, 1983, p. 21.)

EXHIBIT 6-1   **Research Activities of 599 Companies**

Forecasting and studies of business trends are carried out by the vast majority of firms; certain types of specialized studies are more rare. These figures represent averages for both consumers and organizational marketers. Generally, they are higher than average for consumer companies and lower for marketers to organizations.

	Where Research Conducted			
	Market Research Department	Other Department	Outside Firm	Total (%)
Advertising Research				
Motivation research	30	2	15	47
Copy research	30	6	25	61
Media research	22	14	32	68
Studies of ad effectiveness	42	5	29	76
Studies of competitive advertising	36	11	20	67
Business Economics and Corporate Research				
Short-range forecasting (up to 1 year)	51	36	2	89
Long-range forecasting (over 1 year)	49	34	4	87
Studies of business trends	68	20	3	91
Pricing studies	34	47	2	83
Plant/warehouse location studies	29	35	4	68
Acquisition studies	33	38	2	73
Export and international studies	22	25	2	49
Management information system	25	53	2	80
Operations research	14	50	1	65
Internal company employees	25	45	6	76
Corporate Responsibility Research				
Consumers' "right to know" studies	7	9	2	18
Ecological impact studies	2	17	4	23
Studies of legal constraints on advertising and promotion	10	31	5	46
Social values and policies studies	19	13	7	39
Product Research				
New product acceptance and potential	59	11	6	76
Competitive product studies	71	10	6	87
Testing of existing products	55	19	6	80
Packaging research: design or physical characteristics	44	12	9	65
Sales and Market Research				
Measurement of market potentials	88	4	5	97
Market share analysis	85	6	6	97
Determination of market characteristics	88	3	6	97
Sales analysis	67	23	2	92
Establishment of sales quotas, territories	23	54	1	78
Distribution channel studies	32	38	1	71
Test markets, store audits	43	7	9	59

	Where Research Conducted			
	Market Research Department	Other Department	Outside Firm	Total (%)
Consumer panel operations	46	2	15	63
Sales compensation studies	13	43	4	60
Promotional studies of premiums, coupons, sampling, deals, etc.	38	14	6	58

Source: Dik Warren Twedt, ed., *1983 Survey of Marketing Research* (Chicago: American Marketing Association, 1983), p. 41.

estimated at $1.5 to $3 billion per year. Clearly, marketing research itself has become big business.

Exhibit 6-1 shows the broad scope of research in a large sample of companies in the United States. The sample includes marketers of consumer and industrial products (including financial services) and advertising agencies. Marketing research can be broadly categorized into five areas: advertising research, business economics and corporate research, corporate responsibility research, product research, and sales and market research. Each category comprises a variety of research areas. As the exhibit indicates, the companies' own marketing research departments are where almost all these types of research are conducted. Outside research firms are most active in advertising studies; departments other than marketing research dominate certain types of research, such as establishing sales quotas and compensation programs, operations research, and information systems.

In the 1940s, when this picture was taken, marketing research was just getting established and being accepted by both marketers and consumers. From its crude beginnings, marketing research techniques have developed in sophistication as well as market acceptance.
(The Paul B. Sheatsley Library/NORC.)

☐ Research Decisions

The first decision to be made about research, of course, is whether to do it. Marketing research can be thought of as providing the information that reduces (but never eliminates) the uncertainty in marketing decisions. However, the value of reducing that uncertainty must be balanced against the cost (in money and time) of conducting the research. Companies vary a great deal in their willingness to commit money and time to marketing research. On one hand, Procter & Gamble, for instance, might conduct an extensive consumer survey and then offer a product (such as a new liquid Tide detergent) in a test market for 2 to 3 years. On the other hand, General Foods did very little research before taking Folgers Coffee into new markets.

benefit > cost

When their decisions involve many millions of dollars, such as in the introduction of a new product, most marketers will feel more comfortable doing some research. Managers who are adding a new version of a product to an existing line are less likely to see the need. Frequently, time constraints preclude a formal study; by the time research could be executed, the opportunity would be lost or the problem would have gotten out of hand. Although Procter & Gamble carefully carried out its testing of Duncan Hines crisp and chewy chocolate-chip cookies in Kansas City, competitors Nabisco Brands and Keebler introduced their own crisp and chewy cookies nationwide and stole the thunder from the Duncan Hines brand.

In other situations, the costs of research may exceed its value to decision makers. Full-blown research efforts—especially testing of new products—can be very expensive, costing hundreds of thousands or even millions of dollars. Yet, if the time is available, the market is large enough, and the costs seem justified, a marketer will commit resources to a substantial research effort. The crucial next step will be determining what type of research would be best.

EXPLORATORY AND CONFIRMATORY RESEARCH   Symptoms of a problem—for example, decreases in sales—do not tell marketers what is really wrong. The problem may be decreasing product quality, new competitors, or outdated pricing. Marketers turn to **exploratory research,** which consists of informal attempts to identify and define problems. In general, exploratory research uses qualitative rather than quantitative methods; it may take the form of informal surveys of customers or discussions with distributors. Such research does not attempt to provide solutions, which should be developed after more formal efforts. Instead, for example, an informal survey of potential users of word-processing programs will help programmers to identify the most-desired features of such programs. At the same time, this survey will allow marketers to avoid the expense of drafting sample programs at early stages of the research process.

Confirmatory research, in contrast, provides information, usually of a statistical nature, that helps managers reduce risk in decision making. For example, exploratory research might be conducted to identify possible desirable features in a new flashlight battery and to identify what concerns consumers might have about batteries. Such research might reveal the not-so-surprising fact that consumers are mostly interested in reliability and length of service. Turning to a confirmatory (quantitative) study, the battery makers might then do research to determine just how much money members of the target market would pay for a battery with a longer life of 3 to 4 months.

Qualitative and exploratory research are valuable and legitimate tools. Although they may not provide the wealth of statistically based probabilities that can result from quantitative research, qualitative and exploratory methods often help marketers devise a list of alternatives which can be evaluated in measurable ways. Moreover, these methods are likely to lead to the right kinds of confirmatory studies. In fact, full-scale marketing research will commonly include both exploratory and (subsequently) confirmatory studies.[9] The most frequently employed qualitative research techniques are interviews conducted with individuals and with focus groups.

INDIVIDUAL DEPTH INTERVIEWS **Qualitative research** may take the form of detailed interviews with a small number of consumers or organizational buyers. Such sessions are conducted by trained interviewers and are only partly structured; they include considerable probing into the subjects' behavioral and thinking patterns. A company marketing telecommunications equipment, for example, might conduct interviews with buyers for large organizations to pin down organizational needs for systems that can transmit both numerical data and voice communications at high speed. A series of interviews might be conducted in both domestic and international operations to seek information about differing needs for telecommunications services. One major advertising agency, Young & Rubicam, asks the researcher to spend hours with the consumer and examine very personal subjects. One researcher videotaped 200 hours of consumers' diaper-changing techniques![10]

The results from individual depth interviews are reported without statistics and include a large number of direct quotes from respondents' answers to questions. Typically, the interviewer will evaluate the interviews and make judgments about apparent agreement or disagreement over any particular issue. Again, such qualitative research is more useful for identifying and clarifying issues than for defining specific actions to be taken.

FOCUS GROUP INTERVIEWS A **focus group** is a small number of people of similar backgrounds and interests brought together in a comfortable environment to discuss a particular product, idea, or issue. The interviews are conducted by trained interviewers—usually working for independent research firms—who are skilled at probing people's thinking processes. Focus group interviews are frequently watched through a one-way mirror by client personnel. If you could watch through one of these mirrors, the focus group would appear to be a chatty gathering of

Marketing research is nearly always useful in making marketing decisions. But, not only does research cost money, it can delay decisions and allow competitors to move aggressively into a market. (Ken Karp.)

friends talking about soft drinks, video games, disposable diapers, or other goods or services produced by the client. The interviewer encourages all focus group members to participate and interact with one another, attempts to ensure that no one dominates, and tries to keep the conversation on track.

Occasionally, a new product idea will emerge from a focus group. The concepts for Pepsi Light, Charlie fragrance, and Virginia Slims cigarettes and the general plans for Arden's Lip-Fix emerged from such discussions. However, such instances are rare; more commonly, focus groups generate ideas for product repositioning or better promotion. In other words, the creative work remains the responsibility of advertising staff, not research personnel. The comments of focus groups members must be "read" in thoughtful ways that will lead to possible marketing actions.[11]

Qualitative research, as exemplified by individual interviews and focus group discussions, has not received as much attention from marketing scholars as has quantitative research. Yet qualitative research is an important aspect of the research conducted by consumer products marketers, by organizational marketers, and even by certain not-for-profit organizations such as universities.[12] Moreover, the use of qualitative research is growing more rapidly than that of investigations based on statistics.[13]

Quantitative research, by contrast, is based on a statistically valid sampling of a target market. Given a small margin of error, the results of quantitative research should predict how the entire target market will behave. For example, quantitative research can identify the number of working women, ages 24 to 44, who will be potential subscribers to a new magazine focusing on the dual problems of pursuing a career and being a homemaker. The publisher will not wish to launch a new magazine unless it can attract substantial readership; quantitative research should clarify whether this is likely to happen.

Scientific, confirmatory research is conducted by almost all large marketing organizations (or is performed for them by outside agencies). We will now explore the basic ways in which such research is carried out.

CONDUCTING MARKETING RESEARCH

The Lorillard division of Loews Corporation, marketer of Kent and Newport cigarettes, spends a large portion of its marketing research budget on testing the effectiveness of its advertising. The Kimberly-Clark Corporation concentrates on product testing. The expensive machinery used in the manufacture of its paper products is very costly to change, so management wants assurance that a new product will be successful. Japan's Toyota Corporation keeps an ongoing watch on what consumers want in automobiles and how they buy them. Political candidates spend millions of dollars surveying voters' attitudes to tailor their advertising and public statements to sway those voters to their side.

Whatever the goal of marketing research, the process consists of five stages: (1) defining the problem and stating objectives, (2) designing the research study and selecting information sources, (3) collecting the data, (4) analyzing the data, and (5) reporting the results and making decision recommendations (see Figure 6-6).

☐ Stage 1: Define the Problem and State Objectives

Problem definition follows the recognition of the need to make a decision. For example, "Why are sales down in the St. Louis district?" is too broad a question. An

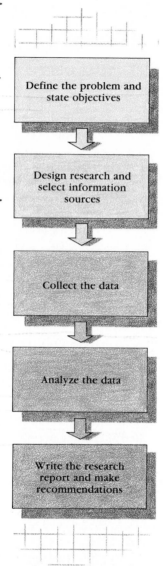

Figure 6-6 *Steps in the marketing research process.* Marketing research is a highly disciplined process. Good marketing research produces dependable information on which important decisions can be based. Poor marketing research can mislead decision makers and lead to damaging consequences.

apparently obvious problem, a drop in sales, may actually be a symptom of a more serious problem. The St. Louis sales decline may stem from an overall weakness in the distribution system. Or it may signal that competitors have reduced prices or increased their advertising. Exploratory research is often valuable in correctly identifying the underlying problem.

Clear communication between marketing managers and researchers is essential. Both should cooperate to ensure that researchers do not study the wrong problem. Thus, if what really caused the problem in the St. Louis district was that a major competitor had cut prices by 20 percent, substantial time and money spent researching consumers' reactions to various advertising campaigns would be wasteful.

☐ Stage 2: Design Research and Select Information Sources

After defining a problem, managers and researchers choose what kind of data to use for their research. If the problem concerns social or demographic trends, they will use information that has already been collected—secondary data; if testing a new product or advertising copy is involved, representatives from the target market will be chosen and new information—primary data—will be collected.

SECONDARY DATA   Marketers at Macy's or McDonald's responsible for finding the best locations for new outlets have much information about population movements already available from the *Statistical Abstract of the United States* published by the U.S. Bureau of the Census. Much of the data compiled by the Census Bureau is available in computer format for ready use in marketing information systems.[14] Such data, previously collected by others, often for another purpose, are called **secondary data.** Researchers will apply new analytical tools and perspectives to such data to serve their own purposes.[15]

Exhibit 6-2 lists selected sources of secondary data. Many are similar to those used for monitoring the environments (as discussed in Chapter 2) and are also

primary data – new – original
secondary " – old

Marketing research supply companies, such as Clark Jones Inc. Market Research of Columbus, Ohio, provide facilities such as those pictured here. In the focus group discussion, note the microphones being used to record the discussion. In the second picture, marketers observe the discussion through a one-way mirror, and a video camera records the session. (Copyright © 1987 High Tides Photography.)

EXHIBIT 6-2	Sources of Secondary Data

Government publications: Statistical publications of the U.S. government, primarily originating from the Bureau of the Census and the Department of Commerce, include such compilations as:

1. *Economic Indicators:* Current information on prices, wages, production, business activity, purchasing power, credit, money, and federal finance, published yearly

2. *Statistical Abstract of the United States:* Yearly summary of statistics on the social, political, and economic organization of the United States

3. *Statistical Yearbook:* International statistics on agriculture, population, manufacturing, mining, finance, trade, and education, published yearly by the United Nations

4. *Survey of Current Business:* Official monthly source of figures for gross national product, national income, and international balance of payments

Census data: In addition to the complete census conducted every 10 years, the Bureau of the Census publishes certain updates at regular intervals (usually every year). These reports include the *Census of Retail Trade, Census of Wholesale Trade, Census of Selected Services,* and the *Census of Manufacturers.*

Internal records: Historical data available from the organization's MKIS may provide records of sales, costs, and promotion expenditures that can be analyzed for perspective and projections. Such data should be easily accessible and may be combined in new ways for research analysis.

Trade associations: Trade groups often compile useful data on markets for an entire industry. For example, the Business and Institutional Furniture Manufacturers' Association (BIFMA) collects information from furniture makers who contribute data anonymously; BIFMA compiles the figures and distributes them to members, who can get industry total sales and their own market-share percentages.

Business and trade publications: Literally thousands of publications serve needs for general business and trade-specific information. A number of magazines issue annual reports on topics of use to researchers. For example, each year *Sales and Marketing Management* publishes a *Survey of Buying Power* and a *Survey of Industrial Buying Power.* The *Survey of Buying Power* provides useful data to marketers of consumer products: population of metropolitan areas, household buying income, and retail sales of various kinds of stores (drug, food, furniture, etc.) in those areas.

Note: Statistics Canada is the government agency in Canada that collects information similar to that compiled by U.S. Bureau of the Census.

useful for more specific marketing research projects. The secondary sources listed only represent the kinds of information available. Thousands of sources are available that may save research groups much time and money. At least one firm, FIND/SVP in New York City, is a business information clearinghouse that specializes in finding already gathered and published statistics and research reports for clients.

PRIMARY DATA   Firms marketing new products and political candidates seeking the latest pulse of the electorate must usually collect their own information. **Primary data are facts collected from original research designed to address a particular problem.** For example, if you respond to a questionnaire from a sporting goods firm about your sports activities and buying habits, your answers become part of the set of primary data for the firm's research project. Like other behavioral scientists,

An important source of secondary data for marketers of products sold to organizations is a group of companies which devote their efforts to supplying specialized information. This ad for one of those suppliers, McGraw-Hill, says that information is better than luck in securing a business future. (Reprinted with permission from McGraw-Hill Publications Company.)

marketing researchers employ three principal methods for collecting primary data: observation, experimentation, and surveys.

Observational Method

The **observational method** of collecting data relies on watching people's behavior. Trained observers may mingle with customers on a supermarket floor to identify and record certain buying patterns. With a view to store location, automatic counters may be set up by a firm to tally a street corner's automobile traffic volume. A specially designed camera tracks the movement of a consumer's eye to record how long they spend on an ad's headline, artwork, or copy.

The observational method is almost bias-free; it merely records what is happening. Since subjects are unaware of the observation, their behavior is assumed to be normal. This technique is rather limited in its applications: Observation merely records what happens; it does not explain *why*. Attitudes, motives, or opinions are not addressed. And some things—decision processes, for instance—cannot be observed.

Experimental Method

The study of the relationship between two or more variables under controlled conditions is the basis for the **experimental method.** A **variable** is a characteristic that can change or differ from one individual or group to another. Differences in social class, sex, race, and age are variables, as are differences in intelligence, sense of humor, nationality, and lifestyle.

Researchers analyze cause-and-effect relationships by showing the influence of one variable on another. For example, one variable—brand name, say—may have an important influence on a second—consumers' perceptions of a product's quality. The variable that causes an effect—in this example, brand name—is the **independent variable.** The variable it influences—perceptions of product quality—is the **dependent variable.**

In an experiment, the researcher manipulates changes in the independent variable and measures any changes that occur in the dependent variable. Marketing researchers may wish to study the impact of price differentials (the independent variable) on consumers' purchasing behavior (the dependent variable). Let us assume they are testing a new household product that would sell in supermarkets and convenience stores. Researchers will assemble three groups of subjects and allow them to inspect the product. Each group will be offered the product at a different price—$1.79, $2.49, and $3.25—and then will be asked whether they intend to purchase the product. If willingness to buy the product differs significantly among the three groups (if, for example, subjects offered the product for $1.79 are somewhat more likely to buy than those offered it at $2.49 and are much more likely to buy than subjects paying $3.25) the independent variable (price differentials) apparently does exert influence over the dependent variable (consumers' purchasing intentions).

Survey Method The means most frequently used to gather primary data is the survey method—the gathering of data from a limited number of people who represent a larger group. The larger group, whose characteristics are of primary interest to the researchers, is called the **population** or **universe**; the smaller group, from which data are actually drawn, is called the **sample.** A very large population might be all females aged 18 to 35 who live in urban areas of more than 500,000 residents. A more specific population might be Hispanic females aged 18 to 24 who hold full-time jobs and reside in Maryland.

A population may also include organizations or institutions: elementary schools in Missouri; businesses with fewer than 100 employees in Washington, Oregon, and Idaho; restaurants in France; or county governments in Alabama. The population is usually the target market for the product in question.

The **sample** is a subset of the population chosen to represent the population. Since it is impossible to ask 235 million people about their preferences in soda or disposable diapers, researchers can draw conclusions about the population through statistical analysis, using the less expensive and more efficient survey of the selected sample. For example, the public opinion polls conducted by the Gallup and Harris organizations generally use samples of about 1500 people to reflect national attitudes and opinions. A sample of this size produces fairly accurate estimates even for a country with a population as large as that of the United States.

Typically, researchers employ one or two basic sampling procedures: **probability sampling,** in which all population members have a known chance of being included in the sample, and **nonprobability sampling,** in which researchers decide which members of a total population are representative. Probability samples can be illustrated by the hypothetical case of choosing county governments for a survey. In a true **simple random sample,** every county government in the country would be assigned a sequential number. Those numbers would be tossed in a barrel, and each number would have an equal and known chance of being selected in a drawing. In a **systematic random sample,** researchers might choose every tenth or fiftieth county after starting with a randomly selected number (say, 4 or 7).

A **stratified random sample** might entail breaking the total population into strata by county size (over 1 million people, 500,000 to 999,999, 200,000 to 499,000, under 200,000). From within each group, counties would be chosen randomly, although it is unlikely that a different number would be chosen from each group to reflect the relative abundance of the groups. Few counties have populations over 1 million; more counties are in the other population ranges. Every county

The observation method of data collection attempts to reduce or eliminate bias by not letting the subject know that he or she is being observed. Here, a researcher observes consumers making choices in a supermarket. (Ken Karp.)

would therefore not have an equal chance of being selected, but the odds for being selected within each population grouping would be known (and the same for each county in the group).

In an **area (cluster) sample,** researchers might choose to select 1 percent of the county governments in the United States. In stage one, the researcher may take a sample of 20 states, where each state has an equal chance of being selected. Within each state (a cluster of counties), the counties are again chosen so that each has an equal chance of being selected. If the study is made of consumers, the process may be to first select blocks from a city map, then select houses on a block, then interview someone at each chosen house.

In nonprobability sampling, the chances of each unit in the population being selected are not known or equal. Sampling error cannot be measured statistically. In the strict statistical sense, nonprobability samples cannot be projected to reflect the total population. However, in reality, researchers do make generalizations from nonprobability samples because they have chosen subjects that they believe represent the target population. In addition, nonprobability samples are usually less expensive to carry out than probability samples and are easier to administer. Researchers may choose one of three nonprobability sampling techniques: judgment, convenience, and quota sampling.

If researchers testing a concept for a new movie (Would you definitely go to see a new domestic comedy starring Dustin Hoffman and Meryl Streep?) decided to survey audiences at movie theaters located within ½ mile of a large university, they would be carrying out a **judgment sample.** They would be assuming that college students represent well enough the target population of young adults aged 18 to 24. Such a method has inherent drawbacks: college students may not be representative of all 18- to 24-year-olds, and patrons of the theater are not necessarily college students.

A **convenience sample** could be obtained by simply sending interviewers to the nearest movie theater and interviewing the first 100 people leaving a showing.

This is an easy way to reach respondents, but little assurance exists that the movie-goers can represent any group but the one attending that particular show at that hour on that day.

A **quota sample,** based on chosen control characteristics, might be carried out by asking each member of the audience leaving the movie theater if he or she is between 18 and 24 years old and enrolled full-time in a college or university. Only those meeting control criteria would be queried.

Marketers will benefit from survey data only if samples are carefully chosen and represent the target market groups. Box 6-1 presents an example of biased sampling used in testing new television programs.

COLLECTING SURVEY DATA   Three basic types of surveys are used to collect primary data: personal interviews, telephone interviews, and mail surveys. Each method has benefits and drawbacks.

Personal interviews elicit the most information, since trained interviewers are able to adjust question guidelines as appropriate and ask for lengthy and complex answers. Typically, individual respondents are visited in their homes or stopped in a shopping mall—in a face-to-face situation. Personal interviewing is the most expensive and time-consuming of the survey methods. Follow-up interviews with missed respondents can be difficult to pursue, reducing accuracy and adding to costs.

Telephone interviews are the most efficient means of surveying relatively large numbers of respondents in a brief time. Calling chosen respondents is fairly inex-

BOX 6-1   A Classic Example of Bad Research

Since 1960, volunteers have been pulled off the streets of New York and Los Angeles by CBS researchers to test the television network's new prime-time shows. Viewers are brought to a CBS screening room and are shown a 30-minute or 1-hour episode of a projected CBS series. While watching, viewers are asked to press green or red buttons whenever they particularly like or dislike something happening on the screen. At the end of the show, they are asked to complete a lengthy questionnaire, filled with questions such as "Would you watch this series if it were on opposite *The Bill Cosby Show*?"

One wonders why CBS bothers. According to Bud Grant, president of CBS Entertainment: "The claim is that the testing process will show what shows will succeed and what shows will fail. The fact is that 70 percent of all network shows fail." Ironically, *All in the Family,* one of the most innovative and longest-running hits aired on CBS, tested *worse* than any show in the history of CBS research.

Why doesn't this type of survey data produce more accurate results? One reason is that U.S. viewers almost always initially reject innovative programming.

Consequently, any one-time test of a show which seems different—as *All in the Family* certainly must have when first tested by CBS—is likely to evoke a negative vote. Interestingly, when allowed 13 or 26 weeks to become accustomed to a new series, viewers may accept (or even come to love) a show that at first seemed too "different."

In evaluating CBS's audience testing, marketing researchers emphasize that there are serious flaws in the way that samples are constructed. The audiences used for testing new shows are not random samples but are self-selected volunteers who agree to take time from their shopping or sightseeing. Even though tourists visiting New York and Los Angeles are included, the samples remain heavily weighted toward residents of the east and west coasts and neglect other parts of the United States (where, it is rumored, people also watch television). CBS does attempt to reduce each sample of 1000 volunteers to about 250 demographically desirable "usables," but the sample remains staunchly middle class.

Source: Sandra Salmans, "At CBS-TV, It's Testing 1, 2, 3...," *The New York Times,* May 2, 1986, pp. D1, D3.

pensive, and calling back missed respondents is easy. Although it is the fastest-growing survey method, the telephone interview still requires training of personnel. Many telephone survey operations now provide computer terminals for interviewers who enter responses directly into the data banks where tabulations are updated as the interviews are completed. Unfortunately, the telephone method has allowed unethical marketers to use a survey as a pretext to launch into a sales call for a product. Enough Americans have been "burned" by such tactics that some are now reluctant to cooperate with callers involved in legitimate marketing research projects.

Mail surveys are the least expensive way to sample large populations. However, mail methods bring slow responses, have the largest number of nonrespondents, and have the highest chance of reaching the wrong person. For example, a survey directed to female heads of household may be answered by a child or male head of household. Also, the number of people on the sample list who simply do not bother to fill out a mail questionnaire is typically so high that doubts may arise as to the similarity of respondents and nonrespondents.

THE QUESTIONNAIRE Whatever the data collection method chosen, a data collection instrument is required. That instrument is almost always the familiar **questionnaire.** Questionnaires are used for all survey methods. In personal and telephone surveys, the interviewer completes the formatted questions; in a mail survey, the respondent fills in the answers.

Effective questionnaire design combines elements of art and science. Marketing managers generally (and wisely) rely on experienced researchers for questionnaire construction. Such experience is valuable, since questionnaires must be structured and worded concisely, with little room for misinterpretation.

In designing questionnaires, marketing researchers may use three types of questions: structured questions, semistructured questions, and unstructured questions. Examples of each technique are presented in Exhibit 6-3. **Structured questions** demand brief and specific answers; respondents are usually limited to a specified number of replies. Dichotomous questions (which allow only two possible answers, such as "yes" or "no"), multiple-choice questions, and simple checklists are common types of structured questions. **Semistructured questions** include sentence-completion items and word association tests.

Unstructured questions allow respondents freedom and creativity in framing answers. Essay questions, picture completion, story completion, and thematic apperception tests (TAT) are among the techniques used in unstructured questions. Such questions may reveal important and sometimes surprising insights, because respondents are not restricted to answers already provided for them. However, although unstructured questioning may be effective in probing respondents' attitudes, feelings, and preferences—all significant aspects of buying behavior—skilled interpreters are needed to analyze results and to identify patterns and trends evident in the responses. Unstructured techniques are most useful in exploratory research aimed at identifying problems and possibilities. By contrast, structured questions can be easily tabulated and yield less ambiguous results than unstructured questions.

Whether contact with respondents is personal, by mail, or by telephone, and whether structured or unstructured techniques are chosen, careful wording of questionnaires is terribly important. The most carefully chosen sample possible will not give useful or correct answers if flaws exist in the questions asked. The pitfalls of questionnaire wording are innumerable, but four warnings are in order for beginning researchers:

EXHIBIT 6-3	Types of Survey Questions

Type	Description	Example
Structured Questioning Techniques		
Dichotomous	Respondent must choose one or two answers.	"Was the decision to attend this college solely yours?" _____ Yes _____ No
Checklist	Respondent may choose as many answers as apply.	"What factors influenced your choice of this college?" (Please check each applicable answer.) _____ Parental influence _____ Academic reputation _____ Friends' influence _____ Sports programs _____ High school teachers _____ Variety of course _____ Proximity to home offerings _____ Tuition costs _____ Other (please elaborate) _____ Availability of financial _____ assistance
Multiple choice	Respondent may choose from three or more answers.	"How many 3-hour courses are you taking for full credit this semester?" ____ 1 ____ 2 ____ 3 ____ 4 ____ 5 ____ 6 ____ More
Semantic differential	Respondent chooses a point on a scale between bipolar (opposite) responses.	"General faculty attitude toward students is—:" Friendly ____:____:____:____:____ Unfriendly Helpful ____:____:____:____:____ Not helpful Committed ____:____:____:____:____ Uninterested to teaching in teaching
Likert scale	Respondents indicate the degree of their agreement or disagreement.	"Students receive more personal attention from faculty at smaller (under 2000 students) colleges than at larger ones (over 2000 students)." _____ Strongly disagree _____ Agree _____ Disagree _____ Strongly agree _____ No opinion
Ranking scale	Respondents rate some characteristic from positive to negative.	"The quality of the marketing faculty is:" Excellent Very Good Good Fair Poor _____ _____ _____ _____ _____
Semistructured Questioning Techniques		
Sentence completion	Respondents complete incomplete sentences.	"When I choose an elective course, the most important factor in my decision is _____ _____."
Word association	Respondents mention the first word that comes to mind when presented with a trigger word or phrase.	"Give the first word that comes to mind when you hear the following:" Introduction to marketing _____ Introduction to psychology _____ Introduction to accounting _____

1. *Don't ask questions the respondent can't answer.* "How many hamburgers have you eaten in the last 6 months?" "What brand of underwear does your mother prefer?"
2. *Don't ask ambiguous questions.* "Are you happy?" "Do you believe that Brand X is expensive?" (as compared to what?)
3. *Don't load the question.* "Should loyal Americans support the government's uncalled-for actions in the Middle East?" "Would you prefer to buy a cheap, foreign-made car as opposed to a high-quality U.S. automobile?"
4. *Don't violate the respondent's right to privacy.* "How much money do you have in a savings account?" "Do you believe that premarital sex is immoral?"

EXHIBIT 6-3   **Types of Survey Questions (Continued)**

Type	Description	Example

Unstructured Questioning Techniques

Type	Description	Example
Essay	Respondent is given great latitude and space to reveal personal feelings.	"Why did you choose to attend this college?"
Picture completion	Respondents to identify with a pictured character and to fill in missing dialogue.	
Story completion	Respondents are asked to complete a story with only a sketchy beginning.	After I had decided to transfer to this college from Northern State University, I was both elated and sad. (Now complete the story.) 
Thematic Apperception Test (TAT)	Respondents are asked to make up a story about what they think is happening in a picture.	

Proper structuring and ordering of questions is also vital to obtaining meaningful data. If possible, the opening question should invite respondent interest. All questions should fall in a logical and cumulative order. Difficult or personal questions should come near the end of the questionnaire, when there is a psychological impetus to finish. Questions concerning demographic information (age, income level, level of education, and the like) should also come at the end, since they are rote and hold little interest for the respondent. These simple guidelines are in no way intended to guide a novice through the construction of a complex questionnaire. Training and a talent for writing are needed to design and construct research instruments.

Pretesting questionnaires is imperative. A pretest of the questions with a small sample may reveal misleading or loaded questions of which the researchers were unaware. Flawed questions can render test results that are harmfully misleading. Researchers in foreign countries must have questionnaires drafted and tested by native speakers of the language who are aware of its idioms and nuances. Similarly, foreign marketers in the United States should pretest research instruments for clarity and faithfulness to the idiosyncracies of colloquial U.S. English. The pretest phase of a survey is often neglected, but most professional researchers regard it as a necessary step in research design.

Stage 3: Data Collection

Data collection is usually the most expensive phase of marketing research. For personal and telephone surveys, interviewers must be recruited, trained, and managed. Organizations may hire outside interviewing services that provide skilled interviewers who need only orientation for the project at hand. Personnel costs make up the largest part of the budget for personal interview projects.

Mail surveys involve countless details to be administered. Timing of mailings and cutoff dates for responses must be established. Return envelopes must be included with the printed questionnaire. Often incentives (or gifts) must be offered to respondents. Finally, for all types of surveys, responses must be tabulated. Today, this almost always involves coding for computer entry.

Two potential threats to the accuracy and usefulness of surveys must be monitored consistently throughout data collection. First, simple errors in marking answers and in computer input can be significant enough to skew results. Although it seems a minor point, inaccuracy can build into a serious problem. Second, personal and telephone surveys need safeguards to minimize interviewer bias.

In recent years, the most prevalent type of personal interviewing has been the "shopping mall intercept" wherein interviewers attempt to question every *n*th shopper, all adult males, or some other specified sample.[16] Bias can easily slip into such a survey through interviewers' failure to choose respondents in the specified group. Interviewer bias can also influence personal and telephone surveys through nothing more than a particular tone of voice employed by an interviewer. To control for interviewer bias, marketing researchers may evaluate the survey results obtained by each interviewer to see, for example, if one person has obtained much more positive (or negative) reactions to a new product than all other interviewers. The interviewer obtaining strikingly different results may be conveying a bias to respondents and influencing their responses.

This scene is becoming more common as data collection methods stress more "shopping-mall intercept" approaches to personal interviews. (Copyright © Bob Daemmrich.)

Stage 4: Data Analysis

After collection, coding, and processing, data must be analyzed. Some research results involve nothing more complicated than studying simple **cross-tabulations**—comparing the responses to one question to the responses to another. For example, researchers might compare brand preferences for men and women. A cross tabulation looks like the following:

High, medium, and low preferences for brand A (percent)				
	High	Medium	Low	Total
Men	40	40	20	100
Women	10	20	70	100

The intent is to see whether men or women like brand A more. As relationships between more variables are compared, the complexity of computation and analysis rises. Most marketing research can be tabulated and analyzed through the use of standard computer software programs such as *SPSS (Statistical Package for the Social Sciences)*. In addition, researchers can make use of many specialized statistical procedures.[17]

If the research project has been properly planned, a decision as to the kinds of analysis and data manipulation needed will be made well before the data are collected. The data should be collected in a form that is consistent with the planned analysis. If one of the goals of the study is to determine the automobile-buying plans of Hispanic females between ages 24 and 36, the data should have been collected in convenient form and provision made for tabulations and cross-tabulations concerning the target group.

Stage 5: The Research Report and Recommendations

After all data are analyzed and conclusions are drawn, researchers and marketing managers must renew their cooperation. Findings must be written up and recommendations for action must be offered. Research results should support marketing decision making. Four general rules should guide researchers and managers as they are formalizing results and recommendations:

1. The report should be written in the language of marketing managers, not in the technical language researchers employ to describe statistical methods. The authors should address the issues managers must face, answering such questions as, "Is the information accurate?", "Can I believe it?", and "Are important findings highlighted?"
2. The report should be completely objective and should present the bad news along with the good. If test market results project that a new product will *not* be successful, the report must present this information candidly.
3. Any recommendations contained in the report should be capable of implementation; that is, they should be "actionable." This is another important area in which researchers and managers must confer and coordinate their efforts. All too often, marketing research reports contain recommendations that are impossible for managers to implement. For example, a marketing research study conducted for a local film-processing lab documents a nationwide shift away from

the drugstore "drop off and pick up" service now offered and toward the 1-hour service provided by the new "minilabs." It would be impractical for researchers to recommend that managers conduct a promotional campaign to reverse this trend; any experienced marketing manager would quickly dismiss such a suggestion. By contrast, a recommendation that the company install one or more of its own minilabs in a local shopping center would be more actionable.

4. The valuable and often expensive information obtained in research projects should be integrated into the organization's MKIS. This data may prove valuable for use in solving future marketing problems.

■ MANAGING MARKETING RESEARCH ■

Marketing research departments in the corporate setting almost always work under the supervision of the organization's marketing department. Typically, the marketing research director reports to the chief marketing officer. Like any other marketing subgroup—promotion, sales, forecasting, brand management, and so on—research is accountable overall to marketing management. Research efforts should be integral parts of the organization's marketing program.

☐ *The Roles of Managers and Researchers*

In the best-managed organizations, marketing managers and researchers act as both catalysts and balances for each other. At times, the differing demands on managers and researchers can lead to conflict that needs to be managed in creative ways. Line managers—charged with a product's sales and profitability—are usually under pressure to produce measurable results, to do so quickly, and to hold down costs. By contrast, researchers are more concerned with the precision and accuracy of their work; they can rarely provide managers with results that remove all uncertainty from decisions.

Managers want research to produce reports that say: "Our new product should gain a 20 percent market share within 6 months." Researchers, well aware of the limitations of their projections, are more likely to say: "Within an error range of 5 percent, there is a probability of gaining market share of 20 percent within 6 months." Obviously, marketing managers and researchers have somewhat different perspectives. Yet it is worth emphasizing that managers' unique perspective may help to get marketing research *used,* which is why it is conducted in the first place.[18]

Studies of the perspectives of managers and researchers reveal that the most serious barriers to effective cooperation between the two groups are failure to involve the research group in strategic planning, inadequate funding of research, a lack of management consistency in expectations of research efforts, and lack of feedback from both groups after completion of a study.[19] Top-level marketing managers should make efforts to ease those problems and to encourage cooperation between these two vital marketing functions.

☐ *Cost and Value: Budgeting for Research*

Research departments, like any other marketing group, must formulate and seek approval of operating budgets. If any generalization can be made about research budgets, it is that most organizations do not spend enough money on research. Although research can be an expensive proposition, inadequate funding may result in inferior research—no real help in reducing the risk of decision making.[20]

In budgeting for research, marketing managers should ask: "What will be the costs of mistakes which result if no (or inadequate) research supports a decision?" Many costly mistakes can be avoided through information generated by research studies. Consequently, top-level managers should avoid viewing the research budget as an easy place to cut costs.

☐ *Using Independent Research Firms*

Some marketing organizations have large, professional research staffs; others have no research personnel. Regardless of how many people are employed in a research department, certain parts of projects or whole projects should and will be carried out by independent research organizations—firms that supply marketing research.

Supplying marketing research has become an industry in itself. The largest company, A.C. Nielsen, measures television-viewing habits and audits the movement of consumer package goods; IMS International specializes in pharmaceutical and health care products. Selling Areas-Marketing Inc. (SAMI) audits warehouse movement of thousands of items sold through food stores.

Marketing research firms offer a wide range of services. Some are specialized and do only part of the research job. Some do only telephone interviewing; others provide sophisticated mathematical models. In contrast, Burke Marketing Services and Market Facts are full-service research suppliers who have the resources to carry out a full-scale research effort from inception to report and recommendations.

Firms are most likely to employ outside research suppliers when adding sufficient staff for research would be more expensive or when the research project calls for expertise beyond that of in-house personnel. For example, only large companies have the resources to carry out a national survey; smaller companies requiring a national survey would probably call on an outside research firm.

Most contracts for research services are based on a bidding process. Costs are likely to reflect the number of experienced researchers the vendor has on its staff and the extent of the tasks required. In addition, provisions for ensuring the accuracy and quality of the work will add to costs. When contracting for outside services, managers should evaluate bids carefully. The lowest bidder may not provide the best solutions to the research problem.[21]

Research suppliers know that their reputations for ethical practices and confidentiality are priceless: Clients must be able to trust their research suppliers, since confidential information is often necessary to the project. Good personal relations and communications are also vital to this working relationship. Management involvement with the research firm will be heaviest at the beginning and end of the research process, but some level of contact will be maintained throughout.

Both supplier and client should plan for postproject evaluations. Suppliers will be measured on adherence to schedule and budget on research design, on the caliber of personnel assigned, and on the quality of the research report and recommendations. Future use of the research supplier will depend heavily on a favorable evaluation.

■ *PROSPECTS FOR RESEARCH* ■

Several thousand families in Midland, Texas; Pittsfield, Massachusetts; Marion, Indiana; Eau Claire, Wisconsin; and other cities are taking part in what appears to be a revolution in market research. These families shop for their food in supermarkets

The future of marketing research is largely tied to future developments of computer hardware and software. One company on the leading edge of such advanced applications of marketing research technology is Adtel. (Courtesy of Sami/Burke, Inc.)

equipped with laser scanners that record all their purchases. Test families present a special identification card that triggers entry of their purchases into computers in Chicago maintained by Information Resources Incorporated or by AdTel (a division of Burke Marketing Services). These two competing research suppliers have lined up such marketing giants as Procter & Gamble, Quaker Oats, and R. J. Reynolds as customers.

All homes in the test groups are wired for cable television, allowing researchers to go an important step beyond recording purchases. Split-cable television facilities allow researchers to beam different commercials into selected homes. For example, commercials for Duncan Hines cake mixes can be shown to users of Betty Crocker cake mixes; purchases can then be tracked to see if any consumers switch brands. In addition, split-cable television allows researchers to test the effects of different commercials for the same product. One advertisement may be shown to families in group A, another to group B, while families in group C will not see either commercial. Information Resources and AdTel also have provisions for ensuring that newspapers with food coupons are delivered to test families. In this way, the effect of sales promotion efforts can be tracked.

Although this kind of test-marketing capability is now limited primarily to grocery items, both companies plan to track drugstore purchases of health and beauty aid products as well as pharmaceuticals. The implications of such research are far reaching, and although questions about the invasion of test families' privacy have been raised, this kind of market testing will probably increase dramatically in the 1990s.[22]

Although new technologies are facilitating many innovative research approaches, new threats to marketing research are surfacing. Some researchers fear that too much market research will turn respondents used time after time into "professional respondents." Such overused subjects might lose their naturalness and bias research findings. The more likely danger, however, is that the public will refuse to cooperate with researchers because they are tired of answering questions that are poorly worded, overly personal, or extremely time-consuming or because they have been conned by those who present themselves as market researchers but who actually are selling products.[23]

At least three general predictions can be made about the future of marketing research in the United States and Canada.[24] First, new data collection hardware such as laser scanners and split- and two-way cable television will have far-reaching impact, allowing researchers to refine information collection. Other electronic media—home computers, direct-broadcast satellites, videocassette and videodisk recorders—will also affect information gathering and analysis in big ways. Second, computing power will become very cheap, and researchers will have greatly increased computational and analytical capabilities at their fingertips. Third, both marketing researchers and managers will have more training and knowledge about research tools and methods. In short, marketing research will move at an increasing rate along the continuum from art to science.

■ SUMMARY ■

1. Managers use both informal and formal sources of information when making decisions.
2. Formal information flows from the organization's marketing information system (MKIS).
3. Hardware and software components of an MKIS include a data bank for storage, a statistical bank with procedures for analyzing relationships among data, a model bank of mathematical models for testing hypotheses, and workstations (or display units) for managerial interaction with the MKIS.
4. Marketing information flows include scheduled information delivery from internal and external sources, marketing intelligence networks, and marketing research findings.
5. Marketing research can be broadly categorized into five areas: advertising, business economics and corporate studies, corporate responsibility, product, and sales and markets.
6. The first decision to be made about marketing research is whether to do it at all.
7. Research may be qualitative or quantitative. In general, qualitative research is exploratory; quantitative research is confirmatory.
8. Typical marketing research follows five steps: (1) defining the problem and stating objectives; (2) designing the research study and choosing information sources; (3) collecting the data; (4) analyzing the data; and (5) writing the report and making recommendations.
9. Researchers may choose to use secondary (collected by other researchers) data or primary (original) data.
10. In an experiment, the researcher manipulates changes in the independent variable and measures any changes that occur in the dependent variable.
11. A sample is a subset of a population that is chosen to represent the population.
12. Three basic types of surveys are used to collect primary data: personal interviews, telephone interviews, and mail surveys.
13. Effective questionnaire design combines elements of art and science. Marketing researchers may use structured, semistructured, or unstructured questions.

14. Data collection is usually the most expensive phase of marketing research.
15. The marketing research report should be completely objective, presenting the bad news along with the good, and should contain recommendations that can be implemented.
16. At times, marketing managers and researchers may pursue conflicting goals. Top-level managers should encourage cooperation between these two vital marketing functions.

Key Terms

area (cluster) sample	judgment sample	qualitative research
artificial intelligence	management information system	quantitative research
confirmatory research	marketing information system	questionnaire
convenience sample	marketing intelligence network	quota sample
cross-tabulation	marketing research	sample
decision support system	MKIS data bank	secondary data
dependent variable	MKIS information flows	semistructured questions
experimental method	MKIS model bank	simple random sample
expert system	MKIS statistical bank	stratified random sample
exploratory research	nonprobability sampling	structured questions
focus group	observational method	survey method
formal information	population (universe)	syndicated research services
independent variable	primary data	systematic random sample
informal information	probability sampling	unstructured questions
information	purchase diaries	variable

Chapter Review

1. Can you turn these data into information: 741776? What differentiates data from information?

2. How do informal and formal sources of information differ? What characteristics give marketing information its value?

3. What are the four hardware and software components of an MKIS? Describe the four basic subsystems of an MKIS.

4. Outline a marketing situation in which decisions must be made without the support of research results. What characteristics differentiate qualitative and quantitative research?

5. List the five stages in the marketing research process.

6. Give examples of secondary and primary data. What are the three basic methods for collecting primary data?

7. Summarize the types of sampling that may be used in conducting surveys. Give an example of a quota sample.

8. What are the three basic types of surveys?

9. Give examples of situations in which questionnaire designers might choose structured questions, semistructured questions, and unstructured questions.

10. Why are independent research firms often employed even by marketing organizations with their own research departments?

11. Identify three likely prospects for the future of marketing research.

References

1. C. Richard Roberts and Louis E. Boone, "MIS Development in American Industry: The Apex," *Journal of Business Strategy,* Spring 1983, pp. 106–112.
2. Robert J. Williams, "Marketing Intelligence Systems: A DEW Line for Marketing Men," *Business Management,* Jan. 1966, p. 32.
3. Adapted from Samuel V. Smith et al., "Marketing Information Systems: An Introductory Overview," in S. V. Smith, R. H. Brien, and J. E. Stafford, eds., *Readings in Marketing Information Systems* (Boston: Houghton Mifflin, 1968), p. 7.

4. See John D. C. Little and Michael N. Cassettari, *Decision Support Systems for Marketing Managers* (New York: American Management Association, 1984).

5. Marc Miller, "Putting More Power into Managerial Decisions," *Management Review,* Sept. 1984, pp. 12–16.

6. Fred L. Luconi, Thomas W. Malone, and Michael S. Scott Morton, "Expert Systems: The Next Challenge for Managers," *Sloan Management Review,* Summer 1986, pp. 3–14. See also "The Leading Edge of White-Collar Robotics," *Business Week,* Feb. 10, 1986, pp. 94–96 and "Artificial Intelligence Finally Hits the Desktop," *Business Week,* June 9, 1986, pp. 68, 70.

7. Paul E. Green and Donald S. Tull, *Research for Marketing Decisions,* 4th ed. (Englewood Cliffs, N.J.: Prentice-Hall, 1978).

8. "Garbage Dump Marks Long Ago Beginnings of Market Research," *Advertising Age,* Apr. 20, 1980, p. 68.

9. Gerald Zaltman and Rohit Deshpande, *The Use of Market Research: An Exploratory Study of Manager and Researcher Perspectives* (Cambridge, Mass.: Marketing Science Institute, 1980), p. 3.

10. Ronald Alsop, "People Watchers' Seek Clues to Consumers' True Behavior," *The Wall Street Journal,* Sept. 4, 1986, p. 25.

11. Frederick D. Buggie, "Focus Groups: Searching for the 'Right' Product," *Management Review,* Apr. 1983, p. 40.

12. Joe L. Welch, "Researching Marketing Problems and Opportunities with Focus Groups," *Industrial Marketing Management,* Nov. 1985, pp. 245–253; see also Amanda Bennett, "Once a Tool of Retail Marketers, Focus Groups Gain Wider Usage," *The Wall Street Journal,* June 3, 1986, p. 27.

13. Alfred E. Goldman and Susan S. McDonald, *The Group Depth Interview* (Englewood Cliffs, N.J.: Prentice-Hall, 1986).

14. Ronald L. Vaughn, "Demographic Data Banks: A New Management Resource," *Business Horizons,* Nov.–Dec. 1984, pp. 38–42.

15. For a comprehensive listing of secondary sources useful to market researchers, see C. R. Goeldner and Laura M. Dirks, "Business Facts: Where to Find Them," *MSU Business Topics,* Summer 1983, pp. 23–26; and Thomas C. Kinnear and James R. Taylor, *Marketing Research: An Applied Approach,* 2d ed. (New York: McGraw-Hill, 1983), pp. 169–184.

16. Alan J. Bush and Joseph F. Hair, Jr., "An Assessment of the Mall Intercept as a Data Collection Method," *Journal of Marketing Research,* vol. XXII, May 1985, pp. 158–167.

17. James J. Minno, "Software Packages for Market Researchers: A Review," *Marketing News,* Sept. 13, 1985, pp. 62 ff.

18. Rohit Deshpande and Gerald Zaltman, "A Comparison of Factors Affecting Researcher and Manager Perceptions of Market Research Use," *Journal of Marketing Research,* vol. XXI, Feb. 1984, pp. 32–38.

19. David J. Luck and James R. Krim, *Conditions Conducive to the Effective Use of Marketing Research in the Corporation* (Cambridge, Mass.: Marketing Science Institute, 1981), p. 26. See also Zaltman and Deshpande, op. cit., p. 45.

20. A. Parasuraman, "Research's Place in the Marketing Budget," *Business Horizons,* Mar.–Apr. 1983, pp. 25–29.

21. For further discussion of buying research services, see David W. Flegal, "How to Buy Marketing Research," *Management Review,* Feb. 1983, pp. 63–66; and David W. Flegal, "Controlling Marketing Research Costs," *Management Review,* March 1983, pp. 52–55.

22. Leonard M. Lodish and David J. Reibstein, "New Gold Mines and Minefields in Market Research," *Harvard Business Review,* Jan.–Feb. 1986, pp. 168 ff. See also Felix Kessler, "High-Tech Shocks in Ad Research," *Fortune,* July 7, 1986, pp. 58–62; and "Big Brother Gets a Job in Market Research," *Business Week,* Apr. 8, 1985, pp. 96–97.

23. Stephan W. McDaniel, Perry Verille, and Charles S. Madden, "The Threats to Marketing Research: An Empirical Reappraisal," *Journal of Marketing Research,* vol. XXII, Feb. 1985, pp. 74–80.

24. B. G. Yovovich, "Shifting Technology, Shifting Power," *Advertising Age,* Oct. 31, 1983, p. M-9.

HEWLETT-PACKARD

Hewlett-Packard (H-P) has been one of the leading Silicon Valley manufacturers for more than 45 years. Well known for its engineering wizardry, the company's early success in making electronic testing devices helped it to become a high-tech, high-growth outfit. Then, in 1968, H-P developed its first minicomputer. The HP 3000 model, introduced in 1972, remains one of the industry's all-time best sellers. In the mid-1980s, computers are H-P's biggest business, accounting for more than half of the company's sales and pretax profits.

As a technologically driven company, H-P's corporate structure long emphasized highly autonomous divisions. For example, one sales force sold test instruments, while a second sold computers. In the process, H-P lost valuable opportunities to coordinate sales of its analytical instruments, test instruments, and computers. However, in July 1984, H-P revised its organizational structure in order to centralize authority somewhat and to move toward a marketing orientation. Among the changes instituted were the appointment of a new chief operating officer, the creation of a new corporate marketing division, and the merger of the computer and instrument sales forces.

Hewlett-Packard's personal computer group, established in 1982, has been a central force in reshaping the way the company conceives, develops, and sells products. "Creating the personal computer group was an extremely good way of getting a focus on marketing," notes the firm's chief executive, John Young. "It was a way of communicating to everyone that this [marketing] was okay: that it's okay to eat quiche."

The personal computer group had to face an unpleasant truth: Hewlett-Packard's efforts to sell this popular product line had been a flop. In fact, H-P held only a 2 percent share of the retail personal computer business in mid-1984. One apparent cause of these failures was H-P's insistence on making engineering-based decisions regarding its personal computers and peripherals. For example, the HP 150 personal computer uses a $3\frac{1}{2}$-inch floppy disk rather than the more popular $5\frac{1}{4}$-inch disk. When it was introduced, only 25 software programs were available on $3\frac{1}{2}$-inch disks that could run on the 150, compared with more than 5000 for the IBM PC. Moreover, the 150 was not IBM-compatible. Despite offering more speed and memory than the IBM PC, the 150 did rather poorly in retail outlets.

With such fiascos in mind, H-P's personal computer group turned to marketing techniques commonly used in the packaged-goods industry, such as focus groups, test marketing, and quantitative market research. H-P's advertising budget for its personal computers and peripherals boosted from about $5 million in 1983 to $30 million in 1984.

New-product development has been another facet of the personal computer group's efforts to reverse H-P's previous disappointments in this market. In 1984, three new products were offered: a lap-size computer named the Portable and two printers, the ThinkJet and the LaserJet. The very names of these products represent an important shift toward a marketing orientation; Hewlett-Packard had traditionally used numbers (such as HP 150) for computers and peripherals. The goal of the personal computer's marketing staff is to create a "brand family" that will be recognizable both by retailers and consumers.

There has been a similar shift in H-P's pricing philosophy. In the past, H-P's orientation was more technological: it simply designed the best possible product and put off pricing decisions until later. H-P's personal computer group specifically designed the Thinkjet—a quiet, ink-jet printer which is IBM-compatible—for low-cost mass production. They hoped that aggressive pricing (list price of $495) would allow a strong challenge to the top-selling competitors in the low-end (under $500) printer market. This strategy indeed achieved initial success. The Thinkjet quickly achieved a 10 percent share of this market.

At the same time, H-P introduced its Laserjet printer, which offers extremely high quality printing at high speeds with almost no noise. The Laserjet was priced at $3495—about half the cost of comparable laser printers.

Dealers are enthusiastic about H-P's new products, among them the 9-pound Portable, H-P's Model 110. This lap-size computer sells for $2995. It offers extensive built-in hardware and software, a modem, a flat screen, word processing, and the Lotus 1-2-3 spreadsheet package. Unlike the 150, the Portable *is* IBM-compatible; Hewlett-Packard's print ads show a Portable next to an IBM PC with the caption, "They talk to each other."

Retailers are equally pleased with H-P's new approach to its channel members. "H-P is more realistic about what kinds of terms and margins it's willing to discuss," says a vice president of merchandising at a Texas-based chain of computer stores. Hewlett-Packard rewrote its dealer agreements, offering both better payment terms and bigger volume discounts. It also doubled its advertising allowances for ads that feature H-P products.

Despite these changes in its marketing mix, H-P faces an uphill battle against industry giant IBM. Whereas IBM registers an impressive 80 percent score in "unaided brand awareness" (a measure of how recognizable a company's name is to the general public), H-P scores only 15 percent. Moreover, IBM has achieved commanding economies of scale: its PC/AT package, with twice the internal memory of a PC as well as a hard disk, was selling for only about $3000 in late 1986.

It will be virtually impossible for Hewlett-Packard to match IBM's low prices; instead, it will have to convince buyers that Hewlett-Packard's technological advantages are worth the additional cost. Cyril Yansouni, the vice president of Hewlett-Packard's personal computer group, admits: "I keep telling my engineers that they now have five minutes to make a sale, not five hours like we used to. We have to focus on apparent user benefits."

Source: Bill Saporito, "Hewlett-Packard Discovers Marketing," *Fortune,* Oct. 1, 1984, pp. 51–52, 54, 56.

1. How do you think it was possible for a company like Hewlett-Packard to be so successful for 45 years before it "discovered" modern marketing?
2. Describe Hewlett-Packard's marketing mix for personal computers and its marketing mix for peripherals such as printers.
3. Explain Hewlett-Packard's version of "marketing myopia."

■ CASE 2

PEPSICO

"Pepsi . . . just kept hammering away," comments a competitor of both Pepsico and Coca-Cola. "They've kept hammering away with a simple lineup and with simple themes: Taste and youth, youth and taste." Indeed, Pepsi-Cola has been warring against arch rival Coca-Cola for more than half a century. Back in the 1930s, in the world's first radio jingle, Pepsi announced that it was cutting the price of its largest serving, then a dime, and offered consumers "twice as much for a nickel, too." So began the soft-drink industry's first price war.

For decades thereafter, Pepsi-Cola continued to be a distant number two to Coke. In the early 1960s, for example, Coke enjoyed a sales lead over Pepsi of more than 2 to 1. However, in 1963 Pepsi began a marketing campaign that has survived in various forms to this day. It announced the birth of "the Pepsi Generation" and launched "lifestyle advertising" aimed at younger viewers.

"We made a decision in the 1960s," recalls Alan Pottasch, Pepsi-Cola U.S.A.'s senior vice president of creative services, "to stop talking about the product and to start talking about the user." Adopting a long-term positioning strategy, Pepsi was fighting not only to improve the brand's market share but to improve its "share of mind." As Pottasch notes, "the word Coke had practically become generic." Pepsi marketers decided that they should position their product with the next generation of consumers, who had not yet become firmly attached to Coca-Cola. Rather than getting Coke loyalists to switch brands, Pepsi hoped to win over an uncommitted and desirable target market.

In retrospect, even Pepsi's rivals admit that this decision was brilliant. John Bergin of McCann-Erickson—who worked on both "the Pepsi Generation" and the "Coke Is It" campaigns—recalls: "Here the world was bursting with teenagers, some 70 million war babies representing the single largest homogeneous group ever assembled on this earth. And then there's Pepsi-Cola—the first marketers ever to recognize them."

Some 25 years later, Pepsi-Cola is still relying on its generational strategy. In 1983, it began using a revised theme, the "Choice of a New Generation," which has continued through the mid-1980s. Pepsi appealed to this new generation with creative, energetic advertising, including television commercials featuring rock stars Michael Jackson and Lionel Richie, television actors Don Johnson and Michael J. Fox, and comedian Billy Crystal. In 1985, Pepsi-Cola spent an estimated $460 million on advertising, up 29 percent from its 1983 spending.

In the history of the cola wars, Pepsi-Cola has successfully attacked Coke's dominant position not only with its "Pepsi Generation" campaign but also with the now-famous "Pepsi Challenge." Begun in Texas in 1974, the "Pepsi Challenge" campaign focused on blind taste tests of loyal Coca-Cola drinkers whose reactions were videotaped through a one-way mirror. Again and again, more than half of the original sample of Coke loyalists declared they preferred the taste of Pepsi in these blind taste tests.

According to various reports, the "Pepsi Challenge" has obsessed Coca-Cola executives ever since its introduction in the mid-1970s. "They never really stopped being mesmerized by it," claims one observer of the soft-drink industry. "Even when Pepsi was willing to move on to other themes, [the Challenge] continued to bug the hell out of Coke. They just can't seem to live with the idea that their product might not be the best on the market."

Apparently, the threat posed by the "Pepsi Challenge" contributed to Coca-Cola's controversial decision to introduce "New Coke" in 1985 as a replacement for the long-familiar Coca-Cola. Coke executives may have come to believe that their brand would have to taste "better" (or at least sweeter) if it was to preserve its historic dominance in the soft-drink industry. As is well known, many devoted Coke drinkers were stunned and outraged by the introduction of New Coke. Tens of thousands called Coca-Cola headquarters to complain; some even formed protest organizations to lobby for the return of traditional Coca-Cola. Within a few months, of course, Coca-Cola brought back "Classic Coke" and then found itself with a new marketing problem: how should it market its two versions of Coke?

By the fall of 1985, both Pepsico and Coca-Cola were pointing to benefits from the two-Coke phenomenon. Reports from retailers and bottlers suggested that Coke's two colas were together gaining a larger following than either would have achieved separately. Yet Pepsi-Cola seemed to finally have the number one cola. While Coke's total market share (combining New Coke and Classic Coke) still appeared to be higher than that of Pepsi-Cola, Pepsi marketers could counter that their brand had a higher market share than either version of Coke when considered individually. This offered a useful weapon for Pepsi in convincing retailers and fast-food chains to carry more Pepsi at the expense of either brand of Coke.

Interestingly, it appeared by early 1986 that America's Coke drinkers were increasingly returning to Classic Coke and abandoning New Coke. Coca-Cola executives had hoped that, over time, the taste of New Coke would become more acceptable to soft-drink consumers. But reports from bottlers across the country suggested that Classic Coke was outselling New Coke by margins ranging from 3 to 2 in Chicago and 3 to 1 in Washington, to 8 to 1 in Dallas and New York and 9 to 1 in Minneapolis.

The cola war which took shape in the 1930s certainly continues as we head toward the 1990s. However, there has been a dramatic change: it is now being fought by two equals. Whereas Coke was clearly dominant until at least the 1960s, Pepsico has mounted a strong challenge and has made substantial gains—in good part through skillful marketing efforts.

Sources: Richard Morgan, "Pepsi's Long March Toward Victory," *Adweek,* Sept. 19, 1985, pp. 2–4, 6; "Pepsi's Marketing Magic: Why Nobody Does It Better," *Business Week,* Feb. 10, 1986, pp. 52–53, 56–57; "Two Cokes Really Are Better than One—For Now," *Business Week,* Sept. 9, 1985, pp. 38–39; "Coke 'Family' Sales Fly as New Coke Stumbles," *Advertising Age,* Jan. 27, 1986, pp. 1, 91.

1. Why is it important to Pepsi management that its market share be as large as that of Coke?
2. Discuss the concept of "share of mind" and compare it with "share of market."
3. Describe the logic behind Pepsi's long-range marketing strategy.

■ CASE 3

HOWARD JOHNSON

In December 1979, Imperial Group Plc., a leading British conglomerate, paid $630 million for one of the best-known consumer franchises in the United States, Howard Johnson. Imperial described its new acquisition as "part of the American way of life . . . attuned to the changing consumer preferences and circumstances. . . ." However, 6 years later, Imperial had abandoned this lofty rhetoric; it sold Howard Johnson for $300 million, less than half of what it had originally paid.

Howard Johnson began his entrepreneurial efforts in 1925 by purchasing a combined patent medicine store and newspaper agency in suburban Quincy, Massachusetts. He soon added store-made ice cream and a soda fountain. Johnson's ice cream became quite popular, and he began to license restaurant franchises. At the time, of course, there were few nationwide chains; most restaurants were small mom-and-pop operations. Things went well for Johnson's franchising outlets until World War II. Because of food and gas rationing, Johnson had to shut down most of his restaurants and survive through his institutional feeding business. These difficult years left the chain's founder and his son forever leery of incurring long-term debts.

As the age of highway building began in the 1950s and continued through the 1960s, the chain's fortunes improved dramatically. The younger Howard Johnson took over the firm's leadership from his father and oversaw expansion of hundreds of company-owned restaurants along highways and toll roads. At the time, there was a shortage of decent places to enjoy a meal or stay overnight on or near the nation's highways. Howard Johnson restaurants benefited not only from their reputation—clean, wholesome family restaurants with the chain's famous 28 flavors of ice cream—but also from business coming from nearby Howard Johnson's franchised motor lodges.

The company's downturn began in the 1970s, spurred for a time by the Arab oil embargo and the threat of gas rationing. Perhaps the most serious cause was Howard Johnson's failure to adjust to the changing nature of the restaurant business. Fast-food marketers such as McDonald's, Wendy's, and Kentucky Fried Chicken were expanding dramatically, as were higher-priced theme and ethnic restaurants. Yet, in contrast to a booming coffee-shop chain such as Denny's, Howard Johnson failed to appeal to specific market segments by offering regionally flavored dinners or low-cholesterol entrees. Instead, it held steadfastly to a rather unexciting and outdated menu. As Vern Curtis, chairman of Denny's, observed: "If you're not willing to adapt to a changing market, the world is going to pass you by. I don't see a lot of difference between the Howard Johnson's of today and that of 10 to 12 years ago."

The same critique could be made concerning Howard Johnson's motor lodges. As franchise operators expanded the lodges to 200 rooms or more, they attracted and came to depend on a new type of customer—the business traveler—whose needs were quite different from those of families patronizing the motor lodges. While families may have been comfortable sharing hot dogs and soda at Howard Johnson restaurants, business travelers wanted hard liquor and steaks. And they didn't want to eat dinner next to noisy young children.

In many respects, the Howard Johnson story is one of wasted opportunities. Howard Johnson was once in a strong position to dominate ice-cream franchising but was surpassed by Baskin-Robbins and later Häagen-Dazs because of its conservative financial outlook. Howard Johnson avoided risks at all costs; the Johnsons were preoccupied with cutting costs, avoiding debts, and accumulating cash assets. Had it risked a major cash outlay to open downtown ice cream parlors, Howard Johnson might have reaped huge profits.

In retrospect, it seems clear that the company was run for decades without the benefit of any marketing orientation. For example, while competitors Marriott and Denny's rely on sophisticated market-testing operations to survey customer satisfaction and changing tastes, Howard Johnson instead chose to use comment cards left at restaurant tables.

By the end of 1985, Howard Johnson's restaurant operations had declined by about 300 locations from its 1975 peak figure. Ironically, 20 years earlier, Howard Johnson's sales exceeded the combined sales of McDonald's, Burger King, and Kentucky Fried Chicken. In the view of Denny's Vern Curtis: "Howard Johnson ought to have been the $4 billion company, not McDonald's."

Source: John Merwin, "The Sad Case of the Dwindling Orange Roofs," *Forbes,* Dec. 30, 1985, pp. 75–79.

1. Describe the forces that were most responsible for the decline in Howard Johnson's fortunes.
2. What should the company have been doing to anticipate and prevent its decline?

■ CASE 4

YOUNG AND RUBICAM ADVERTISING AGENCY

In their efforts to understand consumers' attitudes and behavior, advertising agencies have traditionally relied on such research methods as telephone surveys, focus group interviews, and laboratory experiments. More recently, however, agencies have turned to new techniques that they hope will generate information truer to real life. Among these techniques are observation of shoppers and even motorcycle-group members, cinema verité style filming of families at home, and sifting through garbage to study consumption patterns.

One of the leaders in this effort to observe consumers in natural settings is the New York–based agency of Young and Rubicam (Y&R). This agency employs a research technique known as *ethnography,* actually a branch of anthropology involving the scientific description of cultures. According to Joseph Plummer, Y&R's executive vice president for research and a former graduate student in anthropology: "Ethnography tends to work as a context provider—an enriching, background mosaic—and in that respect it's very powerful. The notion is that in order to study rituals and symbols, one has to go to the environment where the symbols exist and the rituals occur."

In conducting ethnographic research projects, Y&R sends researchers into homes not only to ask questions but to photograph people's behavior and surroundings. Ideally, they will observe telling details that help the agency to understand the needs, wants, and aspirations of the consumer. For example, Y&R's ethnographic study of snack-food consumers—intended to assist its client, Frito-Lay, Inc.—revealed that heavy users included families who typically invited neighborhood children over to watch television and served bowls of snack food. Consequently, Y&R devised an advertising campaign that featured snack foods as a part of family life. In another ethnographic study, conducted for Richardson-Vicks Inc.'s Oil of Olay, Y&R researchers found that mothers were as heavily engaged in beauty rituals as their daughters. As Joseph Plummer recalls: "That gave us the confidence to proceed with developing a new line of products."

Young and Rubicam's competitors have experimented with similar research techniques. One firm films consumers using various products and studies their verbal reactions, body language, and use of the product in order to draw conclusions and develop advertising concepts. Another agency once studied motorcyclists for Harley Davidson by sending a researcher to "hang around" with bikers. He found that "a lot of those guys were fairly straight Monday through Friday, then, for one reason or another, became different on weekends. For them, it was a mental vacation, a weekend away as someone else."

Thus far, however, some clients remain skeptical about the value of ethnography. John Burke, vice president of marketing services for Nestlé Foods, suggests: "I'm going to wait until somebody proves their effectiveness. What we try to do in all research is to assure that it's actionable, that it does lead to some type of sales improvement and franchise building." Yet Young and Rubicam reports that client requests for ethnographic studies are on the rise—both within the United States and overseas. Moreover, Stephanie Kugelman, director of Y&R's Creative Research Services, points out that in some instances the agency conducts ethnographic research—even when it has not been requested—for its own research and development.

Source: Karen Singer, "Ethnography: Research That's Up Close and Personal," *Adweek's Marketing Week,* Sept. 29, 1986, pp. 30, 32.

1. What are the most important benefits likely to result from ethnographic studies?
2. It has been said of this and other qualitative research methods: "If it is qualitative, it is not projectable." Comment on this statement.

■ CASE 5

EASTMAN KODAK

In the highly competitive business environment of the 1980s, incorrect marketplace decisions can be disastrous even for a prestigious and traditionally successful marketer. Consequently, top management at Eastman Kodak Company has made a strong commitment to supporting and *using* market research. Vincent P. Barabba, director of market intelligence at Kodak, states that "top management has invested considerable time to participate in and fully understand the market intelligence function, and to be certain that all information is gathered and reported objectively."

Kodak's market intelligence team must work within limitations of both time frame and cost. In one instance, management asked market intelligence to obtain information by a deadline that researchers found prohibitive. They reported back to management that the quality of information needed could not be assembled unless they had another 6 months. Additionally, they reported the analytical trade-offs that would be required if they met the original deadline. Management ultimately concluded that the deadline should be maintained: the increased level of risk resulting from a lesser quality of information was preferable to the high costs of a 6-month delay. In another case, management initially requested a research effort that the intelligence team projected would cost over $1 million. They reported back to management that if Kodak was willing to give up two percentage points in accuracy, the research cost could be halved. Management then approved the revised research plan.

Kodak's market intelligence system, known as MAIN, integrates problem definition and market information into a unified decision-making process. The system performs five important market intelligence functions:

- It evaluates Kodak's information needs and establishes a priority list of market data needs.
- It assesses the market and collects information in a cost-effective manner.
- It stores, retrieves, and displays information, using a hierarchical data base approach that assures easy retrieval of data.
- It develops descriptive information analyses that can be used by decision makers.
- It improves Kodak's utilization of knowledge by evaluating the impact of information on decision making.

In using its MAIN system, Kodak emphasizes management involvement and interaction in market intelligence processes. As Vincent Barabba observes: "While top management doesn't have to do its own market intelligence work, it must understand how that work was done to eliminate the possibility of information misuse." As a result, market intelligence experts conduct seminars for Kodak decision makers at which they explain how their intelligence models work and underscore the strengths and limitations of the information developed through these models. At the same time, Kodak invites market intelligence staffers to certain higher management "brainstorming" sessions so that the market researchers will be more sensitive to management strategies and priorities.

Another tool used by Kodak's market intelligence team is called SAST, Strategic Assumption Surfacing and Testing. In one use of SAST in the mid-1980s, researchers were asked to evaluate alternative new film products to see which could be successfully marketed. One option was a 35mm color negative film, rated at ISO 200, that would offer twice the film speed of the popular Kodacolor II film (rated ISO 100) without any substantial drop in quality. Another option was a new ISO 100 film that would be ideal for big enlargements because of its sharpness and extremely fine grain.

The market intelligence team developed a survey designed for 35mm film users on six continents. Cultural differences in various nations were taken into account in devising survey questions. After extensive interviewing, it became clear that many users were rather loyal to Kodak's 100-speed film. Yet a significant market segment appeared ready to switch to a 200-speed film with good quality. Researchers became convinced that the market would accept both new products. Eventually, the idea emerged for a Kodak "family" of color negative films, including a 400-speed and a 1000-speed film.

In presenting Kodak's market intelligence process, Vincent Barabba concludes that "implementation is where the value of market intelligence is finally determined. We are concerned with knowledge utilization. Data means nothing until its meaning is converted into work." According to Barabba, Kodak is especially interested in studying its market intelligence efforts *after* decisions have been made in order to determine the actual impact of the information developed by researchers. Only through such postdecision evaluations can Kodak genuinely improve its MAIN system and guarantee better solutions to future problems.

Source: Vincent P. Barabba, "How Kodak's Market Intelligence System Cuts Risk, Speeds Decisions," *Management Review;* Aug. 1984, pp. 8–13.

1. At Kodak, it seems managers who will use the results of marketing research and intelligence gathering actually get involved in understanding research methods. What value do you see in this?
2. Discuss the statement: "Implementation is where the value of market intelligence is finally determined."
3. How does Kodak's market intelligence reduce the risk of new-product introductions?

Analysis for Marketing Planning

TWO

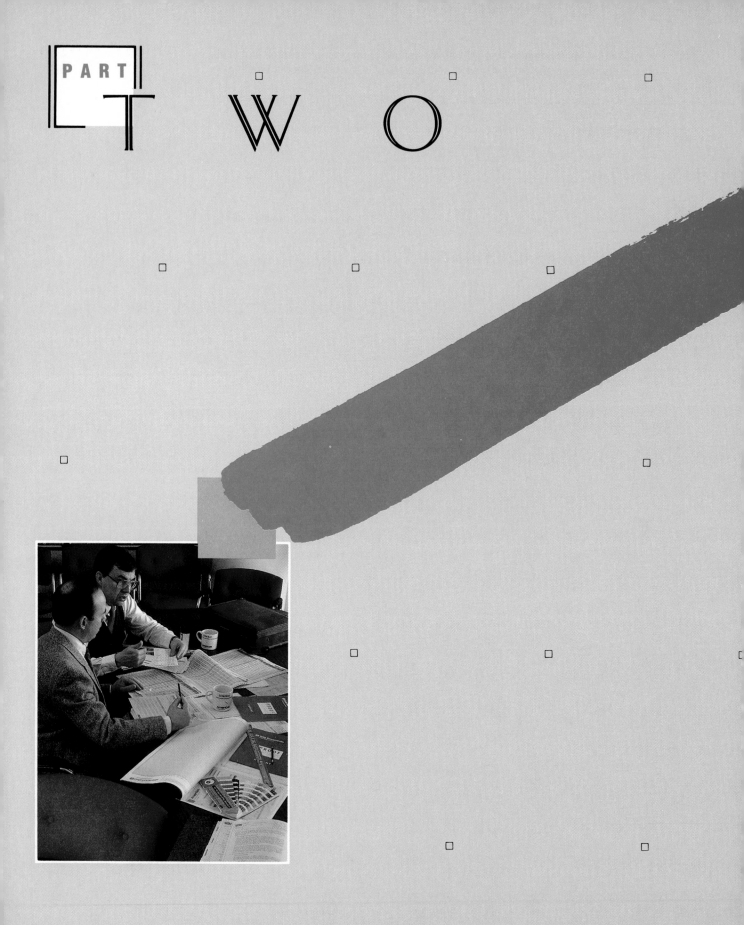

PLANNING THE MARKETING PROGRAM

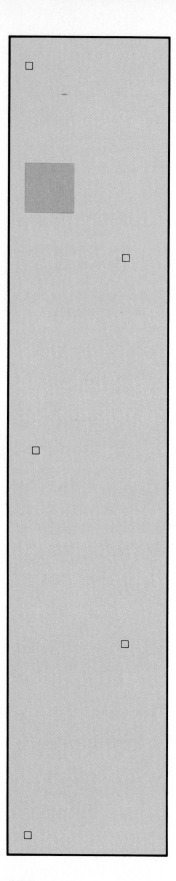

Planning marks the difference between effective and ineffective marketing management. An old saying is, "If you don't know where you are going, there is a good chance you will wind up somewhere else." Effective marketers are as likely to have a marketing plan as airline pilots are to have a flight plan. These plans are based on the *analysis* of environments and markets that we have covered in Chapters 2 through 6.

Chapter 7 covers the topics of market segmentation and product positioning. Market segmentation is the process of breaking down large, complex markets into smaller, more manageable parts, or segments, which are the targets of marketing efforts. Positioning is how marketers present products to selected target markets.

Chapter 8 focuses on issues somewhat broader than marketing. It covers issues of corporate strategy—the strategy of the total organization—as well as marketing strategy. Once strategy is established, it must be translated into concrete operational marketing programs, the subject of Chapter 9. The overall planning process results in the marketing plans that will guide the organization's implementation of marketing programs.

7

Copyright © Naoki Okamoto/Black Star.

SEGMENTING MARKETS AND POSITIONING PRODUCTS

SPOTLIGHT ON

☐ Basic concepts of the segmentation and positioning process

☐ Advantages of segmentation for marketers

☐ Steps in the segmentation and positioning process

☐ Bases for segmentation of consumer and organizational markets

☐ Testing segments for validity

☐ Competitive segmentation strategies

☐ Product-positioning strategies

The Duchess of Windsor, it is said, once observed that no one could be too thin or too rich. To those attributes, many Americans would add another: No one can be too tan. Our belief that the sun is good for us and for our looks has spawned a $230 million suntan product industry. However, we know that the sun's ultraviolet rays are bad for us—overexposure can cause premature aging of the skin and skin cancer—and thus one estimate projects annual suntan product sales of $425 million by 1990.

Two factors have contributed to the extraordinary growth of this industry. In 1978, the Food and Drug Administration (FDA) approved a system of measuring the effectiveness of sunscreens in tanning products: the sun protection factor (SPF, or simply PF) scale. With this encouragement, most manufacturers of suntan oils and lotions quickly adapted their products, adding aminobenzoic acid (PABA), among other ingredients, in varying amounts to fit a PF scale ranging from 2 to 15. The FDA also allowed manufacturers to state on their packaging that "liberal use of this product may reduce the chance of premature aging of the skin and skin cancer." For once, a federal agency had helped to produce a marketer's dream: Industry sales surged 50 percent in the 5 years following 1978.

As the suntan industry began following a more sophisticated marketing approach, it increased its range of offerings to appeal to sun worshipers of all ages and descriptions. Among age groups, teenagers are the biggest users of tanning products. Teenagers tend to prefer oils—"fryers" as they are called in the trade—a preference capitalized on by Tanning Research Laboratories' Hawaiian Tropic line. By contrast, Charles of the Ritz, Revlon, Germaine Monteil, and Clinique offer suntan product lines aimed at adults, with balms, creams, and potions for before, during, and after sunning. Estee Lauder promotes an entire "Solar System" for the over-thirty sun-loving crowd.

(Ken Karp.)

Planning the Marketing Program

The Coppertone line, marketed by Schering-Plough Corporation, sells 45 percent of all suntan products made. In addition to its oils, creams, lotions, gels, and sunscreens (a complete line rated from PF 5 to PF 15), Coppertone also differentiates its products by body part. A survey conducted by Coppertone's advertising agency, Warwick, revealed that many users found the firm's regular products "too greasy" for their faces. As a result, Coppertone introduced For Faces Only and other products especially designed for the lips, nose, and neck. Initially, the firm's managers feared that these new products would cut into the sales of familiar Coppertone offerings, but they soon learned that people were eagerly using two or more lotions at the same time. Coppertone had actually expanded the market for suntan products.

Currently, suntan products take up as much room as hair-care products in many retail stores. This is because marketers have identified so many different groups with distinctive needs and desires concerning suntan products. Marketers view these groups as market segments, and are now developing suntan products to provide the particular benefits valued by each market segment.

Source: Bernice Kanner, "What's New under the Sun," *New York,* Aug. 8, 1983, pp. 19–20.

Few products can satisfy all customers. To implement the marketing concept, thereby placing the buyer at the center of marketing efforts, different products must be offered to satisfy different buyer groups. Thus, before you think of buying a tube of suntan oil, an automobile, or a certificate of deposit, you have already been marked as a member of a specific group—a **target market.**

Marketers use the technique of *segmentation*—the identification of different groups of potential buyers that share similar, definable needs and behaviors—to help them put the customer ahead of the product. We can illustrate segmentation through a visual analogy to a deck of cards. Each of a deck's 52 cards has individual properties, with no other card being exactly like it. Nevertheless, the deck can be segmented by color (26 red cards and 26 black cards), by suit (13 hearts, 13 diamonds, 13 clubs, and 13 spades), and by various formulations reflecting "power" in certain card games (for poker games without wild cards, 2 through 10 have less power than jack through ace). Similarly, marketers can segment potential buyers on the basis of geographic variables (city, state, region, nation), demographic variables (age, sex, marital status), socioeconomic variables (occupation, education, income), or other criteria.

Well aware that different consumers want different benefits from the goods and services that they buy, marketers create different brands, adjust their services, and vary their promotional messages to appeal to target groups. Furthermore, marketers intentionally position their products for comparison with those of competitors. Every time you pick up a new tube of suntan oil, you choose your brand over others on the shelf because of its "feel" (not too greasy), price, and supposed success (in protecting your skin). Strategic positioning of products allows a marketer to appeal to one or more of the identified target market segments.

Chapter 7 discusses the importance of segmentation and positioning applied to the marketing concept and outlines the advantages of segmentation for marketing organizations. An overview of the segmentation process precedes an examination of the ground rules for segmenting consumer and organizational markets. We then outline the steps that marketers take to describe and test the validity of segments within their markets. Finally, we present various competitive segmentation and product-positioning strategies.

■ WHAT IS MARKET SEGMENTATION?

Market segmentation is the process of dividing large, heterogeneous (dissimilar) markets into smaller, homogeneous (similar) submarkets. As noted earlier, marketers of suntan products have segmented the total market into parts, or segments, such as age groups (teenagers and the over-30 crowd), groups with needs for different levels of skin protection (PF 2 versus PF 15), and even groups that want suntan products for particular parts of the body.

The opposite of market segmentation (and far less common) is **undifferentiated marketing,** also called **mass marketing.** Marketers in mass marketing define their product or service as broadly as possible and promote it to anyone able to purchase. Although product characteristics may be emphasized, especially within a competitive context, no differentiation is made among potential buyers. Until when they recently "discovered" marketing (see Chapter 23), U.S. banks accepted the undifferentiated approach and did not offer particular services for distinctive market segments.

Once the marketer has established a market's appropriate segments, particular segments are designated as the firm's *target market.* Target marketing selects which segments the marketer will try to satisfy with particular marketing programs. For instance, the market for automobiles has a number of segments based on levels of luxury and on price needed to get that luxury. General Motors, BMW, and Korea's Hyundai have all segmented the market the same way, but BMW has targeted only the high end, Hyundai has targeted only the low end, and General Motors has targeted *all* segments with products ranging from Chevrolet to Cadillac.

☐ Advantages of Segmentation

During the 1970s, Limited Inc., a successful women's wear chain, grew rapidly by targeting its merchandise to young collegiate and working women. In 1982, chair Leslie H. Wexner decided to enter a different market segment: the 13 million tall or heavy U.S. women, age 16 or older, who buy special sizes. The Limited acquired two apparel chains that already specialized in large sizes: Lane Bryant (207 stores) and Roamans (63 stores). Wexner projects 500 stores for each chain by 1990.[1] Rather than expanding its markets across the board, the Limited has chosen controlled growth by adding new specialty stores catering to carefully identified market segments.

As companies that segment well know, segmentation allows for (1) more precise market definition, (2) better analysis of competition, (3) rapid response to changing market needs, (4) efficient resource allocation, and (5) effective strategic planning.

PRECISE MARKET DEFINITION   Specific descriptions of those in a selected market segment allow the marketer to find the most efficient and effective ways of serving them. Does social class influence their buying decisions? What reference groups are likely to be important to segment members? How do they get product information and arrive at buying decisions? What specific benefits do these people seek from the product type in question? The more accurate and complete the

Perhaps the most spectacular retail growth story of the century is that of The Limited. At least part of the success of this chain is that management has clearly segmented the market and focuses its attention on its chosen target market—young collegiate and working women. (Copyright © Peggy Roberts.)

market definition, the better able the marketer is to design a marketing mix that will lead segment members to the point of exchange.

Tandy Corporation has been able to maintain profitability in the personal computer business because of detailed knowledge of those in its chosen market segment—small businesses with only a few employees. Providing free instruction and carry-in servicing for its TRS line of computers at thousands of Radio Shack Computer Centers has enabled Tandy to hold onto a sizable portion of its base segment in the face of formidable marketing efforts from competitors IBM and Apple. Marketers at Tandy know the characteristics and needs of those in their chosen market segment. By defining their market precisely, Tandy's managers have been able to prevail and to do so profitably.

ANALYSIS OF COMPETITION   Through market differentiation and target marketing an organization can identify and carefully analyze the efforts of its prime competitors—those companies that have targeted the same markets. The organization can focus on its real competitors and relegate to secondary concern those who compete peripherally. When IBM fielded its PC line in the personal computer market, its strategy was to play on its own strengths vis-à-vis Apple and Tandy. Large business firms were IBM's primary target market; small businesses were a secondary market. Consequently, even though IBM established a small number of retail outlets, it did not attempt to rival Tandy's Radio Shack distribution network. IBM's several thousand sales representatives were already calling on large companies and could promote the PC. IBM's new offering held a competitive advantage since it was compatible with the predominant and established IBM large mainframe computers. Since the Apple IIE and the TRS-80 were *not* compatible, many buyers felt compelled to select IBM's PC.

Tandy and Apple were fully aware of the power of the compatibility issue. Tandy focused on small-business customers who could use stand-alone machines for accounting and word processing without the need to tie into an IBM mainframe.

Apple took a different tack, speeding up the introduction of its Macintosh model. The Macintosh was easier to learn and use than the IBM PC, had clearer graphics, and cost less. In other words, Apple countered the compatibility issue by emphasizing the alternative benefits of its Macintosh.

By the mid-1980s, however, Apple decided to go head-to-head with IBM in the battle for large corporate buyers and had to take its compatibility problem more seriously. Yet, to the extent that its small-business and larger corporate segments have different needs, Apple faces a substantial problem in designing its marketing offerings and strategy. In sharp contrast, the latest entry into this field, AT&T, is clearly positioning itself in the large corporate end of the market. However, unlike Apple, AT&T has the vast resources necessary for a direct assault on IBM.

RESPONSE TO CHANGING MARKET NEEDS   Market segmentation enables marketers to sense, analyze, and respond quickly to the changing tastes of people within a target market. Obviously, the needs of a precisely defined, homogeneous group are easier to monitor than those of a sprawling, heterogeneous group. For instance, when many Americans became more health-conscious and weight-conscious, Coke and Pepsi quickly came up with new diet colas and natural fruit juices.

EFFICIENT RESOURCE ALLOCATION   Even giant corporations have limited resources, and none can compete in every market. The resources of any firm—its people, its time, and its money—can be used most effectively when the *right* target markets are clearly limited and defined.

Digital Equipment Corporation, second only to IBM in computer industry sales, tried to compete in the personal computer market in the early 1980s, but Digital was never able to match its main adversaries on price and distribution. Digital finally dropped its Rainbow line of personal computers, refocusing its efforts on its VAX line of minicomputers (almost as powerful, but less costly than mainframes). Digital continues to sell its Decmate line of word-processing stations as support to the profitable minicomputers. The failure to serve a market segment taught Digital managers to concentrate their resources in segments where the firm could not only compete but could lead.

EFFECTIVE STRATEGIC PLANNING   Segment-by-segment analysis of a firm's chosen markets lays the groundwork for strategic planning. Neither Apple, Tandy, nor IBM sets long-range goals for individual products, in units sold, revenues, or profits, without first studying the needs and buying behaviors of the groups of consumers or organizations the company now serves and those it hopes to serve. IBM's overall strategy contains separate strategies built on the needs of potential PC buyers and on the differing needs of the organizational buyers of its Sierra line of mainframe computers. Having analyzed the current markets for its products, planners then consider the makeup and needs of various markets projecting perhaps 20 years into the future. Overall corporate plans are firmly based in exhaustive study of chosen market segments.

☐ The Process of Market Segmentation and Product Positioning

After the basic choice of consumer or organizational markets is made, market segmentation occurs in an orderly sequence. Circumstances may alter specific cases, but marketers generally follow these steps (also diagrammed in Figure 7-1):

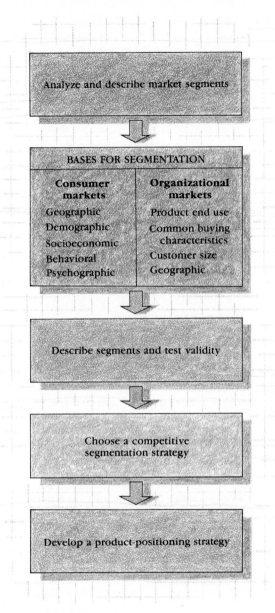

Figure 7-1 *The market segmentation and product-positioning process.* Applying market segmentation and product-positioning concepts requires a disciplined approach. The first step is primarily analytical—selecting from the many available criteria for segmenting and then describing and testing the segments chosen. Management then chooses a competitive segmentation strategy and sets specific marketing mix decisions to position the product strategically.

1. *Analyze and describe market segments.* Many criteria can be used to segment broad markets into smaller, more attractive ones. Drawing on market research and experience, analysts characterize the nature and needs of buyers in their target market (or markets) as specifically and completely as possible. Every competitor engages in such analysis and description of segments. Thus, both General Motors and Rolls-Royce *study* the entire market for automobiles; only later does each firm develop a distinctive marketing strategy.

2. *Choose a competitive segmentation strategy.* At this point, marketers must evaluate their target segments, select a strategy for reaching those segments, and prepare to implement that strategy. General Motors sees its market as many segments and pursues all but the very top and bottom segments. By contrast, Rolls-Royce concentrates on the most affluent segment of car buyers.

3. *Develop a positioning strategy.* Before they can promote a product to its potential users, marketers must position that product within a descriptive or functional category. What is the product? More precisely, how does the consumer perceive the product? Is the automobile basic transportation? Is it an "experience" of driving the best-engineered machine on the road? Is it a luxurious statement of its owner's affluence? The selling theme—which may be product-oriented, buyer-oriented, or both—will emerge from this positioning process.

Keep two factors in mind as we look at various ways to segment consumer and organizational markets. First, the marketing concept should pervade segmentation planning. Buyers' needs, perceptions, and actions should be the foundation for differentiating markets; product characteristics should be secondary to buyer characteristics. Second, logical buyer characteristics that mesh with product characteristics should be the criteria chosen. For example, income is one logical basis for segmenting automobile buyers, but income is not a useful basis for segmenting chewing gum buyers, and personal income is practically irrelevant for segmenting organizational buyers.

■ SEGMENTING CONSUMER MARKETS ■

Although marketers consider and combine many variables in identifying consumer market segments, the most frequently used—geographic, demographic, socioeconomic, behavioral, and psychographic factors—are best examined individually. These factors may seem familiar, because we looked at them in a slightly different perspective in our discussion of consumer behavior in Chapters 3 and 4. Here we look on these factors as **segmentation variables,** because it is the differences among buyers that enable and require segmentation.

☐ *Geographic Variables*

Marketers often identify buyer groups by neighborhood, city, state, region, and nation. Some behaviors clearly are peculiar to regions: Germans drink more beer per capita than any other national group, the French and Italians consume more wine, and Americans brew more coffee. Within the United States, residents of the Sunbelt buy more air-conditioned convertibles; people living along the Atlantic and Pacific coasts purchase more scuba gear. New Englanders bake clams in their seaweed pits, and Texans consider mesquite coals a must for grilling beef. Social scientists have studied value differences among the regions of North America and have identified nine "nations."[2] A major advertising agency has attempted to provide geographic segmentation information for a similar grouping.[3]

Some firms choose to serve only one or a few regions. Black, finely ground Spanish roast Cafe Bustelo coffee appears in supermarkets only in New York and other cities with large Hispanic populations. Martinson's and Savarin are coffee brands distributed only in the northeastern United States. Other firms sell in many areas but adjust their marketing mixes for specific regions. Folgers and Maxwell House vary the coffee blends that they sell to westerners, who like stronger coffee than their eastern counterparts do.

Global communication is expanding markets for certain formerly regional products. French-produced Perrier water now appears on U.S. dinner tables; the Chinese and the Soviets drink Pepsi-Cola; McDonald's hamburgers are popular in Japan. Marketers are constantly on the watch for new geographic market segments.

The glass of wine on a table at a sidewalk cafe on the Champs Elysées in Paris is an expected scene. On a similar table in Stuttgart, Germany, one will more often find beer, and elsewhere yet other beverages. Markets are often segmented on a geographical basis because of the tastes and habits of consumers in different places. (Copyright © John Bryson/Photo Researchers, Inc.)

Marketers who employ geographical segmentation attend carefully to population trends, especially population shifts among regions (such as the migration of Americans to the Sunbelt). Certain products that find markets in heavily populated cosmopolitan areas—for example, custom-tailored dresses or gold-plated faucet handles—attract few buyers in sparsely populated rural areas. Exhibit 7-1 discusses government data available to marketers for their geographical segmentation.

A manufacturer of kitchen and bathroom tiles located in Westchester might want to expand its advertising to the New York CMSA. Information about the Westchester MSA and the New York CMSA such as age, sex, income, and occupation available from the Department of Commerce can be quite valuable in marketing planning. Figure 7-2 shows how a CMSA is composed of smaller parts.

☐ Demographic Variables

Demographic variables—age, sex, marital status, household size—provide the most commonly used criteria for segmenting markets. However, these factors must be monitored carefully, since long-term shifts produce changes in target groups. For example, today's older Americans are physically stronger, live longer, and expect more of life than did elderly persons of previous generations. Even though they buy more prescription drugs than members of other age groups, older Americans

The U.S. Department of Commerce compiles a great deal of information useful to marketers. One program, helpful to both regional and national marketers, amasses facts about urban areas. This information is compiled for three metropolitan categories.

A **metropolitan statistical area** (MSA) has one or more central cities, each with a population of at least 50,000, or a single urbanized area that has at least 50,000 people and that is part of an MSA with a total population of 100,000. An MSA may include several counties that have close economic and social ties to the central urban area[s].

An MSA with more than 1 million people is classified as a **primary metropolitan statistical area** (PMSA) and usually consists of a large, urbanized county or cluster of counties.

An area that includes multiple PMSAs is classified as a **consolidated metropolitan statistical area** (CMSA). For example, the New York City CMSA includes counties in northern New Jersey, nearby portions of Long Island, and parts of Connecticut. Westchester, New York, is an MSA, whereas Newark, New Jersey is a PMSA; both are included in the New York CMSA.

---

have become an increasingly attractive target market for promoters of travel and cruise packages and luxury goods.[4]

As noted in Chapter 2, the relative sizes of age groups in the overall U.S. population are also changing. Figure 2-5 shows that in the period 1980 to 1990 the number of teenagers and young adults (ages 14 to 24) in the United States will decrease while the numbers of very young and of elderly Americans will increase considerably. The largest projected increase, those ages 35 to 44, represents the so-called baby-boom generation, a market segment too large to be viewed as homogeneous.[5]

When viewed as a basis for segmentation, gender has lost some of its traditional meanings and has taken on newer meanings. Over 50 percent of all adult women in the United States are found in the work force; 3 out of 5 wives in upper-income households (incomes of more than $35,000 per year) work outside the home. Such working women represent a market segment with needs (such as office wardrobe and professional child care) and interests (insurance policies and business magazines) different from those of full-time homemakers. The new market segment composed of affluent working women is profiled in Box 7-1.

Men's needs have changed as well.[6] The number of men who wear hats to work has steadily declined over the last four decades. Since the 1931 introduction of Mennen's Skin Bracer, the market for men's grooming aids has grown to become an aftershave and cologne industry with estimated retail sales of $1 billion. Moreover, as men take over more responsibility for household and child care duties, consumer marketers are revising their promotional messages to teach men about "waxy buildup," "ring around the collar," and the uses of Hamburger Helper. Stages of the family life cycle form still another demographic basis for segmentation in some consumer markets. Young adults spend more of their incomes on entertainment and large purchases (cars, new homes, furniture) than do parents in their forties, whose priorities include investments and higher education for their children. Grandparents, as well as young parents, may be targeted by toy makers and by marketers of cameras and film.

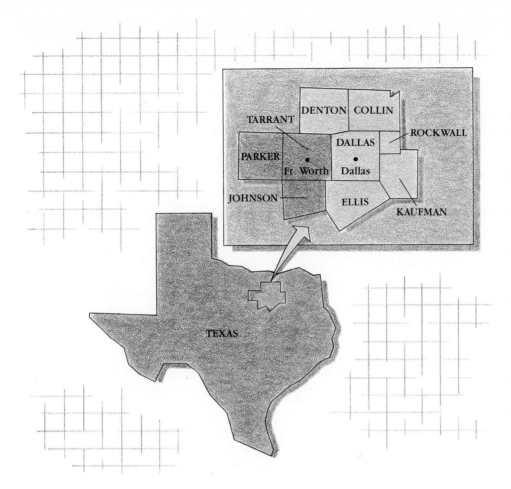

Figure 7-2 *U.S. Census Bureau statistical areas.* The U.S. government reports many statistics by geographic area. The census bureau designates three kinds of statistical areas, two of which are shown in this map of the Dallas–Fort Worth area in Texas. Note that three counties make up the Fort Worth PMSA, shown in purple; while six counties shown in green, make up the Dallas PMSA. PMSAs are large metropolitan centers, while smaller units, such as Austin (not shown, but to the south) are MSAs. Because of the proximity of Dallas and Fort Worth, they are combined into the Dallas–Fort Worth CMSA.

Socioeconomic Variables

Social class indicators—occupation, education, and income—are often used as a basis for market segmentation. Many marketers who segment groups on the basis of income find the growing upper-income segment of the U.S. population to be more and more attractive. In 1980, 13 million households, or 16 percent of the nation's households, had incomes of over $35,000. By 1990, that segment will have grown to 21 million households, or 22 percent of all households.

Still, marketers find that they must subdivide this heterogeneous group. The upper-income market segment now includes the traditional single-income wealthy families as well as newer (usually younger) households who have reached upper-income status only because they benefit from *two* household incomes. In comparison to those in traditional affluent households, the new affluent tend to be less well-educated and not so exclusively managerial or professional.[7] The traditional affluent may buy a BMW, but the new affluent are as likely to buy a Chevrolet pickup truck as a BMW.

Racial, ethnic, and religious groupings provide segmentation bases for certain products. Some hair and skin care products are designed with benefits for inherited racial characteristics, but products that appeal to acquired cultural characteristics are more commonly aimed at ethnic market segments. Indeed, as we pointed out

BOX 7-1   Targeting the Upscale Working Woman

American marketers are increasingly recognizing an important new target market: the affluent working woman with substantial income and the freedom to spend it as she chooses. Consider the following data:

- More than half of all new investors on the New York Stock Exchange are professional or managerial women.
- Women currently account for 36 percent of total business travel; this figure may rise as high as 50 percent by 1990.
- Women are now making almost as many automobile purchases as are men.
- Nearly 40 percent of all dollars spent on stereo speakers, 24 percent spent on cassette decks, and 18 percent spent on videocassette recorders are spent by women.

Marketers have made special efforts to reach these "upscale" professional and managerial women. Chevrolet developed a new advertising campaign to sell its S-10 Blazer station wagon to women. Magnavox, Zenith, and other U.S. electronics marketers have rec-

ognized the profit potential in this affluent female market segment. By contrast, Japanese electronics firms have not taken full advantage of the changing market because they "don't perceive women as making purchase decisions," notes Bobbi Halfin, divisional sales manager for *Working Woman* magazine.

Interestingly, studies conducted by a major New York advertising agency suggest that career women are *least* effectively reached by television. The best advertising medium for reaching this desirable market segment is print journalism, especially magazines aimed specifically at working women. One managerial woman observes that "when I see ads in my magazines, I identify with them because they are part of an editorial environment that talks to me. I see the same ads in other magazines, but they don't have the same impact." Consequently, publications such as *Savvy* and *Working Woman* are attracting an increasing amount of advertising from automobile manufacturers and marketers of business machines. ◾

Source: Peter Oberlink, "Advertisers Home in on Working Women," *Adweek,* July 7, 1986, pp. 44, 46.

Chevrolet. (Courtesy of Chevrolet Motor Division.)

American Airlines. (Copyright © 1985, American Airlines, Inc. Ad courtesy of American Airlines and Bozell, Jacobs, Kenyon & Eckhardt, Inc.)

A particularly important and growing subculture in the United States are Spanish-speaking Americans. Many marketers are making extra efforts to reach this audience by using Spanish advertisements. (Copyright © Susan Van Etten/The Picture Cube.)

in Chapter 3, most identifiable buying behaviors among racial and ethnic group members result from cultural (and not racial) heritage.

Racial and ethnic groups are far too heterogeneous to support and justify most segmentation generalizations. By contrast, income, education, social class, and place of residence are likely to be more helpful in assessing consumer needs and responses to marketing mixes. This combination of variables defines most market segments.

Behavioral Variables

Markets may also be segmented by consumer behavior patterns. Examples of behavioral variables are product usage rates, brand loyalty, and benefits sought.

Marketers who segment on the basis of usage rates categorize consumers as "nonusers," "light users," and "heavy users." When they can identify heavy users of a product, marketers may direct most marketing mix efforts (particularly promotional efforts) toward that category. Among beer drinkers in the United States, those classified as heavy users account for more than 80 percent of beer sales; light users account for less than 20 percent. Marketers segmenting along usage-rate lines often find a well-known **80/20 principle** at work—about 80 percent of a product's sales come from about 20 percent of its market.[8] Figure 7-3 shows other ratios of nonusers to light and heavy users of selected consumer products.

Marketers frequently use either "defense" or "attack" strategies in marketing products to consumers who have been segmented along lines of **brand loyalty.** Defense strategies aim to hold on to users: "Would you trust this moment to anyone but Kodak?" The airlines' "frequent flyer" programs are defense strategies aimed at buttressing brand loyalty by giving away bonus trips as a reward. Attack strategies seek to woo consumers away from other brands. Burger King used one such theme announcing that "the big switch is on." Blind taste tests ("I can't tell it's not butter," "This is instant coffee? I don't believe it!") and direct comparison tests ("The Pampers are definitely softer!") are also attacks.

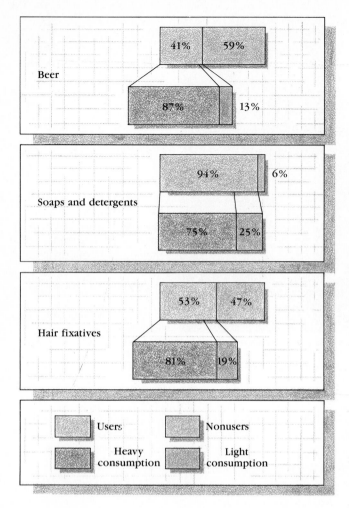

Figure 7-3 *Segmentation by usage rate.* For virtually all products, some consuming units do not use the product at all. Note that in 1982 some 59 percent of households did not consume any beer. For soaps and detergents, the proportion of nonusers was much smaller. Among users, the half that buy the most beer buy 87 percent of all beer purchased. This group is referred to as the "heavy half" (perhaps in more than one meaning). (From Victor J. Cook, Jr., and William A. Mindak, "A Search for Constants: The 'Heavy-User' Revisited," *Journal of Consumer Marketing*, vol. 1, no. 4, 1984, p. 80.)

Marketers engage in **benefit segmentation** because they realize that different consumers seek different benefits when purchasing a product. For example, people have different motives for buying cameras and film. Some are technically sophisticated and wish to express themselves artistically; others like to capture special moments on an instant's notice; still others keep photographic family histories. Each user thus seeks a particular benefit from his or her camera. Camera marketers, of course, tailor their marketing mixes to emphasize various benefits. Expensive cameras with extensive capabilities for fine photography are promoted in special interest magazines such as *American Photographer.* By contrast, Polaroid uses prime-time television commercials aimed at a much wider audience to promote cameras delivering "instant" benefits.

A group of toothpaste users was one of the first to be examined on the basis of benefit segmentation; Exhibit 7-2 presents the results of that research. Those worried about decay prevention favored Crest, whereas those more concerned about appearance preferred MacLeans, Plus White, and Ultra Brite. Benefit segmentation seeks the real reasons people buy rather than the buying likelihoods indicated by demographic segmentation. Demographic characteristics suggest a position in life associated with certain buying behaviors; identification of benefits sought reveals the determinants of buying behavior.

EXHIBIT 7-2 **Benefit Segmentation of the Toothpaste Market**

Benefit segmentation provides a rich picture of the consumers who make up a market segment by including a number of descriptors—demographics, personality, lifestyle—to the segments built on the principal benefit that consumers in that segment are seeking.

	Segment Name			
	Sensory Segment	Sociables	Worriers	Independent Segment
Principal benefit sought	Flavor, product appearance	Brightness of teeth	Decay prevention	Price
Demographic strengths	Children	Teens, young people	Large families	Men
Special behavior characteristics	Users of spearmint-flavored toothpaste	Smokers	Heavy users	Heavy users
Brands disproportionately favored	Colgate, Stripe	Macleans, Plus White, Ultra Brite	Crest	Brands on sale
Personality characteristics	High self-involvement	High sociability	High hypo-chondria	High autonomy
Lifestyle characteristics	Hedonistic	Active	Conservative	Value oriented

Source: Russell I. Haley, "Benefit Segmentation: A Decision-Oriented Research Tool," *Journal of Marketing,* vol. 32, July 1968, p. 33.

☐ *Psychographic Variables*

Demographic surveys can yield rather sterile pictures of consumers:

> The average heavy user of "X" is generally from a large family with an average of 2½ children. She is 33 years of age, lives in the suburbs in a house of 5.3 rooms, has 2.2 baths, 1.7 television sets, ⅔ of a dog, 1.6 automobiles. Certainly, this woman with her unusual dog, ½ of a child, ⅓ of a room, part of a television and automobile is a statistical artifact.[9]

To obtain a richer picture of their target markets and go beyond the rather colorless information provided by the typical demographic study, researchers often turn to lifestyle profiles based on psychographic variables.[10]

Psychographic research is also referred to as *AIO methods*—"AIO" for Activities (how people spend their time), Interests, and Opinions (of themselves and their environment). This information is combined with certain basic demographic variables—income, education, family life cycle stage, and so forth.[11] Exhibit 3-4 lists the elements considered in building lifestyle profiles. As we pointed out in Chapter 3, analysis of consumer traits closely related to personality traits is important in understanding how groups of consumers differ. Such analysis allows us to describe a group's lifestyle as "active, health conscious"—a group distinctly different from the heavy users of beer.[12]

As with any market segmentation process, the marketer begins with a total market, conducts the research needed to define the particular segments, then decides which of these segments to target. Consider the case in which a brewer, Schlitz, segmented the market based on usage and decided to target its efforts toward the heavy users of beer. Rather than using a strictly demographic profile of that segment (42.3 years old, 57.7 percent blue-collar worker, and so forth), the marketer wants a richer psychographic profile. The next step is to conduct a market research study to build that profile.

Subjects of psychographic studies are typically asked whether they "strongly agree," "agree," "are neutral," "disagree," or "strongly disagree" with a list of statements. Individual answers have no importance; rather, the answer patterns that emerge reveal certain personal characteristics which, taken together, form a profile of that consumer. Marketers use these profiles in designing marketing strategies, particularly those behind promotion campaigns. Many television commercials, for example, have their appeals constructed around well-defined psychographic profiles of their target audiences.

Schlitz beer employed lifestyle profiles to get a better understanding of beer drinkers in the heavy users category. Exhibit 7-3 lists some of the statements that subjects were asked to agree or disagree with. Statistical analysis revealed that men

---

EXHIBIT 7-3	**Sample AIO Statements from a Psychographic Profile of Heavy Users in the Beer Market**

Psychographic (or lifestyle) profiles are made up of responses consumers give to a number of questions. The responses are clustered, or grouped together. For instance, the heavy beer drinker answers "yes" to all of the first five statements. This leads the marketer to conclude that this consumer has a masculine self-image. He says "no" to all the last four, which as a group describe him as one who rejects old fashioned institutions/morals. These descriptions (along with more that we don't show here) help the marketer and advertiser to target their efforts more directly on this consumer.

Statement	Evaluation
Beer is a real man's drink. *Playboy* is one of my favorite magazines. I am a girl watcher. Men should not do the dishes. Men are smarter than women.	Masculine self-concept
I would like to be a pro football player. I like bowling. I usually read the sports page. I would do better than average in a fist fight. I like war stories.	Attraction to sports/physical orientation
I like to play poker. I like to take chances. I would rather spend a quiet evening at home than go out to a party. ($-$) If I had my way I would own a convertible. I smoke too much.	Self-indulgent/enjoys himself/ likes risks
I like to work on community projects. ($-$) I'm not very good at saving money. I find myself checking prices, even for small items. ($-$)	Rejects responsibility/a bit impulsive
I go to church regularly. ($-$) Movies should be censored. ($-$) I have old-fashioned tastes and habits. ($-$) There is too much emphasis on sex today. ($-$)	Rejects old-fashioned institutions and morals

Note: ($-$) indicates disagreement with the statement.

Source: Joseph T. Plummer, "Applications of Life Style Research to the Creation of Advertising Campaigns," in W. D. Wells, ed., *Life Style and Psychographics* (American Marketing Association, 1974), pp. 159–169. Used with permission of Joseph T. Plummer.

who drink a lot of beer consider themselves very masculine, like sports, tend to be self-indulgent, reject responsibility, and reject old-fashioned notions and morals. Based on this research, Schlitz chose to position their product through a marketing program which relied heavily on advertising designed to appeal to this masculine fellow. The result was Schlitz's "grab the gusto" and "you only go around once in life" campaigns. Competitors Budweiser and Miller often play on the same themes. In fact, beer commercials over the last two decades have given new life to the careers of a number of past-their-prime athletes.

■ SEGMENTING ORGANIZATIONAL MARKETS ■

The goals of organizational market segmentation closely resemble those of segmenting consumer markets: to identify homogeneous buyer groups that can be reached effectively and persuasively by separate marketing mixes and to provide better service than that afforded by an undifferentiated marketing approach.[13] Competitive advantage is a corollary aim of both goals. As in segmenting consumer markets, organizational markets are first sorted into groups with similar needs and behaviors, then marketing mixes are designed to accommodate the differences and meet the special needs of those groups. White Motor Company, for example, sees the needs of long-distance, heavy-freight haulers as quite different from the needs of an express package delivery service. Trucks powerful enough to pull a 16-wheeler are built for the freight haulers; lightweight, easy-access panel trucks are built for package delivery firms. These are just two market segments served by White.

The most common criteria for segmenting organizational markets are (1) end use—how the customer will use the product, (2) buying characteristics of customers, (3) customer account size, and (4) geography. Organizational marketers, like consumer marketers, often use more than one criterion in delineating market segments. Figure 7-4 illustrates a segmentation strategy for a hypothetical manufacturer of heavy machinery. This marketer, a large, multinational firm, uses all four criteria to segment its complex markets. Separate product-use segments are represented by mining companies and manufacturers. Buying-characteristic segments include western and socialist governments as well as multinational customers. Miners and manufacturers are also segmented by customer account size. Because of its large sales potential and unique legal environment, Japan is identified as a separate geographic segment.

☐ Use of Product

Pinpointing how a buyer uses a product provides marketers with valuable insights into how they can break down organizational markets into manageable segments. One manufacturer of precision motors had always segregated its markets into those who required low-performance motors, those who required high-performance motors, and those who wanted motors for custom applications. Research then revealed that the real difference in how customers used the products lay in what motor speed they needed. At about the same time, the company learned that a new, less expensive motor introduced by a competitor wore out quickly when used at medium and high speeds. With this in mind, the company's marketing staff resegmented the market and pitched its sales efforts toward the segments requiring superior motors that could withstand medium- and high-speed use (see Figure 7-5), thereby emphasizing the life cycle cost advantage of its existing product. The company also began development of a new low-speed motor for that market segment.[14]

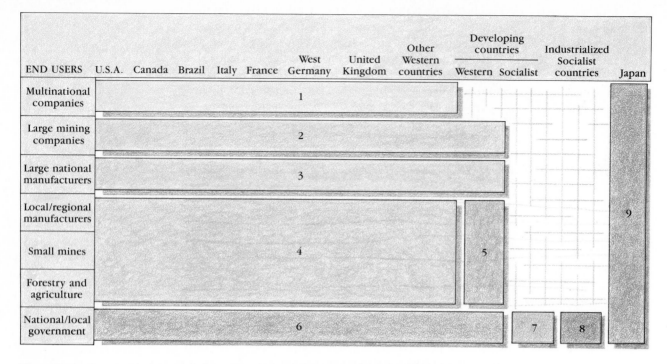

Figure 7-4 *Market segmentation by a heavy-machinery manufacturer*. This company uses multiple variables to segment the organizational market. Note that the two main variables used are countries (across the top) and types of end users (along the left side). The numbered bars illustrate segments, which are considered homogeneous groups. In most segments, the type of end user is the dominant variable. Multinational, large mining, and large national companies make up segments 1, 2, and 3, in large parts of the world. In Japan, the dominant segmentation variable is geography, across all end users. Marketing to national and local governments reveals some homogeneity across several countries (segment 6), but the developing socialist countries (segment 7) and the industrialized socialist countries (segment 8) require special programs. (From Robert A. Garda, "Strategic Segmentation: How to Carve Niches for Growth in Industrial Markets," *Management Review*, Aug. 1981, pp. 15–22. © 1981, AMACOM, a division of American Management Associations. All rights reserved.)

Product use markets can often be identified through the use of Standard Industrial Classification (SIC) and Census of Manufacturer codes (see Chapter 5). Market data are readily available by industry. Buying criteria and decision-making processes, customer size, and geographic location tend to be more homogeneous within an industry.

☐ *Buying Characteristics*

Buying characteristics used to segment organizational markets include price sensitivity, importance of service, purchasing behaviors, and type of customer business. Analyzing these factors, singly or in combination, can help marketers define clear, reachable market segments.

Realizing the waste of developing strategies for each of its 47 SIC markets, one manufacturer of electrical components regrouped its business into four market segments on the basis of shared buying characteristics (see Figure 7-6). Buyers in

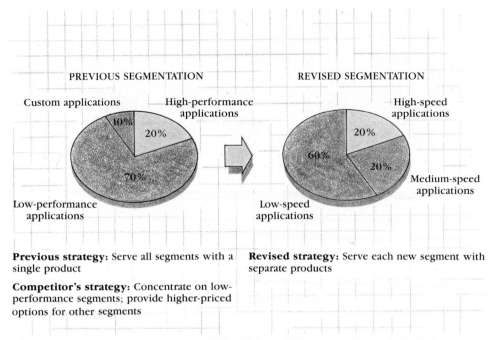

PREVIOUS SEGMENTATION

REVISED SEGMENTATION

Custom applications   High-performance applications

10%
20%
70%

Low-performance applications

High-speed applications

20%
60%
20%

Medium-speed applications

Low-speed applications

Previous strategy: Serve all segments with a single product

Competitor's strategy: Concentrate on low-performance segments; provide higher-priced options for other segments

Revised strategy: Serve each new segment with separate products

Figure 7-5 *Resegmentation through refinement of end-use markets.* In the previous segmentation, this motor marketer attempted to serve all segments with a single product. After revising the segments, the marketer offers different products for the different segments. The new strategy concentrates on the low-performance segment and provides higher-priced options for the other segments. (From Robert A. Garda, "Strategic Segmentation: How to Carve Niches for Growth in Industrial Markets," *Management Review*, Aug. 1981, pp. 15–22. © 1981, AMACOM, a division of American Management Associations. All rights reserved.)

segment A wanted standard motors and were highly sensitive to price; buyers in segment D, however, looked for nonstandard motors first and considered price second. Buyers in segments B and C fell somewhere between these extremes in the importance they attached to product features, price, quality , delivery, marketing and engineering support, and sales coverage. This new segmentation allowed the company to serve its accounts far more profitably than it could with 47 different markets to service.[15]

How purchase decisions are made constitutes another variable in segmenting by buyer characteristics. Does a multimember buying center make the decision or does a purchasing agent? Does the customer have centralized purchasing, or does it give subsidiaries and branches buying authority? Does the buyer take competitive bids? Is the bidding open or closed? Separate marketing mixes are probably in order for each of these buying situations.

☐ *Account Size*

Some marketers find the customer's size, as well as the size of its account, to be a useful basis for segmentation. Large organizations usually have fairly formal buying procedures, and the seller may face the challenge of approaching several members of a buying center. Confronting this problem and the additional task of overcoming an attitude among purchasing agents that "nobody ever got fired for buying IBM,"

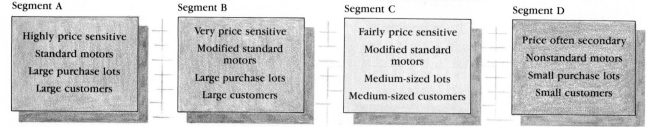

Segment A	Segment B	Segment C	Segment D
Highly price sensitive	Very price sensitive	Fairly price sensitive	Price often secondary
Standard motors	Modified standard motors	Modified standard motors	Nonstandard motors
Large purchase lots	Large purchase lots	Medium-sized lots	Small purchase lots
Large customers	Large customers	Medium-sized customers	Small customers

Figure 7-6 *Segmentation by key buying factors.* Some dimensions of customer groups are shown as examples of buying factors. An important factor in many organizational markets is sensitivity to price. Note that segments A and B are more sensitive to price than the others—and they buy primarily standard motors or modified ones. At the other extreme, customers in segment D are much less sensitive to price as a buying factor. Predictably, they are buying custom, or nonstandard, motors in fairly small quantities. Good market segmentation analysis often leads to segments that make good logical sense, as these do. (Adapted from Robert A. Garda, "Strategic Segmentation: How to Carve Niches for Growth in Industrial Markets," *Management Review,* Aug. 1981, pp. 15–22. © 1981, AMACOM, a division of American Management Associations. All rights reserved.)

Apple Computer set up a special 65-person national accounts team to woo large corporate customers.

The fund-raising staff at the Metropolitan Opera aims its efforts at four market segments, each defined by size and buying characteristics and each demanding separate marketing strategies. Three segments—corporate donors, wealthy individuals, and the federal and New York State governments—are the organization's largest customers. Corporations and individuals who contribute large sums are approached by the influential members of the Met's board of directors—an example of personal selling at its most sophisticated. Staff members prepare the grant proposals and voluminous paperwork required for government funding. Individuals who buy season and individual-performance tickets are pursued via radio and newspaper advertising prepared by the Met's advertising agency; direct marketing (mail and telephone sales) is handled by staff members and volunteers. Segmentation by account size has proved effective for the Met and its Lincoln Center sister and competitor, the New York City Opera.

☐ Geography

Because certain industries cluster geographically—microelectronics, furniture, automobiles, oil, and insurance, for example—marketers of equipment, supplies, components, and services to these industries may segment their markets by region. For example, a supplier of rough-cut hardwood for the furniture industry might treat manufacturers located in North Carolina as an independent market segment. Because geographical segmentation typically means savings on transportation and personal sales calls, it most benefits the distribution and promotion components of the marketing mix.

Multinational marketers almost always employ some form of geographical segmentation. Every nation has different laws, customs, social structures, and economic policies that demand regional adaptations in marketing efforts. Language differences can present traps for unwary marketers. Within any national market, of course, other segmentation variables come into play—account size, buying characteristics, and product use.

206

If this man is representative of the target market for stereo equipment, it is not simply because he is male and relatively young. The marketer of stereo equipment would do well to learn about his lifestyle and preferences. (Copyright © Gabe Palmer/The Stock Market.)

■ DESCRIBING MARKET SEGMENTS ■

After choosing the most appropriate variables for segmenting its markets, a marketing organization should then not only define those segments precisely but also describe them fully, considering as many factors as possible that make that segment unique. The richer the description, the more options the marketers will have in fine-tuning an effective and creative marketing mix that exploits the total potential of the segment or segments chosen.

Markets may be segmented quite simply, perhaps on the basis of a single variable such as age or sex. At other times, marketers may choose to define a market on a number of dimensions, perhaps adding lifestyle profiles to demographic, sociological, and behavioral dimensions. A targeted market segment for high-performance stereo equipment might be defined as male professionals, 24 to 36 years old, earning $25,000 to $45,000 a year, and having at least some college education who enjoy imported wines, tennis, and bridge, and who read either *Time* or *Newsweek*. Although such a description is fairly specific, marketing mix analysis and planning can be enriched and made even more useful by asking other questions that go beyond the variables chosen for segmentation.

The description of the market segment for stereo equipment just outlined might be expanded by asking questions such as what reference groups are likely to be influential for these consumers? Are certain television shows likely to appeal to this group? In what kinds of retail outlets are these men most likely to shop for the equipment? What percentage of the group live in urban areas? What percentage is married? Can other lifestyle dimensions be identified or inferred? Such questions may be almost limitless, but answers may not come so easily.

When additional questions can be answered with reasonable accuracy, practical applications of segmentation analysis can lead to innovative marketing mix design and, in turn, to measurable competitive advantage. Advertising media can be chosen with accuracy. Inspiration for promotional themes can spring from such information. Channels of distribution can be pinpointed. Prices can be fine-tuned. In short, a better marketing mix will almost assuredly follow from going beyond segmentation variables.

■ TESTING SEGMENT VALIDITY ■

Once a target market is defined and described, it should be reexamined closely. Although segments may sound quite attractive to analysts, they must withstand "reality checks." If their dimensions are accurately drawn and their descriptions are realistic, clear directions for an effective marketing mix should emerge.

Four common questions give focus to preliminary analysis of potential market behavior. The answers to these questions tell marketers if they have undersegmented or oversegmented their target markets and if they have delineated these markets correctly.

☐ Can Segments Be Measured?

Marketers must ask the very practical question of whether a dimension, or segmentation variable, is amenable to marketing research and the MKIS. For example, although a cosmetics marketer might wish to segment the market on the basis of "beauty," such segmentation is impossible since beauty is "in the eye of the beholder" and cannot be measured in any simple and objective manner. A segmentation variable *can* be measured if relevant data are already published and available (e.g., census data or data from syndicated services) or if it can be investigated through primary data collection.

☐ Can Segments Be Reached?

Marketers must have access to those in their chosen market segments through their promotion and distribution channels. People who own or know a dog will be reachable by marketers of Milkbones if they watch the same television shows, read the same newspapers, and shop in supermarkets. The essential point is that if marketers do not have a satisfactory means of *reaching* any desirable market segment, then identifying, describing, and measuring the segment has little value.

☐ Do Segments Respond Differently?

validity → act the way segment is supposed to act.

One basic test of segment validity is whether a segment requires a singular blend of product, price, distribution, and promotion—that is, its own marketing mix. If buyers in a segment respond differently to a marketing mix (or if some do not respond at all), then the segmentation or the marketing mix or both need to be changed. If two segments respond the same way to the same marketing mix, then they are probably a single segment.

We have already noted that toothpaste buyers seek different benefits and respond in different ways to marketing mixes. Advertising for Crest features children and parents who want good checkups for them; Ultra Brite commercials promise sex appeal. Obviously, segments of the overall toothpaste market respond in different ways.

Are Segments Large Enough?

To produce results, segmentation must isolate groups of sufficient size and/or purchasing power. A public television station may find that although chamber music afficionados respond to fund-raising appeals, there are too few of them to justify extensive programming of string quartets. Horror-film buffs, however, may contribute less money per person, yet so many may respond so frequently that the station may find it desirable to program 10 hours of horror films each week.

A market segment does not have to be large to be profitable; a small audience for a high-profit product may justify its own marketing mix. For example, although the market for expensive art books about individual painters is small, art book publishers such as Harry Abrams Inc. can sell elaborately designed books filled with color plates at a price high enough to make these buyers a profitable market segment. Similarly, the television networks devote many programming hours to professional golf even though the ratings for golf are rather low (and well below the ratings for other major sports telecasts). Those who watch golf tournaments on television are a very desirable segment for marketers of high-priced cars, air travel, sporting equipment, and other products because of their affluence and spending patterns. Consequently, although golf ratings are low, the networks can profitably sell the advertising time for such programming.

■ CHOOSING A COMPETITIVE SEGMENTATION STRATEGY

If segments can be measured and reached, if they respond individually, if they are large and profitable enough, then it is time to select a competitive segmentation strategy. Marketers hope to gain a competitive advantage by designing a marketing mix, including specific products or product forms, that will be as closely aligned to the needs, wants, and preferences of target market segments as possible. Marketers often think about and talk about segments using a competitive perspective ("That's the segment of the auto market in which Cadillac, Lincoln, and Chrysler compete.") In general, marketing organizations follow one of three strategies in approaching their markets: undifferentiated marketing, concentrated marketing, and differentiated marketing.

Undifferentiated Marketing

Strategists committed to **undifferentiated marketing** take the view that a single marketing mix—one price, promotional campaign, distribution arrangement, and product—can satisfy all markets. This approach emphasizes the similarities among buyers to the exclusion of their differences.

Undifferentiated marketing strategies are rare in contemporary marketing. Beer marketers used such strategies until the 1970s, when new research showed that beer drinkers had different tastes and different perceptions of the products they chose. As a result, premium and imported beers were introduced, and, more recently, light, low-calorie, and low-alcohol brews. For centuries there was just one kind of popcorn. Today market segments have been identified by popping method—over heat or in the microwave, and popcorn marketers tempt snackers with flavors that range from pizza to watermelon.

Undifferentiated marketing persists in certain service areas. The three television networks present similar evening news programs to the mass market. When the United Way launches an appeal for contributions, it seeks donations from everyone.

☐ Concentrated Marketing

After analyzing the total market, a marketer may choose to focus on a single, easily defined, profitable market segment, using **concentrated marketing** strategies. Hewlett-Packard produces only high-quality, high-performance, high-priced calculators; Harley-Davidson markets only large, high-powered motorcycles. Rolls-Royce has long catered to the wealthy, offering only a limited line of cars; Polaroid sells only instant cameras and film. Such strategies are frequently referred to as "niche" strategies, as when a firm chooses to compete in only one particular part of the market rather than competing broadly in the total market. We will discuss these marketing strategies more fully in Chapter 8.

Concentrated marketing allows a firm to establish a strong image and, in some cases, to dominate a market segment. With specialized knowledge, the marketer can respond promptly to the needs of its target audience. It can also achieve economies in production, distribution, and promotion as a result of its specialization. However, concentrated marketing can be risky. Buyers' tastes may change, leaving the marketer with a product that no one wants. Competitors can flood the market segment, thereby destroying profitability for everyone, as Kodak did for years with its instant cameras and film. The disadvantages associated with both undifferentiated and concentrated marketing have led most organizations with the requisite resources to diversify their marketing efforts.

☐ Differentiated Marketing

Differentiated marketing pursues several market segments with particular products and marketing mixes designed for the needs of each. Ramada Inns, for example, has taken a step beyond the addition of its luxury Renaissance hotel chain by

Once markets have been carefully studied and segments identified, the marketers must decide which market segments to target. One marketer, such as Canon, may choose to target many segments, following a differentiated strategy. Another, such as Mita, may choose to follow a concentrated strategy, focusing its efforts on one segment. The latter is often referred to as a niche strategy. (Canon ad courtesy of DCA Advertising; Mita, courtesy of HCM Advertising.)

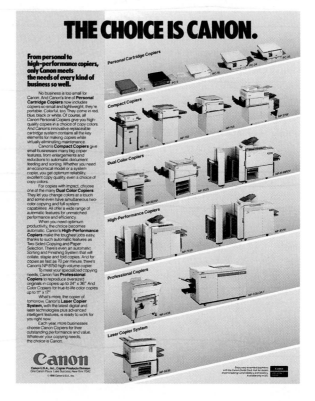

opening a chain of medium-priced Ramada Hotels—another alternative to its budget-priced Ramada Inns. According to Edward Pritchert, a Ramada vice president: "We have the Chevy, the Pontiac, and the Cadillac."

An increasing number of firms are adopting differentiated marketing strategies to increase sales (see Box 7-2). Rising sales, however, are accompanied by increasing expenditures for production, product modification, inventory, promotion, and administration. Marketers must keep an eye on profitability to prevent additional expenses from offsetting increased sales.

No one correct strategy exists for all marketing organizations. An undifferentiated approach may be best in some situations, whereas a concentrated or differentiation strategy may succeed in others.

DEVELOPING A PRODUCT-POSITIONING STRATEGY

When National Cash Register (NCR) billed itself as "the computer company" in a major ad campaign, the promotion died on the vine because everyone knew NCR as a cash register company. IBM might well have made the same claim but didn't have to—the general public already viewed IBM as "the computer company." Organizations that make and sell goods must *position* their products in the marketplace—that is, they must create an image in buyers' minds and control buyers' perceptions of their products relative to competing products. Product positioning

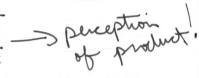
→ perception of product!

BOX 7-2   Differentiated Marketing in the Airline Industry

The airline industry is an example of a service industry which traditionally engaged in little segmentation. Many airlines operated for decades with a small first-class section and a large regular-fare section in each plane. Beyond that, there were few discount fares and only rare attempts to segment the market and target specific groups of air travelers. However, in the last decade, as industry deregulation has proceeded, virtually all air carriers have differentiated air travel service in terms of both price and level of service.

One notable attempt to reach a target market of air travelers is the Get-Up-and-Go Passport program begun by Eastern Airlines in 1983. The program was first instituted as a stop-gap measure to fill underutilized seats. Through marketing studies, Eastern realized that moving travelers into seats outside of peak demand was often difficult. However, consumers over 65 years old were found to be less restricted by normal work schedules. Consequently, for a fee of $1299, Eastern's Get-Up-and-Go program offered elderly customers an Eastern passport allowing almost unlimited travel on the airline for a year.

Eastern introduced this program before the end of

1983 with an advertising campaign on network television and in newspaper advertisements across the United States. Along with many other marketers, Eastern came to view older Americans as a highly desirable market segment for two important reasons: (1) According to the Bureau of the Census, consumers over the age of 55 have more discretionary income than any other age group. (2) By the mid-1990s the population over 55 years old is projected to rise to 56 million, constituting one-fifth of the overall population.

In the 1980s, marketers of services such as air travel and banking are increasingly turning to market segmentation and differentiated marketing strategies. Marketing experts once believed that services could not be differentiated, but this view can now be seen as little more than a "cop-out." Applying the differentiated marketing approach to services may be difficult, but the rewards will be evident for those marketers who can successfully devise and implement such strategies.

Source: "Eastern Finds a Passport to the Mature Market," *Ad Forum,* May 1985, pp. 63, 66.

---

requires that marketing managers first choose a competitive position and then a selling position.

Competitive Positioning

Deciding what a product is (and choosing a category in which it will compete) is not as easy as it appears. Yogurt marketers have wrestled for years with the problem of **competitive positioning.** Is yogurt a snack (like General Mills' Granola Bars) or a breakfast substitute (like Carnation's Instant Breakfast)? Is it a light meal (like hamburgers and sandwiches) or a dessert (like ice cream)?

Lever's Wisk liquid detergent—which removes "ring around the collar"—gained and held an advantage over Procter & Gamble's Era and Colgate's Dynamo by promoting its ability to remove tough stains. Logic might have dictated positioning the product against S. C. Johnson & Son's Shout spot remover. However, Wisk gained an early competitive advantage by building a reputation as the spot remover in the liquid laundry detergent category. This was an example of creative competitive positioning.

Selling Positioning

A **product's selling position** is the specific promotional idea used to present the product to buyers in the target market.[16] Selling concepts can be either product-oriented or buyer-oriented; both concepts keep consumer needs central and position the product against its competitors.

PRODUCT-ORIENTED POSITIONING   Some years ago, Pillsbury reformulated its line of cake mixes to include pudding for extra moistness. The new ingredient was heavily advertised by Pillsbury; it apparently had wide appeal because the market share for the reformulated cake mix doubled in many areas.

Product-oriented positioning rests on some attribute inherent in a product's makeup, packaging, use, or price. Pledge separates itself from other furniture polishes by promoting itself as a dusting aid. Butterball turkeys have a product orientation built into their brand name. The success of L'eggs pantyhose is, in part, attributable to the egg-shaped container that reinforces the brand name. The marketers who chose this uniquely shaped package were well aware of the female associations of an egg (with the reproductive process).

Perhaps the most dramatic positioning of a product was the clear distinction made by 7-Up. As a soft drink, this product was quite different from Coca-Cola and Pepsi; however, if consumers perceived 7-Up as competing with these two popular brands, it would never have been more than a poor third. Consequently, a creative marketing campaign was devised to make the public aware that 7-Up was an "uncola" so different from Coke and Pepsi that there was no competitive problem. The campaign was successful: Among the uncolas, 7-Up is the leader.

CONSUMER-ORIENTED POSITIONING   **Consumer-oriented positioning** aims at getting the consumer to perceive a product in some unique, personally related manner, regardless of the product's characteristics. Nike ran an award-winning series of print and billboard advertisements featuring young athletes who had obviously just run a race. With no ad copy and Nike's name in small letters at the bottom, the ads sought to get runners to identify Nike running shoes with appealing strivers and winners.

Long-running and effective print campaigns for Marlboro and Virginia Slims cigarettes present ideal masculine and feminine self-images rather than product

There is nothing more feminine than an egg. And, when L'eggs began its marketing effort, they astutely used the shape of an egg not only as the package for one pair of pantyhose, but also as the shape of the stand in which they are displayed. (Ken Karp.)

features. Marlboro's identity, in particular, and the way that Philip Morris continues to keep the product positioned are more important financial assets to the company than the factories where the cigarettes are made.

☐ *Analyzing Product Positioning*

In an important series of articles written in the early 1970s, advertising agency executives Jack Trout and Al Reis reflected marketing thinking about positioning.[17] Trout and Reis articulated two fundamental points. First, products are positioned against other products. Consumers compare one brand of insurance or toothpaste with competing brands. Second, the battle for competitive superiority is fought in the "6 inches of gray matter" in the buyer's head. With these thoughts in mind, marketers can analyze their existing positions and positioning plans using two tools: the **product ladder** and the **perceptual map**.

THE PRODUCT LADDER   Marketers not only want their product to be included in the evoked set of acceptable alternatives when buyers approach a purchase, they also want their product to be *high* in that evoked set. The concept of a **product ladder** put forth by Trout and Reis suggests such rankings. On the car rental ladder, Hertz occupies the top rung, followed by Avis, National, and Budget. Interestingly, Avis turned its second ranking into a competitive asset by claiming that as number two, they had to try harder. Faced with this formidable set of brand positions, any new competitor in the car rental market must find a distinctive position.[18]

In most markets, one firm sits on top, with competitors ranged below. A firm's ranking on the product ladder may not match its market share, but it does measure "share of buyers' minds." A product ladder has only a limited number of rungs— perhaps six to eight at most—because buyers keep in mind a limited number of items.

Figure 7-7 *Perceptual map of automobile brands*. A perceptual map summarizes consumers' images of various brands, as does Chrysler's map from the early 1980s. Note that all three Chrysler brands (Chrysler, Dodge, and Plymouth) were seen then as more on the "older, conservative" side than on the "youthful, sporty" side. Note also that the top-of-the-line Chrysler is seen as more "classy" than Buick or Oldsmobile but well below Cadillac, Lincoln, or Mercedes. This kind of picture helps marketers assess their current positions and gives them information to help reposition their products if they think that is appropriate. (Reprinted from "Car Makers Use 'Image' Map as Tool to Position Products," *The Wall Street Journal*, Mar. 22, 1984, p. 33, as rendered by Chrysler Corp.)

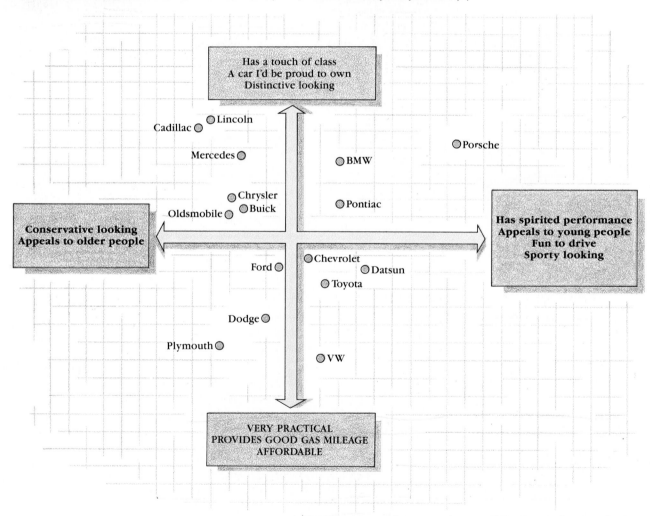

THE PERCEPTUAL MAP Among more sophisticated methods of research and analysis, the most widely used is the perceptual map. A **perceptual map** results when marketers ask a representative group of buyers within a market segment to compare brands in a certain category. Through sophisticated statistical analysis, consumers' perceptions may then be ranked in terms of product attribute—cost, taste, overall quality, and so on.

A perceptual map based on consumer surveys put together by the marketing department of the Chrysler Corporation (see Figure 7-7) shows that consumers perceive the Chrysler as luxurious—but not as luxurious as a Cadillac or Lincoln. Of more interest to General Motors than to Chrysler, the close proximity of Buick and Oldsmobile in the upper left quadrant suggests a marketing battle between these two GM divisions rather than against similar models from Ford and Chrysler.

JOHNSON'S BABY SHAMPOO
JOHNSON & JOHNSON
"Fran Tarkenton, Rev."

Length: 30 Seconds

Comm'l. No.: JJSS3747

(SFX: LOCKER ROOM)
ANNCR: (VO) Fran Tarkenton for Johnson's Baby Shampoo.

FRAN TARKENTON: You may recognize the face...Fran Tarkenton.

But the hair? Huh. This dirty even I don't recognize it.

I've got to shampoo every day ... That's a lot of shampooing.

So I use this ... Johnson's Baby Shampoo.

(VO) It's gentle.

(DV) When you shampoo as often as I do...

it doesn't make sense to use anything harsh.

An' Johnson's makes my hair look thick and healthy. But tomorrow...

(VO) It'll look like this again.

Gentle enough to use every day

(DV) Good thing Johnson's Baby Shampoo is gentle enough to use every day.

Johnson & Johnson

From Johnson & Johnson.

No More Tears shampoo was first positioned as a product for babies. Later, Johnson & Johnson repositioned it as a gentle shampoo that was good for mothers, too. This ad repositioned the product again as appropriate even for masculine athletes—here, quarterback Fran Tarkenton—who must shampoo often. The market for the product has been enlarged to multiple segments. (Reprinted with permission of Johnson & Johnson; storyboard courtesy of SSC&B Advertising.)

Even though perceptual maps plot comparative perceptions and not absolute judgments, they can guide marketers in designing new products, in efforts to change consumers' perceptions, and in reinforcing desirable images. If a new perception of a product seems necessary, the map may be used as a guide in efforts to reposition the product.

☐ *Repositioning Products*

No More Tears, a shampoo that does not sting the eyes, was formulated for babies. Realizing that gentleness might appeal to adults as well, Johnson & Johnson marketers launched a promotional campaign featuring mothers and babies washing their hair together. When a healthy share of the adult female shampoo market came its way, the company added former pro football quarterback Fran Tarkenton as a thinning-hair spokesperson. Apparently gentle hair treatment appealed to middle-aged men, too, and the company captured part of still another market segment.

Such **repositioning**—the conscious effort to change consumers' perceptions of a product—may be in order when marketers discover that a product appeals to other market segments. Other circumstances may also occasion repositioning: Shifts in taste may leave a product behind, or a successful new competitive product may necessitate the creation of a new image for an old product. In the early 1970s, for example, Sherwin-Williams' image slipped with consumers because they perceived the paint manufacturer largely as a contractor's supplier. By redoing its stores and cutting its prices, Sherwin-Williams repositioned itself to compete with home-improvement centers. Although the repositioning was costly, it paid off in increased sales and profits.

■ *SUMMARY* ■

1. Marketers use segmentation to help them put the customer ahead of the project.
2. Market segmentation allows for (1) precise market definition, (2) analysis of competition, (3) rapid response to changing market needs, (4) efficient resource allocation, and (5) effective strategic planning.
3. The steps involved in segmenting markets include (1) analyzing and describing market segments, (2) choosing a competitive segmentation strategy, and (3) developing a positioning strategy.
4. Consumer markets are typically segmented on the basis of geographic, demographic, socioeconomic, behavioral, and psychographic variables.
5. Organizational marketers employ product use, common buyer characteristics, account size, and geography as segmentation variables.
6. After identifying market segments, marketers should amplify and enrich the segment description.
7. Each proposed market segment should be tested against at least four questions: Can segments be measured? Can segments be reached? Do segments respond differently? Are segments large enough?
8. Marketers may choose among three basic competitive segmentation strategies: undifferentiated marketing, concentrated marketing, and differentiated marketing.
9. Through product positioning, marketers attempt to tie their offerings more closely to the needs of specific segments.
10. Product positioning rests on two fundamental concepts: (1) Products are positioned against other products. (2) Competitive superiority is determined in the minds of consumers.
11. Marketers sometimes attempt to reposition a product to change consumers' perceptions of the product.

☐ Key Terms

benefit segmentation
brand loyalty
competitive positioning
concentrated marketing
consolidated statistical area (CMSA)
consumer-oriented positioning
differentiated marketing
80/20 principle

market segmentation
mass marketing
metropolitan statistical area (MSA)
perceptual map
primary metropolitan statistical area
  (PMSA)
product ladder

product-oriented positioning
product positioning
repositioning
segmentation variables
selling position
target market
undifferentiated marketing

☐ Chapter Review

1. Acorn, a British marketer of personal computers, has chosen to focus its selling efforts on schools. Relate Acorn's decision to the concepts of market segmentation, target marketing, and product positioning. What advantages should Acorn realize from its decision?

2. What is the logical progression of steps in the market segmentation and product-positioning process?

3. With what criteria might marketers of American Express cards segment their markets? What criteria might an importer of Italian wines choose?

4. Continental Engineering is a Chicago-based firm that makes and installs heating, ventilation, and air-conditioning systems. Explain how Continental might segment its possible markets by geography, customer size, product use, or customer buying characteristics.

5. How can marketers go beyond chosen segmentation variables in describing a market segment?

6. Against what criteria should a proposed market segment be evaluated?

7. Give examples of situations in which a marketer might choose competitive segmentation strategies of undifferentiated, concentrated, and differentiated marketing.

8. Against what criteria should a competitive segmentation strategy be evaluated? Evaluate Volkswagen's small-car strategy against those criteria.

9. Explain the difference between product-oriented positioning and consumer-oriented positioning. How might the publishers of *Newsweek* use a perceptual map as a guide to reposition their product?

☐ References

1. "Limited Inc.: Expanding Its Position to Serve the Rubenesque Woman," *Business Week,* Nov. 22, 1982, pp. 56–58.

2. Lynn R. Kahle, "The Nine Nations of North America and the Value Basis of Geographic Segmentation," *Journal of Marketing,* vol. 50, Apr. 1986, pp. 37–47. See also Joel Garreau, *The Nine Nations of North America* (New York: Avon, 1981).

3. Ogilvy and Mather, "Ogilvy and Mather's Eight Nations of the United States," *Listening Post,* Dec. 1983.

4. Ganesau Visvabharthy, "The Elderly: Neglected Business Opportunities," *Journal of Consumer Marketing,* vol. 1, no. 4, 1984, pp. 35–46; and Hank Gilman, "Marketers Court Older Consumers as Balance of Buying Power Shifts," *The Wall Street Journal,* Apr. 23, 1986, p. 37.

5. Joe Mandese, "Study Busts Image of the Baby Boomer," *Adweek,* June 9, 1986, p. 6.

6. Valerie A. Zeithaml, "The New Demographics and Market Fragmentation," *Journal of Marketing,* vol. 49, Summer 1985, pp. 64–75.

7. "Affluence: It No Longer Means Easy Money for Marketers," *Ad Forum,* May 1983, pp. 13–18.

8. Victor J. Cook, Jr., and William A. Mindak, "A Search for Constants: The 'Heavy-User' Revisited!" *Journal of Consumer Marketing,* vol. 1, no. 4, 1984, pp. 79–81. This study

is a replication after 20 years of the classic study: Dik Warren Twedt, "How Important to Marketing Strategy Is the 'Heavy User'?" *Journal of Marketing*, vol. 28, Jan. 1964, p. 72.

9. Ruth Ziff, "The Role of Psychographics in the Development of Advertising Strategy and Copy," in William D. Wells, ed., *Life Style and Psychographics* (Chicago: American Marketing Association, 1974), p. 131.

10. John H. Mather, "No Reason to Fear 'Frightening' Reality of VALS," *Marketing News*, Sept. 13, 1985, p. 15. Many marketers still find the use of lifestyle segmentation difficult, however, and rely on demographics. See "Lifestyles: Survey Finds Advertisers Confused," *Adweek*, Sept. 30, 1985, p. 84.

11. Joseph T. Plummer, "The Concept and Application of Life Style Segmentation," *Journal of Marketing*, vol. 38, Jan. 1974, p. 33.

12. Jon Berry, "Flab Is Found in Fitness Fad," *Adweek*, June 30, 1986, pp. 1, 8.

13. Peter Doyle and John Saunders, "Market Segmentation and Positioning in Specialized Industry Markets," *Journal of Marketing*, vol. 49, Spring 1985, pp. 24–32.

14. This example was adapted from Robert Garda, "Strategic Segmentation: How to Carve Niches for Growth in Industrial Markets," *Management Review*, Aug. 1981, p. 19.

15. Ibid., p. 22.

16. These positioning definitions are adapted from F. Beavin Ennis, "Positioning Revisited," *Advertising Age*, Mar. 15, 1982, pp. M43, M46.

17. See Jack Trout and Al Reis, "The Positioning Era Cometh," *Advertising Age*, Apr. 24, 1972, pp. 35–38, "Positioning Cuts Through Chaos in the Marketplace," *Advertising Age*, May 1, 1972, pp. 51–54; "How to Position Your Product," *Advertising Age*, May 8, 1972, pp. 114–116.

18. Lore Crogran, "Positioning Alamo as a Low-Price, Quality Rental," *Adweek*, Aug. 11, 1986, p. 32D.

8

Copyright © Nick Nicholson/The Image Bank.

FORMULATING CORPORATE AND MARKETING STRATEGIES

SPOTLIGHT ON

- ☐ Basic steps in strategic management
- ☐ Strategic-planning framework
- ☐ Organizational mission statements
- ☐ Common business definition techniques
- ☐ Analysis of strengths, weaknesses, opportunities, threats
- ☐ Analysis of a company's portfolio
- ☐ Planning calendars

International Business Machines Corporation—known as "IBM" to most of us and as "Big Blue" to insiders—is the fifth largest industrial company in the United States and the eighth largest in the world. IBM's 1985 revenues were $50 billion; it employs close to 400,000 persons. These impressive statistics are only part of the story; IBM was chosen as the "Most Admired Corporation" for the first several years *Fortune* has recorded that designation.

IBM has long been the leading firm in the computer business. It plans to retain that industry leadership in the coming decades through implementation of a broad business plan set by IBM's powerful corporate management committee. This growth strategy is built around four basic concepts:

1. *Low-cost production:* IBM has made major investments in highly automated plants and equipment—more than $10 billion since 1977. Well-positioned to keep its costs down, IBM will reap the benefits of the microelectronics revolution of recent years.
2. *Low-cost distribution:* To promote its new lines of personal computers and office products, IBM has augmented its own sales force with independent distributors, mail-order catalogs, and IBM-owned retail stores. Such promotion and sales channels would have been unthinkable for the company in past years, but it has become flexible enough to expand its traditional marketing approaches.
3. *Customer-based sales force:* IBM's sales force was traditionally organized by product line: One sales representative was responsible for large, mainframe computer sales; another for sales of office machines such as typewriters and copiers; and still another for sales of small personal computers. Thus several IBM salespeople often called on the same customer. However, the firms' sales force has been restructured around the customer's needs. Consequently, one representative is now responsible for selling all IBM products to each buyer.

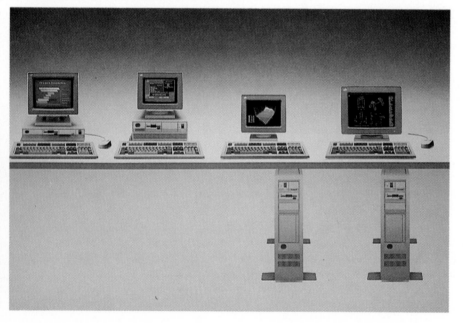

In early 1987, IBM again made a change in the personal computers competitive battle. It introduced the Personal Systems/2, with models 30, 50, 60, and 80 shown here. They made it much more difficult for competitors to produce copies, or "clones." (Courtesy of IBM.)

Planning the Marketing Program

4. *High-growth markets:* IBM views almost every area of the computer business as fair game—from desktop, personal computers to mainframe computers for large corporations and governments. Few industries have the growth potential that the computer industry does; the total computer market was estimated at $145 billion in 1985, compared to only $8.6 billion in 1975. The key to IBM's growth strategy is what chairperson John Opel calls "the limitless demand for information." According to Opel: "You can reach the point where you would prefer not ever to have another bite of watermelon. But when a business manager is dealing with a problem, he rarely reaches the point when he says, 'I don't want to know anything more about this.' "

In building its overall strategy for the 1980s and 1990s, IBM has not lost the basic marketing thrust instilled in the 1930s by founder Thomas Watson, Sr.: an overriding emphasis on customer service. The rise of Opel to IBM's top post continues the firm's tradition of elevating marketing employees to senior management. Opel began his IBM career over 30 years ago as a sales representative in his hometown of Jefferson City, Missouri. Similarly, John F. Akers, Opel's successor as president, first worked for IBM as a sales representative in rural Vermont.

Sources: "IBM: More Worlds to Conquer," *Business Week,* Feb. 18, 1985, pp. 84–98; Myron Magnet, "How to Compete with IBM," *Fortune,* Feb. 6, 1984, pp. 58–71; "The Colossus That Works," *Time,* July 11, 1983, pp. 44–54; "No. 1's Awesome Strategy," *Business Week,* June 8, 1981, pp. 84–90.

As you enter the world of higher education and consider a career, you decide on objectives and make plans to accomplish your goals. Even though you may do so only unconsciously, you probably set long-range, intermediate, and short-term goals. If, for example, your long-term goal is to become the vice president of marketing for an industrial or consumer services corporation—an admirable goal, in our opinion—you will identify particular steps on the road to that position. Your intermediate goals might include a bachelor's degree in marketing and master's degree in business administration (MBA). Your immediate (functional) goals might include successful completion of courses in consumer behavior, advertising, and statistics. In undertaking this career-planning process, you first select your long-range objective and then work backward, proceeding through the short-term steps that will eventually get you to the desired vice presidency.

Just as individuals benefit from setting and pursuing goals, so too do organizations. Virtually all marketing takes place within organizations, and the larger part of marketing emerges from business organizations. These companies may be as large and complex as IBM or as small as a neighborhood drugstore. No matter what their size, organizations need long-range strategies to shape their actions.

Setting corporate strategy is the most important responsibility of top-level executives. But the best managers do not simply dictate "marching orders" to the troops; employees at *all* levels of an organization are involved in devising strategy. In most large firms, strategy formulation takes place at three levels: headquarters (corporate strategy), division (business strategy), and department (functional strategy). The planning processes that lead to the building of these strategies may be similarly labeled as corporate planning, business planning, and functional planning.[1]

At General Motors (GM), the nation's largest business employer, corporate executives first set forth what they think GM's broad objectives should be. The top executives in each GM division (such as Chevrolet, Cadillac, and GM Trucks) then set division objectives which are consistent with the broad corporate objectives. Functional managers—such as Chevrolet's directors of marketing, production, and finance—propose objectives and goals for their functioning areas that support corporate and division plans. As we will see later in our discussion of the planning calendar, strategies at all three levels are refined in a several-stage process until they mesh into a mutually supportive and final form. Note that the overall corporate strategy is more than a marketing strategy, but that marketing is a crucial element in corporate strategy.

Chapter 8 explains why marketers should understand the processes of building corporate (top-level) strategy and why marketing is such an important part of this strategy formulation. We examine the macro environment facing goal setters in marketing organizations around the world and discuss four principles of contemporary strategic management. The bulk of the chapter describes contemporary techniques employed by managers in setting organizational objectives and in laying out strategies to meet these goals. Finally, we will see how corporate strategies direct and are translated into marketing strategies.

THE ROLE OF MARKETING IN STRATEGIC MANAGEMENT

The term "strategic management" has somewhat of a military ring, and well it should. The primary definition of strategy is the science or art of military command or large-scale combat operations. In nonmilitary terms, a **strategy** includes the major objectives of the organization and a general plan for achieving these objectives. By contrast, a **tactic** is a specific set of actions to secure the objectives set forth by a strategy.

Strategic management involves at least four steps.

In a market-driven economy, marketers follow strategies that satisfy consumers' needs. In the case of Procter & Gamble, this has led to multiple brands of laundry products, including powder and liquid versions of the same product. Most of these products can be purchased in a variety of sizes. (Ken Karp.)

1. *Analyzing* internal and external environments and market opportunities → SWOT; Portfolio
2. *Planning* corporate strategies to meet changes in environments and to exploit opportunities
3. *Implementing* such strategies
4. *Controlling* the organization's resources and capabilities to ensure competitive advantage

Admittedly, strategic management is a complex process that goes well beyond marketing, but marketers must grasp and master this critical management function. The marketing concept itself is an integral aspect of strategic management, for it provides the basic focus in the process. Indeed, successful strategic management generally puts the marketplace at the center of the system. Konosuke Matsushita, founder of Japan's giant Matsushita Electric Company, put it this way:

> Our social mission as a manufacturer is only realized when products reach, are used by, and satisfy the customer.... It is therefore vital for an enterprise to have the quickest possible information of what the customer is asking for. We need to take the customer's skin temperature daily.[2]

As a further example, look again at IBM's four objectives for the 1980s and 1990s; you will find the customer or marketplace at the center of each. No doubt IBM's marketers helped formulate those objectives and must now uphold them. Whether at Matsushita, IBM, or any other organization offering products to customers, marketers are vital in setting and managing corporate strategy for three main reasons: (1) Modern business systems are market-driven. (2) Strategic management involves teamwork from all business functions. (3) Market information is the foundation for strategic management formulation.

Market-Driven Business Systems

Since shortly after World War II, business firms have been able to produce more than the marketplace can consume. Thus, we live in a buyer's market, not a seller's market. High prices may lead you to question this assessment, yet prices would be even higher without the mass-production efficiencies brought about (at least in part) by marketing. Moreover, the range of products available to consumers in industrialized nations is enormous. Procter & Gamble alone offers 10 brands of laundry detergents: Bold, Cheer, Dash, Era, Solo, Gain, Oxydol, Tide, Dreft, and Ivory Snow.

If they wish to compete effectively, modern businesses must place the needs and wants of their target market at the center of their marketing efforts. IBM and its competitors—NCR and Digital, for example—have the technical expertise and resources to produce a wide range of computers. To attract a large share of customers from the overall marketplace, these computer firms must base their strategies on satisfaction. IBM became the industry leader not because it had superior technology but because it outmarketed its competitors.

Strategic Management and Teamwork

We noted earlier that IBM's broad strategy is set by its corporate management committee, currently a five-member group consisting of the chairperson of the board, the president, and three senior vice presidents. In modern management systems, no individual completely controls the process of formulating strategy. Rather, individuals representing various areas of expertise (such as finance, production, and legal counsel) are represented on corporate strategy committees. Any such management team will almost certainly include at least one person who represents marketing (and, by extension, potential customers). Therefore, anyone who aspires to work in the field of marketing must understand strategic management. Marketers help to establish corporate strategy, and their activities are guided by long-range corporate objectives.

Strategic Management and Information

Formal planning systems require valid, reliable information. Strategic planning is based not on hunches and guesses but on marketing research—a fact that further brings together marketing and strategic management. If a food-processing company wishes to introduce a new cracker to compete with Nabisco's brand Triskets, that processor will need to know what share of the total market Triskets commands, whether other segments of the market exist, and how consumers feel about Triskets. The primary sources of that information are the firm's marketing research department, which monitors the environments described in Chapter 2 and the marketing information system discussed in Chapter 6.

Contemporary Strategic Management

Most business firms have yet to develop true strategic management, although most firms are striving toward this goal. The concepts that characterize today's strategic management include creating a competitive advantage, a creative planning process, and a supportive value system.[3]

In the business sector particularly, competition is the norm. **Competitive advantage** is that part of the firm's total market offering which is superior to that of its competitors. Superiority may stem from a reputation for quality products (Kodak) or from an ability to offer attractive prices (Fuji).

A creative planning process is equally important. Such a process considers the perspectives and expertise of all organizational levels. People at the corporate level, at the division (or business unit) level, and at the functional level (marketing, production, finance, and so forth) must participate creatively in the planning process.

The strategic management process will flourish when there is a supportive value system. A demonstrated commitment to making things happen must exist. Communication must be free and open; opportunities and dangers facing the firm must be brought out openly in the planning process and must not be hidden. In sum, strategically managed companies display a shared belief that they can create their own futures and will not be forced into a corner by the winds of environmental change.

After years of treating formal strategic planning as though it were a magic cure for how to run an organization successfully, some experts now find it fashionable to criticize the planning process for what are really faults in people's attempts to implement it. In spite of this trend, most top managers and business managers— including those in three-fourths of the companies in the *Fortune* 500—draw on the discipline of the planning process and find it useful. We have learned, quite simply, that although strategic planning is quite valuable, it is not a panacea.[4]

The following sections explore recent developments in strategic planning methods and implementation—methods to maximize the advantages of true strategic managment. These methods will be refined in future years and new ideas will emerge. Yet refinements and new concepts will build on and incorporate the best of previous planning methods. Clearly, not all methods will work for all organizations; managers must adapt planning methods to fit their own marketplaces and environments. The analysis and planning tools that we will discuss are just that—tools. Good tools can lead to (but cannot substitute for) informed decisions and, in turn, successful strategies.

THE MISSION STATEMENT: SETTING GOALS FOR THE WORLD TO SEE

The first task of strategic planning is to develop a statement of the organization's purpose—its reason for being. Whether it is a profit-seeking business or a service-providing nonprofit agency, all organizations have missions. A **mission statement** articulates a firm's philosophy of doing business, sets forth the firm's values and social goals, and addresses the development of its employees.

In *Theory Z,* a widely read book on Japanese management practices, William Ouchi summarized the need for mission statements thus:

> ... the development of a consistent organizational philosophy must begin with an underlying set of values and beliefs that are internally consistent with each other as well as being externally consistent with the realities of the economic marketplace and the social environment.[5]

A well-conceived and well-articulated public statement of a company's broad aims and values can guide the activities of all officials and employees—from the president to the newest clerk-typist. Of course, many organizations do not have mission statements. But, as one authority remarked in describing a firm which has no such statement: "Like a ship without a rudder, this is a company without a mission. And even the most competent executive team will have trouble steering a proper course."[6]

A mission statement must offer an honest picture of a firm for the benefit of its stakeholders. **Stakeholders** are those who use the company's products or services, those who work for the firm, those who own it, and those who are affected (even indirectly) by it. In short, stakeholders include not only owners and stockholders, but also customers, employees, and the general public.

Herman Miller markets furniture for office, light manufacturing, and medical markets. The "Herman Miller Mandate," which follows in its entirety, states the company's purpose in an admirably straightforward way and spells out how it aims to serve its stakeholders:[7]

> Herman Miller must be an international organization in which people define and solve problems. Problem definition, problem solving, through innovation wherever possible, must result in products and service which improve the quality of life in the working and healing environments.
>
> At Herman Miller, people do this through having the responsibility and opportunity to contribute, to participate, to be involved, to own the problem and, indeed, to own Herman Miller.
>
> We are committed to quality and excellence in all that we do and the way in which we do it.
>
> We seek to be socially responsible and we share a concern and responsibility for the quality of the environment in which we and our neighbors live and work.
>
> Profit is an essential and enabling factor in all annual and long-range planning and operations. Specific profit goals will be set annually.
>
> Growth is implicit but must come because of the quality of the problem solution and the potential in our people and our program.

A key part of the Herman Miller mission statement is to serve their markets "through innovation wherever possible." A concrete example of that mission is the famous Eames lounge and ottoman featured here. This product, introduced in 1956, won the Triennale Prize in Milan for design in 1957 and is in the permanent collection of New York's Museum of Modern Art. But just as important to Herman Miller is the less elaborate Ergon desk chair, which ushered in an era of ergonomically designed chairs. Bill Stumpf, the designer, was named "Designer of the 70s" for this and other works. (Courtesy of Herman Miller Inc.)

Why is the "Herman Miller Mandate" such an effective mission statement? It clearly identifies the markets to be served (working and healing environments); it establishes a unique approach to serving its markets consistent with its capabilities (through innovation wherever possible); and it concisely states the basic objectives of the organization (profits, growth, social responsibility, and commitment to its employees).

■ DEFINING THE BUSINESS ■

Chapter 1 discussed Theodore Levitt's concept of marketing myopia—the failure of a company to correctly identify its business. As a consultant to major corporations, Peter Drucker has forced a number of his clients to answer the not-always-simple question, "What business are you in?" In many cases, the correct answer to Drucker's query is: "We are in a number of businesses." Almost all large corporations, most medium-size companies, and even a number of small firms are involved in multiple businesses. They offer many products and services to different groups of customers. Each of a company's businesses requires definition, strategic management, and creative marketing.

□ The Strategic Business Unit

One common business definition technique used by large firms is to separate the entire firm into more coherent business units. A **strategic business unit (SBU)** is, ideally, a single business with its own unique goal or mission, its own products or services, its own identifiable group of customers, its own competitors, its own resources, and a responsible manager. An SBU can be independently run and planned for strategically.

General Electric (GE) pioneered the SBU approach in the 1970s by mapping strategic business areas onto the most suitable units within the organization, disregarding hierarchical level and size.[8] The GE units so identified were given the SBU label. For example, GE's color television division, washer and dryer division, and airplane engine division might be considered as SBUs.

Why is it so important to define businesses and to break them down into SBUs? If we look at businesses separately, examining the problems and opportunities unique to each, we can more easily manage them strategically because:

- The environment can be closely watched.
- Competitors are known.
- Alternative scenarios are realistic.
- Strategic plans can be flexible and can be quickly adjusted.
- Marketing strategy is efficient.[9]

Overall corporate strategy succeeds or fails at the SBU level. It is at this level that strategy becomes action; it is here that the superordinate goals of the corporate mission are translated into the tactics of successful marketing.

The Product-Market Matrix

An easy way to differentiate the separate businesses that make up a large corporation is to lay out a product-market matrix. A **product-market matrix** is a visual means of defining a business by its markets and by the products directed toward those markets. A proper mesh of product and market is crucial for a clear definition of a business.

Figure 8-1 presents a product-market matrix for some of Kodak's nonconsumer businesses. (In reality, Kodak's 17 divisions offer thousands of products to hundreds of market segments.) As the figure shows, Kodak copiers are targeted to industrial firms, universities, and banks, but not to hospitals, whereas Kodak laboratory equipment is targeted to hospitals and universities. Note that Figure 8-1 is a rather simple product-market matrix. Most matrices are more complex and involve multiple factors that must be considered in laying out the boundaries of a business.

■ ANALYZING THE BUSINESS   ■

Before a firm's managers can decide what strategies they will follow, they must begin with the first management step: analysis of the existing situation. Managers must review the firm's capabilities and capacities (or lack of them). Potential operations should be considered as well as existing and potential problems. One systematic method of review is called a **SWOT analysis**—a detailed review of a firm's Strengths, Weaknesses, Opportunities, and Threats.

Strengths and Weaknesses—The Internal Examination

Any formal strategic planning process will typically begin with an examination of the organization, an internal appraisal. Managers must critically and correctly determine the firm's strengths, which should be exploited to their full advantage. Equally important are any weak points to be tackled as problems or in some way negated.

Strengths and weaknesses vary widely; one company's strengths may be viewed as a weakness in another company. For example, as we noted early in

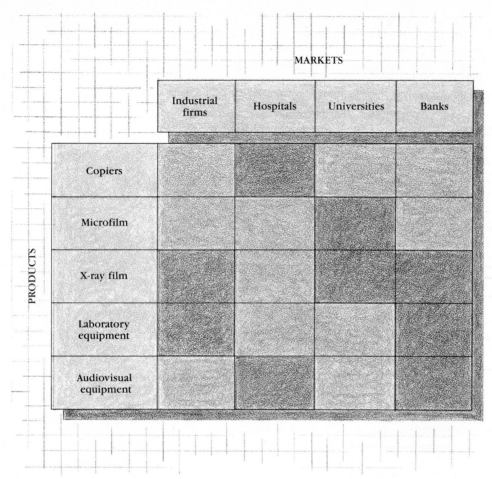

MARKETS

	Industrial firms	Hospitals	Universities	Banks
Copiers				
Microfilm				
X-ray film				
Laboratory equipment				
Audiovisual equipment				

PRODUCTS

Figure 8-1 *Incomplete product-market matrix for Kodak's nonconsumer businesses.* This simple product-market matrix represents four of Kodak's nonconsumer businesses. The blue cells in the matrix represent combinations of products and markets that are target business opportunities, such as laboratory equipment sold to hospitals and universities. The red cells represent poor fits, such as audiovisual equipment for hospitals and banks.

Chapter 1, IBM did not become the leading computer company in the world because of technological superiority. In effect, technology was a weakness at IBM; UNIVAC, General Electric, and RCA all were ahead of IBM in early computer development. But IBM focused on its major strengths: marketing and service. It grew and soon soared past its competitors by placing the customer at the center of its marketing efforts. At the same time, the company attempted to remedy its technological weakness and by the 1960s technology had joined marketing as another IBM strength.

Procter & Gamble, the giant, Cincinnati-based home and personal products marketer, has prospered by emphasizing two important strengths. First, Procter & Gamble has established an extremely strong system of distribution. In its strategic decision making, the company chooses to manufacture and market only those products that go through distribution channels where it is strong. Second, the firm supports its retailers with the largest advertising budget and efforts of any company in the world. The firm spends well over half a billion dollars per year on advertising, 90 percent of which goes to television commercials.

What weaknesses affect Procter & Gamble's marketing strategy? One crucial "weakness" is that any one of its products may be difficult to distinguish from a competitor's or even from a second Procter & Gamble product. Is Camay a "better" bar soap than Safeguard or Zest (all three are Procter & Gamble products)? Is Camay better than Irish Spring or Cashmere Bouquet (both Colgate-Palmolive soaps)? Consumers make such subjective judgments daily. Well aware that it must overcome a "weakness" in product differentiation, Procter & Gamble relies on advertising to create awareness of and preference for its brands.

A critical aspect of analyzing a firm's internal strengths and weaknesses is evaluating these strengths and weaknesses relative to something else—usually a product offered by a competitor. The Cadillac division of GM has strengths and weaknesses relative to Mercedes, Audi, and the Lincoln Continental.

☐ *Opportunities and Threats—The External Examination*

Just as companies must look internally for strengths and weaknesses, they must look externally to the environment for opportunities and threats. Most opportunities and threats evolve from (1) changes in the demographic, economic, political and legal, and cultural environments discussed in Chapter 2; (2) changes in the competitive environment, such as a technological breakthrough by a competitor; or (3) events that may or may not be under the company's control, such as a strike by the work force or a serious fire in an industrial plant.

The OPEC oil embargo of 1973 represented a threat to the U.S. automobile industry, which was primarily producing large, fuel-inefficient cars at that time. By contrast, the oil embargo represented an opportunity for manufacturers such as Toyota, Nissan, and Volkswagen. *Xerography,* the photocopying process that uses

Weather can be one of the most difficult threats to predict. A retail store in the north will suffer if heavy snows keep shoppers bundled up in their homes. That same snowfall, however, may be an opportunity to the maker of snowplows, or to catalog merchants from whom consumers can buy without leaving their homes. (Copyright © David F. Hughes 1983/The Picture Cube.)

ordinary paper, was a technological breakthrough and an opportunity for Xerox. But it was also a threat to Thermofax, whose copying machines required special, heat-sensitive paper.

An industrial strike obviously represents a serious threat to a firm if its operations are shut down for any significant time. Interestingly, for television production companies, the 1981 strike of television writers provided an opportunity to release a backlog of already produced films. The hardest environmental events for marketers to monitor are those in the physical environment. A winter of unpredictably low snowfall will pose a threat to producers of snowmobiles but offers an opportunity for manufacturers of lightweight jackets.

■ ANALYZING THE PORTFOLIO OF BUSINESSES AND PRODUCTS ■

General Mills is usually considered a food-processing company. The Minneapolis-based firm makes cereals (Cheerios and Wheaties), mixes (Bisquick and Betty Crocker), and flour (Gold Medal). In addition, General Mills produces yogurt (Yoplait), frozen seafoods (Gorton's), and a bagful of other packaged foods. However, food processing does not tell the whole story about General Mills. It owns restaurants (Red Lobster) and specialty retailing operations (Talbots and Eddie Bauer). These are only some of the companies and products that fall under the impressive General Mills umbrella.

What business, then, is General Mills in? Like many large corporations, General Mills is in a number of businesses. Its businesses and products constitute a **portfolio**—a collection of businesses owned and managed by a parent corporation. Top-level managers at General Mills, like their counterparts at other multibusiness firms, must analyze each business before they can devise an overall strategy for the entire company. Before these managers decide, for example, to invest in more restaurant chains and to cut back investments in clothing and accessories, they will need to closely examine each business.

Analysis of the businesses in a portfolio typically focuses on such factors as the market share each business holds, the growth rate (or industry attractiveness) of the market, and the strength of the business relative to its competitors.

☐ *Analyzing Growth and Share*

In 1963, Bruce Henderson started a management consulting firm that came to be known as the Boston Consulting Group (BCG). Henderson, who had previously worked for Arthur D. Little Inc., established himself initially as a one-person, general consulting operation. However, he quickly and perceptively concluded that businesses were confusing 5-year budget forecasts with long-range planning; as a result, he decided to specialize in strategic planning. We will draw on Henderson's insights in the following sections as we examine the importance of market growth and market share in long-term planning.

RELATIVE MARKET SHARE Henderson's work involved the study of a large number of industries and individual companies. He devoted particular attention to the **relative market share** held by competitors in an industry. A firm's relative market share (RMS) can be calculated based on the following equation:

$$\text{Relative market share} = \frac{\text{your firm's market share}}{\text{your largest competitor's market share}}$$

Unlike the concept of plain market share (MS), RMS tells you how your firm stands relative to its competitors. For example, you may hold a 30 percent MS in a highly fragmented industry (e.g., beer production) and be the leader, while your closest rival has a MS of only 5 percent. In this case, your RMS is $30 \div 5 = 6$. By contrast, if you hold a 30 percent MS in a highly concentrated industry (such as large mainframe computers), your main rival might have 60 percent of the market. Your RMS might then be $30 \div 60 = 0.50$. As these two examples illustrate, a 30 percent market share can have quite different meanings, depending on your *relative* market position within the industry.

Henderson emphasizes that a firm with a large share of the market *relative to its largest competitors* enjoys a number of substantial advantages. Central among these is the cost advantage held by the dominant firm because it produces and markets a larger volume of products. This concept, which Henderson labeled the "experience curve," suggests that the cost advantage occurs because the larger competitor has had more experience than smaller-share competitors.

The **experience curve** concept states that the costs tend to decrease at a rate described by the slope of the curve. A flat curve would indicate slow cost reduction, whereas a steep curve would indicate rapid cost savings. A particular curve, for instance, could mean that costs would drop 20 percent for every doubling of the firm's *cumulative* experience. For a young, rapidly growing industry such as fiber optics, that 20 percent reduction might occur in 1 year. A highly mature industry, such as vacuum cleaners, might need 10 years to accumulate the same savings.[10]

→ scale economies

The cost advantage resulting from a high RMS permits the dominant firm to lower its prices, thereby making it more difficult for the higher-cost, lower-share competitor to price competitively. Alternatively, the dominant firm can hold prices up and make greater profits, which it can then spend on marketing efforts to raise its market share still higher. Underlying Henderson's experience curve theory is his conclusion that acquiring a dominant share of the market will improve company

John F. Welch, Jr., chairperson and chief executive at General Electric (GE), has bluntly informed managers in each of the company's more than 200 businesses that they must achieve the first or second ranking in their respective industries. If not, GE is likely to divest itself of the business and invest its resources elsewhere. Welch is not making idle threats; in recent years, GE has sold more than 75 businesses worth more than $5 billion.

Welch's dominate-or-die philosophy is gaining wider acceptance among marketing experts. According to this view, correct positioning of a product is essential, since in most markets only the top few competitors can maintain long-term profitability. "My theory is that in the old days you could make money as number three or four," notes Marc Particelli of the management consulting firm of Booz, Allen & Hamilton. "Now it's only one and two (that can be profitable)."

A recent study conducted at the Harvard Business School and supervised by Larry Light, an executive vice president of Ted Bates Advertising, offers solid evidence to support this rather pessimistic conclusion. Researchers studied confidential market share and profitability information supplied by about 250 companies running approximately 2000 business units. On average, according to the data compiled in the survey, a market leader holds a 38 percent market share and shows an after-tax return on investment of 17.9 per-

cent. The second-ranked brand controls 21 percent of the market and produces an after-tax return on investment of 2.8 percent. Number 3 in an industry holds a 12 percent market share but has negative after-tax return on investment of −0.9 percent; for number 4, the figures are 6 percent market share and −5.9 percent return on investment. Light concludes that market *rank* rather than market *share* is the critical determinant of brand profitability. He adds that "one is wonderful, two is terrific, three is threatened, four is fatal."

A number of factors have combined to increase the pressure on second-tier brands. Stockholders may not be satisfied with a respectable but less-than-spectacular return on investment. Retailers—bombarded by a proliferation of brands—may be reluctant to stock any but the industry leaders. Moreover, with the rise of computerized systems such as the Universal Product Code scanner, many retail outlets (among them supermarkets) are immediately aware of which brands are selling and which are not.

Clearly, in a business environment which is increasingly difficult for even the third- and fourth-ranked brands, proper positioning must be a central element in strategic planning and implementation. ▪

Source: Dick Stevenson, "One, Two, Three or Out: Brand Rank Is Everything," *Ad Forum,* Feb. 1985, pp. 22–23, 25, 27.

performance (see Box 8-1). Research indicates that a major financial objective, return on investment, is correlated with relative market share, although not perfectly.[11] We will discuss the experience curve in more detail when we analyze pricing decisions in Chapter 16.

THE GROWTH-SHARE MATRIX Henderson and BCG developed a second analytical tool: the **growth-share matrix.** This matrix attempts to explain how market share, market growth, and cash flows relate. In this second step of portfolio analysis, managers must decide whether their SBUs are in high-, medium-, or low-growth markets. Of course, what is defined as "high" or "low" will differ from industry to industry. In the electronics industry, a growth rate of less than 15 percent per year is probably low. By contrast, in the beer and cigarette industries (which are considered mature), a growth rate of 5 percent is viewed as high.

Using market share and growth rate, BCG developed a four-quadrant matrix that has become a widely used analytical tool in strategic planning. Figure 8-2 presents a hypothetical company's business displayed on the BCG model. The vertical axis represents growth rate; the horizontal axis represents relative market share. Growth rate is shown from 0 to 30 percent with 15 percent as an arbitrary dividing line between high and low growth. The dividing line on the horizontal

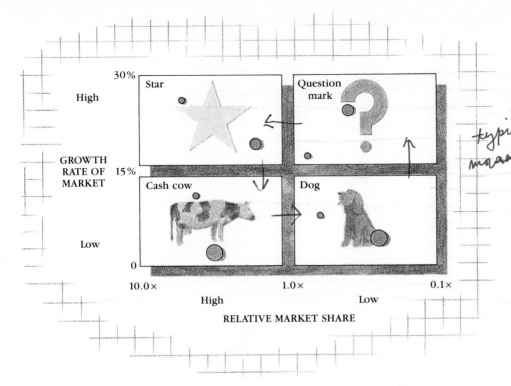

Figure 8-2 *Boston Consulting Group's growth-share matrix*. One chart captures the general assessment of the firm's various strategic business units (SBUs), or product lines, in terms of their competitive position (relative market share) and their attractiveness for the future (growth rate of the market). The size of the circles representing the SBUs are proportional to the SBU's yearly sales.

axis is a 1.0 relative market share. This figure conveniently divides leaders from followers, since, in any industry, only one firm can have an RMS higher than 1.0. Managers are asked to place each of the company's SBUs or product lines in one of the four quadrants. The size of the circles representing each SBU in Figure 8-2 are proportional to the SBU's yearly sales.

Each quadrant has been given a name that conveys a great deal about each SBU. SBUs falling into the lower left square of Figure 8-2 have been designated as "cash cows." **Cash cows** are dominant (high relative market share) and mature (slow-growth) businesses that require minimal reinvestment and can contribute funds for other, growing businesses in the company. Examples of cash cows are Kodak's dominant position in the marketing of consumer film, GE's light bulbs, and Kimberly-Clark's Kleenex tissues. Note that the label "cash cow" is by no means negative: cash cows must be managed as carefully and creatively as businesses in the upper left square—the "stars."

Stars are a company's big winners—businesses that hold high relative market shares in high-growth markets. Examples are IBM's dominance of the personal computer market and Disney's amusement parks. Like cash cows, stars produce large amounts of cash. Unlike cash cows, however, stars typically require large reinvestment and extensive promotion to grow (or even maintain) their market shares. As their businesses mature, stars are expected to eventually become cash cows.

In the lower right square of Figure 8-2 are those businesses known as "dogs." **Dogs** have low relative market shares in markets with low-growth rates. American Motors would be considered a dog in everything but its Jeep business; other dogs include Magnavox television sets and Dutch Boy paint. In these negatively labeled businesses, astute management is essential. One option for managers is to carve out small market segments (or niches) in which these businesses may dominate and be profitable.[12] Some managers simply allow dogs to run their course without any new investment to "harvest" the profits. Or they may decide to sell off the company's dogs.

The final quadrant, the upper right square in Figure 8-2, is reserved for businesses with a low market share in high-growth industries. This investment almost always represents a gamble; consequently, the names given to businesses in this square ("question mark," "problem child," "sweepstakes," and "wildcats") reflect their uncertain futures. Examples of **question marks** include Polaroid's floppy disks, Zenith's videocassette recorders, and Lean Cuisine's frozen dinners. Typically, question marks require large cash inflows to assist growth or maintenance, yet their ability to generate cash is questionable. Such businesses may increase their market shares, move left on the quadrant, and become stars. Or their marketing strategies may not work, their market shares decline, and they become dogs.

Unfortunately, the terms "dog" and "question mark" are often seen as negative. Some people even assume that the businesses in these quadrants are neither profitable nor attractive. There are, of course, "sick dogs," whose entire industry is in decline and a firm other than the leader *is* losing money. But there are just as many examples of "golden dogs," businesses in which competitors other than the leader are quite profitable (refer back to Box 8-1). As for question marks, some certainly will not succeed, but others will.

☐ *Portfolio Strategy*

The BCG growth-share matrix is intended to provide managers with an overview of their business portfolios. Such matrix analysis offers top-level managers certain directions for strategy and for improving both the mix of their businesses and the corporation's cash flow.[13] As an example of strategy implementation, let us now examine certain moves made by Philip Morris, a company whose fortunes have risen dramatically in the last 30 years. Philip Morris grew in sales from $400 million in 1957 (with $17 million in profits) to over $10 billion in 1984 (with $888 million in profits)—even though the firm's main product, cigarettes, was under attack for reasons of health. Our discussion of Philip Morris focuses on five strategic actions identified by the BCG: to build, to acquire, to hold, to harvest, and to divest.

BUILD   *Building* is a strategy generally applied to stars and question marks, the goal being to increase RMS and turn the question mark into a star or to maintain

In managing a portfolio of products, companies use monies generated by mature brands, like Miller's High Life, to fund newer and faster growing brands like Miller Lite. As Miller Lite matures, it can fund the growth of even newer products in the Philip Morris product portfolio. (Photos courtesy of Miller Brewing Company.)

the star's dominant position. This typically requires heavy investments in the business.[14] In the early 1960s, Philip Morris was the smallest of the nation's six major tobacco companies. Today, it is the leader. Through massive advertising (featuring a ruggedly handsome cowboy), Philip Morris and its advertising agency, McCann-Erickson, built Marlboro into the top-selling brand of cigarettes in the United States.

After acquiring the Miller Brewing Company in 1970, Philip Morris's chief executive, Joseph Cullman, III, sent John A. Murphy to Milwaukee to build the company then ranking seventh among U.S. brewers. Murphy did just that—again with the help of McCann-Erickson. By 1975, Miller had moved into fourth place; in that year, Miller introduced a higher-priced but lower-calorie beer, Miller Lite. By 1979, Miller beer itself was the second best–selling brand and Miller Lite was fourth. Even though Miller's sales leveled off in the mid-1980s, its important market share had been well-established through wise investments and strategic moves by Philip Morris.

ACQUIRE *Acquiring,* often an alternative strategy to internal development, happens when managers decide that a certain business is attractive and pursue acquisition of a firm competing in that market. The most likely targets for acquisition are other companies' question marks that can potentially be built into stars.

Just as Philip Morris acquired Miller to diversify its portfolio (and reduce its dependence on the cigarette business), it paid more than $500 million in 1978 to acquire the country's third-selling (at that time) soft drink company, 7-Up. Philip Morris hoped to "build" this acquisition against the market leaders, Coca-Cola and Pepsi, but found the marketing skill and greater knowledge of Coke and Pepsi to be difficult obstacles.

HOLD *Holding,* a strategy best suited for healthy cash cows, is basically a defensive posture in which businesses aim to retain relative market share and keep the cash cows generating large cash flows for use in other businesses. Currently, Philip Morris could be said to be using a holding strategy for its market-leading Marlboro brand while it seeks to build its Merit brand in the low-tar and ultra-low-tar segments of the market. At the same time, Miller's success is funding efforts to build market share for its premium label beer, Lowenbrau.

HARVEST *Harvesting* is generally applied to cash cows and dogs to cut costs and reduce product promotion while generating cash. In the long run, harvesting may kill off the business, yet management may determine that this is the best available option, as Philip Morris seems to have done with one of its dogs: its house-named, unfiltered cigarette, Philip Morris. (Have you seen any Philip Morris ads lately?) The same harvesting strategy could someday be applied to Marlboros.

DIVEST *Divesting* involves getting rid of a business in the most advantageous way. Usually applied to dogs, such a strategy can also be applied to question marks if management believes that other businesses represent better opportunity and use of cash. In 1986, Philip Morris divested itself of 7-Up, a golden dog it had acquired in 1978. The Dallas company that bought it had recently bought Dr. Pepper.

Divesting should not be viewed as an inherently negative strategy or as an admission of failure. A corporation may simply decide to concentrate on those businesses that it knows best. Even with dogs, however, there are alternatives to divesting.[15]

Strengths and Weaknesses of Portfolio Analysis

Portfolio analysis using the BCG growth-share matrix has been applied widely long enough to develop its supporters and critics. On the positive side, the growth-share matrix is simple and graphic, and employs measurable criteria for judgment. This approach allows management to view its businesses or product lines as interdependent parts of a total company. Managers can decide to shift resources away from businesses that are slow in growth (cash cows) or in a weak market position (dogs). These resources can be shifted to question mark businesses, fueling their growth in the hope of making them stars. Alternatively, the resources can be used for research and development operations that may create new products or businesses—the question marks and stars of the future.

On the negative side, many managers feel that the BCG approach is too simple and is not rich enough in its analytical dimensions. A measure of relative market share (the horizontal axis) is really an attempt to assess business strength or the ability to compete. Although relative market share is clearly an important element in defining competitive strength and power, it is not the only one. Similarly, a measure of market growth (the vertical axis) is really an effort to communicate a market's overall attractiveness. For certain companies, some high-growth markets may not be good investments because the firm has no expertise in the market. For example, even though personal computers are currently seen as a high-growth market, it would make little sense for a drugstore chain to add a line of small computers. Customers would not expect to find computers in a drugstore, and employees probably would not know how to sell them.

Another important drawback to the BCG approach is that the assumptions of the experience curve concept do not always hold true. That is, the firm with the largest relative market share may not always be the lowest-cost producer. Later entries into certain markets may be able to purchase more efficient automated equipment than the dominant firm and therefore may have lower costs.

Finally, the strategies that BCG-type portfolio analysis suggests are all rather high-level—what might be called "strategic thrusts." Actions such as building, acquiring, holding, harvesting, and divesting best suit top-level management's resource allocation strategies. Such indicators provide little guidance to division-level managers as to *how* they should build, harvest, and so forth. According to one critic, "though companies have found the matrices useful in helping them think more clearly about their existing businesses, the grids don't suggest ways to find new 'stars.' "[16]

■ INDIVIDUALIZED PORTFOLIO TECHNIQUES ■

In response to criticisms of the BCG approach, other thinkers and firms have developed newer **individualized portfolio techniques.** These new techniques throw out neither the insights of the BCG growth-share matrix nor the basics of strategic planning that have evolved over the years. Rather, individualized portfolio techniques build and expand on these earlier concepts, refining and adding analytical factors to make portfolio analysis both more sophisticated and more useful to managers.

The General Electric Business Screen

Managers and consultants at General Electric—building on the BCG growth-share matrix—have developed a technique, called the **GE business screen,** that includes *multiple* measures of competitive strength and market attractiveness. This approach still assigns a business a place on a matrix, but the measures used in assigning matrix positions are more complex than in the BCG model. Relative market share and market growth rate are retained as underlying bases for judgment and analysis, but other factors are also considered in evaluating an SBU's business strength.

Figure 8-3 presents the GE business screen and lists some of the factors considered in determining a business's location on the matrix. For example, a number of factors come into play on the vertical axis (market attractiveness): total market size, market growth rate, profit margin, competitive intensity, cyclicality, seasonality, scale economies, and company match or appropriateness. On the horizontal axis, business strength is measured by relative market share, price competitiveness, product quality, knowledge of customers and markets, sales effectiveness, and geography.

Figure 8-3 *General Electric's business screen.* Note that the size of the circles on the screen reflects the relative sizes of each business's sales. This method of portfolio planning improves on the BCG approach by providing a richer picture of business or competitive strength (including but not limited to relative market share) and a richer assessment of attractiveness of the market (including but not limited to market growth rate).

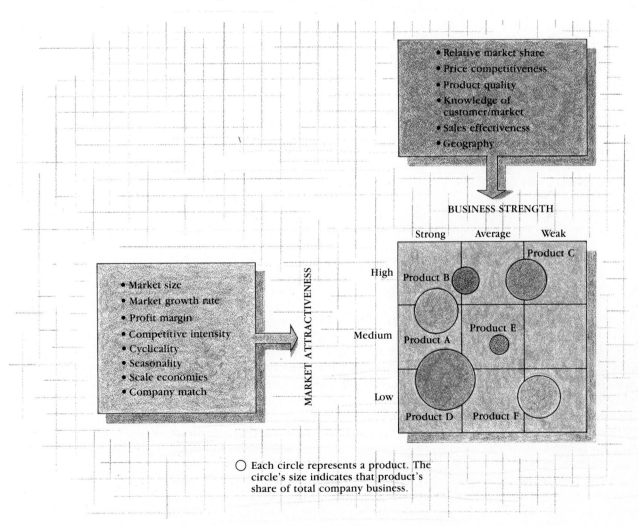

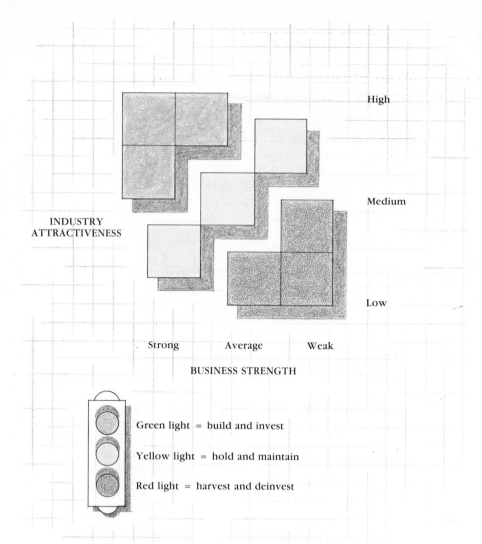

High

Medium

Low

INDUSTRY
ATTRACTIVENESS

Strong   Average   Weak

BUSINESS STRENGTH

Green light = build and invest

Yellow light = hold and maintain

Red light = harvest and deinvest

Figure 8-4 *GE business screen stoplight categories.* When managers of individual strategic business units (SBUs) propose that the corporation invest funds in their unit, the presumption is that they will get a "green light" or "go" signal if their unit is in the upper left segment of the portfolio (and therefore measures well on industry attractiveness and business strength). If the unit is in the lower right, low in both attractiveness and strength, the answer is likely to be a "red light." A strategy of caution, such as holding and maintaining, is recommended for SBUs in the middle boxes of the screen.

Managers using individualized portfolio techniques like the GE business screen must first decide which factors are useful to include—all companies will not find the same ones useful. Then, they must weight each factor's relative importance—advertising would be more important to Procter & Gamble than to a marketer of steel such as USX. Finally, managers must rate how each business stands on each factor. Combining all the results places the business in the portfolio.

The GE business screen takes an additional step by separating the cells in the matrix into groups somewhat analogous to the cash cows, stars, dogs, and question marks of the BCG growth-share matrix. Figure 8-4 illustrates the GE model, which uses the signals of a stoplight: red, yellow, and green. The three cells at the upper left—areas where industry attractiveness is high and business strength is growing—are designated as green-light businesses. Recommended strategy here is to invest and seek growth. The three cells stretching diagonally from the lower left to the upper right represent the yellow, or caution, area. Common strategy here will be to hold and maintain market share; any major investments should be viewed with caution. Finally, the three cells in the lower right represent the red, or danger, area. Businesses in this area are in relatively unattractive markets and have limited business strength. Suggested strategy here is to harvest, divest, or carve out a profitable niche.

☐ *The Benefits of Customized Portfolio Analysis*

The GE business screen and other individualized approaches go further than the BCG growth-share matrix and add considerably to the richness and complexity of portfolio analysis. BCG's approach is "generic"—all firms employing this approach use relative market share as a measure of business strength and market growth as the indicator of market attractiveness. By contrast, the GE business screen approach is "customized"—each company's management team selects its own dimensions for study and assigns its own weights.

Individualized approaches do not have the simplicity nor the clear numerical standards of the BCG analysis. Managers must make *qualitative* assessments of factors contributing to industry attractiveness and business strength and of the factors' relative importance. However, the benefits derived from the creative and interactive aspects of such analysis outweigh the loss of fully quantitative measures and of some degree of specificity.

Managers benefit from individualized portfolio analysis because it provides concrete steps to be implemented. If product quality is the factor that is eroding business strength, then upgrading of product quality can become a priority. If the effectiveness of the sales force is in question, then measures can be taken to improve training programs and supervision. Individualized analysis points to many changes that managers can undertake to improve their businesses, such as selecting a new advertising agency to get a fresh creative approach, reexamining pricing strategy, or using physical distribution as a strategic weapon.[17]

While individualized portfolio techniques provide rich descriptions of the attractiveness of markets and of the company's business strength, they also require that managers have the skill to make qualitative judgments about a host of factors that determine those key dimensions. (Copyright © Dario Perla 1983/International Stock Photo.)

SETTING STRATEGY: TOP–DOWN AND BOTTOM–UP

Good strategic planning is always a two-way process. Top-level management is charged with the high-level decisions: to invest in a question mark, to harvest a cash cow, or to get rid of a dog. Such strategic decisions flow downward from the top level to the division level and eventually to functional-level management. The same downward flow of strategy occurs when the manager of a business—for example, a vice president—works with a functional management team to articulate strategies and plans for carrying out the mission of the SBU. Similarly, a functional manager—for example, the director of marketing—uses such guidance from higher levels in working with a team of marketing specialists in advertising, sales, marketing research, and other areas to develop plans for carrying out strategies.

At the same time, to inform these strategic decisions at the top, information must flow upward from people involved in the marketplace. Top-level management may require plans to be drafted at the functional level before, concurrent with, or after the drafting of overall strategies. Planning takes place at all levels; a coordinated flow of information up and down the management ladder is essential.

Figure 8-5 shows a typical organization chart for a large firm. This chart is drawn as a series of overlapping triangles for two important reasons. First, all persons in each triangle are involved as a team in the planning undertaken at their level. Planning must be viewed as a team or group process involving the participation and commitment of all members. Second, the vice president and the director of marketing are both members of two triangles or teams. Each is a member of one planning team and the leader of another. Consequently, these two managers are vital links in the communications flow of the planning process.

In large diversified companies, long-range planning is a complex and thus a necessarily formal process. Careful coordination is required to ensure that the strategies resulting from top-down and bottom-up information flow are internally consistent. Because of the complexity of the formal planning task, many corporations maintain separate planning staffs who work with and assist managers at each level. Some companies have gone as far as to establish a corporate vice presidency for planning. At the same time, as we show in Box 8-2, small businesses also engage in and benefit from effective planning.

THE PLANNING CALENDAR

Typically, a complete and new set of corporate strategies is not developed every year, but some major objectives and strategies *will* change annually. In general, a long-range plan is laid out for 3, 5, 7, or more years. In the intervening time, business performance is measured against the plan. Adjustments are made as new opportunities or threats appear in the environment. Strategically managed companies will reexamine overall strategy each year in light of the mission statement. Do they still mesh? Does the mission statement still guide the company? Has there been satisfactory progress toward meeting long-range goals? These questions must be asked annually, yet sound strategies will carry the firm for several years.

The process of long-range planning requires specific goals in and of itself: Assignments are made, due dates are established, and arrangements for coordinating the efforts of different management levels are laid out. A **planning calendar** provides a time frame for planning with target dates for initial and revised goals for

240   Planning the Marketing Program

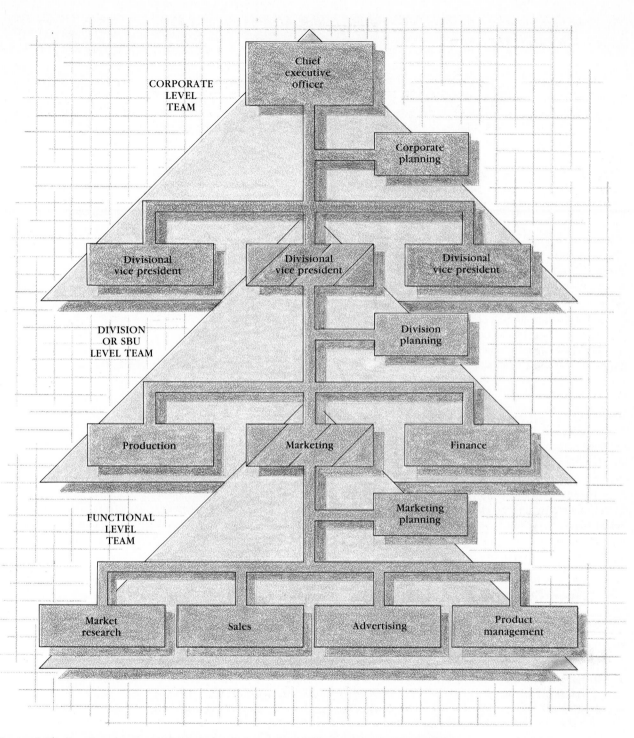

Figure 8-5 *Overlapping teams in the planning process.* Like many business activities, strategic planning is conducted in groups. At the corporate level, the chief executive officer works with a team of divisional managers, each of whom is the leader of a division or unit team of the various functional groups in the division. Each member of the divisional team, including the chief marketing manager, leads still another team at the functional level.

each organizational level involved. Figure 8-6 depicts a planning calendar for a diversified corporation.

Three cycles, covering a period of several months and the interaction of three levels of management, characterize this planning calendar. Top-level management first sets forth corporate objectives which are quite general and broad. Examples might be "grow the video business at an annual rate of 15 percent for each of the next 3 years," "acquire a small, high-technology laboratory instrument company," or "expand banking operations in the Middle East."

Such objectives are examined for practicality at the divisional or SBU level. A star would probably have no problem with an objective of 15 percent annual growth; the manager of a cash cow might express reservations about this goal. However, a corporate objective of improving cash flow might fit in nicely with the capabilities of a cash cow, whereas giving more cash back to the corporation might hurt the efforts of an expanding star. Managers at the divisional level propose goals for their SBUs that are then tentatively approved by corporate management. Indeed, top managers may wish to encourage creative proposals from below in a spirit of **intrapreneurship,** a new business term meaning internal entrepreneurship.[18]

In the second planning cycle, functional departments within divisions—marketing, production, finance, personnel—lay out departmental strategies to meet the goals established in the first cycle. Often these strategies are expressed in the form of alternatives. For example, if corporate strategy called for improved cash flow, the marketing department of an SBU might propose improving cash contribution by (1) raising prices, although market share might drop, or (2) holding prices, investing more in advertising, and boosting sales. These proposals flow back up through the division and to the corporation for approval of one of the alternatives. When strategies, objectives, and goals are approved at all three levels—frequently after some revision and compromise—the third planning cycle begins.

In the final cycle, budgets are called for at the divisional and departmental levels that will allow those units to accomplish the agreed-upon objectives. Again, a back and forth process of negotiation is usually required to match financial resources and strategic objectives. Approved budgets become the quantitative measures against which divisions and departments will be measured and by which they will be controlled. Planning is over (at least for a while), and action begins.

FROM CORPORATE STRATEGY TO MARKETING STRATEGY

Chapter 8 has examined how corporate strategy is developed. Marketing seemingly may have played a secondary role as we have looked at the evolution of business planning. The reason for this rather detailed picture of strategic management is simple: To understand the formulation of marketing strategy and, in turn, the detailed operational plans of a marketing mix, it is necessary to understand the total corporate strategy into which marketing strategy and tactics fit.

Business marketing departments do not take actions in the marketplace; entire firms take action. Another way of saying this is that marketing departments carry out some of the firm's actions, but they do so under the direction of the firm. Marketing actions are an important part—but only a part—of the firm's actions.

Strategic management ensures coordination and consistency across all the firm's operations. Horror stories abound about companies where management failed to place all departments on the same strategic track. Manufacturing divisions have planned production cutbacks at the same time that an advertising group planned a new campaign to increase sales. Marketing groups have cut prices to meet competition while a financial group laid out a budget based on income at the higher price. Few companies can afford such embarrassing errors.

Yet the goal of strategic management is not simply to avoid errors; seeking and seizing business opportunities is even more important. The definition of strategic management presented at the beginning of this chapter deserves another look. Strategic management is the process of (1) *analyzing* the corporation's environment and business opportunities, (2) formally *planning* to meet changes in that environment and to exploit opportunities through corporate strategies, (3) *implementing* such strategies, and (4) *controlling* the firm's resources and capabilities to ensure competitive advantage. Strategic management pursues these four activities with an eye toward the firm's healthy future.

Although marketing is but one arm of business strategy, it is undoubtedly the most visible and arguably the most important. It is no exaggeration to suggest that marketing strategy is at the heart of effective management strategy. Recall the words of Peter Drucker, "the purpose of a business is to create a customer."

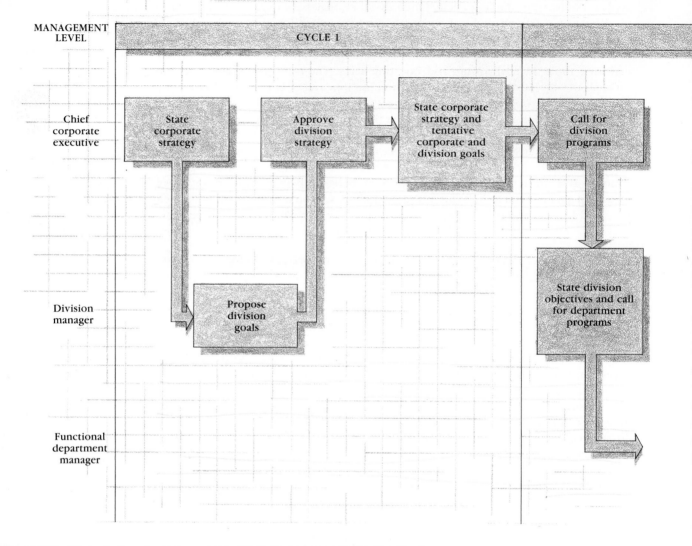

Figure 8-6 *Steps in the planning process*. Strategic and operational planning is a process of considerable importance. A number of organization levels become involved as the process works itself down, then up, then down again. Careful specification of who does what at each stage is frequently referred to as the "plan to plan." Cycles 1, 2, and 3 are described in the text.

◼ SUMMARY ◼

1. Strategic management involves at least four steps: (1) analyzing the internal and external environments and market opportunities, (2) planning corporate strategies to meet changes in environments and to exploit opportunities, (3) implementing such strategies, and (4) controlling the organization's resources and capabilities to ensure competitive advantage.

2. Strategic planning is based on market research and thus helps bring together marketing and strategic management.

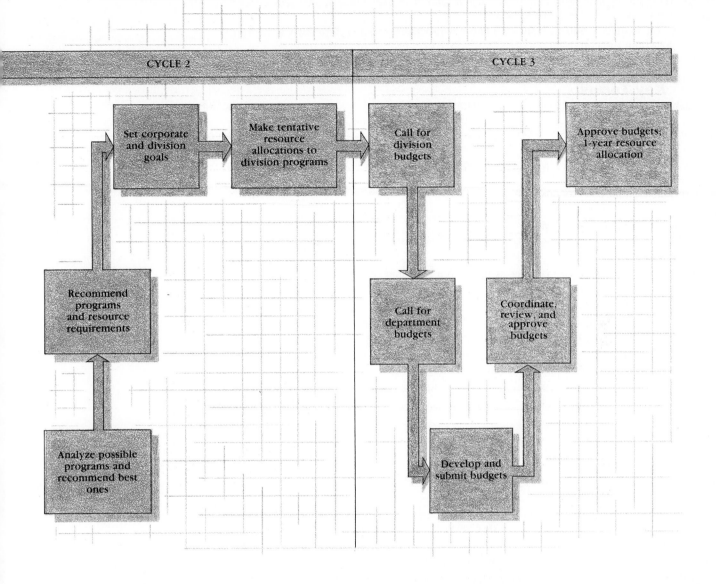

3. The first tool of strategic planning is a mission statement expressing the organization's superordinate goals.

4. Overall corporate strategy succeeds or fails at the strategic business unit level.

5. An easy way to differentiate the separate businesses that make up a large corporation is to lay out a product-market matrix.

6. Any formal strategic planning process will include an internal appraisal of the firm's strengths and weaknesses as well as an examination of opportunities and threats in the environment.

7. The Boston Consulting Group's (BCG's) growth-share matrix attempts to explain how market share, market growth, and cash flow are tied together.

8. The BCG approach identifies businesses as cash cows, stars, dogs, and question marks and establishes five strategic courses of business action: building, acquiring, holding, harvesting, and divesting.

9. The General Electric business screen includes *multiple* measures of competitive strength and market attractiveness.

10. Managers benefit from individualized portfolio analysis because it provides concrete action steps that can be implemented.
11. Good strategic planning is always a two-way process, going both top-down and bottom-up within the corporation.
12. Marketing strategy is at the heart of effective management strategy.

☐ Key Terms

cash cows	intrapreneurship	stakeholders
competitive advantage	mission statement	stars
dogs	planning calendar	strategic business unit
experience curve	portfolio	strategic management
GE business screen	product-market matrix	strategy
growth-share matrix	question marks	SWOT analysis
individualized portfolio techniques	relative market share	tactics

☐ Chapter Review

1. Do you believe that Chrysler Corporation has been strategically managed over the last 20 years?

2. Describe the role of a marketer assigned to a corporate group responsible for setting long-range strategy.

3. What implications did IBM's entry into the small-computer market have for firms that specialize in such computers—Tandy (Radio Shack), Apple, and Commodore? Would changes in corporate strategies be indicated for the smaller companies?

4. Try to draft a one-paragraph corporate mission statement for a large diversified corporation such as General Mills or Procter & Gamble.

5. Would Dodge pickup trucks form an SBU for Chrysler Corporation? Why or why not?

6. Give your own analysis of the strengths and weaknesses, opportunities and threats for one of the following companies:
   a. Sony
   b. Burger King
   c. American Express
   d. Columbia Pictures or 20th Century-Fox
   e. Levi Strauss

7. Draw a growth-share matrix for a hypothetical corporation with 10 separate businesses or product lines. What might be an ideally balanced portfolio of cash cows, stars, question marks, and dogs?

8. Why is a bottom-up flow of information vital to the setting of corporate strategy?

9. If General Foods set a corporate strategy of improving relative market share by 3 percentage points over the next 18 months, what actions (or alternative actions) might the marketing staff in its coffee division (Maxwell House, Sanka, and Brim) propose?

☐ References

1. Richard F. Vancil and Peter Lorange, "Strategic Planning in Diversified Companies," *Harvard Business Review,* Jan.–Feb. 1975, pp. 65–74.
2. Richard T. Pascale and Anthony G. Athos, *The Art of Japanese Management* (New York: Simon & Schuster, 1981), p. 44.
3. Frederick W. Gluck, Stephen P. Kaufman, and A. Steven Walleck, "Strategic Management for Competitive Advantage," *Harvard Business Review,* July–Aug. 1980, p. 157.
4. Daniel H. Gray, "Uses and Misuses of Strategic Planning," *Harvard Business Review,* Jan.–Feb. 1986, pp. 89–97, and Richard G. Hamermesh, "Making Planning Strategic," *Harvard Business Review,* July–Aug. 1986, pp. 115–120.
5. William Ouchi, *Theory Z* (Reading, Mass.: Addison-Wesley, 1981), p. 132.

6. Jerome H. Want, "Corporate Mission: The Intangible Contributor to Performance," *Management Review,* Aug. 1986, pp. 46–50, at p. 47.

7. For an indication of the marketing orientation of this company, see "Customer Service Key to Office Furniture Strategy," *Marketing News,* May 9, 1986, p. 10.

8. Igor H. Ansoff, "The State of Practice in Planning Systems," *Sloan Management Review,* Winter 1977, pp. 1–24.

9. Derek F. Abell, *Defining the Business: The Starting Point of Corporate Planning* (Englewood Cliffs, N.J.: Prentice-Hall, 1980), chaps. 9 and 10.

10. In realilty, the experience curve concept is extremely complex; its full development is beyond the scope of this book. For a more thorough discussion, see George S. Day and David B. Montgomery, "Diagnosing the Experience Curve," *Journal of Marketing,* vol. 47, Spring 1983, pp. 44–58; and Pankaj Ghemawat, "Building Strategy on the Experience Curve," *Harvard Business Review,* Mar.–Apr. 1985, pp. 143–149.

11. See, for instance, Carolyn Y. Woo, "Market Share Leadership: Not Always So Good," *Harvard Business Review,* Jan.–Feb. 1984, pp. 50 ff, and Robert Jacobson and David A. Aaker, "Is Market Share All That It's Cracked Up to Be?" *Journal of Marketing,* vol. 49, Fall 1985, pp. 11–22.

12. Donald C. Hambrick and Ian C. MacMillan, "The Product Portfolio and Man's Best Friend," *California Management Review,* vol. 25, Fall 1982, pp. 84–95.

13. Marian C. Burke, "Strategic Choice and Marketing Managers: An Examination of Business-Level Marketing Objectives," *Journal of Marketing Research,* vol. XXI, Nov. 1984, pp. 345–359.

14. Tom Delaney, "Down Puts $70-Mil. behind Product Line," *Adweek,* July 14, 1986, p. 16; and Sandra D. Atchison, "Kraft Is Celestial Seasonings' Cup of Tea," *Business Week,* July 28, 1986, p. 73.

15. Jagdish Sheth and Glenn Morrison, "Winning Again in the Marketplace: Nine Strategies for Revitalizing Mature Products," *Journal of Consumer Marketing,* vol. 1, no. 4, 1984, pp. 17–28.

16. Walter Kiechel, III, "Playing by the Rules of the Corporate Strategy Game," *Fortune,* Sept. 24, 1979, p. 115.

17. Roy D. Shapiro, "Get Leverage from Logistics," *Harvard Business Review,* May–June 1984, pp. 119–126; and Graham Sharman, "The Rediscovery of Logistics," *Harvard Business Review,* Sept.–Oct. 1984, pp. 71–79.

18. "Intrapreneurship Now Favorite Weapon of Corporate Strategists," *Marketing News,* June 6, 1986, pp. 23, 26.

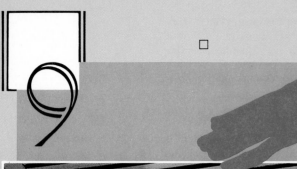

9

PLANNING MARKETING PROGRAMS

SPOTLIGHT ON

Copyright © 1986 Jed Share/The Stock Market.

□ Action plans in marketing

□ How marketing strategy and implementation influence each other

□ Marketing plans

□ Analytical steps in the marketing planning process

□ Advantages and drawbacks of various forecasting methods

□ Common bases for organizing marketing organizations

"**T**his is our proudest moment since 1947, when powdered Tide was born," noted Stephen Donovan, vice president of the packaged-soap and detergent division of Procter & Gamble. The "proudest moment" was the introduction of a new "convenience" liquid detergent, Liquid Tide, in January 1985.

The laundry habits of consumers by two technical breakthroughs: were revolutionized in 1946 when the automatic washing machine became available and in 1947 when granular Tide, the first heavy-duty synthetic detergent, was introduced. Four decades later, Tide remains by far the dominant detergent brand, accounting for more than 20 percent of all detergent sales in the United States.

Why, then, has Procter & Gamble developed Liquid Tide to go along with the already-successful powdered Tide? In the last decade, more and more Americans have turned to heavy-duty liquids (HDLs) to meet their laundry needs; HDLs now account for almost 25 percent of the $2.7 billion detergent business. Liquid detergents are viewed as a time saver by many consumers because the liquid can be poured directly on a stain for extra cleansing power. Reducing the burden of this time-consuming task is especially important for members of the baby-boom generation, whose households are less likely to have full-time homemakers who can spend time doing the laundry.

With this desirable market segment in mind, Procter & Gamble's brand manager for Liquid Tide, Candace McNamara, developed a launch plan for the new brand. Liquid Tide had been created only after 400,000 employee-hours of technical research and 9 months of test marketing. According to McNamara, these tests were remarkably successful. "What we expected to sell in 12 weeks moved out in four," she recalls. "At the same time, sales of regular Tide soared. There was no cannibalization."

Procter & Gamble highly touts its new brand, stating that Liquid Tide has twice as many active ingredients as its competitors, including a newly formed cleaning molecule. The marketer further claims that Liquid Tide outcleaned its competitors by a 9-to-1 margin in blind cleaning tests. For this reason, Procter & Gamble was willing to lend the cherished Tide name to its new product. "We wouldn't have used Tide's name unless [Liquid Tide] could deliver the same breakthrough," suggested Donovan.

Traditionally, marketers of detergents rely primarily on demonstration and testimonial advertising, especially commercials during television soap operas. Such commercial spots are aimed at heavy users of detergent: women 18 to 49 years old with at least two children. In launching Liquid Tide, brand manager Candace McNamara expected Procter & Gamble to spend $40 to $50 million in 1985 alone on advertising for the new brand. Television spots focused on blind tests establishing the superiority of Liquid Tide, with a voice-over reminding viewers that, "You say it cleans better, because you see it cleans better."

At the time of its introduction, Liquid Tide faced some formidable competitors in the liquid-detergent market, particularly Lever Brothers' Wisk, which accounts for about 7.5 percent of overall detergent sales. But, in early 1985, one financial analyst predicted that Liquid Tide would eventually pass Wisk and become the nation's number 2 detergent, trailing only powdered

A typical day's mail might bring you an invitation to subscribe to a news-magazine, a letter from a political action committee asking you to support a congressional candidate, or an envelope containing cents-off coupons for several household cleaning products. These pieces did not reach you haphazardly; extensive marketing efforts went into identifying and selecting the target market to which you belong.

Chapter 9 focuses on the planning of marketing operations; marketing planning is part of corporate strategic planning. Early in the chapter, we will show how strategic marketing plans are transformed into concrete marketing programs capable of implementation. Both strategy and implementation are meaningful at the corporate and marketing levels of an organization. We will show how marketers go through the various steps of the marketing planning process, including the formulation of sales forecasts for current and new products. Finally, we will examine the basic ways in which marketing staffs are organized to carry out strategic plans.

FROM STRATEGY TO IMPLEMENTATION

Peter Drucker says planning is only wishful thinking unless it degenerates into work. An **action plan** is the crucial intermediate step between the formulation and implementation of marketing strategy. Strategies tell organizations where they should go or what they should be; action plans address the questions of what will be done (where, when, how, and by whom). Note the important distinction between *planning* and *a plan.* Planning should be viewed as a *process;* an action plan is a *document* that specifies how marketing strategies will be implemented.

The foundation of almost every good action plan lies in marketing; implementation of the plan falls heavily on working marketers within an organization. Strategies answer the question, "Are we doing the right things?" (For example, should Coca-Cola begin a line of fruit juices?) Implementation answers the question, "Are we doing things right?" (For example, will the copy and illustration in a fruit juice manufacturer's magazine ad get the message across to a target market?) Exhibit 9-1 shows the differences between the marketing strategies and the implementation of strategies at General Mills' Red Lobster restaurant chain.

Chapter 8 emphasized the need to establish broad corporate goals and strategies. Critics of strategic planning insist that too many action plans fail to provide measures for ensuring that strategies will be carried out effectively. Indeed, this is frequently the case. To avoid such implementation failures, careful planning is also needed at the level of the individual business or division and in supporting action (or campaign) plans for actually selling the product.

In his classic article on marketing implementation, Thomas Bonoma discusses how marketing strategy affects implementation and how implementation affects strategy.[1] In many situations, diagnosis of these effects is crucial. Bonoma tells the story of a manufacturer of "dumb" computer terminals (those that cannot be used for anything unless they are hooked up to a mainframe computer). Changes in the

EXHIBIT 9-1

EXHIBIT 9-1 **Strategies and Implementation at General Mills' Red Lobster Restaurant Chain**

In all elements of its marketing mix, an organization (such as the Red Lobster restaurant chain) must differentiate between its marketing strategy (what it hopes to accomplish) and its implementation (tactics or actions used to carry out these strategies).

Marketing Mix Element	Strategy	Implementation
Product	Change menu to attract weight-conscious adults aged 22 to 44 and two-income families	Serve more fresh, broiled seafood entrees; expand salad bars; add cocktail lounges with liquor service
Distribution	Solidify market share in existing locations	Cut expansion plans; add only a few new units per year
Price	Maintain image as a chain of moderately priced, family restaurants	Lower dinner prices; make up lost revenues from liquor sales and appetizer platters at the bar
Promotion	Change image from a fast, efficient place to eat to that of restaurants for leisurely, comfortable dining	Hire new advertising agency (Backer & Spielvogel of Miller Lite fame); promote theme of "the dining experience" to position restaurants above those of McDonald's and Burger King

Source: Bill Saporito, "When Business Got So Good It Got Dangerous," *Fortune,* Apr. 2, 1984, pp. 61–64.

competitive environment clearly began to suggest that the appropriate marketing strategy was a move to "smart" terminals. Forecasts called for the smart-terminal market to grow by over 500 percent during the 1980s. The company subsequently introduced these terminals in a new sales campaign with expected sales of 500 units. However, its 39-person sales force succeeded in selling only 50 terminals during the campaign. Was the problem one of strategy or implementation?

Figure 9-1 shows how strategy and implementation influence each other. Bonoma notes that "the computer terminal example falls in the lower left cell of the matrix and illustrates an important rule about strategy and implementation: poor implementation can disguise good strategy."[2] If both are good, as in the upper left quadrant of the matrix—or if both are wrong, as in the lower right quadrant—the results are usually obvious. But if one is right and the other is a problem, as in the terminal example, the situation requires special care to diagnose. Good execution may cover up poor strategy; poor execution may hamper good strategy.

■ *CONTENTS OF A MARKETING PLAN* ■

With the differences between marketing strategies and implementation in mind, let us turn to the major tasks of planning marketing operations. We begin with a simple yet essential question: What does the marketing plan contain? Kenneth A. Randall, president of the Conference Board, a major association of corporate executives, offers a vivid description of the aims and uses of a marketing plan:

> The marketing plan embodies, in capsule form, a seller's realistic hopes and intentions for competing successfully in the marketplace. . . . As a blueprint for action

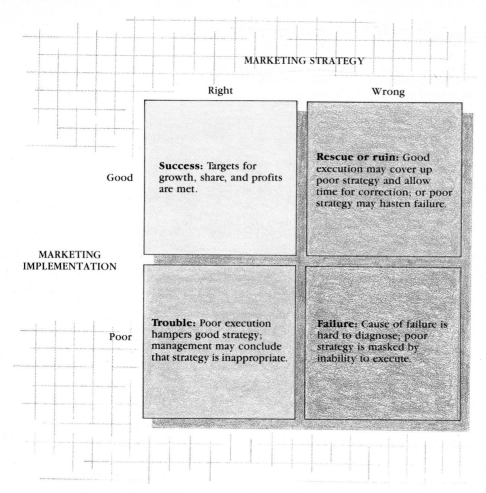

MARKETING STRATEGY

	Right	Wrong
Good	**Success:** Targets for growth, share, and profits are met.	**Rescue or ruin:** Good execution may cover up poor strategy and allow time for correction; or poor strategy may hasten failure.
Poor	**Trouble:** Poor execution hampers good strategy; management may conclude that strategy is inappropriate.	**Failure:** Cause of failure is hard to diagnose; poor strategy is masked by inability to execute.

MARKETING IMPLEMENTATION

Figure 9-1 *Marketing strategy and implementation.* Diagnosing what went wrong, or what went right, must consider both the strategy and the implementation. When the organization is poorly implementing a mistaken strategy, failure is likely to be obvious. A good job of implementing a sound strategy is also likely to be obvious. Good implementation of poor strategy leads to quicker failure than would have come with poor implementation—or the good action will provide time to change the strategy appropriately. Correct strategy and poor implementation lead to problems that obscure how good the strategy really was. (Adapted from Thomas V. Bonoma, "Making Your Marketing Strategy Work," *Harvard Business Review,* Mar.–Apr. 1984, pp. 69–76, at p. 72.)

. . . the marketing plan sets forth marching orders for those units and personnel engaged in product management, sales, advertising, and other marketing-related activities. . . . It is a virtual treaty by which general management and senior marketing management are able to negotiate delegated responsibilities for the company's marketing effort. . . . It establishes agreed-upon targets and benchmarks for the various elements of the marketing operation by which their subsequent performances may be judged.[3]

A **marketing plan,** therefore, is a written document that answers these questions: (1) Where are we now? (2) Where do we want to go? (3) How can we get there?[4] Marketing plans are drafted by product managers, divisional marketing directors, the general manager of a division, or a committee of marketing personnel. Final approval of plans may go as high as the organization's president (or chief executive officer), a divisional general manager, a vice president for marketing, or a corporate executive vice president. Wherever the drafting and approval responsibilities lie, marketing plans are drafted and approved in conjunction with plans from finance, production, research and development, personnel, administration, or other divisions.

Marketing plans follow formats as varied as the companies that employ them, but most firms require some standardized format for all divisions. Planning guidelines are useful because such formats:

252   Planning the Marketing Program

- Ensure that all units cover all pertinent aspects
- Facilitate management review and control
- Provide a road map for novice planners
- Upgrade the quality of marketing plans to a minimal level of competence

Exhibit 9-2 is an example of a marketing plan guideline of a large urban bank. All business units of this well-managed firm are expected to address the topics or answer the questions posed in these guidelines.

Although each organization will tailor the specifications of its marketing plan to meet its particular needs, a typical plan will include at least the following elements in some form:

- *Management summary:* Intended as an aid for top-level management, this summary is a brief (1- or 2-page) overview of the key points and highlights of the plan.
- *Situation analysis:* This section analyzes the organization's strengths and weaknesses, identifies opportunities and problems in the marketplace, sums up environmental trends, and reports on the competitive situation.
- *Specific objectives:* Both quantitative and qualitative objectives are generally included. Quantitative objectives such as profit, sales volume, market share, and return on investment can be measured precisely. Qualitative objectives such as "improved relationships with retail channels" cannot be as precise.

EXHIBIT 9-2	**Marketing Plan Outline:** **The Fidelity Bank, Philadephia**

Fidelity Bank
Philadelphia, PA 19109

Banks are primarily large service organizations. The planning process for this large Philadelphia bank helps its units to focus on issues of importance for the marketing of bank services. The emphasis on environmental forces is evident in this plan outline. It is appropriate that the end of the outline discusses action programs designed to implement the organization's objectives and goals.

1. *Management summary:* What is our marketing plan for this service in brief?

2. *Economic projections:* What factors in the overall economy will affect the marketing of this service for next year, and how?

3. *The market (qualitative issues):* Who or what kinds of organization could conceivably be considered prospects for this service?

4. *The market (quantitative issues):* What is the potential market for this service?

5. *Trend analysis:* Based on the history of this service, where do we appear to be headed?

6. *Competition:* Who are our competitors for this service, and how do we stand competitively?

7. *Problems and opportunities:* Are there internal and/or external problems inhibiting the marketing of this service, or are there opportunities we have not taken advantage of?

8. *Objectives and goals:* Where do we want to go with this service?
   a. Qualitative decisions—reasoning behind the offering of this service and what modifications or other changes do we expect to make
   b. Quantitative issues—number of accounts, dollar volume, share of market, profit goals

9. *Action programs:* Given history, the economy, the market, competition, etc., what must we do to reach the goals we have set for this service?

Source: David S. Hopkins, *The Marketing Plan* (New York: The Conference Board, 1981), pp. 63–64.

- *Marketing strategies:* Market segmentation and product-positioning strategies will be discussed. Any marketing strategies must dovetail with and support overall corporate strategies.
- *Budgets and controls:* Revenues and expenses will be presented for the current year and for specified future years. Some organizations will require a highly specific breakdown of expenses and may require multiple measures of productivity. After the fact, the revenue and expenses sections of the marketing plan will serve a basic control function; that is, revenues can be clearly measured against expenses and plans.
- *Action programs:* These detailed sections focus on marketing mix programs and spell out specific plans, timetables, and responsibilities. Promotion campaigns and advertising programs will be summarized; significant factors or changes in distribution channels and pricing policies will be highlighted.

Failure to coordinate action programs with nonmarketing functions can be damaging. When Coleco announced its budget-priced but multifeatured personal computer, the Adam, initial announcements and plans called for introduction in early Fall 1984. The Adam was to be nationally available, in quantity, for Christmas sales; Coleco hoped to ship 400,000 units by the end of the calendar year. However, the company failed to coordinate its inventory program with its promotional efforts at a key selling time. Production difficulties caused a slippage in availability dates, and only about 90,000 units were available for the holiday rush. Promotion programs had to be altered drastically: Coleco had to take out advertisements apologizing to consumers for its failure to deliver Adams on time.

Coleco learned a painful lesson in 1984, when it failed to coordinate all the elements of the marketing mix on the introduction of the Adam computer. The demand was there, but store shelves just didn't have the product when the consumer went to buy. (Copyright © Robert McElroy/Woodfin Camp & Assoc.)

THE MARKETING PLANNING PROCESS

The content of the marketing plans discussed above is extremely important; it is used to guide the entire organization toward the completion of its marketing objectives. Equally important, however, is the highly disciplined *process by which* these plans are determined. Although it will vary from company to company, the process will closely follow the model presented in Figure 9-2.

Before committing to a formal plan, certain analytical steps are in order. Proceeding through these steps helps to ensure that the action plans for a product or business mesh with the goals and objectives of overall corporate strategy and of marketing strategy. As set forth in Figure 9-2, these steps include a review of market segmentation and product-positioning policies, a market opportunity analysis, and an examination of marketing mix programs. Sales revenues must be forecast, and marketing expenditures must be budgeted. After the plan has been drafted, it will be evaluated as to its effectiveness. Only then will the plan be set into action and implemented. When this process is formalized (but not bureaucratized), managers will believe and therefore use the resulting plans.[5]

Segmentation and Positioning

As we noted in Chapter 7, one advantage of carefully segmenting markets and positioning products is the resulting value for both strategic planning and implementation. Recall that market segmentation is the process of breaking down large, dissimilar buying units into smaller and more similar buying groups. Segmentation is fundamental to the marketing concept because it allows marketers to focus on who their customers really are and what these customers really want. Marketers use product positioning to create favorable perceptions of their products in buyers' eyes relative to buyers' perceptions of competitors' products. A review of the makeup of target market segments and product-positioning philosophy is part of the bottom-up compilation of marketing strategy; for implementation, such a review leads to specific action steps. Thus, analysis of segmentation and positioning is a necessary first step in drafting a marketing plan.

Market Opportunity Analysis

A review of segmentation and positioning encourages planners to explore other markets and products. For instance, in such an analysis, the brand manager for Nestlé's Taster's Choice decaffeinated coffee might want to investigate the institutional market (restaurants and hospitals). The manager should ask at least three basic questions:[6]

1. What is the size of the market (total market demand)?
2. What is the extent and quality of service to the market by other firms?
3. What investments and marketing programs would be required to satisfy market needs and to compete successfully?

For the Taster's Choice brand manager, the answer to the second question would undercut the attractiveness of the market opportunity. General Foods' Sanka brand has a commanding lead in the institutional market. The funds and efforts necessary to compete with Sanka in restaurants might be more profitably spent trying to extend Taster's Choice's lead over Sanka in supermarkets.

Market opportunity analysis sometimes leads to decisions to tackle new markets or to offer new products. During the early 1980s, brand managers for Yuban

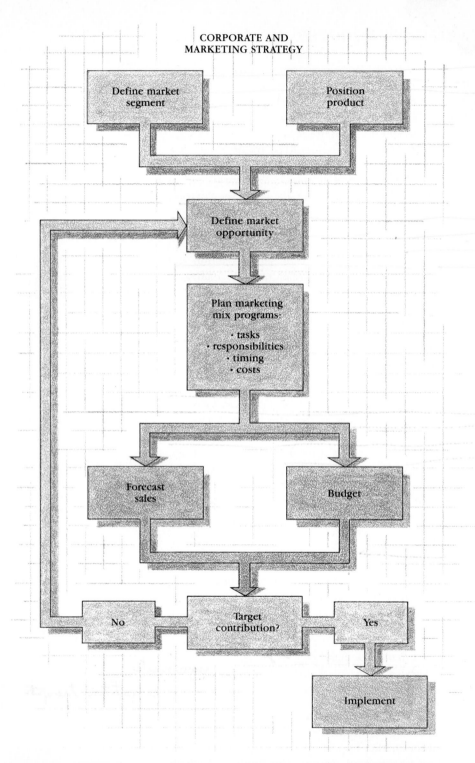

Figure 9-2 *Marketing planning process.* Marketing planning is a highly disciplined process designed to lead to the most effective results. It is useful to distinguish between the process itself (as shown in the figure) and the *result* of that process (published plans). (The process shown here is adapted from that developed and refined by Dr. Stewart W. Bither, Associate Dean, The Pennsylvania State University.)

Even for something as simple as a cup of coffee, competitors provide a wide array of options in the effort to attract consumers. One key to assessing market opportunities is to evaluate how well competitors are now serving segments of the market. (Ken Karp.)

coffee (another General Foods brand) decided to offer a decaffeinated brew. They rolled the product out to national markets in 1984, thereby competing not only with Taster's Choice but also with its sisters brands Sanka, Maxwell House, and Brim.

In answering these three basic questions about market opportunity, planners initially use only rough estimates of market size, marketing program requirements, and competitive strength. However, if preliminary estimates suggest that a market opportunity looks promising, planners will then employ full-scale, formal forecasting techniques before reaching a decision. The real message here is that marketers should always be alert for market or product opportunities. The marketing planning process is one way of ensuring that opportunities are periodically assessed.

Marketing Mix Programs

Once a marketing organization completes segmentation and marketing opportunity analysis, planning becomes specific. Managers spell out detailed plans for product positioning, promotion, distribution, and pricing. The appropriate personnel continue or change promotional messages; choose advertising media and schedules; adjust sales force territories; select new wholesale and retail channels (if necessary); review pricing; and chart any product adjustments and repositioning. Wherever necessary, marketers schedule support activities—from research projects to dealer training.

Whatever the marketing mix plans, four elements of any planned actions must be assigned:

1. *Tasks:* What are the particular jobs to be done?
2. *Responsibilities:* Who in the marketing organization will be given these assignments?
3. *Timing:* When will specific tasks be carried out in order to make subsequent efforts possible?
4. *Costs:* How much of the budget will be assigned to each marketing division? (All expenditures for carrying out the marketing mix programs must be estimated and assigned to various cost centers.)

In short, the marketing mix and support programs set the blueprint for making planning "degenerate into work." And, as retired Army General James Gavin has said, "Nothing chastens a planner more than the knowledge that he will have to carry out the plan."

Forecasting the Market

Ex-Cell-O markets diversified industrial items, but its mainstay is a line of machine tools ranging in price from a few thousand dollars to $400,000 or more. With such high-priced products, Ex-Cell-O must estimate new orders realistically and in some detail. As one input to sales projections, the company asks sales representatives to predict sales for their territories every 3 months. Ex-Cell-O also considers many other factors in its estimates, among them forecasts of general economic trends, a projection of industrywide demand for machine tools, and historical sales data and patterns.

Sales predictions are one of the basic building blocks of all marketing plans. Marketers' action plans most frequently use estimates of sales—given specified levels of marketing effort—as their starting points. One of marketing's basic (and most difficult) tasks is to estimate how much of a product consumers and organizational buyers will actually purchase. **Forecasting** consists of predicting what buyers in a target market are likely to do under a given set of conditions.

Perhaps the one absolute statement we can make about sales forecasts is that they are always wrong. Marketers should make that fact a fundamental assumption of their forecasting. However, the crucial questions for planners are "How *far* wrong is the forecast?" (see Box 9-1) and "*why* is it wrong?" For established products affected only marginally by changes in the external environment—salt, health insurance, or bibles—forecasters' predictions are often quite close to the mark, perhaps within 2 or 3 percentage points of actual sales. For new, innovative products, forecast accuracy varies more widely.

FORECASTING LEVELS   Sales forecasting normally involves a progression through several degrees of specificity, proceeding from a macro view of the external

---

BOX 9-1   **The Perils of Forecasting: A Wall Street Hula**

One corporate executive certainly paid dearly for his skepticism about forecasting. Sam Moore Walton, head of the Wal-Mart chain of some 950 discount stores, simply could not believe a forecast that his company's 1983 profits would top 8 percent. Well aware that profits normally were about 3 percent, Walton impulsively told Wal-Mart forecasters: "There's not a chance, but if you achieve those ridiculous figures, I'll dance a hula on Wall Street."

And so Walton danced! When sales figures for 1983 were compiled, sales had exceeded $4 billion. Profits were 8.04 percent, so Wal-Mart had (barely) reached the "ridiculous figures" offered by its forecasters. "It was so close, I accused them of juggling," noted Walton. Nevertheless, on a chilly winter morning in 1984

(temperature 28°), Walton appeared outside Merrill Lynch's Wall Street office wearing a lei around his neck, a gaudy shirt, and a grass skirt. With the help of Hawaiian dancers hired for the occasion, Walton nervously launched into a less-than-classic hula.

"I just couldn't back out," admitted Walton. He added that he had made no such promises for the following year. One thing is certain: If Walton chooses to make a cash wager against forecasters, he can afford to lose. In 1986, the annual *Forbes* magazine list identified Walton as the richest person in the United States, worth about $4.5 billion.

Sources: "New York Day by Day," *The New York Times*, Mar. 16, 1984, p. B2; "Wal-Mart Founder Tops Rich List," *The New York Times*, Oct. 14, 1986, p. D6.

environment down to the microenvironment of the marketplace for an individual product.[7] The results of environmental monitoring should produce a set of projections concerning the future. These projections inform not only corporate strategy and planning but also the action plans for marketing.

Environmental projections are made at the highest corporate levels and are passed along as a set of operating parameters for planners at the functional level. For example, at Heublein Inc., marketers at the company's decentralized operations are given certain projections about the overall environment: the predicted course of the economy, notable demographic trends, legislative probabilities, social trends, technological breakthroughs, and projections concerning the competitive climate. Heublein planners use the resources described in Chapter 2 along with the company's marketing intelligence reports to build macro-assessments of the overall environment.

Figure 9-3 shows the flow of information and forecasts among levels. Using the assumptions of a general environmental forecast, planners estimate the total market demand. Then, working from that figure, they can formulate a projection of sales by product or product line. These forecasts can subsequently be combined into a company sales forecast. Or planners may use the historical evidence of the company's share of the total market to make a company sales forecast. After that, they will develop forecasts for individual products.

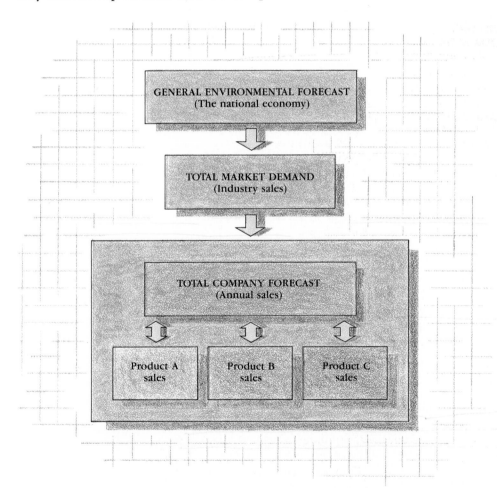

Figure 9-3 *Levels of forecasting*. Forecasts are often made for several levels of aggregation and may include a number of major environmental forces, such as the total economy. Within that large aggregation is the forecast for a particular industry (such as the U.S. automobile industry). This forecast will include the company in question (for example, Chrysler) and all its competitors. The forecast for the company will contain forecasts for each of its product lines (such as Plymouth, Dodge, and Chrysler).

TOTAL MARKET DEMAND   Given environmental projections, forecasters at the strategic-business-unit (SBU) and functional levels compile a picture of the maximum amount of product all competitors in the market could expect to sell at a specified level of effort: "**Total market demand** for a product is the total volume that would be bought by a defined consumer group in a defined geographical area in a defined time period in a defined marketing environment under a defined level and mix of industry marketing effort."[8]

Let's examine the components and projections of an estimate of total market demand as seen through the eyes of William H. Crawley, vice president for international marketing at Rolm Corporation.[9] Rolm, an IBM subsidiary based in Santa Clara, California, is a leading producer of private branch exchanges (PBXs). PBXs are sophisticated electronic switching systems that handle not only voice conversations but also computer data, telex messages, and facsimile images. Sometimes called the "computerized switchboard," the PBX is considered the hub of the automated office.

Crawley estimated the total Japanese market demand for PBXs as follows:

Level and mix of industry marketing effort: Rolm projects that its products, along with those of four competitors (NEC Corporation, Oki Electrical Industry Corporation, Fujitsu, and Hitachi), will be the prime players in the market for PBXs. Each firm is expected to spend promotion monies aggressively.
Marketing environment: Projected favorable economic conditions for capital investments. Japan's gross national product (GNP) expected to grow at an average rate of 3 percent per year.
Time period: 1986 calendar year sales.
Geographical area: Japan.
Customer group: Large companies upgrading telecommunications networks.
Total market demand for PBXs in Japan in 1986: Projected at $500 million (2000 PBX systems at average price of $250,000).

Note that the $500 million figure represents estimated sales for *all* marketers of PBXs in Japan in 1986. But this figure is valid only for the conditions laid out above. Should economic conditions change, should a new competitor enter the market, or (in particular) should the competitors increase their marketing efforts, Rolm's projection would need to be revised to reflect such changes.

TOTAL MARKET POTENTIAL   Should all other market factors remain unchanged (time period, geographical area, economic conditions, and so forth) while each competitor makes a maximum marketing effort, we can estimate a **total market potential**—the total possible sales of the product by all competitors. Total market potential is rarely realized or sought. The additional expenditures necessary to reach marginally interested buyers would very likely lower the profits on such sales (between estimated demand and total market potential) to an unattractive level.

SALES FORECAST   A **sales forecast** represents realistic expectations of a company's sales of a particular product or product line to the chosen target market, over a specified time, in a chosen geographic area, and under a defined marketing program. Note the relationship between the sales forecast and the actions called for in the marketing plan: Additional sales will result from additional marketing efforts. Marketing programs—not forecasts—produce sales.

A **company sales forecast** is the total dollars and units of all the organization's products sold during the time laid out in the forecasts for individual products or businesses. As described in Chapter 8, top-down and bottom-up aspects of planning are involved in constructing estimates of total market demand and total market potential, sales forecasts, and company forecasts. Both techniques are needed to build realistic estimates.

Sales forecasts are the projections used to formulate the action plans for implementation of marketing strategies. These forecasts are most often short-term and quite specific. Marketing managers and statisticians have developed a number of techniques for making sales forecasts.

☐ *Forecasting Methods*

Forecasting options range from the simple to the mathematically complex. The technique chosen will depend on the following factors:

1. What degree of accuracy is required?
2. What is the availability and accuracy of historical data?
3. How far into the future must the forecast extend?
4. How much time is available to prepare the forecast?
5. How often will revisions be required?
6. How experienced are the forecasters?[10]

Answers to these questions will lead forecasters to one of the two broad categories of forecasting techniques: those with a judgmental basis or those rooted in historical data and quantitative methods. In reality, forecasting methods frequently combine a number of different approaches. Useful guides as to how to use forecasting methods are available.[11]

JUDGMENTAL METHODS **Judgmental forecasts** rely on the opinions of informed participants or outside consultants. This is not to suggest that judgmental methods are never quantitative—sales predictions couched in dollars and units will indeed result.[12] The most widely employed judgmental methods include surveys of executive opinion, the Delphi technique, sales force composites, and compilations of customer purchase intentions.

Executive Opinion   Some organizations conduct their forecasting by compiling the views of their own executives. The goal of such a survey is a sounder projection than might be made by a single estimator. Juries of executives may prepare their forecasts independently and without any discussion. More frequently, however, executive panels will meet to discuss their projections and to arrive at a consensus. Executive forecasters are typically furnished background material, including sales histories. In addition, these panels may be given (or asked to agree on) an official set of assumptions about the operating environment to limit divergence on fundamental issues.

The Delphi Approach   The **Delphi technique** (named for a town in ancient Greece which was the seat of an oracle of Apollo) was developed for use in environmental forecasting.[13] Under this procedure, a group of experts are solicited anonymously (usually by questionnaire) and asked to predict the likelihood and time of occurrence of significant events. In some instances, they may be asked to estimate a particular statistic, such as sales in 1995.

Forecasting the future is always difficult, and sophisticated quantitative techniques are helpful. Often, however, forecasts benefit from managers' subjective judgments. The executive opinion method uses such judgments as its main approach. (Copyright © 1984 Stacy Pick/ Stock, Boston.)

These experts cast their opinions in isolation without any discussion; consequently, no respondent can be influenced by the views of a colleague or a higher executive. After the first poll has been tallied, panel members are shown the average judgment and are asked to revise and justify their stance. They may go through several anonymous rounds of estimation and feedback. Members may then have face-to-face discussions and generally reach a consensus about the issues under study.

Sales-Force Composite   Certain organizations (particularly industrial marketers) ask their sales representatives to make short-term sales projections for their territories. The combined totals are useful for estimating national and regional demand. Obviously, salespeople are close to the marketplace; the best representatives can often provide fairly accurate estimates of future sales.

Many companies have found, however, that sales-force composites have their drawbacks. If compensation plans are based on meeting quotas, representatives may have a stake in keeping their estimates low, thereby making it easier to reach the quotas. Other representatives may be overly optimistic in their projections. If a sales-composite system draws on historical data, the biases of individual representatives can be adjusted. Sales managers at the district and regional levels can also factor in adjustments for accuracy based on their knowledge of representatives' sales records and of the history of sales in the area.

Customer-Purchase Intentions   Like sales-force composites, the combined purchase plans of customers are most often used by industrial marketers. Such polls may be taken by the sales force or by the organization's market research staff. Customers tend to overestimate their purchases and often change their minds, especially with regard to the timing of their buying. Here, too, historical data help forecasters to make adjustments: If past projections have been 8 percent over actual sales, current projections can be lowered by that same percentage to ensure greater accuracy.

In the area of consumer products, the University of Michigan's Survey Research Center measures consumers' intentions to purchase durable products such as cars and major household appliances. Those surveyed are asked to state the probability (certain, very likely, slight possibility, and so forth) of the near-term purchase of various items. Similarly, American Airlines has carried out its own surveys to predict consumers' flying plans and has achieved a fair degree of accuracy.

HISTORICAL AND QUANTITATIVE METHODS   Opinions and individual judgments are discounted by estimating through **historical and quantitative forecasts,** which project future sales based on sales patterns and/or mathematical calculations. The most widely employed quantitative techniques include time series models, advanced time series models, leading indicators, and statistical demand analysis.

Time Series Models   Many organizations attempt to project future sales by analyzing factors influencing past sales over successive time periods. **Time series analysis** serves to identify and measure repetitive influences on sales patterns. Four elements are generally studied in a traditional time series analysis of past sales (Y):

Secular (or long-run) **trends** (T) are rising or falling patterns of sales over a period of years. They are based on fundamental changes such as growth in population or decline in sales because customers are switching to a more advanced product.

Cyclical patterns (C) are changes in sales in an industry caused by changes in the macroeconomy as reflected in such factors as GNP or disposable personal income (see Chapter 2). These patterns usually last longer than a year and may be irregular in repetition.

One of the forecasting techniques that is not dependent on historical data is based on consumers' stated intentions to purchase. Such methods employ survey research techniques, and are a way to gauge consumer optimism (or pessimism) about future purchases. (Courtesy of SAMI/Burke.)

Seasonal patterns (*S*) are consistent sales patterns within a year which are based on factors such as weather or holidays.

Irregular events (*I*) are random events such as acts of God (earthquakes, fires, floods) or windfall sales contracts.

Using a time series analytic approach, forecasting studies historical sales patterns to determine how much of each period's change is caused by long-term secular trends, by the economic cycle, and by seasonal patterns—all factors consistent enough to be used to project the future. An example of such analysis is presented in Exhibit 9-3.

Advanced Time Series Models Because time series trends and patterns can be multiple and complex, a number of highly sophisticated models have been de-

---

EXHIBIT 9-3	Time Series Analysis

The local automobile tire retailer, Tire Town, is attempting to plan its cash flow for 1988 and needs to determine cash flow for each month of the year. Total sales in 1987 were 3000 tires.

Trend Effects

T shows a 3 percent per year growth:
$$1988 = 1987 \times (1 + T) = 3000 \times (1.03) = 3090$$

Cyclical Effects

The economy is in a state of healthy growth since the 1981–1983 recession, and consumer spending is projected to improve by 5 percent in 1988. However, the automobile aftermarket should grow even faster because of delayed purchases predicted at 7 percent:
$$3090 \times (1 + C) = 3090 \times 1.07 = 3306$$

Seasonal Effects

Tire sales are affected by a number of seasonal patterns: (1) a rush on snow tires in early winter; (2) heavier purchases in vacation periods; and (3) people's spending for other items around Christmas. This has shown a seasonal pattern as follows:

	Seasonal Index	×	1/12 of Annual (3,306 ÷ 12)	=	Forecasted Monthly Sales
Month					
January	1.05		275.5		289.3
February	0.90		275.5		248.0
March	1.00		275.5		275.5
April	0.95		275.5		261.7
May	0.95		275.5		261.7
June	1.15		275.5		316.8
July	1.10		275.5		303.0
August	1.05		275.5		289.3
September	1.00		275.5		275.5
October	0.95		275.5		261.7
November	1.10		275.5		303.0
December	0.85		275.5		234.2
Year	1.00		3306.0		3306.0

Based on its time series analysis of trend and cyclical effects, Tire Town projects that it will sell 3306 tires in 1988. Based on its analysis of seasonal effects, the company projects that it will show especially high sales in June, July, and August and lowest sales in December. Using these projections, Tire Town can estimate its cash flow for each month of 1988.

---

veloped to project future sales. These methods (most of which require a computer program) place weights on historical data. Advanced time series models include those based on moving averages, exponential smoothing, and the Box-Jenkins technique, all of which are beyond the scope of this text.[14]

Leading Indicators   For certain products, time series trends actually in advance of the product in question serve as reliable indicators of sales. For example, Steelcase and Herman Miller, both marketers of office furniture, closely monitor the issuance of commercial building permits for office buildings. Data on the square footage of future office space have proven to be a useful indicator of future demand for office furniture. Similarly, permits for residential housing can be used to project sales of major appliances and plumbing fixtures. Leading indicators are generally more reliable for industrial products than for consumer packaged goods.

Statistical Demand Analysis   Also known as causal forecasting, **statistical demand analysis** develops relationships among marketing mix factors and environmental circumstances (the independent variables) and sales (the dependent variable). Such analysis assesses the impact on sales of such variables as the cost of materials, personal income, promotional expenditures, and price changes. Statistical demand models are most frequently used to estimate the overall market for a general product class as opposed to the market for a specific brand.

Advanced forecasting techniques depend on sophisticated mathematical models and on the ability of high-speed computers to make necessary calculations. The sophistication, as well as the accuracy of such techniques, is constantly under development. (Copyright © 1985 Walter Bibikow/The Image Bank.)

Forecasting Sales of New Products

When desktop personal computers were introduced in the mid-1970s, marketers had no convenient measures on which to base sales forecasts. Obviously, the new machines had no sales history to use as a basis for projections, nor did the histories of other products offer much enlightenment: The market was not the same as those for electric typewriters or calculators. Only a few people, such as Steven Jobs of Apple Computer, had a vision of the many possible uses of small computers on the job and in the home.

With no sales history available, forecasters must seek alternatives to historical techniques. Judgmental methods are sometimes used; whenever possible, projections from test market results are studied. Mathematical models have been developed to project national sales of new products based on volume and market share achieved in test markets or on early sales of the new product.[15]

Data Sources

Whether estimating sales for products with established sales patterns or for new products, forecasters will generally draw upon a wide range of outside sources of information. The data sources used in environmental monitoring (see Chapter 2) are also used as inputs to the forecasting process.

By combining demographic and economic data, the annual *Forecasting Service* offered by *Sales & Marketing Management* gives current and projected population, households, effective buying income, retail sales, and a "buying power index" for the United States (broken down by state, region, metropolitan area, and county). The trends projected by this service are useful leading indicators for marketers of consumer products. Organizational marketers find the same magazine's annual *Survey of Industrial Buying Power* to be an important source of information.

As you can see, the governmental and trade association publications and syndicated services available to marketers are invaluable tools—not only for environmental monitoring and strategic planning but also for sales forecasting and marketing action planning. This underscores an organization's need for a well-organized marketing information system employing all relevant sources of information.

Using Multiple Forecasting Methods

Few organizations rely on one, all-purpose method of forecasting. Instead, most draw on several methods to check forecast accuracy and to fit individual forecasting tasks. Many companies combine sophisticated mathematical models with those involving managerial judgment.[16]

It is not simple to build and maintain a forecasting system that produces credible estimates. Forecasters continuously search for and experiment with new methods and combinations. Despite the difficulties involved, establishing a forecasting system that is accurate within an acceptable range of error is vital to forecasting's complementary operation—marketing planning.

Budgeting Marketing Expenses

Return for a moment to Figure 9-2. The marketing planning process illustrated in the figure has taken us through the development of detailed marketing mix programs with specific actions that we plan to carry out. In light of these planned programs, we are now able to do the detailed sales forecasting described above. But the sales forecast is only one-half of the picture—the forecast of revenues. To determine that plans are valid, we also need a forecast of expenditures, which we call the budget.

In practice, the balancing of planned revenues and expenditures may involve more than one trial. This is the key point at which marketing action plans and the

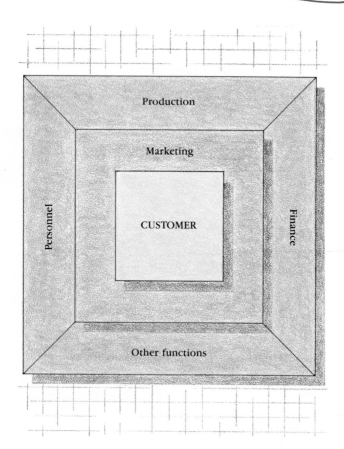

Figure 9-4 *Marketing is the agency for integrating the firm's efforts to meet customer needs.* Production, finance, personnel, and other functions are crucial to a company's success, but marketing integrates all the efforts of the firm. This is especially the case from the customers' point of view. (Adapted from Philip Kotler, *Principles of Marketing*, 2d ed., Englewood Cliffs, N.J.: Prentice-Hall, 1983, p. 544.)

results of such plans come together. In Figure 9-2, we see both the results of the forecasting process and the budget process.

A critical question arises: Does the expected result meet our target contribution? This contribution, an indication of profitability, is the revenue minus the expenditures. Most organizations have pinpointed a target result that they expect to see. The target contribution should be reasonable in light of the specific market conditions facing the business. One helpful resource used by managers in this process is called PIMS. A major ongoing research program, Profit Impact of Market Strategies (PIMS)—now managed by the Strategic Planning Institute in Boston—helps managers to develop quantitative estimates of the impact on their businesses' profitability of various levels of expenditures for marketing efforts.[17]

Regardless of the exact form of a company's financial goal—whether profitability, contribution to margin, or cash flow—if the planner projects the goal will not be met, rethink the action plan. We may then loop back to examine how we might revise the market opportunity that led to the detailed marketing mix program. Planners will develop a new forecast and a new budget. After these are available, we will again ask: Does the plan meet our target contribution?

If there is still no way to bring the marketing mix program's budget into line with the forecasted results, then the entire plan may be scrapped. If the original or revised plan *does* meet the target financial result, a decision to implement the plan will be made. The plan will be written up in an official format—generally following the planning guidelines described on pages 251 to 254.

■ MARKETING ORGANIZATION: IMPLEMENTING PLANS THROUGH PEOPLE ■

Until "planning degenerates into work"—until people perform the tasks called for in the marketing plan—the plan is little more than a sheaf of neatly typed papers. Product managers, advertising copywriters, market researchers, sales managers, and other members of the marketing department must join forces to make the marketing plan work—as laid out, on time, and on budget.

The likelihood of effective implementation of the plan is greatest when members of the marketing staff at all levels have been involved in creating the plan. Participation in this process almost invariably spurs commitment by marketing personnel to make a plan or plans work. However, to implement marketing plans (and carry out other day-to-day operations), marketing personnel must be organized in some productive way. The organization's marketing philosophy and the nature of its business will determine how its marketing operations are structured.

☐ From Sales to Marketing: Underpinnings of Modern Organization

As noted in Chapter 1, organizational philosophies of conducting business have evolved from product orientations ("selling what you know how to make") through sales orientations ("focus on selling what you make") to today's marketing orientations ("make and sell what customers want"). These contrasting philosophies determine the relative importance of marketing in an organization's operations and also influence the structure of the marketing department itself.

Most current producers of goods and services believe that marketing serves a unique, integrative function for a company. Figure 9-4 illustrates this concept: With the customer or consumer as the center of attention, marketing coordinates the firm's attempts to provide what customers want. Externally, marketing functions as the organization's face to and contact with the world of buyers; within a company, marketing is the customer's advocate.

☐ *Types of Marketing Organization*

Although the internal structure of marketing departments varies widely, most marketing organizations are structured around functions, products or product categories, geographical areas, or customer types. Large organizations serving diverse markets with numerous products will often adopt more than one approach. Figure 9-5 presents basic organization charts for each type of structure.

FUNCTIONAL ORGANIZATION   A **functional organization** divides the marketing operation into groups by their assigned tasks: sales, advertising and sales promotion, marketing research and information, product development, marketing logistics, customer services, and so on. Such a structure is shown in Figure 9-5a.

A functional organization works well for small companies or for those larger firms that concentrate on a small number of products or customer types. In addition, organizing by function facilitates the management of marketing areas requiring special skills and training such as marketing research. Holiday Inns, McDonalds, and British Airways are large organizations marketing primarily one product or service on a global scale. A basically functional organization might work efficiently for these companies.

PRODUCT-CATEGORY ORGANIZATION   A **product-category organization** assigns marketing tasks by product category or brand (see Figure 9-5b). Companies which use this form of organization typically reserve some duties for a corporate marketing staff. For instance, a marketing services department may handle advertising services, product promotion, marketing research, and new products. Product managers are able to draw upon the assistance of the corporate staff.[18] Firms generally employ product-category organization when their products are numerous and diverse. In such firms, the differing needs of target markets, distribution channels, promotion avenues, and pricing tactics dictate the product-category form of organization.

When firms use a product-category structure, product managers (whose jobs will be described in more detail in Chapter 11) must have good negotiating and diplomatic skills. They must compete with other brands for company funds; in addition, they are frequently charged with obtaining support and cooperation from staff personnel who do not work directly for them.

GEOGRAPHICAL ORGANIZATION   A **geographical organization**—used in the United States primarily for sales force structure—is based on management by region, state, area, nation, or global sector. For companies operating internationally, functions other than personal selling may also be organized on a geographical basis;

Figure 9-5 *Four bases for organizing marketing operations.* (a) An organization built strictly around the major marketing functions—the traditional and still quite common model; (b) a product line organization, which may include each of the functions within each product divison; (c) how the geography in which a firm conducts marketing operations may shape the organization—both internationally and within the United States; (d) an organization built around consumer groups—a newer organizational form that is growing in popularity. (Shown on page following.)

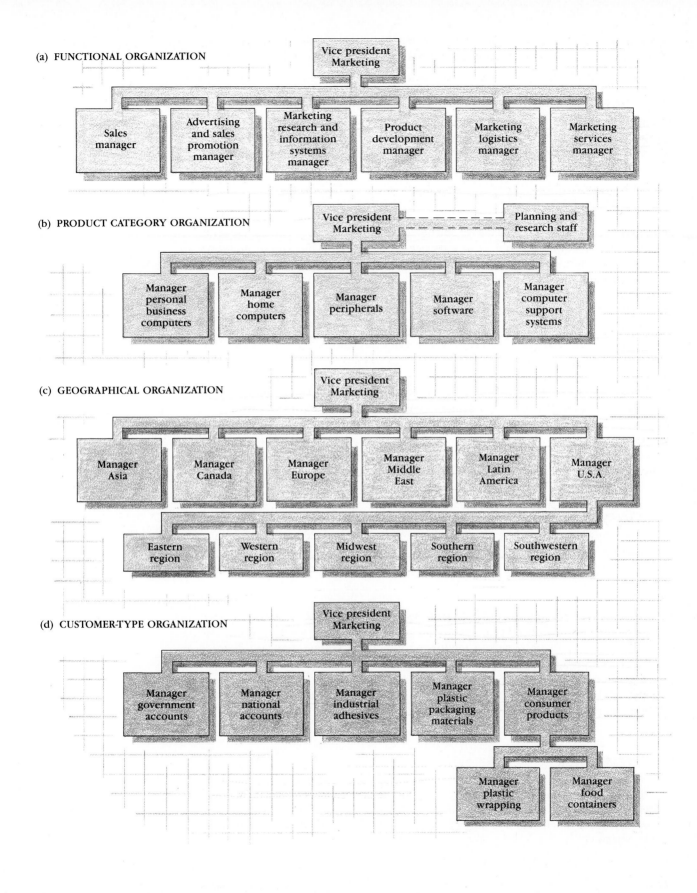

(a) FUNCTIONAL ORGANIZATION

Vice president Marketing

- Sales manager
- Advertising and sales promotion manager
- Marketing research and information systems manager
- Product development manager
- Marketing logistics manager
- Marketing services manager

(b) PRODUCT CATEGORY ORGANIZATION

Vice president Marketing ----- Planning and research staff

- Manager personal business computers
- Manager home computers
- Manager peripherals
- Manager software
- Manager computer support systems

(c) GEOGRAPHICAL ORGANIZATION

Vice president Marketing

- Manager Asia
- Manager Canada
- Manager Europe
- Manager Middle East
- Manager Latin America
- Manager U.S.A.

- Eastern region
- Western region
- Midwest region
- Southern region
- Southwestern region

(d) CUSTOMER-TYPE ORGANIZATION

Vice president Marketing

- Manager government accounts
- Manager national accounts
- Manager industrial adhesives
- Manager plastic packaging materials
- Manager consumer products

- Manager plastic wrapping
- Manager food containers

for example, advertising and promotion responsibility may be assigned in countries of operation. A typical geographical organization for an international marketer is shown in Figure 9-5c.

CUSTOMER-TYPES ORGANIZATION   Like a geographical organization, a customer-types organization is most often used to set up the operations of the personal selling group. Typically, other marketing functions such as advertising and research operate at a corporate staff level. Figure 9-5d illustrates a customer-types organization for a firm serving both consumer and industrial markets.

A customer-types (or market segment) structure encourages the marketing organization to focus its efforts on customer needs. For the past 2 or 3 years, marketers of mainline and business minicomputers have specialized their personal selling efforts by industry (banking, petroleum, insurance), government (federal, state, and local), and by other large national accounts. This specialization allows sales representatives to become expert in their customers' businesses and to function as partners in problem solving.

COMBINED ORGANIZATIONAL BASES   In practice, the organizational forms considered above are usually combined to serve the needs of a particular marketing organization. For example, a firm may have a basic customer-types organization with certain functions operating both at the corporate level and below the market segment level.

A company usually takes a number of years to find the right combination of organizational bases. Even so, changing customer preferences, environmental trends, and competitive actions may require a continuing evaluation of the effectiveness of the organization chosen. By using a combination of organizations, the marketing unit can adapt quickly to change and can develop and implement marketing plans that will effectively meet the needs of target markets.

☐ *Characteristics of an Effective Organizational Structure*

Whatever the personal wishes of marketers—and regardless of the neatness of any organization chart—the underlying focus of a marketing department structure should be serving customer needs. In designing marketing systems, marketers should:

1. Provide a framework for coordinating diverse marketing activities so that specific objectives can be realized through the implementation of marketing action plans
2. Establish a systematic means of identifying which marketing tasks and degrees of specialization are needed
3. Clarify lines of authority and responsibility in the marketing organization
4. Establish formal communications channels and procedures which will facilitate marketing decisions and implementation of marketing plans[19]

■ *SUMMARY* ■

1. Planning should be viewed as a process; an action plan is a document that specifies how marketing strategies will be implemented.
2. Strategies and action plans are not necessarily synonymous with long-term and short-term plans.

3. Annual operating plans are linked to the budgeting process.

4. Borrowing a military term, we can view implementation efforts as marketing campaigns.

5. A marketing plan answers the following questions: (1) Where are we now? (2) Where do we want to go? (3) How can we get there?

6. A typical marketing plan will include the following elements in some form: management summary, situation analysis, statement of specific objectives, marketing strategies, action programs, and budgets and controls.

7. Analysis of segmentation and positioning is the first step in drafting a marketing plan.

8. Whatever the marketing mix plans, these four elements of any planned actions must be assigned: tasks, responsibilities, timing, and costs.

9. One of marketing's most difficult tasks is to estimate how much of a product consumers and organizational buyers will actually purchase.

10. Forecasters are concerned with total market demand, total market potential, and sales forecasts.

11. Sales forecasts are the projections used to formulate the action plans for the implementation of marketing strategies.

12. Judgmental methods of forecasting include executive opinion, the Delphi approach, sales force composites, and customer purchase intentions.

13. The most widely employed quantitative forecasting techniques include time series models, advanced time series analysis, leading indicators, and statistical demand analysis.

14. Most firms draw on several forecasting methods to check accuracy and to fit individual forecasting tasks.

15. Effective implementation of a marketing plan is most likely when members of the marketing staff at all levels have been involved in creating the plan.

16. Most marketing organizations are structured around functions, products or product categories, geographical areas, or customer types.

☐ Key Terms

action plan
company sales forecast
customer-types organization
cyclical patterns
Delphi technique
forecasting
functional organization

geographical organization
historical and quantitative forecasts
judgmental forecasts
marketing plan
product-category organization
sales forecast

seasonal patterns
secular trends
statistical demand analysis
time series analysis
total market demand
total market potential

☐ Chapter Review

1. Give some examples from your own experience of the distinction between strategy and implementation.

2. Why do many organizations have such detailed instructions for how their various units are to prepare their marketing plans?

3. How might Coca-Cola use knowledge about the following market segments in the planning process: (1) heavy users of colas, (2) health-conscious consumers?

4. Explain how a forecast of the U.S. economy might relate to a company's sales forecast.

5. Define and then describe the similarities and differences in the executive opinion and Delphi approaches to forecasting.

6. Why do many organizations use a number of different forecasting techniques to project the same result?

7. How does the marketing planning process consider the expected financial results from implementing the plan?

8. Give examples of conditions that would lead companies to use the functional, product, geographical, and customer-types organization.

9. How would top management determine whether its marketing organization is effective?

References

1. Thomas V. Bonoma, "Making Your Marketing Strategy Work," *Harvard Business Review,* Mar.–Apr. 1984, pp. 69–76.

2. Ibid., p. 70.

3. Kenneth A. Randall, foreword, in David S. Hopkins, *The Marketing Plan* (New York: The Conference Board, 1981), p. iii.

4. This section draws on a number of concepts and examples presented in David S. Hopkins, *The Marketing Plan* (New York: The Conference Board, 1981).

5. George John and John Martin, "Effects of Organizational Structure of Marketing Planning on Credibility and Utilization of Plan Output," *Journal of Marketing Research,* vol. XXI, May 1984, pp. 170–183.

6. Robert B. Woodruff, "A Systematic Approach to Market Opportunity Analysis," *Business Horizons,* Aug. 1976, pp. 55–65.

7. A number of concepts and examples in the section on forecasting have been adapted from David L. Hurwood, Elliot S. Grossman, and Earl L. Bailey, *Sales Forecasting* (New York: The Conference Board, 1978).

8. Philip Kotler, *Marketing Management,* 5th ed. (Englewood Cliffs, N.J.: Prentice-Hall, 1984), p. 228.

9. Steve Lohr, "Japan PBX Market Cracked by Rohm," *The New York Times,* Jan. 16, 1984, p. D9.

10. William Lazer and James D. Culley, *Marketing Management: Foundations and Practices* (Boston: Houghton Mifflin, 1983), p. 323.

11. David M. Georgoff and Robert G. Murdick, "Manager's Guide to Forecasting," *Harvard Business Review,* Jan.–Feb. 1986, pp. 110–120.

12. Mark M. Moriarty, "Design Features of Forecasting Systems Involving Management Judgments," *Journal of Marketing Research,* vol. XXIII, Nov. 1985, pp. 353–364.

13. Norman Dalkey, *The Delphi Method: An Experimental Study of Group Opinion* (Santa Monica, Calif.: Rand, 1969).

14. For a more complete discussion of advanced time series analysis, see Hurwood, Grossman, and Bailey, op. cit., chap. 6, pp. 81–94.

15. Richard Edel, "New Testing System to the Defense," *Advertising Age,* Feb. 20, 1984, p. M44. See also Frank M. Bass, "A New Product Growth Model for Consumer Durables," *Management Science,* vol. 15, Jan. 1969, pp. 215–227.

16. Mark M. Moriarty and Arthur J. Adams, "Management Judgment Forecasts, Composite Forecasting Models, and Conditional Efficiency," *Journal of Marketing Research,* vol. XXI, Aug. 1984, pp. 239–250.

17. Michael Lubatkin and Michael Pitts, "PIMS: Fact or Folklore?" *Journal of Business Strategy,* vol. 3, no. 3, Winter 1983, pp. 38–43.

18. Victor P. Buell, *Marketing Management: A Strategic Planning Approach* (New York: McGraw-Hill, 1984), pp. 389–390.

19. Lazer and Culley, op. cit., p. 265.

CASE 6

ALAMO RENT A CAR

In little more than a decade, Alamo Rent A Car has registered a staggering rise to become number five in the $5-billion U.S. car-rental industry. Back in 1974, Alamo had only four Florida locations and a mere 1000 cars. By mid-1986, it operated in 57 cities, had a fleet of more than 50,000 cars, and was racking up annual sales of more than $300 million.

Initially, Alamo focused on the leisure market and particularly on expansion within the state of Florida. By exclusively targeting tour operators—a group with little allure for the car-rental giants because of wholesale rates—Alamo grew to $30 million in sales by 1979. Then, in 1980, Alamo expanded its leisure operations by purchasing a California company, Trans Rent-A-Car. Alamo further expanded its leisure strategy in 1982 by buying operating rights in Hawaii.

Meanwhile, as its leisure-oriented efforts were paying off, Alamo was simultaneously moving into commercial trade. In 1981, it targeted business trade in Atlanta. Since then, it has expanded its business trade to western cities such as Denver, Seattle, Phoenix, and Portland.

Alamo has faced an uphill battle in expanding into new segments because of its comparatively limited resources. Currently, Alamo spends about $1.5 million per year on advertising, while industry giants Hertz and Avis each spend about $12 million annually. "Until 1980," notes Alamo's director of advertising, "our competitors' ad budgets were greater than our total revenues." Yet, with profits expanding in recent years, Alamo has been able to double its exposure in newspapers, quadruple magazine space, and begin radio advertising for the first time.

Alamo maintains a no-frills, utilitarian approach to advertising. "We have a preference for advertising that will create business," notes the director of advertising. "We like ads that will work hard, and whose prime mission is to sell the product." The account supervisor for BDA/BBDO, Alamo's advertising agency, adds: "Alamo has developed a better way for customers to rent cars, and we tell it like it is."

Alamo's travel trade advertising emphasizes low prices and high quality, with the unifying slogan of "Alamo Rent A Car: The Real Number One Bargain." A major theme is Alamo's free-mileage feature. The headline of one ad notes: "At Alamo, Mileage is Priceless. 0 Cents A Mile." Like its ads for the commercial market, ads for travel trade detail the upgrading that Alamo has been doing since 1983, including "air conditioning, automatic transmission and radio at no extra charge."

Alamo's business trade advertising focuses on the simplicity of its corporate rate program: There is one rate per car size nationwide. This simplified pricing has been a key factor in persuading 100,000 companies to enroll in Alamo's corporate rate program. The general slogan for the company's commercial-trade campaign is "Alamo Rent A Car: A Great Deal More."

Source: Lore Croghan, "Positioning Alamo as a Low-Price, Quality Rental," *Adweek,* Aug. 11, 1986, p. 32D.

1. Over a 12-year period, Alamo enjoyed a spectacular rise and became the number five car-rental company. Why is it important to be ranked high among competitors in an industry?
2. In your view, why has Alamo been so successful? What has been the most important factor in Alamo's success?
3. Alamo seems to be emphasizing both low price and high quality. Does this approach make sense to you?

APPLE COMPUTER

Since its beginnings in 1976, Apple Computer has been the most successful start-up company in the United States. By the mid-1980s, it had won more than a million households with its pioneering personal computer, the Apple II. Along with Tandy's Radio Shack, it assumed a dominant position in the personal computer field. Indeed, for the year ending September 26, 1984, Apple's overall sales had reached $1.5 billion.

Apple Computer has often straddled the delicate line between boldness and arrogance. In discussing the "Apple knows best" attitude that many customers have found offensive, one industry analyst said of Apple's co-founder, Steven P. Jobs: "Jobs judges more on what is right with a capital "R," than on what the market wants and what will sell best. Like many brilliant visionaries, he is arrogant." Whether bold or simply arrogant, Jobs and Apple certainly had reason to be proud of their success in competing with IBM in the home computer market. In view of IBM's difficulties in selling its PC to households and the retailing fiasco of IBM's PC Jr., Apple can claim that it was the first competitor to truly defeat IBM in a head-to-head competition.

By the mid-1980s, however, Apple had focused on an even more ambitious goal: challenging IBM's dominance of the office market for personal computers. According to one estimate, businesses buy about two-thirds of the personal computers sold in the United States. Apple achieved little success in its efforts to win over business buyers with two of its more powerful personal computers, the Apple III and the Lisa. As a result, it has attempted to turn its Macintosh computer, first offered in 1983, into a formidable office alternative to the IBM PC.

In 1984, the first year of this Macintosh campaign, Apple sold 275,000 Macs. While industry analysts view this as a respectable first-year figure, Apple failed to achieve critical sales to the *Fortune* 500 companies. Despite impressive graphics and computing power— despite being somewhat easier to use than the IBM PC—the Macintosh did not "take off" because it lacked business software and was not IBM-compatible.

Initially, Jobs and other Apple executives had brashly predicted that Macintosh would come to rival the IBM PC, which accounts for more than 75 percent of all desktop computers in *Fortune* 500 companies. By 1985, Apple had been forced to scale down its predictions (and its bold rhetoric); its goal was simply to win 50 orders from major corporations during the year that would serve as "showcase accounts." Industry sources suggest that smaller companies account for more than 80 percent of sales of personal computers to businesses. Even while conceding that IBM would continue to dominate sales to the *Fortune* 500, Apple hoped to reach the target market of smaller business buyers by showing that it had at least some impressive big-company Macintosh users. Apple did receive major Mac orders from Federal Express, General Motors, GTE, Honeywell, and Motorola.

Perhaps the critical stumbling block was the issue of IBM compatibility. "What has made the Macintosh seductive is that it's easier to use for basic functions than IBM's PC," noted John Hammitt, vice president of information management at Pillsbury. "But like it or not, we live in an IBM world. People who don't plug into that world are not going to have a long-term place with us." Apple hoped to resolve this problem partly through its Macintosh Office (a device that will allow Macs to communicate with PCs) and other new offerings.

Software was another key problem, and here Apple faced a vicious cycle. Until it sells many more Macintoshes to business clients, it will have great difficulty convincing software writers and producers to develop programs for the Mac. Yet without an extensive array of programs, it will continue to be difficult to sell the Mac to major companies. IBM clearly enjoys a dramatic advantage over Apple in terms of software. In 1983, for example, five times as many programs were written for the IBM PC than for Apple computers.

Apple's advertising has hardly been a spectacular success with potential corporate customers; even the firm's whimsical name seems to contrast unfavorably with that of International Business Machines. A controversial Apple commercial, (aired during the 1985

Super Bowl) showed a procession of apparent business executives blindly following IBM and marching single-file off a cliff. Only the last executive in line, presumably a Macintosh user, pulled off his blindfold and avoided imminent death. Advertising experts were highly critical of the commercial, viewing it as one more example of Apple's arrogance. "It insulted the very people Apple was trying to reach," observed the president of a New York market research firm.

Another key weakness was poor relations with independent dealers. Apple's salespeople were apparently offering cut-rate Macs to potential corporate customers at prices that dealers couldn't match. "We didn't feel we were getting a fair shake," remarks the chairman of a California-based chain. With such complaints in mind, Apple's national salespeople were instructed to seek only "highly visible reference accounts" and to leave smaller orders for dealers.

By mid-1985, it had become clear that Apple was in severe trouble, partly because of the disappointing performance of the Macintosh campaign. The firm was forced to take its first quarterly loss as a public company and to dismiss 20 percent of its employees. Shipments of the Mac were running at only 10,000 per month—far below Apple's 80,000 per month capacity for making the computer. As matters grew worse, chairman John Sculley (formerly a protégé of Donald Kendall at Pepsico) wrestled control of Apple from and ousted co-founder Steven Jobs.

While some business customers advised Sculley to stick to the education market and drop its attempt to challenge IBM with the Macintosh, he rejected such counsel. "The Mac was one of the major reasons I came to Apple in the first place. I had to fall back on what I knew best." He began a new marketing campaign for the Mac, personally lobbied for the machine with buyers for major corporations, and pleaded with software companies to write better programs for the Macintosh.

By early 1987, Sculley's efforts seemed to be paying off. One industry analyst estimates that shipments of Macintoshes doubled in 1986 while worldwide personal computer shipments increased by only 9 percent. Although the Mac still holds only about 7 percent of sales to business firms, its noted user-friendly style is apparently being noticed. Moreover, Apple has benefited from two important developments: the success of desktop publishing, a method for printing typeset-quality documents that the Macintosh pioneered; and the success of Excel, a spreadsheet program that allows the Mac to challenge the Lotus 1-2-3 program which can run on the IBM PC.

While IBM's 1986 earnings fell, Apple's jumped 151 percent, to $154 million, in the fiscal year ending September 30, 1986. By early 1987, Apple's shares on the stock market—which sold as low as 14 in mid-1985—were trading at over 40, a 3-year high. Analysts project that Apple's earnings will rise by 15 percent in 1987; some Wall Street sources claim that the company's stock will reach 60 by the end of 1987.

Of course, Apple still faces a rather formidable threat from the always-dangerous IBM. In early 1987, a leading IBM executive told an industry gathering that future PCs will offer "a new level of user-friendliness." IBM certainly has the potential to coopt the key strengths and selling points of the Macintosh, just as it took business away from the successful Apple II in the early 1980s.

Another lingering question facing Sculley is whether Apple can maintain its present sales approach. "Apple is up against the direct-sales forces of IBM and DEC," notes one industry analyst. "I don't think it's possible to sell successfully in the business market without a direct-sales force." Thus far, Sculley continues to disagree. He insists that Apple can attract business customers by carefully selecting its dealers and by restricting the company's more complex products to the more sophisticated outlets. But Sculley has made one concession: he placed 40 salespeople across the nation to link up dealers with corporate customers.

Sources: "Apple's New Crusade," *Business Week,* Nov. 26, 1984, pp. 146–149, 152, 154, 156; Felix Kessler, "Apple's Pitch to the Fortune 500," *Fortune,* April 15, 1985, pp. 53–56; "Apple's Comeback," *Business Week,* Jan. 19, 1987, pp. 84–89.

1. Why did Apple decide that it was so important to shift its focus from the home computer market to the office computer market?
2. What were the major reasons for Apple's difficulties in penetrating the office computer market?
3. What do you think are two or three major changes that Apple made in its marketing program in order to become more successful in the office computer market?

■ CASE 8

HERSHEY FOODS

Hershey Chocolate Company was founded in 1903 by Milton Snavely Hershey, a Pennsylvania entrepreneur. In 1909, Hershey and his wife, partly because they had no children, decided to donate some of their profits to an orphanage. Indeed, for years, the chocolate company operated mainly to provide funding for the orphanage. Today, the orphanage has evolved into the coeducational Milton Hershey School, and it holds 50.1 percent of the stock in the Hershey Foods Corporation.

In addition to his unusually strong commitment to philanthropy, Milton Hershey implemented his personal values within his company. He emphasized high moral and religious principles; truth, honesty, and integrity; thrift, economy, and industry; the value of education; the importance of maintaining high standards of quality; the rewards of doing good for others; and an emphasis on the family and the community.

By the mid-1980s, Hershey had become a broad-line food marketer, largely through its acquisition of Friendly Ice Cream Corporation, Cory Food Services Corporation, and other firms. By mid-1985, Hershey's sales for the previous four quarters were about $1.9 billion, up 13 percent from a year earlier. The net profit of $111.9 million was up 17 percent. Whereas candy had provided 88 percent of Hershey's sales and 94 percent of its operating profit in 1978, by 1985 candy was responsible for only 68 percent of Hershey's sales and 81 percent of its operating profit.

As Hershey became a larger and more diverse food marketer, top managers began to wonder if the company was changing too quickly. With its new acquisitions, such as Friendly Ice Cream—with its new divisions, among them legal, corporate planning, and public relations—was Hershey losing sight of the core values instilled by Milton Hershey? With this in mind, in 1985 chairman and chief executive officer Richard Zimmerman established a task force to study the situation.

The objectives of the task force's values study were defined as follows:

■ To identify a common set of corporate-wide values that we, as a corporation, wish to publicize. . . .

■ To identify how we can best communicate these values, and how we can gain acceptance and commitment from our employees to them.

■ To identify any internal issues that might hamper success in this area, and how we successfully can deal with them.

It was decided that each task force member would interview Hershey employees on a one-to-one basis and ask them such questions as "What do you think is important to this company?" and "What values do you have to identify with in order to succeed at Hershey?" The interviewing process took about 6 months. Subjects were chosen from all areas and many levels of the company. Results revealed what could be called the "corporate culture" of Hershey, particularly four basic values: people orientation, consumer and quality consciousness, honesty and integrity, and results orientation.

Hershey management has taken a number of steps to underscore its core values. Each of the 20,000 Hershey employees now carries a wallet-sized card stating these values. New management training seminars and house newsletters emphasize Hershey's core values, and an orientation film is being revised to focus on values at Hershey. Chairman and CEO Zimmerman feels this new emphasis on values is critical for the company's future managers. "As time goes by," he suggests, "talking about values will be regarded as absolutely essential. Just as essential as marketing, or logistics, or strategic planning, or thinking, or decision making—as any of those great subjects that they teach in the Harvards and the Stanfords."

Interestingly, Hershey's corporate culture appears to be quite different from that of Mars, its major competitor in the candy business. A 1985 article in *Fortune* reported that "Mars is so secretive that the industry calls it the Kremlin." The article added that the atmosphere at Mars can become bitter when sales are lagging. A former Mars employee reports: "These are people devoted to the company and under a lot of pressure to perform. When market share is growing healthily, everything is okay, but when sales flatten out or even when goals are not quite met, guys can start tearing each other's throats out."

Hershey's Zimmerman believes that the company's values—well founded in the heritage of its founder—will stand the test of time. "Sure, we'll get bigger and more diverse, . . . and will have to change," he acknowledges. "But our values won't change. Instead, values will *guide* change."

Sources: Sally J. Blank, "Hershey: A Company Driven by Values," *Management Review,* Nov. 1986, pp. 31–35; Steve Lawrence, "Bar Wars: Hershey Bites Mars," *Fortune,* July 8, 1985, pp. 52–54, 57.

1. Do you think it possible for a company to maintain very high standards such as those voiced by Hershey and still be successful in the competitive world of business? Why or why not?
2. How will the Hershey corporate culture affect its competitive battle with Mars?
3. Name some ways in which marketing actions could be affected by the four core values of Hershey.

■ CASE 9

TeenAge MAGAZINE

According to *The New York Times,* "Barbara Hannah Marks, who was named a 'young achiever' by *Advertising Age* in 1984, has turned 30, decided that is her fighting age, and is about to take on some heavyweights. As publisher of underachieving *TeenAge* magazine, circulation 200,000, she is declaring war on the well-entrenched forces of *Seventeen,* with a circulation rate base of 1.7 million; *'Teen,* with 1 million; and *YM* (previously *Young Miss*), with 885,000. At her office . . ., Ms. Marks explained her tactic. It's called niche building."

Marks told the *Times* that "teenage girls . . . are not a homogeneous group but, like the adult population, [are] quite segmented. Their numbers and diversity could readily accommodate five magazines."

The *Times* reports that " *'Teen,* from Petersen Publishing, in [Marks'] opinion, is for California-type girls whose three main thoughts are boys, boys, and boys. *YM,* from the United States subsidiary of West Germany's Gruner and Jahr, appeals, she thinks, to conservative middle Americans, is not on the edge of fashion and is the kind of magazine most mothers would be happy to have their daughters read. Both *'Teen* and *YM* are for the younger girls, 11 to 15."

"The older teenager," the *Times* continues, "has *Seventeen* unless she slips up to *Cosmopolitan* or *Vogue,* though Ms. Marks thinks that age group is not interested in all the contents of those two publications. But it is *Seventeen,* the mass-establishment magazine, that advertisers automatically turn to."

The *Times* reports that Ms. Marks is critical of *Seventeen* for being "a bit preachy at times." It adds that Marks is "determined to publish a hipper magazine with the latest fashions, a sophisticated look, and editorial material intended to help young women through the transitional years of 15 to 19, perhaps the most difficult in their lives."

According to the *Times,* Ms. Marks has stated that the seven issues of *TeenAge* put out in 1986 carried only 85 pages of advertising. "By comparison," the *Times* continues, "*Seventeen*'s 12 issues raked in more than 1,376 pages. The young achiever of 1984 has set her six-issue 1987 goal at 200 to 250 pages of advertising, and she is more inclined toward the latter. According to her, certain advertisers are the backbone of the teenage magazine market: Bonne Bell Inc., Maybelline, International Playtex, Johnson & Johnson, Revlon, and Noxell. She said she had received schedules from the first four and that she was optimistic about the last two."

Source: Philip H. Dougherty, "Magazine Seeking Its Niche," *The New York Times,* Dec. 30, 1986, p. D19.

1. If Marks is successful in competing against *Seventeen* and other well-established teen publications, what will be the key to that success?
2. Describe the segmentation approach used by Marks to arrive at her marketing strategy for *TeenAge.*

■ CASE 10

PROCTER & GAMBLE

Procter & Gamble (P&G), the longtime king of consumer marketing in the United States, was clearly beginning to falter in the early 1980s. But fiscal 1985 was especially bitter for P&G: It saw its annual earnings fall 29 percent, the company's first earnings decline since 1952.

Many factors contributed to the disappointing sales performance of P&G products in the early 1980s. With the rise of cable television, network television audiences declined, thereby weakening the effectiveness of P&G's primary marketing tool. Wholesalers and retailers, who have become more independent of manufacturers, became increasingly resentful of the traditionally shabby and high-handed treatment they received from powerful P&G. Moreover, competitors offered new products that narrowed the quality advantage of many P&G items; consumers therefore had less reason to pay premium prices for P&G's products. While these unfavorable trends were developing, P&G's famed laboratories failed to devise major innovative products (except for Rely tampons, which had to be abandoned after they were linked to the toxic shock syndrome).

But Procter & Gamble—dubbed a "wounded lion" by the ad agency Ogilvy & Mather—registered an impressive comeback by mid-1986. In a 12-month period, P&G racked up remarkable market share gains in diapers, toothpaste, and detergents—products that account for over half of the company's earnings. Hercules Segalas, a senior vice president of Drexel Burnham Lambert, suggests: "The market share rebound has been nothing short of phenomenal."

In the detergent market, P&G mounted a new challenge to the dominant liquid detergent, Lever Brothers' Wisk, by offering Liquid Tide. This product features 12 cleaning agents (twice the norm) and a molecule that traps dirt in the wash water. Procter & Gamble drew upon the name of its familiar Tide detergent and placed Liquid Tide in a fire-bright orange bottle—the same orange color as on the Tide box. After only 18 months on the market, sales of Liquid Tide were roughly equal to those of Wisk. Despite the slow-growing nature of the detergent market, Liquid Tide has lifted P&G's overall market share from 49.5 to 51.5 percent.

Procter & Gamble made an even more striking comeback in the disposable diapers market. It first offered new Blue Ribbon Pampers—with a leakproof waistband and elasticized legs—in an effort to wrest sales from Kimberly-Clark's premium-priced Huggies brand. Then, in early 1986, P&G introduced Ultra Pampers, a superabsorbent diaper which reduces the risk of diaper rash. Ultra Pampers, which draws on unpatented technology developed in Japan, offers the further advantage of being thinner than other disposables and therefore easier to carry around. Procter & Gamble boldly spent $500 million to redesign its diaper machines and plants so that Blue Ribbon Pampers and Ultra Pampers could be manufactured. The results certainly justified this investment: Procter & Gamble's share of the diaper market jumped 15 percentage points to 61.5 percent.

In the toothpaste market, P&G lost its dominant position in the early 1980s as competitors offered gels, pump dispensers, and other innovations. But P&G finally countered with a dramatic innovation of its own. Its Crest Tartar Control is the first toothpaste to use the cleansing agent sodium pyrophosphate, which reduces the buildup of tartar. Since the new brand was launched, P&G's share of toothpastes has risen from 32 to 37 percent.

Without question, a crucial factor in P&G's comeback has been a return to one of its traditional strengths—offering superior new products. Liquid Tide, Ultra Pampers, and Crest Tartar Control each had an immediate impact on very lucrative markets. At the same time, however, P&G has apparently learned from some of its mistakes of the early 1980s. In an effort to build better relations with distributors and retailers, P&G instituted various changes, among them new package sizes that are cheaper to handle. Moreover, in a reversal of longtime P&G practice, it began to adapt old names (Tide, Pampers, Crest) for use on new products. The success of existing brands would now be exploited to assist the introduction of new ones.

These were not the only changes in traditional P&G marketing strategy and tactics. While test-marketing was once mandatory at P&G, the company is now bringing out some new products with little or no test-marketing. Although P&G built its reputation on high-quality, premium-price brands, it has begun to offer bargain brands aimed at the lower end of a market. Procter & Gamble has also introduced "me-too" products and product line extensions, among them different "flavors" of dishwashing detergent and cleansers, that essentially trail after consumer trends.

Not surprisingly, many of these changes—especially introduction of major new products—have been costly. For example, in addition to the $500 million needed to redesign its diaper machines and plants, P&G incurred substantial advertising expenditures to launch Blue Ribbon Pampers and Ultra Pampers. But security analysts estimate that P&G's profits for fiscal 1986 will rise by 10 percent. They add that earnings will probably rise a bit faster in 1987 as P&G has already experienced the high costs of new-product introduction in three major markets.

While competitors will undoubtedly challenge Procter & Gamble's successful new products, there is little doubt that Procter & Gamble has effectively flexed its muscles and shown that its slump is over. As a 1986 article in *Fortune* noted: "The aroused lion has ferociously defended its corner of the consumer products jungle."

Sources: Bill Saporito, "Procter & Gamble's Comeback Plan," *Fortune,* Feb. 4, 1985, pp. 30–33, 35, 37; Faye Rice, "The King of Suds Reigns Again," *Fortune,* Aug. 4, 1986, pp.. 130–131, 134.

1. What major changes in the environment led to the slippage in Procter & Gamble's position in the early 1980s?
2. In what ways has Procter & Gamble responded to its disappointing performance in 1985?
3. Should Procter & Gamble abandon its strategy of making innovative and superior products for which they must charge higher prices?

■ ■

IMPLEMENTING AND CONTROLLING MARKETING PLANS

The four components of the marketing mix—product, distribution, price, and promotion—are considered "controllable" in that marketers *create* them through analysis and planning. Now, by implementing and controlling their well-laid plans, marketers compete to convince consumers that their offering provides the most benefits and represents the greatest value. If all goes well, an exchange—a sale—will finally take place.

Although consumers usually perceive the four components of the marketing mix as an integrated whole, we will examine them separately, from a marketer's standpoint:

The *product* consists of core benefits and additional characteristics that consumers must perceive as desirable in quality and value.

Distribution makes products available in useful form where and when consumers want them. Networks of marketing intermediaries channel the product, service, or idea from producer to consumer.

Price is what consumers give up to get the products and services; price tells consumers what to expect in quality and value. For an exchange to occur, price must be perceived as an acceptable risk.

Promotion positions the product in the marketplace. Marketers provide information and make persuasive appeals through advertising, personal selling, publicity, and sales promotion.

THE PRODUCT

10 Managing Products

11 Developing New Products

Of the four components of the marketing mix, the product may be viewed as the starting point of marketing. Although each component contributes to consumers' overall perceptions, decisions about distribution, price, and promotion all revolve around the product itself. Thus, in examining how marketing plans are implemented, we begin with the product.

Chapter 10 views the product as a bundle of benefits that produce satisfaction. We look closely at the marketing of both goods and services, and then we present a framework for classifying products. Decisions about branding, packaging, and the product mix are the essence of product management.

Chapter 11 shifts the focus to new-product development, exploring why marketers seek new products. Important influences include the product life cycle and the processes of diffusion and adoption, whereby innovative products are accepted or rejected by consumers. We describe the strategies and tactics of product development, and we examine how large marketers typically organize to accomplish product management.

10

MANAGING PRODUCTS

Copyright © Donna Ferrato/Visions.

SPOTLIGHT ON

☐ Core products and their transformation to augmented products

☐ Differences between services and physical goods

☐ Special factors affecting the marketing of services

☐ Bases of classification for consumer and industrial products

☐ Branding and packaging decisions and product success or failure

☐ Basic decisions that marketers typically make about the product mix

(Ken Karp.)

If, like so many consumers these days, you prefer to limit your sugar intake, you may drink so-called diet sodas or add a sugar substitute to your coffee. Chances are that you have tasted aspartame, a low-calorie sweetener developed by G. D. Searle & Company. Searle markets aspartame to consumers under the brand name Equal; as an ingredient in food products, aspartame is sold under the NutraSweet label.

Equal/NutraSweet was initially priced two to three times higher than competing products Sweet 'N Low and Sugar Twin. The higher price did not hurt sales: In test markets in Marion, Indiana, and Pittsfield, Massachusetts, Equal expanded the artificial sweetener market by some 27 percent. The reason? Aspartame tastes much more like sugar than its competitors. Searle claimed that aspartame left no bitter aftertaste, and calorie-conscious consumers seemed to agree.

Advertising for Equal featured the theme "Welcome to the sweet life." In an unusual move, Searle also embarked on a consumer advertising campaign for NutraSweet, even though the product is not marketed to the public. Saying "You can't buy it, but you're gonna love it," these ads listed the first products to use NutraSweet as an additive: Kool-Aid sugar-free drink mixes, Lipton iced-tea mix, Quaker Oats' Halfsies cereal, Swiss Miss sugar-free cocoa mix, and Sugar Free Wyler's drink mix. Searle enlisted Lipton's sales force to distribute Equal to grocery outlets, but the company handled its own bulk sales of NutraSweet.

Aspartame became a successful product not only because it was an innovation that offered an attractive benefit—better taste—but also because it was boldly yet appropriately priced, its benefits were communicated through extensive promotion, and it was distributed effectively. Marketing the product under two brand names was an imaginative way to capture different markets. Finally, the consumer version, Equal, was packaged attractively. Equal and NutraSweet truly offered both the public and resale buyers a bundle of satisfactions.

Source: Jennifer Alter, "Something Old, Something New Sweeten Searle's Sales Picture," *Advertising Age,* Feb. 14, 1983, pp. 4, 64.

We have noted that a product may be a tangible good (a camera, a computer, or a can of corn); an intangible benefit in the form of a service (dry cleaning, life insurance, or baby-sitting); or even an idea ("I Love New York" or "Join the March of Dimes"). A product may even be a person "packaged" for the public (political candidates and pop musicians come immediately to mind). In short, products encompass a wide range of goods, services, ideas, and personalities, and managing products of any kind is the focus of this chapter.

First we examine core products and how they can be enhanced by additional characteristics to become augmented products. Then we analyze the differences between the marketing of services and the marketing of tangible goods. A classification of products, focusing on categories of consumer and industrial goods, follows. The remainder of the chapter describes in detail the branding, packaging, labeling, and product mix decisions that marketers face in managing products.

THE PRODUCT: A BUNDLE OF SATISFACTIONS

A **product** is anything an organization or individual offers for exchange that may satisfy customers' or consumers' needs or the marketer's own needs. This is necessarily a broad definition: Whereas many products are as simple as a paper clip or a hairpin, others are quite complex—consider a data-processing system or a pipe-coating and inspection service for an oil field. Whether simple or complex, though, every product is more than what meets the eye.

When you buy a bar of Ivory soap, for example, you buy a package (and not simply the physical wrapping that protects the soap). With Ivory, you purchase an image—a long-standing one—of purity ($99^{44}/_{100ths}\%$ pure, in fact). You pay a reasonable price for the soap, thereby exchanging your money for a history embedded in the U.S. consciousness: a history of pink-cheeked babies being bathed; a history which persuades you that Ivory does more than clean; a history which convinces you that it's nice for a bar of soap to float in your bathtub! In short, you expect and receive a number of interrelated satisfactions from that exchange.

Amazing that a few ounces of vegetable oil with air whipped into it can deliver so much, isn't it? In the marketplace, every exchange of your money, time, opinion,

While the physical ingredients of a bar of Ivory may not be very complicated nor very glamorous, the image of the product has kept people buying. Marketers keep the image fresh; buyers get more for their money than a bar of whipped vegetable oil. (Courtesy of the Procter & Gamble Company.)

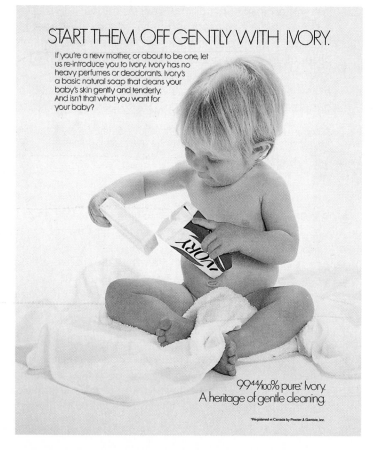

or vote should deliver a bundle of satisfactions: the familiar utilities of form, time, place, and possession. But that bundle of satisfactions begins with a core product and a core benefit.

☐ *The Core Product: What Benefit?*

The **core product** is the basic good or service purchased, aside from its packaging or accompanying services. Ivory soap's core product is the simple, unperfumed bar of oil and air. But few purchases are made because of the core product alone. We purchase a product first because of its **core benefit**—the need that product fulfills or the problem it solves. The core benefit from a bar of soap is obvious: It cleans your skin.

A core product's benefits range from tangible to intangible. Your handheld calculator, for instance, is a tangible fabrication of plastic, metal, electronic circuitry, and a liquid display crystal; the core product must function well to satisfy your demand for its core benefit—speedy calculations. Yet you expect other, less tangible benefits. A product delivers a bundle of such satisfactions related to its package, servicing, warranties, image, and branding.

THE PACKAGE   The **package** comprises the container or wrapping and the graphics and labeling that enclose the product. Packaging's most important function is to protect the product—to get calculators, cookies, and cameras to consumers in proper, useful condition. Any package that fails to satisfy that fundamental purpose is a marketing mistake. But packages have other important and useful functions; they promote the product, provide information, and appeal to buyers' emotions.

Sometimes the package is as important as, or more important than, the core product itself in ensuring buyers' psychological satisfaction. If Esteé Lauder, Revlon, or Dior packaged their most expensive fragrances in plastic, screw-top bottles, customers would move along the perfume counter to other products. In the House of Guerlain plant near Paris, expensive floral oils are piped into exquisite crystal bottles bearing the Shalimar label. Obviously, the Shalimar buyer needs more than aroma for satisfaction.

Packaging is often expensive for mundane products as well. The packaging of a can of beer costs the manufacturer five times as much as the water, barley, hops, and so on that go into the brew. And the packaging for the food and beverages ingested by the average American each year weighs more than 600 pounds.[1]

PRODUCT SERVICING   An important extension of the core product is its **servicing**—maintenance of the product in working order so that its benefits are not diminished. Most physical goods do break down eventually. If the muffler on your car becomes noisy, quick repair is vital to your satisfaction with the entire car. For most consumers, the servicing offered by manufacturers of major appliances is an essential aspect of the product and affects buying decisions. An out-of-service television set on Super Bowl Sunday provides little satisfaction and no core benefit. Servicing is also important to organizational buyers. IBM attained its preeminent position in the computer industry at least in part by having speedy and competent repair service available before its competitors did.

WARRANTIES   A **warranty** is the producer's assurance that the product will meet buyers' expectations or that buyers will be compensated in some way if the product fails to meet expectations. Warranties are either express or implied. An **express warranty** specifies exactly what claims and guarantees the producer is

Beyond the core product, which can sometimes be very similar to the competitors' product, marketers extend the meaning of the product by adding value. These people looking to buy a microwave oven are interested in the brand name of Maytag—known for its lack of repair needs—and in the product warranty. The credibility of the retail store and the retail salesperson are also important. (Copyright © Jeffry W. Myers/The Stock Market.)

offering and adds value to such major purchases as automobiles, appliances, and electronic equipment. Midas Mufflers has long offered an express warranty stating that an installed muffler will last as long as the buyer owns the car or will be replaced free. In Midas's case, the warranty is an important part of the company's promotional message; it affects how consumers perceive the product they are buying.

Implied warranties indicate that the product is in good condition and is suitable for the purpose for which it was bought. Courts imply such warranties largely in response to the Magnuson-Moss Consumer Product Warranty Act of 1975. Implied warranties are considered to go with the product, to be an extension of it. Although this warranty greatly protects consumers in the marketplace, it is the express warranty that concerns most buyers; such specific, stated assurances add even more value to the core product.[2]

IMAGE AND BRANDING   The marketing department of a west coast university conducted a series of taste tests in which panel members ranked five national brands of beer. The beers were presented in plain, identical bottles labeled only A through E. In two tests with different panels conducted 4 weeks apart, brand B received the top ranking and brand A the bottom. A third test included a new variable: The bottles were labeled, but only with typewritten tags spelling out Schlitz, Pabst, Budweiser, and so on. In this round, brand A received the top ranking, and brand

C fell to the bottom. In a fourth test, the beers were presented in their regular retail containers. This time, brand C was rated highest in overall quality, and brand D received the lowest ranking.[3] Clearly, the panelists in these experiments perceived the beers differently when the bottles were labeled with brands.

Brand image is the overall concept of the product as perceived by consumers. It consists of many individual perceptions that together create an aura surrounding the product. Among the major factors that coalesce into a product's image are its inherent quality, its packaging and price, the brand's reputation, and the effectiveness of promotion. Indeed, some product classes, like perfume, rely almost totally on the creation of brand images in selling their products.[4]

Product utility thus stems from more than the core product; the package, servicing, warranties, image, and branding all contribute to an enhanced perception of the product. These benefits must be considered an integral part of the product, because the product and its benefits are inseparable in consumers' minds. Together, they augment the product by enhancing its bundle of satisfactions (see Figure 10-1).

☐ *The Augmented Product*

Chapter 1 cited Theodore Levitt's justly famous aphorism that people buy quarter-inch holes not quarter-inch drill bits. To that insight about a product's core benefit he added these thoughts about enhancing consumers' satisfaction:

> People don't buy products; they buy the expectation of benefits. . . . The marketing view demands the active recognition of a new kind of competition that is in

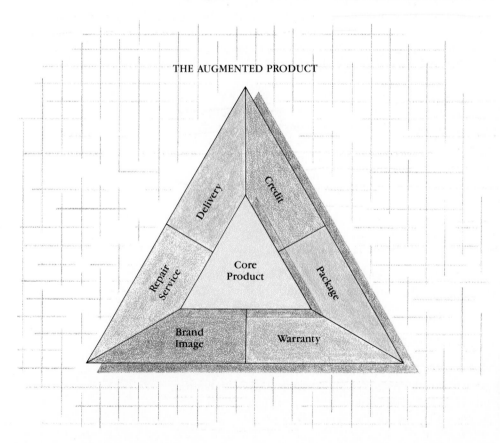

THE AUGMENTED PRODUCT

Figure 10-1 *The augmented product.* The augmented product is what the consumer is really buying. It includes the "expectation of benefits" from the core product and the benefits from all that goes with it.

galloping ascendancy in the world today. This is the competition of product augmentation: not competition between what companies produce in their factories, but between what they add to their factory output in the form of packaging, services, advertising, customer advice, financing, delivery arrangements, warehousing, and other things people value.[5]

The **augmented product,** then, is a good, service, or idea enhanced by its accompanying benefits; it is "a synthesis of what the seller intends and the buyer perceives."[6]

Consider how Kodak has augmented its core product to capture nearly 80 percent of all film sales to consumers. Rather than featuring photographic equipment or film, Kodak's advertising often centers on a family event, such as a child's birthday party or the opening of Christmas presents. In effect, the basic message is, "Would you trust this moment to anyone but Kodak?" Over the years the company has consciously built a reputation for quality and reliability. Through promotion, simple but distinctive packaging, effective distribution, and efficient service added to a quality core product, Kodak has achieved a truly augmented product. To paraphrase Theodore Levitt, Kodak customers don't buy film, they buy memories.

One decision marketers often face is just how much quality to build into a product. The logical answer might seem to be "As much as possible," but would you be willing to buy an electronic typewriter that was unconditionally guaranteed (perhaps you'd get a new machine if yours should malfunction within 25 years) at a price of, say, $22,500? Probably not. The price is too high for an unnecessary level of quality. Moreover, technical advances are certain to produce newer machines with desirable features (such as a large memory capacity) that your very durable model would lack. Marketers are constantly challenged with the question of how much quality to build into a product at a cost that allows a profit. Companies reach different decisions regarding the trade-off between quality and price, but the most successful marketers are those who most accurately measure buyers' perceptions of quality versus price.

Quality is really a complex set of dimensions. When we speak of a product's "quality," we could mean its durability (how long it lasts), its reliability (how frequently it fails), its features (how many "bells and whistles"), or other dimensions—all of which are important.[7] The recent trend suggests consumer preference for higher-quality products. This preference is evident both in what people say (that they intend to buy higher-quality items even it it means buying fewer) and in what they actually buy.[8]

THE MARKETING OF SERVICES

For about two decades, the U.S. role in the world economy has been shifting. More and more, the U.S. business system is dominated by the production of services rather than the manufacturing of physical goods. Consider the following items:

- Only 13 percent of the U.S. labor force is employed in manufacturing; 60 percent of workers either produce or process information.[9] Service industries employ two out of three Americans working in the private sector.
- An era of deindustrialization is beginning in all industrial countries, including Japan and Germany. Estimates are that third-world nations will manufacture as much as 30 percent of the world's goods by the year 2000.

The consumers in this picture are simultaneously buying and consuming haircutting services. Such services are perishable (you can't stock up on them), intangible (you are buying the skills of the barber), not standardized (which one of these is the most skilled?), and require consumer participation (you can't offer to pick up a haircut for your roommate). (Copyright © Miro Vintoniv/The Picture Cube.)

- Services account for more than one-third of U.S. export receipts, 46 percent of the nation's gross national product, and almost 50 cents of every household dollar spent.[10]
- Almost 100 percent of new jobs created between now and the end of the century will be service-related.

The shift to a service economy is real. It will affect the way we pursue our careers and spend our leisure time, and it most assuredly will have impact on what and how marketers sell.

Throughout this book we have considered services—and even ideas, organizations, and people—as products. Like physical goods, services offer benefits for which consumers exchange something of value. The transaction may involve consumers' money (a haircut), time (a typing course), or votes (a political candidate). Services also can be augmented or enhanced by related benefits: The haircut may be scheduled at your convenience; the typing course may include an overview of word processing; and the political candidate may sponsor a neighborhood newsletter. Thus, services also have images and can be positioned, just as physical products can be. Again, marketers must understand consumers' perceptions of services to match products' benefits with people's needs and desires.[11]

Four major characteristics distinguish the marketing of services from that of physical goods: (1) Services are intangible. (2) Buyers and producers participate in service marketing. (3) Services are perishable. (4) Services lack standardization.

INTANGIBILITY   Certain aspects of services cannot be held, touched, smelled, tried on, or placed on a shelf. Consider what happens when you purchase such services as "entertainment" (such as movies), "time and advice" (consulting with a professor), or a "process" (such as dry cleaning). Services are rendered and experienced that often cannot be grasped or inventoried. Services are frequently characterized by *intangibility*—they are not palpable, physical goods. As Figure

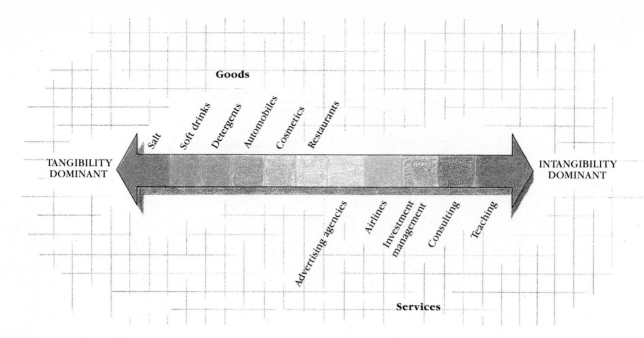

Figure 10-2 *Tangibility of products: goods versus services.* Most physical products, or goods, are more tangible than are services. However, both goods and services have many degrees of intangibility.

10-2 illustrates, intangibility is dominant in services, whereas tangibility dominates most goods. The figure shows a continuum ranging from salt and soft drinks (goods) at the tangible end to teaching and consulting (services) at the intangible end.

PARTICIPATION OF BUYERS AND PRODUCERS   When shoppers pick up a loaf of bread or a package of cereal from the supermarket shelf, those goods' producers are removed some distance in space and time (the less so for the bread, the better). When those same consumers choose a psychiatrist, consult a tax accountant, or begin a course in aerobic dancing, they are very much involved in the creation and production of that service—as are the producing sellers. The interaction of buyer and producer in the production and consumption of many services is thus quite high.

Although buyer and seller participation in the purchase of physical goods may also be low (the loaf of bread) or high (the design and construction of a new home), participation in services is typically higher because buyer and seller actually produce the service. Figure 10-3 indicates the degree of buyer and seller participation in the exchange of various goods and services.[12]

PERISHABILITY   In general, goods are produced, then sold, and finally consumed. Services, however, are usually sold first and then produced and consumed at the same time. As a result of this simultaneous production and consumption, services are often transitory; they have the characteristic of perishability. A hotel room or a seat on a train does not truly provide a service until it is purchased (rented) and used. An empty seat on a flight from St. Louis to Seattle can never be sold again. It may be occupied the next day, but the previous day it represented a loss that the airline can never make up.

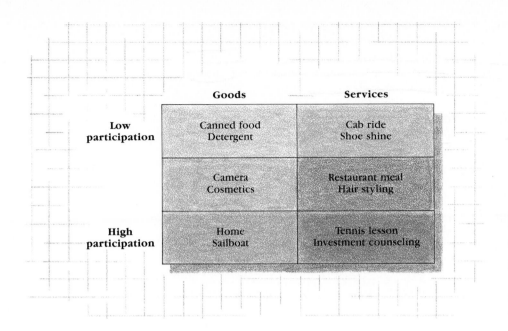

	Goods	Services
Low participation	Canned food Detergent	Cab ride Shoe shine
	Camera Cosmetics	Restaurant meal Hair styling
High participation	Home Sailboat	Tennis lesson Investment counseling

Figure 10-3 *Participation of buyer in the exchange of products: goods versus services.* There is generally greater participation of the buyer in the exchange process for services than for physical goods, but there is variation in both.

LACK OF STANDARDIZATION   A can of Del Monte peas is usually of consistent quality, whereas a waiter's service may be attentive and polite or slow and surly. Consumers of services frequently experience wide variations in the quality of benefits they receive. Services are usually produced and consumed simultaneously and are often uniquely tailored to an individual consumer's needs. Standardization is not always possible or desirable.[13]

PRODUCT CLASSIFICATIONS

Given the vast array of physical products on the marketplace and the many services viewed as products, some method of classification is obviously needed. This method should help us to understand how the groups are—and should be—marketed. Of the many methods used to classify products, two provide the greatest insight to product management: classification by product characteristics and by consumers' perceptions and purchases of products.

Characteristics: Durables, Nondurables, and Services

The U.S. government keeps track of business statistics (gross national product, imports and exports, plant investment, and so on) by classifying products first as **durable goods**—tangible items that can be expected to survive multiple uses, like vacuum cleaners and sofas.[14] **Nondurable goods** are also tangible items, but they normally are consumed in one or a few uses—fresh fruit, shampoo, and razor blades are examples. The government also distinguishes between services and goods in its bookkeeping. In contrast to physical goods, **services** are activities, benefits, or satisfactions that are offered to satisfy consumers' and customers' needs.

Now consider some complications. For example, although many (even most) services are created at the time of transaction and are nondurable, exceptions abound. Whereas a haircut soon outgrows its usefulness, a life insurance policy lasts a lifetime (and beyond). Similarly, your relationship with your bank may last for years, allowing you to use its services hundreds of times. And a service that inspects and maintains industrial pipelines is generally ongoing. Clearly, then, classifying products by characteristics is only marginally useful to marketers. They need a classification system that is more attuned to the marketing concept—one that reflects how use of the product will satisfy consumers' needs.

☐ Consumers' Perceptions and Purchasing Patterns

A more useful classification system is based on how products are perceived and bought. For example, a homemaker and a plant supervisor have different needs when purchasing light bulbs. The two buyers have different attitudes toward the wattage, shape, type of bulb, price, and likely longevity; they also probably buy their bulbs from different sources. The homemaker may pick up bulbs as needed, on the weekly shopping trip, but the plant manager is responsible for stocking bulbs in quantity for all fixtures. The homemaker "knows" all about light bulbs and may even buy them from a charitable group. The industrial buyer, however, is likely to have technical questions, servicing requirements, and financial terms to consider, possibly requiring consultation with a professional sales representative.

To illustrate why marketers need to consider customers' perceptions and buying practices, the following sections explore consumer products and industrial products.

CONSUMER PRODUCTS   A **consumer product** is a good or service purchased by an individual for personal or household use. For example, you, a college student, might own a Bic pen, a Van Heusen or McGregor sweater, and an Accutron watch. You thus would possess what marketers term a "convenience" product, a "shopping" product, and a "specialty" product. If you also have a life insurance policy, you own an "unsought" product. What differentiates these goods and services is how you (the consumer) think (or don't think) about them and how you go about buying them.

Convenience Products   You probably made little effort to get that Bic pen. You may have bought several of them, and you may not even remember where you made your purchase. **Convenience products** are widely available, usually inexpensive, and frequently purchased. "Convenience" is the key word, consumers do not expect to make much effort to get a carton of milk, a newspaper, or a package of chewing gum. In general, accessibility is the key factor in choosing convenience services such as dry cleaning and film processing.

Prices for convenience products tend to be similar wherever they are available, and mass advertising usually promotes the goods directly to consumers. Marketers see convenience goods as staples, as impulse products, and as emergency products.

Consumers buy **staples,** such as bread, flour, salt, milk, and bathroom tissues, routinely and often. Buyers give little thought to the purchase other than noting the need for the item and picking it up.

All those racks arranged prominently and enticingly around checkout counters in supermarkets, drugstores, and variety stores typically feature **impulse products.** Such items are purchased because of an immediate stimulus and without previous planning. Flashbulbs, razor blades, pocket novels and horoscope books, candy, chewing gum, and trial sizes of cosmetics are goods that consumers purchase on impulse. Shoe shines, car washes, and gift wrapping are services often bought on impulse.

Impulse products are those consumers buy on the "spur of the moment." Items bought this way are often found on the racks near the checkout lines in supermarkets. (Ken Karp.)

Unexpected and urgent needs prompt the purchase of **emergency products.** In the midst of a rainstorm, the need for an umbrella may become an emergency. If you forget to pack toothpaste for a trip, the need for it becomes compelling.

Shopping Products **Shopping products** are goods and services that consumers "shop" for, comparing quality, suitability, style, price, and other factors. Products in this category include major appliances, audio and video components, winter coats, home-remodeling services, and investment plans offered by financial institutions. Although advertising is essential for convenience products, it is less important for most shopping products; instead, personal selling plays a major role as salespeople help consumers to make comparisons. Another important point is that shopping products need not be so widely available as convenience items. Consumers will make a trip to learn about videocassette recorders, but they will not go out of their way for a soft drink.

Shopping products may be categorized—according to consumers' perceptions—as either homogeneous (similar) or heterogeneous (dissimilar). Dishwashers are **homogeneous shopping products**—products about which consumers perceive little difference in the core benefits the products they provide. Even the least expensive dishwashers made by KitchenAid, Maytag, and General Electric provide wash, rinse, and dry cycles. Those are the core features or benefits that make the

machines similar to prospective buyers. Price and personal selling are likely to be major influences in purchasing homogeneous products or services. For this reason, Hertz, Avis, and National cannot price their rental cars above the going rate.

Heterogeneous shopping products differ from homogeneous ones primarily in that style, design, and personal taste tend to outweigh price in the purchasing decision. Consumers perceive that core products and their benefits differ between brands. A family shopping for a set of china recognizes the design differences between Wedgewood and Royal Doulton; these differences are crucial in the family's choice of dishes. Furniture, clothing, and the concerts you attend all reflect your personal taste.

Shopping goods are those products sufficiently important to consumers that they will shop around, comparing prices and features. Many shopping goods are relatively homogeneous, such as these television sets; others are more heterogeneous, such as furniture, which involves different styles and fashions. (Left: Copyright © Rob Nelson/Stock, Boston. Right: Copyright © Bohdan Hrynewych/Stock, Boston.)

Specialty Products If you have the money, want to spend it, and decide you would look good behind the wheel of a Jaguar or a Porsche sports car, you won't be satisfied with a Ford Escort or a Chevrolet Citation. Consumers perceive **specialty products** as having unique qualities—to the point that no substitutes are acceptable. As a result, image and reputation usually far outweigh price in the purchasing decision for specialty products. In addition, specialty items need not be widely available. Consumers who want a Prince tennis racquet, Lalique crystal, or a Brooks Brothers shirt will make the effort to find that brand and only that brand. The services of well-known catering firms, hair stylists, photographers, and plastic surgeons also may be considered specialty products.

The promotion of specialty products typically combines well-targeted advertising with a limited number of retail outlets where sales personnel are expected to be knowledgeable and helpful. Potential crystal buyers, for example, will learn about Lalique in the pages of *The New Yorker* or *Gourmet*, but not in *TV Guide*, *People*, or *Sports Illustrated*. And Lalique's imported stemware and vases will be found at only a few outlets located in major cities and fashionable resort areas.

Again, remember that some products fall into categories different from those we have indicated, according to the unique perceptions (and fortunes) of individual consumers. A weekend athlete may grab the first pair of correctly sized tennis shorts in a discount store (a convenience product); more serious tennis players may shop and compare shorts made by Nike and Adidas (a shopping product); style-conscious players may insist on Italian-designed linen shorts available only from an exclusive boutique on Madison Avenue or Rodeo Drive (a specialty product).

Unsought Products In contrast to our examples thus far, consumers do not consciously want or actively seek out **unsought products.** Hence, such a product's characteristics, use, and image mean little; consumers have no intention of buying the product in the first place. Encyclopedias and life insurance are the traditional examples of unsought products. Other items include the wares of street vendors, cemetery plots and tombstones, and emergency medical services. Unsought products are not *unknown* to consumers; they are simply not wanted and not sought unless a need is aroused. Since people often avoid these products, costly personal selling is often required, which may lead to higher markups.

Exhibit 10-1 summarizes the classification of consumer products. Product categories are not always clear-cut; a single product may fit more than one category, depending on consumers' perceptions. However, the traditional groupings of consumer products do help marketers to develop products aimed at specific market segments. A similar approach is useful in considering the categories of industrial products.

INDUSTRIAL PRODUCTS **Industrial products** are purchased by an organization for use either in other products or in its own operations. Organizations that buy industrial products include manufacturers, commercial businesses, not-for-profit institutions, and government agencies at all levels. In Chapter 5, we explained that demand for industrial products is **derived demand**—that is, demand arises from the needs of other organizations and (usually) from ultimate consumers. Thus, when Briggs & Stratton provides the motors for Toro Lawn mowers, demand for those motors depends directly on consumer demand for lawn mowers.

Many industrial products become part of another product, as in the case of Briggs & Stratton motors or the milk and flavorings that go into Howard Johnson's ice cream. Other industrial products are needed for the buying organization's production processes; for example, USX buys iron ore to produce its various grades of steel. Still other industrial items are needed for the buying organization's general operations. Aetna Insurance buys mainframe computers to process data about its thousands of policyholders, and it also buys paper towels for the restrooms in its various office locations.

Whatever their use, industrial products would not be in demand if the buying organization were not, in turn, offering other goods and services for sale. As a result,

EXHIBIT 10-1	**Classification of Consumer Products**		
Convenience Products	Shopping Products	Specialty Products	Unsought Products
Staples: Bread, milk, cigarettes, beer, gasoline	*Homogeneous products:* Refrigerators, washing machines	Health foods, engagement rings, luxury cars	Caskets, self-improvement courses, life insurance
Impulse items: Candy, magazines, flashbulbs, packaged snacks, fortune-telling	*Heterogeneous products:* Pianos, winter coats, dental services		
Emergency items: Medical supplies, repair kits for leaky pipes			

An important category of industrial products includes the parts that make other products. This is a bin full of lock mechanisms, which are needed for the manufacture of locks. (Copyright © Lawrence Migdale 1986.)

the concept of derived demand applies directly or indirectly to all industrial products.

Industrial products may be classified most usefully into five categories:

1. Installations (plant and major equipment)
2. Accessory equipment
3. Components, including raw materials and parts and subassemblies
4. Supplies for maintenance, repair, and operation
5. Various industrial services[15]

To some extent, the first two classifications are defined from an accounting standpoint. The issue is whether major expenditures enter accounting records as capital goods to be depreciated over a period of several years or whether they are to be expensed in the year of purchase.

Installations: Plant and Major Equipment   Typically, a **plant** consists of the site and buildings needed for an organization's manufacturing, processing, service production, or office operations. Plants are costly and are major commitments of an organization's resources against future revenues. As such, they are considered to be capital goods. **Major equipment**—costly durable goods—are also capital expenditures. Examples include spot-welding robots used by automakers, complex data-processing systems, and large machine tools.

Prices for major equipment are usually determined on a bid basis after a period of prolonged negotiations between buyers and sellers. Personal selling is important for such major purchases, and top management is usually involved in these buying decisions. Advertising for industrial equipment is aimed primarily at building the company's image rather than at securing individual orders. Distribution of major equipment is direct, and no intermediaries are involved.

Accessory Equipment   Desk chairs, small power tools, and typewriters are all **accessory equipment**—machines and materials that do not become integral parts of the purchaser's product. Such items are often expensed at the time of purchase and are not depreciated, although exceptions exist. A small business may consider an electronic typewriter to be a capital expense; however, a large organization may buy thousands of typewriters and may expense them in the year of purchase.

Great variety exists in the pricing, distribution, and promotion of accessory equipment. Such items differ in size and use; may be expensive or inexpensive; are distributed directly or by intermediaries; and are sold through personal selling, advertising, or a combination of the two.

Components   **Components** include raw materials or parts and subassemblies that become integral elements of the buying organization's products. Cotton and cottonseeds, oil shale, iron ore, and animal hides are examples of **raw materials**—natural resources and agricultural goods that have been processed only as necessary for economy or physical handling before being incorporated into the buyer's products. Copper ore, tuna fish, and pine trees—resources of the land, sea, and forest—are other examples. Agricultural raw materials range from wheat and mushrooms to eggs and milk, which may be used to produce bread, soup, or ice cream, or may be marketed directly to consumers with little or no processing.

Traditionally, raw materials have been produced and sold in markets of almost pure competition, that is, as commodities. Standard prices are still the rule for resources like copper and iron ores, but buyers increasingly pay different prices for the various grades of agricultural products like peaches, apples, and veal. Advertising and mass promotion have played only minor roles in the marketing of raw materials in the past, but today such agricultural promoters as the New Zealand Lamb Council and the Washington State Apple Growers' Association are seeking to influence industrial buyers by appealing directly to consumers through mass advertising. Distribution of raw materials is most often accomplished through commodity exchanges.

Parts and subassemblies are fabricated items that are assembled into other products; they range from screws and bolts to the complex microprocessor chips that help guide satellites into orbit. Marketing of parts and subassemblies depends heavily on personal selling and competitive pricing; distribution may be direct or through intermediaries.

Companies producing parts and subassemblies are often little known outside their own industries. Borg-Warner has been called an "invisible corporation." Among its many industrial products, the company makes axles, universal joints, transmissions, clutches, and a host of components for automakers and has long been a supplier of valves for plumbing equipment. The company supplies plastics to RCA for radios and to Western Electric for telephones. Borg-Warner's electric motors are found in many air conditioners, including its own York brand.

Supplies   **Supplies** are items that are not incorporated into the buying organization's products; they are the goods needed to keep everyday operations going—everything from typewriter cartridges, computer printing paper, machine oil, and socket wrenches to liquid soap for restrooms and janitorial services. Such products—both goods and services—are referred to as **MRO items:** maintenance, repair, and operations products. Typically ordered by purchasing agents through dealers and distributors, MRO items make up a highly competitive industry. Prices reflect this, for low profit margins are the rule. Personal selling is the major means of promoting MRO items to industrial buyers, although marketers also use catalogs extensively.

Industrial Services   A large and growing part of the U.S. economy, **industrial services** are purchased for use in producing the buyer's products or, more frequently, for use in general operations. Like consumer services, industrial services are not as standardized as goods, nor are they as tangible or as durable. Buyer participation in the creation of industrial services may be quite high (as in management consulting) or relatively low (as in janitorial services).

A large sector of industrial services lies directly in marketing. Advertising agencies, marketing research firms, product-testing groups, brand-name advisers, and individual marketing consultants exist to serve the needs of the nation's producers. Political consulting firms and polling organizations have also expanded their services tremendously in recent years.

Exhibit 10-2 summarizes the classification of industrial products. Remember that exceptions exist in all the categories we have examined. Nonetheless the categories provide good general guidelines for planning, developing, selling, and managing products.

■ BRANDING DECISIONS ■

When you choose Pepperidge Farm chocolate chip cookies over similar treats offered by Keebler's, Nabisco, or Famous Amos, you express, quite concretely, a brand preference. Pepperidge Farm and its many competitors offer specific brands of "chocolate chip" cookies, but the courts have ruled that there will be only one brand of "Toll House" cookies. In the early 1930s, Ruth Wakeman began baking cookies using Nestlé's semisweet chocolate bits at her Toll House Restaurant in Whitman, Massachusetts. After some years, the restaurant was sold, and Nestlé acquired the rights to the Toll House name. Today, each package of Nestlé's Toll House Morsels carries a copy of the original recipe; other bakers are prohibited from using the Toll House name.[16]

What's in a name? When it comes to successful products, a great deal. Consider the following statement from Coca-Cola's legal staff: "The production plants and

EXHIBIT 10-2	Classification of Industrial Products			
Installations	**Accessory Equipment**	**Components**	**MRO Supplies**	**Industrial Services**
Plant:	Desks	*Raw materials:*	Floor wax	Institutional food
■ General Electric's	Delivery vans	■ Bauxite	Pipe wrenches	services
Louisville factory	Drafting tables	■ Copper ore	Company	Accounting
■ Transamerica's	Labeling machines	■ Pacific salmon	stationery	Advertising
San Francisco		eggs	Cleaning fluids	Grounds
headquarters				maintenance
■ Pabst's Milwaukee				
brewery				
		Parts and		
		subassemblies:		
Major equipment:		■ Car stereos		
■ Construction crane		■ Safety valves		
■ Mainframe		■ Refrigerator		
computer		shelves		
■ Oil-drilling rig		■ Microchips		

inventories of the Coca-Cola Company could go up in flames one night, yet the following morning there is not a bank in Atlanta, New York, or any other place that would not lend this company the funds necessary for rebuilding, accepting as security only the goodwill of its trademark."[17] Coca-Cola, Nestlé, Xerox, and other successful marketers go to great lengths to defend their names as valuable parts of their products. That identification, or branding, has value so great that it cannot really be measured. Branding is more complex than it might seem, as the many specific terms in Exhibit 10-3 indicate.[18]

Branding Past and Present

Branding is a centuries-old idea whose time has not yet passed. As early as the middle ages, medieval artisans organized guilds for the distribution of their products. Each guild required individuals to mark their items with a distinguishing symbol. Branding also might be regarded as the beginning of quality control and implied warranties. In the United States, a **brand** identified the producer and made it possible to identify the makers of both superior and inferior products. Sellers of patent medicines began to employ brand names for their wares in the nineteenth century. At that time, most products were sold in general stores, usually in bulk form, and with no identifying name or mark. Consumers simply bought soap (cut from a large cake, weighed, and wrapped in brown paper), salt, flour, meat, or pickles. Beans came to the store in 100-pound sacks, and were put in 1-pound paper sacks by the store owner or employee. Eggs came in from individual farmers, and when con-

EXHIBIT 10-3	Key Terms Related to Branding

Brand   A name, term, symbol, or design or a combination of them that is intended to identify the goods or services of one seller or group of sellers and to differentiate them from products of competitors.

Brand name   That part of a brand which can be vocalized—the utterable. Examples are Kodak, CBS, Kentucky Fried Chicken, Q-Tips, American Express, and United Parcel Service.

Trade name   The name under which a company chooses to conduct its business, which may or may not also be a brand name. "Lever Brothers" and "Procter & Gamble" are trade names, but those companies choose to market their products under different brand names. "Coca-Cola," however, is the trade name both of the company that markets many soft drinks and of that company's leading brand.

Brand mark   That part of a brand which can be recognized but is not utterable, such as a symbol, design, or distinctive coloring or lettering. Examples are Texaco's red star, Ralston-Purina's checkerboard, and Coca-Cola's familiar script lettering.

Copyright   The exclusive legal right to reproduce, publish, and sell a literary, musical, dramatic, or artistic work. This book is copyrighted by McGraw-Hill, Inc., which is noted on the copyright page with the symbol ©. In the United States, copyright extends for 28 years and may be renewed for another 28 years.

Trade character   A brand mark that represents a human being or an animal associated with the products. Examples are Ronald McDonald; the Pillsbury Doughboy; the gentleman from Quaker Oats; Charlie, the Star-Kist tuna; the Playboy bunny; the Smith Brothers; and those imaginary ladies, Betty Crocker and Ann Page.

Trademark   A brand or part of a brand that is given legal protection because it is capable of exclusive appropriation. A trademark protects the seller's exclusive rights to use the brand name or brand mark. Registered trademarks are sometimes followed by the symbol ®, meaning "registered." Examples are Pepsi-Cola® and Xerox®. All trademarks are brands and include the brand name, brand mark, or both.

In the early decades of this century, some products carried brand names—some still known today. Many others, however, arrived at the store in bulk packaging, and were put up in smaller units by the retailer, with no brand names. (Bettmann Archive.)

sumers brought a dozen, they might get some from farmer Jones and some from farmer Brown.

That system of unbranded merchandising has given way to a modern system of branding. The major forces for change were the development of extensive advertising creating brand images, the cost efficiencies of packaging at the manufacturing level, and the development of self-service at the retail level. Today, few goods or services are left unbranded. Even oranges, dental clinics, and peppercorns have brand names. Many familiar brands have been around for more than a century: Gold Medal flour, Ivory soap, Vaseline, Borden's Condensed Milk, and Quaker Oats.

Virtually all products introduced today have brand names (we will look at the exceptions, generic products, shortly). Even raw fruit and vegetables are being branded.[19] In most cases, brand names are also registered as **trademarks** to gain legal and exclusive rights to the name as spelled out in the Lanham Act of 1946, which specifies the kinds of trademarks, **trade names, trade characters,** and brand names that may be protected by law (see Box 10-1). Products are branded for three compelling reasons: (1) the protection of a trademark encourages innovation; (2) brands help consumers make buying decisions; and (3) brands carry meanings that are recognized by consumers and marketers alike.

ENCOURAGEMENT OF INNOVATION Without the protection of a registered brand or trademark, few companies would be willing to invest money in the research and development of new products. Federal registration gives the trademark owner exclusive rights to that name or symbol, protects the owner against infringement from both domestic and foreign competitors, and allows the owner to register for protection in some foreign countries. Since owners can have legal protection for their brand names, branding supports innovation and contributes to better standards of living. It also prods marketers of successful brands to maintain their standards of quality and to improve their brands to hold their market share.

BOX 10-1 BRAND NAMES: The Legal Side

To consumers, the brand is a familiar word or symbol that tells us a lot about what we are buying. It could be a familiar "friend" that has been around the house since before we were born or a new name associated with an exciting innovation. To a lawyer, however, brands carry very special meaning, and marketing managers do well to heed legal advice. The advice recently offered by a well-respected lawyer was to follow these rules:

Rule 1. *"Never select a corporate name or a mark without first doing a trademark search."* A trademark search is quick, inexpensive, and easy for a well-equipped law firm. There are over 600,000 registered trademarks in all 50 states, but the search is worth the effort. In the early 1980s, the NBC television network spent millions developing a new "N" logo only to find later that a local public service television station had one almost like it. It was an embarrassing and expensive mistake.

Rule 2. *"If your attorney says you have a potential problem with a mark, trust that judgment."* Experienced legal talent can help you to clarify the distinction between words that are *suggestive* of the benefits of a product and therefore *can* be protected ("Spic 'N Span" for cleaners or "When It Rains It Pours" for salt) and words that would be considered *descriptive* ("Security" for tires or "Brilliant" for flour) and *cannot* be copyright protected. These distinctions would be difficult for most of us.

Rule 3. *"Seek a coined or a fanciful name or mark before you settle for a descriptive or a highly suggestive one."* Kodak was chosen because George Eastman liked the sound of Ks; it meant nothing about photography. If fanciful names haven't been used, then the money spent on advertising them is not lost. Examples come from astrology (Quasar, Pulsar), botany (Lotus, Apple), and zoology (Cougar, Impala, Mustang).

Rule 4. *"Whenever marketing or other considerations dictate the use of a name or a mark that is highly suggestive of the product, select a distinctive logotype for the descriptive or suggestive words."* The name GE for General Electric would be very easy to copy but the highly distinctive type style of the GE symbol is protected. The Indian Business Machines use of the distinctive IBM letters would most likely not be permitted under U.S. law (see Chapter 2).

Rule 5. *"Avoid abbreviations and acronyms wherever possible, and when no alternative is acceptable, select a distinctive logotype in which the abbreviation or acronym appears."* It is tempting to say that IBM, GM, and GE have done well, so why not use the letters of my company? The trouble is that there are only 676 combinations of two letters each, 17,576 of three each, and fewer than a half million of even four letters each, but there are about 17 million businesses in the United States. There are not enough letters to go around!

To those of us not trained and experienced in the law, especially such a highly specialized segment as trademark law, these issues can seem mysterious. When it comes to legal issues like this, the marketing manager should call upon legal advice.

Source: Thomas M. S. Hemnes, "How Can You Find a Safe Trademark?" *Harvard Business Review,* Mar.–Apr. 1985, pp. 36 ff. See also, Dorothy Cohen, "Trademark Strategy," *Journal of Marketing,* Jan. 1986, pp. 61–74.

AID TO CONSUMERS' BUYING DECISIONS Suppose that you stop at a drugstore on your way home from class to pick up some soap, toothpaste, shampoo, mouthwash, and deodorant. Without the help of brands, how would you decide what to buy? Store employees would be unlikely to let you uncap and taste each toothpaste and mouthwash. And you also might feel silly sniffing each deodorant or soap. Branding helps consumers make buying decisions by giving the product some recognizable, ensured identity.

Your image of a bar of Irish Spring soap or a tube of Ultra Brite toothpaste is a combination of a number of perceptions made up of advertising you have seen, previous experience with the product, packaging, shelf placement, and your current mental and physical state. A brand name helps you to combine your perceptions into an overview that helps you make a decision. Brand perceptions lead to certain expectations and allow you to make buying decisions efficiently.

BRAND RECOGNITION   The perception of a brand comes in stages. Each of us, at some point, learns about a brand for the first time. Before that happens, we have **brand nonrecognition;** we simply do not know that the brand exists. How many of these popular beer brands do you recognize: Schaeffer's, Hamm's, Pearl, Jax, Genessee, Lone Star? Don't be alarmed if you suffer from brand nonrecognition. All these are regional brands that are not advertised or distributed nationally.

At some point, most of us do become aware of nationally distributed brands, at least of products that interest us. **Brand recognition** is the simple awareness that a product exists, apart from competing products. This awareness is neutral; no positive or negative feelings are attached to brand recognition.

Marketers work hard to move consumers from nonrecognition to recognition and on to brand preference and brand insistence. **Brand preference** is established when consumers have tried a brand and have at least moderately positive attitudes toward it. Assume, for example, that you prefer Peter Pan peanut butter and that you will buy the brand if it is in stock. When it is not in stock, however, you will pick up Jif or another brand rather than making a trip to another store.

Marketers next direct their actions toward achieving **brand insistence**— consumers demand a certain product and will go out of their way to get it. If one laundry replaces missing buttons on your clothes, you may insist on that laundry— even though a competitor is two blocks nearer and slightly less expensive. Brand insistence was the goal behind Campbell Soup's campaign for V-8 vegetable juice: "Wow! I could have had a V-8!" The flip side of brand insistence is **brand rejection;** bad experience or overfamiliarity with a specific brand can lead consumers to reject it. The product quality may not have been as expected.

☐ *Choosing a Brand Name*

In the past, brand names were often selected by nonmarketing employees or consumers, through contests, or by whimsey. Today, new brand names are selected and tested carefully. A good name cannot sell a bad product, but it *can* give a good product an edge on competitors. Frito-Lay's Tostitos corn snacks quickly attained crisp and crackling revenues of $160 million a year. The name was a good one and helped considerably in the product's successful introduction. However, a French company experienced widespread failure with pantyhose bearing the unfortunate name Fannyhose.

No hard-and-fast rules guide marketers in the choice of brand names, but the following general principles have emerged:[20]

Be short, memorable, and easily pronounced. "Jif," "Dove," Dreft," "Glade," "Pledge," "Shout," and "Off" are names that meet this goal nicely. Single-syllable names cannot effectively do the job for every product, of course, but briefer generally is better.

Suggest the product's benefit. "Eveready" and "Beautyrest" are good names for batteries and mattresses. "Sizzle" would be a terrible name for a tanning lotion; however, "Coppertone" works well. Hunt-Wesson's "Sunlite" cooking oil communicates several product benefits at once: lightly fried foods, the nutrition of sunflower seeds, and healthful aspects of sunlight. In contrast, what does

Heinz markets a number of food products (shown left) that all carry the Heinz brand, and even have similarly shaped labels. When new products are introduced, the image of quality for which Heinz is known is immediately carried on to the new product. The risk is that any product failure, or major problem with any one product, can hurt the reputation of the others. In contrast to the Heinz branding strategy, Lever Brothers identifies its many brands (shown right) individually, letting each stand or fall on its own. This is similar to the strategy of Lever's major competitor, Procter & Gamble. (Heinz products photo used with permission of H. J. Heinz Co. Lever Brothers photo by Ken Karp.)

the name "Good News" suggest? You might think it's a magazine devoted to the bright side of life, but as a brand name it suggests few of the functions or benefits of the products to which it has been attached: disposable razors, brassieres, and even a cereal.

Distinguish the product from its competition. Names like Imperial, Classic, Mark I, and Diplomat do evoke images, but they do not set those automobiles apart from competitors as well as Volkswagen's "Rabbit" does. Turtle Wax products for cars have an unusual brand name that meets the first two criteria and is certainly distinctive; it suggests a hard, protective shield, whereas "Simonize" implies a process. The brand name Raid for pesticide is brief and memorable, suggests the product's benefit, and is not easily confused with other brands. Drano (a drain cleaner), Easy-Off (an oven cleaner), and Spic 'N Span (a general household cleaner) are three other brand names that meet the criteria suggested.

▢ *Family Brands and Individual Brands*

Family brands employ the name of the parent organization in some way. Campbell and Heinz, for example, use their company names to brand dozens of their products. Kodak reworks its name and initials into all products: *Koda*color, *Koda*chrome, *Ek*tachrome ("Ek" stands for Eastman Kodak). Use of a family name allows the marketers to promote a consistent image and to make all advertising do double duty, promoting the organization's name as well as its individual brands.

Other marketers choose to let brands stand on their own, and follow a multiple brand strategy. **Individual brands** have no obvious connections with the parent company. Thus, General Motors markets Buick and Chevrolet; Procter & Gamble sells Tide and Crest. Marketers use individual brands rather than family brands when they need to differentiate their own products (General Motors), when their products are so diversified that a family name loses meaning (Procter & Gamble), or when they want to protect their family name should one product fail or get negative publicity. In 1981, when Rely tampons were associated with toxic shock syndrome in some women and were withdrawn from the market, few consumers realized that the product was a Procter & Gamble brand. Thus, in 1984, Procter & Gamble was able to introduce a new product aimed at a similar market under the brand name Always.

☐ Manufacturer's Brands, Private Brands, and Generic Products

A&P supermarket shoppers looking for a can of green beans frequently can choose from Del Monte and Ann Page brands or from an unbranded product. These particular items represent, respectively, a manufacturer's brand, a private brand, and a generic product.

MANUFACTURER'S BRANDS   Almost all the brands mentioned so far have been **manufacturer's brands**—the products' makers chose the brand names (Del Monte, Heinz, Green Giant). Such brands are usually distributed nationally, carry higher prices than other brands, and are perceived by most consumers as having superior quality.

PRIVATE BRANDS   Sears' Kenmore appliances and Craftsman tools, A&P's Ann Page canned and baked goods, and any number of Macy's products are examples of **private brands**—products made by manufacturers for sale by intermediaries under a label of the intermediary's own choice. Whether the intermediaries are wholesalers, buying agents, or retailers, they control distrbution and promotion. Private brands are also called "middlemen's brands" or "house brands." These brands are usually priced slightly lower than manufacturer's brands. Distributors that have private brands usually also carry manufacturer's brands. An exception is Sears, which carries only its own Kenmore appliances.

Paper products such as these are still often sold as generics—simple packages with the identification of the package's contents. In spite of their lower price, they still do not sell as well as the branded versions. (Copyright © Bob Daemmrich.)

GENERIC PRODUCTS   **Generic products** are not branded, are simply packaged (usually in white with black lettering), and usually are priced well below both manufacturer's and private brands. Generics are primarily grocery and drug items and are identified only by product class: lemon cake mix, spaghetti sauce, paper towels, shampoo, aspirin, and so on. Generic products are produced by or for large supermarket or discount chains using the most inexpensive processing, packaging, and raw materials and thereby making lower prices possible.

Generics are fairly new to food and drug retailing. Introduced in France in 1976 by the Carrefour supermarket chain, they were somewhat misleadingly called *produits libres*—"free products." Chicago's Jewel supermarket chain introduced generics to the United States in 1977, and such products are now available throughout the country. Contrary to many expectations, generics have not necessarily attracted lower-income, economically disadvantaged consumers; rather, buyers of generic products tend to be younger and better-educated than average consumers.[21] Generics apparently appeal most to middle-income customers.[22]

Generics have one strong advantage over branded products: lower price. The lack of brand names conveys no meaning to consumers other than the product's class and price. In the late 1970s and early 1980s, generics generally held between 1 and 4 percent market shares of the product classes in which they were available.[23] However, recent data suggest a steady decline in sales of generic products since 1983. For example, although generics accounted for about 2.4 percent of all grocery sales in 1982 and 1983, that figure fell to 1.8 percent of such sales by 1985—a 25 percent decline in about 2 years. According to analysts, the decreasing popularity of generics has been influenced by an improved U.S. economy, more price-cutting promotions by brand name products, and continuing consumer doubts about the quality and ingredients used in generic items.[24]

☐ Protected Successful Brand Names

Nylon, shredded wheat, linoleum, escalator, cellophane, zipper, aspirin, kerosene, and celluloid—what do these diverse products have in common? All were once brand names, but now any company may use the names. In some cases, the producers allowed trademark protection to expire. In others, the brand names were used so commonly as general (or generic) words to describe the product class that their makers lost protection in the courts or gave up trying to defend their exclusive legal rights.

Today, marketers go to great lengths to defend their brand names and to keep them from falling into generic usage. Xerox, Band-Aids, and Kleenex are brand names that border on being generic, but they are registered trademarks of Xerox, Johnson & Johnson, and Kimberly-Clark. A photocopy of this page made on a copier other than one manufactured by Xerox is not "a Xerox copy"; legally, it is a photocopy.

■ PACKAGING DECISIONS ■

A product's package is second only to the core product in attracting consumers. The package is a means by which the core product is enhanced to become an augmented product. Consider the importance of packaging a blank 90-minute audiocassette marketed by Sony, TDK, or Maxell. The tape itself (the core product) is protected first by a plastic housing that includes the sprockets which turn the tape during recording and playback. The housing is further protected in a $4\frac{1}{4}$-inch by $2\frac{3}{4}$-inch plastic case. The secondary cases are a standard size for all brands and time lengths, a convenience for distributors and retailers and for consumers who want to store their cassettes in racks designed to hold the standard size. Within the case is a product label identifying the brand, telling how much time is available, and giving product specifications (ferrous oxide or chrome-coated) as well as recording instructions for the particular tape. A warranty is also included on each label. The packaging for audiocassettes, like that for almost all products, adds value and benefits for buyers.

Effective packaging should accomplish at least three basic and critical aims:

- Protect the product
- Facilitate distribution and make consumption convenient
- Promote the product and provide needed information through labeling

Protection

Whatever else a package does, it must protect the core product from breakage or spoilage. Good packaging goes much further than protection, however; it also augments the product. But unless the need for protection is met, anything else a package can do to enhance the product's benefits will have little meaning. Although a colorful Styrofoam package labeled "One Dozen Farm-Fresh Grade AA Eggs" may look attractive in the supermarket display case, if yolks and whites are oozing out of the carton, no benefits are provided.

In recent years, the protectve role of packaging has taken on new meaning. Because of the efforts of some sick minds, packages of Tylenol pain relief capsules, Gerber baby food, Jell-O dessert, and other products have been laced with poison. Designing a package to make these and other products "tamper-proof" has been a major concern of marketers.[25] Packaging (or multiple packages) must be designed to move the product safely from the manufacturer or processor through various distribution channels into consumers' hands.

Convenience

A product's package should enable distributors to ship it safely and conveniently and retailers to display the product efficiently and attractively. Finally, the package should facilitate consumers' convenient and safe storage of the product. In short, whenever possible, packaging should augment the core product by adding convenience for all those who handle it. Making the package convenient for ultimate consumers should be the foremost concern.

Marketers of L'eggs pantyhose made a virtue of necessity with their packaging. The plastic oval containers, which tied in nicely with the brand name and image, obviously would not stack neatly on retailers' shelves. So L'eggs offered store managers a freestanding, eye-catching display unit to hold the oval packages. Ultimately, the packaging was convenient for distributors and consumers alike.

Promotion

Bali Company produces brassieres in four varieties, to fit a woman's body type as well as her bustline. Sales of Bali bras climbed when the company packaged the product in a purse-style folding carton and offered retailers display units similar to those for L'eggs. A card embossed with the Bali logo—containing size, style, and color information—slips into a front panel on the see-through package. Bali's packaging not only offers protection and convenience, it also promotes the product effectively.

With the rise of self-service retail stores, the promotional aspect of packaging has increased in importance. In effect, the package must do a great deal of the selling: Many firms call their package the "silent salesperson." An entire package design industry has developed to meet marketers' needs for better promotion in packaging. Package design companies and special units within advertising agencies offer marketers expertise in developing packages that promote the products.

☐ Labeling Decisions

Labels are an integral part of a product's packaging. A **label** encompasses any printed information on the packaging that describes the product. It can also convey meaning through its size, shape, and color. Labels should promote the product and help consumers make decisions. As a result, typical labels are persuasive or informative (or both).

Persuasive labels are promotional in intent. Words like "new," "improved," and "easy to use" are all too familiar to most consumers, but they can influence buyers positively. The label on a tube of Close-up toothpaste describes the product as a "super-whitening toothpaste and mouthwash in one plus fluoride to fight cavities." The back of the tube adds an **informative label** that tells the consumer about the product's ingredients, use, dating, and so on. Close-up's label says that the active ingredient is sodium monofluorophosphate and then goes on to inform purchasers: "Performance and quality of Close-up unconditionally guaranteed. If not fully satisfied, purchase price will be refunded. Lever Bros. Co., N.Y., N.Y. 10022. U.S. Pat. 3,438,230."

Federal law requires that food and drug items list contents by amount in descending order (see discussion of the Fair Packaging and Labeling Act of 1966, p. 48). Such laws have encouraged the practices of **nutritional labeling** (listing the product's nutrients and the percentage of each), **open dating** (announcing the normal shelf life of the product), and **unit pricing** (stating the cost per standard measure).

Labels are often both persuasive and informative. Because Alka Seltzer is most often sold in self-service stores, the label must act to promote the product. In addition, once the product is bought, the package is the best place to give the consumer information needed to make use of the product. (Ken Karp.)

■ PRODUCT MIX DECISIONS ■

So far, we have seen that marketers must make decisions concerning the classification, branding, packaging, and labeling of products. The results of those decisions should influence buyers' perceptions of the product positively, and they should follow legal requirements carefully. Although these decisions are extremely important to the product's acceptance in the marketplace, they may be seen as micro-level decisions. On a macro-level, marketers must make product line decisions, choosing to add to the organization's product mix or to eliminate products from that mix.

Richardson-Vicks Inc., of Wilton, Connecticut, a subsidiary of Procter & Gamble, is a diversified marketer of a wide range of consumer and industrial products. The company's health care division produces the decongestant VapoRub as well as NyQuil cold medicine, Formula-44 cough syrup, and Tempo antacid. The toiletry products division is responsible for Oil of Olay skin care products, Clearasil acne remedies, and Lavoris mouthwash. Richardson-Vicks' home products division sells Formby's furniture refinisher and Thompson's Seal Stain waterproofing preparations. Tiger's Milk nutritional bars and supplements, Plus nutritional supplements, and Mill Creek hair and skin care products fall under the natural products division. Subsidiary companies of Richardson-Vicks include J. T. Baker Chemical Company, a marketer of laboratory chemicals, and Baker Instruments Corporation, a leading supplier of sophisticated medical equipment. Although this list of Richardson-Vicks products is far from complete, it is sufficient to paint a picture of the company's **product mix—** its total offering of individual products. Richardson-Vicks markets hundreds of individual products. To manage those products, the divisions of the company separate individual items into product lines.

☐ Product Line Decisions: Breadth, Depth, and Extension

A **product line** is a grouping of products managed and marketed as a unit because they have similar functions, are distributed in similar ways, or fall within a certain price range. Richardson-Vicks, for example, places its Oil of Olay skin care products and its Mill Creek skin care items in different divisions and in different product lines because Oil of Olay is sold through drugstores and department stores. Mill Creek products, by contrast, are marketed through health food outlets. Actually, the several skin care items marketed under the Oil of Olay brand make up an individual product line.

Exhibit 10-4 lays out the product lines of Chesebrough-Pond's Inc., which markets Vaseline Petroleum Jelly, Ragú spaghetti sauce, Rave home permanents, Bass Weejun shoes, Q-tips cotton swabs, Prince tennis racquets, and Prince Matchabelli fragrances—among a host of items. Other firms market fewer product lines. Revlon focuses on cosmetics and health care lines. Carnation concentrates on dairy and dairy-based product lines and on pet food.

EXHIBIT 10-4	Chesebrough-Pond's Consumer Product Mix

Packaged Foods:
  Ragú pasta meals
  Ragú spaghetti sauces
  Adolph's meat tenderizer

Health and Beauty Products:
  Rave Hair Care
  Vaseline Hair Tonic
  Vaseline Intensive Care lotions
  Vaseline Dermatology Formula
  Vaseline Petroleum Jelly
  Pond's Angel Face Makeup
  Pond's creams and powders
  Cutex nail products
  Q-tips cotton swabs
  Groom & Clean hair products
  Odorono deodorants

Footwear by G.H. Bass & Company:
  Bass Weejuns loafers
  Sunjun sandals
  Bass Secrets
  Bear Traps
  Ecliase

Prince Matchabelli:
  Aviance
  Cachet
  Erno Lask skin care products
  Wind Song
  Décadence
  Golden Autumn
  Matchabelli after-shave
  Chimère
  Vervé
  Aziza cosmetics

Prince Tennis Rackets

Hospital Products:
  Balls and Fiachney thermometers
  Filac electronic thermometer
  Intersorb and Sta-tite dressings
  Q-tips cotton products
  Pertussin cough syrup

Note: All Chesebrough-Pond's products are international.

Source: Based on Chesebrough-Pond's *Annual Report,* 1985; and Howard Rudnitsky with Jay Glissen, "Chesebrough-Pond's: The Unsung Miracle," *Forbes,* Sept. 28, 1981, pp. 105–109.

PRODUCT LINE BREADTH   The number of product lines in an organization's product mix is the firm's **product line breadth** (or width). Xerox (among other businesses) is a marketer of photocopy machines and has a broad line of tabletop copiers, medium-speed copiers, and high-speed copiers with automatic feed and stapling capabilities. Canon, however, has a narrow product line, marketing only relatively slow, desktop copiers.

PRODUCT LINE DEPTH   Campbell Soup maintains a deep product line in cookies, pickles, and frozen dinners, as well as in soups. **Product line depth** refers to the number of individual items within each product line. Campbell's product line depth in soup is well-known. The company manufactures 54 varieties of condensed soups to which consumers add water. Since 1970, Campbell has also marketed Chunky ready-to-serve soups, which, in addition to being prediluted, carry higher prices and greater profit margins than do condensed soups. As was noted in Exhibit 10-4, Chesebrough-Pond's product mix has a breadth of product lines, but it has more depth in health and beauty products than in foods.

PRODUCT LINE EXTENSION   **Product line extension** develops greater depth by adding new product varieties. This can be accomplished by extending the brand (Coke adding Diet Coke) or by using another brand (Tab). Product lines can be extended relatively easily, since new items are often variations of existing ones. Del Monte extended its product line by offering low-salt versions of its canned vegetables. Deepening a product line thus is usually a risk-free proposition and may exploit excess manufacturing capability.[26] The sales force and distributors may pressure the manufacturer to add items to a successful product line. As a result, firms sometimes have to include or retain items that are not really profitable. Marketers of cosmetics and beauty care lines often derive most of their profits from just two or three of their products, but they maintain the marginal items to offer consumers a range of choices and to preserve brand loyalty.

☐ *Product Elimination*

Marketers sometimes have difficulty with eliminating declining products. They become attached to failing products and are reluctant to let them go. **Product elimination** is the withdrawal (usually in phases) of a product from the normal marketplace. The economics of this withdrawal can be complex. Even though a product may be only marginally profitable or unprofitable, it still may help the firm cover its fixed costs. Deleting it from the product line may harm the firm's overall profitability, because fixed costs cannot be reduced in the short term.[27]

Products may be eliminated for any number of reasons—because they are obsolete (such as mechanical calculators or manual typewriters), because consumers' tastes change (for example, in women's dresses), because the product no longer fits into the organization's portfolio.[28] As noted, however, products sometimes are retained—even when no longer profitable—if the marketers feel that a complete line of products is needed to support other, profitable items.

■ SUMMARY ■

1. Few purchases are made because of the core product alone. We purchase a product first because of its core benefit.
2. A product delivers satisfactions related to its packaging, servicing, warranties, image, and branding.

3. A product's intrinsic quality has an important effect on buyers' perceptions.

4. Service industries now employ two out of three Americans working in the private sector.

5. Four major characteristics distinguish the marketing of services from that of physical goods: (1) service intangibility; (2) buyer and producer participation in service marketing; (3) service perishability; and (4) lack of standardization in service provision.

6. Traditionally, products have been classified by characteristics (durables, nondurables, and services) and by how consumers perceive and purchase them.

7. Consumer products are generally classified as convenience products; shopping products; specialty products; and unsought products.

8. Industrial products may be classified into five categories: installations (plant and major equipment); accessory equipment; components, including raw materials and parts and subassemblies; supplies for maintenance, repair, and operation; and industrial services.

9. Marketers identify and legally protect their products through brands, brand names, trade names, brand marks, trade characters, trademarks, and copyrights.

10. Products are branded because the protection of a trademark encourages innovation, because brands help consumers make buying decisions, and because brands carry meanings that are recognized by consumers and marketers alike.

11. Today, marketers go to great lengths to defend their brand names and to keep them from falling into generic usage.

12. A product's package is second only to the product itself in attracting consumers.

13. Effective packaging should protect the product, facilitate distribution, make consumption convenient, promote the product, and provide needed information through labeling.

14. On a macro-level, marketers must make product line decisions, choosing to add to the organization's product mix or to eliminate products from that mix.

☐ *Key Terms*

accessory equipment
augmented product
brand
brand image
brand insistence
brand mark
brand name
brand nonrecognition
brand preference
brand recognition
brand rejection
components
consumer product
convenience product
copyright
core benefit
core product
derived demand
durable goods
emergency products
express warranty

family brands
generic products
heterogeneous shopping products
homogeneous shopping products
implied warranty
impulse products
individual brands
industrial products
industrial services
informative label
label
major equipment
manufacturers' brands
MRO items
nondurable goods
nutritional labeling
open dating
package
parts and subassemblies
persuasive label
plant

private brands
product
product elimination
product line
product line breadth
product line depth
product line extension
product mix
raw materials
services
servicing
shopping product
specialty products
staples
supplies
trade characters
trademarks
trade names
unit pricing
unsought products
warranty

☐ *Chapter Review*

1. Give an example of a product, identify its core benefit, and specify the additional features that enhance it into an augmented product.

2. "It makes no sense to build more quality into a product than buyers can perceive." Do you agree or disagree with this statement? Why?

3. Give an example of a service, and indicate how intangible and how perishable it is. Can

it be standardized? To what extent does it require the participation of the consumer and the producer?

4. Can you think of a convenience product that also might be classified as a shopping product and a specialty product? How is this possible?

5. Give an example of an unsought product that you or someone in your family has bought. What brought about the purchase?

6. Name an industrial product, and specify why demand for it is derived. Identify the ultimate source of demand for this product.

7. State three reasons that products are branded, illustrating each reason with a specific example.

8. Describe a product of your own invention, and give it a brand name that suggests its benefits.

9. Distinguish between product line breadth and depth by citing examples of each.

☐ *References*

1. Lynn Densford, "USDA Report Compares Cost of Food, Packs," *Food & Drug Packaging,* Sept. 3, 1981, p. 1.
2. Joshua Lyle Weiner, "Are Warranties Accurate Signals of Product Reliability?" *Journal of Consumer Research,* vol. 12, Sept. 1985, pp. 245–250.
3. Walter Stern, "Design Research: Beauty or Beast," *Advertising Age,* Mar. 9, 1981, p. 43.
4. Ronald Aslop, "To Sell Glut of New Perfumes, Firms Stress Image, Not Scent," *The Wall Street Journal,* Mar. 28, 1985, p. 33.
5. Theodore Levitt, *The Marketing Mode* (New York: McGraw-Hill, 1969), p. 1.
6. Ibid., pp. 1–2.
7. David A. Garvin, "Product Quality: An Important Strategic Weapon," *Business Horizons,* Mar.–Apr. 1984, pp. 40–43.
8. Dick Stevenson, "Quality: The New Marketing Imperative," *Ad Forum,* Aug. 1984, pp. 24–26.
9. John Naisbitt, *Megatrends: Ten New Directions Transforming Our Lives* (New York: Warner, 1982), p. 14.
10. U.S. Department of Commerce, Bureau of Economic Analysis, *Survey of Current Business,* vol. 66, Mar. 1986, pp. S-9, 36, 60.
11. Valarie A. Zeithaml, A. Parasuraman, and Leonard L. Berry, "Problems and Strategies in Services Marketing," *Journal of Marketing,* vol. 49, Spring 1985, pp. 33–46; and James L. Heskett, "Lessons in the Service Sector," *Harvard Business Review,* Mar.–Apr. 1987, pp. 118–126.
12. A. Parasuraman, Valarie A. Zeithaml, and Leonard L. Berry, "A Conceptual Model of Service Quality and Its Implications for Future Research," *Journal of Marketing,* vol. 49, Fall 1985, pp. 41–50, and Leonard L. Berry, Valarie A. Zeithaml, and A. Parasuraman, "Quality Counts in Services, Too," *Business Horizons,* May–June 1985, pp. 44–52.
13. For a detailed examination of special factors in the marketing of services, see Eric Langeard, John E. G. Bateson, Christopher H. Lovelock, and Pierre Eigler, *Services Marketing: New Insights from Consumers and Managers* (Cambridge, Mass.: Marketing Science Institute, August 1981), Report no. 81-104. It has even been suggested that in the marketing services, we need to add three new elements to the marketing mix. See A. J. Magrath, "When Marketing Services, 4 Ps Are Not Enough," *Business Horizons,* May–June, 1986, pp. 44–50.
14. The definitions in this section are adapted from *Marketing Definitions: A Glossary of Marketing Terms,* compiled by the Committee on Definitions of the American Marketing Association (Chicago: American Marketing Association, 1960).
15. Adapted from Richard M. Hill, Ralph S. Alexander, and James S. Cross, *Industrial Marketing,* 4th ed. (Homewood, Ill.: Irwin, 1975), p. 37.
16. "A Federal Case for the Cookie Monster," *Inc.,* Oct. 1982, pp. 25–27.

17. *Trademarks: Orientation for Advertising People* (New York: American Association of Advertising Agencies, 1971), p. 1.

18. The definitions in Exhibit 10-1 are taken from or adapted from *Marketing Definitions* (see entry 14).

19. Eleanor Johnson Tracy, "Here Come Brand-Name Fruit and Veggies," *Fortune,* Feb. 18, 1985, p. 105.

20. Adapted from Dennis J. Moran, "How a Name Can Label Your Product," *Advertising Age,* Nov. 10, 1980, pp. 53, 56.

21. Isabella C. M. Cunningham, Andrew P. Hardy, and Giovanna Imperia, "Generic Brands versus National Brands and Store Brands," *Journal of Advertising Research,* vol. 22, no. 5, Oct.–Nov. 1982, pp. 25–32.

22. Robert E. Wilkes and Humberto Valencia, "A Note on Generic Purchaser Generalizations and Subcultural Variations," *Journal of Marketing,* vol. 49, Summer 1985, pp. 114–120; and Martha R. McEnally and Jon M. Haves, "The Market for Generic Brand Grocery Products: A Review and Extension," *Journal of Marketing,* vol. 48, Winter 1984, pp. 75–83.

23. Brian F. Harris and Roger A. Strang, "Marketing Strategies in the Age of Generics," *Journal of Marketing,* vol. 49, Fall 1985, pp. 70–81.

24. Richard W. Stevenson, "No Frills, No Sales," *The New York Times,* Oct. 5, 1986, pp. F12–F13.

25. Trish Hall, "Food Packaging May Be Improved, But Tampering Can't Be Prevented," *The Wall Street Journal,* July 16, 1986, p. 21; Patricia Strand, "Gerber Ignores 'Tylenol Textbook,'" *Advertising Age,* Mar. 10, 1986, pp. 3 ff; and Felix Kessler, "Tremors from the Tylenol Scare Hit Food Companies," *Fortune,* Mar. 31, 1986, pp. 59 ff.

26. Gerald Schoenfeld, "Line Extensions: Milking a Name for All It's Worth," *Adweek,* Nov. 18, 1985, p. 44; and Jack Trout, quoted in, "The Line-Extension Time Bomb," *Adweek,* Nov. 4, 1985, pp. 26–27.

27. Philip Kotler, "Phasing Out Weak Products," *Harvard Business Review,* vol. 43, Mar.–Apr. 1965, pp. 107–118.

28. George J. Avlonitis, "The Product-Elimination Decision and Strategies," *Industrial Marketing Management,* vol. 12, no. 1, Feb. 1983, pp. 31–43, and George J. Avlonitis, "Product Elimination Decision Making: Does Formality Matter?" *Journal of Marketing,* vol. 49, Winter 1985, pp. 41–52.

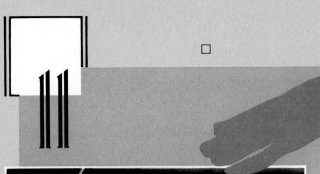

DEVELOPING NEW PRODUCTS

SPOTLIGHT ON

Copyright © Chuck O'Rear/Woodfin Camp & Assoc.

□ Why marketing organizations seek a balanced product portfolio

□ Stages and conditions within a product's life cycle

□ How innovative products are adopted by different kinds of consumers and are spread throughout society

□ Internal and external factors that affect an organization's product strategy

□ Basic steps in new-product development

□ The role of the product manager within a marketing organization

Yoplait and New Country are yogurt brands introduced in the mid-1970s by entrepreneurs with extensive marketing backgrounds: Bill Bennet and David Goldsmith. Both brands became successful, even though the two marketers followed different philosophies of product development.

Bennet acquired the U.S. rights to Yoplait from a French manufacturer whose research showed that Americans preferred the taste of Yoplait to Dannon, the market leader. The unfamiliar shape of the tapered package, however, did not appeal to consumers. Bennett was glad that research supported his judgment about the brand's taste, but he felt that the unusual carton would attract attention in the dairy case. He kept the tapered carton but removed the product's taste enhancers and stabilizers, making it "all natural."

This marketer felt no need to test his changes, but relied instead "on what was in my head and heart, based on observing the marketplace for years." Yoplait moved into a few supermarkets in Michigan, and sales proved Bennet's hunches right: Consumers liked and bought the brand. The waxed-paper carton would sometimes leak, however, and some time passed before it was changed to plastic with an improved seal. During this period, Bennet's coinvestors lost confidence in the product and sold their controlling interest to General Mills, which wanted a new product in its portfolio. General Mills introduced Yoplait first to regional and then to national markets, and by 1980 the brand was second only to Dannon in sales.

David Goldsmith and his partner, Robert Finnie, took a different tack when they unveiled New Country yogurt in 1975. These marketers had spent 18 months and more than $200,000 gathering ideas from consumers and testing the product's concept, package, and taste. Unlike Bennet, they had no product to begin with, so they used marketing research to learn what consumers wanted—before the item was produced.

Working with consumer groups in three cities, Goldsmith and Finnie gleaned 60 ideas for new kinds of yogurt. Next, consultants in food technology and packaging helped them narrow the possibilities to eight samples for testing. Three of the samples received enthusiastic support: a fruit-and-

(Ken Karp.)

nut yogurt, a custardlike yogurt with fruit rippled through it, and a fruit-salad yogurt. Five hundred consumers then reacted to various packaging shapes and graphics, and New Country was test-marketed in 30 supermarkets in Binghamton, New York, for 6 months. Results were encouraging: The brand actually attracted *new* users to yogurt, expanding the market in Binghamton by 30 percent.

In March 1975, New Country was unveiled in the Northeast, and initial sales were strong. The brand captured a 7 percent share of the greater New York market after a year. By 1979, however, its share had declined to around 2 percent, reflecting the proliferation of competing brands and a trend among consumers toward unflavored yogurt. Goldsmith took action to keep his company healthy; he acquired the license to the brand name Sweet 'N Low and began developing a low-calorie yogurt.

Goldsmith still believes in the effectiveness of his approach to product development: "It's easy to say that we may have gone overboard with our market research, but there are a lot of guys who have tried it in this business who aren't around anymore. We're still here, and it's because we did market research."

Source: Susan E. Currier, "Creating a New Product: Two Paths to the Same Marketplace," *Inc.,* Oct. 1980, pp. 95–102.

The introduction of a new product may be filled with the tension and suspense of high drama—or with the errors of low comedy. Exciting success stories (IBM's personal computer, Sony's videocassette recorder, Frito-Lay's Doritos snacks) are matched by a long list of failures (Green Giant's vegetable yogurt, quadraphonic sound systems, and Ford's Edsel). Some new products seem to succeed but then fail. Texas Instruments' 99-4A home computer and the Osborne I portable computer both had high initial sales, but Osborne lacked the resources to beat back competitors. The success of the 99-4A came primarily from its very low price—so low that the product was unprofitable and was dropped in 1983.

Chapter 11 first explores two factors that underlie product development: (1) the need to create a balanced portfolio of products and (2) the existence of the product life cycle. We will see how innovative products spread throughout society as they are adopted at varying speeds by different kinds of people. We then examine some factors within the organization and the marketplace that determine the strategies and tactics of product development and point to the important role of marketing research. The chapter concludes by exploring how marketers can organize to manage products and gives special attention to the role of the product manager.

THE NEED FOR PRODUCT DEVELOPMENT

The needs and wants of both consumers and marketers lead to new products. Consumers want better goods and services; marketers want to conduct profitable, ongoing business by serving the needs of consumers and organizational buyers. There is evidence that the competitor who first offers a new product or service will often have a much more successful entry than will marketers who later introduce copies of a product or service.[1]

This chapter emphasizes *managing* the development process because even the best ideas and products can go awry. Yoplait yogurt almost failed because of a packaging weakness. When new-product development is managed carefully and systematically, good products are given the fighting chance that they deserve.

Two closely related factors impel marketers not only to develop new products but also to manage that development creatively, always with an eye toward consumers' needs. First is the need for a balanced portfolio of products. In Chapter 8, we discussed the concept of an organization's portfolio of businesses (or products), including new high-growth products—"stars" and "question marks," and more mature slower-growth products—"cash cows" and "dogs" (see pages 233–234). The second factor is what underlies the aging process of products, the product life cycle.

☐ *A Balanced Product Portfolio*

Even though Procter & Gamble has a reputation as America's premier marketer, for the past decade profits from its food and beverage division have languished at levels far below its detergent, paper, and soap businesses. Relying on mature, often heavily discounted products like shortening, cake mix, coffee, and peanut butter, Procter & Gamble has been unable to introduce major new products to bolster its earnings. Pringle's potato chips have been a disappointment despite prodigious efforts to boost sales. And a new ice cream dessert mix, Coldsnap, was yanked from the market because of listless consumer response.[2]

Obviously, Procter & Gamble's product mix (Chapter 10) is quite broad, which is in keeping with the company's purpose. However, in terms of strategic marketing (Chapter 8), Procter & Gamble's food product portfolio is not balanced. Whereas a broad product mix concerns the collection of products based on their purpose or use, the balanced portfolio concept refers to the collection of products based on their relative maturity. A **balanced product portfolio** is a proper mix of new, growing, and mature products whose sales provide the cash flow to ensure long-term prosperity.

To repeat Chapter 8 a bit, embryonic products are *question marks*—newly introduced items that require large outlays of cash but whose futures are uncertain. Growing products are *stars*—items that have been introduced successfully, that still require funds for promotion, but that also are bringing in cash and profits. *Cash cows* are mature businesses or products that are profitable and require relatively low levels of reinvestment. Finally, *dogs* are mature businesses or products that have seen better days. Although they may still be profitable and may require only minimal reinvestment, dogs may be harvested, divested, or allowed to die.

Too many of Procter & Gamble's food products are mature cash cows. Although profitable, they are not the stars the company needs to build its future. Procter & Gamble's one truly successful new food product in recent years is Puritan Oil, and the company has spent millions to carve out its leading market share.

However, a portfolio comprising only stars and question marks—winners and potential winners—would not provide the balanced product mix most marketers seek. The typically high investments and low profits that characterize newly introduced and rapidly growing products would place severe financial strains on all but the wealthiest companies. A more desirable situation for most firms is the balanced portfolio in which profits generated by cash cows and carefully harvested dogs are used to fund the development of question marks into stars.

A review of the Boston Consulting Group's growth-share matrix (Figure 8-2) shows that products and product lines almost inevitably move from the top two quadrants down to the bottom two. Successful question marks first move left to become stars and then move downward to cash cow status; unsuccessful ones move directly downward to become dogs. The rarest movement is out of the dog quadrant in any direction. Typical movement on the matrix is from question mark to star to cash cow to dog. Because of this movement, companies need to continually develop new products to keep their portfolios balanced.

☐ *The Product Life Cycle*

In 1913, Gideon Sundback, a young engineer for Judson and Walker's Automatic Hook and Eye Company, developed the first simple, reliable slide fastener—now known as the zipper. Sundback's employer, Lewis Walker, formed a new firm, the Hookless Fastener Company. It set about selling the device, but with little success. Finally, in 1923, B. F. Goodrich Company took a chance and introduced rubber galoshes with the new fastener. Delighted with the boots, a Goodrich executive slid the fasteners up and down, exclaiming, "Zip 'er up!" The name stuck and has now become the generic term for the device.[3]

Today the zipper is no longer a star. It has become a mature product, perhaps even a declining one, since Velcro and other modern fasteners were developed. The zipper has moved through a **product life cycle** (PLC), which, as shown in Figure 11-1, is made up of introductory, growth, maturity, and decline stages. Most products, product lines, and markets pass through such a cycle as reflected in sales and profits over time.

INTRODUCTORY STAGE   Polaroid Corporation sold its first instant camera in 1948, and over the next three decades built its business almost entirely on Dr. Edwin Land's remarkable invention. More recently, Sony Corporation announced the development of a new electronic camera, the Mavica—the first consumer instrument to make images electromagnetically instead of chemically. Both cameras illustrate the typical situations that occur when an innovative product first appears.

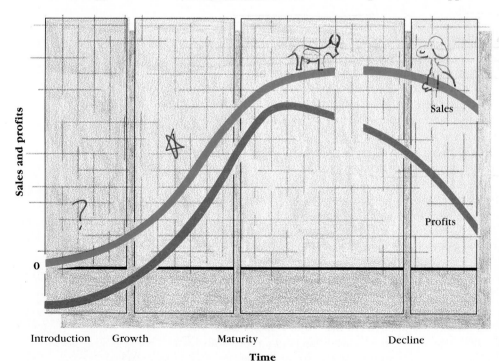

Figure 11-1 *The stages of the product life cycle.* Products tend to have a life cycle, as do plants and animals—from birth to eventual death. The blue curve illustrates that sales of newly introduced products start from 0, rise somewhat during the introductory stage, increase sharply in the growth stage, stop growing in the maturity stage (which often lasts a very long time), and then decline later. The red curve represents profits earned from the product. Note that profits start to decline long before sales decline, due primarily to competitive price pressures on mature products.

In the **introductory stage** of the product life cycle, an innovation is alone in the market. For a time, at least, it has no competitors—a pleasant if short-lived period for the manufacturer. New products do not usually earn a profit in the introductory stage. Investments in research, manufacturing, and marketing often exceed revenues until sales have grown to sizable figures. As a result, the profit curve is typically negative, as shown in Figure 11-1. Because of this unprofitability, the new product's development and production must often be subsidized by the cash and profits generated by older products. In Polaroid's case, the funds came from sales of sunglasses, goggles, and filters developed during World War II. Sony's development of the Mavica was financed by a host of successful products, including television sets.

These characteristics—the initial lack of competitors, negative profit performance, and start-up cash from elsewhere in the corporation—typify the introduction of innovative products. During this stage, the producer establishes the market by creating **primary demand**—demand for the product class as a whole—as Apple Computers did for personal computers in the late 1970s.

If the product is truly innovative, then no competition exists during the introductory stages. Bausch & Lomb, the optical company, had such an innovation when it introduced the first soft contact lens in 1971. This product was the most revolutionary vision aid offered to consumers since the late 1940s, when the much less comfortable hard contact lens appeared. The company enjoyed a particularly favorable competitive advantage: The Food & Drug Administration (FDA) did not approve a competing soft lens until 1974, giving Bausch & Lomb 100 percent of its market for 3 years. From 1974 to 1978, however, its market share fell to less than 50 percent as the product moved out of the introductory stage.[4]

GROWTH STAGE   What went "wrong" for Bausch & Lomb was that the soft lens entered the second stage of its life cycle. The **growth stage** of the PLC is characterized by several new factors. First, sales and profits grow rapidly (profits often grow even faster than sales, since costs may diminish). Second, competitors are attracted to the growing market—often more competitors enter than will survive. Third, cash flow may still be negative because of the firm's efforts to establish a strong market share ahead of competitors. This does not mean that there are no profits. Any resulting profits are used up in reinvestment to further the product's growth. Finally, the market is turbulent during the growth stage as competitors enter and fight for share. Even measuring exact market share is difficult, since the total market—the number of new users—is growing.

As competitors enter the market, however, each attempts to create a **selective demand**—a preference among buyers for its specific brand. In 1974, competitors, led by American Optical Corporation, began to offer the soft lens. Bausch & Lomb did not really react; it held its retail price at a forbidding $400. Other formidable competitors—Revlon, Dow Corning, Ciba-Geigy, and Syntex—not only introduced soft lenses but offered thinner ones or lenses that could correct astigmatism (something Bausch & Lomb's product could not do). And the competitors cut prices.

Bausch & Lomb then began to fight back. Because it had more experience than its competitors, the company could manufacture its lenses at lower unit costs, thereby making it easier to offer discounts to large optical chains. Daniel Gill, a marketing specialist, was appointed president of Bausch & Lomb. He improved services to doctors and optical retailers, pushed the firm into a major new advertising effort, and guided its entry into the related market for contact lens solutions. Bausch & Lomb rebounded and now holds a dominant share of the market.[5]

Bausch & Lomb did the necessary scientific research to make the soft contact lens a reality. When it was introduced, the company enjoyed a period of very profitable sales before competitors were able to produce and market soft lenses. Later stages of the life cycle for soft contact lenses proved much more competitive. (Courtesy of Bausch & Lomb.)

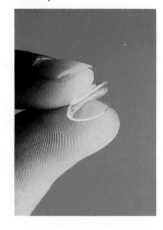

While the bicycle has gone through stages of development—from large balloon tires, to lighter weights, to multiple-speed mechanisms—it is an example of a mature product. Sales are still good but no longer growing rapidly. Profits should be good as well. (Copyright © John Marmaras 1981/ Woodfin Camp & Assoc.)

MATURITY STAGE   The third stage of the PLC usually lasts much longer than the other stages—namely, for years or decades. Mature products like automobiles, beer, and television sets have been around for years and seem likely to survive for many more. The **maturity stage** of the PLC is characterized by a shake-out of competitors: Companies that did not establish a healthy market share during the growth stage drop out. Sales growth slows during product maturity because most potential customers have been reached. The market becomes saturated. Profits are high but begin to decline as market leaders cut prices in a strategy to gain share. Profits remain large, however, and mature products become the cash cows of the company, providing funds for the development of new products.

Mature products are not necessarily static; improvements can be made on the basic product, and variations can be offered. Bausch & Lomb, for example, introduced a refined soft lens in 1980 that is only half as thick as the original and is produced in one standard curvature that fits almost everyone adequately, although not perfectly. ("Their lens is like stretch socks," observed one optometrist.) During maturity, although market leaders generally have the resources to expand their offerings, gaining market share is difficult and expensive. Instead, the best-managed companies try to hold and improve their share slightly while diverting profits from successful mature products into the development and introduction of new ones. Remember that a balanced product portfolio is the goal. As mature products begin to reach the final stage of the life cycle, new strategies must be called into play.

DECLINE STAGE   Kix cereal, Ipana toothpaste, Studebaker and Packard automobiles, Wings cigarettes—you can't buy them today. Most products and brands do eventually pass from maturity to a fourth stage of the life cycle: decline and eventual elimination. The **decline stage** is characterized by a further dropout of competitors until only a few remain. Profits begin to fall sharply, often because of excess production capacity. Promotion of the product is reduced or discontinued. Any remaining profit will not be reinvested in the product; no attempt will be made

While pure-rolled white oats might have "made kids husky," as in this 1919 ad, they have now gone through the decline stage and cannot be found on supermarket shelves today. (New York Public Library, Picture Collection.)

to rebuild demand. However, careful management can extend a declining product's life for some time.

Products decline for a number of reasons. The most common cause is an alternative innovative product. Eastman Kodak's black-and-white film has been replaced, to a large extent, by color film. Long-playing records, and then tapes and discs, replaced earlier recording media. "Ultra-low-tar" cigarettes are replacing filtered cigarettes, which replaced unfiltered brands. And "light" beers, liquors, and salad oils are replacing heavier, darker, richer products (refer to Box 2-1). These are all examples of extending a declining product's life cycle.

☐ *Product Classes versus Brands*

Studebaker and Packard were mentioned here as automobiles that reached the decline stage and were eliminated from the marketplace. In 1930 they were among the 20 top-selling cars in the United States, along with Willys, Terreplane, Nash, DeSoto, Hudson, Graham, Huppmobile, Auburn-Cord, Reo, and LaSalle. Also on the list of best sellers as the United States entered the Great Depression were cars that are still with us: Ford, Chevrolet, Buick, Pontiac, Plymouth, Dodge, and Chrysler.

Life cycles exist for whole classes of products as well as for brands. A **product class** includes all the goods and services offered by marketers to meet a basic

These cars may look strange to our eyes today, but they were real beauties in the 1930s. The brands of autos from that day include some familiar to us still, but also some that have already gone through the decline stage of the life cycle. The life cycle for the automobile product class, however, is still in the maturity stage. (Ken Karp.)

consumer need. Although many brands of cars have been driven their last mile, people's needs for transportation by car have not entered a decline stage. The product class "automobile" may be mature, but it is very much alive, unlike the certain virtually extinct product classes, such as the horse-drawn buggy and the icebox (the forerunner of modern refrigerators).

As these examples have shown, brands also have life cycles, and they are usually shorter than the cycles of product classes. The life cycle of a brand will be influenced by that particular brand's ability to compete; the life cycle of the product class is more influenced by major changes in technology. In terms of automobile brands, DeSotos and Hudsons have declined and are gone; Chevrolets, Fords, and Chryslers are mature products; Toyotas and Hondas are leaving the growth stage and reaching maturity. Brands like the Hyundai (from Korea) and the Yugo (Yugoslavia) are already in U.S. dealerships. What about the introductory stage? Not only new brands of cars but also new technology in personal transportation are on the drawing boards in Detroit, Tokyo, Oslo, and Stuttgart.

When marketers analyze product life cycles, they try to differentiate between the product class and brand. One brand may be rising or falling, growing or declining; but the life cycle of the product class may show different, unconnected movement. In addition, some products have been around for so long—Ivory soap, Quaker Oats, Vaseline Petroleum Jelly—that their existence seems to belie the whole concept of the life cycle, although such products simply are enjoying a longer maturity stage than is normal. Who can predict the sales of Ivory soap in 50 years?

BOX 11-1   Fashions and Fads: Attempts to Control the PLC

When we use the term "fashion," the first thing we usually think of is women's clothing. In reality, many other products, including men's clothing, automobile design, sugar content of soft drinks, and even the architectural appearance of office buildings follow a **fashion** cycle.

The cycle usually starts with a designer's need to be different and his or her sense that the new design will be acceptable to at least a segment of the market. Creating a distinctive new version of a product may be as simple as raising hemlines a couple of inches or as dramatic as the industrial designer genius Raymond Lowey's design of the 1950 Studebaker.

If a design is destined to become a fashion, enough consumers respond favorably to the new design that less bold designers begin making products that are very similar (or exact copies). These are called "knock-offs" in the trade. This development is accompanied by a broad acceptance by consumers. The leaders have legitimized the new design, and it becomes the accepted fashion by the masses.

Then, the process starts over again. This now accepted fashion is challenged by another design change; as it becomes accepted, the first one declines and often dies. The fashion cycle is just a special version of the product life cycle.

Fads differ from fashion only in the length of the cycle. They tend to burst on the scene, are adopted very rapidly and enthusiastically, and then die off in a hurry. Most fail to last because they don't really fit the needs of more than a very small avant garde segment. Topless women's swimsuits made the cover of *Life* but didn't last even one season. These fashion changes apparently were not destined to become fashionable.

One fact about both fads and fashions is that they are deliberate attempts by designers—and the product marketers whom they serve—to manage, or control, the life cycle. Many critics complain that the up and down movement of hemlines, the changes in the width of men's ties, the adding and subtracting of cars' tailfins, and other seemingly random design changes mainpulate the life cycle so that consumers throw out

Fashion is evident in design and architecture as well as clothing. For many years, the fashion in large office buildings has been large square boxes made of glass. The famous architect, Philip Johnson, broke with this tradition in the design of the new AT&T building in New York City. Some predict his leadership will usher in a new design fashion. (Courtesy of AT&T.)

perfectly serviceable products to buy the new fashion. The usual response is, "the consumer isn't being forced to change; she could still be wearing high-buttoned shoes."

☐ *Variation and Extension of the PLC*

Some products have extremely short life cycles: Pet Rocks and Hula Hoops came and went quickly, passing into the littered history of fads (see Box 11-1). Other products, bearing similar earmarks, have surprisingly endured: Wham-O Company has enjoyed steady sales of its Frisbees for almost 30 years. Movie classics like *Gone*

With the Wind and *The Wizard of Oz* still appear regularly on television, although both films were released nearly 50 years ago. More recent successes, like *Raiders of the Lost Ark,* appear to be headed for long lives on videocassettes. In contrast, *Heaven's Gate* cost Universal Studios $36 million to produce and market, was a box-office failure, and disappeared in a few weeks. The staying power of Cabbage Patch dolls remains to be seen, although teddy bears and Raggedy Ann and Raggedy Andy dolls have delighted children for over 70 years.

Cycle lengths for most products are not as volatile and unpredictable as those of films and toys, but they do vary. Recent advances in technology and increased competition among marketers to introduce new offerings have shortened cycle lengths for many products. However, through superior marketing strategy, astute marketers who carefully monitor their products' movement through the PLC can sometimes control and extend the lives of products.

Over several decades, marketers at Arm & Hammer, a division of Church & Dwight Company, have prolonged and expanded the life of their baking soda through research and suggestions from consumers. In its purest form, **life cycle extension** finds new uses for the same product by the same users. As shown in Figure 11-2a, Arm & Hammer baking soda was first packaged and marketed over 130 years ago as a leavening agent for baking. Chemists at the company then suggested that the product—simple bicarbonate of soda—would alleviate heartburn and acid indigestion when half a teaspoon is mixed into a glass of water and the whole is drunk. Some years later, baking soda was discovered to be an effective refrigerator deodorizer: Simply place an open box on a refrigerator shelf and change it every few months. Today, Arm & Hammer also promotes baking soda for eliminating carpet odors: Sprinkle it lightly over a carpet, wait 15 minutes, and vacuum as usual. By suggesting new uses of its product (primarily through information on the familiar yellow box), Arm & Hammer has periodically extended the PLC.

Marketers more frequently extend the PLC by reformulating or slightly altering the product. (How many times have you seen the words "new" and "improved" emblazoned on a product's package?) General Mills took this approach with Bisquick, another baking product, which has been reformulated and altered several times since its introduction in the 1930s. Sales remain brisk 50 years later.

Reformulation as a means of extending the PLC is aimed primarily at retaining present customers who otherwise might try some newer product. Whole product classes—toothpaste, beer, cigarettes—have been reformulated and repackaged regularly to extend their life cycles. Figure 11-2b shows how the life cycle of beer, a mature product class, has been extended over the years by a series of repackaging and reformulation tactics.

Marketers have also extended the PLC by repositioning the basic product, a tactic aimed not only at retaining market segments but also at adding them. Repositioning relies less on actual reformulation of the product than on creative ways to promote the product. Repositioning was the goal of A-1 Steak Sauce marketers, who saw the rising price of beef as an opportunity rather than a threat; they launched a new advertising campaign to promote the product's use on simple hamburgers. The purpose of all these efforts is to extend the mature stage as long as the product remains profitable.

Given the need for a balanced product portfolio and the nature of product life cycles, creative marketers need to understand two basic processes in managing new products: (1) the adoption of innovations by consumers and organizational buyers; and (2) the diffusion of innovations throughout their markets and society.

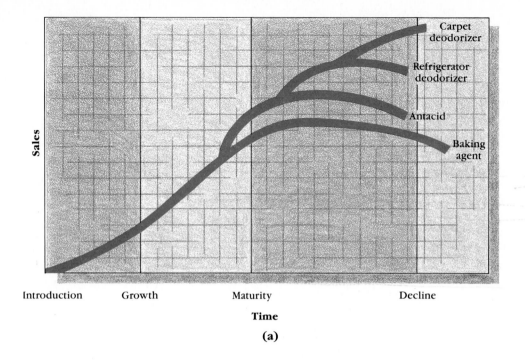

(a)

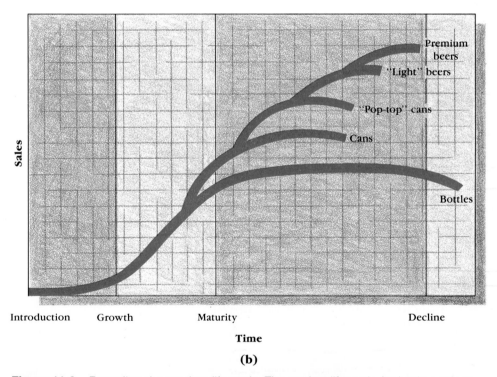

(b)

Figure 11-2 *Extending the product life cycle.* The product life cycle for basic products, such as baking soda or bottled beer, might reach maturity and be headed for decline. Creative marketing might extend the life cycle, perhaps even starting a new growth stage. This can be done by (a) finding new uses for the product, as has been done for baking soda, or (b) actually changing the product or its packaging, as shown in the beer example.

ADOPTION AND DIFFUSION OF INNOVATIONS

During the 1970s, yogurt, an "innovative" food product, was adopted by U.S. consumers and diffused throughout our society. Dannon, the first major market entry, established itself as the leading brand, followed by many competitors, including Yoplait and New Country. Americans perceived yogurt as innovative, even though this custard-like, bacteria-curdled milk had been a food staple in Turkey and other Mideastern countries for centuries.

The **adoption process** includes the stages that individuals, households, or organizations go through in accepting (buying and rebuying) an **innovation.** The **diffusion process** consists of communication about, and acceptance of, the innovation throughout the social system over a period of time. The steps, events, or measures of both adoption and diffusion are the same, but they occur at different levels. Adoption is a micro-level process of individual choice; diffusion is a macro-level process of social choice. Individual consumers adopt an innovation, which then must be adopted by whole segments of society for it to be diffused. Figure 11-3 illustrates the steps we will examine in relation to both adoption and diffusion.

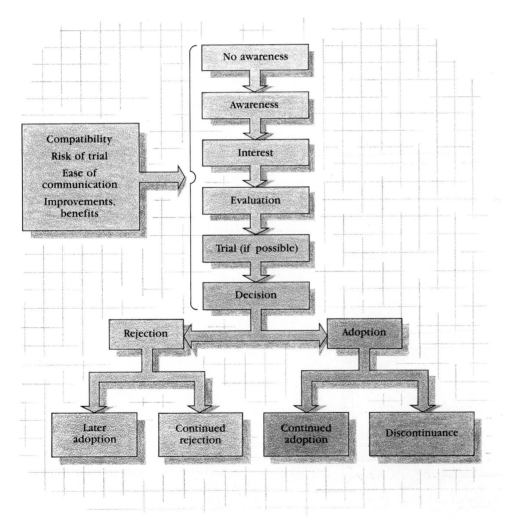

Figure 11-3 *Adoption and diffusion of innovations*. Adoption is a process through which each person moves—from not even being aware of an innovation, to a decision to adopt or reject, and then later confirming or reversing that decision. Diffusion refers to adoption by a large number of people as an innovation is accepted throughout the social system over a period of time. (Adapted from Everett M. Rogers and F. Floyd Shoemaker, *Communications in Innovations*, New York: Free Press, 1971.)

To understand these related processes, we need to establish exactly what an innovation is. What distinguishes an innovation from just another brand?

☐ *Innovations: Defined by the Market*

An electronic typewriter and a pencil are both instruments for printing words. Since they have the same basic function and offer the same core benefit, one might argue that the typewriter is *not* an innovation. Going further, one might argue that the word processor is just a glorified pencil. Such arguments could go on endlessly—if innovations were defined in terms of technology. For our purposes, however, a product is an **innovation** if, and only if, the marketplace perceives it as being innovative. No matter how ingenious a technological change might be, if customers do not perceive it as *truly* new, it is not innovative.

In Chapter 1, we quoted Peter Drucker's conclusion that a business has only two legitimate functions: innovation and marketing. Innovation is the continual supplanting of the old by the new, of providing something that is somehow better. Business attempts to achieve this goal, but the process of innovating is difficult and requires both hard work and the kinds of creativity associated with entrepreneurship.[6] If a large organization is to promote that type of creativity, it must beware of stifling its innovative managers.[7] Of course, all efforts to achieve innovation are futile unless consumers *perceive* the resulting product as new and better.

When Alexander Graham Bell first invented the telephone and made his first call, the telephone was a truly discontinuous innovation. It called on us to change much about the way we communicate. Further developments—electronics, fiber optics, push button, even cellular auto phones—have been innovations, but have not required such dramatic changes. They are examples of continuous innovations. (Courtesy of AT&T.)

Categories of Innovations

"New" means different things to different people. If you are taking notes with a felt-tipped pen, are you using a new product? Or is your pen simply an extension of the pencil, the fountain pen, the ballpoint pen, and the cartridge pen? We have said that a product is an innovation only if the market perceives it as such. Based on consumers' perceptions, we can distinguish two kinds of innovations: continuous and discontinuous.

A **continuous innovation** offers a clear improvement over the product it replaces and yet is enough like the old product that it does not really change how we normally use it. Trading a pencil for a ballpoint or a felt-tipped pen requires little effort. Similarly, the push-button telephone is a continuous innovation; although it did change the way we dial numbers, the change was minor. Although both Yoplait and New Country yogurts represented a truly new food product, they do not require that we change our way of eating.

In contrast, a **discontinuous innovation** truly changes how we do what we have long been doing. Television was a discontinuous innovation. People were accustomed to listening to the radio while they washed dishes, pursued a hobby, drove a car, or took a bath. But television requires us to watch as well as listen, and social scientists are still documenting all the changes this innovation entails. Discontinuous innovations are dramatic and profoundly alter how we live our lives.

This distinction between continuous and discontinuous innovations strongly influences the processes of adoption and diffusion. Since a continuous innovation requires little change on the part of consumers, it may be adopted quickly. But unless a discontinuous innovation offers dramatic advantages or new benefits over other products, consumers may resist it, and diffusion may take more time. Since the goal in marketing an innovation is its acceptance by large numbers of the target market, we will look first at how diffusion occurs.

The Diffusion Process

The extent of diffusion varies greatly across product classes. It is nearly 100 percent for indoor plumbing, refrigerators, and television sets, but it is considerably lower for snowmobiles, sailboats, and golf carts. In other words, a completely diffused innovation may be accepted by nearly everyone (telephones) or by only a small percentage of the population (electric wine cellars).

An innovation's characteristics influence the extent and speed of its diffusion. Widespread, rapid acceptance is more likely when the following questions can be answered affirmatively:

- Is the innovation compatible with existing products and ways of doing things?
- Can consumers try the innovation without making a major commitment (taking a great risk)?
- Can the existence of the innovation, and information about it, be communicated easily? Are its benefits readily observable?
- Does the innovation represent real improvements and benefits over existing products?

COMPATIBILITY An innovation will be accepted faster and more widely if it is compatible with other products and systems and with the consumer's expectations. The radial tire, for example, was compatible from the moment B. F. Goodrich introduced it. Consumers (and distributors) simply put the new tires on the same rims of the same cars. Microwave ovens, by contrast, were not compatible with existing values such as "If it's quick, it's low quality" or "Mothers who use shortcuts don't care about their children." In addition, the microwave oven required extensive relearning about how to cook.

The more an innovation is compatible with existing products and practices, the easier it is to adopt and the greater the likelihood that it will diffuse extensively and rapidly. In other words, continuous innovations are more likely to be diffused more rapidly. Discontinuous innovations need to be very strong on other dimensions to enjoy success.

RISK OF TRIAL   The extent and speed of diffusion are enhanced when an innovation can be tried with relatively little risk and commitment on the part of the adopter. Inexpensive nondurable goods (disposable razors or a new brand of crackers) present new users with negligible financial risk and require little commitment. If you dislike the product, you discard it without hesitation; you paid little for it, and your personal commitment was slight.

However, for most consumers a videocassette recorder or a microwave oven represents a higher degree of financial commitment and risk, since such products usually cannot be tried in the home before making a purchase. Most expensive durable goods—cars, refrigerators, aluminum siding—require a major commitment of both money and personal involvement in the buying decision. The more that marketers make an innovation available for trial with acceptable risk, thus lowering the commitment required, the more likely the innovation will be diffused successfully. Consequently, store and showroom trials assist the overall marketing effort. You can often take a car out for a ride before deciding to buy it; you can sit in various stores and play with personal computers or electronic typewriters. Since the goal is to reduce the consumer's perceived risk, home trials might also be effective in marketing such innovations as video equipment and computers.

EASE OF COMMUNICATION   Diffusion requires that consumers must learn about the innovation through some kind of communication. The rate and extent of diffusion depend on how easily the innovation's existence and benefits can be communicated to consumers. Also important is whether the innovation itself "advertises" its adoption by being highly visible.

In most cases, communicating about the innovation's existence and benefits is fairly easy: "Try Brand A" or "Brand B tastes better." And creative marketers usually can come up with effective communication channels. Both principles are illustrated by Loctite Corporation's communication efforts in introducing Quick Metal, a puttylike adhesive for repairing machine parts, to the product's proper audience—maintenance workers. Sales representatives promoted Quick Metal to retailers such as plumbing-supply houses, which most maintenance workers are likely to patronize. Instead of describing the product in terms traditional for industrial products ("a nonmigrating thixotropic anaerobic gel"), Loctite's advertising agency, Mintz & Hoke, created the slogan: "Keeps machinery running until the new parts arrive." Tubes of Quick Metal were priced high—$17.95 retail. Yet, in the first 5 months, retailers sold $2.2 million of the adhesive.[8] Successful diffusion in this case can be attributed in part to effective communication about the product's benefits and to the use of communication channels most likely to reach the target audience.

The third factor—how visibly an innovation communicates the fact of its adoption—varies from product to product. A Stetson hat is highly visible; designers' names on clothing are prominent; but bifocal contact lenses are intended to go

One determinant of the speed of diffusion of an innovation is how easy it is to communicate its existence. With apparel such as these hats, the product communicates itself—loud and clear! (Copyright © 1984 Lawrence Migdale.)

unnoticed. A related issue is just how much people care about the products or brands they use. Some products (the Stetson hat and designer jeans) are self-expressive; our automobiles, clothing, and even furniture tell others about our tastes and lifestyle. A Volkswagen suggests good sense and practicality, whereas a Bentley represents opulence and luxury. Other products, like refrigerators and contact lenses, communicate little about their owners; what they do express is known to only a few people.

IMPROVEMENTS AND BENEFITS   The degree to which an innovation improves on existing products and offers desirable benefits influences the extent and speed of diffusion. Color television clearly offers benefits over black-and-white television, just as stereophonic sound can be differentiated easily from monaural. But the benefits of rear-screen projection and quadrophonic sound have not yet convinced enough consumers to adopt these new technologies, and the products have not been diffused. Because of their more dramatic break with the products they replace, discontinuous innovations which are eventually successful are usually very high on this dimension.

The characteristics we have just examined all influence an innovation's diffusion, and they operate simultaneously. Sometimes these factors work together to enhance diffusion, and sometimes they work against it; more likely, some factors will be positive and others will be negative. The computer, for example, offers clear benefits over traditional methods of communicating and accounting; but it has problems of compatibility, represents a high degree of risk, and is easily misunderstood by customers. Even so, the benefits of computers are so great that they have quickly diffused through society—so quickly that this innovation has revolutionized our lives.

The Adoption Process

In addition to the characteristics of the innovation itself, the characteristics of the people who adopt new products have a strong impact on their success or failure. The decision to adopt an innovation may be made by an individual, by a household, or by those responsible for purchases within an organization. Individual consumers decide whether to purchase a new kind of camera; household members usually confer before deciding to buy a car; and managers decide which kind of information-processing system a firm should adopt. In every case, adoption is in the decision makers' hands, not the marketers' hands. Moreover, consumers and organizational buyers pass through various mental and behavioral stages before deciding to adopt an innovation. They move from no awareness, to awareness, to interest, to evaluation, to trial, and finally to adoption.

This set of stages is very similar to what we called the consumer decision-making process (see Chapter 4, pages 94–95). The adoption process is a special case of consumer decision making when the product in question is an innovation. Indeed, we need to put the entire process of product development as discussed here in the context of customer analysis we discussed in Part 1:

1. Whether an innovation is continuous or discontinuous, little or no *awareness* of it exists at first. Potential adopters have to be informed about the innovation through publicity, advertising, and other marketing efforts. This is why ease of communication is so important.
2. When the innovation is introduced, decision makers have to determine whether it relates to their needs. *Interest* may or may not be sparked, depending on whether the decision maker perceives the innovation as a relevant, feasible alternative to existing products.
3. Potential adopters of innovations have to establish some measures of *evaluation* in order to compare the new product with existing ones. If the innovation is discontinuous, it may be difficult to evaluate the benefits offered.
4. As we indicated earlier, the *trial* stage for innovations is complex. Successful introduction depends greatly on the new product's characteristics, benefits, and perceived risk. Effective communication is the key to achieving trial by consumers.
5. The final stage, *adoption*, is indicated most directly by sales, but the visibility of the innovation (if it has that attribute) is also a measure of success.

An outstanding example of a relatively expensive innovation that has been introduced successfully is the videocassette recorder. Domestic sales jumped from only 30,000 units in 1976 to 1.4 million units in 1981. By 1983, Japanese manufacturers alone produced over 18 million units; by 1986, VCRs were found in about half of all U.S. homes.[9] So many consumers have moved through the stages of adoption that the product is well on its way to diffusion. The characteristics of the product allowed consumers to move quickly to adoption, and yet they did so at different rates and for different reasons. This points to a third major consideration in introducing new products: Why does one consumer adopt an innovation while another ignores it or waits to see what happens?

Adopters

When we talk of consumers, adopters, or decision makers, we tend to forget that, after all, we are talking about people—living individuals who decide, for various reasons, whether to adopt and consume a product. From a marketer's standpoint,

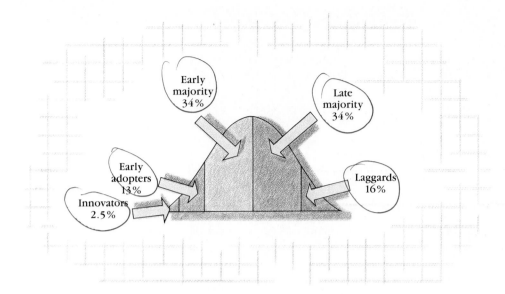

Figure 11-4 *Categories of adopters*. The figure illustrates the very small proportion of eventual users who fall into the category of innovators. These individuals or organizations, along with the "early adopter" category, are crucial to the success of a new product. The first large group to adopt, the early majority, legitimizes the product for the last two groups, who eventually adopt the innovation.

people who share certain characteristics can be grouped into categories of adopters. Everett Rogers and F. Floyd Shoemaker have done that, labeling adopters as "innovators," "early adopters," the "early majority," "the late majority," and "laggards."[10] Figure 11-4 shows the usual breakdown of the total market by these five categories. A popularly priced innovation with clear benefits, for example, can persuade more people to become innovators or early adopters (television sets and videocassette recorders did that as soon as people could afford them). Thus, although these categories of adopters change greatly depending on the product, they do illuminate the adoption process in general. An early adopter of new clothing fashion may be a laggard when it comes to an innovation like microwave ovens, whereas the microwave innovator may have little interest in new clothing fashions.

INNOVATORS   The first users of the new product are called **innovators.** Because of high interest or high need, they may seek out the new offering even before it has been widely promoted or distributed. The first people to buy personal computers were innovators; they tended to have above-average incomes and education, and many worked in the computer industry. Innovators are not always higher-income consumers, however. When Kinder-Care Learning Centers were established across the United States, they were welcomed by thousands of middle-income families who needed two paychecks but could not afford the high costs of child care. Kinder-Care is a chain of franchise operations, but this did not bother innovators. In fact, the perceived reliability of other franchise chains seemed to encourage parents who might have had reservations about commercial child care. Innovators make up a small proportion of the total market, and early adopters follow their lead.

EARLY ADOPTERS   Although they do not move as quickly as innovators, **early adopters** try a new product early in its life cycle without waiting for a large number of people to accept it. Early adopters are opinion leaders who have great impact on later adopters. Indeed, their influence can decide a product's success or failure, and marketers are especially interested in reaching them. First communication efforts are directed at early adopters in attempts to generate favorable word of mouth. When launching a new movie, for example, movie distributors often hold special

Services, like physical products, go through an adoption process. When Kinder-Care Learning Centers were first introduced, parents who were innovators made them successful early, and these were followed by the later categories of adopters. (Courtesy of Kinder-Care Learning Centers, Inc.)

previews for people who have daily contact with the public, such as taxi drivers, waiters, and hairdressers.

Reaching early adopters can be relatively easy. Marketers of home horticultural products (a new type of pruning shears, a new brand of fertilizer, or a new strain of tulip bulbs) know that their early adopters are likely to subscribe to gardening magazines, and so they place their first advertising in such magazines. The marketers at Loctite, however, were not able to reach their early adopters so easily. Sales representatives could not pace factory floors giving away samples of Quick Metal to machinery operators. Instead the company focused on carefully selected retail outlets, hoping that sales clerks would recommend the new product to their customers.

THE EARLY MAJORITY   One of the largest groups of adopters, the **early majority,** adopt the product only after it has been accepted somewhat widely. These consumers perceive more risk in new products than do innovators and early adopters. Because this group is so large, it is the deciding influence on whether the product will succeed in general use or will serve a narrow market niche.

THE LATE MAJORITY   Members of the **late majority** see even more risk in new products than do those in the early majority; they do not adopt an innovation until its use is widespread and thoroughly accepted. In terms of the product life cycle, the late majority tend to adopt late in the growth stage or early in the maturity stage. Members of the late majority do not view the product in terms of its life cycle, of course, but they become comfortable about adopting it only after the innovation is widely accepted. Older consumers, for example, are not as likely to be the early adopters of new products as are younger consumers. Yet, when the new product or service meets their real needs, older consumers will adopt it.[11]

LAGGARDS **Laggards** are individuals, households, or organizations that resist or never adopt the new product. Although laggards may be timid by nature, that is not necessarily the reason they reject an innovation. Some products are of little interest to certain consumers, are not needed, or are simply too expensive. In any case, laggards often make up only a tiny part of the total market (only 1 or 2 percent of U.S. households are without refrigerators, for example). Depending on the innovation's characteristics, the laggard or nonadopter group varies widely.

Remember that categories of adopters differ from product to product. The innovator who rushed to purchase one of the first personal computers from Radio Shack or Apple might have little interest in a new line of sportswear from Calvin Klein. Even people generally receptive to new products are not always among the early adopters; almost everyone has a streak of conservatism when it comes to spending money.

PRODUCT DEVELOPMENT STRATEGY

The complexity and necessity of introducing new products means that, to remain viable, marketing organizations need a solid development process. Close-up was the first gel toothpaste. Lever Brothers introduced it to appeal to "kissers"—mostly young people who are concerned about their breath and the whiteness of their teeth. Encouraged by Close-up's success, Lever Brothers then developed a gel that contains fluoride, Aim, and broadened the market by persuading parents that their children would enjoy its taste and still receive protection from cavities.

The two gels started inching their way into the toothpaste market; their acceptance was helped when Beecham Products introduced Aqua-Fresh, which combined gel and traditional toothpaste. By 1980 gels had captured 32 percent of the market—four times their share a decade earlier. To no one's surprise, Procter & Gamble (with its leading toothpaste, Crest) and Colgate-Palmolive (producer of second-ranking Colgate) entered the "gel war" in the early 1980s with Crest Gel and Colgate's Winterfresh Gel.

By introducing a new product into an existing market, Lever Brothers and the other toothpaste marketers followed the first of four broad strategies shown in Figure 11-5. In general, organizations expand and diversify by one of these strategies: entering a new product in a new market (innovation or diversification), entering a new product in an existing market (product development or extension), promoting an existing product to a new market (market development or extension), or promoting an existing product in an existing market (market penetration).

NEW PRODUCTS IN NEW MARKETS This strategy is the one with the highest risk and, if successful, the highest payoff. It relies on research and development and aggressive strategic marketing because, by definition, the product is an innovation and the market represents a new venture. For example, Kodak's research into imaging technology led to the development of a medical laboratory device—the blood analyzer—which has been a valuable new product.

NEW PRODUCTS IN EXISTING MARKETS Developing a new product for a market which you already know is less risky. There was a great deal of scientific research required to develop Liquid Tide, but the market was one that Procter & Gamble had known for decades. The simplest approach here is one of product line

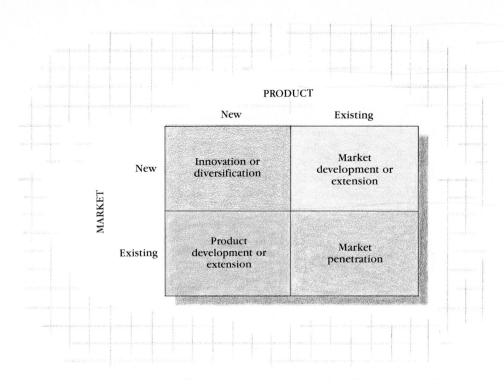

Figure 11-5 *Product and market development strategies.* Any marketer wishing to increase sales can do so through market development, product development, or both. If the effort is to grow with existing products in existing markets (the lower right box), the process is simply to further penetrate the market. The upper right box shows the process of taking existing products into new markets. When marketers develop new products for the same markets they are already serving, they are engaged in product development or extension (the lower left box). The most innovative marketing stance involves developing new products to meet the needs of new markets (the upper left box).

or brand extension. A more complicated approach is when the company develops a completely new method of solving a particular problem. When National Cash Register introduced its electronic check-out systems to familiar supermarkets, it demonstrated this approach.

EXISTING PRODUCTS IN NEW MARKETS This market development strategy places products already in existence in totally new markets. For example, after decades of targeting men as car buyers, automobile marketers began new selling efforts aimed at women in the 1980s. They were careful to be sure that the product itself was acceptable to the broader market, but the product really changed very little.

EXISTING PRODUCTS TO EXISTING MARKETS This market penetration strategy promotes familiar products more heavily to penetrate desirable existing markets more thoroughly. Such a strategy is evident when Levi Strauss increases its advertising budget to further reach the high school and college-age market with ads for its jeans.

When RCA developed the Selectavision video player, it certainly had an innovative new product. The record looked like a phonograph disk but it played back a magnetic recording of video pictures. It was available before the videocassette, but lacked the advantages of the first VCR, the Sony Betamax. It could play prerecorded programs but could not record. As a result, it became an innovation that was never diffused and was abandoned by RCA in 1984. (Peter Roth/Time Magazine.)

■ *PRODUCT DEVELOPMENT TACTICS* ■

Next, managers consider the best tactics for implementing their product development strategy. One central issue involves the timing of new-product introductions. Another is whether the new offering will "cannibalize" the firm's other products by eating into sales or will enhance profitability by regularly replacing outmoded offerings.

When a market has seasonal sales patterns, the introduction of a new product may be delayed if it cannot be produced, distributed, and promoted to take advantage of the peak sales time (for college textbooks, for instance, that time is early spring). It makes little sense to introduce a new snowmobile in January after sales and snowfall have peaked. Similarly, a new brand of frozen pumpkin pie should be in supermarkets well before demand soars in November and December.

If a company offers a new product to a market in which it already competes, it risks **cannibalization;** that is, part of the new product's sales may come from the firm's other products as well as from competitors.[12] When Ragú introduced

When introducing new products, marketers need to consider to what extent the new product will take sales away from an existing product—cannibalization. The various versions of Pepsi—light, caffeine-free, and diet—surely had some of their success at the expense of original Pepsi. (Ken Karp.)

Homestyle and Extra Thick and Zesty spaghetti sauces, managers knew that sales of the new sauces might detract from sales of the regular sauce. But Ragú also had to respond to competition. It was Hunt-Wesson's Prima Salsa that prompted the introduction of Extra Thick and Zesty; Ragú brought out Homestyle sauce to counter Campbell Soup's Prego. As a result of advertising blitzes launched by all competitors, the total market grew to $358 million, and Ragú still commanded nearly 60 percent of that expanded business. By introducing new products, Ragú minimized the total market share lost to competitors.[13] Similarly, Coca-Cola Company knew that Diet Coke would cannibalize sales of its other low-calorie drink, Tab. Tab's sales did fall, but not as much as forecasters feared; a reformulated Tab with aspartame later regained some of its cannibalized market share.

One tactic aimed at holding or expanding market share is **planned obsolescence,** whereby the marketer introduces a new product whose life cycle will be ended by the already-planned introduction of another product or model. This tactic of product development has been widely criticized by consumer organizations, not without reason. The U.S. automobile industry, for example, persuaded consumers to trade in their cars for many years by introducing regular but mostly superficial style changes that made last year's model seem obsolete. Similarly, by such means as raising and lowering hemlines, the women's fashion wear industry has made planned obsolescence highly profitable and even "fashionable."

☐ *The Product Development Process*

Figure 11-6 illustrates the **product development process:** idea generation, screening, feasibility studies, prototype development, test marketing, and commercialization. Though complex, the process is designed to eliminate the greatest risks—as early as possible—from the hundreds of new-product ideas that a firm may consider. The importance of this is obvious in the packaged foods industry: in 1979 the 912 new packaged foods that were introduced had a failure rate greater than 60 percent.[14] This process applies also to industrial products[15] and to the development of new services.[16]

GENERATING PRODUCT CONCEPTS   Ideas for new products come from almost anywhere: from company employees and salespeople, from customers and consumers in general, from vendors,[17] from older products,[18] and from research scientists. Most large marketers establish some formal system to generate and consider ideas. For example, the developers of New Country yogurt set up group discussions among consumers to find out what characteristics would appeal to buyers of a new brand. Some companies use "brainstorming sessions," in which employees from throughout the organization suggest ideas without regard for their practicality or feasibility. The goal is simply to gather as many ideas as possible; criticism of the ideas is deferred until the screening stage.

SCREENING PRODUCT CONCEPTS   The second stage in product development is concerned with eliminating ideas: The **screening process** sifts out all ideas that are not feasible or desirable for the organization. Some product ideas simply do not fit the strategies, capabilities, and expertise of the firm. Revlon, for example, is a successful marketer of beauty and medical products. Although some consumers might be attracted by the idea of motorcycles painted to match eyeliner colors, developing such a line of motorcycles would be senseless for Revlon. Not only is the market most likely minuscule, but the company has no expertise, no production facilities, and no distribution channels for marketing motorcycles. Even if it did,

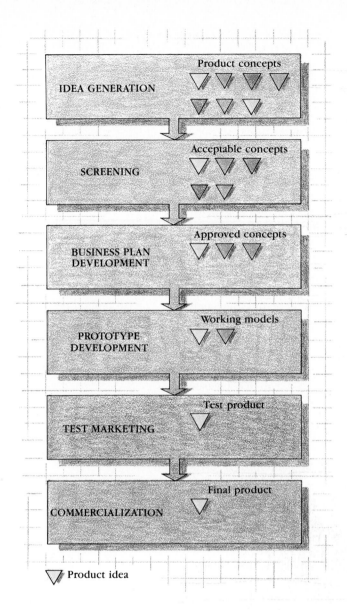

Figure 11-6 *The product development process.* The product development process begins with a large number of product ideas. (In the figure, each triangle represents a product idea.) Each idea is further developed at each stage of the process, but it is also subject to growing tests of practicality. Ideas tend to drop out as these tests get more demanding—as is evident in the decreasing number of triangles—so that only one out of these seven product ideas actually reaches the point of introduction. Note that the product development process *precedes* the product life cycle.

there would still be an image problem: Would *you* trust a motorcycle made by a cosmetics company?

The example is farfetched, to be sure, but it shows why most product concepts are tossed out during screening. Bad ideas sometimes go far, as the failure rate attests, but they are very costly if they make it past the screening stage. Fortunately, marketers are improving and making better use of the screening process. In 1981 an average of only 7 ideas had to be evaluated seriously to find a successful product, compared with an average of 58 ideas in 1968.[19]

Two relatively inexpensive screening methods are concept testing and the use of focus groups. **Concept testing** accumulates and evaluates consumers' reactions to a new-product idea before the product is actually developed. This might be accomplished by a questionnaire or through a guided interview. The emphasis is on quantitative information that can be gathered and compared objectively. (Individual consumers might be asked to indicate on a scale of 1 to 10 how interested they would be in a laundry detergent that comes in tablet form.)

Less formal is the **focus group,** a small number of "typical" consumers who discuss their reactions to a product concept in the presence of a group leader. No attempt is made to quantify the information obtained, since developers are interested in qualitative responses ("A tablet would be much more convenient than a liquid or a powder"). This technique is not as casual as it sounds, however, for the leader of a focus group is highly trained and skillful at eliciting useful information.

ANALYZING THE BUSINESS PLAN   Marketers are important team members in the development of a business plan for the still-hypothetical product. A **new-product business plan** includes estimates from marketing, production, and accounting personnel. Marketers provide projections of sales and market share, advertising and promotion budgets, and pricing information. Engineering and production personnel estimate research and manufacturing costs, and accountants project profit margins. Such thorough economic analysis is expensive and time-consuming but often prevents disaster. In Figure 11-6, only five product concepts made it to the planning stage; two were then dropped after economic analysis revealed that they would be not profitable or only marginally profitable.

DEVELOPING THE PROTOTYPE   Only three products in Figure 11-6 survived the business test, and each will now be developed into a **prototype,** an actual version of the product that will help developers evaluate its feasibility, costs, and characteristics. Prototype costs can run very high, depending on the product. Developing three new flavors of yogurt is relatively inexpensive, but Rockwell International spent several billion dollars in designing and building four prototypes of the B-1 bomber.

By preparing prototypes, developers get solid information about the new product's feasibility and actual costs. Some concepts will be abandoned at this stage (only two remain in Figure 11-6). The costs of manufacturing the product are often found to be more than were projected, thereby making it unprofitable to produce and market.

TEST MARKETING   If product concepts survive the preceding stages of development, they next undergo trial by fire. During **test marketing,** the product is actually introduced into selected geographical markets where developers can observe how consumers and dealers react to the handling, use, and promotion of the product. Test marketing is a form of the experimental method of marketing research (see Chapter 6). The test-marketing process includes several steps:

1. Test-marketing locations are selected to represent, either individually or collectively, the projected total market for the product. Such cities as Pittsfield (Massachusetts), Marion (Indiana), and Orlando (Florida) are used frequently by marketers of consumer goods. They are chosen as test markets because they are very similar to the demographic makeup of the entire country.
2. A small-scale manufacturing line must be set up to supply the product in sufficient quantity for test markets. This can be expensive, too, since high production efficiency is seldom achieved on a limited run.
3. Distributors or users must be sought out and involved in the testing. Most food items, naturally enough, are tested in a number of typical supermarkets. Marketers of major industrial products frequently seek representative companies to

use the product in their facilities (IBM, for example, lets a company use its latest equipment for a modest cost during the test period).

4. Methods must be established to collect feedback (reactions to the product). In-store interviews, questionnaires, telephone surveys, and close observation of actual sales are typical techniques of collecting and analyzing feedback.

5. A variety of approaches to pricing, promotion, and packaging may be used in different testing locations, thereby allowing marketers to analyze and refine their plans for each component of the marketing mix.

Test marketing, therefore, is an opportunity to develop and appraise the entire marketing program in selected geographical areas (see Box 11-2). Marketers are asking the consuming public (the eventual jury) to cast their votes with dollars. Successful test results indicate that plans for the product are on target; disappointments or failures in test markets tell developers either to rethink their plans or to cut their losses by dropping the product. In Figure 11-6, only one product did well enough in test markets to be deemed worthy of full-scale introduction to national markets.

COMMERCIALIZATION   Given success in test markets, during **commercialization** developers establish full-scale production, set prices, lay out a distribution network, and make final promotion plans to introduce the product in all its markets. Refinements may be made in the product's design and packaging; advertising and promotion methods are set; the sales force is trained; and, if necessary, programs are implemented to teach organization buyers how to use the new product.

BOX 11-2   MARKETING ISSUES: Simulated Test Marketing

Simulated test marketing (STM) was introduced in the early 1970s as an alternative to traditional test marketing and has been greatly refined during the 1980s. In a simulation, a few hundred consumers are exposed to ads for a new product—often at a shopping center—and are given either free samples or an opportunity to purchase the product at a laboratory store. The consumers are then questioned over the telephone regarding their reactions to the product and their repurchase intentions. Using the data developed through such interviews, a test-marketing firm predicts the product's potential sales volume.

A growing number of marketers rely on simulated testing techniques—sometimes in combination with more traditional approaches—to test new products (especially packaged goods). In part, this is because traditional test marketing is viewed as slow, expensive, and open to spying by competitors. Certainly the cost comparisons of traditional versus simulated testing can be dramatic. Depending on the size of the test market, traditional test marketing often costs $500,000 to $1 million. By contrast, one marketing services firm estimates that it can use simulated testing to identify

potential product failures at a cost of about $40,000. Two-thirds of the products sampled over a 3-month period will be pinpointed as "duds" that should be reevaluated or simply dropped.

Thomas E. Hatch, vice president for new business at Mattel Toys, observes: "I'm amazed that many companies are not using these [simulated] techniques because the cost of introducing a new product is phenomenal." Yet, according to market researchers, simulated test marketing has yet to win wide acceptance. Some researchers suggest that fewer than 50 percent of marketers use simulated test methods. One important reason, according to Marc Particelli, a vice president of the consulting firm of Booz, Allen & Hamilton, is that although simulations are able to identify potential product failures, "they don't do such a good job predicting the upside potential of products." ▪

Sources: "Many Hesitate to Simulate," *Advertising Age,* Feb. 20, 1984, pp. M42–M43; Nancy Madlin, "Streamlining the Test-Market Process," *Adweek,* Nov. 11, 1985, pp. 10, 12; Eleanor Johnson Tracy, "Testing Time for Test Marketing," *Fortune,* Oct. 29, 1984, pp. 75–76.

Because U.S. consumer markets are so large and complex, new products frequently are *rolled out,* or introduced at different times to different geographic areas. Thus, a product available in Boston in February may not be available in San Diego until November. By rolling out to national markets, the organization gets an opportunity to fine-tune production processes and distribution systems while building inventory and demand. Commercialization leads us back to the introductory stage of the product life cycle. In fact, the introductory stage *is* commercialization, and many new products go no further.

☐ *Successes and Failures: We're Getting Better*

No matter how carefully marketers analyze and plan for new-product introductions, some new products will not succeed. The evidence indicates, however, that certain companies do better than others, with success rates as high as 90 percent of new products introduced. The management consulting firm of Booz, Allen & Hamilton has published two major reports, the latest containing both good and bad news.[20]

The good news reflects on the efficiency of marketing: Not only have we improved the success rate of new products from 1 in 58 to 1 in 7 as mentioned earlier, we are spending our new-product development funds more effectively. Of all the funds expended on new-product development, 30 percent was spent on eventual successes in 1968; that figure rose to 54 percent by 1982. One explanation for this improvement involves the dramatic shift in the proportion of expenditures at different stages in the process of developing new products. In 1968, about half the expenditures were in the last stage, commercialization, a figure which had dropped to one-fourth by 1981. In this same period, the up-front expenditures for generating concepts, screening, and the business plan more than doubled, rising from 10 to 21 percent. The Booz, Allen & Hamilton study also notes that the success

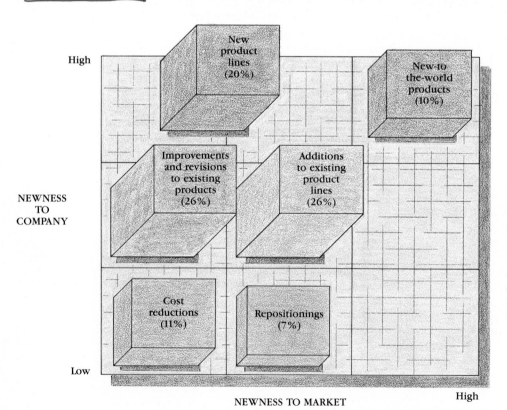

Figure 11-7 *New-product intervention in 5 years (ending in 1981).* A major research effort reports on the newness of new-product development. Only one out of ten products studied was really a new product to both the company and the market. Many more are extensions or improvements of existing products, copies of competitors' products, or simply repositionings of existing products. (From Booz, Allen & Hamilton, *New Products Management for the 1980s,* 1982, p. 9. Reproduced by permission.)

Implementing and Controlling Marketing Plans

rate of new products which *do* make it to commercialization remains almost the same—about 65 percent. It appears that marketers bring out new products at the same rate of success by committing more effort to the less costly up-front analysis of product ideas or concepts.

The researchers classified the new products according to newness to the market and newness to the company. Figure 11-7 illustrates the proportions of the new products falling into these categories. The bad news in the report is that only 10 percent of the new products introduced in the 5-year period ending in 1981 were true innovations. Most new products are (1) improvements to present products, (2) product line extensions, or (3) "me-too" products competitors already have on the market. Roger Bennett and Robert Cooper have chastised the marketing community for letting this happen in the name of the marketing concept.[21]

◼ PRODUCT MANAGEMENT ◼

Whether in development or in one of the stages of the life cycle, most products and product lines in a large organization are the responsibility of a designated manager. In general, a **product manager** (or **brand manager**) is responsible for initiating, developing, and implementing product or product line plans. This manager's responsibilities and level of authority vary from company to company; product management frequently involves the cooperative efforts of managers throughout the organization.[22]

Figure 11-8 shows the typical overlapping (matrix) structure found in many large consumer goods companies. Each of the three product managers is responsible for numerous marketing activities (from research through sales) for a narrow set of products or lines within the company's total product mix. Note, however, that all the managers share these responsibilities with other managers in the organization and have no structural authority over their departments. In small firms and those with very narrow product lines, all the responsibilities and tasks of product management may fall to a single individual.

☐ Consumer Products

At General Foods in White Plains, New York, a so-called category manager (in some companies called a product group manager) is responsible for the overall marketing of several brands and types of a product—for example, coffee. General Foods markets Maxwell House regular, instant, and decaffeinated coffees as well as Sanka, Brim, Yuban, and Mellow Roast. Each item is the responsibility of a brand manager who must compete internally with other brands for marketing dollars and externally with brands from Nestlé, Procter & Gamble, and others. In addition, General Foods has a department for consumer promotions as well as advertising specialists within its coffee division. All the Maxwell House coffees are advertised under one brand name. What, then, does a brand manager at General Foods do?

On a typical day, the brand manager for Maxwell House instant coffee—let's call her Anne Ingrahm—confers with the six regional managers for the coffee division, perhaps to discuss the value of distributing a certain package size in a given market. She may talk with the manager of consumer promotions about ideas for coupons and premiums (should they offer a coupon worth 40 cents or a free coffee mug in return for three labels?). Next she may discuss the advertising strategy with personnel at Ogilvy & Mather, the Maxwell House advertising agency. As much as half of her time is likely to be spent in allocating her large marketing budget.

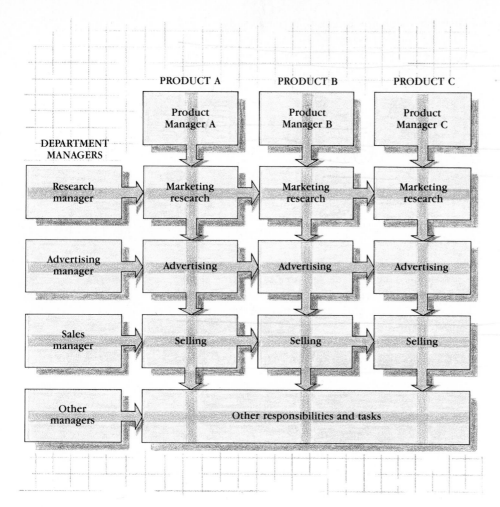

PRODUCT A   PRODUCT B   PRODUCT C

| | Product Manager A | Product Manager B | Product Manager C |

DEPARTMENT MANAGERS

Research manager	Marketing research	Marketing research	Marketing research
Advertising manager	Advertising	Advertising	Advertising
Sales manager	Selling	Selling	Selling
Other managers	Other responsibilities and tasks		

Figure 11-8 *Shared responsibilities in typical organization of product management.* Product managers have some responsibility for a wide variety of marketing functions as they pertain to a narrow range of products. Functional managers, by contrast, have a narrow responsibility for their specific function but manage this function for a broad number of products. The two share the responsibility under a product- or brand-management system.

Ingrahm does not expect to continue as brand manager of Maxwell House instant for more than a year. Very likely she will then manage a new brand of coffee or possibly will work on developing a new product. Such a pattern is typical for brand managers, who usually are young people eager to handle a wide variety of job responsibilities.[23]

☐ *Industrial Products*

The concept of product management is not as widespread in industrial marketing as it is in consumer marketing, but it has been adopted to an extent. Industrial product managers' jobs differ somewhat from those of consumer product brand managers.[24] Industrial product managers generally work very closely with the research and design, engineering, and manufacturing departments to ensure that the product meets the often highly specialized needs of organizational buyers. The job also entails greater responsibility for providing straightforward information about the product's specifications and uses, both to the sales force and to customers. In other ways, industrial product managers function much like their counterparts in consumer marketing, although they may handle a particular product for a longer time, given the higher levels of professionalism and expertise in organizational markets.

One of the most extensive product categories at General Foods (GF) is its lineup of coffee brands. Under the product (or brand) management system, individual marketing managers have extensive responsibility for the marketing programs of individual brands, such as Maxwell House. Another brand manager has responsibility for Sanka, and another for Brim. All three report to a product category manager responsible for all GF coffees. (Copyright © Laura Dwight/Peter Arnold, Inc.)

☐ *The Right Manager for the Right Product*

General Foods classifies Maxwell House instant coffee as a mature or "maintenance" product, since coffee consumption has been slipping steadily for 20 years. Ingrahm, our hypothetical brand manager, thus has to focus on sales volume to retain the product's market share and profitability. Strict financial analysis and planning are in order. In contrast, the brand manager for Procter & Gamble's High Point, a more recent brand of instant coffee, needs to be more entrepreneurial in fighting for a growing niche of the mature coffee market.

During different stages of their life cycles, products require different kinds of management. Some product managers may excel at cost control—so important in harvesting a mature product. Others may be better at handling the high risks of launching a new product. Most good managers develop talents for both types of assignments and any that fall in between.

Higher-level managers must find the right way to reward each product manager, regardless of the assignment. If all product managers are compensated on the basis of profitability or cash flow, those who are assigned to mature, successful products would be favored. More important, the managers of new products, keeping an eye on profitability, might not invest enough to support growth. When managers' rewards are based on the goals associated with each specific product, the organization as a whole should benefit from effective product management.

■ *SUMMARY*   ■

1. Marketers must *manage* the development process, because even the best ideas and products can go awry.
2. The balanced portfolio concept relies on the collection of products based on their relative maturity.
3. The product life cycle is made up of introductory, growth, maturity, and decline stages.

4. Marketers frequently extend the product life cycle by reformulating or slightly altering a product.

5. Both adoption and diffusion depend on moving consumers from no awareness of an innovation to awareness, interest, evaluation, trial, and adoption.

6. The extent of diffusion varies greatly across product classes.

7. Adopters can be subdivided into innovators, early adopters, the early majority, the late majority, and laggards.

8. Organizations expand and diversify by entering a new product in a new market, a new product in an existing market, an existing product in a new market, or an existing product in an existing market.

9. An individual marketer's product development strategy is determined by the characteristics of the company and the market.

10. Important considerations in devising product development tactics are the timing of new-product introductions, cannibalization, and planned obsolescence.

11. The product development process comprises a series of steps: idea generation, screening, feasibility studies, prototype development, test marketing, and commercialization.

12. Commercialization marks the introductory state of the product's life cycle.

13. Most products and product lines in a large organization are the responsibility of a designated manager.

14. During different stages of their life cycles, products require different kinds of management.

☐ Key Terms

adoption process
balanced product portfolio
brand manager
cannibalization
commercialization
concept testing
continuous innovation
decline stage
diffusion process
discontinuous innovation
early adopters

early majority
fad
fashion
focus group
growth stage
innovation
innovators
introductory stage
laggards
late majority
life cycle extension
maturity stage

new-product business plan
planned obsolescence
primary demand
product class
product development process
product life cycle
product manager
prototype
screening process
selective demand
simulated test marketing
test marketing

☐ Chapter Review

1. Why should multiproduct manufacturers seek to balance their product portfolio? How does the portfolio relate to ongoing profitability?

2. Contrast the main characteristics of the introductory and the maturity stages of the product life cycle. What activities should marketers emphasize during each stage?

3. Why do product classes tend to have more stable life cycles than individual brands do? Name a product class that you think is in its decline, and predict its future.

4. Name an innovation, explain why you think it is continuous or discontinuous, and evaluate how it reflects the four factors that influence diffusion.

5. To what extent is the innovation you named in item 4 diffused? Did the factors of diffusion aid or hinder its acceptance by society?

6. Why might a consumer be willing to adopt one product but not another? Give examples to support your view.

7. Explain how company factors and market factors determine product strategy. Characterize the kind of company that, in your opinion, can most afford to be innovative.

8. List the steps in the product development process, and outline the main activities of each step.

9. How do skills needed to manage a new product differ from those used to manage a mature one?

References

1. William T. Robinson and Claes Fornell, "Sources of Market Pioneer Advantages in Consumer Goods Industries," *Journal of Marketing Research,* vol. XXII, Aug. 1985.
2. "Procter & Gamble's Profit Problem—Food," *Business Week,* Jan. 26, 1981, p. 52.
3. Milton Moskowitz, Michael Katz, and Robert Levering, eds, *Everybody's Business* (New York: Harper & Row, 1980), p. 153.
4. "Bausch & Lomb: Marketing Vision Bolsters Its Role in Contact Lenses," *Business Week,* Nov. 17, 1980, pp. 173–184.
5. Ibid., p. 177.
6. Peter F. Drucker, "The Discipline of Innovation," *Harvard Business Review,* May–June 1985, pp. 67–72; and Peter F. Drucker, *Innovation and Entrepreneurship* (New York: Harper & Row, 1985).
7. James Brian Quinn, "Managing Innovation: Controlled Chaos," *Harvard Business Review,* May–June 1985, pp. 73–84.
8. "Consumer Product Techniques Help Loctite Sell to Industry," *The Wall Street Journal,* Apr. 2, 1981, p. 29.
9. "The Anatomy of RCA's Videodisc Failure," *Business Week,* Apr. 23, 1984, pp. 89–90.
10. Everett M. Rogers and F. Floyd Shoemaker, *Communication of Innovation* (New York: Free Press, 1971).
11. Mary C. Gilly and Valerie A. Zeithaml, "The Elderly Consumer and Adoption of Technologies," *Journal of Consumer Research,* vol. 12, Dec. 1985, pp. 353–357.
12. Mark B. Traylor, "Cannibalism in Multi-brand Firms," *Journal of Consumer Marketing,* vol. 3, Spring 1986, pp. 69–75.
13. Howard Rudnitsky with Jay Gissen, "Chesebrough-Pond's: The Unsung Miracle," *Forbes,* Sept. 28, 1981, pp. 105–109.
14. "A Matter of Taste: There's No Way to Tell If a New Food Product Will Please the Public," *The Wall Street Journal,* Feb. 26, 1980, p. 1.
15. Ilkka A. Ronkainen, "Criteria Changes across Product Development Stages," *Industrial Marketing Management,* vol. 14, Aug. 1985, pp. 171–178; and C. Merle Crawford, "Evaluating New Products: A System, Not an Art," *Business Horizons,* vol. 29, Nov.–Dec. 1986, pp. 48–55.
16. G. Lynn Shostack, "Designing Services That Deliver," *Harvard Business Review,* Jan.–Feb. 1984, pp. 133–139.
17. David N. Burt and William R. Sonkup, "Purchasing's Role in New Product Development," *Harvard Business Review,* Sept.–Oct. 1985, pp. 90–97.
18. William Lazer, Mushtaq Luqmani, and Zahir Quraeshi, "Product Rejuvenation Strategies," *Business Horizons,* Nov.–Dec. 1984, pp. 21–28.
19. "Despite Mixed Record, Firms Still Pushing for New Products," *The Wall Street Journal,* Nov. 12, 1981, p. 31.
20. This section is based on Booz, Allen & Hamilton's *New Product Management for the 1980s* (New York, 1982), and Peter D. Bennett, "The Marketing of Consumer Products," in Victor P. Buell, ed., *Handbook of Modern Marketing,* 2d ed. (New York: McGraw-Hill, 1986), pp. 3.1–3.10.
21. Roger C. Bennett and Robert G. Cooper, "The Misuse of Marketing: An American Tragedy," *Business Horizons,* Nov.–Dec. 1981, pp. 51–60. See also Geoffrey Kiel, "Technology and Marketing: The Magic Mix?" *Business Horizons,* May–June 1984, pp. 7–14.
22. Steven Lysonski, "A Boundary Theory Investigation of the Product Manager's Role," *Journal of Marketing,* vol. 49, Winter 1985, pp. 26–40.
23. "Pushing the Maxwell Product at General Foods," *The New York Times,* Aug. 16, 1981.
24. Robert W. Eckles and Timothy J. Novotney, "Industrial Product Managers: Authority and Responsibility," *Industrial Marketing Management,* vol. 13, May 1984, pp. 71–75; and William Theodore Cummings, Donald W. Jackson, Jr., and Lonnie L. Ostrom, "Differences between Industrial and Consumer Product Managers," *Industrial Marketing Management,* vol. 13, Aug. 1984, pp. 171–180.

CASE 11

PEPPERIDGE FARM

What happens when a marketer known for quality products attempts to introduce new lines of moderate-quality goods? In the case of Pepperidge Farm, a subsidiary of Campbell Soup Company, the result was somewhat of a disaster. In fiscal 1984, Pepperidge Farm's operating earnings were down 18 percent, the first such decline in the division's recent history. This decline came about in good part because of three separate but related failures over a period of years.

By the late 1970s, Pepperidge Farm had established a solid reputation as a marketer of old-fashioned, high-quality fresh and frozen baked goods. But focus group research suggested that people's eating patterns were changing: The decline of the traditional family meal had created a need for a tasty, light, fun food for "nonmeal meals" at odd hours. Pepperidge Farm eventually developed a product line of filled puff pastry intended to be more exciting than a sandwich, more convenient than cooking, and less expensive than eating out. This line was tested in Bakersfield, California, in late 1979 and early 1980 and was subsequently named Deli's. A national rollout began in April 1980.

Pepperidge Farm executives had estimated sales of $40 million after a year on the market. However, it soon became apparent that earlier failure to develop a clear positioning strategy—partly because Deli's were supposed to have such a broad appeal—was coming back to haunt Pepperidge Farm. In addition, new flavors were abruptly added to the Deli's line even before the impact of the initial six flavors had been carefully monitored. Most serious, Pepperidge Farm did not include enough meat in Deli's flavors and failed to use high-quality meat. A vice president for marketing at Campbells admits: "I had one of the beef Deli's that I could still be chewing now. While the quality started out fair, it ended up terrible. The worst thing we could do was put out a product that didn't taste good."

Thus, although Pepperidge Farm was successful in persuading consumers to try Deli's—perhaps because of the high quality associated with the Pepperidge Farm name, there were few repeat purchases. By the time the company faced up to its marketing mistakes, a good deal of damage had already been done. Product quality of Deli's flavors was improved, and sales leveled off at about $35 million—still well below Pepperidge Farm's earlier forecasts.

The introduction of Star Wars Cookies was another disappointment. As the dominant marketer of premium cookies, Pepperidge Farm felt confident it could leap into the children's cookie business by capitalizing on the popularity of the *Star Wars* film trilogy. Star Wars cookies were rolled out in the spring of 1983, just as *Return of the Jedi*, the third film in the *Star Wars* series, was released. But, despite good initial sales, the product flopped. The cookies proved to be rather expensive for children's cookies ($1.39), quality was not up to par, and many supermarkets chose not to carry the line. Since use of the name Star Wars cookies involved a licensing agreement with Lucasfilm Company, Pepperidge Farm had not been asked to put up any money up front. Still, it had to continue a mediocre product for a year to get rid of its backlog.

The failure of Pepperidge Farm's apple juice is a somewhat different story. In this case, unlike that of Deli's or Star Wars cookies, Pepperidge Farm originally intended to introduce a new, high-quality product: an unfiltered, premium apple juice. Since 80 percent of apple juice bought by U.S. consumers is filtered (clear), Pepperidge Farm believed that it could differentiate its product by its taste superiority. Testing in June 1982 in Hartford and New Haven, Connecticut, produced somewhat encouraging results.

Then, for reasons that remain unclear, Pepperidge Farm decided to add a filtered juice and go after the larger segment of the juice market (in which apple juice is sold on

Implementing and Controlling Marketing Plans

price as a children's beverage). As one Campbell executive reflects: "That was the beginning of the end. . . . Here we were competing in the commodity end of the business with a premium-price product that had a name which didn't in any way signal it was for kids."

By that time, Pepperidge Farm had already made a substantial investment in its juice line, including purchase of a plant. But sales began to lag, and Pepperidge Farm adopted a strategy of dealing the product. "We were trying to sell cheap apple juice with the Pepperidge Farm name on it," admits the Campbell executive. "It just flies in the face of everything you want to do with Pepperidge Farm." Eventually, the apple juice line was discontinued and the plant was shut down.

Source: Nancy Giges, "Pepperidge Farm's Fallow Ground," *Advertising Age*, Feb. 21, 1985, pp. 2–3.

1. Why do you think Pepperidge Farm management backed three new product lines which proved to be failures?
2. If you had been a supermarket manager with many years of experience selling high-priced, high-quality Pepperidge Farm breads, cookies, and other products and the company offered you a line of cookies targeted to children, what would you have done?

■ CASE 12

HARMAN INTERNATIONAL

The name Sidney Harman is well-known to audio buffs. In the early 1960s, Harman helped to pioneer the high-fidelity sound market by introducing his premium-priced Harman-Kardon line of audio equipment. By mid-1986, Harman International, with Sidney Harman as its chief executive, had annual sales of $180 million.

It was not a simple, steady path to the top for Harman and his firm. After his initial success in building the audio equipment market, Harman sold his company in 1977 to Beatrice. He briefly served as deputy secretary of Commerce in the Carter administration and then moved into management consulting. But, by the 1980s, Harman was disenchanted with the way his firm was being run. Beatrice had attempted to boost sales by cutting prices, thereby undercutting the prestigious image of the Harman-Kardon line. When such moves proved unsuccessful, Beatrice sold the company to Shin Shirasuna Electronic Corporation in 1979.

Harman reentered the audio business in 1981 by purchasing JBL and a number of European audio distribution firms. Then, in 1985, he was finally able to reacquire Harman-Kardon. Since this purchase, Harman has attempted to renew the line's high-quality image by advertising in audio-buff magazines and targeting distribution to audio boutiques.

Already respected as an industry innovator, Harman's current goal is to manufacture all components for his audio lines (including Harmon-Kardon, JBL, and Infinity) inside the United States. In his view, the declining value of the dollar, lower interest rates, and consumers' growing attachment to premium audio names will help him to achieve this goal while competing against lower-cost brands from the Far East. "If you don't manufacture, you forget the art," argues Harman in defense of his bold manufacturing plan. And his efforts are well under way: Harman International is making speakers in the United States for the Japanese firms of Sharp and Mitsubishi and is manufacturing speakers and amplifiers for Ford and Chrysler cars.

Harman's attempt to pursue the higher end of the audio market is also being followed by other U.S. companies, among them McIntosh Labs and Carver. With low-cost, Far East competitors controlling about three-fourths of the overall audio market, these U.S. firms have simply bypassed this difficult challenge and instead aim for an upscale segment interested in premium-priced, top-quality equipment. Although this segment is smaller than the lower-priced end of the audio market, it has at least one compensating advantage: Expensive audio equipment averages up to 32 percent gross margins; lower-priced brands average only 18 to 25 percent gross margins.

Sidney Harman's long-range planning must be viewed in the larger context of a rapidly changing audio industry. Stereo sales in the United States rose 15 percent in 1984, 8 percent in 1985, and 10 percent in 1986. The introduction of compact disc players in 1983 is responsible for this bonanza. In 1985, for example, U.S. consumers bought nearly 1 million CD players. Moreover, such purchases lead many affluent consumers to buy better stereo speakers and receivers as well. "You can't play a CD on cheap equipment," notes one industry analyst. "It would be like driving a Mercedes with retreads."

Worldwide data for CDs are equally impressive. By early 1985, worldwide sales of players reached 1.2 million units, and sales of discs exceeded 22 million. These figures translate into $800 million worth of business, and Americans are providing a hefty chunk of that business: at least 22 percent.

Compact disc systems have been praised by many audio buffs because they offer an extremely high quality sound. They offer another important advantage over conventional long-playing records: They don't break or easily scratch. Leslie Rosen, executive director of the Compact Disc Group, a nonprofit trade association, observes: "I guess you could destroy them if you wanted to, but it's something you would have to deliberately want to do."

Having been disappointed by previous audio technological "revolutions"—among them 8-track cartridges and quadrophonic sound—audio dealers initially took a cautious stance concerning CD technology. However, by 1984, dealers were encouraged by a downward trend in the pricing of both players and discs. By 1985, major dealers such as the 36-unit Tower Records chain were increasing their promotion of CDs and allocating much more store space to the CD section. Bill Silverman, director of communications for the National Association of Recording Merchandisers (NARM), bluntly states: "The compact disc is here to stay. The CD has already passed the point beyond which there's a question of whether it will survive or not."

Sources: Liz Murphy, "Compact Discs Sing a Hi-Tech Success Story," *Sales and Marketing Management*, Feb. 4, 1985, pp. 34–36; Scott Ticer, "High-Tech Music Has the Audio Market Rocking," *Business Week*, July 2, 1986, p. 100, 102, 104; Scott Ticer, "Sidney Harman Loves the Sound of 'Made in the U.S.A.,'" *Business Week*, July 2, 1986, p. 102.

1. Why was 1985 a particularly good year for Sidney Harman to reacquire the Harman-Kardon line and get back into the audio business?
2. As of 1985, how would you characterize the stage of adoption of compact disc technology? Where is that process today?
3. What major factors have helped and hurt the diffusion of compact disc technology in the U.S. market?

■ CASE 13

XEROX

In 1984, Xerox Corporation rolled out three new copying machines—the first results of a new-product development process begun 3 years earlier. Xerox executives hope that this new process will revitalize its troubled copier business, which accounts for roughly three-fourths of the company's overall sales.

The late 1970s and early 1980s were difficult for Xerox. As Japanese firms successfully penetrated the low end of the copier market, introducing reliable and inexpensive machines, Xerox's sales took a nosedive. Although the firm's market share was a staggering 86 percent in 1970, by 1982 Xerox's market share had fallen below 45 percent. Not surprisingly, such figures led to a corporate shakeup. Xerox laid off 17,000 employees and reduced its manufacturing costs by more than 50 percent.

One key element in this shakeup was an effort to overhaul Xerox's cumbersome product development process. The company's complicated matrix organization was scrapped; instead, four strategic business units (SBUs) now run the copier business. General managers for each SBU set long-range strategy and oversee product development. They report to Wayland R. Hicks, head of the Reprographics Business Group, and he reports to a higher executive at corporate headquarters in Stamford, Connecticut.

Under the new product development process, an idea for a new product is typically generated by an SBU. Any such ideas are tested for feasibility by product-synthesis teams. If tests are favorable, an idea is passed along to teams of designers, who then produce a prototype. The prototype must meet certain preestablished goals; if it does not, the project is killed. If the prototype meets Xerox's goals, a product delivery team run by a chief engineer takes it through to manufacturing.

Xerox executives already point to noticeable gains from the streamlined new-product development process. For example, the development of one of the new copiers introduced in 1984—the 9900—took only 3 years. Comparable products developed under the matrix organizational plan had taken more than 5 years. Development of the 9900 might well have fallen behind schedule when Xerox encountered a problem involving software codes for the machine, but a "crisis team" of software designers and manufacturing engineers was quickly assembled and worked through a Labor Day weekend to find a solution. Chief engineer Daniel W. Cholish notes that, under the previous organizational structure, "to get that commitment would have been impossible."

Wayland Hicks claims that instituting the new-product development process allowed an immediate 10 percent productivity gain and shortened engineering cycles for some products by 50 percent. Overall, in his view, Xerox "cut in half the resources and the time we used to require to develop comparable products."

According to Xerox executives, the new-product development process has been noticeably helpful in its work on the company's 10 series of copiers (which includes the award-winning 1075 machine). Xerox reports that it can build copiers in this series for 35 to 75 percent less than the copiers they replaced; one result is that the 1045 machine costs $10,500—42 percent less than its predecessor, the 3450, did in 1979. In addition, Xerox insists that they have been able to reduce production costs and prices while improving the quality of its copiers. Industry experts seem to agree; one consultant maintains that the company "has added strong products at good prices which bring new sophistication to the market."

Source: "How Xerox Speeds Up the Birth of New Products," *Business Week*, Mar. 19, 1984, pp. 58–59.

1. How is Xerox's new-product development process consistent with the process of most companies described in Chapter 11? How is it different?
2. What external pressures forced Xerox to change the way of its development of new products?

■   ■

DISTRIBUTION

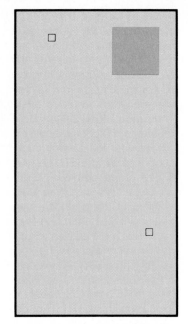

Distribution is the process whereby goods and services are delivered from producers to consumers and to organizational buyers where and when the products are needed. Except for the retail outlets where we make our purchases, most organizations involved in distribution and the distribution process itself are all but invisible to the public. But distribution is as important as the other components of the marketing mix; it is the marketing function that provides time, place, and possession utilities.

Chapter 12 introduces the functions and types of marketing intermediaries—the wholesalers and retailers who, along with producers, form distribution systems—and describes the ownership and control of retailing institutions, including how retail locations are chosen and the changing nature of retailing systems. The chapter ends with some comments about the future of marketing intermediaries.

Chapter 13 looks closely at distribution channels and describes what flows within them—if they are well-managed. The basic structures and designs of distribution channels relate to marketing objectives and strategies, to buying behavior, and to product classifications. The distribution of industrial products is highlighted.

Chapter 14 focuses on marketing logistics, or physical distribution—the actual movement, storage, and handling of finished products. The chapter outlines the objectives of marketing logistics, with an emphasis on balancing costs and levels of service. The chapter ends by describing the specific tasks of transportation and of inventory and warehouse management.

12

Copyright © 1984 Jeff Smith.

MARKETING INTERMEDIARIES

SPOTLIGHT ON

☐ Basic functions of marketing intermediaries

☐ Wholesalers' specific tasks; classification of wholesalers

☐ Retailers' specific tasks; classification of retailers

☐ Ownership, control, and location decisions for retail institutions

☐ Factors that make retailing systems dynamic

☐ The future of marketing intermediaries: Changes in how wholesalers and retailers distribute products

Maria Lopez gets up early 6 days a week to open up the small *bodega* (store) she runs in Saucillo, a village in the state of Chihuahua in northern Mexico. Señora Lopez stocks a limited number of items for her customers: products that require refrigeration, such as milk, eggs, meat, and vegetables, as well as staples like flour, salt, sugar, and canned goods.

Most of Maria's customers work in a nearby oil refinery or are farmers. To help feed their families, many grow some of their own food and raise animals. Maria calls nearly all her customers by their first names and always attends their christenings, weddings, and funerals. She saves the freshest produce and best cuts of meat for her favorite customers and even keeps up with their diets.

Supplies for the Lopez *bodega* arrive twice a week from a wholesale distributor in the state's capital city of Chihuahua. Angelo Martinez, the driver of the refrigerated truck, knows just how much of each product Señora Lopez is likely to need each week. Still, he and Maria go through a 10-minute ritual of filling out her orders, complaining about the weather, joking about music favored by local teenagers, and commiserating about the exchange ratio of the peso to the dollar.

Tony Lopez, Maria's third cousin, manages a large Kroger supermarket on the west side of San Antonio, Texas. Tony's store has just under 200 employees maintaining over 40,000 square feet of shopping space, and sells more than $4 million worth of products per year. Although Tony tries to spend at least an hour a day on the shopping floor chatting with customers and employees, most of his time is generally taken up meeting with route salespeople for various grocery distributors and checking with Kroger's regional buyers.

Left: A bodega in Mazatlan, Mexico. (Owen Franken/Stock, Boston.)
Right: A large Kroger's supermarket in San Marcos, Texas. (Copyright © Bob Daemmrich.)

Implementing and Controlling Marketing Plans

Keeping such a mammoth store fully stocked requires careful planning, buying, and coordinating. Each morning, a computer printout from Kroger's regional office in San Antonio tells Tony the previous day's sales. It also provides a great deal more information: how many quarts of milk, crates of grapefruit, boxes of Tide (in each size), and packages of Green Giant frozen peas were sold. The computerized checkout scanners enable Tony and other Kroger managers to monitor buying trends quickly and adjust orders accordingly. The computer cannot, however, predict how sales of Bounty paper towels will be affected by a cents-off coupon running in the Wednesday editions of San Antonio newspapers. But four years' experience running the store has taught Tony to make accurate estimates. On this particular Wednesday, he makes sure that an order for 50 additional cases of towels is placed with the Procter & Gamble sales representative. Although the demands of their work situations are quite different, both Tony Lopez and his cousin Maria face long, exhausting workdays.

If you have a yen for an orange, a grapefruit, or an avocado—and you happen to live in Florida—you may be able to walk into your backyard and pick the fruit you want. But if you live in Vermont or Montana and have that yen for tropical fruit, someone has to get it to you. Most goods and many services reach us through the efforts of **marketing intermediaries, or middlemen**: the independent business concerns that facilitate the flow of products from producers to organizational buyers or ultimate consumers. These intermediaries—primarily wholesalers and retailers—are the building blocks of distribution systems. We depend on them even for the food we eat.

Chapter 12 discusses the main functions of wholesalers and retailers and the basic tasks they perform. We explore the general nature of wholesaling and retailing, and we look at the great variety of intermediaries available to marketers. The chapter concludes with an appraisal of how wholesaling and retailing are likely to change in the future.

MARKETING INTERMEDIARIES: BUILDING BLOCKS OF DISTRIBUTION

When you buy a pack of chewing gum, a book, an automobile, a kerosene heater, or a personal computer, you make your purchase at a retailing establishment. **Retailers** are merchants whose main business is selling directly to ultimate consumers. Retailing establishments include the stores, shops, supermarkets, discounters, and boutiques where we purchase items almost daily. Indeed, for most consumers, retailers are the most visible units in a distribution channel. By contrast, wholesalers are not as visible to most people outside of marketing. **Wholesalers** are merchants who buy products from producers or other wholesalers and resell them to retailers, organizational buyers, or to other wholesalers. Ordinarily, wholesalers do not sell directly to ultimate consumers.

Although wholesalers and retailers are the primary participants in channels of distribution, other organizations or individuals also serve facilitating functions. Transportation and storage firms play important roles in the physical distribution

Most consumer products travel through marketing intermediaries. Wholesalers buy in large quantity and transport to retailers, where consumers buy in the quantity they want. Such intermediaries provide utility to the product. (Left: Bendick Assoc./Monkmeyer. Right: Copyright © Bob Daemmrich.)

of products. Banks provide financial backing for wholesalers and retailers as well as for producers. Insurance companies underwrite policies providing financial protection for intermediaries and producers. Marketing research firms play vital facilitating roles in developing products, while advertising agencies inform and influence buyers.

This chapter focuses on the intermediaries most directly involved in distribution channels: wholesalers and retailers. Although they serve different purposes in a distribution channel, both share at least three basic functions: sorting out products; providing time, place, and possession utilities; and keeping down costs to buyers.[1]

☐ *Concentration and Dispersal of Products*

Intermediaries resolve two basic discrepancies between producers and purchasers: the discrepancies of volume and variety (or choice). Both discrepancies are resolved by concentrating (or bringing together) certain products and by the dispersal (or sorting out) of other products.

Consider the following examples of volume discrepancy. Procter & Gamble produces millions of boxes of Tide detergent each year; most consumers, however, want to buy only a box or so a month, and in a particular size. Similarly, Singer produces hundreds of thousands of sewing machines annually; but a typical consumer might purchase only one sewing machine—again, of a particular model—every 15 years or so. **Volume discrepancy** is the difference between the amounts produced by marketers and the amounts desired by consumers. Intermediaries resolve this volume discrepancy by "breaking bulk," or dividing large quantities of products into units practical for retail distribution and purchase by consumers.

Variety discrepancy is the difference between the number of different products produced by marketers and the number desired by consumers. To understand variety discrepancy, consider Nabisco Brands. Even that packaged-goods giant can-

Implementing and Controlling Marketing Plans

not produce all the many items that supermarket shoppers want and expect. So intermediaries resolve the second discrepancy: They gather all the products made by different suppliers that shoppers expect to find in a certain type of store, thereby providing the variety and choice consumers want. These discrepancies are so great that it is hard to conceive of marketing taking place without intermediaries.

To resolve volume discrepancy, marketing intermediaries perform two basic functions: They accumulate and allocate. Through **accumulation,** wholesalers and retailers collect quantities of products from numerous sources. The buyers of housewares for Macy's department stores, for example, order toasters, mixers, food processors, and electric skillets from General Electric, Norelco, Sunbeam, and a host of other producers, accumulating the items for allocation to the chain's various stores. Through **allocation,** intermediaries apportion products to their own divisions or to other resellers in quantities they believe consumers will want. A supermarket may need only two 4-foot shelves to display boxes of Tide, since its customers do not want an entire aisle given over to various sizes of those bright orange packages. Thus, intermediaries allocate amounts of products to different buying points.

The discrepancy of variety (choice) between producers and consumers is also handled by intermediaries through two basic functions: sorting out and assorting. Through the process of **sorting out,** wholesalers and retailers separate quantities of products into sizes, colors, quality grades, and so on. This is done with meats, for instance, when we grade them as standard, good, and choice. Then, through **assorting** (handled primarily by retailers) different brands, models, sizes, colors, and price ranges are brought together to come up with an assortment desired by the consumer. This function is performed when a single store brings to one place the products of marketers of suits, dresses, sweaters, hats, and belts.

One major part of sorting out products is that of grading. Here, an official inspector of the U.S. Department of Agriculture stamps meat with its appropriate grade. (USDA Photo.)

☐ *Utility*

Marketing activities give products form, time, place, and possession utilities. Intermediaries, however, have little to do with form utility. Once the distribution point is reached, the good or service is usually already in the form that marketers believe consumers want. But intermediaries are greatly involved with the other utilities and often are the main providers of them. For example, intermediaries ensure that goods and services are available where ultimate consumers and organizational buyers want them, thus providing place utility. They also provide time utility through such activities as transportation, warehousing, and storing. Through concentration and dispersal, intermediaries provide the appropriate volume and variety of products, thereby moving buyers to make the purchase and gain possession utility.

Suppose you want to purchase a Sony Walkman cassette player. As a shopper, you want the product readily available in a range of models, with various capabilities, and in different price ranges. Moreover, you want it *when* you want it. You do not want to wait; you expect to walk out of the store with music playing in your ears. In short, you want the utilities of form, time, place, and possession. Sony provides the first; marketing intermediaries provide the others.

☐ *Saving Consumers Money*

Many people mistakenly assume that intermediaries simply add their markup to the producer's price and thus directly raise the cost of products to consumers. What many fail to realize is that the functions of intermediaries *must* be performed for buyers to get what they want. Someone must concentrate and disperse products and provide time, place, and possession utilities. Although certain intermediaries could indeed be eliminated, either the manufacturer or the buyer would have to assume their activities and the costs of those activities. If manufacturers performed the distribution functions, they would have to add staff and equipment and, in turn, raise prices. If they chose not to, the buyer of a Sony Walkman would have to travel to the factory in New Jersey to get a cassette player—a trip that would add considerably to the product's cost. In other words, intermediaries perform essential functions that cannot be eliminated—although they *can* be passed along to someone else in the distribution channel.

Figure 12-1 illustrates how the number of transactions are usually reduced when intermediaries are part of the distribution channel. If a manufacturer of paintbrushes chose to sell directly to consumers, an army of salespeople would have to be deployed to thousands of street corners—at prohibitive cost. Instead, Figure 12-1a assumes that four different paintbrush manufacturers might deal directly with 10 retailers. This results in only 40 lines of contact, or 40 transactions, each with its own cost. Figure 12-1b adds a wholesaler to help move those paintbrushes to

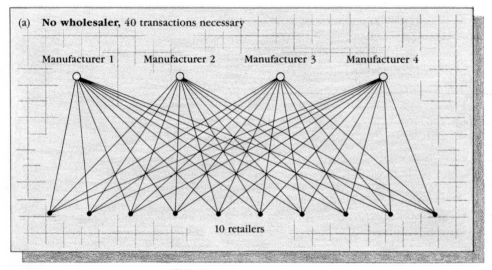

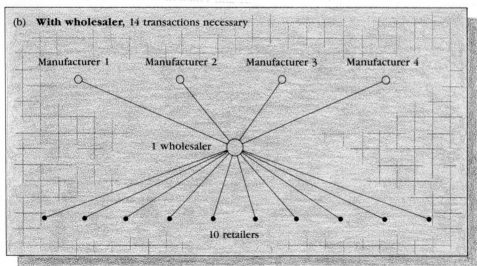

Figure 12-1 *Transactions with and without intermediaries.* As the top figure shows, for four manufacturers to sell directly to 10 retailers, there is a need for 40 transactions. By inserting a wholesaler in the channel, the number of transactions is cut to 14. This decrease of almost two-thirds of the transactions in the channel reduces costs for everyone. You can cut out the channel member, or "middleman," but you cannot eliminate the functions it performs.

Implementing and Controlling Marketing Plans

the retailers; now the number of transactions has been reduced from 40 to 14. Attendant costs, and prices to consumers, are reduced because the costs have been spread across a greater number of products.

The following sections look separately, and in some detail, at wholesalers and retailers as the fundamental building blocks of distribution systems. Many kinds of intermediaries are found in each category. As you will see, they usually perform different functions and are owned and operated differently.

THE NATURE OF WHOLESALING

Houston-based Sysco Corporation is among the most profitable of the 2000 firms in the business of wholesaling food to restaurants and other institutional servers. In an industry with sales of $55 billion a year, Sysco's share is large—close to $2 billion annually. Its profits exceed competitors' too, because Sysco practices the marketing concept and is ever mindful of customers' needs. According to Chief Executive Officer John Baugh, "Our people don't just sell food—they sell peace of mind." A favorite Sysco anecdote backs up Baugh's claim:

> Preparations for a lobster roast at Houston's Inn on the Park were going smoothly until the chef noticed unexpected guests and found he was ten lobsters short. At 5 pm on a Saturday, where was he going to find fresh lobsters? Panic-stricken, the chef called his Sysco representative at home. The salesman jumped into his car, drove to a gourmet store that he knew would be open until 6 pm, bought the lobsters and delivered them to the hotel. He even slapped them on the grill himself.[2]

Essentially, wholesalers provide services; they facilitate the flow of products from producers to resellers to consumers by providing economy and convenience—and peace of mind. In the nineteenth century, wholesalers were the most powerful members of distribution channels, since typical manufacturers and retailers had small operations. As retailers and manufacturers grew, their power increased, and the influence of wholesalers decreased—that is, until recent years. Around the middle of this century, most wholesalers had become passive order-takers, operating on razor-thin profit margins averaging 1 percent. However, as manufacturing became automated, so did wholesaling. Computer-based inventory systems and automated warehouses now allow modern wholesalers to provide fast and efficient service to retailers and other institutions and to increase their own profits.

An example is Lawson Products of Des Plaines, Illinois. This wholesaler sells *17,000* different replacement parts, primarily of the nuts-and-bolts variety. It ships from five regional warehouses but can still boast 99 percent order fulfillment. Lawson's 1100 sales representatives don't talk price to customers; they talk quality and convenience; they sell not nuts and bolts but a "fastener program." Lawson's high-grade parts, crisply packaged in yellow boxes, are displayed in storage bins in retail customers' installations. These bins are labeled neatly and are restocked regularly by a Lawson representative. Retailers pay premium prices for these services. As a result, Lawson, which manufactures none of its products but marks up the ones it distributes by an average of 240 percent, clears a net profit of 9 percent. Yet Lawson's customers also save money by reducing their own inventory carrying and control costs.[3]

Just as retailers provide utilities of time, place, and possession to consumers, wholesalers provide those utilities to retailers and other reselling organizations. Also like retailers—but acting for them—wholesalers resolve the discrepancies of

A key resource of modern wholesalers is an efficient warehouse and transportation system. With very thin profit margins, such businesses succeed or fail based on their efficiency. (Aronson/Stock, Boston.)

Hunt's Point Market, near New York City, is a facility where many wholesalers of fresh foods and food retailers can come together to negotiate and engage in the exchanges that will eventually get those foods to millions of consumers in the city and surrounding areas. (Copyright © Jim Anderson/ Woodfin Camp & Assoc.)

volume and variety; they accumulate, allocate, sort out, and build assortments. In providing these services, wholesalers perform several additional functions. To illustrate these realistically, let's look at the services provided by wholesalers at New York City's Hunts Point market in the Bronx, where the bulk of the fresh food for more than 7 million people is directed to 6000 retail stores.[4]

PROMOTION AND SALES   Many wholesalers provide a sales force to call on retailers and other institutions. Small producers without their own sales representatives thus receive the benefits of an experienced sales group. In addition, wholesalers may promote their wares via telephone sales and through catalogs and fliers mailed to organizational buyers. For some producers, wholesalers provide the product's main promotional thrust. At Hunts Point, Lew Solomon of Goodie Brand Packing Corporation (a wholesaler) sells hothouse tomatoes flown in from Israel; the city's gourmet markets pay about $1.50 a pound for such produce that they could not otherwise offer.

TRANSPORTATION   By buying and shipping in mass quantities, often carload and truckload lots, wholesalers cut transportation expenses. They assume administrative responsibility as well as costs, thus relieving their retail customers of that function. Finally, wholesalers generally are located nearer to customers than manufacturers are. The 125-acre Hunts Point market consists basically of four narrow buildings, each 0.3 miles long. Wholesalers' shipments enter one side of each building by train and large truck, get divided into smaller lots, and move efficiently out the other side in smaller trucks for delivery to retailers.

A short distance south of Hunts Point, at Pier 42 on the East River, two or three large refrigerated freighters arrive weekly with loads of bananas, pineapples, and coconuts from Honduras, Costa Rica, and Equador. Employees of Standard Brands, an importer-wholesaler, can unload more than 5 million pounds of bananas in about 9 hours.

WAREHOUSING Wholesalers provide warehouse storage and delivery facilities. If they did not, manufacturers and/or retailers would have to assume the costs of doing so. At Hunts Point, Ben Zdatny is an independent wholesaler serving the city's independent food stores from a warehouse that covers 600,000 square feet. Cheerios are stacked 12 cases high in its warehouse, as are cartons of tomato sauce, paper towels, and cat litter. Four hundred people work in Zdatny's warehouse, loading cartons with forklifts. Doors on one side of the building open to accept shipments from as many as 20 boxcars at a time. Just as Zdatny warehouses goods for independent grocery retailers, many supermarket chains operate their own warehousing facilities—thus they bypass the intermediary but not the function.

FINANCING By paying suppliers when products are shipped, wholesalers help producers to improve their cash flow; they may also extend credit to retailers. In effect, wholesalers may serve as "bankers" by providing financing for the suppliers and retailers on each side of them in the distribution channel.

RISK BEARING When wholesalers at Fulton Fish Market buy their supplies, they assume the risk that goes with ownership. As a wholesaling service, **risk bearing** involves possible loss of product value, for example, from changes in style or in consumers' preferences, or even from spoiled fish; this loss is borne by the wholesaler instead of the supplier or retailer—*if* the wholesaler has taken title to the products. In other words, the risks of ownership follow the title. As we soon will see, taking title to products is a major differentiation among the many kinds of intermediaries that make up a distribution channel: Not all intermediaries assume the financial risks of ownership.

MARKET INFORMATION Like a supplier's own sales force, wholesalers are an important source of information about customers and, ultimately, about consumers' needs and desires. Thus, they are instrumental in applying the marketing concept. Information about purchasing patterns, pricing, new products, and competitors' activities is crucial to marketing success, and wholesalers are in a unique position to provide it. As they accumulate large quantities of products, they also amass volumes of information. Cholho Kim, a young Korean distributor at Hunts Point, buys produce for a small chain of six retail greengrocers. Not only does Kim supply the best goods for his customers, but he relays information about competitors' prices and recommends fast-moving items to his suppliers.

SERVICING PRODUCTS Some wholesalers assume responsibility for servicing the products that they sell to retailers. Rather than dealing directly with manufacturers, retailers often find it more efficient and more convenient to have wholesalers replace or repair returned goods. Naturally, such services are more important to the retailers of small appliances and tools than to those who sell food items.

◼ WHOLESALERS ◼

Wholesalers fall into three major categories: merchant wholesalers, agents and brokers, and manufacturer-run wholesaling operations. The key distinction is whether the wholesaler takes title to, or legal ownership of, products. **Merchant wholesalers** do take title and therefore carry the responsibility for risk bearing and (usually) for performing the various functions described above. **Agents** and **brokers** are intermediaries who help bring manufacturers and retailers together and arrange sales for a commission payment, but they do not take legal title to products. Under an agent arrangement, title remains with the producer until products are transferred to retailers. *Manufacturer-owned wholesaling operations,* of course, hold title until products are exchanged through payment by retailers.

☐ *Merchant Wholesalers*

Merchant wholesalers take title to products and provide either full service or selected functions. They account for slightly more than half the wholesaling dollar volume in the United States. About two-thirds of the nation's wholesalers are in the merchant category; their share of the wholesaling market has been increasing, primarily at the expense of agents and brokers.[5] There are several types of merchant wholesalers, among them **full-service** and **limited-service wholesalers.**

FULL-SERVICE WHOLESALERS Full-service wholesalers provide almost all the functions described in the previous section and generally are divided into three subgroups: general merchandise wholesalers, single-line wholesalers, and specialty wholesalers.

General merchandise wholesalers handle a broad range of products, from food and drug items to plumbing supplies and automotive accessories. **Single-line wholesalers** restrict their inventories to a single product line such as hardware, appliances, or drugs. David Wexler Company of Chicago, for example, handles only musical instruments and accessories. **Specialty wholesalers** have the most restricted inventories, focusing, for instance, on such items as health foods or electric motors. Within their chosen line, however, they provide great merchandise depth. These wholesalers tend to offer higher levels of technical advice and service than nonspecialized intermediaries do.

Full-service wholesalers charge a higher markup on products than do limited-service operations; they typically concentrate either on consumer products or on industrial products.

Wholesalers of Consumer Products McKesson of San Francisco is the largest wholesaler in the United States; most of its revenues come from distributing consumer products to retailers. Approximately 42 percent of its revenues come from drugs, 25 percent from foods, and 20 percent from wines and spirits. (The company also has an industrial products division specializing in chemicals.) McKesson can stock almost an entire drugstore from the items it distributes, and its recent growth has been fueled by the strategy of adding value to products. For example, McKesson will process insurance claims for drugstores and insurance companies; in fact, this wholesaler is the third-largest processor of insurance claims in the nation. The company also designs drugstores and provides crews to maintain inventory for such outlets.[6]

Industrial Wholesalers Industrial distributors usually handle a broad range of inexpensive, small, frequently purchased items for incorporation into other products or for resale in other markets. In contrast, the marketers of large or expensive industrial products such as bulk plastics or computer systems often assume the intermediary function and bypass these wholesalers.

Vallen Corporation of Houston is an industrial product wholesaler, supplying some 6000 plant safety items ranging from acid hoods to vapor sniffers. For large accounts like Dow Chemical, Vallen assumes the tasks of product safety, inventory, stocking, and staffing from its nearby warehouse in Freeport, Texas, allowing Dow to eliminate the costs of keeping and staffing a stockroom. Thus Vallen adds value to the items it distributes.[7]

LIMITED-SERVICE WHOLESALERS Although they do take titles to products, limited-service wholesalers perform only selected functions. Their functions have evolved to meet special needs rather than to provide a full range of wholesaling services; such wholesalers charge a smaller markup than full-service operators do. Some particular limited-service wholesalers follow:

Cash-and-Carry Wholesalers Offering neither credit nor delivery services, cash-and-carry wholesalers emphasize reduced costs for small retailers. Customers are expected to drive their own trucks to the warehouse, pick out the products they want for their stores, pay cash, and take their purchases with them.

Truck Wholesalers Dealing primarily in perishable goods such as fresh vegetables, candy, snacks, and tobacco products, truck wholesalers pick up quantities of products at commercial markets and deliver them to retailers in case lots. They serve small firms and usually operate on a cash basis only. In effect, the truck is the warehouse.

Drop Shippers Drop shippers take bulk orders from industrial users, other wholesalers, or even retailers; they then order the desired products from manufacturers, who ship directly to the customers. Drop shippers take title to produce, but they do not take physical possession. They may or may not provide credit services, and they obviously perform no delivery tasks.

Rack Jobbers Rack jobbers maintain inventories, primarily for large supermarket and drugstore chains. Some jobbers provide and stock their own display units (L'eggs hosiery and Maybelline cosmetics); some service the retailer's display units (Frito-Lay snacks and Nabisco cookies); and some provide special point-of-purchase promotional displays. Thus retailers are relieved of stocking, removing stale food products, and pricing.

☐ Agent Wholesalers

Working on a commission basis, **agent wholesalers** seldom take title to, or physical possession of, the products they distribute. Instead, agents are sales facilitators—they arrange purchases between manufacturers and retailers or other wholesalers. The major types of agent wholesalers are brokers, selling agents, manufacturers' agents, and commission merchants.

BROKERS **Brokers** are facilitating agents who bring buyers and sellers together, usually on a temporary basis. Used machinery, seasonal food products, and real estate are items commonly distributed in this way. Brokers receive a commission if the transaction between buyers and sellers is completed. Since they seldom actually possess or hold title to the product, what they really have to sell is information. It is their business to know, for example, who has an oil rig or a petroleum tanker for sale or rent and who needs such a product. Similarly, food brokers may bring together sellers from a farmers' cooperative and buyers for a small supermarket chain.

SELLING AGENTS   **Selling agents** distribute the entire output of a manufacturer. They perform a wide range of services (including credit, delivery, promotion, and storage), but they do not take title to products. Selling agents are common in industries such as textiles, canned foods, apparel, home furnishings, and metals.

MANUFACTURERS' AGENTS   **Manufacturers' agents, or manufacturers' representatives,** are promotional wholesalers in a specific geographical area who sell noncompeting products from several manufacturers of related product lines. For example, a single agent might sell swimming pool chemicals, paint, and safety supplies—all from different producers—in the state of Colorado. Most often, manufacturers' agents promote a company's products in areas where the firm cannot afford to maintain its own sales representatives. In cities and other areas of business concentration, however, a producer is likely to employ its own sales force. Manufacturers' agents are paid on commission, and they enjoy a great deal of freedom in their work.

COMMISSION MERCHANTS   **Commission merchants** receive goods on consignment from producers, take the merchandise to a central market, sell at the best price possible, deduct their commission, and remit the balance to the producer. These wholesalers distribute primarily agricultural commodities, seafood products, art, and furniture. Arrangements between producers and commission merchants are usually short-term or seasonal.

☐ Manufacturers' Sales Branches

Manufacturers' sales branches are classified as wholesalers in the *U.S. Census of Wholesaling*. Although they represent only about one-tenth of the nation's wholesaling establishments, they account for well over one-third of the overall dollar volume of wholesale sales. These intermediaries handle product lines that range from paints, chemicals, and auto parts to large farm equipment and computers. A branch that both promotes and stores the product is a *sales branch*. In contrast, a manufacturer's *sales office* is a promotional operation only and carries no inventory.

■ THE NATURE OF RETAILING ■

From Filene's Department Store in Boston to a Safeway supermarket in Sacramento; from a Radio Shack Computer Center on Chicago's Michigan Avenue to an exotic foods shop on North Clark Street a few miles away; from the vast spaces of the Northgate shopping center in Seattle to the cozy confines of Annabelle's Roadrunner card shop in Charleston—U.S. retailers provide consumers with the widest variety of products in the world. And the 2 million or so retail stores in the United States share at least three features:

- They are consumers' primary personal contact with marketing.
- They provide more than strictly economic transactions to satisfy consumers.
- They project some kind of image or personality to consumers.

☐ Contact with Consumers

Because most consumers buy nearly all the items they purchase in retailing institutions, retailers are consumers' primary contact with marketing. Indeed, retailers are in the best position to stay attuned to consumers' needs and buying behaviors, and many of them do. As a result, marketing managers in firms producing consumer goods listen closely to feedback from retailers. Both producers and retailers must be flexible and alert in monitoring the changing tastes and buying habits of consumers. Sears and K mart are two retailers that have read consumers' desires successfully and have devised their marketing strategies accordingly. F. W. Woolworth, however, was unable to translate consumers' feedback into a successful contemporary strategy for its discount stores. The attempt to compete with K mart through Woolco discount stores failed, and Woolworth closed its discount division in 1982.

☐ *More Than Economic Exchange*

"A lot of our business is glamour, theater, and environment, which we feel Fifth Avenue imparts like no other street in America." Thus Helen Galland, president of exclusive Bonwit Teller's in New York, sums up the idea that the store's customers want much more than simply a suit, a scarf, or a tablecloth. They want style, the work of well-known designers, and luxurious surroundings. In choosing Bonwit's, patrons seek the best and pay more for it. The store's location on elegant upper Fifth Avenue contributes in no small way to the pleasurable experience of shopping at Bonwit's. After all, Tiffany & Company is right next door.

Whether they opt for an expensive environment and high prices or for plain decor and bargain lines, successful retailers understand that they are offering more than merchandise. May Company, in opening a new department store in Mission Viejo, California, arranged 65 separate events to herald the opening of the new trading area. Fashion shows, cooking demonstrations, performances by a marching band, daredevil roller-skating acts, a money-management seminar, a sports medicine clinic, and giveaways and prizes were all part of a month-long effort to entice consumers into the new store.[8]

Wouldn't quality merchandise, reasonable prices, and some imaginative advertising attract customers to May Company? Not necessarily. Consumers expect and want more than the basic product in exchange for their money. At large department stores like May Company, promotional events have become commonplace as large-scale retailers attempt to add glamour, excitement, and interest to shopping. For consumers, special events, theme displays, and atmosphere add value to the products that retailers sell.

Retailers add value and augment their products in other ways, too. Special events are not practical for small retailers like Annabelle's Roadrunner in Charleston. But Annabelle's employees know some 70 percent of their customers by name, and they point out new magazines and greeting cards to customers whose tastes and interests they know. The Roadrunner provides personal attention and friendliness to add value to, and augment, the products that it carries.

☐ *Image and Atmosphere*

Retailing firms, like people, have different personalities. K mart stores are large, impersonal, efficient, and plainly decorated to reflect K mart's low prices. In contrast, Neiman-Marcus and Sakowitz compete for customers in Houston and Dallas with luxuriously appointed stores, high-fashion clothing, and expensive furs and jewelry. Costly fragrances waft through the air-conditioned stores; shoppers browse to Mozart's music; salespeople are *very* well dressed. Intimidating? Not to the consumers those upscale retailers seek to attract.

Contemporary retailers do not let their "personalities" evolve by chance, and some marketing consulting firms specialize in creating retail atmospheres.[9] Retailing firms, like products, are positioned carefully to project a desired image. Also like

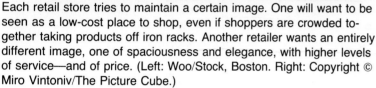
Each retail store tries to maintain a certain image. One will want to be seen as a low-cost place to shop, even if shoppers are crowded together taking products off iron racks. Another retailer wants an entirely different image, one of spaciousness and elegance, with higher levels of service—and of price. (Left: Woo/Stock, Boston. Right: Copyright © Miro Vintoniv/The Picture Cube.)

products, stores are sometimes repositioned (see Chapter 7). Sears, Roebuck, for example, has made concerted efforts in recent years to upgrade its apparel lines by adding designer clothes under the Cheryl Tiegs label. Sears vastly expanded its financial services (taking advantage of the environment of deregulation), acquiring Allstate Insurance and brokerage house Dean Witter Reynolds. It also added specialty departments to market personal computers. All these changes were an effort by Sears to reposition the store's image and attract more affluent customers.

Retailers develop their images primarily to appeal to carefully targeted market segments. Few retailers can appeal successfully to all consumers, and so most focus on selected groups. In addition, retailers want to ensure that their stores will be perceived appropriately by manufacturers whose products they want to carry. Just as consumers do not think of K mart as the place to buy a Blackglama mink coat, so Blackglama is aware that its retailers must have an image of quality and prestige.

☐ *Service versus Price*

Almost without exception, retailers seek target market segments either by providing a high level of service or by offering low prices. Since high levels of service cost money, retailers must trade off: Low prices and extensive service are rarely compatible for profit-seeking organizations. K mart and other discount chains offer low prices with minimal services; in contrast, Tiffany's extends personal charge accounts to qualified customers, provides free delivery, and trains its salespeople to give expert advice to shoppers looking for platinum bracelets or imported crystal stemware.

Thus retailers offer various levels of service. As Figure 12-2 illustrates, services can range from virtually nonexistent ("no frills") to personal sales consultations, financing, free delivery, alterations, gift wrapping, and liberal returns policies. These services are costly. The gross margins and accompanying markups of high-service

Implementing and Controlling Marketing Plans

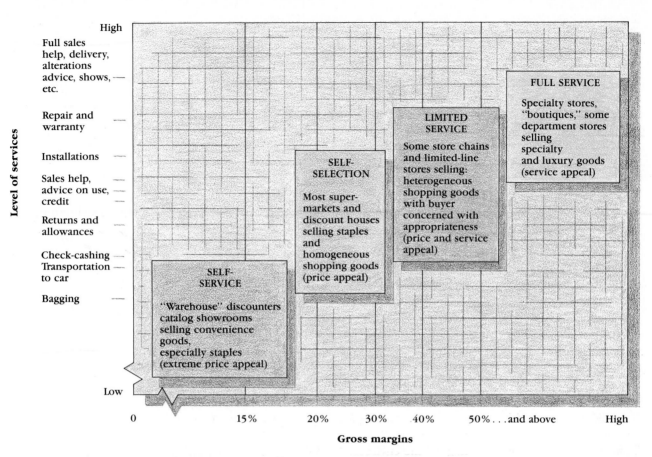

Figure 12-2 *Retailers' service and price levels.* The services listed along the left side of the figure range from simply putting the merchandise in bags to assisting the customer in buying, delivery, alterations, and so forth. As more and more of these services are added, the retailer will have higher costs, and thus will need to earn a larger and larger gross margin. Because consumers differ in their preference for more services or for lower prices, there is a need for a variety of retail types. (Adapted from Dale M. Lewison and M. Wayne DeLozier, *Retailing: Principles and Practices,* Columbus, Ohio: Charles E. Merrill, 1982, p. 66. Reprinted with permission.)

retailers thus rise in proportion to services offered (see the horizontal axis in Figure 12-2). It is this large gross margin (the difference between the selling price they charge and what the product cost them) that provides the funds needed to supply extra services.

Warehouse discounters and catalog showrooms are examples of **self-service retailers** whose customers take care of themselves. Shoppers in discount warehouses make their selections with no sales help. Merchandise, primarily staples and convenience goods, often remains in shipping cartons, and customers may have to furnish their own bags and boxes. Low prices and bulk sales are the main attraction. In catalog showrooms, buyers make their selections from a catalog, give their orders to a sales clerk, pick up their merchandise from a loading dock, and transport their purchases in their own vehicles.

Supermarkets and discount houses fall into the category of **self-selection retailers,** stores that provide few services or sales personnel and sell mostly staples and homogeneous shopping goods. Low prices and a wide assortment of products are the primary appeals to shoppers. **Limited-service retailers** include some department store chains (Sears, Roebuck and Montgomery Ward) and limited-line stores that concentrate on heterogeneous shopping products (major kitchen appliances, television sets, air conditioners, audio equipment). Customers are attracted by appropriate prices but need a certain level of advice and help from sales personnel.

Finally, customer service is the primary attraction of **full-service retailers** such as specialty shops, boutiques, and top-of-the-line department stores. Saks, Macy's, Neiman-Marcus, and Bloomingdale's provide consumers with the services of gift advisers, fashion coordinators, interior decorators, cooking instructors, and makeup consultants. Price is a secondary consideration for shoppers who seek the specialty and luxury goods that such retailers feature.[10]

■ THE SCOPE OF RETAILING ■

By 1982, total sales volume for the almost 2 million retailers was over $1 trillion annually.[11] In other words, retailing is a major part of the U.S. economy. Large retailers—those grossing more than $5 million annually—get the lion's share of those $1 trillion: Only 20 percent of U.S. retailers account for over 70 percent of retail sales. The bottom 30 percent of all retailing establishments are small, with annual sales of less than $50,000, but they account for only 0.9 percent of total retail sales.[12] Exhibit 12-1 displays retailing establishments according to annual revenues.

In general, large retailers have tuned in to consumers' desires quite successfully. Even in an economic environment characterized by ups and downs, huge retailers like Sears, Roebuck and K mart have been able to increase their revenues fairly consistently through strategic management and adherence to the marketing concept. The Great Atlantic & Pacific Tea Company (A&P), however, was once the undisputed leader of food retailers, but misjudgments about demographic trends and consumers' tastes forced the chain to close over half its stores between 1974 and 1980. And Montgomery Ward, once the country's largest general merchandiser, lost its leadership to Sears in the years after World War II. Sears pursued an aggressive, expansionist strategy, while Montgomery Ward, wrongly betting on a stag-

EXHIBIT 12-1	U.S. Retail Trade, Sales by Size of Establishment (1982)					
	Number (thousands)	Percent	Cumulative Percent	Sales ($ millions)	Percent	Cumulative Percent
Total, all establishments*	1,731,055			1,010,355		
Establishments with sales of:						
$5,000,000+	36,026	2.1	2.1	386,726	38.3	38.3
$500,000–4,999,999	350,611	20.2	22.3	443,187	43.9	82.2
$50,000–499,999	837,834	48.4	70.7	171,368	16.9	99.1
Less than $50,000	506,584	29.3	100.0	9,074	0.9	100.0

*Includes only establishments that were open entire year of 1982.

Source: U.S. Bureau of the Census, *1982 Census of Retail Trade: Establishment and Firm Size,* Feb. 1985, pp. 1–3.

nant economy, lost market share. Exhibit 12-2 lists the 10 largest general merchandisers and the 10 largest grocery retailers in the United States.

Small retailers, who typically require larger markups than chain operations do, remain a vital force in retailing. Small stores and boutiques allow entrepreneurs to be their own bosses, to provide personalized service, and to serve as innovative and creative distributors.

■ RETAILERS ■

Retailing includes an enormous variety of merchandisers—the huge Marshall Field store on Chicago's State Street, the multiacre shopping malls dotting the country, the limited-line boutiques on Fisherman's Wharf in San Francisco, and the newsstands on city streets are just a few. Consumers demand high variety in retail stores. They want diverse merchandise, and they want to purchase it in different ways and in different places. One useful approach in exploring this many-faceted world is to break down retailing into its broadest categories: traditional retailers, mass merchandisers, and nonstore retailers.

☐ Traditional Retailers

The major types of **traditional retailers** include specialty, department, and variety stores; supermarkets; and convenience stores. Thus, "tradition" in retailing ranges from department stores like Macy's (founded in 1858) to the Southland Corporation (which in 1946 adopted the name 7-Eleven for its chain of convenience stores). Although most retailers in this category have been around for nearly half a century, "traditional" does not imply an outdated or inflexible approach to retailing. Successful traditional retailers monitor consumers' desires constantly, adjusting their marketing techniques and finding new ways to attract shoppers.

SPECIALTY STORES   Narrow product mixes with deep product lines, a high level of personal service, and relatively high prices characterize **specialty stores.** Examples include retailers that carry only women's footwear, custom-made jewelry, or baked goods. Lawyers and dentists offer specialty services.

EXHIBIT 12-2	Largest U.S. General Merchandisers and Grocery Retailers (1983)		
General Merchandisers	Sales ($ billions)	Grocery Retailers	Sales ($ billions)
Sears, Roebuck	40.7	Safeway Stores	18.7
K mart	22.4	Kroger	17.1
J. C. Penney	13.7	American Stores	13.9
Federated Department Stores	10.0	Southland	12.7
Dayton-Hudson	8.8	Lucky Stores	9.4
Household International	8.7	Winn-Dixie Stores	7.8
Wal-Mart Stores	8.6	Great Atlantic and Pacific Tea Co.	5.9
F. W. Woolworth	6.0	Supermarkets General	5.1
BATUS	5.9	Albertson's	5.1
Montgomery Ward	5.4		

Source: "The Fortune Service 500," Fortune, June 9, 1986, pp. 113–152, at p. 136.

A dramatic example of specialty retailing is the personal computer center. When interest in citizen's band radios peaked around 1976 or 1977, Tandy Corporation was ready with an exciting new item in its Radio Shack stores: the TRS 80 microcomputer. Tandy was following hard on the heels of Apple Computer, which introduced the first widely accepted personal computer in 1976. Chains like Computerworld quickly entered this specialty-store battle, followed by the Sears Business Centers. IBM and Xerox even changed their long-standing strategies of selling directly only to organizational buyers; they, too, opened retail outlets. In one decade, the retailing of personal computers flourished into projected sales of $21 billion for 1986—most of it through specialty stores.[13]

DEPARTMENT STORES   From the turn of the century until after World War II, department stores dominated urban retailing. After World War II, many consumers joined the exodus to the suburbs, and well-managed department stores quickly followed with suburban branch stores, either freestanding or (increasingly) in shopping centers.

Major **department stores**—including Macy's, Bullock's, and Jordan Marsh—feature wide, deep product mixes; individual departments within stores; mid- to upper-level prices; and extensive services. Credit is a major feature of department stores. Over half their sales are made on credit; many stores offer customers their own credit lines and cards (in addition to the MasterCard and Visa accounts that smaller retailers also accept).

Image plays an important role in advancing the strategy of department store operations. Most chains advertise heavily to convey a certain image and appeal to their target audiences. Special events and promotions are central to the retailing strategy of leading chains such as Bloomingdale's, Stix Baer & Fuller, and Lord & Taylor. A number of department stores cultivate a high-fashion image, featuring designer apparel, high-quality furniture, and the most up-to-date houseware items.

VARIETY STORES   Variety stores were practically created by Frank W. Woolworth, who in 1879 opened The Great Five Cent Stores in Utica, New York, and Lancaster, Pennsylvania. All items were priced at a nickel. Although Woolworth soon added products costing a dime, prices stayed at 10 cents until 1932. The retailer's name was changed to F. W. Woolworth Company, and the chain spread rapidly throughout the United States. In 1909, the first Woolworth stores were opened in Britain, under the name Three and Sixpence, and F. W. Woolworth Company went on to become one of the world's largest retail chains.

Traditionally, **variety stores** have sold a wide assortment of low-priced merchandise while offering only minimal personal service. They feature toys, kitchen aids, stationery, toiletries, inexpensive clothing, and hardware. Since the failure of the W. T. Grant chain in 1976, Woolworth has been the undisputed leader among variety chains.

Variety stores do not seem to have a bright future. Their downfall began when S. S. Kresge opened the first discount store, K mart, in 1962. Discount chains have preempted variety stores by offering competitively low prices along with a wider range of merchandise and quality.

SUPERMARKETS   Supermarkets are self-selection stores that sell a complete range of food items and other items from various departments. Such stores have become the dominant form of food retailing in the United States and Canada, selling about 75 percent of all groceries. The first supermarkets appeared in the 1930s as

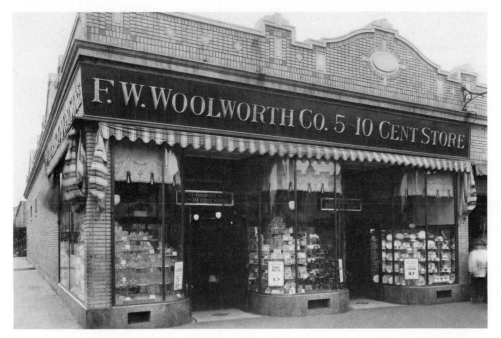

The famous chain of F. W. Woolworth Co. 5 and 10 Cent Stores epitomizes the variety store. This 1925 photo is typical of the stores in that chain, and while not many of its numerous products sell for 5 or 10 cents today, variety stores are still the home of many inexpensive products, often called "notions." (Culver Pictures.)

automobiles and refrigerators diffused throughout society. Refrigeration allowed consumers to store perishable items and eliminated the need for such services as daily milk deliveries to the home. In addition to the once-a-week, one-stop shopping made possible by home refrigerators, the advent of the automobile allowed consumers easy travel from their neighborhoods to the large new stores.

Supermarkets encourage volume sales and impulse buying. Their attractions include low prices, weekly sales, self-selection, and one-stop shopping. Most supermarkets are found in shopping centers or as large, freestanding stores. In inner cities, smaller versions of supermarkets, called *superettes,* offer fewer brands and products but provide essentially the same services. The largest national supermarket chains are Safeway and Kroger (see Exhibit 12-2).

CONVENIENCE STORES   **Convenience stores** feature just what their name implies: ease of access and quick shopping for items such as bread, milk, eggs, cigarettes, and newspapers. The names of convenience store chains reflect this emphasis: 7-Eleven (which originally indicated the hours of operation), Stop 'N Shop, and Unimart. Southland Corporation's 7-Eleven is by far the largest such chain, with almost 7000 stores in the United States and over 600 outlets in Japan (see Box 12-1). Such stores have succeeded because consumers will pay higher prices at convenience stores to avoid time-consuming trips to the supermarket.

☐ *Mass Merchandisers*

Mass merchandisers are retail institutions that have developed primarily since World War II. They operate high-volume, low-overhead, and low-price stores that typically offer less service than traditional retailers. Mass merchandisers include discount houses, off-price retailers, superstores, and warehouse and catalog showrooms.

DISCOUNT HOUSES   Carrying a wide, fairly deep product mix, **discount houses** resemble department stores except that their primary appeal is low price

Southland Corporation's 7-Elevens were among the first convenience stores to install banks of video games and to sell fast foods such as tacos and microwave-heated hamburgers. However, in the last decade, Southland has pioneered an even more dramatic change in the competitive world of convenience store chains by selling gasoline—often at the lowest prices in town—at its 7-Elevens.

By late 1982, about 2700 of Southland's 7400 stores were selling gasoline. Overhead aside, gasoline contributed more than $50 million to Southland's pre-tax earnings in 1981 (or more than 30 percent of total pretax earnings). Not surprisingly, therefore, almost all the 2000 new 7-Elevens added in the years 1974 to 1982 sell gasoline.

Gasoline has provided a double benefit for Southland and other convenience store marketers. First, their costs of selling gasoline are lower than those of traditional gas stations. No additional employees are required (the 7-Eleven cashier turns the pump on and off and collects money without ever leaving the counter), and the stores pay for their overhead by selling 3000 other items. Second, gasoline business generates *added* sales of food and other items, partly because customers must come into the 7-Elevens to pay.

(Copyright © Bob Daemmrich.)

According to a survey by Southland, one in three gasoline customers makes another purchase, averaging about $1. With this double incentive in mind, Southland has become one of the most powerful gasoline retailers in the United States.

Source: Shawn Tully, "Look Who's a Champ of Gasoline Marketing," *Fortune,* Nov. 1, 1982, pp. 149–154.

(made possible partly by self-selection, self-service, and centrally located checkout islands). For heterogeneous products that vary a good deal—clothing, shoes, jewelry—discount houses offer merchandise significantly lower in quality and price than that found in department stores. But for such items as electrical appliances, audio equipment, and cameras, discount houses compete with department stores by carrying major brands priced 10 to 30 percent lower.

OFF-PRICE RETAILERS   **Off-price retailers** differ from other discounters by featuring almost exclusively famous brand and designer-label apparel at prices significantly below those in department and specialty stores. Off-price retailers get their merchandise by buying unsold garments from manufacturers and from other retailers. Filene's, in Boston, has specialized in discounting on its basement floor since 1909 and now has a chain of stores called Filene's Basement. Although Loehmann's, a chain of 61 stores (now owned by Associated Dry Goods), has been in the off-price clothing and accessory business since the 1920s, off-price retailing has emerged as a potent force only in recent years (see Box 12-2). Major chains include Marshalls (owned by Melville Corporation) and Zayre's, T. J. Maxx, and Hit or Miss stores.[14]

SUPERSTORES   At the end of the retailing spectrum opposite to convenience stores are three types of retailers that are larger than supermarkets and carry a greater number of product lines. The most prevalent is the **combination store,**

Alton F. Doody, president of a retailing organization in the Midwest, notes that "off-price is a word that helps us understand a new or at least modified mode of doing business." According to one study, this new form of retailing—based on sales of famous name and designer-label apparel at substantially discounted prices—increased sales at a compounded annual rate of 23 percent from 1978 to 1984. Off-price revenues were estimated at $7 billion in 1983, accounting for almost 8 percent of the total apparel and footwear market. According to projections, off-price retailing could account for as much as 15 to 20 percent of the retail apparel business by 1990.

Ross Stores Inc. is a rapidly expanding off-price retailer based in South San Francisco, California. Ross claims to offer more than 1000 nationally advertised labels in its 48 California units. It carries such prestigious labels as Givenchy, Christian Dior, Yves St. Laurent, Bill Blass, London Fog, and Evan Picone at discounts of 20 to 60 percent off normal prices. The firm's entrepreneurial orientation is viewed as a key ingredient in its recent success. Don Rowlett, president and chief executive officer of Ross Stores, notes that "most buyers have to go back to their company headquarters and get purchase approval from five levels of merchandise people. Because our buyers are able to make decisions on the spot, they can buy good merchandise as soon as it becomes available."

The rise of off-price retailers such as Ross Stores represents a particular competitive threat to department stores and other traditional retailers. In a 1983 speech to the Menswear Retailers of America, Lawrence Phillips, president and chief executive officer of the Phillips-Van Heusen Corporation, stated: "I know of no subject that is commanding as much attention as is the question of the off-price retailer, and how one should compete or defend against them." Certainly no full-price store can casually accept that the same articles it sells at the garment industry's "keystone" price (double the wholesale cost) are being sold nearby by an off-price retailer at 20 to 60 percent off.

As one competitive response, certain stores and manufacturers are going on the offensive against off-pricing. Federated Department Stores announced in 1983 that it would no longer buy goods from manufacturers who sell to off-price shops or who fail to prevent its apparel from being resold to off-pricers. General Mills has informed its retailers that it will immediately sever all ties with any store found to be moving merchandise to discount stores. Some department stores are attempting to fight off-price retailing by returning to a past emphasis on aggressive private-label marketing of quality goods. "The great opportunity is to use the store's name," notes one retail consultant. "Some of these stores have been around for 100 years, and that still means something."

Sources: Alton F. Doody, "The Next Turn of the Wheel," *Advertising Age,* July 25, 1983, p. M-12; Liz Murphy, "Off-price: No Place for the Timid," *Sales & Marketing Management,* Aug. 13, 1984, pp. 61–62; Dick Stevenson, "Retailers Promote Private Labels to Counter Off-Price Threat," *Ad Forum,* Nov. 1983, pp. 13, 15, 19–20.

which carries over-the-counter and prescription drugs in addition to food items. The Kroger chain locates its SupeRx drugstores next to its supermarkets. Supermarkets General has gone a step further by combining the two operations under one roof in its Pathmark chain.

Superstores go well beyond combination stores by carrying such nonfood items as garden supplies, alcoholic beverages (where local laws allow), books, housewares, and hardware. Superstores average 30,000 square feet, almost twice the space of a typical supermarket. Prices are slightly higher than those of conventional supermarkets—a trade-off consumers accept for the convenience of one-stop shopping. Superstores also may offer such services as check cashing, shoe repair, dry cleaning, and film processing.

In 1963 the French firm Carrefour opened the first "super-superstore"—the **hypermarché,** or hypermarket. This is a very large store (80,000+ square feet) that adds furniture, appliances, and clothing to the items found in superstores. Hypermarchés have had some success in France and Germany but are less popular in the United States and Canada, where superstores and discount houses seem to satisfy consumers.

WAREHOUSE SHOWROOMS   Located on low-rent, suburban sites, **warehouse showrooms** focus on medium-priced furniture and appliances. They carry far fewer product lines than do discount houses or superstores, operating instead on the principle of high volume and low overhead. In general, their operating margins are much narrower than department or specialty stores'.

Warehouse showrooms are so named because they are attached to a large warehouse where the products are stored. Shoppers inspect furniture and appliances in the showroom, place their orders, and either pick up their purchases at a loading dock or arrange for delivery (at an extra charge). Levitz Furniture Corporation, with stores along the east coast, pioneered this form of retailing and is among the largest warehouse showroom chains.

CATALOG SHOWROOMS   Carrying a broader range of merchandise than warehouse showrooms, **catalog showrooms** display discounted merchandise in both catalogs and in-store displays. Although they carry general product lines, such stores feature high-markup items that can be discounted significantly: jewelry, luggage, audio and photographic equipment, toys, and sporting goods.

Both catalog and warehouse showrooms have experienced solid growth in recent years, mostly at the expense of discount chains. Few truly national chains have developed, however; different chains dominate various regions of the country.

☐ *Nonstore Retailing*

Consumers do not always have to visit retail stores to make purchases. **Nonstore retailing** may be conducted impersonally (through catalogs, direct mail, and vending machines) or personally (door-to-door selling, in-home retailing, and telephone sales). Direct marketing, a major trend in nonstore retailing, uses both approaches.

DIRECT MARKETING   When you order camping gear or cooking equipment from a catalog delivered to your home or when you call a toll-free number to buy a recording of your favorite musical group's greatest hits, you are taking advantage of the conveniences offered by **direct marketing.** This form of nonstore retailing delivers a promotional message directly to potential customers, who respond directly to the company rather than through a traditional point of sale such as a store.

Direct marketing appeals to consumers who put a premium on their time and is a boon to marketers who want to segment their audiences specifically and efficiently. For example, The Sharper Image in San Francisco mails its slick catalogs of expensive electronic items and athletic equipment to upper-income men aged 25 to 45 years.

A fast-growing form of direct marketing is **mail-order sales,** sold primarily through catalogs. Mail-order sales to consumers exceeded $44 billion in 1984, and large merchandisers like J. C. Penney, Sears, Roebuck, and Montgomery Ward garnered 5 to 6 percent of the total (earning about 25 percent of their revenues).[15] In the 1980s department store chains such as Bloomingdale's, Macy's, Neiman-Marcus, and Saks Fifth Avenue have increased their catalog promotions. Many specialty catalog houses operate in the mail-order market—some with notable success: Spiegel (general merchandise), L. L. Bean (outdoor clothes and gear), Williams-Sonoma (kitchen equipment and gourmet foods), The Sharper Image (luxury gifts), and Charles & Co. (fine foods).

Shopping at home is a rapidly growing form of direct marketing. From catalogs, or more recently by home-shopping television, consumers spend billions of dollars from the convenience of their homes. Nonstore retailing is now growing much more rapidly than store sales. (Copyright © Michal Heron/Woodfin Camp & Assoc.)

Telephone sales—promoting and selling products by telephone—is a second major area of direct marketing. Catalog houses and department and specialty stores encourage consumers to "let their fingers do the walking," and the use of toll-free telephone numbers has become a standard means of personal selling and order taking. Telephone sales allow consumers to shop for countless goods and services from the comfort of home. One new and dramatic approach to direct marketing is in-home television shopping, where consumers watch product demonstrations and sales pitches and phone in orders. From less than $1 billion in 1986, total sales are expected to exceed $6 billion by 1990.[16]

Direct marketing revenues have surpassed $175 billion and are growing faster than in-store sales. Currently, 14 percent of retail transactions result from direct marketing; the figure is expected to rise to 20 percent by 1990.[17]

VENDING MACHINES   Nonstore, nonpersonal selling is taken to the extreme in the transaction between consumer and machine. Today more than 6 million **vending machines** across the country accept consumers' coins and provide convenience items at relatively high prices. Although soft drinks, candies, and packaged snacks account for most of the $13 billion in vending-machine sales, other items such as toiletries and basic hardware are increasingly offered. Food services in hospitals, dormitories, and transportation terminals rely more and more on vending units to offer hot soups, sandwiches that can be heated in a microwave oven, and chilled salads and desserts.

In nonmerchandise vending, electronic video games have joined the more traditional juke boxes and pinball machines. Automated tellers are rapidly replacing their human counterparts in bank branches all over the country. Machines in airports offer insurance policies, traveler's checks, and even a shoe shine. Mass transit commuters in the San Francisco area depend on machines to calculate fares, make change, and collect tickets. Thus, vending machines are becoming an important part of service retailing as well.

PERSONAL SALES AT HOME   Door-to-door selling and in-home retailing allow consumers to enjoy the advantages of personal sales—a service that offers great convenience and requires little travel for the customer. **Door-to-door selling** occupies a small but time-honored niche in retailing. Avon has become the largest cosmetics company in the world through the personal door-to-door and telephone efforts of almost half a million representatives. Electrolux and Kirby vacuum cleaners and World Book encyclopedias have long been sold primarily door-to-door. **In-home retailing** usually takes the form of a small party given by a hostess or host to allow friends and neighbors to examine and order a product line. Tupperware, Just for Play ("sexy" underwear), Mary Kay Cosmetics, Stanley Home Products, and Queen's-Way to Fashion clothes all employ the in-home method of selling. The Direct Selling Association estimates that as many as 50,000 such parties are held nightly across the country.[18]

RETAILING SERVICES   Like physical goods, services are sold through traditional retailers, mass merchandisers, and nonstore retailing. Chapter 10 pointed out that the buying and selling of services involve greater consumer participation than do sales of tangible goods. Intangibility, lack of standardization, and perishability also affect service retailing, and service retailers must consider these differences both in strategic planning and in retailing tactics. Some retailers of services are restaurants, hotels and motels, airlines, shippers and movers, entertainment businesses, hospitals, funeral homes, dry cleaners and laundries, beauty and barber shops, and educational and financial institutions. Service retailing is growing faster than the retailing of goods, and new forms of retailing institutions are likely to develop. Other retailers will probably adjust their merchandising techniques to include more services in their product mix.

■ OWNERSHIP AND CONTROL OF RETAILING ■

In addition to the broad categories we have examined, retailers may be classified by how they are owned or controlled. Most U.S. retailers remain independent and are fairly small operations, even though when combined they account for approximately two-thirds of all retail sales. Networks of retailers—large and small—control an ever-increasing share of the retail dollar in the form of corporate chains, voluntary chains, retailer cooperatives, franchise operations, and consumer cooperatives.

☐ *Corporate Chains*
Corporate chains are multiunit retailing organizations operated under central ownership, management, and control.[19] They range from giant networks of thou-

sands of stores—Sears, K mart, and Safeway are examples—to small, regional organizations with only a few units. In general, stores in such chains carry similar product lines, since centralized buying and warehousing are the basis of efficiency. Corporate chains often employ standardized architectural designs and merchandising techniques as well. For that reason, consumers can purchase a Kenmore washing machine at almost any Sears store in the country; usually even the location of the appliances department is similar from store to store.

Ownership groups are special types of retailing organizations that own a number of corporate chains; each chain is allowed and encouraged to retain its own identity, buying practices, and merchandising techniques. For example, Federated Department Stores is the ownership group controlling such diverse chains as Bloomingdale's, Foley's, Goldsmith's, and Lazarus. Exhibit 12-3 shows some representative ownership groups and the chains each controls, which may include department stores, discount chains, and specialty chains. Dayton-Hudson, for example, controls department stores (Hudson's and Dayton's), discount chains (Target and Lechmere), and specialty chains (B. Dalton booksellers and Shreve's jewelry stores).

☐ *Voluntary Chains and Retailer Cooperatives*

Two kinds of retailing organizations arose in response to the development of corporate chains. **Voluntary chains** are wholesaler-sponsored organizations of independent retailers who practice bulk buying and similar merchandising techniques. Voluntary chains of supermarkets include IGA, Minimax, Thriftway, United Super, and Dixie Dandy stores—all supplied by Fleming Companies of Oklahoma City.

EXHIBIT 12-3	**Selected Ownership Groups of Corporate Retail Chains**

Federated Department Stores
  Abraham & Straus
  Bloomingdale's
  Bullock's
  Foley's
  Lazarus
  Rich's
  Burdine's
  Filene's
  Sanger-Harris
  I. Magnin
  Goldsmith's

May Department Stores
  May Co. (Calif.)
  Hecht
  Famous Barr
  Kaufman's
  May Co. (Cleveland)
  Meier & Frank
  G. Fox
  O'Neils
  May–D & F
  May–Cohens

Dayton-Hudson
  Hudson's
  Dayton's
  Lechmere
  Lechmere
  Target

Allied Stores
  Jordan Marsh (NE)
  The Bon
  Maas Bros.
  Joske's
  Jordan Marsh (Fla.)
  Pomeroy's
  Stern's
  Donaldson's
  Read's
  Brooks Bros.
  Bonwit Teller
  Garfinkels

R. H. Macy
  Macy's (N.Y.)
  Macy's (N.J.)
  Macy's (Calif.)
  Macy's (K.C.)

Carter Hawley Hale
  The Broadway
  Emporium-Capwell
  Neiman-Marcus
  Weinstock's
  Bergdorf Goodman

Associated Dry Goods
  Lord & Taylor
  J. W. Robinson
  Joseph Horne
  L. S. Ayre's
  Sibley's
  Denver Dry Goods
  Hahne
  Robinson's (Fla.)
  Goldwaters

Source: Chain Store Age, June 1986, pp. 19–23.

Retailer cooperatives are centralized buying organizations set up by retailers; Associated Grocer of Seattle, Washington, is one example. Cooperatives are not limited to food retailers, however; Ace Hardware and Western Auto serve independent dealers of hardware and automotive parts.

☐ *Franchisors and Franchisees*

Computerworld stores, Kentucky Fried Chicken outlets, and Holiday Inn motels and hotels are examples of franchise organizations. **Franchisors** supply products and management and marketing expertise to **franchisees** (dealers), and grant them the right to run chainlike retailing establishments usually in return for fee and royalty arrangements. Franchisors insist on strict standardization and quality control; even a few sloppily run outlets can damage their reputation. McDonald's customers expect their Big Macs, Egg McMuffins, and Chicken McNuggets to taste the same in Tallahassee and Tacoma—as well as in Tokyo.

In return for payments to the franchisors, franchisees benefit from mass advertising and promotion campaigns directed by the parent organization. The competitive wars between McDonald's, Burger King, and Wendy's are fueled by multi-million-dollar advertising budgets and constant new product ideas (from McMuffins to Whoppers).

Franchise ownership takes three basic forms: (1) Some are owned by individuals who run their dealerships like entrepreneurs; they operate with a certain degree of autonomy within the constraints of their franchising agreements. Automobile dealerships and service stations fall into this category. (2) Sometimes individuals or groups own multiple franchise outlets, often concentrated in a region. Producers, for example, may franchise wholesalers to sell to retailers. In the soft-drink industry, Coca-Cola, 7-Up, Pepsi-Cola, Dr Pepper, and Royal Crown all grant franchises to bottlers that serve retail markets. (In the large southern California franchise, Coca-Cola is owned by Beatrice Foods, whereas Westinghouse Electric owns 7-Up, A&W

Franchised retailers, of everything from fast foods to automobile oil changes, are an example of entrepreneurship at work. Local business people are able to combine some of the advantages of large chain retailing with the freedom of being in business for themselves. (Copyright © Shelly Katz/Black Star.)

Implementing and Controlling Marketing Plans

Root Beer, and Orange Crush.) ③ Franchisors may choose to retain ownership of some outlets and hire their own store managers. Pillsbury's Burger King chain, for example, retains ownership of a number of its franchises.

Consumer Cooperatives

Consumer cooperatives have been successful in Switzerland, Sweden, and other European countries but have not achieved much success in North America. Formed by consumer groups, they purchase mostly foodstuffs in bulk to get the same discount that business-based intermediaries do. These cooperatives require much volunteer work and coordination. Once again, intermediaries can be replaced, but their functions cannot. Because of the time consumed in sorting and allocating, some cooperatives have had to hire employees to perform such intermediary duties. As a result, savings are eroded, and members find shopping just as thrifty in regular retailing outlets. With the increasing number of dual-career households and women in the paid work force, the prospect for volunteer labor, and thus for successful cooperatives, does not seem bright.

RETAILING LOCATIONS: GOING WHERE THE DOLLARS ARE

A cliché of retailing holds that the three most important things to consider are location, location, and location. That stretches the case, no doubt, but accessibility to consumers can spell the difference between success and failure for retailing establishments.

Until recently, store sites were determined by chance or, at best, by educated guess. Marketing research has changed that process; store locations now reflect sophisticated studies of traffic patterns, consumer behavior, competitors' locations, and business opportunities. Today an individual retailer in the United States generally opens shop either in a central business district or in a planned shopping center.

Central Business Districts

Along with the development of cities in the United States came **central business districts,** areas where many retailers clustered to take advantage of each other's traffic. Large department stores and collections of specialty shops formed central shopping areas along major avenues and streets. Such districts remain primary sites for retailing in Chicago, San Francisco, New York, and Boston, but they have lost much of their market share in Detroit, St. Louis, Dallas, and Miami.

More recently, however, developers in several cities have established the equivalent of a shopping center within the central business area. **Urban shopping malls** are collections of shops and department stores located in or near central business districts. Milwaukee's Grand Avenue complex, Boston's Faneuil Hall Marketplace, and Harborplace in Baltimore are all thriving, in-city shopping malls; more shopping malls are planned for other cities.

Adjuncts to central business districts have been termed **string streets,** major thoroughfares along which are found random collections of almost every kind of store. String streets often turn abruptly into residential areas, since the business district may be only one block deep. Such areas are far from ideal for many retailers; they are often unsightly, and parking space is usually scarce.

Shopping Centers

The Urban Land Institute defines a *shopping center* as "a group of commercial establishments planned, developed, owned, and managed as a unit related in location, size, and type of shops to the trade area that it services, and providing on-site parking in definite relationships to the types and sizes of stores it contains."[20] More simply, a **shopping center** is a planned group of complementary stores that are assessible. Marketers classify such centers by whether they serve a region, a community, or a neighborhood.

Careful planning is the key characteristic of shopping centers. Developers call on a number of research techniques to decide on a center's location, size, and blend of stores. The retailers in a shopping center benefit from each other's traffic, and each attracts customers for the others. Encouraging cross-traffic is a primary goal of shopping center planners, for the drawing power of a shopping center should be greater than the sum of its parts.

The first **regional shopping center,** Northgate, was opened by Allied Stores in Seattle in 1950. In the 1960s, Dayton-Hudson opened the first enclosed and air-conditioned regional shopping mall in Southdale, Minnesota. Such large, planned shopping areas have become a dominant feature of U.S. retailing.

Generally, a regional shopping center is anchored by a large supermarket and branches of one or more major department stores; it has 150,000 or more consumers in its target market and contains 40 or more stores. The large stores draw consumers, who are also expected to do planned or impulse shopping in the center's specialty shops. Conversely, shoppers who come specifically for the smaller shops may be expected to patronize the larger stores. Traffic patterns are planned, and landscaping and maintenance costs are shared by all tenants. If the center is an enclosed mall, air-conditioning and heating costs are also prorated for tenants. The mall may advertise cooperatively as well, and tenant stores may jointly promote special events and "theme" weeks to draw consumers to the center.

Typically somewhat smaller than regional centers, **community shopping centers** have 10 to 40 stores. Again, most include a large supermarket, and some

Shopping centers away from downtown centers range from small neighborhood centers, where parking is provided for only a few shops, to large, multilevel enclosed malls with hundreds of stores surrounded by dozens of acres of parking lot. (Left: Copyright © Bob Daemmrich. Right: Copyright © Arlene Collins/Monkmeyer.)

may be anchored by a department store also. Community shopping centers serve smaller target markets than regional malls do, but they, too, are planned, and the stores are complementary.

A small number of convenience stores clustered around a central supermarket characterizes a **neighborhood shopping center.** Typically such centers are not as well planned as larger community and regional centers. They are more like the central business district but are smaller and are located strategically in residential districts.

◼ THE DYNAMIC NATURE OF RETAILING SYSTEMS ◼

Like products, retailing systems can be said to have life cycles that rise, peak, mature, and decline. The department store has been around for over a century, and it certainly is a mature system. Supermarkets developed half a century ago (King Kullen opened the first one in 1930, in Jamaica, New York) now appear to be reaching maturity. Discount houses first appeared before World War II, but their fastest growth occurred in the 1950s and 1960s, and already they too are reaching maturity. Variety stores seem to have reached the decline stage, and "mom and pop" stores are being replaced by specialty boutiques.

A concept called the **wheel of retailing** has been advanced to explain this dynamic nature of retailing.[21] Simply put, this theory states that entrepreneurs continually find new, usually low-overhead and low-cost ways of bringing products to consumers. Originally, department stores were similar to discount houses: low prices, low overhead, and minimal service. As these stores became more successful, they began to upgrade physical surroundings, merchandise quality, and levels of service. Discount houses then appeared to serve the markets originally sought by department stores. As discounters upgraded their merchandise and service, off-price retailers and warehouse and catalog showrooms offered lower prices to consumers.

Figure 12-3 illustrates the typical movement around the wheel of retailing. Innovative retailers enter the market, upgrade to become traditional retailers, and finally become mature—and vulnerable to new retailing techniques.[22] The evolution of some retailers, however, has been affected both directly and indirectly by two phenomena that have emerged strongly in the 1980s: scrambled merchandising and the polarity of retailing.

☐ Scrambled Merchandising

In dollar volume, the best-selling items in drugstores are not aspirin, shaving cream, and cold remedies but film made by Polaroid and Kodak. **Scrambled merchandising** (or intertype competition) refers to the contemporary practice among retailers of expanding beyond their traditional product lines. We have seen, for example, that superstores carry narrow lines of clothing as well as drugs, liquors, and garden supplies; drugstores sell toys, canned food, and stationery; and convenience stores pump gasoline. Retailers engage in scrambled merchandising both to add higher-profit items to their lines and to generate traffic.

☐ Polarity of Retailing

In about two decades, the continuum of retailing has expanded considerably; the term **polarity of retailing** describes the extremes. At one end of the scale, large mass merchandisers, line superstores, and discount houses have enjoyed healthy growth by offering an ever-increasing variety of items; at the scale's other end, small

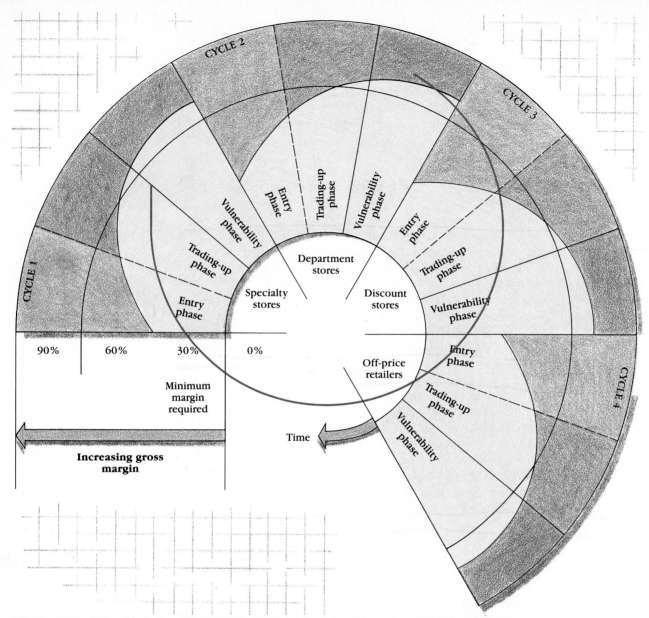

Figure 12-3 *The wheel of retailing.* Starting with specialty stores prior to the twentieth century, continuing through department stores, discount stores, and, more recently, off-price retailers, the wheel of retailing continues to turn. When each new form of retail store begins, it can operate at low margins because it has low costs. As time passes, it upgrades its offering through "trading up" until it becomes vulnerable to the next innovation. (From Jack G. Kaikati, "Don't Discount Off-Price Retailers," *Harvard Business Review*, May–June 1985, p. 87; and Dale M. Lewison and Wayne Delozier, *Retailing*: *Principles and Practices*, Columbus, Ohio: Charles E. Merrill, 1982, p. 37.)

boutiques with narrow but deep product lines (only bathroom items or science fiction books or designer belts) have prospered. This growing polarity of retailing has come at the expense of medium-size, more traditional outlets like hardware, food, and clothing stores. Whether the trend will continue is unpredictable, but its limits do not yet seem to be exhausted.

THE FUTURE OF MARKETING INTERMEDIARIES

Although the basic roles of intermediaries in distributing products have not changed much, their methods, strategies, and structures of marketing efforts have been adjusted continuously. It seems likely that the future will bring even more dramatic shifts than have been seen since the turn of this century. One thing seems certain: Wholesalers and retailers are in no danger of disappearing from the scene. They are the essential building blocks of a distribution system and will be needed as long as producers and consumers of a product are separate. Yet, as the world changes, so must marketing intermediaries. In wholesaling, the major thrust will be toward increased automation and the addition of value to products through processing. In retailing, telecommunications seems sure to revolutionize the ways in which we shop.

Wholesaling Tomorrow

Wholesaling may not be the most dramatic and exciting element in a distribution system, but its functions are essential. The elimination of wholesalers would not bring lower prices to consumers, because producers and retailers would then have to assume the wholesalers' functions and costs. Yet the amount of trade handled by different types of wholesalers has been changing noticeably. Merchant wholesalers, for example, have garnered a steadily increasing share of sales—from 49 percent in 1954 to 58 percent in 1982.[23] Although manufacturers' sales branches and offices have held a steady percentage of sales, agents and brokers have lost ground to merchant wholesalers. Figure 12-4 portrays the changes that have occurred in wholesaling over the last three decades.

Tomorrow's wholesalers will try to hold down costs and increase productivity by expanding automation in warehousing, inventory control, and order services. Between 1976 and 1982, for example, the pharmaceutical wholesaler McKesson established computer links with 32 drug producers and reduced its purchasing staff from 140 to 13. During the same period the firm's sales volume doubled. Increased automation and added value are the earmarks of contemporary wholesaling.

Retailing Tomorrow

Computerized telecommunications technology has already had significant effects on retailing. Almost daily, retail outlets are adding electronic checkout equipment to provide speedier, more efficient service to customers and to implement better inventory control and ordering practices. Most systems employ either the universal product code (UPC) or optical character recognition (OCR) to instantaneously achieve both machine-readable and human-readable pricing and product identification. Such payoffs in efficient operation and customer service are changing the face of retailing.

The following factors seem certain to keep the wheel of retailing in motion, although the timing and extent of changes remain open:

Two-income families: The influx of women into the U.S. work force has given many families more disposable income but less time to shop. Retailing methods that recognize the need for more convenient, less time-consuming shopping will continue to evolve.

Shopping by mail and telephone: Nonstore retailing seems sure to become an even greater factor in the future. Consumers will increasingly choose products from catalogs or other print media and will place orders by mail or telephone.

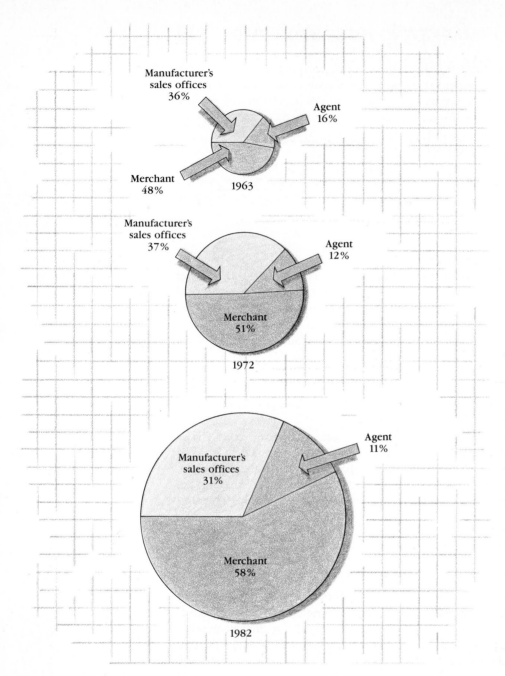

Figure 12-4 *Wholesale trade: 1963 to 1982.* The size of the circles in the figure illustrates the growth in total U.S. wholesale trade from about $0.3 trillion in 1963 to about $2 trillion in 1982. (Consequently, the circle for 1982 is about 6.1 times as large as the circle for 1963.) As shown, the proportion of trade handled by merchant wholesalers has grown at the expense of agents, brokers, commission merchants, and manufacturers' sales branches and offices. (From U.S. Bureau of the Census, *Statistical Abstract of the United States: 1986,* 1985 p. 238.)

Electronic catalogs: Consumers will be able to view merchandise on videodisks (and similar media) and on cable television channels devoted exclusively to product demonstrations and promotional information.

Teleshopping: The Qube division of Warner Communications already allows consumers to shop through interactive, two-way cable television. Shopping from the "electronic cottage" (the wired home envisioned by Alvin Toffler in *Future Shock*) seems inevitable. Major questions remain about who will bear the cost of these retailing structures—consumers, the media, or retailers—and about the methods of such vastly expanded product delivery systems.

Electronic funds transfer: Retailers and financial institutions will increasingly use computerized systems to transfer money directly from consumers' accounts to retailers' accounts, and an electronic exchange system that uses credit cards and bank debit cards will affect retailing and shopping practices. The cashless society seems ever closer.

Other phenomena not yet identified will affect retailing in the years to come. If anything, the list above is short-sighted. But retailing and retailers will not disappear from the world economic system—even though their methods of operation (and the behavior of buyers) will change.[24] Consumers will adopt new buying behaviors that parallel their adoption of innovations (see Chapter 11). Leaders will sample new shopping methods as they are introduced, the majority of retailers and consumers will move more slowly, and others (the so-called laggards) will bring up the rear. The answer for the retailer will be away from the merchant mentality and toward a more progressive style of business management.[25] No one knows when or how dramatically these changes will come, but the direction seems clear.

■ SUMMARY ■

1. Most goods and many services reach us through the efforts of marketing intermediaries—primarily wholesalers and retailers.
2. For most consumers, retailers are the most visible units in a distribution channel.
3. Wholesalers and retailers share at least three basic functions: They sort products; they provide time, place, and possession utilities; and they keep down costs to buyers.
4. Essentially, wholesalers provide services that facilitate the flow of products from producers to resellers to consumers.
5. Wholesalers are grouped into three major categories: merchant wholesalers, agents and brokers, and manufacturer-owned wholesaling operations.
6. Merchant wholesalers take title to products, whereas agents do not.
7. Retailers are consumers' primary personal contact with marketing. They provide more than strictly economic transactions to satisfy consumers, projecting an image or personality.
8. Almost without exception, retailers seek target market segments either by providing a high level of sevice or by offering low prices.
9. Only 7.4 percent of U.S. retailers account for over 60 percent of all retail sales.
10. The broadest categories of retailers are traditional retailers, mass merchandisers, and nonstore retailers.
11. Nonstore retailing may be conducted impersonally (catalogs, direct mail, and vending machines) or personally (door-to-door selling, in-home retailing, and telephone sales).
12. Retailing of services is growing faster than retailing of goods.
13. Networks of retailers—which control an ever-increasing share of the retail dollar—form corporate chains, voluntary chains, retailer cooperatives, franchise operations, and consumer cooperatives.
14. The primary retailing locations in the United States today are central business districts (with their accompanying string streets) and planned shopping centers.
15. The wheel of retailing holds that entrepreneurs will constantly find new, usually low-overhead or low-cost ways of bringing products to consumers.

☐ Key Terms

accumulation
agent wholesalers
allocation
assorting

brokers
cash-and-carry wholesalers
catalog showrooms
central business districts

combination store
commission merchants
community shopping centers
consumer cooperatives

convenience stores
corporate chains
department stores
direct marketing
discount houses
distribution
door-to-door selling
drop shippers
franchisees
franchisors
full-service retailers
full-service wholesalers
general merchandise wholesalers
hypermarché
in-home retailing
limited-service retailers
limited-service wholesalers
mail-order sales
manufacturer's agents or
   representatives

manufacturer's sales branches
marketing intermediaries
mass merchandisers
merchant wholesalers
neighborhood shopping center
nonstore retailing
off-price retailers
ownership groups
polarity of retailing
rack jobbers
regional shopping center
retailer cooperatives
retailers
risk bearing
scrambled merchandising
self-selection retailers
self-service retailers
selling agents
shopping center

single-line wholesalers
sorting out
specialty stores
specialty wholesalers
string streets
supermarkets
superstores
telephone sales
traditional retailers
truck wholesalers
urban shopping malls
variety discrepancy
variety stores
vending machines
volume discrepancy
voluntary chains
warehouse showrooms
wheel of retailing
wholesalers

☐ *Chapter Review*

1. Identify the three basic functions shared by wholesalers and retailers, and give an example of each.

2. Which of the various services offered by wholesalers could be performed by someone else in the distribution system or by consumers themselves? What advantages would you see in bypassing the wholesalers?

3. Give examples of full-service, limited-service, and agent wholesalers. What are the distinguishing features of each group?

4. How can the image and atmosphere of a retail store be compared with product positioning? Give examples to support your claims.

5. What are the main differences between traditional retailers and mass merchandisers? Which group is likely to evolve into the other, and why?

6. What are some advantages and disadvantages of direct marketing from the standpoint of retailers? From the standpoint of consumers?

7. Explain the rationale for grouping retail stores into shopping centers or malls. Do consumers or retailers benefit more from this arrangement?

8. Give examples to support the wheel of retailing theory. Can you think of examples that refute the concept?

9. How do you think consumers' buying behavior will change in the years ahead? What changes will you personally welcome or resist?

☐ *References*

1. These intermediary functions are based on a concept proposed by Wroe Alderson, *Marketing Behavior and Executive Action* (Homewood, Ill.: Irwin, 1957), chap. 7.
2. Anne Bagamery, "Don't Sell Food, Sell Peace of Mind," *Forbes,* Oct. 11, 1982, p. 51.
3. William Baldwin, "Dollars from Doodads," *Forbes,* Oct. 11, 1982, p. 51.
4. Fred Powledge, "How Your Food Gets to You," *New York,* June 13, 1983, pp. 30–38.
5. U.S. Bureau of the Census, *1982 Census of Wholesale Trade: Establishment and Firm Size,* May 1985, pp. 1–3.
6. "Foremost-McKesson: The Computer Moves Distribution to Center Stage," *Business Week,* Dec. 7, 1981, pp. 115–119.
7. Baldwin, op. cit., p. 52.

8. Ann Estes, "How Retailers Promote, Entertain," *Advertising Age,* Apr. 6, 1981, pp. 47–48.

9. David Mazursky and Jacob Jacoby, "Exploring the Development of Store Images," *Journal of Retailing,* vol. 62, no. 2, Summer 1986, pp. 145–165.

10. For a complete discussion of retail services, see Dale M. Lewison and M. Wayne DeLozier, *Retailing: Principles and Practices* (Columbus, Ohio: Merrill, 1982), chap. 4.

11. U.S. Bureau of the Census, *Statistical Abstract of the United States, 1986,* (Washington, D.C., 1985), p. 775.

12. U.S. Bureau of the Census, *1982 Census of Retail Trade: Establishment and Firm Size,* Feb. 1985, pp. 1–3.

13. "The Coming Shakeout in Personal Computers," *Business Week,* Nov. 22, 1982, pp. 72–83.

14. Jack G. Kaikati, "Don't Discount Off-Price Retailers," *Harvard Business Review,* May–June 1985, pp. 85–92.

15. Cara S. Trager, "Corporate Interest Made to Order," *Advertising Age,* Apr. 16, 1984, p. M-24.

16. "TV Home Shopping: Retail's Hottest Pitch," *Sales and Marketing Management,* Jan. 1987, p. 28.

17. Richard Greene, "A Boutique in Your Living Room," *Forbes,* May 7, 1984, pp. 86–94.

18. Sandra Salmans, "Home Parties, Where the Selling Is Easy," *The New York Times,* Sept. 3, 1981, pp. C1, C6.

19. Lewison and DeLozier, op. cit., p. 21.

20. Roger A. Dickinson, *Retail Management: A Channels Approach* (Belmont, Calif.: Wadsworth, 1974), p. 9.

21. The wheel of retailing concept was first proposed by Malcolm P. McNair, "Significant Trends and Developments in the Postwar Period," in A. B. Smith, ed., *Competitive Distribution in a High-Level Economy and Its Implications for the University* (Pittsburgh: University of Pittsburgh Press, 1958), pp. 1–25; see also Malcolm P. McNair and Eleanor G. May, "The Next Revolution of the Retailing Wheel," *Harvard Business Review,* Sept.–Oct. 1978, pp. 81–91.

22. Lewison and DeLozier, op. cit., p. 37.

23. U.S. Bureau of the Census, *1982 Census of Wholesale Trade: Establishment and Firm Size,* May 1985, pp. 1–3.

24. For a discussion of the future of nonstore retailing, see Larry J. Rosenberg and Elizabeth C. Hirschman, "Retailing without Stores," *Harvard Business Review,* July–Aug. 1980, pp. 103–112.

25. Deborah J. Cornwall, "Say Goodbye to the Merchant Mystique," *Business Horizons,* Sept.–Oct. 1984, pp. 78–82.

13

Copyright © Gabe Palmer/The Stock Market.

MANAGING DISTRIBUTION CHANNELS

SPOTLIGHT ON

☐ Effective distribution channels

☐ Movement of goods, ownership, money, and communications through distribution channels

☐ Conflict and resolution within distribution channels

☐ Key considerations in establishing a distribution system

☐ How distribution channels are structured

☐ How industrial distribution channels differ from channels used for consumer products

☐ The role of a channel leader

During the 1970s, sales of Levi Strauss & Company's jeans soared, reflecting their rising popularity among young people all over the world. Model 501 jeans even became a black market prize in the Soviet Union. Perhaps somewhat overconfident, the company expended little effort on keeping its network of retailers happy. In fact, it developed a dangerous reputation for aloofness toward its retailing customers.

Levi's troubles with retailers increased during the early 1980s. The recession from 1981 to 1982, along with increasingly keen competition from Blue Bell's Wrangler jeans and Lee jeans from VF Corporation, forced Levi Strauss to expand drastically its list of retailers. Most notably, Levi jeans became available at Sears and J. C. Penney—adding 2600 outlets for the denim king. However, this move to the large chains angered Levi's traditional customers (department stores and smaller, specialty outlets), and many cut their orders. As a result, Levi Strauss reconsidered its attitude toward the intermediaries in its distribution system.

"We were all on the operations side," notes James A. McDermott, Levi's senior vice president of marketing, "and we forgot about our customers." Obviously taking a new approach, McDermott asserts: "It is the company that provides the most service to retailers that will get the business." Acting on that idea, Levi Strauss has taken the following steps to improve its relations with retailers:

- The company simplified the form that retailers use to get money from Levi Strauss for joint advertising programs.
- The company helps retailers improve their profit margins by installing a computer-based inventory system that eliminates supply bottlenecks, increases sales, and helps retailers to reduce their inventories—a substantial boon in light of high interest rates.
- Ten top executives from Levi Strauss worked on the selling floors of 35 major customers to learn more about retailers' operations and problems.

Levi jeans are an international symbol of both youth and the United States. They are sold openly in shops in France, as shown left. In much of the Socialist world, Levi jeans are forbidden and must be purchased on the black market. The picture of the young people was taken in East Germany. (Left: Copyright © Scott Thode/ International Stock Photo. Right: Arthur Grace/Sygma.)

At the company's headquarters, these executives serve as "account sponsors," fielding questions and complaints from customers.

■ Levi Strauss boosted its advertising budget by 40 percent. Part of this effort was the $50 million contributed to the 1984 Olympics in Los Angeles.

■ The company began offering its traditional 40,000 outlets new clothing lines not available in chain stores, such as menswear by David Hunter and Claude Roegiers.

By offering better service to retailers, Levi Strauss made a determined effort to expand and protect its valuable franchise. Without question, good relations with channel members are an essential element in successful marketing.

Source: "Levi Strauss: A Touch of Fashion—and a Dash of Humility," *Business Week,* Oct. 24, 1983, pp. 85, 88.

This marketing textbook was shipped directly from the publisher's warehouse to the bookstore (a retailer) where you bought it. The notebook and pen or pencil that you use for lecture notes probably got to your college bookstore by way of an office supplies wholesaler. Other goods and services reach you in various ways through the efforts of the wholesalers and retailers described in Chapter 12. These "building blocks" of distribution systems, along with the manufacturers of products, make up the interlocking networks known as channels of distribution.

Distribution channels are made up of manufacturers or service producers and the wholesalers and retailers through which products are marketed to consumers and industrial buyers. The effectiveness of distribution channels strongly influences a marketer's other marketing mix decisions and actions—those concerning the product itself and its pricing and promotion. Distribution is that part of the marketing mix which gives products their time, place, and possession utilities.

All marketers seek to establish the very best ways to move their products to customers. The ideal distribution system—if attainable—would be productive, cost-efficient, and problem-free. In today's world, only strategically managed marketing organizations that truly plan, implement, and control their distribution systems can aspire to developing "ideal" channels.

Chapter 13 looks at the evolution of distribution systems and at the characteristics of effective systems. We examine flows within channels and the contrasting views of channel members (which may produce conflict). Some major considerations concerning distribution follow, and then we describe the design of distribution channels for both consumer and industrial products. The remainder of this chapter explores the ways in which channels are managed.

■ *EFFECTIVE DISTRIBUTION CHANNELS* ■

Forty or fifty years ago, only the most astute marketers truly planned their channels of distribution; channel members were selected only when the product was ready. However, in today's competitive and increasingly global marketplace, managers plan for product distribution *as* they plan their products. The best-designed product, offering the buyer clear benefits, is nevertheless doomed without effective and cost-efficient distribution. Modern distribution systems are based on strategic planning, adhere to the marketing concept, focus on target markets, and are consistent and flexible.

Strategic Planning

One of the first questions marketers must address in considering a new-product area is "Does it fit into our existing channels, or will it require different channels?" To a great extent, the enduring success of Procter & Gamble over the years has resulted from a massive and effective distribution system. Recognizing this fact, Procter & Gamble introduces only those new products that can be efficiently marketed through its distribution system.

A second important question about a new product is "Will the distribution channels remain the same throughout the product's life cycle, or will the product's distribution needs change?" Not surprisingly, the distribution system needed to get a new product introduced may be quite different from that needed after many competitors have introduced similar products in the maturity stage. For example, consumers were willing to go out of their way to find the Sony videocassette recorder (VCR) when it was the only VCR available. However, VCR marketers now realize that they must make their products easy to find and to purchase. As part of effective planning, marketing managers should anticipate future as well as initial needs in designing their distribution channels.

A third pertinent question is "Which intermediaries are needed to provide effective distribution?" Channels are interlocking, highly interdependent, and often complex. Effective distribution is not a patchwork quilt of randomly selected channel members; rather, it requires a carefully planned network whose members have clearly assigned functions. The flow of products from manufacturers to wholesaler to retailer to the final buyer depends on systematic, strategic planning, and management.

Adherence to the Marketing Concept

Marketing managers try to establish channels that focus on the needs of the various intermediaries involved. Ultimately, of course, they want to satisfy final consumers. Coca-Cola and Pepsi-Cola, for example, both want their soft drinks readily available to consumers, and they have established distribution channels to ensure that. Yet they also must consider the needs of their channel members—bottlers and distributors. Through promotional assistance and liberal pricing policies, Coke and Pepsi try to ensure the satisfaction of their intermediaries, knowing that this is the basis of ultimate consumer satisfaction. Channel management thus requires—at least in certain ways—a view of intermediaries as "consumers." The marketing concept should be practiced throughout the distribution channel.

Focus on Target Markets

Channels should be selected and managed so that products are directed to predetermined target markets. In marketing cosmetics, for example, Avon uses personal sales representatives who call on brand-loyal shoppers at home. Maybelline and Cover Girl sell their cosmetics to consumers who shop at a range of retailers—drugstores, variety and discount stores, and supermarkets. Estée Lauder aims for more affluent customers by basing distribution in department stores. Each company's approach to distribution focuses on its main target markets. What works for one marketer would prove disastrous for the others, since they must satisfy different customers.

Consistency and Flexibility

Clearly, the adage that a chain is only as strong as its weakest link applies to distribution channels. An inefficient wholesaling operation will endanger the most successful product and the strongest retailing system. Intermediaries at all levels need to be strong and efficient.

As part of strategic planning, marketers try to keep their distribution channels flexible enough to respond to changing market conditions. When the makers of Metrecal, a diet supplement, expanded their distribution from drugstores to supermarkets (cutting prices and thus lowering drugstore profit margins), drugstore managers were angered. Some drugstores downgraded Metrecal to an undisplayed, under-the-counter item, to be sold only if customers asked for it.

Eastman Kodak, on the other hand, managed change within its distribution channels. Just as Metrecal needed to expand into supermarkets, some years ago Kodak recognized the need to expand its distribution network to include discount retailers as well as its traditional outlets—photographic specialty stores. Long-time distributors objected to the lower prices offered by discounters, who now were competitors. But Eastman Kodak had built such a strong consumer loyalty that traditional distributors could not afford to boycott the company's products. They had to accept Kodak's expansion of its distribution system.

Although most arrangements with channel members are long-term, marketers must watch for new intermediaries and better methods of distribution. The most successful marketers understand that distribution channels are dynamic. Indeed, the successful marketer anticipates and ensures change through strategic planning.

FLOWS WITHIN DISTRIBUTION CHANNELS

Another useful way of examining distribution channels is to trace their flows. As shown in Figure 13-1, at least three major flows can be identified. Physical movement, transfer of ownership and money, and exchange of communications are evident in almost all distribution channels.

Physical Flow

Manufacturers obtain materials and components for the production of goods, which, in turn, are moved physically to consumers. **Physical flow** (or **business logistics**) involves all the steps needed to move raw materials to and through production (materials management) as well as the movement of finished products to consumers (marketing logistics). Transporting, storing, retrieving, and displaying are all part of the physical flow. The logistics may be simple, as when a farmer sets up a roadside stand to sell motorists fresh vegetables from a nearby field. In contrast, consider the complex physical flow of raw materials, parts, and subassemblies into IBM's Boca Raton, Florida, plant for production of its personal computers and the flow of finished goods to buyers at Sears, specialty stores, and IBM's own outlets.

The physical flows related to services obviously differ from those involving goods, but service flows also may be simple or complex. On the one hand, getting a haircut or a shoe shine entails simple, direct physical flows. A flight from Miami to Seattle, on the other hand, involves moving a gigantic aircraft thousands of miles with hundreds of people (and their luggage) on board. Moreover, passengers can select from a variety of beverages, meals, and entertainment—certainly an impressive physical flow in the provision of service.

392   Implementing and Controlling Marketing Plans

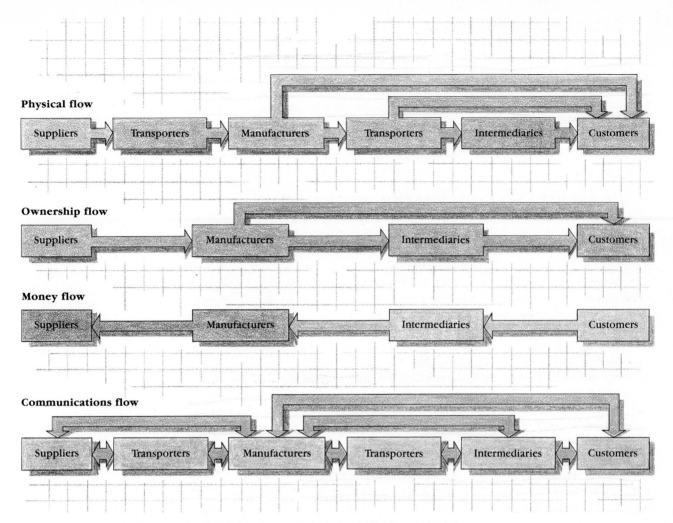

Figure 13-1 *Flows within channels of distribution.* Consider channels as a system through which various flows take place: Physical products flow into the manufacturer from suppliers through the transportation system. Then they flow out from the manufacturer to the consumer through the transporters, often with intermediate stops at wholesalers and retailers. Ownership does not pass to the transporters and other facilitators but through the channel to the ultimate owner, the end customer. In exchange for that ownership, money flows in the opposite direction. To make the system work, information flows in all directions among almost all the parties.

☐ *Ownership and Money Flows*

As products move through channels, **ownership flow** moves forward—from producers or manufacturers, through intermediaries, and to customers. **Money flow,** however, moves backward through the channel—from customers, through retailers and wholesalers, and to producers (see Figure 13-1). Ownership brings financial risks; intermediaries who take title to products assume those risks. Of course, not all intermediaries take title to products, and so ownership sometimes leapfrogs through the channel, as when agents and brokers are involved.

☐ *Communications Flow*

The third major movement in Figure 13-1 is **communications flow.** It moves in two directions. Manufacturers direct promotion and advertising forward to intermediaries and to final customers; at the same time, information about customers' needs and buying behaviors flows back to manufacturers, either directly or through channel members. Marketers cannot function effectively without a speedy, reliable information system that monitors the environment and consumers' desires. Since retailers and sales personnel have daily contact with consumers, they are particularly important in the communications flow between manufacturers and consumers.

■ CONFLICT AND COOPERATION IN CHANNELS ■

Ideally, channels are smoothly functioning systems that facilitate the flows just discussed. That certainly is the goal of marketing managers at the manufacturing end, at least. Some years ago, however, Phillip McVey pointed out that intermediaries do not always view themselves as members of channels. Wholesalers, for example, may see themselves as independent operators whose primary business is buying products for their own customers; they may be less likely to think of themselves as manufacturers' distributors. Retailers also tend to consider themselves as independent organizations. In reality, each channel member is most aware of the other members who are immediately adjacent in the channel.[1]

McVey contended that the distribution channel is an artificial and academic concept. In some respects he was correct, for manufacturers and producers are likely to think of the distribution channel as a system, whereas intermediaries may regard themselves as independent operators. Manufacturers who take an independent view may soon find their products missing from retailers' shelves.

Since members of a distribution channel often lack a systems orientation, they are likely to experience conflict as they pursue individual goals. Like people, organizations often resist integration into larger systems, fearing a loss of identity, self-determination, and power. Unless intermediaries believe that (at the very least) their basic goals will be served, they will be reluctant to cooperate and compromise in the interests of the overall channel system.

Some conflict in channels inevitably arises from the differing goals of members. A manufacturer may have the main goal of establishing as many retail outlets as possible to give its product the widest exposure—Eastman Kodak's objective in adding discount outlets to its channels. Retailers, however, may seek exclusive rights to market the product within a territory. That is why camera specialty stores tried to resist Kodak's new discounting operations. Such conflicting goals are common among the members of a distribution channel.[2]

Conflicts also arise in channels because members are involved in economic exchanges. In reality, these exchanges are not conflicts—they are the resolution of conflicts, although conflicts take place along the road to exchange.[3] Manufacturers seek the highest realistic prices for their products; intermediaries seek the lowest. In a similar way, you naturally want the best (lowest) price you can find when you buy a tape deck, but if you later try to sell that tape deck, you want the highest price you can get.

Conflict along the way to exchange springs primarily from each channel member's attempt to get the largest piece of the profit pie. In the long run, however, compromise and cooperation are in everyone's best interest. All members working to increase the size of the pie is more productive than fighting over the crumb-sized portions of a smaller one. If Burger King and its many franchised outlets squabble with each other all the time, how will they cooperatively counter the threats of McDonalds?

When conflict does arise in a distribution channel, it usually takes one of three forms: horizontal, intertype, or vertical.[4] Figure 13-2 presents examples of each.

☐ *Horizontal Conflict*

<u>Horizontal conflict arises between wholesalers and retailers of the same level and type in a channel.</u> In most consumer goods channels, horizontal conflict is represented by normal competition among retailers (see Figure 13-2). Kroger and Safeway, for example, sell many of the same grocery items. One retailer may put a product on sale, temporarily cutting the price, say, of Swanson's frozen fried

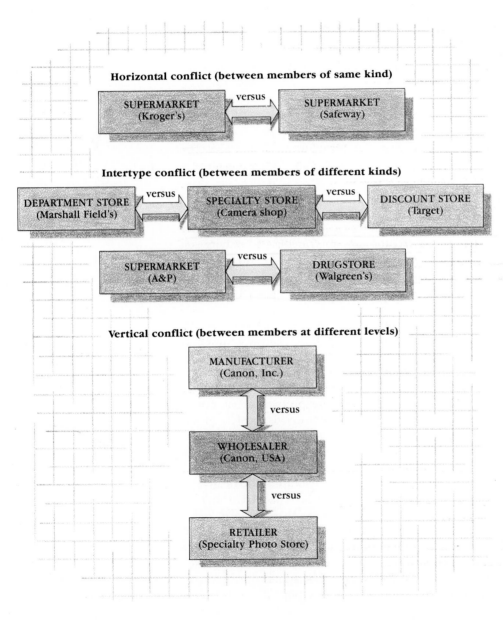

Figure 13-2 *Types of conflict in channels of distribution.* Channel conflict is most obvious between direct competitors within a specific channel. It also occurs between types of channels when, through "scrambled merchandising," one kind of retailer adds merchandise lines previously carried by another type. Vertical conflict occurs between levels within a channel.

Horizontal conflict (between members of same kind)

SUPERMARKET (Kroger's) versus SUPERMARKET (Safeway)

Intertype conflict (between members of different kinds)

DEPARTMENT STORE (Marshall Field's) versus SPECIALTY STORE (Camera shop) versus DISCOUNT STORE (Target)

SUPERMARKET (A&P) versus DRUGSTORE (Walgreen's)

Vertical conflict (between members at different levels)

MANUFACTURER (Canon, Inc.) versus WHOLESALER (Canon, USA) versus RETAILER (Specialty Photo Store)

chicken. This action is a competitive effort to increase store traffic, even at a temporary profit loss. At the same time, the other retailer may offer a special price on Comet cleanser to attract new customers to that store. Such horizontal conflict seems inevitable in multiple channels that distribute products widely.

☐ *Intertype Conflict*

When different kinds of intermediaries are part of the distribution channel, **intertype conflict** is likely to occur (see Figure 13-2). In Chicago, camera buffs can purchase a Nikon 35mm camera for one price at Marshall Field, for a second price at a camera specialty store, or for a third price at a discount store such as Target. Each retailer may buy the Nikon from the same distributor, but because Target and Marshall Field buy in much larger quantities than the specialty store, they receive a larger discount from the wholesaler. Target, as a low-service discount operation with reduced overhead costs, will add the lowest markup on the camera.

Scrambled merchandising has contributed to intertype conflict. Superstores selling drugs, lawn care implements, and clothing lines compete with drugstores, garden centers, and discount clothing stores. Because consumers like to have products available through a wide range of retailers, some intertype conflict is inevitable and produces consumer benefits.

Horizontal and intertype conflict also occur in industrial marketing channels. A small manufacturer of steel cases for blood analyzers used in medical laboratories may buy stainless-steel sheeting from the same manufacturer's branch warehouse that serves National Cash Register and Steelcase, the office furniture producer. The two latter companies are likely to buy the sheeting in larger amounts and thus may receive a larger discount than the small manufacturer.

☐ *Vertical Conflict*

Vertical conflict occurs between members above and below each other in the distribution channel—between the manufacturer and intermediaries or between intermediaries such as wholesalers and retailers (see Figure 13-2). Most vertical conflicts revolve around price, discount levels, or payment terms offered by the manufacturer, but vertical conflicts also arise from how products and communications flow through the channel.

Communication in the form of promotion policies has caused conflict in the wine industry. The advertising of such large wineries as E. J. Gallo and Paul Masson focuses on building consumer demand for their specific brands, but specialty wine retailers complain that such advertising ignores the benefits *they* offer: service, selection, and expertise. Manager Frank Stone of the Skinflint Winestore in Atlanta, however, gives Italian wine marketer Riunite high marks for promotion. He points to Riunite's "aggressive use of instore materials. They've got decals, posters, doormats, maps of Italy with the Riunite logo on them, and even cassette tapes with the Riunite jingle."[5] Apparently, Gallo and Masson decided to risk conflict by supporting supermarkets in their channels at the expense of specialty stores.

Discounting has caused major conflicts between manufacturers and dealers of low-cost, plain-paper copiers. In the early 1980s, Japanese manufacturers such as Canon, Sharp, Minolta, and Ricoh attempted to wrest market share from industry leader Xerox, and price cutting trimmed dealers' profit margins by 25 percent and more. At the same time, the manufacturers themselves took lower profit margins, cut the volume discounts available to dealers, and reduced the allowable time for payment. These actions forced a number of dealers into bankruptcy—particularly the weaker members of the channel. Marketers at the copier companies were aware

Give your customers a whiff of Riunite's great new taste...
with this peach-scented introductory P.O.S. promotion!

Retailers who wish to display Riunite wines have a wide variety of point-of-purchase, or point-of-sale, materials to choose from. The items shown here for their introduction of Natural Peach were printed in ink with a peach aroma built in. (Copyright © Villa Banfi, U.S.A., Old Brookville, NY.)

of this possibility, but they decided to trade the loss of channel members for increases in their market shares.[6]

☐ *Conflict Resolution*

Channel members usually specialize in particular marketing functions. Manufacturers focus on production and national promotion; wholesalers perform distribution tasks; and retailers specialize in distribution, merchandising, and promotion at the consumer level. Such specialization creates a necessary interdependence among channel members. As a result, conflict resolution among channel members becomes imperative. Failure to resolve such conflict results in failure for all, for the weak link undermines the entire distribution effort.

Conflict resolution is the accommodation of various channel members to decisions designed to promote the overall goals of the distribution channel. Members resolve conflict either by accepting the will of the strongest member or by submitting to some "democratic" process involving cooperation and compromise. Following are some typical means of conflict resolution for resolving vertical conflict.[7] (Many of these techniques would be illegal among intermediaries at the *same* level in the channel because they would violate antitrust laws.)

Negotiating committees: Channel members can meet formally and regularly to iron out any differences.

Trade associations: Improved communications among channel members at the same level can prevent certain conflicts.

Financial compromises: Channel members can work out compromises concerning pricing, discounts, payment terms, and financing.

Cooperative promotion: In many channels, manufacturers and retailers jointly plan and pay for promotion and advertising.

Guarantees of quality: If manufacturers guarantee product quality and intermediaries pledge to give proper servicing, conflict should be minimal.

Trade promotion: Some manufacturers agree to promote their products to all intermediaries, regardless of type.

Sales training: Manufacturers may establish training programs for intermediaries' sales personnel.

■ *DISTRIBUTION CONSIDERATIONS* ■

In analyzing and planning distribution networks, marketing managers consider several pertinent factors. First, a general channel strategy and a supporting promotion program must be chosen. Second, the buying behaviors of channel members as well as consumers must be examined. Finally, marketers should set measurable objectives to evaluate the performance of channel members.

☐ *CHANNEL STRATEGY*

Until the introduction of its personal computer in 1981, IBM had sold various computer and office products only through its own sales force directly to organizational buyers. Management realized, however, that a new (for IBM) market segment—small businesses and individuals—could not be reached effectively by personal sales representatives. Before its first personal computer rolled off the assembly line, the company made a strategic decision to seek distribution through retail chains like Sears, through computer specialty stores, and through new retail outlets of its own. This strategy worked. Helped in no small part by its widely recognized name, IBM sold 150,000 microcomputers in the first year of sales. In 2 short years, IBM was the segment leader with a 26 percent market share, passing major rivals Apple and Tandy Corporation.[8] IBM achieved its stunning success through a product that was perceived as the coming standard for microcomputers, through careful target marketing, and through the establishment of different distribution channels—in short, through a shift in channel strategy.

Channel strategy decisions center on choosing and attracting the most effective types and the most efficient number of distributors in the best geographical locations. In addition to reaching the intended target market, the channel strategy should match and support the overall marketing strategy. General Motors, for ex-

398   Implementing and Controlling Marketing Plans

In evaluating the competition between soft-drink brands, one western bottler of Dr Pepper remarked: "The big guys dictate. If you don't follow, they either gobble you up or push you out." The "big guys"—Coca-Cola and Pepsi-Cola—have turned to increasingly aggressive marketing efforts in recent years. One crucial battleground in the soft-drink wars is the display space in supermarkets and grocery stores; here, in particular, Coke and Pepsi have flexed their muscles and fought for greater dominance. In many stores, displays for the two leaders account for as much as 50 percent of overall soft-drink volume.

Coke and Pepsi bottlers across the nation capture high-volume selling ground in supermarkets by essentially buying it. The bottlers offer retailers huge price breaks and promotional allowances in return for valuable display space. Other competitors—such as 7-Up, Royal Crown Cola, and Dr Pepper—do not have the resources needed to compete with these attractive offers. One financial analyst points out that "Dr Pepper probably doesn't spend as much on promotion in one year as Coke and Pepsi do in one month."

After securing precious display space in supermarkets and grocery stores, Coke and Pepsi increase their market shares of soft-drink business. At this point, the two giants benefit from what their competitors undoubtedly view as a vicious cycle. Most grocers divide up store display space on the basis of sales per square foot. Consequently, each time Coke or Pepsi (or both) increases its market share by even a fraction of a percent, it gains more shelf space. Each time 7-Up, Royal Crown, or Dr Pepper loses a bit of its market share, it loses some of its already-limited shelf space. One competitor laments: "Pretty soon Coke and Pepsi are

(*Micheal Simpson.*)

going to squeeze everyone else out—it's just a matter of time."

Source: Ford S. Worthy, "Coke and Pepsi Stomp on the Little Guys," *Fortune*, Jan. 7, 1985, pp. 67–68.

---

ample, maintains a large and varied distribution system to reach numerous market segments with its wide range of products. In contrast, Rolls-Royce needs relatively few dealers to serve its highly affluent audience.

For small organizations or new ones, getting *any* distribution may entail major efforts. Even large, established organizations like Procter & Gamble and General Foods have to compete with thousands of suppliers in distributing packaged goods through supermarkets (see Box 13-1). Channel strategy is often dictated more by what is possible than by what is desirable.

A firm's channel strategy may relate closely to its promotion strategy. Some organizations focus their promotional efforts on channel members rather than on consumers; by aiming sales and promotion campaigns primarily at wholesalers and retailers, the firm enlists their aid in generating demand for the product. Discounts to retailers and incentives for retailers' sales personnel are tactics frequently employed in this kind of promotion. The success of such an effort to push products through the distribution system depends on the nature and philosophies of the channel members selected.

Marketers of packaged and frozen foods, toiletries, and cosmetics are more likely to choose a promotion strategy that focuses on consumers. In this case, advertising through the mass media is used to create demand among final buyers. Such an effort to pull products through the distribution system must be supported by numerous and widespread retail outlets. (A more complete discussion of the "push" and "pull" promotion strategies is contained in Chapter 17).

☐ *Buying Behavior*

As we discussed in Chapters 3, 4, and 5, the purchasing behaviors of consumers differ significantly from those of organizational buyers. In designing distribution channels, marketers keep these differences in mind and attempt to choose proper and effective distributors that suit the buyer's habits and needs. Marketers of consumer products most often seek the widest distribution possible. Convenience items like soda, beer, cigarettes, and snacks require numerous outlets with easy access. Some specialty products, however, are more attractive to consumers when distribution is limited. Mondavi Wineries' Special Reserve Cabernet Sauvignon, which sells for around $40 per bottle, is properly distributed through specialty wine shops, not through supermarkets.

Compared to consumers, organizational buyers are not impulsive; they expect to make purchases from knowledgeable distributors or directly from the manufacturer. As a result, the marketing of industrial products relies more heavily on personal selling than does the promotion of consumer products. In general, industrial marketers choose direct, or at least short, distribution channels that accommodate their target markets.

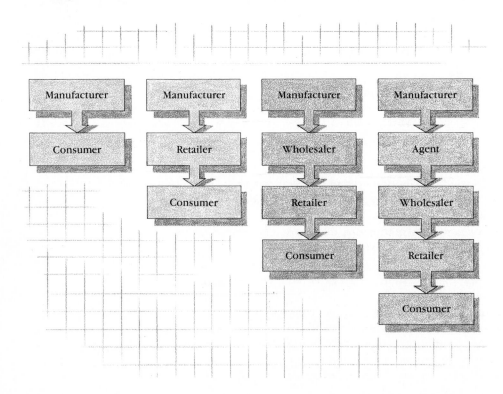

Figure 13-3 *Distribution channels for consumer products.* Channels may be very simple and direct, as when the manufacturer sells directly to the consumer. They grow in complexity as additional members are added.

■ DESIGNING DISTRIBUTION CHANNELS ■

Distribution channels should be designed with buyers' behavior foremost in mind; the product's features and benefits are secondary considerations. Consumer products and industrial products are often distributed through different intermediaries; Figures 13-3 and 13-4 illustrate the channels typically used for each type of product. Although these channels appear similar, we will soon see that the physical flow, the flows of money and ownership, and the communications flow differ within industrial and consumer channels.

□ System Structures

Distribution channels range from direct to multilayered. Using **direct channels** (on the left in Figures 13-3 and 13-4), producers sell directly to final buyers; no intermediaries are involved. Mary Kay Cosmetics and Electrolux use direct channels—their own representatives sell cosmetics and vacuum cleaners to consumers in their homes. A direct channel has no wholesalers or retailers, a common arrangement in marketing industrial products to organizational buyers.

The second channel in Figure 13-3—manufacturer to retailer to consumer—is common in fashion merchandising. Retail corporations like department store chains purchase clothing in large lots from the manufacturers who make Wrangler jeans (Blue Bell Corporation) and Hickey-Freeman suits (Hartmarx). Manufacturers of convenience products—such as Beech-Nut chewing gum (Squibb) and Kool cigarettes (Brown & Williamson)—use multilayered channels to distribute their products. Examples are shown on the right in Figure 13-3.

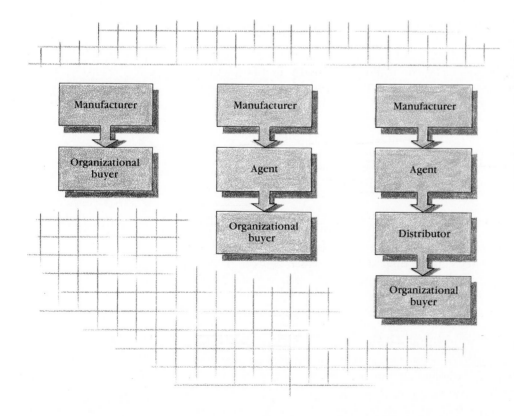

Figure 13-4 *Distribution channels for industrial products.* Whereas direct marketing by manufacturers to consumers is somewhat rare, it is much more common in marketing to organizational buyers. Agents and distributors often act as intermediaries in the marketing of industrial products.

CHANNEL LENGTH AND WIDTH A direct channel from manufacturer to final buyer is considered short, whereas a channel with several intermediaries is considered long. **Channel length** refers to the number of levels in a distribution channel. Marketers of convenience goods, for example, need long channels. They need wholesalers, agents, and brokers to reach the many retailers who sell to ultimate consumers. However, long channels erode the marketer's control over pricing and promotion; since the communications flow is filtered through a number of organizations, long channels frequently require more marketing research. (The longer the channel, the more likely the marketer will get a distorted picture of consumers' wants and needs.)

Typically, channels for convenience products are wide. Width is not an indication of how many sequential members are required in the channel; rather, **channel width** refers to the number of intermediaries found at the same level in the channel. Perishable goods, in particular, require wide distribution channels (although not necessarily long ones), whereas expensive designers' jewelry can be moved to consumers with only a few retailers or even one. Cigarettes, candy, and chewing gum require channels that are both long and wide. In contrast, McDonnell-Douglas can market its F-16 fighter aircraft with a short, narrow channel—from McDonnell-Douglas to the Department of Defense or to a foreign government.

Channel width may be viewed as a continuum ranging from very few to thousands of wholesalers and retailers. A special issue arises when a manufacturer seeks to market its product through more than one type of distribution channel. **Multiple channels** include different kinds of intermediaries at the same level, as exemplified by the channels shown in Figure 13-5. Philip Morris knows that Marlboro cigarettes must be available for sale in supermarkets, drugstores, and convenience stores as well as in vending machines. The company uses multiple channels, and competing retailers accept that fact. In contrast, makers of fine silver tableware such as Cristofle (France) and Tiffany (United States) may grant distribution rights to only one retailer, even in major cities.

Wide channels of distribution are necessary for certain products. However, like long channels, wide channels make controlling price and promotion and collecting market information difficult for marketers. These problems may be alleviated by horizontal or vertical integration of channel members.

HORIZONTAL INTEGRATION **Horizontal integration** brings together a number of channel members at the same level and puts them under single ownership. Horizontal integration often comes about through purchases of competing firms that enable the parent corporation to exercise considerable control over the flows in the distribution channel.

Retailers frequently seek horizontal integration. For example, giant Federated Department Stores, Inc., of Cincinnati owns several retail chains, including Abraham & Straus, Burdines, Foley's, I. Magnin, Rich's, Lazarus, and Bloomingdale's. Retailers as large and powerful as Federated can tell their suppliers which kinds of products to make. At the manufacturing level, Warner-Lambert achieved horizontal integration by purchasing such pharmaceutical companies as Emerson Drug (Bromo-Seltzer), Smith Brothers (cough drops), and Parke-Davis (prescription drugs).

VERTICAL INTEGRATION **Vertical integration** takes place when members of a channel of distribution at different levels merge into one organization. A manufacturer may decide to enter the wholesaling business and buy a large wholesaler. Or, it may open a chain of retail stores. Large retailers may think that it is in their

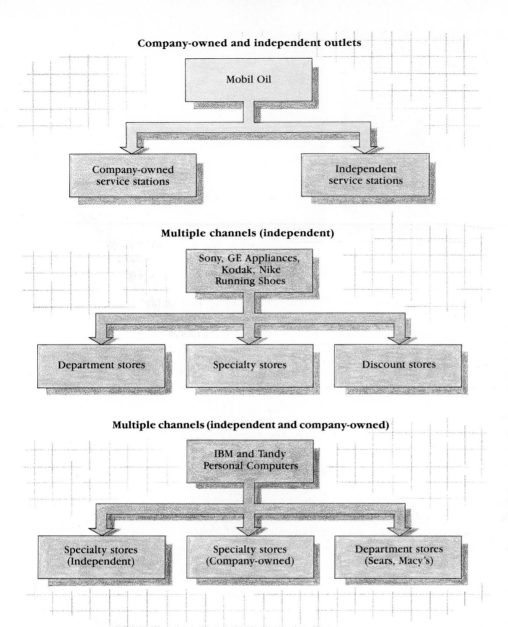

Company-owned and independent outlets

Mobil Oil

Company-owned service stations

Independent service stations

Multiple channels (independent)

Sony, GE Appliances, Kodak, Nike Running Shoes

Department stores

Specialty stores

Discount stores

Multiple channels (independent and company-owned)

IBM and Tandy Personal Computers

Specialty stores (Independent)

Specialty stores (Company-owned)

Department stores (Sears, Macy's)

Figure 13-5 *Multiple distribution channels.* These examples of companies' channels of distribution (simplified here) show how any marketer may use different channels for different purposes. Distinctions among the Mobil service stations are not obvious to consumers. The various kinds of stores in which the consumer may shop for appliances and other products are more obvious. IBM and Tandy, for example, market through channels of different types—some are owned by the company, and some are not.

best interests to own the factories that produce the goods they sell in their stores. If these channel members decide to follow this kind of strategy, they are becoming vertically integrated.

McKesson is one of the nation's largest wholesalers. At various times in its corporate history, it has owned some of the retail stores through which it sold its products. And, it has owned some of the brand names and the facilities for their manufacture—from Dolly Madison ice cream to ORAfix denture adhesive.

The direction of control in a vertical channel can be forward or backward. When manufacturers acquire control over wholesalers and retailers, they achieve

In contrast to many retail chains that put the same name on all their outlets, major department store chains often keep the original names of the stores they buy. Horizontal integration of Federated Department Stores, Inc., retains the well-respected identities of Bloomingdale's in Miami and Lazarus in Indianapolis. (Courtesy of Federated Department Stores, Inc.)

forward integration. When retailers acquire control over manufacturers, they achieve **backward integration**. Wholesalers can integrate either backward or forward in the distribution channel.

☐ *DISTRIBUTION INTENSITY*

Within 10 blocks of where you are right now, you probably can purchase chewing gum, magazines, or soft drinks at half a dozen retail outlets. In the same area, two or three stores probably sell stationery or cassette recordings of your favorite singer. Perhaps you can find a specialty store selling cameras or computers in your neighborhood. But the odds are against finding a Rolls-Royce distributorship nearby. We can make such predictions because the extent of distribution generally relates to product classifications. Convenience items and most shopping products require intensive distribution to make them readily available, whereas consumers are willing to make special efforts to locate some expensive specialty products or items in limited demand. Figure 13-6 arrays product classifications across a distribution continuum ranging from intensive to exclusive.

INTENSIVE DISTRIBUTION   Those easy-to-reach outlets selling chewing gum and soft drinks are designed to achieve **intensive distribution**, a system in which all available and appropriate intermediaries are used. Convenience goods, by nature, must be distributed intensively. Consumers do not want to adjust their buying behavior or make any real effort to get a quart of milk or a felt-tipped pen. As a result, intensive distribution systems typically include thousands of retailers and a strong wholesaling network. Long, wide channels are needed to provide intensive distribution.

SELECTIVE DISTRIBUTION   In **selective distribution**, only a certain number of intermediaries, or those of a certain type, are chosen to distribute the product. "Selective" is a relative term, however; the number and type of outlets depend on the product involved. For instance, Oster makes top-of-the-line, high-priced household appliances and chooses to distribute them primarily through selected depart-

The daily newspaper is the kind of product people won't go far out of their way to buy. This kind of product is distributed intensively. (Copyright © Jan Halaska/Photo Researchers, Inc.)

Implementing and Controlling Marketing Plans

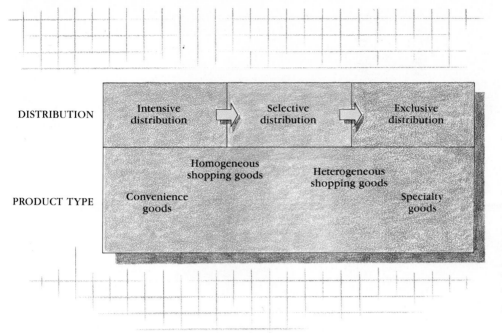

DISTRIBUTION	Intensive distribution	⇒	Selective distribution	⇒	Exclusive distribution

PRODUCT TYPE	Convenience goods	Homogeneous shopping goods	Heterogeneous shopping goods	Specialty goods

Figure 13-6 *Distribution intensity and product classification.* Although the relationship is not perfect—there are exceptions—the types of products are somewhat related to the intensity of distribution required to get those products to consumers.

ment stores rather than through discount outlets or drugstores. Selective distribution allows Oster to maintain its prices and an image of quality. In contrast, General Electric markets middle-of-the-line appliances through practically every department and discount store in the country. Relatively speaking, Oster's distribution is selective, whereas GE's system is closer to intensive.

Marketers of higher-priced specialty and shopping goods are usually quite selective in establishing distribution channels. Producers of homogeneous shopping goods, however, are more likely to move toward the intensive end of the distribution continuum.

EXCLUSIVE DISTRIBUTION To achieve **exclusive distribution**, a manufacturer grants one retailer the sole right to sell a product within a specific geographical area. Caterpillar Tractor Company, for example, allows only one dealer to market its products in any particular area of the United States. In return, Caterpillar expects to exercise some control over that dealer's pricing, promotion, and service policies. Exclusive distribution is an attempt by the producer to integrate and control its distribution channels and, hence, its marketing strategy. For retailers, this arrangement provides a territorial "monopoly" on a desirable product.

Exclusive distribution is used most often for expensive products, when brand preference and even brand insistence play an important role in the buying decision. Such products are purchased infrequently, lend themselves to personal selling, and require a high level of service. Baccarat and Lalique, for example, want their expensive crystal available only in a limited number of outlets so that the product's exclusive image will be enhanced.

Until recently, automobiles were sold almost entirely through a system of tightly controlled dealerships which started out with exclusive rights. That exclusivity weakened as the manufacturers needed more dealers in urban areas. It weakened further when dealers who had been exclusively Buick or Chrysler-Plymouth (both Chrysler Corporation cars) now added Datsun, Toyota, or Fiat to their offer-

When products are very important to the consumer, as automobiles almost always are, the purchase is important enough to take extra effort. Such products are often distributed exclusively. (Copyright © Jon Feingersh 1986/Stock, Boston.)

ings. Since 1979, there has been a further erosion of exclusive dealerships to the point that, according to predictions, about one-third of cars sold in the United States by 1990 will go through "superdealers." These are car dealers with little loyalty to any manufacturer; they handle a dozen or more brands, have formed chains operating in several states, and are taking on the character of large retail chains in other product lines.[9]

Channels for Distributing Services

Because services are usually intangible, the consumer usually participates in the supply of the service; because services cannot be stocked on a retailer shelf, one could conclude (erroneously) that there is no need for channels of distribution for services. Indeed, many services are marketed directly. A physician's or a dentist's treatment rarely involves intermediaries—the same with a haircut or manicure.

Financial services provided by banks, however, often do require channels. Some are the bank's own outlets, as with the many branch locations through which they make their services available. With the advent of automatic teller machines, banks have leased space in other business locations to sell their services. Those banks with credit card services such as MasterCard and Visa depend on retail stores, restaurants, and many other institutions to act as channel members to market those charge card services.

Similarly, large photofinishers use drugstores and other outlets as pickup and delivery points in the marketing of their services; airlines and other travel service industries make heavy use of channels through travel agencies. Much insurance is sold through agents.

In the marketing of services, franchising systems have been used very effectively. Hotels and motels are prime examples of franchised services, as are fast food restaurants like McDonalds, which mix goods and services. In organizational marketing, temporary help franchises like Kelly Services or Manpower Temporary Services are examples. For another example of a franchised service, see Box 13-2.

Box 13-2 The Franchising Bonanza

Well over 2000 franchisors are currently in business in the United States—twice as many as in 1973. Andrew Kostecka, a franchising expert at the Department of Commerce, observes: "Any business that can be taught to someone is being franchised." By 1985, franchised businesses accounted for one-third of retail sales in the United States. According to Commerce Department projections, franchising will account for half of all retail sales by the year 2000.

One aspect of the franchising bonanza has been a dramatic rise in the franchising of services. Banks, accountants, dating services, tub and tile refinishers, tutors, funeral homes, bookkeepers, dentists, nurses, gift wrappers, wedding consultants, baby-sitters, maid services, lawn care specialists—all are being franchised.

An example of successful franchising of services is Gymboree exercise centers for children. Gymboree was founded in 1976 by Joan Barnes, a mother of two. At her first center, located in a San Francisco suburb, Barnes devised Gymboree's basic exercise program for children aged 3 months to 4 years. Once or twice a week for 45-minute sessions, the children perform light exercises with the assistance of a parent. They climb, slide, bounce, and roll on specially designed jungle gyms to the rhythm of music. Special exercises known as "boogies" have been developed for the arm and leg movements of younger babies.

Gymboree was an immediate success in the Bay Area. While refining her exercise program and marketing strategy, Barnes built a solid organization with eight centers. She began franchising in 1980, assisted by early backing from a venture capital firm. As of late 1985, 220 Gymboree centers were in operation, and another 100 had been sold to franchisees. For a cost of $12,000 for a single site plus a royalty of 6 percent of revenues, the franchisee obtains the right to use Gymboree's name and methods, exclusive territory,

(*Copyright © J. Ross Baughman/Visions.*)

and 9 days of training. Gymboree's income from fees and royalties came to almost $1 million in 1985 and was expected to double in 1986. Barnes retains a 50 percent interest in the firm and her personal net worth exceeds $2 million.

Experts on franchising have identified three essential ingredients for success as a franchisor: a sound concept, adequate financing, and a good relationship with franchisees. The last factor can be especially important. Edward Kushell, who heads the Franchise Consulting Group in Los Angeles, states: "Franchisors must understand that their franchisees are not employees. It's a partnership, but some franchisors consider the relationship a feudal system—they are kings and franchisees are serfs." If, however, the working relationship is good, the franchisor can supply valuable financial and marketing expertise. Ultimately, of course, the success of each franchisee will benefit the franchisor as well.

Source: Faye Rice, "How to Succeed at Cloning a Small Business," *Fortune*, Oct. 28, 1985, pp. 60–62, 66.

Legal Considerations

Marketers are not entirely free in selecting intermediaries for their distribution channels. The selection of distributors and agreements with them are subject to federal regulation under the Sherman Antitrust Act, the Clayton Antitrust Act, the Federal Trade Commission Act, and the Robinson-Patman Act (see Chapter 2). A marketer must carefully consider the regulatory environment when it develops what might be viewed as control of those channels.

In general, suppliers can choose the intermediaries they desire, as long as no left-out distributor—or competitors—can prove the supplier intended to create a monopoly. Exclusive dealerships, where all but one intermediary in an area is left out, are basically legal. However, courts have declared them illegal when they affect a substantial percentage of a given market or when the manufacturer is so powerful that exclusive dealerships are deemed a restraint of free trade. A **tying contract** is an arrangement between a supplier and an intermediary which requires the intermediary to buy product B to get product A. Tying contracts are sought when a supplier has a desirable product in short supply, when the supplier is granting a franchise, and when the supplier wants intermediaries to carry a full line of products. Tying contracts are frequently seen as violating antitrust laws unless the supplier can prove that the intent is to maintain quality (as in the case of franchises) or when the supplier is seeking to enter new markets.

Marketers have long assigned "closed" geographic territories to wholesalers and retailers so that particular intermediaries cannot sell outside of their territories, and others cannot sell inside it. In recent years, some closed territories have been declared illegal on the grounds that they restrain trade and competition. Such court decisions have provided an impetus to the establishment of vertical marketing systems.

☐ *Vertical Marketing Systems*

A **vertical marketing system** (VMS) integrates the functions of members at different levels in the distribution channel under the ownership or influence of one member in order to set shared goals and to achieve effective performance. Traditionally, channels consisted of completely independent organizations at each level, and each member focused on its own goals. Traditional channels thus presented the greatest likelihood of conflict and offered the least incentive for cooperation. More recently, marketers have moved toward vertical integration to resolve conflict, increase cooperation among channel members, and achieve control and economy in distribution.

Channel coordination is achieved through ownership, legal contract, or administered leadership, and thus a VMS is classified as corporate, contractual, or administered.[10] The main characteristics of each system are listed in Exhibit 13-1.

CORPORATE VMS In a **corporate VMS**, a channel leader—often the manufacturer—owns all other organizations in the channel. Such an arrangement increases cooperation and reduces conflict, for the parent company sets the goals of the system and coordinates its operation. Sherwin-Williams paint company owns its own distribution channel, made up of almost 1500 retailers throughout the country.

CONTRACTUAL VMS In a **contractual VMS**, channel members are independently owned, but some of the cooperation of a corporate VMS is achieved through legal agreements. Chapter 12 introduced the three main types of contractual systems: franchises, wholesaler-sponsored voluntary chains, and retailer cooperatives.

Franchise systems are evident in 40 different industries and are used by 2000 companies. Franchisees include car dealerships, soft-drink bottlers, and service retailing groups such as Midas Muffler, Ramada Inns, Burger King, Hertz, and H&R Block (see Box 13-2). The best-known wholesaler-sponsored voluntary chains are IGA supermarkets, Ace Hardware, and Ben Franklin stores. Retailer cooperatives are groups of independent retailers who band together to buy in quantity and to advertise cooperatively. Examples include Certified Grocers and Minimax supermarkets.

Exhibit 13-1

Characteristics of Traditional and Vertical Channel Systems			

Conflict among members is more common in traditional channels than in a corporate, contractual, or administered vertical marketing system.

System	Conflict	Controls	Examples
Traditional channels	Conflict likely	None	Completely independent channels
Corporate VMS	No conflict	Channel owner	Singer, Sears, A&P
Contractual VMS	Controlled conflict	Legal agreements	Ace Hardware, Holiday Inns, Wendy's
Administered VMS	Some conflict	Most powerful channel member	Kraft, Procter & Gamble, Henredon (furniture)

ADMINISTERED VMS   Some degree of cooperation and conflict resolution is achieved in an **administered VMS**, which exists primarily because of the power held by the channel leader; it may or may not be based on contractual agreements. Nabisco Brands, Procter & Gamble, and General Electric—by virtue of size alone—obtain and hold a high degree of support and cooperation from the intermediaries in their channels. An administered VMS can achieve such success, however, only if the channel leader is large and powerful enough to impose its own will on other channel members or is regarded by other channel members as providing value through its special knowledge of the market.

In general, vertical marketing systems are increasing in number, size, and power. Small, independent retailers increasingly face the choice of joining a VMS or of becoming a specialty store. Corporate chains now make up more than 30 percent of retail operations, and contractual systems account for an additional 40 percent.[12] In the United States, vertical systems have become the dominant form of channel organization—clearly, distribution channels are not artificial concepts. Marketers and their intermediaries now recognize their mutual stake in operating as integrated systems members.

Direct Marketing Systems

Direct marketing—nonstore sales to consumers and organizational buyers via mail and telephone—was the most striking trend in selling during the late 1970s and early 1980s, growing at an annual rate of about 15 percent (twice the growth rate of traditional in-store retailing). More than 85 percent of adults in the United States have purchased "direct" at least once. Obviously, Americans are shopping at home and liking it.

Distribution management has entered a new era with direct channels that link the telephone, computers, and interactive cable television. Advances in technology have affected how intermediaries perform their functions and forge new links in distribution channels. Although mail-order distribution will continue to increase, its growth will be slower as other direct channels are established. There seems no question that in-home shopping will increase at the expense of traditional retailing. Using interactive cable television or personal computers linked to information systems by telephone lines, consumers can view products at home and—simply by pushing the right buttons—can order virtually any item now found in a store. (As Box 13-3 illustrates, a related development has also become common: home delivery by grocery stores, prepared-food outlets, and other retailers.)

Direct distribution poses some of the brightest challenges to contemporary marketers. It certainly will bring widespread changes in buying behavior, as in-store shopping declines by some unpredictable amount. Many of today's retailers will redirect their efforts, becoming electronic catalog showrooms. Advertisers will devise messages to present more "hard" information about products and to encourage direct action. Refinements in technology will allow marketers to segment populations into increasingly specific target markets and to satisfy an individual customer's needs better. At the same time, however, customers will be more knowledgeable and will demand better, more competitive information.

INDUSTRIAL CHANNELS

Like channels for consumer products, those for industrial products are designed to facilitate physical flow, money and ownership flows, and communications flow (Figure 13-1). They may be direct or may include intermediaries (Figure 13-4), and they may be organized and integrated both horizontally and vertically. Industrial distribution may also be intensive, selective, or exclusive, and the channels may be weakened by conflict among members.

Similarities aside, however, some differences exist between consumer and industrial channels. Among the special factors influencing industrial distribution are the concentration of customers, the technological complexity of products, the use of noncompeting contracts, and product characteristics.

Concentration of Customers

For some industrial products—office supplies and floor wax, for example—distribution channels are wide, as they are for many consumer products. The buyers of such products are scattered throughout the country, and they can be reached and serviced only by a large number of competing distributors. Other industrial markets, however, are concentrated geographically, with many customers in a specific region. The marketers of steel, glass, and plastic used in automobiles, for example, must focus their efforts on the large concentration of decision makers in Detroit and the Midwest. Similarly, producers of materials for the furniture industry—quality woods, upholstery fabrics, and bonding agents—focus on customers concentrated in North Carolina and in western Michigan. Makers of processing machinery for the sugar industry sell their products primarily in Hawaii and Louisiana. And producers of silicon chips and other components for microcomputers have their markets concentrated in "Silicon Valley," a misleading name that includes areas just south of San Francisco, along Route 128 outside Boston, and in Austin, Texas.

Product Technology Complexity

Until Apple launched the first ready-to-use personal computers, almost all computer sales were accomplished without intermediaries. IBM, DEC, and NCR sold powerful computers directly to organizational buyers in business and industry, in large not-for-profit organizations, and in government. The personal computer, however, is a self-contained stand-alone product that does not require the highly complex system components of mainframe computers. So, whether sold to individuals or to small organizations, it can be marketed most effectively through a consumer-like distribution channel. However, complex mainframe computer installations are still sold directly to organizational buyers, because professional, highly trained sales representatives are needed to explain the technical specifications of the product.

Makers of nuclear power installations (Westinghouse and General Electric) and of oil-well drilling equipment (Haliburton and Brown & Root) also distribute their products without intermediaries. Their sales teams include engineers and financial experts to advise customers and arrange for the delivery and installation of highly specific, technologically complex products.

Some complex industrial products *are* distributed through dealers or large wholesalers, of course. Caterpillar Tractor Company markets its earth-moving machinery, diesel engines, and materials-handling equipment through a network of 93 domestic and 137 foreign dealerships. And, although some hospital equipment is distributed directly, other medical technology is handled by expert wholesalers like American Hospital Supply. The more complex the product, the fewer levels and members the channels of distribution are likely to have.

Noncompeting Contractual Arrangements

Marketers of consumer goods expect their products to move through systems of wholesalers and retailers who also distribute competing lines. Procter & Gamble knows, for example, that supermarkets will stock food, paper, and cleaning products from Colgate-Palmolive and General Foods.

Distributors in industrial channels often agree not to carry competing products. Exclusive dealing is the normal arrangement in contracts with manufacturers' representatives.[13] Thus, an independent distributor of specialty chemicals will not carry a competitor's chemicals but may carry complementary products (packaging materials, for example) from a different manufacturer. By contract, manufacturers' representatives limit their promotion to one firm's product lines within a geographical area.

☐ *Product Type*

Recall from Chapter 10 that industrial products are classified into five groups: installations (plant and major equipment); accessory equipment; components (raw materials and parts and subassemblies); supplies for maintenance, repair, and operation (MRO) items; and industrial services. These classifications have major impact on the design of industrial distribution channels.

INSTALLATIONS   Sewage treatment systems, power-generating plants, and large data-processing installations are almost always distributed through the shortest channels—directly from maker to user. The technological complexity and enormous expense of major installations eliminate all but the most expert intermediaries.

ACCESSORY EQUIPMENT   Depending on size and cost, accessory equipment may go directly to users or may flow through some intermediary channel. Recall that accessory equipment does not become part of the finished product but is needed to manufacture it. Anything from forklifts, conveyor belts, robots, and office machinery may be needed. If the accessory is fairly simple and inexpensive, it may be distributed through intermediaries; but if it is complex and costly, it is more likely to be distributed directly.

COMPONENTS   Again, complexity and price determine the distribution of industrial components, including raw materials and parts and subassemblies. Burlington Industries, the world's largest maker of textiles, buys huge amounts of synthetic fibers from suppliers like Du Pont. The quantities and specifications are so unique that direct distribution is negotiated between the two firms. But Burlington then uses wholesalers to distribute its fabrics to retailers.

When any organization in a channel has effective control over the channel, it is referred to as the *channel leader,* or *channel captain.* In franchise channels, the franchisor is nearly always the leader. (Copyright © Bob Daemmrich.)

Implementing and Controlling Marketing Plans

SUPPLIES   Mops and matches, screws and staples, light bulbs and lubricants—the items needed to keep things going—are usually simple, inexpensive purchases and thus are distributed through wholesaling channels. W. W. Grainger Company produces a 1000-page catalog of industrial supplies ranging from electric motors to buckets. Lawson Products carries over 17,000 items in the nuts-and-bolts category. Industrial wholesalers can distribute maintenance, repair, and operation (MRO) items far more efficiently than their manufacturers can.

INDUSTRIAL SERVICES   Most industrial services center on functions like maintenance, inspection, security, and accounting and auditing, and most are sold directly by the producer to the user. Intermediaries can perform few useful functions in distributing these services, which generally are sold on the basis of bids and contracts. Organizational buyers seeking outside services seldom want or need intermediaries. Direct channel flows are more efficient for industrial services.

■ MANAGING CHANNEL RELATIONS ■

A **channel leader**, or **channel captain**, is needed to manage a collection of intermediaries. This organization tends to have the power to establish goals and to monitor outcomes throughout the channel. Various marketing scholars have advanced the leadership case for manufacturers, wholesalers, and retailers. In establishing a distribution channel, the marketer must ask: "Who should the leader be, and how can that leader exercise control?"

□ The Channel Leader: An Active Approach

In reality, only two types of organizations have sufficient power to influence other channel members to accept overriding goals: the manufacturer and what has been termed the **multilevel merchandiser** (MLM).[14] MLMs are represented by those corporate retail chains which, by dint of size, have integrated backward and have achieved strong control over (if not ownership of) their wholesalers as well as their manufacturers.

Leadership in a distribution channel is essentially a question of power relationships.[15] In one sense, power is ascribed—or given—to one member of the channel by the other member (or members) when they perceive that the leader can provide them with the benefits that they desire. This "given" power results in cooperation within the channel.[16] For instance, franchisees will willingly give power to a franchisor when they are convinced that their own success is tied to the franchisor's actions.[17]

The manufacturer's best opportunity to assume channel leadership is through the development of products, particularly unique ones. This results in a consumer franchise that is the manufacturer's strongest path to economic power. However, as competititors enter the market with similar products, the manufacturer loses some of this initial advantage.

The channel leader's tasks may include establishing new channel structures or modifying existing ones. After selecting channel members, the leader should pursue an active management approach. In analyzing and planning a distribution channel, the leader must understand the goals of other members and must devise ways for them to realize their goals within the framework of the leader's objectives. In implementing and controlling the channel, the leader should establish effective and ongoing motivations for other channel members.

Motivating Channel Members

Both new and existing channel members must be motivated to accomplish the objectives established by the channel leader. Typically, channel relations are managed by the manufacturer's marketing organization, especially its sales and promotion departments.[18] Marketers in these organizations motivate channel members through a combination of service; pricing policies; promotion, advertising, and incentives; and sales aids and training.

SERVICE Caterpillar Tractor Company maintains its strong network of dealers by providing services that keep distributors enthusiastic. This manufacturer encourages its dealers to establish a profitable side business in rebuilt parts by providing 2-day delivery of any part to any customer in the world, by introducing new products only after building up a 2-month supply of spare parts, and by repurchasing parts or equipment that dealers cannot sell.[19]

Ideally, such services from the manufacturer will help the entire channel to achieve its goals even as individual members realize theirs. Caterpillar's services keep dealers intensely loyal, and so they act as representatives for Caterpillar products.

PRICING POLICIES As we noted, most channel conflict arises from questions about how much of the profit pie each member will receive. Manufacturers that offer fair and consistent discount policies to distributors maintain good channel relations. In turn, faced with high interest rates on inventory, distributors are encouraged to push products that turn over quickly. To motivate distributors to carry adequate inventory, manufacturers need to consider the higher margin per item, or more rapid turnover for items with lower margins.[20]

PROMOTION, ADVERTISING, AND INCENTIVES Manufacturers should provide effective promotion and advertising for their products. Distributors are motivated by promotion aimed both at consumers and at the distributors themselves. One of the most powerful motivators for channel members is the trend toward cooperative advertising, in which manufacturers and distributors share the expenses. Typically, these programs include rebates or discounts from the manufacturer when the distributor undertakes advertising costs; many manufacturers also help the distributor to develop advertising copy and layouts.

An effective communications flow between the producer and channel member is essential if promotional activities are to advance the objectives of the entire channel. In the case of industrial products, well-informed sales representatives are a major factor in securing the cooperation of distributors.

Incentive programs also play a significant role in motivating channel members. Bonuses, contests, and special promotional programs capture the interest and boost the morale of intermediaries just as they do with consumers. Typical contests for distributors aim at generating additional sales within a certain period. Bonuses and other incentives are awarded for specific achievements, such as securing new accounts or increasing the sales of a particular item.

SALES AIDS AND TRAINING Manufacturers develop and provide aids to help distributors promote the product. Pamphlets, brochures, posters, and displays are typical sales aids; manufacturers are in the best position to see that such aids complement the product and are used effectively.

Perhaps even more important is the training that channel leaders provide to intermediaries' sales forces. More and more suppliers instruct distributors' sales personnel as though they were the supplier's own staff. In industrial channels, detailed sales training and product information for intermediaries are considered crucial to success. In addition, some manufacturers train distributors in business management. By helping intermediaries to manage their operations efficiently, suppliers motivate distributors and achieve better promotion of the product.

☐ *Evaluating Channel Members*

Assuming that measurable objectives have been set for the entire channel as well as for individual members, periodic evaluation is essential in managing the channel and maintaining motivation. Among the criteria often used to evaluate channel members are inventory policies, competency of the sales force, and market share.

INVENTORY POLICIES   Suppliers may set minimum inventory levels for distributors. From the producer's standpoint, inadequate inventories represent lost sales opportunities; for distributors, however, large inventories are costly. As a result, suppliers and distributors may have to compromise on inventory levels. Whatever level they agree upon then becomes the basis for evaluating the distributor's performance.

COMPETENCY OF THE SALES FORCE   Manufacturers may establish standards to measure the effectiveness of an individual distributor's sales force. Are salespeople knowledgeable about the product? Are they trained in selling techniques? Are they effective communicators? Are they well motivated and adequately compensated? Does the sales force have a high turnover rate?

Naturally, the entire channel benefits when the sales personnel of intermediaries are knowledgeable, well-trained, and sufficiently motivated. If a distributor's sales force does not meet standards, the channel leader may seek that distributor's replacement, build its own sales staff, hire professional agents, or perhaps reevaluate the role of personal selling.

MARKET SHARE   If Oldsmobile dealers in the St. Louis area have a 22 percent share of all new-car sales and dealers in San Diego have only a 14 percent share, perhaps the San Diego dealers are not as effective as their midwestern counterparts. However, the discrepancy may mean that foreign automakers are making greater efforts in San Diego than in St. Louis. Regional differences in consumers' preferences may also explain the discrepancy. For most nationally promoted convenience and shopping products, however, regional differences in relative market share are likely to reflect distributors' competency and efforts. Obviously, many factors must be considered in comparing distributors' market shares—especially across regions—but most manufacturers try to make that kind of appraisal in evaluating channel members.

☐ *Adding or Dropping Channel Members*

When marketing managers speak politely of "modifying channels," they are usually speaking, realistically, of adding or dropping members. Distributors who do not measure up to evaluation standards may be fired, just as individuals are. Suppliers naturally want the best intermediaries they can obtain, and they may seek new distributors to replace those who do not achieve objectives. In turn, intermediaries want the most desirable products for their customers. Manufacturers who do not provide appropriate quality and attendant services, or who do not match new offerings from competitors, may find themselves "fired" by their distributors.

SUMMARY

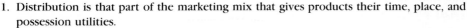

1. Distribution is that part of the marketing mix that gives products their time, place, and possession utilities.
2. Modern distribution systems are based on strategic planning, adhere to the marketing concept, focus on target markets, and are consistent and flexible.
3. Physical movement, transfer of ownership and money, and exchange of communications are evident in almost all distribution channels.
4. Members of a distribution channel often lack a systems orientation and are likely to experience conflict as they pursue individual goals.
5. Conflict in a distribution channel usually takes one of three forms: horizontal, intertype, or vertical.
6. Failure to resolve conflict between channel members results in failure for all, for the weak link undermines the entire distribution effort.
7. Marketing managers must choose a general channel strategy along with a supporting promotion program.
8. Managers must set measurable objectives for later use in evaluating the performance of channel members.
9. Distribution channels range from direct to multilayered and, depending on the number and types of intermediaries involved, are described as having length and width and as being horizontal or vertical.
10. Channel coordination achieved through ownership, legal contract, or administered leadership determines whether a vertical marketing system (VMS) is classified as corporate, contractual, or administered.
11. Special factors influencing industrial distribution are the concentration of customers, the technological complexity of products, the use of noncompeting contracts, and the characteristics of the product itself.
12. Power in a distribution channel is ascribed—or given—to one member of the channel by the other members (or member) when they perceive that the leader can provide them with the benefits that they desire.
13. Marketers for a manufacturer typically motivate other channel members through a combination of service; pricing policies; promotion, advertising, and incentives; and sales aids and training.
14. Among the criteria used to evaluate channel members are inventory policies, competency of the sales force, and market share.

☐ Key Terms

administered VMS	corporate VMS	money flow
backward integration	direct channels	multilevel merchandiser
business logistics	direct marketing	multiple channels
channel captain	distribution channels	ownership flow
channel leader	exclusive distribution	physical flow
channel length	forward integration	selective distribution
channel strategy	horizontal conflict	tying contract
channel width	horizontal integration	vertical conflict
communications flow	intensive distribution	vertical integration
conflict resolution	intertype conflict	vertical marketing system
contractual VMS		

☐ Chapter Review

1. Why should marketers view intermediaries as "consumers" when planning and managing distribution channels?

2. Select a product and describe the three major flows that occur in its distribution channels. What physical flows can you identify? How do ownership and money flow? What communications occur in the channel, and in what directions do they flow?

3. What type of conflict arises between competing retailers in a distribution channel? Between a retailer and a discount store? Between a retailer and a wholesaler?

4. Why does buying behavior lead to different kinds of distribution channels for potato chips, designer jeans, and mainframe computers? Which channel would be longest? Which channel would be widest? Why?

5. Sears, Roebuck manufactures some products, buys others for resale, and retails both. Is this an example of horizontal integration or vertical integration? Of forward integration or backward integration?

6. Is vertical integration most likely to result in intensive, selective, or exclusive distribution? Why?

7. In general, independent retailers are losing business to vertical marketing systems and to direct marketing systems. Do you think independent retailers will eventually disappear? Give examples to support your answer.

8. Why are some industrial products marketed without intermediaries but others are distributed through channels much like those for consumer products?

9. "The manufacturer's best opportunity to assume channel leadership is through the development of products, particularly unique ones." How does a unique product confer power on its manufacturer?

☐ References

1. Phillip McVey, "Are Channels of Distribution What the Textbooks Say?" *Journal of Marketing,* Jan. 1960, pp. 61–64.

2. Jehoshua Eliashberg and Donald A. Michie, "Multiple Business Goals Sets as Determinants of Marketing Channel Conflict: An Empirical Study," *Journal of Marketing Research,* vol. XXI, Feb. 1984, pp. 75–88.

3. Bruce Mallen, "Conflict and Cooperation in Marketing Channels," in L. George Smith, ed., *Progress in Marketing* (Chicago: American Marketing Association, 1964), pp. 68–85; and John F. Gaski, "The Theory of Power and Conflict in Channels of Distribution," *Journal of Marketing,* vol. 48, Summer 1984, pp. 9–29.

4. Joseph C. Palamountain, *The Politics of Distribution* (Cambridge, Mass.: Harvard University Press, 1955).

5. B. G. Yovovich, "Retailers, Miffed at Industry Neglect, Have a Cluster of Gripes (and Praise)," *Advertising Age,* Mar. 29, 1982, p. M22.

6. "The Squeeze on Copier Dealers," *Business Week,* July 6, 1981, p. 78.

7. Louis W. Stern and Adel I. Elansary, *Marketing Channels,* 2d ed. (Englewood Cliffs, N.J.: Prentice-Hall, 1982), pp. 292–299.

8. "The Coming Shakeout in Personal Computers," *Business Week,* Nov. 22, 1982, pp. 72–83; and "Personal Computers: And the Winner Is IBM," *Business Week,* Oct. 3, 1983, pp. 76–95.

9. William J. Hampton, "The New Super-Dealers," *Business Week,* June 2, 1986, pp. 60 ff.

10. Stanley D. Sibley and Donald A. Michie, "Distribution Performance and Power Sources," *Industrial Marketing Management,* vol. 10, 1981, pp. 59–65.

11. R. Richard Bruno and Gerald P. Davey, "Franchising: Business Review," *Journal of Consumer Marketing,* vol. 1, no. 4, 1984, pp. 47–55.

12. Bert C. McCamon, Jr., and William L. Hammer, "A Frame of Reference for Improving Productivity and Distribution," *Atlantic Economic Review,* vol. 24, Sept.–Oct. 1974, p. 12.

13. Joseph A. Bellizzi and Christine Glacken, "Building a More Successful Rep Organization," *Industrial Marketing Management,* vol. 15, Aug. 1986, pp. 207–213.

14. For a detailed discussion of multilevel merchandisers, see Robert W. Little, "The Marketing Channel: Who Should Lead This Extra-Corporate Organization?" *Journal of Marketing,* vol. 34, Jan. 1970, pp. 31–38.

15. John F. Gaski, "Interrelations among a Channel Entity's Power Sources: Impact of the Exercise of Reward and Coercion on Expert, Referent, and Legitimate Power Sources," *Journal of Marketing Research,* vol. XXIII, Feb. 1986, pp. 62–77.

16. Gary L. Frazier and John O. Summers, "Perceptions of Interfirm Power and Its Use within a Franchise Channel of Distribution," *Journal of Marketing Research,* vol. XXIII, May 1986, pp. 169–176.

17. Punam Anand and Louis W. Stern, "A Sociopsychological Explanation for Why Marketing Channel Members Relinquish Control," *Journal of Marketing Research,* vol. XXII, Nov. 1985, pp. 365–376.

18. David D. Shipley, "Selection and Motivation of Distribution Intermediaries," *Industrial Marketing Management,* vol. 13, Oct. 1984, pp. 249–256; and William T. Ross, *Managing Marketing Channel Relations* (Cambridge, Mass.: Marketing Science Institute, July 1985), Report no. 85-106.

19. "Caterpillar: Sticking to Basics to Stay Competitive," *Business Week,* May 4, 1981, p. 74.

20. Dennis A. Zolar, *Motivating the Distributor to Market Your Product* (New York: American Management Association, 1980), p. 24.

14

MANAGING MARKETING LOGISTICS

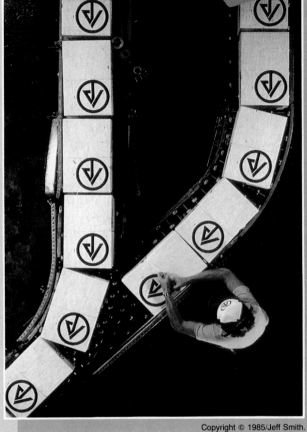

Copyright © 1985/Jeff Smith.

SPOTLIGHT ON

☐ Marketing logistics and the overall process of business logistics

☐ Measuring a marketer's service levels to customers

☐ Compromise between the operating costs and service levels of marketing logistics

☐ Five major transportation modes

☐ Choosing among transportation modes

☐ Achieving the basic aim of inventory management

☐ Warehousing options available to marketers and intermediaries

☐ Marketing logistics as an integral part of marketing strategy

Giant Food Inc., a chain of 142 supermarkets in the Washington, D.C.–Baltimore area, used microcomputers to boost its market share in 2 years from 34 percent to 41 percent. By the end of 1983 it had moved ahead of such established chains as Safeway and Grand Union. This success was achieved in part because Giant Food found high-technology solutions to the industry's traditional problems: the low profit margins of grocery products and the high costs of labor. All Giant's supermarkets use computerized checkout scanners to provide faster service for customers and up-to-the-minute inventory and sales information for store managers.

Technology enables Giant to keep its shelves fully stocked (satisfying customers with product availability) at lower costs. The heart of Giant's distribution system is an 80-acre warehousing operation in Jessup, Maryland, where state-of-the-art moving and storage equipment handle bulk shipments from manufacturers and wholesalers quickly and economically. Desired quantities of products are allocated to individual stores automatically, without human contact. Computerized conveyor belts move cartons of Tide, Nabisco cookies, and Sara Lee frozen croissants to designated shipping docks, where Giant's own trucking fleet takes over.

One aspect of Giant's marketing strategy is to attract single consumers and working couples with fast, one-stop shopping. Among the chain's new enticements are bakeries, deli counters, and pasta shops, providing freshly baked pastries and unusual prepared foods and salads with the convenience

(Giant Food Inc.)

Implementing and Controlling Marketing Plans

of supermarket shopping. Without computer-directed distribution of such highly perishable items, it would be all but impossible to satisfy this market segment profitably.

Computers and automated distribution equipment are becoming necessities for large producers and distributors of food products. Many other industries also are using or exploring technological advances to improve service and lower the costs of transportation, inventory control, and warehousing. The goal of marketing logistics is not only to increase profitability through lower distribution costs but also to satisfy all potential customers by providing what they want, in a desirable form, where and when they want it.

Source: "How Giant Food Harnesses High Tech to Fatten Supermarket Profits," *Business Week,* Dec. 5, 1983, p. 120.

The food you eat, the clothes you wear, and the books you read all travel some distance—short or long—to reach the stores where you buy them. Day and night all over the world, trains, boats, and planes (as well as trucks, pipelines, and even donkey carts) transport products to where buyers want them. In general, this process of physical distribution is unnoticed by the public, yet it is vital in the provision of place utility.

Chapter 14 opens by differentiating among business logistics, materials management, and marketing logistics. Our focus is on the last—all the tasks involved in managing the storage and physical distribution of finished products. We analyze how marketers weigh costs against the levels of service buyers require, and we examine the three major concerns of marketing logistics: management of transportation, inventory, and warehousing. Finally, the chapter explores the relationship between marketing logistics and marketing strategy.

■ AN OVERVIEW OF BUSINESS LOGISTICS ■

Management consultant Peter Drucker has called physical distribution the "dark continent" of business.[1] Drucker was referring not only to the low visibility of product movement for most consumers but also to its neglect by marketers in analyzing and planning their marketing strategies. Until the 1960s, the movement of goods to customers typically was seen as a series of steps that were administered and managed separately. Little attempt was made to integrate the steps into a system of **business logistics**—the overall process of managing the flow of goods from raw materials and components through production, storage, and transportation into the hands of consumers and buyers. But many changes have occurred in the world marketing environment. Stringent profit goals, technological advances, shifts to multinational markets, the lessons learned from military operations, and "reverse" logistics (the recycling of materials) have created an overriding need for all marketers to integrate their logistical efforts.[2]

Consider the complexity of manufacturing an Olivetti typewriter in Italy and transporting it thousands of miles to the desk of a U.S. college student. Many raw materials are needed to produce the typewriter's plastic chassis and printing wheel, its steel bail rod and aluminum type mechanism, and its silicon microcomputer chip. Materials and components must arrive from around the world in specified

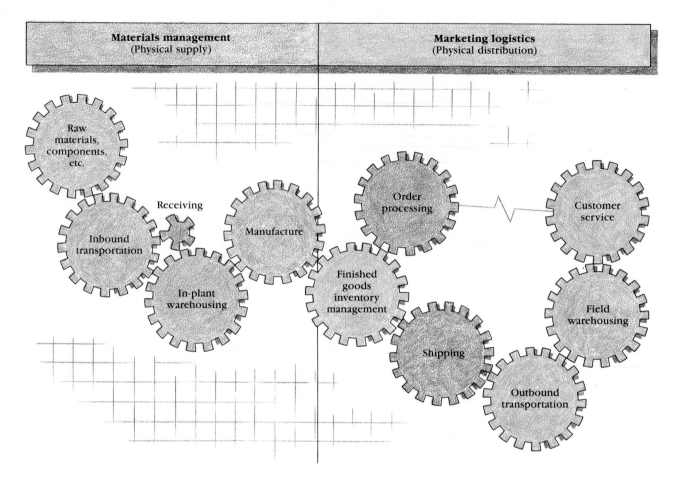

| Materials management (Physical supply) | Marketing logistics (Physical distribution) |

Figure 14-1 *Business logistics.* The business logistics system moves supplies to the manufacturing process and finished goods from manufacturer to consumer. This system is shown as an interlocking set of gears to indicate that it is an interdependent system: Any one activity done poorly can affect the workings of the entire system. (Inspired by Wendell M. Stewart, "Physical Distribution, Key to Improved Volume and Profit," *Journal of Marketing*, Jan. 1965, p. 66.)

quantities and in a highly coordinated sequence to keep the factory's assembly lines moving. Finished products then must be distributed around the world. Olivetti's managers view the flow—from raw materials to assembled machines to overseas transportation—as an integrated system of business logistics. Figure 14-1 depicts this system as a series of interlocking gears, each affecting the others. If one gear freezes, all others stop as well.

Business logistics can be divided into two general areas: materials management and marketing logistics.[3] **Materials management, or physical supply,** involves the procurement, storage, and movement of raw materials and components to and through manufacturing to a finished product. Materials management is the responsibility of those who oversee operations, production, and manufacturing. The left

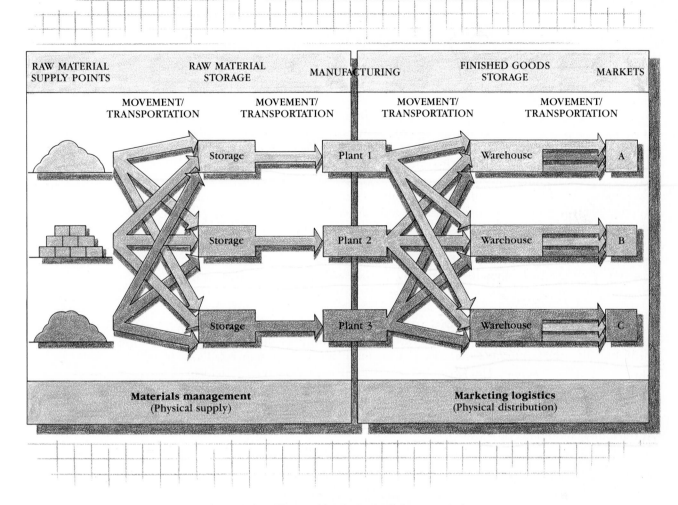

Figure 14-2 *Overview of business logistics.* The total business logistics system involves the physical supply of manufacturing, what is commonly called "materials management," and is usually not considered part of marketing. The physical distribution of the finished product, or "marketing logistics," is the major topic of this chapter. (From John J. Coyle and Edward J. Bardi, *The Management of Business Logistics*, 2d ed., St. Paul: West, 1980, p. 11.)

side of Figure 14-2 shows how physical supply fits into the overall system of business logistics. The right side of the figure shows **marketing logistics,** or **physical distribution,** by which finished products are moved and stored. Since this aspect of business logistics involves assembled products, intermediaries, and final buyers, it is the responsibility of marketing management.

■ GOALS OF MARKETING LOGISTICS ■

According to the National Council of Physical Distribution Management, marketing logistics includes the following tasks:[4]

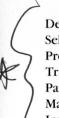

Demand forecasting
Selection of sites
Procurement of inventory
Traffic and transportation
Parts and service support
Materials handling
Inventory control

Warehousing and storage
Packaging
Distribution communications
Order processing
Customer service
Handling of returned goods
Salvage and scrap disposal

Not every marketing organization needs to perform each of these tasks, of course, nor is marketing logistics limited to these areas. But the list does represent the major responsibilities of physical distribution managers. Nearly everything that marketers do to move finished products from the assembly line into consumers' hands is an aspect of marketing logistics.

Almost half of U.S. companies place physical distribution management under the direct control of marketing executives. In addition, well over half the marketing executives polled by the Conference Board claimed to play significant roles in physical distribution, even if they do not directly control those operations.[5] High-level managers view marketing logistics as especially important because a firm's marketing strategy and ultimate profitability are so closely tied to marketing logistics.

□ *Customer Service Levels*

In practicing the marketing concept, marketers seek to satisfy not only their final buyers but also their intermediaries. They must make wholesalers and retailers happy as well as consumers. The key to a large extent is customer service, which intermediaries consider almost as important as product quality and desirability. For wholesalers and retailers, major considerations in evaluating a marketer's service are on-time delivery, consistency and reliability, product protection, order accuracy and reliability, and competitor's service levels.

When a marketer's product is delivered to the customer's warehouse, the customer's inventory costs begin. If it comes too late, it could hamper the customer's production process; if it comes too early, it drives up their inventory costs. What customers want is dependable, on-time delivery. (Courtesy of Fort Howard Paper Company.)

ON-TIME DELIVERY   Fort Howard Paper Company markets its wide range of products through some 2500 distributors, most of whom also carry competing lines. Keeping these intermediaries happy is vital; Fort Howard does so by making sure that distributors have exactly what they want when they need it. Obviously, late deliveries cause problems for intermediaries—in addition to the possibility of lost sales, problems of channel management may arise, and intermediaries may turn to competing suppliers.

In striving for promptness, some organizations set specific shipping and delivery goals. They may decide, for example, that 94 percent of orders must be shipped within 48 hours, or that 90 percent of orders must be delivered within 8 days. Such goals certainly help management to control schedules and ensure on-time delivery. But speed is only one aspect of service; intermediaries also want consistent, reliable deliveries.

CONSISTENCY AND RELIABILITY   "The only thing worse than getting a shipment late is getting a shipment early," says Fort Howard's chief executive, Paul Schierl.[6] Indeed, most distributors do not necessarily require the fastest service, but they do want consistent service. If buyers know that orders placed with a certain supplier will arrive without fail in 10 days, they can plan accordingly and can schedule their orders properly. Intermediaries have businesses to run, and they cannot afford surprises and uncertainty. Orders that arrive early will clutter valuable storage facilities, whereas late deliveries can lead to **stockouts.**

PRODUCT PROTECTION   The marketing logistics staff at Fort Howard is well aware that an on-time delivery of paper towels or napkins is useless to retailers if the cartons arrive crushed or water-damaged. Remember from Chapter 10 that the first job of packaging is to protect the product—an attractive package promotes its contents only if that package arrives at retail stores in perfect condition. Protective packaging for bulk shipments is thus of great concern to physical distribution members. As with delivery schedules, some manufacturers set standards for safe arrival, for example, that no more than 2 percent of goods will be returned because of damage during shipment.

ORDER ACCURACY AND COMPLETENESS   Simply by punching a few wrong keys at a computer terminal, an order-processing clerk can easily misdirect a truckload of facial tissues to San Diego instead of to San Jose. A certain amount of human error is inevitable, but physical distribution managers may also set standards of accuracy for order-processing units.

Completeness of orders is another concern in measuring service levels. Customers are rightly upset when they receive only 42 of the 55 items they ordered. Completeness is crucial for industrial buyers who need subassemblies and components for production. If the correct circuit boards in the exact amount ordered are not delivered at the right time to Zenith's television assembly plant in Glenview, Illinois, Zenith may look for a new supplier.

COMPETITORS' SERVICE LEVELS   To some extent, an organization's service goals are dictated by those of its competitors. A marketer who cannot at least meet the service levels of competing firms may have to offer distributors a price trade-off. In general, the firm that offers the greatest service for the least cost to customers will enjoy a measurable competitive advantage.

EXHIBIT 14-1

EXHIBIT 14-1 — Total-Cost Analysis: Alternative Warehousing Systems

In this example, the two-warehouse system is more cost-effective than the one-warehouse system.

Cost Centers	One Warehouse	Two Warehouses
Transportation	$ 900,000	$ 700,000 (↓)
Inventory	650,000	810,000 (↑)
Cost of lost sales*	300,000	100,000 (↓)
Total cost	$1,850,000	$1,610,000 (↓)

*Reflects levels of customer service based on distance from warehouse.

Source: Based on John J. Coyle and Edward J. Bardi, *The Management of Business Logistics,* 2d ed. (St. Paul: West, 1980), p. 13.

In 1983, Fort Howard advanced its competitive position by acquiring one of its major rivals in the paper products industry, Maryland Cup Corporation. By combining the marketing logistics efforts of the two organizations, the company hopes to cut distribution costs while improving its level of service to intermediaries.

☐ *Balancing Costs and Service Levels*

Any profit-seeking producer finds conflicting organizational objectives when considering marketing logistics. Sales managers, for example, want to maintain the highest inventory levels possible to prevent stockouts and lost sales. Manufacturing units probably support this effort, since long production runs generally cost less per unit than short ones do. Financial managers, however, want it both ways: They seek economies of scale in production but want to avoid the carrying costs and interest associated with large inventories. Marketing logistics managers have to resolve such internal conflicts and turn them into opportunities by maintaining or cutting costs while ensuring or improving customer service levels. Many organizations resolve the conflicting objectives of physical distribution management by considering the total costs of varying levels of service.

THE TOTAL-COST APPROACH   As this term implies, the **total-cost approach** to marketing logistics entails an overall examination of the costs involved in moving finished goods from the end of the production line into customers' hands. All the costs of alternative physical distribution systems that provide a comparable level of service are considered. Since higher levels of service almost always entail higher costs, trade-offs between costs and service are inevitable.

Typically, two comparisons are involved in analyzing total costs. First, costs and revenues are analyzed to determine how different levels of service affect sales. Although higher service levels may cost more, they can produce additional revenues, which may justify the expense. Second, the costs of alternative distribution methods—such as different modes of transportation or warehousing—are compared. Exhibit 14-1 illustrates how increased warehousing capability might affect the total cost of a distribution system. In this case, transportation savings in the two-warehouse system offset higher inventory costs, making that system more cost-effective. Exhibit 14-2 compares the relative costs of railway and truck transportation. Savings in inventory and packaging make shipping by truck worthwhile, although this mode actually costs more than railway shipment.

Distribution costs might be reduced in still another way. Research may show, for example, that customers would be content with lower levels of service—4-day

EXHIBIT 14-2 | Total-Cost Analysis: Alternative Transportation Modes

In this example, the costs of shipping by truck are higher than the costs of railway shipment, but savings in inventory and packaging make it worthwhile to ship by truck.

Cost Centers	Railway	Truck
Transportation	$ 600	$ 700 (↑)
Inventory	1000	900 (↓)
Packaging	400	300 (↓)
Total cost	$2000	$1900 (↓)

Source: Based on John J. Coyle and Edward J. Bardi, *The Management of Business Logistics,* 2d ed. (St. Paul: West, 1980), p. 13.

delivery with 90 percent completeness rather than 2-day delivery with 94 percent completeness. Significant savings can be realized by lowering the level of service if sales and customers' satisfaction are unaffected. However, if research reveals that higher (and costlier) service levels would increase sales by a significant percentage, the additional cost of service may be justified. Balancing all these alternatives may sound complicated, but sophisticated computer models actually perform most of the work.[7]

Marketers will increasingly have to take a total-cost approach to physical distribution. In the food-processing industry, for example, 30 percent of costs relate to physical distribution; for some organizations, distribution costs exceed 50 percent of all operating expenses.[8] Improved management of marketing logistics can affect profits dramatically, since cost savings drop directly to the bottom line. Thus, if profits for some grocery retailers average about 1 percent of net sales, a savings of $1000 in distribution costs would have the same bottom-line effect as a $100,000 increase in sales.

MEASURING COSTS Fortunately for logistics managers, distribution costs and customer service levels can be measured. A total-cost approach need not be based on intuition and hunches; real data are available, and comparisons can be made. Today marketers frequently use computers to determine the optimal balance between distribution costs and levels of service. Programs like IBM's IMPACT and COGS allow logistics managers to analyze and compare the costs of various inventory and service levels. Other computer software is available to analyze the benefits and costs of transportation and warehousing systems.

After setting objectives for customer service, the major decisions for marketing logistics managers center on transportation modes, levels of inventory, and warehousing (including order processing). Figure 14-3 indicates the average proportion of total distribution costs for these areas. Transportation represents the greatest cost in distributing both consumer products (50 percent) and industrial products (35 percent).

▮ *TRANSPORTATION MANAGEMENT* ▮

Since transportation makes up the largest part of physical distribution costs, marketing logistics managers naturally are concerned with finding economical, reliable, and safe methods of moving products to markets. A trade-off between cost and

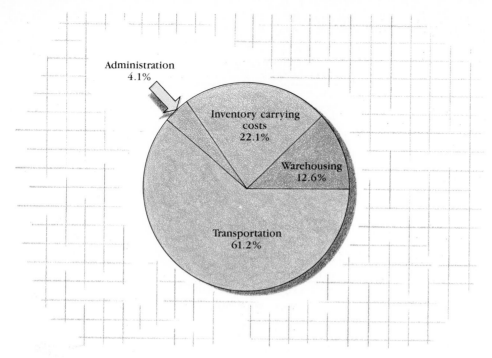

Administration
4.1%

Inventory carrying
costs
22.1%

Warehousing
12.6%

Transportation
61.2%

Figure 14-3 *Physical distribution costs for consumer and industrial products.* Transportation costs, warehousing costs, and inventory carrying costs account for the bulk of all physical distribution costs for a combination of consumer and industrial products. In the past decade, the share going to transportation costs has grown. (From Council of Logistics Management, Oct. 1986.)

speed is often the first issue to resolve. Shipping by barges on inland waterways and by ships at sea is inexpensive but slow; shipping by air is very fast but expensive. Does the need for speed warrant the cost?

At times shipping by air makes economic sense. Such companies as Federal Express, Purolator Courier, Emery Worldwide, Flying Tigers—and the U.S. Postal Service—have capitalized on the need to move documents and small expensive parts rapidly. Air freight companies spend heavily on advertising to consumers, knowing that shipping clerks are often the ones who decide which overnight air service to use. Still, air shipments in the United States account for only 0.2 percent of all *ton-miles* (the movement of 1 ton of freight over 1 mile). Ground and water carriers handle the distribution of most products.

The cost-speed trade-off is complicated by considerations of bulk and weight in relation to product value. Paper towels have large bulk but fairly low value, whereas camera film has little bulk but relatively high value. Weight also must be taken into account: Computer chips have very little weight and bulk but high value; automobiles are heavy and bulky *and* have high value. The more expensive forms of transportation such as air and trucks may be more appropriate for small, light, high-value items like cameras, film, or computer chips. In contrast, coal, fertilizers, and iron ore are low-value, high-bulk commodities for which the cheaper (and slower) modes such as rail and water are more appropriate.

The diversity of the product line and whether foreign markets must be reached are also important considerations for the marketers who make transportation decisions. Organizations that sell just a few products to limited markets can rely on relatively simple distribution channels, but companies with diverse product lines aimed at many markets require multiple channels. In addition, as firms around the world enter global markets, the complexities of international shipping must be considered. Besides cost and speed, such factors as packaging requirements, tariffs, export laws, tax concessions, and cultural and political environments influence transportation decisions.[9]

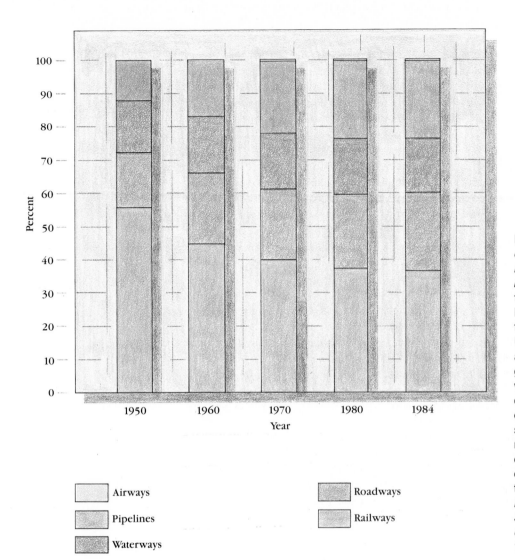

Figure 14-4 *Percent of domestic ton-miles carried by major transportation modes: 1950–1984.* Since the 1950s, railways have lost out in the competition for moving freight in the United States. Pipelines and roadways have gained significantly, while waterways have held their own. Air traffic has increased; however, it is still so small (measured in ton-miles) that it accounts for only a fraction of 1 percent of all domestic freight traffic. (Data from *U.S. Bureau of the Census, Statistical Abstract of the United States, 1986,* 1985, p. 591.)

☐ *Major Modes of Transportation*

Products are transported primarily by rail, road (trucks), water, and air. Pipelines are also important, but they play a more specialized role. Figure 14-4 shows the relative amount of ton-miles carried by each of the major transportation modes in the United States from 1950 to 1984. Railways remain the most frequently used mode of transportation, although the proportion of total freight carried by rail has diminished in recent decades. For distances of fewer than 400 miles, motor carriers are the most common choice. Airlines handle a small but growing percentage of freight in the United States.

RAILWAYS   Rail shipment is most appropriate for raw materials (such as coal, sand, and lumber), for steel and bulk chemicals, and for heavy equipment—for shipping heavy, high-bulk items over long distances. Such goods are typically low in value given their bulk or weight. Railroads still account for more ton-miles than any other transportation mode in the United States.

To compete with more flexible truck transportation, railroads have developed a service known as "piggybacking" in which freight is first loaded onto truck trailers to be driven to the nearest railroad station. There the trailers are loaded, freight and all, onto railroad flatcars and moved to depots near customers, where truck tractors again haul the trailers to their final destination. Piggybacking makes rail shipment more flexible while avoiding the expenses of loading freight more than once.

ROADWAYS   Transportation by motor carriers has become most common for small and medium-size shipments over short distances. The U.S. highway system, rivaled only by those of Canada and Germany, provides great flexibility to motor carriers. Products can be shipped directly from the manufacturer's warehouse to the customer's loading dock or home. Moreover, truck transportation is relatively fast, dependable, and frequent. Some 15,000 trucking companies vie to move products over U.S. roads.

WATERWAYS   The earth's surface is 71 percent water, much of it charted by domestic or international shippers. Inland waterways in this country carry domestic shipments between cities along our rivers and coastlines, on the Great Lakes, and on the St. Lawrence Seaway. Ocean-going freighters and tankers allow international marketers to export and import products of all kinds worldwide. Toyotas arrive from Japan, Volvos from Sweden, and Audis from Germany; meanwhile, U.S. exporters send wheat to the Soviet Union and China, microcomputers to England and France, and telecommunications equipment to nations throughout the world. As more and more marketers take a global perspective, the importance of waterway transportation can only increase.

Waterways are most suitable for transporting heavy, high-bulk items, whether they are relatively low in value (agricultural commodities, lumber, metal ore) or high in value (automobiles, farm machinery). Water shipment is the most economical of the major transportation modes, but it is usually the slowest. It also offers little flexibility to shippers because port sites are limited by geographical factors and water travel is subject to weather conditions.

AIRWAYS   The overriding benefit of air transportation is speed. Jetliners can move even heavy equipment around the globe in hours, but at a very high cost. As Exhibit 14-3 shows, air shipment is by far the most expensive transportation mode, averaging $44.87 per ton-mile in 1983 (compared with $0.89 per ton-mile over water).[10] In addition, air shippers are as tied to airport sites as rail and water shippers are limited by the locations of depots and ports. Still, when a product is needed in an emergency or is small and valuable (or perishable), air shipment is probably the best choice.

PIPELINES   Although pipelines are considered a major transportation mode, only specialized products can move through them. However, despite this limitation, pipelines now carry a significant percentage of freight—more ton-miles than domestic waterways and almost as much as motor carriers (see Figure 14-4).

Pipelines primarily transport oil and gasoline and are not really a shipping alternative for most marketing logistics managers. Some pipelines are used to transport coal and woodchips in a semiliquid state, but few products can be adapted to

EXHIBIT 14-3	Average Cost per Ton-Mile of Major Transportation Modes			

Air shipping is by far the most expensive mode of transportation.

Transportation Mode	1960	1970	1980	1983
Railway	$ 1.40	$ 1.03	$ 2.85	$ 3.11
Roadway	6.31	7.46	12.91	13.55
Waterway	—	0.30	0.75	0.89
Pipeline	0.32	0.27	1.03	1.29
Airway	22.80	21.91	46.29	44.87

Source: Statistical Abstract of the United States, 1986 (Washington, D.C.: U.S. Government Printing Office, 1986), p. 590.

the limitations of pipelines. Nonetheless, vast systems like the Alaskan Pipeline and the TransEuropean-Russian Gas Pipeline carry huge amounts of oil and gasoline thousands of miles across several international borders. No other transportation mode can do this as safely, efficiently, and economically.

☐ *Criteria for Choosing a Transportation Mode*

Expensive, perishable foodstuffs like raspberries and kiwi fruits can be shipped economically by air, but soybeans (low value) and tractors (high bulk and weight) are better shipped by other means. Marketing logistics managers must consider numerous factors in selecting the best transportation mode under the total-cost approach. Cost is usually the prime concern, but a transporter's **speed** (door-to-door delivery time), **accessibility** (number of geographic points served), **capability** (ability to handle various products), and **reliability** (ability to meet planned schedules) are also important. Exhibit 14-4 compares the major transportation modes by these criteria.

COST   Kiwi fruit shipped by ocean freighter from New Zealand to San Francisco would arrive past their prime, although shipping costs would be far lower than if they had been shipped by air. The manager responsible for choosing transportation for this perishable commodity therefore has litte choice—only air transport will ensure safe arrival. More common examples of the choices facing logistics managers can be seen in the distribution of appliances, toys, or clothing. Domestically, the most reasonable transportation choices are rail or truck. If speed is not the most important consideration, the lower cost of rail shipment makes it more attractive. If trucks are the choice, manufacturers can compare competing carriers to find the best shipping rate.

EXHIBIT 14-4	Comparison of Major Transportation Modes			

Transportation Mode	Cost (per ton-mile)	Speed	Accessibility	Capability	Reliability
Railway	Medium	Medium	Good	Good	Good
Waterway	Low	Slow	Poor	Good	Fair
Roadway	High	Fast	Best	Fair	Good
Pipeline	Medium	Medium	Poor	Very limited	Best
Airway	Very high	Fastest	Fair	Limited	Fair

Exhibit 14-3 compared the *average* cost per ton-mile of the major transportation modes over the past three decades. Real comparisons, however, must take into account the quantities and types of products shipped, special handling requirements, and the direction and distance of movement. Slow-ripening bananas can travel at a leisurely speed by boat; strawberries from Florida can be shipped to Philadelphia or Kansas City by train or truck; but hothouse tomatoes from Israel must be flown quickly to the United States. Again, cost and speed are usually closely related.

SPEED   Large freighters plying the Great Lakes with iron ore offer cheap, but slow, transportation, as do the ocean-going freighters carrying lumber from the Pacific Northwest to Japanese ports. Suppliers and buyers of such commodities thus must coordinate and plan their exchange far in advance. In contrast, a replacement part—say, an integrated circuit board for a computer in a Chicago insurance office—may be delivered personally by a courier who flies from the plant. **Transit time** is the time from receipt of the order to delivery of the goods. In gereral, the longer the allowable transit time, the lower the transportation costs. Short transit time usually commands a premium rate.

ACCESSIBILITY   Motor carriers are most accessible to shippers; they can pick up and deliver orders wherever the shipper and customer desire. Waterways have limited accessibility: No boats or barges can deliver goods to Odessa, Texas, or to Reno, Nevada. Pipelines are even more limited, usually offering only a few access points. Railways and airways are tied to their depots and airports, of course, and so motor carriers usually are needed to move shipments to their final destination.

CAPABILITY   A particular carrier's capability is measured by the extent to which it provides appropriate equipment and conditions for moving a specific product. Some railroad cars (the cylindrical ones) are specially constructed to carry gasoline

The large containers such as those on the dock and on board the ship are able to be transported by truck and rail. They can be filled and sealed at the point of origin, transported to the ship, and they can go from the ship to their destination without being opened. (Copyright © Karen Kasmauski/Wheeler Pictures.)

under pressure. Perishable foodstuffs, however, require refrigerated vehicles that can deliver within a specified time. A few superfreighters on the Great Lakes can carry up to 61,000 tons of ore. Although they certainly could carry microchips as well, computer components are too valuable (and their bulk is too little) to make water shipment the best choice.

RELIABILITY   Consistent, dependable delivery is the measure of a carrier's reliability. Few marketers can afford significant variations in delivery schedules. Unreliable carriers force customers to maintain higher and more costly inventory levels, and stockouts frequently result in lost sales. Carriers need not always be fast or inexpensive, but they must be dependable.

SAFETY   Damaged, spoiled, or pilfered shipments plague marketers and carriers alike. In general, marketers provide protective packaging for their products, but the burden of safety and protection from theft during shipment falls upon carriers. Ruined, lost, or stolen goods lead not only to increased costs but to lost sales, since those goods are not available or suitable for sale upon delivery. Unfortunately, the flexibility and accessibility that make truck transportation so attractive also render it most susceptible to thieves: hijacking a truck is easier than a train, plane, or freighter.

☐ Containers and Combined Modes

The use of special containers and combined transportation modes is the most significant modern trend in shipping. **Containerization** is a clumsy term for an elegantly simple concept: consolidating quantities of goods into easily handled, sealed containers. These are usually 8 feet wide and 8 feet high, ranging in length from 10 to 40 feet. Since large quantities are handled as a single unit, containerization saves space, energy, and time and reduces product damage. Costly, repetitive handling is held to a minimum, along with the potential for errors.

Containers can be used with all transportation modes except pipelines. In fact, containerization has been a key element in the development of **combined transportation modes,** which use more than one type of carrier. Sealed containers can be transferred easily from ship to rail to truck and even to airplane (if the weight is within limits). When containers are used in a combination of land and sea modes, shippers refer to the process as *fishyback;* when land and air modes are combined, the term is *birdyback;* and, as we noted earlier, *piggyback* refers to rail and truck combinations.

☐ Government Regulation and the Legal Status of Transporters

Carriers were once strictly regulated by such government agencies as the Interstate Commerce Commission (ICC), the Civil Aeronautics Board (CAB), the Federal Aviation Agency (FAA), and the Federal Maritime Commission (FMC). In 1977 (for airlines) and 1980 (for rail and trucking industries), Congress passed laws removing many but not all regulations governing routes, rates, and schedules. As recently as 1983, the ICC removed restrictions that prohibited railroads from entering the trucking business. Such moves were aimed at creating a freer competitive climate by reducing government's control over private industries. During roughly the same period, Great Britain moved to return some government-controlled industries to private hands, while France took the opposite tack and nationalized a number of major industries.

Even in this climate of deregulation, however, U.S. transportation firms operate under some basic legal restrictions. Those classified as **common carriers,** for example, are required by the federal government to offer their services to all customers. Railroads, airlines, and bus companies (which transport people as well as products) must have government approval to adjust their routes, schedules, and rates. Still, under deregulation, common carriers may make such changes more freely than in the past.

Contract carriers are private businesses that shippers may engage for transportation services under private agreements. Although contract carriers need government certification to operate, they may negotiate their fees and modify their routes and schedules at will. Finally, **private carriers** are manufacturer- or wholesaler-owned shipping fleets (primarily trucks) and are subject only to safety regulations.

Facilitating Agencies

Railroads and motor carriers offer lower rates to shippers who move full loads rather than partial ones. Thus, shippers who transport full-car lots have an edge over competitors who do not. To aid smaller shippers, **freight forwarders** provide a combining service by which partial shipments (usually under 500 pounds) are assembled from several customers. At interim points or at the final destination, the forwarder breaks down these multiple shipments and arranges to transport the smaller lots to their various recipients. Although freight forwarders charge fees, they still save shippers money by assembling full carloads. Therefore, a marketer of diverse products who takes a total-cost approach might use common, private, and contract carriers along with freight forwarders to achieve the lowest costs and a suitable level of service.

INVENTORY MANAGEMENT

As with transportation management, the overriding goal of inventory management is to provide the appropriate level of customer service at the least cost. Inventory managers try to hold down inventory levels and the frequency of orders, with their attendant costs, and still provide an appropriate level of customer service while avoiding lost sales opportunities caused by stockouts. The major inventory expenses are carrying costs, procurement costs, and stockouts (opportunity costs).

Carrying Costs

Inventory **carrying costs** are expenses associated with storage, product depreciation and obsolescence, and taxes and insurance premiums. In some industries, these costs are estimated at as high as 36 percent of the cost of inventory itself.[11] Figure 14-3 revealed that inventory carrying costs alone average 28 percent for industrial products and 15 percent for consumer products—ample reason for managers to seek lower levels of inventory and faster turnover.

The Japanese inventory management system, known as *kanban,* is based on reducing the costs of keeping inventory to the very minimum—even though transportation costs may be raised. In recent years, this system has been adopted in the United States under the name, *just-in-time inventory system.* Such a system requires close cooperation with suppliers so that inventories arrive "just in time" for their use.[12]

Implementing and Controlling Marketing Plans

Procurement Costs

Inventory expenses that arise from the ordering process itself are **procurement costs.** These accrue from filling out forms, performing quality inspections on shipments, supervising clerical personnel, and, increasingly, paying for computer equipment and time-sharing systems. As more firms order through computerized networks, physical distribution managers may be able to achieve procurement savings by using personnel more effectively, by achieving greater speed through automation, and by reducing the paperwork of inventory management.

Stockouts (Opportunity Costs)

If a firm cannot fill an order because its inventory is not adequate—a *stockout*—the major costs to the firm are a lost sale or maybe even a lost customer. Although these are not costs the firm has to pay "out of pocket," they nonetheless represent **opportunity costs**—lost revenues and profits that may never be regained. To prevent stockouts, some firms set a policy of carrying **safety stock** (a higher level of inventory than is thought necessary to meet demand forecasts), a policy that merely leads to higher carrying and procurement costs. To balance the trade-offs, logistics managers try to determine the most economical amounts of inventory to carry and how frequently to order additional quantities. An objective approach to this problem is outlined below.

■ WAREHOUSE MANAGEMENT ■

The general goal of warehouse management, like transportation and inventory management, is to provide an appropriate level of customer service at the most economical cost. Too often, storage costs are not presented to managers comprehensively and systematically. Yet warehousing represents 18 percent of the distribution expense for industrial products and 25 percent for consumer products (see Figure 14-3). In attempting to control the expenses of marketing logistics, many organizations forget that service enhances sales. The task, again, is to balance costs against the most important goal: customer service.

Warehouses

Logistics managers decide whether storage is needed near production lines or distributors—or both. **Plant warehouses** are located near manufacturing operations and are used to store incoming raw materials and parts as well as finished products before they are shipped to distributors or customers. By contrast, **field warehouses** are located near distribution points to provide fast delivery to wholesalers, retailers, and customers. Decisions about field warehouses center on the types of facilities needed and on their number and location. We will describe various types of field warehouses below; the type selected depends on the nature of the product, the organization's service goals, and financial considerations.

PUBLIC WAREHOUSES More than 15,000 **public warehouses** rent space to manufacturers or distributors for the storage of general merchandise. Most have no specialized facilities but handle a variety of items: tires, furniture, appliances, clothing, paper goods, and so on. Public warehouses assume responsibility for the safety of stored products. Although marketers who use public facilities lose some flexibility and give up some control over their products, renting has an important advantage.

Marketers can apply capital to other purposes rather than investing it in storage space, which they may need only temporarily or intermittently.

PRIVATE WAREHOUSES   **Private warehouses** are owned or leased by the firm, which gives logistics managers maximum control and flexibility but requires a large capital investment. The cost may be warranted, however, since private warehouses usually enable the firm to provide the highest level of customer service. The effects on sales can be dramatic. American Hospital Supply Corporation, the largest wholesaler of its kind in this country, owns 159 private warehouses as well as a fleet of delivery trucks. By directly controlling its marketing logistics and providing unusually responsive service, the company moved from sixth to first place in its industry during the 1970s.

Some organizations decide to use a combination of warehouse types. General Electric, for example, buys warehouses in its major markets but chooses to use public warehouses in its smaller markets. As with transportation and inventory management, decisions about storage and product movement should be based on a total-cost approach.

BONDED WAREHOUSES   When inventory is stored in public **bonded warehouses,** taxes become due only when the products are released for sale. The primary users of bonded warehouses are distributors of liquor and tobacco products and importers/exporters. Firms using these facilities can retain working capital and defer taxes which then can be paid by receipts from sales.

SPECIAL WAREHOUSES   Public or privately owned **special warehouses** are designed and constructed to store goods that have exceptional configurations and characteristics. Silos, for example, store commodities like corn and grain; refrigerated or heated facilities are needed for perishable goods and livestock; and pressurized tanks are in demand for storing gasoline, oil, and chemicals.

Large, modern distribution facilities, such as W. W. Grainger's Chicago facility shown here, are known as *distribution centers*. The efficiency of such physical distribution facilities is a key to W. W. Grainger's success. (Courtesy of W. W. Grainger, Inc.)

Handling of products in the warehouse must be as efficient as possible. Trucks that lift and transport heavy pallets of materials from the warehouse to the overland carrier are common in modern warehouses. (Copyright © Richard Pasley 1984/ Stock, Boston.)

DISTRIBUTION CENTERS Typically larger than regular warehouses, **distribution centers** are organized to process and move goods quickly—to provide fast inventory turnover rather than inactive storage. These centers perform such tasks as bulk breaking, assembling, computerized accounting, price marking, and packing and unpacking. Goods may be shipped from distribution centers to conventional warehouses or directly to wholesalers and retailers. W. W. Grainger, an industrial wholesaler, distributes 14,000 products and 15,000 parts from large distribution centers located in Chicago, Illinois, and Kansas City, Missouri. Each day, truckload shipments are dispatched to Grainger's 197 branches throughout the United States from these highly automated facilities; stacks of cartons move in and out of storage on conveyer belts without ever being touched by employees.[13]

Materials Handling

The old multistory warehouses commonly found in urban areas are rapidly becoming obsolete. Intensive labor is needed to move goods between floors, and city transportation systems are congested. Consequently, typical modern storage facilities are one-story buildings in suburban areas that permit the high level of automation achieved in Grainger's distribution centers.

Materials handling—all the processes involved in the physical movement of products—is affected greatly by the product's characteristics (weight, bulk, and fragility) as well as by packaging requirements. Efficiency and economy can be achieved through **unit handling,** whereby multiple cartons are placed on pallets or skids that can be moved easily by forklifts. Hundreds of pounds can be lifted and transported by conveyor belts in a single operation. When warehouses become fully automated, materials handling will be performed almost completely by machines and robots under the direction of a single operator at a computer terminal.

Order Processing

Another important function of warehouse and inventory management is **order processing:** receiving and recording orders, expediting them, and billing cus-

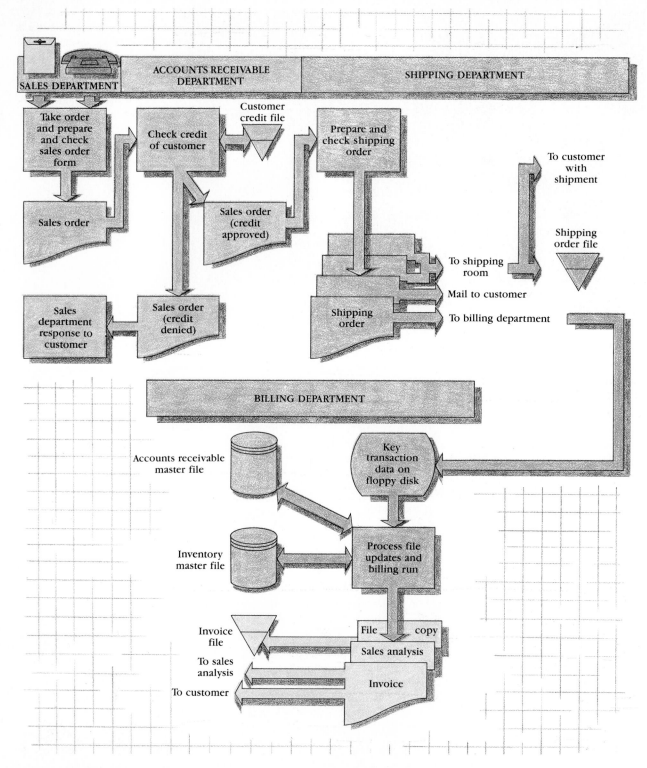

Figure 14-5 *Computer-based order processing system.* In addition to the physical movement of finished product to customers, information flow and accounting transactions must be managed: Orders flow in to sales and credit is checked; after approval, shipping orders instruct the warehouse to ship to the customer; finally, the billing department issues invoices for payment. (From Donald H. Sanders, *Computers Today*, New York: McGraw-Hill, 1983, p. 77.)

tomers. Efficient, accurate order processing is one basis of customer satisfaction and competitive service. Like materials handling, order processing today is highly automated and will get more so as new technology becomes available and is accepted. Many large manufacturers already provide customers with terminals linked directly to the company's computer. Figure 14-5 shows how a typical order-processing system can be linked by computer technology.

The best-managed companies realize that an overall plan for physical distribution is an integral part of marketing strategy. With increased competition, firms are learning that distribution costs can affect their company's position in the market. The total-cost approach to marketing presented in this chapter can be a key element in marketing strategy.

■ *SUMMARY*   ■

1. Profitability, technological advances, and the shift to multinational markets demand an integrated approach to marketing logistics.
2. Business logistics covers two broad areas: materials management and marketing logistics.
3. Nearly everything that marketers do to move finished products from the assembly line into consumers' hands is an aspect of marketing logistics.
4. Almost one-half of U.S. companies place physical distribution management under the direct control of marketing executives.
5. For wholesalers and retailers, major considerations in evaluating a marketer's service are on-time delivery, consistency and reliability, product protection, order accuracy and reliability, and competitor's service levels.
6. Many organizations resolve the conflicting objectives of physical distribution management by considering the total costs of varying levels of service.
7. The major costs and activities of marketing logistics relate to transportation, inventory, and warehousing.
8. The primary means of transporting products are by rail, road (trucks), water, and air. Pipelines play a more specialized role.
9. Cost is usually the prime concern in choosing a transportation mode, but a transporter's speed, accessibility, capability, and reliability are also important.
10. The use of special containers and combined transportation modes is the most significant modern trend in shipping.
11. Even in the present climate of deregulation, U.S. transportation firms operate under some basic legal restrictions.
12. The major components of inventory expenses are carrying costs, procurement costs, and stockouts (opportunity costs).
13. From the broad range of warehousing facilities available, logistics managers basically decide whether storage is needed near production lines or distributors—or both.
14. The best-managed companies realize that an overall plan for physical distribution is an integral part of marketing strategy.

☐ *Key Terms*

bonded warehouses
business logistics
carrying costs
combined transportation modes
common carriers
containerization
contract carriers
distribution centers
field warehouses
freight forwarders

just-in-time inventory system
marketing logistics
materials handling
materials management
opportunity costs
order processing
physical distribution
physical supply
plant warehouses
private carriers

private warehouses
procurement costs
public warehouses
safety stock
special warehouses
stockouts
total-cost approach
transit time
unit handling

Chapter Review

1. Is the purchase of iron ore by a steel mill an aspect of marketing logistics or materials management? For the *seller* of the iron ore, does the transaction represent marketing logistics or materials management? Support your answers.

2. Why is consistent, reliable delivery often more important to intermediaries than speed?

3. What two factors of marketing logistics must be monitored and modified to achieve efficient distribution? Why are these two factors at odds, and how can logistics managers bring them into line?

4. Which two transportation modes are used most widely in distributing products, and what advantages do they offer? Give examples to explain why the other three modes are limited.

5. Identify six criteria for choosing a transportation mode. Which factors are likely to be most important to a firm shipping lumber? To a firm shipping mushrooms?

6. How does containerization help shippers equalize the differences among transportation modes?

7. Identify the three costs associated with inventory. Which two of these costs do inventory managers try to control in taking a total-cost approach? How do they do that?

8. What distinguishes a plant warehouse from a field warehouse? Of the many types of warehouses available, which gives the marketer the greatest flexibility and control? Why don't all marketers use that type of warehouse?

9. Outline the technological changes that are occurring in materials handling and in order processing. Why are such changes so important in practicing the marketing concept profitably?

10. Why does the total-cost approach to marketing logistics have such dramatic impact on profits?

References

1. Peter F. Drucker, "The Economy's Dark Continent," *Fortune,* Apr. 1962, pp. 265–270.
2. See Lewis M. Schneider, "Milestones in the Road of Physical Distribution," in David McConaughy, ed., *Readings in Business Logistics* (Homewood, Ill.: Irwin, 1969), pp. 51–63.
3. See Donald J. Bowersox, *Logistical Management,* 2d ed. (New York: Macmillan, 1978), p. 13; and John J. Coyle and Edward J. Bardi, *The Management of Business Logistics,* 2d ed. (St. Paul: West, 1980), p. 10.
4. National Council of Physical Distribution Management, general information pamphlet, 1977.
5. David S. Hopkins and Earl L. Bailey, *The Chief Marketing Executive: A Profile* (New York: Conference Board, 1971), pp. 13–16.
6. "Tinkering with Success," *Forbes,* Oct. 10, 1983, p. 179.
7. David J. Armstrong, "Sharpening Inventory Management," *Harvard Business Review,* Nov.–Dec. 1985, pp. 42 ff.
8. William H. Joubert, *Profit Potentials in Physical Distribution* (New York: American Management Association, 1972), p. 2.
9. William Lazer and James D. Culley, *Marketing Management: Foundations and Practices* (Boston: Houghton Mifflin, 1983), p. 651.
10. *Transportation Facts and Trends,* 17th ed. (Washington, D.C.: Transportation Association of America, 1981), p. 8.
11. "Leaner Inventories in Prior Slumps Could Lessen Impact of This Recession," *The Wall Street Journal,* May 23, 1980, p. 48.
12. Hal F. Mather, "The Case for Skimpy Inventories," *Harvard Business Review,* Jan.–Feb. 1984, pp. 40 ff.
13. William Baldwin, "Dollars from Doodads," *Forbes,* Oct. 11, 1982, p. 56.

CASE 14

F. W. WOOLWORTH

"For the past 20 years, Woolco has been an albatross around our necks," recalled Richard L. Anderson, president of F. W. Woolworth Company, as he explained the firm's decision to shut down its 336 ailing discount stores just before Christmas of 1982. Woolworth thereby "pulled the plug" on its largest division, which accounted for almost 30 percent of overall sales. Some 35,000 to 40,000 employees abruptly lost their jobs. The closing of Woolco followed shortly after Woolworth's top management decided to sell its majority interest in F. W. Woolworth PLC, the British subsidiary.

Woolworth began as a five-and-dime variety chain in 1879. As the decades passed, the successful, New York–based chain expanded into new businesses (Woolco, Kinney Shoe Corporation, the J. Brannam chain of off-price apparel outlets, and the Richman Brothers specialty apparel chain) and new, international markets (Great Britain, West Germany, Mexico, and Canada).

By the 1980s, it became clear that some of these ambitious moves—most notably Woolworth's commitment to Woolco—were proving costly. By 1982, hurt along with other retailers by a period of worldwide recession, the Woolco division was losing more than $1 million per week, and sales in the international Woolworth stores and in other Woolworth divisions were slumping. "Woolco was running out of money," reported one Woolworth source to *Business Week*. "Woolworth's other businesses weren't doing well enough to help Woolco's cash position, and we knew it would be three years before Woolco returned a profit. We began to realize that Woolco could bring down the whole company."

To figure out why Woolco failed, we need to consider some aspects of retailing. Retailing is a tough business affected by many factors. One factor is real estate—the need for a location in exactly the right place. A second is merchandising—staying with the changing trends and offering just what the clientele really wants to buy. A third is price—being able to offer consumers what they want and need at a competitive price. And a final factor is store design or layout—an internal store management issue that can ultimately make or break a retail outlet. Even if you offer the right merchandise at the right price in the right location, you are sure to fail if customers find your store unappealing or unpleasant.

In the case of Woolco, industry observers go back to the 1960s to pinpoint a critical failure in marketing strategy. When discounting became the hot new concept in retailing in the early 1960s, S. S. Kresge "rolled the dice" and committed all its efforts and resources to this new form of retailing. It even changed its long-familiar name to K mart, which symbolized Kresge's total commitment to this bold marketing gamble.

By contrast, Woolworth executives were ambivalent and unsure of how to deal with the discounting boom. "We couldn't decide which way we wanted to go—variety, discount store, medium-priced—right from the start," admits one Woolco official. This confusion was carried into purchasing procedures: All buying for both the Woolco discount stores and the Woolworth variety outlets was consolidated into one operation, weakening the distinctive identity of each division.

Woolworth's blunders in California typified its marketing mistakes. Initially, it planned to open 17 Woolco stores in the state, but ended up with only 6 because the operation proved to be too costly. Since expenses could not be economically shared, advertising and other operating costs for the 6 stores were excessive. One consequence was that Woolco goods in the state were often priced higher than those of other discounters.

By the late 1970s and early 1980s, the discounting end of retailing had changed somewhat, but Woolco had failed to adapt. Aggressive discounters such as Target Stores and Caldor were offering cut-rate goods in plush environments; specialized discounters such as Toys 'R' Us were cutting into the sales of more broadly focused discounters. Both of these trends hurt Woolco. Woolworth management took various steps to improve Wool-co's financial position—among them reducing the stores' size by renting space to outside retailers—but achieved little success.

Reflecting on Woolco's demise, one competitor stated: "Woolco had a lot of potential that was never exploited. I can remember people at K mart considering them a sleeping giant. But the giant never woke up."

Source: "Finally, Woolworth Wields the Ax," *Business Week,* Oct. 11, 1982, pp. 118–119, "Woolworth Is Still Rummaging for a Retail Strategy," *Business Week,* June 6, 1983, pp. 82–83.

1. What historical forces help to account for the difficulties of the Woolco division of F. W. Woolworth Company?
2. At about the same time that Woolworth began Woolco, S. S. Kresge began its K mart operations. In your view, what accounts for the dramatic difference between Woolco's failure and Kresge's success?

■ CASE 15

PORSCHE

Conventional marketing wisdom certainly emphasizes the importance of good channel relations. However, Peter Schutz, president of Porsche, boldly challenged this conventional wisdom in 1984, provoking intense conflict, when he decided to build an independent distribution network in the United States to handle Porsche sports cars. As part of this change, Schutz planned not to renew the contract under which Volkswagen of America had been distributing Porsches. Not surprisingly, however, Volkswagen and car dealers angrily revolted against Schutz's plans.

Schutz's goal was to replace dealers (who buy Porsches for resale) with agents (who would order Porsches as they sold them and work on commission). In addition, Schutz intended to develop 40 Porsche centers in the United States that would not only distribute cars but also sell them in direct competition with agents. In the process, the traditional U.S. practice of selling automobiles through independent franchised dealers would be abolished.

Ironically, Schutz favored this controversial plan not because Porsche was doing poorly in the U.S. market, but rather because Porsche had become a smash hit. By 1983, sales of Porsches in the United States had reached 21,800 cars, more than double the sales from only 3 years earlier. This increase meant that the U.S. market had become larger than Porsche's next three markets combined (West Germany, Great Britain, and France).

Faced with these sales figures, some top executives might have decided to simply "stand pat" and allow a favorable situation to continue, but Schutz felt that Porsche could do even better with new distribution arrangements. He had many reservations about extending the 1969 contract delegating Volkswagen of America to handle all aspects of Porsche's automotive business in the United States, including importing, advertising, sales, and service. Schutz was unhappy about having no voice in the selection of dealers, some of whom sold Audis (made by a Volkswagen subsidiary) in addition to Porsches. He also viewed a large mass retailer as the wrong outlet for his low-volume, high-priced ($21,400 to $44,000) cars.

Schutz and his staff presented Porsche's revolutionary distribution plan to 300 U.S. Porsche and Audi dealers at a meeting in Reno, Nevada, in early 1984. They argued that the new Porsche centers would supply dealers with the exact cars they needed much more quickly than was possible under the traditional distribution arrangements. Schutz invited the independent dealers to invest in limited partnerships that would bankroll the Porsche centers.

Dealers reacted bitterly to Porsche's offer. They felt betrayed by the proposed abolition of their franchises and insulted by the limited partnership scheme. Soon after the Reno meeting, the dealers struck back. The American International Automobile Association, a trade association for imported car dealers, helped a Porsche action committee undertake a federal class action lawsuit. Schutz suddenly found himself facing lawsuits by dealers all over the United States, who were seeking total damages exceeding $3 billion. Volkswagen, too, was heading for court battles against Porsche. Volkswagen took in more than $40 million in 1983 by importing Porsches to the United States, and it filed lawsuits in four states to protect this lucrative business.

Three weeks after the disastrous Reno meeting, Schutz began to back down. While holding firm to his intention of breaking ties with Volkswagen, Schutz scrapped his plans for Porsche company centers and a dealerless car company. A letter to dealers explained that the franchising system would continue but aroused further controversy by failing to guarantee all 323 independent dealers that they would be given new franchises. Distrustful dealers saw this as a veiled attempt to reduce the number of independent dealers handling Porsches. They noted, as well, that Schutz was continuing (although in a rather slow and muddled manner) his efforts to build a new distribution company, Porsche Cars North America.

By spring 1984—about 2 months after the Reno meeting—the situation was far from resolved. Ferry Porsche, chair of the board, indirectly acknowledged that Schutz had made glaring errors and suggested that Schutz deserved a "second chance." Meanwhile, Schutz was having buttons made to give out to friends and foes, reading "Nobody's perfect."

Source: David B. Tinnin, "Porsche's Civil War with Its Dealers," *Fortune,* Apr. 16, 1984, pp. 63– 64, 68.

1. How could an experienced marketing executive make the kinds of mistakes that Peter Schutz made?
2. Could Schutz have ignored dealers' complaints and simply set up the distribution system he wanted?
3. Do you think the compromise system of distribution being worked out will be successful? Why or why not?

■ CASE 16

CALIFORNIA COOLER

Michael Crete created his first batch of cooler at a beach party during his college years in the early 1970s. For years afterward, he made up small batches of wine cooler for friends' parties. Finally, after enough people suggested that his drink might be commercially viable, he raised $5000, teamed up with his high school friend, Stuart Bewley, and formed a company to sell their cooler. To suggest that they have been successful would be quite an understatement; in 1984, their sales were expected to exceed $100 million.

How were two unproven entrepreneurs with little capital able to turn a virtually un- known drink—a lightly carbonated wine and fruit juice mix—into somewhat of a national craze? Quite simply, the crucial element in the astonishing success of California Cooler was a surprising marketing decision: to package their cooler like beer and sell it through beer distributors.

Back in 1981, Crete and Bewley were selling California Cooler from the back of a pickup truck. But they made their first breakthrough in 1982 when several distributors of the Adolph Coors Company agreed to handle their product. There was no advertising for California Cooler, yet somehow it sold well. "It developed a mystique," recalls one Oakland distributor. "We expected it to pass in 90 days, but it kept going."

Word spread throughout the northern California network of Coors distributors. "When they get something that works," says Bewley, "they call their buddies." Soon the little- known product was spreading downstate to southern California markets. Whereas Crete and Bewley sold only 700 cases of California Cooler off their truck in 1981, the growing distribution network sold 80,000 in 1982. By the spring of 1983, the brand had moved out of state to Arizona and Texas. By 1984, California Cooler had gone national, with 500 distributors handling it in every part of the nation and sales up to 6.7 million cases in the first 8 months of the year.

Previous cooler-type drinks, such as Boone's Farm Apple Wine, had been packaged and distributed like wine. However, Crete and Bewley realized that their cooler should be positioned as (in Crete's words) "a thirst-quencher you consume just like a soft drink, versus something you swirl with a steak or lobster." Their target market was not a snobbish elite of wine sippers, but rather a broader array of beer and soda guzzlers. Consequently, California Cooler *looks like* an imported beer. It is packaged in a 12-ounce green bottle with gold foil around the neck, and typically is sold in four-or six-pack cartons or 24-bottle cases.

Crete and Bewley realized that beer distributors—rather than wine distributors—could most effectively reach the target market they sought. Beer distributors often call on every outlet in a district, including mom-and-pop grocery stores and even bait shops. "If you go with a major beer distributor," argues Bewley, "he's in virtually all the accounts, where a wine distributor may be in only a third of the accounts."

Beer distributors offered other important advantages for the new product. In general, they carry far fewer items than wine distributors, which meant that California Cooler would get much more attention. Moreover, beer distributors were much more comfortable with the "cold box" (or refrigerated case) that Crete and Bewley felt essential for marketing an item that would sell better if it was chilled. "Wine people," explains Crete," had an aloof attitude and wouldn't consider working in a cold box."

Although brilliant channel strategy brought California Cooler two-thirds of the growing market for a previously unknown drink, California Cooler's success brought new problems. By the mid-1980s, 40 brands had quickly emerged to challenge Crete and Bewley's creation, some backed by major wine and beer markets. As 1986 ended, California Cooler had lost its dominant position in the cooler market due to strong competition from new leader Gallo's Bartles and Jaymes (with its striking advertising campaign featuring Frank Bartles and Ed Jaymes), from Seagram's Golden Wine Cooler (relying on commercials in which television star Bruce Willis sings), and from Canandaigua's Sun Country Wine Cooler (using celebrity endorsements from Donna Mills, Vincent Price, and others—all in bear suits!).

In 1986, the wine cooler industry topped $1 billion in sales, and advertising spending exceeded $100 million. Ironically, just as this innovative product was becoming remarkably successful, creators Stuart Bewley and Michael Crete were leaving the industry. Brown-Foreman purchased California Cooler in late 1985, leading to the resignation of Crete. Then, when Brown-Foreman reorganized the company in 1986—spurred on by heavy investment-spending losses—Bewley resigned.

According to projections, there will be 20 to 25 percent growth in the wine cooler category in 1987, and advertising spending will be more than $200 million. Many new products are expected in 1987, including Gallo's Bartles and Jaymes Blush wine cooler, Canandaigua Wine's Sun Country Classic (a drier-tasting cooler targeting consumers 30 years and older), and a peach variety of California Cooler.

Sources: "The Concoction That's Raising Spirits in the Wine Industry," *Business Week,* Oct. 8, 1984, pp. 182, 186; Peter Dworkin, "Strange Brew," *Inc.,* Jan. 1985, pp. 99, 101–102; "Forecast and Review: 1986–1987," *Advertising Age,* Dec. 29, 1986, pp. 3 ff; Patricia Winters, "Coolers Boil," *Advertising Age,* Dec. 22, 1986, pp. 2, 38.

1. What were the major advantages of using beer distributors—rather than wine distributors—for this new product?
2. Now that competitors (including Bartles and Jaymes) are advertising heavily on television, will dealers' expectations of California Cooler change? If so, in what ways?
3. What should California Cooler do now to continue its success with its channels of distribution?

PRICING

15 Price Theory: A Concise Review
16 Establishing and Managing Prices

Once products are developed, and the plan for their distribution to the market set, they have a value to consumers and customers. In an exchange economy, that value is expressed as a price. The price is what the consumer must give up in order to get the product—so it is what the marketer will get in return for the product. But the actual price the consumer pays is only the most visible part of the pricing process.

Chapter 15 is largely a review for students who have taken a course in economics. Although the real world does not always operate as the economic theory says it does, or says it *should*, the forces described in economic theory do operate to some extent. The effective marketing manager has a good understanding of the economic theory that affects prices.

Chapter 16 makes use of economic theory, but goes beyond it to describe what managers must actually do to establish and manage prices, including setting pricing objectives, strategies, and the specific pricing decisions.

15

Copyright © 1983 Joel Gordon.

PRICE THEORY: A CONCISE REVIEW

SPOTLIGHT ON

☐ What price means to consumers and to marketers

☐ Degree of competition and market settings

☐ Laws of supply and demand as a framework for marketers' pricing decisions

☐ Influences on elasticity of demand

☐ Interaction of costs and revenues as they affect pricing decisions

☐ Marginal analysis and prices that yield the greatest profit

☐ Pricing decisions that are inconsistent with economic theory

You might think it would be difficult to sell expensive ice cream to a mass market. Why, after all, should consumers spend $2 per pint for a "super-premium" ice cream when other brands are available at about $4 per half-gallon? But Myron Jennings, manager of a South Carolina supermarket, reports that costly Frusen Glädjé ice cream is the most popular item in his store's freezer. "It's the quality and name," suggests Jennings. "People don't care what it costs."

One of the most dramatic trends in the generally sluggish food business has been the boom in superpremium ice creams such as Frusen Glädjé and Häagen-Dazs. Sales of these ice creams—which contain twice the butterfat of regular ice cream, less air, and usually only natural ingredients—have doubled since 1980. According to a New York research firm, the market for superpremiums is approaching $2 billion and sales of superpremium ice creams will grow at double-digit rates through 1990.

Häagen-Dazs, the leading superpremium brand, was purchased in 1983 by Pillsbury Company, a giant packaged goods marketer. Since then, sales of Häagen-Dazs products have more than doubled. In early 1986, Häagen-Dazs introduced ice cream bars coated with Belgian chocolate and a number of sorbet-and-cream flavors. Frusen Glädjé, one of Häagen-Dazs' main competitors, has followed a similar path. In 1985, it was acquired by the giant food marketer, Dart & Kraft. A year later, Frusen Glädjé's market share had tripled.

Advertising has been a key factor in the success of the superpremiums. Consumers clearly are attracted not only by the high quality of these ice creams but also by the classy image, complete with European-sounding

(Ken Karp.)

names. (Note that both Häagen-Dazs and Frusen Glädjé are domestic, not European, products; Häagen-Dazs was initially manufactured in the Bronx!) Frusen Glädjé has boosted its market share via a lavish advertising campaign emphasizing the theme of "enjoy the guilt."

Distribution remains a major hurdle for certain superpremium brands as they struggle against more powerful competitors. According to one estimate, 70 percent of the nation's supermarkets were carrying superpremiums by mid-1986, up from 45 percent in 1985. Pillsbury and Kraft are improving the marketing mixes for their brands by adding new flavors, building new plants, and adding the superpremiums to their supermarket routes. Smaller superpremium marketers, such as Ben and Jerry's, DoveBar International, and San Francisco's Double Rainbow Gourmet Ice Cream, do not have the extensive distribution networks or substantial distribution budgets needed to compete with Pillsbury (Häagen-Dazs) and Kraft (Frusen Glädjé).

As the battle of the superpremiums continues, one overriding pattern seems clear: The high prices of these brands are not driving consumers to less expensive ice creams. Indeed, if anything, the high prices of Häagen-Dazs, Frusen Glädjé, and other superpremiums appear to be a central element of their marketing appeal.

Source: "Pricey Ice Cream Is Scooping the Market," *Business Week,* June 30, 1986, pp. 60–61.

When unusually cold weather damages the Florida citrus crop, you would naturally expect the price of orange juice to rise. But it may not—if processors have a stockpile of frozen concentrate. And if the price does rise, it may not come back down to the level you expect when orange growers recover and produce a bumper crop.

Economic theories relating to price are rooted in the assumption that factors in the marketing mix other than price remain constant. This assumption, however, rarely holds true. Even so, economic theory forms an important base for the price-setting actions of marketers—and for the resulting amounts that consumers pay for products.

Chapter 15 opens by examining the different meanings of price for consumers and for marketers. We then survey the bases of competitive market settings, supply and demand, and demand elasticity. The roles of costs and revenues in price setting are summarized, and we look at marginal analysis as a tool for balancing costs and revenues. The chapter concludes by explaining why variations from the assumptions of economic theory occur and how these variations affect marketers' pricing decisions.

THE MEANING OF PRICE

Just what "price" means depends on point of view. When consumers pay for a good or service, they typically (and unconsciously) base their buying decision on more than their need for the basic product. They buy an augmented product: the core product and its accompanying benefits. To get the utilities represented by that augmented product, buyers must give up something, most often money. In doing so, they give up the use of money that might obtain other products.

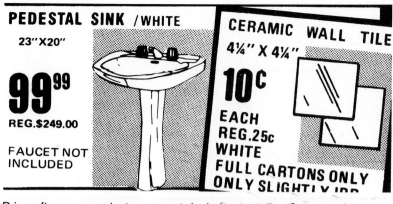

Price often communicates a great deal about quality. Compare the strong price-oriented nature of the products on the left with the emphasis on artistic design on the right. Most people would conclude the products on the right to be of higher quality. (Right photo: Copyright © Kohler Co.)

☐ *To Consumers and Marketers*

To consumers, price is what they must exchange for a product's utilities and value. Price indicates the priority that they assign to that product among the general range of products. For some consumers, a speedy sports car is important, and they are willing to give up a large sum of money to get that type of car. For others, the security of a substantial savings account has priority; they pay the price of walking or taking the bus so that they can invest money in an interest-yielding account. For organizational buyers, priority (and price) is likely to be based on a systematic analysis of the product's actual worth.

Marketers look at price in many ways. One approach divides price into two elements: the basic, or commodity, price and the premium price differential.[1] The **basic price** is the amount marketers estimate consumers will pay for the core product—a plain white bathtub, for example. The **premium price differential** represents the additional money consumers will pay for the augmented product—in this case, a pastel tub with plated faucets bearing the Kohler brand name. Similarly, a car buyer may choose to pay the basic price for a Yugo or a Hyundai with no accessories or may decide to pay the higher premium price differential for a Mercedes sports model with air conditioning and a sunroof.

A major challenge facing marketers is to influence consumers to pay the premium price differential. The basic price is subject to laws of economics governing supply and demand. However, by successfully establishing a premium price differential, marketers free themselves from some of the constraints of those laws. If the annual market for ice cream in the United States is not growing, the superpremium marketer who can provide extra value and convince customers of the product's worth will succeed at the expense of competitors.

The variance between the basic price and the premium price differential ranges widely across product categories. As Figure 15-1 illustrates, the basic and the premium price for true commodities like wheat and other agricultural products is the same. (Farmer Smith's bushel of wheat is the same as Farmer Brown's bushel.) Thus, the basic price is the total price. For commodities like rolled steel, the basic

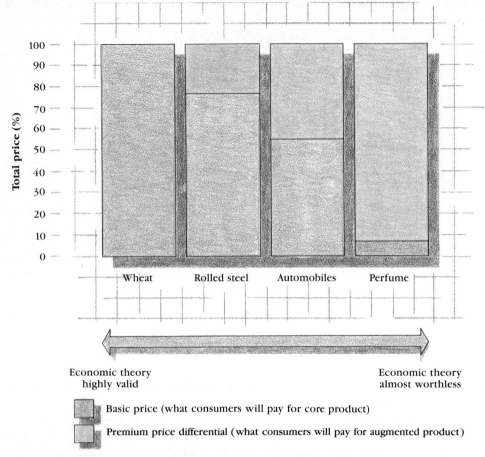

Figure 15-1 *Basic price and premium price differential for different products.* The basic price, represented here in blue, is what consumers will pay for the core product, and the premium price differential, in orange, is what they will pay for the extended or augmented product. One farmer's wheat is just like another's—there is no opportunity to add value beyond the core product. At the other extreme, the chemicals in perfumes have little value. What consumers will spend for perfumes is largely a function of the image created by brand names and advertising, packaging, or other elements of the marketing mix other than price. Most products, sold to both organizations and ultimate consumers, fall somewhere in between. The laws of economics discussed in this chapter are applicable to products like wheat but do very little to explain the purchase of perfume; they are more or less valid for most products in between.

price makes up most of the total price. For perfumes, however, the premium price differential makes up most of the total price. When a consumer decides to buy Revlon's Charlie or Chanel No. 5, the product's packaging, image, and reputation far outweigh the basic cost of ingredients. For automobiles and many other products, the proportion of the total price based on the core product and the proportion based on its augmented features are more in balance.

For the most part, consumers see only the total price and base their economic exchanges on that price. Marketers arrive at the total price by building the premium price differential onto the basic price. Thus, **price** reflects both the value that buyers place on what is exchanged and the marketers' estimates of that value. Price differs from other components of the marketing mix—product, distribution, and promotion—because it is not an out-of-pocket cost. Marketers spend money on research and product development; on establishing and managing channels of distribution; and on advertising, promotion, personal selling, and publicity. Investments for those activities are intended to stimulate an increase in the quantity of products demanded by consumers. By contrast, a price reduction designed to stimulate purchases affects revenues, not costs.

☐ *Price Theory*

Price theory and business decisions are intertwined. Although this chapter focuses primarily on economic concepts, keep the concerns of marketing in mind: Prices are set within an economic environment bounded by theories; marketers need to understand these boundaries when setting prices. The goal is to choose the right theory for a particular situation and to apply it correctly.

Disregarding economic concepts and theories invites disaster. In the market-place, economic principles never operate as precisely as economists describe them, but they do help us to understand the complexities of markets. For that reason, the following sections review market settings and types of competition, the laws of supply and demand, the concept of demand elasticity, and the interplay of costs and revenues in pricing decisions. Finally, we return to the marketer's role to look at the effects of economic theory in real-world pricing situations.

■ *MARKET SETTINGS: DEGREE OF COMPETITION* ■

Prices are set in (or even produced by) the marketplace for a specific product. Market settings can be classified into three broad categories by the number of competitors and their power or lack of it: perfect (or pure) monopoly; perfect (or pure) competition; and imperfect competition, which includes monopolistic competition and oligopoly. Exhibit 15-1 sets forth the characteristics of these market settings.

☐ *Perfect Monopoly*

A **perfect monopoly** is a marketplace where only one producer supplies the good or service. If not controlled in some way, that producer could exercise enormous

EXHIBIT 15-1	Characteristics of Market Settings		
Market settings are classified by their power or lack of it.			
Market Setting	Competition, Differentiation	Economic Sector	Price Control
Perfect monopoly	Single producer, unique product	Utilities, cable TV	Government restriction
Perfect competition	Numerous producers, identical product	Primarily agriculture	None
Imperfect competition			
Monopolistic competition	Numerous producers, perceived differences in products	Packaged goods, general retail trade	Some
Oligopoly	Few producers, little or some differentiation	Aluminum, steel, automobiles	Some

Source: Adapted from Paul A. Samuelson and William D. Nordhaus, *Economics,* 12th ed. (New York: McGraw-Hill, 1985), p. 510.

sway over the marketplace and its prices. As a result, the government usually institutes price restrictions to check the producer's power. The most visible monopolies in the United States are the utility companies that supply electricity. Whether owned privately or by government agencies, they alone produce electric power for specific regions of the country. Consumers must buy electricity from them or do without this essential product. Because of the costs and complexity of installing wiring for these services, a monopoly is an efficient way to provide electric power. Local telephone service—also dependent on wiring—is another instance of monopoly. When competition among multiple producers would result in gross inefficiencies and wasted resources, the marketplace tends to permit monopolies.

In practice, modern monopolies do not operate unchecked; price restrictions are in place. Public utilities must have their rate changes approved by local government commissions. Thus U.S. monopolies are controlled to some extent—especially their price setting.

☐ *Perfect and Imperfect Competition*

When numerous sellers offer numerous buyers an identical product and no single seller can influence the product's price, the market setting is labeled **perfect competition.** These conditions typify the marketing of homogeneous (similar) products whose start-up costs are relatively low, thereby making it easy for new competitors to enter the market. Modern economies like that of the United States have perfect competition almost exclusively in agricultural sectors. In the production of soybeans and cotton and in the fishing industry, so many sellers market identical products that prices are set by the quantity demanded. With the exception of commodities graded by quality levels (eggs and veal, for example), similar agricultural products generally command similar prices.

Between the extremes of perfect monopoly and perfect competition lies the broad setting in which most marketers operate: imperfect competition. Although **imperfect competition** may be characterized by a large number of sellers and

This farmer combining his wheat must sell his product in a market of perfect competition. A bushel of his wheat will be treated just like all other bushels, and he will be paid a market price over which he has no control. (Copyright © Earl Roberge/Photo Researchers, Inc.)

buyers, fewer producers compete than in agricultural markets, where thousands of farmers supply essentially similar products. In settings of imperfect competition with only a few producers, some may command relatively large market shares and thus may influence the industry's price levels. Within this middle range of the competitive spectrum, economists have identified two distinct market settings: monopolistic competition and oligopoly.

MONOPOLISTIC COMPETITION   A large portion of the U.S. economy is characterized by **monopolistic competition**, in which large numbers of firms market heterogeneous (dissimilar) products. In this setting, the degree of product differentiation is the key to price levels. Thus, Stouffer's frozen dinners command higher prices than dinners from Swanson, and sofas made by Knoll and Henredon cost more than sofas from Sears. This setting is known as "monopolistic" competition

---

BOX 15-1   COMPETITION IN MARKETING: Profits from Popcorn

Movie theater owners don't make their profits from the dollars you pay at the box office. Although film goers spent almost $4 billion on tickets in 1984, over half that money had to be returned to producers and distributors. After deducting operating costs, theater owners had to look elsewhere for their profits—specifically, to the concession stand, where cash registers ring up approximately $750 million per year. According to Alan Friedburg, president of the Sack chain of 59 theaters in Massachusetts: "Without concessions, no theater could remain in business. That's the profit margin."

Popcorn accounts for slightly more than 40 percent of all concession sales. Soft drinks bring in another 40 percent, and candy and other items garner the remaining revenues. Clearly popcorn is the profit king. Major theater chains offer small, medium, and large containers of popcorn. The medium-size box holds 8.5

ounces; the container, the popcorn, and the oil and salt for which a customer pays $1.75 cost the theater owner about 17 cents. Soft drinks also are highly profitable, costing the theater owner about 16 cents for each $1 soda purchase. By contrast, candy is less profitable. The concessionaire pays 20 cents for a 1¼-ounce Hershey bar that is sold to customers for 60 cents.

Movie theaters can sell popcorn and soft drinks at such high markups because customers are truly a captive audience after buying their tickets. Movie fans will not choose to see a different film simply to get lower prices at the concession stand, but if the cost of admission increased dramatically, patrons might forgo snacking during the movie. Consequently, theater owners would like to hold ticket prices relatively stable while enticing as many customers as possible into visiting the concession stand.

In terms of market settings, the market for movie theater tickets is one of monopolistic competition. Consumers have many types of entertainment alternatives, including multiple movie theaters in most markets, which helps to explain why the profit margin on movie tickets is not all that high: If it were too high, people would simply opt for another alternative (such as renting films and watching them on videocassette recorders). By contrast, the market for popcorn and other food items sold *within* movie theaters is one of monopoly. Because theater owners enjoy this monopoly, they can maintain extremely high profit margins in selling popcorn and soda.   ■

Source: "For Theater Owners, Many Flavors of Profit," *The New York Times,* Nov. 5, 1983, p. 17.

(Ken Karp.)

because each product (even Stouffer's frozen dinners) is perceived to be so unique that it more or less "owns" a certain portion of the market.

In settings of monopolistic competition, the greater the degree of product differentiation perceived by buyers, the greater the disparity among prices set by competitors. Some marketers in this setting can influence prices substantially, either because of their dominant position in an industry (IBM and Procter & Gamble) or because of the perceived quality of their products. Similarly, because of their specialized expertise, orthodontists can charge higher fees than dentists; corporate lawyers who arrange mergers can charge higher fees than lawyers in general practice.

OLIGOPOLY In the second type of imperfect competition, an **oligopoly,** a few sellers dominate the marketplace. They control the means of production and thus have substantial influence over the prices of product. Oligopolies arise primarily because the need for large economies of scale in certain industries discourages competition. Some commodity markets—copper and aluminum, for example—are oligopolistic. So, too, are the automobile and machine tool industries and the markets for cement and for paperboard boxes.

The increasingly global perspective of many marketers has tended to move oligopolies toward the setting of monopolistic competition. Imported automobiles,

Many commodities are marketed through the buying and selling of future exchanges. Much like the market for corporate stocks, special markets such as the Chicago Commodities Exchange pictured here are the centers of most transactions. (Copyright © Craig Aurness/ Woodfin Camp & Assoc.)

cameras, and electronic equipment have increased the choices available to consumers, thereby making it less likely that a few producers can strongly influence price.

◼ SUPPLY AND DEMAND: THE LAWS THAT CANNOT ◼ BE REPEALED

Whether one, a few, or many producers are operating in a marketplace, their pricing decisions are influenced to some degree by the economic laws affecting supply and demand. Everyone knows the "laws" of supply and demand: If the price of something people want goes down, they will buy more of it; if the price of that product goes up, they will buy less. Right? Well, not exactly. Marketers have learned (sometimes the hard way) that a product will not be sold unless consumers will exchange money for it, will forgo other things that they might buy with that money, and have the money to buy the item.

Suppose you want to purchase an ocean-going yacht. Your desire is only a dream unless you have a million dollars or so to spare on that investment. To use a more likely example, suppose you have several hundred dollars in savings and want to buy a $600 tape deck. Again, your desire for the product will not lead to an exchange until your tuition and other expenses are covered and you can afford to tie up your money in audio equipment. Your purchase depends, then, not only on your desire to buy at a certain price but also on your ability and willingness to buy.

☐ The Law of Demand

For economists, "demand" has a special meaning that gives rise to a specific law. Many businesspeople misleadingly speak of demand as a *number* rather than as a relation. To an automobile executive, for example, demand is the number of cars that can be sold in a given period. An economist more technically refers to this number as the "quantity demanded" and defines demand as the relation between this number and price. **Demand** is a relation among the various amounts of a product that buyers would be willing and able to purchase at possible alternative prices during a given time, all other things remaining the same. According to the **law of downward-sloping demand,** when a good's price is raised (at the same time that all other things are held constant), less good is demanded.[2]

The inverse relation between the quantity demand and the price of a product holds true more consistently in commodity markets, where many producers offer a similar product in a setting of perfect competition. Typically, economists illustrate this relation with examples of agricultural products like wheat and corn. Staying within this tradition, Exhibit 15-2 shows how the law of demand applies to soybeans.

This exhibit represents a **demand schedule; it specifies the quantities demanded at various prices at given times.** Note that the quantity demanded varies from 7 million to 20 million bushels per month at prices ranging from $10 to $2 per bushel. When the price drops from $10 to $8 per bushel, the quantity demanded increases, and total revenue (price multiplied by quantity) also increases. However, at the lower price of $6 per bushel, total revenue decreases. Although the quantity demanded is greater than at $8 per bushel, the increase does not offset the lower price.

Economists depict the demand schedule as shown in the graph in Figure 15-2. Note that the **demand curve slopes downward and to the right,** where

EXHIBIT 15-2 |

Total revenue for soybeans reaches its highest point at a price of $8 per bushel. The quantity demanded is 10 million bushels and total revenue reaches $80 million.

Price per Bushel (P)	Quantity Demanded (Q)	Total Revenue (P × Q = TR)
$10	7 million	$70 million
8	10 million	80 million
6	12.5 million	75 million
4	15 million	60 million
2	20 million	40 million

increasing quantities demanded are shown on the horizontal axis. The quantity demanded rises with diminishing price not only because current buyers increase their consumption but also because new buyers who would not afford soybeans now enter the market. The opposite also holds true. If the price rises, the quantity demanded will decrease both because some buyers drop out of the market and because buyers who remain will purchase fewer soybeans.

The effects of the law of downward-sloping demand on soybean growers are clear: When farmers produce a bumper crop—in this case, an excess of soybeans relative to the quantity demanded—prices will drop. That, in turn, will lead to an increase in the quantity demanded. Conversely, a bad crop will produce a shortage of soybeans relative to what buyers want. Prices will then rise, causing the quantity demanded to fall. In both cases, the quantity of soybeans demanded varies inversely with its price, just as economists predict.

☐ *The Law of Supply*

The law of demand governs only one side of the economic coin: how much of a product will be bought at various prices. The coin's other side relates to how much

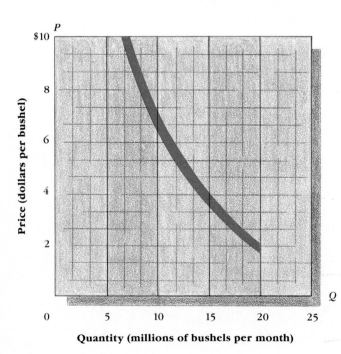

Figure 15-2 *The demand curve for soybeans.* The lower the price of soybeans (and almost any other product), the more soybeans customers will demand. The demand curve represents the quantities demanded at different prices.

Quantity (millions of bushels per month)

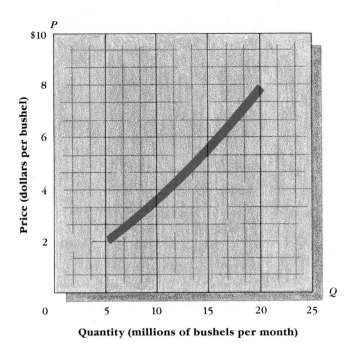

Figure 15-3 *The supply curve for soybeans.* The higher the price offered for a product, the more of that product will be made and offered for sale. The supply curve represents the quantities supplied at different prices.

of a product will be made available at various prices. Economic theory holds that, as a product's price increases, producers will be willing to supply more of it. Thus, a continuing upswing in soybean prices may encourage farmers to switch from production of wheat or cotton to soybeans.

Again, economists assign a special meaning to supply, which gives rise to a second economic law. **Supply** is a relation showing the various amounts of a commodity that a seller would make available for sale at possible alternative prices during a given period of time, all other things remaining the same. According to the **law of upward-sloping supply,** when the price of a good is raised (while all other things are held constant), more will be produced.

Economists depict the **supply schedule** by an upward-sloping curve on a graph. The **supply curve** in Figure 15-3 thus indicates rising production by sloping upward and to the right, where increasing quantities supplied are shown on the horizontal axis. At the low price of $2 per bushel, farmers might produce only 5 million bushels of soybeans per month. As the price rises, however, more farmers switch their acreage to soybean production and the quantity supplied increases (the curve moves upward and to the right on the graph). If the price rises to $8 per bushel, the quantity supplied will increase to 20 million bushels per month.

In the case of supply, notice that price and quantity vary directly (not inversely). Thus, if the price of a dozen eggs at the supermarket climbs to $8.50, thousands of farmers will race to enter or increase poultry production. They will, that is, if the price of chicken feed has not also risen to levels as high as the price of eggs. This is why the laws of supply and demand specify "all other things remaining the same." In economic theory, things are always "remaining the same," but real-life economic conditions cannot be held so constant.

☐ *Equilibrium: The Intersection of Supply and Demand*

The demand and supply curves presented in Figures 15-2 and 15-3 do not show what actually happens in a market, whether for soybeans or any other commodity.

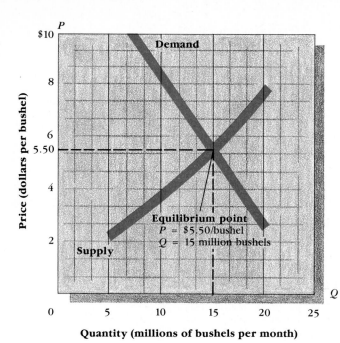

Figure 15-4 *The equilibrium point for soybeans.* When both the demand curve and the supply curve are plotted on the same chart, they will intersect at the price at which the quantity demanded by consumers is the quantity supplied by producers. This is called the *equilibrium point*. To find the equilibrium point, read the price from the vertical axis and the quantity from the horizontal axis.

Instead, at some point the two curves intersect, and equilibrium is established between supply and demand. At that intersection we find the **equilibrium or market price** in a perfectly competitive setting. As shown in Figure 15-4, the demand and supply curves for soybeans intersect at an equilibrium price of $5.50 per bushel, where quantities demanded and supplied equal 14 million bushels per month. In this case, no single soybean producer can ask more than $5.50 per bushel, since buyers can get all the soybeans they want at that market price. But if farmers supply more than 14 million bushels per month, a new equilibrium will be reached at a lower price.

We must emphasize that the economic laws illustrated by this soybean example are based on simplified assumptions which do not always describe the changing world. Disequilibrium is quite common. When it occurs in the United States, the government may step in and buy up surplus commodities. By stockpiling wheat, cotton, cheese, butter, and the like, the government supports prices at a level higher than the theoretical equilibrium price of a perfectly competitive marketplace. Similarly, in the face of commodity shortages, the government may sell off its surpluses to keep prices from going too high. Even with such intervention, however, the opposing forces of supply and demand operate much as economists theorize.

■ *ELASTICITY OF DEMAND*   ■

In the real world, practical applications of economic theory require marketers to understand a related concept that greatly influences prices: Demand for a particular product is relatively "elastic." Economists use **elasticity of demand** to describe the degree to which the quantity produced and sold will increase or decrease in response to changes in price. On the one hand, a small decrease in the price of coffee or chocolate may yield a relatively large increase in sales. On the other hand, a small decrease *or* increase in the price of salt or flour may bring little fluctuation in sales. Thus, elasticity of demand is relative and is usually product-specific. Three major environmental factors interact to determine a product's relative demand elasticity: the availability of close substitutes, consumer's ability or option to defer purchasing, and a given product's relative importance in the consumer's overall budget.

Determinants of Demand Elasticity

The most important determinant of a product's demand elasticity is the availability of close substitutes. Were public utilities unregulated, for example, and prices for electric power doubled overnight, consumers' howls of protest would be accompanied by only small reductions in demand. No close substitutes exist for this product. Reading by kerosene lanterns and candles is difficult; only electricity can light up our television screens and computer terminals. Lacking a substitute for electric power, we reduce consumption only slightly when prices rise. By contrast, large price increases for a brand of underwear, lip gloss, or breakfast cereal would spur us to buy other brands. Close substitutes *are* readily available for these products, so price increases might lead us to reduce our consumption of them.

The second basic determinant of demand elasticity is consumer ability or option to postpone purchases. As automobile prices rose drastically in the mid-1970s, consumers began to hold on to their old cars longer. In fact, between 1970 and 1984, the age of the average car on U.S. highways rose from 5.6 to 7.5 years. More dramatically, the proportion of cars over 12 years old rose from 6.1 percent in 1970 to 17 percent in 1984.[3] Potential buyers delayed purchasing a new car in hopes of lower prices and lower interest rates for auto loans. Dealers enjoyed brief periods of increased sales only when they offered special rebates and other concessions.

Conversely, when consumers cannot postpone or avoid a purchase, rising prices have only limited effects on sales. Homeowners in the northern United States

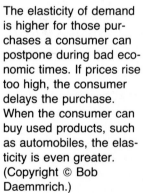

The elasticity of demand is higher for those purchases a consumer can postpone during bad economic times. If prices rise too high, the consumer delays the purchase. When the consumer can buy used products, such as automobiles, the elasticity is even greater. (Copyright © Bob Daemmrich.)

can lower their thermostats in response to the high cost of fuel oil or natural gas, but they are unlikely to stop heating their homes in the middle of winter. The ability to postpone or avoid heating costs is quite limited. We can put off buying a new car as long as the old one still functions, but we must have life's necessities, regardless of cost.

Going a step further, we see that marketers of nonessential durable products are hit particularly hard by recessionary and inflationary times. As prices rise, consumers will postpone purchasing such items as video equipment, pianos, and trash compactors. Similarly, they will forgo such services as life insurance and lawn maintenance until prices come down or purchasing power rises.

The final determinant of demand elasticity is the relative importance of an individual purchase within the buyer's overall budget. Typically, the cost of a sailboat or bedroom furniture represents a large portion of a family's budget, whereas the price of a bottle of wine, a subscription to *Time* magazine, or the services of an exterminator are relatively insignificant. For major purchases, fluctuations in price can lead to large changes in quantities produced and sold, but for relatively unimportant purchases, price changes do not have significant effects.

Organizational buyers make similar judgments. Thus, expenditures for major installations—such as a data-processing system or a robotic assembly line—make up an imposing part of the overall budget and are greatly influenced by price changes. An organization's minor purchases—for example, filing cabinets and desk lamps—are usually not as crucial within the total budget. Consequently, sales of such items are not influenced as strongly by price increases.

The availability of close substitutes, the option to postpone purchases, and the relative importance of an individual's purchase together determine a product's relative demand elasticity. When the determinants interact so that purchases are highly affected by price changes, economists say that demand is relatively elastic. When price fluctuations influence purchases only in minor ways, demand is deemed relatively inelastic.

☐ *Elastic, Inelastic, and Unitary Demand*

Since demand elasticity is relative, various goods and services show a spectrum of price sensitivity. One end of the spectrum can be labeled as **elastic demand**, in which a given percentage change in price results in a greater percentage change in the quantity demanded. These changes are generally in opposite directions. Small-appliance markets, for example, have been characterized by elastic demand: Lower prices result in larger sales increases (on a percentage basis) than the percentage of the price cut.

The markets for automobiles, designers' clothing, and personal computers are also characterized by elastic demand. In such markets, elasticity of demand is greater than 1 ($E_d > 1$). As shown in Figure 15-5a, a price change from $1000 to $500 increases the quantity demanded from 1000 to 3000 units. Total revenue thus rises from $1 million to $1.5 million. (Of course, the total cost of producing the additional units also rises.)

Under conditions of **inelastic demand**, a given percentage change in price results in a smaller increase in the quantity demanded. In such markets, a decrease in price brings so small an increase in quantity demanded that total revenue actually falls. In markets characterized by inelastic demand, E_d is less than 1 but not less than 0 ($E_d < 1$). As Figure 15-5b shows, a price cut from $1000 to $500 increases the quantity demanded from 1000 units to only 1500 units. Thus, total revenue declines from $1 million to $750,000. A price increase under conditions of inelastic

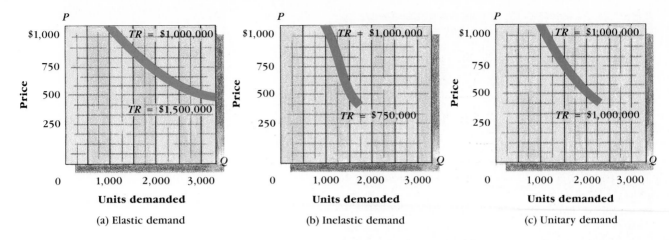

(a) Elastic demand   (b) Inelastic demand   (c) Unitary demand

Figure 15-5 *Effects of demand elasticity* E_d *on total revenue* TR. The curve for elastic demand, represented in the far left chart, is relatively flat. When price is reduced, the demand increases enough to increase total revenue; when price is raised, total revenue goes down. Under inelastic demand, the center chart, the curve is relatively steep. When prices are reduced, the increase in demand is not enough to maintain revenues, so they go down. When price is raised, total revenue goes up. When the demand curve shape is neither flat nor steep—and when any price-multiplied-by-quantity calculations lead to the same total revenue—the demand is said to have *unitary elasticity*.

demand would lead to greater total revenue. The quantity demanded would not decrease enough to lower total revenue.

Unitary demand exists when a decrease in price produces a rise in the quantity demanded that exactly compensates for the price cut. In other words, changes in price and quantity cancel each other out, leaving total revenue unchanged. Such an elasticity is numerically equal to unity ($E_d = 1$). As shown in Figure 15-5c, a price cut from $1000 to $500 increases the quantity demanded from 1000 to 2000 units, thereby producing the same total revenue of $1 million.

Some examples should make these concepts less abstract. We have already noted that demand for nonessential durable products is generally inelastic. Thus, price cuts on Jaguar sports cars or on Philipe Patek watches would result in little or no increase in sales, and price increases would not cause a major sales decline. Inexpensive staple goods also show inelastic demand; fluctuations in the price of milk, salt, flour, and sugar have little impact on sales.

A notable example of elastic demand can be seen in the markets for business-oriented personal computers and for the less powerful home machines. As competitors Apple, Tandy, and Victor dropped prices in response to the introduction of IBM's personal computer, hundreds of thousands of new buyers entered the market. The quantity demanded increased by a greater percentage than the price changes. Prices in the home computer market eventually dropped to the point that Texas Instruments pulled its model 99-4A off the market. Although lower prices of computers led to increased sales, not all marketers were able to hold costs down to profitable levels.

☐ *Cross-Elasticity of Demand*

The quantity demanded can be influenced not only by the product's price but also by the price of another product. **Cross-elasticity of demand** is the degree to which

As the price of personal computers declined, the demand grew much greater. With more personal computers being bought, the demand for software from Microsoft increased without it having to lower its prices. This illustrates cross-elasticity of demand between two *complementary* products. (Ken Karp.)

the quantity of one product demanded will increase or decrease in response to changes in the price of another product. Cross-elasticity affects demand primarily in two situations: when close substitutes are available for the product and when products are complementary (that is, when they are consumed together).

SUBSTITUTE PRODUCTS   When products are similar in use, quality, and price, a change in one brand's price will significantly influence the sales of other brands. Some products with close substitutes include color television sets, soft drinks, life insurance policies, and lumber. Should Sony drop the price of its 19-inch color television sets by a substantial amount—say, $100—that change would affect sales of 19-inch models of RCA, Panasonic, and Zenith.

Products that can be readily substituted for each other are said to have high cross-elasticity of demand. This applies not only to brands within one product class but also to different product classes. For example, as the price of ice cream goes up (fueled by the rise of superpremium brands), consumers may switch to cakes for dessert, thereby increasing the sales of cake mixes. By contrast, completely dissimilar products—lettuce and soap, beer and books—have no cross-elasticity of demand.

COMPLEMENTARY PRODUCTS   Watches and watchbands, dress shirts and neckties, and cameras and film are all complementary products. Because such items are typically consumed together, price changes for one product affect sales of the other. Personal computers again offer a ready example. As their prices dropped dramatically in the early 1980s, sales of complementary software programs that increased the benefits of computers rose just as dramatically.

Complementary products may be offered by a single marketer or by competing firms. Consider cameras and film. Traditionally, Eastman Kodak has held its camera prices down to encourage sales of its film and processing services. Kodak's sales have been spurred as well by lower prices for cameras marketed by Canon and Olympus, among others.

For many products, the quantity demanded may be influenced as much by cross-elasticity as by relative elasticity, but even when substitute and complementary products are not involved, the laws of supply and demand and the concept of demand elasticity shape the economic environment in which prices are set. These external, independent factors affect all marketing organizations, and they should be monitored. To offset or overcome their influence, marketers have to manage factors *within* the organization. They respond to external economic forces by understanding and controlling two internal influences on pricing: costs and revenues.

■ *COSTS AND REVENUES IN PRICING DECISIONS* ■

We will return to the role of demand in price setting, but for the time being, we will assume that a certain quantity of the product is demanded (an assumption we do not recommend to marketers in the real world). This assumption will allow us to turn our attention to the costs associated with producing goods and services and to the revenues derived from sales.

Costs naturally play an important role in pricing decisions. At times they play the dominant role. To understand why costs are so influential in price setting, we need to examine just what costs are. At the most basic level, costs consist of either fixed or variable expenses, which together make up total costs.

In a plant such as this one, the wages paid to laborers are often a variable cost; they will go up or down based on the level of production. The salary of the manager of the plant is a fixed cost because it stays the same at all levels of production. (Copyright © Raoul Hackel/Stock, Boston.)

Fixed, Variable, and Total Costs

Certain production expenditures remain the same, whether ten units or millions are produced. Included in this cost category are items such as property taxes, executives' compensation, mortgages, leases, insurance, and amortization of capital equipment. Such **fixed costs** *FC* are recurring expenses that are not tied to the level of production. Taxes, some salaries, and insurance premiums must be paid no matter how many units roll off the assembly line. Fixed costs are designated by price setters as **total fixed costs** *TFC*—the sum of all recurring and constant expenditures—and as **average fixed costs** *AFC,* attained simply by dividing *TFC* by the number of units produced. An automobile assembly line, a movie theater, a hospital, and a newspaper all have fixed costs that can be divided by the units produced to determine average fixed costs.

A **variable cost** *VC* is an expense that does change directly with the number of units produced. The variable costs of a business may include hourly wages for labor, employee benefits, and costs of materials, fuel, and utilities. Variable costs all rise or fall depending on the production level—up to a point, and together they make up the **total variable costs** *TVC.* By dividing *TVC* by the quantity of a specified production level, planners obtain the **average variable cost** *AVC.* Thus, if a production run for 10,000 units has total variable costs of $9900, the *AVC* is 99 cents.

If we add the total fixed costs and total variable costs at a specified level of production, we can determine **total costs** *TC.* In other words,

$$TC = TFC + TVC$$

Since fixed costs do not change (by definition), any fluctuations in total costs can be attributed to changes in variable costs.

Figure 15-6 depicts the basic relationship among fixed, variable, and total costs. A stationary, horizontal line represents *TFC.* By contrast, *TVC* increases with the quantity produced; as a result, *TC* also increases. Let's see what happens to these cost relationships when we know actual units of production and can determine average costs.

Economies of Scale

Figure 15-7 shows average costs for specific levels of production. Because fixed costs are spread over an increasing number of units, *AFC* is a constantly declining curve (compare it with the horizontal *TFC* in Figure 15-6). And because of **economies of scale,** by which more efficient and multiple uses of resources result in decreased costs, *AVC* and thus *ATC* also decline (compare them to *TVC* and *TC* in Figure 15-6). At some point, however, **diseconomies of scale** set in; the effort to increase production results in inefficiencies, such as having to pay higher labor costs for overtime or having to pay more for scarce resources. Average and total costs will then begin to rise again. Thus, as we will see shortly, the highest point of profitability is not necessarily found at the highest levels of production or sales.

Revenues

Offsetting an organization's incurred costs are **revenues**—payments received for the sale of goods and services. Just as we must consider total and average costs in the pricing equation, so must we project total and average revenues. This is the same as estimating demand. Recall that **total revenue** *TR* is simply the price per unit multiplied by the quantity sold (*TR* = *P* × *Q*). Thus, **average revenue** *AR* is exactly the same as the unit price and is calculated by dividing total revenue by

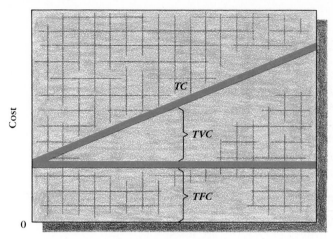

Figure 15-6 *Fixed, variable, and total cost:* TFC + TVC = TC. Consider *TFC* the vertical distance, at each level of production, from 0 to the *TFC* curve (which is flat, since fixed costs are by definition fixed at all levels of production). *TVC* is the distance from the *TFC* curve to the *TC* curve—variable costs increase with greater production. *TC = TFC + TVC* at every production level.

the quantity sold, which is equal to the unit price. The average revenue curve, then, is identical to the demand curve.

Profit is obviously total revenue minus total costs. Less obvious—and often elusive—is the point of *maximum* profit, where the difference between *TR* and *TC* is greatest. Marketers in search of that point need to understand the process of marginal analysis.

☐ *Marginal Analysis*

When something is "marginal," it is on the edge or border, verging on something else. Through **marginal analysis,** price setters consider the effects of one additional increment of costs or revenues on profit. Will the extra unit of cost or revenue

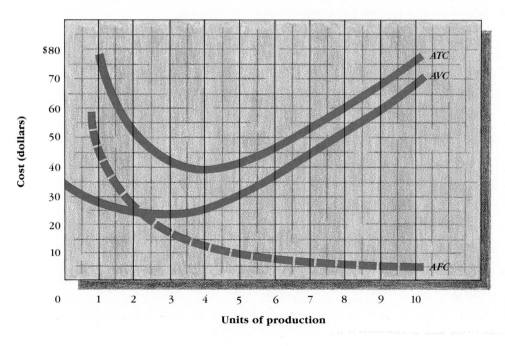

Figure 15-7 *Average costs:* AFC + AVC = ATC. Average fixed costs decline as units of production increase. The fixed costs are spread over larger quantities. Average variable costs tend to decline over some range of production as the firm is enjoying economies of scale. At some production level, the economies of larger scale disappear, and diseconomies begin to cause the average variable costs to rise, as represented by the *AVC* curve. Average total costs are the sum of average fixed and variable costs, as represented by the *ATC* curve.

increase profits? The goal of marginal analysis is to find the best price, the one at which additional revenues will still exceed additional costs, resulting in the greatest profit. The first step, then, is to determine how one extra increment of costs or revenues will affect profit.

Marginal cost MC is the additional cost incurred by producing and selling one more unit of a product. Since that one extra unit raises variable costs and thus total costs by the same amount, marginal cost may also be defined as the increase in total variable costs brought on by producing one additional unit. In a typical situation, MC will fall rapidly at low production levels as economies of scale are realized. Then MC will level off and rise sharply again as production quantities increase and diseconomies set in.

Marginal revenue MR is the additional revenue received from selling one more unit of a product; it constitutes the increase (or decrease) of revenue that results from producing and selling one additional unit. If a product's price were always the same, MR would always be the same, but changes in quantity are associated with changes in price, so MR does decline as lower prices bring on greater quantity. As prices decline, marginal revenue will fall below average revenue (remember that AR is analogous to the demand curve). Income is therefore lost not only from the lower-priced unit but also from the lower price on all previous units.

Profit reaches its most desirable point when marginal cost and marginal revenue are the same; that is, profit is maximized when $MC = MR$. As long as producing additional units leads to more revenue than costs, profit increases and the firm will continue to produce more. But whenever MC exceeds MR, profits decrease and can eventually disappear. Thus, maximum profit is found where $MR = MC$.

EXHIBIT 15-3	Marginal Analysis to Achieve Maximum Profit

As this marginal analysis shows, maximum profit is found where marginal revenue MR is equal to marginal cost MC. If the firm produces 4000 units and sells them at $120 per unit, it will reap a profit of $230,000.

Quantity	Price per Unit	Total Revenue TR	Total Cost TC	Profit (TR − TC)	Marginal Revenue MR	Marginal Cost MC	
0	$200	$ 0	$145,000	$ − 145,000	$ + 200	$ 34	
					+ 180	30	MR > MC
1,000	180	180,000	175,000	+ 5,000	+ 160	27	
					+ 140	25	
2,000	160	320,000	200,000	+ 120,000	+ 120	22	
					+ 100	20	
3,000	140	420,000	220,000	+ 200,000	+ 80	21	
					+ 60	30	
4,000	120	480,000	250,000	+ 230,000	+ 40	40	MR = MC
					+ 20	50	
5,000	100	500,000	300,000	+ 200,000	0	60	
					− 20	70	
6,000	80	480,000	370,000	+ 110,000	− 40	80	
					− 60	90	
7,000	60	420,000	460,000	− 40,000	− 80	100	
					− 100	110	MR < MC
8,000	40	320,000	570,000	− 250,000			

The two columns of numbers at the right in blue represent the *marginal* revenues and costs, the revenues and costs of the last unit produced and sold.

Implementing and Controlling Marketing Plans

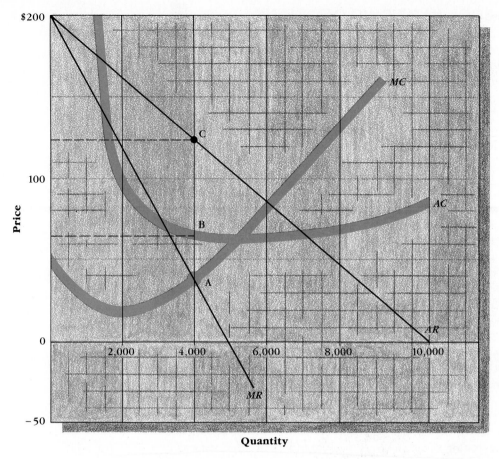

$200 |

100

Price

0

−50

Quantity

2,000 4,000 6,000 8,000 10,000

MC

C

AC

B

A

AR

MR

Figure 15-8 *The point of maximum profit:* MC = MR. This figure brings together both the cost and revenue analyses for the first time. When they are combined, it is possible to determine the price and quantity level where the firm's profits are maximum. That point is where marginal costs and marginal revenues are equal.

Exhibit 15-3 and Figure 15-8 clarify these concepts. Note in Exhibit 15-3 that the highest possible profit is $230,000, which occurs upon sale of 4000 units priced at $120 each. That is the point with the largest difference between *TR* ($480,000) and *TC* ($250,000); it coincides with the point where *MC* and *MR* are equal. If instead the firm produces and sells 5000 units at $100 each, *TR* rises (to $500,000), but so does *TC* (to $300,000). Profit is thus $200,000—a smaller gain than is realized at the point where *MC* equals *MR*. Profit diminishes further for every quantity and price below that point in the table. If 7000 units are produced and sold, profits are actually negative. No longer is the firm merely losing some potential profit by marketing an additional 3000 units; now it is losing $40,000—*real* dollars!

Figure 15-8 graphically presents marginal analysis. Profit is highest at point *A*, where *MC* = *MR* at a quantity of 4000 units. Moving up to point *B* (average costs) and still higher to point *C* (average revenues), we trace the right side of a box whose area represents total profits. Any movement up or down that line from point *A* will result in smaller profits.

Having examined marginal analysis as a means of maximizing profit, we must note that increased profit is not always an organization's goal. Nor are the major economic concepts we have examined always relevant to price setters. The following section explores how marketing managers adjust economic theory to fit a world where "other factors" do *not* remain the same.

ECONOMIC THEORY IN PRICING DECISIONS

"In economic theory, it is always assumed that the firm's underlying objective is to maximize profit. The reason is that this assumption ... enables us to evaluate the social performance of the firm as a resource allocator."[4] For most marketing organizations, realizing the greatest possible profit is certainly an important goal. But it is only one goal that an organization may have. Other objectives may conflict with the attempt to maximize profits, thereby bringing about compromises in profit goals. In fact, some firms have valid reasons for limiting profits:

To achieve long-term benefits: Short-term profit maximization may not be in the best long-term interests of a firm. At certain periods, some organizations choose to invest heavily in research and development for future products or to make capital investments that will make the firm more productive in the years ahead. Such investments may cut heavily into short-term profits, but they are part of a calculated strategy aimed at long-term profits and a healthy, long-lived organization.

To discourage competitors: Companies with strong market positions may accept lower profits (from lower prices) to discourage new competitors from entering the market. A pricing policy that is in line with the rest of the industry may thus be more advantageous than one that exploits current conditions to gain short-term profits.

To maintain goodwill: Managers may choose to limit profits for the sake of good, ongoing relations with customers. Some firms try to identify and adhere to prices that consumers perceive as "fair."

Two other factors complicate the use of economic theory in marketing decisions: the difficulty of estimating demand and the assumption that all factors will remain constant.

Estimating Demand

Marketing research techniques are improving, and better forecasting methods are available every year. Nevertheless, the economic models we have reviewed are predicated on absolute accuracy. Even improved forecasting techniques do not achieve the accuracy required by economic theory.

For some established products with a substantial history, marketers can estimate demand fairly accurately, but estimating demand at changing price levels is extremely difficult. In a relatively elastic market, managers can confidently predict that lowering a product's price will increase the quantity demanded, but estimating the magnitude of the change remains difficult.

It is certainly worthwhile for marketers to apply the kinds of calculations we have discussed in connection with costs, for these data approach the degree of accuracy required by economists. However, since all calculations of revenues are based only on *estimates* of demand, sales forecasts cannot be expected to be totally accurate.

Constancy of Factors

Economists often employ the Latin phrase "ceteris paribus"—literally, "other things being equal"—when setting forth economic models. In moving from theory to application, however, price setters find that in the real world, other things do not remain the same. Many factors change because of environmental influences beyond the control of marketers or even because marketers themselves keep changing their goals and tactics.

Estimates can be thrown off by the unexpected influence of some environmental factor. Competitors may change their prices unexpectedly or may change their advertising expenditures; members of the distribution channel may exert pressure for additional discounts. The assumption that such factors will be constant is rarely borne out by reality; consequently, pricing decisions cannot be based on that condition. In addition to changes arising from the environment, certain factors change because of what marketers do with other elements of the marketing mix—such as improving their products, expanding their distribution systems, or increasing their budgets for advertising and sales promotion.

☐ *Economic Theory Cannot Be Ignored*

Traditionally, many marketing experts believed that pricing was not an issue for the brand-conscious smoker. It was assumed that the addictive nature of cigarettes and the heavy promotion campaigns of manufacturers combined to create a product that consumers would buy at virtually any price. However, between late 1982 and late 1983, the average cost of a pack of cigarettes rose from 73 cents to 93 cents—in part because of increases in cigarette taxes. In response to rising prices, domestic shipments of cigarettes slumped in 1983. The message seems clear: When prices become too high, *any* product is subject to the laws of supply and demand. No product, not even cigarettes, can maintain perfect inelasticity over all price ranges.[5]

As we have seen thus far, marketers make determined efforts to differentiate their products or to build what we have called the "extended product." They may do so by distributing the product through appropriate retail outlets, by offering a special warranty, or by building an image through advertising—all for the purpose of freeing them from the problems of marketing a pure commodity (which leads to the economics of pure competition). However, despite all their attempts to bypass economic theory, marketers must not conclude that these economic principles are meaningless. Although such theories do not describe the way the real world of business always works, they nevertheless suggest general tendencies that *are* relevant in developing an ideal marketing mix for a product.

■ *SUMMARY* ■

1. To consumers, price is what they must exchange for a product's utilities. To marketers, price has two essential elements: the basic price for the core product and the premium price differential for the augmented product.
2. Price differs from other components of the marketing mix—product, distribution, and promotion—because it does not represent an out-of-pocket cost.
3. Market settings fall into three categories: perfect (or pure) monopoly; perfect (or pure) competition; and imperfect competition, which includes monopolistic competition and oligopoly.
4. In the large portion of the U.S. economy characterized by monopolistic competition, large numbers of firms market heterogeneous (dissimilar) products.
5. According to the law of downward-sloping demand, when the price of a good is raised (and all other variables hold constant), less of it is demanded.
6. According to the law of upward-sloping supply, when the price of a good is raised (and all other variables hold constant), more of it will be produced.
7. Elasticity of demand is relative and is usually product-specific. Three major environmental factors determine a product's relative demand elasticity: the availability of close substitutes, the ability or option of a consumer to defer purchasing, and the relative importance of a given product in the consumer's overall budget.

8. Cross-elasticity affects demand primarily in two situations: when close substitutes are available for the product and when products are complementary.

9. At the most basic level, costs consist of either fixed or variable expenses, which together make up total costs.

10. The point of maximum profit is that point where the difference between total revenues *TR* and total costs *TC* is greatest.

11. Some firms have valid reasons for limiting profits: to achieve long-term benefits, to discourage competitors, or to maintain goodwill.

12. These factors complicate the use of economic theory in marketing decisions: the difficulty of estimating demand and the assumption that all factors will remain constant.

☐ *Key Terms*

average fixed costs	fixed costs	premium price differential
average revenue	imperfect competition	price
average variable cost	inelastic demand	revenues
basic price	law of downward-sloping demand	supply
cross-elasticity of demand	law of upward-sloping supply	supply curve
demand	market price	supply schedule
demand curve	marginal analysis	total costs
demand schedule	marginal cost	total fixed costs
diseconomies of scale	marginal revenue	total revenue
economies of scale	monopolistic competition	total variable costs
elastic demand	oligopoly	unitary demand
elasticity of demand	perfect competition	variable cost
equilibrium price	perfect monopoly	

☐ *Chapter Review*

1. Compare the different perceptions of price held by consumers and marketers. As the buyer of a television set, what features and benefits do you think should be covered by the core price? By the premium price differential?

2. Identify and characterize the market settings for the following organizations: an automobile producer; a dairy farm; a marketer of laundry detergents; a cable television service. Which of these marketers has the greatest freedom in pricing? Why?

3. Why do economists define supply and demand as a relation rather than as the number of units produced or sold? Can equilibrium occur in a market setting of perfect monopoly? Why or why not?

4. What three factors determine the demand elasticity of a product? In which market setting are these factors most likely to arise? Why?

5. Describe two situations that give rise to cross-elasticity of demand. What is the common factor in these situations?

6. Explain why average revenue is exactly the same as unit price.

7. Why is it not always profitable to produce and sell additional units of a product? What action would you advise if marginal revenue falls below marginal cost? Why?

☐ *References*

1. Irwin Gross, "Insights from Pricing Research," in Earl L. Bailey, ed., *Pricing Practices and Strategies* (New York: Conference Board, 1983), pp. 34–39.

2. Paul A. Samuelson and William D. Nordhaus, *Economics,* 12th ed. (New York: McGraw-Hill, 1985), p. 61.

3. U.S. Bureau of the Census, *Statistical Abstract of the United States, 1986* (Washington, D.C.: U.S. Government Printing Office, 1986), p. 596.

4. Milton H. Spencer, *Contemporary Economics,* 5th ed. (New York: Worth, 1983), p. 519.

5. "Smokers Are Starting to Choke on Soaring Prices," *Business Week,* Dec. 19, 1983, pp. 62–63.

16

ESTABLISHING AND MANAGING PRICES

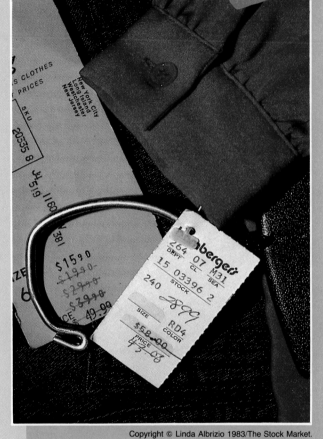

Copyright © Linda Albrizio 1983/The Stock Market.

SPOTLIGHT ON

□ Top-level managers and pricing decisions

□ Environmental forces influencing pricing decisions

□ Main basis for pricing objectives

□ Pricing strategies used by marketers in seeking a competitive advantage; pricing policies used to implement these strategies

□ Marketer-initiated price changes; why firms choose to lead or follow competitors in changing prices

The success of the South Korean Hyundai and the Yugoslavian Yugo in the U.S. new-car market has forced a radical shift in the thinking of this country's "Big Three" automakers. Traditionally, General Motors, Ford, and Chrysler have placed little emphasis on offering smaller, lower-priced cars, in good part because small cars are almost as expensive to design and produce as larger models and yield far less profit. Consequently, U.S. automakers targeted affluent buyers who could afford more expensive models with higher profit margins. Even despite the impressive sales of the Volkswagen Beetle in the late 1950s and 1960s—and the introduction of cheap, fuel-efficient Japanese cars in the mid-1970s—the Big Three continued to concentrate on large, expensive cars.

Now, however, Detroit automakers have finally accepted the fact that the U.S. auto market includes a sizable proportion of buyers who are price sensitive. One California consumer, considering replacing her 1978 Toyota with a Hyundai, admits: "They aren't exactly really pretty or anything, but I have to be practical." Inexpensive models appeal primarily to three types of buyers: a consumer who wants a new car but cannot afford the typical price tag ($12,000), a family looking for a second car, and a buyer unhappy with the average $5400 price of a used car and therefore willing to purchase a lower-priced new car.

According to one industry analyst, the growing availability and interest in inexpensive models suggests that by 1990, U.S. consumers may buy as

During the 1950s and 1960s, the success of the homely VW Beetle (lower left) was a warning that price was important to U.S. car buyers. The same message is being given by the more stylish, but quite inexpensive, Hyundai and Yugo in the 1980s. (Credits, lower left, clockwise: Claus Meyer/Black Star. Courtesy of Hyundai Motor America. Copyright © Rick Browne/Stock, Boston.)

Implementing and Controlling Marketing Plans

many as 1 million cars annually with price tags below $6500—up from the current figure of about 200,000 per year. As one example of this trend, sales of America, Chrysler's new subcompact economy car—whose base price was $5499—accounted for almost 30 percent of all new-car sales at a Detroit dealership in mid-1986. With such data in mind, the Big Three automakers are adopting more efficient, high-technology production methods; importing low-priced minicars; and revamping older subcompact models.

This pricing strategy has both a short-term and a long-term rationale. In the short run, U.S. automakers hope to make immediate sales of inexpensive models rather than lose out to Hyundai, Yugo, and other foreign competitors. In the long run, U.S. automakers fear that the customer lost now may be lost forever. By contrast, if consumers buy Chrysler's America and are satisified with their purchase, they may "trade up" to a high-priced Chrysler model in the future.

As we saw in Chapter 15, economic theory projects that demand for a product will increase as the price drops. Although the major U.S. automakers have long resisted this formulation, they have clearly begun to reshape their pricing strategies. In the auto industry, as in others, offering a bigger and better product is not a guaranteed path to success. Proper market segmentation by price—offering a range of models, including lower-priced cars that certain consumers prefer—seems likely to bring good results.

Source: Melinda Grenier Guiles, "Auto Makers Scrambling to Enter Growing Market for Cheap Wheels," *Wall Street Journal,* July 21, 1986, p. 15.

During the course of any day, the cost of living is tallied in many ways. Perhaps you pay a *fare* to ride a bus to work, where you earn a *salary* or *wages*. You may also pay your college *tuition* and write checks to pay your *rent* and MasterCard *bill* (which includes monthly interest *charges*). If you shop in a clothing store, you may pay *cash* (*dollars* and *cents*) for a sweater, and the clerk may receive a *commission* on the sale. If you happen to be criminal by nature, you may *bribe* a customs official to avoid paying an *import tax* on a camera brought into the country from Japan.

Even though these payments are quite different, they all represent **prices**. Prices are established—and changed—by marketers. Setting prices is a complex process that is central to providing exchange utility and to designing a successful marketing mix. In Chapter 15, we showed how the economic forces of supply and demand influence prices in various market settings. Essentially, marketers account for and respond to economic influences, but they exercise little control over them. Other environmental forces change constantly; price setters must monitor and respond to these forces as well.

By looking within the organization to examine the price-setting process, we can see that the numerous marketers who vie for sales in the prevalent U.S. settings of imperfect competition do, in fact, have some control over prices. Marketers are not merely pawns subject to the whims of supply and demand. Instead, a setting of imperfect competition allows marketers to *administer* prices—to manage them in a way that achieves the organization's goals.

Price administration is a deliberate effort by marketers to determine what price, sequence of prices, or price adjustments are appropriate for a specific product, given market conditions. This approach is common in today's business world. The seller sets the price and buyers either accept or reject it. A specific price is deemed successful (or unsuccessful) to the extent that it advances (or hinders) the organization's goals. In short, price is managed: The price setter calls the shots, judges their accuracy, and makes adjustments when goals are not achieved.

Chapter 16 begins by looking at who sets the prices that we pay for goods and services. The price-setting process is described within the context of several environmental influences. We then examine pricing objectives, strategies, tactics, and policies. Finally, we explore how marketers administer price changes to achieve their organizations' objectives.

WHO MAKES PRICING DECISIONS?

In 1964, researcher Jon Udell reported that a sample of business executives ranked price as only the sixth most important item in a list of marketing success factors.[1] Studies conducted since then, however, have revealed different attitudes. More recently, marketing managers have ranked price as the most imporant element of the marketing mix—even more important than product planning and management.[2] Because price is crucially important, top management usually is deeply involved in pricing decisions.

In marketing-oriented firms, pricing is an effective means of implementing and controlling strategy. When properly administered, it can help marketers make the most of the product's perceived value, to increase or create markets, and to optimize use of capital.[3] Such strategic use of pricing requires that decisions be made by top-level managers.

The price-setting process also requires the joint effort of both marketing and accounting managers. Accountants are best able to provide the detailed financial information on which pricing decisions rest and can project the results of price changes on the company's financial returns. Similarly, sales and marketing managers have the most accurate information about the effects of price on a product's acceptance by customers—what price the market will bear.[4] As we will see, one important issue in pricing is concern over the discounts made available to members of the distribution channels. It is marketing's role to maintain relations with these intermediaries. Finally, once prices have been set, marketing personnel monitor and adjust them in response to marketplace changes.

Because pricing decisions are so crucial to the financial success of the company, they are often made by fairly high-level executives. (Copyright © Jeff Smith.)

THE PRICE-SETTING PROCESS

In the best-managed organizations, price setters make decisions systematically by balancing the variables of cost and demand. Because it is a complex process, many firms establish formal procedures for price setting. Among the marketing scholars who have proposed influential models of the pricing process are Alfred Oxenfeldt and Kent Monroe.[5] Monroe's model is highly formal and provides guidance for the more advanced student of marketing. Figure 16-1 illustrates the simpler approach proposed by Oxenfeldt; we will use this model as the structure for the rest of Chapter 16.

We will begin, as price setters do, by looking outside the organization at environmental influences on costs and demand (the orange arrows). Once these influences are taken into account, price setters proceed in increasingly specific steps

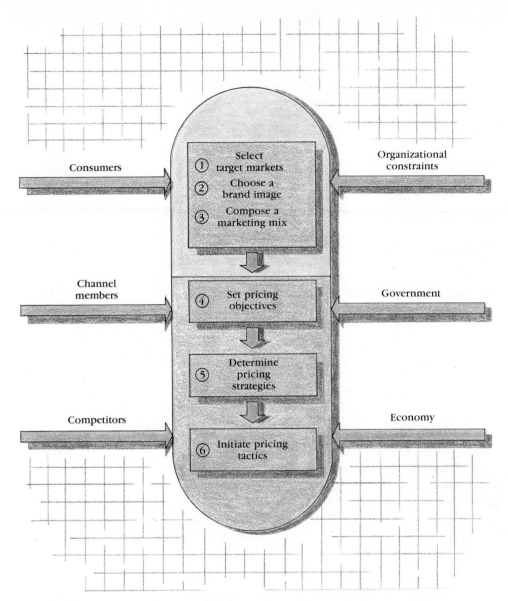

Figure 16-1 *The environment and structure of the pricing process.* The figure illustrates Alfred Oxenfeldt's model of the pricing process. Pricing decisions take place within the context of a number of environmental forces (orange outside arrows). The decision process itself is composed of two parts, the first (upper area in yellow) is a part of all marketing decision making, and the second (lower area in purple) is the pricing decision-making process itself.

(the green arrows) to arrive at pricing objectives, strategies, and tactics. Note that Oxenfeldt's first three steps—selecting target markets, developing a brand image appropriate for those target markets, and building a complete marketing mix consistent with that brand image—are all outside the pricing decision process per se. Consequently, these steps are treated not as items to be determined but rather as constraints or "givens" to price setting.

ENVIRONMENTAL INFLUENCES ON PRICING

Prices are not set in a vacuum. Marketers must consider many factors—both inside and outside the organization—before determining final prices for their products. All components of the marketing mix are subject to environmental influences, but pricing is perhaps most susceptible. Among the variables that come into play during the various stages of the pricing process are the organization itself, consumers and customers, channel members, competitors, government, and the economy.

☐ Organizational Constraints

A marketing organization's overall objectives have major impact on the prices it sets. If a product is in the maturity or decline stage of its life cycle, the goal may be to harvest what was sown by keeping prices at high levels, thereby reaping as much profit as possible. However, when introducing a new product, the marketer may establish a low initial price to enter the market strongly. This was the objective of Texas Instruments and Societe Bic in pricing their calculators and pens. By setting low initial prices for these new products (and lowering them further as experience and economies of scale accrued), both companies captured relatively large market shares and forced competitors to follow their market leads. Other firms may use high initial prices to recover their investment or to realize a specific (target) return on investment. Still other marketers will set middle-level prices in an effort to maintain their existing market share. Whatever a company's objective, it will influence pricing decisions and is likely to be reflected in final prices.

The organization's costs of manufacturing and marketing can significantly influence pricing decisions. Costs tend to limit a firm's pricing options—perhaps forcing an increase in price or permitting only a limited price cut. A forced price increase may actually work against the company's objectives, yet decision makers sometimes have to raise prices simply to maintain profitability.

The other components of the marketing mix created by the organization—product, distribution, and promotion—all affect pricing. The nature of the product, for instance, may make high prices not only possible but desirable. This is certainly the case in marketing custom-made furniture and tailored clothing. Similarly, the image of the organization can influence pricing. Porsche and Rolls-Royce have images of high status and quality; pricing of their products supports this overall image.

Firms that market their products primarily to upper-income consumers with an image of elegance will prefer selling to high-priced retail outlets such as Saks or Bonwits. By contrast, marketers targeting a broad segment of "average consumers" who prefer "popular" brands may sell directly to K mart stores or use wholesalers who service a variety of retail outlets. Finally, promotion costs influence the price-setting process. It is especially costly to advertise and support a new product, but even well-established brands need ongoing expenditures to maintain their market share.

☐ Consumers

Chapters 3 and 4 examined how consumers and organizational buyers make purchasing decisions. Price setters take careful account of the factors and patterns of buying behavior. They focus particularly on the characteristics of target markets, the product's position, and the perceptions of price and quality held by consumers.

TARGET MARKETS   Although organizational buyers tend to be more rational than consumers in their purchasing decisions, the importance of price to organi-

For those firms that have targeted the elderly, price is an especially important element of the marketing mix. Retired people on fixed incomes watch their spending very carefully—and they have time to check competitors' prices. (Copyright © Tom McHugh/Photo Researchers, Inc.)

zations varies according to the situation. Some buyers are simply looking for a bargain. Others are more influenced by a product's installation, servicing, and replacement costs than by the initial price. It often makes good sense to pay considerably more for a product that includes complete servicing provisions than to buy a cheaper product that does not. Marketers of industrial products investigate how important price is to their target markets.

Of course, the importance of price to consumers varies as well. Members of some market segments base their buying decisions primarily on price. Elderly persons living on fixed incomes, for example, may seek out generic drugs and inexpensive eyeglasses, whereas members of other market segments may prefer brand-name drugs and designer eyeglass frames with polarized lenses. In market segments that view products as undifferentiated commodities, price often plays the major role in buying decisions. By contrast, buyers of luxury cars and fur coats are influenced less by price than by a product's status, image, and styling.

THE PRODUCT'S POSITION A product's **position** refers both to its category and to its relative standing within that category. For example, the owner of a tree nursery may view a pickup truck as necessary equipment, whereas a young couple may see the same truck as a recreational vehicle. Moreover, within these categories, one buyer's sporty model may be seen as practical and durable by another buyer.

BOX 16-1   COMPETITION IN MARKETING: Pricing Ice Cream

There are many ways to control the competitive position of a product. In one well-known example, 7-Up, facing the formidable task of competing against Coca-Cola and Pepsi-Cola, attempted to use a new promotional campaign to reposition its product as an "uncola." Use of promotional tactics is a common means of repositioning a product, and marketers also use pricing and product features to shape a competitive positioning strategy.

In Chapter 15, we discussed the rise of "super-premium" ice cream brands such as Häagen-Dazs and Frusen Glädjé. If pure economic theory were to hold true, there would be no market for such costly brands. Yet, as the accompanying figure shows, the entire

arena of ice cream competition can be appropriately subdivided into various brackets based on product quality and consumer price. An expensive, high-quality brand like Häagen-Dazs does not really compete against lower-quality, less expensive brands such as Foremost or Borden. Instead, through a positioning strategy in which price and quality are central elements, Häagen-Dazs has narrowed its field of competitors. As the figure reveals, its true competitors are Schrafft's and Howard Johnson's (and we could probably add Frusen Glädjé)—brands which, like Häagen-Dazs, rate high both in product quality and in price per serving. ▪

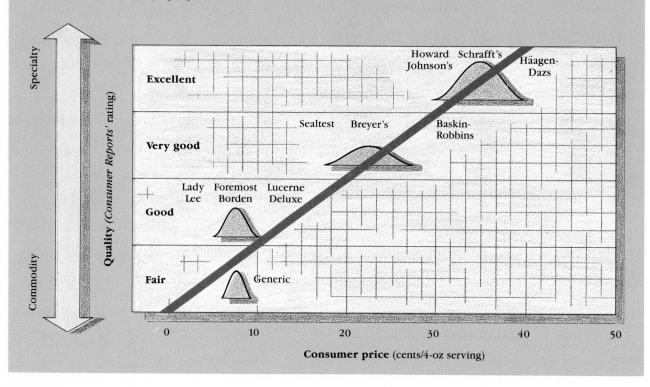

Such perceptions often reflect tradition or the history of a specific brand; they may also be tied to the effectiveness of promotional campaigns.

Consumers' perceptions of products allow for different pricing levels (see Box 16-1). Miller Brewing Company commands a premium price for Lowenbräu, a slightly lower tab for Miller High Life, and the lowest ("popular") price for Meister Brau. Brewing methods for the three brands differ and ingredients vary, but the cost of ingredients is virtually the same. Can we assume, then, that Lowenbräu is the most profitable brand? Not when we realize that Miller High Life sells in far greater quantities than Lowenbräu and that the latter carries higher packaging costs (for its foil-wrapped cap and other niceties).

To a large extent, consumer perceptions allow firms to charge a premium price for benefits that augment the core product (such as image, servicing, or warranties). Very often, such perceptions are based on expectations of quality.

PRICE AND QUALITY PERCEPTIONS   Would you buy a package of aspirin that costs only 30 cents? Would you be happy to find this bargain, or would you suspect that the product is inferior to more expensive brands? In fact, manufacturers could probably produce and price aspirin for the costs of ingredients and packaging—totaling perhaps 25 cents. But the marketers of Bayer and Excedrin know that consumers assign meaning to price; as a result, they price their products within the range that people expect to pay.

Price tells consumers what value marketers assign to the product, and consumers often equate price with quality. Researchers have found that when consumers lack other cues or information about quality—such as when a brand is unknown—they look to price as the basis for evaluation.[6] The extent to which higher prices are interpreted by consumers to mean higher quality differs for different products, but is a general tendency that marketers must consider.[7] Marketers must price products within the range that consumers consider reasonable. Several studies report that shoppers approach a purchase with both an upper and a lower price limit in mind. They are unwilling to pay more than their upper limit and are suspicious of products (such as the 30-cent aspirin) that cost less than their lower limit.[8]

☐ Channel Members

A third major influence on pricing comes from members of the distribution channel: the intermediaries who move products from manufacturers to consumers. Marketers whose pricing policies fit the needs and objectives of channel members can "grease the wheels" of distribution. Later in this chapter, we will look at a number of discounts commonly offered to wholesalers and retailers. Discounts are vital to intermediaries' profits; pricing decisions often reflect this concern.

Moreover, since members of a complex channel are likely to have different objectives, price setters must understand how distributors view price and how they will establish their own prices to consumers. Unless legal agreements are involved, manufacturers cannot dictate the final prices that intermediaries charge. But they can *suggest* retail prices that allow channel members a fair markup without adversely affecting consumers' perceptions. The trick is to deliver the product to the target market while maintaining a price that correctly represents the product.

☐ Competitors

Most products are exchanged in a relatively competitive market setting; thus, price setters keep a close watch on competitors' prices. In markets where one company commands a dominant share, that firm is usually the leader. When it raises or lowers prices, other companies follow suit. But in markets in which no single firm dominates, marketers generally monitor and react to the prices of all major competitors.

Price is the most readily changed component of the marketing mix. A company cannot change its brand images and product quality overnight; nor can it abruptly change its distribution channels or even its promotional efforts. It *can* adjust prices quickly—especially when pricing is computerized. Price is therefore a handy competitive weapon. Like a sword, however, it can cut both ways: Overreacting to

Consumer expectations about prices often set a range which will be considered reasonable. A moccasin-style slip-on priced at $29.90 is likely to be perceived as within reason. The $69.90 price on the dress shoe might be within the range, but would be too high for the moccasin. (Copyright © John Coletti/Stock, Boston.)

When price becomes the central issue in competitive battles, such "price wars" may drive down the price of the product so low that no competitor is able to make a profit. (Copyright © Donald Dietz/ Stock, Boston.)

competitors' prices is a danger. In many industries, including supermarkets and gasoline, prolonged price wars have resulted from intense competition. When these battles have become especially severe, deep price cuts have wiped out profits and forced some competitors out of business. Such overreaction to competitors' prices is not good for anyone.

☐ *The Government*

Chapter 2 discussed important government legislation affecting marketing. Three of the laws identified apply especially to price setting. The Robinson-Patman Act applies generally to restraint of competition and specifically to pricing practices that lessen competition. Basically, it forbids **price discrimination,** making it illegal to sell the same product to different customers for different prices. The Sherman Act and the Clayton Act make it illegal for competitors to enter into agreements that restrain or monopolize trade. This antitrust legislation outlaws **price fixing,** whereby competitors, through formal contracts or collusive actions, agree on prices.

PRICE DISCRIMINATION   The Robinson-Patman Act was passed in 1936 to protect small, independent retailers from being charged more for products than large retail chains paid. Sellers can, however, defend themselves against discrimination charges by showing that their costs of selling vary from customer to customer. Cost savings can then be passed along to individual buyers in the form of lower prices. The Robinson-Patman Act therefore permits pricing inconsistencies in the following cases:

1. If the firm can demonstrate that it saves money by selling large quantities to certain customers, it can offer these buyers discounts equal to the amount saved.
2. Long-term sales agreements with customers also reduce costs; again, discounts may be granted equal to the amount saved.
3. In cases where competitors' prices in a particular market must be met, it is legal to lower prices in such a market while charging regular prices in other markets.

Marketers are well aware of the provisions of the Robinson-Patman Act; any pricing variances or discounts offered must comply with the dictates of this law.

PRICE FIXING   The Sherman Act (1890) and the Clayton Act (1914) bar competitors from agreeing on prices. Such obvious **horizontal price fixing** conjures up images of a smoke-filled room in which business tycoons gather to sip aged bourbon and make unethical deals. In truth, an informal but legal type of **horizontal price fixing** does, at times, occur.

Vertical price fixing—whereby manufacturers and wholesalers set prices charged by retailers—was legal until 1976 when the Consumer Goods Pricing Act took place. Until then, producers were free to control the retail prices of their products if they so desired. This practice, known as **fair trade,** was criticized by retailers and some consumer groups for keeping retail prices artificially high. Today, manufacturers and wholesalers cannot force retailers to accept their suggested prices.[9] They can only control retailers' prices by printing prices on products, by carefully screening their retailers, and by persuading retailers.

UNFAIR PRICING POLICIES   In addition to price discrimination and price fixing, certain other pricing policies are illegal under state and federal laws. These include bait-and-switch promotion, predatory pricing, and loss-leader pricing.

Have you ever been lured to a store by advertisements promising an unusually low price for a specific product—only to learn that the item is out of stock or is of very poor quality? Perhaps a sales clerk then tried to shift your interest to a more expensive product. If so, you were deceived by an illegal **bait-and-switch promotion.** In general, local ordinances and agencies require that sellers have a "reasonable" amount of the advertised product on hand; if they make no real effort to do so, they may be forced to sell the more expensive product for the advertised "special price."

A number of states have enacted **unfair-sales acts** (also known as "minimum price" laws) which prohibit retailers from selling products at less than cost plus a percentage for profit and overhead. Unfair-sales acts aim to prevent predatory pricing and loss-leader sales. Under **predatory pricing,** large firms set extremely low prices in an effort to undercut small competitors and drive them out of business. Such pricing is illegal when the intent is to drive out competition and then raise prices once competitors have been reduced or eliminated. Because predatory pricing injures competition, it is also forbidden at the federal level by the Sherman and Clayton Acts. Unfair-sales acts are also intended to discourage the sale of products below cost as **loss leaders**—products advertised below the retailer's cost to increase customer traffic. These laws are seldom enforced, since consumers benefit from the low prices of loss leaders.

As one response to the abuses associated with unfair pricing, many states require grocery retailers to establish **unit pricing,** whereby each product's price is expressed per standard measure (ounce, pound, gram, liter, pint, and so on). This allows consumers to compare the prices of competing brands, which are often packaged in different sizes. Thus, if a 12-ounce package of laundry detergent sells for $1.99 and a competing 18-ounce package costs $2.49, shoppers must be told that the respective prices per ounce are 16.6 cents and 13.8 cents. All other factors being equal—and they may not be—the larger package is the better buy.

Unit prices are typically posted on the shelf, directly in front of each brand

Unit pricing is an attempt to provide consumers with meaningful information about price. Note that the can has 10.50 ounces of soup, and costs 49 cents. That gives a unit price of 74.7 cents per pound. That price can be compared on a cost-per-pound basis with other soups of different sizes and prices. (Copyright © Laura Dwight/Peter Arnold, Inc.)

and size, but sometimes they are quoted on a product's regular price label. Not all shoppers use unit pricing; few take it into account for every purchase. Unit pricing is valuable for price setters because it allows price-conscious shoppers to quickly compare competing brands.[10]

The Economy

One key influence on pricing decisions is the health of the economy. In prosperous times, when productivity and the gross national product are high, and inflation, interest rates, and unemployment are low, price decisions are simpler. Sales are easier to forecast and stability dominates marketplaces. However, in troubled economic times, many firms find it impossible to hold their normal prices and yet remain in business. Of the various influences on the pricing process, the state of the economy is the hardest for marketers to predict, control, and deal with successfully. Monitoring the general economic environment occupies a large part of marketing managers' time and has a major impact on pricing decisions.

In summary, environmental influences on the pricing process come from within the organization; from consumers and customers; and from channel members, competitors, government, and the economy. Assuming that the marketing organization has mechanisms in place to monitor the environment—and thus has a context for pricing decisions—we can now turn to the actual decision-making processes. As Figure 16-1 illustrates, the environment establishes the setting in which decisions are made about pricing objectives, strategies, and tactics (steps 4, 5, and 6 in the figure).

PRICING OBJECTIVES

As we explained in Chapters 8 and 9, an organization's objectives for any particular element of a marketing program should flow from at least two prior levels of planning. First, overall corporate objectives must be considered. Even as broad a goal as being the industry leader will affect pricing objectives. Second, the organization's specific marketing objectives are based on those corporate objectives. Finally, the third level of planning involves setting objectives for one element of the marketing mix, such as pricing. Pricing objectives should be consistent with and should advance corporate and marketing objectives. If a firm simply wishes to maintain its market share and preserve the status quo, that goal will help to determine its pricing objectives. Probably the firm will attempt to hold prices steady or keep them in line with competitors' prices.

In practice, of course, most organizations have multiple objectives, which makes analyzing each objective separately somewhat artificial. Nevertheless, pricing objectives can be classified according to profitability or financial goals, sales volume, and competitive factors.

Profitability Objectives

As is true of most marketing objectives, pricing objectives need to be measured precisely. Performance can then be compared with objectives to assess results. **Profitability objectives** allow such assessment; they are expressed in specific dollars or as a percentage of sales. Thus, a firm may seek average profits of $1.1 million for 5 years, or an 11 percent increase in total revenues before taxes. Profitability objectives usually reflect varied financial goals for a number of product lines or strategic business units.

PROFIT MAXIMIZATION   **Profit maximization** through price setting discussed in Chapter 15—remember that profit is highest at the point where marginal costs equal marginal revenues ($MC = MR$)—is rarely found in the real world. In practice, maximum profits may be realized in different ways. In markets where demand is elastic, low prices result in greater sales and higher profits. But when demand is inelastic, even though higher prices lead to slightly decreased unit sales, total revenues increase. Thus, the profit margins of some firms may be predicated on low prices, high turnover, and high sales volume. A&P and K mart, for example, expect low profit margins because of their low prices; they also expect to maximize cumulative profits because of their high product turnover. In contrast, Tiffany's and Neiman-Marcus aim to maximize their profits through a strategy of high prices and high profit margins, which will offset relatively low sales and turnover.

Typically, profitability objectives focus on current, rather than long-term, performance. Although such goals yield the greatest immediate cash flow, they may influence the firm to neglect such long-range goals as improved market share, competitive dominance, and necessary capital investment.

TARGET RETURN ON INVESTMENT   A common pricing objective is some form of **target return on investment,** that is, regaining a specified percentage of investment as income. **Return on investment** (ROI) is expressed as the ratio of profits to investments. For manufacturers, investments include capital, machinery, buildings, and land—as well as inventory. For wholesalers and retailers, inventory constitutes the bulk of investments; consequently, an ROI objective is a specific percentage of the revenues above the cost of products purchased for resale. Of course, this calculation must be based on a forecast of demand, which is always open to change. Manufacturers base their ROI targets on capital investments, inventory, and demand. In each case, a systematic and reliable accounting system is necessary.

Typically, target ROI objectives are set by organizations that hold a dominant position in their markets. General Motors, for example, has traditionally targeted a 20 percent ROI (after taxes), whereas International Harvester has sought a 10 percent return. Competitors not dominant in their markets can also set target ROI objectives; however, they are less able to use these objectives, since the dominant firm sets the pricing lead.

A variation on ROI objectives is **target return on sales,** whereby the firm sets a profit goal for each unit sold. Thus, if a manufacturer sells a product to intermediaries for $1 per unit, the target profit (return on sales) may be set at 14 cents per unit. For fast-food chains such as Burger King and Wendy's that deal in high sales volume, the return on sales per unit is quite low. By contrast, for expensive restaurants like Ernie's in San Francisco or Windows on the World in New York, the return on sales per unit is high. Ernie's seeks profits based on high margins but low turnover; Burger King's objectives are based on low margins but high turnover.

☐ *Volume-Based Objectives*

Some organizations set pricing objectives in terms of sales volume. A common goal is sales growth, in which case the firm sets prices that will increase demand. Other firms may seek sales maintenance, knowing that growth does not ensure higher profits and that the organization may not have the resources needed to pursue sales growth. Still other firms may only seek survival—at least for a time. For example, Chrysler Corporation in the late 1970s was faced with dwindling sales and spiraling costs, Chrysler offered substantial rebates (promotional discounts) to buyers to move costly inventory and improve cash flow. With the federal government stepping in to guarantee some of the automaker's loans, Chrysler survived.

THE CORPORATE PORTFOLIO   An organization's pricing objectives may follow the dictates of its corporate portfolio and advance broad strategies (see Chapter 8). For example, low prices may be set for certain product lines or strategic business units to achieve faster sales growth than the market in general is experiencing. Alternatively, a strategy of slower growth may dictate higher prices and profit margins than are common in the industry. Perhaps a harvesting strategy will be set for a mature product or for a division that the company plans to close down; the sales objective will then be based on low investment and maximum cash flow rather than on growth. In all these cases, prices are influenced more by corporate strategy than by sales objectives.

MARKET SHARE   Washington-based USAir is the only carrier offering nonstop service on some of its main routes. Where this is true, the company keeps its prices high. However, on other routes, such as between Buffalo and Newark, the airline matches the fares of low-cost carriers like Continental and New York Air. In other words, USAir prices for lower profits when this strategy is necessary to maintain market share.[11]

As reported in Chapter 8, market share and profitability are correlated. If capturing a high market share is a key objective of the overall marketing program, pricing objectives will reflect this goal. In general, companies achieve a high market share by holding down prices to increase sales. Such a strategy, often practiced successfully by Texas Instruments over the years, is based on a long-term view of profitability. The company is willing to accept lower initial profits in exchange for the profits produced over time by increased volume and high market share. By contrast, Hewlett-Packard has achieved a strong position in selected markets by setting high prices for its calculators and small computers. Through pricing, Texas Instruments has sought a high share in mass markets, whereas Hewlett-Packard has aimed for a high share in smaller, specialty markets.

☐ *Competitive Objectives*

In certain situations, firms base their marketing and pricing objectives on competitive strategies, most often when marketers aim to achieve price stability and engage in nonprice competition or when they want to take advantage of market turbulence by pricing aggressively.

PRICE STABILITY AND NONPRICE COMPETITION   When marketing a mature product whose sales growth has peaked, a company's objective may be price stability. In general, the firm marketing such a product is the market leader; competitors tend to follow the leader's pricing. This is especially true in oligopolies dominated by one or a few firms—examples include U.S. Steel, General Motors, and R. J. Reynolds (cigarettes). In effect, market leaders can enforce price stability: Competitors stay in line because the leader's objective benefits everyone. Aggressive pricing would lower profit margins for all competitors, and no one wants that.

In many cases, price stability leads to **nonprice competition** in which a firm's strategy is advanced by other components of the marketing mix: the product itself, the distribution system, or the promotional campaign. Promotion is typically the main tool of nonprice competition. Although the goal is to maintain profitability through stable prices, the effort to increase sales through expensive promotion may erode that profitability. Still, the risks would be even greater if pricing were used to compete; a price war might destroy everyone's profits.

AGGRESSIVE PRICING AND TURBULENCE   In some markets, a firm may choose to price aggressively to take advantage of turbulence: when products are in early stages of the life cycle, when markets are still growing, and when there are opportunities to establish or gain a large market share. Never is competition so keen.

In the first half of the 1980s, the market for personal computers was quite turbulent. Market leaders Apple, Tandy, and IBM offered increasingly sophisticated models at lower and lower prices. They aggressively sought not only to strengthen their market shares but also to outsell the many new competitors. In 1981 alone, some 50 small companies challenged the leaders and held 36 percent of the market. By the end of 1983, three times as many firms were fighting for a slice of the market but held only a 19 percent share. The market leaders were able to survive the shake-out battle among competitors; their positions of strength had been solidified earlier through aggressive pricing strategies. In the coming years, the market for personal computers is likely to enter a phase of stability in which fewer firms will jockey for position and they will primarily engage in nonprice competition.

PRICING STRATEGIES

We have seen that pricing objectives may be based on profit, volume, or competitive factors. In practice, most companies have multiple pricing objectives. A firm may seek to realize a 12 percent target return on investment (profit), to gain 2 percentage points in market share (volume), and to achieve dominance in a selected market through aggressive pricing (competition). To reach such goals, marketers establish pricing strategies—broad plans that flow directly from the pricing objectives. In turn, these strategies give rise to specific pricing tactics and policies. For now, though, our focus is on step 5 of Figure 16-1. We will consider the pricing strategies used for introducing new products, for obtaining a competitive advantage, and for capitalizing on the experience curve.

New-Product Pricing Strategies

Pricing strategies for new products generally aim either to "skim" or to "penetrate" the market. A skimming strategy usually results in higher prices, whereas a penetration strategy tends to establish lower prices.[12] Each of these strategies may be desirable under different circumstances.

SKIMMING   Innovative products and those that represent measurable improvements in fulfilling needs are often introduced by a skimming strategy. **Skimming is characterized by high initial prices and promotional expenditures; the intent is to "skim the cream" from the market before anyone else can serve it.** The following situations often give rise to skimming:

1. There are no competitors or they are rather weak; buyers are therefore willing to pay a premium price for a unique product.
2. Market segments differ in their sensitivity to price (elasticity of demand); initial high prices skim the segments that are relatively insensitive to price.

3. Pricing objectives are aimed at rapid return on investment—high short-term profits that can finance expansion into larger, perhaps more price-sensitive, markets.
4. The innovator holds a monopoly or even patent protection and can gain a competitive advantage while such protection is in effect.
5. The organization sees an opportunity—through skimming—to rapidly recover the large investment it has made on a new product.

Skimming is not always appropriate in these situations, and it does have drawbacks. A skimming strategy will not entice buyers *into* the market and it does not encourage rapid adoption or diffusion of the product. Moreover, skimming may attract competitors who recognize that the product promises high profit margins.

PENETRATION   In following a strategy of **penetration,** marketers set low initial prices to capture mass markets. This approach is often desirable in the following situations:

1. No elite market segment of buyers will pay a premium price for the newest or best product.
2. The product will attract large market segments in which buyers are sensitive to price.
3. Significant economies of scale can be realized in production and distribution.
4. It is advantageous to discourage competitors from entering the market; low prices and low profit margins are unlikely to attract new producers.

A penetration strategy encourages both rapid adoption and diffusion of new products. An innovative firm may thus be able to capture large market segments before its competitors can respond. One disadvantage of penetration, however, is that low prices and low profit margins must be offset by extremely high sales. It may be some time before enough profits accrue to recover the costs of product development, production, distribution, and promotion.

To avoid the disadvantages of skimming and penetration, some firms employ both alternatives. They pursue a skimming strategy after a product is first introduced—typically, until competitors enter the market. Then they switch to a penetration strategy by lowering prices to build market share and volume. As one example, pharmaceutical companies often introduce prescription drugs with high prices and keep them high until shortly before the patent period runs out. At that point, since competitors enter the market and offer lower prices, the original marketer will cut its prices to remain competitive and maintain a high market share.

☐ *Pricing in Relation to Competitors*

As we noted earlier, pricing objectives may be based on competition, as when the goal is to achieve price stability or to take advantage of market turbulence. The decision is seldom simple. A number of key issues must be resolved in competitive pricing strategies:

1. Are there different market segments with different pricing expectations and different competitors?
2. How do consumers perceive the product's quality in relation to other products? Do they view it as "good" (low price), "better" (medium price), or "best" (high price)?

Packaged goods marketers generally have three options in pricing a new product: (1) sell it as a generic or private brand at the lowest possible price; (2) raise the price slightly, using a moderate amount of promotion that still features low price as the primary benefit; or (3) establish a higher price by finding a meaningful product benefit and promoting it heavily. The largest profit per unit is secured by this last option.

Helene Curtis Corporation has utilized all three pricing strategies. It entered the hair care field in 1927 by supplying its private label products to beauty salons. Then, in the 1940s, it took the low-price, moderate-promotion approach by introducing its successful line of Suave products. Finally, in 1982, Helene Curtis pursued the high-price, intensive-promotion approach with Finesse conditioners and shampoos. Its efforts to attain growth objectives were successful: Finesse products captured 5 percent of sales in both markets within a year.

The perceived benefit of Finesse is that its products are formulated to respond to the changing amount of dirt in a person's hair. This benefit inspired the company's advertising agency, Backer & Spielvogel, to develop a single theme that fits both the shampoo and conditioner: "Sometimes you need a little Finesse, sometimes you need a lot."

Establishing correct prices for Finese products was the second critical element in their success. Both the shampoos and conditioners were priced above the

(*Ken Karp.*)

company's Suave line but still below many best-selling brands. For example, Finesse shampoo's price per ounce was lower than Prell and Head & Shoulders but higher than Flex and Suave. By positioning Finesse near the higher end of the market while promoting its distinctive benefit, Helene Curtis spurred the product's growth at the expense of its competitors.

Source: "Curtis: In Search of Big Profts," *The New York Times,* Apr. 1, 1983, p. D4.

---

3. Is there already a market leader with the ability to force a certain price level? Or does the product have few or no competitors?

Pricing in relation to competitors is an important strategy for almost all marketing organizations. To use an example from the auto industry, Chevrolet and Honda both set relatively low prices and offer periodic rebate programs. By contrast, Cadillac and Mercedes-Benz carry high price tags and offer no discounts. The pricing strategies of these automakers make it clear just who their competitors are. Box 16-2 examines how the Helene Curtis Corporation decided to position Finesse conditioners and shampoos against competitors and how it used pricing to reach its growth objectives.

☐ *Pricing and the Experience Curve*

Chapter 8 discussed the importance of the experience curve in the relationship between costs and price—particularly for new products. Basically, the earliest producer in a market can learn through experience to lower production costs quickly. Then, having attained lower costs, that producer can dominate the market because

For years, Kodak held the price of film at a level so high that less efficient competitors could profit under their umbrella. On the other hand, as Texas Instruments proceeded along the experience curve, they dropped their prices as their costs dropped. (Ken Karp.)

it can afford to lower prices and still make a profit, which discourages competitors. Thus, **experience-curve pricing** accounts for the costs of competing firms based on their experience in producing goods.

RIDING THE EXPERIENCE CURVE   For a time after introduction of a product, a manufacturer's costs usually are higher than the product's price. When costs fall sufficiently that profits are adequate, the market leader cuts prices and continues to do so as costs fall. By the time competitors, who must start high on the cost curve, can enter the market, the leader has "ridden the experience curve" and pushed prices down to a point where the market is not so attractive to competitors.

Pricing on the experience curve is really a form of penetration pricing based on cumulative experience and cost reduction. Although Texas Instruments is the firm most often cited for practicing this strategy, other marketers, particularly in the electronics and computer industries, use experience-curve pricing to penetrate new markets.

UMBRELLA PRICING   Another pricing strategy based on the experience curve is **umbrella pricing;** in this case, the firm also cuts prices but not as rapidly as costs fall. Prices are held relatively high for some time before they are reduced. This strategy holds an "umbrella" over the industry, keeping prices high enough that competitors are attracted—although this is not the purpose, of course. Ideally, by the time that such new competitors have made a dent in the market, your firm has already amassed substantial profits and a strong market share.

IBM and Eastman Kodak have both used umbrella pricing. They so effectively dominated the markets for some of their products that they did not fear the inroads of competitors. They enjoyed large profit margins and felt assured of holding their dominant market shares. Until recently, Xerox also practiced umbrella pricing for its photocopying machines, but when Japanese copiers came on the market with lower prices, Xerox was forced to lower its prices.

We come at last to the final step of our pricing model (see Figure 16-1). Marketers put the price tag on the product—and implement their objectives and strategies—by using pricing tactics. In this section, we will evaluate three methods of price determination and a variety of discount structures. We will also examine the impact of geography on pricing.

☐ *Techniques for Determining Price*

Three basic techniques are used to determine which price best achieves the organization's objectives and strategies: the cost-plus approach, breakeven analysis, and cost-volume-profit analysis. Although these analytical methods often employ complex financial data, we will deal with them in their basic forms. Appendix A provides additional detail concerning these methods.

COST-PLUS APPROACH   The simplest and most common method of determining price is the cost-plus approach. **Cost-plus pricing** assumes a basic cost per unit and then adds a markup to provide a margin that covers overhead costs and returns a profit. For a simple example, assume that a department store purchases Variblo hair dryers from the manufacturer at $20 each. Taking a markup of $12.95 per unit, the store prices the hair dryers at $32.95. (The $12.95 figure reflects this retailer's overhead costs of $9.35 per unit; per-unit profit is $3.60.) The markup percentage is calculated as follows:

$$\text{Markup on cost} = \frac{\text{amount added to cost}}{\text{cost}}$$

$$= \frac{\$12.95}{\$20.00}$$

$$= 64.75\%$$

Markups may also be calculated as a percentage of the selling price using the same example:

$$\text{Markup on price} = \frac{\text{amount added to price}}{\text{retail price}}$$

$$= \frac{\$12.95}{\$32.95}$$

$$= 39.3\%$$

Obviously, when referring to a markup percentage, it is essential to state whether the calculation is based on cost or on selling price (in this example, the difference is more than 25 percent).

Cost-plus pricing is most commonly used by wholesalers and retailers. However, manufacturers also use this approach when their pricing objective is simply to maintain margins on specific product lines. Both manufacturers and wholesalers often suggest standard markups, which are calculated to allow a reasonable profit for retailers. Faced with an entire store of products to price, retailers are often inclined to welcome the convenience of standard markups.

Markups vary widely according to the product in question and its turnover rate. Luxury products—fur coats, perfume, and jewelry—typically carry markups as high as 75 to 100 percent of cost. Staples like canned foods, however, may have markups of only a few percentage points. Textbooks—including this one—carry a standard industry markup of 20 percent.

BREAKEVEN ANALYSIS   Price setters use **breakeven analysis** to calculate what quantity of product the firm needs to sell just to cover all costs, that is, the firm suffers no loss but makes no profit; it "breaks even."

Breakeven analysis requires price setters to know their fixed and variable costs. As we stated in Chapter 15, **fixed costs** include such expenditures as managers' salaries, building maintenance, insurance, mortgage payments, and debt service—costs that stay constant whether 5000 or 10,000 units are produced. **Variable costs,** however, include such expenses as hourly wages, raw materials, parts and subassemblies, and commissions paid to sales representatives—all of which are relative to increases or decreases in production and sales.

Breakeven calculation can be illustrated by a simple formula or a graph. The formula is:

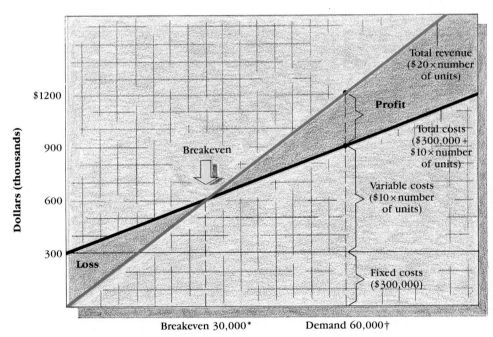

Figure 16-2 *Breakeven analysis.* A simple breakeven analysis shows how many units of a product must be sold to exactly break even, given specific fixed and variable costs and a given price. Note that any unit sales below the breakeven point will result in a loss, represented by the red shaded area, and any sales above that point will result in profits, as represented by the gray shaded area.

* Revenues ($20 × 30,000 units)	= $600,000	† Revenues ($20 × 60,000)		=	$1,200,000
Fixed costs	= 300,000	Fixed costs		=	300,000
Variable costs ($10 × 30,000 units) =	300,000	Variable costs ($10 × 60,000)	=		600,000
Profits	$ 0	Profits		=	$ 300,000

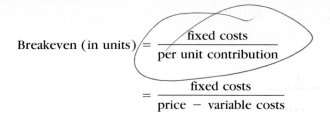

$$\text{Breakeven (in units)} = \frac{\text{fixed costs}}{\text{per unit contribution}}$$

$$= \frac{\text{fixed costs}}{\text{price} - \text{variable costs}}$$

If Variblo Corporation sells its hair dryers to retailers for $20 each, that is Variblo's selling price. If its fixed costs are $300,000 and its variable costs per unit are $10, we can compute the breakeven point using the equation presented above:

$$\text{Breakeven} = \frac{\$300,000}{\$20 - \$10}$$

$$= \frac{\$300,000}{\$10}$$

$$= 30,000 \text{ units}$$

Variblo must sell 30,000 units to break even. If it sells fewer hair dryers, it loses money; it if sells more, it makes a profit.

Figure 16-2 shows the same information graphically. Note that Variblo must sell 30,000 units to reach the breakeven point at which revenues ($600,000) exactly equal total costs ($600,000). However, if Variblo can sell 60,000 units at $20 each, its revenues will exceed costs and result in a profit of $300,000.

COST-VOLUME-PROFIT ANALYSIS   A major drawback of both cost-plus pricing and breakeven analysis is that they do not explicitly consider differences in demand but concentrate on the cost side of the profit equation. The demand side of this equation is given its due in **cost-volume-profit analysis** (or flexible breakeven analysis). This approach calculates the effect on profits of different prices, given different levels of demand in response to those prices. (A quick review of Figure 15-2 will remind you of the downward-sloping character of the demand curve: As prices rise, quantity demanded falls.)

Suppose price setters at Variblo want to determine the best price for their hair dryer and wonder whether to charge retailers $15, $20, or $25. Figure 16-3 shows the results of cost-volume-profit analysis. Demand is estimated to be 70,000 units at the $15 price (shown in blue); 60,000 units at $20 (shown in gray); and 35,000 units at $25 (shown in red). At the highest price of $25, the breakeven point A is 20,000 units. This is lower than breakeven at the $20 price—point B— 30,000 units.

$$\text{Breakeven } A = \frac{\$300,000 \ (FC)}{\$25(P) - 10 \ (VC)}$$

$$= \frac{\$300,000}{\$15}$$

$$= 20,000 \text{ units}$$

At the $20 price, the breakeven point is 30,000 units.

$$\text{Breakeven } B = \frac{\$300{,}000 \ (FC)}{\$20(P) \ - \ \$10(VC)}$$

$$= \frac{\$300{,}000}{\$10}$$

$$= 30{,}000 \text{ units}$$

At the lowest price of $15, the breakeven point is 60,000 units.

$$\text{Breakeven } C = \frac{\$300{,}000 \ (FC)}{\$15(P) \ - \ \$10(VC)}$$

$$= \frac{\$300{,}000}{\$5}$$

$$= 60{,}000 \text{ units}$$

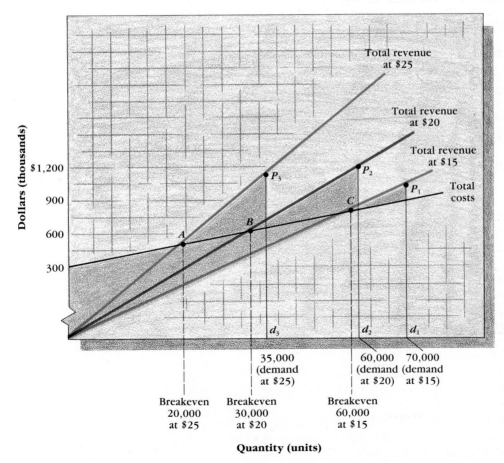

Figure 16-3 *Cost-volume-profit analysis.* When the methodology of breakeven analysis includes estimates of the quantity that would be demanded (d_1, d_2, and d_3) given different prices (P_1, P_2, and P_3), it becomes a price determination method that considers both costs and demand.

Since demand estimates vary with price, we can compare profitability at each level:

$15 Price

Total revenue ($15 × 70,000 units)	$1,050,000
Fixed costs	(300,000)
Variable costs ($10 × 70,000 units)	(700,000)
Profit	$ 50,000

$20 Price

Total revenue ($20 × 60,000 units)	$1,200,000
Fixed costs	(300,000)
Variable costs ($10 × 60,000 units)	(600,000)
Profit	$ 300,000

$25 Price

Total revenue ($25 × 35,000 units)	$ 875,000
Fixed costs	(300,000)
Variable costs ($10 × 35,000 units)	(350,000)
Profit	$ 225,000

If based on realistic demand estimates, cost-volume-profit analysis not only accounts for the likelihood of demand varying at different prices but also shows the price at which profits are highest (in this case, at $20). Though complex, such analysis gives marketers meaningful comparisons on which to base pricing decisions.

☐ *Price and Discounts*

A product's **list price** is the product's price to final buyers. Throughout the distribution system, manufacturers grant intermediaries **discounts,** or deductions from the list price. These price concessions from producers may be seen as payment to intermediaries for performing the distribution function and for providing time and place utilities. The difference between the list price and the amount that the original producer receives represents the total discounts provided to channel members. Exhibit 16-1 describes the five primary forms of discounts: functional, quantity, cash, promotional, and seasonal.

Functional (or trade) discounts compensate intermediaries for performing such services as storage, handling, and selling. These discounts allow wholesalers and retailers to cover their overhead costs and secure a profit. Producers may also offer **quantity discounts** to buyers who purchase in multiple units or above a specified dollar amount; they may offer **cash discounts** to buyers who pay for their purchases within a specified time. **Promotional discounts** take many forms; in general, they help intermediaries pay the costs of local advertising and other promotional activities. Finally, **seasonal discounts** are granted to early or off-season buyers of products that have peak selling periods. Exhibit 16-2 calculates the discounts for a product that qualifies for all five types of price reduction; the discounts are figured backward from the manufacturer's suggested list price.

Channel members themselves employ discounts in various ways. Wholesalers pass on discounts to retailers just as manufacturers pass along discounts to wholesalers. Retailers may offer promotional discounts to consumers in the form of sweepstakes, contests, and free samples. Some stores offer quantity and cash discounts to regular customers. Even seasonal discounts may be passed along—for example, to reduce inventory of Halloween candy or Christmas cards.

EXHIBIT 16-1   **Characteristics of Major Discounts**

Functional (Trade) Discounts

Functional discounts compensate intermediaries for the various distribution and selling functions they perform; they are typically figured as a percentage off the list price. Such trade discounts vary from industry to industry and are based on the degree of service the intermediary provides as well as on industry norms.

Quantity Discounts

Quantity discounts are based either on the number of units purchased or on the total dollar amount; they are used to encourage larger orders from a single buyer. Quantity discounts may apply to one product, to a particular product line, or to all the products of a given producer.

Two types of quantity discounts prevail in business: noncumulative and cumulative. **Noncumulative discounts** are offered on each individual sale. Alternatively, a producer may set up a **cumulative discount** schedule that applies to one buyer's orders over a specified time—perhaps a 6- or 12-month period. For example, a producer may set up a discount schedule (applied either noncumulatively or cumulatively) like this:

Number of Units	Discount
0–9	20%
10–19	25
20–29	30
30 or more	35

Cash Discounts

Cash discounts are price reductions given to buyers who pay for purchases within a stated period; they are *not* cash payments. A typical cash discount is stated as "2/10, net 30," indicating that the buyer may take 2 percent off the invoice price if the bill is paid within 10 days of delivery. However, the total invoice amount is due if the bill is paid between 10 and 30 days after delivery.

Even though cash discounts are usually small, they add up for buyers who make many or large purchases. Producers offer such price reductions to encourage prompt payments and improve their cash flow.

Promotional Discounts

Producers give promotional discounts to encourage promotion and sales efforts by intermediaries. In addition to a percentage off the list price, promotional discounts may take the form of free merchandise, cash payments (for local advertising expenses), in-store displays, or special discounts to be passed along to consumers to encourage sales.

Seasonal Discounts

Air conditioners, resort hotel space, greeting cards, and home insulation all have strong seasonal demand. To keep production facilities operating year-round and to shift storage charges into the distribution channel, producers of such goods may offer seasonal discounts to off-season buyers.

Note: All discounts must follow the nondiscriminatory provisions of the Robinson-Patman Act as discussed earlier. In practice, the Federal Trade Commission has not pursued the complex issues raised by the use of functional discounts.

EXHIBIT 16-2	Calculation of Possible Discounts

List price (producer's suggested selling price): $100.00
Discounts:

Functional	33%
Quantity	10
Cash	3
Seasonal	3
Promotional	6

Price paid to producer:

List price	$100.00
Less functional discount ($100.00 × 33%)	− 33.00
	67.00
Less quantity discount ($67.00 × 10%)	− 6.70
	60.30
Less promotional discount ($60.30 × 6%)	− 3.62
	56.68
Less seasonal discount ($56.68 × 3%)	1.70
	54.98
Less cash discount ($54.98 × 3%)	1.65
	$ 53.33

Final price paid to producer by intermediary:	$ 53.33
Total dollar discount:	$ 46.67
Total discount percentage:	46.67%

☐ The Impact of Geography on Pricing

As well as the discounts discussed above, price reductions may be based on the physical distance between producers and intermediaries. Sellers may try to "equalize" the distance between themselves and various buyers through **geographic pricing,** in which responsibility for transportation charges is assigned to either the

When the costs of shipping goods to the point of consumption is a major part of the total cost of a product, prices are likely to differ in different geographical areas. This can become a competitive issue among suppliers from different locations. (Copyright © Tom Tracy/Black Star.)

| EXHIBIT 16-3 | Geographic Pricing Policies |

FOB Pricing

FOB stands for "free on board" and is followed by the designation "factory" or "destination" to indicate at what point the buyer assumes freight costs and title to the product. If the product is sold "FOB factory," for example, the buyer pays all freight costs beyond the factory. This can be a real disadvantage for sellers with distant customers, who may avoid freight costs by buying from nearby producers. To counter this problem, some sellers choose a pricing policy of "FOB destination," in which they absorb transportation costs and retain title to the product until it is delivered to the buyer. Although this practice can cut sharply into profits, it may be the only way to attract distant customers.

Uniform Delivered Pricing

Some sellers establish a standard freight charge which they add to the base price of the product. This uniform rate applies to *all* customers, regardless of geographic location or actual freight costs. The charge is usually an average of all the producer's shipping costs. As a result, nearby customers actually pay more than the true freight costs (the difference is referred to as "phantom freight"). Distant customers, by paying the standard rate, are thus subsidized by the producer and by nearby customers.

Zone Pricing

With zone pricing, the seller sets up two or more geographic areas and establishes uniform freight charges within each. For example, a seller in Boston may set up three zones across the United States. The most distant customers on the west coast pay the highest freight charges, but all customers within that zone pay the same rate. Other customers, such as all those between the Rocky Mountains and the Mississippi River, pay a lower common price. Finally, all those east of the Mississippi pay an even lower common rate.

---

seller or the buyer. Many marketers ship products nationwide or even worldwide, and freight costs can have major impact on a product's price. As we saw in Chapter 14, transportation costs for some products run as high as 50 percent of their cost. Standards and norms for geographic pricing policies prevail within most industries. Exhibit 16-3 describes the main types of geographic pricing in the United States.

■ SELECTED PRICING POLICIES ■

In employing tactics to carry out their pricing strategies, marketers establish various policies that affect the list price. Naturally, certain policies are appropriate for some products but not for others. The most common policies can be classified into four categories: psychological pricing, promotional pricing, flexible pricing, and pricing arrived at through negotiation and bidding.

☐ Psychological Pricing

Psychological pricing is intended to appeal to buyers' emotions rather than their logic. Used most often by retailers, psychological pricing is rarely effective in swaying organizational buyers. Consumers, by contrast, may be responsive to various forms of psychological pricing—among them odd-even pricing, prestige pricing, customary pricing, and price lining.

ODD-EVEN PRICING   Why are so many products priced at $9.99 or $14.95 rather than at $10 or $15? In fact, why are so few products priced in even dollars? The theory known as **odd-even pricing** assumes that consumers will perceive prices as being "$9 and something" rather than as "almost $10." Somehow, the pennies-lower price is seen as attractive—even as a bargain.

Gabrielle Brenner and Reuven Brenner have proposed that odd-even pricing is effective because of human memory limits: "When a price is $398, the digit 3 is more significant as information than the digit 9, which in turn is more significant than 8. Thus the consumer will act so as to remember first that the price is $300, then maybe that it is $390, but rarely that it is exactly $398."[13] Given our limited short-term memory storage, we retain the most important information, but we seem to prefer to round prices downward rather than upward. There is also evidence that we perceive an odd price to be further below the even price than it actually is.

PRESTIGE PRICING   Expensive luxury items frequently carry even-numbered prices, such as $4000 for a mink coat. A high price is part of the image that certain buyers seek. Hence, **prestige pricing** intentionally sets prices at levels high enough to connote an image of quality and status. Consumers often associate quality with price; the demand for some products would actually fall if they were priced lower.

Figure 16-4 shows the demand curve for prestige products. If the price goes below P_1, demand will decrease because buyers feel that product quality has been

For some products, price is a sign of prestige. The demand for a fine perfume, for instance, would likely go *down* rather than up if the price is dropped too low. (Reprinted with permission of CHANEL, Inc.)

compromised. This type of demand situation occurs with items like emeralds, aged whiskies, foreign sports cars, and fine china. Prestige pricing communicates that the product is exceptional; the high price tells buyers that they can expect equally high quality.

CUSTOMARY PRICING   Buyers' expectations about price also affect sales of candy bars, chewing gum, and newspapers, as well as mass transit fares. Competing brands of many inexpensive products or services typically carry the same price even though they come from different producers. **Customary pricing** matches buyers' expectations about the cost of certain items; prices reflect custom and tradition, and price changes are infrequent.

Hershey's chocolate bars are an often-cited example of customary pricing. Their prices have changed only a few times over four decades—inching up from a nickel to their current cost. Although price increases were necessary from time to time, Hershey maintained its profit margins (and stayed within custom) by varying the size of the candy bar. In general, the bar shrank gradually as each price held. Then, when the price was raised, the size of the candy bar was increased.[14] At each stage, prices matched buyers' expectations about what a candy bar *should* cost.

PRICE LINING   Another form of psychological pricing is **price lining,** in which a manufacturer or a retailer sets a limited number of prices for selected lines of products.[15] Brooks Brothers, for example, may decide to sell men's neckties at only four prices: $55, $40, $30, and $18. This approach assumes that distinct market segments exist and can be matched to the limited number of price levels. It also assumes that demand is inelastic for products priced in this manner. Consequently, if the necktie lines were priced at $53, $38, $28, and $17, quantity demanded at each level would increase only slightly, if at all.

Price lining is relatively easy to implement, and it simplifies decision making for consumers. Shoppers can select a comfortable price level and look for items only at that level, while ignoring products at other price levels. Price setters, however, face the important task of assessing their market segments accurately. The differences in price levels must be great enough that consumers can perceive and accept them readily. However, the price levels should not be too far apart; if they are, some market segments may be missed. For example, if Brooks Brothers priced its neckties only at $55 and $18, buyers in the middle, who prefer to purchase ties in the $30 to $35 price range, would be lost.

The demand curve for line-priced products resembles a staircase, as shown in Figure 16-5. Note that quantity demanded does not increase within one price range until the next lower range is almost reached.

☐ *Promotional Pricing*

Promotional pricing paves the way for a good old-fashioned sale; prices of selected items are lowered to attract customers. Retailers hope that the traffic generated by the special, temporary prices will lead to increased sales of other products priced at the regular markup. The sale items, called **loss leaders** or **price leaders,** are offered at close to cost. They may even be priced slightly below the merchant's cost.

Another promotional pricing tactic is **multiple-unit pricing,** best known as the "2 for 1" sale. With this approach, beer and soft drinks, chewing gum and candy, pet food, and even motor oil are packaged in multiple units at a price slightly lower than for a single unit purchased separately. Multiple-unit pricing does increase the

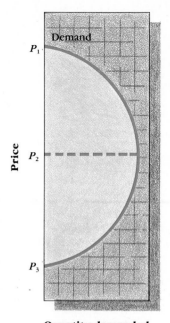

Figure 16-4   *Prestige pricing and the demand curve.* As in Chapter 15, demand curves usually slope down to the right, indicating more of something will be demanded as its price drops. With certain "prestige" products, such as perfumes or mink coats, that relationship tends to hold true at higher price levels, as between P_1 and P_2. However, if prices go too low, consumers assume the product is not of high quality and actually buy less of it at a lower price, as between P_2 and P_3.

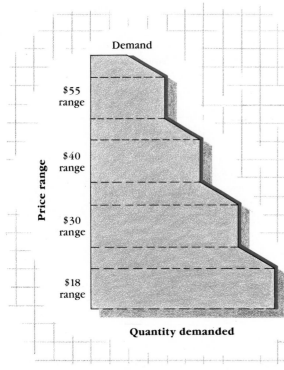

Demand

$55 range

$40 range

$30 range

$18 range

Price range

Quantity demanded

Figure 16-5 *Price lining and the demand curve.* The concept of price lining refers to providing a line of products with different prices, based on consumers' expectations of price ranges. These expectations lead to demand being highly inelastic within the specific ranges, but elastic between the ranges.

quantity sold in an individual transaction, but it is not particularly effective for new products or for items consumed slowly (such as ketchup and peanut butter).

Flexible Pricing

The prices of most products sold in the United States are set by the final seller. As a result, buyers cannot negotiate a price with sellers in department stores, discount stores, or supermarkets. The use of a single fixed price allows retailers to count on a consistent profit margin. In addition, most U.S. consumers prefer the one-price tactic because they are uncomfortable haggling over prices. In other countries, however, where there are fewer mass-merchandise retailers, shoppers still enjoy the time-honored practice of bargaining with merchants. Negotiating over price is regarded as a normal part of shopping.

Flexible pricing—charging different prices to different customers—is rare but not unknown in this country. Buyers of automobiles, homes, and major appliances are looking for a price break; salespeople in these markets are often allowed some leeway in negotiating the final price. In fact, some sellers would be surprised if a buyer did not try to get a better price. Even so, flexible pricing makes it difficult to predict profit margins; sellers also run the risk of losing customers who learn that a neighbor got a better deal. In view of these many uncertainties, flexible pricing in the United States functions more as a tactic to secure an individual sale than as an overall policy.

Pricing through Negotiation and Bidding

Price negotiation is far more common in industrial and organizational purchasing. Those who buy large amounts of industrial products may be able to negotiate quantity discounts from sellers. Buyers of specialized products like industrial chemicals and waste-management services can negotiate price breaks based not only on quantity but also on the length of a contract.

Large industrial marketers such as Westinghouse, General Electric, and Rockwell International often negotiate the prices of multimillion-dollar installations; this bargaining process has become quite formal. Typically, the customer provides specifications for the equipment needed or outlines the problems to be solved. For something as complex and specialized as an entire assembly line, the customer is likely to request proposals from several potential suppliers. This leads to competitive bidding in which each seller estimates and presents its costs, overhead, and a target profit. A low bid increases the probability of getting the contract but may not result in desired profits; a high bid ensures attractive profits but lowers the probability of making the sale.

Bidding on a cost-plus basis is standard procedure for companies seeking government contracts. In the case of government buying under cost-plus bids, the government agrees to pay the costs of building, for example, a missile guidance system on a tank. It also agrees to pay a certain sum over costs. This arrangement protects the bidder from losing money if costs increase during the time covered by the contract, which is often lengthy. Whether cost-plus arrangements protect taxpayers as ultimate buyers is another matter: The federal government sometimes pays millions of dollars in cost overruns.

■ ADMINISTERING PRICE CHANGES ■

Shaklee Corporation is the largest U.S. marketer of vitamins and dietary supplements made from only natural sources. During the 1970s, America's love affair with all things "natural" helped the California company to expand its sales from $10 million in 1969 to $318 million in 1979. Shaklee not only added customers using a door-to-door sales force but also raised its prices by 1977 to a level 50 percent above competitors. However, sales increases began to falter as Shaklee's market share was eroded by competition from vitamins produced by Miles Laboratories (One-A-Day brand) and Squibb Corporation (Theragran). Alarmed by its slide in market share, Shaklee ordered a price freeze on all nutritional products until June 1980. Although the company did have to accept lower profit margins on its still-increasing sales, its market share began to climb. Shaklee administered its prices in an unusual way: simply by holding them.[16]

Until now, we have focused on how marketers set initial prices for products. Yet, in a dynamic business world, price administration cannot end with the setting of an initial price. Changing marketplace conditions often require the organization to increase or cut prices or, as in Shaklee's case, to stop making changes. Price administration—monitoring market conditions and responding through price adjustments—falls heavily on marketers in most organizations.

☐ Initiating Price Changes: Leading
Tradition holds that any competitor can lead prices down, but only dominant competitors can lead prices up. This rule of thumb holds true *some* of the time. A small competitor may institute price cuts to gain market share; however, a large competitor will follow price reductions only if a greater amount of profit will be lost by not doing so. Only companies with relatively large market shares are likely to be successful in leading price increases.[17]

Perhaps the key issue for price leaders is how competitors will respond to a price change. This will depend on the competitor's history of price responses, its current relative market share and profit margins, and the likely consequences of following (or not following) the leader's price change. Anticipating competitors' price changes is an important but difficult undertaking for both leaders and followers. Many firms establish contingency plans for reacting to such changes. Plans are formulated in advance simply because changes may occur so rapidly that there is little time for careful consideration of pricing responses.

If the impetus for a price change comes from increased costs, price setters can generally anticipate that competitors face the same problem and are likely to adopt a similar solution. The risks are higher, though, if the impetus comes from an expected change in demand—particularly for the leader with a large market share. If IBM raises prices, its competitors are likely to follow the leader. However, if competitors do not follow, IBM stands alone charging a higher price, risking its hard-won market share.

Responding to Price Changes: Following

Following price changes is usually less risky than leading. If a dominant firm increases its prices, smaller competitors can hold steady and hope to gain market share. If they follow the leader's increases, they are likely to at least hold their current shares. They may even improve their profits with little risk.

What if relative market shares are fairly even among a number of competitors? In this case, the firm that leads with price increases takes the greatest risk. Customers obviously favor price cuts, but they have to be educated about increases. It is always safer, therefore, to follow, but this is not always an option. A firm's survival may hinge on leading with a price increase at the right moment.

Competitors' pricing actions are sometimes impossible to predict, but they can have devastating effects. Marketers face difficult pricing decisions and must make them quickly. Like so much else in marketing, price administration is only part science; much depends on intuition, preparedness, and art. Certainly, pricing is not a dull aspect of marketing; it is sometimes exasperatingly exciting.

SUMMARY

1. Setting prices is a complex process that is central to providing exchange utility and to designing a successful marketing mix.
2. Recently, marketing managers have ranked price as the most important element of the marketing mix—as even more important than product planning and management.
3. More than half of all decisions affecting price administration are made by chief marketing officers.
4. The price-setting process should systematically focus on at least six areas: (1) target markets, (2) brand image, (3) the marketing mix, (4) pricing objectives, (5) pricing strategies, and (6) pricing tactics that advance their corporate and marketing objectives.
5. All components of the marketing mix are subject to environmental influences, but pricing is perhaps most susceptible to them. Among the factors that come into play during the pricing process are the organization itself, consumers and customers, channel members, competitors, government, and the economy.
6. Various federal, state, and local laws prohibit price discrimination, price fixing, and unfair pricing policies such as bait-and-switch promotion and predatory pricing.
7. Pricing objectives should be consistent with and should advance corporate and marketing objectives. In general, such goals are based on profitability, sales volume, and/or competition.

8. Pricing strategies for new products generally aim either to "skim" or to "penetrate" the market. A skimming strategy usually results in higher prices, while a penetration strategy tends to establish lower prices.

9. Three basic techniques are used to determine which price best achieves the organization's objectives and strategies: the cost-plus approach, breakeven analysis, and cost-volume-profit analysis. The first two methods emphasize cost factors, and the third takes into account the demand size of the profit equation.

10. Manufacturers allow intermediaries deductions from the list price in the form of discounts. There are five primary types of discounts: functional, quantity, cash, promotional, and seasonal.

11. The most common pricing policies can be classified into four categories: psychological pricing, promotional pricing, flexible pricing, and pricing arrived at through negotiation and bidding.

12. Pricing strategy generally dictates that a firm either lead or follow competitors' prices.

☐ Key Terms

bait-and-switch promotion
breakeven analysis
cash discounts
cost-plus pricing
cost-volume-profit analysis
cumulative discounts
customary pricing
discounts
experience-curve pricing
fair trade
fixed costs
flexible pricing
FOB pricing
functional discounts
geographic pricing
horizontal price fixing
list price

loss leaders
multiple-unit pricing
noncumulative discounts
nonprice competition
odd-even pricing
penetration
position
predatory pricing
prestige pricing
prices
price administration
price discrimination
price fixing
price leaders
price lining
profitability objectives
profit maximization

promotional discounts
promotional pricing
psychological pricing
quantity discounts
return on investment
seasonal discounts
skimming
target return on investment
target return on sales
umbrella pricing
unfair-sales acts
uniform delivered pricing
unit pricing
variable costs
vertical price fixing
zone pricing

☐ Chapter Review

1. What are the roles of accounting and finance personnel and marketing experts in making pricing recommendations to top-level management? What advice is marketing uniquely prepared to offer?

2. Explain the logic of the six steps of the price-setting process set forth in Figure 16-1.

3. Summarize the major environmental influences on pricing. Why are antitrust laws the vehicles for most price constraint legislation?

4. What are the major pricing objectives employed by most organizations? Cite an example of a firm seeking price stability and nonprice competition.

5. Give examples of firms that would be likely to employ a pricing strategy of skimming and of penetration pricing. Why might the first firm to enter a market pursue a pricing strategy based on the experience curve?

6. Summarize the primary techniques for price determination. How does cost-volume-profit analysis account for different probable sales at different prices in a way that cost-plus analysis and breakeven analysis do not?

7. Summarize the techniques of psychological pricing. Give an example of a product that might lend itself to price lining.

8. Contrast the flexibility of pricing in consumer markets and organizational markets.

9. Characterize the philosophies of leading and following in price administration.

References

1. Jon G. Udell, "How Important Is Pricing in Competitive Strategy?" *Journal of Marketing,* Jan. 1964, pp. 44–48.

2. Robert A. Robichaux, "How Important Is Pricing in Competitive Strategy, Circa 1975?" in Henry W. Nash and Donald P. Ribin, eds., *Proceedings of the Southern Marketing Association* (Atlanta, Ga.: Nov. 1976), pp. 55–57; and Richard Fleming, "Pricing Competition Is Shaping Up as '84's Top Marketing 'Pressure Point,' " *Marketing News,* Nov. 11, 1983, p. 1.

3. Thomas G. Paterson, "Pricing Is Marketing, Costing Is Accounting," *Vantage Points,* ref. I-81.

4. Russell Abratt and Leyland F. Pitt, "Pricing Practices in Two Industries," *Industrial Marketing Management,* vol. 14, Nov. 1985, pp. 301–306.

5. Alfred R. Oxenfeldt, "Multistage Approach to Pricing," *Harvard Business Review,* July–Aug. 1960, pp. 125–133; and Kent B. Monroe, *Pricing: Making Profitable Decisions* (New York: McGraw-Hill, 1979), pp. 277–278.

6. Jerry C. Olson, "Price as Informational Cue: Effects on Product Evaluation," in Arch G. Woodside, Jagdish N. Sheth, and Peter D. Bennett, eds., *Consumer and Industrial Buying Behavior* (New York: North Holland, 1977), pp. 277–286; Kent Monroe and Susan Petroshius, "Buyers' Perceptions of Price: An Update of the Evidence," in Harold Kassarjian and Thomas Robertson, *Perspectives in Consumer Behavior,* 3d ed. (Glenview, Ill.: Scott, Foresman, 1978), pp. 43–55; and Steven M. Shugan, "Price-Quality Relationships," in Thomas Kinnear, ed., *Advances in Consumer Research,* vol. 11 (Ann Arbor, Mich.: Association for Consumer Research, 1984), pp. 627–632.

7. Eitan Gerstner, "Do Higher Prices Signal Higher Quality?" *Journal of Marketing Research,* vol. XXII, May 1985, pp. 209–215; and Gary M. Erickson and Johny K. Johansson, "The Role of Price in Multi-Attribute Product Evaluations," *Journal of Consumer Research,* vol. 12, Sept. 1985, pp. 195–199.

8. Andre Gabor and C. W. J. Granger, "On the Price Consciousness of Consumers," *Applied Statistics,* Nov. 1961, pp. 170–180.

9. Mary Jane Sheffet and Debra L. Scammon, "Resale Price Maintenance: Is It Safe to Suggest Retail Prices?" *Journal of Marketing,* vol. 49, Fall 1985, pp. 82–91.

10. For a more thorough discussion, see Kent B. Monroe and Peter LaPlaca, "What Are the Benefits of Unit Pricing?" *Journal of Marketing,* vol. 36, July 1972, pp. 16–22.

11. "USAir's High-Yield Strategy," *The New York Times,* Dec. 22, 1982, pp. D1, D5.

12. Kent B. Monroe, "Techniques for Pricing New Products and Services," in Victor P. Buell, ed., *Handbook of Modern Marketing* (New York: McGraw-Hill, 1986), pp. 32-1–32-13.

13. Gabrielle A. Brenner and Reuven Brenner, "Memory and Markets, or Why Are You Paying $2.99 for a Widget?" *Journal of Business,* vol. 55, no. 1, 1982, pp. 147–158.

14. "Misadventures of Cocoa Trade," *The New York Times,* Feb. 25, 1979, pp. F1, F4.

15. David J. Reibstein and Hubert Gatignon, "Optimal Product Line Pricing: The Influence of Elasticities and Cross-Elasticities," *Journal of Marketing Research,* vol. XXI, Aug. 1984, pp. 259–287.

16. "Shaklee: Curbing Profits to Gain New Vigor in the Vitamin Market," *Business Week,* June 9, 1980, pp. 108, 110.

17. S. E. Heymann, "Cost Considerations," in Earl L. Bailey, ed., *Pricing Practices and Strategies* (New York: Conference Board, 1978), pp. 4–42.

18. "What Blew the Head off Miller's Profits?" *Business Week,* Feb. 15, 1982, pp. 39–40.

MOTEL 6

The Motel 6 economy chain opened its first inn in Santa Barbara, California, in 1961. Rooms cost only $6, thereby providing the chain with an appropriate name. Some 25 years later, Motel 6 owns 401 properties in 39 states but still emphasizes economy in its pricing: A typical room goes for a low $15 in Texas and $25 in California.

Motel 6 has certainly been part of the boom in budget inns across the United States. Such inns feature bargain accommodations, charging 20 percent to 50 percent less than the average rates in their areas. In 1980, the 1500 economy inns accounted for less than 10 percent of all U.S. hotel rooms. By mid-1986, 3500 economy inns accounted for more than 12 percent of the nation's 2.7 million hotel rooms. The growth in this part of the industry has brought with it a flurry of new competitors, including Econo Lodges of America, Red Roof Inns, and Days Inns. One result of this new challenge is that Motel 6's occupancy rate fell from 81 percent in 1981 to only 59 percent in mid-1986.

In 1985, Kohlberg Kravis Roberts & Company (KKR) bought the Motel 6 chain for $881 million. The new owners faced not only the chain's declining occupancy rate but a host of other problems. According to a 1986 *Consumer Reports* survey, customers rated Motel 6 last among 14 budget chains. Even the low prices offered by Motel 6 (about $5 less than competitors) were not enough to offset customers' negative feelings about the Motel 6 facilities.

KKR has taken steps to improve the Motel 6 chain, adding such amenities as phones and color televisions to Motel 6 rooms. The company plans to renovate run-down rooms and is considering installation of a toll-free reservation system. Expansion is another part of the picture: KKR will build 30 motels per year, particularly in the Northeast, where Motel 6 has few facilities.

Motel 6 will also benefit from a new marketing campaign. Remarkably, apart from billboards near its inns, the Motel 6 chain has never advertised. "I find that astonishing," admits Joseph W. McCarthy, hired by KKR as the chain's new president. McCarthy intends to target a new market—business travelers with limited expenses—as a balance to Motel 6's primary market of weekend pleasure travelers.

Motel 6 faces an especially serious challenge from the Days Inn of America chain. Days Inn has 390 inns in 44 states and offers and average $34 room rate. It has derived significant benefits from its toll-free reservations lines, which produced 44 percent of all bookings in 1984. Days Inn targets senior citizens, the military, school sports teams, educators, and business travelers as the key markets for its budget rooms.

Days Inn has adopted a number of unusual marketing approaches. Using no television advertising, Days has arranged promotions with such firms as K mart Corporation and Keystone Camera Products Corporation. A 1985 promotion through which Blue Bonnet margarine users could exchange proof-of-purchase seals for a free night at Days Inn led to sales of 10,000 extra rooms. Moreover, Days pioneered an innovative pricing approach, becoming the first hotel company to offer "supersaver discounts similar to those used by airlines. If guests book rooms 30 days in advance, they pay only $19 to $29. This program has produced 220,000 bookings thus far.

Industry analysts expect that the boom in economy lodging will continue. Many Americans cannot afford the lavish prices of full-service hotels and do not need such amenities as plush lobbies and restaurants. Motel 6 hopes that it can meet the challenge of Days Inn and other competitors and increase its share of the market.

Source: "Cheap Dreams, the Budget Inn Boom," *Business Week*, July 14, 1986, pp. 76–77.

Implementing and Controlling Marketing Plans

1. When the total package of services provided by Motel 6 (and other economy chains) is so different from the package provided by such chains as Holiday Inn or Sheraton, is the price comparison meaningful?
2. Should Motel 6 begin offering such services as a central reservation system? If so, how would this affect the chain's pricing decisions?
3. Given the current state of the economy motel industry, what pressures on prices of its motel rooms should managers expect over the next few years?

■ CASE 18

TEXAS AIR

During the late 1970s and early 1980s, the United States went through a wave of deregulation in such industries as airlines, railroads, trucking, and long-distance telephone services. Advocates of deregulation commonly argued that an unrestrained free market in these industries would increase competition, enhance productivity, and reduce prices. Through the first decade of deregulation, these predictions seemed on target. Airline fares, for example, declined 13 percent (when adjusted for inflation) from 1978 to 1986. But, as in other deregulated industries, developments in the airline industry in the mid-1980s suggested that the long-term results of deregulation might well be greater concentration and *less* competition.

Certainly one of the key players in the now-deregulated airline industry has been Frank Lorenzo, chair of Texas Air Corporation. In the early 1970s—well before deregulation began—Lorenzo's Texas International shocked the industry by offering "peanut fares." After failing to acquire both National Airlines and TWA in the late 1970s, Lorenzo created New York Air in 1980 to challenge Eastern's lucrative east coast shuttle service and took over Continental Airlines in 1982.

In early 1986, Lorenzo's Texas Air tripled its size by taking over Eastern Airlines. This move meant that Lorenzo's operations now combined to form the nation's largest airline, with 451 planes, or 15 percent of the country's commercial airline capacity. But Texas Air acquisitions were not over: by early 1987 it had taken over People Express and merged People and New York Air into Continental. Continental thereby became the third-largest airline in the United States, behind only United Airlines and American Airlines.

Interestingly, with these acquisitions completed, Texas Air began to reposition Continental. In the early 1980s, Continental had aggressively promoted itself as an irreverent, fare-slashing upstart. By 1987, however, Continental initiated its first-ever corporate image advertising campaign, promoting the airline as a benevolent, service-oriented giant. The carrier's new theme was: "Up where you belong."

Industry analysts suggest that Continental's shift to image advertising could lead to a move away from its traditional discounting stance. As an example, fares to certain People Express destinations were expected to more than double when the Continental takeover was completed. One marketing executive for Continental noted: "We want to expend less energy talking price, where we think we already have a strong identity, and more on the feel-good intangibles." Quite a change indeed from the "peanut fares" that Frank Lorenzo emphasized in building Texas International!

Just as Texas Air has vigorously enlarged itself during the years of deregulation, the industry as a whole has clearly become more concentrated than before. In 1978, the six largest carriers controlled 73 percent of the market; by 1986, they controlled 84 percent. One consultant projects a "tight oligopoly" by 1990 with the top six holding more than 90 percent of the market.

Contrary to the earlier optimistic predictions of deregulation advocates, this new concentration may result in *higher* airline prices. Economist Alfred E. Kahn, former chair of the Civil Aeronautics Board, observes: "When you have the same six carriers meeting each other in market after market, there is danger of softer competition. It's not in their interest to insult one another excessively." Harold J. Pareti, president of the new discount-oriented Presidential Airlines, adds that control of the industry by "a handful of large national airlines" would allow them to "increase prices to the detriment of the American consumer."

Sources: "Frank Lorenzo, High Flier," *Business Week,* Mar. 10, 1986, pp. 104–107, 110, 112; George Getschow and Steve Frazier, "Changing Skies: Texas Air's Managers Pushed Deregulation, Then Put It to Work," *The Wall Street Journal,* Mar. 14, 1986, pp. 1, 12; "Is Deregulation Working?" *Business Week,* Dec. 22, 1986, pp. 50–55; Brian Moran, "Texas Air Repositions Lines," *Advertising Age,* Jan. 19, 1987, pp. 1, 90.

1. According to economic theory, what should happen to prices in a deregulated airline industry?
2. Why is Frank Lorenzo changing the "peanut fare" approach that he pioneered in the past?
3. Are consumers likely to continue to benefit from the lower fares that initially resulted from deregulation? Why or why not?

■　　■

PROMOTION

Promotion is the last of the four elements of the marketing mix to be covered. Essentially, promotion is the way marketers attempt to influence the customer and consumer to take the desired actions in the marketplace. The promotion mix includes a variety of ways the marketer communicates with the market.

The task of Chapter 17 is twofold. It first presents a conceptual view of promotion as communication. Regardless of its form—advertising, selling, direct mail—promotion *communicates*. Chapter 17 discusses the ways to do this effectively and covers two of the forms of communication: publicity and sales promotion.

Chapter 18 covers the many issues involved in managing the advertising program. In many companies, especially those marketing frequently purchased consumer products, advertising is often the most important promotion tool available. For those marketing other kinds of products, advertising is less central but almost always important.

Chapters 19 and 20 deal with managing the personal selling process. Chapter 19 deals with this from the perspective of the sales manager, who must deploy a trained and competent sales force and manage this major marketing effort. Chapter 20 discusses selling from the perspective of the professional salesperson, who is the manager of a territory, a part of the organization's total effort.

17

DESIGNING THE PROMOTION MIX

SPOTLIGHT ON

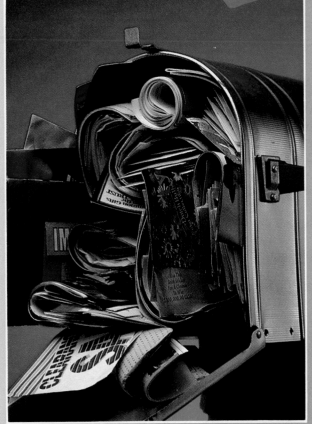

Copyright © 1986 Joel Gordon.

- The aims of promotion
- The steps of the communication process
- Major influences on promotion strategy
- Sales promotion contrasted with other elements of promotion
- Promotion campaigns aimed at consumers and channel members
- Sales promotion campaigns
- The nature and functions of publicity

(Copyright © Mark Greenberg, Visions.)

Coca-Cola Company and Coca-Cola Bottling Company of New York launched diet Coke with music and celebrities, with skyrockets and Rockettes—that is, with a carefully orchestrated event followed by an all-out campaign to push the new soft drink. The New York bottler invited 4000 employees, retailers, distributors, route salespeople, and members of the news media to a 4-hour gala at Radio City Music Hall. As the orchestra struck up the new "Coke is it!" theme, 36 Rockettes precision-kicked their way across the great stage. Famed café singer Bobby Short performed several songs from *Encore,* a Music Hall production sponsored by Coca-Cola. Officers of the company then introduced a 60-second diet Coke commercial featuring former football quarterback Joe Namath. For the finale, New York employees joined the Rockettes onstage, singing: "Just for the taste of it, introducing diet Coke." The entire production was taped for use in later commercials.

But this spectacular party wasn't over yet. All 4000 guests were bused to a pier on the Hudson River, where they feasted on the perfect accompaniments for a diet drink: pizza, hot dogs, baklava, and other ethnic delights. For the evening's climax, fireworks were set off from a barge on the river. In red and white letters, "diet Coke" illuminated the New York skyline and rocketed into the public eye.

During the weeks following the party, Coca-Cola of New York placed coupons in major newspapers to encourage consumers to try the new soft drink. Retailers were offered special incentives to prominently stock diet Coke, sometimes at the expense of Pepsi-Cola's shelf space. And the message "Coke is it!" filled the airwaves.

All these activities were carefully coordinated, of course. Coca-Cola's longtime advertising agency, McCann-Erickson, oversaw development of the new slogan, which replaced "Have a Coke and a smile." The gala itself was arranged by the company's public relations firm, Burson-Marsteller. With their help, the launching was *certain* to be a success: Even before the hoopla began, news releases had been written proclaiming that "more than 4,000 in the audience gave rave reviews to the 'star' of the evening, diet Coke. . . ."

Source: "Coca-Cola Kicks Off Diet-Coke Campaign with $100,000 Party," *The Wall Street Journal,* Aug. 20, 1982, p. 1.

On a given day, you might do any of the following:

- Ask a salesperson for help in selecting a new videotape
- See at least one television commercial for an automobile, perhaps Volvo or Mercury
- Clip a newspaper coupon worth 30 cents off the purchase price of a gallon of Sealtest ice cream
- Read a *Time* or *Newsweek* interview in which an Exxon executive explains the company's oil exploration policies

If you did all these things, you would have been exposed to the four major elements of promotion: personal selling, advertising, sales promotion, and publicity.

Chapter 17 begins by defining promotion and discussing its main purposes. Promotion aims basically to communicate; and we examine it in light of a widely accepted model of communication. Then we describe the elements of promotion and explore how to blend these elements into an effective promotion campaign. The rest of the chapter looks in detail at sales promotion and at publicity. The other two elements of promotion—advertising and personal selling—are studied in Chapters 18 through 20.

■ PROMOTION IS COMMUNICATION

The product offers benefits; distribution gives it place utility; price points out the product's value; promotion communicates these other factors to potential buyers. Diet Coke's launch party was obviously a celebration, but its organizers also hoped to promote an important message to guests and members of the media. Although information about diet Coke was communicated, the message was primarily one of confidence, enthusiasm—in a word, success.

Promotion has its own task in the marketing mix: to communicate to consumers and customers what the other marketing elements offer. Consumers needed to know that diet Coke was now available and that it promised the well-known and popular Coke taste with low-calorie advantages. Newspaper advertisements let the public know where diet Coke could be purchased at an introductory bargain price. But, above all, Coke wanted consumers, bottlers, and retailers to associate instant success and unquestionable desirability with its new product. One simply *had* to try diet Coke.

For many consumers, promotion is more visible and immediate than anything else marketers do. Consumers are far more aware of promotion than of distribution or even pricing. The promotion of a product communicates what marketers have done to satisfy consumers' needs; it is marketing made tangible.

☐ The Aims of Promotion

The promotion component of the marketing mix includes four major elements: (1) personal selling, (2) advertising, (3) sales promotion, and (4) publicity. These elements are often used in concert. Basically, **promotion** includes all aspects of the marketing mix designed to communciate with and influence target markets. In general, promotion has four aims: to inform, to persuade, to remind, and to reinforce.

INFORMING   Almost all promotion conveys some kind of information about the product: availability, features, name, use—in short, what functional and psychological needs the product is designed to satisfy. A television commercial for a videocassette recorder (VCR), for example, tells the viewer that the machine will record while the buyer is away from home and that it can be operated by a remote control device. The commercial also demonstrates that VCRs are easy to use by showing a 10-year-old girl putting on a movie. Information is therefore provided both directly and indirectly.

PERSUADING   In addition to informing, promotion attempts to persuade the audience to move toward some action or attitude. When sales representatives for Xerox point out the features of the latest copier to potential buyers and emphasize how economically it operates, they are trying to persuade prospects to buy the copier.

REMINDING   A third aim of promotion is to remind consumers that a product is still available. Reminder promotion is often used for products in the latter stages of their life cycles to offset competition from newer products. Heinz has used newspaper coupons as part of a promotional effort to remind consumers that its vinegar has been "America's Favorite Since 1880." Although the savings offered were slight (10 cents off the pint size and 15 cents off the quart size), Heinz's slogan reinforced the product's delivery of satisfaction to generations of customers.

Promotion reinforces consumers' satisfaction after a purchase is made. Much of the advertising for automobiles is designed to strengthen the satisfaction of car buyers who are recovering from "sticker shock" and thus reinforce their pride in owning a new Dodge, Pontiac, or Honda. The automobile manufacturers are taking the long view: They want new owners to feel and talk favorably about their purchases. When car-buying time rolls around again, these reinforced customers will be more likely to drive back to their previous dealers.

☐ Promotion and Other Components of the Marketing Mix

Promotion is designed to communicate directly and indirectly through words, images, sounds, and incentives. But product, price, and even location convey important ideas. For example, the elegant simplicity of a Cartier watch signals an image of quality to an affluent market. A two-pack of Gillette disposable razors, priced at under a dollar, suggests a bargain. The place of sale also tells consumers something. Whereas Cartier limits its distribution to exclusive outlets, Gillette razors may be picked up in almost any drugstore or supermarket.

All four components of the marketing mix communicate to inspire action by consumers and intermediaries and to provide them with functional and psychological satisfaction. Keeping that interaction of the marketing mix in mind, let us look briefly at the elements of promotion.

☐ Elements of Promotion

Marketers use four complementary methods to communicate through promotion: personal selling, advertising, sales promotion, and publicity. Most promotion campaigns use all four methods to some degree. Before we see how they work together, however, we need to look briefly at each element as a separate tool of communication.

PERSONAL SELLING   Approximately 8 million women and men are engaged in personal selling in the United States—or about 10 percent of the U.S. work force. In retailing alone, the number of salespeople totals around 4 million. **Personal selling** includes all promotional efforts made by the organization directly to reach individuals, or groups of individuals, on a personal basis. This form of promotion embraces the full spectrum of human interaction—from a team of highly trained engineers explaining a sewage system to a city council to a single salesclerk suggesting a Lacoste shirt to someone browsing in a clothing store. Chapter 20 explores why personal selling is such a rewarding career for so many Americans. Among other advantages, it represents an entry-level job for numerous other positions in the field of marketing.

Burger King had a major advertising campaign in the mid-1980s about a character who was such a nerd that he had never eaten a Whopper. The person in the ads visited many Burger King restaurants, and any consumer who could identify him was given a prize. Local media picked up on the story, resulting in good publicity for Burger King. (Carol Rosegg.)

ADVERTISING   Advertising is the most visible element of the promotion component. In the mid-1980s, advertising expenditures in the United States reached an annual level of $100 billion. **Advertising** is any paid form of nonpersonal communication, usually delivered through mass media by an identified sponsor. Chapter 18 describes the great variety of methods, tools, and practitioners in the world of advertising.

SALES PROMOTION   From cents-off coupons to premiums, sweepstakes to sponsorship of sports events, display racks in your local store to trade shows, marketers employ a multitude of methods to promote their wares. **Sales promotion** consists of short-range tactics that are intended to achieve specific objectives within a target market. Later in this chapter, we will examine how sales promotion complements the other elements of promotion as one of the most flexible tools available to modern marketers.

PUBLICITY   When a song called "Pac-Man Fever" hit the music charts in the early 1980s, marketers at Atari could not have been more delighted. The Pac-Man video game was already enormously successful; having a song on the air that (in effect) promoted the game was icing on the cake. An unusual aspect of this publicity was that it came from two young songwriters who were cashing in on the popularity of the video game. More typically, large organizations establish public relations departments to generate their own publicity.

Publicity is a form of promotion composed of newsworthy messages sent through the media on a nonpaid basis. It typically aims at a broader public than would be targeted in an advertising campaign. Like advertising, publicity is transmitted by the media, but it is not controlled by its subject as easily as advertising. Although publicity is considered to be "free" because the media are not paid, costs *are* incurred by marketers.

The elements of promotion are potent means of communicating an organization's message. Remember that they are usually used in concert to complement and reinforce each other.

☐ *An Overview of Communication*

Theorist Frank Dance has counted more than 90 definitions of communication, which indicates the complexity of this seemingly simple process.[1] For our purposes, however, a simple definition seems best: **Communication** is the process of sharing meaning through the use of symbols.

The most widely cited model of the communication process was proposed in the 1940s by Claude Shannon, an engineer at Bell Laboratories. Shannon's goal was to find the most efficient way to transmit electrical signals from one location to another.[2] Figure 17-1 illustrates Shannon's model, which postulates a sequential process to explain how communication takes place. This process warrants careful attention from marketers.

SOURCE   The **source** is the communicator sending a message to another party or parties. The effectiveness of communication depends greatly on the credibility, or believability, of the communicator. **Source credibility** hinges on at least four factors:

1. *Competence* is the degree to which the source is perceived as knowledgeable or expert about the topic at hand. For instance, John McEnroe is one of the many tennis pros who endorse brands of tennis racquets. Ford Motor Company has used a race car driver to promote the design and performance of its cars.
2. *Trustworthiness* is the extent to which the source is perceived as honest, fair, and objective. When calling on prospective buyers, salespeople know that they must first "sell themselves" before anyone will believe the points they wish to make about their company and products.
3. *Similarity* is the extent to which the source and the audience are similar in outlook, lifestyle, and beliefs. The greater the similarity, the more likely it is that the communication will have its intended effects. In an attempt to establish similarity between source and audience, cereal commercials often feature healthy, pert children and their harried but loving parents.
4. *Attraction* refers to the physical characteristics of the source as perceived by the audience. Cheryl Tiegs and Brooke Shields have been in great demand as advertising communicators for cosmetics and clothing, and James Garner and Mariette Hartley were extremely effective for many years in portraying a handsome, humorous couple featured in Polaroid commercials.

Other factors such as prestige and charisma also influence the credibility of a source.[3] Degree of credibility is obviously difficult to measure precisely, yet it is vital to effective communication. Not all marketers rely on spokespeople to lend credibility to their messages, of course, but all marketers need credibility in their communication. Some organizations have achieved impressive credibility: IBM, the American Cancer Society, and American Express among them. Their names alone infuse their promotional efforts with valuable credibility.

ENCODING   The words, images, and even music used in promotion are all symbolic; human beings, after all, communicate by means of symbols. The process by which a source chooses signs and symbols—words, images, and sounds—to con-

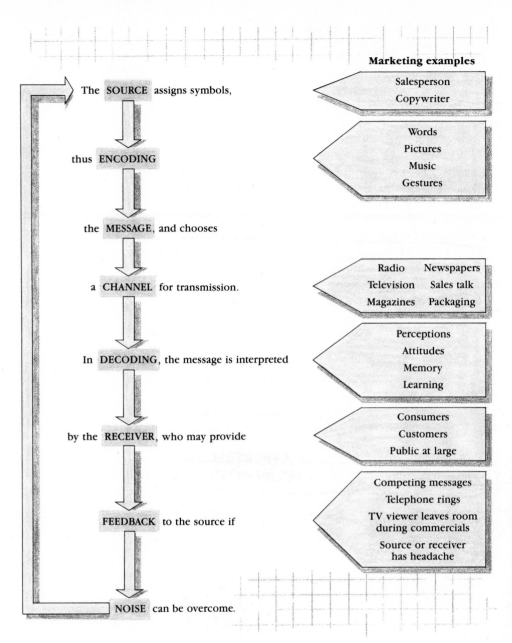

The SOURCE assigns symbols,

Marketing examples

Salesperson
Copywriter

thus ENCODING

Words
Pictures
Music
Gestures

the MESSAGE, and chooses

a CHANNEL for transmission.

Radio   Newspapers
Television   Sales talk
Magazines   Packaging

In DECODING, the message is interpreted

Perceptions
Attitudes
Memory
Learning

by the RECEIVER, who may provide

Consumers
Customers
Public at large

FEEDBACK to the source if

Competing messages
Telephone rings
TV viewer leaves room
during commercials
Source or receiver
has headache

NOISE can be overcome.

Figure 17-1 *The communication process.* The left side of Figure 17-1 displays the theory of how communication works. On the right are examples of communication in a marketing setting. Both personal selling and mass selling efforts are included. (Adapted from Claude Shannon and Warren Weaver, *The Mathematical Theory of Communication*, Urbana, Ill.: University of Illinois, 1949, p. 98.)

struct a message is **encoding.** Although encoding is the most important step in the communication process for marketers, it can be treacherous. If the wrong symbols are chosen, the message will not be perceived as intended.

Marketing communicators must choose symbols that will be understood by at least a majority of the target audience. Consider what happened when Lever Brothers sent hundreds of thousands of free samples of Lemon Light dishwashing detergent to consumers. The initial package design prominently featured a bright, juicy-looking lemon to convey the ideas of freshness and cleanliness. But some consumers took the message literally and sprinkled Lemon Light onto their salads and other foods. The marketers thought they had encoded the message "lemon-scented," but some receivers apparently read that message as "lemon-flavored." Lever Brothers was forced to redesign its package and include a label warning against eating Lemon Light.

MESSAGE   A **message** is a set of verbal and/or nonverbal signs and symbols transmitted by the source. Promotional messages often include words (spoken writ-ten, or sung), images, gestures, movements, and background music. Messages may be straightforward or subtle. "Tide gets the dirt out!" is certainly direct. But "Reach out and touch someone" (AT&T) and "Times like these were made for Taster's Choice" convey more subtle messages: moods. Consumers are encouraged to share these moods by calling a distant loved one or by using a cup of coffee to help create a warm, intimate atmosphere with a special friend.

CHANNEL   A communication **channel** is the vehicle for transmitting a message. In communication theory, the term "medium" is sometimes used interchangeably with "channel" to identify the means by which information is conveyed. Promotion uses an endless variety of channels: the broadcast media (radio spots and television commercials); the print media (newspapers, magazines, direct mail); and special channels (posters, T-shirts, shopping bags, matchbooks, the Goodyear blimps, or an airplane skywriting "Coppertone" above a crowded beach). The product and its packaging are also channels for promotional messages, as the marketers at Lever Brothers were reminded in the Lemon Light fiasco. (Note that, in personal selling, the channel is merely the space between the salesperson and the buyer.)

Chapter 18 will explore commercial messages further in discussing advertis-ing. Most often, the specific channels for a given product are selected by media-buying departments in advertising agencies or by independent media consultants.

DECODING   As discussed earlier, **decoding** is the process of translating or in-terpreting the symbols of a message to derive its meaning. Decoding is complicated

For many years, if you saw a blimp in the sky, it was sure to be that of Goodyear. Now, Fuji, the film marketer, is using this distinctive channel of com-munication. (Copyright © 1987 Lawrence Migdale.)

because there is no guarantee that the symbols encoded by the source will be perceived as intended. To a large extent, consumers perceive selectively; they attend to and remember some cues but not others (see Chapter 4). Hence, all, some, or none of the message may be decoded correctly. For this reason, much advertising research tests consumers' perceptions of promotional messages. Marketers wish to learn, for example, if an announcement of lower prices will affect consumers' perceptions of product quality. They want to be sure that consumers decode what marketers believe has been encoded.

RECEIVER   The person who decodes the message transmitted by the source is the **receiver.** The receiver's interpretation (decoding) of the message is critical to the success of the communication. If the source effectively encodes the message by anticipating the receiver's encoding process, the intended communication occurs.

All of us constantly receive promotional messages; the typical American is exposed to hundreds of messages per day. In our daily interactions, such as talking with a friend, the responsibility for successful communication falls equally on the source (encoder) and the receiver (decoder). In marketing communications, however, the source (marketer) bears the responsibility for ensuring that the message is understood by a not-always-cooperative receiver. To be effective, television commercials, newspaper advertisements, or any other promotional message must be understood by and capable of influencing a large percentage of the target audience. Reaching that predetermined sector of the audience is the marketer's primary promotional task.

FEEDBACK   Communication is a transaction, a two-way process. **Feedback** is the receiver's response or reaction to a message. The source uses this response to adapt, adjust, or recast subsequent messages. Thus, feedback may be used as a corrective mechanism that tells communicators how successful they have been. The most obvious response to a marketer's message occurs when a customer purchases the promoted product. However, the goal of the message may not be to move the consumer to purchase; instead, the message may be intended simply to promote awareness or to move the receiver to seek more information ("send for our free brochure").

Feedback may be positive or negative. Positive feedback occurs when a message gets through, is understood, and achieves its intended effect. Negative feedback occurs if a message does not get through, if it gets through but is not understood, or if it gets through and is understood but does not achieve its intended effect. Consequently, *not* responding to a marketer's message may represent a form of negative feedback. The receiver may be saying: "I got your message, but I wasn't impressed."

Even negative feedback is useful to marketers. If enough receivers misunderstand a message or fail to react as intended, the marketer is likely to adjust the promotion to yield more satisfactory results. Prudential Insurance changed an advertising campaign when research showed that consumers reacted negatively to commercials in which the insured person died. The company's revised campaign showed a person surviving a "close call" to enjoy the security of family and home.

Finally, feedback differs in levels of immediacy among the various elements of promotion. For example, in personal selling the salesperson gets direct feedback from the potential customer, whose verbal comments, body language, and facial expressions all indicate how the message is being received. Thus, in face-to-face selling, the salesperson can adjust the message on the spot. By contrast, copywriters in an advertising agency do not get immediate feedback from consumers and must rely on marketing research and results of advertising tests to learn whether their messages are decoded as originally intended. Feedback is a natural part of the transaction in personal selling, but it must be sought out when advertising is used. As a result, the promotional message of a salesperson is often different from the message devised by a copywriter—even when the intent is the same.

NOISE Many factors can inhibit or impede communication, both in daily life and in marketing campaigns. Communications theorists use the term **noise** to refer to anything that interferes with accurate, successful transmission of a message. Noise can be actual sound, such as the wail of an ambulance siren when you are listening to a lecture or a television commercial. However, noise can also be an ambiguous, misused, or misheard word. External noise comes from outside the communication process, but internal noise may arise within one or both parties, as when a salesperson is distracted by a headache or a potential customer's prejudices lead him or her to distort a message.[4] Even a competitor's messages may be considered noise. "Coke is it!" is noise to marketers for Pepsi-Cola, who are trying to send a message of their own.

Marketing communications should anticipate noise and encode messages to minimize its effects. This is one reason that feedback is so important in the communication process: It indicates how much noise occurred. The existence of noise also explains why many marketers repeat promotional messages so often and in so many ways. They hope that one of these many transmissions will get through to receivers as intended.

☐ *Marketing and the Communication Process*

Obviously, communication is not a simple process; none of the steps shown in Figure 17-1 can be eliminated. The encoding and decoding steps of this process contain inherent difficulties. Effective messages must be structured and assembled clearly. The most appropriate channels must be selected; noise must be minimized; feedback must be provided for. Marketers must carefully assess the challenges posed by the communication process and must design each promotion component to communicate effectively.

The right side of Figure 17-1 places this theoretical model of communication within the day-to-day context of marketing. Although effective communication is vital in all aspects of business, it is especially important in marketing. Through marketing, a company communicates directly with consumers and potential customers—with those on whom its existence depends. The value of effective communication cannot be emphasized enough when it comes to promotion, a primary task of marketing. Keep the communication process in mind as we take a closer look at promotion in action, beginning with the formulation of promotion strategy.

■ *SETTING PROMOTION STRATEGY* ■

Marketers face a complex yet exciting task in devising the most effective blend of promotional elements. Success or failure in marketing communications depends greatly on selecting the proper blend of personal selling, advertising, sales promotion, and publicity. To that end, **promotion strategy**—governed by the overall marketing strategy—is a communication plan designed to bring about desired buyer behaviors by employing a mix of the four elements of promotion. The blend of promotional elements selected and the extent to which each is used is the **promotion mix.** In general, marketers consider at least five factors in setting promotion strategy and devising the promotion mix: the nature of the product, the stage of the product's life cycle, the stage of the exchange process, channel strategy, and the promotion budget.

The Nature of the Product

Boeing's promotion of a new jetliner to Air France or TWA will differ dramatically from Lever Brothers's introduction of a new mouthwash to U.S. consumers. Similarly, a bank's promotional efforts to attract customers for individual retirement accounts (IRAs) will differ radically from the promotional activities of a lawn-care service. In other words, the nature of the product being promoted dictates, to a large extent, how marketers will blend the elements of promotion. We can see dramatic differences in promotion strategies by comparing the typical promotion mix for consumer products and industrial products.

CONSUMER PRODUCTS   A common but not always reliable rule of thumb is that promotion strategies for consumer goods and services rely heavily on advertising and sales promotion, whereas strategies for industrial products depend more on personal selling. This generalization holds true for a large number of consumer products, including nondurables, convenience goods, and low-cost, high-volume services. Thus, film-processing firms like Fotomat rely heavily on advertising (broadcast and print media as well as direct mail) and on sales promotion (coupons and premiums) to promote their services. Procter & Gamble, the world's largest marketer of packaged consumer goods, spends more money on advertising and sales promotion (about $1.3 billion per year) than any other company.[5] Yet Procter & Gamble also fields a large and efficient sales staff to promote its products to retailers. Even though the firm's promotional expenditures emphasize media communications, personal selling is not ignored in the company's promotion mix.

Organizations that market shopping products, specialty goods, or higher-priced services are more likely to focus on advertising and personal selling and to put less emphasis on sales promotion. Examples of such service marketing include commercial health care and nursing homes, building maintenance, and pest control services. Typically, shoppers want sales assistance when making these purchases. Personal selling is also important to comparison shoppers who seek the best price for a major appliance or advice about the styling and fit of a business suit. Those consumers looking for specialty goods such as antiques, golf clubs, and designer clothing are often influenced by personal selling and advertising.

INDUSTRIAL PRODUCTS   Much of Texas Instruments's business comes from the sale of low-cost semiconductor chips to makers of such products as electronic games and digital watches. But when a manufacturer needs a nonstandard component, engineers at Texas Instruments help design it—and thus help sell it. Specialized sales representatives are used by Waste Management, the nation's largest disposer of industrial and residential trash, in marketing its services to corporations and municipalities. In cases like these, personal selling makes up the lion's share of the promotion mix.

It is important to add, however, that many organizational marketers stress advertising in their promotion mix. Industrial advertising is often aimed at professional buyers through special-interest magazines (refer to Box 5-2); moreover, many corporations seek to enhance their image by appealing directly to consumers through the mass media. Rockwell International promotes itself as a company "where science gets down to business."

Advertising for industrial products viewed as commodities (cleaning compounds, floor wax, light bulbs) is typically limited to brochures and catalogs. The promotion mix for such familiar standardized products is likely to emphasize the personal sales call as the best way to communicate with purchasing agents and distributors. Overall, the nature of the product and attendant concern for the nature of its markets probably exert the greatest influence on the makeup of the promotion mix. We can conclude by revising the rule of thumb about promotion strategies presented earlier. Strategies aimed at organizational markets rely heavily on personal selling and only lightly on other elements of the promotion mix. By contrast, in consumer marketing, advertising and sales promotion receive more equal weights; personal selling is somewhat less important; and publicity is the "lightest" element of promotion.

Balance
- A well-ordered integration of elements; e.g., combining the sales from diverse businesses into ten years of uninterrupted earnings growth.
- Stability produced by distribution of weight; e.g., planned diversification between commercial and government business.
- A harmony; one encouraging divisional entrepreneurship with strong financial support—like $2.5 billion in capital expenditures over the last five years.

Ours is a strategic balance. Between commercial and government business. Between down-to-earth management and opportunities as limitless as space. This balance has been the key to our consistent growth, contributing to annual sales in excess of $11 billion.

Our Allen-Bradley subsidiary contributes in a major way to Rockwell's strategic balance. It increases significantly our capabilities in industrial automation and electronics equipment and systems. This further establishes Rockwell's leadership position in applying electronics technology for diverse areas of business, giving us a $3.4 billion share of electronics markets. To learn more about us, write: Rockwell International, Department 815N-2, 600 Grant Street, Pittsburgh, PA 15219.

 **Rockwell International**

...where science gets down to business

Aerospace / Electronics / Automotive
General Industries / A-B Industrial Automation

Rockwell International markets to organizations—mostly government and industry. The bulk of the marketing effort of this kind of company is in personal selling, but advertisements such as this one supplement that effort. (Courtesy of Rockwell International.)

The Product Life Cycle

The product life cycle also helps to shape marketers' use of promotional elements. The promotion mix may shift over the span of a product's introduction, growth, maturity, and decline.

INTRODUCTION   New goods and services are clearly newsworthy. Consequently, when Sony introduced its Mavica electronic camera, it held press conferences in both Tokyo and New York. Polaroid likewise held press conferences to introduce its Spectra camera. Such publicity is a vital part of the promotion mix during a product's introductory stage, when the marketer's goal is to make consumers aware of the product and its benefits. Advertising is also essential at this stage, since it puts the product in the public eye most effectively. Finally, marketers use certain forms of sales promotion for product introduction, as when packaged foods are introduced through the use of newspaper coupons and free samples. Large food companies like Nabisco Brands and Beatrice Foods have developed a sophisticated blend of advertising and sales promotion to persuade consumers to try a new product. Trade shows where buyers and sellers come together are an important sales promotion tool for introducing industrial products.

GROWTH   During the growth stage, competing products usually have entered the picture, the market becomes more turbulent, and competitors use promotion to create selective demand (buy our brand instead of theirs). At this stage, sales promotion frequently dominates the promotion mix. Marketers of packaged goods employ a mix of premiums, coupons, and in-store displays—all coordinated with advertising—to win the fight for shelf space. During the turbulent growth years for low-priced personal computers, Atari, Commodore, and Timex launched massive campaigns combining television and newspaper advertising with rebate programs to cut the final cost to consumers. This battle for market share was waged through promotional efforts. As we will see shortly, trade promotion to retailers takes on added importance during a product's growth stage.

MATURITY   When a product is mature, its sales growth has slowed, market shares of competitors have stabilized, and demand may even be in decline. At this stage, advertising often serves as a reminder or reinforcement of the product, and sales promotion and promotion to intermediaries are aimed at retaining market share. The packaging of mature products often promotes repeat sales; trade discounts are common. Competing retailers like Scott and Procter & Gamble may offer retailers a free case of Viva or Bounty paper towels for every 24 cases they purchase. There is less emphasis on personal selling during the maturity stage; the sales force is turning its attention to promoting newer products.

DECLINE   The promotional budget is much smaller for declining products. In such cases, marketers may use a modest amount of remainder advertising, reduce personal selling to bare maintenance, and cut back sales promotion drastically in an effort to secure all possible profits from the product. Publicity is rarely sought, since a product's decline is seldom good news for the marketer.

The Purchase Process

Marketers design the promotion mix based on judgments about how much of each promotional element is needed during the stages prior to, during, and after the purchase.

PRIOR TO PURCHASE When consumers are learning about products, acquiring knowledge or beliefs about them, or developing attitudes toward them, advertising and publicity are generally the major elements of the promotion mix. However, personal selling may also play a role during the early stages. Although consumers may not decide to buy a product when they are browsing in a store and a salesclerk calls attention to the product, that mild form of personal selling often piques a shopper's interest. Sales promotion can also make consumers aware of the product and build demand. Marketers of packaged goods, for example, may offer free samples to attract consumers' attention, encourage them to try the product, and move them toward making a purchase. Similarly, in marketing industrial goods, advertising to professional buyers can be quite important in preselling.

PURCHASE During the actual transaction, personal selling and sales promotion reach peak importance. An effective salesperson is often the crucial element in closing the sale for shopping goods, specialty products, and relatively expensive services. For nondurable consumer goods, sales promotion in the form of point-of-purchase displays and cents-off coupons may be pivotal in moving the consumer to complete the transaction. For industrial products, personal selling is nearly always crucial at the purchase stage.

AFTER THE PURCHASE Once the exchange has been made, the role of personal selling shifts to emphasize follow-up services. Sales promotion encourages repeat purchases through coupons and the like. Advertising again takes on greater importance in reminding the consumer about the product and in reinforcing both the marketer's message, and the consumers' judgment that they have made wise purchases.

☐ Channel Strategy

The marketer's distribution strategy determines the makeup of the promotion mix. That strategy can be aimed at "pulling" the product through distribution channels, at "pushing" it through by enlisting the support of channel members, or at pulling and pushing at the same time. All three approaches can be used to promote both industrial and consumer products.

In adopting a **pull strategy,** marketers aim promotional efforts at creating demand among consumers and customers. This strategy is most common in consumer goods promotion, which emphasizes mass media advertising and direct sales promotion designed to spur consumers into asking for the product, which encourages retailers to carry it. Frito-Lay often uses a pull strategy in promoting its packaged snack foods: Demand is created through advertising and sales promotion, and the product is pulled through the distribution channel.

Marketers may choose instead to aim promotion (or a large part of it) at intermediaries. In a **push strategy,** personal selling and sales promotion are directed at channel members, who then promote the product to consumers. Trade promotions—such as price reductions to retailers and contests among salespeople—are often emphasized in a push strategy.

Figure 17-2 summarizes these two strategies and their promotional emphasis. In effect, a pull strategy gets around the need to influence intermediaries by creating demand among consumers, largely through advertising. In contrast, push strategy enlists the aid of intermediaries in creating demand. Although most marketers of

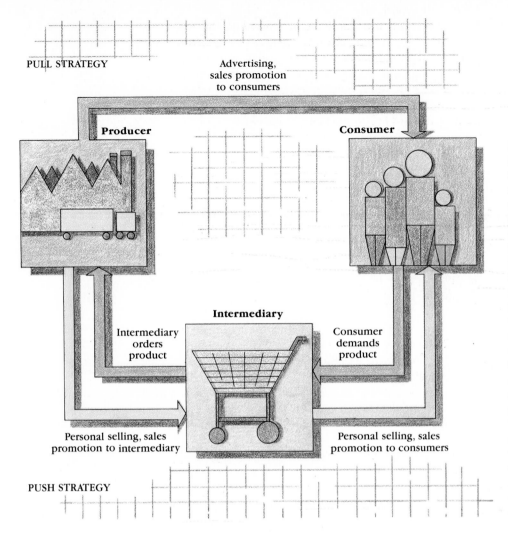

PULL STRATEGY

Advertising,
sales promotion
to consumers

Producer

Consumer

Figure 17-2 *Promotional emphasis of channel strategies.* Under a push strategy, the manufacturer directs promotional efforts such as personal selling and sales promotion and, to a lesser extent, advertising at the intermediaries such as wholesalers and retailers. The expectation is that the intermediary will, in turn, promote to the next member of the channel until there is selling effort directed at the final consumer. Under a pull strategy, the manufacturer directs promotional efforts, predominantly advertising and sales promotion, to the final consumer to build demand directly. The consumer then "pulls" the product through the channels.

Intermediary

Intermediary
orders
product

Consumer
demands
product

Personal selling, sales
promotion to intermediary

Personal selling, sales
promotion to consumers

PUSH STRATEGY

consumer goods combine these promotional approaches, some companies favor one strategy over the other. Thus, Frito-Lay typically emphasizes advertising to pull its products through distribution channels, whereas archrival Nabisco Brands concentrates on promoting products directly to wholesale distributors and supermarket chains.

☐ *The Promotion Budget*

Ideally, the amount of money budgeted for promotion should be a direct result of a particular strategy—not vice versa. The best promotion blend should be allotted the right amount of funds (not always the largest amount) to achieve stated goals. Allocation of funds for each element of promotion should be dictated primarily by the strategy factors discussed earlier: the product, the stages of the product life cycle and purchase process, and channel considerations.

In reality, few organizations can devote the amount of money to promotion that advertising, promotion, and sales staffs honestly believe is optimum. Network television advertising may be most efficient in the number of persons reached per dollars spent, but a small manufacturer of sportswear is unlikely to have the necessary resources to pay for a 30-second spot on *The Bill Cosby Show* or *Miami Vice*. This marketer may have to adjust its strategy to what can realistically be accomplished by a small sales force and carefully targeted newspaper advertising in a few geographical areas.

Whether strategy sets the budget or the budget puts constraints on strategy, financial planning is a key factor in promotion strategy. Moreover, the budget can be used for promotion evaluation. If funds spent on a sales promotion campaign did not produce the desired results, the company's promotion mix may need adjustments.

Promotional Consistency

The aim of promotion is to communicate, but inconsistent promotion sends conflicting messages that are likely to confuse the audience. The marketing manager should ensure that each element of the promotion component complements and reinforces the others. A company's publicity, advertising, sales promotion, and personal selling efforts should communicate the same message and should be coordinated to advance specific goals. When properly planned and executed, the promotion campaign creates opportunities for sales and dramatically increases the likelihood of an exchange.

One good example of promotional consistency is the long-time campaign developed by the Leo Burnett agency for Marlboro cigarettes. The target audience, male smokers aged 21 to 35, responded impressively to the Marlboro Man's cowboy image by making Marlboro the best-selling brand of cigarettes in the world. All elements of promotion are chosen to reinforce the masculine and western theme. Premiums tied to sales promotion have included such items as western-style belt buckles, sheepskin coats, and bandanas. The colors, images, and messages of Marlboro's promotion campaign have been coordinated carefully over the years—so successfully that Winston and Camels have imitated Marlboro in competing for the same target audience.

SALES PROMOTION

If you have ever clipped a newspaper coupon and redeemed it at the supermarket for a lower price on a can of coffee or a tube of toothpaste, you have taken part in a sales promotion campaign. You have done exactly what the marketer wanted you to do: You took action. Without sales promotion, you might never have made that purchase or might have bought another brand. By redeeming that coupon (or entering a sweepstakes or trying a free sample), you join the millions of consumers who respond to sales promotions. According to A. C. Nielsen Company, 76 percent of all U.S. households use **cents-off coupons.** In 1985 alone, 179.8 million coupons were issued, and the number redeemed led to discounts totaling $2.24 billion.[6]

The use of sales promotion has increased dramatically over the last decade, especially among marketers of packaged goods. As can be seen in Figure 17-3, the growth of sales promotion from 1975 to 1985 averaged 12 percent per year, whereas advertising grew at 8 percent per year. By 1985, sales promotion accounted for 63 percent of the mass promotion expenditures of manufacturers, as opposed to 37 percent for advertising. Interestingly, sales promotion aimed at the trade (intermediaries) was greater than that aimed at the ultimate consumer. Whereas 15 years ago advertising accounted for the bulk of most national advertisers' budgets, sales promotion has since become the dominant promotion element.[7]

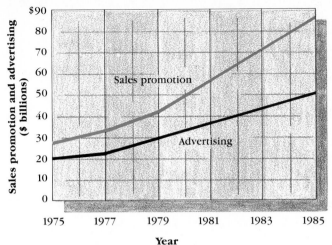

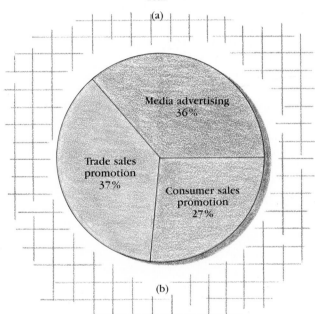

Figure 17-3 *Growth of advertising and sales promotion.* It is difficult to track with accuracy the proportion of promotional budgets going to various forms of promotion because of the differences among reporting sources. (a) More money is spent on sales promotion than advertising, and the gap continues to widen. This bothers some marketers because money spent on advertising is felt to build long-term consumer loyalty, whereas that spent on sales promotion is felt to have only very short-term effects of shifting demand from one brand to another. (b) The figure illustrates how the promotional budget spent on the three most costly forms of mass promotion was spent. (Data from Don E. Schultz, "Why Marketers Like the Sales Promotion Gambit," *Advertising Age*, No. 7, 1983, p. M-52; Kevin T. Higgins, "Sales Promotion Spending Closing in on Advertising," *Marketing News*, July 4, 1986, pp. 8, 10; and *Donnelley Marketing Seventh Annual Survey of Promotional Practices*.)

Recall that sales promotion consists of tactics designed to achieve specific objectives in a limited time in a target market. Sales promotions are directed at two primary audiences: consumers and the trade.

☐ *Consumer Promotions*

Promotions directed at consumers typically have one or more of the following objectives:

- To entice nonusers to try the brand
- To reward users for their loyalty (and thus maintain market share)
- To increase perceptions of brand differentiation in markets where products are basically similar
- To encourage impulse purchases
- To create excitement
- To promote off-season products

The variety of ways in which marketers carry out consumer promotions is dizzying. The following tactics are hardly an exhaustive survey, but they provide a glimpse of the fertile imaginations of modern marketers.

PRICE-OFF PROMOTIONS   Aimed at both consumers and distributors, **price-off promotions** involve temporary price reductions to retailers with the intent that savings will be passed along to consumers. In an immediate price-off promotion, the marketer usually affixes a special label to the product's package to indicate the percentage or cash savings, which the retailer then honors. In a delayed price-off promotion, the consumer has to pay the normal price but can send the marketer a proof-of-purchase label or a UPC label to claim a cash rebate (refund) of a few cents or dollars. Marketers are increasingly offering coupons toward the next purchase of the product or even toward the purchase of another product. For example, marketers of small appliances, such as Sunbeam and Norelco, offer rebates of several dollars on purchase of items like toasters, irons, and mixers.

sales → % off price

REBATES   During the 1981 to 1982 recession, automobile companies turned to the use of large **rebates** to promote their cars. Chrysler employed this tactic by offering cash rebates of more than $500 to buyers. Although the rebates reduced profits for the company and its dealers, this promotional effort helped move inven-

Coupons are an important part of the sales promotion efforts of consumer goods marketers. Coupons offering price off the purchase can come in the mail, in the package, and in the company's advertising, as shown here. (Courtesy of Alley Marketing.)

tory, kept production lines open, and may have been crucial to Chrysler's survival. Producers of major appliances have also used large cash rebates as an effective promotional tool.

COUPONS   Cents-off coupons offer buyers minor price reductions at the point of sale (most often at a supermarket checkout counter, since couponing has proven to be especially effective in promoting food products and other products sold in supermarkets and convenience stores). Coupons are made available to consumers in a variety of ways. Some can be clipped from daily newspaper ads for supermarkets; some come as colorful freestanding inserts in Sunday newspapers; and some are distributed as fliers to homes within a store's immediate vicinity. Coupons are also mailed directly to consumers, often in booklets or packets assembled by distributors or companies specializing in such promotions. Finally, **in-pack** and **on-pack coupons** may be affixed to the product and allow savings on a future purchase.

When marketers redeem a coupon, they have to pay retailers its face value (say, 20 cents) plus a handling charge (say, 7 to 9 cents). Aside from the costs of coupon promotion, some marketers question the effectiveness of this tactic, claiming that coupons undercut the brand loyalty that advertising seeks to establish.[8] Another serious problem associated with coupons is **misredemption,** which involves improper claims by consumers at the checkout counter or improper handling of coupons by retailers and distributors. The magnitude of misredemption is troubling for marketers. One Procter & Gamble executive has estimated that up to 20 percent of all coupons are redeemed improperly.

CONTESTS, SWEEPSTAKES, AND GAMES   Promotional **contests** require consumers to compete for prizes, typically by completing some type of puzzle or stating why they like the product "in 25 words or less." In **sweepstakes,** consumers fill out a form to enter a random drawing for prizes ("Win a free trip for two to Hawaii!"). **Games** require consumers to take specific actions, such as determining whether the card they received with the product contains a winning number by rubbing it with the edge of a coin or collecting several cards to produce the winning combination. Variations on this kind of promotion are endless.

Just as marketers intend, these promotional tactics often generate interest and excitement among consumers. In-pack games are increasingly used for promotion because they are tied directly to the product. However, sweepstakes remain popular: The number of nationally advertised sweepstakes tripled from the mid-1970s to the early 1980s. One well-publicized sweepstakes used to promote magazine subscriptions, the Publishers' Clearing House Giveaway, receives millions of entries each year.

SAMPLES   The most effective way to encourage consumers to try a new product—as well as the most expensive—is to give away free **samples.** To hold costs down, marketers may mail trial-sized versions of the product to consumers or give them away in retail stores. Another approach is to offer samples only to those persons who make purchasing decisions. Your marketing instructors, for example, regularly receive complementary copies of textbooks from publishers; these samples are provided to promote each publisher's books. Copies of the marketing text selected by the instructor are then sold to students taking the course. Many services can also be promoted through sampling. Potential customers can be offered a free car wash at a service station, a month of free cable television service, or a free 2-week introductory period at an exercise studio.

PREMIUMS   Premiums are gifts to paying customers; in general, they are claimed through the mail by sending the marketer a number of proof-of-purchase labels or box tops. In many cases, the consumer must pay a small charge for the premium to help cover the marketer's expenses. If this charge completely covers a marketer's costs, the premium is called a **self-liquidator.**

Johnson & Johnson mounted a premium campaign to reinforce its image as a caring, trustworthy marketer of baby products. The company hired experts in child development to write *The First Wonderful Years,* a book that customers could buy through the mail for only $4.95. This premium appealed to new parents (potential new customers); the offer was supported by coupons promoting Johnson & Johnson's baby products. In a less successful example of use of premiums, the four major rental car companies engaged in a promotion war from 1982 to 1983 that helped no one (see Box 17-1).

JOINT PROMOTIONS   A growing form of consumer promotion is the joint promotion, in which two brands of the same manufacturer or the products of two manufacturers are promoted together. For example, Lever has jointly promoted two of its products, Aim toothpaste and Signal mouthwash. By carefully pairing noncompeting products, a marketer like Lever can get two promotions for the price of one. In another example, Dannon Yogurt and Post's Grape Nuts, each marketed by different companies, have been jointly promoted. Not only does each company get wider exposure, but they share the promotional costs.[9]

Pepsi-Cola Company has found joint promotions to be a useful marketing tactic. Pepsi-Cola joined No Nonsense Panty Hose in a campaign in which Pepsi buyers could claim a free pair of panty hose by sending in an order form available at point-of-purchase displays. Advertising supported the campaign, as did in-pack coupons in Pepsi cartons, and No Nonsense display racks promoted the offer and encouraged purchases of Pepsi. Both marketers reported substantial sales increases during this campaign. More recently, television commercials have announced the

The packaging that includes the "Sculpt and Hold" product is a *premium*—offered free with the purchase of Dep shampoo and conditioner. (Copyright © Bob Daemmrich.)

BOX 17-1   COMPETITION IN MARKETING: Avis and the Premium War

Tired of being "number two" in the rental car business, Avis launched a major promotional campaign in September 1982, by offering its customers free luggage, calculators, and blow dryers. For a few months, competitors failed to counter the Avis premium blitz, and Avis raised its market share from 26 percent to 29 percent. However, beginning in late 1982 and continuing well into 1983, Hertz, National, and Budget all matched Avis gift for gift. The industry found itself in the midst of an all-out promotion war.

When the dust finally settled in mid-1983—as all four marketers ended their premium offers—Hertz had spent $25 million on this program, Avis $15 million, and National and Budget a combined $10 million. What had these marketers received in return for their $50 million in promotional expenditures? Essentially noth-

ing. Partly as a result of the economic recession, the industry had failed to attract new customers. Moreover, during the 9-month period in which the premium war took place, Hertz's market share rose by 0.3 percent, National's increased by 0.1 percent, Budget's rose by 0.3 percent, and Avis's fell by 0.9 percent. In other words, the $50 million in spending brought virtually no change in the market shares of the four leading rental car companies. Yet each firm's profits were substantially reduced because of the dramatic increases in promotional costs. "We all went out and spent a great deal of money on frills, and didn't get anything out of it," acknowledged one Hertz executive. "It didn't help anybody."

Source: "Car Renters Go Back to Basics as Business Travel Rebounds," *Ad Forum,* Feb. 1984, pp. 43, 45–46.   ■

"great romance" between Pepsi and Burger King (as lovers are shown embracing on a deserted beach), and Pepsi's two-time sponsorship of Michael Jackson promoted both the musical star and the soft drink to "a whole new generation."

Our examples emphasize the most common methods of consumer promotion, which are extended and varied almost daily by some enterprising promoter. Indeed, the opportunities for sales promotion are limited only by marketers' imagination, daring, and good taste. As a result of such ingenuity, 20-foot hot dogs are pulled by helicopter over the San Diego freeway, scratch-and-sniff samples of perfume are tucked into the pages of a fashion magazine, and contributors to public television stations can claim a new tote bag or umbrella along with a tax deduction.

☐ *Trade Promotions*

Marketers not only mount promotion campaigns aimed at consumers, they also aim at marketing intermediaries. **Trade promotions** spur action on the part of channel members, such as additional orders from retailers or a special push by a wholesaler to promote one manufacturer's products. Following are some typical methods of trade promotion.

PRICE-OFF PROMOTIONS   Marketers offer intermediaries a reduced price (perhaps $1 off the cost of each case or 13 cases for the price of 12) through **price-off promotions** or **trade allowances.** These savings are not intended to be passed along to consumers; they represent a bonus to the intermediary and serve as an incentive to increase the size of the order.

CONTESTS   Trade promotion often takes the form of contests offering bonuses or prizes to retailers and dealers who sell the most of a manufacturer's product within a given period. Automakers and insurance companies have long sponsored such contests for dealers' sales representatives; they send winners on free vacations to Hawaii or Bermuda. Eastman Kodak also holds frequent contests for its retailers.

PUSH MONEY   Special bonuses paid by a marketer to an intermediary's sales force are called **push money** because they advance the strategy of pushing the product through the distribution channel. For example, Zenith may pay sales personnel at Macy's or Burdine's a $40 bonus for every Zenith television set sold during a specific period. Or Loctite may pay salesclerks in a hardware or plumbing outlet $1 in push money for each sale of Quick Metal, the company's adhesive for machinery repair. Many retailers dislike push money, however, since it tends to make the sales force loyal to that promoter's brand and may undermine the retailer's own goals.

TRADE SHOWS   Important promotional events for both industrial and consumer marketers, known as **trade shows,** are typically organized by an industry's trade associations and are held yearly (or more often) in different cities.[10] Trade shows allow marketers to display all their wares—especially new products—to a well-defined group of current and potential new customers. This opportunity is especially attractive for companies with a small sales force, because important potential customers are gathered together under one roof in a large exhibition hall like New York's Jacob Javits Convention Center or Chicago's McCormack Place.

One believer in the effectiveness of trade shows is Plaskolite, a $30-million firm in Columbus, Ohio, that markets do-it-yourself plumbing supplies and "window weatherization" products. Plaskolite exhibits both at the National Hardware Show

Hundreds of manufacturers and thousands of retailers attend the annual consumer electronics shows in major cities. These *trade shows* play an important role in the marketing of these products. (Copyright © Barrie Rokeach 1986/The Image Bank.)

in August and at the National Home Center/Home Improvement Congress in March. Luis Weil, the company's vice president of marketing, sums up their view: "Exhibiting at a trade show gives us a chance to meet with major decision makers in one location."[11]

POINT-OF-PURCHASE DISPLAYS   **Point-of-purchase** (POP) or **point-of-sale** (POS) **displays** are self-contained, specially designed shelves or racks used to display one manufacturer's products. The manufacturer gives or sells the display units to retailers and also assumes the responsibility of keeping them stocked. POP displays offer marketers an opportunity to promote their products to the trade and to consumers at the same time. These displays help retailers because the manufacturer assumes certain inventory tasks and, of course, because prominent display of products results in additional sales. Food marketers are particularly eager to place POP displays at the end of a supermarket aisle or at the checkout counter to encourage consumers to make impulse purchases. Candy, magazines, razor blades, batteries, film, and panty hose are often promoted through eye-catching displays placed near the cash register.

COOPERATIVE ADVERTISING   **Cooperative advertising** is promotion that the manufacturer makes available to the wholesaler—or more commonly to the retailer—through a fund intended to help cover the cost of the channel member's advertising which features the manufacturer's brand. For example, a newspaper ad may feature the names of both the manufacturer (Minolta cameras) and the local photo retailer. Minolta will pay part, perhaps 50 percent, of the cost of the ad. This form of promotion encourages the retailer to feature the manufacturer's brand and helps the retailer to offer more advertising than would otherwise be possible.

As in our survey of consumer promotions, we have looked only at the most common methods of trade promotion. Besides these devices, marketers use a variety of discounts and services that encourage intermediaries to carry and promote their

Point-of-purchase (or point-of-sale) promotional materials are an attempt to remind the consumer of the name of the brand, and often its advertising theme, right at the point of purchase—inside the retail store. (Courtesy of Villa Banfi, U.S.A., Old Brookville, N.Y.)

products. (We didn't even mention the people in clown costumes who wave cereal boxes at you in the supermarket—or the smiling people who offer you a piece of cheese or salami on a toothpick!)

PLANNING SALES PROMOTION CAMPAIGNS

Consumer, trade, and sales force promotions must be planned and coordinated to achieve a unified program supported by advertising and publicity. Once again, we can apply the marketing management model of analyzing, planning, implementing, and controlling. For the promotion component to take its place effectively in the overall marketing mix, it should be planned and implemented just as rigorously as the product, pricing, and distribution components.

Until recent years, sales promotion efforts were regarded by most marketing firms as an adjunct of either advertising or personal selling. Even though sales promotion efforts and expenditures have grown enormously, the need for close attention to strategic planning, implementation, and control has traditionally lagged behind the more sophisticated management and measurement of areas such as advertising. Yet today more persons trained in sales promotion are entering marketing, and the effectiveness of sales promotion departments is being watched carefully by skilled managers.

Setting Objectives

What is to be accomplished by a sales promotion? Is the objective a sales increase of 6 percent over a 2-month period? An increase in market share of 0.5 percent within 4 months? Is it to persuade 2 million new customers to try the product? Perhaps the goal is to get retailers to increase their inventory by 500,000 cases in a 6-week period. Whatever the objectives of sales promotion, they should meet two basic criteria: (1) Objectives should support and be an integral part of the overall corporate marketing strategy. (2) To the extent possible, objectives should be quantifiable and measurable.

Spur-of-the-moment promotion campaigns may be effective, but all too often their impact is temporary. The best campaigns have long-lasting effects that result from careful analysis and planning of the marketing mix. When objectives can be quantified and measured, managers can learn which specific promotional efforts were successful and justified their costs.

The Body Centers—located in Los Angeles, San Francisco, New York, and Fort Lauderdale—have a well-coordinated promotion campaign. Their yearly marketing plan calls for a special, once-a-year promotional effort aimed at enrolling a specific number of new members at each gym. The promotion mix includes sales force bonuses, supporting newspaper ads, flyers distributed on the street, and direct mail to former members. Most important, Body Centers can easily measure the results of promotion: Did each gym enroll the target number of new members during the 1-month campaign? The organization carefully attempts to measure the effectiveness of the various promotional elements used in each city. Only the sales force bonus is held constant; other elements of the promotion mix are altered and evaluated.

Assigning Responsibility

The growing importance of sales promotion is evidenced by its new prominence within marketing organizations. Many large companies have established sales promotion divisions, although responsibility for sales promotion is still commonly given to the director of advertising or to the sales force manager. Some organizations turn to outside firms that specialize in particular kinds of sales promotion. For example, D. L. Blair Company offers expertise in sweepstakes promotions; Donnelly Marketing specializes in cooperative coupon mailings; A. C. Nielsen monitors product movement during promotion campaigns; and SPAR (Sales Promotion Analysis and Reporting) measures and analyzes the effectiveness of sales promotion. In addition, many large advertising agencies now have their own promotion departments. Today, even small marketers have opportunities to support their products with effective sales promotion.

The Overall Plan: Selecting the Tools of Promotion

Which promotional elements produce the most effective campaign? Quite simply, the ones that best fit the promotional objectives. If the marketer's goal is to encourage consumers to try the product, sampling is most effective (even if also the most expensive). If the objective is to hold market share, promotions that require multiple purchases may be tried. And if a straightforward sales increase is the goal, then sales force incentives may be the answer. Marketers can expect to become increasingly sophisticated in their ability to choose the right tool for the intended objective. As the measurement of promotional effectiveness becomes more of a science than an art, even the highly creative aspects of promotion will be analyzed and appraised.[12]

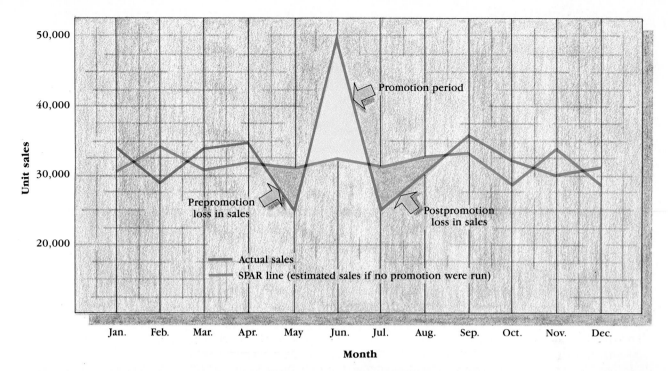

Figure 17-4 *Evaluating effectiveness of promotions.* It is important to carefully evaluate how effectively sales promotions improve profitability. One method for doing so has been developed by Sales Promotion Analysis and Reporting (SPAR). A key to whether the promotion is successful comes from answering the question: Did the firm make more profit in June when sales were higher but the margin was lower (represented by yellow) than it lost in May and July when sales were lower (dark gray) and the margins were normal? (From *Sales Promotion Analysis and Reporting.*)

☐ *Implementing and Controlling the Campaign*

Whatever the objectives chosen, whatever the theme and tools and media selected, whatever group is the target of the campaign, promotion must be monitored and controlled to ensure some measure of success. If display units do not reach retailers in time, if brochures are not attention-getting, if budgets are not enforced, promotion campaigns can easily backfire. Responsibility for promotion should be assigned to a specific individual (or group) who also has the authority to carry out the campaign successfully.

If the objectives of promotion are tied closely to sales, measuring success can be fairly straightforward, but this is not always the case. Suppose, for example, that intermediaries or consumers know in advance that prices will be cut as part of a promotion campaign. As shown in Figure 17-4, they may hold back on purchases before the campaign starts and then may buy heavily *during* the campaign at the lower promotional price. Afterward, sales may again decline. Marketers must assess whether the campaign itself increased sales, or whether such purchases were simply delayed from previous months to take advantage of the reduced price. Sales must be monitored before, during, and after the campaign to answer such questions.

In the example illustrated here, the marketer runs a promotion during June. The line *S* on the chart is the forecasted sales that would take place if no promotion were held. This forecast is based on historical conditions and relies on the forecasting methods discussed in Chapter 9. The line marked *A* represents the actual sales.

Note that sales dropped off in May as retailers got word of the impending promotion. They began buying fewer cases of the product and instead used up inventory. Then, during the promotion in June, the retailers bought much more than normal at the lower promotional price. They sold more goods to consumers but still had large inventories of the promoted product at the end of the promotion. Consequently, their purchases are lower in July when the price has returned to normal.

In addition to monitoring sales effects, marketers keep track of the redemption rates of coupons and premiums and of the receipt of sweepstakes and contest entries. Surveys of channel members or consumers are also used to evaluate the effectiveness of promotion, and they may uncover ways to improve a campaign.

▮ *PUBLICITY* ▮

"Advertising has never had credibility and never will have. With advertising, people are always on their guard. They're always wary because they know the purpose of advertising is to sell. But public relations—that's something different."[13] These comments were made by Jack O'Dwyer, publisher of a public relations and publicity newsletter, who is obviously biased in favor of his field. But O'Dwyer makes an important point: Public relations *is* "something different" from advertising. Actually, **public relations** is the broader term of which publicity is a part. In general, **publicity** is an intentional effort to produce favorable, unpaid-for communication with the organization's "stakeholders": employees, stockholders, customers, clients, as well as consumers and the public at large.[14] By contrast, advertising is paid for and controlled by its sponsor and is typically aimed at a specific audience rather than the larger public.

Publicity can be a useful promotional device for both organizational and consumer marketers.[15] Most sizable organizations, whether profit-oriented or not, have publicity departments (which is one reason why publicity is not really "free"). Others hire outside firms to handle their normal, day-to-day publicity or engage such firms for special projects. Large advertising agencies usually have experts to provide publicity services along with advertising.

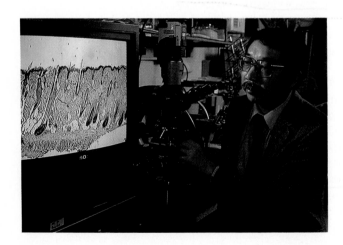

In developing new products for the market, scientists in a company's research laboratories often make important new discoveries. Such breakthroughs can be the source of favorable publicity for the company, as when Upjohn Co. developed Minoxidil, a heart disease drug that makes hair grow. (Copyright © Melford/Wheeler Pictures.)

In the mid-1980s, the publicity experts of Humana Inc. used the company's heart implant program to engineer a mountain of favorable publicity. Humana's promotional objective was to gain visibility and recognition so that Humana would become "a national brand of health care." The central event in Humana's media blitz was the implantation of an artificial heart into William Schroeder in November 1984 at the Humana Heart Institute International in Louisville. This procedure, financed by Humana, was only the second such heart implantation ever performed.

Even before the surgery took place, Humana conducted a 1-day briefing on its artificial heart program at the Louisville Convention Center. Humana used the center as its media headquarters and went to great lengths to assist visiting reporters by installing telephones, lighting for electronic coverage, and other equipment. Publicity staff provided extensive background material, arranged regular briefings by medical specialists and interviews with the patient and his family, and issued timely bulletins about Schroeder's condition. Some negative publicity developed—critics called the affair "a Roman circus" and accused Humana of caring more about

Publicity can cut both ways. Bad publicity, such as the suffering caused by the accident in the Union Carbide plant in Bhopal, India, can hurt the company seriously. (Copyright © Raghu Rai/Magnum.)

profits than about research—but, in general, Humana scored a smashing success in terms of worldwide favorable publicity in the print media, radio, and television. The company's costs for communications were between $250,000 and $300,000, leading one columnist to conclude that "purely in terms of media exposure, it's got to be the biggest steal since the Brink's caper."[16]

The ultimate test of any publicity campaign is whether it enhances or damages a firm's reputation. When publicity is good, it is very very good; when it is bad, it is awful. In either case, as in the Humana example, publicity generally gets wide attention at relatively little cost. Remember that people tend to believe what the media report—even if the story was supplied by a publicist. Good publicity may be taken with a grain of salt, and bad publicity may be believed no matter how outrageous ("Where there's smoke, there's fire"). But the attention-getting power of publicity is so great that no marketer can afford to ignore this unique element of the promotion mix.

◼ SUMMARY ◼

1. The four elements of promotion are personal selling, advertising, sales promotion, and publicity.
2. In general, promotion has three aims: to inform, to persuade, and to remind.
3. The other components of the marketing mix—product, price, and distribution—are the subjects of promotion.
4. Advertising is the most visible element of the promotion component.
5. Typical publicity aims at a broader audience than would be targeted in an advertising campaign.
6. According to the most widely cited model of the communication process, a source or sender encodes a message and sends it through some channel to a receiver, who then decodes the message and gives the source some type of feedback.
7. In general, marketers consider at least five factors in setting promotion strategy and devising the promotion mix: the nature of the product, the stage of the product's life cycle, the stage of the exchange process, channel strategy, and the promotion budget.
8. Ideally, the amount of money budgeted for promotion should be a direct result of chosen strategy—not vice versa.
9. The use of sales promotion has increased dramatically over the last decade, especially among marketers of packaged goods.
10. Sales promotions are usually directed at two primary audiences: consumers and the trade.

11. Tactics of consumer promotion include price-off promotions; large rebates; coupons; contests, sweepstakes, and games; samples; premiums; and joint promotions.

12. Typical methods of trade promotion include price-off promotions, contests, push money, trade shows, point-of-purchase displays, and cooperative advertising.

13. Sales promotion objectives should support and be an integral part of overall corporate marketing strategy. Objectives should be as quantifiable and measurable as possible.

14. Promotion must be monitored and controlled to ensure some measure of success.

15. Publicity can be useful for both organizational and consumer marketers.

16. Almost all organizations view public relations as a direct responsibility of top-level management.

☐ *Key Terms*

advertising	noise	push strategy
cents-off coupons	personal selling	rebates
channel	point-of-purchase displays	receiver
communication	point-of-sale displays	sales promotion
contests	premiums	samples
cooperative advertising	price-off promotions	self-liquidator
decoding	promotion	source
encoding	promotion mix	source credibility
feedback	promotion strategy	sweepstakes
games	publicity	trade allowances
in-pack and on-pack coupons	public relations	trade promotions
message	pull strategy	trade shows
misredemption	push money	

☐ *Chapter Review*

1. Cite the four major aims of promotion. Identify a newspaper or television advertisement that focuses on each of the aims. How do elements of the marketing mix other than promotion convey important information? Give examples.

2. Contrast the four elements of promotion. Which element would be the likely choice to emphasize in promoting (1) an automated assembly line to a maker of household appliances, (2) a new headache remedy, (3) a new flavor of an established yogurt brand, and (4) a new corporate name?

3. How is packaging (the "silent salesperson") closely related to the four elements of promotion?

4. Diagram the process of communication. Break down a television commercial for a pain remedy into the steps of the communication process.

5. What major factors influence the establishment of promotion strategy? Give examples of products that marketers might choose to pull through channels and of products that marketers might choose to push through channels.

6. Differentiate sales promotion and advertising. Explain how a 25-cents-off coupon for a detergent is part of a sales promotion campaign.

7. What are the differing aims of consumer and trade promotions?

8. What might be some logical objectives for a promotion campaign for Dial bath soap? For Chevrolet pickup trucks? For a supplier of lumber to contractors?

9. Why is publicity considered "free"?

References

1. Frank E. Dance, "The Concepts of Communication," *Journal of Communication,* vol. 20, 1970, pp. 201–210.

2. Claude Shannon and Warren Weaver, *The Mathematical Theory of Communication* (Urbana, Ill.: University of Illinois, 1949), p. 98.

3. James C. McCroskey and Lawrence Wheeless, *Introduction to Human Communication* (Boston: Allyn & Bacon, 1976), p. 102.

4. Shannon and Weaver, op. cit.

5. R. Craig Endicott, "Advertisers Cut Spending Space," *Advertising Age,* Sept. 4, 1986, pp. 1 ff.

6. Kevin T. Higgins, "Sales Promotion Spending Closing in on Advertising," *Marketing News,* July 4, 1986, pp. 8, 10.

7. F. Kent Mitchell, "Advertising/Promotion Budgets: How Did We Get Here, and What Do We Do Now?" *Journal of Consumer Marketing,* Fall 1985, pp. 45–47.

8. William Nigut, Sr., "Is the Boom in Cents-Off Couponing Going to Burst?" *Advertising Age,* Dec. 15, 1980, p. 42.

9. P. "Rajan" Varadarajan, "Horizontal Cooperative Sales Promotion: A Framework for Classification and Additional Perspectives," *Journal of Marketing,* vol. 50, Apr. 1986, pp. 61–73; and P. "Rajan" Varadarajan, "Cooperative Sales Promotion: An Idea Whose Time Has Come," *Journal of Consumer Marketing,* Winter 1986, pp. 15–33.

10. Joseph A. Bellizzi and Delilah J. Lipps, "Managerial Guidelines for Trade Show Effectiveness," *Industrial Marketing Management,* vol. 13, Feb. 1984, pp. 49–52.

11. Rayna Skolnick, "Why Trade Shows Are Big with Small Companies," *Sales & Marketing Management,* Feb. 8, 1982, pp. 72–74.

12. For discussions of recent developments in such analysis, see Patrick McIvor, "Simple, Inexpensive Method Analyzes Promotion," *Advertising Age,* Aug. 15, 1985, pp. 35–36; "Marketers Calculate Return on Promotion," *Advertising Age,* Feb. 6, 1986, pp. 26–27; and "Modified Computer System Helps Kraft Make Plans," *Marketing News,* May 23, 1986, p. 31.

13. Quoted in Theodore J. Gage, "PR Ripens Role in Marketing," *Advertising Age,* Jan. 5, 1981, p. 5.

14. John E. Marston, *Modern Public Relations* (New York: McGraw-Hill, 1979), p. 6.

15. Jerome D. Williams, "Industrial Publicity: One of the Best Promotional Tools," *Industrial Marketing Management,* vol. 12, no. 3, July 1983, pp. 207–211.

16. Jack Bernstein, "Anatomy of a Public Relations Bonanza," *Advertising Age,* Feb. 18, 1985, p. 66.

18

MANAGING THE ADVERTISING PROGRAM

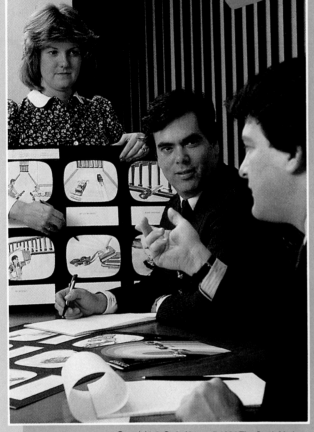

SPOTLIGHT ON

- ☐ Functions of advertising
- ☐ Relationships among advertisers, advertising agencies, and the media
- ☐ Services that advertising agencies offer to their clients
- ☐ Setting objectives and budgets as initial steps in the advertising process
- ☐ Creative strategy for and creative execution of advertising
- ☐ Requirements of an effective advertisement
- ☐ Selection of media for an advertising campaign
- ☐ Evaluation of advertising

539

"Do you know me?" asked a vaguely familiar face in a 1974 television commercial. "People often look at me and say, 'You're somebody,' but they haven't the foggiest idea who." So began the first of more than 60 American Express commercials to use the now-trademarked phrase "Do you know me?" The late John McGiver, a respected character actor, explained how he often needed an American Express card to get recognition. Since then, he has been followed by an assortment of distinguished but not necessarily recognizable figures, including astronaut Charles Conrad, opera star Luciano Pavarotti, former Senator Sam Ervin of North Carolina, comedians Bob & Ray, and Dallas Cowboys' football coach Tom Landry.

The "Do You Know Me?" commercials were created by William B. Taylor, senior vice president and executive creative director of Ogilvy & Mather, a major New York advertising agency. Taylor has written that "anyone who dreams up a TV campaign, gets it on the air, and then dares to imagine it might run for 10 years is certifiable." But in 1987, more than 12 years later, this campaign was still going strong with remarkably few changes.

In 1974, Ogilvy and Mather and American Express were faced with the need to replace the "real people" spot commercials for American Express cards that had been popular for a few years. This successful campaign had involved short endorsements from actual card members filmed in cities like Rome, London, and Dubrovnik. Many other advertisers had copied the approach, weakening the effectiveness of the American Express spots. Moreover, marketing research suggested a possible weakness in terms of prestige, an attribute viewed as vital to the success of American Express cards.

Jim Henson, inventor of the Muppets, put his own face in front of the camera in an American Express Commercial. (Courtesy of American Express.)

JIM HENSON: Do you know me?

To get any recognition at all, I either have to travel with one of my muppets
MUPPETS: Yea!

or with this: The American Express Card.

Don't leave home without it.

Ogilvy & Mather experimented with three new approaches; a commercial was written and shot for each. One of these, involving character actor Norman Fell, made a game out of identifying someone whose face was well-known but whose name wasn't. Fell stated: "Thanks to TV, lots of people know my face, but not many know my name." The commercial established the American Express card as a heroic product which brought the actor the recognition (and services) that he needed.

The advertising agency tested all three commercials, and the Norman Fell spot was the winner. Ogilvy & Mather then produced the John McGiver commercial, introducing the familiar, "Do you know me?" opening. As the campaign evolved, American Express representatives began to worry about the effectiveness of a series of commercials featuring obscure Hollywood actors. At this point, Ogilvy & Mather's creative staff realized that the campaign could be expanded to include people whose faces weren't famous but whose *names* (author Robert Ludlum), *voices* (Mel Blanc, the voice of Bugs Bunny), or *accomplishments* (musician Benny Goodman) were.

Ogilvy & Mather concluded early on that it needed to change commercials often if the campaign was to be successful. Over the years, it not only shot a wide array of show business professionals, business leaders, politicians, and sports figures; it also achieved success by shooting some personalities in unfamiliar settings. Thus, golfer Jack Nicklaus was filmed playing tennis, and quarterback Fran Tarkenton was shot on a rugby field. The publicity value of the American Express campaign was enhanced by television "Do You Know Me?" comedy takeoffs: Johnny Carson as Hamlet, Rich Little as President Nixon, even Bob Hope as the Pope (complete with an American Express card reading, "Pope Hope").

In the view of creator William B. Taylor, four important reasons explain the success of this advertising campaign: (1) Frequently changing spots keep the campaign current and fresh. (2) The campaign is credible: You can believe that the personalities shown may not be recognized in all situations and therefore may need an American Express card. (3) The campaign is involving and entertaining. (4) The campaign is relatively intelligent, with a tone that is respectful toward the audience.

Source: William B. Taylor, "We Know Them Now, American Express," *Advertising Age,* Aug. 27, 1984, p. 34.

Displayed on coffee-shop windows and theater marquees; highlighted in newspapers and magazines; broadcast on television and radio; blazoned on billboards, printed on matchbooks, and stuffed into mailboxes—advertising messages surround us daily. Advertising is ever-present in modern society and influences people's lives around the world. Although advertising is only one of the tools and tasks of marketers, it is the most visible: Advertising is marketing seen and heard.

As defined by the American Marketing Association, **advertising** is "any paid form of nonpersonal presentation and promotion of ideas, goods, or services by an identified sponsor."[1] The first key word in this definition is "paid." Advertisers must pay for advertising time or space in the media—as opposed to publicity, where that time and space is free (see Chapter 17). Another key word is "nonpersonal," which distinguishes advertising from personal selling, which involves a face-to-face presentation. The final key word in the AMA definition is "sponsor." In advertising, the sponsor of the ad must be clearly identified for the consumer to see (or hear).

Chapter 18 examines the functions and scope of advertising and introduces its practitioners: advertisers, advertising agencies, and the media. We will see how marketers choose their audiences and set objectives for advertising and how they develop creative strategies and creative executions for use in various media. Finally, we will review techniques used to evaluate the effectiveness of advertising.

ADVERTISING: MARKETING BROUGHT HOME

Rosie the waitress, Ed and Frank, and Mr. Whipple the grocer were all familiar faces on television in the recent past—so familiar that you can probably name the products they promoted (Bounty paper towels, Bartles and Jaymes wine cooler, and Charmin toilet paper). Animals and cartoon characters have also been imprinted on the U.S. consciousness. Advertising has made household pets of Morris the cat (9-Lives), Charlie the tuna (Star-Kist), and Tony the tiger (Kellogg's Frosted Flakes). Smokey the bear (U.S. Forest Service) is recognized by 98 of 100 people. He receives so much mail that he needs his own zip code (20252); use of his image has been regulated by an act of Congress.

Newer to the television screen and magazine pages are such spokespeople as Lionel Richie (Pepsi-Cola), Bill Cosby (Jell-O pudding), John Houseman (for the investment firm of Smith Barney), daytime-television star Susan Lucci (for the Revlon fragrance Scoundrel), and *Moonlighting*'s Bruce Willis (Seagram's Golden Wine

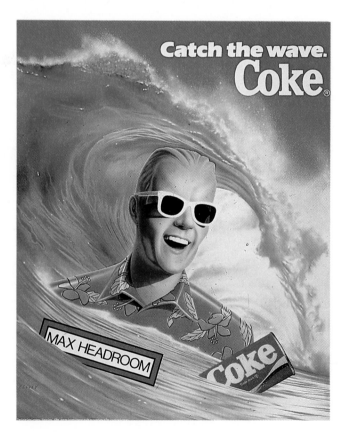

McCann-Erickson advertising agency found a unique spokesperson for Coca-Cola in the form of Max Headroom, a part human, part computer-generated character who made a big splash in 1987. (Courtesy of Coca-Cola.)

Cooler). We recognize them as would our neighbors and relatives; we can predict what these celebrities will say. Even a computer-generated talk-show personality, "Max Headroom," became a promotional hit on Coca-Cola television commercials and on music videos in the mid-1980s.

Like them or loathe them, advertisements are the most visible aspect of marketing in general and of promotion. Yet, advertising practice remains mysterious to most people. Behind the scenes, advertising professionals combine science and art into messages of great power, creating ideas and images that sometimes interest us, sometimes annoy us, and often become firmly embedded in our psyches. (Test yourself: "It's a good time, for a great taste, at . . ."; "Give me a light, no a. . . .")

Why do marketers seem to rely so heavily on advertising? What special purposes does advertising have as an element of promotion? How are they achieved? Who decides which messages to send and how to present them? Is there really any difference between good and bad advertising? These are the main questions that we will explore in looking at one of the most creative and controversial aspects of marketing.

The Functions of Advertising

Advertising is unique as an element of promotion in that it communicates a specific, controlled message to an entire group of people—some of whom may not be the intended audience. Our look at sales promotion and publicity in Chapter 17 revealed that the former is a short-range tactic designed to influence members of a particular target market, whereas the latter is often outside the marketer's control (since the message is created and delivered at the discretion of the media). The other element of promotion, personal selling, most often involves one-to-one communication. Such use of individually directed, interactive messages is probably the most effective way to sell homes, financial counseling services, and complex industrial products like assembly lines. However, marketers of laundry detergents, toothpaste, soft drinks, and fast foods have found that mass communication is the most efficient way of promoting their products.

By its very nature, then, advertising directs controlled messages to entire target markets—to groups. The group addressed may be large or small. Janco Greenhouses of Laurel, Maryland, expects to reach only a small but affluent market segment with its column-width ads in the back pages of magazines like *House Beautiful.* By contrast, Chrysler Corporation expects millions of car buyers to see Lee Iacocca's gruff, straightforward commercials on prime-time network television.

Unlike publicity, which also aims impersonal messages at groups, advertising is created and paid for by an identified sponsor. Because advertisments are aimed at groups whose members cannot respond directly to them, advertising functions quite differently from personal selling. The one-sided nature of advertising messages and their persistent presence in daily life make advertising a uniquely powerful element of promotion. Yet these very factors also limit advertising's impact and make it suspect.

Sid Bernstein, a popular columnist who writes in *Advertising Age,* the ad industry's most popular magazine, admits: "Advertising is not impartial or unbiased; its function is to present the advertiser's story or product as alluringly as possible, without overstepping the bounds of honesty, truthfulness, and good taste."[2] Consumers realize, of course, that advertising is biased and that it attempts to present the product in the best possible light. By the time they reach third grade, almost 90 percent of U.S. children know that advertising is attempting to persuade them

HOW TO PEDDLE A ROSE.

Some say advertising is an illusion. Wrong. Good advertising is an imaginative representation of things familiar that puts product or service in its best light, makes you see it, smell it, reach for it . . . want it. There's nothing illusory about it. The product is there. To view again and again. And nothing sells better than advertising printed on Howard Papers.

Advertising can be used to sell anything—including advertising itself. This ad for Howard Paper is designed to appeal to the advertising professional who might influence the purchase of paper. (Courtesy of Howard Paper Mills, Inc.)

of something.[3] But advertising also supports the other basic aims of promotion: In addition to persuading consumers to act, it informs, reminds, and reinforces. Consumers cannot buy a product unless they know about it, and they need to be reminded of the product and its benefits. Finally, advertising seeks to reinforce our satisfaction with products already purchased; marketers are well aware that satisfied customers are likely to buy again.

Certain advertising is directed not to consumers but to intermediaries within distribution channels, as when a company places a "Don't Be Out of Stock of . . ." ad in media read by the managers of supermarkets and drugstores. The intent is to remind the store manager to maintain an adequate stock of the product. Other ads aimed at intermediaries may attempt to inform, to persuade, or to reinforce. Distributors are also influenced by effective consumer advertising; they certainly recognize the advantage of stocking and supporting products that consumers want.

☐ *The Scope of Advertising*

With only 6 percent of the world's population, the U.S. receives a staggering 57 percent of the world's advertising. Television alone accomplishes much of this: By the time typical students graduate from high school, they have spent 11,000 hours in classes but have watched 25,000 hours of television. Almost 6000 of these television hours were devoted to commercial messages. The cost of advertising is another eye-opener. Worldwide expenditures have passed the $150 billion mark annually and are projected to double by the year 2000. Agencies handle most of the advertising in the U.S. and about one-third of global advertising.

EXHIBIT 18-1 **Top Advertisers in the United States**

In 1985, Procter & Gamble was the leading advertiser in the United States in "measured" media, spending about $1.6 billion to advertise its many consumer products. As these data illustrate, the leading advertisers tend to be companies selling products that are consumed on a regular basis, such as foods, beverages, and cigarettes. Of the top 10 advertisers, only two (General Motors and Ford) sell products of a more durable nature.

Rank	Company	1985 Advertising Expenditures ($ thousands)
1	Procter & Gamble	1,600,000
2	Philip Morris Cos.	1,400,000
3	R. J. Reynolds/Nabisco	1,093,000
4	Sears, Roebuck & Co.	800,000
5	General Motors Corp.	779,000
6	Beatrice Cos.	684,000
7	Ford Motor Co.	614,600
8	K mart Corp.	567,000
9	McDonald's Corp.	550,000
10	Anheuser-Busch Cos.	522,900
100	George A. Hormel & Co.	70,700

Note: The most authoritative source for advertising expenditures is *Advertising Age,* which annually surveys the 100 leading national advertisers. Its data, however, include only eight "measured" media: newspapers, magazines, farm publications, spot (local) television, network television, spot (local) radio, network radio, and outdoor advertising. Cable TV, cooperative advertising, direct mail, national retail advertising, and local newspaper expenditures are *not* included in this survey. The cost of sales promotion is also omitted. In 1983, *Advertising Age* estimated that the 100 leading national advertisers spent $7.2 billion on unmeasured media (besides the $11.7 billion devoted to measured media).

Source: R. Craig Endicott, "Advertisers Cut Spending Pace," *Advertising Age,* Sept. 4, 1986, pp. 1 ff.

Exhibit 18-1 lists the top 10 advertisers in the United States in 1985, as well as number 100. Procter & Gamble has headed this list for a number of years, but if local newspaper advertising were included, the leader would be Sears, Roebuck. As a percentage of sales, advertising expenditures vary widely from industry to industry and among companies within industries. In general, marketers of beauty care products, pharmaceuticals, and toys spend a relatively high percentage of sales on advertising. Industrial marketers typically budget a lower percentage of their sales to advertising; they reach their markets through ads in specialized magazines but also rely more heavily on personal selling to promote their products. Exhibit 18-2 lists advertising expenditures as a percentage of sales for selected industries.

The data in Exhibits 18-1 and 18-2 make it clear that advertising not only represents vast expenditures but has great impact on the economies of the United States and the world as a whole. The influence of advertising is unlikely to diminish in the near future. Yet advertising is not without its critics; Box 18-1 presents both criticisms of advertising and the responses of some marketers.

■ THE ADVERTISING BUSINESS ■

The main participants in the advertising business, as we will see shortly, are advertisers, advertising agencies, and the mass media. Other groups also have an impact on advertising: regulatory agencies such as the Federal Trade Commission and the Food and Drug Administration; unofficial regulators such as consumer advocate Ralph Nader and television consumer reporters; organizations such as the Better Business Bureau; and, on occasion, the U.S. Congress.

EXHIBIT 18-2

Advertising Expenditures as a Percentage of Sales in Selected Industries, 1985

In general, marketers of consumer products spend a higher percentage of their sales on advertising than do industrial marketers.

Industry	Ad Dollars as Percentage of Sales
Consumer Markets	
Retail mail-order houses	13.2
Perfumes, cosmetics, toiletries	13.1
Toys, amusements, sporting goods	10.0
Phonograph records	9.1
Prepared feeds for animals	8.9
Malt beverages	8.4
Soap and other detergents	7.9
Books, publishing, and printing	4.0
Hotels and motels	3.5
Household furniture	2.6
Motor vehicles	1.6
Convenience stores	0.4
Organizational Markets	
Computers: mini and micro	6.5
Office furniture	1.6
Computers: mainframe	1.5
Sanitary services	0.7
Management consulting, PR services	0.2
Water transportation	0.1

Source: "Ad Study Uncovers Spending Patterns," *Advertising Age,* Sept. 15, 1986, p. 60.

☐ *Advertisers*

Advertisers—referred to by their agencies as client organizations—are the "identified sponsors" who pay to promote their goods, services, and ideas to target audiences. Business firms pay for the bulk of advertising, but advertising is also sponsored by trade associations (such as the American Association of Manufacturers, by retailers and wholesalers (often in cooperation with manufacturers), and by a host of nonprofit organizations (among them the Better Vision Institute, the Congress for Jewish Culture, and the St. Louis Symphony Orchestra). In fact, the U.S. government ranked as the thirty-third largest advertiser in the nation in 1985, spending over $259 million.[4]

The advertiser is responsible for the goals of, the strategy behind, and the budget for any advertising campaign. Although most large-scale advertising is conceived and carried out by outside agencies, final decisions concerning advertising rest with the organization that pays for it.

☐ *Advertising Agencies*

Manhattan's Madison Avenue has traditionally been regarded as the center of the nation's advertising business. Eight of the ten largest agencies have their headquarters there, although they also have offices in other major U.S. cities and across the world. All the most populous cities in the United States have thriving, homegrown advertising agencies as well. Interestingly, the largest advertising agency in the world is based not in New York but in London: Saatchi and Saatchi.

BOX 18-1 MARKETING ISSUES: Criticisms of Advertising

The advertisement below enumerates and addresses the main criticisms that have been directed at the advertising industry. Among other charges, critics have claimed that advertising (1) unduly influences "ignorant" consumers and persuades them to buy unneeded products, (2) merely increases the costs of products, (3) can foist second-rate products on an unsuspecting public, and (4) is a nonproductive activity that absorbs valuable economic resources.

Take a moment to consider how the ad answers these charges. Like other ads this one reflects the sponsor's point of view. It faces criticisms head-on and suggests that such views are baseless. But are they? Does the ad persuade you that criticisms are unfair?

The four objections to advertising addressed in the ad are, of course, not the only potential objections.

Advertising is often intrusive and annoying; its potential effects on children deeply concern many parents and educators. No one discounts the seriousness of these issues, but many marketing and advertising professionals feel that advertising is criticized because it is an easy, visible target. They point out that revenues from advertising "pay the freight" for print and broadcast media, thereby contributing to diversity of expression by enlarging the number of media outlets.

Advertising is a human activity and thus can be used positively or negatively. When advertising is misleading, unethical, or manipulative, it *should* be criticized. But, sweeping attacks often ignore the benefits that advertising provides. The overall effect of advertising is to broaden our choices and inform our decision making.

THIS AD IS FULL OF LIES.

LIE #1: ADVERTISING MAKES YOU BUY THINGS YOU DON'T WANT.
Advertising is often accused of inducing people to buy things against their will.

But when was the last time you returned home from the local shopping mall with a bag full of things you had absolutely no use for? The truth is, nothing short of a pointed gun can get *anybody* to spend money on something he or she doesn't want.

No matter how effective an ad is, you and millions of other American consumers make your own decisions. If you don't believe it, ask someone who knows firsthand about the limits of advertising. Like your local Edsel dealer.

LIE #2: ADVERTISING MAKES THINGS COST MORE. Since advertising costs money, it's natural to assume it costs *you* money. But the truth is that advertising often brings prices down.

Consider the electronic calculator, for example. In the late 1960s, advertising created a mass market for calculators. That meant more of them needed to be produced, which brought the price of producing each calculator down. Competition spurred by advertising brought the price down still further.

As a result, the same product that used to cost hundreds of dollars now costs as little as five dollars.

LIE #3: ADVERTISING HELPS BAD PRODUCTS SELL.
Some people worry that good advertising sometimes covers up for bad products.

But nothing can make you like a bad product. So, while advertising can help convince you to try something once, it can't make you buy it twice. If you don't like what you've bought, you won't buy it again. And if enough people feel the same way, the product dies on the shelf.

In other words, the only thing advertising can do for a bad product is help you find out it's a bad product. And you take it from there.

LIE #4: ADVERTISING IS A WASTE OF MONEY. Some people wonder why we don't just put all the money spent on advertising directly into our national economy.

The answer is, we already do.

Advertising helps products sell, which holds down prices, which helps sales even more. It creates jobs. It informs you about all the products available and helps you compare them. And it stimulates the competition that produces new and better products at reasonable prices.

If all that doesn't convince you that advertising is important to our economy, you might as well stop reading.

Because on top of everything else, advertising has paid for a large part of the magazine you're now holding.

And that's the truth.

ADVERTISING.
ANOTHER WORD FOR FREEDOM OF CHOICE.
American Association of Advertising Agencies

(Courtesy of American Association of Advertising Agencies.)

☐ *Profile of a Full-Service Agency*

Backer & Spielvogel, one of New York City's more powerful advertising agencies, was founded in 1979 by William Backer and Carl Spielvogel. Backer had been the creative director at McCann-Erickson and was responsible for its Coca-Cola ad campaigns; Spielvogel was the vice chair of Interpublic, the parent corporation of McCann-Erickson. Shortly after the new agency was established, Miller Beer moved its multimillion-dollar account from McCann. Obviously, Miller had great faith in William Backer and Carl Spielvogel. Such account shifts give credence to the old saying that an ad agency is the only business where the inventory goes down in the elevator every evening after work.[5]

Backer & Spielvogel grew quickly, adding major clients such as Campbell Soup Company, NCR Corporation, United States Data Processing Group, Paddington Corporation (liquor importers), and Red Lobster Inns. In short order, the firm developed into a **full-service advertising agency** that offered its clients a wide range of services, including (at a minimum) the four most basic: account management and marketing, creative, media, and research services. Certain full-service agencies offer additional services such as packaging design, promotion development and execution, public relations, new-product development, and specialized advertising such as direct response and recruitment (of employees).[6]

Figure 18-1 illustrates a typical organization of a full-service agency. Let's take a more in-depth look at the services offered to clients by such agencies.

ACCOUNT SERVICES An advertising agency's **account services department** helps the client to devise an overall campaign strategy that determines a product's target market, how to position the product, and which aspects of the product to stress. After these basic decisions have been made, the information is passed on to the creative services staff. **Account executives** (or supervisors) therefore serve as liaisons between the client and the agency. After working with the client on a day-to-day basis, the account executive interprets the client's needs for other agency personnel and assists them in devising programs that the client will approve.

A successful account executive must be an effective salesperson, especially in winning new clients for the agency. When a client is ready to assign a new account, to select an agency for a new product, or to switch accounts, a competition is often held in which three to five agencies make presentations. In "selling" the agency to a client, account executives call on top managers of the agency—from creative directors to marketing research specialists—to participate.

As the main contacts between client and agency, account executives have good interpersonal and communication skills. Good agency-client relations often depend not only on the actual work of the agency but also on building and sustaining friendship and respect. Consequently, account executives must effectively play the roles of salesperson, agency-client contact, and account coordinator.

CREATIVE SERVICES Typically, an advertising agency's **creative services department** is responsible for the creation, design, and production of whatever will appear or be heard on radio or television or in print. Creative services may also design packages and may write, design, and produce sales promotion materials. The work of this department involves the services of composers, musicians, directors, producers, actors, announcers, photographers, writers, and so forth. They may be hired for a particular project or may be full-time agency staff members. To produce its ads, J. Walter Thompson employs over 1300 writers, art directors, and television

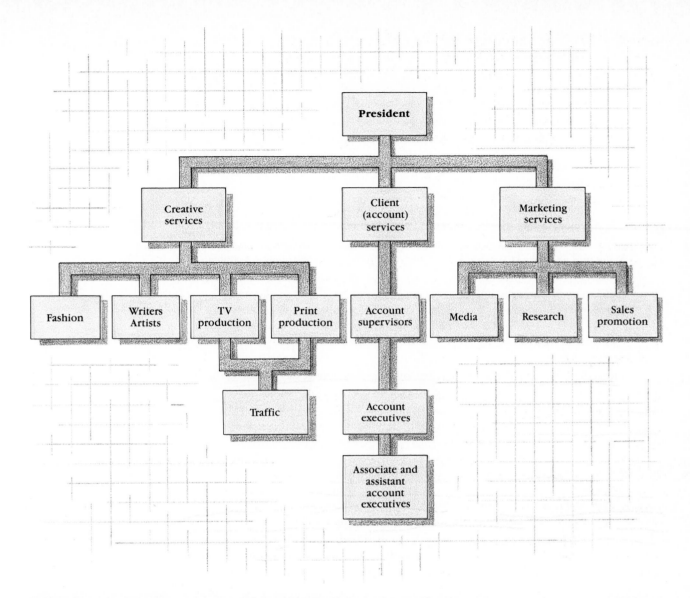

Figure 18-1 *Organization of a full-service advertising agency.* A full-service advertising agency provides answers for most of its clients' needs. As the figure illustrates, one major agency division is that of client (or account) services. These employees work with the advertiser (client) and others to develop the total advertising strategy and to decide how much to spend on the advertising program. They serve as the key link between the agency and the advertiser. The creative services division of the agency—the group that originates and executes the ads themselves—has the most employees. Other marketing services provided by a full-service agency include media scheduling, marketing research, and management of sales promotions. (Adapted from material supplied by the American Association of Advertising Agencies. Used by permission.)

producers. An official at Thompson has pointed out that large advertising agencies "employ more creative people than any other social institution"—more than newspapers, magazines, broadcasting stations, or book publishers.[7]

Advertising themes such as Coca-Cola's "Catch the Wave" and Kodak's "Pours on the Colors" are developed by imaginative copywriters and artists. After discussions with the client and the account executive about product strategy, a copywriter—who creates the promotional concept and writes the text or dialogue to be used—comes up with ideas for the client's approval. In getting to know a target audience and devising an idea for an advertising campaign, account executives and copywriters draw on extensive product, market, and demographic research. Advertising copy is often tested with a sample of the target audience, much as a product is tested, to see if it is likely to accomplish its goals.

David Ogilvy, former head of Ogilvy & Mather and a highly regarded writer of advertising copy, described the creation of effective advertising this way:

> First, do your homework. Soak yourself in the product and the research. Review the precedents. It is dull work, but do it you must.
>
> Shove all this in your mind, then switch off. Now the rational process ends and the unconscious takes over. Big ideas come only from the unconscious—in all fields of endeavor.
>
> After a while you get a telephone call from your unconscious, saying, "Hey, I've got an idea." The trick is to keep the telephone line open. People who are 100% rational have lost touch with their unconscious and don't take the calls. All big ideas have come this way."[8]

Television advertisements, the most widely seen products of creative services departments, are made in the same way movies are. In lieu of a script, however, a commercial is based on a series of **storyboards**—sketches, written copy, and directions used to communicate a commercial's message. Figure 18-2 presents a sample storyboard.

MEDIA   An advertising agency's **media group** is staffed by specialists who analyze, plan, select, and obtain time or space in various media in accordance with the client's advertising program. In its choice of broadcast or print, in its timing of advertising, and by the nature of its budget guidelines, the media group is the most scientifically oriented of the agency groups. Media buyers deal with the facts and figures of demographics, readership studies, and costs. As a result, their work is closely tied to that of the research department.

MARKETING RESEARCH   An advertising agency's **marketing research department** may research consumer attitudes for the client, perform demographic studies, test the effectiveness of advertising copy or packaging, or conduct research for the agency itself. In short, this department is a vital arm of the agency, responsible for whatever marketing research is needed to help produce effective advertising. Some full-service agencies emphasize their research capabilities: Batten, Barton, Durstine, & Osborne (BBD&O), for example, employs a large staff of statisticians, psychologists, and computer specialists. By contrast, other agencies stress their creative strengths, among them Wells Rich Greene Inc. and Della Femina, Travisano & Partners.

SPECIAL FUNCTIONS   Full-service agencies may offer still other services to clients. A number have public relations groups, either within the agency or as subsidiary companies. Some agencies also offer sales promotion services. In other words, these full-service agencies present clients with a complete promotion package that stops short only of fielding a personal sales force.

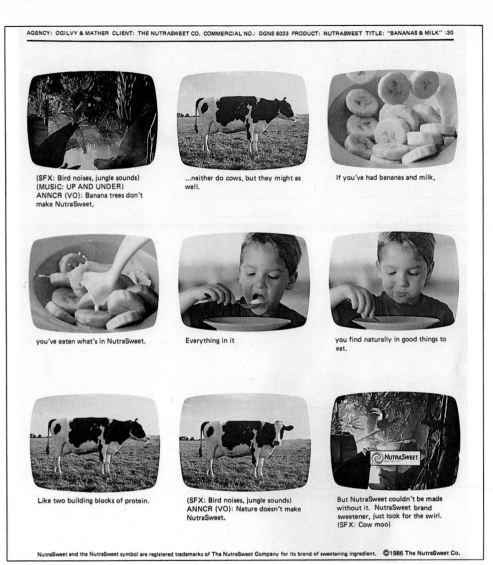

(SFX: Bird noises, jungle sounds) (MUSIC: UP AND UNDER) ANNCR (VO): Banana trees don't make NutraSweet,

...neither do cows, but they might as well.

If you've had bananas and milk,

you've eaten what's in NutraSweet.

Everything in it

you find naturally in good things to eat.

Like two building blocks of protein.

(SFX: Bird noises, jungle sounds) ANNCR (VO): Nature doesn't make NutraSweet.

But NutraSweet couldn't be made without it. NutraSweet brand sweetener, just look for the swirl. (SFX: Cow moo)

NutraSweet and the NutraSweet symbol are registered trademarks of The NutraSweet Company for its brand of sweetening ingredient. ©1986 The NutraSweet Co.

Figure 18-2 *Storyboard for a NutraSweet commercial.* This storyboard, developed by the Ogilvy and Mather advertising agency, is the way a television commercial is first presented to the client for approval before the money is spent to produce it. Note that it starts out and ends with sound effects (SFX), and that the words spoken are from an announcer (ANNCR) in what is termed a "voice over" (VO), as opposed to the consumer actually seeing the announcer speak the words. Note also that the commercial is given a name, "Bananas and Milk," and that it will be a 30-second ad.

☐ *Specialized Agencies*

Whereas full-service agencies offer diverse clients a wide range of services, certain advertising agencies are more specialized—in terms of either who they work for (in-house agencies) or the services they offer (media buyers and creative boutiques).

IN-HOUSE AGENCIES Marketers as diverse as General Electric, Ralston Purina, and Nabisco Brands have their own agencies, termed **in-house agencies**, which perform the functions of a full-service agency. Some companies believe that an in-house agency ensures stricter control over advertising, but the primary objective is to spend advertising dollars more efficiently by controlling expenditures and by eliminating as a cost the profit that an independent advertising agency would make.

Those critical of the in-house concept believe that the objectivity an independent agency would bring to the appraisal of an advertising strategy is likely to be lost. Critics add that in-house creative service departments may become stale or inbred and often get caught up in the internal affairs of the larger organization. Partly in response to such concerns, certain marketers maintain in-house advertising agencies for a few products while retaining independent agencies for others.

MEDIA BUYERS   **Media buying organizations** do just what their name implies: They select, schedule, and purchase media. Advertisers use media buyers when other sources—such as in-house agencies, creative boutiques, or other firms—provide the creative work and the necessary research.

CREATIVE BOUTIQUES   **Creative boutiques** are small agencies specializing in the creative work for an advertising campaign. Such firms are typically established by creative people who leave full-service agencies to concentrate on what they do best. Della Femina, Travisano & Partners began as a creative boutique but has since grown into a full-service agency.

> independent creative dept.

☐ Media and Vehicles

The third major component of the advertising business is a group of organizations collectively referred to as the media. The **media** are print or broadcast firms that carry advertising messages in addition to their news, editorial, and entertainment material. Television, radio, newspapers, and magazines are the major media involved in transmitting promotional messages. Other media include direct mail, business publications, outdoor (billboards) ads, transit cards (buses and subways), telephone directories, and flyers. When we refer to **vehicles**, we mean specific outlets within a larger advertising medium. *Better Homes and Gardens* and *Popular Computing* are vehicles within the magazine medium; a particular FM station is a vehicle within the radio medium.

☐ Advertiser-Agency Relations

Contractual arrangements between agencies and their client advertisers are written so that fast exits are possible (and frequent). Agencies can be fired at will by advertisers, and agencies occasionally resign from accounts. As a result, stable relations between the two must be built on trust and respect. Their working relationship is so close—agency personnel are as privy to information about the advertiser's marketing strategy for the next 5 years as anyone in the advertiser's own organization—that confidentiality is an absolute necessity.

Another important aspect of the advertiser-agency relationship is **product line exclusivity**—an agreement that the agency will not work on a competing product for the duration of the relationship. Ogilvy & Mather has the Maxwell House coffee account from General Foods and therefore cannot take on the Folgers coffee account from Procter & Gamble. Young & Rubicam will be free, however, to take on Procter & Gamble's Ivory Liquid dish detergent—if the agency has no other dish detergent accounts. When an agency resigns an account, it frequently does so in order to take on a more lucrative assignment that conflicts with the previous account. In Box 18-2, we examine the conflicts of interest that arise when two advertising agencies (who may handle competing brands of the same product) merge.

Box 18-2   MARKETING ISSUES: Agency Mergers and Conflicts of Interest

One of the most dramatic (and controversial) recent trends in the advertising business has been mergers involving large or medium-size advertising agencies (sometimes known as "megamergers"). For example, in two of the largest such mergers of the 1980s, Saatchi & Saatchi Company bought Ted Bates Worldwide, and Batten, Barton, Durstine & Osborne (BBD&O), Needham Harper Worldwide, and Doyle Dane Bernbach combined to form the new Omnicom Group.

Such mergers have raised many sensitive issues of conflict of interest. To do its job effectively, an advertising agency needs detailed knowledge of a client's marketing strategy and even its larger corporate strategy. Naturally, this involves highly secretive and valuable information that must be kept in strict confidence. If a competitor learned your firm's marketing plan, it could begin to counterattack or defend its position even before your advertising campaign reached the public through the mass media. With this in mind, how would you feel if your agency suddenly merged with an agency handling advertising for a major competitor? Obviously, the merger would make you rather uneasy.

Agencies involved in such situations may argue that conflicts of interest can be avoided. They may promise to assign completely different creative services personnel to each competitor's account and insist that there be no communication between these staffers concerning the two clients. Consequently, they will argue, neither marketer's secrets will be compromised by the potential conflict of interest.

But many marketing executives find this position far from convincing. They point out that the merged agency will undoubtedly wish to take advantage of any opportunity for economy of scale. Suppose it does research on beer consumers for one of its clients, a domestic beer manufacturer. Won't the agency use the same research for another beer marketer if it has that account as well? It hardly seems likely that the agency will double its costs by having similar studies conducted by different market researchers to service each client separately.

A number of major marketers have taken business away from merged agencies because they find such conflicts of interest to be inevitable when the agency represents a competitor. In particular, Procter & Gamble has taken a strong stand against agencies with dual loyalties. It has a strict policy barring agencies from handling any brand that competes with any product in the Procter & Gamble divisions assigned to that agency. Thus, an agency handling Procter & Gamble paper towels cannot take on another advertiser's sanitary napkins or disposable diapers because all these products are produced by Procter & Gamble's paper division. In mid-1986, Procter & Gamble implemented this policy rather dramatically by removing $85 million in business from the Saatchi agencies. Saatchi's DFS Dorland Worldwide lost Procter & Gamble's Luvs baby pants and Bounty paper towels accounts, and Saatchi & Saatchi Compton lost Crisco oil and shortening and Duncan Hines baking mixes—all because one or another of the merged Saatchi agencies handled products for Procter & Gamble's competitors such as Johnson & Johnson and Nabisco.

Marketing and advertising professionals seem divided over the viability of Procter & Gamble's antimerger stand. When questioned about the company's "punishment" of the Saatchi network, Elizabeth Harris, president and creative director of a Philadelphia agency, wondered: "Now where will P&G go? They'll have to look hard to find another big agency not affected by mergers." But Paul Mulcahey, president of Campbell Soup Company's in-house advertising agency, replies: "There is no such thing as agency business other than its service to clients. A client has to control its own destiny, and you can't abdicate that to any agency."

Interestingly, it is the small and medium-size marketers who seem most likely to suffer from advertising agency megamergers. Just after the merger of BBD&O, Needham Harper, and Doyle Dane Bernbach in April 1986, the president of BBD&O appeared unannounced at the office of Stroh Brewery Company's president to inform him that BBD&O was dropping the Stroh account. "We were thrown out," charges Stroh's executive vice president, "because Anheuser Busch, a Needham account, insisted there would be a conflict." Despite a mutually satisfactory and profitable business relationship over 7 years—during which Stroh had provided BBD&O with about $20 million in annual billings— Stroh abruptly learned that they were expendable. When agency mergers create such conflicts of interest, bigger clients with spending clout will often have their way, and smaller marketers may find their marketing strategy in ruins. ◾

Sources: Aimee Stern, "Agency Mergers: The Perils for Advertisers," *Dun's Business Month,* July 1986, pp. 48–49; "Why P&G Wars on Megamergers," *Advertising Age,* Sept. 29, 1986, pp. 3, 84; "Street Talk," *Advertising Age*, Sept. 29, 1986, p. 84.

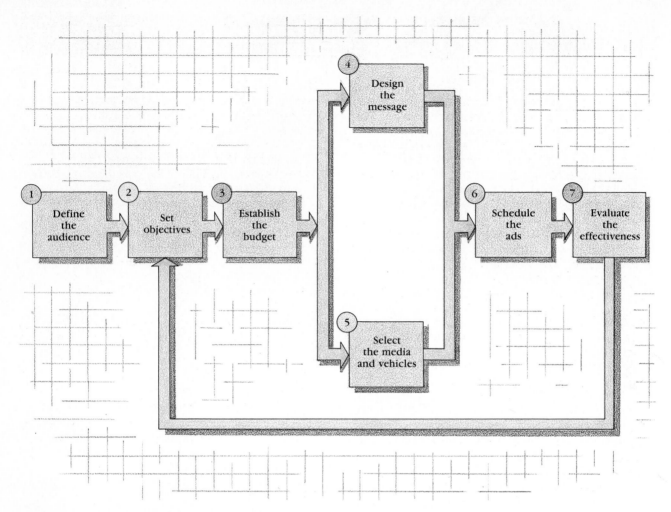

Figure 18-3 *Steps in advertising.* Advertising is accomplished through a series of seven steps, beginning with defining the audience and concluding with evaluating the effectiveness of advertisements.

■ *THE ADVERTISING PROCESS* ■

Advertising is accomplished through a series of seven steps: (1) define (target) the audience; (2) set objectives; (3) make a budget; (4) design advertisements and commercials in conjunction with (5) the media mix selection; (6) make schedules and produce the advertisements; and (7) evaluate and measure the advertisements' effectiveness. Figure 18-3 illustrates these steps in the advertising process.

□ *Choosing the Basic Audience*

Advertising is generally directed to one of three audiences: consumers, the trade (members of distribution channels), or organizational buyers. The messages and media chosen vary for each audience.

CONSUMER ADVERTISING We daily see consumer advertising on television, in newspapers, and in magazines; we also hear it on the radio. **Consumer adver-**

"Memorex is my tape."

"When it comes to tape, only Memorex® CDX II fits me right. It delivers my music pure.
Every note. Every time. And I can record at incredible levels without distortion.
"Compare CDX II to the best compact disc. You may have to. 'Cause it flat outperforms all
those other, ordinary high bias tapes. It's simple. If I put something on over and over again,
it'd better be good. That's why Memorex is my tape." **IS IT LIVE...OR IS IT MEMOREX?**
© 1986 Memtek Products

**What do grocers
make of our new
six-bar packaging?**

About 50% more profit.

Dole has just put together a new package deal. We've gone from
4 to 6 bars per box of Fruit 'N Juice and Fruit & Cream bars. The extra
two bars guarantee about 50% more profit with each sale.
Two more bars and a more impactful box convey Dole quality
even better. Our new advertising campaign with Kenny Rogers will
attract more customers to your store and our strong retail programs
will ensure customer sales.
So, stock up today. And enjoy pure profit. From Dole.
© 1987 Castle & Cooke Inc.

Dole
pure pleasure

The bulk of advertising expenditures is spent to communicate to consumers. An ad such
as the one on the left for Memorex tapes might be placed in dozens of consumer magazines. But, advertising can also have as its audience the retailer or some other intermediary who is part of the channel of distribution for the product. In the ad on the right,
Dole wants the retailer to give its products special treatment. (Left: Courtesy of Memtek
Products © 1986. Right: Copyright © 1987 Castle & Cooke, Inc.)

tisements are directed at those persons who might want the product for their own
use, for household use, or as a gift. Aimed at large target markets, consumer advertising in general is placed in the mass media.

TRADE ADVERTISING   **Trade advertisements** try to influence intermediaries
either to stock a product (pull strategy) or to advance it through distribution
channels on its way to ultimate consumers (push strategy). Trade advertisements
are most likely to appear in specialized magazines such as *Progressive Grocer* or
Beer Distributor. These ads may report on upcoming manufacturer-sponsored promotional campaigns intended to support retailers' efforts; they may announce special discounts offered to encourage intermediaries to stock up on a product. At
times, manufacturers launch tandem advertising campaigns aimed at both consumers and the trade.

INDUSTRIAL ADVERTISING   Sometimes called "business-to-business advertising," **industrial advertisements** promote goods and services for business or organizational use (refer back to Box 5-2 on page 130). Marketers of word-processing
equipment advertise their products in magazines directed at business people in

charge of information systems and offices. Large corporations use *The Wall Street Journal* and the business section of *The New York Times*—as well as such magazines as *Fortune, Business Week,* and *Forbes*—to promote their products and enhance their corporate identities. The readers of these publications include managers who influence the buying decisions of their companies.

◻ *Setting Advertising Objectives*

After choosing the general audience, the advertiser's next step is to set realistic advertising objectives, that is, to establish specific and measurable goals for the overall advertising campaign and perhaps even for specific advertisements. Advertising objectives are part of a promotion plan that flows from the organization's marketing objectives, which are based, in turn, on overall corporate strategy.

Remember two requirements: (1) Advertising objectives must support and add detail to corporate objectives. (2) Those objectives, to the extent possible, should be measurable (unmeasurable objectives are difficult to evaluate). Advertising objectives can be broadly divided into sales objectives and nonsales objectives.

SALES OBJECTIVES Most advertising is aimed at initiating sales, increasing sales, or stemming a decline in sales. And most consumer, trade, and industrial advertising is still based on sales objectives. Sales objectives are frequently tied to the product life cycle; the product's stage in the cycle affects both the message and the media chosen.

Introduction Advertising for the introduction of a new product to the market usually takes one of two forms. **Informative advertisements** aim simply to create

When a product or brand is mature and is well known by the target market, marketers often use reminder advertising. This ad for Coke is an example. There is little need for long copy—there's just a reminder to buy the product. (Courtesy of Coca-Cola.)

awareness that the product now exists. **Pioneering advertisements** are meant to increase primary demand for the product—that is, to bring nonusers into the user category. For example, advertising may aim to make consumers aware of a new computer-controlled lawn mower that "remembers" the layout of any lawn so that it can repeat the task without assistance after only one mowing. Objectives for these advertisements can be fairly specific and measurable; expenditures at this stage of the product life cycle are likely to be high.

Growth and Maturity   When a product should be reaching its sales potential, sales objectives usually dictate the use of two types of advertisements. **Competitive advertisements** seek to create selective demand—that is, to create a preference for the advertiser's brand as opposed to a competitor's. **Reinforcement advertisements** attempt to bolster and enhance satisfaction with purchases already made. Such messages are often based on status appeals ("Move Up to Ford").

Late Maturity and Decline   The late maturity of a product's life may last for years or even decades, during which sales may remain steady or sometimes increase, as has been the case for Prell Shampoo, Crackerjacks, and Band-Aids. In such instances, **reminder advertisements,** like those that aim at reinforcement, attempt to keep the product in buyers' minds. In general, reminder advertising does not focus on specifics about the product and says little about the brand's advantages over competitors. After all, "Coke Is It" doesn't tell us much about Coca-Cola, but it nevertheless does its job very well simply by showing us images of healthy people in happy situations.

Direct- versus Delayed-Action Advertising   Advertisements may also be characterized as either direct or delayed action ads. **Direct-action advertisements** are designed to move consumers and customers to take some immediate action. The message is probably one of straightforward persuasion: "On sale, buy now" or "Send in this coupon for more information." By contrast, **delayed-action advertisements** attempt to influence consumer attitudes and preferences, thus helping to set the stage for a purchase. A beer ad says simply: "The night belongs to Michelob." No request for action here, but, rest assured, bottles of Michelob will be ready for purchase when you are. Delayed-action advertising may be tailored for early or late stages of the product life cycle; it is the most common form of advertising.

NONSALES OBJECTIVES   Some advertising campaigns do not focus directly on increasing sales. The campaigns may aim instead at increasing the number of people who are aware of the product or at enhancing the advertiser's public image.

Awareness   Increased public awareness, the simple knowledge of a product's or service's existence, may be an advertising objective. Let's assume that Andy Steinfeld, brand manager for Danskin Panty Hose, receives a marketing research report revealing that 22 percent of the consumers in the target audience (women aged 18 to 45) are aware of Danskin. Sales obviously cannot increase without consumer awareness, so Steinfeld may propose an advertising campaign aimed at increasing awareness among the target audience from 22 to 40 percent.

Beliefs or Knowledge   A related aim may be to *decrease* the percentage of consumers in the target audience who believe that Danskin is the most expensive brand of panty hose. Thus awareness may be the primary goal of the firm's advertising, and altering an inaccurate perception may be a secondary goal. If such a campaign can fit within overall promotion, marketing, and corporate goals, a go-ahead will be likely. The campaign itself will probably include broadcast and print media as well as sales promotion. Although such an advertising campaign is harder to evaluate than direct-action advertising, its effectiveness can be assessed through surveys of attitudes in the target audience before, during, and after the campaign.

Corporate Image   Many leading companies have marketing objectives that fall outside of normal product advertising. Campaigns formerly known as public opinion, image, or institutional advertising are now simply called **corporate advertising**—media space or time bought for the benefit of the corporation rather than any of its products. Corporate advertising may be divided into three categories: corporate image building, financial or investor relations campaigns, and advocacy or issue advertising.

Image advertising aims to establish a positive identity for the corporation or to rebut criticism. Many diverse corporations employ image campaigns to clarify or improve their public images. For example, Exxon may run ads telling the public about how its research is finding ways to decrease the total consumption of petroleum products and thus save on the nation's negative trade balance.

Financial relations advertising portrays the corporation as fiscally sound and run by forward-looking management. Advertising for Santa Fe Industries emphasizes the company's strength in transportation, natural resources, forest products, real estate, and construction. Santa Fe's aim is to be perceived as a sound company for investment; readers are asked to write to the company for a copy of its annual report. The goal of this advertising campaign is to attract potential investors and to receive favorable recommendations from stockbrokers.

Advocacy advertising, or issue advertising, is highly visible, even though less than 5 percent of the money spent on corporate advertising is devoted to such ads. In general, companies employ issue advertising in response to what they perceive as threatening legislation or social activity. For example, Mobil Oil and United Technologies have both sponsored advertising campaigns in major newspapers which extol the virtues of the free enterprise system and warn of the dangers posed by government regulation of business.[9] In other cases, advocacy advertising is designed to support popular ideas, thereby providing evidence of the firm's concern and enhancing its image.[10] General Motors ran a series of print ads giving information on topics such as how to wear a seat belt and the damaging effects of alcohol consumption on driving.

Under the right conditions, corporate advertising may accomplish some or all of the following objectives: (1) increase sales, (2) recruit new employees and raise the morale of current employees, (3) boost the price of stock, and (4) foster a better public understanding of the company.

☐ *Setting the Advertising Budget*

After an organization's advertising objectives are set, the next step is to construct an advertising budget. Such budgets, typically prepared annually, are part of the overall promotion budget and are designed to further corporate strategy.

An often-repeated quote in advertising circles has been attributed to early retail merchant John Wanamaker. He is supposed to have said: "I know that 50 percent of my advertising is wasted, but I don't know which 50 percent." His dilemma remains a problem for contemporary marketing organizations: Planning

We're also interested in computers.

These are some of the many art exhibitions, musical events, and
television specials that IBM has supported over the years.
Which goes to show that a company known for state-of-the-art technology
can also be interested in the state of the arts.

IBM

IBM spends millions of dollars supporting the arts. They also spend millions of dollars telling the public that they spend millions on the arts, or we wouldn't know about it. This is known as *corporate advertising*. (Courtesy of IBM.)

for advertising expenditures is not easy. Managers obviously don't want to spend too much, but they also don't want to spend too little.[11] Consequently, sophisticated and rather complex approaches to advertising budgeting continue to be developed.[12]

We will focus here, however, on less elegant models of budgeting for advertising. Because sales promotion and advertising are often handled by a single marketing department, their budgets may be constructed simultaneously or even as one entity. Several methods are used to construct these budgets, as we will see in the following sections.

PERCENTAGE OF SALES   One of the most common methods of setting the advertising budget is to forecast sales for the coming year (using the forecasting methods discussed in Chapter 9) and to make the advertising budget equal to some percentage of that figure. This is not the most logical system of budgeting, but certain firms use it because it is so simple and because they know that many competitors will budget advertising at about that same percentage (as the data in Exhibit 18-2 illustrate).

COMPETITIVE PARITY Some companies choose the **competitive parity approach** to budget setting, typically used when firms wish to equalize the impact of advertising so that they can compete on some other marketing mix variable, such as price or distribution. When using this method, marketers will carefully monitor competitors' advertising, estimate their advertising expenditures, and then set their own advertising budgets at about the same level (the word "parity" means "equal to"). Again, this system of budgeting lacks logic; it gives competitors' budget decisions great influence over their rivals' budget setting.

ALL-YOU-CAN-AFFORD Another common budgeting approach is to set the advertising budget as high as possible. Marketers using this method essentially take the view that it is impossible to *overspend* on advertising, so therefore a firm should spend all that it can afford to spend. The firm forecasts sales, cost of goods sold, and operating costs other than advertising. It then sets a target profit on the expected sales and treats that figure as a cost. All forecasted sales are subtracted from forecasted revenues; the remaining sum becomes the advertising budget.

OBJECTIVE AND TASK Under an **objective-and-task approach,** marketers establish advertising objectives and then calculate the costs of the methods selected to achieve these goals to arrive at a budget. For example, two objectives may be set: to introduce a new product and to gain a 3 percent market share for it and to increase the sales of an existing product by 7 percent. The marketer must assess the costs of all tasks deemed necessary to reach objectives: design, production, media placement, and so forth. The budget figure resulting from this method reflects the costs of the advertising believed necessary to achieve these objectives and to accomplish all required tasks.

Among the tools used in setting advertising objectives are the concepts of reach, frequency, and gross rating points. **Reach** is the proportion of the target audience that will see an advertisement at least once. An objective may be to reach, say, 40 percent of the audience. **Frequency** is the number of times, on average, that each person reached will see the advertisement. Conventional wisdom holds that a frequency of fewer than 3 is not effective and that more than 10 is wasteful. However, a major study conducted by Joseph E. Seagram's and Time Inc. indicated that awareness increases after only one exposure and can continue to increase for as long as 48 weeks through multiple exposures.[13] A **gross ratings point** (GRP) is a unit of reach times frequency; thus, a GRP of 1 indicates that 1 percent of the target audience saw the ad once. If the goal is to reach 40 percent of the target audience an average of four times, marketers must purchase 160 GRPs. Media buyers decide on the proper media mix to attain the desired number of GRPs.

CREATING AN ADVERTISING MESSAGE

In general, the copywriters and art directors who create advertising campaigns are better than most of us at making associations—at mentally joining verbal and nonverbal symbols to form concepts that effectively deliver the intended message. In their work for a client, creative personnel must first develop a creative strategy for advertising and then must devise creative executions that implement the overall strategy.

☐ *Creative Strategy*

The **creative strategy** for a product or service is the primary message to be communicated by the advertising campaign. Devising such a strategy with the advertiser is one of the agency's major responsibilities.[14] A creative strategy is based on knowledge of what is to be accomplished by the ads and understanding of how the consumer or customer will react to advertising messages. Devising a creative strategy involves choosing among possible approaches to the communication message, including which of a product's attributes should be featured prominently. Should the advertising message emphasize the product's functional attributes, its physical attributes, or its characterizational attributes?

FUNCTIONAL ATTRIBUTES   What a product or service does for consumers or customers are its **functional attributes.** One toothpaste prevents cavities (Crest) while another freshens breath (Close-Up); a word processor increases communications efficiency; a window-cleaning service gets the grime off office windows. If the creative strategy is to emphasize one or more functional attributes in the message, the advertisement is likely to be fairly straightforward.

PHYSICAL ATTRIBUTES   In addition to its primary function, a product or service offers certain inherent benefits or **physical attributes.** A toothpaste may taste like peppermint; a word processor may have 256,000 bits of memory; a window-cleaning service may use only the best ammonia-based cleaners.

CHARACTERIZATIONAL ATTRIBUTES   Some messages are designed to get the reader or viewer to identify with the product or service. These methods focus on **characterizational attributes**—in other words, on what kinds of people use the product. Advertisements for vintage wines, expensive liquors, luxury cars, and fine china frequently display their products being used in elegant or romantic settings by sophisticated men and women. Soft-drink ads on television often show attractive, healthy young people cavorting in outdoor settings. Industrial firms often list prestigious users of their products. The unstated message in this strategy is that the product or service is used by the kinds of people shown in the ads and that we should identify with these desirable people and places by using the sponsor's product.

☐ *Creative Execution*

Just as creative strategy involves deciding what a message is to say, **creative execution** decides how to say it. Creative personnel must select verbal and nonverbal elements to communicate the message as well as pass judgments concerning use of humor, sex appeal, celebrities, and so forth. Verbal elements used in creative execution include headlines, slogans, copy, and brand names. Nonverbal elements include illustrations, layout, typography, trademarks, color, motion, and sound effects.[15] These elements are blended into an approach or "slant" for the message.

Among the commonly used approaches to the execution of advertising are reason-why advertisements, humorous advertisements, testimonial advertisements, slice-of-life advertisements, comparative advertisements, and emotional advertisements.

Raisins don't dance, and they don't sing either. In this successful television commercial for the California Raisin Advisory Board by the Foote, Cone and Belding agency, they do dance and sing across the picture tube. The result is a humorous execution. (Courtesy of the California Raisin Advisory Board.)

REASON-WHY ADVERTISEMENTS **Reason-why advertisements** explain what the product will do and why its use will be particularly beneficial for the buyer. Typically, reason-why advertisements use simple declarative statements proclaiming why the product will perform better than its competitors. Examples include, "Tylenol has 100 milligrams more pain killer," "You can take better photographs with Kodak's K-12 camera because it has automatic focusing," and "Sanka brand caffeine-free coffee won't keep you awake."

HUMOROUS ADVERTISEMENTS Humor is frequently used in advertising to communicate a message persuasively; Polaroid, Volkswagen, Blue Nun Wines, and Culligan Water Softeners have all used it effectively. Interestingly, the use of **humorous advertising** can be dangerous; humor can overcome the message and become "noise," thus interfering with the attempt to communicate a specific, product-related idea.

TESTIMONIAL ADVERTISEMENTS **Testimonial advertisements** attempt to get the consumer to identify with people who claim that they use and like the product. Some testimonials use celebrities, as when Bill Cosby tells us that he prefers the E. F. Hutton brokerage company.[16] Other testimonial ads feature unknown people like those in the intended audience in the hope that consumers who see the advertising will identify with these unknown persons.

SLICE-OF-LIFE ADVERTISEMENTS Some ads show the product being used by "ordinary people" in very common settings or engaged in everyday activities. The family eating cereal at the breakfast table before going off to work and to school, the married couple discussing dishwashing detergents while washing and drying dishes after a meal, the office workers enjoying a cup of coffee together at the end

Implementing and Controlling Marketing Plans

When the advertiser openly names a competitor, the execution results in a *comparative ad.* This ad for Blue Chip, a marketer of "IBM-clone" personal computers, communicates the key advantage they claim over IBM—low price. (Courtesy of Blue Chip Electronic.)

When the message in an advertisement is designed to just make you feel good, or tug at your heart strings, it is an emotional execution. The intent in this ad is to make you feel as good about New York Telephone as this young woman does about getting the call. (Courtesy of New York Telephone.)

of the day—these are all examples of **slice-of-life advertisements** highlighting some brand of breakfast cereal, detergent, or coffee.

COMPARATIVE ADVERTISEMENTS   Some ads name a specific competing brand and compare it (unfavorably, of course) to the advertiser's brand, as in "Wendy's has more meat than Big Mac or Whopper." **Comparative advertisements** are of fairly recent vintage. Until a few years ago, they were discouraged by the Federal Trade Commission (FTC); advertisers could only refer to competitors as "Brand X."[17] But the FTC reversed itself, ruling that such messages encourage healthy competition, and today's comparative advertisements are quite explicit in naming and criticizing competitive brands.

EMOTIONAL ADVERTISEMENTS   Rather than carrying much specific information, **emotional advertisements** attempt to create moods that will subsequently be associated with the product. Typically, these moods are positive and pleasant, as in AT&T's "Reach out and touch someone" and "Mean Joe" Greene's famous football jersey toss for Coca-Cola. The intent is to create a good feeling in the consumer which will become linked to the product in the consumer's mind.

☐ *Requirements of an Effective Advertisement*

Whatever strategy is chosen and whatever execution is used, an advertisement will accomplish its purposes only if it fulfills three basic requirements: It must get attention, it must be understood, and it must show a solution to a problem.

The average U.S. adult is exposed to almost 500 advertisements per day but attends to or is conscious of only about 76 of these messages.[18] Consequently, to have any effect, an ad must first get our attention.[19] A television commercial for a brand of panty hose began by showing a pair of shapely legs. The camera then panned up the legs—slowly—until the model's entire body and the face were revealed: Joe Namath, the famous football quarterback. Marketing research revealed that the percentage of people who remembered seeing the commercial was phenomenally high, but only a small proportion of those polled could remember the brand of panty hose being advertised. This commercial met the first requirement for an effective ad—it got attention—but it failed to meet the second because it was not understood.

The concept of Joe Namath wearing pantyhose was certainly an attention getter, but the gimmick overshadowed the product and the message. Because any advertising message must be readily understood, most messages—especially those used in the broadcast media—must be fairly simple. A television commercial has only 10, 15, 30, or 60 seconds to make its point. Messages in the print media can be slightly more complex, but, on the whole, commercial messages are rather simple.

The final requirement for an effective ad is that it show a solution to a problem. Effective advertising reminds consumers of a need and demonstrates how the product can fill that need—that is, solve the problem.[20] For example, a highly successful advertising campaign for American Express travelers' checks shows people on vacation who have either lost their billfold or purse or had it stolen. They are understandably quite upset about losing their money while far away from home, but their problems are solved when they learn that a nearby American Express office will replace all their travelers' checks. Then actor Karl Malden reminds us: "Don't leave home without them."

■ SELECTING MEDIA AND VEHICLES ■

Media planners are familiar with the characteristics of the various media (such as numbers of readers or viewers) and the costs of each. They must decide on a media mix within the allocated budget. For example, a firm seeking to increase market share for a spaghetti sauce may choose to allocate funds in the following way: $1.6 million to four-color advertising in women's magazines ($1 million for *Redbook* and $600,000 for *Woman's Day*), $2.4 million to network television spots (for daytime commercials on soap operas and game shows), and $850,000 to a program using newspaper advertisements in 23 major markets.

☐ *Cost per Thousand and Vehicle Selection*

When considering advertising in the print media, media planners can draw upon measures of magazine and newspaper circulation and readership. For example, *Standard Rate & Data Service* supplies reliable information on the number of copies sold of most publications. In the area of broadcast media, the A. C. Nielsen Company and Arbitron provide data on numbers of viewers.

Selecting vehicles within a print or broadcast medium usually involves a cost associated with the number of people reached by ads in different vehicles. It is common to refer to these costs as the **cost per thousand** (CPM) and to use this device to compare vehicles (see Exhibit 18-3). Thus, the estimated cost of a 30-second ad on NBC's *The Bill Cosby Show* in the 1986 to 1987 season was $380,000, whereas the cost of the same 30-second spot on ABC's *Our World* was only $30,000. By dividing these cost figures by the number of viewers Nielsen and Arbitron say are watching these shows, you get an estimate of the cost per thousand people you reach with your commercial.

This approach to the selection of media and vehicles is useful but has its limitations. The measures used for television viewing report how many sets were turned on at a given time but not how many people were actually watching (although this figure is also estimated). Moveover, demographic information concerning the media may or may not match up with any particular marketer's target market selection. A typical report will indicate the CPM reached, whereas the market may wish to know the CPM of 18- to 35-year-old females with college educations who reside in urban areas.

Another limitation of the CPM method is that it does not measure how many people actually paid attention to an ad. For example, concern has been expressed that viewers engaged in "zapping," or fast-forwarding through commercials while playing recorded programming on a videocassette recorder, will not be aware of the commercial messages (though a 1986 study for *Advertising Age* suggested that "zapping" was not seriously reducing the effectiveness of advertising.)[21] The CPM approach also does not tell us how believable our ad was perceived to be by the

EXHIBIT 18-3	Media Costs

Network television is generally the most expensive advertising medium; even a 30-second spot is quite costly.

Medium	"Approximate" Cost To Reach Each 1000 Adults
Network television (30-second spots)	$4.05–$7.75
Radio (1-minute spots)	3.50– 4.75
National magazines (full-page, 4-color)	2.50– 4.00
Newspaper (1000-line ad)	3.50– 4.50
Outdoor billboard	
Painted bulletin	1.25– 1.50
30 sheet poster	.45– .50
Outdoor metal sign (3′ × 5′ wall-mounted sign, $20 cost, 500 daily adult exposure, 3-year life)	0.04
Outdoor metal curbstand sign ($50 cost, 2500 daily adult exposure, 3-year life)	0.03
In-store permanent product merchandiser or sign (cost range of $5 to $20, exposure range 200 to 1000/ day depending on type of outlet, 1-year life)	0.03– 0.37
In-store temporary product merchandiser or sign (cost range $2.50 to $10, exposure range 200 to 1000/ day depending on type of outlet, 2-week life)	0.18– 3.00

Note: Figures are approximate.

Source: "Merchandising Power: Maximizing Consumer Potential at Retail," *Advertising Age,* Jan. 10, 1983, p. 8P.

reader or viewer. Some evidence indicates that the editorial quality of the vehicle will affect the believability of the advertising appearing in it. Thus, while the quantitative CPM is clearly useful in media selection, advertisers still need other media and vehicle selection determinants.[22]

☐ *Media Decision Determinants*

In addition to the statistical bases for determining media and vehicle choice, media planners and buyers consider a number of more qualitative factors. Among these are target audience, product characteristics, the competition, message constraints, and budget constraints.

TARGET AUDIENCE   Television is often the most cost-effective choice for products with broad target audiences, such as automobiles, aspirin, and antacids. By contrast, if the audience is narrow, magazines would be logical vehicles—particularly special-interest magazines. Thousands of these magazines cater to virtually every personal and business interest, from *Gourmet* to *Fleet Owner, Cycle World* to *American Photographer, Personal Computing* to *Sales and Marketing Management.* Marketers of specialty products are usually assured of very little waste when they place appropriate advertising in these special-interest publications.

PRODUCT CHARACTERISTICS   A company that sells liability insurance to firms with 500 or more employees has a complex story to tell its potential customers. This sales message cannot be contained in a short television spot; the waste percentage would be extremely high. Obviously, the characteristics of the product itself largely determine which media and vehicles are appropriate. If Polident, a cleanser for dentures, were advertised in the pages of *Seventeen*, the marketer would be promoting the product to the wrong audience.

Media buying decisions are also affected by the constraints imposed on advertising of certain products. Liquor and cigarettes may not be advertised on television in the United States. Moreover, many media will not accept ads that they consider controversial or in poor taste, such as for certain feminine hygiene products.

THE COMPETITION   Companies are certainly aware of the advertising of their competitors. They usually, but not always, use the same vehicles as their competitors to compete directly. Thus, advertisements for Kitchen Aid and Maytag dishwashers sometimes appear side-by-side in newspapers.

MESSAGE CONSTRAINTS   If the advertising message is simple and can be communicated visually through demonstration, television would seem to be the appropriate medium. If the message is complex and needs careful explanation, then a print medium would be the natural choice. Broadcast media do not easily lend themselves to complex messages.

BUDGET CONSTRAINTS   Exxon can and does advertise as extensively as it pleases in the media of its choice. By contrast, the advertising budget for Annabelle's Roadrunner card shop in Charleston is only a few thousand dollars a year. The store would be using its funds wastefully if it spent the entire budget on two 30-second commercials on local television; local newspapers or radio stations are more appropriate media to use. No matter what the size of the advertiser, media planners attempt to get the most effective vehicles for the money allotted.

SCHEDULING THE ADVERTISING PROGRAM

Schedules for advertising in any medium are usually planned in one of two ways (or a combination of both). **Continuity** is the strategy of scheduling the advertising evenly over the weeks and months of the years: **pulsing**, or **flighting**, refers to unevenly timed exposures. The aim of continuity is to maintain a constant exposure to the target audience. By contrast, pulsing has more impact during certain stages of the life cycle, such as product introduction. The use of pulsing may also be dictated by the product's seasonal appeal; Toro doesn't advertise its snow plows in May.

Large-scale advertisers typically employ both continuity and pulsing when appropriate. Figure 18-4 presents a sample media schedule for a consumer product, using both techniques.

EVALUATING ADVERTISING EFFECTIVENESS

As mentioned earlier, effective evaluation of an advertising campaign requires measurable objectives. Credible evaluation is difficult—even with clear objectives—but some good techniques are currently being used for evaluation, and more sophisticated techniques are being developed.

Pretesting

There are two reasons for testing the effectiveness of an ad before it is broadcast or printed. First, pretesting alternative advertisements and commercials on sample

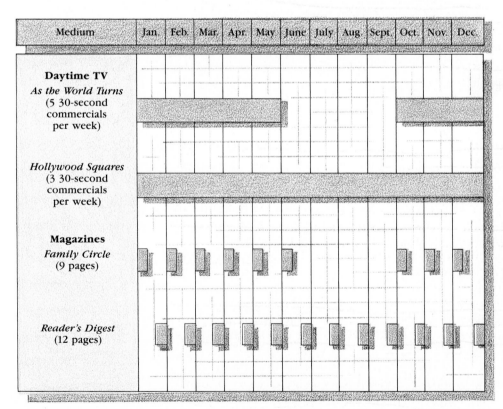

Medium	Jan.	Feb.	Mar.	Apr.	May	June	July	Aug.	Sept.	Oct.	Nov.	Dec.
Daytime TV *As the World Turns* (5 30-second commercials per week)												
Hollywood Squares (3 30-second commercials per week)												
Magazines *Family Circle* (9 pages)												
Reader's Digest (12 pages)												

Figure 18-4 *A sample media schedule.* In this sample media schedule, the advertiser uses commercials on *Hollywood Squares* and print ads in *Reader's Digest* throughout the year. In all but the summer months, the advertiser uses commercials on *As the World Turns* and print ads in *Family Circle*. (From S. Watson Dunn and Arnold M. Barban, *Advertising: Its Role in Modern Marketing*, 4th ed., Hinsdale, IL.: The Dryden Press, 1978, p. 523.)

audiences allows advertisers to get some measure of which presentation is most effective. It was through pretesting that Ogilvy & Mather decided upon the advertising approach that evolved into the highly successful "Do you know me?" campaign for American Express. In general, pretesting is unlikely to identify great ads, but it can screen out ads that generate weak or negative responses from test groups. Second, pretesting is used to gauge consumer awareness and attitudes before an advertising campaign begins. The findings can later be compared with postcampaign results.

Several methods are used to pretest advertisements to predict which will be the most effective. Two frequently employed methods are **theater tests** and **psychophysical measures**. Neither is entirely reliable, and marketers tend to suspect their results. They do, however, represent efforts to ensure that advertising campaigns will meet their objectives.

THEATER TESTS These tests are an expensive method of judging the effectiveness of television commercials. Consumer groups are brought into theaters, supposedly to see pilots of forthcoming television series. Test commercials are also shown to these viewers. They are asked their opinions not only of the pilots but of the impact and effectiveness of the commercials. Then other groups are brought in to see the pilots, but this time they are shown along with different versions of ads for the same products. For example, the first ad for a product may feature a testimonial from a celebrity, the second a testimonial from an "unknown" person. Researchers tally the responses to each ad to see which is most effective.

PSYCHOPHYSICAL TESTING Under such testing, procedures similar to those employed in lie detector tests are used to assess people's reactions to print or broadcast advertising. Physiological reactions, such as pupil dilation, brain waves, blood pressure, perspiration, and galvonic skin response (a flow of electric current across the skin that increases with emotional reaction), are monitored as subjects see, hear, or read alternate advertisements. Such tests may indicate the attention-getting power of an ad, but little can be learned in this way about the ad's effect on attitudes and beliefs.

Posttesting

Recognition tests and recall tests are two common measures of an advertisement's impact and effectiveness *after* it has been run.

RECOGNITION TESTS The Starch readership scores are among the most widely used measures for testing the effectiveness of print advertising. These **recognition tests**, developed by Daniel Starch, involve showing people an advertisement and asking if they recognize it. If they do, the interviewer probes further to determine if they have noted it in passing, have read at least part of the copy, or have read most of it. The researcher then matches the most effective ads with their cost to determine the cost effectiveness of an advertisement.

Starch scores are broken down into age groups, male-female groups, and so on. Average scores are provided for product classes and for individual magazines. As a result, advertisers can compare the effectiveness of their efforts with those of their competitors.

RECALL TESTS Unlike recognition tests, **recall tests** do not assist the respondent's memory by providing the ads themselves. If the person has seen a magazine, for instance, he or she is asked which products have been advertised there. If the consumer mentions any, the interviewer asks what the ad looked like, what the brand name was, and so forth. Recall tests are obviously more rigorous in testing the impact of an ad than are recognition tests; if the consumer can recall the ad without assistance, then it has hit home in some way.

A special version of the recall method is the *day-after-recall* test, in which the consumer is called and asked about a commercial run the evening before on television. This test aims to assess the strength of the advertising message by studying its immediate impact.

Evaluating Advertising Campaigns

We have discussed several methods of evaluating the effectiveness of individual components of an advertising campaign—that is, individual ads. At least as important, however, is the evaluation of a complete advertising campaign. To do so, we must return to the second step in the advertising process: the setting of objectives.

As noted earlier, advertising objectives should be clear and easily measured. In order to evaluate the effectiveness of an advertising campaign, we must determine if objectives have been met by studying whether the specific measures used have been achieved. Has market share grown from 15 percent to our objective of 20 percent? Did sales grow from 1.7 million units to 1.9 million units?

Even though advertising is sometimes cute, humorous, or even dramatic in its ability to touch our hearts, its central purpose is to accomplish marketing objectives—eventually the sale of the product or service. Marketers need to know whether an advertising campaign has, in fact, accomplished its purposes.

SUMMARY

1. Advertisements are the most visible aspect of marketing in general and of promotion in particular.
2. In addition to persuading consumers to act, advertising informs, reminds, and reinforces.
3. In general, marketers of beauty care products, pharmaceuticals, and toys spend a relatively high percentage of sales on advertising, and industrial marketers typically budget a lower percentage of sales to advertising.
4. The main participants in the advertising business are advertisers, advertising agencies, and the mass media.
5. The advertiser itself is responsible for the goals of, the strategy behind, and the budget for any advertising campaign.
6. A full-service agency offers its clients four basic services: account management and marketing, creative, media, and research services.
7. Television, radio, newspapers, and magazines are the major media involved in transmitting promotional messages.
8. Confidentiality is an absolute necessity in the delicate advertiser-agency relationship.
9. Advertising is accomplished through a series of sequential steps: (1) define (target) the audience; (2) set objectives; (3) make a budget; (4) design ads and commericals in conjunction with (5) the media mix selection; (6) make schedules and produce the ads; and (7) evaluate and measure the advertisements' effectiveness.
10. Advertising is generally directed to one of three audiences: consumers, the trade (members of distribution channels), or organizational buyers.
11. Advertising objectives must support and add detail to corporate objectives; to the extent possible, they should be measurable.
12. Most advertising is aimed at initiating sales, increasing sales, or stemming a decline in sales.

13. Some methods used to set the advertising budget are percentage of sales, competitive parity, all-you-can-afford, and objective-and-task.

14. Creative strategy must determine whether the advertising message should emphasize the product's functional, physical, or characterizational attributes.

15. Just as creative strategy involves what a message should say, creative execution involves deciding how it is to be said.

16. An effective advertisement must get attention, must be understood, and must show a solution to a problem.

17. Large-scale advertisers typically employ both continuity and pulsing strategies when scheduling advertising.

18. Both pretesting methods (theater tests and psychophysical testing) and posttesting (recognition tests and recall tests) are used to evaluate advertising effectiveness.

☐ *Key Terms*

account executives	direct-action advertisements	percentage-of-sales approach
account services department	emotional advertisements	physical attributes
advertiser	financial relations advertising	pioneering advertisements
advertising	flighting	product line exclusivity
advocacy advertising	frequency	psychophysical testing
all-you-can-afford approach	full-service advertising agency	pulsing
characterizational attributes	functional attributes	reach
comparative advertisements	gross ratings point	reason-why advertisements
competitive advertisements	humorous advertisements	recall tests
competitive parity approach	image advertising	recognition tests
consumer advertisements	industrial advertisements	reinforcement advertisements
continuity	informative advertisements	reminder advertisements
corporate advertising	in-house agencies	slice-of-life advertisements
cost per thousand	issue advertising	storyboards
creative boutiques	marketing research department	testimonial advertisements
creative execution	media	theater tests
creative services department	media buying organization	trade advertisements
creative strategy	media group	vehicles
delayed-action advertisements	objective-and-task approach	

☐ *Chapter Review*

1. The aims of advertising are to inform, persuade, remind, and reinforce. Does the phrase, "Hallmark, when you care enough to send the very best" satisfy those goals?

2. How does advertising differ from personal selling? From sales promotion? What is the primary influence on a consumer's choice of a new automobile? Of a shampoo? Of an institution in which to open a savings account?

3. How does advertising help to create a mass market for a product category such as personal computers? Has advertising been a factor in lowering the price of such computers?

4. McCann-Erickson created the "Coke Is It" campaign for Coca-Cola, which reaches the public on the three national networks. Identify the roles of each organization in this example of the advertising business.

5. What are the four basic services provided to clients by a full-service advertising agency? What additional services may a full-service agency offer?

6. Give examples of each of the four major advertising media. Why do Pepsi-Cola and Miller Brewing Company devote such a large part of their advertising budgets to network televisions?

7. What are the first three steps in the advertising process? Why are advertising objectives frequently tied to the product's life cycle?

8. Describe the four methods used to set an advertising budget.

9. Explain the difference between an advertising strategy and an advertising tactic.

10. What are the three basic requirements for an effective advertisement? Give examples of print and radio ads that meet these requirements.

11. Marshall McLuhan once said that "the medium should fit the message." How does this statement apply to the choice of media and vehicles for promotion of American Express credit cards?

12. Give the three main reasons for sponsors to evaluate advertising.

☐ *References*

1. *Marketing Definitions: A Glossary of Marketing Terms*, compiled by Ralph S. Alexander and the Committee on Definitions of the American Marketing Association (Chicago, 1960), p. 9.

2. S. R. Bernstein, "What Is Advertising?" *Advertising Age*, Apr. 30, 1980, p. 28.

3. Scott Ward, Daniel Wackman, and Ellen Wortella, *Children Learning to Buy: The Development of Consumer Information Processing Skills* (Cambridge, Mass.: Marketing Science Institute, 1975), pp. 75–76.

4. R. Craig Endicott, "Advertisers Cut Spending Pace," *Advertising Age,* Sept. 4, 1986, pp. 1 ff.

5. Milton Moskowitz, Michael Katz, and Robert Levering, *Everybody's Business: An Almanac* (New York: Harper & Row, 1980), p. 340.

6. Nancy L. Salz, *How to Get the Best Advertising from Your Agency* (Englewood Cliffs, N.J.: Prentice-Hall, 1983), pp. 12–14.

7. Moskowitz, Katz, and Levering, op. cit., p. 342.

8. Carl Hixon, "A Conversation with the 'Scottish Blade' David Ogilvy," *Advertising Age*, Sept. 14, 1981, p. 64.

9. Robert L. Heath and Richard Alan Nelson, "Image and Issue Advertising: A Corporate and Public Policy Perspective," *Journal of Marketing*, vol. 49, Spring 1985, pp. 58–68.

10. Thomas R. Garbett, "When to Advertise Your Company," *Harvard Business Review*, Mar.–Apr. 1982, pp. 100–106.

11. David A. Aaker and James Carman, "Are You Overadvertising?" *Journal of Advertising Research*, vol. 22, Aug.–Sept., 1982, pp. 57–70; and Donald S. Tull et al., " 'Leveraged' Decision Making in Advertising: The Flat Maximum Principle and Its Implications," *Journal of Marketing Research*, vol. XXIII, Feb. 1986, pp. 25–32.

12. Albert C. Bemmaor, "Testing Alternative Econometric Models on the Existence of Advertising Threshold Effect," *Journal of Marketing Research*, vol. XXI, Aug. 1984, pp. 298–308, and Lakshman Krishnamurti and S. P. Raj, "The Effect of Advertising on Consumer Price Sensitivity," *Journal of Marketing Research*, vol. XXII, May 1985, pp. 119–129.

13. Stuart Emmrich, "Major Study Details Ads Effect on Sales," *Advertising Age*, June 21, 1982, pp. 1, 80.

14. Thomas W. Hizer, "Two Questions Almost Everyone Forgets to Ask Their Advertising Agency," *Journal of Consumer Marketing,* Summer 1985, pp. 45–53.

15. S. Watson Dunn and Arnold M. Barban, *Advertising: Its Role in Modern Marketing*, 5th ed. (Hinsdale, Ill.: Dryden Press, 1982), p. 301.

16. Lynn R. Kahle and Pamela H. Homer, "Physical Attractiveness of the Celebrity Endorser: A Social Adaptation Perspective," *Journal of Consumer Research*, vol. 11, Mar. 1985, pp. 954–961.

17. Bruce Buchanan, "Can You Pass the Comparative Ad Challenge?" *Harvard Business Review*, July–Aug. 1985, pp. 106–113; and Gerald J. Gorn and Charles B. Weinberg, "The Impact of Comparative Advertising on Perception and Attitude: Some Positive Findings," *Journal of Consumer Research*, vol. 11, Sept. 1984, pp. 719–727.

18. Raymond A. Bauer and Stephen A. Greyser, *Advertising in America: The Consumer View*, (Cambridge, Mass.: Harvard University, 1968), pp. 173–176.

19. Anthony G. Greenwald and Clark Leavitt, "Audience Involvement in Advertising: Four Levels," *Journal of Consumer Research*, vol. 11, June 1984, pp. 581–592.
20. John Deighton, "The Interaction of Advertising and Evidence," *Journal of Consumer Research*, vol. 11, Dec. 1984, pp. 763–770.
21. Craig Reiss, "Fast-Forward Ads Deliver," *Advertising Age,* October 27, 1986, pp. 3, 97.
22. Roland T. Rust and Robert P. Leone, "The Mixed-Media Direchlet Multinomial Distribution: A Model for Evaluating Television-Magazine Advertising Schedules," *Journal of Marketing Research*, vol. XXI, Feb. 1984, pp. 898–899.

19

MANAGING THE SALES FORCE

Copyright © Janeart Ltd. 1986/The Image Bank.

SPOTLIGHT ON

☐ The responsibilities of a sales manager

☐ Sales management systems

☐ Sales objectives related to corporate and marketing objectives

☐ Size and structure in an organization's sales force

☐ Sales force recruitment, training, motivation, and compensation

☐ Evaluating sales force performance

Is teamwork an important part of effective marketing? It certainly is—at least in the opinion of top marketing executives at Campbell Soup. According to Carl V. Stinnett, president of Campbell Sales Company, the sales arm of Campbell Soup: "Complete teamwork doesn't exist in any company in the grocery industry." But, in his view, once Campbell's teamwork-oriented restructuring of its sales force goes into effect, "there'll be nobody who can beat us."

Campbell had previously structured its sales force by product line, which meant that as many as four or five Campbell representatives made separate sales calls to a single retailer. However, in early 1986, Campbell reorganized its sales force, emphasizing a regional structure under which a field salesperson in a territory would sell the full Campbell line. R. Gordon McGovern, president and chief executive officer of Campbell Soup, notes: "We were coming out with all these new products, and our sales force . . . couldn't take them. . . . It's more efficient to put it all in one focus so the buyer can talk to one person."

One key factor that contributed to Campbell's restructuring was the changing nature of the grocery retailer. "We used to view the grocery trade as merchants," admits Carl Stinnett. "Now we view them as marketers." Because they have made such effective use of technology, especially scanner technology, retailers have gained some degree of power at the expense of manufacturers. Campbell hopes to respond to such changes by training its field staff to use personal computers to create local marketing programs.

Campbell's restructuring will allow regional brand managers (a newly created position) and field salespeople to become much more involved in developing promotions aimed at local target markets. In recent years, the influence of national television advertising on local marketing has noticeably declined. Yet Campbell's previous product line structure allowed little room for local promotions. One Campbell executive points out that he "never had the structure to address Hispanic markets, and you certainly need that in the West and the South."

Under Campbell's new structure, field salespeople will become a much more important part of the marketing team than they were before. The new structure will increase both the authority and accountability of the field staff, particularly in developing local promotions. "You give them a budget," says Carl Stinnett, "they develop a promotion, you approve it, they execute it, and you hold them accountable for results." Viewed from the perspective of the contemporary marketing concept, Campbell has clearly recognized that its field sales organization must fit the overall marketing plan of the company. Moreover, it has recognized that its field salespeople are really marketing people whose expertise can be valuable in *all* aspects of Campbell's marketing effort.

Source: Rayna Skolnik, "Campbell Stirs Up Its Sales Force," *Sales and Marketing Management,* Apr. 1986, pp. 56–58; and Christine Dugas et al., "Marketing's New Look," *Business Week,* Jan. 26, 1987, pp. 64–69.

Even if you are marketing a desirable product, even if you have established an efficient distribution system, even if the price is reasonable, even if you have a strong promotion mix—all this can be negated by poor sales force performance. As the *personal* side of the promotion mix, the sales organization plays a vital role in the total marketing effort. It is Campbell's field salespeople, for example, who must ultimately convince local retailers that they should stock and even promote new Campbell food products.

Chapter 19 focuses on the organization and responsibilities of the sales force. We first examine the nature of the sales manager's job and the skills needed to perform it. Then we look at the primary methods of organizing a sales management system and how the objectives of a sales plan carry out corporate and marketing objectives. Next, we describe factors affecting the size and structure of a sales force and discuss the recruitment, training, motivation, and compensation of sales personnel. The chapter concludes by showing how specific objectives are used to evaluate the performance of the sales force.

THE SALES MANAGER

A sales manager's job is ever-changing, challenging, and complex. At whatever level in the organization, the **sales manager** is directly responsible for the day-to-day analysis, planning, implementation, and control of the marketing division's personal selling arm. Not surprisingly, this broad definition includes many types of sales organizations and various levels of sales management within the same firm.

The typical sales management team includes persons who have territorial responsibilities ranging from the entire national market, to regions of the country (usually three or four), and finally to districts (often located in major cities and their major markets). The role of the sales force has traditionally involved implementing marketing plans developed by marketing managers. However, as we saw in our discussion of Campbell Soup's regional brand managers and field salespeople, a company's sales management team may now be involved in developing—as well as implementing—marketing plans and programs.

As in other chapters describing the elements of promotion, our discussion of personal selling starts with top managers and moves down to those working most closely with customers. These managers are the front line of a marketing organization; their main assignment is to translate a selling plan into specific actions in the field.

The Nature of the Job

Suppose that the top marketing executives for a manufacturer of consumer products—the vice president of marketing and the national sales manager—set a strategic target of $400 million in yearly sales. Each district manager will be charged with meeting some specific part of that goal: For example, the manager for the southwest district (Texas, Louisiana, Oklahoma, New Mexico, and Arizona) may be given a goal of $50 million in yearly sales. The district manager must then motivate sales representatives to bring in that revenue. The sales team for that district must accomplish its goal within the expense budget set for that district.

Thus, a **district sales manager** is a line executive who plans, directs, and controls the activities of field salespeople.[1] Success in sales management on this level depends greatly on one's ability to provide astute, individually tailored motivation to a diverse group of salespeople, many of whom may be geographically separated from the sales manager. Not everyone can be flexible and still motivate individuals to accomplish group goals; sales managers must be.

Traditional Skills Needed for the Job

Successful sales managers come in all types: They may be extroverts or introverts, excitable or restrained, exciting or dull. They may be cool and analytical decision makers, or they may "shoot from the hip." However they express their strengths, good sales managers share certain abilities.

Throughout this century, sales organizations have sought managers with specific behavioral traits that are still considered fitting for the job. Sales managers are expected to be self-starters, effective motivators, and action-oriented.

SELF-STARTERS   District sales managers may work out of an office or out of their homes. They do not punch time clocks (nor do the salespeople they manage). Because of the geographical spread of the typical sales organization, sales managers are not closely supervised on a day-to-day basis. In fact, their regional managers are usually located in another city. Given such loose supervision, district sales managers must be self-starters—must have strong internal motivation—to do their jobs well.

EFFECTIVE MOTIVATORS   The success or failure of sales managers is tied directly to how the people they manage perform. Since individual sales representatives may be motivated by status, money, the need for self-esteem, peer recognition, or the opportunity for promotion, effective sales managers must recognize the employees' different motivations and use individualized techniques to get them to perform their best.[2]

ACTION-ORIENTED INDIVIDUALS   Sales management and personal selling require action. Most sales managers are evaluated on the basis of net sales, and they must be ready to take many direct and indirect actions to secure those sales. A

Sales managers often work without direct supervision. Most companies have only one home office, but many sales offices spread across the country. The sales managers in charge of those offices are self-starters. They are increasingly expected to be analysts and planners, as well as managers of the salespeople in their district. (Copyright © Barry O'Rourke/The Stock Market.)

direct action might be a sales manager helping representatives to close important sales. Less direct actions include hiring and firing sales personnel, conducting on-the-job training for representatives, and providing higher-level managers with information about customers' needs; all can contribute to improved sales performance.

Analysis and Planning Skills

Contemporary sales organizations are increasingly involving district managers in the processes of strategic marketing. This involvement requires both traditional managerial skills, based mainly on implementing and controlling, and skills in analysis and planning.

ANALYSIS   Managers frequently conduct studies to determine if resources (people, materials, and money) are being used most efficiently. A manager may be asked to consider whether a sales promotion campaign has been effective, whether a territory should be realigned, or whether telemarketing techniques have been beneficial.

PLANNING   Since effective marketing strategy is based on the input and involvement of managers at all levels, district sales managers are increasingly being asked to propose annual (and even longer-range) sales goals and plans for their areas of responsibility. Clearly, the district sales manager is becoming an active participant in setting marketing strategy.[3] As a result, the manager needs the education, training, and ability to interact with managers at higher levels. As practiced today, sales management requires a thorough understanding of marketing research and testing, market segmentation, product positioning, and the coordination of personal selling with advertising and sales promotion. The district manager adds a unique perspective to the strategy-setting process with first-hand, day-to-day knowledge of the customer and the marketplace.

THE SALES MANAGEMENT SYSTEM

The **sales management system** encompasses the policies, procedures, and practices that enable and encourage salespeople to carry out their roles in the organization's marketing strategy.[4] The structure and management of the sales force is a fundamental aspect of this system. Organizations are usually divided by geographic area, by product line, or by customer type, although many companies combine these types.

Geography

Sales organizations are structured geographically because representatives need to be physically close to the customer. Managers and representatives are often located in or near large cities where industries or large numbers of consumers are located, and thus customer concentration can be a factor in geographical organization. For example, organizations selling products to the petroleum industry place representatives in Texas and Oklahoma, whereas those supplying the furniture industry will concentrate salespeople in North Carolina and western Michigan.

Typically, one sales executive is responsible for all of a company's domestic sales. Individual managers are then assigned to specific regions, each of which is divided into districts. Sales representatives are assigned to territories within each district. Figure 19-1 shows how a sales management system may be organized geographically. Although sales territories may also reflect product lines or market segments, geography nearly always influences the number and structure of territories.

Product Line

Marketers of diverse goods and services or complex products often organize their sales forces around products or product lines. Eastman Kodak, for example, has several sales organizations: one for consumer products—the cameras, film, and processing services used by professional and amateur photographers; one for business systems products such as photocopiers and microfilm; one for medical equipment and supplies and X-ray film; another for professional photofinishing; yet another for graphic arts; and, finally, a sales force responsible for Eastman chemical products—the plastics used for soft-drink containers, vitamin E, a bread softener for the baking industry, acetate fibers for clothing and cigarette filters, and other specialty chemicals.

The complexity of Kodak's offerings demands organization by product line. To be effective, sales representatives must know their products and attendant services; no single representative could be knowledgeable about all the company's products and their uses. Consequently, Kodak organizes, trains, and fields different sales forces to sell its divergent products to divergent markets.

Customer Type

A third way of organizing and managing a sales force is by customer type or market segments. This structure is best suited for organizations whose product line is used

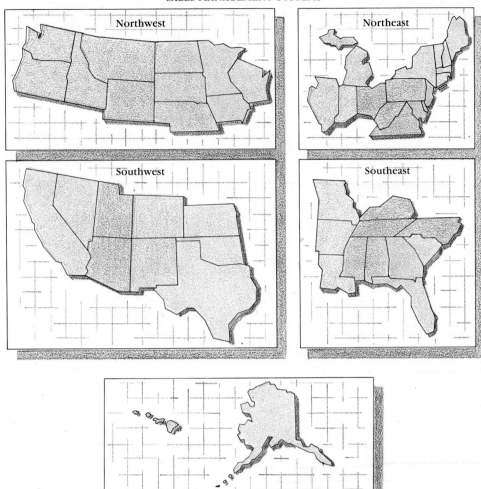

Figure 19-1 *Typical geographic organization of a sales force.* Every company will have its own way of deploying its sales force. This figure illustrates a typical organization, which breaks up the United States into five regions and separates each region into districts. Within each of these districts, the geography is further broken into sales territories, for which one salesperson usually has responsibility.

differently by different customers. For example, marketers of business forms—invoices, order forms, interoffice memos, and the like—such as Moore Business Forms or NCR would number among their present or potential clients banks, insurance companies, hospitals, and many other organizations. Such a company's sales force would be best organized according to customer type, since the salesperson has to understand the customer's business needs to serve each firm effectively.

A customer-based sales force often includes a **national account representative**—a person who has special sales and servicing responsibilities for a specific large customer. Miles Laboratories, the producer of Alka-Seltzer and the largest U.S. marketer of vitamins (One-A-Day), would designate as national accounts those major drug and supermarket chains which use centralized purchasing. Then an account representative (or a team) would be assigned to serve specific large chains like Walgreen drugstores and the Southland Corporation (7-Eleven stores). For a look at the role of a national accounts manager for Xerox, see Box 19-2.

Christine M. Lojacono manages five national accounts out of Xerox's Rochester, New York, branch office. For her, serving as a national account manager (NAM) means "building a rapport with the customer, hanging around their headquarters as much as possible, and finding out their particular problems for which Xerox can provide solutions." In building such rapport, Lojacono stresses that she must be sensitive to the particular needs and style of the account: "Some are highly centralized; they want everything done through headquarters. Others are very decentralized and give you complete freedom to call on satellite offices."

Lojacono maintains a close relationship with Xerox's field sales representatives. She regularly visits the account's largest locations and, in some instances, will have a field salesperson accompany her. More-over, when a representative needs her assistance with a client, she will fly out to support the sales effort. "Sales reps welcome a NAM's presence," notes Lojacono, "because it means someone is coming down who understands the account."

Like other national account managers for Xerox, Lojacono holds quarterly review sessions with all sales representatives who deal with her accounts. At these meetings, she reviews the marketing strategy developed to take advantage of the national contract, discusses difficulties that have arisen, and helps representatives to evaluate their performance.

Source: Thayer C. Taylor, "Xerox's Sales Force Learns a New Game," *Sales & Marketing Management,* July 1, 1985, pp. 48–51.

Complex Sales Organizations

Most multidivision companies organize a sales force by combining geographical, product line, and customer-based structures. The San Francisco conglomerate McKesson markets food items (Mueller pastas), bottled water (Sparkletts), wines and spirits (Folonari Italian wines and Liquore Galliano), health-care products and drugs (Sun Mark, McKesson, and Valu Rite), and even costume jewelry (Hi Lights).[6] Given its size and diversity, McKesson needs not only different sales forces but also different structures within them. Thus, several representatives may be assigned to major cities; some may handle only certain product lines (bottled water, wines, spirits), and others may specialize in certain types of customers (health-care professionals or jewelry retailers). In less populous areas, a single representative may be responsible for most of the marketer's offerings—from food to drugs to jewelry.

In the beginning of the chapter, we discussed Campbell Soup's shift away from a product-based sales organization. Campbell's new structure (see Figure 19-2) combines geography-, product-, and customer-based forms of organization. The sales force is organized first by geography (four sectors and then regions within sectors), then by product (brand managers), and finally by customer (headquarters or national accounts versus retail operations). This organizational structure is normal for marketers with large sales forces.

THE SALES PLAN: SETTING OBJECTIVES

Whether the sales force is organized along one dimension, such as geography, or along all three (geography, product line, and customer type), contemporary sales management is guided and bounded by the objectives spelled out in a company's sales plan. Like all managers, sales managers analyze, plan, implement, and control. Their first responsibility, whatever their level in the organization, is to set forth sales objectives for the year (or longer) and to plan specific actions to attain these goals. Sales plans should complement and advance the overall corporate and mar-

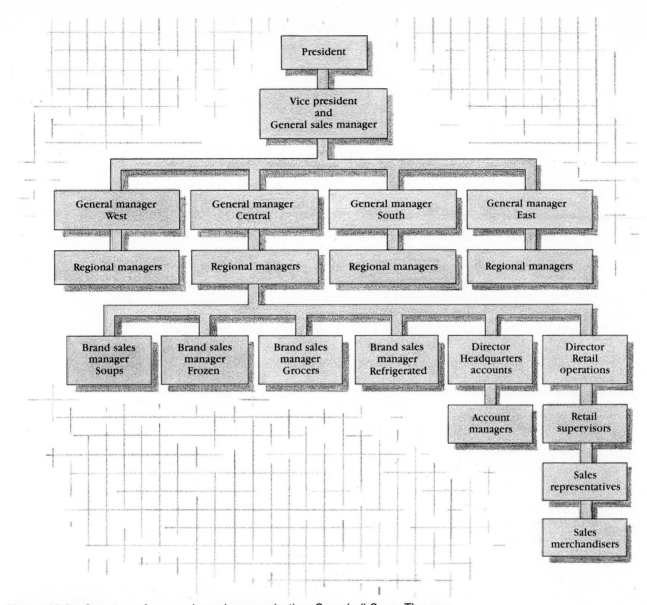

Figure 19-2 *Structure of a complex sales organization: Campbell Soup.* The new sales organization of Campbell Soup, implemented in 1986, combines geographical, product-based, and customer-based forms of organization.

keting strategies of the organization. Of course, development of sales plans and objectives is ideally a two-way process. There is a flow down the organization from top management and another up the organization from the field salespeople.

☐ Corporate Strategy to Marketing Strategy to Sales Planning

To establish a sales program for the current year, companies translate their corporate strategy into marketing strategy, into promotion strategy, and finally into specific sales strategies and actions. Let us take, for instance, the hypothetical but realistic example of the Acme Chemical Company.

Three years ago, Acme's executive committee approved total company sales goals of $650 million, $725 million, and $800 million for the coming years. District sales managers were required to submit a set of sales goals and plans last January. They started work on their plans the previous fall by meeting with individual representatives in their districts. Because they believe that representatives should function as managers of their own territories, Acme's district sales managers asked each salesperson to project sales for the coming year. These projections added up to $104.5 million for the northwest district, managed by Sam Costanzo. After a morning-long conference with his boss, regional manager Angela Bonterre, this projection of $104.5 million was approved. Costanzo's projection fits in rather well with Bonterre's projection of $221 million in sales for the western region, which was subsequently approved after some heated argument (Acme's national sales manager initially wanted $235 million from the region).

National sales were projected at $802 million for the coming year, once people in marketing research, forecasting, financial planning, and other groups at the company's headquarters coordinated their efforts. Acme's president and vice president of marketing, in turn, were satisfied that the company would reach its corporate domestic goal of $800 million with some ease.

In fact, Acme's international sales manager forecast revenues of $42 million from operations in West Germany, Belgium, Great Britain, and Japan—some $1.5 million more than originally expected. Barring uncontrollable forces, Acme will have a good year and shareholders will be happy with their dividends.

In addition to its dollar sales goal, Acme wants to increase its domestic and international market shares for carbon fiber by 5 percent and 10 percent, respec-

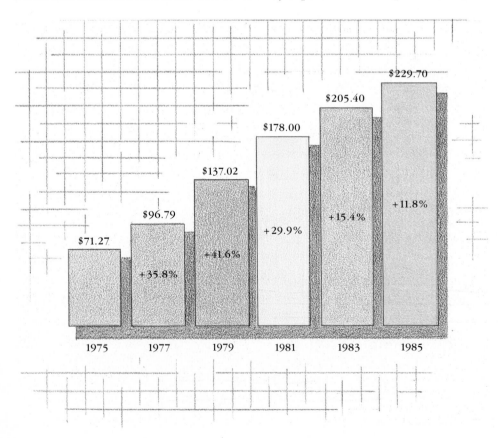

Figure 19-3 *The growing cost of a sales call.* The cost of keeping a sales representative in the field includes the salesperson's salary, travel, entertainment, and other factors. When divided by the number of calls salespeople can make, the cost per call has increased dramatically during the last decade. (From McGraw-Hill Research, *Cost of an Industrial Sales Call* 8013.8. © Sales and Marketing Management.)

tively. Money has been budgeted for the advertising and promotion required to secure this growth; a special 2 percent commission on sales of carbon-fiber products will be offered to the sales force between April and September as an incentive to coordinate personal selling with these advertising and promotion campaigns. At the same time, expenditures for Toughkote, an industrial adhesive, will be cut back. Since Toughkote is a mature product in a mature market, Delancey hopes to hold profits steady or experience only a slight decline as a result of cutbacks in promotion.

In these ways, Acme translated its corporate strategy into marketing strategy and then into promotion strategy. After this planning was completed, Acme developed a sales plan based on specific goals and tactics.

☐ Sales Objectives

Modern organizations frequently set sales goals after consulting individuals at various levels, including sales representatives. The aim is to give representatives and managers at each level the opportunity to set goals that are challenging but reasonable. Unrealistic goals, arbitrarily dictated from above, run the risk of being unattainable and may result in unhappy salespeople and disappointed managers. Although a dollar sales figure is the most common sales objective, goals such as those discussed below are often part of the sales plan agreed upon by managers and representatives.

NET SALES   For most sales representatives, the basic objective consists of the annual sales total for a territory, district, or region after returns and discounts, without consideration of expenses or profits. Even though other, more sophisticated measures of performance are being used in managing a territory, dollar sales still lie at the heart of most sales plans. Usually sales reports are structured and issued quarterly or monthly so that sales can be monitored throughout the year.

MARKET SHARE   Goals concerning the market share for a territory, district, or region may be established to support corporate objectives, to challenge representatives, and to evaluate performance. Thus, district sales managers for Acme Chemical might meet with each representative in their districts about increasing the market share for Acme's carbon fiber by 5 percent annually in each territory.

EXPENSE CONTROLS: PROFITABILITY AND PRODUCTIVITY   In recent years, the cost of fielding a sales force has increased dramatically. Between 1975 and 1985, the Consumer Price Index rose by 96.3 percent. During those same years, the cost of keeping an industrial sales force in the field has increased by 222 percent. As a result, the average cost of an industrial sales call is now over $230 (see Figure 19-3). When closing one sale averages several calls, the cost to close one sale to an organizational buyer can run well over $1000.

Faced with such large and continually rising costs, many firms set expense goals all the way down to the territory level. Moreover, although representatives and sales managers tend to focus on the "top line" (net sales), more and more firms are using profitability and productivity goals (the "bottom line") to help evaluate the performance of their sales force.

CUSTOMER SERVICE AND CHANNEL RELATIONS   Special objectives may be set for improving customer service, such as reducing complaints by a certain percentage or gaining a specific number of new accounts through superior service.

The cost of keeping a salesperson in the field includes salary and a host of expenses. Salespeople nearly all travel; some have company cars, some travel by train, and many cover their territories by air. Careful control of the total costs of selling is a major task of the sales manager. (Copyright © P. Zachmann/Magnum.)

Such objectives can be set even at the territory level and foster good channel relations. Promotional activities and pricing tactics (cooperative advertising, discounts to distributors, and so forth) are essential in maintaining smooth channel relations, but it is the sales representative who makes daily face-to-face contact with buyers and purchasing agents. Good service and relations at the territory level support the attainment of other goals throughout the organization.

MARKET INFORMATION The sales force can and should be the eyes and ears of the marketing organization. Although a company's marketing information system routinely gathers and assesses information—and many firms conduct sophisticated research and special studies—the sales force's fingers are on the market's pulse. Representatives in the field provide management with the information needed to put the marketing concept into practice and truly satisfy customers. Even in marketing packaged goods to consumers, where retailers are closest to customers, the sales representative calls on the retailer and learns what customers want. Contact is more direct in industrial markets, since buyers are often users.

Traditionally, sales force feedback has been seen as a weak link in sales management. Representatives frequently complain that their managers do not really use or respond to the information gathered in the field. Well-managed organizations, however, have refined their management information systems to incorporate and formalize sales force information. Companies that make a special effort to gather and respond to sales information, whether formally or informally, have improved their sales effectiveness.[7] The goal of securing market information will undoubtedly become increasingly common for both representatives and managers.

■ *SIZE AND STRUCTURE OF THE SALES FORCE* ■

Personal selling has become so expensive that marketing organizations must analyze and justify the number of sales representatives in the field. The costs of employing and supporting a sales force (salaries, commissions, travel expenses, and support personnel) directly affect the bottom line—profits. But, although fielding too large a sales force negatively affects profitability, missed sales resulting from too small a sales force have negative effects on the top line—net sales.

No simple formula can determine the correct size for a sales force, although rigorous computer models have been developed to attack the problem. In general, the goal is to balance selling costs against potential sales.[8] If the cost of additional representatives is covered by the sales that they secure, the top line minus the bottom line will still yield profits. The scales can tilt quickly, however; sales managers need to constantly monitor and analyze performance and costs.

Besides determining the number of representatives and territories that will be most effective, managers attempt to structure territories to produce optimal sales and profits. The typical criteria considered in structuring sales territories are work load, market potential, and the experience and talent of individual representatives.

☐ *Work Load*

A **sales territory**, geographically based or otherwise, includes the current and potential accounts assigned to an individual sales representative or territory manager. Assume that a typical territory has 100 accounts: 20 large, 30 medium, and 50 small or marginal accounts. Large accounts require 20 calls per year; medium accounts 10 calls per year; and small accounts 4 calls per year. Thus 900 sales calls are needed each year to service all accounts in the territory. Since a typical representative is estimated to have 230 calling days per year, this hypothetical territory requires about 4 sales calls per day.

These numbers, however, tell only part of the story. We cannot determine whether this or any particular call schedule is reasonable and efficient simply by analyzing the work load. Although managers do consider work load requirements as one factor in structuring territories, they also weigh other less measurable factors. Among these are the complexity and nature of the product, the flexibility demanded by various accounts, the market potential of the territory, and personal aspects of the individual sales representatives.

☐ *Market Potential*

Stable, long-established territories can be effectively worked and prospected by an experienced sales representative with a suitable work load. However, newer, less stable territories need attentive management. Accounts are gained and lost more frequently in such territories, and the market potential can change radically as a result. In addition, the potential of any territory can be affected by the introduction of new products. Current accounts may expand or contract in response to new offerings; customers may be added or lost.

Sales territories must be developed and monitored carefully by the sales manager to ensure that the work load assigned to each salesperson is appropriate. If a territory is too large, it won't be adequately covered; if it is not large enough, the salesperson's time will not be well utilized. (Copyright © Charles Feil 1983/Stock, Boston.)

Since the sales representative is closest to the events and influences that affect a territory's market potential, the sales manager also analyzes information from the field to determine the best structure for the company's needs. (Chapter 20 looks more closely at a territory's market potential.) Management collects and appraises information about market potential from all territories and relates it to work loads and individual talents. The optimal structure should be efficient in serving current accounts and aggressive in securing new ones.

☐ *Individual Experience and Ability*

In general, a salesperson with 15 years of experience can be expected to manage a territory more effectively than a trainee will. However, the years also take their toll. An experienced representative may lack the energy and enthusiasm of a new rep and may be inclined to rely on past methods and achievements. Again, the sales manager must consider *individual* experience in structuring territories. Which sales representative is best able to handle the work load and exploit the market potential of a territory? Which is best able to hold current accounts or to secure new business?

Increasingly sophisticated computer models are helping managers to analyze quantitative information about the size and structure of sales territories.[9] However, human, qualitative factors remain the major challenge confronting sales managers. Various recruitment and selection tools aid managers in finding the right person for the job.

■ SALES POSITIONS ■

The U.S. Bureau of Labor Statistics estimates that well over 6 million Americans work in some type of sales job. That figure, however, does not include all the service providers—the dentists, cashiers, manicurists, electricians, and others who have daily face-to-face contact with those to whom they "sell" their services. (To a certain extent, we all sell our talents and services to employers, but here we focus on positions in which selling is the primary task.) We can classify sales positions usefully by distinguishing between industrial and consumer sales and by considering the level of professionalism needed for each job.

☐ *Industrial and Consumer Sales*

One million U.S. women and men are engaged in "selling business to business." As **industrial salespeople, they sell** goods and services used for producing other goods or for rendering other services. The products they handle are not intended for ultimate consumers.

In comparison to consumer sales, industrial selling usually requires higher levels of education and professionalism as well as greater technical and financial expertise. Indeed, providing accurate, informative advice is an essential part of industrial selling; poor advice can jeopardize a customer's business. One chemical producer outlined the current situation facing industrial sales representatives:

> If they're trying to sell plastic film to a packager who has several million dollars of packaging equipment designed to use some other material, they must now know how to unload the present equipment, purchase new equipment, and work out the intricacies of amortization. Without that background, they cannot persuade the customer to accept delivery of a single carload of plastic film.[10]

Implementing and Controlling Marketing Plans

Industrial salespeople often must have special knowledge in order to be able to sell. Some sales positions, for instance, require an engineering degree just to understand the product. Regardless of how technical, industrial selling often means calling on high-level executives. (Woo/Stock, Boston.)

Consumer salespeople, in selling goods and services to intermediaries or directly to ultimate users, may not need such a high level of expertise, but they, too, must know their products and their customers' needs. Such jobs range in complexity from pumping gasoline at a service station, to selling appliances and furniture, to advising individual investors about the purchase of stocks and bonds, to helping store managers control their inventories.

Del Monte Corporation employs two levels of consumer salespeople: account representatives and sales representatives. Account representatives make direct calls on retailers and write up orders, as any salesperson would. But they also inform store managers about cooperative advertising programs and special promotional activities and use a computerized system to report on their products' shelf position, pricing, advertising support, and other basic information affecting sales and profitability. In short, they supply the raw data of sales management. Their field work is supported by sales representatives who work with store managers on such merchandising tasks as shelf management, restocking, and display. Del Monte regards this position as a training ground for future account representatives.[11]

A second method of classifying sales positions focuses on the requirements of a particular job. Based on standards of education and training, the diversity of skills needed, and the degree of commitment required, salespeople may be grouped as (1) professional sales representatives or territory managers, (2) special sales representatives, (3) order takers, or (4) support personnel.

☐ *Professional Sales Representatives*

Although they increasingly rely on the telephone for initial prospecting and for handling routine inquiries and orders, **professional sales representatives** are territory managers whose primary task is persuasive and creative face-to-face selling and account management. Because professional buyers expect a high degree of expertise from sellers, professional sales representatives are found in consumer marketing, where they call on buyers in large chain organizations, and in industrial marketing, where buyers tend to be professionals and are often engineers or scientists. Today's sales jobs usually require a college degree; some firms seek representatives who hold a master's degree in business administration or an applicable scientific or technical degree.

Professional selling is a lifelong career for some representatives; annual compensation can exceed six figures. For others, professional sales serves as a stepping-stone to higher management positions.

☐ *Special Sales Representatives*

Also true professionals, **special sales representatives** promote the product directly to those who purchase it to intermediaries, or to those who recommend purchases but do not actually take orders. These representatives establish goodwill for the marketer and provide customer service. Special sales representatives work in both consumer and industrial marketing; they are generally classified as missionary salespeople or as technical specialists.

MISSIONARY SALESPEOPLE   In consumer marketing, special sales representatives often function as **missionary salespeople** who perform such diverse tasks as building the organization's image, cultivating relations with decision makers, giving away samples, and presenting in-depth information about the product. Among

Representatives of pharmaceutical companies often call on physicians to keep them informed of new developments or new test data on prescription drugs. These representatives are often referred to as *missionary salespeople*. (Copyright © Christopher Springman/The Stock Market.)

those classified as missionary salespeople are the representatives of pharmaceutical companies, who call on physicians; of clothing manufacturers, who call on retailers; and of textbook publishers, who call on teachers and professors. Such salespeople do not take orders but do influence doctors prescribing drugs for patients, retailers purchasing from wholesalers, and educators selecting textbooks.

TECHNICAL SPECIALISTS   Because they are equipped with technical and scientific expertise beyond that of professional sales representatives, **technical specialists (or sales engineers)** function as consultants and provide specific information about the product's capabilities, specifications, installation, use, and maintenance. They are especially knowledgeable about applications—how a particular product can be used, such as computers for word processing or microfilm equipment in libraries. Technical specialists support and augment the efforts of sales representatives, most often in selling to industrial customers.

☐ *Order Takers*

The majority of selling positions fall into the order-taker category. These jobs range from the routine to the creative—from supermarket and variety store cashiers to travel agents, bank officers, and wine stewards. In general, **order takers** help customers shop and complete the sale. Although some of these jobs are repetitive, like a supermarket cashier, the work must be done in a friendly and pleasant manner, or customers will go elsewhere. Other positions, such as a travel agent, require a fair amount of training, creativity, and persuasiveness in selling. Unlike the professional and special representatives, order takers often do not have to have a college degree.

☐ *Support Personnel*

Working by telephone or direct mail from central or district offices, **support personnel** aid the efforts of professional and special sales representatives and order takers. They follow up orders, answer inquiries, handle marginal accounts, qualify prospects, and, in general, allow sales representatives to spend more time in face-to-face selling with important customers. Sales support personnel are in training-level positions that often lead to more demanding, professional sales jobs.

■ RECRUITING AND SELECTING SALES PERSONNEL ■

Sales managers need to attract, identify, and hire the most qualified and most talented applicants for sales positions, especially for positions requiring a high level of professionalism. Yet determining what makes an effective salesperson is quite difficult. Important factors are the individual's aptitude, motivation, skill, and other personal variables as well as factors within the organization.[12]

Alan Dubinsky and Thomas Barry surveyed 121 chief sales executives of industrial companies with annual sales ranging from $1 million to $8.5 million. The procedures used by those companies to select promising job applicants are summarized in Exhibit 19-1. The most common selection tool by far is the personal interview of the applicant by the sales manager.[13] Next to interviews, managers rely on application blanks, personal reference checks, and lists of job qualifications.

The typical personal interview includes two stages. First, qualified applicants are screened and evaluated. (These initial interviews often take place on college campuses, to recruit new graduates. Interviews with applicants who have work

EXHIBIT 19-1 | Use of Various Tools for Selecting Sales Personnel

In selecting sales personnel, industrial companies rely most frequently on personal interviews of applicants, application blanks, personal reference checks, and lists of job qualifications.

Tool	Firms that "Extensively Use" Tool (%)
Personal interviews	93
Application blanks	72
Personal reference checks	67
Lists of job qualifications	38
Job descriptions	38
Psychological tests	26
Credit reports	23

Source: Adapted from Alan J. Dubinsky and Thomas E. Barry, "A Survey of Sales Management Practices," *Industrial Marketing Management,* vol. 11, 1982, p. 136.

experience take place in a variety of settings.) Second, additional or final interviews are conducted in the hiring firm's offices under the direction of the sales manager. Wesley Johnson and Martha Cooper found that the following behaviors were considered most important by sales managers in interviewing applicants: (1) the desire and willingness to make sacrifices for a sales career; (2) inquisitiveness about the job and the company; (3) specific personal goals and ambitions; and (4) friendliness.[14]

TRAINING THE SALES FORCE

IBM has had a long-standing belief in extensive training for its sales force. An old company joke puts it: "No one ever retires from IBM; eventually, one just graduates." Depending on an organization's needs and resources, training programs for sales representatives vary widely in duration, content, and setting.

The most common duration of training programs is something less than 6 months, but a considerable number of companies have programs lasting longer than a year. There is some consistency in the content of training programs, although each company must of course design its own. In general, the content will include product knowledge, selling techniques, markets and competition, and company policies and practices. As settings, on-the-job training, classroom study, and coaching sessions with sales managers and senior sales personnel are clearly favored. The general view is that at least a portion of formal classroom training is best left until sales trainees have spent some time on the job.

On-the-Job Training

On-the-job training consists of actual sales calls made with a senior sales representative or the district manager. This process gives the trainee firsthand insight into the challenges and opportunities of selling the company's product. Besides serving as a dress rehearsal for new personnel, on-the-job training introduces newcomers to the company's clients and exposes them to the professionalism of seasoned representatives. On-the-job training also prods recruits to formulate questions so that they can make the most of their classroom training.

Formal Sales Training

In classroom courses of varying lengths, **formal sales training** gives new salespeople product knowledge, skill in selling, information about markets and compe-

The need for learning by professionals never ends. One of the sales manager's major responsibilities is the coaching of the salespeople in their territories. (Copyright © Stacy Pick/Stock, Boston.)

tition, and guidance on company policies and practices. In a typical training program, formal study and fieldwork might alternate. Trainees would first undertake a week or so of classroom study to orient them to the company; the classroom study would be followed by a few weeks of on-the-job training. Trainees would then return to the classroom for training in product knowledge or markets and competition. After some more weeks of on-the-job training, they would return again to the classroom for work on skills needed for selling. This pattern of classroom and fieldwork helps trainees to relate their formal instruction to the experience of actual sales calls.

☐ Coaching

Like on-the-job training, **coaching** consists of making sales calls under the supervision of a sales manager or a trainer. However, here the trainee actually makes the sales presentation to customers. Periodically through the day or at its end, the manager evaluates the trainee's efforts and suggests improvements. Coaching is a major responsibility of sales managers; it allows trainees to apply their classroom instruction realistically in a relatively safe setting.

☐ Other Training Techniques

In addition to their initial training, sales personnel may be observed from time to time by experienced salespeople, and many pursue individualized study at home or in courses outside the company. Sales training is an educational process that continues throughout a person's career; there is always something new to master and bring to the sales call. Many companies offer periodic refresher courses and seminars to upgrade or update their staff's selling techniques. Most organizations also schedule two or more sales meetings per year, primarily to improve salespeople's knowledge of existing products or to introduce new products.[15]

MOTIVATING THE SALES FORCE

Contrary to the popular belief that salespeople are driven primarily by money, they are quite concerned about nonfinancial incentives as well. Figure 19-4 summarizes a survey in which 127 sales and marketing executives rated the effectiveness of various **sales force motivators**—incentives, both tangible and intangible, for excellent performance. From the viewpoint of sales and marketing executives, the best ways to motivate the sales staff are to offer (1) special recognition for outstanding performance, (2) an opportunity for promotion and advancement, and (3) encouragement from and contact with a supervisor (recall that many sales representatives are geographically separated from their sales managers). Some research indicates that money does enter the list (in the form of bonuses, commissions, and finally overall compensation) only after these psychological motivators. Obviously, status and peer recognition motivate today's salespeople more effectively than compensation alone, although a different study of salespeople's preferences for rewards did show pay ranked above other rewards.[16]

As a representative's immediate supervisor, the district sales manager is the person most directly concerned with motivating the salesperson. In their supervision and coaching, the best sales managers emphasize the dignity and importance of being a sales representative, thereby providing the official recognition that tops the list of motivating factors. Creative managers recognize individual differences among their employees and devise effective methods of motivating each of them. An ambitious representative who seeks advancement and promotion (and shows the potential for it) will probably be best motivated by a sales manager who delegates certain training responsibilities to that person. Another representative may respond better to simple encouragement and contact with the supervisor. For still others, incentive bonuses and commissions may be the most effective motivators.[17]

COMPENSATING THE SALES FORCE

No matter what motivator is most meaningful to a particular representative, compensation still plays an important role as an incentive to improve performance. Like other aspects of sales management, compensation can be tailored to the selling situation and the individual. Most employees in both business and not-for-profit organizations are paid a straight salary; most get yearly raises based on performance. Sales representatives, however, are typically compensated in direct proportion to performance—in other words, according to how much they sell. Thus, most salespeople have a financial stake in making that extra sales call and working just a little bit harder. Marketers use a variety of compensation plans to support other sales force motivators. The normal, expected methods of compensating salespeople involve a salary, a commission, or a combination of the two.

SALARY   A **salary** is a regular, specified amount of compensation based on minimal performance. This compensation method is employed when the sales force must perform many nonselling tasks, when salespeople are new, or when new territories require extensive development. About one in five salespeople works in such markets and is paid a straight salary. Although this approach to compensating salespeople allows the organization to project and monitor selling costs, salary plans alone provide poor financial incentive. Salary is tied to minimal performance—and often ensures just that.

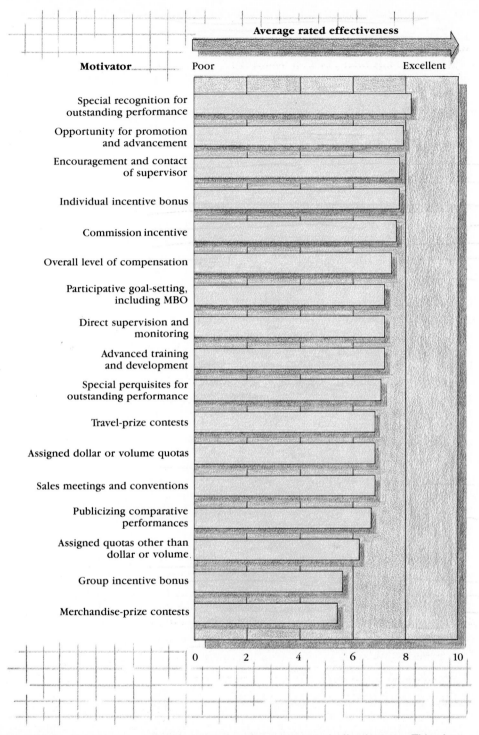

Figure 19-4 *Sales force motivators, in order of average rated effectiveness.* This chart summarizes the views of 127 sales and marketing executives regarding the most effective sales force motivators. Contrary to popular expectations, salespeople apparently can be effectively motivated by nonfinancial incentives as well as by bonuses, commission, and other forms of financial compensation. (From Mary Lynn Miller, *Motivating the Sales Force*, New York: Conference Board, 1979, p. 3.)

STRAIGHT COMMISSION   A **straight commission** is a financial incentive based solely on sales results; each increment of sales increases the commission. This was once a fairly common method of compensating salespeople, but today less than 10 percent of organizations rely solely on straight commissions. Most people need a more stable form of income than commission arrangements provide (although such compensation is still used for many real estate agents and for independent representatives or manufacturer's agents who sell products for more than one marketer). In general, since commission plans are based on sales—which can only be projected—they do not permit tight control over selling expenses. Costs can be predicted only insofar as sales can be predicted. Yet commissions do provide a strong incentive for salespeople and often lead to aggressive selling efforts.

COMBINATION PLANS   About three-fourths of sales representatives are currently paid through a **combination plan**—salary plus some type of bonus or commission. Salespeople thus receive both a stable financial base (salary) and an incentive to perform (bonus or commission). This compensation mix is useful when territories have similar potential. The salary provides an equitable base for all representatives; the incentive spurs individuals to aggressively pursue their best sales opportunities. Combination plans provide relatively tight control over selling costs even as they allow costs to fluctuate with sales.

Under a typical combination plan, the sales manager and each representative decide on a sales target or quota for each territory. If the goal is $500,000 and that target is reached in October of the calendar year, all sales beyond the target may yield a 2 percent commission. If the representative's annual salary is $35,000 and post-October sales are $100,000, then the representative's combined compensation for the year would be $37,000 (salary of $35,000 plus commission of $2000, based on 2 percent of $100,000).

Less common combination plans include a salary plus a commission based on territory profit. In such instances, the commission is some percentage of net sales minus selling expenses for the territory. This method of compensation encourages representatives to concentrate on the most profitable products and accounts and to control costs. Consequently, the goals of sales representatives are closely tied to the organization's profit goals.

SPECIAL INCENTIVES   Besides the regular compensation plans, marketers may offer **special incentives**—usually for a brief period—to strengthen representatives' efforts to achieve specific sales goals. Special incentives are often part of an overall promotion strategy; bonuses may be offered for additional sales of a particular producer during a period, or sales contests may be used to encourage competition among salespeople. Marketing organizations may use cash prizes, vacations, and merchandise as short-term sales incentives.[18]

EVALUATING SALES FORCE PERFORMANCE

Standards used to appraise an individual representative's performance usually reflect the specific objectives set jointly with the sales manager. The following are some of the measurable standards used:

- *Net sales:* Did the representative meet, fail to meet, or exceed sales goals for the territory?

- *Market share:* If specific goals relating to market share were set, were they achieved?
- *Expense controls:* Did the representative cover the territory within the budget set? Were selling costs under or over budget? If the budget was exceeded, were net sales also greater than targeted goals?
- *Customer service and channel relations:* If objectives in these areas were set, were they met? Unless such goals are specified carefully, performance may be difficult to measure.
- *Market information:* Did the representative provide systematic feedback about trends in the territory?

Of course, objectives other than these may be agreed upon—depending on the territory, the firm's product, and the talents and experience of the representative. Special research projects may be assigned and become another basis of evaluation, as can the manager's impression of sheer effort and hard work.[19] The sales manager and the representative should discuss all goals frankly, both to agree on realistic goals and to evaluate to what extent the goals were attained. Performance evaluations are essential to effective coaching, since they allow the manager and representative to refer to specific, measurable aspects of performance.

Not all goals, however, are easily measurable, and a representative's personality may affect performance as much as a manager's appraisal. As a result, subjective evaluations should be balanced with objective ones. Then, whether a manager recommends that a representative be promoted, penalized, or even fired, the basis of the evaluation will be as reasonable, unbiased, and accurate as possible.

■ SUMMARY ■

1. As the personal side of the promotion mix, the sales organization plays a vital role in the total marketing efforts.
2. The main assignment of the sales manager is to translate a selling plan into specific actions in the field.
3. Sales managers are expected to be self-starters, effective motivators, and action-oriented; they also must be skilled in analysis and planning.
4. The three most common methods of organizing a sales management system are by geographic area, by product line, and by customer type. Many companies use a combination of these organizational forms.
5. In establishing a sales program, companies translate their corporate strategy into a marketing strategy and a promotion strategy and finally into specific sales strategies and actions.
6. Sales objectives may focus on net sales, market share, expense controls, customer service and channel relations, or market information.
7. The typical criteria considered in structuring sales territories are work load, market potential, and the experience and talent of individual representatives.
8. Sales positions can be classified in terms of industrial versus consumer sales or by considering the level of professionalism needed for the job.
9. The most common tool in selecting personnel for a sales force is the personal interview of the applicant by the sales manager.
10. In training a sales force, companies rely on a combination of on-the-job training, formal sales training, coaching, and other training techniques.
11. Contrary to the popular belief that salespeople are driven primarily by money, they are quite concerned about nonfinancial incentives as well.
12. Methods of compensation for sales representatives include salary; straight commission;

a combination of the two; and special incentives such as bonuses, cash prizes, and vacations.

13. In evaluating sales force performance, managers should balance subjective evaluations with objective ones.

☐ Key Terms

coaching	on-the-job training	sales manager
combination plan	order takers	sales territory
consumer salespeople	professional sales representatives	special incentives
district sales manager	salary	special sales representatives
formal sales training	sales engineers	straight commission
industrial salespeople	sales force motivators	support personnel
missionary salespeople	sales management system	technical specialists
national account representative		

☐ Chapter Review

1. Explain why today's sales managers often must do analysis and planning. Why is being a self-starter important for a sales manager?

2. What type of sales force organization would be most logical for a manufacturer of automotive machine tools? For a producer of a wide line of diversified food and drug products?

3. How do an organization's marketing and sales objectives affect each other?

4. Cite some factors that influence sales force size and structure. What is the primary disadvantage of a sales force that is too small?

5. Give examples of some products that require the skills of highly trained, professional representatives. Would a stockbroker be considered a sales representative?

6. Why is on-the-job performance the most frequently employed training setting? Describe some of the ways in which a sales manager's coaching might improve employee performance.

7. Support or criticize the following statement: "Sales managers should always regard financial compensation as a sales representative's primary motivator."

8. Why is evaluation against set goals so important to effective sales management?

☐ References

1. American Marketing Association, *Marketing Definitions: A Glossary of Marketing Terms* (Chicago, 1960).

2. Robert E. Hite and Joseph A. Bellizzi, "A Preferred Style of Sales Management," *Industrial Marketing Management,* vol. 15, Aug. 1986, pp. 215–223.

3. Bert Rosenbloom and Rolph E. Anderson, "The Sales Manager: Tomorrow's Super Marketer," *Business Horizons,* Mar.–Apr. 1984, pp. 50–56; and Raymond W. LaForge, David W. Cravens, and Clifford E. Young, "Improving Salesforce Productivity," *Business Horizons,* Sept.–Oct. 1985, pp. 50–59.

4. Gilbert A. Churchill, Jr., Neil M. Ford, and Orville C. Walker, Jr., *Sales Force Management: Planning, Implementation, and Control* (Homewood, Ill.: Richard D. Irwin, 1985), pp. 20–23.

5. John Barrett, "Why Major Account Selling Works," *Industrial Marketing Management,* vol. 15, Feb. 1986, pp. 63–73.

6. Milton Moskowitz, Michael Katz, and Robert Levering, *Everybody's Business: An Almanac* (New York: Harper & Row, 1980), p. 816.

7. Don Waite, "When Salespeople Talk, Does Management Listen?" *Sales and Marketing Management,* Oct. 7, 1985, pp. 43–45.

8. Arthur Meridan, "Optimizing the Number of Industrial Salespersons," *Industrial Marketing Management,* vol. 11, no. 1, Feb. 1982, pp. 63–74.

9. William K. Fudge and Leonard M. Lodish, "Evaluation of the Effectiveness of a Model-

Implementing and Controlling Marketing Plans

Based Salesman's Planning System by Field Experimentation," *Interfaces,* vol. 8, Nov. 1977, p. 104; and Gary M. Armstrong, "The SCHEDULE Model and the Salesman's Effort Allocation," *California Management Review,* vol. 18, Summer 1976, pp. 43–51.

10. "The New Supersalesman," *Business Week,* Jan. 6, 1973, p. 45.

11. Ibid., pp. 46–47.

12. Gilbert A. Churchill, Jr., Neil M. Ford, Steven W. Hartley, and Orville C. Walker, Jr., "The Determinants of Salesperson Performance: A Meta-Analysis," *Journal of Marketing Research,* vol. XXII, May 1985, pp. 103–118.

13. Alan J. Dubinsky and Thomas E. Barry, "A Survey of Sales Management Practices," *Industrial Marketing Management,* vol. 11, 1982, pp. 131–141.

14. David S. Hopkins, *Training the Sales Force: A Progress Report* (New York: Conference Board, 1978), p. 6.

15. Ibid., p. 13.

16. Neil M. Ford, Orville C. Walker, Jr., and Gilbert A. Churchill, Jr., "Differences in the Attractiveness of Alternative Rewards among Industrial Salespeople: Additional Evidence," University of Wisconsin Working Paper no. 1-84-4, Jan. 1984.

17. Z. S. Demirdjian, "A Multidimensional Approach to Motivating Salespeople," *Industrial Marketing Management,* vol. 13, Feb. 1984, pp. 25–32.

18. See André J. San Augustine and Joel N. Greene, "The Psychology of Noncash Incentives," *Sales and Marketing Management,* Apr. 5, 1982, pp. 112–118.

19. John C. Mowen, Janet E. Keith, Steven W. Brown, and Donald W. Jackson, Jr., "Utilizing Effort and Task Difficulty Information in Evaluating Salespeople," *Journal of Marketing Research,* vol. XXII, May 1985, pp. 185–191; and Harish Sujan, "Smarter versus Harder: An Exploratory Attributional Analysis of Salespeople's Motivation," *Journal of Marketing Research,* vol. XXIII, Feb. 1985, pp. 41–49.

20

MANAGING THE SALES TERRITORY

SPOTLIGHT ON

☐ Professionalism in personal selling

☐ Sales representatives as marketers

☐ Traditional steps of the selling process

☐ Territory managers performing account and work load analysis

☐ Sales plans and effective territory management

☐ Territory managers' implementation and control of sales plans

Copyright © Craig Aurness/Woodfin Camp & Assoc.

To illustrate the workings of the personal selling process, we present the following hypothetical case study. Friday, May 21, was not a typical day for Kimberly Ann Hall—it was a day of celebration. Her district manager, Carlos Ruiz, and her regional manager, Paula DeVito, were taking her to lunch at New Orleans' famed Antoine's restaurant. Hall's first 2 years as the New Orleans sales representative for Delancey Inc. had been good ones: Her territory's sales had increased 11 percent in her first year and 22 percent in the second year. The luncheon celebrated not only her generally fine sales record but also her persistent and astute work in landing a major new account.

Hall's predecessors in the New Orleans territory had all attempted without success to land at least part of the chemical and plastics business of Whittier Inc., a large supplier of packaging materials for the local food-processing industry. The director of materials management at Whittier, Dan McCartney, was his own purchasing agent and had been buying needed chemicals from Rising Star Corporation in Houston. Bob Wjoljack, Rising Star's local representative (and Kimberly Ann Hall's direct competitor) had 10 years' experience in the territory and a solid working relationship with McCartney. Yet Hall was able to capture a substantial part of Whittier's business for Delancey through some alert professional sales work.

Some 18 months earlier, Hall had read a brief article in the *New Orleans Times-Picayune* about Whittier's success in winning a federal contract to provide protective storage packaging for aircraft engine parts processed through the U.S. Air Force near St. Louis. She realized that the contract represented a new direction for Whittier and a new opportunity for Delancey; obviously, different materials would be needed for packaging the engine parts. As it happened, just a few days earlier Delancey had sent out a product bulletin describing a new plastic bubble sheeting that Hall thought might fit Whittier's needs.

Hall met with McCartney to discuss specifications for the new supplies that Whittier would require. With these "specs" in hand, she discussed the situation with Carlos Ruiz, who approved a special sample shipment of the new bubble sheeting for McCartney. Over the next few months, Hall met with McCartney several times, providing him with test results of the bubble sheeting's capabilities.

Although a price advantage helped secure the Whittier order for Delancey, Dan McCartney later admitted to Carlos Ruiz that the clincher was Hall's help in negotiating a guarantee of 30 days' delivery time on future orders of at least 100,000 square yards. Perhaps even more important was her suggestion that Whittier use the plastic bubble material as protection for several lines of foodstuffs that they sell packaged in glass jars. The cost per carton for the plastic sheeting was approximately three cents less than the cardboard material then in use. In addition, Delancey's tests showed that Whittier could expect an 8 to 10 percent reduction in breakage if they used the bubble sheeting. Kimberly Ann Hall got Whittier's business because she did more than ask for an order—she helped her customer solve a problem.

You purchase goods and services from sales personnel almost every day: items as diverse as records and rubber bands, insurance policies and dry-cleaning services, food, clothing, and shelter. But you probably don't make purchases from the professional sales representatives who are the focus of this chapter. Sales professionals, selling consumer products to intermediaries like wholesalers or retailers, or to customers in an industrial setting, are highly educated and skilled; in a genuine sense, they serve as the managers of their own territories.

Chapter 20 opens with an examination of sales professionalism and of the roles that sales representatives play as marketers. A look at the traditional steps in personal selling follows. We describe the processes of territory management and planning in some detail and suggest ways in which territory plans may be implemented and controlled. The chapter concludes with a brief discussion of the career move from territory manager to sales manager.

THE PROFESSIONAL SALES REPRESENTATIVE

Like Kimberly Ann Hall, sales professionals are problem solvers and consultants for their customers. Do they still *sell* products? Of course, but they do so in creative ways that go far beyond merely touting their wares. They show how their company's products can meet needs and solve problems. And, like Hall, they may suggest innovative uses for products.

Sales professionals are trained in selling techniques, of course, but they also become increasingly expert about their products. They know which offerings will help customers and which will not. They see customers on a long-term basis and do not try to sell the wrong product just to make a quick sale. Over time, their attitude of service and helpfulness produces greater sales because customers know that they can depend on the sales representative to give honest, practical advice. We will use the terms "professional sales representative" and "territory manager" interchangeably in this chapter; managing a sales territory clearly requires the skills and training of a professional.

An Undeserved Legacy

Professional sales representatives, as we will see, use modern techniques to manage their territories through analysis, planning, implementing, and controlling—just as top-level executives manage companies. Yet professional sales representatives often feel misunderstood and are perceived inaccurately by many. Novels, movies, and television frequently portray salespeople as glad-handing backslappers (like Professor Harold Hill in Meredith Willson's *The Music Man*) or as pitiable losers (Willy Loman in Arthur Miller's *Death of a Salesman*). In truth, however dramatic and moving these portraits are, they do not depict typical sales representatives, even those of the past.

Backslappers, losers, and charlatans can indeed be found among salespeople—just as they are found in the legal profession, medicine, architecture, manufacturing, politics, and education. No doubt human frailty exists in every profession (even though some might say that politicians have a slight edge). Yet the majority of today's professional salespeople are well-educated and well-trained; they are dedicated to performing their jobs imaginatively and honestly. Salespeople practice an honorable, challenging, and rewarding trade. In truth, the complexities of modern economics, marketing environments, products, and buying situations have rendered the Willy Lomans of the world obsolete. Today's sophisticated customers—both

Arthur Miller's *Death of a Salesman* is one of the great American play. Its latest revival on Broadway starred Dustin Hoffman as the play's tragic hero, Willy Loman. Unfortunately, this pitiable character has led many people to believe that his was the typical life of a salesman. That image, regardless of its inaccuracy, has plagued the profession for years. (Copyright © Inge Morath/ Magnum.)

professional buyers and final customers—demand the help of equally sophisticated salespeople.

Sales Representatives as Marketers

Each year, *Purchasing* magazine asks the people who deal with sales representatives most directly—purchasing agents—to nominate one representative who calls on them as the "outstanding salesperson" and to provide reasons for their selection. An analysis of their responses has shown that every year since 1977 the following traits have been the top four: (1) thoroughness (or follow-through), (2) product knowledge, (3) willingness to go to bat for the buyer with the representative's own company, and (4) market knowledge.[1] These are certainly not the traits of an old-fashioned peddler.

A nationwide survey of 1400 salespeople under age 30 revealed that one-third are women (see Box 20-1), 63 percent are college graduates, 11 percent hold MBA degrees, and less than 2 percent have no college training.[2] These people all consider themselves marketers and are, in fact, key members of marketing teams. Increasingly, sales representatives are becoming directly involved in such activities as coordinating promotion efforts, consulting, making a total offer, assuming a profit orientation, and providing market intelligence—all tasks which had traditionally been the responsibility of marketing managers.[3]

Kimberly Ann Hall, the sales representative featured in our opening vignette, was merely a character in a story about a fictitious company. However, in the real world of sales, more and more women are moving into positions that were formerly the exclusive domain of men. For example, Brown & Bigelow, a manufacturer of advertising specialty items, had virtually no women in its sales force until the late 1970s. By 1985, 25 percent of the company's salespeople were women. Johnson & Johnson—best known for its medical and pharmaceutical supplies and consumer products—has seen the proportion of women in its field sales force increase from 17.6 percent in 1978 to 31 percent in 1984.

Despite their growing numbers in sales positions, women continue to face difficulties in gaining respect and equal treatment. "Credibility is still a problem," notes Dr. Barbara Pletcher, founder of the National Association for Professional Saleswomen (NAPS). She suggests that the expertise of saleswomen is often questioned—and sometimes challenged—by men who doubt that women could possibly understand their business. Linda Crocker, a sales representative who has specialized in selling data communications net-

works, recalls that one male customer, a civil engineer, treated her "like a bit of fluff" and asked questions with a tone indicating that "he just didn't expect me to know the answers."

In general, however, women in sales positions appear optimistic that they will overcome any initial prejudices against them. For example, Cindy Fleming of G. Heileman Brewing describes herself as the only woman in a beer company who travels to the port cities of the United States to sell to suppliers of foreign ships. Fleming remarks: "I know my business as well as my competitors do. When people find out you can handle your business, they don't care if you're male or female." Dr. Pletcher adds that business firms will continue to hire more women for sales positions simply because they need talented employees who demonstrate both competence and commitment to their work. In her view, "Companies can't refuse people who can do the job." ∎

Source: Rayna Skolnik, "A Woman's Place Is on the Sales Force," *Sales and Marketing Management,* Apr. 1, 1985, pp. 34–37.

COORDINATING PROMOTION EFFORTS   Besides making personal contact with customers, many salespeople coordinate their sales activities with other elements of the promotion mix (advertising, sales promotion, and publicity). Chapter 17 stressed that all promotional efforts must be coordinated and blended to ensure maximum effectiveness. More than ever before, professional salespeople implement the components of promotion strategy. For example, a team of Frito-Lay's territory managers may serve as an advisory board for the company's promotion managers, recommending the best time to mail new-product brochures. Many representatives also plan and manage their own personalized-letter campaigns.

CONSULTING   Salespeople must know the needs of their customers. In the long run, they will be most successful by acting as consultants—that is, by helping customers decide what, when, and how to buy. By studying markets and customers' buying habits, salespeople can offer "packages" to solve buyers' problems and satisfy their needs. Representatives may forgo urging an immediate sale because they know that building trust as knowledgeable advisers will lead to greater future sales.[4]

MAKING A TOTAL OFFER   When a sale is made, more than the core product is sold. The customer also pays for the marketer's reputation and servicing as well as for dependable support from the salesperson. Cincinnati Milacron, a manufacturer purchasing assembly line robots and numerically controlled machine tools, wants to know that its large investment will ensure the on-call services of a knowledgeable customer representative. Similarly, investors in stocks and bonds are "buying" the astute, readily available advice of a broker. Potential home buyers expect real estate agents to know the ins and outs of home financing. In all these instances, professional salespeople are prepared to serve the needs of the customer beyond merely providing the core benefit represented by the product itself.

ASSUMING A PROFIT ORIENTATION Salespeople can directly influence the organization's profits by deciding which accounts to emphasize and by spending money wisely. In the future, sales force competition will be increasingly tied to the profitability of sales rather than simply to their total volume.

PROVIDING MARKET INTELLIGENCE As the members of the organization most closely in touch with markets, salespeople advance the marketing concept by systematically reporting information about changes in customers' and consumers' attitudes and buying patterns. Another vital aspect of the sales professional's market reporting involves keeping tabs on competitors' products and their performance in specific markets.

■ *PERSONAL SELLING* ■

At the time of the latest census, more than 10 million Americans were employed in direct selling to businesses and the public.[5] These people range from retail sales personnel to industrial sales representatives responsible for multimillion-dollar technical products. Not included in these figures, however, are millions of other Americans who have daily face-to-face persuasive contact with the users of countless goods and services. From this vast array of sales personnel, we will focus especially on the one million or so **professional sales representatives**—those sellers who

Professional sales representatives manage their own time, and often find their work challenging. They must plan their own work and must be active in arranging the opportunities for calling on customers. Rarely do the customers come to the salesperson. (Copyright © Brett H. Froomer/The Image Bank.)

Although the focus of this chapter is on the professional selling position normally held by college graduates, the total scope of selling includes the retail sales clerk and the route salesperson. They, too, make important contributions to their companies. (Left: Copyright © Craig Hammell 1984/The Stock Market. Right: Copyright © 1986 John Keating/Photo Researchers, Inc.)

view their jobs as lifelong careers or as experience vital to management careers in other aspects of marketing or business.

Some companies insist on sales experience as a prerequisite for advancement into managerial ranks. In fact, a large proportion of entry-level jobs open to college graduates in business administration today are professional sales positions. Of the chief executive officers included in *Fortune*'s 500 largest (industrial) corporations, many began their careers as sales representatives. Moreover, a survey of recently promoted executives asked which entry field they would choose if they had to start over; the largest number of respondents replied that they would choose marketing and sales.[6]

Broadly defined, **personal selling** is an element of the promotion mix that involves personal and persuasive efforts by the seller. Traditionally, sales experts have divided the selling process into seven steps: (1) prospecting and qualifying, (2) approaching customers, (3) preparing for customers, (4) presenting products, (5) handling objections, (6) closing, and (7) following up.

Prospecting and Qualifying

A **prospect** is a potential (but not current) customer; thus, **prospecting** is a systematic process of identifying new buyers. In the past, industrial salespeople prospected through a technique known as "smokestacking"—they simply dropped in on potential customers whose smokestacks could be spotted along the highway. Such hit-and-miss methods are far too time-consuming and costly for today's sales professionals.

Contemporary prospecting is conducted in many ways, with an emphasis on systematic approaches. Sales representatives screen and contact respondents to advertising; they watch for announcements in trade journals to learn about new companies and divisions; they seek referrals from current customers; they use secondary information sources such as business licensing bureaus or listings from the local Better Business Bureau. In general, they carefully monitor their territory for new business leads. Even an unobtrusive item in a local newspaper or radio show may trigger an alert sales professional to investigate new possibilities.

Effective prospecting is often a process of screening potential clients to identify those who genuinely are prospects. Business and industrial publications are filled with advertisements with coupons inviting the reader to request more information about the product. Those who send in coupons (or call a toll-free number, or write for information using their company's letterhead) are more accurately viewed as "suspects" rather than "prospects." Although a personal sales call may be in order, the representative will view them as prime prospects only if they meet an important test: not only are they interested in buying but also they are able to buy. One basic screening goal is to identify which decision makers in an organization are responsible for buying. Thus, the emphasis is on *evaluating* prospects: screening out those who are not likely buyers and focusing attention on those who are.

Approaching Customers

Typically, a prospect who requests more information will receive a telephone call from a sales support person. Printed information—brochures, catalogs, and the like—may also be mailed out. At this point, the sales representative often steps in and requests an interview with the prospect, either by mail or by telephone. This is called the **initial approach.** During this approach, the representative seeks to heighten interest in the product by mentioning a feature or service likely to attract that particular prospect. It is essential—and far more than a courtesy—that the

A salesperson's presentation is based on study of the customer's needs and knowledge of the company's products. The sales presentation is much like an actor going on stage—it is done with careful preparation, and often even rehearsal. (Copyright © 1986 Jon Feingersh/Stock, Boston.)

salesperson establish an appointment time which is convenient for the potential buyer.

Preparing for Customers

While the prospect is being approached, the sales representative seeks all available information about that buyer. This may include checks on the prospect's financial history and stability. Certainly the representative will attempt to learn as much as possible about the prospect's needs and problems. If a competitor now has the account, the representative assesses the likelihood of winning the account—and what may be needed to do so. Complete, accurate information is difficult to obtain at this point, but sales professionals know that the more information they have at their disposal, the better their chances for identifying the buyer's needs and, in turn, for securing the account.

Presenting Products

During the preparation stage, the sales representative must begin to tailor a presentation for the first meeting with a prospect. A **sales presentation** usually is a face-to-face discussion of the product between the salesperson and the prospect (or buying group). When armed with background information, a sales professional can develop a good idea of what a prospect's needs are and of what materials may be needed to inform and persuade the prospect.

Displays, printed materials, audiovisual cassettes, and other presentation aids may be used, but the key to an effective sales presentation is personal communication between seller and buyer. The intangibles of communication—facial expressions, vocal inflections, body language—come into play as the salesperson attempts to identify the keys to persuading a particular buyer. That, of course, is what makes selling personal. Such feedback gives personal selling an advantage over advertising as a promotional tool.

The best salespeople are skilled listeners. They probe prospects, seeking out their real problems and needs, and then tailor their sales presentations to emphasize the benefits of the product that best address each customer's concerns.[7] In focusing on a certain product benefit—perhaps cost, durability, or style—the salesperson is not ignoring or hiding what might be considered a weakness of the product. Instead, the aim of the sales presentation is to draw the prospect's attention to valuable benefits and features of a product that solve problems or satisfy needs.

In a real sense, a sales presentation is a consultation. By identifying the pros-

---

BOX 20-2   **COMPETITION IN MARKETING:**
Avoiding Business Defamation

When comparing their company's products with those of competitors during sales presentations, representatives do not enjoy complete freedom of speech. There can be serious legal consequences (including huge awards for damages) if a firm or its salesperson is found to have slandered or libeled another company's business reputation, dishonestly disparaged a competitor's products, or engaged in unfair and deceptive sales practices.

There are four broad types of business defamation: business slander, business libel, product disparagement, and unfair competition:

1. **Business slander** is making an unfair or untrue oral statement about a competitor.
2. **Business libel** is making an unfair or untrue written statement about a competitor (for example, in your promotional literature).
3. **Product disparagement** is making false or deceptive comparisons or distorted claims concerning a competitor's product, services, or property.
4. **Unfair competition** is falsely advertising a product, misrepresenting its qualities or characteristics, or engaging in related deceptive trade practices.

In addition to these categories, salespeople can run into trouble if they make statements during or after sales presentations that personally defame a competitor. Examples include *untrue* statements that a com-

petitor engages in illegal or unfair business practices; that it is financially unstable or going bankrupt; or that one of its officers is incompetent, unreliable, or dishonest.

How can a company protect itself against lawsuits or actions by the Federal Trade Commission that may result if a sales representative or a piece of promotional literature is implicated in any form of defamatory advertising? Attorney Steven Mitchell Sack, who conducts seminars for the American Management Association on "Selling within the Law," offers four recommendations for companies wishing to avoid such costly problems:

1. Review your correspondence and promotional material before distribution. This will reduce the chance that defamatory material is inadvertently distributed by your sales force. . . .

2. Instruct the sales staff to avoid repeating unconfirmed gossip, particularly about the financial condition of a competitor.

3. Tell salespeople to avoid statements that may be interpreted as impairing the reputation of a business or individual.

4. Ensure that the staff avoids making unfair or inaccurate comparisons about a competitor's product.

Source: Steven Mitchell Sack, "Watch the Words," *Sales and Marketing Management,* July 1, 1985, pp. 56, 58.

---

pect's needs, the sales representative may find that the product does not solve the problems at hand. Even so, successful sales professionals try to help prospects find solutions. They build good relationships with accounts based on helpfulness and trust—with the hope of eventual (if not immediate) sales.

In a sales presentation, interpersonal and managerial skills are required—on the spot. The sales representative must choose the right questions to ask and must evaluate the prospect's responses, sometimes shifting direction to move toward a positive decision. Throughout the presentation, the sales representative must be ready to overcome any objections the prospect may raise.

Handling Objections

"Your price is simply higher than your competitor's." "I'm sorry, but I need faster servicing than your company can provide." "Your multipack is nice, but my customers prefer large, single portions."

Such responses are common in personal selling; experienced salespeople expect and even anticipate them. More important, they acknowledge objections and try to turn them around by pointing to other product benefits that the prospect *does* want (such as quality, dependable delivery, or consumer appeal). An objection gives the sales representative an opportunity to provide more information. A prospect who says, "I really don't like the casing color," may be trying to learn whether alternatives are available. In fact, by allowing the exchange of more information, many objections provide new opportunities to persuade the prospect to move toward closing.

Closing

When sales representatives ask prospects to make positive exchange decisions, the sales representatives are closing. Trial closings may be employed first: "How many cases should I ship?" "Will delivery by May 1 be soon enough?" "Will you want to take advantage of the thousand-unit discount?" Trial closings may ease the prospect into making a positive decision; they may also uncover hidden objections that the representative must address.

Because successful closings challenge the salesperson to be creative and persuasive, they must be seen as victories. Yet negative decisions by prospects are but small defeats—and are only temporary. The sales professional will be back again with more ideas and solutions.

Following Up

If the sales call and presentation resulted in a successful closing, the representative moves to the final selling step, **follow-up,** by ensuring after the sale that the order is received on time and as specified. Follow-up is an opportunity to thank the customer for the order, to gain feedback about the product and its level of satisfaction, and to suggest other products or services that may fit the buyer's needs. Even if a trial closing was unsuccessful, sales professionals may still perform a follow-up to thank prospects for their time and interest and, if it feels comfortable, to mention other products. In this case, follow-up sets the stage for a later sales call, thereby reinforcing the representative's image as a consultant who offers service, help, and solutions to problems.

Because personal selling is a human interaction, it requires an immediate, person-oriented kind of management. Sales professionals *manage* their sales calls—not manipulatively, but in ways that lead to effective and efficient use of time for buyer as well as seller.

THE TERRITORY MANAGEMENT PROCESS

Louis Manara is a professional sales representative—so successful that he has won American Cyanamid's highest sales award, the Golden Oval, three times in his years with the chemical company. Manara achieved his remarkable record during a decade of change for the U.S. sales representative. Gordon Sterling, the division president for American Cyanamid, pinpointed the basic changes: "Ten years ago, it was sales, sales, sales. . . . Now we tell our salespeople: 'Don't just sell—we need information. What do our customers need? What is the competition doing? What sort of financial package do we need to win the order?' "[8]

Probing for market intelligence is not Louis Manara's only new duty; he is also expected to mediate disputes between slow-paying customers and Cyanamid's credit department, to handle customers' complaints, and to keep abreast of changing government regulations and worldwide chemical markets. Life has clearly changed for this salesperson. As Manara recalls: "Ten years ago we had backup people to handle all this. But most of them have been let go. We have to be far better informed than we were then."[9]

Manara is just one of many contemporary sales representatives who manage their territories. They have to be managers; pressures of time and money demand that they be analytical and organized and ensure that their sales calls are as productive as possible. As one researcher has suggested, salespeople need to work smarter rather than harder.[10] In their work as **territory managers,** they must analyze, plan, implement, and control their own sales activities. Figure 20-1 shows a model of territory management and what each managerial task encompasses. The analysis phase of the figure focuses on both accounts and work load.

☐ Account Analysis

An **account** is a buying organization to which one is already selling (a customer) or to which one would like to sell (a prospect). **Account analysis,** therefore, is the evaluation of all accounts in a territory. Such analysis identifies customers and prospects, estimates account potentials, and classifies accounts. Unless the market is opening a completely new territory, lists of current customers and even of prospects should be available to the territory manager, along with the sales histories of current accounts. Territory managers continually update lists of prospects and systematically explore opportunities to turn prospects into customers.

As skilled representatives are well aware, the potential in an account is not, in most cases, what existing sales *are.* Rather, **account potential** is the total amount of goods and services purchased by the buyer that *could* be purchased from the seller. In other words, if Coca-Cola purchases one-half of the artificial sweetener for its diet sodas from Searle Laboratories and one-half from another supplier, then Searle is realizing 50 percent of its Coca-Cola account potential.

The most difficult and uncertain step in estimating a customer's potential is projecting the probability of increasing sales and account share. An imperfect but nonetheless useful method bases projections on a territory's history. Thus, if the territory has increased sales and share by an average of 3 percent per year over the last 5 years, then the territory manager might project a 3 percent increase in sales and share for the coming year.

Estimating customer and prospect account potentials is not an idle exercise in crunching numbers nor does it establish sales goals that might be guessed. Instead, careful analysis and accurate estimates of account potentials become the basis for classifying accounts, classifying which is vital to later work load analysis. Selling

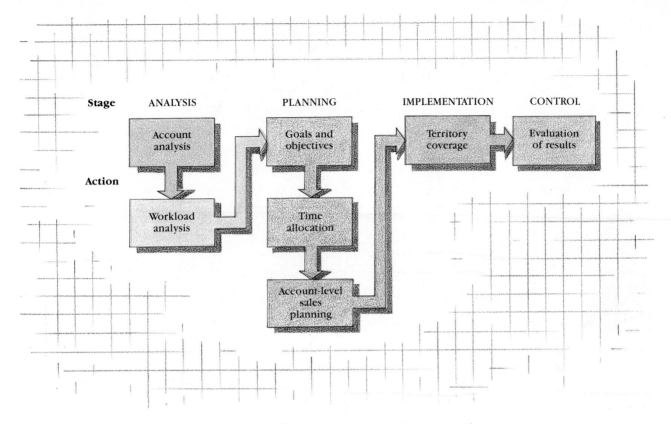

Figure 20-1 *A model of territory management*. Professional salespeople carry out the marketing management process of analysis, planning, implementation, and control as they manage their territories.

lore holds that one accurate predictor of account activity is the **80/20 principle.** This "law" states that 80 percent of business in a territory comes from 20 percent of accounts and, conversely, that only 20 percent of business comes from the other 80 percent of accounts. Concentrating on the accounts that produce 80 percent of business obviously makes good sense.

For most territory managers, estimates of account potentials are essential in classifying their most important accounts. Konica USA used such a classification system in helping the company to enter the U.S. market for copying machines.[11] In one way or another, most organizations categorize the 20 percent of accounts that bring in 80 percent of business as *A* accounts. *B* accounts are of moderate size, and *C* accounts are small buyers whose business is marginal. Even this simple model allows territory managers to identify major accounts for special attention. Along with estimates of account potential, this classification scheme can be used to pinpoint *B* accounts that may be moved into the *A* group. The remaining *C* accounts may be handled by telephone or mail or may be delegated to sales support personnel at a regional or district office.

☐ *Work Load Analysis*

The territory management process moves from account analysis to work load analysis, which determines how the allotted territory can be covered effectively within the time available during the workweek and work year. **Work load analysis** estab-

Salespeople often must spend the majority of their time calling on important customers. The cost of calling on small customers (those who are not among the 20 percent who provide 80 percent of sales) has made regular sales calls impossible. Telemarketing is a system in which persons located at central headquarters communicate with such small customers by telephone. (Copyright © Bob Daemmrich.)

lishes standards for the number of sales calls required and the time needed to make those calls. To better understand this process, let us return to the hypothetical company, Delancey Inc., that we introduced at the beginning of the chapter.

After a few weeks of calling on accounts for Delancey in her New Orleans territory, Kimberly Ann Hall met with Carlos Ruiz, her district manager, to do an account analysis of her territory. This analysis led Hall to classify 20 customers as *A* accounts, 30 as *B* accounts, and 50 as *C* accounts. Together, Hall and Ruiz decided that the optimal number of calls on *A* accounts would be one per month, allowing an average of 2 hours per call. The *B* accounts were allotted one call every 2 months, with an average length of 1½ hours. Hall and Ruiz agreed that the marginal *C* accounts could be handled with only two calls per year, allowing but a half-hour for each visit. The arithmetic looks like this:

$$
\begin{array}{llll}
20\ A\ \text{accounts} & \times\ 12\ \text{calls at 2 hours each} & = & 480\ \text{hours/year} \\
30\ B\ \text{accounts} & \times\ \ \ 6\ \text{calls at 1½ hours each} & = & 270\ \text{hours/year} \\
50\ C\ \text{accounts} & \times\ \ \ 2\ \text{calls at ½ hour each} & = & \underline{\ 50\ \text{hours/year}\ } \\
& & & 800\ \text{hours/year}
\end{array}
$$

At first glance, 800 hours per year for sales calls does not sound like much. It represents only 16 hours per week for 50 weeks. However, marketers are well aware that selling consumes only part of a sales representative's time. Travel between calls, waiting for appointments, servicing accounts, handling paperwork and reports, and other nonselling activities significantly erode the time available for face-to-face sales calls. McGraw-Hill's Laboratory for Advertising Performance regularly monitors how salespeople allocate their time; the latest figures are presented in Exhibit 20-1.

Almost all estimates report that salespeople spend about 25 to 40 percent of their time actually selling products or services.[12] If Kimberly Ann Hall works 50

EXHIBIT 20-1	Allocation of Salesperson's Time

Taken together, face-to-face selling and selling by telephone still constitute less than half (42 percent) of a salesperson's time.

Task	Percent of Time
Face-to-face selling	25
Selling by telephone	17
Traveling, waiting	25
Reports, paperwork, meetings	22
Servicing accounts	8
Other tasks	3

Source: McGraw-Hill Laboratory for Advertising Performance, *How Salespeople Spend Their Time,* LAP #7023-2 (New York, 1986).

weeks per year and 40 hours each week, she has 2000 work hours available per year. Using the 25 to 30 percent figure, she will have between 500 and 600 hours available for sales calls—considerably less than the 800 hours that her work load calls for.

Almost invariably, representatives have more accounts than can be reached as ideally planned. Here managerial judgment comes into play: Territory coverage calls not for the ideal but for the most effective and efficient scheduling possible. To achieve this goal, certain adjustments are inevitable. In the example, the discrepancy between Hall's call standards (800 hours) and the likely hours available (perhaps 550 hours) is much too great. Kimberly Ann Hall and Carlos Ruiz will have to devise some compromise that allows her not only to cover current accounts but also to search out and land new accounts.

■ THE TERRITORY SALES PLAN ■

After analyzing accounts and work load, the territory manager's next important responsibility is planning (refer back to Figure 20-1). Such planning sets out objectives and specific actions to realize the most effective territory coverage. The **territory sales plan** specifies which activities the territory manager will perform to achieve sales and other objectives. Obviously, the first planning step is to determine which objectives are desirable and feasible.

The territory sales plan is where the buck stops. Corporate strategy has been transformed into marketing strategy, into promotion strategy, and into sales strategy. It arrives, finally, for actual implementation at the territory level. The aim of all this strategy, after all, is to sell something. As one experienced sales representative told a group of top-level executives: "You people owe your jobs to me. When I make a sale, I give meaning to your existence."

☐ *Establishing Territory Objectives*

As we pointed out in Chapter 19, setting objectives has increasingly come to involve negotiation between sales representatives and management. Typically, there are multiple objectives: Objectives are set for sales (units or dollars), for market share, for new accounts, and for other concerns. All these aspects of objective setting are applicable at the territory level.

| ACCOUNT | PRODUCT | | | | TOTAL |
	A	B	C	D	
1	$100,000	$ 0	$ 50,000	$ 25,000	$ 175,000
2	0	25,000	50,000	100,000	175,000
3	25,000	50,000	50,000	0	125,000
4	75,000	0	0	125,000	200,000
5	25,000	75,000	100,000	0	200,000
Other	75,000	50,000	100,000	75,000	300,000
Total	$300,000	$200,000	$350,000	$325,000	$1,175,000 **Grand total**

Figure 20-2 *The account/product matrix.* The account/product matrix allows territory managers to combine the account potential, determined in the account analysis process, and product line projections. In this example, sales of four product lines for five major accounts (and other accounts) are projected in dollars. Product and account totals are the same—$1,175,000.

No matter what the difference in companies' priorities, almost any firm is likely to consider sales results an important objective. In setting such objectives, companies use the account-product matrix shown in Figure 20-2. This matrix is similar in concept to the product-market matrix discussed in Chapter 8 (see page 227). The account-product matrix allows territory managers to combine two measurable factors in selling: the account potential determined in the account analysis process and product line projections. The projected total for all product lines should be the total for all accounts—which is the objective (or quota) for the sales territory.

☐ *Allocating Time*

As we have seen, a sales representative's most valuable resource is time. Because limited hours are available for face-to-face persuasive selling and for solving customers' problems, time wasted or spent on an unproductive account can have devastating effects on sales goals. Consequently, a critical factor in successful territory management is deciding just how, when, and where to allocate selling time.

RETURN ON TIME INVESTED   In Chapter 16, we explained why return on investment (ROI) is an important measure of the success or failure of a business organization. Just as the president of a company is evaluated on the firm's measure of profit compared with an investment base or the use of resources, a territory manager may be evaluated on the return on time invested.

A few simple calculations can tell a territory manager how effectively selling

Time is the territory manager's most valuable resource. Careful creative time management assures the manager of the greatest return on time invested in the territory. (Copyright © Jeff Smith.)

time was spent on each account. The first step is to total all costs the organization incurs simply by having the representative in the field for a year: salary, commission, travel and entertainment expenses, fringe benefits, and miscellaneous expenses. Assume, for instance, that the yearly cost to Delancey Inc. for each field representative is $100,000. If a salesperson spends 50 weeks a year on company business and works 40 hours a week, then 2000 hours divided into $100,000 yields a cost of $50 per hour for that representative. In other words, each salesperson's time is worth $50 per hour regardless of the activity involved—whether selling, waiting, traveling, preparing reports, entertaining, or even being trained.

The next step in determining return on time invested is figuring the cost per call hour. Returning to our earlier example, Kimberly Ann Hall spends between 25 to 30 percent of her time actually selling, or between 500 and 600 hours. Let's assume 550 hours for our calculations here. By dividing 550 hours into the yearly $100,000 cost of a field representative to Delancey, we get a cost per call hour of $181.82—an expensive 60 minutes.

Return on time invested (ROTI) is obtained by dividing the gross margin of an individual account by the cost of time invested (recall that gross margin is sales minus cost of goods or services sold):

$$\text{ROTI} = \frac{\text{gross margin}}{\text{cost of time invested}}$$

If Kimberly Ann Hall sells $60,000 worth of carbon fiber to Velco Industries (an *A* account for Delancy Inc.) and the cost of producing that carbon fiber is $40,000, the gross margin figure for the Velco account is $20,000. Since Velco is an *A* account, Hall plans to spend 24 hours calling on that account (12 calls per year at 2 hours per call). Thus, the ROTI for the Velco business is 4.6:

$$\text{Velco ROTI} = \frac{\text{gross margin}}{\text{cost of time invested}}$$

$$= \frac{\$20,000}{\$181.82 \times 24 \text{ hours} = \$4363.68}$$

$$= 4.6$$

In and of itself, the 4.6 figure is meaningless. Is that a good return on time invested or a poor one? Only by comparing the ROTI on other accounts in this territory is the computation useful in setting priorities. For example, another *A* account that Kimberly Ann Hall serves is Westco Inc. Her sales goal for the year is $96,000 worth of plastic film packaging. The gross margin for that projected sale is $48,000. Thus, the ROTI for the Westco account is 11.0:

$$\text{Westco ROTI} = \frac{\text{gross margin}}{\text{cost of time invested}}$$

$$= \frac{\$48,000}{\$181.82 \times 24 \text{ hours} = \$4363.68}$$

$$= 11.0$$

When compared with the 4.6 ROTI figure for the Velco account, this 11.0 figure for Westco tells Kimberly Ann Hall and her manager, Carlos Ruiz, that it may be fruitful to adjust her time allocation. Hours spent on accounts with higher ROTIs obviously bring greater returns. Of course, other factors—especially account potential—are also important in setting priorities. ROTI is not the sole answer in setting time priorities; it is but one tool that territory managers use in allocating total time for sales calls.

SALES RESPONSE FUNCTION   Another useful tool for allocating time is the **sales response function**—a curve that shows the relationship between the number of calls made on an account and the sales to an account. Figure 20-3 illustrates a typical sales response function. Such response functions can be found empirically, though much of the value lies in understanding the concepts surrounding them.

Note the following key points about the curve. There is some level of sales greater than 0 that the account will buy even if no calls are made on it, here shown as X dollars for purposes of illustration. Even if no one from IBM calls on a certain company, they may nevertheless order one or more microcomputers. This concept is especially valid in consumer marketing. Although a Procter & Gamble representative may decide not to call on a particular grocery store in his or her territory, the store will likely buy some Tide detergent because advertising has made some of the store's customers aware of and anxious to buy Tide.

The second key point is that of the **threshold effect**, illustrated by the shape of the curve at point A. Note that even as a very few calls in a period of time (say a year) are made on the account, sales do not rise above the original X dollars. In other words, when making so few calls, the salesperson does not really gain the account's attention. However, once this threshold number of calls is reached, sales begin rising dramatically with an increased number of calls.

Finally, note that the shape of the curve is such that sales begin to rise at a

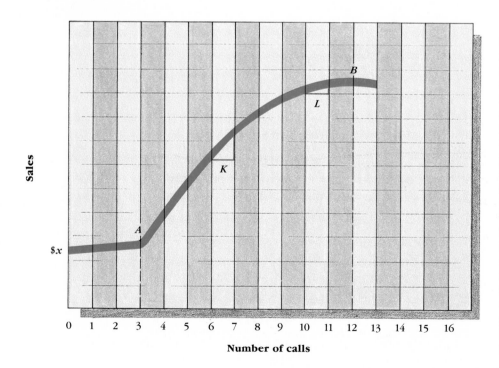

Figure 20-3   *Sales response function*. The blue curve shows how sales typically relate to the number of calls made on an account. After reaching a threshold level at point *A*, sales increase rapidly at first, then continue to rise at a decreasing rate until some saturation level of calls is reached at point *B*. The return on invested time is improved if calls are reallocated among customers shown in red, taking time away from customers higher on the curve (customer L) and giving that time to customers low on the curve (customer K).

Implementing and Controlling Marketing Plans

decreasing rate for much of the time until finally, at some level of calls (illustrated here at point *B*), no additional sales result from increasing the number of calls. (One can even imagine sales going down after point *B* if the customer feels the salesperson is making too many calls and is becoming a pest.)

Figure 20-3 is a single sales response function, which means it is for a single account. In a territory with 20 accounts, there would be 20 different sales response functions. They would not be identical, but would be similar in shape. The way the concept is used is to imagine the call frequency on two accounts, represented by *K* and *L* shown here in red. If the salesperson has time for 16 calls—and is now making 11 on account *L* and 5 on account *K*—he or she can improve the results by reallocating time, making fewer calls on *L* and more on *K*. Note that the loss of sales when moving from 11 to 10 calls on *L* is much less than the sales increase when moving from 5 to 6 calls on *K*. This type of reallocation of the representative's time can take place until the optimum time allocation is reached.

OPTIMAL CALL PLAN An **optimal call plan** is one in which no further reallocation of time can improve the return. But how is an optimal plan established? Couldn't the analyses of ROTIs and sales response functions indicate different time allocations for accounts in a territory? Absolutely. But here modern technology enters the picture to assist territory managers. Computer models have been developed that assemble all the data needed for territory analysis and calculate mathematically which call plan should yield the best time allocation for each account.[13]

Such software models aid the territory manager who wants to manage systematically and efficiently and to base decisions on solid data whenever possible. The use of these models is merely one aspect of the growing importance of sales-oriented software. For example, the SAS 4 (Sales Analysis System), or SALES MANAGER, developed by the California firm, Precision Logic, helps the representative to maintain files on accounts, develop plans for selling to them, evaluate sales plans against objectives, and assess the results of such plans. The same firm's SAS 5, or SALES SUMMARY, allows district sales managers to analyze individual sales plans in their districts and measure their results against company goals.[14] A 1986 report by the Conference Board, *Computers and the Sales Effort,* observes: "The emphasis has shifted from using the computer to do a variety of jobs, one of which *might* benefit the sales organization, to that of using the computer to reinforce and optimize the sales process itself."[15]

Of course, computer models cannot replace the creativity, judgment, and flexibility demanded of professional sales representatives; but they do provide an orderly and scientific basis for territory planning. For professional sales representatives, the days of hitting the road haphazardly and randomly "scouting for smokestacks" are over.

☐ *Account Planning*

The territory management concept leads to account-level sales planning. **Account planning** is a detailed analysis of the buying organization in which the marketer prepares a set of specific actions to achieve account objectives. Different accounts often require different strategies. Even so, territory managers probably use detailed account planning of the sort that follows only on the largest and most productive accounts: the 20 percent of accounts that deliver 80 percent of the business.

CUSTOMER PROFILE The first step in account planning is the **customer profile,** which is a written record of an account. It includes information such as type

EXHIBIT 20-2   **Customer Profile of a Small Manufacturer**

This is a simplified version of a customer profile form for a manufacturer of "widgets." The information on these forms can help the territory manager and the sales manager develop action plans for individual accounts. The hand-drawn form shown here is rapidly giving way to computer-based versions.

Name: *White Machine Works*

Address: *707 University Avenue*

Type of Business: *Narrow line of high-precision instruments*

Buying Influences (names and titles of people to be called on):

Name	Title
Peter White (wife, Mary)	President
Jane Smith (son, Bob) *No smoking*	Chief Engineer
Bill McGee (Notre Dame grad.)	Purchasing Agent

Product Analysis:

Product	Market Sold To	Approximate Sales
Can extruder	Packaging	$2,000,000
Cutting blades	Bindery mach.	1,500,000
Tube extenders	AV manufacturers	1,000,000
Misc. (50)	Many small markets	1,250,000

Total Sales: *$5,750,000*

Buying Policies and Practices:

(1) *Prime contact with purchasing agent*

(2) *Open contact on new-product development*

(3) *Second source on all purchases over $500,000*

Environmental Influences (economic, legal, social, technical, political):

Potential Pennsylvania "bottle" law would damage can extruder business. Growth in magazine business should help bindery sales. Demographics already hurting audiovisual sales to public schools and universities.

Purchasing Criteria:

	Important	Neutral	Unimportant
Price			X
Delivery	X		
Product Availability	X		
Technical Service		X	
Product Service			X
Product Quality & Performance		X	

Problems/Opportunities: *Customer views all widgets alike, considers them "commodities"; price and quality differences don't exist. Potential problem.*

Competitive Analysis (list competitors selling to this account, approximate sales, reasons customer buys from them):

Competitor's Name	Competitor's Sales	Competitor's	Advantages	Disadvantages
Acme Widget Division	$250,000	Price		
		Delivery		X
		Product Availability		
		Technical Service		
		Product Service		
		Product Quality and Performance		

Competitor's Name	Competitor's Sales	Competitor's	Advantages	Disadvantages
Sam's Widget Company	0	Price	X	
		Delivery		X
		Product Availability	X	X
		Technical Service		X
		Product Service		X
		Product Quality and Performance		X

Other Competitive Advantages and Disadvantages: *Customer happy with Acme; Sam's trying to displace us or Acme on price basis, but Jane Smith doesn't trust them.*

of business, buying influences, the product mix, buying policies and practices, environmental influences, purchase criteria, and competitor analysis. Exhibit 20-2 presents such a profile. The layout of the form is not important, but the information conveyed is. The profile varies, of course, from industry to industry. The characteristics listed in Exhibit 20-2 are fairly typical of a small industrial manufacturer; the profile of a consumer goods company would emphasize different characteristics.

Maintaining and consistently updating a customer profile is important for two reasons. First, the territory manager uses this document in day-to-day planning and work and in consultations with the district sales manager. Second, the customer profile provides a record of the account that is invaluable if the territory manager leaves or is replaced. The new manager will depend heavily on customer profiles to learn about the new territory. No doubt, such profiles will increasingly be maintained using personal computer programs or by portable terminals that allow managers access to the company's central data banks.[16]

To illustrate the value of a customer profile, let's look briefly at the information in Exhibit 20-2.

Type of Business   White Machine Works makes a narrow line of high-precision instruments: can extruders, cutting blades, and tube extenders. As in other sections of the profile, information listed here should be precise. Whenever the account enters new areas or drops product lines, the customer profile must be updated.

Buying Influences   The profile lists individuals who make or influence buying decisions. Recall from Chapter 4 that an organization's buying center may include buyers, influencers, decision makers, users, and a gatekeeper. At White Machine Works, Bill McGee, the purchasing agent, is the prime contact; but President Peter White and Chief Engineer Jane Smith often influence McGee's decisions. Even personal notes about such people may prove to be valuable. Jane Smith, for example, prefers that you not smoke in her office and likes to talk about her son Bob. The profile includes the name of the president's wife, along with the information that McGee is a graduate of Notre Dame.

Product Analysis   It is vital to know the customer's products, services, and markets. If White Machine builds a new product or enters a new market, an opportunity for additional sales may well appear. Such information helps the territory manager to be a creative consultant and a problem solver for the customer. If the salesperson can suggest new business opportunities or ways to cut expenses, the customer will usually be impressed and will be favorably disposed toward the seller.

Buying Policies and Practices   White Machine requires a second source on all purchases over $500,000. Consequently, no one supplier can have all the business on White's large purchases. Note, too, that when a new product is being developed, White encourages calls on personnel other than the purchasing agent, including engineers, production supervisors, and top-level managers.

Environmental Influences   Territory managers must monitor any environmental influences that may affect accounts. In this case, a Pennsylvania law under consideration would require all beverage bottles to be recycled. If enacted, this law would damage White's can-extruding operations. Declining sales of audiovisual equipment to schools and colleges because of smaller enrollments are already hurting White's sales of tube extenders to manufacturers of such equipment. On a more positive note, increased magazine sales should boost White's paper-cutting-blade business.

Knowing how the environment may affect an account enables the territory manager to estimate sales. Environmental influences present opportunities and problems, both of which may change rapidly. As a result, this section of the customer profile often needs extensive updating. In a way, the profile is a tool of environmental monitoring, as described in Chapter 2. The territory manager monitors influences on the account just as the organization monitors the environment on a broader level. This process requires a two-way flow of information. Reports from several territory managers can be the basis for a regional or national picture of environmental trends; the resulting analysis can then be relayed to the field staff, thereby alerting them to influences on their individual accounts.

Purchasing Criteria   What are the customer's criteria for making decisions? How important is each? Criteria other than those listed in Exhibit 20-2 can be used;

EXHIBIT 20-3	An Account Action Plan

A professional sales representative carefully plans his or her course of action. A plan such as this one is the result of hard thinking and analysis, and is more likely to lead to success than making sales calls without a plan.

Territory manager: Kimberly Ann Hall

Account: Westco Industries "A" account #7

Account objectives for year:

1. Increase sales of carbon fiber to $165,000 (12.5%)
2. Sell 500 cases of Sure Bind epoxy sealer ($22,000 in new account revenue)
3. Get account to improve payment from 60 to 30 days

Action plan:

1. 15 calls - twice a month in Feb., April, June
2. Ask our technical specialist to join me in call on chief engineer to achieve Sure Bind sales; aim for February
3. Ask district manager to join me in call on Westco's president to discuss payment schedule
4. Get specifications of new formula for carbon fiber to purchasing agent by March 1
5. Close sale of Sure Bind by April 1

the most important consideration for analysis is how much each criterion influences purchase decisions. White Machine certainly wants its supplies when it wants them—delivery and availability are its most important purchasing criteria, whereas price appears to be of little importance. When territory managers know a customer's purchase criteria, they can structure sales messages with these considerations (benefits) in mind.

Competitive Analysis   Just as the company's top-level marketing group keeps tabs on competitors in general, territory managers should perform continuing competitive analyses of individual accounts. As in Exhibit 20-2, each competitor's advantages and disadvantages should be noted. Obviously, such competitive analysis helps the territory manager in planning sales calls, but it is also a vital aid whenever a new representative takes over the account. The combined analyses of territory managers keep the district sales manager informed about competitive activity throughout the district.

ACCOUNT ACTION PLAN   For major accounts, some companies may require a written **account action plan** specifying which steps the territory manager intends to take (and when) to achieve account objectives. As shown in Exhibit 20-3, these steps include the number and timing of calls, the persons to call on, and the resources needed to reach the account objectives. As territory managers increasingly concentrate their personal visits on large accounts and handle smaller accounts by telephone and mail, detailed action plans will become even more common.[17] Large accounts are too important—and influence overall business too much— to be handled without careful, point-by-point planning.

◼ IMPLEMENTING AND CONTROLLING SALES PLANS ◼

All this analysis and planning of territory management must ultimately lead to action: the implementation and control phases shown in Figure 20-1. Now the territory manager puts the sales and account plans to work. Since valuable hours for personal selling are limited, salespeople must systematically and creatively implement plans.

☐ *Implementation*

Common sense and experience are the basis of the territory manager's routing patterns and scheduling, but objective tools are also available to assist in implementing sales plans.

Attempting to cover a geographically dispersed territory without some plan for allocating time and money makes little sense. Time wasted in travel may be the most persistent problem of sales representatives. Obviously, logic suggests calling on closely situated accounts during a single trip. Computer models can be particularly helpful in determining the most cost-effective patterns for routing a salesperson through a territory.

Following a typical routing plan, sales representatives may decide to call on all *A* accounts each time the representatives are in a particular part of the territory. *B* accounts may be seen every other trip, and *C* accounts less frequently. Although they must maintain flexibility to handle unforeseen problems or opportunities, experienced territory managers plan and follow a basic call schedule. They make appointments to visit important decision makers, thereby cutting down on missed calls and wasted travel time. In such instances, a 30-second telephone call can ensure that a 50-mile trip is worthwhile.

Control

In any managerial process, the controlling phase stems directly from the setting of objectives. Implemented sales plans can be controlled only if careful, measurable objectives were set earlier. Territory and account objectives are thus the standards against which the territory manager's work can be measured and then controlled.

Sales, market share, new business, market research, channel relations—all the territory objectives discussed earlier—are the performance standards against which territory managers measure themselves and are evaluated by their district sales managers. Progress toward sales goals can be measured daily, but most organizations use weekly or monthly reporting systems.[18] When sales or other objectives are being exceeded, territory managers can enjoy the satisfaction of a job well done. When objectives are not being met, territory managers must decide whether the lapse is significant and corrective action is needed.

When performance lags behind objectives, territory managers can take a number of corrective steps. They may call more often on behind-goal accounts and spend less time with accounts that are on target. Besides seeking the advice of their district managers, representatives may call upon technical specialists or other support personnel for help with a difficult account. In some cases, they adjust their sales presentations or take other actions to compete more effectively.

Whatever approach they take, typical professional territory managers are self-starters who not only want the approval of their district managers and peers but also measure themselves rigorously against their own performance standards. As a result, they often take corrective action without waiting to be told to do so. The best territory managers engage in honest and objective self-evaluation.

ON BECOMING A SALES MANAGER

In the field of personal selling, a talented and successful salesperson (in other words, a real-life Kimberly Ann Hall) will often receive a promotion to a sales management position. Yet some representatives choose selling as a lifelong career. The job offers freedom, challenges, and, often, large financial incentives: Some sales representatives earn more than $100,000 a year. Others, having obtained valuable experience in practicing the marketing concept in the field, then move from selling into related business or marketing careers.

Effectively managing others requires special skills and personal traits. The best territory managers do not always make the best sales managers, although the experience of working as a territory manager provides analytical as well as sales training. For those who aspire to higher sales management positions, time spent as a successful territory manager is a must.

SUMMARY

1. Professional sales representatives manage their territories through analysis, planning, implementing, and controlling—the same techniques that top-level executives use to manage companies.
2. Increasingly, sales representatives are becoming directly involved in such activities as coordinating promotion efforts, consulting, making a total offer, assuming a profit orientation, and providing market intelligence.
3. Most professional sales jobs are either in the industrial sector or in consumer goods settings.

4. Sales experts have traditionally divided the selling process into seven steps: (1) prospecting and qualifying; (2) approaching customers; (3) preparing for customers; (4) presenting products; (5) handling objectives; (6) closing; and (7) following up.

5. Effective prospecting is often a process of screening potential clients to identify those who are genuine prospects.

6. The aim of the sales presentation is to draw the prospect's attention to valuable benefits and features of a product that solve problems or satisfy needs.

7. An objection gives the sales representative an opportunity to provide more information.

8. Account analysis is used to identify customers and prospects, to estimate account potentials, and to classify accounts.

9. Selling lore holds that one accurate predictor of account activity is the 80/20 principle.

10. Work load analysis determines how the allotted territory can be covered effectively within the time available during the workweek and work year.

11. Almost all estimates report that salespeople spend about 25 to 30 percent of their time actually selling products or services.

12. The territory sales plan is where corporate, marketing, promotion, and sales strategy arrive for actual implementation.

13. A critical factor in successful territory management is deciding just how, when, and where to allocate selling time.

14. Tools used by managers in allocating time include return on time invested, the sales response function, and an optimal call plan.

15. The first step in account planning is the customer profile.

16. For major accounts, some companies may require a written account action plan, specifying which steps the territory manager intends to take (and when) to achieve account objectives.

17. In implementing sales plans, managers use routing patterns and scheduling as well as common sense and experience.

18. For those who aspire to higher sales management positions, time spent as a successful territory manager is a must.

☐ Key Terms

account	customer profile	prospecting
account action plan	80/20 principle	return on time invested (ROTI)
account analysis	follow-up	sales presentation
account planning	initial approach	sales response function
account potential	optimal call plan	territory managers
account-product matrix	personal selling	territory sales plan
business libel	product disparagement	threshold effect
business slander	professional sales representative	unfair competition
closing	prospect	work load analysis

☐ Chapter Review

1. Cite some actions that sales representatives take that fall into the overall realm of marketing. Why should representatives see themselves as problem solvers?

2. Summarize the traditional steps in the personal-selling process. Would it ever be possible to skip the step of "handling objections"?

3. Give some reasons for performing account and work load analysis. Why is a territory work load plan often subject to adjustment?

4. What are the most commonly set territory objectives? Explain how return on time invested may be calculated.

5. Explain why a beginning sales representative would find carefully maintained customer profiles useful.

6. What goes into implementing and controlling a sales plan?

7. Do you find the job of a professional sales representative attractive? Why or why not?

☐ *References*

1. Alvin J. Williams and John Seminerio, "What Buyers Like from Salesmen," *Industrial Marketing Management*, vol. 14, May 1985, pp. 75–78.
2. *Industrial Marketing*, July 1981, p. 91.
3. *Marketing News*, Jan. 8, 1982, p. 6.
4. Mack Hanan, "Consultative Selling: Get to Know Your Customers' Problems," *Management Review*, Apr. 1986, pp. 25–31.
5. U.S. Bureau of the Census, *Statistical Abstract of the United States, 1982–1983* (Washington, D.C.: U.S. Government Printing Office, 1983), p. 400.
6. Floyd A. Bond, Herbert W. Hildebrand, Edwin L. Miller, and Alfred W. Swinyard, *The Newly Promoted Executive: A Study in Corporate Leadership, 1981–1982* (Ann Arbor, Mich.: University of Michigan, Division of Research, Graduate School of Business Administration, 1982), p. 14.
7. Kaylene C. Williams and Rosann L. Spiro, "Communication Style in the Salesperson-Customer Dyad," *Journal of Marketing Research*, vol. XXII, Nov. 1985, pp. 434–442.
8. Hugh D. Menzies, "The New Life of a Salesman," *Fortune,* Aug. 11, 1980, p. 173.
9. Ibid.
10. Harish Sujan, "Smarter versus Harder: An Exploratory Attributional Analysis of Salespeople's Motivation," *Journal of Marketing Research*, vol. XXIII, Feb. 1986, pp. 41–49.
11. Brian L. Merriman, "Konica Uses Total Account Management to Capture a Large Share of Copier Market," *Marketing News*, May 23, 1986, pp. 14–15.
12. Robert F. Vizza, *Time and Territorial Management* (New York: Amacom, 1979), pp. 3–1 to 3–4.
13. Leonard M. Lodish, "CALLPLAN: An Interactive Sales Call Planning System," *Management Science*, Dec. 1971, pp. 25–40, and Peter D. Bennett et al., *Territory Optimization Planning System: A User's Manual* (Interactive Management Systems, 1982).
14. Thayer C. Taylor, "Is There Life after IBM?" *Sales and Marketing Management*, Nov. 12, 1984, pp. 141–142.
15. Thayer C. Taylor, "Marketers and the PC: Steady as She Goes," *Sales and Marketing Management*, Aug. 1986, p. 54.
16. Lindsay Meredith, "Developing and Using a Customer Profile Data Bank," *Industrial Marketing Management*, vol. 14, Nov. 1985, pp. 255–268.
17. John I. Coppett and Roy Dale Voorhees, "Telemarketing: Supplement to Field Sales," *Industrial Marketing Management*, vol. 14, Aug. 1985, pp. 213–216.
18. Hal Fahner, "Call Reports That Tell It All," *Sales and Marketing Management*, Nov. 12, 1984, pp. 50–52.

CASE 19

DOM PERIGNON

In the 1980s, the name "Dom Perignon" is synonymous with a long tradition of producing the highest-quality champagne. Actually, Dom Perignon was a seventeenth-century monk believed to be the first person to make wine "with constant froth." His wine was named after the French region of Champagne and soon became popular with France's royalty. Somewhat later, the champagne house of Moet & Chandon, founded in 1743, named its premiere product for the pioneering monk.

Americans associate Dom Perignon with an image of quality and affluence, partly because a top-of-the-line bottle costs $65 or more. But the pricing of Dom Perignon is merely one aspect of an overall marketing effort to promote the first-class mystique of the brand. Interestingly, Moet & Chandon and Schieffelin, the brand's U.S. importer, face a difficult challenge in maintaining this image: How do you make a premium product widely known and available without eroding its exclusive appeal?

Schieffelin promotes Dom Perignon in the United States with almost no paid advertising; occasionally, you will see an ad for the brand in an exclusive magazine during June (wedding month) or December holidays. More often, Schieffelin is actually trying to *prevent* Dom Perignon bottles from being used in ads for other products. In 1985, for example, a Schieffelin executive revealed that he had recently turned down $3 million worth of advertising, presumably because he did not want Dom Perignon associated with a less-than-prestigious airline, hotel chain, or automobile line. Schieffelin also institutes legal actions to prohibit advertisers from comparing their products to Dom Perignon without authorization.

How, then, does Dom Perignon receive a promotional boost? The answer apparently lies in a rather ingenious publicity campaign. When a prominent New York society hostess throws a benefit for her favorite charity, Dom Perignon is everywhere. On the fashion-conscious television series *Dynasty,* Dom Perignon is the only champagne served at the Carrington mansion. From such carefully chosen publicity opportunities, Schieffelin is able to send a message across the country: Dom Perignon is *the* champagne of the super-rich, of those with real class. "It's all word of mouth," notes a New York public relations expert, "and it's better than advertising."

Schieffelin is quite secretive about exactly how these publicity opportunities magically appear, but, according to the anonymous New York public relations source, the heart of these arrangements is a delicate and informal give-and-take. Moet & Chandon learns about charity events and—where the event seems to fit the proper image—offers a donation (perhaps $200,000) along with free Dom Perignon for the event. According to the source: "The hostess knows that if she announces she chose the champagne in return for a contribution, it would be the last contribution she'd get."

Both sides benefit from this arrangement. The charity gets both a substantial contribution and an abundance of free, top-quality champagne. Dom Perignon's marketers benefit because the brand name will sometimes be mentioned in a society columnist's account of the party in a newspaper or pretigious magazine. Even an occasional and brief mention of Dom Perignon can have great impact on the target market. "You want the product seen in the right places," suggests the public relations expert.

Dr. Scott Ward, professor of marketing at the Wharton School of the University of Pennsylvania, points out that Dom Perignon's marketing strategy is successful—despite the virtual absence of advertising—only because the product already has "mystique, history, and tradition." Dom Perignon surely has all these precious marketing assets; it also has a team of experts working quietly and carefully to get Dom Perignon just the right amount of publicity in just the right media and vehicles.

Source: Rose DeWolf, "Dom Perignon Markets with a Whisper That Roars," *Adweek,* Oct. 14, 1985, pp. 16–17.

1. Reporters and editors of major media are at least indirectly helping to generate free publicity for products like Dom Perignon champagne. Why do you suppose they participate in arrangements that lead to "free advertising" for a company that is buying very little advertising space?
2. People often refer to a favorable publicity mention as being worth 1000 ads. What is the rationale for this position?

■ CASE 20

TYLENOL

In 1975, McNeil Consumer Products, owned by Johnson & Johnson, began aggressively advertising Tylenol as an alternative pain reliever to aspirin. Within 7 years, this remarkable product had captured 37 percent of the $1.2 billion analgesic market. The Tylenol product line was reportedly contributing an estimated 8 percent of Johnson & Johnson's worldwide sales and 15 to 20 percent of its profits. Tylenol was clearly an astonishing success story.

But all that success was threatened in 1982 by a terrifying tragedy: Seven people in the Chicago area died after taking Tylenol capsules that had been contaminated with cyanide. In the days after the public learned of these deaths, Tylenol was pulled off store shelves, and some experts suggested that the product line might have to be scrapped altogether. Instead, Johnson & Johnson successfully confronted this public relations challenge and managed to save its popular and profitable product.

Johnson & Johnson's corporate credo, written by its late chairman, Robert Wood Johnson, emphasizes the social responsibility of business. It states in part: "Every time business hires, builds, sells or buys it is acting for the people as well as for itself and must be prepared to accept full responsibility." This credo formed the basis for the company's responses to the Tylenol crisis.

In the immediate aftermath of the Tylenol scare, Johnson & Johnson took the following steps:

■ It recalled all Tylenol capsules on the market, at a pretax cost of $100 million.
■ It tested more than 8 million Tylenol capsules to see if there had been other tampering.
■ It fielded more than 2000 calls from the press in the days following the poisonings.
■ It pulled all Tylenol commercials off the air and stopped newspaper and magazine advertising wherever possible.

Perhaps most important in these difficult days was the forthright, "open door" attitude of Johnson & Johnson executives in dealing with the press. For example, the company's public relations department was forced to contradict an earlier (and incorrect) statement by David E. Collins, chair of McNeil Consumer Products, denying that cyanide was used on the premises where Tylenol was made. Although the admission was embarrassing, it underscored Johnson & Johnson's commitment to candor.

The company hoped that the actual facts of the tragedy—while certainly distressing—would demystify the incident. "There was a lot of noise out there, most of it associating Tylenol with death," recalls one McNeil executive. "We wanted to clear up any misunderstanding, to make sure everyone had all the facts we did, that the problem was limited to one area of the country, and only a few bottles of Tylenol capsules were contaminated."

Six weeks after the poisonings, Tylenol was reintroduced in a new triple-sealed container. Johnson & Johnson took steps to win reacceptance for the product by blanketing the nation with newspaper coupons worth $2.50 off the price of Tylenol. In effect, this made the smaller bottles cost-free. Johnson & Johnson's sales force made more than 1 million visits to physicians and other medical personnel to seek their support for Tylenol. In addition, the company began a careful public-service advertising campaign, with a pointedly discreet tone. "We're coming back against a tragedy," admitted McNeil's David E. Collins, "so there's no way we can come riding in on elephants, blowing horns and saying here we are."

Apparently, all these efforts were successful. By the end of 1982, the company's tablets—thought to be in danger simply because, like the capsules, they carried the Tylenol name—were registering a 29.9 percent market share, even higher than the 22.2 percent share before the poisonings. By mid-1983, Tylenol had recaptured about 80 percent of its previous market share and was once again the leading pain reliever in the nation.

"It's been a remarkable recovery," noted one industry analyst. "I definitely think Johnson & Johnson is as strong as before," said another. "If anything, it has solidified the company's corporate strategy and their confidence and ability to deal with adversity."

Source: Nancy Giges, "J&J Begins Its Drive to Keep Tylenol Alive," *Advertising Age,* Oct. 11, 1982, pp. 1, 78; Thomas Moore, "The Fight to Save Tylenol," *Fortune,* Nov. 29, 1982, pp. 44–49; Nancy Giges, "Tylenol Tablets Lead Rebound," *Advertising Age,* Dec. 13, 1982, pp. 1, 55; Gail Collins, "J&J Turned the Tylenol Tragedy into a Triumph," *Elizabeth Daily Journal,* Aug. 15, 1983, pp. 9–10.

1. Negative publicity can have as much impact on a product's market performance as can positive publicity. Could Johnson & Johnson have done anything to prevent this kind of negative publicity?
2. In the weeks just after the tragedy, competitors increased their advertising budgets, some even alluding to their product as "safe." What is your opinion of this type of competitive behavior?
3. Was Johnson & Johnson basically correct in becoming very proactive in trying to convince the public through the media that their brand was still the right one to use?

■ CASE 21

ADVERTISING AGENCY REGISTER

It is vitally important that a business firm have the right advertising agency handling its accounts. With this in mind, an increasing number of companies—among them Miller Brewing, Mattel, Honda, and Hallmark—have relied on consultants to assist them in their agency searches. "It's a business-like way of approaching the situation and minimizing risk," argues Spencer Boise, vice president for corporate affairs at Mattel.

Consultants offer a number of distinctive advantages, especially for smaller companies without huge marketing staffs or relationships with many agencies. A consultant has detailed knowledge of each agency's strengths and weaknesses and can evaluate the specific personnel likely to work on an account. Moreover, consultants establish systematic and objective criteria for choosing among agencies. "The days are gone when you can give your business to your golfing buddy," notes one consultant. "When you're dealing with millions of dollars, it's a serious proposition."

Advertising Agency Register (AAR)—established in Great Britain in 1975 by Lyndy Payne—presents itself as an "information service" rather than a consultant. Its primary business is handling advertising agency switches. More than 70 percent of all British agency switches are conducted through AAR. The firm began its U.S. operations in 1980; according to current estimates, AAR handles between 10 and 20 percent of agency switches in the United States.

AAR functions as a clearinghouse. It charges each advertising agency a yearly fee of $5000 to maintain a file with the agency's video presentations and information on its clients and personnel. Advertisers pay a fee of $1500 to $2500 to review this material and develop a "short list" of agencies under consideration for the account. AAR then sets up meetings with these agencies, who make presentations for the client. It is only at this final stage of the selection process that agencies learn who the client is.

AAR receives high praise from Walter Layton, advertising and sales promotion manager at the KitchenAid division of Hobart, which chose a new agency in 1983. "It was a good way to go," says Layton. "It enabled us to trim down a large number of agencies in a short period of time to a few that met all our requirements. It also helped us to do it without publicizing the search. Once it's public, the phone starts ringing off the hook, and we didn't want that."

Some advertising agencies, however, are less enthusiastic about AAR's methods. "I don't like the whole concept because I don't think someone else can present your agency for you," states the chair of one New York agency that dropped out of AAR after belonging for 2½ years. "The method they use is not in the best interests of the agency business or the client. They call you up and say, 'We've got an airline or a hotel, give us a paragraph on your hotel experience, a summary of your approach and some success story.' It's a *Reader's Digest* approach to selecting an ad agency."

Despite such criticisms, AAR claims it has more than 100 U.S. ad agencies as members, including 48 of the top 50. Although the firm has concentrated on its London and New York operations, in the mid-1980s it opened offices in various locations in Western Europe to better service international advertisers.

Source: "Madison Avenue Matchmakers Help More Clients Pick Agencies," *Ad Forum,* Jan. 1985, pp. 41–43.

1. Changing advertising agencies is a task that arises only once every several years. What are the benefits that a consultant or the AAR can supply to a company seeking a new agency?
2. What do you think are the agencies' real reasons for opposing the trend toward use of consultants?
3. Is it likely that the marriages made between advertisers and their agencies will be better because of the services of a consultant or AAR?

CASE 22

IBM

IBM is the premiere sales organization in the United States. The founder of IBM, Thomas J. Watson, Sr., was a super salesperson and served as the national sales manager for NCR before he left to set up the new company that became IBM. Watson's legacy at IBM, above all, is that the sales representative is valued highly and viewed as crucial to the company's success. Consequently, all sales representatives know that they can call any plant in the IBM system and get instant attention from managers or technical experts. Given Watson's legacy, it is no surprise that all the firm's succeeding chief executive officers have come up through the sales organization.

IBM's sales force is well known as being the best in the computer industry. As one industry researcher notes: "It starts with the caliber of people they hire, high achievers; [IBM] then nurtures them with a constant effort to keep them above their peers." According to an IBM spokesperson, the firm's college recruiters seek out "highly motivated people with a technical background, a 3.5 or better college average, and communications skills. All candidates take the Information Processing Aptitude Test (IPAT) to determine if they have a knack for learning and understanding technical information."

IBM views training as an essential element in the success of its sales force. Basic training—which combines classroom work, hours in sales offices, and on-the-job training working with senior sales representatives in the field—lasts anywhere from 9 to 15 months. A former sales representative for IBM recalls this period as "a pressure-filled existence designed to make the survivors feel they are part of a special elite. . . . By the time you went on quota, you were convinced you were the best of the best, filled with a missionary zeal to bring the world's best products to prospects."

IBM monitors and motivates each sales representative through a personal performance plan drawn up and signed by sales representatives and their branch managers.

The plan lists specific revenue goals and nonrevenue objectives. However, each sales representative is also evaluated on such criteria as territory management, marketing management, customer satisfaction, and leadership among peers.

No one would question the talent and dedication of IBM's sales force. Yet even these strengths are no guarantee of successful selling. "In the '70s we focused on the competitiveness of each individual computer and lost a little sight of the customer's needs," admits one IBM executive. As a result, chair John F. Akers issued a directive: "Get inside the customer's head, focus on his problem, and solve it." At the same time, a new "customer sector" marketing team was established to assist customers in installing computer and software systems—even systems which include products marketed by IBM's competitors.

IBM's shift to a more customer-oriented marketing approach led to a major reorganization in the 1980s. Previously, IBM's Data Processing Division sold large computers, its General Systems Division sold small computers, and its Office Products Division sold office products such as typewriters, dictating machines, and copiers. In the reorganization, these product-oriented divisions were replaced by two customer-oriented divisions which sell the full spectrum of IBM products. The National Marketing Division sells to small, medium, and large customers; the National Accounts Division targets selected large accounts with "complex information needs."

By 1986, IBM had begun to establish separate sales offices along industry lines. It had a New York office for finance and brokerage customers, a Detroit office for General Motors, and a Dearborn, Michigan, office for Ford Motor Company. In many respects, IBM was moving increasingly toward a sensitivity to customers as a more central element in its marketing strategy. One executive of an insurance firm praised this trend, remarking: "There's much more responsiveness and much less trying to ram a product down your throat."

Sources: "Alternative Selling Marks the New IBM," *Sales & Marketing Management,* Jan. 17, 1983, pp. 26–27; "The IBM Salesperson Is King," *Sales & Marketing Management,* Dec. 3, 1984, p. 39; "How IBM Is Fighting Back," *Business Week,*" Nov. 17, 1986, pp. 152–157.

1. IBM says that, in its recruiting, it looks for college graduates with an aptitude for learning technical information. Why do you suppose they want this type of person?
2. What are the key experiences that an IBM salesperson gets before moving into management that lead the company to continually select former sales representatives as its chief executives?
3. When IBM switched its sales force from one based on product lines to one based on customer size, all salespeople had to learn about a wider range of products. Do you see this as a potential problem?

■ ■

21

Copyright © Gabe Palmer 1986/The Stock Market.

CONTROLLING THE MARKETING FUNCTION

SPOTLIGHT ON

☐ Accounting and marketing in the marketing control process

☐ Implementation control and strategic control

☐ Control of marketing programs through sales analysis, cost analysis, and profitability analysis

☐ Requirements and components of the marketing audit

Does "bigger" necessarily mean "better" in the world of contemporary marketing? Top executives of Chalone Inc., a California winery noted for its premium wines, would certainly say not. In fact, Chalone is relying on small production units in its battle to capture the premium end of the wine-making business.

Thus far, its efforts have been successful: Chalone's sales doubled every year in the period 1980 to 1986. Currently, about 60 percent of Chalone wine is sold in restaurants, 15 percent in mail-order sales, and 25 percent in retail stores. Chalone brands are sold by a network of independent distributors in 40 states and 6 foreign countries; most of the company's brands are priced from $10 to $20.

"The strategy I had from the beginning," recalls Philip Woodward, president and chief executive officer of Chalone, "was to grow by staying small, to keep the production facilities separate and limited, and to build a different winery in each of the four premium wine-growing areas of California." Chalone is committed to the view that keeping quality high means keeping its wineries small; no winery is expected to produce more than 50,000 cases per year.

Chalone's limited, decentralized production offers distinct marketing advantages. "There's a lot of image in this thing," notes Woodward. "Once you get up there [in price], you're paying for more than the liquid in the bottle." Consequently, it is to Chalone's advantage to maintain an image as an elite wine producer more concerned with quality than with mass production goals. Moreover, by running four wineries in different parts of California with distinct labels, Chalone offers a varied product line. This is especially important to restaurants, Chalone's largest market. "If Chalone had funneled all its products into one label," says a distributor, "it would not have met with the success it has."

But Chalone's decentralized production system brings with it a severe financial burden. The small winemaker has had to duplicate costly resources; each of Chalone's wineries must maintain its own crushing, pressing, and bottling equipment. Chalone's resources were further strained in building its new Carmenet winery in Sonoma County. The final cost was $3.1 million—almost twice the planned expense. Moreover, sales of Carmenet brands have been disappointing, which contributed to the 12 percent decline in Chalone's 1986 profits.

Chalone's internal production problems come at a poor time—competition is intense in the lucrative premium wine market. (As a result, Chalone had to drop the price of its Carmenet sauvignon blanc from $11 to $9 per bottle.) Although sales of table wines in general have fallen, sales of premium wines have increased at a compounded annual rate of 22 percent since 1979. Small winemakers like Chalone face a serious challenge from the Ernest and Julio Gallo winery, the largest winemaker in the world, which is placing growing emphasis on the higher end of the market. At the same time, major corporations such as Nestlé and United States Tobacco are buying premium wineries. Whether Chalone's decentralized, "smaller is better" strategy will prove viable in the face of such powerful competition remains to be seen. The company will have to evaluate that strategy against the production and marketing results of the strategy.

Source: Joe Rosenbloom, III, "Sour Grapes," *Inc.*, Jan. 1987, pp. 66–67.

As far back as Chapter 1 of this book, we have emphasized the managerial process—the sequential steps of analysis, planning, implementation, and control. First, markets are analyzed, as are environments and buyers' behaviors—usually through marketing research and information systems. Next, planning for both corporate and marketing strategy and actions takes place. These first two steps can be seen as taking place *before* the fact. Once planned, marketing programs are implemented *during* the fact. Finally, the control process occurs *after* the fact. Just as planning looks to the future to decide what should be done (or implemented), control looks back to the past to see if things have gone well or ill.

In the early 1980s, Coleco Industries had two grand objectives: to become a leader in the market for dolls and to gain a significant share of the home computer market. Cabbage Patch Kids, an appealing product with a "must-have" allure, assured Coleco success in its first goal. But Coleco's Adam computer—seemingly a sure-fire, popularly priced, all-in-one package—was a failure. Production of the machines fell behind schedule, and many were defective when they finally reached the market. In 1984, Coleco lost $55 million on the Adam and ceased production of the computer; by contrast, 1984 sales of the cuddly Cabbage Patch dolls topped $500 million.[1] The critical factor in both Coleco's success and its failure was control of the marketing process.

Chapter 23 ends the management process with the fourth and final stage, just as a college class usually ends with an examination to assess the students' learning during the semester. We will first look at the role of control in the marketing process, including just how control ties into the earlier stages. Then we will examine the kinds of control—often exercised by accounting personnel—that target the details of the marketing program. This includes analyses of sales, of costs, and of profitability. The chapter ends by examining a method of controlling strategy known as the marketing audit.

Coleco's president Arnold C. Greenberg sits with two of his main product lines: Cabbage Patch dolls and the Adam computer. The marketing plans for both were grand, but the dolls were a spectacular success, while the computer was a disaster. The control process is designed to tell management whether the plan's objectives were reached—and *why*. (Copyright © John McGrail/*Time Magazine*.)

CONTROL IN MARKETING

No management process can be complete without an evaluation: How well did the individual or organization accomplish the goals and objectives that had been set? **Marketing control** is the process of evaluating achieved results against established standards and of taking corrective action to exploit opportunities or solve problems. For example, Chalone winery initially set an objective of selling its Carmenet white wine at $11 per bottle, but competition then forced the winery to lower the price to $9. The result of that action must be determined and studied. If Chalone set an objective of increasing its profitability by some amount and then experienced a 12 percent *loss* in profitability, the causes must be investigated.

Marketing control is applied to issues as large as the organization's very mission and as detailed as the number of calls territory managers plan to make on their A accounts. The process can be applied frequently or only periodically. Marketing control is carried out by managers with marketing titles as well as by accounting and financial managers.

In fact, control is one of the crucial functions where accounting and marketing come together in the total management of the organization. The entire control function simply cannot be accomplished without the kinds of information that accountants are skilled at providing. Although some organizations attempt to control subjective (or qualitative) objectives, the most common control compares quantitative results to quantitative objectives.

The Control Process

The control process is tightly woven into the processes of planning and implementation. Figure 21-1 shows just how these processes relate. We have stressed throughout the book that all marketing and sales objectives should be as specific—and, if appropriate, as quantitative—as possible. A major objective for a product line, for instance, should not be "to increase market share" but rather "to raise market share of cases shipped from 24.5 percent to 28 percent." Instead of setting an objective to "improve profitability," we might set an objective to "increase profitability from a return on investment of 14.2 percent to a return of 17.5 percent."

Clear and measurable objectives come from the planning process (shown in the upper left box in Figure 21-1). When we have implemented the marketing plans, we will see the results of implementation in the ongoing accounting or marketing information system (MKIS) reports. Actual market share data will tell us if we achieved the 28 percent share objective, if we fell short, or if we surpassed our objective. Accounting data will tell us if our return on investment is less than, equal to, or greater than the 17.5 percent goal.

As we pointed out in the chapters on planning (Chapters 7 through 9), some objectives are difficult—if not impossible—to state quantitatively. In the early 1980s, for example, Procter & Gamble decided that it had a problem in its relations with channel members, many of whom viewed the company as arrogant and high-handed.[2] The company set an objective of improving channel relations—clearly a difficult-to-quantify objective. A similar problem might occur if a marketer set an objective of "increasing consumer satisfaction levels." In such cases, market research surveys of consumers' or distributors' attitudes—both at the beginning and the end of the year, for instance—might create quantitative measures of essentially qualitative objectives.

Whether it is a before-after research measure or a comparison of a quantitative objective against the actual result, the control process involves evaluating results

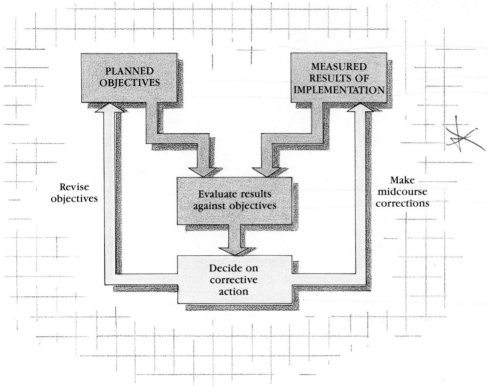

Figure 21-1 *The marketing control process.* The control process uses the output from planning (the objectives) and implementation (the actual results), comparing the planned versus actual results. Based on those results, corrective actions include revision of the objectives or corrections in planned implementation.

against objectives (the center box in Figure 21-1). Although this stage of the process is crucial—it tells us if we have met, exceeded, or fallen short of objectives—this determination is not enough. Perhaps the most creative aspect of control involves establishing *why* those results were achieved and what we should do in response—in other words, what, if any, corrective action should we take (the lower box in Figure 21-1)?

Suppose, for example, that John, the marketing manager for a division of a furniture manufacturer, has established a sales objective of $60 million for the year. The goal for the first quarter was set at $12.5 million, but the results reported by the accounting department show sales of only $10.5 million. John will therefore have to take a hard look at the assumptions made in the planning process and at how the marketing plan has been implemented. He will look for data on total industry sales compared with those forecast by the furniture industry. John will reevaluate the company's plan to add salespeople and probably a dozen other aspects of the marketing plan.

The results of all this effort may lead John and other executives to the conclusion that environmental factors (a downturn in the economy) have depressed the entire furniture industry and that the original objective of $60 million is no longer realistic. If that is the case, they may revise the planned objectives accordingly. However, their study may reveal that the industry as a whole is doing well and that the problem is more specific to their firm. Perhaps the sales department has failed to add salespeople as planned and in fact has failed to replace some who have quit or retired. In this case, a mid-course correction might be in order: The firm may wish to hire a new sales manager who will be more successful at replacing personnel.

The marketing manager on the left has established specific goals for the sale of his fashion merchandise. The buyers for department stores will determine the success of his plans. By following careful control procedures, through reports and in personal contact with buyers, he will be able to assess the success of his plan. (Copyright © Bob Daemmrich.)

Still a third conclusion may be reached: The original marketing plan may be found to be valid. The $2 million shortfall in sales may be simply a technical problem (perhaps the purchases of a large account should have been recorded by March 30 instead of on April 2). Clearly, these are very important parts of the control process; managers must not only measure the results but also decide what to do about them.

☐ *Types of Marketing Control*

Two major types of marketing control are common: The first is the control of day-to-day operations; thus, **implementation control** involves ongoing activities and uses the organization's regular accounting and reporting procedures to analyze the implementation of marketing plans and actions. Primarily, implementation control seeks to answer the question, "Are we doing things right?"

Strategic control involves major strategy directions. This process seeks to answer the question, "Are we doing the right things?" Rather than relying on regular ongoing reports, in general strategic control involves special studies and procedures.[3] In the 1980s, Apple Computer shifted its strategy from a concentration on sales to homes and schools to one of increased sales efforts to large companies. Apple will succeed or fail in its strategy by closely controlling the work of a newly formed national accounts sales team and by measuring the effectiveness of its advertising aimed at these large-potential accounts.

■ *CONTROLLING IMPLEMENTATION* ■

Implementation control is the responsibility of functional-level managers within a marketing organization. A product manager may be responsible for a sales promotion campaign for a toilet soap; an advertising manager will monitor the execution of programs created by an advertising agency. If one objective is to increase the number of sales calls by 5 percent, the sales manager is accountable for ensuring that sales representatives actually make those additional calls. Each marketing manager is assisted by the work of accountants in their organization.

We would need a number of books simply to present a thorough discussion of the processes of implementation control. (If you are planning to become an accountant, you may read some of these books.) Certain elements of implementation control are contained in the ongoing reports prepared by the MKIS operations, but much of it is the work of the accounting department directly. Modern accounting practitioners usually separate their efforts into two parts: financial accounting (the reporting of the financial results for government, stockholders, and so forth) and managerial accounting (the reporting of financial information to aid the decision making of the organization's managers). The latter type is essential to implementation control.

The following sections investigate three major methods of controlling marketing programs: sales analysis, cost analysis, and profitability analysis. Each type of analysis has its own goals up to a point, yet the three methods are cumulative as well. Since sales minus cost equals profits, these factors clearly interrelate. As we discuss each method, their cumulative nature should become clear.

Sales Analysis

In 1986, AT&T's share of the long-distance phone market dropped to about 82 percent, down from over 90 percent 2 years earlier.[4] Merck and Company, the pharmaceutical giant, saw its 1986 sales climb about 15 percent over 1985 sales of $3.55 billion.[5] These results may be good news or bad, but they certainly become more meaningful when analysis compares these results with expectations and establishes in what product lines, sales territories, channels, or markets these results were accomplished. Sales analyses can look at a company's sales alone, generally referred to as "sales analysis," or they can compare a company's sales to competitors' sales, usually called "market share analysis."

Sales analysis compares actual with estimated sales. Sales are analyzed on both an ongoing (weekly, monthly, quarterly) and cumulative (year-end) basis. Overall corporate or business unit sales are evaluated at strategic levels. By contrast, operational and functional managers analyze sales at a micro-level of component factors—for example, by product, by region, or by sales territory.

Sales analysis gives experienced managers much more than a simple measurement (sales were 93,000 units versus a goal of 100,000 units). If sales of one product are up by 30 percent while another product's performance is 12 percent behind goals, managers will study the reasons for the first product's success and the second product's less-than-desirable performance. If sales of the latter product in the Southeast region are found to be 20 percent behind target while other regions are within goals, corrective action will be indicated in the Southeast.

Market share analysis is an evaluation of the firm's performance in comparison to that of its competitors. Such analysis gives executives a broad view of the company's performance. For example, suppose that sales are exactly as forecast: up 3 percent over the previous year. However, if industry sales are up 7 percent, then the organization is actually losing market share and is falling behind its competitors. This comparative picture will serve as another indicator of the need for corrective action.

Market share may be measured in revenue dollars or in units sold, or both. Changes in unit market share indicate volume changes among competitors. Because of price increases and cuts, a company's dollar market share reflects a combination of price and volume changes. These factors must be considered—as must any growth or decline of the market as a whole.

Marketers compile information for sales analysis from their internal records; it flows automatically from the MKIS. However, market share figures are more difficult to obtain since they are based on sales outside the organization. Overall market share may be calculated with relative ease if a trade association reports industry totals. In other cases, an industry's sales (such as that of the housing industry) are tracked by the federal Department of Commerce. Marketers of consumer goods are able to accurately estimate competitive performance through reports from market information firms such as Nielsen, MCRA, SAMI, and others described in Chapter 6.

SALES COMPONENT ANALYSIS   Overall company sales can give only a general notion of marketplace performance, trends, and market share. Both sales analysis and market share analysis are more valuable when data can be broken down into various sales components. Managers are better able to plan and to take corrective action if they can analyze sales by components such as product line, products, region, district, sales territory, customer type or size, method of size, and discount class. Micro-level analysis uncovers opportunities and problems that can be more easily handled than larger components can. Thus, sales of a lagging product can be boosted through a special promotion campaign; action can be taken to boost the performance of an individual representative whose sales are down.

The sales invoice, completed as transactions are made, is the basic source of information—from customer name to order date to salesperson—for all the sales components listed above. Computer programs easily summarize sales of any component or combination of components (for example, large accounts in the southern Louisiana territory) that managers think will be important in marketing control. The importance of modern computer systems in rapid summarizing of sales components cannot be overstated. Today's managers can have sales broken down on a scheduled basis and at a speed impossible only 20 years ago.

Again, we must emphasize the role of the MIS in providing disaggregated (broken down) sales information. Managers with access to the MIS can get regular reports for the time periods considered useful. Marketing managers need to work with information systems planners to ensure that they get the kinds of decision-support reports that they need. One company's managers may find that product line sales are important control units; another organization may wish to analyze sales not only by individual products but also by package size, color, flavor, and design.

Historical analysis requires standard and consistent units of analysis. If at all possible, the units of analysis should match those used by the trade association or in government publications. One way to make outside data meaningful is to use the government-developed Standard Industrial Classification system (see Chapter 5).

DISAGGREGATED SALES ANALYSIS   Sales analysis can be performed with large or small units. As an example, let us look at a quarterly performance analysis of sales of the hypothetical Walden Corporation at the regional level. In Exhibit 21-1, objectives and actual sales in Walden's six regions are compared along with a measure of deviation between the two. The northwest, southwest, and south central regions are nicely ahead of target, and the south central area leads the country at 13.8 percent ahead of target. The southeast region is right on its estimated course, whereas the north central and northeast regions are not meeting their objectives. Although Walden as a whole is running just ahead of objectives,

	EXHIBIT 21-1	Sales Performance, First Quarter 1987		

Region	Objective ($ thousands)	Actual ($ thousands)	Deviation ($ thousands)	Percent Deviation
Northwest	2,100	2,300	200	+ 9.5
Southwest	4,200	4,500	300	+ 7.1
North central	3,700	3,500	(200)	− 5.4
South central	2,900	3,300	400	+13.8
Northeast	6,500	5,900	(600)	− 9.2
Southeast	5,100	5,100	0	0
Totals	24,500	24,600	100	+ 0.4

the national sales manager will probably do further investigation of individual territories in the north central and northeast regions to determine if some corrective action is warranted. An obvious goal would be to get these two lagging regions up to standards by the end of the second quarter.

A similar analysis could be done of individual customers in a sales territory to give the salesperson or the sales manager for the territory more information to correct any problems. This type of disaggregated sales analysis could also have been done by product line or product, discount class, customer size, or any one of a number of ways. Individual organizations will choose for analysis those units that allow the best opportunity for control.

☐ Cost Analysis

Just as sales analysis deals with revenues, cost analysis deals with expenses. **Cost analysis** involves the reallocation of the natural accounts of financial accounting

One major purpose of sales analysis is to diagnose the cause of problems. If the analysis shows that results are on target in the Atlanta region and below target in the New York region, for instance, that will prompt special and more detailed analysis of the results in New York to determine the cause. (Left: Copyright © 1983 Jim Anderson/ Woodfin Camp & Assoc. Right: Copyright © Meri Houtchens-Kitchens/The Picture Cube.)

Implementing and Controlling Marketing Plans

to the functional accounts of managerial accounting so that managers can control marketing costs. This process involves breaking down marketing costs and then assigning them to specific marketing activities or units, such as products, geographic units, channels of distribution, or market segments.

NATURAL ACCOUNTS AND FUNCTIONAL ACCOUNTS **Natural accounts** are the usual financial accounting units found on the official statements of an organization. Our interest here is in the expense accounts, such as rent, salaries, advertising, marketing research, and supplies. Most of these accounts do not show for what purpose—for what product—these expenses were incurred.

The first step in cost analysis typically requires that some of the costs in natural accounts be reclassified into **functional accounts,** which divide expenditures by their purposes. A certain proportion of rent, for example, would be assigned to marketing research. Some costs, such as supplies, must be reclassified among various functions; supplies are obviously needed by advertising, the sales force, marketing research, and order processing, among others.

Exhibit 21-2, an abbreviated income statement, presents an example of natural accounts. These natural accounts are then reclassified into functional accounts in Exhibit 21-3. In a large marketing organization, natural accounts would be much more detailed, and the number of functional accounts would be larger. However, for the sake of simplicity, we have limited the exhibit to four functional accounts: sales force, advertising, marketing research, and order processing. Additional functions commonly analyzed include transportation, storage, sales promotion, and customer credit. Note that in Exhibit 21-3, salaries, rent, and supplies have all been allocated across the four listed functions. Advertising and research expenses, by contrast, have been allotted to natural accounts.

ALLOCATING COSTS Typically, functional costs are allocated to products, to geographic areas, to market segments, and even to specific customers.[6] Exhibit 21-4 continues our example by assigning functional costs in a firm that handles three product lines: typewriters, copiers, and supplies. Sales force costs for this reporting period have been allocated based on the number of calls made on customers. Advertising expenses have been allocated on the number of pages devoted to each product line (70 pages divided into $77,000 in costs). Marketing research costs are split between the typewriter and copier lines. Assignment of order-

EXHIBIT 21-2	Abbreviated Income Statement of Natural Accounts	

Sales		$1,000,000
Cost of goods sold		(600,000)
Gross margin		400,000
Marketing costs		
Salaries	$100,000	
Advertising expenses	50,000	
Marketing research	20,000	
Rent	30,000	
Supplies	10,000	
Total		(210,000)
Net profit (before taxes)		$ 190,000

EXHIBIT 21-3 | **Natural Accounts to Functional Accounts**

		Functional Accounts			
Natural Accounts	Cost	Sales Force	Advertising	Marketing Research	Order Processing
Salaries	$100,000	$50,000	$20,000	$20,000	$10,000
Advertising expenses	50,000		50,000		
Marketing research	20,000			20,000	
Rent	30,000	5,000	5,000	5,000	15,000
Supplies	10,000	500	2,000	1,000	6,500
Total	$210,000	$55,500	$77,000	$46,000	$31,500

processing costs rests on the sales percentage for each product line (40 percent each for typewriters and copiers, 20 percent for supplies). This allocation assigns all costs to each product line by breaking down costs into units ($203.55 per sales call, $1100 per advertising page, $23,000 per research project, $315 for each percent of orders processed).

Allocation of marketing costs usually requires the advice and counsel of the organization's accounting department. Accountants have the specialized training necessary to decide the fairest and most useful method of allocating functional costs.

☐ *Profitability Analysis*

Sales analysis and cost analysis are both very useful in diagnosing how well a company's marketing plan is being implemented. The third type of analysis used for implementation control uses a combination of sales and costs to determine profits.[7] **Profitability analysis** provides information on the profit performance of individual units within an organization to determine appropriate corrective action.

Note that the far right column in Exhibit 21-5 lists the same total company sales and net profit (before taxes) shown in Exhibit 21-2. We still have the same total company financial performance. However, Exhibit 21-5 also shows the profitability of the company's three major product lines. We include this as an illustration; we could just as easily have shown profitability by different channels of distribution, by different market segments, or by any other marketing issue of interest.

EXHIBIT 21-4 | **Allocating Functional Expenses to Products**

Product	Sales Force (Number of Sales Calls in Period)	Advertising (Pages of Advertising)	Marketing Research (Specific Research Projects)	Order Processing (Percentage of Sales Processed in Period)
Typewriters	150	25	1	40
Copiers	80	35	1	40
Supplies	40	10	0	20
Total	270	70	2	100
Functional expenses (divided by number of units equals cost/unit)	$205.55 per call ($55,500/270)	$1100 per page ($77,000/70)	$23,000 per project $46,000/2	$315 per percent $31,500/100

Implementing and Controlling Marketing Plans

EXHIBIT 21-5   **Income Statements for Products**

	Typewriters	Copiers	Supplies	Total Company
Sales	$400,000	$400,000	$200,000	$1,000,000
Cost of goods sold	230,000	190,000	180,000	600,000
Gross margin	170,000	210,000	20,000	400,000
Marketing costs				
Sales force ($205.55 per call)	$ 30,833	$ 16,445	$ 8,222	$ 55,500
Advertising ($1,100/page)	27,500	38,500	11,000	77,000
Marketing research ($23,000/study)	23,000	23,000	0	46,000
Order processing ($315/ percent of total sales)	12,600	12,600	6,300	31,500
Total cost	$ 93,933	$ 90,545	$ 25,522	$ 210,000
Net profit (or loss) before taxes	$ 76,067	$119,455	($ 5,522)	$ 190,000
Net profit as percentage of sales	19	30	(−3)	19

So let's look at these results. As shown in Exhibit 21-5, copiers seem to be very profitable, typewriters have a profitability level equal to that of the company as a whole, whereas supplies are losing money.[8] But it is not easy to answer the key creative question: What should the company do with this information? One could jump at a quick solution and advocate dumping the unprofitable product, supplies. Yet offering these supplies—even in the face of these profitability figures—may be necessary to maintain sales of the company's other products. Would customers buy typewriters from an organization that didn't also sell supplies? Also, if the supplies product line is dropped, the other product lines would have to bear some of the costs now allocated to supplies.

In reality, profitability analysis provides vital information which allows marketing managers to more effectively control the future of their marketing units. This form of implementation control goes beyond sales analysis (did we sell what we expected to?) and beyond cost analysis (did we keep our costs in line?). It reaches all the way to the ultimate questions, taken together: Did the margins and profits during the specified period show the healthy base of profits to which we have become accustomed?

◼ CONTROLLING STRATEGY ◼

The control of marketing implementation is an ongoing process designed to keep the organization on course. While it is obviously essential to regularly ask if we are doing things right, on occasion it is important to ask if we are doing the right things.[9] This requires a broad overview of the entire marketing organization. Hard questions must be asked about the strategy being followed; the fundamental assumptions guiding management of the organization must be reevaluated.

One key problem in trying to control an organization's strategy is that its management team is so involved in *setting* that strategy—in determining the mission and objectives of the organization—that they find it difficult to call the strategy into question. A formal set of procedures is needed to ensure that managers will carry out a genuine control of marketing strategy. This set of procedures is known as the "marketing audit."

☐ *The Marketing Audit*

Two analogies should be helpful in illustrating the meaning of a marketing audit. One is the familiar financial audit, from which the marketing audit gets its name. Every corporation's annual report includes a statement from an independent accounting firm that the financial records of the corporation have been investigated and found to be in accordance with standard accounting practice. These accountants have literally gone through the corporation's accounting records looking for any problems (or misrepresentations) that would be misleading to present and potential stockholders or to others. The law requires this type of independent financial audit.

The second analogy to the marketing audit is that of the physical examination. Here your doctor takes all kinds of information—blood tests, heart signs, x-rays, and so forth—to determine the state of your health. Like the accountants, the doctor is looking for any indications of problems that may require treatment. The law doesn't require physical exams, yet the wise adult gets such examinations regularly as part of a preventative health program.

Similarly, a periodic examination of an organization's marketing health is in order:

> A marketing audit is a *comprehensive, systematic, independent,* and *periodic* examination of a company's—or business unit's—marketing environment, objectives, strategies, and activities with a view of determining problem areas and opportunities and recommending a plan of action to improve the company's marketing performance.[10]

Four key words in this definition deserve elaboration; they spell out the key requirements of an effective marketing audit.

The audit is *comprehensive* in that it covers the complete marketing program of the organization. We will end this chapter with the components of a marketing audit; notice that they include all the topics covered in this book, from the examination of the marketing environment to strategy to elements of the marketing mix. A marketing audit is (and must be) thorough.

To be *systematic,* the audit must include a sequence of investigations which are developed and conducted with great care. The audit cannot be a random set of questions asked of whomever the auditor wishes to talk with at a given moment. Rather, the intent is to be as "scientific" as the financial or medical audit. Since marketing is not totally scientific, this goal cannot be fully achieved, but it remains a worthwhile goal that should be kept in mind in conducting an audit.

The marketing audit is *independent,* which means that the marketing manager in charge of the operation being audited cannot run the audit. (Who would believe a financial audit if it were conducted by a firm's own accountants instead of an independent CPA firm?) If Procter & Gamble wishes to conduct an audit of its Liquid Tide brand, it will not ask the brand manager for Liquid Tide to conduct the audit. The company may, however, ask other knowledgeable marketing personnel within the company (such as the brand manager for Pampers) to handle the Liquid Tide audit. Even more independence in the auditing process is achieved through the use of outside consultants.

Finally, the audit should be conducted on a *periodic* basis. Unfortunately, this is rarely the case; marketing audits are too often done only after there are already trouble spots on the horizon. If sales or profits have taken a downward turn or market share is being lost to a competitor, an audit may indeed be helpful. But, like a physical examination by your doctor, an audit will be especially useful if it pinpoints likely difficulties *before* serious symptoms develop. This will happen if marketers insist on periodic audits rather than waiting for signs of trouble.[11]

☐ *Components of a Marketing Audit*

The marketing audit is conducted across the full spectrum of marketing factors and programs. A company should choose to carry out a vertical audit focused solely on its distribution system, for example, but the audit that we are discussing here is much broader in nature. Its components include the macro-environment, the task environment, marketing strategy, the marketing organization, marketing systems, marketing productivity, and marketing functions.

MACRO-ENVIRONMENT The marketing audit must include study of the demographic, economic, technological, political/legal, and social/cultural environments. It will be designed to ensure that the company has actually monitored these environments and that the company has identified the environmental forces impacting on its marketing programs. The intent is to see that the assumptions supporting marketing plans and programs are sound.

TASK ENVIRONMENT Here the focus is on forces which are outside the direct control of the firm but are close to the marketing operations. Included are the study of markets, customers, and market segmentation. Auditors also study the firm's channel members, its suppliers, its facilitating organizations (such as advertising agencies and transportation services), and its competitors. This part of the audit answers questions such as "What are the needs and satisfactions of market segments? and "How are our relations with dealers?"

MARKETING STRATEGY Marketing strategy in the audit is concerned with such fundamental issues as the appropriateness of the organization's mission statement, its objectives, and its strategic plan to achieve these objectives. A key question is whether the resources budgeted to accomplish objectives are in fact adequate.

MARKETING ORGANIZATION The audit will take a hard look at the company's formal organization. Is the organizational structure appropriate given the marketing tasks that must be fulfilled? Is the firm adequately staffed? The informal organization and the relationships among personnel in the organization will also be studied.

MARKETING SYSTEMS A thorough audit evaluates the firm's marketing research and information system, its strategic and tactical planning systems, and any systems designed to develop new products. Even the control systems, which are the subject of this chapter, will be studied. The purpose of this component of the audit is to determine whether the most up-to-date and appropriate systems are in place to carry out the marketing task.

MARKETING PRODUCTIVITY Here the audit focuses on such issues as whether the firm is operating in a profitable and cost-effective manner. The kinds of analyses discussed in this chapter make up the information basis for this component.

MARKETING FUNCTIONS   The final component of the marketing audit is the total marketing mix. Auditors will evaluate products and product lines (should products be added or dropped?), prices and price-setting methods, the appropriateness of the company's channels of distribution, and the total promotional program (including the sales organization, advertising, sales promotion, and publicity). Critical questions include: "Have we set good objectives for the various promotional tasks?" "Have we committed the proper amount of resources to these tasks?" and "Are they being carried out effectively?"

If this list of components of the marketing audit sounds like the entire contents of this book, it is not by accident. The book is designed to be a comprehensive treatment of marketing; similarly, the marketing audit should be comprehensive.

■ SUMMARY ■

1. Control is one of the most crucial places where accounting and marketing come together in the total management of the organization.
2. The most common control involves comparison of quantitative results with quantitative objectives.
3. The most creative aspect of control is figuring out *why* results are as they are and what a firm should do in response.
4. Implementation control is the responsibility of functional-level managers within a marketing organization. Managerial accounting is essential to implementation control.
5. Market share analysis gives executives a broader view of the company's performance than does sales analysis alone.
6. Both sales analysis and market share analysis are more valuable when data can be broken down into various sales components.
7. The first step in cost analysis typically requires that some of the costs in natural accounts be reclassified into functional accounts.
8. A formal set of procedures, known as a marketing audit, is needed to ensure that managers will carry out a genuine control of marketing strategy. The audit should be comprehensive, systematic, independent, and periodic.
9. The components of a broad marketing audit include the macro-environment, the task environment, marketing strategy, the marketing organization, marketing systems, marketing productivity, and marketing functions.

☐ Key Terms

cost analysis	marketing control	profitability analysis
functional accounts	market share analysis	sales analysis
implementation control	natural accounts	strategic control
marketing audit		

☐ Chapter Review

1. Describe how the marketing control process might be applied to a college or university.
2. In what ways are the processes of planning, implementation, and control connected?
3. Describe the distinction between implementation control and strategic control.
4. Other than by product line, how might a firm like Procter & Gamble break down its sales for analysis?
5. What might a marketing manager do if profitability analysis has indicated that five of the company's products are profitable but a sixth is losing money?
6. Describe how a natural expense account like salaries might be reclassified to functional accounts.

7. Why would it not be appropriate for the advertising agency to audit the advertising program of one of its clients with whom it had been working for some time?

8. Discuss the rationale for the statement: "A marketing audit should be conducted on a regular basis, not just when the company is in trouble."

☐ *References*

1. David E. Sanger, "Coleco Gives Up on the Adam," *The New York Times,* Jan. 3, 1985, pp. D1, D6.

2. "Why P & G wants a mellower image," *Business Week,* June 7, 1982, pp. 60, 64.

3. Subhash Sharma and Dale D. Achibal, "STEMCOM: An Analytical Model for Marketing Control," *Journal of Marketing,* vol. 46, Spring 1982, pp. 104–113.

4. "Is Deregulation Working?" *Business Week,* Dec. 22, 1986, pp. 50–55.

5. Michael Waldholz, "New Cholesterol Drug Enhances Merck's Role as a Leader in Research," *The Wall Street Journal,* Dec. 23, 1986, pp. 1, 14.

6. Patrick M. Dunne and Harry I. Wolk, "Marketing Cost Analysis: A Modularized Contribution Approach," *Journal of Marketing,* vol. 41, July 1977, pp. 83–94.

7. Robert F. Lusch and William Bentz, "A Marketing-Accounting Framework for Controlling Product Profitability," in Stanley J. Shapiro and V. H. Kirpalani, eds., *Marketing Effectiveness: Insights from Accounting and Finance* (Boston: Allyn and Bacon, 1984), pp. 481–506.

8. The allocation represented is only one approach, that of full allocation. More complex approaches include contribution margin analysis. For discussion of the controversies in cost allocation, see John J. Wheatley, "The Allocation Controversy in Marketing Cost Analysis," *University of Washington Business Review,* vol. 30, Summer 1971, pp. 61–70.

9. James M. Hulbert and Norman E. Toy, "A Strategic Framework for Marketing Control," *Journal of Marketing,* vol. 41, Apr. 1977, pp. 12–20.

10. Philip Kotler, William Gregor, and William Rodgers, "The Marketing Audit Comes of Age," *Sloan Management Review,* vol. 18, Winter 1977, pp. 25–43.

11. Based on Kotler et al., op. cit.

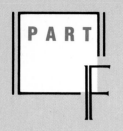

PART

FOUR

MARKETING IN SPECIAL SETTINGS

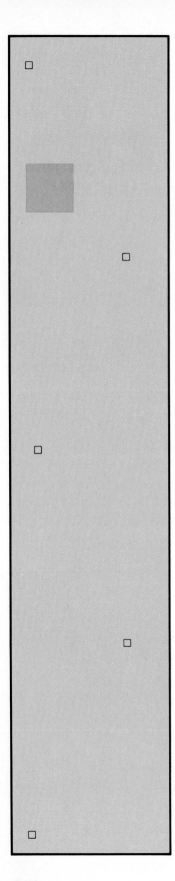

Thus far, we have discussed the entire marketing process of analyzing markets, planning and implementing marketing programs, and controlling marketing operations. This final part of the book discusses some special issues of applying this process to some special settings. We have used throughout the text examples of marketing by nonprofit organizations and within international settings. But, we have not gone into detail on how these special settings require different marketing approaches.

Chapter 22 focuses on the global scene. Many of the marketing principles we have covered apply in all settings, but some have to be given special attention for marketing outside of one's own country. The differences of languages and currencies are obvious, but many other factors are just as important. The need for U.S. marketers to think globally has never been greater.

The final chapter, Marketing in Newer Settings, covers a variety of organizations that have recently recognized the usefulness of marketing approaches in their own efforts. These include many nonprofit organizations such as hospitals, universities, and symphony orchestras. Also included are organizations such as banks, utilities, and other formally regulated businesses, which are learning more and more every day that the marketing principles discussed in this book are applicable to them too.

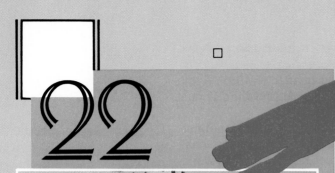

$\mathcal{22}$

Copyright © J. Andanson/Sygma.

GLOBAL MARKETING

SPOTLIGHT ON

☐ Major forces influencing global marketing

☐ Marketers' initial involvement in global marketing

☐ Marketers' analysis of international markets

☐ Marketing research's role in global marketing

☐ Entry strategies for global marketing

☐ Global markets segmented by geography, culture, and stage of development

☐ Global pricing and distribution decisions

☐ Control of global marketing

Is the Apple computer as American as apple pie? Not entirely, for Apple is the leading seller of computers in France and Australia. Apple sells computers to 80 international markets; by the second quarter of 1987, Apple International accounted for 29 percent of the company's projected annual sales of $2.3 billion.

Of course, Apple faces formidable obstacles in its international operations, including the powerful appeal of archrival IBM. To meet this challenge, Apple has instituted a new international structure, centering all worldwide marketing activities in Apple's Silicon Valley headquarters. All foreign marketing campaigns can now be better coordinated to solidify Apple's identity as a "world brand."

While Apple intends to keep that persistent brand and corporate image throughout the world, president Mike Spindler prefers to call their strategy "multi-local" rather than "multinational." They want to maintain local nation autonomy, putting the decision making where the action is—near the markets.

Apple International has repositioned its computer products to bypass the distinction between professional and personal computers. Peter Gilson of BBDO International, one of the leading agencies handling Apple's overseas campaigns, emphasizes: "The solution for us is not to suddenly go on the professional side of the equation, because that's where you can die going head-to-head with IBM. And it's not to emphasize the personal side more, either. Rather, it's to talk to those people who see a link between personal and professional."

In managing its international advertising and promotion program, broad global positioning strategies are developed, and local marketing managers around the world are able to contribute and agree with the strategy. Working with its advertising agency in San Francisco, BBD&O, corporate management develops specific advertising materials for all or part of the world, and sends these to local management to use or adapt to their local markets.

(Courtesy of Apple Computer, Inc.)

Local managers do make adaptations, but most will be working with local offices of BBD&O International, and this helps maintain worldwide consistency—but consistency with a local touch.

Source: Richard Morgan, "Apple Puts New Polish on Its International Image," *Adweek,* Nov. 4, 1985, pp. 24, 26; and personal correspondence with William Holtzman, manager of marketing communications, Apple Computer International, May 21, 1987.

Whether based in California's Silicon Valley (as is Apple) or in office buildings near the harbor in Hong Kong, a growing number of companies are engaging in marketing efforts across the globe. Chapter 22 will explore the special problems and opportunities that surface in worldwide marketing or marketing activities conducted outside your own domestic market.

We will begin by examining the major forces which influence marketing in the international arena. Next, we will discuss certain conditions of the global environment that become especially important as you move out of the familiar U.S. market. We then look at a number of alternative strategies that might be used in entering markets abroad. These strategies carry with them organizational implications as well. Finally, we will focus on planning and implementing international marketing mix programs.

FORCES SHAPING GLOBAL MARKETING

First, what do we mean by "global marketing"? Although in the complex language of the business world certain distinctions are made when referring to marketing that is international, multinational, foreign, transnational, or global, we will use these terms interchangeably. For our purposes, **global marketing** refers to any marketing that involves two or more nations. It can be as simple as a company selling its products to a buyer located in another country or as elaborate as a large multinational corporation arranging to manufacture its products in 30 different nations and sell these products all over the world.

The U.S. market is so huge and attractive that many corporations prefer to deal with the challenges of that substantial market only. When the United States was formed in the eighteenth century, the new nation's founders ensured that there would be no barriers to trade across state lines; the result, two centuries later, is the largest market in the world. Thus, in terms of yearly sales, the state of Pennsylvania is about equal to Australia as a market; California is a larger market than the entire continent of Africa.

Why, then, are more and more U.S. managers deciding that their corporations should enter international markets? Among the forces shaping such decisions are international competition, world products, market growth rates, and international trade control.

International Competition

In the post–World War II era, managers of many U.S. firms had difficulty meeting the demands of their domestic markets. Then, as they experienced a need to expand, many firms simply moved into foreign markets where competitors were very weak or nonexistent. However, in the last few decades, U.S. companies have faced a growing challenge from foreign competitors. For example, West Germany, Great

Britain, and France all became stronger after recovering from World War II, and Japan developed into an especially powerful manufacturing and marketing nation.

The changes in the U.S. auto market have been among the most dramatic. In the 1940s, foreign cars were rare in this country. By the 1950s, Volkswagen had climbed all the way to about 10 percent of the U.S. market; by the 1980s, the foreign makes (mainly from Japan) had captured one-fourth of our auto market. According to the latest projections, the impact of other Asian nations on the U.S. auto market will be even greater in the years ahead.[1] A similar story could be told for other industries. As foreign competitors continue to effectively penetrate U.S. markets, U.S. marketers may compensate by taking greater interest in global markets. Increases in international sales can thus offset a company's declining market share at home.

☐ World Products

Until recently, we could usually speak with considerable accuracy of a product's country of origin: Italian shoes, U.S. blue jeans, German cameras, and so forth. However, attaching a simple national label to a product is becoming much more difficult. Consider the shoes made from the hides of cows slaughtered in the United States: The leather is tanned in Brazil; leather for the uppers is cut in one place and that for the lowers in another. It is all sewn together in Barbados and then is brought back to be marketed inside the United States. Can we call these U.S. shoes.?

To take another example, a company may take a silicon chip from Texas Instruments for a calculator, buy steel for the housing from a plant in India, assemble these and other parts in Singapore or Indonesia, put a Japanese brand name on it, and market the calculator all over the world. Does it make sense to call this a Japanese calculator? Obviously, to participate in this new type of economy, you have to be involved in international business.[2]

☐ Market Growth Rates

Viewed from a global perspective, the market for many products has slowed down in the United States (and in many Western European nations) just as it has begun to grow rapidly in certain countries of the developing world. As we pointed out in Chapter 2, population changes in this country include a slowing of the birth rate and therefore a slowing of population growth; the same phenomenon is affecting most of Western Europe. Although these nations are experiencing market maturity, many Asian and Latin American countries have high population growth rates because of higher birth rates, dramatic decreases in infant mortality, and better health care in general.

When such population growth is matched with improving economies—as it is in much of Asia and parts of Latin America—these markets will grow at rapid rates. Such markets become highly desirable for U.S. marketers hoping to maintain their desired growth rates. As these marketers face slower growth (or even stagnation) in domestic markets, they can shift some of their attention to the growing international markets. As the soft-drink market has become saturated in the United States, Coke, Pepsi, and others seek consumers who have yet to learn of their products.

☐ International Trade Control

The fourth major force influencing global marketing began shortly after World War II, when many of the most powerful nations of the world met to try to rebuild the international trade that had been interrupted by the war. As part of this effort, they signed the General Agreement on Tariffs and Trade (GATT).

Trade between nations is conducted under strict controls, treaties, and other agreements. One of the major responsibilities of international trade organizations is to provide the forum through which these agreements are reached. Apart from this, any two nations can establish special bilateral agreements that apply only to them, and groupings of nations, such as those in Europe, can reach agreements that apply only to them. (M. Grant/United Nations.)

Most economists agree that all nations benefit from an opportunity to trade with each other. We cannot present such economic theory in full detail, but in general it concludes that all countries benefit when each makes more of whatever it does best and then trades the surplus it doesn't need to other nations for the things that *they* do best. In line with this theory, the original intent of GATT was to reduce tariffs, the kinds of taxes that nations use to discourage imports. GATT, which has grown to 85 member nations, last met in Tokyo in 1977 and reached agreement on the reduction of nontariff barriers to trade. The dream of completely free trade among the world's nations has not yet been achieved, but despite many setbacks, the long-range trend is certainly encouraging for companies engaged in global marketing.

→ comparative advantage

☐ *The Global Marketing Process*

Is there a fundamental difference between international and domestic marketing? Yes and no. One important difference is that marketing rules are set partially by governments. Consequently, the rules of marketing in Korea are not the same as the rules in the United States. Indeed, major multinational corporations like Kodak and IBM, which market all over he world, have to learn the rules in dozens of markets. In another sense, however, the answer to the question *is* no: Marketing is marketing wherever it is practiced.

Figure 22-1 shows the process that marketers go through as they become involved in global marketing. Note that this process is very similar to the marketing process described in the first 21 chapters of this book. First, a company must analyze

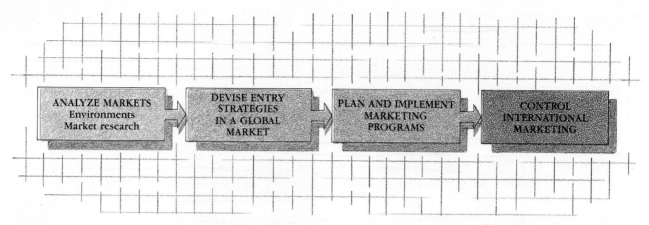

Figure 22-1 *The global marketing process.* The figure shows the four sequential steps that marketers go through as they engage in global marketing.

the markets and environments of the world. Then it must plan strategy and marketing operations and must implement marketing programs. Finally, the firm must devise some method to control for effective implementation.

■ ANALYZING INTERNATIONAL MARKETS ■

Marketing goods or services internationally involves environments—the markets themselves—that are different, sometimes dramatically so. A major task facing marketers, therefore, is to assess these environments—the same types of broad environments discussed in Chapter 2.

☐ *Economic and Market Conditions*

In evaluating the economic and market conditions which affect global marketing, a company will be particularly concerned with a market's income and economic development, its income distribution, and its economic integration.

INCOME AND ECONOMIC DEVELOPMENT   For a nation's markets to be attractive, a nation's people must have incomes adequate to buy a firm's products. One difference among the countries of the world involves their level of economic development. Among the many scholars who have studied this subject, Walt W. Rostow has presented a particularly useful set of stages which nations go through on their way to economic development.[3] A nation at one stage today may be at another stage next year. The five stages presented by Rostow are:

1. *The traditional society:* Countries at this stage cannot improve their own productivity; they do not make extensive use of modern science and technology. Literacy levels tend to be low. Certain African nations, such as Ghana, Ethiopia, and Tanzania are representative of this stage, as are Laos and Bangladesh in Asia.
2. *The precondition for takeoff:* At this stage, the advances of modern science are beginning to be applied to agriculture and production. The development of transportation, communication, power, education, health care, and other public undertakings are evident. Most Latin American countries are at this stage, as are Kenya in Africa and such Asian nations as Burma and the Phillipines.

652   Marketing in Special Settings

The nations of the world are found at various stages of economic development, which invites markets for different kinds of products. The traditional society of Ghana needs mostly food. China is establishing the preconditions for takeoff, demanding mostly transportation and communications, but demands for durable consumer goods, such as this refrigerator, are beginning to emerge in the cities. Hong Kong is one of several countries that is in a drive toward full economic maturity. (Clockwise from top, left: Copyright © Stuart Franklin/Sygma. Copyright © J. P. Laffont/Sygma. Copyright © Robert Frerck/Woodfin Camp & Assoc.)

3. *The takeoff:* When growth has become a normal condition in a country, it has reached the takeoff stage. Human skills and public facilities (such as transportation) support economic growth; agriculture and industry have become modern. Examples of this stage of development include Mexico, India, and Thailand.

4. *The drive to maturity:* Nations at this stage maintain sustained progress, in good part by applying modern technology and science on all fronts. The nation now becomes an active participant in international commerce; its technological and entrepreneurial skills are adequate for producing and marketing an assortment of goods. South Korea, Singapore, Australia, and Israel are prime examples of this stage of development.

5. *The age of high mass consumption:* At this stage, a nation's economy shifts emphasis from industrial consumption to consumer durable goods and services. Incomes are high, and a large proportion of the population enjoys discretionary income. Countries at this stage include the United States, Canada, most of Western Europe, the Soviet Union, and Japan.

A key step in assessing the attractiveness of a foreign market is pinpointing the nation's current position on the developmental ladder and evaluating its prospects for moving forward. Although the discussion above underscores the complex nature of economic development—involving such issues as the development of a nation's infrastructure, transportation, and communications—one measure often used to indicate level of development is per capita gross national product (GNP). Exhibit 22-1 shows a sampling of the world's nations on that important measure.

Unfortunately, even this measure has its difficulties, since it does not indicate all that we need to know before deciding whether a national market is genuinely attractive. In fact, measures of per capita GNP can sometimes be misleading. The United Arab Emirates (UAE), the tiny oil-producing nation in the Mideast, has a per capita GNP higher than that of the United States or any other nation. Yet multinational corporations engaged in global marketing hardly consider the UAE to be the most desirable national market on the planet. Data on per capita GNP—as in this example—will often mislead if a nation's distribution of income is not considered.

INCOME DISTRIBUTION   A country's **income distribution** involves how evenly the income of the nation is distributed throughout the population. In the UAE, the vast majority of income is concentrated in the hands of a very small number of individuals and families, and the number of people with limited incomes is high. This condition tends to characterize less developed countries at the first two (or possibly three) stages of development.

As a nation's economic system matures, land reforms spread ownership of farms to more people, labor unions help to raise the pay of manual workers, and progressive tax systems further distribute the wealth. Thus, nations at the fifth stage of development tend to have more equitable distribution of income. Clearly, for most marketers, a nation's wealth is best divided among many consuming units.

ECONOMIC INTEGRATION   One of the most perplexing problems of international marketing for many years has been how to deal with over 100 individual (national) markets, with all the resulting complexities and paperwork. (As of 1987, 159 nations were members of the United Nations.) Some markets are so small that the payoff is not worth the marketer's effort.

EXHIBIT 22-1	Per Capita Gross National Product of Selected Countries, 1980		
Country	GNP per Capita ($)	Country	GNP per Capita ($)
United Arab Emirates	30,070	Venezuela	3,630
Kuwait	22,840	Uruguay	2,820
Switzerland	16,440	Chile	2,160
West Germany	13,590	Mexico	2,130
Belgium	12,180	Ivory Coast	1,150
United States	11,360	Kenya	420
Japan	9,890	China	290
United Kingdom	7,920	Uganda	280
Soviet Union	4,550	Haiti	270
Singapore	4,480	Ethiopia	140
Hong Kong	4,210	Bangladesh	120

Source: George Thomas Kurian, *New Book of World Rankings* (New York: Facts on File Publications, 1984), pp. 98–99.

Certain countries have entered into agreements with their neighbors to create larger regional markets. These agreements provide for common barriers to trade with countries outside the region, but they lower or eliminate barriers *within* the region. The most important of these efforts is the European Economic Community (EEC), often referred to as the European Common Market. Other examples include the Latin American Integration Association, the Central American Common Market, the Afro-Asian Organization for Economic Cooperation, and the Council for Mutual Economic Assistance (made up of the socialist nations of Eastern Europe).

Obviously, these regional blocks of countries function as more attractive markets than would any nation alone. When a marketer has successfully entered goods into a Western European country that belongs to the EEC, these goods can move freely throughout *all* the EEC member nations. In fact, if a marketer establishes a manufacturing facility in one of the EEC countries, the output of that facility is considered local to all EEC nations. In analyzing international markets, the impact of such economic integration agreement must be considered.

☐ *Political and Legal Conditions*

A second major environment involves the laws and politics of a potential host nation. Many countries are friendly and welcome global marketers from the United States and other nations. Others (notably Iran in the 1980s) can be quite hostile to foreign corporations.

POLITICAL STABILITY **Political stability** refers to the degree of conflict and cooperation within a particular nation and between that nation and others. In a recent study, researchers found that when the level of conflict within a nation was high—and when the level of conflict between the nation and the United States was high—firms made fewer investments in marketing activities. By contrast, when the levels of cooperation were high, greater investments were made.[4] Marketers generally assume that their efforts will be more successful where such political relationships are positive. In other words, stability is good for business; conflict is not.

As multinational corporations make decisions about investing in foreign markets, one essential factor to consider is political stability. Most managers think their investments are safer in a market where the political process is orderly than in one where protests, riots, and violence predominate. (Copyright © Charlyn Zlotnik/Woodfin Camp & Assoc.)

PROTECTIONISM   We discussed earlier the efforts to free international trade from the restrictions of tariffs and other barriers. Although most major trading nations signed the GATT agreements, some still retain serious barriers to trade. **Protectionism** refers to any of a number of efforts a nation might use to "protect" its businesses from the competition of other nations' businesses.

One important tool of protectionism is a **tariff,** a tax on imports that raises the consumer price high enough to make a foreign brand more expensive than a domestic product. Another tool is the **quota,** a direct control on the number of units of a product that may be imported. **Administrative measures** are also used to discourage imports by requiring an enormous amount of paperwork, by requiring importers to deal only with a government agency as their distribution channel, or by dozens of other requirements.

In some cases, protectionist measures effectively bar products from some markets: You can go to jail in South Korea for smoking a U.S. brand of cigarettes.[5] Although the United States is often viewed as being committed to free trade, its law books contain a set of protectionist measures designed to discourage Japanese car imports. Consequently, Japanese auto manufacturers have built plants within the United States and are now making a sizable proportion of all cars manufactured here.[6]

In general, protectionist issues are less significant if you market a product that is not made in the local market. Most protectionist measures are designed to preserve the jobs of a country's own workers. If South Korea had no tobacco industry, it would not have anything to protect.

SPECIFIC MARKETING CONTROLS   Across the many sovereign nations of the world, thousands of specific laws control specific marketing practices. We cannot present all these laws here, but a small sampling will be instructive. In West Germany, advertising cannot use comparative language, such as "better" or "gets your clothes cleaner." In Kuwait, it is illegal to advertise cigarettes, lighters, pharmaceuticals, alcohol, airlines, chocolates, and other candy.[7] Advertising in the Middle East can never show a woman in a "sexy" role; by contrast, nudity is the norm in Brazilian advertising.

Many countries control when stores can (and cannot) be open. Price controls are in effect in many nations; in some cases, it is simply not possible to charge prices high enough to return any profit.[8] The international marketer must study any such legislation that will restrict marketing mix decisions. Interestingly, although socialist countries have traditionally frowned upon marketing as the epitome of capitalism, that attitude has begun to change recently, even in the Soviet Union (see Box 22-1).

☐ *Social and Cultural Conditions*

The laws of any land are largely a product of its distinctive cultural norms, folkways, values, and taboos. However, the buying behavior of consumers and organizational customers is also influenced by the surrounding culture. As a result, the global marketer must analyze any culture to which it directs its marketing efforts.

NORMS, FOLKWAYS, TABOOS, AND LANGUAGE   Chapter 3 discussed the important role of culture and subcultures in the consumer behavior process, emphasizing that marketers must be knowledgeable about and sensitive to the norms and folkways of distinctive consumer segments. This is certainly true in conducting global marketing. As McDonald's goes abroad, it must contend with cultures in

Can you imagine the golden arches of McDonald's or the red roof of Pizza Hut in Moscow, Leningrad, Kiev, and other Soviet cities? Remarkably, they may actually be on the way. The regime of Soviet leader Mikhail S. Gorbachev has shown a surprising interest in Western marketing and management techniques and even in joint ventures with multinational marketers.

By early 1987, more than 30 U.S. companies were negotiating with the Soviets about establishing operations in Moscow and other cities. "There's a whole new dimension" to U.S.-Soviet trade relations, says Dwayne O. Andreas, cochair of the U.S.-U.S.S.R. Trade and Economic Council. Andreas, head of a firm which exports grain to the Soviet Union, is exploring an agribusiness venture with the Soviets involving oil-seed-processing plants and grain-storage systems.

There is great diversity in the kinds of business ventures being discussed by Soviet officials and U.S. corporate leaders:

- A spokesperson for General Electric reports that "we are exploring opportunities for links in gas turbines or pipelines, industrial equipment, and engineering plastics for automobiles."
- PepsiCo is hoping to open 100 Pizza Huts in the larger Soviet cities.
- Coca-Cola already sells Coke and Fanta in the USSR and is reportedly close to announcing investment plans in the Soviet Union.
- Occidental Petroleum Corporation's Armand Hammer, a pioneer in U.S.-Soviet trade, is weighing a new chemicals and plastics venture with the Soviets.

The most difficult issue complicating U.S.-Soviet business dealings involves how to get profits out of the Soviet Union. However, the Soviets have established a new Foreign Economic Relations Commission, headed by Deputy Prime Minister Vladimir Kamentsev, to resolve such problems and accelerate the negotiations. James H. Giffin, president of the U.S.-Soviet council, reports that Kamentsev said to him: "We're not interested in short-term links. We're interested in stable cooperation with U.S. companies, with good profits to the partners."

Meanwhile, as these negotiations continue, the Soviets are beginning to adopt U.S. marketing techniques in their own ventures. As one striking example, more than 100 municipal buses in Moscow have been decorated with transit boards advertising such items as Pepsi-Cola, Soviet-made televisions and radios, and fresh fruit juices. Advertising of any kind has traditionally been a rarity in the Soviet Union, but it may become much more common in the next few years as part of a 5-year plan to produce and sell more consumer goods.

Sources: "Ads Make Marx on Buses," *Advertising Age,* Aug. 25, 1986, p. 62; "Fast Food Is Coming, Fast Food Is Coming," *Business Week,* Dec. 1, 1986, p. 50.

---

which people are more accustomed to eating pig's intestine or snake than hamburgers. Procter & Gamble must keep in mind that in some countries clothes are washed at about 185° Fahrenheit while in others the norm is only 100°. Moreover, in many cultures across the world, the role of women differs markedly from their role in U.S. culture. To market a sewing machine in some countries, convincing a husband that his wife will be more efficient is more important than convincing her that her life will be easier.

Along with local norms, folkways, and taboos, language poses particular problems for international marketers. If your brand name is Cue and you are marketing in French-speaking countries, your name is actually a slang expression for someone's rear end. In Spanish, the brand name Nescafé is heard as "no es cafe," which means "it is not coffee."[9] To further compound the language difficulties facing global marketers, idiomatic use of a language varies from culture to culture. For example, Mexicans and Argentinians use the Spanish language differently, thus making it dangerous to assume that a very good—even a fluent—knowledge of Spanish is sufficient for writing advertising copy for diverse Latin American markets.

When U.S. marketers go abroad, they should be well versed on the different customs and practices of the people with whom they will work. In dealing with people in the Arab world, for example, North Americans often are in too much of a rush to get down to business. Saudis prefer to spend some time in general social conversation before mentioning business. (Copyright © 1984 J. Barry O'Rourke/The Stock Market.)

BUSINESS CUSTOMS AND PRACTICES   The issues raised above relate more to marketing to individual consumers and households than to organizations. You may wonder if the more systematic buying of organizational customers is affected by cultural norms, values, and folkways. The answer is a resounding yes.

Although some global similarities exist in certain buying practices, there are enough differences to make international marketers wary.[10] One such difference is how businesspeople communicate with each other. North Americans—along with Germans, Swiss, and Scandinavians—can get together, exchange a few pleasantries, and get down to business within a few minutes. Indeed, we can become anxious if too much time is devoted to "small talk." By contrast, the Japanese, and the Saudis and other Middle Easterners need to spend a good deal of time in nonbusiness conversations before they are comfortable talking business.

Another difference in business practices concerns business ethics, specifically bribery. In the United States, any type of bribe, if made public, can lead to serious legal problems. It is against U.S. laws for a U.S. marketer to bribe an official of another country. Yet the Italian or West German marketer finds bribery not only legal, but a legitimate deduction as a business expense. While bribery is not explicitly sanctioned in most nations, it is accepted as a way of life, especially if limited amounts of money are involved. Small bribes are commonly referred to as the "grease" that makes things work more smoothly; they are often paid as "fees" to an agent who actually makes the payment. Thus honest executives of a marketing organization may face situations in which bribes are an expected part of making a sale—and where competitors are perfectly willing to offer a bribe.[11]

☐ *Competitive Conditions*

Chapter 2 noted that one of the major environments that marketers must monitor is the competitive environment; this need is no less important in international marketing. The global arena includes two distinct types of competition: that between major multinational companies and that between multinational companies and local marketers.

Among the best-known global battles are those between Kodak and Fuji, between Coca-Cola and Pepsi-Cola, and between Procter & Gamble and Lever. Sometimes these competitive battles somewhat mirror the domestic situation, but sometimes they are quite different. For example, although Coke and Pepsi are running about equal within the United States, Coke has a 3-to-1 edge in the international battle for market share.[12] Coke leads Pepsi in nearly all the 134 nations in which it markets.

Pepsi's response is typical of the competitive strategy of firms other than the leader. Such companies pick their spots to concentrate their efforts, rather than spreading their efforts across all the markets covered by the leader. By using this strategy, Pepsi passed Coke in 1986 sales to the Canadian market, and Fuji follows a similar strategy in its competitive battle against Kodak. Procter & Gamble is the leader in the United States, but Lever leads in Europe, its home ground.

In those instances in which a multinational company finds that its competitors are not other multinationals but rather local marketers, the battle is often fought on different grounds. Sometimes it is not fought at all, as when the protectionist measures discussed earlier are effective in keeping foreign firms out of the market (as with cigarettes in South Korea). In other cases, it is fought on an uneven basis, as with the marketing of automobiles inside the United States. Foreign manufacturers must increase the prices of their cars to cover the taxes they must pay to bring cars into the country.

The difficulties of competing against local marketers are evident in Procter & Gamble's experience in Japan. By the early 1980s, the firm held about 90 percent of the market for disposable diapers in Japan; however, that share had dropped to about 15 percent by 1986. One cause was Procter & Gamble's loss of product quality leadership, but another was that Japanese competitors simply understood their country's consumers better than did Procter & Gamble's international marketers.[13]

□ *International Marketing*

Until the late 1960s or early 1970s, multinational marketers based in the United States were able to sell effectively to foreign markets without substantially tailoring their products to the needs of foreign consumers. A standard practice was simply to have packaging printed in local languages. If the product was electrical, the necessary parts were changed from a 110-volt, 50-cycle to a 220-volt, 60-cycle. Even without any significant adjustments for specific foreign markets, consumers would buy these products because they were the best (and sometimes the only) products available.

In recent years, however, Japanese companies have presented a challenge that is affecting all multinational marketers:

> Japan is one of the few foreign countries where the marketing philosophy is well-understood, widely accepted, and effectively applied. Japanese market management success has been described as a "classic textbook case" of applying the marketing philosophy—carefully studying consumer wants and needs in international markets, developing products incorporating desired features, and putting effective marketing into place to support them.[14]

To compete in the current environment, all firms will need to learn from the Japanese successes and apply the marketing philosophy more effectively. As a result, marketing research is expected to play a larger role in global marketing efforts. In 1986, three-fourths of the 500 largest manufacturers in the United States were involved in marketing abroad. Over 80 percent of these firms maintained international divisions, but only two-thirds had conducted overseas marketing research in the past year, and only 28 percent had an international marketing research director.[15] All these numbers are higher than in an earlier study; clearly, interest in multinational marketing research is growing.

Unfortunately, in spite of the new interest in international marketing research, certain barriers restrict the possibilities for research in foreign markets. Three are especially serious: lack of skilled personnel to conduct research, limited secondary sources of information, and problems in collecting primary data.

A high level of training and skill is required to conduct marketing research. In general, researchers who design and run marketing studies have at least a master's degree. However, outside of North America, education in marketing is a fairly recent phenomenon. Although Japan, many countries of Western Europe, and other nations past the takeoff stage of economic development are now offering college-level courses in marketing—including marketing research—there is not yet an adequate supply of trained researchers around the world.

Secondary-data problems are not uniform throughout the world. Marketers are accustomed to obtaining and relying on data on markets in the United States. Government reports, private data banks, industry association data, and other sources identified in Chapter 6 make marketing research both possible and dependable. Similar, equally trustworthy data are available in Canada and in most of Western Europe.

In those countries at earlier stages of development, secondary data tend to be both less available and less accurate. In really primitive markets, even good data on such factors as gross national product or personal income are rare. For many nations, the most dependable secondary data are those reported by the United Nations, other international agencies, or the U.S. government. In addition, many private organizations—Business International is an example—make secondary data on international markets available. But even these agencies find it difficult to develop trustworthy data when some countries have never conducted a census of the population or have economies where only a small proportion of residents participate in the money economy at all.

Not surprisingly, the problems of collecting primary data are also acute in many of the same countries where it is difficult to obtain secondary data. Consider the task of selecting a good sample of consumers or potential consumers of a product. If little or no census data are available, it is hard to develop a sampling plan that will generate results representative of the population. A U.S. researcher can nearly always find a mailing list for a certain market segment. In many other nations, obtaining such a list would be much more difficult or even impossible.

Just as language barriers pose a problem in international advertising, they also complicate global marketing research efforts. A multinational marketer may need a research team fluent in many diverse languages as well as distinctive local idioms. For example, to do a study of the broad European market, it is not enough to know major languages such as English, French, German, Dutch, Spanish, and Italian. You also need to know many variations of these languages, including French French, Belgian French, Swiss French, German German, Austrian German, and so forth.

Even if a researcher can make respondents understand questions perfectly, answers may not be given or may not be given honestly. For instance, tax evasion is an accepted (even admired) way of life in many countries of the world. Interviewers for a market research study are often suspected of being spies for tax collectors; honest answers are hardly likely under these conditions.

In many countries—most notably, in the Middle East—a male interviewer should not ask questions of a female householder. Moreover, in some countries it is nearly impossible to hire female interviewers. Researchers have also found that certain subjects of discussion are off-limits in traditional cultures, thereby limiting the scope of marketing research. Clearly, international marketers face many for-

Marketing in Special Settings

midable challenges in conducting research, yet the costs of not attempting marketing research are also high.

ENTRY STRATEGIES AND ORGANIZATION IN GLOBAL MARKETS

At any particular time, the state of a company's involvement in international marketing can be assessed by looking at the methods through which it is pursuing foreign sales and by how it is organized to do so. As shown in Figure 22-2, the stages discussed below represent increasing degrees of involvement in global marketing.

☐ *Passive Exporting*

The very first step in exploiting foreign markets may occur almost without the marketer's knowledge. **Indirect exporting** takes place when a firm's products are purchased by some form of marketing intermediary, such as an export agent, and then are sold in a foreign market. This often happens even without any marketing effort by the manufacturer. If the intermediary takes the initiative, the marketer is merely filling an order that will be shipped further than a domestic sale.

The organizational consequences of passive exporting are minimal or nonexistent. The firm does not maintain a special export department or foreign sales representatives. No one is likely to be monitoring international sales or analyzing foreign markets.

☐ *Active Exporting*

Once a firm becomes convinced that it should attempt to expand its markets beyond domestic boundaries, it may enter the second stage of global marketing—active exporting. The most common form of active exporting is **direct exporting**, which refers to the marketing firm's active efforts to sell its products, made domestically, in foreign markets. This may be handled through intermediaries such as export merchants or agents, through distributors in foreign markets, or directly to customers abroad. This process is "exporting" because the product is made in one country and transported through international trade to one or more countries. It

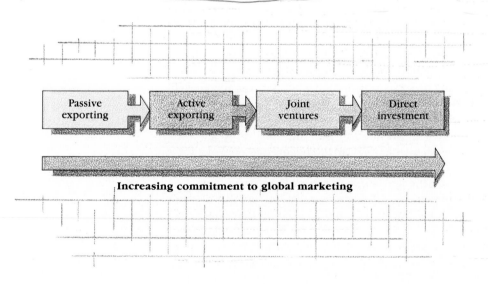

Figure 22-2 *Depth of commitment to global marketing.* The four stages presented in the figure represent progressively greater commitment to international marketing.

Increasing commitment to global marketing

is "active" because the marketer is aggressively working to exploit these foreign markets.

In comparison with passive exporting, active exporting represents a deeper involvement in global marketing. The risks are usually higher, but so are the potential rewards. If a company decides to engage in direct exporting, it will incur higher costs. It must collect information about overseas markets, authorize international travel, hire personnel with exporting responsibilities, and begin other new activities.

New organizational issues face marketers when they reach this second stage of global marketing. Most often, a marketer will establish an **export department,** which has specific responsibilities for managing the company's export markets. This department sends personnel to importing markets to conduct studies; works with facilitating organizations such as advertising agencies and marketing research suppliers; maintains relations with intermediaries in the exporting and importing countries; and supplies these intermediaries with advertising and other promotional literature.

A global marketer reaching the second stage may decide to use a **foreign sales force** responsible for selling directly to customers abroad. This approach is attractive to marketers of industrial products requiring large purchase outlays by customers and/or complex selling tasks. In certain cases of active exporting, these selling and marketing activities are carried out by **foreign subsidiaries,** which are separate corporations located in the host market but owned by the international marketing firm. (When this occurs, others will begin to refer to the parent company as a "multinational corporation.")

☐ *Joint Ventures*

The first two stages of involvement discussed above are considered exporting because the product is made in one place and exported to another. (It is also imported into the latter.) At the next level of commitment to global marketing, a company begins to actually produce the product abroad. This occurs immediately in the case of most services. The service is often produced and consumed simultaneously, as when the London branch of the Chase Manhattan Bank loans funds to its customers.

The least risky method of producing abroad that requires the least investment is to enter into a **joint venture.** This is an agreement with another organization through which the tasks of producing and marketing a product are shared.[16] A joint venture generally involves either a licensing agreement or a joint ownership agreement.

Under a **licensing agreement,** an organization in the host country is given the right to make the marketer's patented (or patentable) product for sale in that market. In many cases, the agreement spells out just how the local company will make and market the product. The host organization, as the licensee, pays a royalty to the company with the patentable product (the licensor). As one example, Coca-Cola licenses bottling plants all over the world. They buy the Coke syrup and then produce and sell the finished product under a Coke label. The international marketer (licensor) makes a low investment in the actual production of the product under such licensing agreements. However, the licensor may incur a large part of the costs of advertising and other marketing efforts. Licensing agreements involve another significant risk: The marketer has less control over the licensee than it would over its own production operation.

Another type of joint venture, known as **joint ownership,** involves more commitment than licensing. Under joint ownership, an international marketer and an organization in the host country create a third organization which they own jointly. These partners share all the profits (or losses) of the new organization.

Joint ownership arrangements can occur for any number of reasons. Occasionally, two large multinational firms will join because each has something that the other needs. By working as partners, the companies may be able to overcome the weaknesses of each. For example, Siecor is a company jointly owned by Siemans (a West German firm) and Corning Glass Works (based in the United States). Siecor was created to make and market optical cable; it represents a marriage of the two companies' technological skills.

In some instances, a joint ownership is the only means of entering a particular market, as when Procter & Gamble finally cracked the Taiwanese market. Local manufacturers of soaps and toothpaste wanted to keep Procter & Gamble out of Taiwan altogether. After threats that Taiwan's favorable U.S. import position could be endangered, the Taiwanese government permitted a compromise solution. Procter & Gamble and a local manufacturer, Namchow Chemical Industrial Co., were allowed to form a third company, Modern Home Products, to make and market soaps, detergents, feminine napkins, disposable diapers, shampoos, and toothpastes.[17] As part of this compromise, the new company agreed not to exceed 10 percent of Taiwan's soap or toothpaste market during its first 3 years of operations.

Certain host governments permit joint ownership only when the local firm owns more than 50 percent of the business. India, for example, insists on this type of jointly owned operation. When it began enforcing this approach, some companies—among them Coke and IBM—decided to abandon the Indian market entirely. By contrast, Kodak chose to stay and now owns less than half of the Indian company which markets Kodak products.

The organizational ramifications of joint venturing can be quite varied. At the lowest level, a firm may license foreign organizations to produce and market its products, doing little more than receiving reports on the volume produced, and accepting royalty payments based on that volume. They need no special organization. This arrangement is most likely in marketing industrial products where there is little chance of damaging a well-known brand name. By contrast, when a familiar brand name (such as Coca-Cola) is to be licensed—and major marketing responsibilities are to be carried out by the licensor—there will almost certainly be a major organizational requirement. This can involve complex issues of international divisions and marketing subsidiaries abroad.

☐ *Direct Investment*

The deepest level of commitment to global marketing is that of **direct investment,** in which the organization invests the funds necessary to build or purchase its own facilities in the host country, most often creating wholly owned subsidiaries. This highest level of commitment is characteristic of the major, recognizable, truly multinational corporations (MNCs): IBM, Kodak, Fuji, Matsushita, Unilever, General Motors, and so forth.

The subsidiaries created by these multinational corporations fall into two categories. A **marketing company** markets, sells, and services the firm's products in the host country. Typically this type of company has a sales organization, an advertising department, a service organization, and customer relations personnel, as well as its own support operations (including warehouse, finance and accounting, and personnel). A MNC establishes a marketing company in a market when it does not wish to actually manufacture its products at that location.

When multinational corporations such as Gillette make direct investments in foreign markets, they may establish subsidiary companies that are predominantly marketing organizations, or ones that are both manufacturer and marketer. Such investments represent the deepest commitment to global marketing. (Copyright © 1986 Viviane Holbrooke/The Stock Market.)

A **marketing and manufacturing company** handles all the functions of a marketing company but also maintains a production facility for the manufacture of the product. Kodak offers a good example of this type of arrangement. In Europe, Kodak has marketing and manufacturing companies in England, France, and West Germany. It reaches all its other markets through marketing companies. In Latin America, Kodak manufactures its goods in Mexico, Brazil, and Argentina, but it markets them all over the region. Through such arrangements, Kodak can rationalize its overseas production. Thus, Kodak Pathe (Paris) primarily makes photographic paper; Kodak Limited (London) primarily makes film; and Kodak A. G. (Stuttgart) makes cameras, projectors, and other equipment.

Although the direct investment approach clearly requires the heaviest drain on a global marketer's financial resources—and thereby places the marketer at greatest risk—it does give the company the greatest control over its destiny. The international marketer can determine how to conduct its marketing efforts without the approval of an export intermediary, a licensee, or a joint ownership partner. This independence is one reason that many large multinational companies have chosen this deep commitment to global marketing.

The organizational implications of direct investment are especially complex: Such involvement in international operations raises the maximum possibilities for special organizational forms. An initial question is how the various foreign marketing, and marketing and manufacturing, companies around the world will be tied into the parent company. One common approach is to establish an **international division** of the company with total commitment to global affairs. This division is usually headed by a senior vice president who reports to the company's president (see Figure 22-3a). Many international marketers have vice presidents for Europe, Latin America, and the Far East, but each MNC must divide the world into regional groups that are most useful for its distinctive operations.

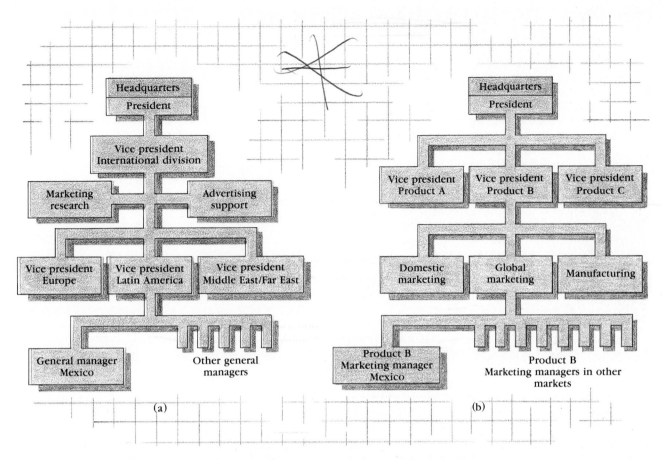

Figure 22-3 *Organization alternatives for multinational corporations.* (a) An organizational framework in which a multinational marketer has established an international division with a total commitment to global affairs. The division has a vice president for Europe, one for Latin America, and one for the Middle East and Far East. (b) The organizational relationships for a global marketer using worldwide product divisions.

Note that the organizational model laid out in Figure 22-3a includes certain staff departments that carry out parts of the marketing task in support of the entire international organization. This is a fairly typical arrangement in international divisions. The expertise of the marketing research staff, the advertising staff, and so forth can be used by all of the company's international regions.

The key advantage of maintaining an international division and regional management teams is that specialized knowledge of global marketing is concentrated in a team of experts. This part of the organization becomes especially knowledgeable about the world outside the United States and is sensitive to the problems and opportunities faced by managers at distant locations. The support of these remote management teams is vital to the company's global marketing.

As an alternative to the international division, certain global marketers establish **worldwide product divisions.** Under this form of organization, each of the company's major product lines, or business units, is responsible for the marketing of its product throughout the world. Each business manager must become knowledgeable about multinational marketing, and less control is exercised by personnel

Box 22-2 MARKETING ISSUES: Standardized versus Customized Marketing

Should international marketers attempt to standardize their marketing efforts for the entire world, or should they customize marketing efforts for each distinctive market?

In an important 1983 article for the *Harvard Business Review*, marketing professor Theodore Levitt put forward the case for standardized multinational marketing. In his view, technological changes (especially the emergence of inexpensive air travel and the new telecommunications technology) have set the stage for true global marketing. Consumers all across the world have similar tastes, needs, and buying behaviors. Consequently, according to Levitt, the "new global realities" dictate that companies should sell the same product in essentially the same way in diverse international markets.

"A lie has been perpetuated for years and years," argues Norman Vale, Grey Advertising's international area director for Europe. "The lie is that people are different. Yes, there are differences among cultures, but a headache is a headache, and people brush their teeth the same way all over the world." Echoing such reasoning, advocates of standardized marketing and advertising point to standardization's four important advantages: cost reduction (or greater efficiency) in planning and control; building of international brand and company image; simplification of coordination and control; and utilization of good ideas across the globe.

But many experts are far from convinced by the arguments offered on behalf of standardization. "You don't sell to people in Salonika, Greece the same way as Delhi or Tulsa, Oklahoma," suggests Stewart Long, senior vice president for marketing for TWA. Jerry Wind of the Wharton School adds that there is no firm evidence to show that consumers around the world are

actually becoming more alike. In fact, he contends, most academic and market research documents that as people in various international markets become better educated and more affluent, their tastes tend to diverge.

Supporters of a customization approach to global marketing insist that this strategy is preferable to standardization because it considers cultural differences, restrictive legislation, variations among local media, and different stages of the product life cycle. They note that two of the examples most commonly cited by advocates of standardization are Coca-Cola and Levi jeans, yet neither company genuinely applies a standardized marketing program worldwide. Each markets under an approach which is adapted to local conditions.

In a 1985 survey of senior marketing executives of major U.S. corporations, only 9 percent indicated that their companies were officially pursuing a global marketing strategy for their products. Asked about product categories particularly appropriate for standardized marketing, these executives pointed to computer hardware, airlines, photography equipment, heavy equipment, and machine tools. The product categories viewed as least appropriate for standardization were beer, household cleaners, toiletries, food, confections, and clothing.

(continued following page)

In some cases, the same advertising and promotional theme may be used all over the world for specific products, leading to significant savings in marketing costs (as in these Playtex bras from England, Spain, and France). In other cases, the marketing efforts must be adjusted to fit the local culture. (Courtesy of Playtex.)

These data suggest that marketers should avoid the simplistic question of standardization versus customization and should instead ask: "In what conditions should marketing programs be standardized or customized?" If a single advertising campaign will work well in all countries—or if a single product design seems appropriate for diverse international markets—then the costs of global marketing will be substantially reduced. Yet these savings may be meaningless if the company loses important sales because it fails to adapt to local tastes and conditions. We can conclude that standardized marketing programs are a worthwhile goal only where they are truly effective. ■

Sources: Theodore Levitt, "The Globalization of Markets," *Harvard Business Review*, May–June 1983, pp. 92–102; Yorum Wind and Susan Douglas, "The Myth of Globalization," working paper of the Wharton Business School, August 1985; Philip Kotler, speech at the American Marketing Association's 1985 educators' conference; Philip R. Cateora, *International Marketing*, 6th ed. (Homewood, Ill.: Irwin, 1987), p. 422; Anne B. Fisher, "The Ad Biz Gloms onto 'Global,'" *Fortune*, Nov. 12, 1984, pp. 77–78, 80; Anthony J. Rutigliano, "Global vs. Local Advertising," *Management Review*, June 1986, pp. 27–31; Nancy Giges, "Executives Say Global Strategies Are Limited," *Advertising Age*, June 3, 1985, p. 56; "Global Marketing: How Marketing Executives Really Feel," *Ad Forum*, Apr. 1985, pp. 30–31.

whose full-time work focuses on global sales. The marketer still requires a local general manager of each subsidiary to supervise all support functions (customer service, government relations, personnel, and so forth). The local company, then, will have marketing managers responsible for the products of each of the worldwide product divisions. Figure 22-3b shows how these relationships are formalized.

Which organizational form is best for an international marketer? Perhaps the critical issue is whether more effective marketing decisions are made through strong worldwide product management or through strong local control. Either answer could be right for a particular multinational marketer, depending on whether the marketer's programs for various parts of the world should be standardized or customized, an issue discussed below.

■ PLANNING AND IMPLEMENTING GLOBAL MARKETING PROGRAMS ■

Most marketers are concerned primarily with the ongoing management of the multinational marketing efforts of the organization. And, as mentioned, marketing is marketing wherever it is practiced. The major differences between domestic and global programs involve the uncontrollable environmental forces discussed earlier—these are the forces that define the rules by which competitive battles are fought. With environmental forces in mind, marketers still segment markets, position products, and plan and implement marketing mix programs (which they later control).

☐ Segmenting Global Markets

The methods of developing a market segmentation program within any market of the world are so similar to those discussed in Chapter 7 (see pages 190–211) that we will not repeat them here. Rather, our concern is segmenting across world markets. If segmentation is unnecessary, a standardized global marketing strategy would be appropriate; if extreme segmentation is needed, a customization strategy might be more effective. (For a discussion of the current debate on this issue, see Box 22-2.)

Regardless of whether the marketing *program* is standardized or customized, the *process* of planning the market should be standardized.[18] That process is somewhat like the marketing planning process discussed in Chapter 9; a simplified model

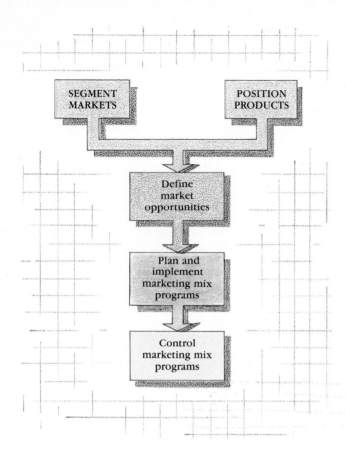

Figure 22-4 *Planning, implementing, and controlling global marketing programs.* Like domestic marketing, the global marketing process begins with analyzing market segments, and product positioning. It includes planning, implementing, and controlling marketing mix programs.

adapted for the global setting is shown in Figure 22-4. As with marketing planning for domestic programs, this process begins with market segmentation and product positioning.

The key segmentation question marketers face is what bases to use to segment markets. The answer is as varied as the creativity of individual marketers, but a few basic methods apply to most marketing situations. International markets may be segmented on the basis of geography, culture, or stage of economic development.

Many companies practice geographic segmentation of international markets. One key advantage of this segmentation strategy is that the global organization is laid out by regions of the world: Western Europe, Eastern Europe, Africa, the Middle East, the Far East, Latin America, and North America. This type of segmentation is efficient for those who must travel within a region. Moreover, in certain regions, particularly in Europe, mass media reach across national boundaries to neighboring countries. As a result, advertising can easily reach geographically defined markets.

Despite the obvious advantages of geographic segmentation, it does raise a few problems. For example, Australia and New Zealand are located in the Far East region, yet in many important ways they resemble Canada or the United Kingdom more than their neighbors in the region. At a more individual level, French-speaking Belgians are culturally closer to France than to the northern part of Belgium (where the Flemish-speaking population may feel more akin to Holland). Consequently, dividing the world into geographic market segments may be both efficient for travel and for physical distribution of products and inefficient for designing products or promotional programs where cultural issues are important.

Cultural segmentation of international markets would place national markets into homogeneous segments based on their basic societal norms, customs, and value systems. Such issues as language, religion, and racial origin become the primary bases for segmentation. In Latin America, for example, Mexico, most of the Central American nations, and the countries in the northern part of South America speak Spanish and are predominantly Roman Catholic. The peoples of these countries are a racial mixture of the Spanish settlers who conquered the region and the advanced Indian nations (mostly Aztec and Inca) that they conquered (and with whom they intermarried). By contrast, residents of Chile, Argentina, and Uruguay are Spanish-speaking, primarily Roman Catholic, and predominantly of European descent. The Indians native to this area were more similar to those of North America and were largely killed off by settlers. The other major nation of Latin America is Brazil, which is mostly Roman Catholic. Here the natives speak Portuguese, and the racial mixture is much more varied than in most Latin American countries.

We introduce this information to show that *careful* study of cultures is essential in grouping homogeneous clusters of nations. Marketers can easily run into trouble if they make incorrect assumptions about groups of nations; as we have shown, it would be wrong to assume that the many Latin American countries have a similar cultural makeup. There is simply no substitute for the serious study of cultures suggested on pages 47 to 52.

Given the problems of geographic and cultural segmentation, some global marketers group nations by stage of economic development. This is especially true in marketing products to organizational buyers, but it can be effective in consumer marketing as well.[19] When countries are building the preconditions for takeoff, they need communications equipment and systems to provide basic connections of people and organizations. For transportation, they need highways and railroads more than new lines of automobiles. At a takeoff stage, the demand turns more to factories and the equipment needed to run them, as well as the equipment used to modernize farming. Nations in the age of high mass consumption are the prime markets for consumer durables like appliances and for such luxuries as expensive cars and audio and video systems.

When segmenting by level of development, many marketers mistakenly assume that markets with very low per capita income are not appropriate for their products—that other markets are better. Figure 22-5 shows the proportion of people in selected nations who have sufficient income to be appropriate market targets for Kodak film. Note that the segment in India that can afford Kodak film is only about 10 percent, while it is 60 percent in France. But 10 percent of India's population comes to more than 90 million people, whereas 60 percent of France's population is only about 15 million.[20] In light of these data, it would be a mistake for Kodak to assume that market potential is great in France (because of the 60 percent figure) but is weak in India.

☐ *Positioning Products*

Any international marketer will probably face different competitors in different markets. For example, Kodak holds a dominant position in many markets and concentrates on defending its impressive market share. In other markets such as Japan and India, Kodak has only a small share and focuses on taking business away from the market leaders.

In the global marketing process, positioning refers in good part to how various competitors are perceived. Fuji film was perceived as less expensive than Kodak 10 years ago, but also of lower quality. However, by the late 1980s, Fuji's image had

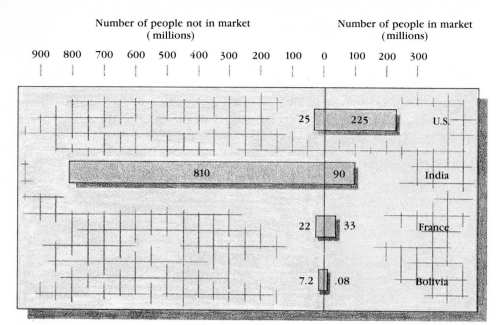

Number of people not in market (millions)

Number of people in market (millions)

| 900 | 800 | 700 | 600 | 500 | 400 | 300 | 200 | 100 | 0 | 100 | 200 | 300 |

25 | 225 | U.S.

810 | 90 | India

22 | 33 | France

7.2 | .08 | Bolivia

Figure 22-5 *Market segments for a Kodak product in selected countries.* The danger of using simple measures of markets is that real market potential could be misrepresented. In both India and Bolivia, only about 10 percent of the population can afford to purchase a particular Kodak product, while that proportion is about 60 percent in France and 90 percent in the United States. But, 10 percent of India's almost 900 million people make up a greater market potential than 60 percent of France's 55 million.

shifted: it is now viewed as less expensive but of equal quality. Kodak is perceived as a high-quality product, and at a higher price, in almost all markets. Managers at Kodak (and at other companies) must continually assess their products' positions in each market; they cannot assume that any product is viewed in the same way across the world.

☐ *Defining Market Opportunities*

The process of defining market opportunities depends on the results of the segmentation and positioning processes. First we answer these questions: "What can we do to improve our product's position in this market segment? Does our analysis show that we can increase our market share by changing our advertising program? Will the market accept a new brand?" To resolve such issues, the marketer must assess how well competing brands are satisfying the needs of the market and must determine what marketing mix elements can be developed to exploit existing opportunities.

☐ *Planning and Implementing Marketing Mix Programs*

The marketing mix we have discussed throughout the book—product, promotion, price, and distribution—is also used to structure marketing programs for international marketing.[21] Of course, the multinational setting offers special opportunities and presents distinctive problems.

Product and promotion decisions are dictated by the resolution of the standardization versus customization issue discussed in Box 22-2. Warren Keegan has suggested a set of alternatives along a scale that ranges from extreme standard-

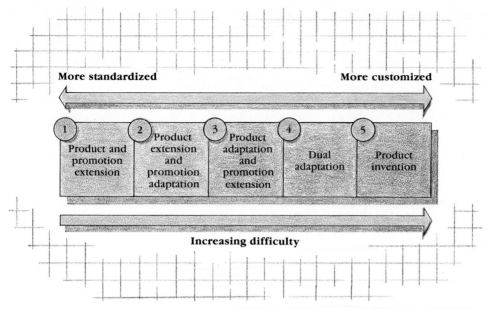

More standardized   **More customized**

| 1 Product and promotion extension | 2 Product extension and promotion adaptation | 3 Product adaptation and promotion extension | 4 Dual adaptation | 5 Product invention |

Increasing difficulty

Figure 22-6 *Alternative global product and promotion strategies.* Moving from left to right, the alternative strategies for product and promotion efforts start with extending our current product and promotion, without modification, into foreign markets. The second stage is to keep the product as is, but adapt the promotion; then, adapt the product but keep the promotion. The fourth stage is to adapt both; and the fifth is to invent and develop entirely new products and their promotion for the needs of the local market. These strategies are both easier and more standardized at the beginning, and more difficult and more customized at the end. (Adapted from Warren J. Keegan, *Multinational Marketing Management*, 3d ed., Englewood Cliffs, N.J.: Prentice-Hall, 1984, pp. 317–322.)

ization on one end to total customization on the other.[22] Such a scale, shown in Figure 22-6, can also be viewed as strategies of geographic expansion ranging from that of the greatest ease to the most difficult.

Straight extension offers the product marketed in the domestic market to the global market, using the same promotional program. This approach is very rare, since the dictates of foreign markets almost always require some degree of adaptation. Straight extension would be appropriate for marketing French-made Exocet missiles or Mirage fighter planes to foreign government military forces. Products purchased by organizations, such as laboratory instruments, might also be marketed in this manner.

Product adaptation adapts a product to local needs or tastes, but the promotional program remains essentially the same. As an example, Coke blends its mixture with different formulas in different markets to fit the tastes of consumers, but its promotions carry a highly standardized message across the world. For example, Coke made good use of a highly successful U.S. television commercial featuring "Mean Joe" Greene of the Pittsburgh Steelers football team—the same advertising message was repeated, changing only the sports figure to a local star, in 14 world markets.

Promotion adaptation by multinational marketers does not alter the product in any important way, but market communications are adapted to local conditions. This means not merely translating promotional messages into local languages and idioms but also developing new creative approaches and media strategies. For example, Kodak has advertising managers and sales managers in its marketing subsi-

The classic Coke commercial featuring Mean Joe Green was so successful that it was repeated with local athletic celebrities in many countries around the world. This example is often cited as evidence that it is possible to follow essentially the same marketing programs anywhere, but Coca-Cola executives will point to the need to make many adaptations to local conditions. (Courtesy of Coca-Cola and McCann-Erickson Worldwide.)

diaries around the world. They work with local advertising agencies, drawing on suggested approaches from corporate headquarters but devising promotional programs suitable for their specific markets.

Dual adaptation adapts both product and promotion to local conditions. Procter & Gamble has learned that people wash their clothes differently in different countries, for example, using dramatically different levels of water heat. To be most effective, therefore, detergents' chemical makeups must be well suited to the particular water temperature. Procter & Gamble's promotional programs are also tailored to the competitive conditions of different international markets: If a Procter & Gamble detergent is a leader in one market and a follower in another, advertising campaigns and other promotional efforts will probably be different in these markets.

Product invention creates a new product to meet a local market's needs and then promotes it to that market. There is no adaptation of an existing product or its promotional programs. Like any product development process, product invention intends to solve the problems of some target market. For example, in the early 1980s, Kodak realized that its existing cameras were too expensive for most of the market in Latin America, the Middle East, and the Far East. As a result, Kodak worked with a Japanese camera manufacturer to develop a new 35mm camera that was simple and inexpensive enough to become a formidable competitor in these markets.

PRICING DECISIONS Pricing policies may be standard across world markets, but individual prices must be based on local conditions. For instance, a policy of pricing at, above, or below the market price may be carried out in all European markets, but the actual price level will be set in the local currency after considering the competitive situation—especially when a company must face local competitors rather than simply other multinational marketers.

In global marketing, the complications of foreign exchange rates affect pricing decisions. A U.S. marketer will want to eventually receive dollars for the goods a consumer in France must buy with francs, and one in Mexico must buy with pesos. If it takes 6 francs to buy 1 dollar, and 1200 pesos to buy the same dollar, the complexities of pricing are clear. In a straight export situation, a U.S. company might price its product which costs $100 in the United States at 600 French francs in France, so that the francs received can be exchanged for the 100 U.S. dollars. In a direct investment situation in Mexico, some costs will be in dollars, and some in pesos. Prices in Mexico will be based partly on this need to exchange currencies.

Where profits are made is a key pricing issue in global marketing. Many countries, primarily in the developing world, have controls on what a multinational corporation can do with the profits it makes in the local economy. These nations set limits on **profit repatriation** (how much profit can be carried out of the country rather than reinvested locally). As a result, an international marketer often will charge local subsidiaries inflated prices so that profit will be made at the headquarters rather than the local level. The local company therefore makes lower profits, but the larger multinational corporation avoids the restrictions of the repatriation laws and makes higher profits.

Dumping is another issue in global marketing. Products are said to be "dumped" when they are sold in a market other than the home market at prices below the cost of making and delivering them to that market. For example, a company may engage in dumping to keep its production facilities going at full capacity. Dumping is also used to build market share in a market where the firm is at a competitive disadvantage, with the intent of raising prices to a profitable level once your products are well-established.

DISTRIBUTION DECISIONS Multinational marketers almost always tailor their distribution decisions to the needs of local markets. Industrial or organizational marketers may make decisions about direct channels versus use of intermediaries in much the same way that they do in domestic marketing. However, any channels selected which do use intermediaries will reflect the local conditions: Obviously, marketers must use the existing channels, and they tend to reflect the local economy and culture. Creating an entirely new global distribution system would be a massive and prohibitively expensive undertaking.

In studying retailing across the world, we can see that successful retailing developments in one country are often copied elsewhere. The department store and the supermarket are U.S. inventions, but they have been adopted throughout the developed nations of the world and in certain developing countries. The hypermarché, or superstore, is of French origin, but it is now spreading to such nations as the United States and Canada. Retailers in many countries seem willing to learn from innovations in other nations. However, local adaptation is still essential; and the structure of retail distribution continues to reflect cultural differences from country to country.

Multinational marketers typically find that the proportion of products sold through different distribution channels will vary widely. For example, a substantial proportion of Canadian food sales occur in large supermarket chains; by contrast, the small specialized store (such as the meat market, fish market, or bread store) remains the dominant food retailing outlet in Mexico. Global marketers must be aware of such differences and must learn to use the channels available within any market.

Large multinational companies usually have rather simple channel decisions; they sell most of what they produce outside their home market to their own subsidiaries abroad. However, smaller international marketers face more difficult distribution problems. As discussed earlier, many marketers rely on export and import agents to assist them in their global marketing efforts.

This is an open market in Djeune, Mali. It is not immediately clear, but many exchanges are being made here. This is a form of retailing that is quite different from what most U.S. marketers know; but when marketing abroad, the marketer must adjust to the retail system that is available. (Copyright © Enrico Ferorelli/DOT.)

An extremely important channel intermediary pioneered in Japan is the **export trading company (ETC)**. This organization—known as a *sogo shosha* in Japan—provides its exporting expertise and facilities to many small and medium-size firms that could not otherwise engage in multinational marketing. From Japan, "the 'Big Nine' ETCs maintain over 1000 overseas offices plus 365 in Japan, and their combined annual transactions top $350 billion."[23] By contrast, such companies were prohibited by the United States until 1982, when the Export Trade Company Act was passed. In spite of the phenomenal record of ETCs in Japan—some experts consider them one of the key reasons for that country's success in global marketing—this type of marketing organization is not well developed elsewhere.[24] In the future, however, ETCs promise to be an effective channel for global marketing for smaller U.S. firms.

Physical distribution in international markets is another function new to the domestic marketer. Since moving products globally involves vast distances, special treatment is obviously required. Typical transportation options change from truck and rail to air and ocean. Except for products with extremely high value-to-weight ratios, ocean transportation is the usual choice. However, because ocean transportation is slow, careful planning and forecasting of inventory needs are essential. Foreign freight forwarders—organizations with expertise and facilities in export movement of products—are very useful in transporting goods overseas.

Marketers in some global markets, especially the less developed ones, find that their inventory needs are greater than they are at home. Where large chains of retailers (with their own warehouses and sophisticated inventory management systems) are not the norm, marketers may need to supply small quantities of goods, often on a rapid-delivery basis, to small and underfinanced retail customers. These problems often lead to increased marketing costs.

CONTROLLING GLOBAL MARKETING

The control process serves the same basic purpose in international marketing as it does in domestic marketing. The distinctions between control of the two markets reside primarily in differences in world money systems, in the great distances characteristic of global operations, and in the many problems of communication across cultures and economic conditions.

One method of controlling worldwide operations in multinational companies is the **annual operating plan** (AOP). Through this process, local subsidiaries develop forecasts of their revenues and expenses and then project their profits; also included are plans for the marketing mix programs, for marketing research and marketing training, and for related activities. The AOP becomes the central management control document, and it contains the company's budgets as well as its plans. Each year—or at intervals during the year—managers at headquarters or regional levels will meet with managers of the local subsidiary to review the company's progress in light of its annual operating plan.

Just as concern over whether to standardize or customize marketing programs is a key strategic issue in global marketing, so too is the extent of headquarters control over local subsidiaries. Most of the larger U.S. multinational companies hire managers for their subsidiaries within the local country. They apparently agree with the founder of IBM, Thomas J. Watson, who is reported to have said: "It is easier to teach a German about IBM than it is to teach an IBMer about Germany." This preference for using local people in key global marketing posts is now fairly standard practice. A few of the highest-level managers in subsidiaries in the less developed countries may be U.S. expatriates, but most members of the management team are local citizens.

This situation often engenders some conflict: Local personnel desire local control of marketing activities, whereas officers in corporate headquarters see a simultaneous need for international control. In one study of this issue, about two-thirds of the firms surveyed allowed a high degree of local autonomy in developing marketing programs. However, the typical result was fairly standard marketing practices with local adaptations.[25] The control process is a major reason for local marketing efforts to stay fairly close to the larger global themes and priorities.

Through the use of common control systems such as the AOP, the regular meetings of managers on a regional or worldwide basis, and the sharing of a common "corporate culture" and communication network, managers of an MNC's local subsidiaries begin to view the world in similar ways. Advertising managers at Kodak Thailand may be Thai, but they will also come to look at marketing issues through Kodak's red and yellow glasses.

SUMMARY

1. Some forces that shape global marketing decisions are international competition, world products, market growth rates, and international trade control.
2. In evaluating the economic and market conditions which affect global marketing, a company will be particularly concerned with a market's income and economic development, income distribution, and economic integration.
3. A key step in assessing the attractiveness of a foreign market is pinpointing the nation's current position on the developmental ladder and evaluating its prospects for moving upward.
4. Most marketers are best served if a nation's wealth is divided among many consuming units.

5. In general, political stability is good for business, and conflict is not.
6. Important methods of protectionism include tariffs, quotas, and administrative measures.
7. The global marketer must analyze the distinctive cultural norms, folkways, values, and taboos of any culture to which it directs its marketing efforts.
8. The global arena includes two distinct types of competition: that between major multinational companies and that between multinational companies and local marketers.
9. Interest in multinational marketing research is clearly growing.
10. In order of increasing degrees of involvement in global marketing, a company may engage in passive exporting, active exporting, joint ventures, or direct investment.
11. Although the direct investment approach clearly establishes the biggest drain on a global marketer's financial resources, it also provides the company the greatest control over its destiny.
12. Companies involved in direct investment abroad may establish (1) an international division with a total commitment to global affairs or (2) worldwide product divisions.
13. International markets may be segmented according to geography, culture, or stage of economic development.
14. One key pricing issue in global marketing concerns *where* profits are made.
15. Multinational marketers almost always tailor their distribution decisions to the needs of local markets.
16. The annual operating plan is used to control worldwide operations in multinational companies.

☐ Key Terms

administrative measures
annual operating plan
direct exporting
direct investment
dual adaptation
dumping
export department
export trading company
foreign sales force
foreign subsidiaries

global marketing
income distribution
indirect exporting
international division
joint ownership
joint venture
licensing agreement
marketing and manufacturing company
marketing company

political stability
product adaptation
product invention
profit repatriation
promotion adaptation
protectionism
quota
straight extension
tariff
worldwide product division

☐ Chapter Review

1. Why might economic theorists conclude that Japan should concentrate on light manufacturing and exporting its surplus to import Argentina's meat, while Argentina concentrates on raising cattle to export in order to import Japanese manufactured goods?

2. How might knowing a nation's stage of economic development be useful to a global marketer?

3. Why should Spain object to the free marketing in Europe of U.S. farm products?

4. Most U.S. managers would not consider paying a bribe to a U.S. government official, but some would pay such a bribe in a less developed country. What accounts for this apparent conflict?

5. Discuss how cultural differences among nations could affect marketing research opportunities in different countries.

6. If a marketer of telephone switching equipment has succeeded in exporting products to foreign markets, why might it move to make direct investments in those markets?

7. Discuss the relative merits of an international organization that emphasizes strong local country management versus one that emphasizes worldwide product divisions.

8. For a marketer of women's cosmetics, what international segmentation approaches might be most effective?

9. In developing the channels of distribution in foreign markets for consumer packaged goods, why might a multinational marketer have different approaches in each market?

⬜ *References*

1. Joel Kotkin, "The Real Threat from Asia," *Inc.,* Jan. 1987, pp. 23–26.
2. Peter F. Drucker, *Managing in Turbulent Times* (New York: Harper & Row, 1980), pp. 96–97.
3. Walt W. Rostow, *The Stages of Economic Growth,* 2d ed. (London: Cambridge University, 1971).
4. Peter D. Bennett and Xiaohong Sun, "The Effect of Political Events on Foreign Direct Investment in Marketing," Working Paper, Pennsylvania State University, Jan. 1987.
5. Louis Kraar, "Smoking U.S. Cigarettes Is Dangerous in Korea," *Fortune,* May 28, 1984, p. 89.
6. Kenneth Gooding, "There's a Trojan Horse in the Garage in Detroit," *Adweek,* Sept. 16, 1985, pp. 22–24.
7. Philip R. Cateora, *International Marketing,* 6th ed. (Homewood, Ill.: Irwin, 1987), p. 424.
8. Victor H. Frank, Jr., "Living with Price Controls Abroad," *Harvard Business Review,* Mar.–Apr. 1984, pp. 137–142.
9. Much of this section is based on Cateora, op. cit., chap. 4.
10. Peter Banting, David Ford, Andrew Gross, and George Holmes, "Similarities in Industrial Procurement across Four Countries," *Industrial Marketing Management,* vol. 14, May 1985, pp. 133–144.
11. Michael G. Harvey and Ilkka Ronkainen, "The Three Faces of the Foreign Corrupt Practices Act: Retain, Reform, or Repeal," *Proceedings of the Educators' Conference* (Chicago: American Marketing Association, 1984), pp. 290–293.
12. Jeffrey Scott, "The Cola Wars Go Global," *Adweek,* Sept. 22, 1986, p. B.R. 18.
13. Barbara Buell and Zachary Schiller, "How P&G Was Brought to a Crawl in Japan's Diaper Market," *Business Week,* Oct. 13, 1986, pp. 71, 74.
14. William Lazer, Soji Murata, and Hiroshi Kosaka, "Japanese Marketing: Toward a Better Understanding," *Journal of Marketing,* vol. 49, Spring 1985, pp. 69–81, at p. 71.
15. Jack Honomichl, "U.S. Companies Go International," *Advertising Age,* Nov. 24, 1986, p. S-6.
16. F. Kingston Berlew, "The Joint Venture: A Way into Foreign Markets," *Harvard Business Review,* July–Aug. 1984, pp. 48 ff.
17. Kenneth Liu, "How P&G Cracked Taiwanese Market," *Advertising Age,* May 21, 1984, p. 52.
18. Michael E. Porter, "Changing Patterns of International Competition," *California Management Review,* vol. XXVIII, Winter 1986, pp. 9–40; and Sandra M. Huszagh, Richard J. Fox, and Ellen Day, "Global Marketing: An Empirical Investigation," *Columbia Journal of World Business,* Twentieth Anniversary Issue, pp. 31–43.
19. John S. Hill and Richard Still, "Adapting Products to LDC Tastes," *Harvard Business Review,* Mar.–Apr. 1984, pp. 92–101.
20. Eugene Seyna, recently retired from Kodak's international division, in personal correspondence with the author.
21. John A. Quelch and Edward J. Hoff, "Customizing Global Marketing," *Harvard Business Review,* May–June 1986, pp. 59–68.
22. Warren J. Keegan, *Multinational Marketing Management,* 3d ed. (Englewood Cliffs, N.J.: Prentice-Hall, 1984), pp. 317–322.
23. A. E. Klausner, "Trading Companies: Japanese Models, American Responses," in Leo G.B. Welt, ed., *ETCs, New Methods for U.S. Exporting* (New York: American Management Associations, 1984), p. 67.
24. David C. Bello and Nicholas C. Williamson, "The American Export Trading Company: A New International Marketing Institution," *Journal of Marketing,* vol. 49, Fall 1984, pp. 60–69; and W. Chan Kim, "Global Diffusion of the General Trading Company Concept," *Business Horizons,* Summer 1986, pp. 35–43.
25. Ralph Z. Sorenson and Ulrich E. Weichmann, "How Multinationals View Marketing Standardization," *Harvard Business Review,* May–June 1975, pp. 38 ff.

23

Copyright © Steve Smith/Wheeler Pictures.

MARKETING IN NEWER SETTINGS

SPOTLIGHT ON

☐ Use of the marketing philosophy by profit-seeking organizations new to marketing and by nonprofit organizations

☐ Special characteristics of nonprofit marketing

☐ Newer marketers' use of market analysis and strategic and operational planning, implementation of the marketing mix, and control of marketing implementation

☐ Social marketing applied through social advertising and the marketing of causes

According to one industry expert, Republic Health Corporation was the first hospital owner-operator "to market health-care services as though they were products." Since 1984, Republic Health has developed special marketing campaigns to promote such "products" as cataract surgery ("the gift of sight"), plastic surgery ("you're becoming"), foot surgery ("step lively"), ophthalmology tests, and solutions to male impotence.

As the hospital industry has grown more competitive, Republic Health has resorted to a more aggressive marketing approach. Many of the firm's 90 facilities—primarily in the southwest and the southeast—are psychiatric or drug-abuse treatment centers. There is intense competition to fill beds in such centers, and Republic Health's occupancy rate is in the low 40 percent range, much lower than the industry's 60 percent average.

With these statistics in mind, the company opted for a brand management approach to market its health-care services. The approach has been particularly successful in promoting solutions to medical problems that untrained consumers can spot without consulting a physician. Republic Health's advertising campaigns have a number of marketing payoffs. They build awareness in target markets of the firm's services and facilities, cement relationships with local doctors (who play a crucial role in filling the beds of any health-care facility), and even lead to pressure on doctors from patients interested in Republic Health's services.

Other health-care providers are certainly following Republic Health's lead. In 1986, the Louisville-based Humana Inc. launched a $20-million national image campaign created by Grey Advertising. There is good reason

(Copyright © Republic Health Corporation 1985.)

for such investments; the $420-billion U.S. health-care industry ranks in size only behind education and automobiles and accounts for 11 percent of the gross national product. Competition for these dollars is contributing to the growth of the health marketing phenomenon at Republic Health and other companies.

Source: Candace Talmadge, "Republic Health Scores in Medical Marketing," *Adweek,* June 2, 1986, p. 42.

In 1905, E. W. Kreusi offered a course at the University of Pennsylvania called "The Marketing of Products." In 1910, the University of Wisconsin's Ralph Starr Butler taught a class on "Marketing Models." These were the first academic studies of marketing. The Curtis Publishing Company established the first marketing research department in 1911 under the leadership of Charles C. Parlin; U.S. Rubber and Swift and Company established marketing research operations before 1920. Prototypes of modern marketing departments then developed as research groups took on such tasks as advertising, sales analysis, customer service, and marketing operations.

Marketing is most sophisticated in large corporations in the United States, Canada, and Western Europe. In the United States, academic studies of marketing have contributed greatly to the knowledge and practice of marketing at companies offering consumer and industrial goods and services. Until about 20 years ago, marketing was basically confined to such enterprises. However, in the last two decades, a wide range of profit-making and nonprofit organizations have embraced marketing as a philosophy of business and have instituted the principles and practices of marketing.

Chapter 23 looks at marketing in some of its newer settings. We will begin by looking at the activities of newcomers to marketing, such as professionals, the health-care industry, and entertainment industries. Next we examine marketing by nonprofit organizations such as higher education, public service organizations, government organizations, and religious organizations. The special characteristics of nonprofit marketing, such as multiple publics and public scrutiny, will be assessed. We will then show *how* the tools of marketing (market analysis, strategic and operational planning, implementation of the marketing mix, and control) have been applied in newer settings. Finally, we will discuss a special application of marketing methods known as **social marketing.**

NEWER APPLICATIONS OF MARKETING

Recall that we define marketing in managerial terms as:

- *Analyzing* markets for opportunities
- *Planning* marketing mix programs for target markets
- *Implementing* marketing mix programs
- *Controlling* implementation of plans and programs to ensure that strategy

Many organizations have recently found it desirable or necessary to adopt a marketing philosophy because of increased supply and decreased demand for their offerings along with increased competition. For many of them, that increased level of competition is a direct result of the deregulation of such industries as airlines, utilities, and banks. Some organizations have instituted only certain aspects of marketing, typically advertising; others have wholeheartedly embraced marketing as a philosophy of business (or operations).

As Figure 23-1 shows, marketing's newer adherents fall into two broad categories: (1) profit-seeking organizations (or individuals) that have realized the importance of marketing in reaching their goals, and (2) nonprofit organizations that have reached similar conclusions. Both these newer marketers may practice a somewhat recent development, social marketing (discussed later in the chapter). In some instances, as we will see, profit-seeking and nonprofit organizations compete for the same consumer's dollars and attention.

Three groups constitute striking examples of for-profit service providers that are newcomers to marketing: professionals, health-care providers, and entertainment industries such as movies, music, and sports.

Figure 23-1 *Marketing's newer settings.* During the twentieth century, the practice of marketing has grown in sophistication in the private business setting. In recent years, however, a number of organizations that either did not or could not apply this approach have begun to do so. Some are profit-seeking organizations providing professional services or mass entertainment; others are nonprofit organizations in a variety of fields. Health-care organizations fall into both the profitmaking and nonprofit categories. Both for-profit and nonprofit groups may engage in social (or cause) marketing.

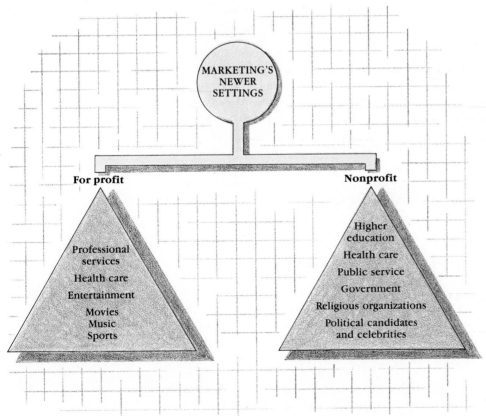

Professional Services

Many professionals have turned to marketing efforts, including lawyers, accountants, management consultants, architects, engineers, dentists, and doctors. Three influences contributed to the increase in marketing by providers of professional services:[1]

1. Consumerism and malpractice suits have diminished professionals' public image. As a result, certain professionals have employed marketing techniques to increase client and patient satisfaction and to enhance the public's perceptions of their services.
2. A series of court cases in the late 1970s struck down existing legal sanctions against such marketing tools. As a result, many physicians, dentists, and lawyers took the first steps toward a marketing orientation for their services by placing discreet advertisements in local newspapers and in the yellow pages.[2]
3. An oversupply of professionals in medicine, dentistry, architecture, and law has forced professionals to compete for customers. (Even though they are not in oversupply, professional accountants can profitably apply the marketing philosophy.[3]) For example, some 17,000 new physicians are graduating each year from U.S. medical schools. In 1980, the United States had 433,000 active physicians; by the year 2000, according to an estimate by the Department of Health and Human Services, the nation will have 700,000 doctors, an increase far above the rate of population growth.[4] Faced with such oversupply, doctors and other professionals can no longer be secure that their reputations and country-club contacts will provide a steady stream of patients or clients.

Health Care

As discussed in our examination of Republic Health Corporation, the 7000 hospitals of the United States have more beds available than the nation needs. The rise of investor-owned, for-profit hospital chains such as Hospital Corporation of America (HCA), Humana Incorporated, and American Medical International (AMI) has forced nonprofit chains and individual hospitals to compete for patients. As one result, over 60 percent of the nation's hospitals now have one or more persons employed to market the hospital's services.[5]

Soaring medical-care costs have fueled the growth of health maintenance organizations (HMOs), which sell prepaid medical-care programs to companies and individuals.[6] Over 20 million Americans now belong to an HMO. According to projections, by the mid-1990s as much as half the population of the United States may be enrolled in HMOs.[7]

Entertainment: Movies, Music, and Sports

Motion-picture advertising has been a feature of U.S. newspapers for many years; banners emblazoned with the names of favorite sports teams still decorate the bedrooms of U.S. teenagers. Recordings of popular musicians have long been promoted indirectly but effectively through air time on youth-oriented radio stations. Today, marketers of movies, music, and sports have moved far beyond unsophisticated advertising efforts; they now market their products much like the producers of other consumer items.

MOVIES   Since 18- to 24-year-olds make up the largest segment of moviegoers, most Hollywood movies are developed to appeal to that age group. Producers sometimes test the interest in a movie's basic concept before giving a production go-ahead; alternative advertising campaigns are also tested even before shooting on the film begins.

Interestingly, films with more "serious" themes (examples include *An Officer and a Gentleman, Platoon,* and *Terms of Endearment*) may be candidates for an introduction strategy technique known as **platforming.** According to Gordon Weave, president of marketing for Paramount Pictures, platforming typically begins by introducing the film in a selected number of theatres in major cities in December. (This makes the film eligible for the next spring's Academy Awards.) In January and February, the film is then released to a much larger number of outlets, with advertising featuring quotes from earlier positive reviews. These stages of distribution allow word of mouth to build interest in the over-25, mostly female audience segment that gives crucial support to more "serious" films. If the film or its stars receive Academy Award nominations or actually win Oscars, the movie will receive

The reviewers praised *Tin Men*. But critical kudos aren't all that is necessary for success in the motion picture business. Major film makers have marketing organizations to establish plans for marketing their products to theaters, to television showings, and to video rental establishments. (Copyright © Touchstone Pictures.)

Even superstars like Bruce Springsteen must be marketed. The forms in which music is recorded lead to a variety of products, which get to consumers through a variety of channels of distribution, at different prices, and with a variety of advertising and promotional programs. The marketing of music is becoming as sophisticated as the marketing of soft drinks. (Bettmann Newsphotos.)

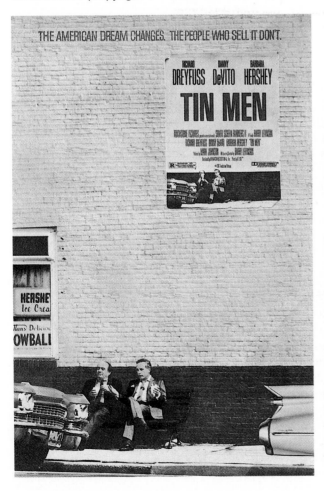

a new promotional push ("Eight Oscar Nominations, Including Best Director and Best Actress").

Three characteristics differentiate movie marketing from other consumer products. First, moviegoers have no brand loyalty to a particular studio and producer, although some actors and even directors develop loyal followings. Promotion for films that star Tom Cruise, Eddie Murphy, Meryl Streep, or Paul Newman—or that are directed by Steven Spielberg or Woody Allen—will naturally focus on these names. Movies lacking the "product benefit" of a big star depend for their success on the overall quality of the film and the public's interest in the subject matter—attributes difficult to measure and forecast.

Second, most movies succeed or fail within a very short time. According to William Soady, a marketing executive at MCA/Universal Pictures, "a film is a retail product, but unlike toothpaste or panty hose, it has only one or two weeks to convince a distributor to keep it on the shelf." Film critic Vincent Canby of *The New York Times* adds that, thanks to computerized tracking of ticket sales, it is now possible "virtually from the first hour of the first day of the first engagement of any movie in any city . . . to predict what that movie will earn during the next 20 years."[8] With production costs for films averaging around $14 million and marketing costs reaching $6 to $7 million, substantial investments ride on a movie's initial impact.

Third, word of mouth generated by reviews in the media and by publicity most affect a movie's success or failure. Advertising stimulates consumer interest, but favorable word of mouth among moviegoers is necessary to sustain that interest. Contrary to the picture painted by television commercials for many consumer products, people do not congregate in kitchens to discuss the merits of one brand of floor wax over another, but they *do* talk about movies.

In recent years, the marketing of movies has taken on a new complexity with the advent of the videocassette recorder (VCR). The movie companies originally viewed the VCR as a threat. Today, they are carefully timing the release of their products in that medium to maximize their returns from the sale of theater tickets, the revenues from television showings, plus the rental of tapes. The video rental outlets have become an important new channel of distribution for movie makers.

MUSIC   Marketing is also spreading in the world of popular music. Will you love Michael Jackson, Cyndi Lauper, and Bruce Springsteen tomorrow as you do today? You can be sure that their managers, publicists, and record companies are hard at work developing marketing strategies to ensure that you will.

Record promoters no longer rely almost entirely on key radio stations around the country to boost a new song or recording artist. Today, advertising and publicity campaigns are combined with the powerful promotional tool of the music video. MTV, Warner Amex's 24-hour music cable network, and a number of network and local television "copycat" shows appear to be spearheading a surge in recorded music sales in the 1980s.

Another aspect of music marketing aims to sustain the popularity (and profitability) of an individual recording artist or group. Some musicians become famous with a hit single or two and then quickly disappear. By contrast, Diana Ross, Lionel Richie, Barbra Streisand, Dolly Parton, Willie Nelson, Chicago, and Pink Floyd have sustained their careers and record sales through careful planning, selective exposure, and astute choice of songs that fit their respective talents.

Celebrities—most often entertainers or sports figures—want to market themselves first to benefit their primary careers. Singers and bands want to sell their recordings; athletes want lucrative professional contracts. Other goals of celebrity marketing include attracting corporate sponsors for concert tours: Jovan has subsidized tours by the Rolling Stones and Kenny Rogers, and Jordache underwrote touring costs for Air Supply. Finally, many celebrities want to sign hefty contracts to serve as the spokesperson for a commercial product. Bill Cosby, O. J. Simpson, and Arnold Palmer are all reputed to earn several million dollars a year for their advertising work alone. In Canada, hockey star Wayne Gretzky has endorsed products ranging from 7-Up to General Mills cereal. Although technically a celebrity is not a for-profit organization, unlike the other examples presented in this section, celebrity marketing tends to have clear for-profit goals, most notably the personal enrichment of the stars and their managers.

SPORTS   Sports marketing has come into its own in the 1980s. The San Francisco Giants and the Oakland Athletics baseball teams are only two examples of sports businesses that have developed marketing strategies. Sports marketers have a special challenge in improving or even maintaining their sales (measured in paid admissions to home games): They don't have a predictable and consistent product.

Winning seasons have been sparse in recent years for both the Giants and the A's, so these teams have chosen promotional themes emphasizing the pleasure of the entertainment experience rather than of being a winner. Thus, the Athletics' advertisements ask: "Wouldn't you rather be at an A's game?" The A's thereby position themselves as a competitor with any other entertainment option in the San Francisco Bay Area. Andy Dolich, the team's vice president for business operations, put Oakland's marketing challenge this way: "The philosophy is that we're entertainment, not just baseball—because our competition isn't the Giants or even other sports, but the 10,000 other things that a Bay Area family can choose to do within an hour's drive of us."[9]

The A's have identified families as their target audience. Special promotions are developed for the entire family, including free pregame barbecues, free A's workout gear (donated by Adidas) for the kids, and free transportation on the Bay Area Rapid Transit (BART) system. Low ticket prices are designed to entice families to the Alameda County Coliseum for an A's baseball game when they might otherwise go to a movie.

The Giants rely on a unique approach: They attempt to turn a liability into an aspect of their appeal. The team's promotional theme, "The Giants Hang in There," is designed to appeal to a market segment of 18- to 35-year-old, blue-collar males who come to a game with their buddies. Gary Freeman, president of Freeman Marketing, the Giants' advertising agency, notes: "The fan image we're promoting is a tough, hang-in-there, no-nonsense kind of guy."

Giants' fans have to be tough! The weather at Candlestick Park, the team's home stadium, is often cold and blustery. With this in mind, recent Giants' promotions have included:

- Beverage Warmer Night, sponsored by Budweiser Beer: The first 15,000 fans of drinking age to enter the park received insulated sleeves which slip over beer cans "to keep them from freezing." At any other park, of course, these sleeves might have been billed as beverage *coolers.*
- Glow Glove Night: The first 15,000 fans were given gloves that glow in the dark.
- Ski Hat Night, sponsored by Pacific Gas & Electric: What could be more appropriate for keeping baseball fans warm than a ski cap?

In the areas of professional services, health care, and entertainment, businesses new to the marketing concept are conducting marketing research, focusing on market segments, positioning their products against competitors, and developing sophisticated marketing mix programs. In coming years, as consumers we will be even more carefully catered to when we visit the dentist, go to the hospital, or decide how to spend our entertainment dollars.

■ MARKETING IN NONPROFIT ORGANIZATIONS ■

Nonprofit organizations are tax-exempt providers of services whose varying goals do not include profit. Such groups have adopted and implemented marketing concepts and practices in response to rising operating costs and uncertain funding. However, the primary impetus is competition for funding and for consumers' time, attention, and dollars. Competition comes from other nonprofit organizations and, in some markets, from for-profit businesses. For example, the Oakland Symphony vies for attendance dollars with the Oakland Athletics baseball team, and public and voluntary hospitals compete against investor-owned hospital chains for patients.

Market and marketing research, advertising, and other promotional efforts are the marketing tools that have been employed most widely by nonprofit organizations. In the future, such organizations are expected to institute strategic planning, to develop marketing information systems, and to plan complete marketing mix programs. Before examining some of the particular characteristics of nonprofit marketing, let's briefly survey some of the applications of marketing in nonprofit settings.

☐ Higher Education

As a result of the decline in the U.S. birthrate from 1960 to 1975, U.S. colleges and universities faced smaller markets for their services beginning in 1978. This led to active competition for enrollments by the 2500 public and private institutions of higher education. Many of these institutions have developed programs to segment the student markets, to position the school against others, and to promote enrollments through advertising campaigns. The University of Wisconsin at Milwaukee combines 10-second testimonials from alumni, students, and faculty to produce 30-second television spots. Fontbonne College, located in St. Louis, supports its MBA program with radio advertising and direct mail; it targets potential students over the age of 24 with family incomes over $25,000.

Willis J. Stetson, dean of admissions at the University of Pennsylvania, points out that colleges need to understand marketing to ensure success in recruitment: "Not too long ago," he recalls, "admissions people who were actively marketing were seen as Madison Avenue hucksters. Now, everyone's doing it because they have to."[10]

☐ Nonprofit Health Providers

Despite the rise of profit-seeking hospital chains, the largest proportion of acute-care hospitals in the United States remain nonprofit in their orientation. Many are tied to their communities, from which they receive the bulk of their support. In general, these institutions are managed as single stand-alone units, although many are joining voluntary chains for such purposes as group buying and management training. Most nonprofit hospitals and clinics have been slower than for-profit hospitals in adopting more modern marketing practices.

EXHIBIT 23-1	Types of Public Service Organizations

Cultural Enrichment	*Social Service and Education*	*Public Well-Being*
The Minnesota Orchestra	Carnegie Corporation	American Lung Association
San Francisco Opera	Ford Foundation	American Diabetes Association
The Asia Society	Girl Scouts of America	American Foundation for the Blind
Art Institute of Chicago	Literacy Volunteers	Red Cross
Kennedy Center for the	American Society for the Prevention	United Fund
Performing Arts	of Cruelty to Animals (ASPCA)	Meals on Wheels (for the elderly)
San Diego Zoo	American Marketing Association	
American Ballet Theater		

Public Service Organizations

The Minnesota Orchestra, the San Diego Zoo, the Girl Scouts of America, the American Diabetes Association, and other **public service organizations** have general objectives of cultural enrichment, social service, or the improvement of the public well-being. More specific aims of such groups are widely diverse, as shown more fully in Exhibit 23-1.

Organizations focusing on public enrichment include symphony orchestras, some theater companies, dance troupes, museums, zoos, and public gardens. Such organizations often run educational programs in addition to their primary functions of performance or exhibition. Cultural institutions need not limit their programs to "high art": the Ravinia Festival presents summer concerts by popular recording artists and performances by the Chicago Symphony, and the Indianapolis Museum of Art sponsors film festivals and jazz programs.

In general, social service and educational organizations attempt to address social needs and the quality of life. The Carnegie Corporation, a nonprofit foundation, funds studies on ways to improve education. Literacy Volunteers run programs to teach illiterate adults to read and write. The American Psychological Association publishes several research-oriented journals. The Big Brothers/Big Sisters organization coordinates volunteer programs in guidance for youths.

Those groups which we term rather broadly as having goals of "public well-being" typically focus their efforts on medical research, disease education, or raising and distributing funds for charitable causes. The March of Dimes originally focused on eradicating polio; after that goal was achieved, it switched its goal to the prevention of birth defects. The American Cancer Society sponsors "stop-smoking campaigns," as does the American Lung Association. Restaurants in New York City donate food and employee time to Meals-on-Wheels, a service providing in-home, hot meals to the needy elderly.

Government Organizations

As marketing techniques have spread throughout the nonprofit world, government agencies have begun using marketing research to target and serve their audiences better and have developed advertising programs to promote these services. The U.S. Postal Service competes with a number of for-profit companies for the business of overnight package delivery.[11] The Bureau of the Census uses advertising to encourage citizen compliance with its surveys.

With the advent of the all-volunteer army, the various branches of the U.S. armed services no longer could rely on the military draft to help recruit personnel.

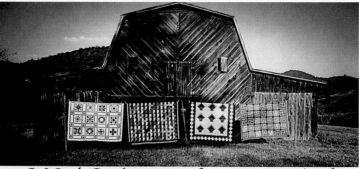

In North Carolina, some of our greatest works of art never hang in a museum.

North Carolina

Whether it is the federal government responding to competitive pressures from Federal Express and Purolator, or a state like North Carolina promoting tourism, modern marketing methods can enhance government's ability to meet its objectives. (Reproduced with the permission of the United States Postal Service; and reprinted with permission of the North Carolina Division of Travel & Tourism.)

As a result, they began to target their audience for enlistment and conducted research to learn more about the desires of potential enlistees. Some branches then embarked on aggressive and successful advertising campaigns to assist their recruiting. The Marine Corps defended its purchase of a very expensive 30-second television spot during the Super Bowl, arguing that the commercial was cost-effective in reaching a target audience of young, single, lower middle-class males who live at home with their parents.

We could speculate that the U.S. Army recruiters have carefully studied consumer behavior. Their "Be All That You Can Be" campaign appears to be an appeal to the highest level of Maslow's need hierarchy (see p. 98)—the need for self-actualization.

☐ *Religious Organizations*

Churches and synagogues use marketing tools not only to increase attendance at services and to gain adherents but also to pinpoint members' concerns and needs. One major religious denomination relied on results of congregational surveys to guide ministers in their selection of sermon topics. The Riverbend Baptist Church in Austin, Texas, used television commercials to increase membership from 60 to 1000 over a 5-year period. One notable ad featured Pastor Gerald Mann and local comedian Cactus Pryor on a golf putting green. Pryor says, "Preacher, you sink that putt and I'll join your church!" Mann looks heavenward, then strokes a 40-foot shot into the cup. In the next scene, Pryor is seated in church before a robed Mann, who exclaims: "At Riverbend, we'll take 'em any way we can get 'em!"[12]

☐ *Political Candidates*

Almost all Americans would agree that Ronald Reagan's communications skills contributed mightily to his landslide presidential reelection in 1984. The talents of the "Great Communicator" were slickly showcased in $20 million of television advertising developed by the "Tuesday Team"—a collection of the nation's top advertis-

Come *home* all ye faithful.

Come home at Christmas— find what you're missing.

The Catholic Archdiocese of New York.

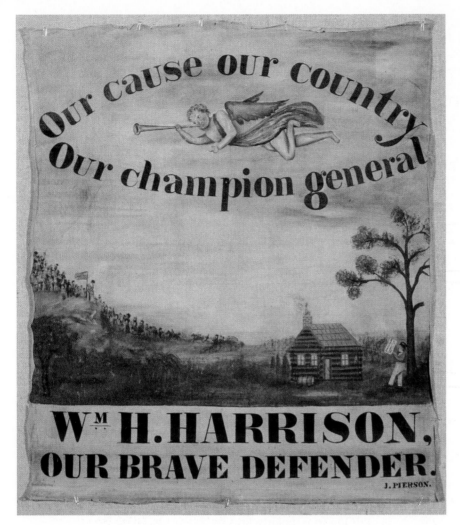

Political candidates have used mass promotion methods for over a century. In recent years, the marketing of political candidates has become quite sophisticated, involving market research, segmentation, and other modern marketing methods. (Courtesy of the President Benjamin Harrison Memorial Home, Indianapolis, IN.)

ing executives. Television spots were carefully coordinated with the issues the candidate was addressing during a particular week. And the issues addressed were selected through a sophisticated research and polling operation directed by Richard Wirthin. With a theme of "Leadership That's Working," the president's reelection was strategically planned in a way that would do credit to the most advanced business marketing. Reagan had no qualms about the need to sell himself to the voters. "I understand you're all here selling soap," the president told the Tuesday Team at a meeting, "so I thought you'd like to see the bar."[13]

The positioning of the political product—the candidate—depends increasingly on skillful use of television. Campaign strategists try to create favorable images through press conferences, photo opportunities, paid-for commercials, and news coverage of the campaign. In addition to the growing importance of political advertising, marketing now plays a leading role in elections through the use of professional campaign management firms, scientific opinion polling and issues analysis, and computer analysis of voting patterns.

The marketing of political candidates, combined with the marketing of celebrities is referred to as **person marketing**—programs designed to cultivate the attention, interest, and preference of a target market toward a person.[14] Although political candidates have adapted the more scientific tools of marketing, personal promotions for celebrities depend more heavily on the celebrity's ability to generate excitement and on astute personal management and public relations programs.

◼ CHARACTERISTICS OF NONPROFIT MARKETING ◼

Although nonprofit organizations increasingly employ marketing concepts and practices, certain characteristics of nonprofit marketing distinguish such efforts from the marketing carried out by business organizations selling products to consumers and organizations. In general, nonprofit marketers confront both problems and opportunities that differ from the challenges faced by business marketers.

☐ Adopting a Marketing Management Orientation

The chief officers of nonprofit institutions are rarely trained in marketing or in business. No one expects a university president, an opera impressario, a museum curator, a symphony conductor, a chief of surgery, or a U.S. senator to be experienced in marketing management. However, such administrators increasingly are aware of the need for staff members who are highly skilled in marketing. Consequently, many large nonprofit organizations now employ a director or vice president of marketing. Years will pass before a marketing management orientation fully permeates the workings of such institutions, but marketing is no longer regarded as too crass and commercial to play an important role in nonprofit operations. As Al Louer, director of public relations for the Indianapolis Museum of Art, put it: "Our survival depends on public perception, so we have to communicate effectively with all our publics. To do this, we must use all the proven marketing tools."[15]

Nonprofit organizations cannot—and should not—practice the marketing concept as fully as businesses do. University administrators would be remiss in allowing students to take only the courses they want; symphony conductors have a responsibility to present some contemporary music in addition to popular works by Bach, Beethoven, and Brahms; brain surgeons do not ask patients what operations they prefer. However, these professionals are learning to lean on advice from marketing managers about how to involve students, subscribers, and patients in the design of curricula, musical repertoire, and health-care programs.

Whenever the marketing concept can be responsibly practiced, administrators will find that they better serve their publics. Like business firms, nonprofit organizations must innovate or face the possibility of losing public interest and support.

☐ Multiple Publics

The marketing concept emphasizes that business marketers should maintain a clear focus on customers, yet nonprofit organizations often have several groups of customers, or **publics,** each of which must be served. Almost all nonprofit institutions must direct their marketing activities at two broad groups: donors, who include individuals, foundations, corporations, and government agencies; and clients, who include audiences, clients, patients, and beneficiaries.[16] To effectively reach these two key groups, organizations often break them down even further.

As shown in Figure 23-2, a symphony orchestra must satisfy at least five groups:[17]

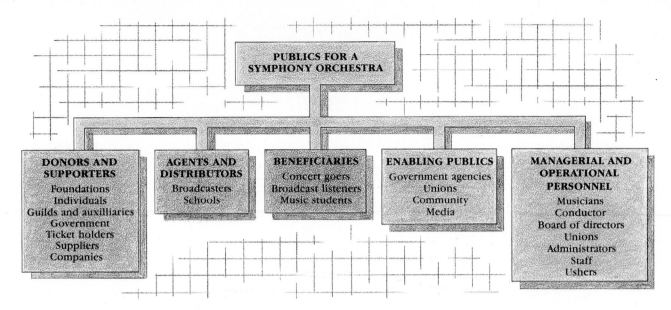

Figure 23-2 *Publics for a symphony orchestra.* The management of nonprofit organizations is made more complex by the number of publics to satisfy. A symphony orchestra must satisfy not only its beneficiaries (such as concert goers and broadcast listeners) and its donors and supporters, but also its managerial and operational personnel, its agents and distributors, and its enabling publics (including government agencies, unions, the community, and the media). (From William Lazer and James Culley, *Marketing Management,* Boston: Houghton Mifflin, 1983, p. 827.)

1. The clients or beneficiaries of the orchestra's performances, including concert goers and students who attend free concerts for young people
2. Donors and supporters who give time and money to fund and assist operations
3. Organizational personnel, including musicians, paid soloists, conductors, administrative staff, and the board of directors
4. Agents and distributors, including broadcasters and schools
5. Enabling publics, such as government agencies and community groups, which lend and build support for the symphony.

These multiple publics are not mutually exclusive; for example, board members may also be major donors to the orchestra.

☐ *Complex Objectives*

The needs and goals of different publics of a nonprofit organization may conflict at times, thereby complicating the setting of objectives for the organization. For example, a hospital's medical staff urges the establishing of a psychiatric counseling program for patients with terminal diseases, and the board of directors and top administrators are feeling pressure to hold down operating costs. These objectives are in conflict and must be resolved through negotiation and compromise among the hospital's publics.

Nonprofit organizations' goals are often difficult to measure, which makes evaluation of alternative marketing strategies difficult. For example, the programming director for a public television station may wish to spend funds on a new series presenting news of particular interest to the Hispanic community. Yet some station executives may feel that the money and air time should instead go to a weekly broadcast reviewing community arts events. Which is the better goal? How should the success of either program be measured? Although a goal of X thousand viewers for either series can be set, the overall benefits of one program versus the other are not easy to assess. Almost all nonprofit organizations face some degree of conflict in choosing their goals; success in achieving targeted objectives frequently must be measured by quantitative means.

Public Scrutiny

Nonprofit organizations' difficulties in choosing goals and measuring success are often further complicated by the pressure of public interest and scrutiny. For instance, trustees of a state university system are elected or appointed to represent the interests of residents of that state. Along with the universities' administrators, the trustees face constant and conflicting pressures on their decisions. For example, keeping tuition low for in-state residents (almost certainly popular with the public) may limit the resources of the state university campuses and therefore hamper the hiring of noted scholars who would enhance the system's reputation. Another example is the pressure on many college and university administrators and trustees from students, faculty, and community groups to sell the college or university's stock in firms doing business in South Africa. Colleges may face contrary pressure from the firms themselves, who may be important donors to the institutions.

Provision of Services

A museum may run a retail shop and sell gift items (physical goods) through direct-mail operations, but its primary task, like that of other nonprofit organizations, is providing services. In developing their marketing efforts, nonprofit organizations consider the basic characteristics of services: intangibility, the participation of the buyer and producer, perishability, and lack of product standardization (see Chapter 10). A visitor to a zoo takes home information and memories, but no physical good. Both performers and audiences are needed to provide the experience of a concert. An unsold ticket for a ballet performance cannot be sold again. And the experience of viewing a Picasso painting in a museum varies widely, depending on the particular tastes of the viewer. Marketing strategies and tools for nonprofit groups need to provide desirable experiences rather than physical possession of a product.

Although nonprofit marketing has its distinctive characteristics, it is based on the same concepts and principles used in marketing for the business world. In the next section, we will apply the marketing management functions of analysis, planning, implementation, and control in newer settings.

■ MARKETING MANAGEMENT FUNCTIONS IN NEWER SETTINGS ■

When an organization turns to marketing as a philosophy of operation, a first step requires determining just who is to develop and carry out a marketing program. Three options are common: (1) The organization may bring in an outside marketing consultant. Usually a temporary measure, hiring a consultant allows the company to get instant expertise in marketing. (2) Efforts will be made to educate existing staff members, often by sending employees to concentrated marketing courses. (3) Most frequently, marketing staff positions are approved and a marketing director is hired. This latter approach has resulted in new job opportunities for trained marketers.

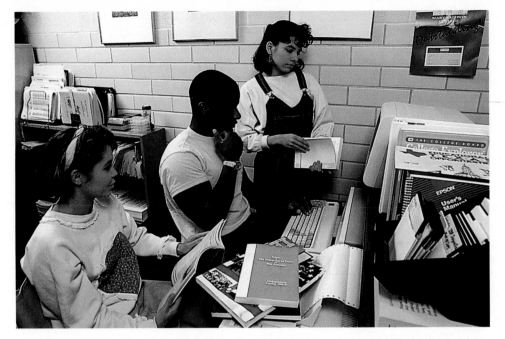

These high school students are examining college brochures and calling up information provided by colleges and universities by computer. As the competition for students becomes more heated, higher education administrators are seeking more and more ways to market their institutions to this market. They are also doing research into how these consumers make their choice of schools. (Copyright © Bob Daemmrich.)

When these personnel are in place and ready to begin work, the organization will begin to move—usually in a step-by-step process—toward a marketing orientation and marketing action. In the following sections, we will see how the tools of each major area of the marketing process can be and have been applied in newer settings.

☐ *Market Analysis*

In analyzing markets for nonprofit organizations, remember the split between client markets on the one hand and donor markets on the other. Indeed, the market analysis task as it relates to clients, students, and other "customers" is not really different from market analysis of for-profit organizations. Those colleges and universities that can better understand the consumer behavior of "selecting a school" are in a better position to attract more (and better-qualified) high school graduates. Austin Peay State University in Tennessee studied 35 different variables in students' school choice to develop more effective promotional programs.[18]

A more challenging task is to sort out the multiple publics of the nonprofit organization and focus on their often quite different needs. One view of a university's functions is that the real customers are the organizations that hire its graduates. Students, then, are the "product" that the university turns out for these customers. According to another view, the real customers of the university are its students, and the curriculum planned and implemented by the faculty is the product. Obviously, the actual workings of a university may be quite different, depending on which of these views it adopts.

In conducting the research needed to understand the market for a university (or for most other nonprofit organizations), remember that different publics are operating from different needs. Each public evaluates the organization using its own distinctive yardstick. Students care about such factors as nearness to home, academic reputations of specific departments, sports programs, and living facilities. Research sponsors (donors) are also interested in the academic reputations of specific departments or scholars but may have little interest in sports or dormitories. It is a challenge for an organization's marketers to sort out the multiple needs of appropriate market segments, but this effort is necessary to properly position the organization to these many publics.

As each type of nonprofit organization analyzes its market, it must develop an understanding of the consumer behavior most relevant to its operations. For instance, the hospital patient is the consumer (end user) but is not always the person making the decision about choice of a hospital. In many cases, the physician actually makes this decision for the patient.[19] In fact, if the patient is covered by health insurance (as many Americans are), the hospital choice may have to come from a list of preferred providers. The hospital marketer will need an understanding of this process to develop appropriate marketing programs for each segment.

☐ *Strategic and Operational Planning*

Experience and skill in developing strategic and marketing plans is not nearly as well refined in most nonprofit settings as it is in the business world. But, just as marketing approaches to running these organizations are spreading, so too is an interest in strategic planning. In many cases, planning methods are borrowed from the for-profit sector and applied to the nonprofit sector. For instance, one of the books read most widely by university administrators in the mid-1980s discussed how to formulate strategic plans in that setting.[20] Hospitals and other nonprofit organizations are following suit and are finding strategic planning as challenging as have their counterparts in business firms.[21]

In general, the planning process for a nonprofit organization will include a clear statement of purpose: the mission statement discussed in Chapter 8 (see page 225). An example of a college's mission statement is shown in Exhibit 23-2. By working through its management team—deans and department heads—a college can develop long-range goals and strategies based on careful analysis of strengths and weaknesses. Should more funds be diverted into areas where student interest is high, such as computer science, engineering, and business? Or should the school give additional funds to its particularly strong chemistry department, where the opportunity for research grants is excellent? Museums and hospitals face similar choices. In setting broad planning goals, nonprofit organizations can then move toward specific marketing mix programs to achieve these goals.

EXHIBIT 23-2	Mission Statement for a College

Like businesses, nonprofit organizations use mission statements to guide their strategic planning process. The mission statement is the most fundamental statement of an organization's purpose.

Organization Purpose

The fundamental purpose of _____ College is to develop a more effective learning community in which all individuals appreciate and learn a number of desired qualities such as: a greater understanding of self and world, personal and intellectual skills for a responsible and satisfying life, potentialities for more productive thinking and for moral commitment, and imaginative capacities for aesthetic expression and appreciation. Another aim is to establish a community which incorporates principles of self-criticism and innovation as integral parts of its life. Furthermore, the College should seek to be in close touch with the needs and changes of society and to utilize more effectively the resources which are close at hand.

Source: Arthur X. Deegan and Roger J. Fritz, *MBO Goes to College* (Boulder, Colo.: University of Colorado, 1975), p. 63.

Marketing in Special Settings

Implementing the Marketing Mix

Nonprofit marketers have been uneven in their use of the four elements of the marketing mix (product, price, distribution, and promotion). Indeed, many have mistakenly equated promotion or even advertising with marketing. When that happens, the organization does not get the full benefit of a marketing orientation.

As we have pointed out, most nonprofit organizations produce a service. The services provided usually have life cycles very much like the product life cycle of business products. For instance, the current life of acute-care hospitals is clearly at the maturity stage, whereas alternative-care facilities such as ambulatory-care centers and mental health hospitals are in the growth stage. Systems of service delivery such as HMOs (health maintenance organizations) and PPOs (preferred provider organizations) are also in the growth stage. As is true of products in different stages, managers must carefully consider the strategic implications of these life cycle stages. During a period of rapid growth of HMOs, market share will change rapidly. Loyalties are not as high as they will be in the future, when the change from one HMO to another will not be as common.

Again like business marketers, nonprofit organizations must examine their "product lines" and develop new products when needed. In the 1970s and early 1980s, colleges and universities established many programs designed to make their students computer-literate, but by 1990, almost all students will be familiar with computers through their exposure during high school. Until recently, no specialized facilities existed within hospitals for the treatment of AIDS. As these examples suggest, nonprofit organizations must remain up-to-date on the services needed and demanded by their customers.

In the field of health-care services, even branding methods are being used. Humana Incorporated, the second-largest private hospital chain, has been working for years to develop national name recognition. We noted earlier in the chapter that in 1986 Humana launched a $20-million national image advertising campaign. But Humana and other chains face a serious problem in applying the brand-name approach. The brand name has meaning—at least in theory—because it communicates consistency in quality. Yet, with its highly decentralized operations, a hospital chain cannot expect to deliver such consistent quality of health care.[22]

Pricing decisions by nonprofit organizations require special treatment. For most, the profit motive and the economy theory of profit maximization simply are not appropriate. Nevertheless, nearly all nonprofit organizations must make pricing decisions. The revenues they receive come primarily from contributions and other public support, from government grants, and from fees for the services provided. The fees for such services constitute the "prices" of the organizations. Revenue from such fees ranges from only 1 percent of total revenues for fraternal and political organizations to 88 percent for hospitals. For all nonprofit organizations except hospitals, the proportion of revenues resulting from fees is less than 50 percent.[23]

Obviously, the pricing problems of such organizations vary substantially, although a key tends to be the availability of support from other sources. Public universities, for instance, often set tuitions as low as possible, depending on the level of funding support from the state legislature. A similar process is followed by private colleges, but here the condition of the school's endowment fund influences tuition rates. Hospitals, which depend primarily on their revenues to provide services, are commonly guided in their pricing by the rates at which Medicare and other health insurance providers will reimburse them for specific types of care.

Distribution channels for nonprofit organizations are usually quite short, as they are for all services. The client, patient, student, or performance-goer must be right there to get the service, so distribution must be fairly direct. However, such organizations must think creatively about how to deliver their services with the convenience that consumers need. In recent years, hospitals have developed satellite ambulatory-care facilities in several locations, sometimes called a "doc in a box," so that patients will not have to come to the acute-care hospital for minor problems. The Pennsylvania State University has 18 campuses all over the state where more than half of its undergraduate students spend the first 2 years of their programs. This system allows most of them to live at home 2 years longer, thereby reducing the total cost of their college educations. These are examples of creative solutions to the delivery of services—an issue that all nonprofit organizations need to consider.

Promotion is the marketing mix element most readily adapted by nonprofit organizations. In response to the rapidly growing advertising budgets of U.S. hospitals, some advertising agencies now specialize in health advertising. The largest portion of hospitals' advertising budgets goes to print media advertising, but a growing proportion goes to television.[24] Other types of nonprofit organizations spend much less on media advertising. Universities use direct mail to high school seniors for much of their admissions recruiting effort. But they also engage in personal "selling" in the form of visits to high schools (frequently by volunteer alumni) to recruit students.

One promotional tool used with great frequency by nonprofit organizations is publicity. As we discussed in Chapter 17, Humana Incorporated used the company's heart implant program to get the Humana name known all across the United States and throughout the world.

Controlling Marketing Implementation

Just as is true of profit-seeking businesses, nonprofit organizations need to compare their performance with established goals and to take corrective action when these objectives are not met. Many of the methods developed in managerial accounting that were discussed in Chapter 21 are also used by nonprofit organizations. However, two factors complicate control by such organizations: the multiple objectives needed for multiple publics and the absence of a clear marketplace measure of success.

As noted earlier, the needs of a nonprofit organization's donors often differ from the needs of its clients. The federal funding agency which supplies large research grants to universities and hospitals wants scholars and researchers to be in their laboratories doing their research. By contrast, the clients of the university—its students—want faculty members to be teaching. The clients of the hospital—its patients—want doctors to be on the floors curing their ills. It can be difficult to balance these multiple and often conflicting objectives.

If an organization's goal is to make a profit, one criterion for measuring success is abundantly clear: how much profit (if any) it made. However, when the very mission of an organization is a bit vague—for example, "to enhance the cultural appreciation of fine music in our city"—measures of success are imprecise. However, nonprofit organizations should not abandon the goal of measuring their performance. Students in colleges and universities are regularly asked to evaluate courses and instructors. Some hospitals have developed similar evaluation forms to be completed by patients at the end of their hospital stay. No matter what the setting, responsible managers wish to learn how their "customers" perceive the quality of the services they are offered.

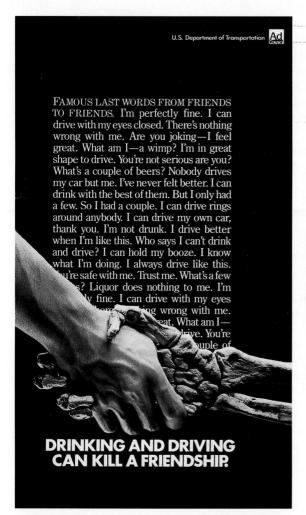

FAMOUS LAST WORDS FROM FRIENDS TO FRIENDS. I'm perfectly fine. I can drive with my eyes closed. There's nothing wrong with me. Are you joking—I feel great. What am I—a wimp? I'm in great shape to drive. You're not serious are you? What's a couple of beers? Nobody drives my car but me. I've never felt better. I can drink with the best of them. But I only had a few. So I had a couple. I can drive rings around anybody. I can drive my own car, thank you. I'm not drunk. I drive better when I'm like this. Who says I can't drink and drive? I can hold my booze. I know what I'm doing. I always drive like this. You're safe with me. Trust me. What's a few ___s? Liquor does nothing to me. I'm ___ly fine. I can drive with my eyes ___ wrong with me. ___ eat. What am I— ___ rive. You're ___ uple of

DRINKING AND DRIVING CAN KILL A FRIENDSHIP.

IT IS BETTER TO HAVE ONE CHILD ONLY

Social marketing uses marketing techniques to promote socially desirable behavior. The ad by the Ad Council is an attempt to get friends to not let friends drive while drunk. The other is a billboard in the Peoples Republic of China, where the government has decided that control of the birth rate is in the nation's best interests. (Left: Courtesy of the Advertising Council. Right: U.N. photo by John Isaac.)

◼ *A SPECIAL CASE: SOCIAL MARKETING* ◼

One additional application of marketing methods deserves special mention. **Social marketing** (also known as **cause marketing**) is the design, implementation, and control of marketing programs calculated to influence the acceptability of social ideas.[25] It is practiced by governments, nonprofit organizations, and profit-seeking business firms. The practice of social marketing predates its first major recognition in marketing literature.[26] It has flourished throughout the last two decades, and is now generally viewed as a useful activity by a substantial majority of marketing personnel.[27]

Social marketing has been applied in a number of ways. Its most visible element is social advertising, which has been used to promote birth control in certain developing countries, to get people to stop smoking cigarettes, to encourage parents to have their children immunized against diseases, and to recruit young men and women to serve as "big brothers" and "big sisters" for lonely boys and girls. Such social advertising will undoubtedly be used in the future for many other worthwhile events and goals.

The marketing of causes can take the form of promoting more controversial issues. Advertising and publicity campaigns have been waged by both sides on controversial issues such as abortion and gun control. In addition, certain corporations (following Mobil Oil's lead) run "issue advertisements" in which they take public stands on broad questions affecting business and government. The increase in cause advertising has provoked the suggestion that marketing could be applied to U.S. foreign affairs policy, including issues of war and peace.[28] In fact, advertising was heavily used by private organizations in the United States to raise funds for the Nicaraguan "Contras" in their war against the Sandanista regime.

■ SUMMARY ■

1. Marketing's newer adherents fall into two broad categories: (1) profit-seeking organizations (or individuals) that have realized the importance of marketing in reaching their goals; and (2) nonprofit organizations that have reached similar conclusions.
2. In the areas of professional services, health care, and entertainment, businesses new to the marketing concept are conducting marketing research, focusing on market segments, positioning their products against competitors, and developing sophisticated marketing mix programs.
3. Market and marketing research, advertising, and other promotional efforts are the marketing tools that have been employed most widely by nonprofit organizations.
4. In nonprofit settings, marketing has been applied by higher education staff, by nonprofit health providers, by public service organizations, government organizations, religious organizations, and political candidates.
5. Many large nonprofit organizations now employ a director or vice president of marketing.
6. Nonprofit organizations often have several "customers" (or publics) to serve whose needs and goals may conflict at times, thereby complicating the setting of objectives for the organization.
7. Nonprofit organizations' difficulties in choosing goals and measuring success are often complicated by the pressure of public interest and scrutiny.
8. In developing their marketing efforts, nonprofit organizations consider the basic characteristics of services: intangibility, buyer and producer participation, perishability, and lack of product standardization.
9. As each type of nonprofit organization analyses its market, it must develop an understanding of the consumer behavior most relevant to its operations.
10. The planning process for a nonprofit organization will generally include a clear statement of purpose, such as a mission statement.
11. Promotion is the marketing mix element most readily adapted by nonprofit organizations.
12. Social marketing is practiced by governments, nonprofit organizations, and for-profit business firms; its most visible element is social advertising.

☐ Key Terms

cause marketing	platforming	public service organizations
nonprofit organizations	publics	social marketing
person marketing		

☐ Chapter Review

1. Describe the marketing mix that a firm of certified public accountants would use.

2. Both profit-seeking and nonprofit hospitals are new to marketing, but both are adapting rapidly. In what ways are their marketing efforts likely to differ?

3. What marketing approaches might be used to market a star group such as The Bangles?

4. Name three government organizations and discuss the products or services that they market.

5. In your view, is it appropriate to use marketing and advertising techniques to "sell" political parties to the voters?

6. What would you expect to find in the mission statement of a symphony orchestra?

7. What is the major distinction between social marketing and other types of marketing?

☐ *References*

1. Paul N. Bloom, "Effective Marketing for Professional Services, *Harvard Business Review,* Sept.–Oct. 1984, p. 102; Doris C. Van Doren, Louise W. Smith, and Ronald J. Biglin, "The Challenges of Professional Services Marketing," *Journal of Consumer Marketing,* Spring 1985, pp. 19–27.

2. Robert E. Hite and Joseph A. Bellizzi, "Consumers' Attitudes toward Accountants, Lawyers, and Physicians with Respect to Advertising Professional Services," *Journal of Advertising Research,* June–July 1986, pp. 45–54.

3. Susan A. Lynn, "Segmenting a Business Market for a Professional Service," *Industrial Marketing Management,* vol. 15, Feb. 1986, pp. 13–21.

4. "Doctors Are Entering a Brave New World of Competition," *Business Week,* July 16, 1984, pp. 56–61.

5. M. Lynn Folse, "Marketing Staffs Give Hospitals a Shot in the Arm," *Advertising Age,* Nov. 8, 1984, p. 14.

6. Mitchell Shields, "HMO: Does Anyone Really Know What It Is?" *Adweek,* May 5, 1986, pp. 38, 40.

7. Richard Edel, "HMO Growing Pains Felt Industry Wide," *Advertising Age,* Dec. 15, 1986, p. S-6.

8. Louis Wershing, "Stage and Screen Put to the Test," *Advertising Age,* Dec. 12, 1983, pp. M-9, M-10.

9. Lynn Berling-Manuel, "Giants Weathering Bay City Blues, Family Fun Comes to the Forefront," *Advertising Age,* Aug. 2, 1984, pp. 10–11.

10. Liz Murphy, "Market or Perish!" *Sales and Marketing Management,* May 13, 1985, pp. 50–53.

11. "Bob Tisch Is Putting More Zip in the Post Office," *Business Week,* Nov. 24, 1986, p. 72.

12. Kevin McManus, "Ads Replace Bell for Modern Mann," *Advertising Age,* Jan. 14, 1985, p. 48.

13. "Making of a Landslide," *Newsweek,* Nov.–Dec. 1984 (Special Issue), p. 87.

14. Philip Kotler, *Marketing for Nonprofit Organizations,* 2d ed. (Englewood Cliffs, N.J.: Prentice-Hall, 1982), p. 482.

15. Quoted in Alan Rosenthal, "Museums Jump into the Marketing Game," *Advertising Age,* Sept. 27, 1982, p. M-2.

16. Benson Shapiro, "Marketing for Nonprofit Organizations," *Harvard Business Review,* Sept.–Oct. 1972, pp. 123–132.

17. Adapted from William Lazer and James D. Culley, *Marketing Management* (Boston: Houghton Mifflin, 1983), p. 827.

18. Charles W. Strang, "Research Gives Schools Competitive Edge," *Marketing News,* Sept. 12, 1986, p. 30.

19. Brett C. Johnson, "Variables of Health Care Demand Cautious Branding," *Marketing News,* Feb. 28, 1986, pp. 10–11.

20. George Keller, *Academic Strategy: The Management Revolution in American Higher Education* (Baltimore: Johns Hopkins, 1983).

21. "Skillful Marketers Will Survive Health-Care Shakeout," *Marketing News,* Sept. 26, 1986, pp. 4, 14.

22. Arthur C. Sturm, Jr., "Hospitals Developing Brand Strategies," *Advertising Age,* Oct. 7, 1985, p. 44.

23. Charles B. Weinberg, "Marketing Mix Decision Rules for Nonprofit Organizations," in Jagdish N. Sheth, ed., *Research in Marketing* (Greenwich, Conn.: JAI Press, 1980), pp. 191–234.
24. Kari E. Super, "Hospitals Seek Diagnosis for Chronic Targeting Ills," *Advertising Age,* Dec. 15, 1986, pp. S-3, S-5.
25. Karen F. A. Fox and Philip Kotler, "The Marketing of Social Causes: The First 10 Years," *Journal of Marketing,* vol. 44, Fall 1980, pp. 24–33.
26. Philip Kotler and Gerald Zaltman, "Social Marketing: An Approach to Planned Social Change," *Journal of Marketing,* vol. 35, July 1971, pp. 3–12.
27. Mona Doyle, "Cause Marketing Wins 3-1," *Adweek's Marketing Week,* Nov. 17, 1986, p. 24.
28. Michael H. Morris, "Is the Cold War a Marketing Problem?" *Business Horizons,* Nov.–Dec. 1985, pp. 55–59.

CASE 23

PARKER PEN

Global marketing has had its success stories, but Parker Pen is not one of them. The company's experiment in centralized and standardized international marketing came to a crashing halt by the end of 1984.

Parker Pen had long been one of the world's best-known brands. By the 1980s, Parker was selling writing instruments in 154 countries. Parker's multinational operations had traditionally been successful in part because of the company's decentralized approach. In the early 1980s, for example, more than 40 advertising agencies around the world were working on various Parker Pen accounts.

But everything changed in 1982 when James R. Peterson became Parker's chief executive. Peterson, previously with R. J. Reynolds, was a staunch advocate of a unified global marketing approach. In his view, Parker's packaging, pricing, promotional materials, and especially its advertising should all be centralized and standardized. With this in mind, Peterson hired Ogilvy & Mather in mid-1982 to handle all Parker's worldwide accounts. One especially damaging consequence of this decision was evident in the United Kingdom, Parker's largest profit center. The London-based Lowe-Howard Spink agency—headed by Frank Lowe—had produced remarkably successful ad campaigns for Parker Pen. But Frank Lowe was fired by Peterson, a move greeted with dismay by many within the company.

Peterson also raised eyebrows by deciding to vigorously pursue the lower end of the market. Along with Manville Smith, whom he had hired to serve as president of the writing-instruments group, Peterson drew up "the Janesville strategy." Lower-priced pens were to be produced in volume at Parker's new and fully automated plant at its Janesville, Wisconsin, headquarters.

By early 1984, Peterson and Smith were ready to focus on their global marketing plan. Three new executives were brought in to help define and implement Parker's international marketing efforts: Richard Swart, Jack Marks, and Carlos Del Nero. These executives, known formally as Group Marketing, ran a gathering of the firm's international managers in March 1984. Swart later wrote of the meeting: "The concept of marketing by centralized direction has been discussed and consensus was reached."

But failure was just ahead. The company's new $15-million plant in Janesville suffered repeated production problems. Costs skyrocketed as the factory turned out a staggering number of defective products. Jack Marks recalls that at one point Parker sent out a shipment of new pens to Ogilvy & Mather, but "they came back to us and said, 'My God, these pens don't write.' " The agency then discovered that Parker's refills, made of a new ink formula, also didn't work.

The disarray at the plant contributed to the firing of Manville Smith in April 1984. Smith, however, had been the only member of the new management team who resisted the notion of "one-look" advertising. With Smith's departure, Peterson took charge of the company's advertising and insisted that pens be sold the same way everywhere. Directives were issued from Janesville, stating:

> Advertising for Parker pens . . . will be based on a *common* creative strategy and positioning. . . . The worldwide advertising theme, "Make your mark with a Parker," has been adopted. . . . [It] will utilize similar graphic layout and photography. It will utilize an agreed-upon typeface. It will utilize the approved Parker logo/graphic design. It will be adapted from centrally supplied materials.

Many Parker subsidiaries and distributors protested this policy, arguing that advertising should be developed with the needs of local markets in mind. Even Ogilvy & Mather personnel strongly opposed Parker's "one world, one brand, one advertisement" standard. But, as one long-time Parker veteran reflects: "Centralization was . . . rigidly enforced. A country manager responsible for millions of dollars of business was told, ' "There's your book [of advertising]; get on with it.' "

According to Mitchell Fromstein, president of Parker's Manpower subsidiary: "That advertising hit the wall and crashed." Fromstein adds that the Janesville strategy of producing low-cost pens for the world was ill-advised because it ran counter to Parker's tradition and image. In his view, "Wrong thinking led to flawed strategy, and the flawed strategy was rejected by the Parker culture." Instead, management should have realized that the pen business consisted of "little pockets of entrepreneurial activity around the world" that were not susceptible to a centralized, standardized approach.

With ad campaigns failing, sales of pens lagging, and production difficulties persisting at the Janesville plant, Parker reached a crisis point. Peterson resigned under pressure in January 1985 and was replaced as chief executive officer by Fromstein. He immediately brought together the pen group's country managers and told them: "Global marketing is dead. You're free again." The trio of Del Nero, Swart, and Marks was gone within months, and the writing instruments group was eventually sold to a group of Parker's international managers and a London venture capital company.

Source: Joseph M. Winski and Laurel Wentz, "Parker Pen: What Went Wrong? Why Company Global Marketing Plan Foundered," *Advertising Age*, June 2, 1986, pp. 1, 60–61, 71.

1. Did the campaign at Parker Pen fail as a result of fundamentally flawed strategy, poor implementation of the strategy, or both?
2. What do you consider the major advantages and the major disadvantages of a global marketing strategy such as that attempted by Parker Pen?

■ CASE 24

McDONALD'S

If you visit Japan, you can stop at a *Makudonarudo* for a *biggu makku* and a milkshake. You can also order a Big Mac in Mexico, Switzerland, and Thailand. If current negotiations are successful, you may even be able to get McDonald's specialties in Hungary and Yugoslavia. In short, McDonald's has become a global marketer. In 1985, the company opened 220 restaurants outside the United States, almost 40 percent of all new McDonald's locations. It now operates in 42 countries, and foreign sales account for one-fifth of the overall $11-billion yearly figure.

McDonald's has taken this course primarily because foreign expansion is viewed as the central element in the firm's future growth. The domestic fast-food market has reached a stage of maturity, growing at a real rate of only 1 percent per year; and Burger King, Wendy's, and other chains are offering serious competition for the U.S. fast-food dollar. For these reasons, McDonald's has placed new emphasis on the untapped potential of the international market.

There are difficulties, of course, in taking McDonald's food products across the world—even to countries where few citizens have ever eaten a hamburger. Thus far, the cost of doing business overseas tends to be higher than in the United States, reducing profits. For example, although international operations produced 24 percent of corporate revenues in 1985, they accounted for only 18 percent of operating income and a still lower percentage of net profit.

Another difficulty faced by McDonald's global operations is the strength of local competitors. Even if the company opens stores in a foreign country not yet penetrated by Wendy's or Burger King, it must compete with local restaurants whose offerings are closely tied to the native culture. In Singapore, for example, street vendors in open-air stalls sell roughly $1 billion per year of noodles, chili, crab, and Chinese vegetables. Patrons of these stalls will not necessarily give up these local specialties for a Big Mac and an order of fries.

In one response to the cultural differences among its international markets, McDonald's permits certain menu modifications to serve particular markets. In a Brazilian McDonald's, you can buy a soft drink made from the guaraná, an Amazonian berry. In Southeast Asian stores, you can get milkshakes made of durian, a local fruit rumored to be an aphrodisiac. At the same time, however, most international McDonald's outlets largely stay with the food products that have made McDonald's successful. "If I wanted to do something with shark fin, I would fail miserably," admits the managing director of a McDonald's in Hong Kong. "People know we don't know how to make shark's fin here."

Local input—with substantial autonomy—has been a critical aspect of McDonald's global expansion. The company operates wholly owned subsidiaries in such countries as Canada, West Germany, and Australia, but it relies more frequently on joint venture partners to assist its entry into new markets. These partners, usually local businesspeople, typically are granted a 50 percent interest in the new business. "They drive us with new ideas and more stability," reports Jack M. Greenberg, McDonald's chief financial officer. "They are more aggressive and more innovative because their stake is greater." Such arrangements underscore the company's long-term success in building mutually profitable relationships with its franchisees—a legacy of McDonald's founder, Ray Kroc.

The company franchises not only its well-known products but also its standardized procedures. The rules for operating a McDonald's outlet are detailed in lengthy operating manuals; they cover such details as how often bathrooms must be cleaned and how hot the grease should be when frying potatoes. McDonald's sets exacting standards as well for its international suppliers. "McDonald's maintains very rigid specifications for all the raw products we use, which is the key to consistency," suggests Robert Kwan, the managing director of a McDonald's outlet in Singapore.

Although international outlets are expected to adhere to these strict standards, McDonald's managers are given leeway to use their entrepreneurial skills to develop marketing methods best suited to the local culture. As one part of this effort, McDonald's usually hires a local corporate staff, in part to improve relations with the country's public officials and entrepreneurs. "We try to come on like a local company, not 'Big Mac Yankee dog,'" notes McDonald's president, Michael R. Quinlan.

The success of McDonald's operations all across the world has shown that there is indeed a sizable foreign market for U.S. fast food. "The fact that [because] it's U.S., it's magic . . . , that wore off a long time ago in Singapore," says Robert Kwan. "The key now is the total experience of coming to McDonald's."

Source: "McWorld?" *Business Week*, Oct. 13, 1986, pp. 78–82, 86.

1. In your own words, describe the McDonald's strategy for penetrating foreign markets.
2. Name three or four major reasons for McDonald's success as a multinational marketer.

CASE 25

SAVE THE CHILDREN FEDERATION

"Imagine, the cost of a cup of coffee can help save a child," pleads Paul Newman or Bonnie Franklin. We have all seen such print ads or television commercials in which major Hollywood stars ask us to help needy children by contributing to the Save the Children Federation (SCF). But, despite their admirable goal, these public service ads have come under fire in recent years for misrepresenting the nature of SCF's aid program.

Save the Children Federation, now the nation's oldest and best-known private child sponsorship agency, was established in 1932. In its early decades, the agency grew primarily through its one-to-one direct sponsorship approach whereby donors could provide cash and clothing to particular children. In return, donors receive snapshots of the children they were aiding as well as brief biographies and quarterly progress reports. Correspondence between donors and the children was encouraged; some relationships continued as the children went through school and became adults.

By 1986, Save the Children Federation was running projects in 43 countries and had a budget of $62 million. It claimed 126,000 child sponsorships across the world and in Indian reservations within the United States. But, since the mid-1970s, the agency has moved away from its direct sponsorship approach—a relatively ineffective method of improving the lives of the needy—to more broadly defined community development work. For example, SCF funds were used in the creation of agricultural and nutrition training centers in the Dominican Republic and the digging of wells in drought-plagued Cameroon.

Why, then, has the agency continued using ads which suggest that it is primarily engaged in direct sponsorship of children? Quite simply, other marketing approaches have proven to be unsuccessful. "We certainly have no intention of deceiving anybody," claims a top SCF executive. "We've got to be sufficiently interesting to get people's attention. It's a real problem for us."

Yet many contributors and even SCF staffers are critical of the misleading ads. One field director admits that "many [staffers] have asked that the ads be more representative of what we're actually doing." Through pressure from New York State regulatory agencies, SCF advertisements now include a disclaimer that donors do not sponsor individual children. But the ads still underscore the message of direct support by asking donors to check boxes on mail-in forms concerning the preferred sex, race, and nationality of the child whom they wish to sponsor.

Source: Richard Behar, "SCF's Little Secret," *Forbes*, Apr. 21, 1986, pp. 106–107.

1. What is your assessment of the effectiveness of the SCF marketing program?
2. In light of the good being done for needy communities, should SCF's less-than-candid advertising be continued?

CASE 26

BOY SCOUTS OF AMERICA

In 1984, the Boy Scouts of America asked its advertising agency—Foote, Cone & Belding (FCB)—to devise a public service campaign aimed at obtaining more corporate backing. And, for 1985, the Boy Scouts needed a campaign that would help local Scout councils to attract new scouts. Consequently, the FCB team developed a recruitment campaign linking Boy Scouts to a group widely viewed as the last U.S. heroes: the nation's astronauts.

"We were looking for something with a broad base of appeal," notes FCB account supervisor Paul Iffland. While researching alternatives, the agency discovered that 90 of the 120 astronauts had been Boy Scouts. This solidified the agency's decision to introduce a campaign connecting the two groups. "We were looking for truly heroic aspiration figures, and there are so few these days," recalls copywriter Bill Hentz. "[The astronauts] have got more of 'The Right Stuff' than any other group America has going. The pieces fell together very naturally."

The agency's creative team worked up a poster and print ad that assembled the commemorative insignia patches designed for the 47 NASA space missions from 1961 through mid-1985. Hentz pointed out that a connection could be made between the NASA patches and the Boy Scouts' own patches. Therefore, the print ad informs readers that "Before they wore these . . . " (before the astronauts wore their NASA mission patches), "they wore this" (the Boy Scouts' patch). It concludes with the message: "Join the Boy Scouts of America."

After developing the poster and print ad, FCB's creative team then produced television and radio spot commercials using the same themes. The radio spot used the astronauts' names (rather than their patches) to establish the link between the astronauts and the Boy Scouts.

The initial response to this public service campaign—from the astronauts asked for permission to use their names, from the national board of the Boy Scouts of America, and from the viewing public—was extremely positive. FCB executive art director Arnie Blumberg observed that the campaign "helps bring Scouts into the twentieth century. You don't get the feeling of old-fashioned when you look at this." Account supervisor Paul Iffland adds that "we're making a long-term commitment to this theme."

Source: Debbie Seaman, "FCB 'Patches Up' Boy Scouts' Image," *Adweek*, Sept. 23, 1985, p. 62.

1. What, if anything, do you see as the weakest part of this public service advertising campaign for the Boy Scouts?
2. Major advertising agencies often work without fees for public service clients such as the Boy Scouts. In this case, do you think the campaign will be done as well as the agency's commercial advertising?

■   ■

APPENDIX A

Financial Implications
of Marketing Decisions

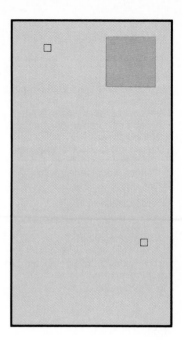

This book is about marketing, and the things men and women who work in marketing do to carry out that major function in organizations. In the real world of business, or of other organizations, marketing and other business functions (such as manufacturing and finance) must work together to achieve the organization's objectives. An especially important interface is the one between marketing, on the one hand, and accounting and finance on the other.

Marketing managers must keep in mind that there are financial implications in all their actions. From setting prices to establishing advertising budgets, marketing actions affect the financial health of the organization. This appendix clarifies the financial implications of marketing decisions.

☐ *Operating Statement*

The major financial statements of any organization are its operating statement, sometimes referred to as the income statement or the profit and loss statement, and the balance sheet. Exhibit A-1 is a typical operating statement for a small retail shop, Beth's Bicycle Barn.

The operating statement is the more important one in viewing the financial effects of marketing actions. We will look closely at three elements of the operating statement: sales, gross margin, and income from operations.

SALES   The top line on the operating statement concerns marketing. The sales organization, the advertising efforts, and the other aspects of the marketing program have a direct effect on the sales of the firm. Note that Beth's sales for the year were $108,000, but with a reduction for returns and allowances of $8000 she was left with net sales of $100,000.

That figure of $108,000 is the result of selling some number of bicycles, parts, and repair services in Beth's Bicycle Barn. Each one of those sales to customers resulted in a pricing decision—2 bicycles at $125 is sales of $250; 10 tires at $12.95 is sales of $129.50. The $108,000 for the year is the sum of all those transactions at specific prices. So price, as an element in the marketing mix, has a key role to play in determining the level of sales.

Where do the "returns and allowances" come in? For a variety of reasons, some customers returned the products they purchased. If the product was faulty, or damaged, then

Operating statement for the year ending December 31, 1987.

Sales		$108,000
Less sales returns and allowances		8,000
Net sales		100,000
Less cost of merchandise sold		
Merchandise inventory, January 1	$ 9,400	
Net purchases	76,600	
Merchandise available for sale	86,000	
Merchandise inventory, December 31	11,000	
Cost of merchandise sold		75,000
Gross margin		25,000
Operating expenses		
Selling expenses	$ 7,700	
General expenses	9,000	
Interest expense	3,000	
Total operating expenses		19,700
Income (loss) from operations		5,300
Less income tax		1,300
Net income (loss)		$ 4,000

Beth very likely gave the customer full credit on the merchandise, which is referred to as a *return.* If the product was only slightly damaged, such as a scratch in the paint, Beth may have arranged to let the customer keep the merchandise but returned some of the money, which is an allowance. The sum of all those transactions resulted in the $8000 for the year.

We have stressed throughout the book that customer service is important to the success of marketing efforts. Part of the cost of providing that service shows up as returns and allowances. In discussing product decisions, we mentioned that deciding about product quality is important. The higher the product quality, the less likely the product will be returned. Product returns will also depend on ability to satisfy customers.

COST OF GOODS SOLD   In any organization, a key to financial results is in the cost of the products sold. In a retail store such as Beth's, the cost of goods sold is figured on the inventory of products she offers for sale. (If Beth were a manufacturer, she would have inventories of raw materials, work in process, and finished goods.)

When the year began, Beth had an inventory valued at $9400. During the year, she made purchases of additional products totaling $76,600 and was left with an inventory of products at the end of the year of $11,000. The result is that the cost of the merchandise which she actually sold during 1987 was $75,000. When that cost is subtracted from her net sales of $100,000, she is left with a gross margin of $25,000.

Just as sales are a result of some quantity multiplied by Beth's selling price, her cost of goods sold is a result of a quantity purchased multiplied by a cost figure, which is her supplier's price. The difference between her cost and price is made up of various kinds of discounts, which we discussed in Chapter 16. Beth's financial success will be strongly affected by the skill she shows in buying the right merchandise—the products her customers want to buy—at a cost which will give her an adequate gross margin to operate her store profitably.

OPERATING EXPENSES   Operating expenses are the costs, other than for merchandise sold, which Beth must incur to operate a retail store. Selling expenses include advertising, wages for a salesperson, and other marketing costs. General expenses include rent, a salary for Beth, and other operating costs. In 1987, these costs totaled $19,700. When that amount is subtracted from the $25,000 gross margin, Beth was left with a profit from operations of $5,300. After paying her income tax, Beth had a net income of $4,000.

Of particular importance to marketing is the control of the selling expenses. In discussing the marketing planning process in Chapter 9, we showed how firms must carefully forecast sales and use those forecasts to develop marketing mix programs which meet target financial returns. For instance, if Beth had been incurring advertising and other selling expenses during the year based on a sales forecast of $200,000 instead of the sales she actually had, she could very well have lost money in 1987 instead of making a profit.

☐ *Analytical Ratios*

The financial statements of an organization provide more than just a record of the results of operations. They are used to make a number of calculations designed to tell the managers in the organization how well they are doing. We will show some of these calculations and discuss how they can be used to evaluate the results of marketing efforts.

RETURNS AND ALLOWANCES TO SALES   The formula for this ratio is:

$$\frac{\text{Returns and allowances}}{\text{Net sales}}$$

In the case of Beth's Bicycle Shop, that is:

$$\frac{8000}{100,000} = 8 \text{ percent}$$

That figure of 8 percent is not very meaningful by itself, but it can be used in various ways. When compared with a similar ratio computed in prior years, it can be seen to go down, which is desirable, or to go up, which can be a sign of declining product quality or lower customer satisfaction levels. It can be computed for different suppliers' products. If the returns and allowances for one brand of bicycle are significantly above or below the average, Beth can use that fact in future buying decisions.

STOCKTURN RATE   It is useful to know how well inventory is turning over. The stockturn rate is a measure of the relationship between what is sold for the year, and the average inventory during the year. The formula is:*

$$\frac{\text{Cost of goods sold}}{\text{Average inventory (at cost)}}$$

Since there is no figure for average inventory (at cost) in the operating statement, we need to show how it is calculated. The formula becomes:

$$\frac{\text{Cost of goods sold}}{(\text{Beginning inventory} + \text{ending inventory})/2}$$

For Beth's, that is:

$$\frac{\$75,000}{(\$9400 + 11,000)/2} = \frac{75,000}{10,200} = 7.4$$

This means that Beth was able to sell 7.4 times her average inventory. Since it costs money to keep merchandise in inventory, as we discussed in Chapter 14, the stockturn rate should be appropriate to the particular kind of business. Again, the number 7.4 is not particularly meaningful by itself, but it allows Beth to compare her results with those of other businesses like hers. She can compare it with the figures reported by the trade association to which she belongs, the American Association of Bicycle Shops.

---

*Other ways to compute the stockturn rate would be to divide sales by average inventory at selling price, or to divide the units sold by the average number of units in inventory.

GROSS MARGIN PERCENTAGE   The formula for this ratio is:

$$\frac{\text{Gross margin}}{\text{Net sales}}$$

which in Beth's case is:

$$\frac{25,000}{100,000} = 25\%$$

This figure tells the manager what the average margin is on all merchandise sold during the year. It may be that bicycles have a gross margin on 20 percent, tires on 35 percent, and so forth. Again, the real value in knowing this is that Beth can compare her results with others in similar businesses. As much as any other factor, knowing the gross margin percentage is useful in making pricing decisions.

OPERATING EXPENSE RATIOS   The purpose of computing operating expense ratios is to control costs and to evaluate performance. As we pointed out in Chapter 21, usually there are standards to use for comparison. These can be similar figures from previous years or industry averages reported by trade associations. The formula is:

$$\frac{\text{Total operating expenses}}{\text{Net sales}}$$

which in Beth's case is:

$$\frac{\$19,700}{100,000} = 19.7\%$$

Managers compute a number of similar ratios. The purpose is to control individual expense categories, such as selling expenses, which were 7.7 percent for Beth's in 1987. It is useful to compute advertising costs as a percent of sales, and other such ratios, which can be compared with those of previous years or with industry standards.

NET PROFIT PERCENTAGE   Finally, it is often useful to know the ratio between net profits (the bottom line) and net sales. It is the ratio which takes into consideration not only prices and gross margins but also expenses and net profit or income. The formula is:

$$\frac{\text{Net income}}{\text{Net sales}}$$

which in Beth's case is:

$$\frac{\$4,000}{100,000} = 4\%$$

This tells Beth that for every dollar in sales during 1987, she made a profit of $.04. While that doesn't sound like very much, it is common for many kinds of retail operations.

RETURN ON INVESTMENT   Many managers believe that the most useful financial ratio is to compare the return they earn, the net income in a particular year, with the amount of money that is invested in earning that return. There are several similar ratios, and all require that the manager look not just at the operating statement, but also at the **balance sheet.** Exhibit A-2 shows a simplified balance sheet for Beth's Bicycle Barn.

EXHIBIT A-2	**Beth's Bicycle Barn**

Balance Sheet, December 31, 1987.

Assets

Current assets	$36,000
Store and equipment	49,000
Total assets	$85,000

Liabilities

Current liabilities	11,500
Long-term liabilities	40,000
Total liabilities	$51,500

Owner's Equity

Paid-in capital	30,000
Retained earnings	3,500
Total owner's equity	$33,500
Total liabilities and owner's equity	$85,000

In computing return on investment, it is important to define carefully what you mean by "investment." This is accomplished by labeling the kind of return in which you are interested. For example, one measure of interest is to compare what was earned, the $4000 from the operating statement, with the total assets that were employed to earn that amount. That is the more traditional return rate commonly referred to as return on investment, or ROI. The formula is:

$$\text{ROI} = \frac{\text{net income}}{\text{average assets}} \times 100$$

As with the operating statement, the balance sheet reports the condition of the firm at a specific point in time; there is no "average assets." The total assets of $85,000 on December 31 is composed of a collection of items—inventories, accounts receivable, cash, and others. Because those numbers change every day, to compute ROI it is necessary to compute average assets. One common way of doing that is to take an average of the assets at the beginning and end of the year. For our purposes, we can assume that they were the same, so average assets are $85,000. Beth's ROI by this method is:

$$\frac{\$4000}{85,000} \times 100 = 4.7\%$$

Put another way, for each dollar of assets at Beth's Bicycle Barn, the earnings for 1987 were 4.7 cents. It is useful to compare this figure with those from prior years, and with similar figures for other bicycle retailers. By accounting standards, assets equal liabilities plus owner's equity. This is a measure of the return on assets regardless of the source of those assets—the owner's equity or debt (liabilities).

Another useful way to look at return is in terms of return on the owner's equity, ROE. This is a measure of the return, again in the net income of 1987, with the amount of money the owner has invested in the business. The formula is:

$$\text{ROE} = \frac{\text{net income}}{\text{owner's equity}} \times 100$$

In Beth's case, that is:

$$\frac{\$4000}{33,500} \times 100 = 11.9\%$$

This figure is particularly useful for any owner, because it can be compared to any alternative investment. If that measure of return falls below what Beth could earn on her money in a bank's certificates of deposit or a money market fund, then she would be better off not being in business.

☐ *Markups and Markdowns*

Marketing intermediaries, wholesalers and retailers, make use of financial analyses which are especially important to businesses that buy finished products to resell. Those are measures of **markups** and **markdowns.**

MARKUP   A markup is based on the difference between the cost of an item and the selling price. For instance, assume that Beth purchases an individual item, a bicycle, for $100 and sells it for $140. The **dollar markup** is $40. The percentage markup is computed two ways, as a *markup on cost,* and as a *markup on sales.* They are computed as follows:

$$\text{Markup on cost} = \frac{\text{dollar markup}}{\text{purchase cost}} \times 100$$

For the bicycle in question, that is:

$$\frac{\$40}{\$100} \times 100 = 40\%$$

$$\text{Markup on sales} = \frac{\text{dollar markup}}{\text{sales price}} \times 100$$

For our bicycle example, that is:

$$\frac{\$40}{\$140} \times 100 = 28.6\%$$

Both of these figures are used in various ways by wholesalers and retailers. Markup on cost is often used as a method of setting prices. Retailers, for instance, establish standards for markups which can be used by employees to price merchandise. If Beth has established standard markups on cost such as 40 percent on bicycles, 50 percent on repairs, and 60 percent on parts, then as merchandise arrives, any employee can calculate selling prices to put on the merchandise.

Since many retailers use markup on sales as a measure of their own margin, it is useful to be able to convert from one markup to the other. The following formula is used to convert a markup on cost to a markup on sales:

$$\text{Percentage markup on sales} = \frac{\text{percentage markup on cost}}{100\% + \text{percentage markup on cost}} \times 100$$

Using our bicycle examples:

$$\frac{40\%}{100\% + 40\%} \times 100 = 28.6\%$$

Similarly, the formula used to convert from markup on sales to markup on cost is:

$$\text{Percentage markup on cost} = \frac{\text{percentage markup on sales}}{100\% - \text{percentage markup on sales}} \times 100$$

Using the bicycle example:

$$\frac{28.6\%}{100\% - 28.6\%} \times 100 = 40\%$$

MARKDOWN   Markdowns are downward adjustments on prices of goods already in the store. Usually they are made on products which have not sold very well. They are particularly common in the retailing of merchandise which has a fashion cycle, such as clothing. For instance, when retail stores will have an end of season sale, they "mark down" the goods in the store. Markdowns are usually based on selling price, not cost. The percentage markdown is the measure of how well the inventory planning has been done. This markdown percentage, or ratio, is computed as follows:

$$\text{Markdown percentage} = \frac{\text{dollar markdown}}{\text{net sales in dollars}}$$

Beth's has purchased 40 bicycles at $100 each, and has sold 35 of these at the regular price of $150. The end of the season has arrived and the remaining 5 bicycles will be considered last year's models next spring. Beth marks these 5 bicycles down to $110, and is able to sell all 5.

   Since Beth has marked the 5 bicycles down $40 each, total dollar markdowns are $200. Net sales in dollars is the sum of the sales of 35 bicycles at $150 ($5250) and the sale of the 5 bicycles at $110 ($550), or $5800. The markdown percentage calculation is:

$$\frac{\$200}{\$5800} = 3.4\%$$

These markdown calculations allow managers to measure the effectiveness of buying decisions. In a large department store, it is common to use measures of percentage markdowns as comparisons across departments. At Beth's Bicycle Barn, the comparison may be across product lines or from year to year.

APPENDIX B

Careers in Marketing

□ ***The Most Important Product You Will Ever Market—Yourself***

When you finish this book, and the course in which it is used, you will have a good idea of what marketing products and services involves. We now invite you to think of yourself as a service to be marketed. For your entire career, you will provide a service to your employer, for which you will be paid. Just as introducing any product on the market without a good marketing plan doesn't lead to success, nor will managing your career without a good plan produce the results you want.

□ ***Analyzing the Career Opportunities***

Environmental changes will affect the success of a marketing plan for your career, and you should carefully assess these. At a minimum, you should carefully assess yourself, the state of the economy when you seek the job, and the industry and organization in which you might like to work.

SELF-ASSESSMENT   You should analyze your strengths and weaknesses in relation to a professional career. One goal should be finding a career that fits both your capabilities and your interests. Your formal education is an obvious place to start—clearly, you cannot be a brain surgeon without proper training; but formal education is only part of the story. Your own personality, interests, and problem-solving styles are also important. Some people are extroverts; some are oriented to analytical tasks; some work better with people than with numbers. There are ways to find out what is right for you. Perhaps your guidance counselor in high school has already helped you with this kind of assessment. Perhaps your college or university can provide you with that kind of opportunity. Your family, close friends, and faculty advisor are sources of insight that can be part of your self-assessment.

This appendix is based largely on works prepared for student use by the Office of Career Development and Placement Services of the Pennsylvania State University. Special thanks are due to Dr. Jack R. Rayman, director.

ECONOMY   The laws of supply and demand affect the outcome of exchange relations in the world of products, and they will affect your job search—employment tends to follow the economic cycle. When the economy is healthy—interest rates low, gross national product (GNP) on the rise, inflation under control—then employment prospects are good. When the country is in a recession, the outlook is bleaker, and jobs are less plentiful.

Assess the state of the economy and research how that state has affected the climate for professional employment in the career to which you are drawn. Current issues of regular publications such as *Business Week Careers* (published six times per year) or *Peterson's Business & Management Jobs* (published annually) will be useful. If your college or university has a placement service, the professionals there can be most helpful.

INDUSTRY AND ORGANIZATION   When starting a career, one normally starts fairly low on a career ladder that will include several promotions to higher levels of responsibility and reward. The speed with which those advances come will depend on many things, including your own performance. Another important determinant of how fast you are promoted is the growth of the organization in which you work. To some degree, picking a company and industry which are growing over ones whose major growth is over may be wise.

For instance, in early 1987, one study projected the 10 "best" industries for the future: (1) restaurants, (2) food stores, (3) electronic components, (4) data processing and computer services, (5) securities brokers and dealers, (6) hotels and motels, (7) plastic products, (8) nonfood retailing, (9) communication equipment, and (10) accounting and bookkeeping.[1] Not only are these industries likely to hire graduates for management careers, but also their growth will provide more opportunities for advancement.

Within any industry, whether growing rapidly or more mature, some organizations are doing better than others. In most cases, working for winners is better than working for losers. Some research into the health and growth of individual companies is likely to be well worth the effort. Look for a competitive winner in a high-growth industry. Information on the performance of individual companies can come from faculty members who read the business press regularly and from a library search. The *Business Periodicals Index* is a good source for tracing what has been written about individual companies. Sometimes the best growth outlook is for smaller companies rather than for the well-known large corporations, and a search there may be fruitful.[2]

☐ *Planning the Job Search*

Before jumping into the job market in your last semester in school, develop a plan for the first step in your career. Develop some realistic long-term goals for your career as well as short-term goals for the first job. One very useful point to keep in mind is that the first job is just the start of a career and as such is a continuation of your education. Many companies like to start new marketing professionals in a selling position, because people in the sales organization are the closest to the customers, calling on them directly. That firsthand knowledge of customers is a very valuable asset throughout a career in marketing.

As you develop your plan, the key ingredient will be your understanding of the alternative career paths in marketing. Exhibit B-1 lists positions in marketing and describes each position's major duties.

Experts say that the job search process takes at least 6 months, so start early and give yourself plenty of time. Your job search plan should state your goals and address your own career aspirations. Consider the long-term financial rewards you expect and the projected balance between the demand for and supply of individuals in that career path. Consider the following in developing your career goal statement:

1. What do you want to do? Identify the skills you would like to use and the interests you would like to incorporate. Define one, two, or three types of jobs you would like.
2. Where would you like to live? Identify your ideal geographic location.
3. What type of an employer would you like? Identify the desirable type of organization, e.g., large corporation, university, nonprofit organization.

Marketing Research

- Assists managers with defining problems and identifying the information needed for their solution
- Designs studies
- Collects and analyzes data
- Prepares reports and presentations of findings and recommendations to management
- Uses background in statistics, psychology, and sociology for job-related tasks

Advertising

Advertising Manager
- Heads advertising department of retail organizations, manufacturing companies, and other business organizations
- Works with the advertising agency employed by their company

Account Executive
- Works for an advertising agency
- Acts as liaison between the agency and the client

Copywriter
- Creates ideas, images, and slogans
- Provides advertising content

Media Buyer
- Purchases ad space and time
- Works with media representatives to get the best visibility (reach, frequency) for dollars spent

Customer Relations

- Responds to customer complaints and questions
- Follows up sales
- Acts as liaison between company and customer

Distribution

- Gets goods to the right place at the right time
- Takes responsibility for varied tasks, including: customer service, demand forecasting, distribution communications, inventory control, materials handling, order processing, parts and service support, location analysis, procurement, packaging, salvage and scrap disposal, traffic and transportation, and warehousing and storage

Public Relations

- Plans and carries out a broad variety of activities designed to enhance communications between a business and society, including the organization's employees, stockholders, customers, and governments
- Writes reports, press releases, and speeches; edits employee publications; works with media, makes appearances; supervises advertising concerned with the company's name or image; and develops and implements communication goals
- Uses a strong background in journalism, English, and public speaking

Sales

Wholesale
- Calls on retailers and buyers
- Represents wholesale organization which purchases for resale
- Negotiates transactions
- Handles transportation and storage
- Gives customers technical advice

Retail
- Assists customers
- Demonstrates merchandise
- Arranges for delivery of goods
- Records sales

☐ *Implementing the Job Search*

If your college or university has a placement service, its professional staff will help implement your job search. Indeed, seeking their help may be the most important step you take in the job search. The following steps should help you make the process work:

1. Develop a list of prospective employers.
   a. Find resources to use to identify possible employers, e.g., directories, telephone books, professional associations, journals.
   b. Write your list of prospective employers.

Purchasing
- Buys raw materials, machinery, supplies, and other services required for the business
- Negotiates cost, quality, quantity, and timing

Product Management
- Takes responsibility for success or failure of a single product or product line
- Handles research and development, packaging, manufacturing, sales and distribution, advertising, and analysis and forecasting
- Usually starts out in a sales position
- Receives what is considered good training for future corporate officers

Retailing

Buyer
- Deals with assortment and selection of goods
- Travels frequently

Section Manager
- Takes responsibility for inventory and promotions

Regional Manager
- Runs activities of several stores within a certain geographic area

Department Manager
- Manages sales force

Industrial Marketing
- Works with sales, service, product design, and marketing research
- Frequently requires a technical background
- Usually starts out in sales

International Marketing
- Has experience in domestic operations
- Speaks foreign languages fluently

Direct Marketing
- Interacts directly with seller
- Uses direct mail, telephone, and television
- Participates in exciting, growing field (projections by the year 2000 are that half of all consumer dollars will be spent through direct marketing)

Buyer
- Carries on much research
- Uncovers unmet needs
- Predicts fads

Catalog Manager
- Coordinates entire marketing campaigns
- Ensures that correct audience is picked, right products are offered, and right message is presented

Research/Mail-List Management
- Determines what products will sell and what mailing lists are valuable

Order Fulfillment and Management
- Ensures that orders get where they should when they should

Fund Raising
- Most all nonprofitable organizations are direct marketing
- Uses the same tools as direct marketers—mail, telephone, and television—for raising funds

Marketing Management Science/Systems Analysis
- Acts as consultants to managers
- Works with model building, forecasting, new-product evaluation, and market structure analysis
- Usually has an MS or MBA

---

    c. Write a list of people who might be helpful in your job search, e.g., alumni, friends and family members, colleagues, members of clubs and organizations.

    d. Write a list of contacts who can help expand your list of prospective employers.

2. Gather information about your prospective employers.

    a. Who do you know who works there, has contact with someone who works there, or knows about the employer? Write their names under the name of the prospective employer they are linked to.

    b. Identify the questions you want to ask them.

    c. Contact them and arrange for a brief interview to obtain information about the employer.

d. Read the literature you have compiled about employers, e.g., from public relations offices—annual reports, brochures, company magazines, newsletters; from a chamber of commerce; from newspapers; from libraries.

3. Prepare to meet employers.

   a. Compose a current résumé cover letter.

   b. Practice your interview skills. Make sure you can:

      (1) Initiate contact for an interview.

      (2) Discuss your skills.

      (3) Relate your experience to the job.

      (4) Maintain good eye contact, relaxed posture, and enthusiasm.

      (5) Follow up with a phone call for information.

   c. Know the employer. Review the preliminary background research, your conversations with people who work there, and all the printed material you read.

   d. Decide if you are interested enough in the organization to want to work there.

4. Contact target employers.

   a. Initiate interviews.

      (1) Arrange for the interview in advance. Know the name and title of the person to whom you wish to speak—a person who has the power to hire you. Ask for at least 30 minutes.

      (2) Explain the purpose of your meeting as soon as the interview begins, e.g., "I have spoken with several people in your organization and done some reading about it. From all I have heard and read, I am interested in discussing the professional opportunities available here."

      (3) Ask a few questions, but let the interview progress smoothly. Don't come on too strong; let your assertive statements about your skills experiences do the work.

      (4) Take your cues from the employer. Don't push for an answer about employment. Ask what you should do to enter the profession. Let your interest in the organization shine through.

      (5) Keep in touch if nothing happens immediately.

   b. For employer-initiated interviews, plan your response:

      (1) Identify resources which list job vacancies.

      (2) Set up a specific time which you will devote to sending cover letters and résumés to the advertised employees.

      (3) Assess your progress frequently.

☐ *The Résumé: A Key to Communicating Your Skills*

The résumé is often the most critical item in determining whether you will obtain an interview. It usually represents the initial screening, so you need to demonstrate in your résumé that you have the knowledge, abilities, and experience for the job you seek. You may need several versions of your résumé for different types of jobs. Tailor the résumé to each type of job; a general, "generic" résumé gets far fewer interviews.

There is a variety of résumé formats. Ideally, your résumé should emphasize your strong points while expressing your individuality. Choose and arrange categories so that the most relevant information is placed to catch the reader's eye. Don't copy a friend's résumé just because it worked for her or him. Instead, read other résumés as sources of ideas for yours.

The three most popular résumé formats are chronological, functional, and targeted. The *chronological résumé* presents your education, extracurricular activities, and work experience with skills and achievements described in reverse chronological order under each category (See Exhibit B-2). An objective can be included but is not required. The advantages of a chronological format are that employers are comfortable with it—it is the most widely used format; it is easy to write; you can display solid achievements whether you state a job objective at the outset or not.

The *functional résumé* organizes your skills and accomplishments into functional (job task) groupings that support your job objective, which should be stated. A functional résumé

GEORGE BLACKWELL

Campus Address (until 5/15/86)
817 Academy Avenue, Room 10B
Indianapolis, Indiana 46208
(317) 283-9962

Home Address
25 Veronica Road
Newton, Massachusetts 02165
(617) 332-3426

EDUCATION

BUTLER UNIVERSITY, Indianapolis, Ind.; BA expected May 1988 Major in *psychology* with a broad range of courses, including statistics, social psychology, organizational development, and economics
GPA: 3.2 in major
Melanie Cottle Award for best psychology project: "A Marketing Plan to Attract More Applicants to the University"

CAMPUS ACTIVITIES

- Residence hall counselor, 1987–1988; supervised and planned activities for 300 undergraduates
- Selection committee for dean of students, Spring 1987
- Varsity swim team, 1984–1986
- Area coordinator of Campus Fund Drive: raised $18,000 after developing marketing strategy and training volunteers

WORK

MARKETING CONCEPTS, INC., Boston, Mass.
Research assistant, Summer 1987
- Persuaded customers to respond to a 20-minute phone interview on home finance
- Coded and tabulated research questionnaires
- Drafted research report for management

HAGLAND'S DEPARTMENT STORE, Housewares Department, Newton, Mass.
Assistant manager, Summer 1986
- Supervised and trained sales staff members
- Researched suppliers and introduced new line of disposable dinnerware
- Provided merchandising department with suggestions about customer preferences

Salesperson, Summer 1985
- Recognized for tactful dealings with difficult customers
- Opened highest number of new charge accounts in 1 month
Earned 60 percent of college expenses through summer jobs and school-year employment as a pizza deliverer, cashier; worked 10 to 15 hours per week

PERSONAL INTERESTS

Backpacked through Scotland and Wales, traveled in England, France, and western United States; played roles in student Gilbert & Sullivan productions

REFERENCES

Available upon request

---

draws attention to what you've done rather than when or where you did it; it allows you greater flexibility in presenting skills gained through personal experience (spending a junior year abroad) or through low-paying or unpaid jobs (baby-sitter, Sunday school teacher); and it works well for entry-level or reentry employees whose employment histories are brief or scattered.

The *targeted résumé* focuses on a specific position or job target, presenting your capabilities and accomplishments supporting that position, eliminating all unrelated data. A job target or objective is, of course, required. A targeted résumé is very powerful because it is very focused—you look like a "natural" for the position if you have done the necessary background research. This résumé projects your ability to do the job even if you don't have directly related experience, and you can easily prepare a different version for each position for which you apply.

1. Name and address
   a. Avoid labels such as "résumé," "personal data sheet," or "vita."
   b. While in school, include both a permanent and local address and a telephone number where you can be reached easily.
   c. Consider irrelevant in most cases: age, health, marital status.
2. Job objective (also called "career objective," "position desired," etc.)
   a. Keep to one or two concise, easy-to-read sentences.
   b. Focus on a type of job—avoid a too general description.
   c. Avoid clichés or jargon, such as "to contribute to the profitability of my employer," or "challenging position."
3. Education
   a. Don't include high school and colleges you transferred from unless necessary; but do include study abroad if relevant.
   b. List degrees in reverse chronological order—most recent first. Mention grades if to your benefit—they are optional information.
   c. Keep the information concise and easy to scan.
   d. Include details relevant to the job you are seeking, such as those courses, special projects, minor, area of emphasis that the employer would not automatically know you've had.
4. Experience
   a. Do not limit your experience to paid employment—include relevant extracurricular activities and volunteer positions.
   b. Reverse chronological order for usual form.
   c. If necessary, break into two major categories, such as "related work" and "other work," to put the most relevant items together.
   d. Give details of your accomplishments and responsibilities rather than a general list of duties: "supervised eight cashiers" or "worked hotline at all hours, responding to crises such as drug overdose, suicide threats, husband abuse, problem pregnancy."
   e. Include only information and skills that relate to the position you are seeking; omit irrelevant facts.
   f. Make the format scannable and put the most relevant words first.
   g. Do not be discouraged if you have never had employment in your field, since most students lack this; instead focus on your strengths, skills, and accomplishments.
5. Activities
   a. List the most relevant activities and offices held first.
   b. Add brief explanatory details of the position and your accomplishments if helpful.
   c. Add individuality and flavor to your résumé by including unusual or interesting items.
   d. Include college, community, and, occasionally, outstanding high school activities.
6. Honors
   a. Include only if you have several honors.
   b. Include in the activities section if desirable.

Cover and Other Letters

Personally delivering your résumé to a prospective employer is usually preferable, but today's job candidate will not be able to do so in every instance. However, never mail a résumé without a cover letter. The primary purpose of the cover letter is to acquaint the prospective employer with your unique talents and skills and to arrange an interview to discuss employment possibilities. Because a résumé is included with each cover, do not duplicate what it says. The cover letter should highlight your résumé by identifying how you are qualified for the position and why hiring you will be advantageous. State the reasons for your interest in that particular employer.

The cover letter should be as brief as possible, usually limited to one page. If possible, the letter should be addressed to the individual responsible for hiring. A description of the important elements to include in the letters to prospective employers follows:

1. Tips for preparing a cover letter
   a. Never mail a résumé without a cover letter.
   b. Address by name and title the individual with the power to hire you, if at all possible.
   c. Plan your letter before you write it.
   d. Adapt the letter carefully to conditions of job opportunity.
   e. Open with an idea that captures the attention of the prospective employer so that the letter and résumé are considered worth reading.
   f. Highlight the points in your résumé that make you uniquely qualified for the position.
   g. If you are unsure what jobs are available, include one or more questions in the cover letter that require a response to preclude a form letter reply.
   h. Close your letter with a request for an interview.
   i. Avoid jargon and trite language.
   j. Use a good stationery and type the letter in a professional manner—never use mimeographed form letters.
   k. Finally, pay special attention to grammar, spelling, and neatness. Consider having a friend or relative review your letter prior to sending it.
2. Acceptance letter of second interview or job offer
   a. Be businesslike, but tailor your letter to the specific employer so that you sound sincere and genuinely interested in the company and job; never copy example letters.
   b. Write to the person who wrote and/or interviewed you.
   c. Thank the person and/or show your enthusiasm for the offer.
   d. State what you are accepting.
   e. Concisely yet descriptively give some details about what has impressed you about the company and/or interview.
3. Rejection letter—be courteous by turning down a plant trip or job offer graciously.
   a. Write to the person who wrote you.
   b. Thank her or him for the offer.
   c. Briefly state that you are declining and why (don't get too personal).
4. Thank you letter (optional)—after you have had a campus interview and especially after an interview associated with a company visit, sending a thank you letter is a simple matter of courtesy.
   a. Send the letter as soon after the interview or visit as possible; express your appreciation for the opportunity to present yourself.
   b. Express your continued interest in the position and company; include some details that impressed you; find a nice way to personalize your letter and convey your interest.
   c. Supply any additional information requested at the visit or interview.
5. Letter of acknowledgement—when an offer is received, pay special attention to the preparation of your response letter.
   a. Transmit prompt acknowledgment of receipt of offer to the prospective employer.
   b. Express your appreciation for the offer.
   c. Notify the company of the date by which you expect to make your decision so that you respond within their time limitations.
   d. Acknowledge receipt of a rejection letter—Don't take this rejection letter as a definite no! A demonstrated interest in the company and respectful letter may lead to further consideration for other positions as they become available. Thank the interviewer for considering your application, indicate that you are still interested in a position with the company, and give some specific information to illustrate what you like about the company, position, or both.
6. Letters of inquiry of application's status
   a. Request an explanation of the status of your application.
   b. Recap the history of your application, including the date your cover letter was sent to the company.

c. State why you need clarification of the status of your application.

d. Include thanks for their cooperation.

7. Letter seeking additional information

    a. Indicate interest in the company and its offer.

    b. Ask for the information which you need. Be as specific as possible!

    c. Express your appreciation for the cooperation that you receive.

☐ *Interview Skills*

The interview is the single most important step in the job search process, and thorough preparation is essential. To be interviewed effectively you need to know the employer and the kind of position you want. You must be able to answer questions with relevant details and in a conversational manner. Exhibit B-3 lists questions you might ask and be asked.

What is the purpose of an interview? All interviews have two major questions in mind: (1) How suited are you for the job? (2) Are you genuinely interested in the employer and position? Interviewers try to get enough information about your background, strengths, and level of interest to answer these questions. In addition, as a prospective employee, you need to learn as much as you can about the position and workplace to decide if they are what you want.

What can you expect in an interview? You need to be ready to handle a variety of interview formats, from the highly structured to the unstructured. Most initial, 30-minute interviews are semistructured and include ice breaking for 2 to 3 minutes, interviewer's questions for 10 to 12 minutes, applicant's questions for 8 to 10 minutes, and closing remarks for 2 to 3 minutes. Most interviewers are friendly and want you to feel relaxed. There are many styles of interviewing, just as there are many styles of teaching, and some recruiters will make you more comfortable than others.

What is the best approach to answering questions? Recruiters are surprisingly accurate in sensing "canned" answers that give no interesting or reliable information about you. When you answer, remember these guidelines:

- There is no single right answer. *How* you answer often is more important than what you say.

- Be honest. Don't pretend, for example, that you were sure about your major from the very start if, in fact, you weren't. The details about how you did choose your major may be much more interesting and communicate some very positive things about how you make decisions.

- Don't look for ulterior motives—some questions are asked purely out of curiosity or to help you relax. Recruiters are not going to conclude that you lack sufficient interest in the field if your favorite course was not related to your major. A genuine answer is almost always more interesting.

- Give details and examples. General responses are boring and don't help the recruiter get to know you. Be specific. Details illustrate your points and make answers more vivid and memorable. When discussing one of your strengths, give an example or two to illustrate that strong point. When mentioning the course you liked most, give some details to illustrate what you liked and why.

- Stay focused and don't ramble. Give details that are relevant, but don't tell long stories that include unnecessary details. Some candidates repeat themselves when they haven't thought of how to wrap up the answer. Respond directly and succinctly.

- Keep the position in mind. What details can you give that are relevant to the type of job you are interested in? When you think of some, remember to include them. For example, if you worked at a summer camp and are now looking for a sales position, mention how you persuaded participants to enjoy your programs.

What is the interviewer usually look for? Most employers seek signs of preparation, pleasant personality, specific career goals, good communication skills, a professional appearance, and relevant experience. The following include some typical employer comments:

Questions Job Hunters Ask	What You Might Be Asked
■ What is the principal job of this department?	Tell me about yourself.
■ What are the duties of the person in the job?	Why should I hire you?
■ What kind of person are you looking for?	What do you want to do?
■ How do the people in the job allocate their time?	Why do you want to work in this field (job, company)?
■ What is the job's most important responsibility? The least?	What do you know about our company?
■ Where are the last three people who held the job working now?	Why did you major in _____?
■ What is your biggest problem?	What was your favorite course?
■ What might be my role in solving it?	What is more important to you—the salary or the job itself?
■ To whom would I report?	What are your greatest strengths? Weaknesses?
■ What is the background of my potential boss?	Which two or three accomplishments have given you the most satisfaction? Why?
■ Who are the other people with whom I would work?	What contributions could you make to this job (department, company)?
■ What are the job holder's most important relationships—clients, customers, other employees?	How have you handled a major crisis or problem?
■ Where would I be situated? What kind of equipment is there?	What are your short-term and long-range goals?
■ Are there performance reviews?	What do you expect to be doing in 5 years? in 10?
■ What kind of schedule do you work? How flexible is it?	How much would you like to be earning in 5 years?
■ What is the job's salary range?	What do you like to do in your free time?
■ What about bonus, profit sharing, and pensions?	What books or magazines do you read?
■ Does the company pay for insurance, vacations?	Are you willing to relocate?
■ What professional associations and publications are important?	What three people in public life do you most admire?
■ What learning opportunities are there?	Why did you decide to interview with our company?

1. Preparation: Knowledge of, and interest in, the employer. "Had researched our company and was prepared with questions about job duties and how she would be evaluated." "Had a genuine interest (as opposed to I need any job) in my company." "The interviewee was prepared with intelligent questions that he had written down."
2. Personality: Confidence, friendliness, enthusiasm, poise, assertiveness. "She enjoyed the interview." "Showed enthusiasm for an opportunity to work in an area he has studied and liked." "Sincere and honest. Not a 'snow job.'"
3. Career goals: Interest in specific jobs or job types. "She had a definite idea of what they wanted. She demonstrated this in the nature of her direct questions." "Had talked with people in the field and knew what the work involved." "Had specific, sincere reasons why he was interested in the position."

4. Communication skills: Conversational and nonverbal skills. Good posture, plentiful eye contact, and tone of voice are as crucial as content of conversation. "Relaxed, smiled, and appeared to be following what was said. Gave the impression of being compatible with fellow employees." "I don't like a hard-sell type of candidate, but I like people who come in talking and really take off with my questions. I want students to take control of the interview up to a point." "Gave specific and examples that were relevant but did not ramble."
5. Appearance: Neat, professional dress. Not overly flashy or made up. "Well-groomed and businesslike dress." "Neat appearance, conservatively attired."
6. Experience: Awareness of own skills and how they relate to the world of work. "He can relate just a little job experience to long-term employment." "The best candidates were active in sports or clubs, or had work experience. They were comfortable interacting with people." "Undertook responsibilities other than just being a student."

What reasons do recruiters give for rejecting candidates? Negative impressions often result from the following:

1. No enthusiasm: Answers often short; tone of voice lacks interest or color.
2. Vague answers: No details given, words are general and not relevant to the type of job.
3. Very fidgety: Little eye contact, many nervous mannerisms such as playing with hair and rubbing hands.
4. Know-it-all attitude: Lack of sincerity; attempts to show off all knowledge about the field; superficial remarks to impress the interviewer.
5. No career direction: No idea what they want in a job. Unable to show how their skills and experiences prepared them for work in any field.

New Advances in the Job Search Process

COMPUTERIZED RECRUITING   Computerized recruiting matches job candidates and employers through résumé databases. To list your credentials on a résumé database, you fill out a form which asks for information such as job objective, area of study, degree(s), geographic preferences, special skills, and date that you are available. A printout of your electronic résumé is sent to you for your approval.

Getting your résumé listed is relatively inexpensive (around $8, and sometimes free, depending on the service you sign up with). The employers who subscribe to the résumé database services cover the costs by paying for on-line computer access time and/or annual fees. With its growth in popularity, computerized recruiting could be a valuable asset to your job search process. For additional information on computerized recruiting contact: Career Placement Registry, Inc., 302 Swann Ave. Alexandria, VA 22301, 800-368-3093; CARI, Inc., 1501 Woodfield Rd. Schaumburg, IL 60195, 1-800-221-5637; or JobNet, Inc., 10 De Angelo Dr., Bedford, MA 01701, 1-617-275-3010

COMPUTERIZED JOB SEARCH   Another computer aid in the job search process is computerized job search. Companies and organizations pay to run job advertisements or company background information on computer terminals located at colleges and universities. The student can find data on potential employment based on such information as educational standing (junior, senior, graduate, etc.), major field of study, geographic preference, and type of work desired (full-time, summer, internship, etc.).

After narrowing the possibilities, the computer presents the choices most closely matched to the job seeker's preferences. Job advertisements are updated on a regular basis, and thus students are always presented with new opportunities. Computerized job search is relatively new in many areas, but it is sure to become an invaluable tool in the job search process.

☐ *References*

1. Steven S. Ross, "10 Top Industries for the Future," *Business Week Careers,* Spring–Summer 1987, pp. 21–24.
2. Mark O'Brien, "How to Pick a Growth Company," *Business Week Careers,* Oct. 1984, pp. 75–76. *Inc.* Magazine is another good source for smaller high-growth companies.

Dictionary of Marketing Terms

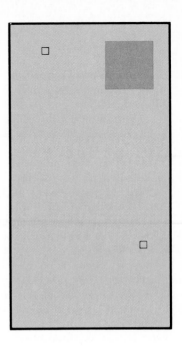

A

Accessory equipment The machines and materials that do not become integral parts of the purchaser's product.

Account A buying organization to which one is already selling (a customer) or to which one would like to sell (a prospect).

Account action plan A plan specifying which steps (and when) the territory manager intends to take to achieve account objectives.

Account analysis Evaluation of all accounts in a territory.

Account executives Advertising agency personnel who serve as liaisons between the client and the agency.

Account planning A detailed analysis of the buying organization in which the marketer prepares a set of specific actions to achieve account objectives.

Account potential The total amount of goods and services purchased by the buyer that could be purchased from the seller.

Account/product matrix A method that allows territory managers to combine two measurable factors in selling: the account potential determined in the account analysis process, and product line projections.

Account services department A section of an advertising agency which helps the client to devise an overall campaign strategy that determines a product's target market, how the product is to be differentiated from those marketed by competitors, and which aspects of the product should be stressed.

Acculturation The process of learning the values and norms of a culture other than the culture in which one was first socialized.

Accumulation The process through which wholesalers and retailers collect quantities of products from numerous sources.

Action plan The crucial intermediate step between the formulation of marketing strategy and the implementation of that strategy, the action plan sets forth specific steps which lead to implementation.

Administered VMS An informal vertical marketing system in which the channel leader exercises power through persuasion, or through providing something which the other channel members value.

Administrative measures (on imports) Methods of limiting importation of goods into a country that take the form of excessive paperwork, delay of approvals, and other similar practices.

Adoption process A process which is made up of the stages that individuals, households, or organizations go through in accepting an innovation.

Advertisers The identified sponsors who pay to promote their goods, services, and ideas to target audiences.

Advertising Any paid form of nonpersonal communication, usually delivered through mass media by an identified sponsor.

Advocacy or issue advertising Advertising which takes a stand on some issue on behalf of the advertiser; is not designed to promote products.

Ageism Prejudice and discrimination against the elderly.

Agents (brokers) Intermediaries who help bring manufacturers and retailers together and arrange sales for a commission payment; they do not take legal title to products.

All-you-can-afford approach   The strategy of setting the advertising budget as high as possible.

Allocation   The process through which intermediaries apportion products to their own divisions or to other resellers in quantities they believe consumers will want.

Annual operating plan   A method through which global marketing organizations control their worldwide subsidiaries; the subsidiaries operate under plans which have been approved by the parent company.

Area (cluster) sample   A process in which researchers choose a sample based on geographical location, such as counties within a state, or blocks within a city.

Artificial intelligence (AI)   The science of getting computers to simulate human thought processes.

Assorting   The process by which different brands, models, sizes, colors, and price ranges are brought together to arrive at an assortment desired by the consumer.

Attitude   A predisposition toward some aspect of the world that is positive or negative, but never neutral.

Augmented product   A good, service, or idea enhanced by its accompanying benefits; a synthesis of what the seller intends and the buyer perceives.

Average fixed costs (AFC)   The result of dividing total fixed cost (TFC) by the number of units produced.

Average revenue (AR)   The same as the unit price, calculated by dividing total revenue by the quantity sold.

Average variable cost (AVC)   The result of dividing total variable costs (TVC) by the quantity of a specified production level.

B

Backward integration   The approach by which the intermediaries acquire control over manufacturers.

Balanced product portfolio   A proper mix of new, growing, and mature products whose sales provide the cash flow to ensure long-term prosperity.

Bait-and-switch promotion   A practice through which the retailer brings buyers to the store with advertising for a bargain price on a product which is not in adequate supply with the intent of switching the buyer to a higher-priced product.

Basic price   The amount marketers estimate consumers will pay for the core product.

Benefit segmentation   The process of segmenting markets based on the benefits sought by consumers.

Benefits   Those attributes which satisfy the perceived needs of a target market and stimulate those consumers to act.

Biogenic needs   Human needs which are inborn and have their genesis in the physiology of the organism, such as needs for food, water, and protection from extreme temperature.

Birthrate   The number of births that occur in a given year per 1000 people in the population.

Brand   A name, term, symbol, or design or a combination of them that is intended to identify the goods or services of one seller or group of sellers and to differentiate them from products of competitors.

Brand competitors   Other companies which also manufacture the same product.

Brand image   The overall concept of the product as perceived by consumers.

Brand insistence   The phenomenon that occurs when consumers demand a certain product and will go out of their way to get it.

Brand mark   The part of a brand which can be recognized but is not utterable.

Brand name   The part of a brand which can be vocalized—the utterable.

Brand nonrecognition   The fact that people do not know the existence of the brand.

Brand preference   The attitude taken by consumers who have tried a brand and have at least moderately positive attitudes toward it.

Brand recognition   The simple awareness that a product exists, apart from competing products.

Brand rejection   The rejection of a brand by a consumer who has had negative experience with it.

Breakeven analysis   A method for calculating what quantity of product the firm needs to sell just to cover all costs.

Business libel   Making an unfair or untrue written statement about a competitor.

Business logistics   The overall process of managing the flow of goods from raw materials and components through production, storage, and transportation into the hands of consumers and buyers.

Business slander   Making an unfair or untrue oral statement about a competitor.

Buy-phase concept   The concept that views organizational purchasing as a series of sequential steps proceeding from recognition of a need through evaluation of the product's performance in satisfying that need.

Buyers   Those who carry out the formal arrangements for purchase, service, delivery, and financial terms.

Buying center   The collective term for people who participate in purchase decisions.

C

Cannibalization   The situation that occurs when part of the new product's sales come from reductions in sales of the firm's other products.

Carrying costs   Expenses associated with storage, product depreciation and obsolescence, and taxes and insurance premiums.

Cash cows Dominant and mature businesses that require minimal reinvestment and contribute funds for other, growing businesses in the company.

Cash discounts Price reductions given to buyers who pay for purchases within a stated period; they are not cash payments.

Cash-and-carry wholesalers Wholesalers who emphasize reduced costs for small retailers, but do not provide credit or delivery.

Catalog showrooms Stores that display discounted merchandise in both catalogs and in-store displays, carrying a broader range of merchandise than warehouse showrooms.

Central business districts Areas where many retailers are clustered together to take advantage of each other's traffic.

Central values The deeply held, enduring beliefs that guide our actions, judgments, and specific behaviors, and that support our efforts to realize important aims.

Cents-off coupons Coupons that offer buyers minor price reductions at the point of sale.

Channel (medium) The vehicle for transmitting a message.

Channel length The number of levels in a distribution channel.

Channel strategy Decisions which center on choosing and attracting the most effective types and the most efficient number of distributors in the best geographical locations.

Channel width The number of intermediaries found at the same level in the channel.

Characterization attributes Those attributes used in advertising which associate the product with the kind of people who use it.

Closed bidding The bidding in which contract terms are kept secret, and suppliers are expected to make their best bids first.

Closing The step of the selling process in which sales representatives ask prospects to make positive exchange decisions.

Coaching A process consisting of making sales calls under the supervision of a sales manager or a trainer.

Cognitive dissonance Psychological discomfort produced by doubts about the wisdom of something we have done.

Combination plan Salary plus some type of bonus or commission.

Combination store Stores that carry over-the-counter and prescription drugs in addition to food items.

Combined transportation modes A transportation method which utilizes more than one type of carrier.

Commercialization A process in which marketers establish full-scale production, set prices, lay out a distribution network, and make final promotion plans to introduce the product in all its markets.

Commission merchants Merchants who receive goods on consignment from producers, take the merchandise to a central market, sell at the best price possible, deduct their commission, and remit the balance to the producer.

Common carriers Those transportation providers which offer their services for the use of others, and are under certain governmental regulations concerning the provision of such services.

Communication The process of sharing meaning through the use of symbols.

Communications flow The movement of information through the channels of distribution; includes the flow of promotion from manufacturers through intermediaries to consumers, and the flow of market information from consumers back through intermediaries to manufacturers.

Community shopping centers Shopping centers which typically have 10 to 40 stores; most include a large supermarket and also may be anchored by a department store.

Company sales forecast The total dollars and units of all the organization's products sold during the time specified in the forecasts for individual products or businesses.

Compensatory model A model which assumes that consumers judge a limited number of product attributes, that the attributes vary in importance to the consumer, and that strength in one area compensates for weakness in another.

Competitive advantage That part of a firm's total market offering which is superior to that of its competitors.

Competitive advertisements Advertisements that create selective demand—that is, a preference for the advertiser's brand as opposed to a competitor's.

Competitive parity approach A method used for budget setting when firms wish to equalize the impact of advertising so that they can compete on some other marketing mix variable, such as price or distribution.

Components Raw materials or parts and subassemblies that become integral elements of the buying organization's products.

Concentrated marketing The strategy of focusing on a single, easily defined, profitable market segment.

Concept testing A process involving the accumulation and evaluation of consumers' reactions to a new-product idea before the product is actually developed.

Confirmatory research Research performed to provide information, usually of a statistical nature, that helps managers reduce risk in decision making.

Conflict resolution Accommodation of various channel members to decisions designed to promote the overall goals of the distribution channel.

Consolidated metropolitan statistical area (CMSA)

An area that includes more than one metropolitan or primary statistical area.

Constant dollar The report of economic variables after they have been adjusted for inflation so they can be compared across many years.

Consumer advertisements Those advertisements directed at people who might want the product for their own use, and for use by the household.

Consumer behavior The acts of individuals that involve buying and using products, including the decision processes that precede and determine these acts.

Consumer cooperatives Organizations that are formed by consumer groups to purchase (mostly) foodstuffs in bulk in order to receive the same discount that business-based intermediaries do.

Consumer markets The most visible markets, which consist of individual customers who buy products for their own use or for use by other members of their households.

Consumer-oriented positioning The strategy aimed at getting the consumer to perceive a product in some unique, personally related manner, regardless of the product's characteristics.

Consumer product A good or service purchased by an individual for personal or household use.

Consumer salespeople People who sell goods and services to intermediaries or directly to ultimate users.

Containerization The practice of consolidating quantities of goods into easily handled, sealed containers.

Contests Strategy that requires consumers to compete for prizes, typically by completing some type of puzzle or stating why they like the product "in 25 words or less."

Continuity The strategy of scheduling the advertising evenly over the weeks and months of the year.

Continuous innovation A product that offers a clear improvement over what it replaces and yet is enough like the old product that it does not really change how we normally use it.

Contract carriers Private businesses that shippers may engage for transportation services under private agreements.

Contractual VMS Members of a channel are independently owned, but some of the cooperation of a corporate vertical marketing system is achieved through legal agreements.

Controllable variables Those factors directly or primarily under the control of the marketing organization, e.g., product distribution, pricing, and promotion.

Convenience products Products that are widely available, usually inexpensive, and frequently purchased.

Convenience sample A sample chosen at the convenience of the researcher, such as the first 100 individuals to be found who are members of a population.

Convenience stores Stores featuring convenience: long store hours (often 24 hours each day), ease of access, and quick shopping for items such as bread, milk, eggs, cigarettes, and newspapers.

Cooperative advertising A form of promotion in which the manufacturer makes available to the wholesaler—or more commonly to the retailer—a fund intended to help cover the cost of the channel member's advertising which features the manufacturer's brand.

Copyright The exclusive legal right to reproduce, publish, and sell a literary, musical, dramatic, or artistic work.

Core benefit The need that a product fulfills or the problem it solves.

Core product The basic good or service purchased, aside from its packaging or accompanying services.

Corporate advertising Campaigns formerly known as public opinion, image, or institutional advertising—media space or time bought for the benefit of the corporation rather than any of its products.

Corporate chains Multiunit retailing organizations operated under central ownership, management, and control

Corporate vertical marketing system (VMS) A channel leader—often the manufacturer—owns all other organizations in the channel.

Cost analysis The reallocation of the natural accounts of financial accounting to the functional accounts of managerial accounting in order to allow managers to control marketing costs.

Cost per thousand (CPM) The media cost of reaching 1000 persons, used to compare across media vehicles.

Cost-plus pricing A strategy that assumes a basic cost per unit and then adds a markup to provide a margin that covers overhead costs and returns a profit.

Cost/volume/profit analysis An approach which calculates the effect on profits of different prices, given different levels of demand in response to those prices.

Countercultures Subcultures whose values are in conflict with those of the wider society.

Creative boutiques Small agencies specializing in the creative work for an advertising campaign.

Creative execution The process involved in deciding how the message is to be said in an advertisement.

Creative services department The section of an advertising agency which is responsible for the creation, design, and production of whatever will appear or be heard on radio or television or in print.

Creative strategy The primary message to be communicated by the advertising campaign. This is the major responsibility of the advertising agency.

Cross-elasticity of demand The degree to which the quantity of one product demanded will increase or decrease in response to changes in the price of another product.

Cross-tabulation   The method of comparing the responses to one question with the responses to another.

Cues   The minor stimuli that shape people's responses and that support the original stimulus.

Culture   All the things, abilities, and ideas that human beings use, do, know, and believe—everything that one generation of a society transmits to the next.

Cumulative quantity discount   A discount that applies to one buyer's orders over a specified time—perhaps a 6- or 12-month period.

Current dollar   The report of economic variables in actual dollar amounts for the year in which the economic activity takes place.

Customary pricing   Pricing that matches buyers' expectations about the cost of certain items; prices reflect custom and tradition, and changes are infrequent.

Customer profile   A written record of an account, including information such as type of business, buying influences, the product mix, buying policies and practices, environmental influences, purchase criteria, and competitor analysis.

Customer types organization   The organization method which is based on customer groups, such as departments responsible for marketing to each segment.

Cyclical patterns   Changes in sales in an industry caused by changes in the macroeconomy as reflected in such factors as the gross national product or disposable personal income.

D

Death rate   The number of deaths that occur in a given year per 1000 people in the population.

Deciders   Those who have the power and the responsibility to approve a product and select final suppliers.

Decision support system (DSS)   A set of software that allows managers to utilize the capabilities of the other banks without having much computer training and to do so from their own terminals.

Decline stage   A stage in which total demand decreases, leading to a further dropout of competitors until only a few remain.

Decoding   The process of translating or interpreting the symbols of a message to derive its meaning.

Delayed-action advertisements   The advertisements which attempt to influence consumer attitudes and preferences, thus helping to set the stage for a purchase.

Delphi technique   The procedure of environmental forecasting by a group of experts who are solicited anonymously and asked to predict the likelihood and time of occurrence of significant events.

Demand   A relation among the various amounts of a product that buyers would be willing and able to purchase at possible alternative prices during a given period of time, all other things remaining the same.

Demand curve   A curve that specifies the quantities demanded at various prices at a given time.

Demographics   A catchall term referring to particular variables describing populations, such as age or sex.

Demography   The study of the changing characteristics of human populations—factors such as vital statistics, growth, size, density, and distribution.

Department stores   Stores characterized by wide and deep product mixes; individual departments within store; mid- to upper-level prices; and extensive services.

Derived demand   The demand based on expectations of upcoming demand for other industrial or consumer products.

Differentiated marketing   The strategy of pursuing several market segments with particular products and marketing mixes designed for the needs of each.

Diffusion process   A process consisting of communication about, and acceptance of, the innovation throughout the social system over a period of time.

Direct-action advertisements   Advertisements designed to move consumers and customers to take some immediate action.

Direct channels   The channels in which producers sell directly to final buyers; no intermediaries are involved.

Direct exporting   Refers to the marketing firm's active efforts to sell its products, made domestically, in foreign markets.

Direct investment   An arrangement under which an international marketer invests the funds necessary to build or purchase its own facilities in the host country.

Direct marketing   (1) A form of nonstore retailing in which a promotional message is delivered directly to potential customers, who respond directly to the company rather than through a traditional point of sale such as a store. (2) Nonstore sales to consumers and organizational buyers via mail and telephone.

Discontinuous innovation   An innovation which truly changes how we do what we have long been doing.

Discount houses   Stores that are much like department stores except that their primary appeal is low price.

Discounts   The reduction from the list price to be paid by consumers which represents the revenue source for intermediaries.

Discretionary income   The amount of personal income left after paying taxes, and after paying for necessities such as food, shelter, and clothing.

Diseconomies of scale   The effort to increase production results in inefficiencies, such as having to pay higher labor costs for overtime or having to pay more for scarce resources.

Disposable income   The amount of personal income left after taxes.

Distribution channels   Channels that are made up of manufacturers or service producers and the wholesalers and retailers through which products are marketed to consumers and organizational buyers.

District sales manager   A line executive who plans, directs, and controls the activities of field salespeople.

Dogs   Those businesses which have low relative market shares in markets with low growth rates.

Door-to-door selling   A form of direct marketing which involves personal selling to individuals in their homes.

Downward-sloping demand, the law of   The law predicting that when the price of a good is raised, less of it is demanded.

Drop shippers   Organizations which take bulk orders from industrial users, other wholesalers, or retailers; they then order the desired products from manufacturers, who ship directly to the customers.

Dual adaptation   A global marketing strategy whereby both the product and the promotional programs are adapted to foreign market conditions.

Dumping   Selling a product in a market other than the home market at prices below the cost of making and delivering them to that market.

Durable goods   The tangible items that can be expected to survive multiple use.

E

Early adopters   People who try a new product early in its life cycle without waiting for its acceptance by a large number of people.

Early majority   People who adopt the product only after it has been accepted somewhat widely.

Economies of scale   More efficient operations and multiple uses of resources result in decreased costs; average variable costs (AVC) and thus average total costs (ATC) also decline.

80/20 principle   A "law" which states that 80 percent of business in a territory comes from 20 percent of accounts—and, conversely, that only 20 percent of business comes from the other 80 percent of accounts (which is, in reality, only approximate).

Elastic demand   A given percentage change in price results in a greater percentage change in the quantity demanded.

Elasticity of demand   The degree to which the quantity produced and sold will increase or decrease in response to changes in price.

Emergency products   Those products that are usually purchased as the result of urgent needs.

Emotional advertisements   Advertisements that attempt to create moods that will subsequently be associated with the product.

Encoding   The process by which a source chooses signs and symbols to construct a message.

Environmental monitoring   A systematic group of activities designed to anticipate changes in external variables that will affect the organization's ability to meet its goals.

Equilibrium (market) price   The price at the point where supply equals demand.

Ethnic group   The social group determined by culturally transmitted, learned traits.

Evoked set   The subset of available brands of a product class which a consumer considers appropriate alternatives, and from which a choice is made.

Exchange   A transaction between two or more persons, groups, or organizations in which each party gives up something of value and receives something of value.

Exclusive distribution   A system in which a manufacturer grants one retailer the sole right to sell a product within a specific geographical area.

Experience curve   A curve reflecting the fact that the costs of doing something tend to decrease as the organization gains experience doing it.

Experience-curve pricing   A strategy that takes into account the costs of competing firms based on their experience in producing goods.

Experimental method   The method based on the study of the relationship between two or more variables under controlled conditions.

Expert system   A software package that includes a stored base of knowledge in a specialized area, and that has the capability to probe this knowledge base and make decision recommendations.

Exploratory research   Research that consists of informal attempts to identify and define problems.

Export department   An organizational form used by firms which are primarily exporting their products to foreign markets, rather than maintaining marketing organizations abroad.

Export trading company   An organization which provides its exporting expertise and facilities to many small and medium-size firms that could not otherwise engage in multinational marketing.

Express warranty   A warranty written in terms that specify exactly what claims and guarantees the producer is offering.

Extended family   A family including relatives other than parents and their children and spanning all generations of living members, derived from the nuclear family.

F

Fad   A cycle that is different from fashion only in the length of time, which is relatively short.

Fair trade   The practice through which producers attempt to control the retail price of their products.

Family brands   The assignment of the same or similar names to multiple products made by the same company in which the name of the company is often employed.

Family household   A household consisting of two or

more persons living together who are related by marriage or birth.

Family life cycle   Various stages in family life, each with its own characteristics.

Family of orientation   The family into which an individual is born; the family that cares for and socializes us as children and gives us our initial class status.

Family of procreation   The new family established by choosing a mate and rearing children.

Fashion   A cycle usually starting with a designer's need to be different, and his or her sense that the new design will be acceptable to at least a segment of the market.

Feedback   The response or reaction that a receiver may give the source as a result of a message.

Fertility rate   The average number of births per woman.

Financial-relations advertising   Advertising which portrays the corporation as fiscally sound and run by forward-looking management.

Fixed costs (FC)   (1) Recurring expenses that are not tied to the level of production. (2) Expenditures such as managers' salaries, building maintenance, insurance, mortgage payments, and debt service—costs that stay constant whether 5000 or 10,000 units are produced.

Flexible pricing   Charging different prices to different customers usually based on negotiation and bargaining; it is rare but not unknown in the United States in consumer marketing, but is more prevalent in organizational marketing.

Flighting (or pulsing)   The strategy of unevenly timed exposures of advertisements.

F.O.B. pricing   F.O.B. stands for "free on board" and is followed by the designation "factory" or "destination" to indicate at what point the buyer assumes freight costs and title to the product.

Focus group   A small number of 'typical' consumers who discuss their reactions to a product concept in the presence of a group leader.

Follow-up   The final selling step which involves actions after the sale to ensure that the order is received on time and as specified.

Forecasting   The prediction of what buyers in a target market are likely to do under a given set of conditions, such as the prediction of how much of a product will be purchased by a particular market segment given a particular price of the product.

Foreign sales force   An organizational form for global marketing in which the marketer maintains a sales organization abroad to sell to foreign markets, but does not have its own subsidiary companies abroad.

Foreign subsidiaries   An organizational form in which the global marketer establishes its own companies in foreign markets in order to market, and sometimes manufacture, in those markets.

Form utility   The usefulness attributable to the form or design of something received.

Formal information   Information designed as such by the organization; it is received in a planned and systematic manner on a scheduled basis.

Formal sales training   A process used to give new salespeople product knowledge, skill in selling, information about markets and competition, and guidance on company policies and practices.

Forward integration   The approach in which the manufacturers acquire control over wholesalers and retailers.

Franchisors   Suppliers of products and management and marketing expertise that grant *franchisees* (dealers) the right to run chain-like retailing establishments in return for fee and royalty arrangements.

Freight forwarders   Agencies which provide a combining service by which partial shipments (usually under 500 pounds) are assembled from several customers.

Frequency   The number of times, on average, that each person reached will see or hear the advertisement.

Full-service advertising agency   The type of advertising agency that has the resources to offer its clients a wide range of services, including the four most basic services: account management/marketing, creative, media, and research.

Full-service retailers   Specialty shops, boutiques, and top-of-the-line department stores.

Full-service wholesalers   Organizations which provide almost all the functions of intermediaries and generally are divided into three subgroups: general merchandise wholesalers, single-line wholesalers, and specialty wholesalers.

Functional accounts   Accounting units which divide expenditures according to their purpose.

Functional attributes   Things that a product or service does for consumers or customers.

Functional (trade) discounts   Price concessions which compensate intermediaries for providing such services as storage, handling, and selling.

Functional organization   The organization method which divides the marketing operation into groups according to their assigned tasks.

G

Games   Promotional methods that require consumers to take specific actions, such as determining whether the card they received with the product contains a winning number by rubbing it with the edge of a coin, or collecting several cards to produce the winning combination.

Gatekeepers   Those who can control information flow to members of the buying center—and to prospective suppliers.

GE business screen   A technique, developed by General

Electric Company, that includes multiple measures of competitive strength and market attractiveness.

General merchandise wholesalers Wholesalers who handle a broad range of products, from food and drug items to plumbing supplies and automotive accessories.

Generic competitors Organizations which do not offer customers either direct brand or even product form alternatives, but do compete for customers' available funds by providing different solutions for a particular need, such as home repair.

Generic products Products which are not branded, are simply packaged, and usually are priced well below both manufacturers' and private brands.

Geographic pricing Pricing decisions which account for who takes responsibility for transportation charges—the seller or the buyer.

Geographical organization The organization method based on management by region, state, area, nation, or global sector.

Global marketing Refers to any marketing that involves two or more nations.

Government markets The purchasing or leasing of goods and services in order to carry out government functions and to further the public purpose.

Gross national product (GNP) The total market value of all goods and services produced in an economy in a given year.

Gross ratings point (GRP) A unit of reach times frequency; thus, a GRP of 1 indicates that 1 percent of the target audience saw the advertisement once.

Group Two or more people, with related statuses and roles, who interact on the basis of shared expectations about each other's behavior.

Growth-share matrix A matrix that explains how market share, market growth, and cash flows are related.

Growth stage A stage in a product's life in which sales and profits grow rapidly, competitors are attracted to the growing market, and cash flow may still be negative because of the firm's efforts to establish a strong market share ahead of competitors. The market is usually turbulent in this period.

H

Heterogeneous shopping products Products that differ from each other on important dimensions, such as style, design, and personal taste, for which such dimensions tend to outweigh price in the purchasing decision.

Hierarchy of needs A system of needs which includes physiological needs, the need for satisfaction, the need for belonging and love, the need for esteem, and the need for self-actualization.

High-involvement decisions Decisions that generally involve a large sum of money, have personal relevance, demand a search for information, and produce some degree of anxiety about the correctness of the product chosen.

Historical and quantitative forecasts A projection of future sales based on sales patterns and/or mathematical calculations.

Homogeneous shopping products Products among which consumers perceive little difference in the core benefits.

Horizontal conflict The conflict which arises between wholesalers and retailers of the same level and type in a channel.

Horizontal integration The process which brings together a number of channel members at the same level and puts them under single ownership.

Horizontal markets Markets on which products are sold to a wide range of industries.

Hypermarché A very large store (80,000 square feet and up) that adds furniture, appliances, and clothing to the items found in superstores.

I

Ideal self-concept A view of ourselves as we would like to be.

Image advertising Advertising which aims to establish a positive identity for the corporation or to rebut criticism.

Imperfect competition A marketplace where a number of sellers and buyers participate. No single seller or buyer can control the market price, and there is opportunity for differentiation of product offerings.

Implementation control The control of ongoing activities which uses the organization's regular accounting and reporting procedures.

Implied warranties Unwritten warranties that indicate that the product is in good condition and is suitable for the purpose for which it was bought.

Impulse products Those products which the consumer buys without having established intention to buy, often featured on racks arranged prominently and enticingly around checkout counters in supermarkets, drugstores, and variety stores.

In-home retailing Selling that usually takes the form of a small party given by a hostess or host to allow friends and neighbors to examine and order a product line.

In-house agencies Advertising agencies owned by the advertiser, which perform the functions of a full-service advertising agency.

In-pack (on-pack) coupons Coupons that are affixed to the product and allow savings on a future purchase.

Income distribution How thoroughly the income in a nation is spread through the population.

Independent variable The variable that causes an effect.

Indirect exporting A form of global marketing that takes the least effort on the part of the seller; relies on the efforts of export agents who sell the product abroad, often without the specific knowledge of the manufacturer.

Individual brands   Brands which have no obvious connections with the parent company.

Individualized portfolio techniques   Portfolio techniques which develop specific company definitions of business strength, and of market attractiveness, rather than using the simpler definitions of the Boston Consulting Group for those factors of market share and market growth.

Industrial advertisements   Advertising to promote goods and services for business and organizational use.

Industrial markets   Markets made up of organizations which buy in order to produce goods.

Industrial products   Products purchased by an organization for use either in other products or in its own operations.

Industrial salespeople   People who sell goods and services used for producing other goods or for rendering other services.

Industrial services   Services purchased for use in producing the buyer's products or, more frequently, for use in general operation.

Inelastic demand   A given percentage change in price results in a smaller percentage change in the quantity demanded.

Inflation   The rise in the general price level of all goods and services.

Influencers   People whose expertise or opinions have a bearing on the purchase decision.

Informal information   The mixture of unorganized, irregular daily communications which flows to most of us in contemporary society.

Informative advertisements   Advertising for the purpose of creating awareness that the product exists or creating knowledge of the product.

Informative labels   Labels that tell the consumer about the product's ingredients, use, dating, and so on.

Initial approach   The first contact by a salesperson with a prospect, usually to arrange a meeting.

Innovation   A product which is perceived in the marketplace as being innovative.

Innovators   The first users of the new product.

Intensive distribution   A system in which all available and appropriate intermediaries are used.

Interest   The price paid for loaned funds over a period of time, usually expressed as percent per year.

International division   A form of organization under which a special division of the company is responsible for the marketing of all the firm's products throughout the world.

Intertype conflict   The conflict which occurs when different kinds of intermediaries are part of the distribution channel.

Intrapreneurship   A new business term meaning internal entrepreneurship.

Introductory stage   A stage in a product's life in which an innovation is alone in the market.

Irregular events   (1) Random events such as acts of God (e.g., earthquakes, fires, floods). (2) Windfall sales contracts.

J

Joint ownership   An arrangement whereby an international marketer and an organization in the host country create a third organization which they own jointly.

Joint venture   An agreement between a marketing organization and another organization, in the host country, through which the tasks of producing and marketing a product are shared.

Judgment sample   A sample chosen simply by the judgment of the researcher as to which individuals would be representative of the population, and about which no statistical analyses would be appropriate.

Judgmental forecasts   The predictions rely upon the opinions of informed participants or outside consultants.

"Just-in-time" inventory system (or kanban system)   A Japanese inventory management system which is based on reducing the costs of keeping inventory to the very minimum—even though transportation costs may be raised.

L

Labels   A label encompasses any printed information on the packaging that describes the product.

Laggards   Individuals, households, or organizations that resist or never adopt the new product.

Late majority   People who do not adopt an innovation until it is in widespread use and is thoroughly accepted.

Learning   The relatively permanent changes in thought and behavior that result from experience.

Licensing agreement   An agreement under which an organization in the host country is given the right to make the marketer's patented (or patentable) product for sale in that market.

Life cycle extension   The process of finding new uses for the same product by the same users.

Lifestyles   Preferred patterns of living as expressed in a person's activities, interests, and opinions, taken as a whole.

Limited-service retailers   Some department store chains and limited-line stores that concentrate on heterogeneous shopping products.

Limited-service wholesaler   Wholesalers who perform only selected functions.

List price The amount at which a product is priced for final buyers, whether individual consumers or organizations.

Loss leaders (or price leaders) Products advertised below the retailer's cost to increase customer traffic.

Low-involvement decisions Decisions generally made in an instant with little or no influence from social or cultural forces.

M

Macroeconomists Theoreticians who measure, explain, and predict the performance of national and international economies—focusing on the relationships among large units within these systems.

Macromarketers People who examine processes whereby exchanges are created to satisfy the needs and wants of individuals and organizations within a national marketing system.

Mail-order sales A fast-growing form of direct marketing which is carried out primarily through catalogs.

Major equipment Those costly durable goods used in a plant which are also capital expenditures.

Manufacturer's agents (representatives) Promotional wholesalers in a specific geographical area who sell noncompeting products from several manufacturers of related product lines.

Manufacturer's brands Brand names chosen by the products' maker.

Manufacturer's sales branches The form of organization that is owned by the manufacturer and sells to retailers, as do other forms of wholesalers.

Marginal analysis Analysis of the effects of one additional increment of costs or revenues on profit.

Marginal cost (MC) The additional cost incurred by producing and selling one more unit of a product.

Marginal revenue (MR) The additional revenue received from selling one more unit of a product; it constitutes the increase (or decrease) of revenue that results from producing and selling one additional unit.

Market A group of people or organizations that have similar needs and wants, the desire to satisfy those needs and wants, the means of exchange (money) to satisfy their needs and wants, and the ability and authority to make the exchange (purchase).

Market segmentation (1) The division of large, dissimilar populations into smaller, more similar groups. (2) The process of subdividing large, heterogeneous (dissimilar) whole markets into smaller, homogeneous (similar) parts of submarkets.

Market share analysis An evaluation of the firm's performance in comparison to that of its competitors.

Marketing audit A set of procedures which ensures that managers will carry out a genuine control of marketing strategy.

Marketing company A form of subsidiary organization which markets, sells, and services the firm's products in the host country.

Marketing concept The philosophy that business organizations achieve their profit and other goals by satisfying consumers.

Marketing control The process of evaluating the achieved results against established standards, and of taking corrective action to exploit opportunities or solve problems.

Marketing information system (MKIS) The continuously interacting structure of people, machines, and procedures that produces information pertinent to marketing decisions.

Marketing intelligence network A set of procedures and sources designed to monitor the organization's external environments, particularly the competitive environment.

Marketing intermediaries (middlemen) Independent business concerns that facilitate the flow of products from producers to organizational buyers or ultimate consumers.

Marketing logistics See **Physical flow.**

Marketing and manufacturing company A form of subsidiary organization which handles all the functions of a marketing company but also maintains a production facility for the manufacture of the product.

Marketing mix Marketing programs including product conception (and development), pricing decisions, promotion of the product, and distribution to consumers.

Marketing orientation An approach to business that focuses primarily on what a firm does to satisfy consumers' needs.

Marketing plan A written document that contains the firm's marketing strategy and tactics.

Marketing planning The process through which an organization designs the offerings that will satisfy the needs of its target markets.

Marketing research The systematic and objective search for and analysis of information relevant to the identification and solution of any problem in the field of marketing.

Marketing research department (agency) The organization within an advertising agency which researches consumer attitudes for the client, performs demographic studies, tests the effectiveness of advertising copy or packaging, or conducts research for the agency itself.

Marketing strategy An overall statement of an organization's goals in terms of markets (Who are our customers?) and products (What are we selling?).

Mass merchandisers Retailing institutions that have developed primarily since World War II. They operate under the concepts of high volume, low overhead, and low pricing, and typically offer less service than traditional retailers.

Material culture All the tangible things that human beings make, use, and give value to.

Materials handling All the processes involved in the physical movement of products.

Materials management (or physical supply) The procurement, storage, and movement of raw materials and components to and through manufacturing, up to the point at which there is a finished product.

Maturity stage A stage in which sales growth slows, the market becomes saturated, and profits are high but begin to decline as market leaders cut prices in order to gain share.

Media Print or broadcast firms that carry advertising messages in addition to their news, editorial, and entertainment material.

Media buying organizations Organizations which select, schedule, and purchase media.

Media group A group within an advertising agency which is staffed by specialists who analyze, plan, select, and obtain time of space in various media in accordance with the client's advertising program.

Memory The ability to summon past thoughts and events to mind.

Merchant wholesalers Organizations which take title to goods, and which carry the responsibility for risk bearing and usually for performing various functions.

Message A set of verbal and/or nonverbal signs and symbols transmitted by the source.

Metropolitan statistical area (MSA) The area which has one or more central cities, each with a population of at least 50,000 or a single urbanized area that has at least 50,000 people and that is part of an MSA with a total population of 100,000.

Micromarketing Activities that deal with how individual organizations solve their particular marketing problems.

Misredemption A problem associated with coupons, which involves improper claims by consumers at the checkout counter or improper handling of coupons by retailers and distributors.

Mission statement An articulation of a firm's philosophy of doing business, setting forth the firm's values and social goals, and addressing its relationships with its publics.

Missionary salespeople People who perform such diverse tasks as building the organization's image, cultivating relations with decision makers, giving away free samples, and presenting in-depth information about the product.

MKIS (marketing information system) data bank That part of the MKIS which contains the facts, or data, which are to be analyzed and reported.

MKIS information flows A system that comprises scheduled information flows from internal and external sources, marketing intelligence networks, and marketing research findings.

MKIS model bank A set of methods for data analysis that provides the capabilities of more sophisticated analyses than is usually provided by the statistical bank.

MKIS statistical bank A system that contains programs for performing routine computations such as advertising spending projections and sales tracking.

Modified rebuy The buying situation in which the buying organization has some familiarity with the product but needs some assistance; it is buying behavior between a straight rebuy and a new-task purchase.

Money flow Backward movement through the channel of money—from customers, through retailers and wholesalers, to producers.

Monopolistic competition A market situation in which large numbers of firms market heterogeneous (dissimilar) products.

Motivation Persons' impulses to take action and the internal and external forces that energize, mobilize, and direct their behavior toward goals.

Multilevel merchandiser (MLM) Those corporate retail chains which, by dint of size, have integrated backward and have achieved strong control over (if not ownership of) their wholesalers as well as their manufacturers.

Multiple channels Channels which include different kinds of intermediaries at the same level.

Multiple-unit pricing A form of promotional pricing where the product is priced for more than one unit, such as a "two for one" sale.

N

National account representative A person who has special sales and servicing responsibilities for a specific large customer.

Natural accounts The usual financial accounting units found on the official statements of an organization.

Neighborhood shopping center A small number of convenience stores clustered around a central supermarket.

New-product business plan A plan that includes estimates for new-product development, submitted by marketing, production, and accounting personnel.

New-task buying The situation generated by an unfamiliar problem with an old product or the need for a new product in the buying process.

Noise Anything that interferes with accurate, successful transmission of a message.

Noncompensatory model A model of information processing in which a high rating for one attribute does not offset a low rating for another.

Noncumulative quantity discounts Price concessions based on quantity ordered on each individual sale.

Nondurable goods Goods consumed in one or a few uses.

Nonfamily household   Two or more unrelated persons sharing living quarters.

Nonmaterial culture   The values, beliefs, and rules by which a society directs people's interactions.

Nonprice competition   When a firm's strategy is advanced by components of the marketing mix other than price: the product itself, the distribution system, or the promotional campaign.

Nonprobability sampling   The process in which researchers decide which members of a total population are representative.

Nonprofit organizations   Tax-exempt providers of services with varying but nonprofit goals.

Nonstore retailing   Retailing that may be conducted impersonally (through catalogs, direct mail, and vending machines) or personally (door-to-door selling, in-home retailing, and telephone sales).

Norms   Rules and guidelines setting forth proper attitudes and behaviors for specific situations.

Not-for-profit markets   "Institutional" markets that exist in order to serve society, such as universities, public hospitals, and museums.

Nuclear family   The basic family unit with two parents and their children.

Nutritional labeling   The listing of the product's nutrients.

O

Objective-and-task approach   An approach in which marketers establish advertising objectives, then calculate the costs of the methods selected to achieve these goals in order to arrive at a budget.

Observational method   A data-collecting method which relies on watching people's behavior.

Odd-even pricing   The practice which assumes that consumers will perceive prices such as $9.95 as being "$9 and something" rather than as "almost $10."

Off-price retailers   Stores that differ from other discounters in that they feature, almost exclusively, name-brand and designer-label apparel at prices significantly below those in department and specialty stores.

Oligopoly   The marketplace which is dominated by only a few sellers who control the means of production and thus often have substantial influence over the prices of products.

On-the-job training   A training process consisting of actual sales calls made with a senior sales representative or the district manager.

Open bidding   The bidding situation in which prospective suppliers are allowed to examine their competitors' proposals.

Open dating   That part of the product's package which announces the normal shelf life of the product.

Operant conditioning   The process through which people learn not to simply respond to stimuli but to perform operations on their environment, that is, to actively manipulate things in order to produce desired consequences or to avoid undesired ones.

Opinion leader   Someone in a group to whom other members look for expert advice, usually on particular subjects.

Opportunity costs   Lost revenues and profits that may never be regained.

Optimal call plan   A plan in which no further reallocation of time can improve the return.

Order processing   The process of receiving and recording orders, expediting them, and billing customers.

Order takers   People who generally help customers shop and complete the sale, but who do little creative selling.

Organizational buying behavior   The decision-making process by which a buying group establishes the need for goods and services and identifies, evaluates, and chooses among alternative brands and suppliers.

Organizational marketing   All marketing efforts directed at buyers for formal institutions, including industrial, service, reseller, government, and not-for-profit groups.

Organizational markets   Markets which include businesses, institutions, and governments that buy products or raw materials for their own use or to make other products that they, in turn, sell.

Others self-concept   A third self-image in which people see themselves as they believe others see them.

Ownership flow   The change of ownership from producers or manufacturers, through intermediaries, to customers.

Ownership groups   Special types of retailing organizations that comprise a number of corporate chains—each of which is allowed and encouraged to retain its own identity, buying practices, and merchandising techniques.

P

Package   The container or wrapping and graphics and labeling that enclose the product.

Parts and subassemblies   Fabricated items that are assembled into other products.

Penetration   Marketers set low initial prices in an attempt to capture mass markets.

Perceived risk   The risk that an incorrect buying decision may result in undesired consequences.

Percentage-of-sales approach   The method of setting the advertising budget by forecasting sales for the coming year and by making the budget equal to some percentage of that figure.

Perception   The process of becoming aware of phenomena, whether internal or external, tangible or intangible.

Perceptual map   The results of the process when marketers ask a representative group of buyers within a market segment to compare brands in a certain category.

Perfect competition A marketplace in which numerous sellers offer numerous buyers an identical product and no single seller can influence the product's price.

Perfect monopoly A marketplace in which only one product supplies the good or service.

Peripheral values Values which reflect, but are not as deeply embedded or as fundamental as, central values.

Person marketing Programs designed to cultivate the attention, interest, and preference of a target market toward a person.

Personal income A person's total income from all sources.

Personal selling (1) All promotional efforts made by the organization directly to reach individuals, or groups of individuals, on a personal basis. (2) An element of the promotion mix involving personal and persuasive efforts by the seller.

Personality The composite of a person's patterned enduring and interacting characteristics.

Persuasive labels Labels which have promotional intent.

Physical attributes Inherent benefits offered by a product or service.

Physical flow (or business logistics) All the steps needed to move raw materials to and through production (materials management) as well as the movement of finished products to consumers (marketing logistics).

Pioneering advertisements Advertisements that increase primary demand for the product—that bring nonusers into the user category.

Place utility The usefulness gained when something of value is received where it is wanted.

Planned obsolescence The tactic by which the marketer introduces a new product whose life cycle will be ended by the already-planned introduction of another product or model.

Planning calendar A time frame for planning with target dates for initial and revised goals for each organizational level involved.

Plant The site and buildings needed for an organization's manufacturing, processing, service production, and office operations.

Point-of-purchase (P-O-P) or point-of-sale (P-O-S) display Self-contained, specially designed shelves, racks, stands, and so forth, used to display a manufacturer's product at the retail level.

Polarity of retailing The concept stating that the successful and growing forms of retailing is at the extremes; either the large mass merchandisers with highly efficient operations, or the very small "boutique" retailers with a very deep line of merchandise in a very limited product line.

Political stability Refers to the degree to which the so-cial and political events in a country are marked by peace or friction—the more unstable the country, the less attractive it is as a market, other things being equal.

Population (universe) The larger group whose characteristics are of primary interest to the researchers.

Portfolio A collection of businesses owned and managed by a parent corporation.

Position A product's category and its relative standing within that category.

Possession utility The usefulness gained with the transfer of ownership of a good or with the actual consumption of a service.

Predatory pricing The practice by which large firms set extremely low prices in an effort to undercut small competitors and drive them out of business.

Premium price differential The additional money consumers will pay for the augmented product.

Premiums Gifts to paying customers; they are generally claimed through the mail by sending the marketer a number of proof-of-purchase labels or box tops.

Prestige pricing When the seller intentionally sets prices at levels high enough to connote an image of quality and status.

Price Both the value that buyers place on what is exchanged and the marketers' estimates of that value.

Price administration A deliberate effort by marketers to determine what price, sequence of prices, or price adjustments are appropriate for a specific product, given market conditions.

Price discrimination Selling the same product to different customers for different prices.

Price fixing When competitors, through formal contracts or collusive actions, jointly agree upon prices.

Price lining A manufacturer or a retailer sets a limited number of prices for selected lines of products.

Price-off promotions A strategy which involves temporary price reductions to retailers with the intent that savings will be passed along to consumers.

Primary data Facts collected from original research designed to address a particular problem.

Primary demand Demand for the product class as a whole.

Primary metropolitan statistical area (PMSA) An MSA with more than 1 million people.

Private brands Brands of products made by manufacturers for sale by intermediaries under a label of the intermediary's own choice.

Private carriers Manufacturer- or wholesaler-owned shipping fleets (primarily trucks) which are subject only to safety regulations.

Probability sampling The process in which all members of the population have a known chance of being included in the sample.

Procurement costs Inventory expenses that arise from the ordering process itself.

Product Anything an organization or individual offers for exchange that may satisfy customers' or consumers' needs or the marketer's own needs.

Product adaptation A global marketing strategy whereby the product is adapted to foreign market needs, but the promotional program used in the domestic market is used in foreign markets.

Product category organization The organization method that assigns marketing tasks by product category or brand.

Product class All the brands of a good and service offered by all competitors to meet a basic consumer need.

Product competitors Companies which are filling the same market needs with a slightly different offering.

Product development process The process which comprises a series of steps involved in getting a product on the market: idea generation, screening, feasibility studies, prototype development, test marketing, and commercialization.

Product disparagement Making false or deceptive comparisons or distorted claims concerning a competitor's product, services, or property.

Product elimination Withdrawal of a product from the normal marketplace.

Product invention A global marketing strategy whereby a new product is created specifically for the needs of the foreign market, and is then promoted to that market.

Product ladder The concept that states that consumers perceive brands of a product to be arrayed from top to bottom in terms of their familiarity and preference.

Product life cycle The product's stages of development, which consist of introductory, growth, maturity, and decline stages.

Product line A grouping of products managed and marketed as a unit because they have similar functions, are distributed in similar ways, or fall within a certain price range.

Product line breadth The number of product lines in the product mix of an organization.

Product line depth The number of individual items within each product line.

Product line exclusivity An agreement that the agency will not work on a competing product for the duration of the relationship.

Product line extension Development of greater depth by adding new product varieties.

Product manager (brand manager) The person who is responsible for initiating, developing, and implementing product or product line plans.

Product-market matrix A visual means of defining a business by its markets and by the products directed toward those markets.

Product mix A company's total offering of individual products.

Product orientation A philosophy of business which focuses primarily on a firm's own resources and products.

Product-oriented positioning The strategy that rests on some attribute inherent in a product's makeup, packaging, use, or price.

Product positioning The process by which marketers create an image in buyers' minds and control buyers' perceptions of their products.

Professional sales representatives Territory managers whose primary task is persuasive and creative face-to-face selling and account management.

Profit repatriation Refers to how much of the profits earned through marketing in a foreign market are permitted to be carried out of the country rather than reinvested in the host country.

Profitability analysis Analysis designed to provide information on the profit performance of individual units within an organization in order to determine appropriate corrective action.

Promotion All aspects of the marketing mix designed to communicate with and influence target markets.

Promotion adaptation A global marketing strategy whereby the product sold in domestic markets is not altered in any important ways, but market communications are adapted to local conditions.

Promotion mix The blend of promotional elements selected and the extent to which each is used.

Promotion strategy A communication plan designed to bring about desired buyer behaviors by employing a mix of the four elements of promotion.

Promotional discounts Discounts for encouraging promotion and sales efforts by intermediaries.

Promotional pricing Pricing that paves the way for a good old-fashioned sale; prices of selected items are lowered in an effort to attract customers.

Prospect A potential (but not current) customer.

Prospecting A systematic process of identifying new buyers.

Protectionism Any of a number of efforts a nation might use to "protect" its businesses from the competition of other nations' businesses.

Prototype An actual version of the product that will help developers to approve its feasibility, costs, and characteristics.

Psychogenic needs Needs which arise from learning and socialization.

Psychographics The system of measurement of lifestyles.

Psychological pricing Pricing intended to appeal to buyers' emotions rather than their logic.

Psychophysical testing A procedure, similar to those employed in lie detector tests, which is used to assess people's reactions to print or broadcast advertisements.

Public service organizations Organizations that have general objectives of cultural enrichment, social service, or the improvement of the public well-being.

Publicity A form of promotion composed of newsworthy messages sent through the media on a nonpaid basis.

Pull strategy A strategy through which marketers aim mass promotional efforts at consumers and customers with the intent to create demand which pulls the product through the channels.

Pulsing (or flighting) A strategy of unevenly timed exposures of advertisements.

Purchase diaries Regularly reported data drawn from consumers' purchases, including brands purchased, prices paid, package sizes, special promotions, and so forth.

Push money Special bonuses paid by a marketer to an intermediary's sales force.

Push strategy A strategy through which personal selling and sales promotion are directed at channel members, who then promote the product to consumers.

Q

Qualitative research Research which takes the form of detailed interviews with a small number of consumers or organizational buyers.

Quantitative research Research based on a statistically valid sampling of a target market.

Quantity discounts Price concessions that are based either on the number of units purchased or on the total dollar amount; they are used to encourage larger orders from a single buyer.

Questionnaire A data collection instrument that is used for all survey methods.

Quota A form of control of imports by governments which places specific quantitative limits on the quantity of products which may be brought into a market.

Quota sample A sample selected by giving the interviewer a quota of a certain number of individuals with some specific characteristic, such as a quota to interview 50 men and 50 women.

R

Racial group A social group determined by genetically transmitted, physically observable traits to which people attach social meaning, both within the group and outside it.

Rack jobbers Organizations which place sales racks or stands in retail stores; they provide inventory maintenance and charge the retailer for what has been sold from the rack. They sell primarily to large supermarket and drugstore chains.

Raw materials Natural resources and agricultural goods that have been processed only as necessary for economy or physical handling before being incorporated into the buyer's products.

Reach The proportion of the target audience who will see an advertisement at least once.

Real self-concept A realistic self-appraisal of who we are and what we are capable of accomplishing.

Rebates A promotional method which provides for financial returns to buyers from the manufacturer after the purchase has taken place.

Recall tests Tests of print advertisements which do not assist the respondent's memory by providing the ads themselves.

Receiver The person who decodes the message transmitted by the source.

Recession A downward phase of a business cycle resulting in a falling off of business and consumer optimism.

Reciprocity A practice of buying from organizations which buy from your organization.

Recognition tests A test of the effectiveness of print advertising which measures the ability to recognize an advertisement when presented.

Reference groups Groups to which people turn in order to measure the acceptability of what they do.

Regional group The social group determined by certain values and tastes that are prevalent within the geographic area.

Regional shopping center A large supermarket and branches of one or more major department stores; it has 150,000 or more consumers in its target market and contains 40 or more stores.

Reinforcement advertisements Advertisements that bolster and enhance satisfaction with purchases already made.

Relative market share A firm's market share divided by the market share of its largest competitor.

Reminder advertisements Advertisements that aim at reinforcement by keeping the product in the buyers' minds.

Repositioning The conscious effort to change consumers' perceptions of a product—may be in order when marketers discover that a product appeals to other market segments.

Reseller markets Firms that acquire goods and services in order to sell them again.

Retailer cooperatives Centralized buying organizations set up by retailers themselves.

Retailers Merchants whose main business is selling directly to ultimate consumers.

Return on investment (ROI) The ratio of profits to investments.

Return on time invested (ROTI) A measure of the return in sales results of a measure of time spent to achieve those results.

Revenues Payments received for the sale of goods and services.

Risk bearing   Any loss of product value because of factors such as changes in style or consumers' preferences (or spoilage) which is borne by the wholesaler instead of the supplier—as when the wholesaler has taken title to the product.

Robot   Any machine that performs jobs previously assigned to human beings, is self-operating, and is "intelligent."

Roles   A set of proper behaviors specified by culturally defined rules.

S

Safety stock   A higher level of inventory than is thought necessary to meet demand forecasts.

Salary   A regular, specified amount of compensation based on minimal performance.

Sales analysis   A comparison of actual versus estimated sales.

Sales force motivators   The incentives, both tangible and intangible, for excellent performance.

Sales forecast   The realistic expectations of a company's sales of a product or product line under a defined marketing program.

Sales management system   The policies, producers, and practices that enable and encourage salespeople to carry out their roles in the organization's marketing strategy.

Sales manager   The person most directly responsible for the day-to-day analysis, planning, implementation, and control of the marketing division's personal selling force.

Sales orientation   An approach to business that focuses primarily on how a firm promotes and sells its products.

Sales presentation   A face-to-face discussion of the product between the salesperson and the prospect (or buying group).

Sales promotion   Short-range tactics that have an effect over a limited time period and are intended to achieve specific objectives within a target market.

Sales response function   A curve that shows the relationship between the number of calls made on an account and the sales to an account.

Sales territory   The area, geographically based or otherwise, which includes the current and potential accounts assigned to an individual sales respresentative or territory manager.

Sample   (1) A subset of the population that is chosen to represent the population. (2) Free gifts of the product (usually in small quantity sizes) designed to persuade the consumer to try it.

Scrambled merchandising   The contemporary practice among retailers of expanding their product lines beyond those traditionally carried, leading to competition between types of retailers.

Screening process   The process which sifts out all ideas that are not feasible or desirable for the organization.

Seasonal discounts   Discounts granted to early or off-season buyers of products that have peak selling periods.

Seasonal patterns   The consistent sales patterns within a year which are based on factors such as weather or holidays.

Secondary data   Facts previously collected by others, often for another purpose.

Secular trends   The rising or falling patterns of sales over a period of years.

Segmentation variables   Factors by which market segments are formed, e.g., geographic, demographic, socio-economic, behavioral, and psychographic variables.

Selective demand   A preference among buyers for specific brands.

Selective distribution   A system in which only a certain number of intermediaries, or those of a certain type, are chosen to distribute the product.

Self-liquidator   The consumer must pay a small charge for the premium to help cover the marketer's expenses; if this charge completely covers a marketer's costs, the premium is called a self-liquidator.

Self-selection retailers   Stores that provide few services or sales personnel and sell mostly staples and homogeneous shopping goods.

Self-service retailers   Retail establishments in which the consumer is responsible for serving him- or herself, such as in supermarkets and other forms of retailing—commonly used in drug retailing.

Selling agents   Agents who distribute the entire output of a manufacturer.

Selling position   The specific promotional idea used to present the product to buyers in the target market.

Semistructured questions   Questions that include sentence completion items and word association tests.

Service market   All organizations that buy in order to produce services.

Services   Activities, benefits, or satisfactions that are offered to satisfy consumers' and customers' needs.

Servicing   The maintenance of the product in working order so that its benefits are not diminished.

Shopping center   A group of commercial establishments planned, developed, owned, and managed as a unit related in location, size, and type of shops to the trade area that it services, and providing on-site parking in definite relationships to the types and sizes of stores it contains.

Shopping products   Goods and services that consumers shop for, comparing quality, suitability, style, price, and other factors.

Simple random sample   The process in which individual members of a population would have an equal and known chance of being selected as part of a sample.

Simulated test marketing   An approach to new-product testing that does not involve the actual marketing of a new product in test cities as in traditional test marketing, but uses special consumer reaction research instead.

Single-line wholesalers Wholesalers who restrict their inventories to a single product line such as hardware, appliances, or drugs.

Single-person household An individual who lives alone in a separate residence.

Situational influences Events beyond consumers' or the marketers' control which sway consumers' behavior from the expected path.

Skimming A strategy that is characterized by high initial prices and promotional expenditures; the intent is to "skim the cream" from the market before anyone else can serve it.

Slice-of-life advertisements Advertisements that show the product being used by 'ordinary people' in very common settings or engaged in everyday activities.

Social class A category made up of people who share similar opportunities, economic positions, lifestyles, attitudes, and behaviors.

Social marketing (or cause marketing) The design, implementation, and control of marketing programs calculated to influence the acceptability of social ideas.

Social mobility The ability of a person or a category of people to move from one level to another within the social system.

Social stratification The social system through which members of the society are assigned ranks, grades, or positions.

Socialization The process through which we learn the entire range of physical, intellectual, and social skills needed to function as members of our society.

Societal marketing orientation An approach that adds a consideration to the marketing concept: the impact of a firm's activities on societal well-being, the very quality of life.

Sorting out The process by which wholesalers and retailers separate quantities of products into sizes, colors, quality grades, and so on.

Source The communicator sending a message to another party or parties.

Source credibility The extent to which the source of a communication is believable to the target audience.

Special incentives A motivator usually used for a brief period to strengthen representatives' efforts to achieve specific sales goals.

Special sales representatives People who promote the product directly to those who purchase it, to intermediaries, or to those who recommend it, but who do not actually take orders.

Specialty products Products perceived by consumers as having unique qualities, to the point that no substitutes are acceptable.

Specialty stores Stores characterized by narrow product mixes with deep product lines, a high level of personal service, and relatively high prices.

Specialty wholesalers Wholesalers who have the most restricted inventories, focusing on items such as health foods or electric motors.

Stakeholders Those who use the company's products or services, those who work for the firm, those who own it, and those who are affected by it.

Standard industrial classification manual The Federal Office of Management and Budget's manual which classifies every kind of economic activity in the United States; it uses a four-digit system to assign increasingly explicit code numbers to each economic unit.

Staple Goods which buyers give little thought when purchasing, other than noting the need for the item and picking it up.

Stars A company's 'big winners'—businesses that hold high relative market shares in high-growth markets.

Statistical demand analysis Analysis that develops relationships among marketing mix factors and environmental circumstances and sales.

Status The socially defined positions held by members of a society.

Stimulus Anything that elicits or accelerates a physiological or psychological activity.

Stimulus-response (SR) theory The theory which holds that organisms learn first to associate an original stimulus with another, adjacent stimulus and then to respond to that second "conditioned" stimulus with the behavior formerly induced by the original stimulus.

Storyboards Sketches, written copy, and directions used to communicate a television commercial's message.

Straight commission A financial incentive based solely on sales results; each increment of sales increases the commission.

Straight extention A global marketing strategy whereby the product offered in the domestic market is offered to foreign markets using the same promotional methods.

Straight rebuy A routine purchase with which a buyer has had substantial experience.

Strategic business unit A single business with its own unique goal or mission, its own products or services, its own identifiable group of customers, its own competitors, its own resources, and a responsible manager.

Strategic control The control of major strategy directions.

Strategic management The management of a strategy; it involves at least four steps, i.e., analyzing, planning, implementing, and controlling.

Strategy The major objectives of the organization and a general plan for achieving these objectives.

Stratified random sample A process that entails breaking the total population into strata, such as by age groups or income levels, in order to select samples within strata.

String streets   Major thoroughfares along which are found random collections of almost every kind of store.

Structured questions   Those questions that demand brief and specific answers.

Subcultures   Groups that share the values and artifacts of the larger society but also have distinctive practices, preferences, and beliefs.

Supermarkets   Self-selection stores that sell a complete range of food and other items from various departments.

Superstores   Stores that go well beyond combination stores by carrying such nonfood items as garden supplies, alcoholic beverages, books, housewares, and hardware.

Supplies   Items that are not incorporated into the buying organization's products; goods needed to keep everyday operations going.

Supply   A relation showing the various amounts of a commodity that a seller would be willing and able to make available for sale at possible alternative prices during a given period of time, all other things remaining the same.

Support personnel   People who aid the efforts of professional and special sales representatives and order takers.

Survey method   A research method based on data gathered by asking respondents to supply facts, opinions, or other information.

Sweepstakes   A promotional method in which consumers fill out a form to enter a random drawing for prizes.

SWOTs analysis   A detailed review of a firm's strengths, weaknesses, opportunities, and threats.

Syndicated research services   The scheduled reports which spell out what consumers are buying and what is happening to a product in the marketplace.

Systematic random sample   The process in which researchers choose every nth (such as every tenth or fiftieth) number after starting with a randomly selected number.

T

Tactic   A specific set of actions to secure the objectives set forth by a strategy.

Target market   (1) Particular segments which the marketer will try to satisfy with particular marketing programs. (2) Specific groups of consumers that a firm proposes to serve.

Target return on investment   A common pricing objective which returns a specified percentage of investment as income.

Target return on sales   A profit goal, set by the firm, for each unit sold.

Tariff   A tax levied on the import of items from another nation; it has the effect of increasing the cost of foreign products.

Technical specialists (or sales engineers)   People who function as consultants and provide specific information about the product's capabilities, specifications, installation, use, and maintenance.

Telecommunications   A blanket term for the electronic transmission of data whether through wires, cables, fiberoptics, or broadcast.

Telephone sales   A second major form of direct marketing, which promotes and sells products directly by telephone.

Territory managers   People who must analyze, plan, implement, and control their own sales activities.

Territory sales plan   A plan that specifies which activities the territory manager will perform to achieve sales and other objectives.

Test marketing   The process in which the product is actually introduced into selected geographical markets where developers can observe how consumers and dealers react to the handling, use, and promotion of the product.

Testimonial advertisements   Advertisements that attempt to get the consumer to identify with someone who claims that he or she uses and likes the product.

Theater tests   An expensive method of judging the effectiveness of television commercials. Consumer groups are brought into theaters, supposedly to see pilots of forthcoming television series. They are asked their opinions not only of the pilots but of the impact and effectiveness of the commercials.

Threshold effect   The concept that very few calls on any account tend not to have any effect on sales until the level of calls reaches a certain level.

Time series analysis   Analysis that identifies and measures repetitive influences on sales patterns over time.

Time utility   The usefulness gained when something of value is received at the time it is wanted.

Total-cost approach   An overall examination of the costs involved in moving finished goods from the end of the production line into customers' hands.

Total costs (TC)   The sum of total fixed costs (TFC) and total variable costs (TVC) at a specified level of production.

Total fixed costs (TFC)   The sum of all recurring and constant expenditures.

Total market demand   The total volume that would be bought by a defined consumer group in a defined geographical area in a defined time period in a defined marketing environment under a defined level and mix of industry marketing effort.

Total market potential   The total possible sales of the product by all competitors.

Total revenue (TR)   The price per unit multiplied by the quantity sold ($TR = P \times Q$).

Total variable costs (TVC)   The sum of all costs which rise or fall depending on the production level.

Dictionary of Marketing Terms

Trade advertisements   Advertisements for the purpose of influencing intermediaries either to stock a product or to advance it through distribution channels on its way to ultimate consumers.

Trade character   A brand mark that represents a human being or an animal associated with the product.

Trade name   The name under which a company chooses to conduct its business, which may or may not also be a brand name.

Trade promotions   Promotional methods that spur action on the part of channel members, such as additional orders from retailers or a special push by a wholesaler to promote one manufacturer's products.

Trade shows   Special gatherings of buyers and sellers of a line of products, usually once per year, where new products can be shown and orders taken for a selling season.

Trademark   A brand or part of a brand that is given legal protection because it is capable of exclusive appropriation.

Traditional retailers   Specialty, department, and variety stores; supermarkets; and convenience stores.

Transit time   The time from receipt of the order to delivery of the goods.

Truck wholesalers   Wholesalers who pick up quantities of products at commercial markets and deliver them to retailers in case lots.

Two-step flow of mass communications   The notion that communications flow from the media to opinion leaders, and then from opinion leaders to other members of society.

Tying contract   An agreement between a supplier and an intermediary which requires the intermediary to buy product B in order to also get product A.

U

Umbrella pricing   The firm sets prices at a level high enough to allow inefficient competitors to remain in business.

Uncontrollable variables   Those forces outside the organization over which managers have little or no control in the short term.

Undifferentiated marketing   The process opposite of market segmentation; i.e., marketers define their products as broadly as possible and promote a product or service to anyone capable of making a purchase.

Unfair competition   Falsely advertising a product, misrepresenting its qualities or characteristics, or engaging in related deceptive trade practices.

Unfair-sales acts   The law which prohibits retailers from selling products at less than cost plus a percentage for profit and overhead.

Uniform delivered pricing   Freight charges are added to the base price of the product such that all buyers pay the same price regardless of their location.

Unit handling   The process whereby multiple cartons are placed on pallets or skids that can be moved easily by forklift trucks.

Unit pricing   Each product's price is expressed per standard measure (ounce, pound, gram, liter, pint, and so on).

Unitary demand   A given percentage change in price results in an identical percentage change in the quantity demanded.

Unsought products   Those products that consumers do not consciously want or actively seek out.

Unstructured questions   Questions that allow respondents a great deal of freedom and creativity in framing answers.

Upward-sloping supply, the law of   The law stating that when the price of a good is raised (at the same time that all other things are held constant), more of it will be produced.

Urban shopping malls   Collections of shops and department stores located in or near central business districts.

Users   Persons within an organization who actually put a purchased product to work.

Utility   A measure of the satisfaction obtained through the receipt of something of value in an exchange.

V

Value analysis   A cost-reduction program in which customers study each component of a supplier's product to determine whether it can be redesigned, standardized, or produced more cheaply.

Values   Shared standards of what is acceptable and unacceptable, good and bad, desirable and undesirable.

Variable   A characteristic that can change or differ from one individual or group to another.

Variable cost (VC)   (1) An expense that changes directly with the number of units produced. (2) Costs that include such expenses as hourly wages, raw materials, parts and subassemblies, and commissions paid to sales representatives—all of which are relative to increases or decreases in production and sales.

Variety discrepancy   The difference between the number of different products produced by marketers and the variety desired by consumers.

Variety stores   Stores which sell a wide assortment of low-priced merchandise while offering only minimal personal service.

Vehicles   Specific outlets within a larger advertising medium.

Vending machines   A form of nonstore, nonpersonal selling which takes to the extreme the transaction between consumer and machine.

Vendor analysis   The buying organization's systematic evaluation and rating of prospective suppliers.

Vertical conflict   The conflict which occurs between

members above and below each other in the distribution channel—between the manufacturer and intermediaries, or between intermediaries such as wholesalers and retailers.

Vertical integration The approach of owning or controlling members at all levels of one's distribution channels.

Vertical marketing system (VMS) A system in which the functions of members at different levels in the distribution channel have been integrated under the ownership or influence of one member in order to set shared goals and to achieve effective performance.

Vertical markets The markets on which products are tailored for specific industries.

Volume discrepancy The difference between the amounts produced by marketers and the amounts desired by consumers.

Voluntary chains Wholesaler-sponsored organizations of independent retailers who practice bulk buying and similar merchandising techniques.

W

Warehouse showrooms Stores that are located on low-rent, suburban sites, and focus on medium-priced furniture and appliances.

Warranty The producer's assurance that the product will meet buyers' expectations or that buyers will be compensated in some way if the product fails to meet expectations.

Wheel of retailing A concept which states that entrepreneurs continually find new, usually low-overhead and low-cost ways of bringing products to consumers; that as they prosper they increase their services and their costs; and that they are eventually challenged by other forms which follow a similar pattern.

Wholesaler Organizations which buy products from producers or other wholesalers and resell them to retailers or organizational buyers, or to other wholesalers.

Work load analysis A method which establishes standards for the number of sales calls required and the time needed to make those calls.

Worldwide product division A form of organization under which each of the company's major product lines, or business units, is responsible for the marketing of its product throughout the world.

Z

Zone pricing When the seller sets up two or more geographic areas and establishes uniform freight charges within each.

Indexes

Name Index

Company and Brand Index

Subject Index